ELEMENTS OF WRITING

Annotated Teacher's Edition

JAMES L. KINNEAVY
JOHN E. WARRINER

Fifth Course

Holt, Rinehart and Winston
Harcourt Brace Jovanovich
HBJ
Austin • Orlando • San Diego • Chicago • Dallas • Toronto

Critical Readers

Gayle Gaither
Durant High School
Durant, Oklahoma

Releah Hawks
A. Crawford Mosley High School
Lynn Haven, Florida

Kristi Lechner
Oregon City Senior High School
Oregon City, Oregon

Anita Martin
Stillwater Central School
Stillwater, New York

Deborah McGinn
Lincoln High School
Lincoln, Nebraska

Herbert Welch
Cedar Springs High School
Cedar Springs, Michigan

Acknowledgments: See pages 1080–1092, which are an extension of the copyright page.

Printed in the United States of America

ISBN 0-03-047159-1 2 3 4 5 6 062 94 93

Authors

James L. Kinneavy, the Jane and Roland Blumberg Centennnial Professor of English at The University of Texas at Austin, directed the development and writing of the composition strand in the program. He is the author of *A Theory of Discourse* and coauthor of *Writing in the Liberal Arts Tradition*. Professor Kinneavy is a leader in the field of rhetoric and composition and a respected educator whose teaching experience spans all levels—elementary, secondary, and college. He has continually been concerned with teaching writing to high school students.

John E. Warriner developed the organizational structure for the Handbook of Grammar, Usage, and Mechanics in the book. He coauthored the *English Workshop* series, was general editor of the *Composition: Models and Exercises* series, and editor of *Short Stories: Characters in Conflict*. He taught English for thirty-two years in junior and senior high school and college.

Professional Essays

Donald M. Murray is Professor Emeritus of English at The University of New Hampshire, where he served as director of Freshman English and as English Department Chairperson. As a journalist, he won a number of awards including the Pulitzer Prize for editorial writing on the *Boston Herald* in 1954.

Lee Odell has a Ph.D. in English and Education from The University of Michigan. A former middle school and high school teacher of English, he now teaches writing at Rensselaer Polytechnic Institute. He has published frequently on the teaching of writing and is interested in the processes of writing, talking, and thinking.

Maxine C. Hairston has a Ph.D. in English from the The University of Texas at Austin, where she served as Director of Freshman English. She is the author of several texts on writing theory and the teaching of writing, including *A Contemporary Composition*.

Barbara J. Shade has a Ph.D. in Educational Psychology from The University of Wisconsin-Madison. She is a Professor and Dean of the School of Education at The University of Wisconsin-Parkside. She specializes in the social and psychological attributes of people with high academic achievement with an emphasis on African Americans. She has written extensively on culture and its impact on learning and achievement. She also served as consultant for this series.

Wanda B. Schindley has an Ed.D. in Composition and Rhetoric from East Texas State University. She teaches at Northeast Texas Community College and serves as coordinator and curriculum specialist for the Workplace Partnership program. She coauthored a teacher's resource series, *The English Teacher's Guide to the Essential Elements.*

Charles W. Leftwich has an Ed.D. in Educational Administration from Harvard University. He is a professor in the Department of Educational Administration at East Texas State University. He worked in public schools for over twenty-five years as a teacher, a vice-principal, a principal, and a superintendent.

Patricia G. Tweeddale has an Ed.D. in Educational Administration from East Texas State University. She has taught at-risk students in high school and has written about the impact of public education policy on such students. She is a partner in an educational consulting service that focuses on helping teachers to teach at-risk student populations.

Norbert Elliot has a Ph.D. in English from The University of Tennessee. A director of the writing program at New Jersey Institute of Technology, he is a specialist in test development and writing assessment.

Karen L. Greenberg has a Ph.D. in Linguistics from New York University. She is an Associate Professor of English at Hunter College of The City University of New York, where she directs the Developmental English Program and teaches courses in writing and linguistics. She is a director of the National Testing Network in Writing, and she has authored numerous books and essays on writing instruction and assessment.

David A. England has a Ph.D. in English from Indiana University. He is the Associate Dean of Teacher Education at Louisiana State University. A former high school English teacher, he has served as a director for the National Council of Teachers of English and was active in the National Writing Project.

Writers and Editors

H. Edward Deluzain has a Ph.D. in English Education from Florida State University. He teaches at A. Crawford Mosley High School in Panama City, Florida. He is a writer of educational material in literature and composition.

Dorothy Frew has a B.A. in Humanities from Shimer College and is completing an M.A. in Applied Linguistics at Portland State University. She teaches English as a Second Language at Clackamas Community College in Clackamas, Oregon.

Mary Hynes-Berry has a Ph.D. in English from The University of Wisconsin-Madison. She is an educational consultant for public schools in Chicago, Illinois. She has been a writer of educational materials for over fifteen years.

Marsha Lippincott has an M.A. in English from Mississippi University for Women and has studied English at Oxford University. She is a teacher who has written educational materials for twelve years.

Sylvia Teague has an M.A. in economics from the University of Texas, where she also taught economics for two years. She has been writing educational materials in composition and literature for five years.

Glenda A. Zumwalt has an Ed.D. in Teaching Composition and Rhetoric from East Texas State University. She teaches composition at Southeastern Oklahoma State University. She is a writer of educational material in composition and literature.

Acknowledgments

We wish to thank the following teachers who participated in field testing of pre-publication materials for this series:

Susan Almand-Myers
Meadow Park Intermediate School
Beaverton, Oregon

Theresa L. Bagwell
Naylor Middle School
Tucson, Arizona

Ruth Bird
Freeport High School
Sarver, Pennsylvania

Joan M. Brooks
Central Junior High School
Guymon, Oklahoma

Candice C. Bush
J. D. Smith Junior High School
N. Las Vegas, Nevada

Mary Jane Childs
Moore West Junior High School
Oklahoma City, Oklahoma

Brian Christensen
Valley High School
West Des Moines, Iowa

Lenise Christopher
Western High School
Las Vegas, Nevada

Mary Ann Crawford
Ruskin Senior High School
Kansas City, Missouri

Linda Dancy
Greenwood Lakes Middle School
Lake Mary, Florida

Elaine A. Espindle
Peabody Veterans Memorial High School
Peabody, Massachusetts

Joan Justice
North Middle School
O'Fallon, Missouri

Beverly Kahwaty
Pueblo High School
Tucson, Arizona

Lamont Leon
Van Buren Junior High School
Tampa, Florida

Susan Lusch
Fort Zumwalt South High School
St. Peters, Missouri

Michele K. Lyall
Rhodes Junior High School
Mesa, Arizona

Belinda Manard
McKinley Senior High School
Canton, Ohio

Nathan Masterson
Peabody Veterans Memorial High School
Peabody, Massachusetts

Marianne Mayer
Swope Middle School
Reno, Nevada

Penne Parker
Greenwood Lakes Middle School
Lake Mary, Florida

Amy Ribble
Gretna Junior-Senior High School
Gretna, Nebraska

Kathleen R. St. Clair
Western High School
Las Vegas, Nevada

Carla Sankovich
Billinghurst Middle School
Reno, Nevada

Sheila Shaffer
Cholla Middle School
Phoenix, Arizona

Joann Smith
Lehman Junior High School
Canton, Ohio

Margie Stevens
Raytown Middle School
Raytown, Missouri

Mary Webster
Central Junior High School
Guymon, Oklahoma

Susan M. Yentz
Oviedo High School
Oviedo, Florida

Contents in Brief

Table of Contents

PROFESSIONAL ESSAYS

A TEACHER'S GUIDE TO ELEMENTS OF WRITING

PART ONE WRITING

CHAPTER 2 UNDERSTANDING PARAGRAPH STRUCTURE

CHAPTER 3 UNDERSTANDING COMPOSITION STRUCTURE

CHAPTER 4 EXPRESSIVE WRITING

CHAPTER 5 CREATIVE WRITING

CHAPTER 6 WRITING TO INFORM

CHAPTER 7 WRITING TO EXPLAIN

CHAPTER 8 WRITING TO PERSUADE

CHAPTER 9 WRITING TO EXPLORE

CHAPTER 10 WRITING ABOUT LITERATURE

CHAPTER 11 WRITING A RESEARCH PAPER

TEACHING CHAPTER 11 **401A-401D**

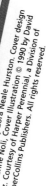

Their Eyes Were Watching God by Zora Neale Hurston. Cover design by Suzanne Noli, cover illustration © 1990 by David Diaz. Courtesy of Harper Perennial, a Division of HarperCollins Publishers. All rights reserved.

Mules and Men by Zora Neale Hurston. Cover design by Suzanne Noli, Cover Illustration © 1990 by David Diaz. Courtesy of Harper Perennial, a Division of HarperCollins Publishers. All rights reserved.

CHAPTER 12 ENGLISH: HISTORY AND DEVELOPMENT

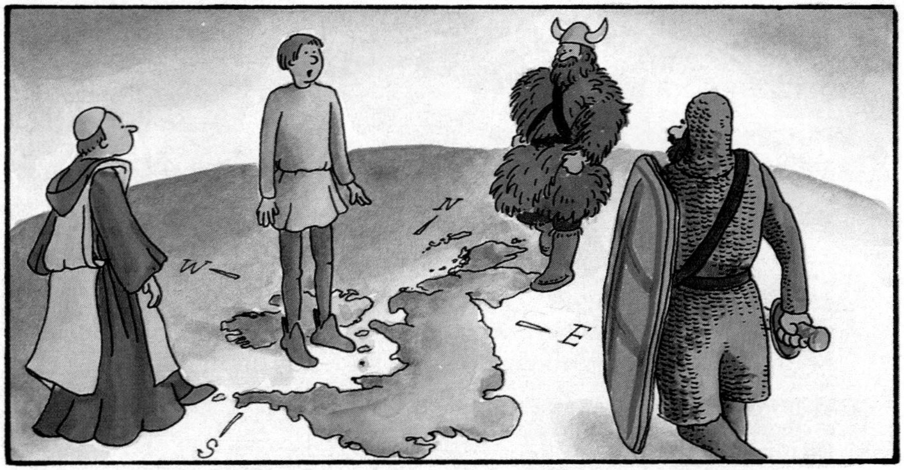

CHAPTER 13 STYLE IN WRITING

CHAPTER 14 WRITING CLEAR SENTENCES

CHAPTER 15 COMBINING SENTENCES

CHAPTER 16 IMPROVING SENTENCE STYLE

CHAPTER 17 THE PARTS OF SPEECH 552

Their Identification and Function

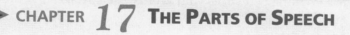

M.C. Escher, Symmetry Work 91: ©M.C. Escher/Cordon Art—Baarn—Holland.

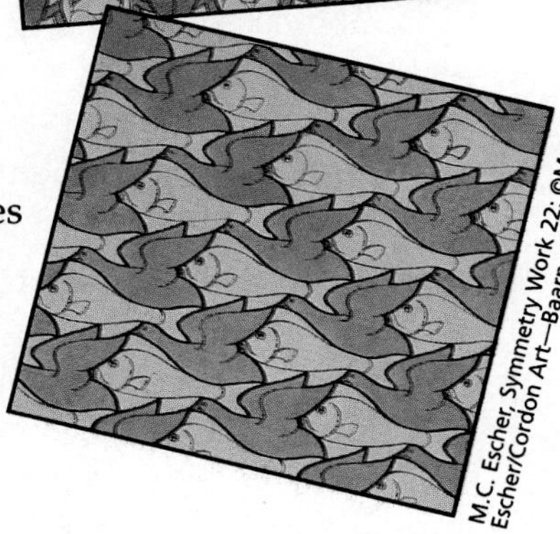

M.C. Escher, Symmetry Work 22: ©M.C. Escher/Cordon Art—Baarn—Holland.

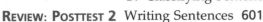

CHAPTER 19 THE PHRASE 603

Kinds of Phrases and Their Functions

CHAPTER 20 THE CLAUSE 626

Adjective, Noun, Adverb Clauses

CHAPTER 21 AGREEMENT 647

Subject and Verb, Pronoun and Antecedent

CHAPTER 22 CORRECT PRONOUN USAGE 672

Case Forms of Pronouns

CHAPTER 30 PUNCTUATION 864

Other Marks of Punctuation

CHAPTER 31 SPELLING 902

Improving Your Spelling

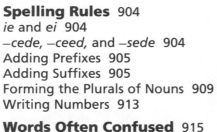

PART THREE RESOURCES

CHAPTER 32 FORMAL SPEAKING AND DEBATE 932

CHAPTER 33 COMMUNICATION SKILLS 948

Types and Techniques

CHAPTER 34 THE LIBRARY/MEDIA CENTER 959

Finding and Using Information

ollegiate Dictionary

Fiction

Ray Bradbury, *The Toynbee Convector*
Lewis Carroll, *Through the Looking-Glass*
James Fenimore Cooper, *The Deerslayer*
Louis Dollarhide, "The Gift," *The Georgia Review*
Michael Dorris, *A Yellow Raft in Blue Water*
Zora Neale Hurston, *Jonah's Gourd Vine*
Cynthia Kadokata, *The Floating World*
David Long, "Blue Spruce," *The New Yorker*
Ruthanne Lum McCunn, *Thousand Pieces of Gold*
Mike Montgomery, *It Was a Dark and Stormy Night: The Best(?) from the Bulwer-Lytton Contest*
Leslie Norris, "A Flight of Geese," *The Girl from Cardigan*
Katherine Anne Porter, "The Jilting of Granny Weatherall," *Flowering Judas and Other Stories*
V. S. Pritchett, "The Wheelbarrow," *Selected Stories*
Hyemeyohsts Storm, *Seven Arrows*
Amy Tan, *The Joy Luck Club*
Sabine Ulibarrí, "My Wonder Horse," *Tierra Amarilla: Stories of New Mexico*
Kurt Vonnegut, Jr., "Tom Edison's Shaggy Dog," *Welcome to the Monkey House*

Nonfiction

Tom and Jane D. Allen, *Dinosaur Days in Texas*
Isaac Asimov, "Learning Science," *The Tyrannosaurus Prescription and 100 Other Essays*
Dave Barry, "Car-Buying: The Compleat Guide," *The Washington Post Magazine*
Joan Benoit with Sally Baker, *Running Tide*
"Black, Blue and Gray: The Other Civil War," *Ebony*
Daniel J. Boorstin, "Making Time Portable," *The Discoverers*
Virginia Buckley, "American Robin: *Turdus migratorius*," *State Birds*
Mark Coleman, review of *Christgau's Record Guide: Rock Albums of the '80's*, *Rolling Stone*
Alistair Cooke, *Alistair Cooke's America*
Edward Corsi, "I Behold America," *In the Shadow of Liberty*
James West Davidson, "The Frontier Kitchen of the Plains," *Nation of Nations: A Narrative History of the American Republic*
Annie Dillard, *Pilgrim at Tinker Creek*
W.E.B. Du Bois, "Galileo Galilei," *"The Education of Black People: Ten Critiques 1906–1960*
Roger Ebert, review "Star Wars," *Roger Ebert's Movie Home Companion*
Paul R. Ehrlich, David S. Dobkin, Darryl Wheye, "Visual Displays," *The Birder's Handbook*
"Eliot Porter," *Life*
Richard P. Feynmann, "The Making of a Scientist," *What Do You Care What Other People Think?*
Adrían Fisher & Georg Gerster, *Labyrinth: Solving the Riddle of the Maze*
Ernesto Galarza, *Barrio Boy*
Mary Hager, et al., "'Dances With Garbage,'" *Newsweek*
Robert E. Henenway, *Zora Neale Hurston: A Literary Biography*
Alton Hornsby, *The Black Almanac*
Langston Hughes, *I Wonder as I Wander*
Jesse Jackson, *Jesse Jackson: Still Fighting for the Dream*
Andy Jacobs, Jr., "Replace 'The Star-Spangled Banner,'" *USA Today*
Chief Joseph, "An Indian's View of Indian Affairs," *Red & White: Indian Views of the White Man*
Linda Kanamine, "Wyoming Dinosaur Find May Be a Fossil First," *USA Today*
Jean Kerr, *Please Don't Eat the Daisies*
Henry Kisor, *What's That Pig Outdoors? A Memoir of Deafness*
James Kotsilibas-Davis, "Sands of Time," *Travel-Holiday*
John Lahr, "Introduction," *Baby, That Was Rock and Roll*
William Langewiesche, "The World In Its Extreme," *The Atlantic*
Gary Larson, *The Far Side Gallery*
William Least Heat-Moon, *Blue Highways*
Shannon Long, "Wheelchair Hell: A Look at Campus Accessibility, *"The Great American Bologna Festival and Other Student Essays*
Robert McCrum, et al., "From Japlish to Franglais," *The Story of English*
Marya Mannes, "How Do You Know It's Good?" *But Will It Sell?*
James Martin, "The Engaging Habits of Chameleons," *Smithsonian*
Mark Mathabane, *Kaffir Boy in America: An Encounter with Apartheid*
Pat Mora, "Why I Am a Writer," *The Horn Book Magazine*
Jane O'Connor and Katy Hall, "Once Is Not Enough," *Magic in the Movies: The Story of Special Effects*
S. J. Perelman, "Insert Flap 'A' and Throw Away," *The Most of S. J. Perelman*
Lila Perl, *From Top Hats to Baseball Caps, From Bustles to Blue Jeans*
Turk Pipkin, "Three Great Homemade Props," *Be a Clown!*
Spencer Reiss, "The Last Days of Eden," *Newsweek*
David Roberts, "The Decipherment of Ancient Maya," *The Atlantic*
Tony Seddon and Jill Bailey, "Animal Senses," *The Living World*
Alvin & Virginia Silverstein, *Dogs: All About Them*
"The Talk of the Town," *The New Yorker*
Paul Theroux, *Riding the Iron Rooster: By Train Through China*
Matt Tomlinson, "A Sit-Down Tour," *New Jersey Monthly*
Mark Twain, "Fenimore Cooper's Literary Offenses," *Laughing Matters: A Celebration of American Humor, Roughing It*
Fred Ward, "The Timeless Mystique of Emeralds," *National Geographic*
Geoffrey C. Ward with Ken Burns and Ric Burns, *The Civil War: An Illustrated History*
Peter Watrous, "Típica Sound of Cuba," *The New York Times*
"Whatzat? An Odd Bird with a Cow's Stomach," *National Geographic*
Vicki Williams, "Keep 'The Star-Spangled Banner,'" *USA Today*
Richard Wright, *American Hunger*
Mitchell Zuckoff, "Lax Regulation, Inadequate Laws Promote Insider-Lending Abuse," *The Boston Globe*

Poetry

Lucille Clifton, *An Ordinary Woman*
Anita Endrezze, "Sunset at Twin Lake," *Harper's Anthology of 20th Century Native American Poetry*
Emma Lazarus, "The New Colossus"
John Travers Moore, "Jet," *Town & Countryside Poems*
Dorothy Parker, "One Perfect Rose," *The Portable Dorothy Parker*
Ishmael Reed, "Beware: Do Not Read This Poem," *Catechism of a Neo-American Hoodoo Church*
John Updike, "Ex-Basketball Player," *The Carpentered Hen and Other Tame Creatures*

Drama

Lorraine Hansberry, *A Raisin in the Sun*

A Teacher's Guide to

ELEMENTS OF WRITING

CONTENTS

JAMES L. KINNEAVY

DONALD MURRAY

KAREN GREENBERG

Lee Odell

Barbara Shade

Maxine Hairston

Norbert Elliot

Patricia Tweeddale
Charles Leftwich

Wanda Schindley

A LETTER TO THE TEACHER FROM THE NEW AUTHOR JAMES L. KINNEAVY

HOW DARE THEY?

. . . IN THE SPIRIT OF MAINTAINING THE LASTING VALUES AND STANDARDS OF THE SERIES . . .

Certainly when teachers saw a new name listed as a coauthor with John E. Warriner, some of you must have said, "How can the editors dare do this?" Like the editors, I am fully aware that Warriner has been a legendary name in high school English composition and grammar books since 1941, the year of the first edition of his series, till the present. His high school textbooks have changed somewhat through the decades, but they have stood the test of half of a century—despite many educational trends and fashions—because they have incorporated important values and standards. I am aware of all of this, aware that Warriner's texts have almost a biblical authority.

But even the Bible is translated anew for different generations. So it is in the spirit of maintaining the lasting values and standards of the series while bringing a few further changes that this new edition of the series is published with a new name listed as coauthor. I was properly flattered when the company's editors asked me to be the consultant for the composition sections of the books in the new series. But I was also in awe of this long tradition of excellence and can only hope that this tradition can be upheld.

Like John E. Warriner, I have a long and varied experience as a teacher. He taught in junior high, high school, and college. I have taught in elementary school, high school, and college. He taught for many years; I have been teaching since 1941 and continue to teach today. For the past twenty-five years I have given workshops to high school students involved in statewide competitive contests in extemporaneous writing. Like Warriner, I have attempted to keep up with the profession and to reflect in my writings what we have learned and continue to learn about teaching the language arts. I have trained students to teach at all grade levels from elementary school through graduate school. I have also observed student teachers for years at the high school and college levels.

You will find in this series, therefore, an attempt to maintain the best values of the Warriner series and to add to it a few new features that teachers, administrators, scholars, and editors think will make it an even better set of books.

THE TEACHER'S EDITION IS A *GREAT* HELP

I know that teaching school combines the blue and white collar syndromes: You're there at 8:00 and leave at 4:00; then you take on extra-hour professional chores in the evening and on weekends of correcting papers, reading to keep up professionally (which you are doing right now), working on extracurricular activities,

James Kinneavy, with students at The University of Texas at Austin.

attending conventions, etc. You need all of the timesavers you can find.

You will find many of them in this edition. On each page you will find that your objectives, your lesson plan, and your resources are packed around the student text. Questions you can ask the students are provided (with answers). Vocabulary items are defined. Adaptations to more-advanced students, to less-advanced students, and to ESL students are suggested. Special exercises supplementing those in the textbook are provided. Student responses to questions are foreseen and reactions suggested. Applications to critical thinking and to cooperative learning are continually provided.

All in all these helps are a treasure trove. Before spending hours looking up supplementary materials for a class, look in your teacher's edition. Someone else may have done your work already and saved you hours. When I look at the wealth of all of these materials and contrast them to what I had to teach with in my early teaching years in both elementary and high school, I am green with envy.

Beginning teachers especially should exploit these materials, built upon the experiences of hundreds of their predecessors. These experiences can help new teachers avoid some all-too-common problems. Let me point out some of them.

RELATIONSHIP BETWEEN COMPOSITION AND GRAMMAR

You will find in the new series the same close relationship between composition and grammar that has characterized the series since its inception. You can see this by simply looking at the table of contents.

Such a look makes quite clear that the primacy and the preponderance of attention is given to writing, and that grammar is a handmaid to writing. But both are covered extensively.

Given the increasing importance of rhetoric in public schools and in college, you will find more depth in the composition section of this textbook. There is a more discernible structure to the various chapters on writing. These chapters reflect the concern for certain important kinds of writing—concerns that are reflected in many state writing tests. Thus, there is a chapter devoted to each of the major aims of writing: to inform, to persuade, to explain, to prove, to entertain, and to allow the students to express themselves. Each of the modes of writing usually gets a chapter at each grade level: narrating, describing, classifying and defining, and evaluating. This structure is more explicit in the new series than it was in the earlier ones.

In each of these chapters, however, the close relationship between composition and grammar

WHAT THIS TEXTBOOK DOES NOT WANT TO DO IS TO ENCOURAGE THE ISOLATED TEACHING OF GRAMMATICAL SKILLS IN A ROTE MANNER.

is maintained. There is a grammatical issue covered in each chapter, particularly relevant to the kind of writing being covered. Thus, a chapter on persuasion can consider the problem of fragments, often seen in advertisements. A chapter on description can consider the importance of adjectives and adverbs. Finally, nearly all of these chapters refer to the grammar chapters for coverage of issues that relate to the kind of writing under consideration.

This careful attempt to relate grammar to composition was explicit in the longtime title of this series, which has linked grammar to composition for years.

This linkage is confirmed by seventy years of *empirical research*. Studies at all levels, from elementary school through college, confirm that grammar is learned best when taught in conjunction with composition, as well as with speaking and with literature. These studies have been made in the United States, in Canada, in the British Isles, and in Australia. What this textbook does not want to do is to encourage the isolated teaching of grammatical skills in a rote manner. This is called the formal teaching of grammar. Sometimes, it has to be done. But most of the time, the grammar is linked to a writing assignment and even motivated by it. For instance, consistent fragments in a formal paper suggest a lesson in the sentence, emphasizing its elements and its completeness. This improves the composition and also teaches the grammar in a manner that gives it meaning.

THE PROCESSES OF COMPOSING

In keeping with the emphasis in the schools and in college writing courses, you will find a continuation of the unremitting concern with the processes of writing in every writing chapter of the series—a concern begun several years ago. The stress on process will be evident in the structuring of the chapters by the stages of the writing process; in the frequent use of support groups of students to react to each other's plans, drafts, and papers; and in teacher and peer interventions in the writing process. The idea that writing is a solitary, sedentary process, as a poet once said, is not at all adhered to in this textbook. Rather writing is viewed as a collaborative and cooperative action.

A COOPERATIVE ATMOSPHERE

The process view of writing that sees the writing place as a happy, cooperative workshop rather than a silent dungeon enables the students to get support and help from one another and from the teacher.

The students are usually divided into *peer support groups* of three or four, all working on similar projects, and all trying to help each other turn out better work. The members of the groups help one another plan the papers, critique each other's rough drafts, and provide a real audience for the final version. The members of the group are like a miniature research group working on a common project.

THIS *DOMINANCE OF THE WHOLE OVER THE PARTS* EXPLAINS THE GENERAL STRUCTURE OF THE BOOK. THE WRITING CHAPTERS COME AT THE BEGINNING OF THE BOOK, AND THE GRAMMAR, USAGE, AND MECHANICS MAKE UP THE LAST SECTION OF THE BOOK.

The *teacher* moves from group to group, helping in the planning, discussing problems, critiquing rough drafts, and grading the final drafts. Like the members of the peer support groups, the teacher fulfills different functions: at times the teacher is a motivator, a source of ideas, a theorist who has general ideas that apply to the current situation, a careful listener, a constructive critic of plans and rough drafts, a sympathetic reader and grader of the final version, and above all, a fellow writer.

With this view of the writing process, the teacher with a *heavy paper load* can find help from the students. The teacher isn't the only person who reads a student's paper. The other members of the support group can assist the teacher with useful feedback to the author at any level of the writer's concerns with mechanics, with word choice, with organization, with ideas, and with style. If the teacher trains support groups to be helpful and constructively critical, a good deal of the drudgery of grading papers can be avoided.

Finally, the writing process often results in some kind of *publication*, possibly in a public speech (or in a performance in the case of creative writing), sometimes in a class newspaper put out by desktop publishing on a computer, sometimes in a school newspaper, or maybe just in a permanent portfolio that the student keeps of his or her better work.

THE WHOLE AND THE PARTS

Another motif that you will see given more prominence from the very beginning and running through all of the writing chapters is the insistence on the relationship between the whole and the parts in the composing process. A theme is like a sentence: It is made up of parts that are uttered in a chronological sequence, but the whole is greater than the parts because it also includes the relationships among the parts and with the whole. We don't begin a sentence with no idea where it is going to end or what it is going to say; we begin with a whole and choose the parts to articulate it. We may change our minds halfway through a sentence and adjust to our new idea; the same phenomenon often happens with a whole theme.

THE IDEA IS TO SUPPORT THE WRITING PROCESS AS A CREATIVE SURGE IN THE BEGINNING. THE MECHANICAL MATTERS ARE OFTEN BETTER HANDLED IN THE REVISION.

In other words, a theme begins with a vague but somewhat distinct idea of a whole and looks around for the parts that will embody that idea. The parts are single words, phrases, sentences, paragraphs, even large sections of the theme.

Consequently, in the writing chapters, each of these parts is treated as a part of a whole. A composition is not an expanded word or phrase or paragraph. An expanded paragraph is a big paragraph, just as an expanded wheel is just a big wheel, not suddenly a complete automobile. To use another metaphor, a student setting out to write a composition is like an architect who draws up a plan of the whole building; it's going to be a home or a department store or a restaurant or a sports coliseum or whatever. But the architect doesn't haphazardly gather bricks and steel and staircases and chimneys and just throw them together.

With this idea of the dominance of the whole over the parts, each of the writing chapters pursues the writing process through to the production of a complete theme. There are writing activities throughout addressing the parts, but they are all orchestrated to the final whole.

This *dominance of the whole over the parts* explains the general structure of the textbook. The writing chapters come at the beginning, and the grammar, usage, and mechanics make up the last section.

In fact, the suggested treatment for writing encourages the students to write rapidly and enthusiastically in their first plans, sketches, and drafts, without stopping to check spelling, word choice, or grammatical purity. The idea is to support the writing process as a creative surge in the beginning. The mechanical matters are often better handled in revision.

AIMS AND MODES AS WAYS OF THINKING

The close connections among the aims and modes of writing and rather different ways of thinking have been emphasized in the introduction to the student's edition, so these will not be repeated here in any detail. But at the heart of the series is the notion that writing involves thinking all of the time; and different ways of writing involve different ways of thinking. Expressive writing is quite different from expository writing, and some students can do one type better than another. Nevertheless, a minimum competence in each aim and mode is necessary to the development of a full mental life. You are encouraged to reread the **"Introduction to Writing"** chapter to see the development of this notion.

THE AIMS OF WRITING AND DIFFERENT DIALECTS

You will undoubtedly notice that different levels of formality are suggested with the different aims of writing. In the chapters on expressive writing, a casual, personal, and familiar style is suggested. At the other extreme, in the chapters on information and proof, a more formal sense of grammar and word choice is expected. This is true in real life and in the classroom. In between self-expression and these types of expository writing, there are various shades of formality in persuasive, creative, and exploratory writing.

The model adopted here is that of Martin Joos, whose book *The Five Clocks* distinguishes five different levels of formality that nearly all of us use, depending on the circumstances. Joos calls these the intimate, the colloquial, the consultative, the formal, and the ritual levels. We speak to our family members (and sometimes our pets) in the familiar dialect. We speak to our friends in an ordinary conversation on the colloquial level. We adopt the consultative tone usually when we are teaching class. We use our formal dialect when we are giving speeches at a convention. And we use the ritual level of formality when we are at church or are graduating or are being initiated into a society.

But teachers are not the only people who have their five levels of formality. Teenagers also have their own dialects for intimacy—I say dialects because girls have a different intimate dialect than do boys. Teenagers also have their own colloquial, consultative, formal, and ritual dialects. Mature people have their own five levels. Finally, the elderly have their own five dialects, often quite different from the other age levels.

Being aware of the different purposes for writing and the various levels of formality also helps the teacher be more aware of ***minority dialects***, such as those used by Hispanic, Asian, and African Americans. The use of these dialects in expressive and sometimes in creative writing is often to be encouraged. On the other hand, the dialect of the targeted audience is to be encouraged in persuasion. In expository writing, there is more emphasis on the standard dialect.

WRITING AND LITERATURE

While you are teaching this book on handling writing and grammar, you are also using a separate textbook for literature. But the necessity of putting the major readings in different literary genres covered in the eleventh grade in a special book should not at all imply a separation of the study of literature from that of writing or grammar. All through the literature book, there are writing assignments that cover the same purposes that are taught in the writing book. Students are asked to react expressively, persuasively, creatively, and informatively to literary selections. Thus the literature textbook resonates the same tones and rhythms as the writing textbook.

Conversely, this series is permeated with reading and literature. Each writing chapter includes models of the type of writing that is being studied. Many samples are drawn from the literary canon. In one of the textbooks, for instance, to illustrate the aims of writing, there is an excellent poem by William Stafford. Nearly every chapter in the student's edition contains similar material. Of course, all of these selections are annotated.

Further, in this edition, in each chapter of the book there are **Literature Links**, which take common literary selections and relate them to the material being studied in the chapter. Besides the **Literature Links**, there is the **Quotation for the Day**, a writing prompt drawn from literature.

Some writing chapters are almost completely devoted to literary writing, especially the chapters on creative writing, narration, and description.

Thus writing and literature are highly integrated by a common underlying philosophy of language.

WRITING AND THE OTHER LANGUAGE ARTS

In addition to being highly integrated with literature, this writing textbook is also tightly integrated with reading, speaking, and listening.

Each chapter contains several reading samples of the type of writing being studied. These are carefully analyzed by the students by means of questions after each selection. These questions are usually answered in an oral forum. The oral emphasis continues throughout the chapter because each stage of the writing process is carried out by means of small support groups of three or four students helping each other in planning, organizing, writing, and revising, as explained above. Frequently the publication of the paper takes an oral form. Thus persuasive speeches are delivered in front of the class.

The support group is clearly as much of a listening group as it is a speaking group. Students learn to listen carefully to each other in order to make constructive suggestions for improvement.

Thus the four language arts are carefully interwoven into the structure of each chapter at each stage of the writing process.

WRITING AND NEW TECHNOLOGIES

Whenever possible, teachers should take advantage of the new technologies that are increasingly becoming available at the high school level. Consequently, throughout this edition, there are continual reminders of these possibilities. Let us mention a few of them.

Networking with Computers

Some high schools have word processors available for use in teaching some writing classes. A few of these are even networked to allow student interactions with each other, either with the entire class or with selected support groups. The simultaneous writing reactions of all members of the class to a common reading assignment is one of the most effective methods to insure one hundred percent participation in group discussions, especially if the right questions are asked. And the use of computers to set up small support groups for the different stages of the writing process is also an exceptionally efficient technique of using small groups in teaching writing.

Revising and Word Processors

Even without networking, however, the use of word processors is to be commended whenever possible, particularly because of the manner in which revising is accomplished on computers. Students who formerly hated to revise now see revision as an easy and enjoyable manner to improve their work, not just at the level of vocabulary or mechanics, but even at the level of full discourse changes.

Spelling, Vocabulary, Grammar, and Word Processors

Word processors also bring substantial help to the poor speller and to the student having trouble finding the right word. Nearly all word-processing programs have some type of spell-check feature that shows students which words are incorrectly spelled. Thus each student can keep a list of his or her own problem words. This is acknowledged by nearly all spelling research as the single best way to improve spelling. Most spell-check programs are accompanied by programs that properly hyphenate words at the end of a line. This is an additional bonus for students who use word processors.

In addition, most word processors now come with a thesaurus of some size. This enables the students to look for options in vocabulary, even while working at the computer.

Thirdly, some word processors now have grammar programs that can check tense, case, subject-verb agreement, fragments, etc. These are not as common as spell-check features or thesauruses, but they are becoming available.

Publishing and Word Processors

Even if there is not a full classroom of word processors, it is possible to use a word processor as a desktop publisher to enable students to see some of their writings in elegant print and format. These can be put into portfolios for permanent records. Frequently throughout the annotated teacher's edition you are reminded of this option as one method of publishing the students' papers.

A FINAL WORD: USE YOUR OWN PERSONAL STAFF

Possibly after reading this essay, which brings together many of the rather complex tasks of the writing teacher, you may have been somewhat intimidated. But luckily you don't have to solve all of these problems overnight. The teaching of writing is a slow and cumulative process. Each chapter of this textbook focuses on a very specific issue and tries to teach just that particular skill. Following chapters build on the skill just learned. The student is slowly building up a range of abilities, not suddenly moving from barbarism to literacy.

Of course, in the preceding grades, your predecessors have worked with the students whom you now face, just as your colleagues will pick up where you leave off. And you are not alone at the present time: Your current colleagues are working with the same students in other classes.

In other words, just as writing is a cooperative endeavor among the students with each other and with you in your classroom, so also is it a cooperative endeavor among a sequence of teachers from year to year and among a group of teachers one year at a time. In many cases, parents are also willing cooperators.

Put Your Staff to Work

This textbook adds several more dimensions of helpmates. The authors are seasoned professionals who have faced many of the issues of these chapters before. These authors draw on other textbooks with which they are familiar. They also draw heavily on scholars that they have consulted. Thus, when I said earlier that the best way for a poor speller to improve spelling skills was to keep a journal list of personal mistakes, add to it when new mistakes are made, and consult this personal list regularly, this statement was drawing on ten years of research at two major universities with thousands of students. The marketing staff of this series is also made up of seasoned professionals who make it their business to find out what teachers want in a textbook. The teaching consultants who tried out the materials for these chapters were chosen because of their experience and knowledge. Finally, the editors of this series are acknowledged masters in their field—they have marketed the best-selling series in writing and grammar for almost half of a century.

Thus, you the teacher are backed by a phalanx of authors, scholars, market experts, teacher consultants, and editors all trying to assist you as you work with your students and other teachers. They are really your own personal staff. Use this book intelligently and this staff springs to life at your command. Donne's statement particularly can be applied to teachers: "No teacher is an island."

This textbook tries to put you in touch with all of these other helpers in the business of education. It can take a good deal of the loneliness out of teaching.

No One Does A More Important Job

Finally, you should be assured that your task is at the top of educational priorities. No one does a more important job than the teacher of writing. Throughout history, people who can write have been considered educated. Writing, in fact, has been the hallmark of the educated person in antiquity, in the Middle Ages (they were called clerks at that time), and in the modern period as well. A person who teaches students how to write is at the forefront of the educational enterprise. Such a person is also teaching students how to think in ways that will enable them to cope with a complex modern society as full human beings. ❦

ELEMENTS OF WRITING addresses the ***aims*** and ***modes*** of writing and the ***writing process*** in the following ways:

Pupil's Edition

Demonstrates and teaches writing skills, focusing on the aims (the *why*) and the modes (the *how*) of writing

Provides an organized, easily understood approach that allows students to gain and sharpen writing skills

Annotated Teacher's Edition

Gives instructional strategies on how to teach the aims and modes

Offers lesson plans based on each stage of the writing process

Teacher's ResourceBank ™

Offers materials keyed to the writing process that assist students in achieving the aims and modes

BY DONALD M. MURRAY

USE GENRE AS LENS

"WE WRITE ABOUT WHAT WE DON'T KNOW ABOUT WHAT WE KNOW."

Students are usually introduced to each genre—essay, narrative, poem—in isolated units, as if one form of writing would contaminate another. But each genre is a lens, a way to observe, record, and examine the world. Students should be encouraged to use each genre to explore a single important experience.

Student writers and their teachers should begin the exploration with a personal experience—an event, a person, a place—that holds a significant mystery for them. Mystery is the starting place for most writing, what Grace Paley described when she said, "We write about what we don't know about what we know." Invite your students to explore a moment in their lives to which they keep returning in memory, the way the tongue seeks the missing tooth.

Encourage your students to play with the fragments of language connected with that experience in their minds and on paper to discover a line, a phrase, or a word that contains a tension or conflict within the experience. The "line" might be a word—*Christmas*—that might have special implications for a student with a Catholic mother and a Jewish father. It might be a phrase—*the debts of Christmas*—to a person whose family spends too much money to make up for their true family feelings. The "line" could be a sentence—"Each Christmas I remember my sister who will never grow old"—for someone who lost a sister years before. Each "line" has a tension and mystery the writer needs to understand by writing.

Before your students begin, it is important to remind them that all writing is experimental, that experimentation implies failure, and that failure is instructive. It is not possible they will fail; it is imperative that they fail. We do not improve our writing by avoiding failure, but by making use of it.

To guarantee failure, urge students to write the first draft fast. Velocity is as important in writing as it is in bicycle racing. Speed will produce the accidents of language, connection, and insight that will propel the draft forward towards meaning. And velocity allows students to escape, for the moment, the censor that demands premature correctness.

They should allow their drafts to instruct them. The evolving text will take its own course, exploring the experience as it is relived. If they are patient, receptive, and open to surprise, the text will tell them what they have to say. You may want to write two statements by E. M. Forster on the chalkboard:

Think before you speak is criticism's motto; speak before you think creation's.

and

How do I know what I think until I see what I say?

Students should write out loud, hearing the text as they write it. They may actually do this—it is your classroom—or read silently but *listen* to the text. As they tune their voices to the story being told, the voice—angry, nostalgic, humorous, sad, analytical, instructive, argumentative, poetic, even narrative—will reveal the meaning of the draft to the writer.

I invite you to stand beside me at my workbench and to observe me

AT HOME ON A WINTERY MORNING, DON MURRAY ENJOYS HIS FAVORITE TIME OF THE DAY.

as I use genre to explore an experience of mine.

THE ESSAY

I prefer the term *reflective essay* to *personal essay* because the writer reflects on personal experience, or on a topic of personal interest. The essay is neither a simple narrative of experience nor of thought unanchored by experience, but a combination of thought and experience, an effort to discover and share meaning in experience. The essay is a demonstration of critical thinking.

Some notes on the craft of the essay.

- Narrow the territory to be explored so you can achieve depth.
- Be specific. The specific will instruct. The more specific you are, the more universal your audience will be.
- Work locally; the paragraph you have just written contains the seed of the next paragraph. For example, if you have said the experience was important, show how it was important in the next paragraph.
- Answer the reader's questions. Writing is a conversation between reader and writer.
- When the draft surprises you, pay attention. Develop the surprise to discover its meaning.

On April 21, while visiting a daughter and her husband in their new home, I got up early without the alarm, as is my habit, and ended up sitting at the top of the stairs waiting for my family to wake, and I found mystery in the experience. It was a moment full of emotion, and I needed—not wanted, but needed—to explore that moment through writing.

I made a few notes in my daybook:

I can remember myself as a small boy in Doctor Denton's trying to be quiet sitting at the head of the stairs (night) waiting for the family to get up

I can remember my own daughter's impatient waiting

Sunday morning I sit at the head of the stairs a good place to read, a good place legs waiting, wife, behind me in the room, my wife

It is 8 AM and they plan on rising 9 AM, I've been up at 5:33, explored town, coffee, read Sunday NY Times

The next day I wrote the column that was published in *The Boston Globe*, April 30, 1991:

I am once again a small boy in Dr. Denton's sitting at the top of the stairs waiting for the snoring to stop and another day to begin.

I am, at the same time, an old man sitting at the top of the stairs in the new home of a daughter and her husband, waiting once more for the snoring to stop and a new day to begin.

Minnie Mae and I, on our first visit, have taken their bed, and they sleep on the hide-a-bed in the living room. They work in the theatre and have agreed to get up early—at 9 o'clock on Sunday morning—because the old folks are here.

But I followed the custom of many old men and was up at 5:33 AM. I tiptoed downstairs, went out to the car, explored Mount Kisco, sipped a cup of coffee at Dunkin Donuts—yes, and had a doughnut, and yes, juice to get down my six pills I take because of previous doughnuts—bought the Sunday *New York Times*, sat in the car reading it, and now, at eight AM sit at the head of the stairs where I can stretch my legs, flex my football knee, and read my book and wait.

It has been a good morning, and I feel little guilt that I have not been able to sleep in. They will laugh at my compulsion to be up and doing, and I will tease them for their laziness, but they will not understand the joy I, like many over sixties, experience when I am up in the lonely hours of dawn.

I ruminate—early morning is ideal for rumination—on the fact that as a child I was always up early when I could lose myself in a book—no TV then—explore the backyard or the vacant lot where the morning glories grew.

Awake before the grown-ups, I could be what I needed to be: Lindbergh crossing the Atlantic alone, Admiral Byrd isolated in his tiny room under the Antarctic ice, the unnamed Indian scout watching the palefaces land on the Maine coast.

As a teenager I bicycled my route for Gallagher's News Agency in Quincy finishing before the sun was up, drove Miller's grocery truck to market in Boston or cleaned the vegetables and laid them out in rows on the boxes balanced in front of the small store on Beach street.

Only now I confess that when I nicked myself trimming the lettuce that was packed in ice, my hands numb and clumsy, I would turn that lettuce head so the blood did not show. I was apprentice to Miller's game: profit through deceit.

I still remember playing grown-up early in the morning, the grocer's apron twice tucked so it did not sweep the sawdust strewn floor. The profit would be Miller's not mine, but I anticipated the customers who might, this Depression Saturday, pay cash. That anticipation would last until midnight when Mr. Miller would go out and scan the street right and left and reluctantly, when no one was on the street, give the command to close.

In combat I preferred the early morning patrols, guard duty when I was alone to watch the theatre of morning's change from dark to light, the promise of a new day even when the landscape was littered with last night's dead.

After college I worked for a morning newspaper and liked the mystery and companionship of the night worker, enjoyed the coming home at dawn. Eventually I returned to days, and morning became my best writing time as it is for most writers.

Goethe advised, "Use the day before the day. Early morning hours have gold in their mouth."

John Hersey testified that "To be a writer is to sit down at one's desk in the chill portion of every day, and to write." A few years ago poet Donald Hall said, "I get up at 5 without an alarm. This morning I didn't get up until 5:45, because I stayed up until 11:15 watching the NCAA basketball. But in summer I'll be up at 4:30, make coffee, let out the dog, go pick up *The Boston Globe*. Then I write."

In retirement I, like so many other over sixties, still get up early when there are no cows to milk, no commuter train to meet, no factory shift to join. It is habit, but for me a habit built not from compulsion but delight.

Sitting at the top of the stairs waiting for the young—and the not-so-young Minnie Mae—to wake, I try to define the strange emotion I feel. At last it comes to me. I am, after a lifetime of chasing the carrot, content.

I have another day to celebrate. Sitting here alone, I can enjoy the feeling of this house that is turning so quickly into a home. I am comfortable in this home and know that soon my wife will wake with a groan and a smile, and downstairs I will hear conversation and music, smell coffee and we will all make plans for the day not too far off when a grandchild will sit where I sit, perhaps beside me, waiting for another day to begin.

The grandchild has arrived. His name is Joshua. I have not yet sat beside him at the top of the stairs but I will.

THIS MORNING I DIDN'T GET UP UNTIL 5:45, BECAUSE I STAYED UP UNTIL 11:15 WATCHING THE NCAA BASKETBALL. BUT IN SUMMER I'LL BE UP AT 4:30, MAKE COFFEE, LET OUT THE DOG, GO PICK UP *THE BOSTON GLOBE*. THEN I WRITE."

THE NARRATIVE

There are many wonderful ways to tell stories, but I suggest student fiction writers begin with the scene.

Conrad is supposed to have said that a novel is a series of scenes of confrontation. The writer experienced in nonfiction tells *about* the story; the fiction writer *reveals* the story. That is an enormous difference, and the writing of a scene is the best way to cross the divide. Students can draw on their experiences with TV and film. The reader observes a room with the fourth wall removed; the action within the room tells the story and the reader discovers its meaning. As the short-story writer Becky Rule points out, students think that fiction has no rules, but the rules come from the story, and they are established early; if Hamlet is an indecisive prince he can suddenly become a king but not a decisive one.

Some notes on the craft of narrative.

- Start with character, not theme. The story and its meaning are revealed through the interaction of the characters.
- Write in the third person. It gives you more room and detachment.
- Dialogue is action, what the characters do to each other. Joan Didion says, "I don't have a very clear idea of who the characters are until they start talking."
- Point of view is where the camera is positioned to record the scene. In the beginning, stick with one point of view, perhaps entering into one head but not jumping in and out of every head. If you are in one sister's head, you don't know Frank is in the freezer; in the other sister's head, you do.
- Kurt Vonnegut counsels, "Don't put anything in a story that does not reveal character or advance the action."

In writing a draft of my novel, I found myself stealing the experience from my own essay and began a scene:

Melissa found Iain sitting in the shadows at the top of the stairs, "It's 5:30 in the morning."

He nodded.

"On guard duty?"

"In a way. I often sit here in winter, watch the light just before dawn, the woods, the field that goes down to the lake."

She thought for a moment of what it would be like to be a spy to your life, always on guard and asked, "You said last night that wherever you are, you see a field of fire, are aware of where to dig in, put the machine guns, even after all these years?"

"I'm not proud of it, Melissa. It's just my geography, an infantryman's geography."

"Do you always see a geography of war?"

"Always first, then I can make it go away. Most times. It's natural, just the way I see things. The doctor sees you as kidney or a colon; I'm an old soldier, I see a field of fire, where the attack would come from."

"That's sad."

"Tedd's a soldier too, Melissa."

They hear the key probe for the lock, at last find it, and hurried down the stairs....

That is just a small fragment of narrative, and yet you can see how the story is revealing itself dramatically to the writer and the reader.

THE POEM

Poetry is the most disciplined and difficult form of writing. It is also the most fun. Experience is distilled by the writing of poetry. Poetry is always play—play with image and language so that meaning is revealed directly without rhetoric getting between the writer and reader or between experience and reader. Inexperienced poets often write with adjectives and adverbs, trying to describe their own feelings. The experienced poet writes with information, revealing specifics, provocative details, and compelling images that make the reader feel and think. The meaning is rarely stated but always there. In the poem, even more than fiction, the meaning is implied. The poem is the stimulus to the reader's thinking.

Some notes on the craft of poetry.

- Forget, for the moment, rhyme, meter, and traditional verse forms.

• Brainstorm images and other specifics, creating a list that may become a poem.
• Draft lines—not sentences but fragments of language—that capture an event, person, or place.
• Rearrange the lines until they reveal a meaningful pattern.
• Pay attention to the line breaks, trying to end on a strong word that causes the reader to read on.

The morning I wrote the column, I also wrote, on the computer, what might become a poem for my poetry group that was meeting that Thursday evening. I pasted this in my daybook:

Sitting at the top of the
stairs
I listen to the silences
to understand Grandma's
war with Mother

Sitting at the top of the
stairs
I tune
train myself to 1
elinesss

Later that day I made a handwritten note I also cut out and pasted in the daybook:

I lived at the top of the
stairs, behind the living room
couch, under the dining room
table, the tent of tablecloth–
in the apple tree, under the
porch,

And still later I drafted a poem that went through one radical and three or four extensive revisions (periods of word play) until it became the following completed poem:

Childhood Espionage

Spy to my life, I lived at the
top of the stairs, recorded
silence, mapped how hurt was
done. Under the porch, at the
bedroom door, behind living
room

sofa, I filled notebooks with
what was not said, not done,
escaped to the sidewalk, tried
to read the shades drawn
against my life. It must be
Mother's shadow

sitting on the edge of the
double bed, must be father's
kneeling to pray. I cannot be
sure, circle the block,
listen to the neighbor's opera
of argument , stand under

an open window where
conversation will pour over me
Once I saw my friend's older
sister. She never pulled the
shade. The dogs learned my
smell

and let me patrol back yard,
alley, vacant lot, in silence. I
found the room where the
Beckers kept the boy with the
enormous head, watched
comfort flow

from a priest's dancing hands
as he gave the last rites to
Vinnie's grandma, swayed to
the rhythm of the Mitchells'
bedroom dancing, lying down.
Late, I returned to the home

of closed doors where we
passed each other without
touching. We never raised our
voices, never stood between

light and shade, never let a
secret fall out a window.

Students should be encouraged to take central experiences from their lives—Willa Cather said, "Most of the basic material a writer works with is acquired before the age of fifteen"—and explore them with an array of genre, using each lens—essay, narrative, poem—and then examining the subject through other genre, perhaps argument, report, screenplay, or news story, to discover the many meanings in their lives.❦

Sources quoted include Grace Paley, Joan Didion, and Kurt Vonnegut cited in the following work: Donald M. Murray, *Shoptalk: Learning to Write with Writers*, Boynton/ Cook Publishers, Inc., 1990.

ELEMENTS OF WRITING addresses the *aims* and *modes* of writing and the *writing process* in the following ways:

Pupil's Edition
Demonstrates and teaches writing skills, focusing on the aims (the *why*) and the modes (the *how*) of writing
Provides an organized, easily understood approach that allows students to gain and sharpen writing skills

Annotated Teacher's Edition
Gives instructional strategies on how to teach the aims and modes
Offers lesson plans based on each stage of the writing process

Teacher's ResourceBank ™
Offers materials keyed to the writing process that assist students in achieving the aims and modes

By James L. Kinneavy

Meet the Aims and Modes of Writing

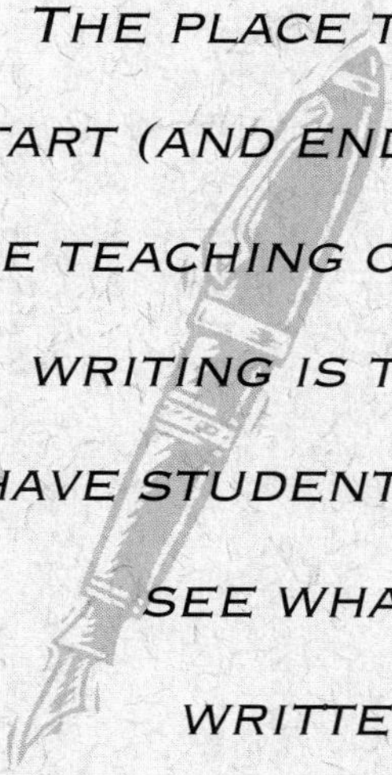

The place to start (and end) the teaching of writing is to have students see what written language can do for them.

Why Write? Where Do I Begin?

Writing is a very complex activity, and so is the teaching of writing. I admit these facts, and I have been teaching writing for fifty years. You may be teaching your first class this year, and you probably have the same problem: In the face of this complex process, where do you start?

Some teachers recommend what may seem to be a very simple and logical approach: Start with the simple building blocks of writing and gradually work up to more complex blocks. In other words, teach students some elementary things about words, then move up to phrases, afterwards teach sentences, eventually work up to paragraphs, and finally, have students write full themes. Some say that this is how children learn to use language orally. At first blush this theory has a kind of plausible simplicity to it. Years of research, however, have shown that it doesn't work and that it isn't the way children learn language.

Language Gets Things Done

Babies see that family members around them accomplish things by using language, and they quickly learn to use it themselves to get food, drink, or attention. This is the motivation behind all language acquisition and usage, from cradle to grave—language gets things done.

Consequently, if we can keep this elementary driving force behind our attempts to teach writing (or any language art for that matter), we can draw on a basic incentive that even babies understand. But when language teaching is divorced from getting things done, students rightly find it boring and uninteresting.

For this reason, the place to start (and end) the teaching of writing is to have students see what written language can do for them. What can writing do? In one introductory chapter, we attempt to get students to look around and see what language is getting done. We call language-users the hidden agents behind many of the miracles of our age, we say that language is where the action is, and we call language-users the movers and shakers of the world.

We focus the student's attention on the different kinds of things that language accomplishes, using very concrete examples. But the principle is the same at every grade-level and on into the college educations, careers, and adult lives of our graduates: The central concept in the teaching of writing at every level is an awareness of the aims or purposes of writing.

The Four Major Aims of Writing

Luckily for you, as well as for the students, these aims are not infinite, unpredictable, and unmanageable. They can be reduced to a few basic categories, and both you and the students have a good deal of practical experience with the categories in general. For example, one kind of language experience with which you are very familiar has to do with attempts to explain to or inform an audience about something of which it is partially or totally ignorant. You do this daily in the classroom and the students are the targets of this use of language. Other examples of this kind of writing are news stories in newspapers and magazines, encyclopedia articles, reports, textbooks, discussions, proposed solutions to problems, research studies, etc. The emphasis is always on the subject matter, considered more or less objectively. *This kind of writing is generically referred to as expository writing.*

As a teacher, you are only too aware of a second kind of writing that places more emphasis on the writer. In this case, the writing reveals the feelings of the writer, allows the writer to voice his or her aspirations or reactions to something in a quite personal way, or gives the writer a chance to articulate important beliefs. Examples of this kind of writing are journals, diaries, myths, prayers, credos, and protests. Of course, some of this writing may also overlap with other kinds. The major emphasis in this kind of writing is on the writer. *This kind of writing is often called expressive writing.*

As a teacher, you often try to convince your students of the importance of an education and of their duties as citizens. As a matter of fact, in our culture we are bombarded with attempts to get readers to vote a certain way, to change attitudes or beliefs, to buy certain products, to switch allegiances, etc. Examples of such writing are advertising, political speeches, legal oratory, editorials, and religious sermons. In all of these cases, the focus of the use of language is on the receiver of the message. *Usually, this kind of writing is called rhetorical or persuasive writing.*

A fourth kind of writing, probably your favorite, is literature. This type of writing is given an honored place in English classes. We read selections of literature. They are intended to delight us and sometimes to teach us lessons. Examples of literature range from simple jokes, funny stories, ballads, small poems, and TV sitcoms to serious dramas, movies, novels, and epics. We try to get students to write this way when we teach creative writing. *Although all writing involves originality, we usually reserve the term* creative writing *for this kind of writing.*

THE COMMUNICATION BASIS OF THE AIMS OF WRITING

As a perceptive reader, you may have noticed as we went through the four major aims of writing that each one emphasized a different element of the communication process. It is not accidental that the major purposes of writing generally can be reduced to four. The structure of the written communication process is based on a writer, a reader, a language, and the subject matter; you may have seen these elements presented in a graphic form, such as the communication triangle shown below.

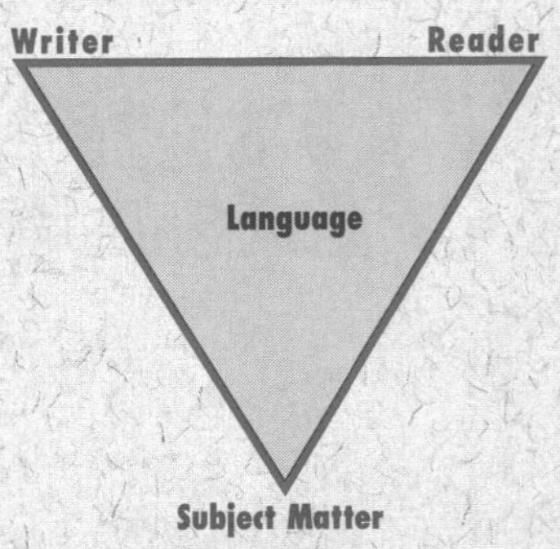

The major parts of the communication process.

You will find that students usually recognize that these four elements all play an important role in the writing process, but it is more difficult to get them to see that the role of each element changes in the different aims of writing.

CHANGING ROLES OF ELEMENTS IN DIFFERENT AIMS

In the expressive aim, as we pointed out above, the major focus of the attention is on the writer; the reader, language, and subject matter take on secondary roles. In persuasion, on the other hand, the reader takes center stage; the writer, though present, wants to get the message acted upon and uses language and subject matter to achieve this end.

In expository writing, the subject matter is given the lead role in the communication drama; the writer, reader, and language are subordinate to the explanation, proof, or communication of information that is involved. In literature, finally, the emphasis is on the beauty of the literary craftsmanship as an object of delight to the reader; the subject matter and the author, though present, are not as important as the literary object. When we are studying *Huck Finn*, the novel is more important than either Mark Twain or life on the Mississippi as experienced by a young white boy and a black man.

To assist you to get students to see these differing roles, the relationship between the elements of the communication process and those of the aims of discourse is expressed graphically below (the major aims of writing and the main parts of the communication process).

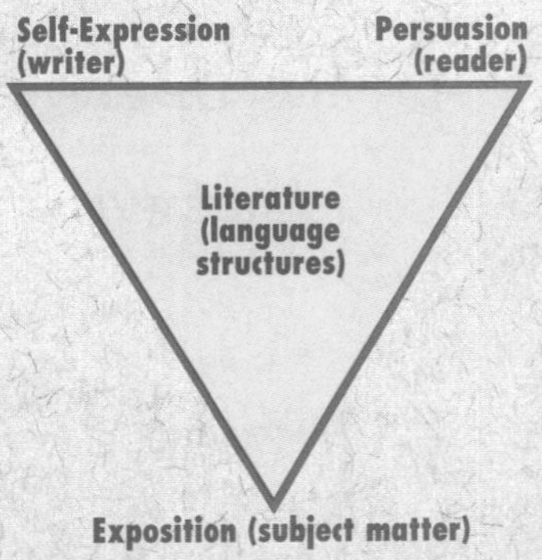

The major aims of writing.

Consequently, from aim to aim there is a continual shifting of roles in the communication process. The lead role determines the major purpose of the writing and the other roles become subordinate. Many teachers have found that this simple diagram enables students to grasp the changing dynamics of language use.

AS A TEACHER, YOU OFTEN TRY TO CONVINCE YOUR STUDENTS OF THE IMPORTANCE OF AN EDUCATION . . .

JAMES L. KINNEAVY
AUTHOR OF
ELEMENTS OF WRITING

DOMINANT AIMS AND OVERLAP

As a teacher, you have probably written one or two of these different kinds of writing, but you may not have written all of them. In your own writing you are certainly aware that most writing does not attempt to achieve all of these aims at the same time. A specific piece of writing usually has a single dominant aim, subordinating the others to avoid conflicts and confusion. Though subordinate, the other aims are still present. Thus, movie ads in the newspaper contain important information about actors, actresses, directors, titles, show times, etc., but the information is there to persuade people to come to the movies.

Similarly, a scientific report proving that smelters of Sudbury, Ontario, affect the ecology of the area emphasizes in an objective way the evidence for this hypothesis. But there is clearly the implicit notion that something ought to be done about it (a persuasive strain). Indeed, all the aims overlap each other.

WHY ARE THE BASIC AIMS IMPORTANT?

Despite overlaps, however, it is quite important to distinguish the various aims. It is crucial that both teachers and students understand why.

As a teacher, you are very aware that the criteria by which one kind of discourse is judged are different from the criteria by which another kind of discourse is judged. You know and try to impress upon your students that expository writing is judged on the basis of objective evidence; the appeal of the writer as such is not relevant to the final proof or explanation, nor is the use of emotion or humor. For this reason, you know that when you teach expository writing, it is important to discourage the use of these other kinds of appeal—they are, in fact, considered inappropriate in news stories, scientific reports, or textbooks. Thus the pedagogy of expository writing follows from the nature of this kind of writing.

But when you switch to teaching other kinds of writing, these other appeals are positive and important. In persuasion, for example, the emphasis is on the appeal of the writer and the appeal to the interests of the audience. The differences among exposition, persuasion, literature, and self-expression force you to emphasize different criteria when teaching these different kinds of writing. There is no single criterion of aim which makes all writing good. That is why the different aims are taught separately.

THE MODES OF WRITING

After all this talk about the aims of writing, you, as a teacher, might very well say to me, "Well, Mr. Kinneavy, all this may be very true. But are you maintaining that if I get students to pay attention to the aims of their writing, all other problems will disappear? There are many other facets of the process of writing to which we teachers have to pay attention. Grammar is clearly a persistent concern, as are spelling, vocabulary, sentence structure, paragraphing, genres of writing (letter, report, story, poem, speech, ad, etc.), subject matter, and last but not least, the modes. What do you propose to do with all of these issues?"

I recognize all of these concerns and reply that they will be given close and continuous attention throughout the entire course, but in this introduction I would like to stress the last dimension, that of the modes of writing.

This dimension bridges the two mentioned just before it—genre and subject matter, and it implicates a major concern of all writing teachers—organization. More than any other aspect of writing, modes determine overall organization. This particular essay, for example, is a series of classifications and definitions.

At times in the history of writing, modes have been given almost as much attention as the aims, but most of the time they have been a serious second candidate. The modes are listed differently in various books. In this textbook we call narration, description, classification, and evaluation the modes. They could be called the genres of writing, and they could be called ways of looking at subject matter.

USE THE NEWSPAPER TO DISPLAY THE MODES

When I want to introduce students to the modes, I use a newspaper. I ask students to find examples of news stories (narratives). I ask them to find classifications, especially in the classifieds, as they are called. I ask the students to examine individual items within each section of the classifieds and to tell me what the details are. It becomes clear to them that there are hundreds of specific descriptions of cars, houses, lost dogs, jobs, etc., in the classifieds. Finally, I have the students check reviews of books, movies, television programs, concerts, football games, etc. These are all evaluations. Modes are as ubiquitous as the aims of writing.

Like the aims, the modes have to be taught separately. What makes a good narrative is not what makes a good evaluation or a good description or a good classification. The rules of defining are not at all the rules of narrating. As with the aims of writing, the modes of writing are different in nature and require different pedagogies. Consequently, the modes are given careful consideration in the following chapters.

THE PHILOSOPHIC BASIS OF THE MODES

You are probably wondering if there is a neat graphic structure that you can use to help students with the modes. Yes, there is. But, before it can be presented, let us ask the preliminary question, "What is a mode?"

WHAT IS A MODE?

A mode is a different perspective on a given subject matter. Take George Washington or a razor, two very different kinds of subject matter. I can write a history of George Washington or a history of the development of a given razor. I can describe the individuating characteristics of both. I can classify George Washington or a razor from several different viewpoints. Finally, I can evaluate George Washington, and I can evaluate the razor. Each of these discourses is a very different kind of writing.

What explains the differences? In other words, what differentiates narration from description, for example? Narration is always dynamic; it is concerned with change, whereas description is static. A narrator looks at the changing aspects of something, whereas a describer looks at the static aspects of the same thing.

When you are trying to get students to see the difference between description and classification, ask them what a description of Washington entails and what a classification of Washington would require. In description, the individuating characteristics of his personality are stressed (the father of our country, for example), but a classification of Washington pays attention to the different roles he assumed (president, general, husband, etc.). Both pay attention to Washington as static, and are therefore not like narration.

When you are trying to get students to differentiate narration from evaluation, first have someone tell a little of the history of Washington at Valley Forge. Then have someone evaluate Washington as a general. They will see that narration as such, simply details change in something, whereas evaluation considers that thing's performance against some norm and makes a judgment of approval or disapproval. Both narration and evaluation are dynamic: Narration details change, and evaluation considers performance.

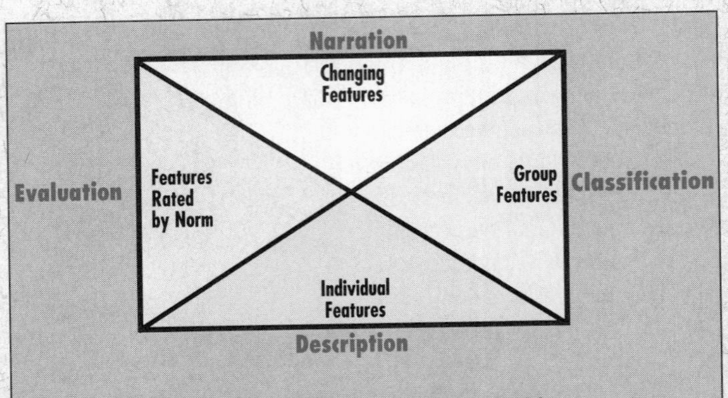

The Modes as Four Ways of Looking at Objects

These differences are shown above in **The Modes as Four Ways of Looking at Objects**.

In the textbook, these four modes will be continuously related to the aims. Anything that is written will always involve both an aim and a mode. Together, they solve nearly all of the organizational problems of writing, for either the aim or the mode determines the way the theme is laid out, as the following chapters will show. The aim especially determines the style, as will be made clear in each chapter. Thus, the aim and the mode of a given piece largely determine the main ideas, the overall organization, and the direction of the style.

ELEMENTS OF WRITING addresses the *aims* and *modes* of writing in the following ways:

Pupil's Edition
Demonstrates and teaches writing skills, focusing on the aims (the *why*) and the modes (the *how*) of writing
Provides an organized, easily understood approach that allows students to gain and sharpen writing skills

Annotated Teacher's Edition
Gives instructional strategies on how to teach the aims and modes

Teacher's ResourceBank ™
Offers materials keyed to the writing process that assist students in achieving the aims and modes

BY LEE ODELL

SHOWING VS. TELLING:

Using Models in Teaching Writing

MAKE US SEE WHAT YOU'RE TALKING ABOUT.

For some time now, teachers of writing have made a point of exhorting students to make their writing "show, not tell." Don't just tell us your reactions or opinions, we say to them. Make us see what you're talking about. If you're trying to describe a person, let us see facial expressions, details of clothing, mannerisms, actions; let us hear exactly what the person says. Or, if students are trying to write persuasively, we insist: Don't just give us your generalized conclusions. Give us some specific information that lets us see what you base your judgment on and that lets us decide for ourselves whether your judgment makes sense.

This advice is not an infallible, inflexible rule. Writers can't elaborate on everything. Furthermore, readers sometimes let a generalization pass unchallenged because it seems to ring true or because writers have sufficient authority for us simply to take their word on the matter. But if we are judicious in asking students to "show, not tell," the phrase constitutes good advice for writers and excellent advice for teachers. If we want students to make significant progress as writers, we will have to show them—not just tell them, *show*

LEE ODELL OPENS HIS CLASSROOM DOOR AT RENSSELAER POLYTECHNIC INSTITUTE.

them—what we mean. In effect, we need to make sure they have models, not just of the kinds of writing they will do but of the writing processes.

There is, of course, a long history to the practice of working with models. For centuries, teachers of rhetoric and writing have required students to study the works of great writers, sometimes having students copy model texts word for word or asking students to imitate the sentence structures they found in these works. Indeed, a version of this practice persisted through the middle 1980s in the form of sentence combining. This system did not ask students to emulate one specific writer, but it did show them frequently used sentence patterns in the works of highly admired professional writers so students could construct their own sentences based on a wide variety of these patterns.

Traditional approaches to using models have their uses, but these approaches are not what I'm talking about here. I'm suggesting that we depart from traditional practice in several ways. For one thing, the model should come not solely from famous authors but rather from books and magazines students read willingly and have readily accessible. Also, teachers don't have to provide all the models; students should be asked to bring in articles or excerpts from books that they personally find engaging and effective. Finally, these models should not be treated as though they are sacred; they are, instead, objects for analysis—for criticism as well as for praise. We and our students need to examine entire models where writers have used successful strategies that students might incorporate into their own writing, as the occasion warrants. But we and our students also need to identify things that don't work and maybe even to collaborate on devising ways to improve the model.

There are several ways we might use models, but my favorite is to use them to help students solve their own writing difficulties. For example, a number of my students can't figure out how to begin a piece of writing, what Donald Murray would refer to as a "lead." When this is a problem, I ask students to bring in copies of the first pages of articles that they somehow found themselves reading, even though the topics might not normally have concerned them.

For example, one student brought in an article entitled "Hell on Wheels," which began this way:

Almost from the time the downtown No. 4 subway train began its 21-mile run below New York City at 11:38 p.m. on the night of Tuesday, Aug. 27, something seemed amiss. Heading from the Bronx to Manhattan, the train overshot the platform at a couple of stations. At times it slowed to a crawl and then accelerated to breakneck speeds. The conductor contacted the motorman, Robert Ray, 38, several times on the intercom to find out if everything was all right. Ray replied that he was fine. But that was clearly not the case....

This article begins, of course, with a claim about a specific event ("something seemed amiss") and then illustrates this claim with a series of incidents. It mentions specific, troubling things that happened (for example, the train "slowed to a crawl and then accelerated to breakneck speeds"); it reports what people said to each other; and then it challenges what one of the people said ("But that clearly was not the case...."). In this last sentence, the author creates a conflict that engages the reader and lets the reader know what the rest of the article will be about (i.e., it will show how the driver's claim was "not the case").

Other articles brought in by the students began quite differently—by citing troubling statistics, for example, or by describing general trends in society that a reader was almost certain to know and be concerned about. These differences are important. I don't want students to think there is just one way to begin a piece of writing. Consequently, I photocopied a variety of examples and asked students to talk them through to identify the strategies writers had used to engage readers. My goal was to help students recognize some of the options that are open to them in doing their own writing.

In addition to bringing in models written by professionals, it can be extremely useful for us to bring in copies of our own efforts to do the same kind of writing students are working on. And once we have developed an atmosphere of trust, it can be useful to bring in effective examples of student work, continually asking such questions as these: What did the writer do here? How did he or she go about capturing our interest and letting us know what to expect in the rest of the text? Is there anything that this writer is doing that you might profitably do? Again, the goal is not to provide recipes or rules chiseled on tablets of stone but to get students to see what is possible.

MODELING THE COMPOSING PROCESS

Thus far, I have been describing ways we might use written products as models. In addition, we also need models of the composing processes of writers. This modeling can be as sophisticated or as rudimentary as our students need. It can focus on the work of an individual writer as Donald Murray shows in his "Use Genre as Lens" essay or on the efforts of peers as they revise their initial drafts. That is, we need to let students see the processes professional writers and students go through in doing their own writing and even in responding to classmates' writing.

There are several activities teachers can use that allow students to observe their peers' writ-

I DON'T WANT STUDENTS TO THINK THERE IS JUST ONE WAY TO BEGIN A PIECE OF WRITING.

ing processes. For example, a colleague was concerned that her tenth-graders would have difficulty passing the state basic competency test that is required for high school graduation. Knowing that one of the questions on that test was likely to require students to report information in a well-organized form, she could have concentrated on paragraph form and the proper use of transitions. But suspecting that her students' difficulties were more profound than that, she decided that her students weren't paragraphing because they did not understand that certain kinds of expository paragraphs require writers to group facts by setting up categories that the paragraphs would be about.

Consequently, she asked students to watch a videotape of a movie that she was fairly certain they would find moving, an account of the difficulties encountered by a child who had been classified as mentally retarded but who had, nonetheless, a number of good traits and who was personally likable. After students had watched the videotape, she asked them to write down every fact they could remember from the movie and to collaborate as a class to make the list as complete as possible. That night she typed a complete list of facts, made an overhead transparency of them, and then cut the transparency into strips, each strip containing one fact.

The next day, she asked students to collaborate on ways to group these facts. For instance, students noticed that many of the facts pertained to ways people reacted to the young boy, while others could be grouped under such headings as the boy's reactions to other people or his abilities. As students discussed ways of grouping facts, the teacher reflected what they were saying by moving the transparency strips around on the overhead projector. She was showing, not telling, her students about the basic process they needed to create one type of organized paragraph.

Another approach to modeling the composing process comes from a ninth-grade teacher concerned that her students' descriptive writing was bland. She believed their real problem was not a lack of descriptive adjectives and adverbs but that students weren't really looking closely at the people or objects they were describing.

She also knew that television programs routinely provide excellent examples of the process of observing. That is, as a rule, television cameras do not stay in one spot to observe everything from the same angle and distance. Instead, the cameras change position to vary the angles and the distances from which they view things. For example, one detective program began with a close-up shot of a ringing phone. Then the camera moved back so that the viewers could see a well-dressed man hurrying across an elegant apartment toward the phone. Next, the camera moved in to focus on the man's trembling hands as he nervously dried his sweaty palms on his handkerchief before picking up the phone. Finally, the camera shifted focus again, to show the head and shoulders of a burly, unshaven man speaking into a pay phone. These shifts in focus set the scene for the entire episode.

To help students understand this process of observing by shifting focus, the teacher asked students, as part of their homework, to watch one of their favorite TV programs and to count the number of times the camera shifted its focus in a two-minute period. She also asked them to make notes about the different things they saw every time the camera shifted focus. The next day they discussed these episodes and concluded that a program in which the camera did not shift focus would almost certainly be dull.

To help students see how this process applied to writing, the teacher gave students the following description:

She probably has false teeth and wears glasses. She wears her hair up in a bun and wears dresses from the 1930s. She has a habit of tapping her pencil on her desk.

Students readily agreed that this passage was uninteresting. To help them see why, the teacher asked students to think of the grammatical subject of each sentence as the visual focus of the sentence. (In response to the predictable question, the teacher told students that, for this passage, they could think of the grammatical subject as "how the writer begins each sentence.") Students saw readily that this writer's "camera" was standing in one place, not shifting at all. So the teacher asked students to work in groups to revise the passage so that the grammatical focus reflected changes in visual focus.

As one group collaborated on revising the passage, the following discussion took place:

"OK. Let's start with her false teeth—yeah—write that down."

She has false teeth.

"No, dummy. We gotta start the sentence with 'her false teeth'."

Her false teeth.

"OK, now what?"

"Oh, no. If we start with that we gotta add stuff. Like....'Her false teeth look funny'."

"Yeah, put that down."

"No, you gotta tell what 'funny' means. She'll [the teacher] only ask 'What's funny mean?'"

"I got it." Her false teeth look yellow. *"My grandma's are."*

"Yeah, 'cause they're old, like her."

"Hey. Who's writing?"

"I am." Her false teeth are yellow because they're old.

"That's good."

"OK, now the stuff on glasses. Oh, gosh. We're gonna have to add stuff to everything!"

Indeed, they would. And that was just the point. Their teacher wanted them to see that as they shifted visual focus, they would have to explore their subject further. Not only was their teacher showing these students a fundamental process of observing, but also she was showing them how the process of observing translated into the process of writing.

In addition to modeling the writing process, we also need to model the process of responding to writing. It is true that students can learn to make very helpful comments about their peers' writing. But the important phrase here is *learn to*. As Karen Spear has pointed out in her excellent book *Sharing Writing*, working in response groups is a complex process. It requires that students be able to go beyond uninformative, global comments ("Yeah, it's pretty good." "I guess it's OK.") and do two things: pay attention to specific words, phrases, or ideas and explain why and how they personally react to those things. The ninth-grade class I've just described illustrates one way to model the process of responding. When the teacher asked students to revise the bland description, she was showing them a process they could use in responding to each other's drafts. That is, she was helping them see that when they responded to a classmate's descriptive writing, they might consider whether the student had shifted focus and whether the shifts in focus helped give the reader a clearer visual picture of the person, object, or place being described. Indeed, the teacher made sure students worked as a class to give this sort of response to one or two students' subsequent drafts.

But modeling the response process may not be enough. It may also be necessary to model the processes of listening to and using those responses. Listening can be especially difficult when the response implies that a writer's work is unclear or in need of further effort. In such cases, any writer—and students are no exception—may well become defensive, more eager to prove that responses are invalid or irrelevant than to listen to those responses and consider the uses they might have. In other words, students may need to learn how to respond to responses.

If so, teachers may need to model the way we want student writers to react to their classmates' comments. Specifically, we should bring in our own efforts to do some of the same writing students are doing and ask students to respond to it. Where is it clear or unclear? What sort of personality or attitude is our writing conveying? At what points have we said things that seem appropriate or inappropriate for the audience we are addressing? My experience in doing this sort of work with students is that if they trust us, they can be very perceptive and painfully direct. If they don't get it, they can tell us so in no uncertain terms. In doing so, they give us a chance to show how a writer listens to readers, not by arguing but by attempting to find out why readers react as they do and then using that information to revise a subsequent draft.

❦

The process of modeling is, like everything else about teaching writing, a slow business. One example rarely does the trick. But if we are persistent in showing students what is involved in producing good writing through the writing process, we can usually count on results. But if we don't model, we should expect our distinction between *showing* and *telling* to fall on deaf ears. If we don't follow our own advice, why should they?❦

ELEMENTS OF WRITING addresses the *writing process* and *cooperative learning* in the following ways:

Pupil's Edition

Provides students with detailed instruction for each stage of the writing process

Provides numerous activities and exercises in the writing chapters for students to work cooperatively

Annotated Teacher's Edition

Offers lesson plans based on each stage of the writing process

Offers *COOPERATIVE LEARNING* features that suggest activities for teaching writing and grammar

Teacher's ResourceBank ™

Furnishes materials that can be used for peer evaluation

BY MAXINE HAIRSTON

THE JOY OF WRITING

STUDENTS NEED TO GET SOME FUN OUT OF WHAT THEY'RE DOING.

MAXINE HAIRSTON TAKES A BREAK FROM CLASSES.

In recent years I have come to believe that the most important job I can do as a writing teacher is to help my students enjoy writing. I say this because I'm convinced that unless students find some pleasure in their writing classes, most of them will not be willing to invest the time and energy required to turn out work that they—and we, as their teachers—can be proud of. Few adults are disciplined and determined enough to drudge away at some project—whether it's exercising or learning Spanish verbs—simply because someone else tells us that it will be good for us in the long run. We just won't stay with such projects unless there's some satisfaction in the process itself. How much harder it is, then, for youngsters to whom college or even next fall seems light years away to subject themselves to the hard work of learning to write if they get no pleasure from it at the time. Deficit motivation, working to avoid penalties or simply for a passing grade, isn't enough; students need to get some fun out of what they're doing. Fortunately, given what we now know about teaching the writing process, it's quite possible to create a writing classroom in which many students work from growth motivation; that is, they work at their writing because they enjoy doing it for its own sake.

Cognitive studies, ethnographic studies about writing, and the national projects argue that four characteristics define the congenial writing classroom, the kind in which students are likely to enjoy writing and to flourish as writers.

First, teachers provide a low-risk environment that encourages students to write without fear. Second, teachers have students develop their papers through a series of drafts and revisions. Third, teachers honor the students' right to their own writing, allowing students to choose their own topics and encouraging them to write about their interests. Fourth, teachers create and support a collaborative learning environment.

> IN THE FIRST WEEK OF A WRITING CLASS SOMETIMES I FEEL AS IF I WANT TO WEAR A BANNER ACROSS MY CHEST, EMBLAZONED WITH "TRUST ME! IT'S GOING TO BE ALL RIGHT!"

ESTABLISHING A LOW-RISK CLASSROOM

Creating a low-risk environment in the writing classroom may seem like a formidable challenge, and indeed it can be at the beginning of a new term when many students are as wary as stray cats. They're nervous for fear someone is going to try to trap them. In the first week of a writing class sometimes I feel as if I want to wear a banner across my chest, emblazoned with "Trust me! It's going to be all right!" But I can understand students' anxiety. Students who have come from writing courses with a heavy emphasis on rules and form, courses in which they did badly, have good reason to see a composition course as a high-risk situation. No wonder they start out by trying to stay in the safety zone of rules and formulas.

The humanistic psychologist Abraham Maslow theorizes that all people have two sets of forces operating within them: a need for safety and a fear of risk on one hand and an urge toward growth and autonomy on the other hand. Maslow also believes that every individual has an innate urge to create, to grow, to discover new abilities and talents. I agree; I think all children want to communicate, to write something that catches the interest and attention of others, but most will hesitate if they think they will be punished for breaking rules. As Maslow points out, "Safety needs are prepotent over growth needs....[and] in general, only a child who feels safe dares to grow forward healthily" (49). He adds, "Only the [teacher] who respects fear and defense can teach; . . . " (53).

The writing teacher's challenge is to foster the low-risk environment that will encourage creativity and expression but at the same time to work toward helping students master the writing conventions that they must know to be accepted as writers. There are several ways teachers can do this. First, of course, is to emphasize that we write in stages; we plan, we draft, we read and reread, and we revise. Final details matter when a writer gets ready to publish, but the most-productive writers learn how to suspend their error monitors in the early stages.

I have found it helps me to suspend my own error monitor when reading early drafts if I can put down my pencil and force myself to read strictly for content, good practice for trying to become a courteous reader. I ask myself, what is this writer trying to express? Why? How? Then I make only a large-scale response, focusing on being positive and on asking questions that could help the next draft. I emphasize that I hope to see substantial change and development in that draft. It would waste time even to mention error at this stage. When students realize that I really am not looking for mistakes in their drafts, they begin to relax and become more venturesome.

On second drafts, I still try to avoid writing on the paper, but focus on more specific suggestions for improvement. I also make checks in the margins to indicate potential trouble spots that the writers need to be aware of when they begin to polish their papers, sometimes adding a comment that the writer should be alert for problems with commas, subject-verb agreement, or whatever area seems most troublesome. This gives the writer specific areas to concentrate on at proofreading/editing time.

Probably one of the best ways to reduce risk in the writing classroom is to set up a portfolio system that allows students to draft a variety of papers over a period of time and then to choose a limited number to develop fully and submit for final evaluation. This method has become increasingly popular for a number of reasons. For one, student writers can work more as adult working writers do. They can attempt different kinds of writing, can stay with those projects that go well and, putting the others aside, they can invest as much as they like in them. It also gives students more control over the evaluation process. They decide which pieces they want evaluated; the teacher doesn't even have to see the others. There is considerable literature on the portfolio system if you find it an attractive option. (See also Elliot and Greenberg's essay "The Direct Assessment of Writing: Notes for Teachers.")

A final specific suggestion for reducing your students' anxieties is to establish a hierarchy of errors. We know from research that not all errors are created equal. Some are truly damaging: for instance, wrong verb forms, egregious sentence fragments, double negatives, and faulty parallelism. Errors like these set off alarms for most readers. Others, such as split infinitives, comparison of absolutes, or misusing *lie* and *lay* cause scarcely a riffle with most audiences. We should be lenient about such lapses and reduce the number of things our students have to worry about.

We should also remember that the more a writer attempts, the more mistakes he or she is likely to make. But if we are encouraging growth, we need to let student writers know that we regard such mistakes as the natural accompaniment of growth and as less important than the students' fresh ideas.

TEACHING THE WRITING PROCESS THROUGH A SYSTEM OF DRAFTS

Because this textbook so strongly emphasizes that drafting, evaluating, and revising are essential parts of the writing process, I don't feel I need to build an elaborate case for having students develop their papers in drafts. Fortunately, with most writing teachers and curriculum supervisors embracing the concept of writing as a process, students accept drafting as a routine practice. I hope so, because students write more freely and more confidently when they know that their readers view their drafts as "work in progress," not as finished products to be critiqued and judged. Under such a system, knowing they're not irrevocably committed to what they've written, writers can afford experiments. Writing tentatively, they can count on getting help from their readers to help them work out their ideas. That's very reassuring, particularly to students who haven't written much and aren't sure they have anything to say.

The less articulate, inexperienced writers are probably those who get the most out of numerous drafts because they have the opportunity to improve first attempts substantially before they must submit the papers for evaluation. They also have the chance to get feedback *during* the writing process, feedback that is far more valuable than comments on a paper that has already been graded. We know that many students, perhaps even most, pay scant attention to comments written on graded papers, especially negative comments. But when they get comments—both written and oral—on drafts, they are likely to pay attention because they use them to real advantage.

> WRITING CAN BECOME A GENUINE JOY FOR GOOD WRITERS WORKING AT THEIR PEAK.

Good students also benefit from drafts, although sometimes they may resist doing them because the system requires more work than they've usually had to do in order to get good grades. But for some good writers, developing a paper through drafts can be a heady experience as they tap into talent they didn't know they had and then earn new recognition from their peers. Writing can become a genuine joy for good writers working at their peak.

In my opinion, the worse possible system for having students write papers is to give a fresh assignment each week, have everyone write the paper only once and turn it in for a grade, and then return the graded papers and repeat the process. Under such circumstances, the anxiety level skyrockets for all but the most able students, writers get no help during the process (when they need it most), and teachers never learn what most students can really do. Even when students write in class, those papers should be drafts that they can work on again during the next class periods. Only then are students likely to develop their potential.

LETTING STUDENTS CHOOSE THEIR OWN TOPICS FOR WRITING

After several years of having students choose their own writing topics, I am committed to the practice because it has several invaluable benefits. First, most students have never had an opportunity to write about matters they're genuinely interested in and can write about with authority. Too often they see traditional assignments that ask everyone to write on the same topic as meaningless exercises in which the teacher seems to be forgetting that students are individuals.

Second, students are more likely to put time and energy into their writing when they can explore topics that interest them. When students are writing on their own topics, they may also discover a potent truth: Writing is a powerful tool for learning, one that will serve them well.

Third, when students choose their own topics, a rich diversity can develop as they write about their own special interests. Some students may write about family rituals that come from their ethnic heritages or about unusual people in their families; others may write about living in another country or on a military base; others may write about hobbies—bicycling or scuba diving or canoeing. The possibilities are almost endless. In many schools, a rich multicultural tapestry can emerge as students from diverse backgrounds and cultures read each other's work and share stories.

Fourth, students will become more-confident writers because they have more control over their writing. As they develop their expertise in some area, they begin to realize how much they know about something, whether it's car stereos or cooking hamburgers. They can take on a new identity in the class and find that people pay attention to what they have to say. That's good for all of us.

Finally, when students choose their own writing topics, the class simply becomes more interesting for everyone. Students may cover a remarkable range of subjects, and even those writing on similar topics bring different perspectives to them. Boredom drops quickly because everyone is constantly learning directly from other people's experiences. Perhaps the greatest bonus is to teachers, who not only garner a wealth of information about their students, but also over a period of years become mini-experts on numerous topics. Furthermore, they are spared trying to think up a good writing topic and then having to read fifty papers on that topic.

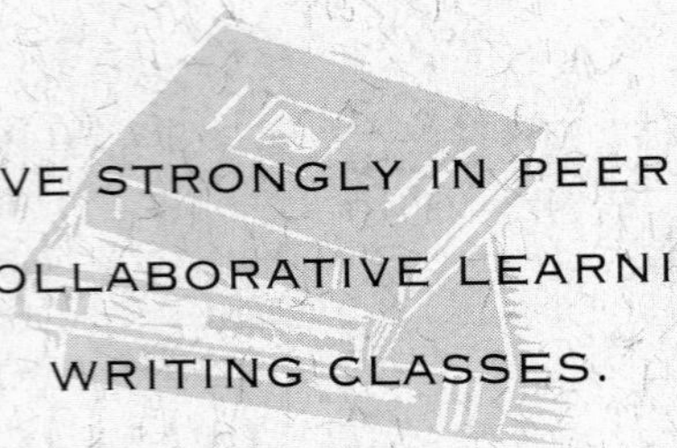

I BELIEVE STRONGLY IN PEER GROUPS AND COLLABORATIVE LEARNING IN WRITING CLASSES.

It does take considerable class time to help select topics, since many students will protest that they have nothing to write about, but such obstacles can be overcome in a few days of brainstorming and group work in class. As teacher, you can come in with a list of possible topics and then work with the class to generate subtopics. Or ask everyone to bring in a list of fifteen things to write about, encouraging the concrete and specific rather than large, abstract categories.

I have had good success with asking students to choose a general topic to write on for the whole term and then to pick subtopics for individual papers. That way they get into their topics in some depth and eliminate the process of having to work through choosing a fresh topic for each paper. You may want to specify the kinds of papers students write within their topics—informative, expressive, persuasive, and so on—to focus the class within the formats they're learning from the textbook.

ESTABLISHING A COLLABORATIVE-LEARNING CLASSROOM

I believe strongly in peer groups and collaborative learning in writing classes. Perhaps their greatest advantage is that they give students an immediate sense of audience, something that's hard to achieve when the teacher is the only reader for the drafts. Usually they respect each other's opinions; in fact, they may take their peers' responses more seriously than they do the teacher's because they feel closer to peers and they genuinely want to communicate.

Students also begin to see how useful collaboration can be for generating ideas. Most students in writing groups readily admit how much their classmates have contributed to the final versions of their papers. Each class period when I hand back graded papers, I pick two or three of the best ones to read aloud and then ask the writer and the writer's group to comment on how the paper developed through drafts. Their accounts are revealing, and the investment they feel in each other's work is truly gratifying.

I favor randomly chosen groups of at least four students so if someone is absent, the discussion doesn't break down. I reorganize groups to allow working with as many writers as possible. This arrangement also enhances every student's exposure to diverse cultural experiences as they get to know other students more closely. Managing groups in the classroom may not be easy, although I suspect trained secondary teachers know considerably more about it than most college teachers do. For the teacher who doesn't feel comfortable with groups, there is considerable literature on the concept. (See the professional bibliography on p. T74.)

Ultimately, groups help to establish the whole class as a community of writers who work together, feel a common sense of purpose, and see writing as a shared enterprise that's important to everyone. We all know intuitively that the most important element for achieving a congenial writing classroom is the teacher's attitude, and for that reason it's important for the teacher to be a part of that community, not to be an outside authority and a judge. Teachers need to write with students during writing workshops and share writing with them—its joys and frustrations. With luck and time, I am convinced that both teachers and students will enjoy being in a writing classroom more than they might have thought possible.

Work Cited

Maslow, Abraham. Toward a Psychology of Being, 2nd ed. New York: D. Van Nostrand Company. 1968.

ELEMENTS OF WRITING addresses students' understanding of the *writing process*, acceleration of learning through *cooperative group work*, and feedback to students through effective *assessment* in the following ways:

Pupil's Edition

Provides detailed instruction for each stage of the writing process

Provides numerous activities and exercises in the writing chapters for students to work cooperatively

Annotated Teacher's Edition

Provides students with detailed instruction for each stage of the writing process

Offers *COOPERATIVE LEARNING* features that suggest activities for teaching writing and grammar

Gives helpful assessment ideas in the *TIMESAVER*, *A DIFFERENT APPROACH*, and *ASSESSMENT* features

Teacher's ResourceBank ™

Offers materials keyed to the writing process that assist students in achieving the aims and modes

Furnishes materials that can be used for peer evaluation

Provides an **Assessment Portfolio** section and **Holistically Graded Composition Models** for the writing chapters

By Barbara J. Shade

Teaching for Learning's Sake

This approach to teaching will empower students as learners.

Helping students incorporate ideas, skills, and concepts that will improve their ability to perform tasks and to solve problems is the ultimate goal of teaching. Teachers who achieve this goal effectively find ways to accommodate students' different learning styles so that the teaching-learning process works more efficiently.

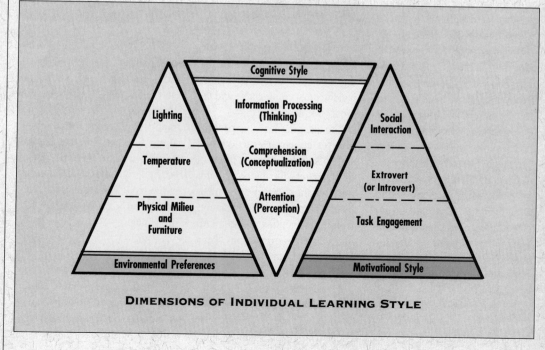

What do we mean by *learning styles*? Over the years, researchers have identified three dimensions in which students have specific learning preferences: (1) their preferences for various environmental factors that influence the learning climate; (2) their preferences about the ways they choose to engage in the learning process (motivational style); and (3) their preferences for the various ways in which they process information (cognitive style).

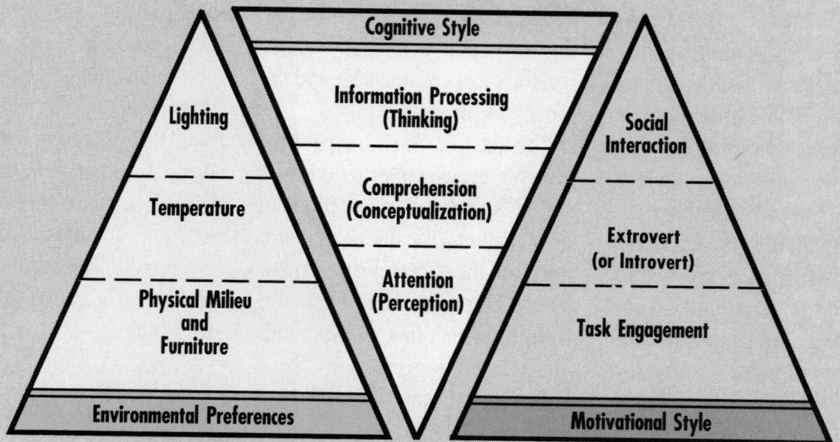

Dimensions of Individual Learning Style

ENVIRONMENTAL PREFERENCES

Individual environmental preferences focus on the lighting, temperature, and furniture used in the learning process. For example, some individuals might prefer bright light while others prefer it muted; some might prefer a warm room while others like it cool. A variation in studying postures has also been noted, with some individuals preferring to sit in a traditional classroom desk while others prefer to stand or recline when engaged in a learning task.[1]

MOTIVATIONAL STYLE

The second dimension of learning style focuses upon the extent to which students take responsibility for their own learning. Teachers often incorrectly assume that students' desire to engage in work is inherent. As with other aspects of learning, the extent to which individuals become involved in work depends upon how they have been socialized to respond to work. Some students, for example, have been taught to rely on others for assistance, to follow directions as given, and to perform the task as modeled. Others have been made more independent of others and have been taught to work alone, to find their own solutions, and to decide whether or not they can complete the work before asking for assistance. Corno and Mandinach refer to this stylistic dimension as a preference for resource management, and students tend to use the approach that makes them feel the most comfortable and the most competent.

[1] For a more detailed description of the social and physical environment preferences of students, the reader should examine the writings of Kenneth and Rita Dunn.

BARBARA SHADE AT UNIVERSITY OF WISCONSIN-PARKSIDE CAMPUS.

The teaching-learning process involves human interaction, and students prefer different levels of involvement with others, depending upon the social and personality development that emanates from their families and communities. Families stressing prosocial behavior encourage children to help, to share, and to work toward benefiting others.

These students are more likely to give and receive assistance in the learning process and to like cooperative-learning ventures. Children trained to be highly individualistic and self-oriented are less likely to cooperate and offer help. Learners with this orientation function well in a competitive setting because they prefer to work alone and are less likely to enjoy cooperative-learning activities unless there is a reward or a method of accommodating their need for individuality.

COGNITIVE STYLE

The least discussed dimension of learning style—that of cognitive style—represents individually preferred ways of perceiving, organizing, and evaluating information so that it can be learned.

Three cognitive processes influence the way individuals acquire and produce knowledge. These are the perceptual, the conceptual, and the evaluative processes.

1. Perceptual Processes: The most recognized area in learning-style literature, this area focuses on the sensory modalities. Through cultural socialization, learners develop a preference for either the visual modality (photographs, graphs, art, texts); the aural modality (records, tapes, lectures); the haptic/kinesthetic modality (group discussions, interactive debates, drama); or some combination of these. Instruction delivered through the preferred modality establishes an instant rapport that allows students to process information more easily.

Different cultures socialize their children to attend to different cues in the environment; therefore, students have selective attention. Some students focus their attention on the task or idea being presented. For others, the people, their peers, their self-evaluation, or even the teacher's reaction to them are the most important elements on which to focus. How children choose to attend to cues is an important dimension of learning, and teachers who wish to ensure cognitive engagement find ways to influence the perceptive focus of the students.

2. Conceptual Processes: Having focused on an idea that must be learned, students must then classify it based upon prior experiences. The techniques involved include assessing similarities and differences to prior knowledge, as well as determining how best to define or describe the concepts. Again, the extent to which students can manipulate various concepts depends upon whether or not the ideas can be communicated to them using a common language with commonly accepted images.

Some students prefer to have ideas presented in a hierarchical manner, beginning with the big picture followed by the details involved (whole to part). Other students prefer to have the information presented in a more sequential approach, beginning with the minute details and building toward the larger concept (part to whole). Regardless of the technique used, teachers must include methods of helping learners make connections with prior knowledge.

3. Evaluative Processes: The third aspect of cognitive style focuses on the processes of thinking about the information. *Thinking* is difficult to define, but many researchers define it as "comprehension monitoring." The major focus of thinking centers on the individual's ability to plan, monitor, and evaluate his or her learning and understanding about the information he or she is seeking to learn.

Again, teachers should look for variations in the way individuals approach thinking. On one hand, individuals may spend time using their imaginations to create ideas based upon personal views or beliefs. On the other hand, some individuals will engage in a more formal logic, which requires familiarity with the rules in order to select the correct problem-solving strategies. In the first type of information processing, individuals seem to arrive at their decisions rather intuitively, using a process that seems to be generated from an internalized logic. In the second type, the one most influenced by instruction, students learn to organize and review their approach to information or problems through an analytical process.

ACCOMMODATING VARIATIONS IN LEARNING STYLES

When teachers are first introduced to the concept of learning styles, they immediately conjure up visions of having to construct thirty different learning plans to accommodate their students. *Learning styles* is not another euphemism for individually guided education. Instead, it is an entreaty to teachers to provide different approaches and strategies that individuals can use as they work at learning.

In today's classrooms, there are basically *two distinct modes of learning*: the *traditional orientation*, the one to which most instruction is geared; and the *community orientation*, the one more likely to be displayed by African American, Hispanic American, Native American, and immigrant Asian students who identify closely with the culture of their ethnic communities.

Particular suggestions to enhance the instructional process for the community-oriented students who are often ignored in instructional delivery system include the following ones:

Environment Style Accommodation: For the community-oriented students, the classroom should become inviting and supportive as an experiential setting in which students can use various media to explore concepts that may be foreign to them because they are not prevalent in their communities or because their economic situation does not permit the type of travel or involvement in enrichment activities that is true of the more successful, economically affluent students. Being able to see an enlarged picture of the Eiffel Tower in the classroom can provide an important conceptual image that might be needed to foster comprehension. Because learning centers permit self-exploration, they should also become important aspects of the classroom design for all levels of students in all types of classes.

Motivational Style Accommodation: Having the opportunity to participate in a good class discussion on lesson content motivates community-oriented students, satisfying their needs to share information with others and to obtain feedback. Moreover, it provides them an opportunity to listen to different perspectives. Teachers should note, however, that group discussion is not the same as class recitation in which students are asked to recite facts and information to the teacher from a textbook. For example, it is not enough to discuss nouns as a part of speech without leading students through the concept of a complete sentence and of the purpose of using nouns within sentences and paragraphs. Moreover, students need to be able to identify nouns within the framework of their own speech and written narratives as well as to determine how and why they have used a particular word as a noun.

The key to a good group discussion is a teacher who is an excellent questioner, who is reflective, who can lead students to reflect and inquire, and who has an excellent understanding of the broad structure and relationships within the lesson content.

Information Processing Style Accommodation: Teachers can facilitate the processing of information by students through the use of some of the following techniques:

1. Present concepts with multimedia using a variety of modalities.

THE KEY TO A GOOD GROUP DISCUSSION IS A TEACHER WHO IS AN EXCELLENT QUESTIONER, WHO IS REFLECTIVE, WHO CAN LEAD STUDENTS TO REFLECT AND INQUIRE, . . .

TEACHERS MUST REMEMBER THAT STUDENTS HAVE DIFFERENT PERCEPTIONS OF THE WORLD AND TEACH TO THESE PERCEPTIONS.

2. Assist the students in identifying the relationships of concepts through cognitive mapping, brainstorming, or reciprocal teaching in which you ask them to predict possible answers in stories.

3. Take time to ensure there is a common understanding of words, concepts, or ideas. Bilingual students should be encouraged to interpret the words in their languages. Students should also be encouraged to develop art projects as representations of the ideas and to use new words in their oral interactions with you.

4. Model the thinking processes that are needed to complete tasks successfully. Most importantly, provide students the time to think about a problem or to complete an assignment so that they grasp the underlying meaning. Students learn best when they can perform a task with the teacher available to provide feedback.

Teachers must remember that students have different perceptions of the world and teach to these perceptions. Assisting students in

The stylistic differences of these two preferences seem to lie along the following continuum:

School-Oriented Students	Community-Oriented Students
Environmental Preferences: Prefer less intense, perhaps earth-oriented colors or plain whites. Seem able to work well in classrooms in which seats are in rows.	*Environmental Preferences:* Prefer warm, bright colors—blues and yellows are particularly soothing. Seem to prefer groupings of desks or tables, which perpetuate cooperation.
Motivational Style: Are individualistic and prefer to work alone on tasks. Are competitive and self-regulated in resource management.	*Motivational Style:* Are prosocial, more cooperative, and prefer to work with others on tasks. Are more dependent and like to have help from peers with constant reinforcement from the teacher or adult.
Cognitive Style: Learn well through auditory senses and function well with print media. Are able to focus attention on a specific task or object. Can focus on a single task for a sustained period of time. Understand American English used in textbooks, magazines, newspapers, and television, which facilitates comprehension. Backgrounds are closer to the writers of the curriculum materials, which facilitates meaning. Prefer or can handle material well when presented in a linear-sequential manner. Have been taught to use formal logic, algorithms, and analytical thinking. Are more likely to present written and spoken thoughts in a sequential manner. Are likely to function in a low-context fashion and to explain all variations of meanings because they assume the meaning is not shared.	*Cognitive Style:* Prefer visual material to emphasize oral presentation. Like group discussions, debates, and projects. Prefer to constantly scan room or object for new features, nonverbal cues, or contextual features. Prefer a variety of tasks in a relatively short time to maintain attention. Can focus on several tasks at one time. Likely to speak dialect or community-oriented language or are bilingual, which creates different orientation to words and meanings. Backgrounds usually differ from that of texts, requiring reinterpretation of the material within the context of the communities from which students come. Prefer to have material presented in a holistic, relational, or contextual manner, a presentation from whole to part. Are more intuitive and synergistic and may not have been taught to use formal logic to approach objects and problems. Have been exposed to more observational learning. Are more likely to present thoughts in a spiral or episodic fashion. Are likely to function in a high-context fashion and to assume that the meaning is shared by all individuals with whom they are communicating.

learning requires lots of talking—talking between students and teachers and between students. Expressing ideas orally allows better processing and comprehension.

When considering the use of learning styles, teachers must confront three important perceptions. First, teachers should understand that the identified style preference should not and cannot be used as evidence of deficiencies. Being different does not mean that the child is deficient in ability. Second, teachers should not think that the community-oriented style reflects all members of a group. It is merely behavior that is most likely to be found within the community. Third, teachers who use the concept of learning styles should do so as indicators of approaches to lesson design and to the selection of methods of instruction, not as the basis for judging intellectual potential.

A FINAL CAVEAT

Developing a successful learner is the ultimate goal of a successful teacher, and ensuring that children become successful learners requires that teachers see themselves not as the ultimate purveyors of knowledge, but as guides through the learning process. This approach to teaching will empower students as learners. By incorporating various learning-style approaches in the classroom and in the curriculum, teachers will assist students to maximize the energy they spend in the learning process. This permits students to approach the learning process in their own words and to use the information as a bridge. When learners grasp the ideas and really know that they know, their sense of self-worth and confidence and their intellectual strength improve tremendously. It is at this point teachers know they, too, have been successful. What a great sense of accomplishment!❦

Additional Readings

Grossman, Herbert. *Educating Hispanic Students.* Springfield, Illinois: Charles C. Thomas Publisher, 1984.

Henson, Kenneth T. *Theory Into Practice: Matching Teaching and Learning Styles*. Columbus, Ohio: Ohio State University, 1984.

Shade, Barbara J. *Culture, Style, and the Educative Process*. Springfield, Illinois: Charles C. Thomas Publisher, 1989.

Tharp, Roland and Ronald Gallimore. *Rousing Minds to Life*. New York: Cambridge University Press, 1988.

Trueba, Henry T., Lila Jacobs and Elizabeth Kirton. *Cultural Conflict and Adaptation: The Case of Hmong Children in American Society*. New York: Falmer Press, 1990.

ELEMENTS OF WRITING addresses the needs of America's diverse student populations and the range of students' *learning styles* in the following ways:

Pupil's Edition

Represents a wide range of ethnically diverse cultures in the literary models and a broad selection of topics in the exercises and examples

Accomodates a range of learning styles by providing a variety of student activities

Offers teachers a flexible program that can be easily adapted to suit a variety of situations

Annotated Teacher's Edition

Provides specific *MEETING INDIVIDUAL NEEDS* features such as *Learning Styles, Less-Advanced, Advanced, Students with Special Needs, LEP/ESL,* and *At-Risk*

Suggests ways for language teachers to address language diversity in the multicultural classroom

Teacher's ResourceBank ™

Meets individual needs of students with graphic organizers and reinforcement practice activities

WANDA B. SCHINDLEY

INTEGRATING THE LANGUAGE ARTS

INTEGRATING THE TEACHING OF THE LANGUAGE ARTS CREATES THE MAGIC THAT HELPS STUDENTS LEARN.

Thirty-five years ago in a rural classroom, a creative woman integrated the teaching of reading, writing, speaking, listening, and even math. Her second-graders built a playhouse-size cardboard post office, made block-letter signs, wrote and read letters, counted tokens to buy and sell stamps, and spoke and listened as postmaster and customer. That teacher had not read research on the integration of skills or on using whole-language methodologies, but she knew intuitively what worked. I don't remember much about my experiences in kindergarten, first grade, third grade, or even fourth grade, but I remember well that second-grade classroom; I remember the magic of learning.

Integrating the teaching of the language arts creates the magic that helps students learn. It creates a context for developing language proficiency and relevancy for reading, writing, speaking, and listening activities. Students grow through active participation in language activities. Although categorizing the language arts may be necessary for describing curricula, in the classroom language skills are best learned through doing—through seeking meaning from texts, through writing and revising, and through sharing ideas and opinions.

WANDA SCHINDLEY IS A SPECIALIST FOR THE WORKPLACE PARTNERSHIP.

WANDA STILL LIVES IN THE RURAL AREA WHERE SHE WENT TO SCHOOL AS A CHILD.

SUGGESTIONS FOR INTEGRATING THE LANGUAGE ARTS

- Involve students in prereading activities such as discussion, writing, research, and sometimes, vocabulary development. Creating a context for reading involves discussing themes and related issues, making predictions, recalling prior knowledge and related experiences, and searching out related information.
- Involve students in prewriting activities such as discussion of possible topics and details, reading model essays, searching out and reading informative pieces, reading literary writing, interviewing others, and sentence-combining or sentence-revision activities. Like the writing process itself, development of language proficiency involves a recursive practice in reading, writing, thinking, speaking, and listening.
- Make writing assignments relevant by having students write for and share with real audiences for meaningful purposes. Have students share their writing with peers.
- Relate correctness—development of conventional usage, spelling, grammar, and punctuation—to the revising and proofreading stages of the writing process. Correctness becomes important to students when it helps them communicate their ideas clearly. Class review of grammar, usage, and mechanics can be done with sentences from student papers and with sentence-combining, sentence-manipulation, and vocabulary activities.
- Approach standard usage in speech as appropriate for use in business and academic situations, not as a replacement for all vernacular expression.
- Encourage student involvement in class discussion, team study groups, cooperative research projects and presentations, group creative writing, and role playing.
- Foster an atmosphere in which students feel free to respond to, to evaluate, and to critique literature.
- Act as facilitator in students' discovery processes through activities that encourage creative and critical thinking—decision making and problem solving—and allow students to take more responsibility for their own learning.
- Create an atmosphere of cooperation, caring, and high expectations.

> LIKE THE WRITING PROCESS ITSELF, DEVELOPMENT OF LANGUAGE PROFICIENCY INVOLVES A RECURSIVE PRACTICE IN READING, WRITING, THINKING, SPEAKING, AND LISTENING.

USING THE TEXTBOOK IN AN INTEGRATED APPROACH

Literature selections are provided in each chapter to give students opportunities to read before writing. However, this book can be used in a literature-driven approach as the springboard to writing by incorporating into the study of each chapter ample readings from literature anthologies, magazines, and student papers. The features in each chapter of the *Teacher's Edition* contain suggestions for integrating additional literature selections **(Integrating the Language Arts: Literature Link)**, using a variety of group activities **(Cooperative Learning)**, and encouraging students to use higher-level thinking skills to contribute to class discussion **(Critical Thinking)**.

Throughout, the textbook guides students through the prewriting, writing, evaluating, revising, proofreading, and publishing phases of the writing process. It also instructs students in the dynamics and behavior involved in group work with ample opportunities for group writing, revising, speaking, and listening activities. The chapters on speaking and listening help students develop skills that will serve them throughout their school years and later as citizens.

The **Common Error** and **Integrating the Language Arts** features in each chapter of the *Teacher's Edition* contain suggestions for integrating the teaching of grammar, usage, and mechanics into the stages of the writing process, as do the suggestions for integrating the language arts in the introduction of each composition chapter.

Sample Integrated Lesson Plan

A lesson on creative writing might begin with a class discussion about stories and poems.

Guiding questions encourage students to share attitudes (What kinds of stories/poems do you like?)
—in order to recall prior knowledge about the structure of stories (What happened toward the end of a favorite story? How did you feel as your read? What name do we use for the most exciting or scary part of the story?)
—and of poems (Can you think of a favorite poem? What do you like about the poem?)
—and to synthesize knowledge about fiction and poetry (What characteristics do stories and poems have in common? What other forms might a writer use to tell about an event or to express an idea?)

Students might then read the stories and poems and discuss their responses and evaluations of each. Volunteers might bring their favorite stories, poems, or lyrics to share with the class before beginning to write original stories and poems.

Teachers can use group stories and poems as guided practice and as a non-threatening introduction to creative writing. Students working in groups to create story lines and to describe characters and setting will quickly learn literary terminology to use within the group. A group activity in which students write noun poems might begin informal grammar instruction as the class brainstorms a list of words that name people, places, things, or ideas. Small groups can then choose from the list of topics for noun-metaphor poems.

Example: Dreams are
Envelopes of hope,
Fluffy clouds that
disappear in daylight,
Stars to reach for.

As groups begin to revise and proofread their poems for class presentation, teachers might focus on the use of commas and end marks.

When students begin the creative writing assignments, they are again given opportunities to write, discuss, read, think, talk, revise, and so on. Instruction in usage and mechanics can be provided to the class as the need arises, to partners as they debate an issue of correctness, and to individuals in one-on-one conferences.

Finally, students share their work with the class—perhaps anonymously at first, but eventually as accomplished and proud authors who share a firsthand knowledge of the creation of literature and a greater understanding of language.

ELEMENTS OF WRITING addresses the *integration* of the various aspects of language in the following ways:

Pupil's Edition
Connects the study of writing to reading, speaking, listening, grammar, usage, and mechanics
Reinforces in the language-structure chapters the fundamentals of effective communication, stressing application and proficiency.

Annotated Teacher's Edition
Provides features that give a variety of strategies to link every aspect of language diversity instruction—*INTEGRATING THE LANGUAGE ARTS: Literature Link, Library Skills Link, Mechanics Link, Grammar Link, Usage Link, Technology Link*

Teacher's ResourceBank ™
Offers supplemental materials on every aspect of the language arts

BY CHARLES W. LEFTWICH & PATRICIA G. TWEEDDALE

ACCEPTING THE DIFFERENCES:

Teaching the At-Risk Student

> ...IT IS UNLIKELY THAT AT-RISK STUDENTS WILL LEAVE SCHOOL WITH THE BASIC SKILLS OUR EDUCATION SYSTEM SHOULD PROVIDE.

Teachers are facing a growing population of students for whom a minimal success such as completing high school is not probable. These students comprise the group known as at-risk, a label that can be acquired for reasons ranging from race and socioeconomic background to being a teenage parent or coming from a single-parent home, from having a parent or sibling incarcerated to being a latchkey child. Whatever the reason for the categorization, it is unlikely that at-risk students will leave school with the basic skills our education system should provide.

The task of teaching the at-risk student must begin with knowledge of individual student characteristics that are relevant to the instructional objective at hand. A focus upon stereotypical characteristics denies attention to the in-

PATRICIA TWEEDDALE AND CHARLES LEFTWICH IN THEIR OFFICE.

CHARLES AND PATRICIA POSE WITH A FAVORITE QUOTATION AND THEIR CANINE FRIEND SPRIGER.

"FEAR OF DIFFERENCE IS DREAD OF LIFE ITSELF."
- mary parker follett
TEACHING & LEARNING

dividual learner and what that student brings to the classroom. Because teaching and learning are highly interactive social encounters, the efficacy of any given encounter may be dependent upon the emotional response of both parties to their first contact.

The initial response by a teacher is often conditioned by previous exposure to learners similar to the one in question. Positive previous exposure leads to a sense of confidence in the ability to successfully foster and facilitate learning. However, if a teacher has had negative previous exposure, the quality of the initial encounter may be tainted by the teacher's lack of confidence in effecting learning or establishing a positive social interaction.

There are at least two sources for interference in the initial interaction between the teacher and the at-risk student, the vicarious and the real. Vicarious sources are grounded in images created by other teachers, the school organization, and community expectations, as well as portrayal in print and electronic media by editorial and entertainment entities.

The real source of interference in the initial interaction may well be so subtle as to escape recognition, and yet it seems to be pervasive. It is a fundamental rejection of differences. The nonverbal language exhibited by the at-risk student is different or at least unfamiliar, and this may reinforce the teacher's sense of being called upon to do an impossible task. The student's verbal language may also be unfamiliar, and the clash between assumptions of what students ought to sound like and what the teacher actually hears further frustrates and impedes the teaching process.

Interaction between the teacher and the learner should focus upon the individual student's characteristics with the intention of discovering what sets that individual apart from others. New learning is built upon old learning, and new knowledge is supported by old; therefore, the teacher of the at-risk student must concentrate on discovering what the student knows. Often this can be a difficult task since that knowledge may be communicated in a different mode. The teacher should be aware of some characteristics of the at-risk student: negative self-image, a heavy dependence upon and rigid adherence to a distinct mode of concrete thinking, a unique dialect of spoken language, low motivation, and a lack of positive response to constructive criticism. Any at-risk student may exhibit one or all of these characteristics in varying degrees. What is important is to recognize and appreciate the student as an individual. Whatever the individual's characteristics, they are an integral part of the learner and as such must be taken

FOR THE TEACHER TO INTERACT SUCCESSFULLY WITH THE AT-RISK STUDENT, A SENSE OF TRUST AND ACCEPTANCE MUST BE ESTABLISHED.

into account in structuring interaction. And that structuring is solely the responsibility of the teacher; the structure must be the product of informed assessment rather than reactive judgment.

For the teacher to interact successfully with the at-risk student, a sense of trust and acceptance must be established. The student must suspend any suspicions of the teacher's intentions, which is no small accomplishment given the student's probable historical experience with schools. The teacher must overcome any negative preconceptions of the nature of the at-risk student that may stem from some students' appearance. In fact, teacher response to the appearance of the at-risk student may be a much larger barrier to a positive interaction than any of the student's other characteristics. The student cannot help but sense rejection by the teacher and will respond in kind. The student, being less sophisticated, frequently manifests inner anger and frustration by overt, socially unacceptable behavior. Administrators and teachers may deal with this behavior as if it were the real problem rather than a symptom. However, if the teacher is well aware of the differences that are brought to the classroom and can accept them, there can develop an interaction in which the teacher and the student are focused on, rather than distracted from, their respective tasks—teaching and learning.

Another difficulty in developing meaningful interaction is overcoming the sense of hopelessness that at-risk students feel. At-risk students know they are at-risk; they have been told this from the beginning. Innumerable sights and sounds reinforce an absence of control over their environment. Hopelessness often pervades the neighborhoods in which they live. Past experience has probably taught them that high hopes and effort more often than not lead to disappointment and heartbreak. The challenge for the teacher is to identify the students' strengths though they be disguised or denied beneath the protective facade of bravado and coolness, and to try to inspire and motivate students who have little or no expectation of success and who outwardly signal an intense desire to be left alone. To meet this challenge, the teacher more than ever before must be a thinker, a planner, and a decision maker. Then, drawing on a rich professional knowledge base, the teacher can serve as a model and mediator.

It is one thing to understand intellectually that at-risk students bring to the classroom with them entirely different bents and behaviors. It is another, however, to confront these differences and to view them as starting points for teaching. If we are to succeed in teaching this segment of our student body, we have to understand and accept these differences and to exercise our expertise as planners and implementers of instruction.

Successful teaching continues to hinge on the characteristics of the learner, the material to be learned, the specific tasks to be mastered, and the strategies utilized by the teacher. No one ever said it would be easy. Surprisingly though, many have found it to be professionally fulfilling and personally rewarding.

ELEMENTS OF WRITING addresses the needs of America's diverse student populations and the range of student *learning styles* in the following ways:

Pupil's Edition

Represents a wide range of ethnically diverse cultures in the literary models and a broad selection of topics in the exercises and examples

Accomodates a range of learning styles by providing a variety of student activities

Offers teachers a flexible program that can be easily adapted to a variety of situations

Annotated Teacher's Edition

Provides specific *MEETING INDIVIDUAL NEEDS* features such as *Learning Styles*, *Less-Advanced, Advanced, Students with Special Needs, LEP/ESL*, and *At-Risk*

Suggests ways for language teachers to address diversity in the multicultural classroom

Teacher's ResourceBank ™

Meets individual needs of students with graphic organizers and reinforcement practice activities

BY NORBERT ELLIOT & KAREN GREENBERG

THE DIRECT ASSESSMENT OF WRITING:

Notes For Teachers

HOW CAN ASSESSMENT STRATEGIES BE MODIFIED TO HELP BOTH TEACHERS AND STUDENTS?

Teachers spend a great deal of time assessing students' writing; they correct errors, offer suggestions, and assign grades. This process can be exhausting to teachers and discouraging for students. How can assessment strategies be modified to help both teachers and students?

Instruction and assessment can be aligned so that the two work together. To enable instruction and assessment to complement each other, teachers have turned to two relatively new methods of direct assessment: holistic scoring and portfolio assessment.

HOLISTIC SCORING

One of the most common methods of scoring writing samples is holistic scoring, a procedure based on the responses of concerned readers to a meaningful whole composition. Holistic scoring involves reading a writing sample for an overall impression of the writing and assigning the sample a score based on a set of consistent scoring criteria. Most holistic scoring systems use a scoring scale, or guide, that describes papers at six or eight different levels of competence.

Holistic scoring has many advantages:

1. It communicates to students that writing is a process leading to a unified, synergistic piece of writing.

2. Writing samples that have been holistically scored provide students with clear information about the quality of their writing, but they are less intimidating than grades or written critiques.

NORBERT ELLIOT, DIRECTOR OF THE WRITING PROGRAM AT THE NEW JERSEY INSTITUTE OF TECHNOLOGY.

3. Holistic scoring is rapid. Readers spend only minutes judging the total effect of a paper.
4. The criteria on a holistic scoring scale give teachers a vocabulary to use in discussing essays with students and their parents.
5. The process of developing holistic scoring guides and scoring writing samples enables teachers to share their unique responses to writing, as well as their evaluative criteria. If an entire department uses the same scoring guide, students will realize that effective writing has definable features upon which all of their English teachers agree.

Nevertheless, there are weaknesses to this method. It alone cannot, for instance, provide diagnostic information about specific writing proficiencies and deficiencies. The score cannot substitute for a teacher's detailed responses to an essay—the provocative notes in the margin, the encouraging comments at the end, etc. This weakness, however, can be overcome if teachers review papers with their students in light of the scoring criteria.

Another weakness is more serious. Using holistic scoring, teachers often consider only one piece of writing during assessment. If only one sample of writing is evaluated, then teachers may not get a representative idea of students' writing ability, because this ability does not exist in a vacuum but varies from day to day and across the aims and modes of writing. In response to this concern, teachers have investigated a second method of direct assessment.

KAREN GREENBERG, DIRECTOR OF THE NATIONAL TESTING NETWORK IN WRITING.

PORTFOLIO ASSESSMENT

Portfolio assessment allows writing teachers to evaluate various samples of students' work, taken at various times under various conditions. Consequently, portfolio assessment can provide a fuller portrait of writing abilities.

To begin portfolio assessment, teachers develop a series of writing assignments that express the goals of a course. For instance, a group of teachers might require their students to write papers based on each of James Kinneavy's aims: expressive writing (a journal entry), informative writing (a summary of a news article), literary writing (a short story), and persuasive writing (an editorial). Over time, students work on these papers both at home and in class. Portfolios can include other forms of communication that students have produced, such as artwork, audio recordings, or videotapes.

Teachers need not assess everything that is included in a portfolio. In fact, it is often preferable not to evaluate every piece of a student's writing. This strategy allows teachers to separate instruction and response from formed evaluation. Portfolio assessment, therefore, can be based on samples that the teacher, the student, or both consider to be the student's best writing.

Clearly, there are advantages to this method:
1. Because multiple samples are assessed, portfolio assessment is a valid, authentic evaluation.
2. Because the authenticity of the assessment is increased, the curriculum becomes enriched.

As teachers plan tasks, they debate curricular values and strategies, devise workable instructional schemes for the classroom, and design thoughtful evaluative criteria for assignments.

With portfolio assessment, students gain a more positive attitude toward writing. Because they invest in their writing, students seek both teacher and peer response, create multiple drafts, and revise for their readers. Over time, a school's entire writing program can become an exciting adventure in communication and critical thinking.

CONCLUSION

There is still much to be investigated about the evaluation of writing. What kind of assessment best suits the multiple literacies on which our democratic society rests? What kind of local assessments will best supplement large-scale assessment? How can assessment reveal more about effective teaching? Answers will have to come from those who know students best: their teachers.❦

ELEMENTS OF WRITING addresses *holistic evaluation* and *portfolio assessment* in the following ways:

Annotated Teacher's Edition
Offers a wide variety of assessment ideas in the *TIMESAVER, A DIFFERENT APPROACH*, and *ASSESSMENT* features

Teacher's ResourceBank ™
Provides an **Assessment Portfolio** section and **Holistically Graded Composition Models** for the writing chapters

BY DAVID A. ENGLAND

PROFESSIONAL BIBLIOGRAPHY

COMPOSING PROCESSES

Belanoff, Pat, Peter Elbow, and Sheryl I. Fontaine, eds. *Nothing Begins with N*. Carbondale and Edwardsville, IL: Southern Illinois University Press, 1981. An overview of what we know about the uses of freewriting in the classroom, with major sections on strategies and benefits for teachers and students.

Berthoff, Anne E. *The Making of Meaning*. Upper Montclair, NJ: Boynton/Cook Publishers, Inc., 1981. Suggesting that classrooms can become philosophical laboratories, Berthoff shows the way to practical approaches for thoughtful teachers.

Brannon, Lil, and C.H. Knoblauch. *Rhetorical Traditions and the Teaching of Writing*. Upper Montclair, NJ: Boynton/Cook Publishers, Inc., 1984. Staying with the theory and history provided in this book's early chapters rewards readers who come to understand better the basis and rewards of teaching in nontraditional ways.

Caplan, Rebekah, and Katherine Keach. *Showing-Writing: A Tutoring Program to Help Students to be Specific*. The University of California, Berkeley, CA: Bay Area Writing Project Publications. This nicely focused monograph is itself a good illustration of "showing, not telling," and it explains how the author tested her program for helping students learn to be more specific in their writing.

Dellinger, Dixie Gibbs. *Out of the Heart: How to Design Writing Assignments for High School Courses*. The University of California, Berkeley, CA: Bay Area Writing Project Publications. The author provides several examples of assignment sequences, each reflecting a solid discourse theory, for teachers who want to move beyond disconnected assignments in writing classes.

Kinneavy, James L., William J. McCleary, and Neil Nakadate. *Writing in the Liberal Arts Tradition* (2nd ed.). New York, NY: Harper & Row, 1990. This book is the basis for the writing chapters in the *Elements of Writing* series.

Kirby, Dan, and Tom Liner. *Inside Out: Developmental Strategies for Teaching Writing*. Upper Montclair, NJ: Boynton/Cook Publishers, Inc., 1981. *Developmental* aptly describes the authors' approach as they explain and demonstrate teaching strategies designed to help writers at all levels of sophistication improve their writing processes.

Kutz, Eleanor, and Hephzibah Roskelly. *An Unquiet Pedagogy: Transforming Practice in the English Classroom*. Upper Montclair, NJ: Boynton/Cook Publishers, Inc., 1991. This seminal book will challenge traditional assumptions about learners and literacy as it explores how imagination and learner-constructed knowledge undergird any meaningful writing in classes where the development of true literacy is the goal.

Mohr, Marian M. *Revision: The Rhythm of Meaning*. Upper Montclair, NJ: Boynton/Cook Publishers, Inc., 1984. This book defines and exemplifies revision in terms that teachers will understand, adapt, and use as they help their students improve initial drafts.

Murray, Donald M. *Learning by Teaching*. Upper Montclair, NJ: Boynton/Cook Publishers, Inc., 1982. The author connects his process model for writing his thoughts on the processes of teaching writing in a readable text with useful examples and illustrations from the author's experiences as a teacher and writer.

———. *A Writer Teaches Writing* (2nd ed.). Boston, MA: Houghton-Mifflin, 1974. This early "writing process" work was designed to show how real writers write and to make that knowledge useful and powerful for teachers of writing.

Romano, Tom. *Clearing the Way: Working with Teenage Writers*. Portsmouth, NH: Heinemann, 1987. Especially helpful chapters on conferencing and evaluation distinguish this book, which is written in a lively style and which is supported with examples of students' writing and clear insights into a writing teacher's learning.

Willis, Meredith Sue. *Personal Fiction Writing: A Guide for Writing from Real Life for Teachers, Students, and Writers*. New York, NY: Teachers & Writers Collaborative, 1989. An experienced writer and teacher shares classroom-tested ideas on helping students to describe places, people, and action; to write dialogues and monologues; to create structure; and to revise what they have written.

Ziegler, Alan. *The Writing Workshop*, Vol. 1. New York, NY: Teachers & Writers Collaborative, 1981. This description of a workshop method for individualizing writing instruction includes ample references to students' work and sharp observations by the author.

———. Vol. 2. New York, NY: Teachers & Writers Collaborative, 1984. This is an excellent catalog of assignments exemplified by students' responses to them, along with the author's observations—a sequel to Vol. 1, which describes a writing environment conducive to such assignments and approaches.

Cooperative Learning

Elbow, Peter. *Writing Without Teachers*. New York, NY: Oxford University Press, 1973. The title of the book should not suggest that teachers are not necessary, but rather that they assume different roles in nurturing students' group processes and peer-response activities.

Eubanks, Ilona M. "Nonstandard Dialect Speakers and Collaborative Learning." *The Writing Instructor* Vol. 10 (Spring 1991): 143-148. This article examines features of the traditional language-and-writing classroom that lead to difficulty, frustration, and often failure for speakers of nonstandard dialects.

Golub, Jeff, ed. *Focus on Collaborative Learning: Classroom Practices in the Teaching of English 1988*. Urbana, IL: National Council of Teachers of English, 1988. In compiling this collection of best practices, the editor includes pieces from teachers who describe general collaborative-learning skills before moving to others who discuss how these skills are applied in literature study and various writing activities, from prewriting through revision.

Healey, Mark K. *Using Students' Writing Response Groups in the Classroom*. The University of California, Berkeley, CA: Bay Area Writing Project Publications. In a monograph that realistically assesses problems often associated with response groups, the author provides practical suggestions on how to help students become more helpful in fostering growth in peers' writing.

Rabkin, Eric S., and Macklin Smith. *Teaching Writing That Works*. Ann Arbor, MI: The University of Michigan Press, 1990. In a step-by-step process for breaking the cycle of one individual student writing for a teacher, the authors move from the development of ideas in group settings through group editing and evaluation. Writing designed to help students accomplish "real work" is central to all group activities.

Spear, Karen. *Sharing Writing*. Upper Montclair, NJ: Boynton/Cook Publishers, Inc., 1988. This most practical guide to forming and nurturing response groups could only have been written with the benefit of this teacher's broad and thoughtful experience with response groups in writing courses. The book begins with an honest and promising appraisal of "challenges in peer response groups."

Individual Needs/Language Diversity

Brooks, Charlotte K., ed. *Tapping Potential: English and the Language Arts for the Black Learner*. Urbana, IL: National Council of Teachers of English, 1985. In addition to explaining why many African American children have not responded to the standard curriculum taught in traditional ways, contributors to this collection offer specific suggestions for classroom practices.

Cleary, Linda Miller. "A Profile of Carlos: Strengths of a Nonstandard Dialect Writer." *English Journal* 77 (September 1988): 59-64. A case study in which the language barriers and biases faced by one writer prove instructive for his teachers and for all teachers.

Allaei, Sara Kurtz, and Ulla Maija Connor. "Exploring the Dynamics of Cross-Cultural Collaboration in Writing Classrooms." *The Writing Instructor* 10 (Fall 1990): 19-28. After reviewing what is known about cross-cultural writing, the authors provide guidelines and recommendations for establishing collaborative groups in multicultural writing classes.

Daniels, Harvey, and Marcia Farr. *Language Diversity and Writing Instruction*. New York, NY: ERIC Clearinghouse on Reading and Communication Skills, National Council of Teachers of English: 1986. This book succeeds in providing just enough theory and background of teachers seeking to improve the writing of students who are native speakers of nonstandard dialects.

Gonzalez, Roseann Duenas. "When Minority Becomes Majority: The Changing Face of English Classrooms." *English Journal* 79 (January 1990): 16-23. Even though the recommendations in this article are for all the language arts, applications to writing instruction will be easy and crucial to teachers in multicultural classes.

Marik, Ray. *Special Education Students Write: Classroom Activities and Assignments*. The University of California, Berkeley, CA: Bay Area Writing Project Publications. Case studies of students with special learning needs are the bases for the author's advocacy of well-sequenced, developmentally appropriate writing activities for all learners.

Rose, Mike. *Lives on the Boundary*. New York, NY: Penguin Books, 1989. The author's experiences as a remedial student contributed to his sensitive understanding of the educational underclass about which he writes so effectively.

Shade, Barbara J. Robinson, ed. *Culture, Style and the Educative Process*. Springfield, IL: Charles C.Thomas, 1989. This book provides insight into various cultures' learning styles as well as methods for enhancing students' retention by addressing their learning styles.

Shaughnessy, M.P. *Errors and Expectations: A Guide for the Teacher of Basic Writing*. New York, NY: Oxford University Press, 1977. The author's strategies for unlocking expression and clarity for basic college writers are helpful to high school writers as well.

Stottlar, James, ed. *Teaching the Gifted*. Urbana, IL: National Council of Teachers of English, 1988. Ways to identify students with special talents in the language arts, to individualize instruction to meet their needs, and to encourage independent thinking in academically advanced students are among topics in this collection.

Urzua, Carole. "'You Stopped Too Soon': Second Language Children Composing and Revising." *TESOL Quarterly* 21 (June 1987): 279-304. This research report shares what six months of careful observations of Southeast Asian students' writing taught teachers about how second-language children learn to write.

ASSESSMENT

Belanoff, Pat, and Marcia Dickson. *Portfolios: Process and Product*. Portsmouth, NH: Heinemann, 1991. In a good blending of theory and practice in how to use writing portfolios for assessment in many settings, this book allows teachers to plan strategies unique to their own purposes.

Clay, Marie M. "Research Currents: What Is and What Might Be in Evaluation." *Language Arts* 67 (March 1990): 288-298. After discussing problems and limitations of standardized testing, the author makes recommendations toward more useful assessment models and philosophies across the language arts and into high school.

Holmes, Ken. *Perspectives on Teaching and Assessing Language Arts*. Urbana, IL: National Council of Teachers of English, 1990. These essays include a rationale for multiculturalism in reading materials as well as a timely consideration of assessment in whole-language approaches.

Najimy, Norman C. *Measure for Measure: A Guidebook for Evaluating Students' Expository Writing*. Urbana, IL: National Council of Teachers of English, 1981. By using examples of students' writing, this guide suggests how teachers' responses can enhance instruction instead of threatening students.

Posner, Richard. "Life Without Scan-Tron: Tests as Thinking." *English Journal* 76 (February 1987): 35-38. This author demonstrates how six types of written, in-class tests improve his students' writing, thinking, and mastery of subject matter.

Robinson, Joy L., et al. *Creating Writers: Linking Assessment and Writing Instruction*. White Plains, NY: Longman, 1990. This book helps students and teachers agree on attributes of good writing and has scoring guides that help link instruction to assessment.

RESPONDING TO WRITING

Belanoff, Pat, and Peter Elbow. *Sharing and Responding*. New York, NY: Random House, 1989. This book provides useful examples of students' responses to peers' writing along with clear rationales and activities designed to increase the value of peer responses.

Freedman, Sarah Warshauer. Response to Student Writing. Urbana, IL: National Council of Teachers of English, 1987. This research report on the state of the art in response to writing not only indicates what teachers do and how students feel about it, but offers clear ideas on best practices in providing students with feedback.

Harris, Muriel. *Teaching One-to-One: The Writing Conference*. Urbana, IL: National Council of Teachers of English, 1986. The author provides a strong justification for one-on-one conferencing in the writing classroom and provides useful strategies and insights that can help writing teachers at all levels.

Sommers, Nancy. "Responding to Student Writing." *College Composition and Communication* 33 (May 1982): 148-56. The author encourages teachers to respond to the ideas, meanings, and purposes in students' papers before error hunting in order for students to engage in meaningful revision.

Sullivan, Patrick, "Responding to Student Writing: The Consequences of Some Common Remarks." *English Journal* 75 (February 1986): 51-53. The author describes the hidden messages behind four types of comments teachers frequently make in responding to students' writing.

Whole Language/Integration

Cronin, Hines, David Meadows, and Richard Sinatra. "Integrating Computers, Reading, and Writing Across the Curriculum." *Educational Leadership* 48 (September 1990): 57-60. Good illustrations suggest how visual maps can be constructed via computers to enhance students' thinking and organizational skills in all school subjects.

Kroll, Barry M., and Roberta J. Vann. *Exploring Speaking-Writing Relationships: Connections and Contracts*. Urbana, IL: National Council of Teachers of English, 1981. A precursor of many whole-language texts and approaches, these essays provide instructive analysis of how speaking and writing can be composed and contrasted toward better understanding and teaching of both.

Martin, Nancy, et al. *Writing Across the Curriculum*. Portsmouth, NH: Boynton/Cook Publishers, Inc., 1983. Each pamphlet in this series suggests ways to integrate the teaching of writing by "writing to learn" in various school subjects.

Newkirk, Thomas. *Only Connect: Uniting Reading and Writing*. Upper Montclair, NJ: Boynton/Cook Publishers, Inc., 1986. An excellent middle section on "Reading, Writing, and Interpreting" will help teachers see possibilities for reading in the writing classroom and vice versa.

Petersen, Bruce T, ed. *Convergences: Transactions in Reading and Writing*. Urbana, IL: National Council of Teachers of English, 1986. This collection of essays cuts across several fields in contemporary writing theory and research to explain the logic of integrating reading and writing in the classroom.

Shuman, Baird R., and Denny Wolfe. *Teaching English Through the Arts*. Urbana, IL: National Council of Teachers of English, 1990. In this "Theory and Research into Practice" (TRIP) booklet, the authors provide teachers with classroom-tested ways to connect reading and writing in English classes to popular culture and traditional art forms.

Self, Judith. *Plain Talk About Learning and Writing Across the Curriculum*. Urbana, IL: National Council of Teachers of English, 1987. Teachers of different subjects demonstrate how writing can provide a helpful way for students to think about content and experiences in all subjects.

Writing Across the Curriculum

Fulwiler, Toby. *Teaching with Writing*. Upper Montclair, NJ: Boynton/Cook Publishers, Inc., 1987. An especially strong chapter on writing and testing helps make this treatment of process writing in the content areas valuable for teachers in all subject areas.

Gere, Anne Ruggles, ed. *Roots in the Sawdust: Writing to Learn Across the Disciplines*. Urbana, IL: National Council of Teachers of English, 1985. The editor has compiled essays on how writing can improve thinking and enhance learning in all the traditionally included subjects such as science and math with the added bonus of thoughtful essays on writing in art and foreign-language classes.

Kiniry, Malcolm, and Ellen Strenski. "Sequencing Expository Writing: A Recursive Approach." *College Composition and Communication* 36 (May 1985): 191-202. Though the model described here is based on a college program, the rhetorical strategies and discipline-specific approaches to writing are applicable to high school writers.

Talbot, Bill. "Writing for Learning in School: Is It Possible?" *Language Arts* 67 (January 1990): 47-57. The author describes his experiences in observing students who were learning how to use writing for learning and raises both concerns and hopes based on his observations.❦

ELEMENTS OF WRITING

A Full Range of Components to Meet Your Students' Needs

The materials that accompany ***Elements of Writing*** have been designed to help teachers in real classrooms—where the demands on their time and energy are great—to deal with each student as an individual. Regardless of your students' learning styles, ***Elements of Writing*** has a variety of materials to meet their needs.

Pupil's Editions

The *Pupil's Editions* for ***Elements of Writing*** combine the latest educational research with practical teacher input. Extensive surveys of both teachers and students, as well as field testing across the nation, were used to verify and validate the instructional design.

Annotated Teacher's Editions

The *Annotated Teacher's Editions* that accompany each level of ***Elements of Writing*** suggest lesson plans and a variety of teaching strategies for all types of students.

Teacher's Resource Banks™

The blackline-masters in the *Teacher's ResourceBanks* provide practice and reinforcement for every chapter in the *Pupil's Editions.* Each binder is divided into nine sections which correspond to specific chapters in the *Pupil's Edition:* Process and Structure, Aims for Writing, Language and Style, Grammar, Usage, Mechanics, Resources, Holistically Graded Composition Models, and Assessment Portfolio.

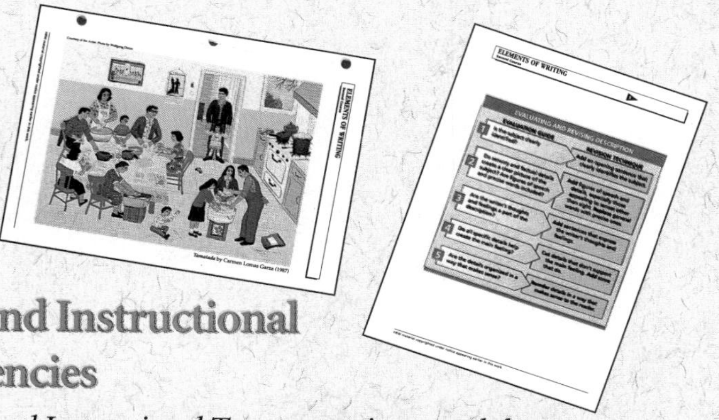

Fine Art and Instructional Transparencies

The *Fine Art and Instructional Transparencies* extend the strong visual program in the *Pupil's Editions* and integrate the study of composition with art history.

For each grade level, there are three types of transparencies: *Fine Art Transparencies, Graphic Organizer Transparencies,* and *Revision Transparencies.* Each transparency is supported by *Teacher's Notes* which suggest ways to use the transparencies in the classroom.

Vocabulary Workshop, Grades 6-12

Vocabulary Workshop is based on the word lists included in the *Teacher's ResourceBanks.* Each level of *Vocabulary Workshop* uses a variety of new student-centered activities to help students develop their ability to understand new and unfamiliar words.

Holt Writer's Workshop 1 and 2

The *Holt Writer's Workshop* is a software program for IBM® PC and Compatibles and Macintosh® computers that provides students with opportunities to develop expository, persuasive, expressive, and literary writing. *Holt Writer's Workshop 1* is designed to be used with Grades 6-8 and *Holt Writer's Workshop 2* is designed to be used with Grades 9-12.

Test Generators

The *Test Generators* are user-friendly software programs that enable teachers to create customized worksheets, quizzes, or tests for each grammar, usage, and mechanics chapter in the text. The *Test Generators* are available for Apple® II Series, IBM® PC and Compatibles, and Macintosh® computers.

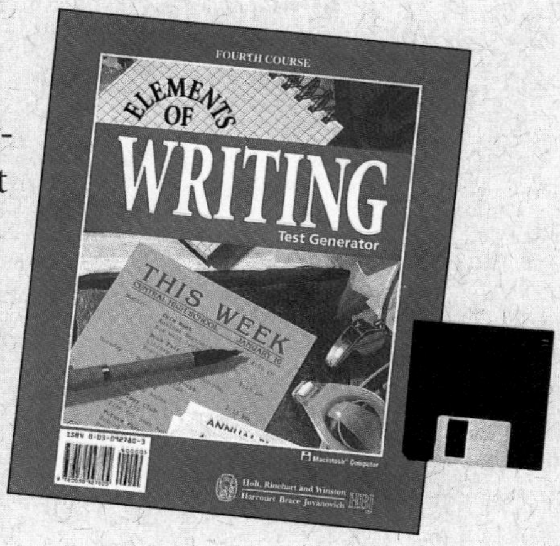

ELEMENTS OF WRITING

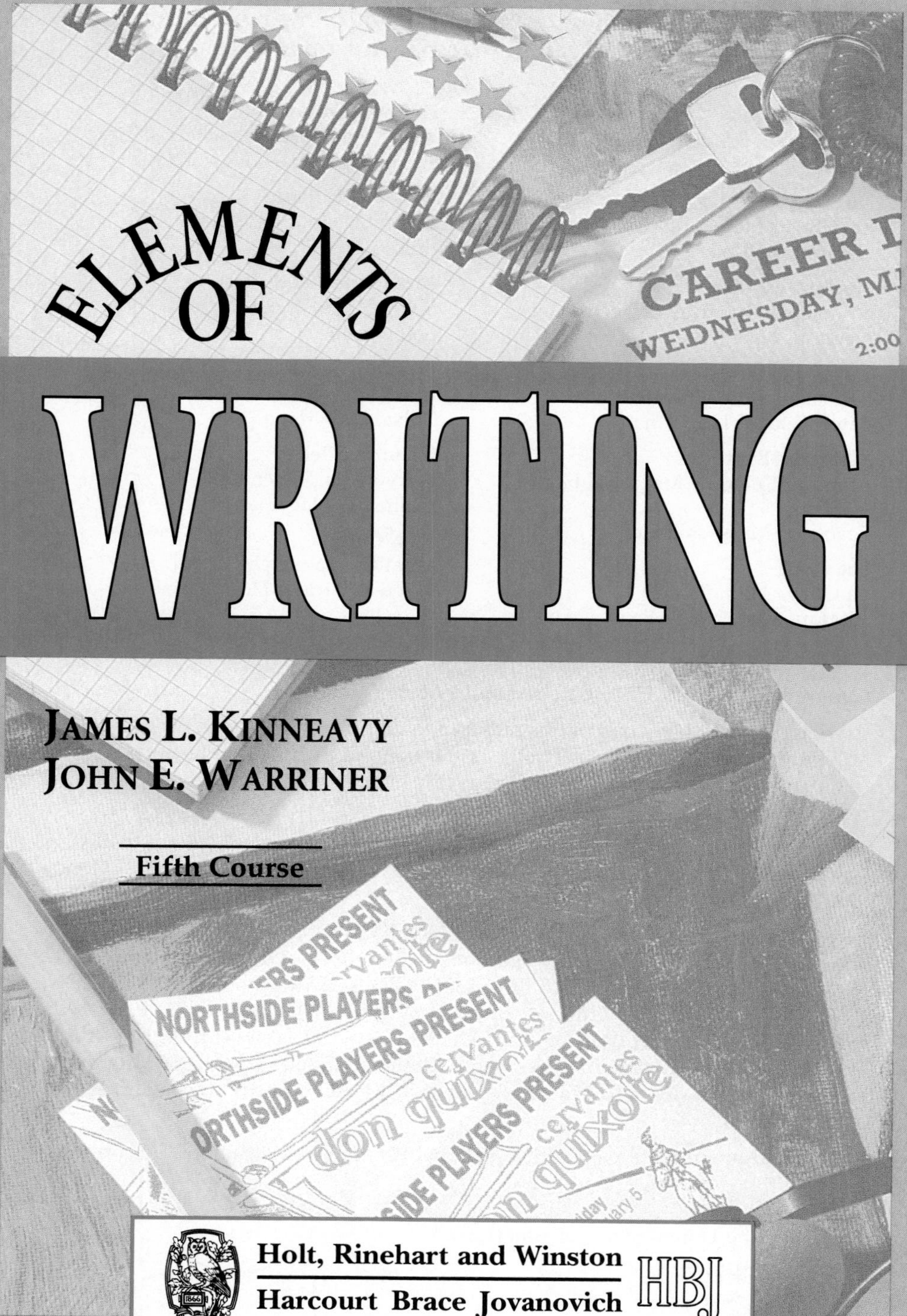

JAMES L. KINNEAVY
JOHN E. WARRINER

Fifth Course

Holt, Rinehart and Winston
Harcourt Brace Jovanovich
HBJ
Austin • Orlando • San Diego • Chicago • Dallas • Toronto

Critical Readers

Grateful acknowledgment is made to the following critical readers who reviewed pre-publication materials for this book:

Donald Baker
Peoria High School
Peoria, Illinois

Anthony Buckley
East Texas State University
Commerce, Texas

Norbert Elliot
New Jersey Institute of Technology
Newark, New Jersey

David England
Louisiana State University
Baton Rouge, Louisiana

Elaine A. Espindle
Peabody Veterans Memorial High School
Peabody, Massachusetts

Pat Graff
La Cueva High School
Albuquerque, New Mexico

Dennis Hannon
Wappingers Central School District
Wappingers Falls, New York

Ronald Murison
Riverdale Country School
Bronx, New York

Mary Jane Reed
Solon High School
Solon, Ohio

Linda E. Sanders
Jenks High School
Tulsa, Oklahoma

Victoria Skelley
Fairview High School
Cullman, Alabama

Kay Tanner
West Orange High School
Winter Garden, Florida

Printed in the United States of America

ISBN 0–03–047148–6

1 2 3 4 5 6 7 8 9 062 95 94 93 92

Authors

James L. Kinneavy, the Jane and Roland Blumberg Centennial Professor of English at The University of Texas at Austin, directed the development and writing of the composition strand in the program. He is the author of *A Theory of Discourse* and coauthor of *Writing in the Liberal Arts Tradition*. Professor Kinneavy is a leader in the field of rhetoric and composition and a respected educator whose teaching experience spans all levels—elementary, secondary, and college. He has continually been concerned with teaching writing to high school students.

John E. Warriner developed the organizational structure for the Handbook of Grammar, Usage, and Mechanics in the book. He coauthored the *English Workshop* series, was general editor of the *Composition: Models and Exercises* series, and editor of *Short Stories: Characters in Conflict*. He taught English for thirty-two years in junior and senior high school and college.

Writers and Editors

John Algeo is Professor of English at the University of Georgia. He is coauthor with Thomas Pyles of *The Origins and Development of the English Language*.

Ellen Ashdown has a Ph.D. in English from the University of Florida. She has taught composition and literature at the college level. She is a professional writer of educational materials and has published articles and reviews on education and art.

John Roberts has an M.A. in Education from the University of Kentucky. He has taught English in secondary school. He is an editor and a writer of educational materials in literature, grammar, and composition.

Alice M. Sohn has a Ph.D. in English Education from Florida State University. She has taught English in middle school, secondary school, and college. She has been a writer and editor of educational materials in language arts for twelve years.

Carolyn Calhoun Walter has an M.A.T. in English Education from the University of Chicago. She has taught English in grades nine through twelve. She is a professional writer and editor of educational materials in composition and literature.

Glenda A. Zumwalt has an Ed.D. in Teaching Composition and Rhetoric from East Texas State University. She teaches composition at Southeastern Oklahoma State University. She is a writer of educational materials in composition and literature.

PART ONE

WRITING

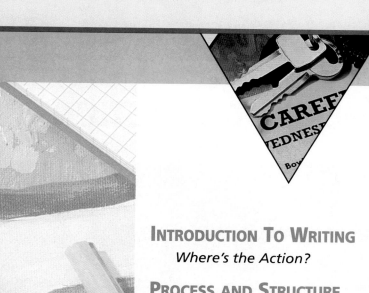

WHERE'S THE ACTION?

(pp. 2–13)

OBJECTIVES

- To explore the ways that writers and writing affect the world
- To identify and analyze the aims of writing
- To compare and contrast the aims of writing

USING THE INTRODUCTION TO WRITING

This introduction to writing is just that—an introduction. It starts by talking briefly about the power of writing in peoples' lives to emphasize that writing is more than just schoolwork. Next, the introduction touches upon the two central focuses of the

INTRODUCTION TO WRITING

WHERE'S THE ACTION?

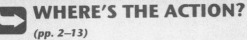

James L. Kinneavy

writing chapters in the textbook—the "how" of writing (modes) and the "why" of writing (aims).

The communication triangle graphically reflects the four major aims of James Kinneavy's theory of discourse. For more information, refer to the essay in the front of this book, **"Meet the Aims and Modes of Writing,"** or to Dr. Kinneavy's two books, *A Theory of Discourse* and *Writing in the Liberal Arts Tradition.* ■

The ocean seems to stretch forever. Whether a sheet of shimmering blue or a tangle of fierce waves, its surface gives no hint of what lies below. We don't see the treasures, the eerie life forms, the **action** lurking beneath the surface.

Away from the ocean, we are still mesmerized by surface features. We judge people by the way they look. We judge a house by its front door, a neighborhood by its streets, and the art of communication by what we see and hear via electronic media.

And the electronic media surround us. Politicians campaign and advertisers push their products on radio and television; CDs, audio and video cassettes, radio, and television entertain us; and telephones and computers satisfy our other information needs.

On the surface of our world, written words hardly seem a ripple; writing is a thing of the past. We get what we need by watching, listening, speaking, and pushing buttons. Isn't that where the action is? Hasn't writing lost its power?

The Action Below the Surface

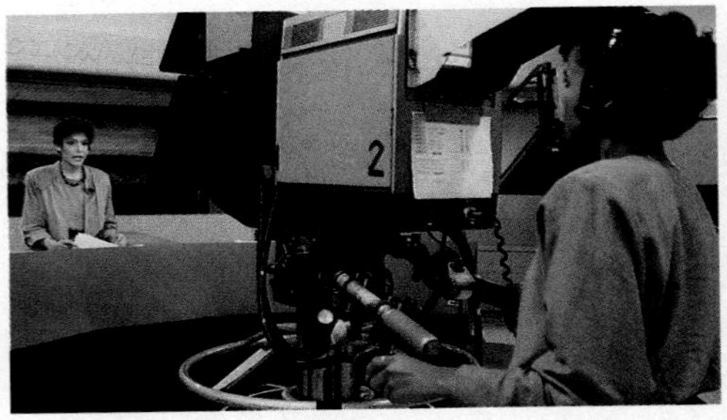

You know that writing hasn't lost *all* of its power; after all, here you sit, reading a book about writing. But, you may well think that written words aren't very important in your life, at least your life outside of school. On the surface, the action seems to be elsewhere.

But peer through your diving mask and you'll see where the action is. On the surface, you see the actors, but behind the scenes scriptwriters write the dialogue and stage directions that the director, actors, and countless crew members work from. On television, you see the politicians, but they are supported by staffers who write and edit their speeches. TV anchors deliver news reports written by researchers and reporters; and those funny, powerful commercials are created from scripts hammered out by copywriters and art directors.

Even forms of communication that seem nonverbal are based on writing that lurks below the surface. Someone wrote a computer program for stock market reports and the year's most popular video game; someone wrote a playbook for the Super Bowl champions; and someone wrote a job training manual for workers in a factory.

Yes, much of the action is below the surface and much of it is dependent on writing. And if you don't have strong writing skills, you won't be part of the action.

To live life completely—not just as an observer but as an active participant—you need to be able to write effectively. Whether you are expressing your emotions and thoughts, sharing your ideas and knowledge, convincing others to share your opinions, or expressing your own creativity, writing is where the action is. Its power is yours to command.

The Writer's Power

It doesn't matter whether you are writing an opera, a business memo, or a letter to your brother, you are exercising a power that is common to all writers and speakers. That power, the power of communication, is basically very simple. Communication requires only the ***writer***, a ***subject,*** (something to say), an ***audience*** (someone to say it to), and ***language*** (a way to say it). It helps to think of these elements in terms of a communications triangle with language—both written and spoken—at its very center.

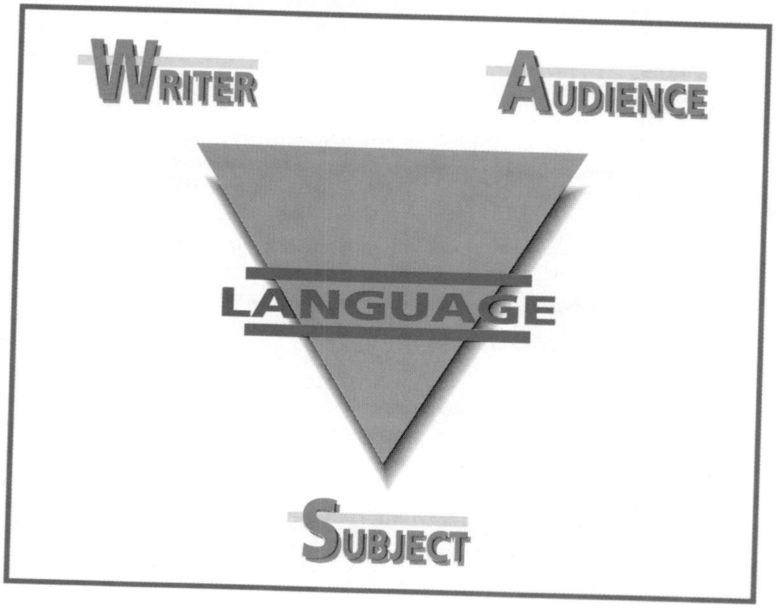

How Writers Communicate

The Writing Process

By being able to affect the action both above and below the surface, writers share a power. But if all writers share a power, they also share a ***process:*** a way of moving from idea to action; from first thought to first words to final writing. As your own experiences may show, there's no right or wrong way to go through the process. Each writer uses the process differently, but most writers work through the same basic steps.

Prewriting	Thinking and planning: thinking about your purpose and audience; deciding what to write about; developing ideas and gathering details; creating a plan for presenting ideas
Writing	Writing a first draft: expressing ideas and details in sentences and paragraphs; following a writing plan; incorporating new ideas
Evaluating and Revising	Reviewing the draft: deciding what works and what doesn't; changing the draft to improve it
Proofreading and Publishing	Finding and correcting mistakes: writing or printing out a final copy; sharing the writing with an audience

Why Writers Communicate

The Aims of Writing

Whether writing a fast-paced TV script, a powerful political speech, or a private diary, every writer has a reason for writing—a ***purpose,*** an ***aim.*** And when you look at all of those reasons and see how they're alike and different, you'll find that every piece of writing has one of four basic ***aims,*** or purposes.

Expository	**Informative:** Writers may want to give facts and information. **Explanatory:** They may want to explain something, using evidence. **Exploratory:** They may want to investigate complex ideas or find solutions to problems.
Persuasive	Sometimes writers want to convince people to accept an idea or take action.
Self-Expressive	Writers may want to express personal feelings and thoughts, for themselves alone or for others.
Literary	Sometimes writers want to create imaginative works, such as films, stories, poems, novels, and plays.

Next you'll read four pieces of writing, one for each aim. All four are on the same topic and illustrate how writers participate in the action. What does each writer want to accomplish?

EXPOSITORY WRITING

American Immigration: *Always Constant, Always Changing*

Except for Native Americans, every person in the United States descends from an immigrant. Yet immigration has not been a single and unbroken stream since the first Europeans arrived. From only a brief overview, it's clear that immigration to the United States, while continuous, has constantly changed, with U.S. attitudes and policies toward immigrants also changing.

Before 1880, most immigrants came from western and northern Europe, followed by southern and eastern Europeans in the 1890s. By 1880, 75,000 Chinese immigrants lived in California, and by 1900, about 80,000 Mexicans lived in the Southwest. Between 1880 and 1920, over twenty-three million immigrants had arrived to begin new lives in America.

This wave ended in 1921 when Congress sharply limited annual immigration and established quotas by nationality, favoring northern Europeans. Asian immigrants were banned altogether, and Mexicans were admitted to work but not allowed to become citizens. Their labor was wanted, but as immigration after World War I rose to one million per year, opinion to restrict non-white groups mounted.

It was not until 1965 that a "Great Society" initiative abolished the national origins system, ended restrictions on Asian immigration, and enacted new provisions for accepting political refugees. . . .

Reader's Response

1. What do the words *immigrant* and *America* mean to you personally? Freewrite about one or both in your journal.
2. The excerpt from this report ends with 1965. What factual information about world events since 1965 and U.S. population today would you expect to find in the remainder of the report?

ANSWERS

Reader's Response

1. Responses will vary. Encourage students to share in a class discussion any personal experiences with immigration or strong feelings about America they may have.
2. Students will differ in their opinions of what factual information about world events since 1965 should be included in the remainder of the report. Ask students to provide support for their suggestions.

EXPRESSIVE WRITING

April 17, 1912—Today was the most exciting and frightening day of my life. We arrived in America! The boat trip over was a nightmare. So dirty, terrible food, many sick people crowded into so little space. The sun was just coming up when Mama woke me. She was very excited. We went up on deck and I saw the beautiful Statue of Liberty, her torch burning brightly, welcoming us majestically. And the "skyscrapers"! I could not believe my eyes.

Our first steps in America were onto Ellis Island. We had name tags pinned to our clothes. Papa clutched our ID papers. We awaited our turns to see the doctors, Papa very anxious. The worst thing that could happen was to have the doctor write a chalk letter on your clothes. That meant you had a disease, and you would be detained, maybe sent back home. We all made it through.

Then we were led to a huge three-stories-high hall—giant half-moon windows and globed chandeliers and a tiled ceiling. We joined many people on the long rows of wooden benches. Three hours later we were called to the inspector's desk. What's your name? age? Where will you live? Do you have work waiting for you? Do you have any money? Papa's answers must have been right—we were told we could stay in the United States. Then the train, New Jersey, Uncle Alfred's house (and bakery), my cousins. It is more than I can write tonight. I am bursting with—everything.

Reader's Response

1. Do you think an immigrant arriving in New York today would share these feelings? What might be the same or different? Why?
2. Is this writer writing only for himself or possibly for others? And *why* do you think he is writing? Explain.

ANSWERS

Reader's Response

Responses will vary.

1. Feelings that might be the same for an immigrant today include fear of a new place, excitement of arrival, awe at the Statue of Liberty, surprise at the size of the skyscrapers, anxiety over seeing a doctor, and worry that the questions would not be answered correctly. Feelings that might not be present for a young immigrant arriving in New York today include distaste and revulsion at the dirty conditions, crowded spaces, poor quality of food, and sick people. (Ellis Island served as the chief immigration station of the country from 1892 until 1943.)
2. The writer probably writes mostly for self-expression, but he may also realize that recording his thoughts and feelings is a good way to remember how he felt during those first few minutes after he arrived. With his perceptions recorded he can share his impressions with others—possibly his children and grandchildren—at a later date.

ANSWERS

Reader's Response

Responses will vary.

1. Many student will think Li's letter would convince Kim to come to the United States. The letter addresses ways the family can feel at home, as well as learn about abundant new things in the new country; it mentions that many people from Li's and Kim's homeland live nearby and that work for Kim's father and a temple would be easy to find; and it explains that the immigrants have freedom from war and from fear. Some students will say Kim and his family might have questions about leaving their homeland or worries about feeling unwelcome in a new land.
2. Li's letter depends on both logical reasoning and facts and appeals to emotion to persuade his friend. Facts include the following: food, clothing, jobs, schools, and temples are all easily accessible; special classes at which one can learn English are available; and this country is safer than Kim's. Emotional appeals include appeals to friendship, freedom, and fun.

PERSUASIVE WRITING

Dear Kim:

I hear your parents are trying to decide upon coming to the United States. At last! I am praying they will do it. How can we help to make up their minds?

Of course you know I like my new life very much--movies, pizza. There is so much. Stores are filled with food (our country's food, too), clothes, everything you'd want. Your parents won't have to search far for what they need.

And they will not feel alone. Many people from our homeland live nearby. My father knows the resettlement group that will help your father find work. You will first live with us. That way it will not be so shocking!

Your parents are probably scared too about not knowing the language and about your school. Yes, learning to speak is hard. But I take special classes, and in less than two years, I hear and read almost everything well and even speak English out of school.

I will not say it is easy to leave a country you have loved. I do not always feel welcome here, and I know my parents are more comfortable keeping to our group. But they do not regret their choice and do not want to give up freedoms after a life of war and fear. Truly, it is every day more our home.

Tell them! Tell them! May my words ease their fears and bring you to us soon.

Your friend,
Li

READER'S RESPONSE

1. What if Kim himself is not absolutely sure about coming to the United States? Do you think Li's letter would convince *him*? Do you think he might have other worries or questions? Explain.
2. Does Li's persuasion depend on logical reasoning and facts, appeals to emotion, or a combination of the two?

LITERARY WRITING

This poem is inscribed on the base of the Statue of Liberty.

THE NEW COLOSSUS

BY EMMA LAZARUS

Not like the brazen giant of Greek fame,
With conquering limbs astride from land to land;
Here at our sea-washed, sunset gates shall stand
A mighty woman with a torch, whose flame
Is the imprisoned lightning, and her name
Mother of Exiles. From her beacon-hand
Glows world-wide welcome; her mild eyes command
The air-bridged harbor that twin cities frame.
"Keep, ancient lands, your storied pomp!" cries she
With silent lips. "Give me your tired, your poor,
Your huddled masses yearning to breathe free,
The wretched refuse of your teeming shore.
Send these, the homeless, tempest-tost to me,
I lift my lamp beside the golden door!"

READER'S RESPONSE

1. A few words from this poem are quoted frequently: " 'Give me your tired, your poor, / Your huddled masses yearning to breathe free. . . .' " How do these words make you feel? Why is it significant that these words greeted immigrants?
2. When a writer's aim is to create literature, the choice of words—language itself—is extremely important. What examples can you find in this poem that illustrate Emma Lazarus's concern for language—for example, a musical effect or an unusual image?

ANSWERS

Reader's Response

Responses will vary.

1. Most students will feel it is significant that the words of the poem greet new immigrants, but their personal responses will vary. If students have visited the Statue of Liberty, ask them to share their individual reactions to the poem and the experience.
2. Lazarus uses unusual images such as "brazen giant of Greek fame,/With conquering limbs astride from land to land," "mighty woman with a torch, whose flame/Is the imprisoned lightning," and "her mild eyes command/The air-bridged harbor that twin cities frame." She creates a musical effect by using rhyming stanzas and alliterative phrases such as the following examples: "sea-washed, sunset gates shall stand," "world-wide welcome," "wretched refuse," and "tempest-tost." She also stresses related phrases with the repetitious use of "your."

ANSWERS

Writing and Thinking Activities

1. **a.** Li's letter to Kim is written primarily to persuade.
   b. The essay **"American Immigration: Always Constant, Always Changing"** uses facts and details to inform readers about American immigration.
   c. Emma Lazarus's poem **"The New Colossus"** uses words differently than ordinary speech.
   d. The immigrant's journal entry of April 17, 1912, expresses the writer's personal thoughts, feelings, and experiences.

Questions 2 and 4 might be journal activities. Question 3 is a group activity. You might want to save these projects to work on at a later date.

Writing and Thinking Activities

1. Look over the four models again, and then meet with two or three classmates to discuss these questions about the writers' aims.
   a. Which writer wants primarily to persuade?
   b. Which one uses facts and details to inform readers about something?
   c. Which one uses words in a way that is different from ordinary speech?
   d. Which one wrote for him- or herself, to express personal thoughts, feelings, and experiences?
2. What aims do you have when you write? Do you use some more than others? Keep track of how you communicate during a typical day. Jot down all your uses of language: writing, reading, speaking, and listening. Notice how much of your communication is informative, persuasive, self-expressive, or creative. Then get together with two or three classmates to discuss what you've learned about your own communication patterns.
3. What are the aims of people who try to communicate with you? For forty-eight hours, keep track of the reasons people are communicating with you. Include oral discussion and comments, telephone calls, television, radio, as well as anything you read for school or for pleasure. Keep a little notebook and jot down the type of communication and its purpose, for example, "TV ad, to persuade; phone call, to inform." At the end of the forty-eight hours, do a tally and allocate percentages to each of the four aims. Then share what you've learned with your classmates, attempting to discover whether you all experienced similar patterns.
4. Emma Lazarus's poem, "The New Colossus," is obviously creative writing. So are novels, short stories, and plays. But are these the only kinds of writing that can be called creative? Do you see creativity of language or thought in any of the other models? Think of any nonliterary writing you've done—a book report, science report, journal entry—that you consider creative in some way, and explain why.

All photos: The Granger Collection, New York

Chapter 1

WRITING AND THINKING

OBJECTIVES

- To discuss author's purpose, audience, and tone
- To write about a surprising experience or event
- To practice brainstorming and clustering
- To use the *5W-How?* questions
- To listen for specific information
- To describe an event or place by using the five senses
- To arrange details in order
- To classify information in chart format
- To arrange notes to write the first draft of a paragraph
- To prepare for peer and self-evaluations
- To evaluate and revise the first draft of a paragraph
- To proofread for errors in grammar, usage, and mechanics
- To publish an essay
- To write a parody of any genre

Motivation

To motivate students for writing and thinking, begin by discussing how writing affects everyday life. Ask students where they find writing and in what forms. What kind of writing is the most enjoyable to read and why? Ask students to think of reasons why writers write. [Students might suggest that writers want to convey messages, save feelings on paper, share experiences with a reader, or sort out feelings.] To motivate students for Pat Mora's essay, ask students to prepare family trees. Discuss how being part of a family influences people. Point out that often writing will be influenced by culture, beliefs, feelings, attitudes, and experiences.

Introduction

Discuss with students the purposes of writing (expressive, literary, informative, and persuasive). Explain to students that in this chapter they will learn several general approaches to writing that they can use for many different types of writing. Tell students that they will begin with the expressive aim and use the first-person point of view to describe sensory impressions.

Integration

This chapter integrates many areas of learning. If your students are reading Thoreau, you could have them read an essay and discuss the writer's tone, style, and ability to unify his writing. At the end of the chapter, students will write parodies of literary genres; you could discuss Thoreau's genre as an example.

Students can use the guidelines charts in this chapter for any writing assignments for any class. They can use what they have learned from a writer's perspective to appreciate and understand a reader's point of view. Students will also learn that a reader's reactions are shaped by his or her feelings, attitudes, and experiences. In this chapter students will learn to revise writing by adding, replacing, deleting, or inserting information. Students can apply these skills to writing answers on essay questions. Students will learn how to divide information into pros and cons and can apply critical-thinking skills to history by acknowledging the pros and cons of elections, wars, or explorations.

The chart on the next page illustrates the strands of language arts as they are integrated into this chapter. For vocabulary study, glossary words are underlined in some writing models.

QUOTATIONS
All **Quotations for the Day** are chosen because of their relevance to instructional material presented in that segment of the chapter and for their usefulness in establishing student interest in writing.

INTEGRATING THE LANGUAGE ARTS

Selection	Reading and Literature	Writing and Critical Thinking	Language and Syntax	Speaking, Listening, and Other Expression Skills
"Why I Am a Writer" by Pat Mora **16-18** from **"The engaging habits of chameleons suggest mirth more than menace"** by James Martin **35** from ***It Was a Dark and Stormy Night: The Best (?) from the Bulwer-Lytton Contest*** by Mike Montgomery **55**	Analyzing an author's opinion **19** Responding personally to literature **19** Reading for specific information **28** Analyzing purpose, audience, and tone **37** Examining parody in literature **54-55**	Responding personally to literature **19** Writing a journal entry **19, 25, 54** Applying interpretive and creative thinking **19, 27, 31, 32, 37, 41-42** Freewriting **25** Brainstorming and clustering **27, 39, 52** Using the *5W-How?* questions **27** Using research resources **28, 52** Taking and using notes for an oral report **28** Observing and imagining **31** Using descriptive language and sensory details **31** Asking "What if?" questions **31** Analyzing subjects and topics **32** Analyzing purpose, audience, and tone **37** Arranging the order of details **39, 44** Classifying and charting information **41-42** Writing a first draft **44** Evaluating and revising a paragraph **49** Imitating a writing style **55**	Proofreading for errors in grammar, usage, and mechanics **49, 51**	Brainstorming and clustering with classmates **27** Preparing *5W-How?* questions for an interview **27** Presenting an oral report **28** Listening for specific information **29** Sharing an analysis with classmates **32** Talking with classmates to compare purpose, audience, and tone in written material **37** Discussing order of details with classmates **39** Working with a classmate to evaluate and revise a paragraph **49** Brainstorming publishing ideas with classmates **52**

CHAPTER 1

SEGMENT PLANNING GUIDE

Whether you are planning for a quick review of a writing concept or preparing an extended lesson on composition, you can use the following Planning Guide to adapt the chapter material to the individual needs of your class.

SEGMENT	PAGES	CONTENT	RESOURCES
1 *Looking at the Process*	*15-19*		
Literary Model **"Why I Am a Writer"**	16-18	Guided reading: a model of an expressive essay	
Reader's Response	19	Model evaluation: responding to literature	
2 *Aim and Process*	*20-21*		
3 *Prewriting*	*22-42*		Freewriting and Brainstorming 1 Clustering and Questioning 2 Purpose, Audience, and Tone 3 Reading and Listening with a Focus 4 Arranging Ideas 5
Finding Ideas for Writing	22	Introduction: finding ideas for writing	
Chart: Prewriting	23	Guidelines: examining techniques for finding ideas	
Keeping a Writer's Journal	23-24	Guidelines: starting a journal	
Freewriting	24-25	Guidelines: using criteria to focus freewriting	
Exercise 1	25	Applied practice: freewriting in a journal	
Brainstorming	25-26	Guidelines: using criteria to brainstorm	
Clustering	26	Guidelines: using criteria to make connections	
Exercise 2	27	Cooperative learning: brainstorming and clustering	
Asking Questions	27	Guidelines: using the *5W-How?* questions	
Exercise 3	27	Applied practice: using the *5W-How?* questions	
Reading with a Focus	28	Guidelines: using criteria to find information	
Exercise 4	28	Applied practice: reading for specific information	
Listening with a Focus	29	Guidelines: using criteria for critical listening	
Exercise 5	29	Applied practice: listening for specific information	
Observing	30	Guidelines: analyzing examples	
Imagining	30-31	Guidelines: using creative questioning	
Exercise 6	31	Applied practice: observing and imagining	
Critical Thinking: Analyzing a Subject	32	Guidelines: narrowing a subject	
Critical Thinking Exercise	32	Applied practice: analyzing subjects and topics	
Considering Purpose, Audience, and Tone	33-34	Guidelines: writing for specific situations	
Critical Thinking: Analyzing Purpose, Audience, and Tone	35-36	Guidelines: analyzing and selecting purpose, audience, and tone	
Literary Model from **"The Engaging Habits of Chameleons"**	35	Guided reading: examining a model for purpose, audience, and tone	

All the resources listed in this chapter are located in the *Teacher's ResourceBank*™.

SEGMENT	PAGES	CONTENT	RESOURCES
Critical Thinking Exercise	37	Cooperative learning: analyzing purpose, audience, and tone	
Arranging Ideas	38	Guidelines: arranging information	
Chart: Arranging Ideas	39	Guidelines: examining methods of order	
Exercise 7	39	Applied practice: arranging the order of details	
Using Charts	39-41	Guidelines: arranging notes in charts	
Critical Thinking: Classifying	41	Guidelines: using criteria to classify information	
Critical Thinking Exercise	41-42	Applied practice: classifying and charting	
4 *Writing*	*43-44*		Writing a First Draft 6
Writing a First Draft	43	Guidelines: examining a first draft	
Exercise 8	44	Applied practice: writing a first draft	
5 *Evaluating and Revising*	*45-49*		Peer Evaluation 7 Revising by Adding and Cutting 8 Revising by Replacing and Reordering 9
Charts: Evaluation Guidelines	45-46	Guidelines: using criteria for peer and self-evaluation	
Chart: Evaluating/Revising	47	Guidelines: applying evaluation and revision techniques	
A Paragraph Revision	48	Example: analyzing a writer's revisions	
Critical Thinking: Evaluating and Revising	49	Guidelines: using criteria to evaluate and revise a paragraph	
Critical Thinking Exercise	49	Cooperative learning: evaluating and revising	
6 *Proofreading and Publishing*	*50-53*		Proofreading 10 Manuscript Form 11
Chart: Proofreading	50-51	Guidelines: using criteria to proofread	
Exercise 9	51	Applied practice: proofreading a paragraph	
Publishing	51-52	Publishing ideas: reaching a specific audience	
Chart: Manuscript Form	52	Guidelines: using good form	
Exercise 10	52	Cooperative learning: brainstorming publishing ideas	
Chart: Proofreading Symbols	53	Guidelines: analyzing editing symbols	
7 *Making Connections*	*54-55*		
Exploring the Creative Process	54	Guidelines: approaching writing creatively Applied practice: writing a journal entry	
Imitating a Writing Style	54-55	Cooperative learning: writing a parody	
Literary Model from ***It Was a Dark and Stormy Night***	55	Guided reading: examining a parody	
WHOLE-CHAPTER RESOURCE Chapter Review			

SEGMENT 1 *(pp. 14–19)*

LOOKING AT THE PROCESS

OBJECTIVES

- To respond personally to literature
- To write a brief journal entry about a surprising experience or event
- To analyze emotions encountered in reading personal essays

MOTIVATION

To interest students in the interrelationship between writing and thinking, ask them to jot down as many words as they can to represent who they are. Have them fill in the blank, "I am a ____." Allow them to write for a few minutes and then have them discuss what they wrote. Did writing one idea lead to another?

VISUAL CONNECTIONS
Drawing

About the Artist. Jack Beal, a realist painter, is noted for the use of perspective in his paintings. To achieve a three-dimensional effect, Beal often places objects in front of the picture plane. An example of this technique in *Drawing* is the paper that falls over the front of the table. The paper seems to reach out from the painting toward the viewer. Another example is the front leg of the table, which extends past the edge of the painting, creating the illusion that the table exists not only within the painting but also beyond it.

Other Expression Skills. Several artists can use the same model, yet each interprets the work through a unique and personal perspective. Writers can also select the same subject, follow the same research path, and yet develop distinct and personal compositions. Each person renders the subject through his or her own interpretation of stored memories and new awarenesses. You might have students design a book cover for a book they are all familiar with. Have them compare the results to see what different interpretations each has.

1 WRITING AND THINKING

TEACHING THE LESSON

Begin the lesson by continuing the discussion of the interrelationships between writing and thinking. Use the information in **Looking at the Process** as a springboard for discussion. Introduce Pat Mora's essay as the way one writer sees the relationship.

Have a volunteer read the essay aloud and allow time for students to respond to the essay. What reactions do they have to the essay? Use the annotations to guide the discussion further.

Looking at the Process

Consider this: Perhaps the title of this chapter should really be WRITINGANDTHINKING. When you write, what comes out on the paper just can't be separated from what goes on in your head. Analyzing, researching, sifting notes, even daydreaming: They're all part of the writing **process.**

Writing and You. A good way to see how these two interact is to look at your personal writing and thinking process. Do you play with different ideas before settling on a topic? When you're drafting, do you mentally weigh each word? Or do you spit out sentences so that your thoughts keep flowing? Have you ever been *surprised* by what you actually write? Probably you have. Because writing is thinking, writing is discovery—for each writer in a different way.

As You Read. A young girl once asked poet Pat Mora why she writes. As you read Mora's answer, notice what she believes that writing can both discover and *do.*

Jack Beal, *Drawing* (1974). Oil on canvas, 60″ × 68″. Courtesy of the Frumkin/Adams Gallery, New York.

QUOTATION FOR THE DAY

"Reading furnishes the mind only with materials of knowledge; it is thinking makes what we read ours." (John Locke, 1632–1704, English philosopher)

Share the quotation with students and ask them to work in pairs to create statements that explain the quotation's meaning. Tell students that, like thinking and reading, thinking and writing must go together.

MEETING INDIVIDUAL NEEDS

LEP/ESL

General Strategies. When ESL students are able to discuss the content of their reading material before they read, their comprehension generally increases. So, before students read the essay by Pat Mora, you may want to discuss some of the main ideas and invite commentary and questions from students.

GUIDED PRACTICE

To guide students in analyzing the professional model, use the first **Reader's Response** question as a group activity. Ask students to think of other examples of personal essays having social consequences [essays of Anne Frank, Abraham Lincoln, or Martin Luther King, Jr.].

INDEPENDENT PRACTICE

After the class discussion, students should be able to answer **Reader's Response** questions 2 and 3 independently. Explain to students that when they write, ideas might come rapidly to mind. Suggest that students list in journals ideas for future writing topics.

Why I am a Writer

by Pat Mora

VISUAL CONNECTIONS

Exploring the Subject. Pat Mora writes poems and stories about her Mexican American heritage and the Southwestern landscape that she loves. She has authored books of poetry, which include *Chants* and *Borders,* and a children's book, *Tomas and the Library Lady.*

ASSESSMENT

Assess students' performance by evaluating their discussion of **Reader's Response** questions and by their willingness to explore ideas in their journals. To help ease students into sharing their writing with classmates, ask students to share their responses to question 3 with the class.

RETEACHING

If students have difficulty understanding the relationships between writing and thinking, you might reword the questions. Using **Reader's Response** question 2 as a guide, have each student describe an exciting place he or she would like to visit and have the student explain why. Adapt **Reader's Response** question 3 by focusing ☛

I like people. I like long, slow lunches with my friends. I like to dance. I'm no hermit, and I'm not shy. So why do I sit with my tablet and pen and mutter to myself?

There are many answers. I write because I am a reader. I want to give to others what writers have given me, a chance to hear the voices of people I will never meet. Even if I met these authors, I wouldn't hear what I hear alone with the page—words carefully chosen, woven
1 into a piece unlike any other, enjoyed by me in a way no other person will enjoy them. I love the privateness of writing and reading.

I write because I am curious. I am curious about me. Writing is a way of finding out how I feel about anything and everything. Now that I've left the desert where I grew up, for example, I'm discovering
2 how it feels to walk on spongy autumn leaves and to watch snow drifting up on a strong wind. I notice what's around me in a special way because I am a writer. I notice my world more, and then I talk to
3 myself about it on paper. Writing is a way of saving my feelings.

I write because I believe that Hispanics need to take their rightful place in American literature. We need to be published and to be studied in schools and colleges so that the stories and ideas of our people won't quietly disappear. Although I am happy when I finish the draft of a poem or story, I always wish that I wrote better, that I could bring more honor and attention to the *abuelitas*—grandmothers—I write about. That mix of sadness and pleasure frequently occurs in a writer's life.

"I write because I am curious. I am curious about me."

USING THE SELECTION

Why I am a Writer

1

What does Mora mean by ". . . enjoyed by me in a way no other person will enjoy them"? [Everyone reacts to the words on the page differently. People bring their own experiences to reading.]

2

How has Mora used sense words to describe new feelings in this description? [She tells what it feels like to walk on spongy autumn leaves and she describes how she watches snow drifting.]

3

Mora states that writing is a way of saving her feelings. Is she saving these feelings for herself or for a larger audience? [Mora is saving her ideas for herself and trying to attain recognition as a Hispanic writer by a larger audience.]

on literature the class has read. You could also stimulate ideas by reading your responses to the questions.

CLOSURE

To close the lesson, discuss the following questions with the class:

1. What is Mora's purpose in writing?
2. Why might writers want to share their experiences with readers?
3. How does reading and writing make you aware of the world?

Although we don't discuss it often because it is depressing, my people have been and sometimes still are viewed as inferior. We have all been hurt by someone who said, "You're not like us; you're not one of us. Speaking Spanish is odd; your family looks funny." Some of us decide we don't want to be different; we don't want to be part of a group that is often described as poor and uneducated. I spoke Spanish at home to my grandmother and aunt, but I didn't always want my friends at school to know that I spoke Spanish. And I didn't like myself for feeling that way. I sensed it was wrong, but I didn't know why. Now I know.

I know that the society we live in affects us. It is not easy to learn to disregard the unimportant things about people—the car they drive, the house they live in, the color of their skin, the language they speak at home. It takes courage to face the fact that we all have ten toes, get sleepy at night, get scared in the dark. Some families, some cities, some states, and even some countries foolishly convince themselves that they are better than others. Then they teach their children this
4 ugly lie. It is like a weed with burrs and stickers that prick people.

How are young people who are Hispanic or members of an ethnic group supposed to feel about themselves? Some are proud of their cultural roots. But television commercials are busy trying to convince us that our cars, clothes, and even our families aren't good enough. It is so hard to be yourself, your many interesting selves, because billboards and magazine ads tell you that being beautiful is being thin,
5 blond, and rich, rich, rich. No wonder we don't always like ourselves when we look in the mirror.

So I write to try to correct these images of worth. I take pride in being a Hispanic writer. I will continue to write and to struggle to say what no other writer can say in quite the same way.

"I write because I believe that Hispanics need to take their rightful place in American literature."

4
Mora uses a simile to describe racism. Do you think the comparison to stickers and burrs is appropriate? Why? [Racism causes pain just as thorns and stickers do and both keep people away.]

5
Why does Mora repeat the word *rich*? [She wants to emphasize the importance that modern society places on material success.]

ENRICHMENT

Remind students that in this essay Mora explains why she is proud to be Hispanic, even though in the past she has tried to hide her culture to help her fit in. Ask students to explore the topic in short journal entries. ■

READER'S RESPONSE

1. Pat Mora says she writes because she loves the "privateness" of writing and reading, but another reason is a very public one: to "correct . . . images of worth" for Hispanics. Is this a contradiction? Can an extremely personal experience like reading have social consequences? Say what you think, and use examples from your own life if you can.
2. Mora also says writing is a way of "saving" new feelings—like her discovery of snow after a life in the desert. What things in your life surprised you when you first saw or experienced them? Recapture one of your surprising experiences in a brief journal entry.
3. Mora believes writers frequently feel a "mix of sadness and pleasure." What mix of feelings has a piece of writing caused you (delight and tear-out-your-hair? fear and then pride?), and why?

LOOKING AHEAD

This chapter will take you through a general approach to writing that you can apply to many different types of writing. You'll learn some specific writing techniques and explore how they can work for you. As you read and experiment, remember that

- writing and thinking are inseparable
- the writing process isn't an unchanging set of steps: it's both flexible and personal
- your topic, purpose, and audience are connected: they shape and influence each other

ANSWERS

Reader's Response

Answers may vary.

1. Students might say that reading can have social consequences when the reader learns something about society that was not known before or when the reader sees a side of society that is unfamiliar and begins to understand other cultures better.
2. Encourage students to respond freely and not to worry about errors as they try to recall surprising experiences. To help inspire confidence in students, recognize and compliment their ability to express ideas.
3. Encourage students to explain their reactions and to be creative in combining the emotions.

MEETING INDIVIDUAL NEEDS

AT-RISK STUDENTS

To help students who are at risk feel like they are part of the group, form discussion circles with desks arranged so that students cannot get lost in the crowd. Until students feel comfortable reading their own writing to the class, encourage them to participate by asking them to comment on what other students have written.

SEGMENT 2 *(pp. 20–21)*

THE "WHY" AND "HOW" OF WRITING

TEACHING THE AIMS AND PROCESS

To introduce the aims of writing to students, explain that all writers have at least one purpose when they begin—expressing themselves, sharing information, persuading people, or creating literature. Use the **Why People Write** chart to expand on the aims and have students give examples of each. Explain that although some writing may have more than one purpose, usually one aim predominates.

To help students think about writing as a process, have them discuss projects

COOPERATIVE LEARNING

Have students work in groups of four to analyze television programming to show how subject, audience, and purpose are related. You might give them the following categories: Saturday morning network shows, prime time network shows, cable television, and public television. Have each group list at least two shows from each category. The groups should identify the subject, audience, and purpose of each show. Allow time for each group to present its analysis.

One way to present the process of writing is with the pie chart. But students may have other ideas about representing the writing process, especially their own writing processes. Brainstorm for a few minutes with the class to start students thinking about how they approach the writing task. Then have students create artistic representations of their writing processes. Encourage original approaches.

Aim—The "Why" of Writing

Consider the types of writing you see and hear about almost every day—ads, postcards, school essays, love letters, protest signs, movie scripts. With all the different writing everywhere around you, you would think the purposes for writing are limitless. Well, yes and no.

It's true that every writer writes for a very specific reason—for example, to say "I love you" to a heartthrob. But even though each writer has a particular intent for writing, each specific reason will fall within four basic purposes for all writing.

WHY PEOPLE WRITE	
To express themselves	To get to know themselves better; to find some kind of meaning in their own lives
To inform, to explain, or to explore	To give other people information that they need or want; to provide an explanation; to explore an idea or problem
To persuade	To convince other people either to do something or believe something they'd like
To create literary works	To be creative with language; to say something in a unique way

Probably everything written has one of these purposes, but it's also true that much writing has a combination of purposes. Someone may write about a strong opinion both to persuade others and to know her own values better. Someone may write a story both to be creative and to share special knowledge.

Your personal message will never be exactly the same as anyone else's, but you will share with all other writers the essential "why" of writing.

they've undertaken that required following steps or establishing procedures, such as running a computer program or planning a school event. Lead students to understand that although there are basic steps that should be followed, individuals must adapt the process to suit their own needs.

Explain that the writing process also has stages of development. Refer students to the writing process pie graph to explain the four stages of the process. You might mention that the process is recursive and the emphasis each writer places on each stage varies. ■

Process—The "How" of Writing

A ***piece*** of writing might be simply defined as words on some surface. But the ***process*** of writing always involves more than the typing, scratching, or crayoning of those words. Writing moves in stages (you don't go from idea to finished paper in one flash), and writing requires thinking (sometimes you may spend more time thinking than setting down the words).

In this chapter you'll have to think and write, because it's really impossible to separate the two. And you'll be working through the basic stages of the writing process, as shown in the diagram that follows. But note what the diagram shows: The process isn't a straight line. As a writer, you always have, and need, the freedom to jump forward, go back, or start over again.

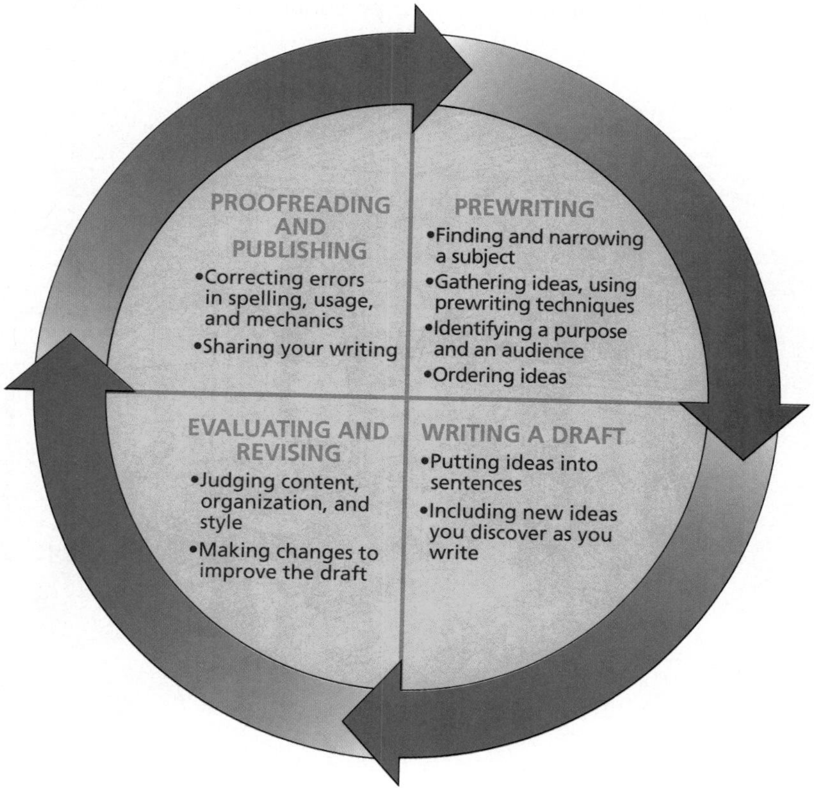

PROOFREADING AND PUBLISHING
•Correcting errors in spelling, usage, and mechanics
•Sharing your writing
PREWRITING
•Finding and narrowing a subject
•Gathering ideas, using prewriting techniques
•Identifying a purpose and an audience
•Ordering ideas
EVALUATING AND REVISING
•Judging content, organization, and style
•Making changes to improve the draft
WRITING A DRAFT
•Putting ideas into sentences
•Including new ideas you discover as you write

MEETING INDIVIDUAL NEEDS

AT-RISK STUDENTS

Almost all writers, even professional ones, experience some anxiety about writing. You can help allay students' anxiety by explaining that every student has special talents and requires an individualized approach to the writing process. Some people work quickly in the prewriting stage, while others work very slowly in planning their writing. Some experienced writers collect information for years before writing a word. Some evaluate and revise as they complete sections; others revise all at once.

Remind students that your goal for them is to develop their skills as writers to the best of their abilities. Writing is not a competitive activity, but an opportunity to improve skills that will be required throughout their lifetimes.

SEGMENT 3 *(pp. 22–42)*

PREWRITING

OBJECTIVES

- To freewrite a journal entry
- To brainstorm and cluster ideas
- To design *5W-How?* questions for an interview
- To research a topic and to present the information orally
- To listen for specific information
- To describe an event or a place by using the five senses
- To arrange details in order

Teacher's ResourceBank™

RESOURCES

PREWRITING

QUOTATION FOR THE DAY

"There is an art of reading, as well as an art of thinking, and an art of writing." (Isaac D'Israeli, 1766–1848, English author)

Discuss with students qualities that "an art" suggests. Include the idea that any expression according to aesthetic principles is an art. Explain that this chapter will introduce composition skills that develop the three arts listed by D'Israeli.

MEETING INDIVIDUAL NEEDS

LEP/ESL

General Strategies. You might remind ESL students that experiences in their native countries or their encounters learning a new language and culture are good choices for writing topics. Assure them that American students are interested in life in faraway places.

Prewriting

Finding Ideas for Writing

Writing is built on ideas. The blank page is a terror to many writers, even professional writers, not because they lack the words but because they lack a workable idea. Writing starts with getting an idea and collecting information about it.

"Easily said," you may be thinking, "not so easily done." Well, there are practical helps: prewriting techniques for stirring up ideas. The following chart shows several. And these techniques aren't closed little boxes. You can use a combination of techniques for the same assignment. You may get an idea for a paper from your **writer's journal** and then use **imagining** to explore it and get started. You'll discover which techniques work for the task and your personal writing approach.

"Write about dogs!"

MOTIVATION

To interest students in this lesson, read an excerpt from a writer's journal, such as that of Thoreau or Sarah Kemble Knight. Point out that the everyday experiences people encounter make interesting reading because everyone's experiences and their reactions to the experiences are different.

TEACHING THE LESSON

This segment may require several days to teach, depending upon your class structure and the needs of your students. Many of your students will be familiar with prewriting techniques. If they are, you may want to discuss several techniques and follow up with exercises. If not, you may want to spend more time on each method. ☛

PREWRITING TECHNIQUES		
Writer's Journal	Recording personal experiences, perceptions, and ideas	Pages 23–24
Freewriting	Writing for a few minutes about whatever comes to mind	Pages 24–25
Brainstorming	Listing ideas (alone or with others) as quickly as they occur	Pages 25–26
Clustering	Drawing lines and circles to show connections between ideas	Page 26
Asking Questions	Using the news reporter's *5W-How?* questions: *Who? What? When? Where? Why?* and *How?*	Page 27
Reading with a Focus	Reading efficiently to locate and collect specific information	Page 28
Listening with a Focus	Listening attentively to locate and collect specific information	Page 29
Observing	Noticing details through the senses: sight, hearing, smell, taste, touch	Page 30
Imagining	Probing your imagination for ideas, often using a "What if?" approach	Pages 30–31

Keeping a Writer's Journal

Writers from antiquity to the present day have kept journals, and for a very good reason. A ***journal***—a daily log of happenings—is a great way to keep a record of experiences, observations, feelings, opinions, original ideas, and unanswered questions. You can put anything you want into your journal: newspaper and magazine articles, interesting quotations, songs, poems, photos, dreams. Any of these bits and chunks may fit into some later piece of writing. On the following page are some suggestions for getting started.

MEETING INDIVIDUAL NEEDS

ADVANCED STUDENTS

Advanced students probably have experienced writing success and have developed their own unique prewriting strategies. Have some students share with the class the prewriting strategies that work best for them and have them explain how they adapt the prewriting strategies to suit their own writing styles and needs.

STUDENTS WITH SPECIAL NEEDS

Students with learning disabilities often have difficulty getting their ideas on paper. To assist them with this chapter, you might let them pick several of the techniques in this segment and concentrate on the development of ideas in the ones they select.

Since spelling problems can create major hindrances to the flow of creative ideas, have students keep spiral notebooks to record relevant words that are difficult to spell.

Three **Critical Thinking Exercises** are interspersed in the segment. They use prewriting techniques but require greater analysis and classificatory skills.

Give students an overview of the segment by having them read the **Prewriting Techniques** chart on p. 23. Explain that over the next several days they will be practicing several of these techniques.

As you read through the material in this segment, you might want to model each technique on the chalkboard to help students visualize the application of the concept. Remind students that the prewriting technique is only the first part of the writing process; refer them back to the pie graph of the writing process on p. 21 if necessary.

COOPERATIVE LEARNING

To analyze the role each sense plays in providing information, divide the class into groups of four or five (taste may be too difficult to arrange) and assign each group one location on campus. Allow groups to go outside, to a lab, or to the school cafeteria.

Designate one student in each group to concentrate on a different sense and to freewrite about the experience. Then have the group combine notes and present the notes to the class. Students might determine which senses provide them with the most information to capture the essense of the site and which ones give more subtle clues.

1. Use a notebook, scrapbook, or file folder.
2. Try to add something to your journal every day, and date your entries. Consider writing at the same time every day, early in the morning or late at night perhaps. (But you can jot down notes any time on anything, and insert them later.)
3. Don't worry about punctuation, grammar, or usage.
4. Use your imagination. Be creative. Write original poems or song lyrics if you want. Jot down story ideas.
5. For paste-in entries, write notes beside them. Why did you like a particular poem, quotation, or cartoon?

Freewriting

When you're ***freewriting,*** you jot down whatever pops into your head.

1. Decide on a time limit of three to five minutes. Keep writing until your time is up.
2. Start with any topic or word, such as *photography* or *sports cars* or *honesty*.
3. Don't worry about complete sentences or proper punctuation. Your thoughts may be disorganized. You may repeat yourself. That's perfectly okay.
4. Occasionally, choose one key word or phrase from your freewriting and use it as a starting point for more writing. This ***focused freewriting,*** or ***looping,*** allows you to "loop" from what you've already written to something new.

As students do the exercises, encourage them to save their work in notebooks or files so that they can refer to the notebooks when they are stuck for writing ideas. Students can personalize the covers and include drawings, cartoons, or other idea starters. Notebooks can also be beneficial because they enable students to compare their work in the early part of the year to the projects they undertake later.

HERE'S HOW

What's the thing about jogging. Dad says it's better to walk. Some doctor said it. Akechi jogs and Fumiyo. I bought running shoes. Jogging, jogging. Maybe jogging hurts your feet. How? First time I jogged—sore legs. Some guy made jogging popular, don't know his name. Got to have good running shoes. That's me. I ran three miles a week ago and my legs still hurt. Jog tomorrow.

EXERCISE 1 **Freewriting in a Journal**

You can freewrite anywhere, but since you have started a journal, you can freewrite there. Start with this question: What's your favorite song? Write a couple of lines of the lyrics. Then give yourself exactly three minutes to write whatever comes into your head about the song.

Brainstorming

Another way to generate ideas is through ***brainstorming,*** or using free association. You can brainstorm alone or with others by using the following steps:

1. Write a word, phrase, or topic on your paper or on the board.

ANSWERS

Exercise 1

You will probably want to evaluate students' journal freewriting on completion rather than on content. However, you might check to see if students have included lyrics to their favorite songs.

GUIDED PRACTICE

During this stage of learning, students often benefit from directed guidance on the prewriting techniques. Using the **Here's How** sections as guides, work with the class to generate class or small-group samples. You might assign different volunteers to work at the chalkboard while the other students supply ideas. As students make suggestions, guide the work and point out alternative ways of recording and grouping ideas.

Because each of the exercises involves a different technique, you may want to have students work on the exercises in class with your assistance. Although several of the techniques are independent in nature and require independent thinking, students need

MEETING INDIVIDUAL NEEDS

LESS-ADVANCED STUDENTS

Some students may have difficulty with the free-association techniques demonstrated in this prewriting section. Emphasize that each technique benefits some (but not all) writers and that the goal for using these exercises is to experiment with what works best for finding ideas.

Students are asked to try using each of the techniques to determine which help stimulate ideas the best for each student. If students have difficulties with some of the techniques, point out that the difficult methods are probably not the best ways for them to generate ideas.

LEARNING STYLES

Kinetic Learners. Kinetic learners might benefit from writing their ideas on circles and clustering them on a wall.

2. Without any careful thought, begin listing every related word or idea that enters your mind. One person can write for a group.
3. Don't stop to evaluate the ideas. Anything goes, even jokes and ideas that seem to be *off* the topic.

Clustering

Clustering is another free-association technique. Like brainstorming, it is used to break up a large subject into its smaller parts or to gather information, but it also shows connections. Clustering is sometimes called *webbing* or *making connections*.

1. Write a subject in the center of a sheet of paper. Draw a circle around it.
2. In the space around the circle, write all the words or ideas that come to mind. Circle each addition, and then connect it to the original circled subject with a line.
3. Create offshoots by adding and connecting related ideas. Then circle each related idea and connect it to the appropriate circle.

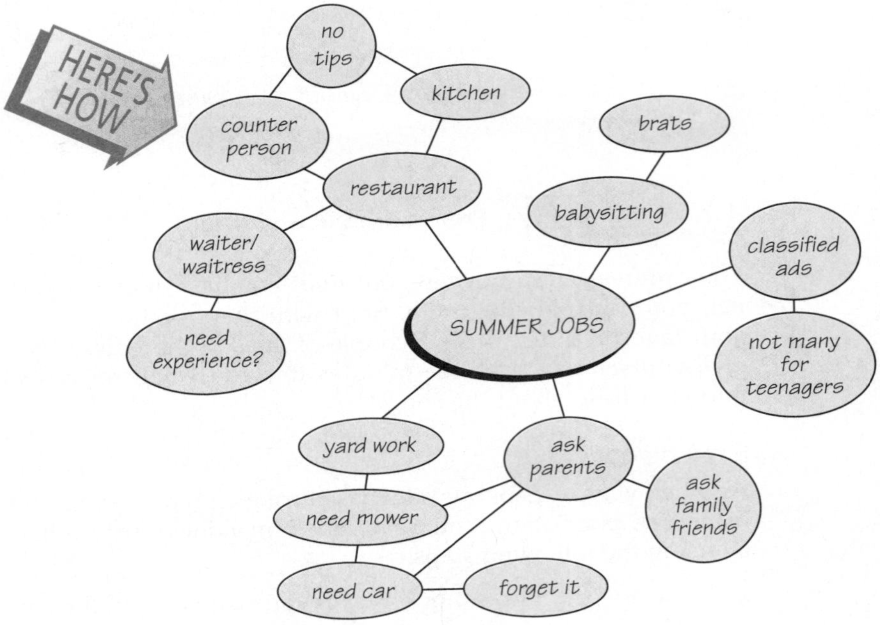

encouragement, as well as guidance, at this stage.

INDEPENDENT PRACTICE

Many of the exercises in this segment lend themselves to independent practice and should be handled as such if your students are capable.

When students are completing **Exercise 5** on p. 29, suggest that if they do not know shorthand, they might abbreviate words or phrases to help them keep up ☛

EXERCISE 2 **Practicing Brainstorming and Clustering**

Get together with another student, or form a small group, and choose one of the following subjects to brainstorm together. Keep going until you've exhausted every possible idea. Then, on your own, choose one of the other subjects and build a cluster diagram.

1. movies
2. the U.S. president
3. advertising
4. professional wrestling
5. vacations
6. automobiles

Asking Questions

The motto of the *New York Times* is "All the News That's Fit to Print." How do reporters for the *Times* go about finding "all the news"? Like reporters everywhere, they start with the *5W-How?* questions: *Who? What? Where? When? Why?* and *How?* Although not every question applies to every situation, the *5W-How?* questions are a good basic approach. You can also ask the same *5W-How?* question more than once, about various aspects of your topic.

HERE'S HOW

Topic: Today's Most Popular Recording Artist

Who?	*Who is number one on the pop charts?*
What?	*What record or album won this year's Grammy Award?*
Where?	*Where do most people see or hear this artist's music performed?*
When?	*When did the artist first achieve stardom?*
Why?	*Why do so many people like this star?*
How?	*How did the star get his or her start in popular music?*

EXERCISE 3 **Using the *5W-How?* Questions**

Responses will vary. Each student should include at least one of the *5W-How* questions.

You are a television news reporter and have been assigned to interview a scientist who has discovered a low-cost, highly efficient new source of energy. Prepare a list of *5W-How?* questions you intend to ask during the interview.

ANSWERS

Exercise 2

Cluster diagrams will vary. You might evaluate students' diagrams on completion rather than on content. However, you might check to see if students are successful in linking their ideas.

COOPERATIVE LEARNING

Students could develop their questioning techniques by using a game-show format. A panel of students could pretend to have unusual occupations that are unknown to the classroom questioners. By preparing questions to ask of the panel, students could polish their questioning strategies and learn interviewing skills.

when listening for specific information. Stress that this approach can be personal and that they can abbreviate any way that will help them remember because they are the only ones using the notes.

As students work independently to complete **Exercise 6** on p. 31, you might let them choose other familiar places.

ASSESSMENT

Read over students' writing to evaluate their ideas and their willingness to present the ideas. Ask a few volunteers to write their answers on transparencies for **Exercises 4, 5,** and **6.** Have the class evaluate the writing in terms of detail and interest.

INTEGRATING THE LANGUAGE ARTS

Library Link. Exercise 4 requires some research, so you might want to have a biographical dictionary available for students. Other possibilities include a desk encyclopedia or desk reference books. If your students are unfamiliar with the newer one-volume references, you might want a few students to familiarize themselves with the contents and to give short reports to the class.

ANSWERS

Exercise 4

Responses will vary. You may want to have students list the references they used for information.

Reading with a Focus

When you read a novel, you can sit back, relax, and enjoy the story. But when you read to gather information—for instance, for a paper on Dixieland music—you have to use a different approach. Here are some hints for finding and collecting information on a specific topic.

1. First, give the source of information a "once-over." Look for key words in the index (*jazz, Dixieland*), check the table of contents, and look through chapter headings and subheadings.
2. Skim passages until you find something about your topic; then slow down and take notes in your own words. Be sure to record publishing information for later use.

EXERCISE 4 **Reading for Specific Information**

Your task is to find material for a report on a famous African American in our nation's history. Some possibilities include Benjamin Banneker, Sojourner Truth, Rosa Parks, Frederick Douglass, Jackie Robinson, and Martin Luther King, Jr. Choose one. Next, find a source—perhaps your American history textbook or a biographical dictionary. Time yourself to see how long it takes to locate the material and to make notes answering the following questions.

1. When and where did the person live?
2. For what is he or she famous?
3. What was one major event in the person's life?

Then, using your notes, prepare a brief oral presentation in which you share with your classmates some of the information you have discovered.

RETEACHING

To reteach how prewriting methods can lead to writing ideas, share the insights of a professional writer with students. Use excerpts from Donald Murray's essay, **"Use Genre as Lens"** on p. T44 of the Annotated Teacher's Edition. Murray tells how a few journal notes led to an essay, a narrative, and a poem.

CLOSURE

To close the lesson, discuss the following questions with students:

1. What strategies help in the prewriting stage of the writing process? [journal writing—recording daily happenings; freewriting—jotting down whatever comes to mind; clustering—showing

Sojourner Truth Jackie Robinson Rosa Parks Frederick Douglass

Listening with a Focus

Your ears are another powerful prewriting tool, but they can't do the work all by themselves. It pays to *prepare* to listen.

Listening for information may include listening to a tape recording, a radio or television program, a speech, or an expert during a personal or telephone interview.

1. Think ahead. Make an outline of information you need, or prepare questions to ask.
2. In an interview, concentrate on the question the person is answering. Don't allow your mind to wander to the next question.
3. Take notes even if you are also recording. However, don't try to write every word—use phrases and abbreviations and listen for main ideas and significant details.

REFERENCE NOTE: For information on interviewing, see pages 950–952.

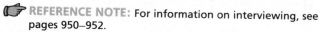

EXERCISE 5 **Listening for Specific Information**

Tune in to a local evening news broadcast on television. Listen for answers to these questions.

1. What is the lead news story—the event covered first? How much time does the station devote to the lead story?
2. What is the first feature story presented—that is, a story that isn't "hard" news?
3. How much air time is devoted to each kind of news: local, state, and national?

A DIFFERENT APPROACH

Exercise 5 requires students to listen to an evening news broadcast. Because auditory information is temporal and cannot be checked, students with difficulty in processing auditory information may feel unsure of their information. If you have equipment available, you might want to videotape a newscast for students to work on in class. Then the information can be rechecked and students can repeat what they need.

ANSWERS

Exercise 5

Responses will vary. You might want students to indicate what news programs they watched and listened to.

connections in ideas; brainstorming—using free association; asking questions—using *Who? What? Where? When? Why?* and *How?* questions to query a subject; listening with a focus—planning ahead and taking notes; observing—using the five senses to collect descriptive details; and imagining—asking "What if?" questions]

2. Which techniques work best for you? Why? ■

CRITICAL THINKING
Evaluation

Have students determine which prewriting techniques work best for them by writing down the nine methods on p. 23 and listing (or using their best means of organization) what they liked or disliked about each. Have students defend their choices with their listed reasons.

Observing

You can gather great writing material just by observing, but you need to remember that observation is purposeful and deliberate; it is not a passive activity. Here are some examples showing how one writer used his observation skills on a camping trip.

HERE'S HOW

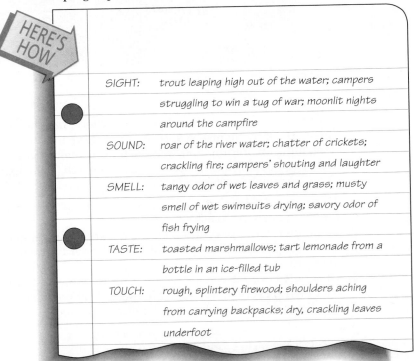

SIGHT:	*trout leaping high out of the water; campers struggling to win a tug of war; moonlit nights around the campfire*
SOUND:	*roar of the river water; chatter of crickets; crackling fire; campers' shouting and laughter*
SMELL:	*tangy odor of wet leaves and grass; musty smell of wet swimsuits drying; savory odor of fish frying*
TASTE:	*toasted marshmallows; tart lemonade from a bottle in an ice-filled tub*
TOUCH:	*rough, splintery firewood; shoulders aching from carrying backpacks; dry, crackling leaves underfoot*

Imagining

Creative writers have active imaginations. How often have you heard about something that happened, then wondered, "Well, that's interesting, but what if . . . ?" You can put that same creative questioning into your search for writing ideas.

1. *What if I could change my circumstances?* (What if I were an only child or what if I were *not* an only child? What if I had lived during the Middle Ages?)

2. *What if a familiar thing in our world no longer existed?* (What if we had no music? What if we had no public schools?)
3. *What if major social changes were made overnight?* (What if racial prejudice no longer existed? What if everyone earned the same amount of money?)

You can take this "What if?" approach and apply it to any subject. Here are some "What if?" questions you might apply to the subject of environmental control.

HERE'S HOW

- *What if we outlawed the manufacture of all nonbiodegradable products, such as plastics and disposable diapers?*
- *What if we permitted no lumbering at all for a period of five years?*

EXERCISE 6 **Observing and Imagining**

A good story can be about almost anything. Think about the four places listed below. Then choose one and observe it carefully. Write down some descriptive details about each event or place as you imagine it through your five senses. Finally, go one step further by writing a few "What if?" questions that might lead to good story plots.

1. a bus or subway train
2. a city park
3. a shopping mall
4. a river

EXAMPLE ***Inside an airplane: sensory perceptions***
blue sky; deep roar of the engines on takeoff; swaying sensation as the plane hits turbulence; inviting smell of the in-flight meal

Inside an airplane: "What if?"
What if hijackers with a time bomb were on the plane?
What if the plane had to make a forced landing in a cornfield?

ANSWERS

Exercise 6

Suggest that students structure their observations like **Here's How** on p. 30. Then encourage students to include "What if?" questions that pertain to the plot, such as character development, conflict, and setting.

CRITICAL THINKING
(p. 32)

OBJECTIVE
- To analyze subjects and topics

TEACHING *ANALYZING A SUBJECT*
Students learn how to analyze a subject and determine if it is too narrow or too broad in this lesson. To assist students in this process, suggest that they use questions to narrow their focus, such as "What kind?" "What about it?" and "What possibilities does it suggest?"

COOPERATIVE LEARNING
To provide practice in analyzing subjects and narrowing topics, have students play a game of writing roulette. Organize students in groups of four and have each student write five broad subjects on different slips of paper. Have students pass one slip at a time to the next group member to narrow until all the topics have been analyzed and narrowed. Have the class discuss the process and the topics that result.

ANSWERS
Critical Thinking Exercise

Responses will vary. Here are some possibilities:

1. subway systems or busing in urban settings; air pollution from automobile emissions or bicycling in the city
2. More narrow subject: ocean transportation

   Topic: modern ships
   More narrow topics:
   (1) hydrofoils and hovercraft
   (2) submarines and submersibles

CRITICAL THINKING

Analyzing a Subject

An editor once asked a famous football coach if he'd like to write a how-to book for other coaches. "Sure," the coach replied. "I'd love to."

"Okay," the editor said. "On what?"

The coach looked puzzled. "On football. What else?"

Now, the coach was right in a way. The editor did want him to write a book on the broad subject of football. But the editor also expected the coach to ***analyze*** his subject a bit—to break it down, to select the various possibilities from among his best tricks of the trade—things other coaches might benefit from.

When you're preparing to write, you, too, should subdivide, or analyze. For example, you may be interested in transportation, but you can't begin writing on that broad subject. You need to find and explore a narrower, more manageable topic for the length of paper you plan.

Broad subject: transportation
More narrow subject:
  urban transportation
Topic: mass transit systems
More narrow topics:
  (1) history in U.S.
  (2) new and experimental systems

CRITICAL THINKING EXERCISE:
Analyzing Subjects and Topics

Answer each of the following questions. You might want to compare your answers with a classmate's.

1. Other subdivisions are possible at every level of the sample analysis. Under "mass transit systems," what subdivisions can you add to the two listed? Under "urban transportation," can you think of topics other than "mass transit systems"?
2. Take the analysis of "transportation" in another direction entirely. Instead of "urban transportation," choose another subdivision and analyze it through all the levels shown.

Prewriting

Considering Purpose, Audience, and Tone

Purpose. You always have a reason, or *purpose,* for writing. Maybe you want to explain something to someone. You may want to persuade someone to come around to your way of thinking, or you may want to create a story or a poem. You may want to put your thoughts and feelings down on paper, just to see what you think. (You may even have a combination of purposes.) And just as you can have various reasons for writing, you can use various forms. The following chart shows some of the forms of writing in which you can achieve your purpose.

MAIN PURPOSE	FORMS OF WRITING
Self-Expressive	Journal, letter, personal essay
Literary works	Short story, poem, play
Expository: Informative, Explanatory, or Exploratory	Technical or scientific report, newspaper or magazine article, biography, autobiography, travel essay, brochure
Persuasive	Persuasive essay, letter to the editor, pamphlet, advertisement, political speech, poster

Audience. You don't talk the same way to everyone, nor do you write the same way for everyone. You adjust your writing for your *audience.* Ask yourself the following questions to find out more about your audience.

- How much does my audience already know about the topic? Do I need to give background information or explain technical terms?
- What strong feelings might my audience have about the topic?

CRITICAL THINKING
Analysis

To illustrate the importance of considering audience and tone, have students determine appropriate audiences and tones for the following subjects:

1. expressing your concerns about global warming
2. explaining how to tell a joke effectively
3. describing the pleasures of sailing
4. discussing the growing number of teenage runaways
5. convincing others of the importance of becoming volunteers
6. relating the economic effects of illiteracy in the United States

[Responses will vary, but students should choose audiences and tones that correspond.]

- What level of language should I use? Should the level be formal or informal? Should the writing be simple or complex?
- How can I make my message interesting and worthwhile to this particular audience?

Tone. When you are speaking to someone, your tone of voice usually contributes meaning to what you say. It tells your listener how you feel about your subject, as well as how you feel about the listener. Your writing also takes on a *tone,* whether you create it deliberately or not. But unlike your speech, in which tone is partly created by the way you control your voice (shouting or soothing, for example), tone in writing is created by choice of words, choice of details, and sentence structure.

- **Word Choice.** The choice of formal language (see pages 484–485) will convey a more serious tone than informal language. Generally, the use of contractions and colloquial language creates a more personal, friendly tone, while the use of polysyllabic words and impersonal language creates a less friendly, more serious tone. You also create a tone when you use objective, unemotional words or words with emotional connotations ("the old goat" or "the pleasant gentleman").
- **Choice of Details.** As you've seen in your reading, a list of facts creates a rather serious tone, while a set of personal examples or reminiscences creates a friendlier, perhaps even playful tone.
- **Sentence Length and Structure.** Long, involved sentences can produce a serious and weighty tone or even a lush tone. (Think of the kinds of sentences participants use on television news and public affairs programs.)

Whenever you write something, you should review and think about its tone. Will your readers object to it? Does it show how you feel and think about both the subject and your audience? The best approach is always to be honest and natural. When you feel anger, show it. When you feel that your subject and your audience should be taken seriously, show that. When you want to have fun and share that fun with your audience, be playful.

CRITICAL THINKING
(pp. 35–37)

OBJECTIVE
- To analyze purpose, audience, and tone

TEACHING *ANALYZING PURPOSE, AUDIENCE, AND TONE*

In this activity students will analyze writing to determine the intended readers, purpose, and tone. You might want to start the lesson by asking students if they always act the same way no matter whom they are with. Discuss how they adjust their speech, mannerisms, and intensity according to who

CRITICAL THINKING

Analyzing Purpose, Audience, and Tone

When you ***analyze*** something, you try to learn more about it by looking at its parts. You can learn more about writing by analyzing it, looking at purpose, audience, and tone.

You instinctively adjust your writing to your purpose and audience. Consider, for example, how a friendly letter to a favorite aunt differs from a chemistry lab report. The purpose, the audience, the tone—all are different. Let's look at how this adjustment works in practice. Read the following article about chameleons. Then read the newspaper advertisement on the next page for chameleons as pets.

> Chameleons live solitary lives. Males, in particular, guard their territory jealously. Any intruder merits vigorous countermeasures. For most, territorial battles consist of aggressive displays, not physical contests. When two rivals meet, they turn sideways to the threat, flatten their bodies, curl their tails and thrust out their throats. They puff themselves up, presenting a literally inflated image. They replace mundane colors and patterns with a vibrant combination intended to intimidate. Both contenders understand the symbolism.
>
> Finally they open their mouths, exposing the contrasting colors of their mucous membranes: this is often accompanied by a choreography of swaying and bobbing, punctuated by soft hisses. In most species, this signals the end of the conflict, as one of the antagonists will usually concede esthetic defeat and slink away. . . .
>
> James Martin, "The engaging habits of chameleons suggest mirth more than menace," *Smithsonian*

MEETING INDIVIDUAL NEEDS

ADVANCED STUDENTS

Students might experiment with purpose, audience, and tone by using the two chameleon pieces as a guide to construct an excercise. Assign them to small groups to rewrite published or familiar works. Each student in the group could rewrite the piece for a different purpose, audience, and tone.

Then students could present their work to the class and have class members answer the questions in the **Critical Thinking Exercise.** Encourage students to use artwork or design elements if the selected purpose, audience, and tone warrants.

SELECTION AMENDMENT
Description of change: excerpted and modified
Rationale: to focus on the relationship of writing and thinking presented in this chapter

their companions are, what they are doing, and how they feel.

Explain that, in the same way, writers adapt their material depending upon their audience, purpose, and tone. Allow students to read the text and discuss with them how audience, purpose, and tone vary for the two pieces written about chameleons. Guide students in using the three questions in the excercise to evaluate a piece of writing. You might use the two chameleon pieces to model your answers to the questions.

Use these questions to close the lesson:

1. How can a writer convey the purpose of writing? [by establishing what the focus of the communication is—the audience (persuasive), the topic (informative),

INTEGRATING THE LANGUAGE ARTS

Speaking Link. One way for students to become aware of the need to tailor what and how they write to an audience is to have them role-play situations involving different audiences. For example, you might ask volunteers to act out a scene in which a student is involved in an automobile accident.

First, the student could describe the accident to the investigating officer. Then the student could explain the same accident to a parent, a group of friends, and an insurance investigator.

Discuss how the descriptions differed in terms of the student's vocabulary, tone of voice, selection of details, and body language. Remind students that the audience controls much of what a speaker (and writer) says and does.

Why in the world would anyone want a chameleon?

You say you're satisfied with that old basset hound of yours? Fine. Dogs are wonderful pets. No one knows that better than the folks down at ***The Pet Set***. Dogs are loyal, friendly, and lovable.

- But can they change their colors in the twinkling of an eye?
- Do they dance, hiss, and puff up like balloons?
- Do they make strangers say, "Boy, is that weird!"

If you answered "No" to any of these questions, perhaps the next question is: "Why don't you have a chameleon?"

Because, really and seriously, folks, chameleons are marvelous pets.

- They're neat, clean, and easy to care for.
- They don't bark, meow, chatter, or warble.
- Plus . . . They're the darndest conversation starters this side of a red turbo sports car.

The Pet Set

Everything in Pets . . . and Then Some

Harborview Mall

the words (creative), or the writer (expressive)]

2. How can a writer adjust writing for an audience? [by asking questions about the readers' backgrounds, their strong feelings, and their reading levels]
3. How can a writer adjust tone in writing? [by choosing words, details, and sentence structures that are appropriate for formal or informal uses]

You can see that there's a world of difference between the paragraphs on chameleons and the advertisement for them. The paragraphs are intended for adults with good reading skills. The writing is informative and precise, with a fairly difficult vocabulary and an objective but admiring tone. In contrast, the ad attempts to persuade a general audience to buy chameleons. Its tone is humorous but sincere.

CRITICAL THINKING EXERCISE:
Analyzing Purpose, Audience, and Tone

The following list identifies several different types of writing you see around you all the time. Choose any two from the list and find examples of them. For an ad, for example, look in a magazine. For a news article, look in the newspaper. After you have found the two examples, use the questions that follow to analyze them. When you've finished your analysis, get together with two or three classmates and discuss the differences you found between the two types of writing you examined.

Types of Writing

a news article	a newspaper editorial
an advertisement	an informative article
a lesson in a textbook	an autobiography (or excerpt)
a comic strip	a recipe or set of instructions
a short story	a poem

1. Who are the intended readers? What are their probable ages? interests? needs? concerns?
2. What is the writer's purpose? What is he or she trying to do? How can you tell?
3. What is the writer's tone? Is it serious, humorous, bitter, worried, light? What words or sentences show this tone?

ANSWERS
Critical Thinking Exercise

Answers may vary. Students should explain the reasons why they decided upon the audience, purpose, and tone of the selected types of writing.

INTEGRATING THE LANGUAGE ARTS

Vocabulary Link. You might want to point out that writers use transitional words to connect their ideas and that transitions are often clues to the type of order used. Brainstorm with the class for words and phrases that can be used as transitions to show chronological order, spatial order, logical order, or order of importance.

Prewriting

Arranging Ideas

By the time you have gathered enough information to begin writing, you're likely to have your notes in various forms: on notepaper, on 3″ × 5″ cards, on photocopies. How do you bring order to this chaos? No, the answer isn't "Sleep on it."

When you step back and look, your information may be easier to arrange than you think. Much writing falls into clear patterns. For example, to explain how to enlarge a photograph, you'll put the explanation in step-by-step, or ***chronological,*** order. If you are describing the stage set for a play, you'll almost automatically arrange the description in ***spatial*** order—left to right, perhaps, or front to back.

If you're writing a campaign speech and want to make a strong impact, you may arrange points using ***order of importance***—from the least important to the most important—to end on a rousing note. But if you want to emphasize the difference between yourself and another candidate, you may swing back and forth between points: "My opponent promises this; I promise that." This is ***logical order***—the order that falls naturally out of your purpose for writing. The chart on the following page shows four common ways of arranging ideas.

Shoe, by Jeff MacNelly, reprinted by permission: Tribune Media Services.

ARRANGING IDEAS		
TYPE OF ORDER	DEFINITION	EXAMPLES
Chronological	Narration: Order that presents events as they happen in time	Story; narrative poem; explanation of a process; history; biography; drama
Spatial	Description: Order that describes objects according to location	Descriptions (near to far; left to right; top to bottom; and so on)
Importance	Evaluation: Order that gives details from least to most important or the reverse	Persuasive writing; descriptions; explanations (main idea and supporting details); evaluative writing
Logical	Classification: Order that relates items and groups	Definitions; classifications; comparisons and contrasts

REFERENCE NOTE: For more information on arranging ideas, see pages 75–77.

EXERCISE 7 **Arranging the Order of Details**

Do you remember the first time you tried to ride a bike, or attempted to roller skate, or boarded a roller coaster? First, brainstorm your memories of such an event for two different paragraphs: (1) a description of the skates, bike, roller coaster, or whatever, and (2) the story of what happened. Then arrange each set of details in a clear order, and discuss with some classmates the order you used.

Using Charts

Charts are a practical, graphic way to arrange your prewriting notes. They group related bits of information, allowing you to "see" the overall arrangement clearly. Sometimes charts are as

A DIFFERENT APPROACH

To make learning ways to arrange ideas more concrete, have students illustrate the types of order with drawings or charts. For example, students could depict chronological order with time lines that highlight the major events in their lives. For spatial order, they could draw pictures of their rooms at home, their lockers, or a park they are familiar with. To illustrate order of importance, students could draw pictures to show the goals they wish to achieve in the next few years. To portray logical order, students could draw Venn diagrams to compare or contrast traits that describe themselves.

ANSWERS

Exercise 7

Responses will vary. Students should arrange each set of details—both the description and the story—in an order that is appropriate for the details.

simple as lists, but they can be more complex. Here's a chart for a student's paper on the inhabitants of Mexico before the Spanish conquest. Notice how the chart has both horizontal and vertical headings.

HERE'S HOW

MAJOR CULTURES OF MEXICO IN 1500		
PEOPLE	LOCATION	CHARACTERISTICS
Aztecs	Central Mexico	centralized government; large, efficient army; 365-day solar calendar; advanced engineering and architectural skills
Mayas	Yucatán peninsula	written language; base-20 mathematical system; 365-day calendar; sophisticated artistry, especially sculpture
Mixtecs	Southwest Mexico	fine stone and metal work; beautiful carvings in wood; painted polychrome pottery
Zapotecs	Oaxaca and Isthmus of Tehuantepec	priestly hierarchy; ancestor worship; artistic heritage influenced by the early Maya

Another graphic way to organize notes is a ***time line***—a chart showing information in chronological order. On the next page is a time line showing the periods of dominance of the four major cultural groups in Mexico.

CRITICAL THINKING
(pp. 41–42)

OBJECTIVES

- To classify information by grouping ideas as favorable or unfavorable
- To classify information by grouping ideas in chart format

TEACHING *CLASSIFYING INFORMATION*

To introduce classifying, have a student read the introductory information. Then have another volunteer read through the lettered facts about college football. Discuss the two grouping assignments as ways to organize ideas.

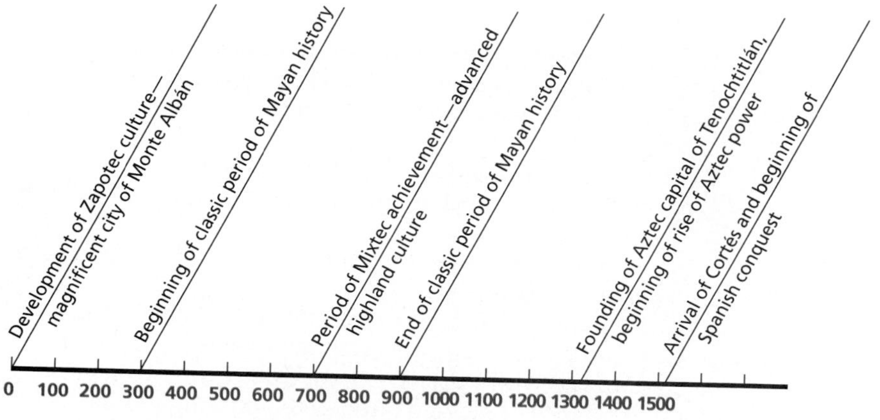

Stages of Pre-Columbian Cultures of Mexico

CRITICAL THINKING

Classifying Information

To make many kinds of charts, you're using the skill of ***classifying:*** grouping related information. When classifying information, ask yourself these questions:

- Which items are similar in some way? What heading will show what they have in common?
- Do some items *include* other items? Which ones?
- Do you have any items left over? Should you create another heading? Should you eliminate the leftovers?

CRITICAL THINKING EXERCISE:
Classifying and Charting Information

Look at the following ideas for a paper on college football, and then answer the questions.

a. Teaches teamwork
b. Encourages school spirit
c. Many football players on scholarship not completing their degrees

MEETING INDIVIDUAL NEEDS

LEARNING STYLES

Kinetic Learners. One way to help students use charts to organize ideas is to have them write the information individual cells should contain on different index cards. Have students spend time maneuvering the cards until they are satisfied with the arrangement. Then tell them to transpose the cards onto a chart or to paste the cards onto poster board and add horizontal and vertical lines.

LESS-ADVANCED STUDENTS

When students are using charts to organize ideas for their writing assignments, you might provide the headings for students' charts and let them fill in the information.

You might want to mention that the presentation of positive and negative details about a proposal, plan, or idea can help an audience make a decision. The audience will have the needed information but can make up their own minds.

If students need help getting started, use the chalkboard to show how you might set up a pro and con, players and schools classification system. Students should then be ready to work independently on their own charts.

To assess understanding, ask students what the advantages of grouping information by topic are. [Grouping helps organize ideas for writing and helps establish paragraph divisions.]

INTEGRATING THE LANGUAGE ARTS

Technology Link. Many computer programs can be used to create charts. Have students work in pairs to organize their information and to design a grid. Then have them type in their organizational information. Remind them to include their names on the printouts to hand in for evaluation.

ANSWERS

Critical Thinking Exercise

1. Pro: a, b, d, f, h, i, l
   Con: c, e, g, j, k, m
2. All items in the list fit in the chart.

	Pro	Con
Players	a, d, i	c, j, k
School	b, f, h, l	e, g, m

d. Scholarship program intended to offer a college education to economically disadvantaged students
e. Competition encouraging colleges to violate recruiting rules
f. Can give a college national recognition
g. Colleges needing to emphasize academics more than sports
h. Alumni fans donating money to alma maters with good football teams
i. Prepares players for professional football careers
j. Good football players often allowed to take easy courses; won't prepare them for life after college
k. Star football players often given passing grades for poor academic work; some players actually illiterate
l. Football very profitable for colleges; helps pay for academic courses and other sports programs
m. Alumni pressure and money possibly corrupting to college football; alumni known to reward star players with money and cars

1. One natural way to classify the information is in two groups: favorable ideas about college football and unfavorable ones. Do this: List all the positive details under *Pro* and all the negative details under *Con.*
2. Another classification is items about players and items about schools. Make a chart that shows all four groupings: *Pro, Con, Players, Schools.* Does every item in the list fit in the chart?

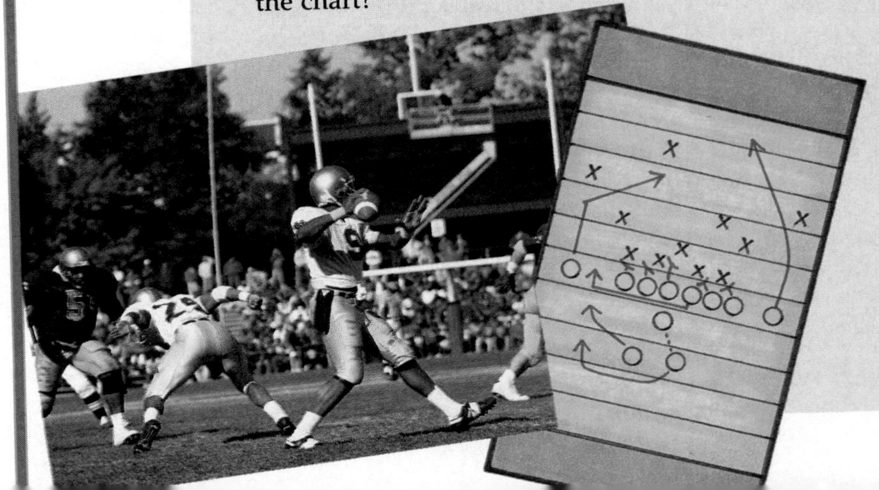

SEGMENT 4 *(pp. 43–44)*

WRITING A FIRST DRAFT

OBJECTIVE

- To arrange notes to write the first draft of a paragraph

TEACHING THE LESSON

The textbook emphasizes the need to begin a draft after prewriting exercises and notes have been completed. The assignment in **Exercise 8** on p. 44, however, is independent of the work students have done in the prewriting segment of this chapter. Remind students that they can use the prewriting notes given, but they can also

Writing a First Draft

W. Somerset Maugham, the English author, wrote a short story about a man who spent a lifetime gathering information for his *magnum opus,* or masterpiece. The man had stacks of information—but he died before getting a word of his book written. The moral is this: Prewriting is important, but at some point you've got to get a first draft on paper.

There is no magic formula, no one right way, to write a first draft. Your prewriting notes may be rough, or you may create a detailed outline. You may like to write *fast*, or you may slowly, carefully shape each sentence. Whatever feels right for your style of writing a draft, consider these suggestions:

- Use your prewriting notes or outline as a guide.
- Write freely. Concentrate on expressing your ideas.
- Include any new ideas that come to you as you write.
- Don't worry about making errors in grammar, usage, and mechanics. You can fix them later.

Here's a first draft of a paragraph on dogs and politics. Notice how the writer makes a few revisions and also writes some personal notes and questions right in the draft.

Dogs and politics go together like ham and eggs. Apparently there's something about a dog that makes its politician-owner more human, lovable, and electable. A first rule of politics would seem to be--own a dog. You've just got to own a dog. In 1944 the opponents of President Franklin D. Roosevelt claimed that Fala, FDR's Scottie [check breed], had been brought back from Alaska on a U.S. Navy destroyer sent especially for the purpose. The story was a lie, and Roosevelt's "Fala speech" of September [?] seriously hurt Thomas E. Dewey, his opponent. So a second rule is never to criticize someone else's dog. When Richard Nixon ran into trouble over the gift of a dog [was that all?] in his 1952 vice-presidential campaign, Nixon responded with his famous "Checkers speech"--Checkers being the dog in question. This speech, delivered eight years to the day after FDR's Fala speech, saved Nixon [how?]. Who can doubt that other dogs will arrive in the future to help other threatened politicians?

Teacher's ResourceBank™
RESOURCES

WRITING A FIRST DRAFT
- Writing a First Draft 6

QUOTATION FOR THE DAY

"If all the earth were paper white/And all the sea were ink/'Twere not enough for me to write/As my poor heart doth think." (John Lyly, 1554(?)–1606, English writer of romances and plays)

You may want to have students use the poem as the basis for a journal entry.

MEETING INDIVIDUAL NEEDS

LEP/ESL

General Strategies. When students begin **Exercise 8** on p. 44, a paragraph-drafting activity, you may want to assist ESL students in organizing the notes about rock stars. For example, they might organize notes into advantages and disadvantages of being a rock star and write a paragraph about each.

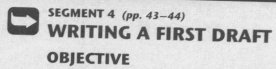

generate their own ideas to add to the details before they start.

Remind students that they will also have to decide how to organize the material they have selected to use before they begin the drafts.

Collect drafts to assess students' understanding. You might want to spend some class time talking about the process so far and how following an organized process makes writing easier. ■

INTEGRATING THE LANGUAGE ARTS

Test-taking Link. Point out to students that when they have to answer essay questions, they might try prewriting techniques first before they write their drafts, if time permits. Jotting down their ideas can help them plan what they want to say and organize the presentation.

ANSWERS

Exercise 8

Responses will vary. Each student should write a first draft that arranges the notes in an organized manner. You probably will not want to penalize students for errors in grammar, spelling, or punctuation at this stage.

EXERCISE 8 **Writing a First Draft**

Have you ever daydreamed about being a famous performer like Hammer or Gloria Estefan? Here are some prewriting notes about the imagined life of a performer. Arrange or group the notes, and add to them if you like. Then use the details to write the first draft of a paragraph.

make millions of dollars
can't safely go out alone in public
own big house and expensive clothes
difficult to have personal relationships
people love you who don't even know you
travel a lot
sleep in strange hotels all over the country
followed by groupies everywhere he or she goes
have to have bodyguards for personal protection
great satisfaction performing before crowds of people

SEGMENT 5 *(pp. 45–49)*

EVALUATING AND REVISING

OBJECTIVE

- To evaluate and revise the first draft of a paragraph

MOTIVATION

Ask students if they have ever spoken before they had time to think about what they were going to say. Explain that although thinking and writing go hand in hand, writing has an advantage in that a writer can take time to revise.

Evaluating and Revising

Evaluating and revising go hand in hand. ***Evaluating*** means deciding what changes need to be made. ***Revising*** involves making the changes.

Evaluating

When you comb your hair in the morning, you look closely into a mirror. You decide what looks okay. You notice what's wrong. You use a similar process when you evaluate your first draft. What seems to be good about it? What changes will make it better?

Self-Evaluation. Seeing what needs improvement in your writing can be difficult, but the following techniques will help.

TIPS FOR SELF-EVALUATION

1. **Reading Carefully.** Read your paper several times. First concentrate on ***content*** (what you say), next on ***organization*** (how you've arranged your ideas), and then on ***style*** (how you've used words and sentences).
2. **Listening Carefully.** Read your paper aloud, "listening" to what you've written. What looked all right on paper may sound awkward or unclear when read aloud.
3. **Taking Time.** If possible, put your paper aside for a while. A day or two (or even a few hours) will give you some mental distance from it and help you to see flaws you didn't notice before.

Peer Evaluation. Every writer needs an editor—a person who can read critically and with a different viewpoint. You can get an editor (or editors) of your own through peer evaluation. Members of a peer-evaluation group read and comment on each other's papers. The group may consist of as few as two people or as many as four or five. Part of the time you'll be the writer whose work is being evaluated, and the rest of the time you'll be evaluating someone else's writing.

Teacher's ResourceBank™

RESOURCES

EVALUATING AND REVISING

QUOTATION FOR THE DAY

"I always began my task by reading the work of the day before, an operation which would take me half an hour, and which consisted chiefly in weighing with my ear the sound of the words and phrases." (Anthony Trollope, 1815–1882, English novelist)

Discuss with students how they must be alert listeners when they read their writing aloud to evaluate it. After several readings they will be able to listen carefully to individual words and decide if they express exactly the right shade of meaning.

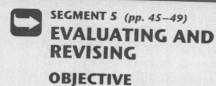

TEACHING THE LESSON

The skills taught in this segment are practiced in the **Critical Thinking Exercise** on p. 49. Therefore, you may want to review the guidelines and go directly to **Critical Thinking.** Some students will need more guidance in reading through the information.

You might want to discuss the interrelationship between evaluating and revising and explain the two types of evaluation students can use, peer and self-evaluation. Have a volunteer read the **Tips for Self-Evaluation** chart and have another read the **Peer-Evaluation Guidelines.** If you have any of your own peer-evaluation guidelines, you might want to post them in the room so all students will understand the goals for peer evaluation.

MEETING **INDIVIDUAL** NEEDS

ADVANCED STUDENTS

Challenge advanced students to find copies of first drafts of famous essays along with the revised work. Ask students to write critical paragraphs explaining the major revisions and how the changes have enhanced the writing. Students could provide examples to support what they write.

AT-RISK STUDENTS

At-risk students are often absent from school and are not always able to benefit from group activities. You might emphasize self-evaluation skills with students who are at risk so that they begin to be more independent in their schoolwork. Make copies of the evaluation guidelines available to students to keep at home for reference.

PEER-EVALUATION GUIDELINES

Guidelines for the Writer

1. Tell the evaluator what bothers you most about your own paper. Point out anything that has caused you difficulty.
2. Don't be defensive. Keep an open mind and make good use of the evaluator's comments.

Guidelines for the Peer Evaluator

1. Be sure to tell the writer what's right as well as what's wrong.
2. Make suggestions for improvement. If you see a weakness, give the writer some suggestions to correct it.
3. Concentrate on content and organization. Don't worry about mechanical errors such as spelling or punctuation.
4. Be sensitive to the writer's feelings. Make sure that your comments are constructive—that means offering solutions, not criticism.

Revising

Revision is one of the most important parts of writing—and one you may be tempted to skip because it's so difficult. Even if you identify some problems with your writing, you may have trouble deciding how to fix them. Take heart: Just as with prewriting, some directed practice makes this writing stage easier. The four basic ways to revise are to ***add, cut, replace,*** and ***reorder.*** The following chart shows how these techniques can be applied. In later chapters, you'll find similar charts that focus on specific types of writing.

The **Guidelines for Evaluating and Revising** chart is the basis for much of the evaluating and revising work students will do in their writing. You might want to duplicate it and post it in the room so that it can be a ready reference.

To reinforce the methods shown on the chart, analyze the writing sample on dogs and politics on p. 48 by going through the **Evaluation Guide** to determine how the revision techniques were applied.

You might want to emphasize that the **Guidelines for Evaluating and Revising** chart is divided into three parts—content, organization, and style. To strengthen students' understanding of the value of each, have them critique the writing sample by giving it three scores: one for content, one ☛

GUIDELINES FOR EVALUATING AND REVISING

	EVALUATION GUIDE	REVISION TECHNIQUE
	CONTENT	
1	Is the writing interesting?	**Add** examples, an anecdote, dialogue, or additional details. **Cut** repetitious or boring details.
2	Does the writing achieve the writer's purpose?	**Add** explanations, descriptive details, arguments, or narrative details.
3	Are there enough details?	**Add** more details, facts, or examples to support your ideas.
4	Are there unrelated ideas or details that distract the reader?	**Cut** irrelevant or distracting information.
5	Are unfamiliar terms explained or defined?	**Add** definitions or other explanations of unfamiliar terms. **Replace** unfamiliar terms with familiar ones.
	ORGANIZATION	
6	Are ideas and details arranged in the best possible order?	**Reorder** ideas and details to make the meaning clear.
7	Are the logical connections between ideas and sentences clear?	**Add** transition words to link ideas: *therefore, for example, because,* and so on.
	STYLE	
8	Is the meaning clear?	**Replace** vague or unclear wording. Use words and phrases that are precise and easy to understand.
9	Does the writing contain clichés or overworked phrases?	**Cut** or **replace** with specific details and fresh comparisons.
10	Is the language appropriate for the audience and purpose?	**Replace** formal words with less formal words and phrases to create an informal tone. To create a more formal tone, **replace** slang and contractions.
11	Do sentences read smoothly?	**Reorder** to vary sentence beginnings and sentence structure.

INTEGRATING THE LANGUAGE ARTS

Vocabulary Link. The **Guidelines for Evaluating and Revising** chart includes several techniques for improving style. Explain to students that one important element of style is choosing the best words to convey the intended meaning.

To help students become aware of how variety in their choice of words improves their writing, have them generate lists of synonymous terms for common adjectives. Suggest that they replace overused words in their writing with words from their lists. A list of synonyms for *said* is also a good preparation for later writing assignments.

Students could also rewrite overused clichés and generate their own lists of similes or metaphors to replace them. Students might want to keep their work in notebooks or in their writing journals so that the vocabulary work is as handy as their ideas for writing are.

for organization, and one for style. As they evaluate the paragraph, have them make suggestions for improvement.

To close, ask students what they have learned about evaluating and revising writing. Have them discuss the advantages of self-evaluation and peer evaluation. ■

Here is the first-draft paragraph on dogs and politics (from page 43), revised according to the chart guidelines. To understand the changes, look at the chart of symbols for proofreading and revising on page 53. As you read this revision, notice how the writer has answered the questions noted on the draft.

Dogs and politics go together like ~~ham~~ [fireworks] **replace**
~~and eggs.~~ [and the Fourth of July.] Apparently there's something
about a dog that makes its politician-owner
more human, lovable, and electable. A first
rule of politics would seem to be [to] own a dog. **replace/reorder**
~~You've just got to own a dog.~~ In 1944 the **cut**
opponents of President Franklin D. Roosevelt
claimed that Fala, FDR's Scottie[sh terrier] ~~[check~~ **replace**
~~breed]~~, had been brought back from Alaska **cut**
on a U.S. Navy destroyer sent especially for
the purpose. The story was ~~a lie,~~ [untrue,] and **replace**
Roosevelt's "Fala speech" of September ~~[?]~~ [23] **replace**
seriously hurt [the chances of] Thomas E. Dewey, his **add**
opponent. ~~So~~ [Other politicians learned from that incident.] a second rule [—discovered in the presidential election of 1944—] is never to **add/cut/add**
criticize someone else's dog. When Richard
Nixon ran into trouble over the gift of a dog
~~[was that all?]~~ [(among other things)] in his 1952 vice-presidential **replace**
campaign, he responded with his famous
"Checkers speech"--Checkers being the [cuddly little] dog **add**
in question. This speech, delivered eight
years to the day after FDR's Fala speech,
saved Nixon ~~[how?]~~['s nomination.] Who can doubt that **replace**
other dogs will ~~arrive~~ [wag into view] in the future to help **replace**
other threatened politicians?

CRITICAL THINKING
(p. 49)

OBJECTIVE

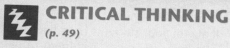

- To evaluate and revise the first draft of a paragraph

TEACHING *EVALUATING AND REVISING A PARAGRAPH*

Explain to students there are several ways to correctly revise a paragraph. You might refer them to the editing symbols on p. 53 and explain what the symbols mean. Make sure students are able to explain why they make the alterations and what criteria they use.

CRITICAL THINKING

Evaluating and Revising a Paragraph

The **Guidelines for Evaluating and Revising** (page 47) show you that *evaluating* is more than uttering a judgment: *This is OK. This is the pits. This is to die for.* A useful judgment is made by using clear criteria, or standards. When you evaluate your own writing or someone else's, you shouldn't simply react. You should have in mind concrete elements of strong writing—and to specify where you see them and where you don't.

CRITICAL THINKING EXERCISE:
Evaluating and Revising a Paragraph

Work with a partner to evaluate and revise the following first draft of a paragraph. Focus on organization, content, and style, using the guidelines on page 47. If you find mechanical and grammatical errors, you can correct them, but that's not your main task. When you've finished, check with another revision team to see if the problems and solutions they found match yours.

Can you imagine being alive in world that does not have trees? You could say that trees are good to look at, and essential to our very lives. We use trees for paper, books, and the shelves and desks and tables and cabinets that we put them on to hold them. Some woods, such as ebony, mahogany, and rosewood, are gorgeous. As a matter of fact, just one ordinary average tree takes in a lot of carbon dioxide. About twenty-six pounds a year, much of it caused by automobile junk and other pollutants around. That same tree puts out enough oxygen to keep four persons breathing for about fifty-two weeks. Trees make shade. When they get planted around homes and other bildings, they lower the need for air conditioning plenty. Chairs, tables, picture frames, and pencils all started as plain, ordinary trees. So did boats, musical instruments, tennis rackets, etc.

ANSWERS

Critical Thinking Exercise

Paragraphs will vary. Here is a possibility:

Can you imagine living in a world without trees? Trees are magnificent to look at and essential to our way of life. Just think how many ways we depend upon trees. Schools certainly wouldn't be the same. We use trees for paper, pencils, and books, and for the shelves, desks, table, and cabinets that we rest them on. Homes and offices wouldn't be the same. Some woods, such as ebony, mahogany, and rosewood, make handsome and warm home and work environments. Trees are also protection for the environment. Just one average tree takes in about twenty-six pounds of carbon dioxide a year, much of it caused by automobile emissions and other pollutants. That same tree gives off enough oxygen to keep four persons breathing for a year. Trees also provide shade. When people plant trees around homes and buildings, they reduce the need for air conditioning. The next time you look at chairs, tables, picture frames, or even pencils, think trees. Remember that your boat, musical instrument, or tennis racket was once a plain, ordinary tree.

SEGMENT 6 *(pp. 50–53)*

PROOFREADING AND PUBLISHING

OBJECTIVES

- To proofread a paragraph for errors in grammar, usage, and mechanics
- To brainstorm for publishing ideas

MOTIVATION

If any of your students have had their work published, you might ask them to tell the class about the experience. What did they publish and where was it printed? Ask them to explain the procedure for getting their work into print. How important was it to submit an impeccable paper?

Teacher's ResourceBank™

RESOURCES

PROOFREADING AND PUBLISHING

QUOTATION FOR THE DAY

"I hope the candid reader now and then calls to mind how much more nimbly he travels over these pages than the writer of them did." (Richard Cumberland, 1732–1811, British dramatist)

You might ask students to compare how much easier it is to read over their papers than it was to write the papers, now that they have almost completed the process. Remind the class that completing the proofreading stage will enable the reader to travel nimbly over the words also.

MEETING INDIVIDUAL NEEDS

LEP/ESL

General Strategies. Publishing papers, despite any flaws in language the work may have, is important to ESL students. Like all students, they need to know that the most important part of their essays—the content—is thought to have value.

Proofreading and Publishing

Proofreading. Once you're finished revising anything you've written, you may think it is perfect. Sometimes it may be—but you'll do well to take one last look. This final look is called ***proofreading.*** When you proofread, you catch and correct any remaining errors in grammar, usage, and mechanics (spelling, capitalization, punctuation). If you've been able to put aside your paper for a while, you'll find it easier to spot these mistakes. Here are some techniques for proofreading:

1. Focus on one line at a time. Use a sheet of paper to cover all the lines below the one you're proofreading. Or try beginning at the bottom line and working your way to the top. That way you'll be forced to concentrate on mechanics, not content.
2. Consider peer proofreading. Exchange papers with a classmate and proofread each other's papers.
3. When in doubt, look it up. For spelling, use a college dictionary. For grammar, usage, and punctuation, use a handbook like the one on pages 550–929.

Some kinds of errors occur again and again, so the following guidelines are designed to help you handle a few of them. By going over these guidelines before you begin to proofread, you'll have a head start on getting your paper exactly right.

GUIDELINES FOR PROOFREADING

1. Is each sentence a complete sentence? (See pages 515–519 and 582–583.)
2. Does every sentence end with the appropriate punctuation mark? (See pages 842–845.)
3. Does every sentence begin with a capital letter? Are all proper nouns and proper adjectives capitalized when necessary? (See pages 820–828.)
4. Does every verb agree in number with its subject? (See pages 649–662.)
5. Are verb forms and tenses used correctly? (See pages 715–747.)

(continued)

TEACHING THE LESSON

To begin the lesson, have a volunteer read **Proofreading.** As you read over the techniques, stop and discuss each one. Have students offer any other techniques or ways to help with each technique that they have found beneficial.

Focus on **Guidelines for Proofreading** by using a completed paper, perhaps from a student's **Exercise 8** revisions. Go over the guidelines as you examine the sample. Explain that each student can adapt the guidelines to create the best proofreading process. Some may prefer checking grammar, spelling, and then punctuation; others may prefer checking each sentence individually.

☛

GUIDELINES FOR PROOFREADING *(continued)*

6. Are subject and object forms of personal pronouns used correctly? (See pages 675–681.)
7. Does every pronoun agree with its antecedent in number and gender? Are pronoun references clear? (See pages 664–666 and 701–707.)
8. Are frequently confused words (such as *slow* and *slowly, imply* and *infer*) used correctly? (See pages 792–809.)
9. Are all words spelled correctly? Are the plural forms of nouns correct? (See pages 902–929.)
10. Is the paper neat and in correct manuscript form? (See page 52.)

EXERCISE 9 **Proofreading**

The paragraph below has ten errors in grammar, usage, and mechanics. Use a college dictionary and the handbook at the back of the book to identify and correct each mistake.

Most people have strong feelings about ~~there~~ pets; Especially when it comes to dogs and cats. Both María and Fran said ~~she~~ preferred dogs because dogs are friendlier than cats. Chad disagreed, pointing out that he had never been chased or ~~bite~~ by a cat. Jennifer asked Chad if he had ever heard of a cat ~~who~~ had tried to save someone's life. After listening to what Jennifer had to say, Chad said that she had a good arguement. Just between you and ~~I~~, I'm glad that each kind of pet ~~are~~ admired by somebody. The important thing is to love and take care of your pet, ~~weather~~ ~~its~~ a dog, a cat, or some other kind of animal.

their **they** **bitten (or bit)** **that** **me** **whether** **it's**

Publishing. Your readers should always be on your mind, but the publishing stage is the time you can finally reach out to them. Here are a few suggestions for sharing your writing.

- Submit your writing for publication in the school newspaper or magazine. Or, send it to your local newspaper. Most newspapers publish letters to the editors, and many accept feature stories.

INTEGRATING THE LANGUAGE ARTS

Technology Link. If students have access to computers at home, the library, or school, try an experiment with **Exercise 9.** Have students input the paragraph and run spell-check and grammar-check features to see if the computer program will detect all the errors in grammar, usage, spelling, and mechanics. After the experiment, explain to students that although the program can help them find errors, they are ultimately responsible for the correctness of their papers.

COOPERATIVE LEARNING

As students begin proofreading their papers, you might want them to work in proofreading teams of four. When students have work to proofread, they could attach checksheets that include the **Guidelines for Proofreading** to their papers. One student could be responsible for guidelines 1–3, the second for guidelines 4–6, and the third for guidelines 7–9. Then the writer could check for guideline 10, neatness and format.

If you have modeled the proofreading process with students, have them work independently on **Exercise 9.** To assess students' proofreading skills, evaluate their papers by writing down the number of the guideline that tells students what to improve.

For **Publishing,** follow the same procedure—have a volunteer read the introduction and pause to discuss suggestions. When you discuss **Guidelines for Manuscript Form,** mention any policies you require students to follow when they submit papers.

Exercise 10 is a brainstorming activity that also requires students to work in small groups to gather information. You could have on hand either a list of publications that accept student writing or examples of published student work. Students may need

A DIFFERENT APPROACH

To show how writers get published, have students invite local writers to speak to the class. The group might include newspaper writers, local college professors, short-story writers, or book authors. Encourage students to research the guests' work and to prepare questions in advance.

ANSWERS

Exercise 10

Make sure students include ideas for publishing their work outside the classroom as well as in school. They might include class magazines, bulletin boards, story booklets for nonnative speakers, and family scrapbooks, as well as publications like the following magazines:

Scholastic Scope
Scholastic Magazines, Inc.
730 Broadway
New York, NY 10003

Odyssey
21027 Crossroads Circle
P. O. Box 1612
Waukesha, WI 53187

- Look for writing contests. A few are specifically for high school students. Some offer prizes or certificates. Ask your teacher or counselor for information.
- Compile a class anthology of each student's favorite piece of writing. Donate it to your school library. If possible, make a copy for each contributor.

When someone else reads your paper—whether that person is your teacher, another student, or an adult outside of school—appearance is important. If you follow these guidelines for your final copy, your paper will look its best.

GUIDELINES FOR MANUSCRIPT FORM

1. Use only one side of a sheet of paper.
2. Use a typewriter or a word processor, or write in blue or black ink.
3. If you type, double-space the lines. If you write by hand, don't skip lines.
4. Leave margins of about one inch at the top, sides, and bottom of each page.
5. Indent the first line of each paragraph.
6. Number all pages (except the first page) in the upper right-hand corner.
7. Be sure all pages are neat and clean. You can make a few changes with correction fluid, but they should be barely noticeable.
8. Follow your teacher's instructions for placement of your name, the date, your class, and the title of your paper.

EXERCISE 10 Publishing

With your classmates, brainstorm ideas for publishing your writing. Anyone who has already been published should share his or her experiences. Work in smaller groups to gather specific information on each possibility—names and addresses of potential publishers, types of material each accepts, length and manuscript form required, and so on. Then compile the information from the different groups into a resource booklet.

some time to research names and addresses of publishers. When they finish their exploration, gather the information they collect into a central file to refer to during the year.

To close the lesson, ask students to recall the proofreading techniques they might consider using [focus on one line at a time, use a peer proofreader, and look information up to be sure]. ■

SYMBOLS FOR REVISING AND PROOFREADING

SYMBOL	EXAMPLE	MEANING OF SYMBOL
cap ≡	Spence college	Capitalize a lowercase letter.
lc /	our Best quarterback	Lowercase a capital letter.
^	on the Fourth of July	Insert a missing word, letter, or punctuation mark.
/	endurence (a)	Change a letter.
^ (with line)	the capital of Iowa (Ohio)	Change a word.
ℓ (delete)	hoped for to go	Leave out a word, letter, or punctuation mark.
ℓ (close)	on that occassion	Leave out and close up.
⁀	today's home work	Close up space.
∿	nieghbor	Change the order of the letters.
tr ∿	the counsel general of the corporation	Transpose words. (Write tr in nearby margin.)
¶	¶ "Wait!" I shouted.	Begin a new paragraph.
⊙	She was right⊙	Add a period.
^,	Yes that's true.	Add a comma.
#	centerfield (#)	Add a space.
⊙:	the following items:	Add a colon.
^;	Evansville, Indiana; Columbus, Ohio	Add a semicolon.
=	self=control	Add a hyphen.
˅'	Mrs. Ruiz's office	Add an apostrophe.
stet	a very tall building	Keep the crossed-out material. (Write stet in nearby margin.)

MEETING INDIVIDUAL NEEDS

AT-RISK STUDENTS

Seeing their papers displayed around the room can help build students' confidence. Make sure you have plenty of room to showcase work so that not only the best writers have their work displayed. You might reserve display room for "Most Improved Writer" or "Feature Writer of the Week," or you could save some awards for unusual personal stories or topics.

LEARNING STYLES

Kinetic Learners. Have students create a bulletin board that includes the proofreading symbols. Encourage originality in the presentation.

A DIFFERENT APPROACH

The editing symbols are the basic ones that students will use throughout their school years. Explain that the marks are correcting shortcuts that are recognized by most writers. Some students may be unfamiliar with the symbols and might benefit from a demonstration. A large chart or individual copies for students' desks might also be helpful in learning the symbols.

SEGMENT 7 *(pp. 54–55)*

MAKING CONNECTIONS

EXPLORING THE CREATIVE PROCESS OBJECTIVE

- To write a journal entry that explores the creative process

IMITATING A WRITING STYLE OBJECTIVE

- To write a parody of a genre

EXPLORING THE CREATIVE PROCESS

Teaching Strategies

You may want to brainstorm with students about times they are called upon to write. Help students realize that writing is not restricted to formal situations such as taking tests and writing research reports. Remind students that expressive writing has certain characteristics: The emphasis is on the writer; thoughts, feelings, and emotions are recorded; and natural language is used.

GUIDELINES

You could assess students' journal entries on effort rather than on content. Encourage students who feel comfortable with their writing to share their experiences with the rest of the class.

AMENDMENTS TO SELECTIONS

Description of change: excerpted
Rationale: to focus on the relationship of writing and thinking presented in this chapter

MAKING CONNECTIONS

Exploring the Creative Process

In the writing process, the more a story cooks, the better.
Doris Lessing

I don't dawdle. I'm a surgeon. I make an incision, do what needs to be done and sew up the wound. There is a beginning, a middle and an end.
Richard Selzer

Two writers, two very different writing approaches. Does one of those quotations hit home for you? Do you let your drafts "cook," or do you simply "get it over with"? Or do you alternate between the two approaches?

Write in your journal about whether, and when, writing flows for you or seems like a nightmare. (And you may have another metaphor for how writing feels.) Then, if it's comfortable, share your experience with others. You may get ideas for freeing up your writing.

Imitating a Writing Style

The annual Bulwer-Lytton Fiction Contest asks contestants to write "the worst possible opening sentence to a novel." (Edward Bulwer-Lytton wrote the infamous opening sentence "It was a dark and stormy night.") For example, the novel can be "mainstream," detective, espionage, science fiction, or romance. Here is a recent winner (loser?) in the science fiction category.

"*Meteor storm!*" Sparks cried, almost throwing the professor's frail body against the bulkhead in zero-grav haste, ignoring Zortran Threndoran's flailing purple tentacles in his fruitless effort to reach the null-space communicator as Bob Star slammed thruster levers into maximum and hoped against impossible odds that their shuddering, nearly fuelless Starcruiser would reach light-speed before the juggernautlike space rocks smashed them, along with the Federation's last hope for peace and Bob Star's only hope for real love, the professor's beautiful daughter Diana, into the cold oblivion of deep space.

Mike Montgomery

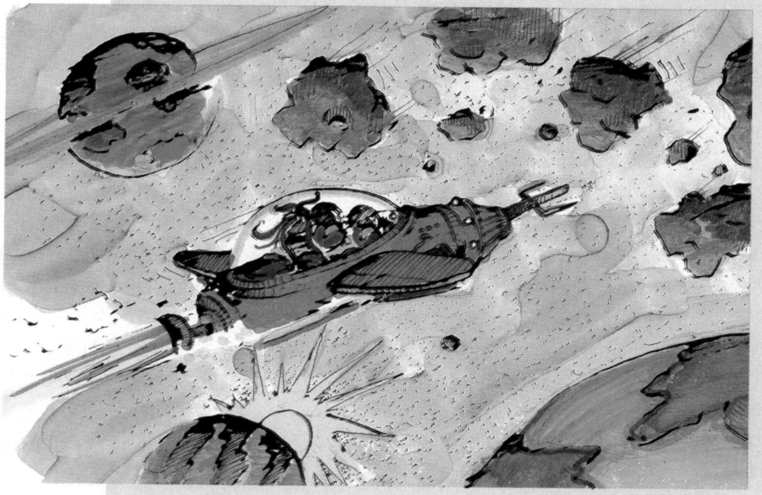

This paragraph is a ***parody*** of science fiction writing. A parody imitates the style of a writer or a type of writing, exaggerating its essential characteristics. The usually funny result is also "bad" writing because the quirks of the author or genre are pushed to an extreme.

What's bad about Mike Montgomery's parody of science fiction writing? Study this parody to see what makes it work. Is it the language? Is it exaggeration? Then use what you've discovered about Montgomery's parody to write a "Bulwer-Lytton" paragraph of your own, parodying any genre. For a double-bad paragraph, work with a partner.

IMITATING A WRITING STYLE

Teaching Strategies

Ask a volunteer to read aloud the paragraph by Mike Montgomery. Discuss the characteristics that add humor to the paragraph, and lead students to see that the writer had to be familiar with the elements of science fiction before he could write his parody.

Brainstorm with students to create a list of genres that would make good subjects for parodies (such as mythology, romance, mysteries, or fairy tales). You might let students who choose the same genre work together. Suggest that students list characteristics of the genre and then decide how they can poke fun at the elements they've listed. Students might have difficulty identifying characteristics, so circulate through the room and offer assistance as students work.

GUIDELINES

An effective parody should humorously imitate or exaggerate the genre's characteristics. If students share their completed parodies with the rest of the class, you may want to have students rate each parody's humor on a scale of 1–5.

SELECTION AMENDMENT
Description of change: excerpted
Rationale: to focus on the relationship of writing and thinking presented in this chapter

Chapter 2 UNDERSTANDING PARAGRAPH STRUCTURE

OBJECTIVES

- To analyze the form and structure of a paragraph
- To analyze the relationship between a paragraph's main idea (topic sentence) and the supporting information
- To evaluate the unity and coherence of paragraphs
- To arrange paragraph ideas in an order that makes the main idea clear
- To analyze the use of direct references and transitions
- To use appropriate strategies for developing main ideas
- To write and revise paragraphs intended for different purposes

Motivation

You may want to begin the lesson by asking your students to tell you what a paragraph is. Some of your students probably have been told that certain rules such as "A paragraph must have at least three sentences" or "A paragraph must begin with a topic sentence" govern all paragraphs. Explain to students that such rules are designed only to help students who are beginning to learn about paragraphs. More-advanced writing does not necessitate exact rules. You may want to have students look through a few magazine or newspaper articles and note the variety in paragraphs. Point out that some paragraphs have topic sentences and some do not. Some paragraphs have three sentences and some have thirteen. This chapter will help students understand how they can and should structure and use paragraphs.

Introduction

In this chapter, students initially will learn about the components of a paragraph—the main idea, topic sentence, supporting details, and clincher sentence. They will also study the importance of unity and coherence in paragraphs. The remainder of the chapter focuses on the writing modes—description, narration, classification, and evaluation. Finally, the pieces are brought together with assignments in which students are asked to write paragraphs for each of the writing aims—expressive, informative, persuasive, and creative.

Integration

This chapter may be used to enhance other activities in your classroom. For example, students could analyze how novelists combine strategies of development, explain how poets use the principles of comparison and description to create striking images, and evaluate an essay by inferring the author's aim.

You may also find the material in this chapter helpful to students who are writing for other courses such as science or business. **Strategies of Development** provides universal writing guidelines for paragraph support.

The chart on the next page illustrates the strands of language arts as they are integrated into this chapter. For vocabulary study, glossary words are underlined in some writing models.

QUOTATIONS
All **Quotations for the Day** are chosen because of their relevance to instructional material presented in that segment of the chapter and for their usefulness in establishing student interest in writing.

Integrating the Language Arts

Selection	Reading and Literature	Writing and Critical Thinking	Language and Syntax	Speaking, Listening, and Other Expression Skills
FROM *Running Tide* 58-60 "Wyoming dinosaur find may be a fossil first" 62-63 *The Story of English* 65 "The World in Its Extreme" 65-66 "Galileo Galilei" 66 *I Know Why The Caged Bird Sings* 67 *Reading the Numbers* 68 *Labyrinth: Solving the Riddle of the Maze* 69 "Men at War: An Interview with Shelby Foote" 69 *Alistair Cooke's America* 71 *The Living World* 72 *From Top Hats to Baseball Caps…* 72-73 "Emeralds" 73 "Blue Spruce" 75 "Black, Blue and Gray: The Other Civil War" 76 "Introduction" to *Baby, That Was Rock and Roll* 77 "Flight" 79 *Blue Highways* 83 *Seven Arrows* 84 *Be a Clown!* 85 *The Black Almanac* 85-86 *Dinosaur Days in Texas* 87 Dogs: *All About Them* 87-88 *"The Great Figure"* 94	Responding personally to literature **61** Finding main idea **61, 64-66** Analyzing paragraphs **61, 63, 64-66** Locating different types of paragraphs **63** Identifying topic sentences **64-66** Identifying paragraph order **77-78** Identifying direct references and transitional expressions **81**	Writing a journal entry **61** Using literature as a catalyst for personal expression **61** Analyzing paragraph structure **61, 77-78** Evaluating paragraph function **61, 63** Analyzing a variety of paragraphs **63, 64-66, 77-78** Identifying main ideas and topic sentences **64-66** Applying interpretive and creative thinking **64-66, 73-74, 77-78, 83, 88, 89, 90-91, 91-92, 93, 95** Writing topic sentences **64-66** Developing supporting details **70, 90** Researching for supporting details **70** Analyzing notes for unity **73-74** Ordering information within a paragraph **77-78** Revising paragraph structure **77-78** Identifying direct references and transitional expressions **81** Developing sensory details **83** Using narration as a writing strategy **86** Using classification as a writing strategy **88** Using evaluation as a writing strategy **89** Using the writing process to write an expressive paragraph **90-91** Using the writing process to write an expository paragraph **92** Using the writing process to write a persuasive paragraph **93** Using the writing process to write a literary paragraph **94-95**	Ordering sentences in a paragraph **77-78** Identifying direct references and transitional expressions **81** Proofreading for errors in grammar, usage, and mechanics **91, 92, 93, 95**	Working with classmates to analyze paragraphs **62** Working with classmates to analyze notes for unity **73-74** Sharing evaluations with classmates **89** Sharing a persuasive paragraph with classmates and getting their opinions **93**

CHAPTER 2

SEGMENT PLANNING GUIDE

Whether you are planning for a quick review of a writing concept or preparing an extended lesson on composition, you can use the following Planning Guide to adapt the chapter material to the individual needs of your class.

SEGMENT	PAGES	CONTENT	RESOURCES
1 *Looking at the Parts*	*57-61*		
Literary Model from ***Running Tide***	58-60	Guided reading: a model of paragraph form	
Reader's Response/Writer's Craft	61	Model evaluation: responding to literature and analyzing paragraphs	
2 *The Uses of Paragraphs*	*62-63*		Using Short Paragraphs Effectively 17
Literary Model from **"Wyoming dinosaur find may be a fossil first"**	62-63	Guided reading: examining paragraphs in a model	
Exercise 1	63	Cooperative learning: surveying the uses of paragraphs	
3 *Paragraphs That Develop a Main Idea*	*64-71*		Main Ideas and Topic Sentences 18 Using Details 19 Using Examples and Anecdotes 20 The Clincher Sentence 21
The Topic Sentence	64	Guidelines: developing and placing a topic sentence	
Exercise 2	64-66	Applied practice: identifying main ideas and topic sentences	
Supporting Sentences	67	Guidelines: writing supporting sentences	
Sensory Details	67	Guidelines: examining the use of sensory details in a model	
Facts and Statistics	68	Guidelines: examining the use of facts and statistics in a model	
Examples	68-69	Guidelines: examining the use of examples in a model	
Anecdotes	69	Guidelines: examining the use of an anecdote in a model	
Exercise 3	70	Applied practice: collecting supporting details	
The Clincher Sentence	71	Guidelines: examining a clincher sentence in a model	
4 *Unity*	*72-74*		Achieving Unity 22
Unity	72-73	Examples: relating sentences	
Exercise 4	73-74	Cooperative learning: analyzing notes for unity	
5 *Coherence*	*75-81*		Achieving Coherence 23
Coherence	75-77	Guidelines: examining models for various types of order	
Exercise 5	77-78	Applied practice: arranging paragraphs	

All the resources listed in this chapter are located in the *Teacher's ResourceBank*™.

SEGMENT	PAGES	CONTENT	RESOURCES
Connections Between Ideas	79-81	Guidelines: using direct references and transitional expressions to achieve coherence	
Chart: Transitional Words and Phrases	80	Guidelines: examining transitional words and phrases	
Writing Note	80	Writing suggestion: using transitional expressions sparingly	
Exercise 6	81	Applied practice: identifying direct references and transitional expressions	
6 *Strategies of Development*	*82-89*		Using Description and Narration 24 Classification and Evaluation 25
Chart: Strategies of Development	82	Guidelines: examining strategies of development	
Description	83	Guidelines: examining order in a descriptive paragraph	
Exercise 7	83	Applied practice: using description as a strategy	
Narration	84-86	Guidelines: examining narrative paragraphs	
Exercise 8	86	Applied practice: using narration as a strategy	
Classification	86-88	Guidelines: examining paragraphs that classify	
Exercise 9	88	Applied practice: using classification as a strategy	
Evaluation	89	Guidelines: examining a paragraph that evaluates	
Exercise 10	89	Applied practice: using evaluation as a strategy	
7 *Making Connections*	*90-95*		
Writing Paragraphs for Different Purposes	90	Introduction: examining purposes for writing	
A Self-Expressive Paragraph	90-91	Applied practice: writing an expressive paragraph	
An Expository Paragraph	91-92	Applied practice: writing an informative paragraph	
A Persuasive Paragraph	93	Applied practice: writing a persuasive paragraph	
A Literary Paragraph	94-95	Applied practice: writing a descriptive paragraph	
Literary Model **"The Great Figure"**	94	Guided reading: examining a poem	
WHOLE-CHAPTER RESOURCE Chapter Review			

SEGMENT 1 *(pp. 56–61)*

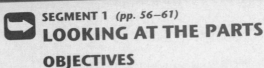

LOOKING AT THE PARTS

OBJECTIVES

- To respond personally to literature
- To identify the main idea of a paragraph
- To analyze a model composition's paragraph usage

TEACHING THE LESSON

After having a student read the introductory text, ask students how they have used paragraphs in their writing. Have several students explain how they decide when to begin new paragraphs as they write compositions. Students might suggest that they begin a new paragraph every five or six

VISUAL CONNECTIONS

Trinity

About the Artist. Richard Anuskiewicz, inspired by studies on color and perception done in the early 1950s, began experimenting with color in his paintings in the late 1950s. By the 1960s, the term *op art* (short for optical art) was being applied to Anuskiewicz's work and the work of other artists who used color to create odd visual effects and optical illusions. Op art relies on the discovery that color is perceived relative to its background and to its neighboring colors. For example, a white piece of paper can seem either yellow or gray when placed near another white object. Anuskiewicz often uses calculated symmetrical geometric compositions to heighten the effects of the color juxtapositions in his paintings.

2 UNDERSTANDING PARAGRAPH STRUCTURE

sentences, whenever the general topic changes, or just whenever it seems they should. Many of your students will have no clearly defined method for paragraphing. As you read the literary selection with students, pause occasionally to analyze the writer's use of different types of paragraphs. Have students consider the differences in length and content of the paragraphs.

You may want to use the first **Reader's Response** question as an oral activity in which volunteers share their responses with the rest of the class. Initiate the journal-writing activity in the second **Reader's Response** question by modeling an experience of your own. Emphasize that competition is not only a characteristic of athletics, but is present in test situations and ☛

Looking at the Parts

You won't find paragraphs in poems or plays, but you'll find them in almost every other kind of writing—novels and short stories, articles, ads, business reports, petitions. They're the **parts** that make up the whole.

Writing and You. In some ways, paragraphs are as elusive as they are essential. There is so much variety in their structure and use that it is difficult to pinpoint their common characteristics. They can be as short as one sentence or as long as many pages; they can show a transition from one idea to the next or develop a single idea; and they can break up long passages to make them easier to read. How have you used paragraphs in your own writing?

As You Read. As you read the following selection from the autobiography of an Olympic runner, notice the different uses of paragraphs.

Richard Anuszkiewicz, *Trinity* (1970). Acrylic on canvas, 42″ × 72″. Collection of Alcoa Collection of Contemporary Art, Pittsburgh, PA. © 1993 Richard Anuszkiewicz/VAGA, New York.

QUOTATION FOR THE DAY

"The purpose of paragraphing is to give the reader a rest." (H. W. Fowler, 1858–1933, British lexicographer)

Ask your students how they would feel if they opened a book and saw no paragraph breaks in the text. Would they feel tired before they even started to read? Then ask students to volunteer other reasons why writers use paragraphs.

MEETING INDIVIDUAL NEEDS

LESS-ADVANCED STUDENTS

You may want to show students a short poem, an excerpt from a play, a stanza of song lyrics, a page from a book, and a newspaper article to illustrate where paragraphs are and aren't found. Discuss the fact that the writings that don't use paragraphs still have meaning and main ideas; their packaging is just different.

in academic, musical, and dramatic events. Most students have been involved in competition even if they are not athletically inclined.

Before having students independently complete the **Writer's Craft** questions, you may want to display a multi-paragraph composition on an overhead projector (or you could use the excerpt from *Kaffir Boy in America* on pp. 242–245) and guide students in a discussion about main idea and the function of paragraphs.

USING THE SELECTION
from Running Tide

1
Joan Benoit is an American long-distance runner who is famous for her marathon records. In 1984 she won the first Olympic women's marathon.

2
Technically, burnout is the point at which a rocket or jet engine uses up all its fuel and stops operating. With people, *burnout* refers to emotional or physical exhaustion and, often, quitting.

from RUNNING TIDE

by Joan Benoit with Sally Baker *1*

Athletes who start young in their chosen sport can point to an early determination to excel in that sport alone. Tennis players, swimmers, and gymnasts begin intensive training when they are little more than babies; which is why, I believe, so many of them fall by the
2 wayside so early. If you start working hard at seven, burnout is a real possibility by thirteen or fourteen. Long-distance runners shouldn't begin so early, as they could do permanent harm to developing bones and muscles, so they should experience a variety of sports and pursue other activities. I always knew I wanted to be an athlete because I loved to be active and to compete, but running wasn't a sport I gave much attention to as a child. So I can't look back and trace my primal devotions step by step, backing them up with training logs and competition results. There was no Little League for runners in my hometown and

ASSESSMENT

You could use students' answers to the **Writer's Craft** questions to assess comprehension of main idea and the uses of paragraphs.

CLOSURE

Ask students to discuss what they learned about paragraphs from an examination of the literary model. [Students should mention that paragraphs vary greatly in length and that length depends on function.]

☛

none was needed. A kindergarten teacher remembers that I used to hang on the fringes of the older kids' group in the playground and run away with their kickball when I got a chance. My childhood was filled with athletic endeavors, none of which would mean anything if I hadn't gone on to pursue a career in running.

3 But a career has to start somewhere, and, as nearly
4 as I can tell, mine started at a gymkana in Norfolk, Connecticut.

It was the summer after my eighth birthday. My brother Peter and I were invited to drive to Norfolk with our aunt and uncle and several cousins. Peter and I would return home on a bus by ourselves. He was eleven and probably very reluctant to look after me, but it was a chance to travel and he grabbed it.

"I used to hang on the fringes of the older kids' group in the playground and run away with their kickball when I got a chance."

On Saturday the Norfolk country club held its annual gymkana. My cousins were anxious to compete and I was eager to find out what a gymkana was (it sounded like an antelope), so their parents got us to the club early that morning. It slowly dawned on me that a gymkana was basically a track and field competition. Anyone could take part, so I signed up for everything appropriate for my age group.

One of the first events was an 880 for teenaged boys. Because I was small enough to wriggle to the front of the crowd without bothering anyone, I had a good view. Separated from Peter and my cousins, I was able to watch without distraction. I was fascinated. One young man took a quick lead in the race and maintained it to the end. He seemed confident; when he crossed the finish line he was winded, but I could tell he wasn't in as much pain as the other runners.

3

The author narrates as a developmental strategy.

4

gymkana: a contest involving a display of skill; refers in Britain to a local sports meeting for horse racing, horse jumping, and competitions for horse and carriage

ENRICHMENT

The excerpt from ***Running Tide*** may intrigue some students. Encourage them to read the entire book and to research the life of Joan Benoit. They can share their findings with the rest of the class. ■

5
The author uses description as a developmental strategy.

6
A ringer is a person who enters a competition dishonestly. In the selection, the aunt refers to the fact that Joan was not supposed to win all of the races; it seemed unfair.

7
The clincher sentence summarizes the intent of the excerpt.

SELECTION AMENDMENT
Description of change: excerpted
Rationale: to focus on the concept of paragraph structure presented in this chapter

This race has stayed in my memory so long because I got my first good advice on running while watching it. I was trying to figure out what it was that made the lead runner look so good when a woman behind me said, "You can tell Jim runs for the high school team. Look at
5 the way he carries his arms." Jim kept his arms close to his sides and ran with his elbows tucked in to his waist. His head and upper body hardly moved—he used his energy to power his legs. That was what made him look so good.

I remembered Jim's style when I ran my races later that day. I signed up for five running and two jumping events; holding my arms as the boy had, I won five blue ribbons.

No big deal, I thought, it was fun. My cousins, on the other hand, were none too pleased with my day's work; I couldn't understand why. The ride back to their house was silent. My aunt was mortified: her guest had 6
turned out to be an eight-year-old ringer.

"Other people loved to win just as much as I did. Until that day I had not considered the costs of competition. Somebody had to lose."

After a time I couldn't stand the silence, so I made the mistake of admiring the red and white ribbons the others had won. I said I thought they were very nice. My cousins hissed at me. "Second place!" they screamed. "Third place! Hon-or-a-ble mention!"

Now I understood. Other people loved to win just as much as I did. Until that day I had not considered the costs of competition. Somebody had to lose. I
7 didn't mind if I lost after doing my best, but I preferred to win and so did everyone else. I have my cousins to thank for an early lesson in the importance of winning with modesty.

Reader's Response

1. In her autobiography, Joan Benoit reveals some of her own thoughts about what makes a winning athlete. Based on your own experience, what do you think are some qualities or characteristics of an athlete who wins?
2. Benoit says that the fact that someone has to lose is one of the "costs of competition." In your journal, write about one of your own competitive experiences. What were the costs? the rewards?

Writer's Craft

3. Longer paragraphs are often used to develop a main idea. What idea does the writer develop in the first paragraph?
4. Shorter paragraphs often emphasize a point or provide a transition from one idea to the other. What's the function of the second paragraph in the selection?
5. Which paragraphs seem to be more effective, the shorter ones or the longer ones? What do you think makes a paragraph effective?

LOOKING AHEAD

In this chapter, you'll study some of the principles of paragraph form and structure. As you work through the chapter, keep in mind that

- paragraphs have many uses
- one important use of a paragraph is to develop a main idea
- sensory details, facts and statistics, examples, and anecdotes are often used to develop a paragraph's main idea
- the strategies of description, narration, classification, and evaluation are ways of developing paragraphs

ANSWERS

Reader's Response

Responses will vary.

1. Possibilities include determination, confidence, dedication, natural skill, concentration, and adaptability.
2. Each response should describe the competitive experience and include both the costs and the rewards of the experience. The emphasis should be on self-expression, not mechanics.

Writer's Craft

3. Although active and competitive as a child, Joan Benoit did not plan to be a long-distance runner.
4. The second paragraph introduces the anecdote about Benoit's first experience with competitive running.
5. Students should support their opinions with details. Students should conclude that the effectiveness of a paragraph depends on its purpose.

SEGMENT 2 *(pp. 62–63)*

THE USES OF PARAGRAPHS

OBJECTIVE

- To survey the way writers use paragraphs

TEACHING THE LESSON

Before having students read the introductory material, write the following uses for paragraphs on the chalkboard:

1. develop a main idea
2. show a transition
3. emphasize a point
4. indicate a change in speakers
5. create visual appeal

Teacher's ResourceBank™

RESOURCES

THE USES OF PARAGRAPHS

- Using Short Paragraphs Effectively 17

QUOTATION FOR THE DAY

"The paragraph is a convenient unit; it serves all forms of literary work. As long as it holds together, a paragraph may be of any length—a single, short sentence or a passage of great duration." (E. B. White, 1899–1985, American humorist, essayist, and novelist)

Ask students to use this quotation to think of short definitions of the word *paragraph.* [A possible response is "a literary unit of varying length with one main idea."]

USING THE SELECTION

Wyoming dinosaur find may be a fossil first

1

Paleontologists: scientists who study fossils

2

Jurassic period: the second period of the Mesozoic era, 190 million years ago, marked by the presence of dinosaurs and the appearance of primitive birds

The Uses of Paragraphs

In school assignments, you most often think of paragraphs as a group of sentences that work together to develop a main idea. But in many other kinds of writing, such as popular magazines and newspapers, ads, and "how-to" manuals, you often find short—even one-sentence—paragraphs that don't really develop a main idea. They're used for a different purpose. Here's a newspaper article that's made up of ten very short paragraphs. What purpose do these short paragraphs serve?

Wyoming dinosaur find may be a fossil first

by Linda Kanamine

1 No bones about it. Paleontologists are jumping for joy over the discovery of an intact dinosaur skeleton.

The recent find in northern Wyoming may be one of the oldest intact dinosaur skeletons ever found in the USA.

Paleontologists from Montana State University, the University of Wyoming and the Royal Tyrell Museum in Canada left Wednesday on a mission to rescue the partly exposed allosaurus, hoping to preserve it before winter hits.

Allosaurus—among earliest meat-eating dinosaurs—was a ferocious predator that roamed the Earth 136 million to 190 million years ago.

The dinosaur predates Tyrannosaurus Rex by 80 million years. Allosaurus walked on huge hind legs, but stood horizontally and didn't drag its tail.

"It's something you hope to see in a lifetime," says Patrick Leiggi, assistant to the curator at MSU's Museum of the Rockies in Bozeman, Mont.

While other allosauruses have been uncovered in Utah, they've been in bits and pieces. And most have been adult dinosaurs up to 35 feet long—not an 18-foot teenager like this rare find.

"It's really neat to look at," Leiggi says.

The fossil, Leiggi says, is another piece in the puzzle of
2 the Jurassic period, when allosaurus roamed, and should give insights to the beast about which so little is known.

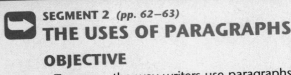

After students read the introductory material, ask volunteers to read aloud the literary model one paragraph at a time. After each paragraph is read, use the list on the chalkboard to help students determine the paragraph's use. (The text that follows the literary model explains the uses of some of the paragraphs.)

Then group students to complete **Exercise 1.** You will probably want to circulate throughout the room to offer assistance and assess progress as the groups survey the way writers use paragraphs. To close, have groups share their surveys with the rest of the class. ■

> "People believe we know all about dinosaurs," Leiggi says. "But what we know is just a drop in the bucket."
>
> *USA TODAY*

Three of the article's short paragraphs (the longest have only two sentences) show that a person is speaking, but the rest make the article seem easy to read—they're visually appealing. Short paragraphs can also catch a reader's eye and make a point stand out or provide a transition from one idea to another. Reread the following paragraph from the opening selection.

> I remembered Jim's style when I ran my races later that day. I signed up for five running and two jumping events; holding my arms as the boy had, I won five blue ribbons.

If you look back to see how this paragraph fits into the opening selection, you'll see that it marks the shift from the idea of studying a runner's techniques to Benoit's idea of becoming a winning runner herself.

EXERCISE 1 Surveying the Uses of Paragraphs

Get together with two or three classmates, and, as a group, make a survey of the way writers actually use paragraphs. Look at sources such as popular magazine and newspaper articles, ads, CD and album cover notes, "how-to" manuals, and movie, book, and restaurant reviews. Take notes about the different uses of paragraphs and the sources where you find them. You might find paragraphs that develop a main idea or that (1) emphasize a point, (2) show a transition from one idea to another, (3) indicate a change in speakers, or (4) create visual appeal.

MEETING INDIVIDUAL NEEDS

LESS-ADVANCED STUDENTS

You may want to schedule conferences throughout the year with students who seem to have difficulty with paragraphing their writing. Help them to understand that paragraphing in expressive and literary writing often reflects the writer's style; however, in expository and persuasive writing, paragraphs generally develop main ideas and advance understanding.

ANSWERS

Exercise 1

To save time, you may want to provide students with a collection of sources such as newspapers, advertisements, magazines, and album covers. Each of the group's example paragraphs should be accompanied by a description of exactly how that paragraph was used and a listing for the source in which it was found.

SEGMENT 3 (pp. 64–71)

PARAGRAPHS THAT DEVELOP A MAIN IDEA

OBJECTIVES

- To identify main ideas and topic sentences
- To provide supporting details for main ideas

TEACHING THE LESSON

You could begin the lesson by having students analyze the structure of several of the main idea paragraphs they found in **Exercise 1** on p. 63. How do these paragraphs begin? How do they develop ideas? How do they end? Emphasize that main idea paragraphs are not always identical in

Teacher's ResourceBank™

RESOURCES

PARAGRAPHS THAT DEVELOP A MAIN IDEA

QUOTATION FOR THE DAY

"A paragraph should not be an accident; it should be carefully thought out and polished." (Dean Memering and Frank O'Hare, university educators and writers)

Explain to the class that clearly communicating an idea in paragraph form involves careful planning. A paragraph's structure, as well as its content, can be included in such a plan.

MEETING INDIVIDUAL NEEDS

LESS ADVANCED STUDENTS

Give students a list of related phrases such as "chew on rawhide bones, chase cats, fetch sticks, and guard the house." Ask students to write a sentence explaining what the phrases describe. ["These are things that dogs like to do."] Explain to students that a main idea is simply what all of the sentences in a paragraph have in common.

Paragraphs That Develop a Main Idea

Paragraphs in thoughtful articles and other works of nonfiction, including essays that you write in school, usually develop one main idea. These main idea paragraphs are often—but not always—made up of a topic sentence and several supporting sentences that support, or prove, the main idea. The paragraphs that you'll read in this part of the chapter appeared originally as part of a longer piece of writing where they worked together to separate and to link ideas. They stand alone here so you can study their structure.

The Topic Sentence

Experienced writers have many options in writing paragraphs. One option is to put, somewhere in the paragraph, a single sentence that states the main idea of the paragraph. This ***topic sentence*** is a specific, limiting statement about the subject of the paragraph.

Location of a Topic Sentence. You'll often find the topic sentence as the first or second sentence of a paragraph (sometimes following a catchy, inviting first sentence). But you can find a topic sentence any place in a paragraph. To create surprise or to summarize ideas, writers sometimes place topic sentences at or near the end of a paragraph.

Importance of a Topic Sentence. Not all paragraphs have or need topic sentences. Paragraphs that relate sequences of events or actions in stories, for example, frequently don't contain topic sentences. In the writing that you do in school, however, you'll find that topic sentences are useful. They provide a focus for your reader, and they keep you from straying off the topic as you develop the rest of your paragraph.

EXERCISE 2 **Identifying Main Ideas and Topic Sentences**

By now you're probably an old hand at identifying main ideas and topic sentences, but you can refresh your skills by tackling the three paragraphs in this exercise. While all three of the paragraphs have a main idea, only two have topic sentences.

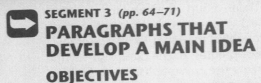

structure but they do share certain characteristics that this segment will explain.

After students read the introductory material and **The Topic Sentence,** point out that purpose often influences the choice of location for the topic sentence. Frequently, writers who want to inform place the topic sentence at or near the beginning of a paragraph. This placement helps readers understand the significance of each supporting detail. Writers who want to entertain will sometimes place the topic sentence near the end of a paragraph to build a dramatic effect or to add an unexpected twist.

Guide students in their reading of **Supporting Sentences** on pp. 67–69. Often,

First, state the main idea in each paragraph, and then identify the topic sentences in the two paragraphs that have them. Make up a topic sentence for the other paragraph. [Hint: To state the main idea of a sequence of events or actions, give a one-sentence summary of what happens in the paragraph.]

1. English as the language of international pop music and mass entertainment is a worldwide phenomenon. In 1982, a Spanish punk rock group, called Asfalto (Asphalt), released a disc about learning English, which became a hit. The Swedish group Abba records all its numbers in English. Michael Luszynski is a Polish singer who performs almost entirely in English. There is no Polish translation for words like "Baby-baby" and "Yeah-yeah-yeah". Luszynski notes wryly that a phrase like "Słysze warkot pociągu nadjedzie na torze" does not roll as smoothly in a lyric as "I hear the train a-coming, it's rolling down the line . . ."

Robert McCrum, William Cran, and Robert MacNeil, *The Story of English*

2. The captain was disgusted by the place. He said, "You let a sheet of paper fall and it takes forever to hit the ground. It's the heat." He tried to be polite. He asked me about the condition of the road. He asked me where I had

INTEGRATING THE LANGUAGE ARTS

Technology Link. Many word-processing programs include cut-and-paste features that allow the simple rearrangement of information. You may want each student to write a paragraph and to move the topic sentence to various locations within the paragraph. If students print each of the possibilities, they could then analyze which placement of the topic sentence was most effective for that paragraph.

ANSWERS

Exercise 2

Responses may vary.

1. Main idea: English is the language of choice for pop musicians around the world.
   Topic sentence: "English as the language of international pop music and mass entertainment is a worldwide phenomenon."

SELECTION AMENDMENT

Description of change: excerpted

Rationale: to focus on the concept of main idea and topic sentences presented in this chapter students have difficulty supplying adequate supporting detail when they are writing. This section provides examples of some of the most common types of detail students need to be able to include. You may want to read the four model paragraphs in this section aloud so that you can help with references and discussion. Ask volunteers to point out all of the sensory details in the first paragraph, all of the statistics in the second paragraph, and all of the examples in the third paragraph. Lead students to see that a writer traditionally gives at least three supporting details to support the main idea of a paragraph.

Have a volunteer read aloud **The Clincher Sentence** and the model paragraph on p. 71. Emphasize to students that

2. Main idea: The protagonist is thorough in his search.
   Possible topic sentence: "If he found no sign of what he was looking for, it wasn't because he didn't try."
3. Main idea: Galileo's accomplishments include an amazing amount of scientific discovery and invention.
   Topic sentence: "To few human beings has it been given, in a life of four-score years, to advance so momentously the sum of human knowledge."

INTEGRATING THE LANGUAGE ARTS

Listening Link. Tell students that when they listen to lectures, news reports, or even friends' conversations, they are probably listening for main ideas. By identifying a speaker's main ideas, the listener is more able to evaluate the information. Remind students that speakers often use certain verbal clues such as *most importantly, first, second, next,* and *remember that* to emphasize main points.

You may want to read aloud several paragraphs and have students listen for the main ideas. Or if the school's daily announcements are broadcast, you could have students jot down the main idea of each announcement.

AMENDMENT TO SELECTIONS
Description of change: excerpted
Rationale: to focus on the concept of main idea and topic sentences presented in this chapter

been and where I was going, and why. He knew I was a writer, and also a pilot, and this made him doubly distrustful. Why would a pilot travel so much by ground? And what was there to say about such emptiness? I tried to explain. He seemed worried about me.

William Langewiesche, "The World in Its Extreme"

3. He became a learner and teacher of men and in this life career what did he accomplish three hundred years ago? The simple unexplained record is in itself wonderful: he found the law of falling bodies; he invented the telescope; he discovered the moons of Jupiter, he explained the reflected light of planets; he laid down the laws of cohesion; he studied the law of the pendulum and applied it to the clock; and above all he adduced irrefragable proof of the correctness of the Copernican doctrine that the sun and not the earth is the center of our universe. Simply and barely stated this accomplishment is tremendous. To few human beings has it been given, in a life of four-score years, to advance so momentously the sum of human knowledge.

W.E.B. Du Bois, "Galileo Galilei"

clincher sentences shouldn't be overused—especially in paragraphs that work with other paragraphs to develop a main idea. Steer students away from weak and unnecessary clinchers such as "Those are the reasons I dislike vacations."

GUIDED PRACTICE

Help students identify the main idea and the topic sentence in the first paragraph of **Exercise 2** on p. 65. To prepare students for **Exercise 3** on p. 70, have them suggest examples as support for the following topic sentence: "Team sports develop skills that you'll use throughout your life." ☛

Supporting Sentences

Imagine what communication would be like if people wrote only in topic sentences.

> Some scientists believe that birds are the modern descendants of dinosaurs.
>
> When Abraham Lincoln first delivered his famous Gettysburg Address, many critics considered it a disgrace.
>
> We are selling the United States to the highest bidder.

These are surprising statements, and few readers would accept these generalizations without ***supporting sentences*** that give details to support, or prove, them. Even when topic sentences are not so surprising *(most Americans know little about geography; the planets revolve around the sun in elliptical orbits)*, they still need support.

Supporting sentences often consist of sensory details, facts or statistics, examples, or an anecdote. A paragraph may be developed with one type of detail or with a combination of types.

Sensory Details

Sensory details are images of sight, sound, taste, smell, and texture that bring the subject to life for readers. In this paragraph, notice how sensory details help you see and hear the children, as well as smell the evening's refreshments.

> The weeks until graduation were filled with heady activities. A group of small children were to be presented in a play about buttercups and daisies and bunny rabbits. They could be heard throughout the building practicing their hops and their little songs that sounded like silver bells. The older girls (nongraduates, of course) were assigned the task of making refreshments for the night's festivities. A tangy scent of ginger, cinnamon, nutmeg and chocolate wafted around the home economics building as the budding cooks made samples for themselves and their teachers.
>
> Maya Angelou, *I know why the caged bird sings*

INTEGRATING THE LANGUAGE ARTS

Test-taking Link. The information on using supporting sentences might be helpful to students when they are asked to develop answers to essay questions on tests. Suggest to students that they introduce each paragraph with a clear topic sentence. Although this format isn't always the most effective in other types of writing, beginning each paragraph of a test essay with a topic sentence identifies the main idea of the answer for the reader.

You may want to work with a teacher of another subject to provide students with essay questions for practice in developing main ideas.

A DIFFERENT APPROACH

You could suggest that before students develop paragraphs with sensory details, they make prewriting charts with the five senses as headings. Using such charts might keep students from relying mainly on visual details.

SELECTION AMENDMENT

Description of change: excerpted
Rationale: to focus on the concept of sensory details presented in this chapter

INDEPENDENT PRACTICE

Assign the remaining excerpts in **Exercise 2** as independent practice. To verify student understanding of main ideas and topic sentences, have each student locate a paragraph that contains a clear topic sentence and a paragraph that contains a clearly stated main idea but no topic sentence. Students might use a local newspaper, magazines, pamphlets, newsletters, or other textbooks.

Before assigning **Exercise 3,** you could discuss with the class possible resources for each topic sentence that requires research.

MEETING INDIVIDUAL NEEDS

ADVANCED STUDENTS

Some advanced students may have difficulty providing enough supporting detail without giving too much information. Just because a fact is interesting does not mean it should be included in the paragraph.

Have students work in pairs to find and evaluate the use of facts and statistics in periodicals. Ask each pair to find a paragraph in which the reader could become bored or confused by too many facts and statistics. In contrast, ask each pair to find a good example of a paragraph whose topic sentence is supported by facts and statistics. Have students write notes that point out similarities and differences between the two paragraphs.

SELECTION AMENDMENT
Description of change: excerpted
Rationale: to focus on the concept of facts and statistics presented in this chapter

Facts and Statistics

Another way to support and clarify a main idea is to use facts and statistics. A ***fact*** is something that can be proven true by concrete information: *Archbishop Desmond Tutu, a South African civil rights leader, received the Nobel Prize for peace in 1984.* A ***statistic*** is a fact based on numbers: *The United States border with Mexico is 1,952 miles long.* To verify the accuracy of facts or statistics, you can cross-check them in reference materials. In the following paragraph, the writer uses statistics to illustrate the popularity of pencils.

> You'd think that the pencil would just fade away, what with pattering keyboards and ubiquitous ballpoint pens. Pencil popularity, however, seems here to stay—more than 2 1/2 billion pencils are produced in America every year. The U.S. government uses 45 million of them a year, and the New York Stock Exchange more than a million. Perhaps it's because the pencil's an old-fashioned hard worker—one standard pencil can leave a 35-mile trail, or about 45,000 words. At least forty materials from twenty-eight countries go into one.
>
> Mary Blocksma, *Reading the Numbers*

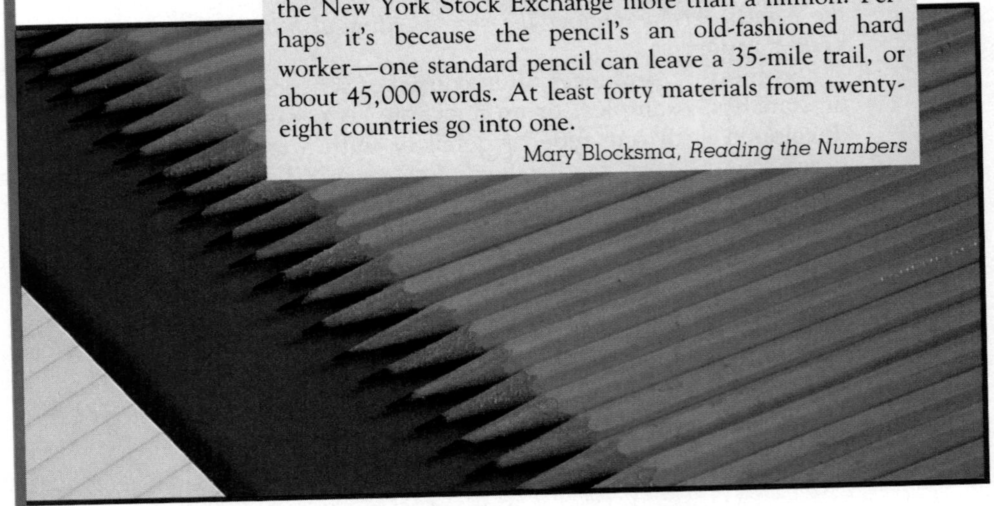

Examples

Many newspapers of the day called Abraham Lincoln's Gettysburg Address a disgrace; one example is the *Times* of London, which referred to the speech as "dull and commonplace." ***Examples*** are specific instances or illustrations of a general idea. The following paragraph (for example) uses specific examples to support the writer's main idea about the modern interest in mazes.

ASSESSMENT

Assess students' mastery of the segment concepts through an evaluation of **Exercises 2 and 3.** In addition, you may want to evaluate the topic sentences and supporting details of paragraphs students have written.

RETEACHING

Give students paragraphs from newspapers and magazines in which you have highlighted the main points covered in this segment. Have students identify the highlighted sections as main ideas, topic sentences, supporting sentences, or clincher sentences.

Since the 1970s, there has been a revolution in innovative puzzle mazes. Greg Bright's puzzle maze at Longleat had curving paths, wooden bridges, a complete lack of symmetry, and, above all, immense size. Stuart Landsborough's wooden mazes triggered off a maze craze in Japan, resulting in the construction of over two hundred three-dimensional wooden mazes during the 1980s. Our own puzzle innovations have encompassed traditional, interactive and color mazes, within a diverse range of landscape settings.

Adrian Fisher and Georg Gerster, *Labyrinth: Solving the Riddle of the Maze*

Anecdotes

An ***anecdote,*** a little story that is usually biographical or autobiographical, can also be used to support, or prove, a main idea. In this paragraph, for example, the writer uses an anecdote to help support a point about General Stonewall Jackson's ability to ignore the suffering of his men.

He had a strange quality of overlooking suffering. He had a young courier, and during one of the battles Jackson looked around for him and he wasn't there. And he said, "Where is Lieutenant So-and-so?" And they said, "He was killed, General." Jackson said, "Very commendable, very commendable," and put him out of his mind. He would send men stumbling into battle where fury was and have no concern about casualties at the moment. He would march men until they were spitting cotton and white-faced and fell by the wayside. He wouldn't even stop to glance at one of them, but kept going.

Geoffrey C. Ward et al., "Men at War: An Interview with Shelby Foote," *The Civil War*

INTEGRATING THE LANGUAGE ARTS

Literature Link. You may want to have students read an informational essay from their literature books, such as William Faulkner's "Nobel Prize Acceptance Speech." As students read, have them analyze the purpose of each paragraph. How does Faulkner emphasize his main points? Does the fact that the speech was written to be presented orally influence his paragraph structure? Students might notice that many of his paragraphs begin with clear topic sentences. Why is this so? [In an oral presentation, the audience does not have the ability to reread. The main ideas must be presented very clearly.]

AMENDMENTS TO SELECTIONS
Description of change: excerpted and modified
Rationale: to focus on the concepts of examples and anecdotes presented in this chapter

CLOSURE

Ask students to define *main idea* and *topic sentence.* Then ask a volunteer to list the various ways to supply supporting information for a topic sentence [sensory details, facts and statistics, examples, and anecdotes]

EXTENSION

Have each student evaluate a paragraph that develops a main idea from one of his or her writing assignments. Tell students to identify their main ideas, topic sentences, and clincher sentences. (Remind students that topic sentences and clincher sentences are not always necessary.) Then have students determine whether they used sensory

ANSWERS

Exercise 3

Answers will vary. Here are some possibilities.

1. *Family Circus* shows familial relationships, especially from children's points of view. *B.C.* often comments on how our activities might seem utterly ridiculous to people elsewhere. *Garfield* looks at life's situations from a cat's point of view.
2. The band's rhythm combines with the chants from the cheerleaders. The sweaty student bodies sway to the loud noises. The teachers and administrators patrol the rows of students. Anticipating the night's game, the players stand tall and proud.
3. Jupiter orbits the sun at a mean velocity of 8.1 miles (13 km) per second. Mercury orbits the sun at a mean velocity of 29.8 miles (48 km) per second. Venus orbits the sun at a mean velocity of 22 miles (35 km) per second. Earth orbits the sun at a mean velocity of 18.5 miles (29.8 km) per second.
4. To fulfill both parts of the assignment, each student should provide two anecdotes—one dealing with friendship in good times and another dealing with friendship during bad times.

EXERCISE 3 Collecting Supporting Details

Now that you have looked at different kinds of supporting details, try creating your own. Here are four main ideas that you might use for paragraphs. Choose two of the ideas, and then list at least three details that support, or prove, the main idea. Use the type of detail—sensory details, facts and/or statistics, examples, or an anecdote—indicated after each main idea. You'll probably have to do a little research to supply most of the details.

EXAMPLE **1. Roller coasters have an interesting history. (facts and statistics)**

a. Forerunner of roller coaster was Russian ice slide, built as early as the fifteenth century in Saint Petersburg

b. First roller coaster at Coney Island constructed in 1884

c. Before Depression of 1930s, 1,500 roller coasters existed; during Depression, number gradually declined

d. Roller coaster began to make a comeback, with numbers rising from 147 in 1979 to 164 in 1989

1. Comic strips aren't just funny; sometimes, they teach important lessons about life. (examples)
2. A high school pep rally has a life of its own. (sensory details)
3. Planets revolve around the sun at different rates. (facts and statistics)
4. Good friends are there to share the good times and to help in the bad times. (anecdote)

details, facts, examples, or anecdotes as supporting information. Finally, have students suggest and explain changes that they would make to their paragraphs to make the paragraphs clearer or more interesting. ■

The Clincher Sentence

A ***clincher sentence,*** a final sentence that emphasizes or summarizes the main idea, can help readers grasp the main idea of a paragraph, especially a longer paragraph. In the following paragraph, for example, the writer uses a clincher sentence to summarize and emphasize his main idea about Native American cultures. Notice that the topic sentence at the beginning of the paragraph also expresses the main idea.

> In the past forty years, however, anthropologists have done some very thorough digging into the life of the North American Indians and have discovered a bewildering variety of cultures and societies beyond anything the schoolbooks have taught. There were Indian societies that dwelt in permanent settlements, and others that wandered; some were wholly democratic, others had very rigid class systems based on property. Some were ruled by gods carried around on litters, some had judicial systems, to some the only known punishment was torture. Some lived in caves, others in tepees of bison skins, others in cabins. There were tribes ruled by warriors or by women, by sacred elders or by councils. . . . There were tribes who worshiped the bison or a matriarch or the maize they lived by. There were tribes that had never heard of war, and there were tribes debauched by centuries of fighting. In short, there was a great diversity of Indian nations, speaking over five hundred languages.
>
> Alistair Cooke, *Alistair Cooke's America*

MEETING INDIVIDUAL NEEDS

LEARNING STYLES

Visual Learners. You could use the following diagram to help students see the function of a clincher sentence in a paragraph. The diagram shows how a clincher sentence brings the discussion full circle.

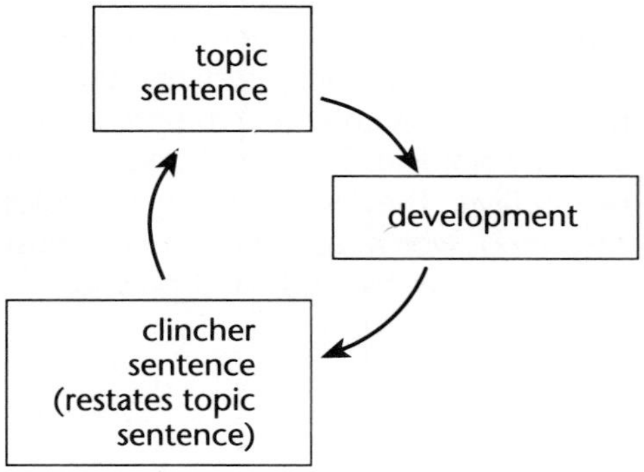

SELECTION AMENDMENT
Description of change: excerpted and modified
Rationale: to focus on the concept of the clincher sentence presented in this chapter

SEGMENT 4 *(pp. 72–74)*

UNITY

OBJECTIVE

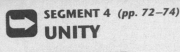

- To analyze the unity of information in paragraphs

MOTIVATION

You may want to introduce this lesson in a humorous way to get students' attention. Add a bizarre item of clothing or a funny hat to your outfit. Point out to students that not only does the item look out of place, but also your entire outfit is overshadowed by the item that does not match or does not belong. Tell students that, similarly, a

Teacher's ResourceBank™

RESOURCES

UNITY

• Achieving Unity	22

QUOTATION FOR THE DAY

"Writing has laws of perspective, of light and shade, just as painting does, or music. If you are born knowing them, fine. If not, learn them." (Truman Capote, 1924–1984, American writer)

Reassure your students that as they practice seeing unity in paragraphs, they are not learning something difficult or intuitive. They are learning the rules of writing, which, as Capote notes, most people master by study and practice.

SELECTION AMENDMENT

Description of change: excerpted

Rationale: to focus on the concept of unity presented in this chapter

Unity

Unity simply means that the paragraph "hangs together." In other words, all the supporting sentences work together to develop the main idea. A paragraph should have unity whether the main idea is stated in a topic sentence or is implied (suggested). In paragraphs that relate a series of actions or events, the main idea is often implied rather than stated. You can achieve unity in these kinds of paragraphs by the very sequence of the actions or events.

All Sentences Relate to the Main Idea Stated in the Topic Sentence. In the following paragraph, the topic sentence states the main idea—that animals' eyes tell a lot about them. Each of the following sentences give some specific information about what you can see in their eyes.

> You can tell a lot about an animal's way of life by looking at its eyes. If it relies a lot on sight, its eyes will be relatively big. If it is a hunting animal, like the tiger, its eyes will be placed toward the front of its head, so that the fields of view of the two eyes overlap. This allows it to judge distance accurately for pouncing on prey. Animals with many predators, like the rabbit, usually have eyes at the sides of their heads. They can spot a predator coming from almost every angle, but they are not very good at judging distance.
>
> Tony Seddon and Jill Bailey, *The Living World*

All Sentences Relate to an Implied Main Idea. The following paragraph doesn't have a topic sentence, but all the sentences support an implied main idea—American women began experimenting with shorter hairstyles during the early 1900s.

> One of the first women to commit the shocking act of cutting her hair was the famous American ballroom dancer Irene Castle. In 1913 she popularized a very short hairstyle called the Castle Clip, worn with a string of pearls around her forehead. It wasn't until after World War I, though, that most women found the courage to bob their hair and exchange their hairpins for the new spring-clip "bobby pin." The shortest cuts of the 1920s flapper age were the

sentence that does not relate to the main idea in a paragraph can cause distractions. The reader is left wondering "What's that doing there?" Tell students that for a paragraph to have unity, all sentences must relate to the main idea.

TEACHING THE LESSON

After a student reads aloud the excerpt from ***The Living World,*** have volunteers identify the three examples that support the topic sentence and contribute to the paragraph's unity [if the animal relies on sight, if it hunts, if it is preyed upon]. Follow the same procedure with the remaining two excerpts and emphasize that a paragraph ☛

"boyish bob" and the "shingle," for which the hair was actually shaved at the back of the neck. For women who wanted their short hair frizzy-curly rather than sleek, there was a new hair treatment called a permanent wave.

Lila Perl, *From Top Hats to Baseball Caps, From Bustles to Blue Jeans: Why We Dress the Way We Do*

All Sentences Relate to a Sequence of Events. The writer of the following paragraph achieves unity through the sequence of events and actions. You won't find a topic sentence in this paragraph, but you will find that all sentences relate to the experience of entering an emerald mine on a tire attached to a steel cable.

First came a drizzle. Then groundwater poured from the walls, and I was plunging through a waterfall. The darkest darkroom doesn't begin to compare to the pitch-black inside the mine shaft. I couldn't look upward at the patch of daylight above for fear of drowning. After about three minutes—an eternity—the unseen operator threw on the brake, jerking me to a stop two feet above the mud. To no one in particular, I sighed, "Welcome to the glamorous world of emeralds."

Fred Ward, "Emeralds"

© Fred Ward

EXERCISE 4 **Analyzing Notes for Unity**

Here are some notes, in the form of a cluster, for a paragraph on the infamous Trail of Tears. The writer's topic sentence is "Thousands of Native Americans, of several groups, died from hardships on the Trail of Tears." In a group of three or four classmates, try to determine which notes should be discarded because they would destroy the unity of the paragraph.

MEETING INDIVIDUAL NEEDS

LEP/ESL

General Strategies. Be aware that rhetorical patterns differ from culture to culture. For a paragraph to have unity in English, all supporting sentences must relate directly to the main idea, which is usually stated in the topic sentence. In Spanish, on the other hand, digression is more common and is not seen as disrupting the unity of a paragraph. A supporting sentence in Spanish, for example, is usually longer and more detailed and might not explicitly refer to the topic sentence. Likewise, African Americans who engage in expository narrative may follow similar paragraph conventions.

AT-RISK STUDENTS

Students might better grasp the concept of unity in paragraphs if they can compare it to something familiar to them. For example, students who are active in sports will probably understand the unity that a team must have to play its best. Most fashion-conscious students practice unity when they get dressed each morning; they are careful to choose components that contribute to the desired look.

AMENDMENTS TO SELECTION
Description of change: excerpted
Rationale: to focus on the concept of unity presented in this chapter

does not need a stated topic sentence to achieve unity.

To prepare students for **Exercise 4** on pp. 73–74, suggest a sentence that destroys the unity of the paragraph from ***The Living World*** on p. 72. For example, you could add "Tigers prefer large prey such as deer, antelope, and wild pigs" before the sentence "Animals with many predators . . . ." You may want to have students suggest sentences that would destroy the unity of the other two paragraphs in the segment. Then assign **Exercise 4** for independent practice. Use class performance on this exercise as assessment or check for unity in students' writing. To close, have students define *paragraph unity.* ■

ANSWERS

Exercise 4

Answers may vary, but students must support their choices. Possible notes to be discarded include "national proposal to designate route of trail," "some still live in Everglades," "moved into Florida during 1700s," and "some owned slaves."

VISUAL CONNECTIONS
Trail of Tears

About the Artist. Jerome Tiger was born in 1941 in eastern Oklahoma. A Creek-Seminole Native American, Tiger is an innovator in Native American art, and his style continues to influence painters today.

From an early age, Tiger exhibited a love and an amazing aptitude for drawing. He pursued his talent and became a successful artist by his mid-twenties. Because he did not have access to the artwork of others, he was mostly self-trained. However, this did not keep him from developing a technical virtuosity, and when his works deviate from the established conventions of composition, they do so successfully.

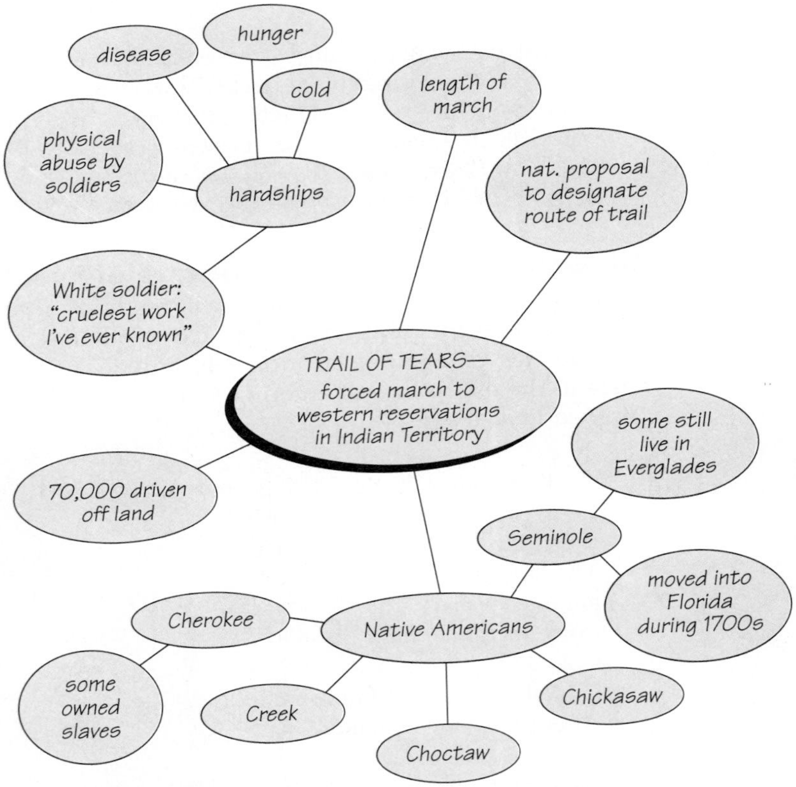

Jerome Tiger, *Trail of Tears* (16¼″ × 18⅞″). Courtesy of The Five Civilized Tribes Museum, Muskogee, Oklahoma.

SEGMENT 5 *(pp. 75–81)*
COHERENCE

OBJECTIVES

- To arrange ideas in paragraphs so that the order makes sense
- To identify direct references and transitional expressions in a paragraph

MOTIVATION

Tell students that they could compare writing a coherent paragraph to building a brick wall. The builder must first determine an order for laying the bricks that suits his or her style and purpose. While laying the bricks, the builder must use mortar to hold them together. Similarly, a writer must determine the order for arranging his or her ideas ☛

Coherence

Unity isn't the only quality of a good paragraph; *coherence* is also important. In a ***coherent*** paragraph, the relationship between ideas is clear—the paragraph flows smoothly. You can go a long way toward making paragraphs coherent by paying attention to two things: (1) the order you use to arrange your ideas, and (2) the connections you make between ideas.

Order of Ideas

When you create a paragraph, you need to arrange ideas so that the order will make sense to your readers. Four types of order that writers often use are *chronological order, spatial order, order of importance,* and *logical order.*

Chronological Order. When you tell how things change over time, you usually give actions or events in the order they happen, or in ***chronological*** (time) ***order.*** You use chronological order to tell a story, to explain a process, and to explain cause and effect.

For an example of chronological order, see the paragraph on entering an emerald mine (page 73).

Spatial Order. Description focuses on the subject itself and often calls for ***spatial order,*** the order of details by their location. You might describe details from left to right, from near to far, from front to back, from top to bottom, and so on. Note the spatial order in the following paragraph.

near	Laurel is up in the cool shadow on the porch roof, in dungarees and a sweatshirt, scraping off pine needles with a snow shovel.
farther away	Below, an old garden hose snakes across the knobby dirt, its pinhole leak shooting up a spray that fizzes in a slash of sunlight. There's a breath of wind, a commotion in the lilacs.
still farther away	Down the lane, stones are finally warming in their sockets.
farthest distance	Between branches, she can see the water tower on Buffalo Hill, the long gravel slide below the golf course, the blinding curlicues of the river.

David Long, "Blue Spruce"

Teacher's ResourceBank™
RESOURCES

COHERENCE
- Achieving Coherence 23

QUOTATION FOR THE DAY

"That may be the reason that a man has to rewrite and rewrite—to reconcile imagination and pattern." (William Faulkner, 1897–1962, American novelist and short-story writer)

You could use this quotation to initiate a discussion on coherence. Lead students to see that it is the writer's responsibility to make his or her thinking clear to the reader. A logical pattern or order can help clarify a writer's ideas, no matter how imaginative the ideas may be. And to establish such a logical pattern, a writer must often rewrite.

SELECTION AMENDMENT
Description of change: excerpted
Rationale: to focus on the concept of special order presented in this chapter

and must use linking devices to hold the ideas together.

TEACHING THE LESSON

Emphasize the two aspects that contribute to coherence—order and connections. Before you examine the types of paragraph order, list them on the chalkboard so students can follow along as you explain the differences among the approaches. Then guide students through the example

MEETING **INDIVIDUAL** NEEDS

LEP/ESL

General Strategies. To demonstrate visually the difference between unity and coherence, hold up four different-colored pieces of chalk and explain that if each piece were a sentence, the four together could form a unified paragraph. Hold up a pencil together with the chalk to show lack of unity. Next, tape the pieces of chalk together and explain that coherence is the tape that holds the sentences together in a paragraph. Such strong visuals generally help ESL students better understand abstract concepts.

SELECTION AMENDMENT
Description of change: excerpted
Rationale: to focus on the concept of order of importance presented in this chapter

Order of Importance. When your purpose is to inform or to persuade, you'll often arrange ideas or details in ***order of importance.*** At times you may find it most effective to begin with the most important detail and move to the least important. Other times, you may want to reverse the order and start with the least important.

In this paragraph, the writer gives information about the help provided by black soldiers and sailors during the Civil War. The article begins with their least important contributions.

Long before Fort Pillow, and long before Sherman's dagger thrusts in Georgia, Black soldiers and sailors became indispensable elements in a war that could not have been won without their help. In the fall of 1862, they participated in minor actions at Island Mounds, Mo., and in skirmishes in Georgia and Florida. But their first major battles came in the summer of 1863 at Port Hudson, the last Confederate obstacle to the capture of Vicksburg, and in the famous "Glory" charge of the Fifty-fourth Massachusetts Volunteers at Fort Wagner in the Charleston, S.C., harbor.

"Black, Blue and Gray: The Other Civil War," *Ebony*

Logical Order. When you use strategies of classification, including definition and comparison/contrast, you will usually find it makes sense to group related ideas together in ***logical order.*** The following paragraph, comparing two types of young adults during the 1950s, shows logical order.

paragraphs that exhibit the four different kinds of order.

Explain to students that the writer of a paragraph must make clear to the reader the relationships among the sentences. One way to clarify the interrelationships among the details is to give the reader clues. Such clues can be in the form of direct references or transitional expressions. To help students understand the three different kinds of direct references, work through the excerpt from **"Flight"** on p. 79. Allow students time to review the **Transitional Words and Phrases** chart on p. 80. Then ask volunteers to explain how each underlined word in the paragraph preceding **Exercise 6** on p. 81 contributes to the paragraph's coherence.

Our world was divided into Tweeds and Greasers, both wanting to be "tough" and irresistible. The Tweeds were would-be Ivy Leaguers who bought Hollywood's Tab Hunter-Robert Wagner hard-sell—white bucks, khaki pants, button-down shirt, red-striped tie. We were shiny, formal, and eager. We trusted our façade to work for us as successfully as it had worked for our film heroes. They wore make-up; we had Clearasil. We wanted to be perfect. The Greasers swallowed James Dean and Marlon Brando whole. They were big on silence and scruffiness. They were losers in life, and, what's more, they didn't care; they gloried in it. That's why they were dangerous—they had nothing to lose. With their leather jackets, DA's, T-shirts with cigarette packs rolled in the turned-up sleeves, they wanted to be left alone. We wanted to be accepted.

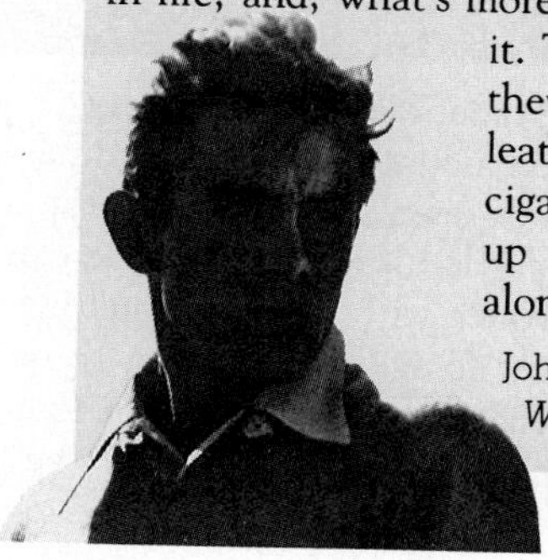

John Lahr, "Introduction" to *Baby, That Was Rock and Roll,* by Robert Palmer

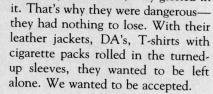

EXERCISE 5 **Arranging Paragraphs in Order**

Revisions will vary.

The ideas in these three paragraphs aren't arranged in an order that makes sense. Identify the type of order that would work for each paragraph, and then revise each paragraph by re-arranging sentences into an appropriate order.

1. order of importance

1. [1]Much evidence may be cited to show George Washington's enormous popularity immediately following his leadership and victories during the colonies' War of Independence.[2] People generally thought of Washington as a genuine hero and model citizen.[4] The most important testament of Washington's esteem came from Congress.[5] Members of that body approved a bronze equestrian statue of Washington for the future capital in which the general was to be dressed in Roman clothes and wear a laurel wreath on his head.[3] In addition, many cities, including Boston and Richmond, celebrated Washington's birthday, February 22.

COOPERATIVE LEARNING

Explain to students that organizing details from more to less important is the traditional method used by writers of newspaper articles. Often called inverted-pyramid organization, this method gives readers the most important information in the headline and the first paragraph of the article. The following paragraphs generally give supporting information in descending order of importance.

Provide copies of recent newspapers and have pairs of students analyze some of the lead articles. Have each pair choose one article and determine if the writer used inverted-pyramid organization. Have the pairs support their decisions with examples from their articles.

MEETING INDIVIDUAL NEEDS

LEARNING STYLES

Kinetic Learners. You may want to reproduce the paragraphs in **Exercise 5** and have students cut the sentences apart. Then students can manually rearrange the sentences into an appropriate order.

SELECTION AMENDMENT
Description of change: excerpted
Rationale: to focus on the concept of logical order presented in this chapter

GUIDED PRACTICE

Guide students through the first paragraph (p. 77) in **Exercise 5** by reading aloud the paragraph and emphasizing the key words and phrases that offer clues for ordering the paragraph's ideas [*generally, most important,* and *in addition*]. Explain that such words indicate order of importance.

To prepare students for **Exercise 6** on p. 81, choose one of the paragraphs from this chapter, such as Lila Perl's excerpt on pp. 72–73, and help students identify the direct references and transitional expressions.

INTEGRATING THE LANGUAGE ARTS

Literature Link. In the writings of Edgar Allan Poe, setting, chronology, and imagination play vital roles. You may want to have students read one of his works, such as "The Fall of the House of Usher," "The Masque of the Red Death," or "The Pit and the Pendulum." Have students look carefully at the manner in which Poe orders his paragraphs. Does he rely on one particular order? How much detail does he provide? Are paragraphs where he uses both spatial and chronological order effective?

2. [1] In the distance, the mountain towered above the landscape.[3] Halfway down the mountain, the timberline began, the trees almost buried in deep snowdrifts.[5] At the foot of the mountain, the boy made his camp.[6] Near the camp, an icy stream rushed by, swollen with the slowly melting snow. [4] The boy knew that deer foraged for food in those drifts and that some had already starved during that long, cold winter.[2] Wreaths of heavy, smoky clouds hid the heavy rocks at the top that would make the ascent so dangerous. [7] At night, curious animals came close on all sides of the camp—the boy often saw the fresh tracks in the snow the next morning.

2. spatial order **3.** chronological order

3. [1] Chad sat on the sidewalk outside the grocery where he had just finished working and changed shoes.[3] Chad met Coach and the other cross-country runners in front of the gym.[2] He then tossed his good shoes into the car and drove the mile to school.[4] They were ready when he got there, late from work as usual.[6] They turned from Harrison onto Bell Street, which contained Killer Hill.[5] The group of twelve runners warmed up with leg exercises before heading slowly down Harrison Street.[7] Just as they started going up the hill, Chad heard Eric call to him, but he was busy thinking that working and running were getting too much for him, and didn't reply.[8] "Chad," Eric yelled again.[10] Chad was tempted, but shook his head.[11] "No," he said. "We signed up to run, and we can't back out now."[9] Chad finally turned toward Eric, who said, puffing, "Let's cut out."

INDEPENDENT PRACTICE

Assign the remaining paragraphs in **Exercise 5** and the paragraph in **Exercise 6** as independent practice. You may want to circulate among students to answer questions and offer assistance as they work on both exercises.

ASSESSMENT

You can use **Exercises 5** and **6** to assess students' understanding of paragraph coherence, or you can evaluate ordering and use of transitions in their original paragraphs.

Connections Between Ideas

Arranging ideas in an order that makes sense helps to make paragraphs coherent, but *direct references* and *transitional words and expressions* can also help. These words and phrases act as connectors between and among ideas so that the paragraph is clear to readers.

REFERENCE NOTE: For help on using direct references and transitional words and expressions to connect ideas *between* paragraphs, see pages 117–118.

Direct References. Referring to a noun or pronoun that you've used earlier in the paragraph is a ***direct reference.*** You can make direct references by (1) using a noun or pronoun that refers to a noun or pronoun used earlier, (2) repeating a word used earlier, or (3) using a word or phrase that means the same thing as one used earlier.

In the following paragraph, the superscript numbers indicate the type of direct reference the writer is using.

> Pepé drank from the water bag, and he[1] reached into the flour sack and brought out a black string of jerky. His[1] white teeth gnawed at the string[2] until the tough meat[3] parted. He[1] chewed[3] slowly and drank[2] occasionally from the water bag[2]. His[1] little eyes were slumberous and tired, but the muscles of his[1] face were hard-set. The earth of the trail was black now. It[1] gave up a hollow sound under the walking hoofbeats.
>
> John Steinbeck, "Flight"

Transitional Expressions. Words and phrases that make a transition from one idea to another are called ***transitional expressions.*** These words and phrases include prepositions that indicate chronological or spatial order, as well as conjunctions, which connect and show relationships. The following chart includes some frequently used transitional expressions,

INTEGRATING THE LANGUAGE ARTS

Grammar Link. Although using pronouns in writing improves coherence by referring to nouns in previous sentences, many writers fail to have a clear antecedent for each pronoun. For example, in the sentence "Elise wrote to Maria every day when she was in the hospital," *she* is not clearly identified.

Have students check the pronoun references in their writing. Suggest that they circle all pronouns and draw arrows to the correct antecedents. The revision stage of the writing process is a good place to incorporate this procedure.

SELECTION AMENDMENT
Description of change: excerpted and modified
Rationale: to focus on the concept of direct references presented in this chapter

RETEACHING

Creating a paragraph that flows might still seem difficult for some students; therefore, you could work with the class through each stage of paragraph development. First, have the class decide on a subject and a topic sentence. List on the chalkboard the supporting sentences that students suggest. (Remind students to consider audience and purpose.) Then have the class decide upon the best order for arrangement of the details. As you arrange the details in the prescribed order on the chalkboard, help students see how adding direct references and transitional expressions can clarify the interrelationships among the details.

CRITICAL THINKING
Evaluation

Give each student a paragraph to critique in terms of unity and coherence. Use various sources, such as paragraphs from newspapers, magazines, travel brochures, and textbooks. Have students use the following guidelines:

1. Do all sentences relate to the main idea? If so, explain how. If not, give specific examples that show unrelated sentences.
2. Does the paragraph seem to flow smoothly? How does the order contribute to coherence? What direct references or transitions has the writer used?
3. Rate the paragraphs on a scale from one to ten. How could the writer increase this score? Give at least two suggestions for improvement.

When students have finished their critiques, you may want to divide the class into small groups to share their findings.

grouped according to the relationships they indicate. The chart also indicates how the expressions are most often used.

TRANSITIONAL WORDS AND PHRASES		
Comparing Ideas/Classification and Definition		
also	another	similarly
and	moreover	too
Contrasting Ideas/Classification and Definition		
although	in spite of	on the other hand
but	instead	still
however	nevertheless	yet
Showing Cause and Effect/Narration		
as a result	consequently	so that
because	since	therefore
Showing Time/Narration		
after	eventually	next
at last	finally	then
at once	first	thereafter
before	meanwhile	when
Showing Place/Description		
above	down	next
across	here	over
around	in	there
before	inside	to
beyond	into	under
Showing Importance/Evaluation		
first	mainly	then
last	more important	to begin with

WRITING NOTE

Transitional expressions can help give your writing coherence. But don't overdo them. The result can be writing that sounds artificial and stilted.

CLOSURE

Have a volunteer explain the difference between unity and coherence and the importance of both to good writing. ■

Transitional words and phrases are underlined in the following paragraph about a woman who was paralyzed as a result of a diving accident. Notice how the words help to show relationships of time and space.

> At first, when Marca Bristo was injured, she couldn't see what she could do beyond that time. Later, as she mastered coping with life in a wheelchair, she decided to fight for more opportunities for disabled people. Then she became executive director of Access Living, an organization that works to remove any barriers that prevent disabled people from becoming independent and taking part in society. Eventually, she co-founded the National Council on Independent Living and afterward prepared a report that resulted in the Americans with Disabilities Act.

EXERCISE 6 **Identifying Direct References and Transitional Expressions**

The following paragraph about volcanoes has both direct references and transitional expressions. Make one list of the direct references and another list of the transitional expressions. You may need to refer to the three kinds of direct references, discussed on page 79, as well as to the chart of transitional expressions.

> The earth is full of volcanoes, which are named after Vulcan, the Roman god of fire. Some volcanoes are extinct and, therefore, pose no threat. Many of them, however, are dormant, and they could explode. Moreover, Mount St. Helens did erupt in Washington in 1980. Of course, you know that volcanoes are found mostly on land. But did you know that they are also on the ocean floor? Because most of the land volcanoes circle the Pacific Ocean, they are known as the Ring of Fire. An ancient Roman probably would have called the circle Vulcan's Ring.

TIMESAVER

If you are planning to use **Exercise 6** for assessment purposes, you may want to have students work in small groups to locate and record the direct references and transitional expressions. Each group can submit one paper. Not only will this help students to find and understand the references and expressions, but it will also cut your grading time substantially.

SEGMENT 6 *(pp. 82–89)*

STRATEGIES OF DEVELOPMENT

OBJECTIVE

- To use description, narration, classification, and evaluation as strategies for paragraph development

TEACHING THE LESSON

Students may need some background information about how the four strategies of development fit into the overall picture of the writing process. First, you may want to review **AIM—The "Why" of Writing** on p. 20. Then write the following chart on the chalkboard:

Teacher's ResourceBank™

RESOURCES

STRATEGIES OF DEVELOPMENT

QUOTATION FOR THE DAY

"Good writing is supposed to evoke sensation in the reader—not the fact that it's raining, but the feel of being rained upon." (E. L. Doctorow, 1931–   , American novelist)

Write the quotation on the chalkboard and ask the students which strategy of development is most likely to evoke sensation in the reader [description]. Remind students that the strategies for development are not necessarily separate entities, but often work together to yield good writing.

MEETING INDIVIDUAL NEEDS

LEP/ESL

General Strategies. One way to introduce description is to read descriptions of objects—without naming them—and to have students guess what the objects are. After students have practiced, have them come up with their own descriptions. Then pair students and have the partners guess what each other describes.

Strategies of Development

Why are you writing your paragraph? What is its purpose? Who will read it? These are questions to consider when choosing a strategy, a method of development, for a paragraph. As you've seen, the type of strategy you select to develop an idea can influence the order you use to arrange ideas. It can also affect the kind of information with which you develop the paragraph.

Depending on your main purpose for writing the paragraph, you could choose from among the four strategies of development shown in the chart below. Remember that you can have more than one purpose (and more than one strategy of development) in a paragraph. For example, writers often combine description and narration in the same paragraph.

STRATEGIES OF DEVELOPMENT	
Description	Looking at individual features of a particular subject
Narration	Looking at changes in a subject over a period of time
Classification	Looking at a subject in relation to other subjects
Evaluation	Looking at the value of, or judging, a subject

Expository	Persuasive	Self-Expressive	Literary
description narration classification evaluation	description narration classification evaluation	description narration classification evaluation	description narration classification evaluation

Description

Have you already picked out the car that you hope to own someday? What does it look like? Is there a food that you especially dislike? What does it look, smell, or taste like?

When you need to focus on a subject, to tell what it's like, you have to examine its specific features. Then you select description as your strategy of development, using sensory details (details of sight, sound, taste, touch, and smell) for support. You'll often use spatial order to organize a description, but, depending on your subject or purpose, you might also use order of importance or chronological order. The writer of the following paragraph uses spatial order to describe a store in Nameless, Tennessee.

> The old store, lighted only by three fifty-watt bulbs, smelled of coal oil and baking bread. In the middle of the rectangular room, where the oak floor sagged a little, stood an iron stove. To the right was a wooden table with an unfinished game of checkers and a stool made from an apple-tree stump. On shelves around the walls sat earthen jugs with corncob stoppers, a few canned goods, and some of the two thousand old clocks and clockworks Thurmond Watts owned. Only one was ticking; the others he just looked at.
>
> William Least Heat-Moon, *Blue Highways*

EXERCISE 7 **Using Description as a Strategy**

Choose one of the following subjects and list five sensory details (details of sight, sound, taste, smell, and touch) that you could use to describe the specific features of the subject.

1. your yard—when you're faced with raking or mowing it
2. the kitchen—when you have to clean it up
3. a character from *Star Trek* or another science fiction book or movie
4. an old, abandoned house
5. a disgusting insect

MEETING INDIVIDUAL NEEDS

LEARNING STYLES

Visual Learners. When students are describing with sensory details, encourage the use of graphic devices similar to the following cluster. The graphic reminder will keep students from relying mainly on visual details.

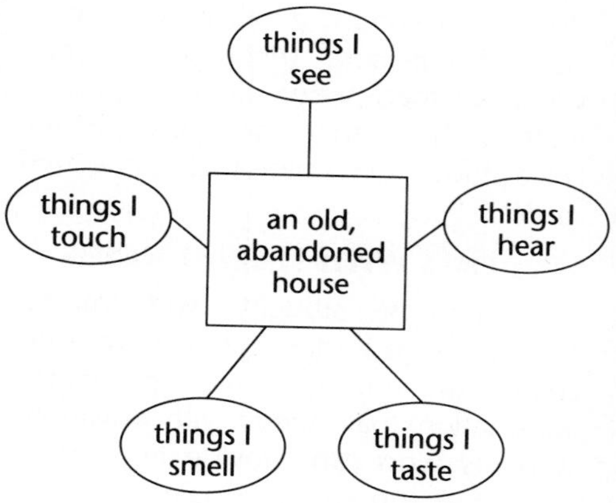

ANSWERS

Exercise 7

Responses will vary. Check to see that students have used details that appeal to all five senses. If many students did not, you could allow them to work in pairs to find more details.

SELECTION AMENDMENT

Description of change: excerpted

Rationale: to focus on the concept of description presented in this chapter

The chart indicates that any (or all) of the strategies of development can be used for each aim. For example, a writer who is attempting to persuade readers to buy a certain car might use two strategies: The writer might first describe the car and then classify it by comparing it to other cars.

Have a volunteer read aloud **Description** and the excerpt from ***Blue Highways*** on p. 83. Have students locate the sensory details in the model. Point out the transitional expressions that indicate spatial order. Although the model doesn't contain examples, tell students that metaphors, similes, and analogies are often used in descriptive writing. You may want to model the procedure of listing sensory details for one of the

MEETING **INDIVIDUAL** NEEDS

ADVANCED STUDENTS

In addition to discussing the role of narration in telling a story, you may want to address point of view. Have students review the **Point of View** chart on p. 170 in **Chapter 5: "Creative Writing."** Then give each student the same picture from a book or magazine. Ask each student to choose a different point of view—first-person, third-person omniscient, or third-person limited—and to write a short story about the picture. Have students compare their completed stories.

STUDENTS WITH SPECIAL NEEDS

Because students with mixed-dominance disorder might have difficulty sequencing and processing information, pair them with advanced students who can provide encouragement and support. The pairs can work together to analyze the professional models and to complete **Exercise 8**, p. 86.

SELECTION AMENDMENT
Description of change: excerpted
Rationale: to focus on the concept of narration presented in this chapter

Narration

What happened during the 1991 Communist coup against Mikhail Gorbachev? How do you replace a lost driver's license? What are the effects of peer pressure on teenagers?

Answering these questions requires the strategy of narration, of looking at changes over time. You may use narration *to tell a story or incident* (what happened during the coup), *to explain a process* (how to replace a driver's license), or *to explain causes and effects* (what the effects of peer pressure are). You usually use chronological order to present ideas and information in paragraphs of narration.

Telling a Story. Writers use the strategy of narration to tell stories, either true or fictional, about incidents and events over time (what happened). In this paragraph, the writer tells part of a Native American story.

> The Youngman Started Out to Look for Wood. It was not long Before he Saw Wood that would Make a Beautiful Warm Fire, and he Began to Busy himself Gathering the Wood. Suddenly he Felt the Presence of the Owl. The Owl Reached Down and Put the Youngman in its Ear. The Youngman Strung his Bow and Fitted One of his Arrows, Letting it Fly from his Bow Deep Into the Ear of the Owl. And the Youngman was Free.
>
> Hyemeyohsts Storm, *Seven Arrows*

Explaining a Process. Explaining a process—telling how something works or telling how to do something—is similar to telling a story. With each type of writing, you look at a subject items in **Exercise 7** on p. 83 before you assign the exercise for independent practice.

To illustrate the differences between description and narration, have the class contrast a still photo with a movie. Elicit the idea that a still captures a moment in time (like description); the movie looks at actions over a period of time (like narration). Reinforce the time factor involved with all three narrative strategies—telling stories, explaining processes, and explaining causes and effects. Help students analyze how narration differs in the three professional models. Then assign **Exercise 8** on p. 86 for independent practice.

Tell students that using the strategy of classification to organize a paragraph is an effective method for achieving clarity. Ask volunteers to read aloud the information ☛

as it changes over time. A writer explaining a process also uses the strategy of narration to tell what happens next or what is to be done next. In the following paragraph, for example, the writer explains how to perform the "Violin with Cord Elastic Strings" clown trick.

> You enter with a violin and prepare to play some lovely music. Taking out a pocket handkerchief, you fold it carefully and place it on your *right* shoulder as a violin rest. You then put the violin under your chin on your *left* shoulder (or vice versa if you are left-handed). Drawing the bow back on the [elastic-cord] strings, you suddenly send the bow flying offstage into the wings like an arrow! Dismayed, you produce a second bow and repeat the action, launching this bow offstage as well. You investigate the violin and discover the elastic strings, reacting with either embarrassment or delight (perhaps even leading into a full demonstration of target practice with "violin and arrow").
>
> Turk Pipkin, *Be a Clown!*

Explaining Causes and Effects. You also look at the way things change over time when you explain causes and effects. Here again, you use the strategy of narration to develop the paragraph. For example, the following writer explains the causes and effects of changes in free black and slave populations.

> The great increase in the free black population in America came after the Revolutionary War. In appreciation of the service of some 5,000 blacks in the War for Independence and as a result of the libertarian and egalitarian spirit that the Declaration of Independence and the war inspired, many masters, especially Northerners, freed their slaves. Soon individual states in the North decreed the gradual abolition of the institution, beginning with Vermont's action in 1777. In 1776 the population of the United States was about 2 1/2 million, more than 500,000 black slaves and approximately 40,000 free blacks. More than one half of these free blacks lived in the South. The Revolutionary leaders, including Washington and Jefferson, anticipated a continuation of the trend toward emancipation until eventually slavery would disappear from the

SELECTION AMENDMENT

Description of change: excerpted and modified

Rationale: to focus on the concept of narration presented in this chapter about dividing, defining, and comparing and contrasting. Guide students through each of the models as illustrations of those concepts. Then assign **Exercise 9** on p. 88 for independent practice.

After students read **Evaluation** on p. 89, discuss the model. Help students locate the specific reasons that the writer gives to support his or her evaluation. Before assigning **Exercise 10** on p. 89 as independent practice, you may want to choose one of the items and model the steps of the exercise. Emphasize to students that the reasons chosen as support for an evaluation should not be opinions.

TIMESAVER

Both **Exercises 8** and **9** may require that students complete outside research. To save research time either in or out of class, have the appropriate research tools available in class. Your librarian or a history teacher may allow you to borrow resources for studying John F. Kennedy's assassination and its surrounding events, and a set of encyclopedias should be sufficient for researching **Exercise 9**.

ANSWERS

Exercise 8

Responses will vary. Students should use chronological order to list actions for the first item. Likewise, the second item should have the steps listed in the order they happen. Students should clearly show the relationship of cause-and-effect in the third item.

SELECTION AMENDMENT

Description of change: excerpted
Rationale: to focus on the concept of narration presented in this chapter

land. This expectation was to be drowned, almost literally, by the whirring noise of Eli Whitney's cotton gin. The invention of this native of Massachusetts made cotton production increasingly profitable and caused rapid and substantial increases in the slave population, so that on the eve of the Civil War there were 4 million black slaves in the South.

Alton Hornsby, *The Black Almanac*

EXERCISE 8 **Using Narration as a Strategy**

You have probably used the strategy of narration many times, perhaps without even being aware that you were doing so. Now practice the strategy by following the three sets of instructions given below.

1. Give the major actions that preceded and followed the assassination of President John F. Kennedy. (If you don't remember, go to your library and research the subject.)
2. Imagine that you are telling a fourteen-year-old the basics of how to drive. List the major steps involved in starting up a car, moving forward, and coming to a smooth stop.
3. Give at least three causes for the popularity of credit cards, and then identify three potentially harmful effects.

Classification

What are the different departments of the CIA? The word *glasnost* became popular during the late 1980s—what does it mean? How is the appearance of poisonous snakes different from that of nonpoisonous snakes?

When you answer questions like these, you're using the strategy of ***classification.*** You can classify a subject by dividing it into its parts (the departments of the CIA), defining it (the term *glasnost*), or comparing and contrasting it with something else (poisonous snakes/nonpoisonous snakes).

Dividing. Classifying by ***dividing*** means looking at the parts of a subject in order to understand the subject as a whole. For example, to explain what woodwind instruments are, you could discuss the different kinds of woodwind instruments,

ASSESSMENT

You could assess students' understanding of the developmental strategies from their performances on **Exercises 7–10.**

CLOSURE

To review the segment, write the following outline on the chalkboard and ask students to volunteer things they remember about each item:

I. description
II. narration
  1. telling a story

such as clarinet, flute, and recorder. In the following paragraph, the writers divide dinosaurs into two groups in order to explain their characteristics.

> To begin with, dinosaurs fell into two groups: the bird-hipped ones, or *ornithischians,* and the reptile-hipped ones, or *saurischians.* (*Ornith–* is Greek for "bird," and *saur–* is Greek for "reptile.") The bird-hipped dinosaurs were almost all herbivores, or plant-eaters, while the reptile-hipped group contained both meat eaters (carnivores) and plant-eaters.
>
> Tom and Jane D. Allen with Savannah Waring Walker, *Dinosaur Days in Texas*

Defining. To ***define,*** you first identify a subject as a part of a larger group or class (a *pediatrician* is a doctor). Then you discuss some features that make the subject different from other members of the class (who specializes in the treatment of children). In the following paragraph, the writer defines pikas.

> Pikas are mountain-dwelling mammals that are tiny relatives of rabbits and hares. Pikas are only about seven inches long and have short, rounded ears. They live in colonies in rocky areas. They prepare for winter by gathering grass and spreading it out to dry in the sun. Then they make little haystacks near their dens, and eat the dried grass throughout the winter.

Comparing and Contrasting. You also use the strategy of classification when ***comparing*** subjects (telling how they're alike), ***contrasting*** them (telling how they're different), or when both comparing and contrasting. The following paragraph compares and contrasts the heads of dogs and wolves.

> A dog's skull is generally somewhat smaller and rounder than a wolf's and its brain is about twenty percent smaller. Wolves and all the other kinds of wild dogs have upstanding ears, which act as sound funnels. Like antennas, they

INTEGRATING THE LANGUAGE ARTS

Literature Link. Explain to students that the developmental strategies discussed in this segment are also used by poets. You may want to have students read poems that use each of the writing strategies. Some possible poems include Edwin Arlington Robinson's "Richard Cory" or "Miniver Cheevy" for description; Edgar Lee Master's "Lucinda Matlock" or Robert Frost's "Out, Out-" for narration; Archibald MacLeish's "Ars Poetica" or Langston Hughes's "Harlem" for classification; and Carl Sandburg's "Chicago" for evaluation. Ask students to evaluate how each poem fits into the category given. Could any of the poems be put into more than one category?

SELECTION AMENDMENT
Description of change: excerpted
Rationale: to focus on the concept of classification presented in this chapter

2. explaining a process
3. explaining causes and effects

III. classification
1. dividing
2. defining
3. comparing and contrasting

IV. evaluation

ENRICHMENT

Have students complete surveys of the types of developmental strategies required for tests in other subject areas. Have each student analyze three different tests in at least two other subject areas. You can then combine the students' answers in a chart that shows the surveys' results. ■

A DIFFERENT APPROACH

As a reteaching strategy, give students several broad topics and have them suggest ways in which the topics could be approached by using each of the four writing strategies. For example, if you gave students the general topic "volleyball," they might suggest the following approaches:

1. description: the atmosphere in the locker room before a big game
2. narration: the play-by-play of a game
3. classification: how volleyball compares with other team sports
4. evaluation: the pros and cons of playing volleyball in high school

ANSWERS

Exercise 9

Responses will vary. You may want to suggest that students use complete sentences when listing the details asked for in the second and third items. Encourage students to list any resources they use.

SELECTION AMENDMENT

Description of change: excerpted and modified
Rationale: to focus on the concept of classification presented in this chapter

gather sound waves from the air and direct them down the ear canals into the inner ear. Most domestic dogs have lop ears: at rest their ears hang limply down, although they can be pricked up to listen to interesting sounds. . . . For all of the dogs, both wild and domestic, the ears are not only organs of hearing but also organs of expression. The position of a dog's ears can communicate a great deal about its mood.

Alvin and Virginia Silverstein, *Dogs: All About Them*

EXERCISE 9 **Using Classification as a Strategy**

What parts does it have? What is it? How is it like or different from something else? The same subject may be handled using different ways of classification. For practice, try classifying an animal of your choice according to the following directions. Use the library or your textbooks to find information.

1. Divide the animal group by listing three different types of animals within the group. (What are three kinds of sharks, giant snakes, bats?)
2. Define the animal group. Put it into a larger group (is it a reptile, a mammal, what?) and then list three details about it that make it different from other members of the group.
3. Compare and contrast the animal with another animal. List three major ways the animals are alike and three major ways they are different. (Both humpbacks and blue whales are types of whales. How are they similar? different?)

Evaluation

Is spanking a good punishment for children? Was the movie *Robin Hood: Prince of Thieves* worth the cost of renting the tape?

Evaluation means judging the value of something. You often evaluate a subject in order to inform readers or to persuade them to think or act differently. An evaluation should be supported with reasons showing *why* you made the judgment about the subject.

The following paragraph is part of a review of recent movies. Notice the reasons the writer gives for the evaluation of the three movies.

> "Movies are better then ever" can usually be regarded as nothing more than a slogan to sell tickets, but now there are some movies that may make it a slogan to believe. After several years of movies of doubtful mentality, the early 1990s gave us some surprisingly intelligent, beautifully filmed, thought-provoking films, such as *Dances With Wolves, Fried Green Tomatoes,* and *Cinema Paradiso.* These go back to the artistry of the best movies of the past and go against the tendency to film everything in closeup, with the eventual (or immediate) transfer to videotape in mind. Movies should be movies, made as these are for large screens, and should give audiences something to admire and think about as these do. Not all movies are better than ever, but some are. Let's hope it's a trend.

EXERCISE 10 **Using Evaluation as a Strategy**

It's your turn to be an entertainment critic. Start by identifying three subjects from the following list.

1. a movie you've seen (at the theater or on videotape)
2. a television special or series you have watched
3. a book or story you've read
4. a recording (tape or CD) you have listened to

For each subject, state your overall opinion (good, bad, somewhere in between), and then list three reasons why you hold this opinion. Share your evaluations with a classmate.

MEETING INDIVIDUAL NEEDS

LEP/ESL

General Strategies. To teach students the kind of functional speech necessary to express their opinions in English, give them the following list:

1. In my opinion, ...
2. It seems to me . . . .
3. I think . . . .
4. I believe . . . .
5. Would you agree that . . . ?

ANSWERS

Exercise 10

Answers may vary. Each student must clearly identify three subjects, state an opinion about each subject, and support each opinion with three reasons. Be sure students use facts and not opinions to support their evaluations.

SEGMENT 7 *(pp. 90–95)*

MAKING CONNECTIONS

WRITING A SELF-EXPRESSIVE PARAGRAPH

OBJECTIVE

- To write a self-expressive paragraph by using the steps of the writing process

WRITING PARAGRAPHS FOR DIFFERENT PURPOSES

To help students understand the different purposes of paragraphs, share the following communication triangle. Explain that the focus of each aim is in parentheses. (For more information about the communication triangle, see p. T50.)

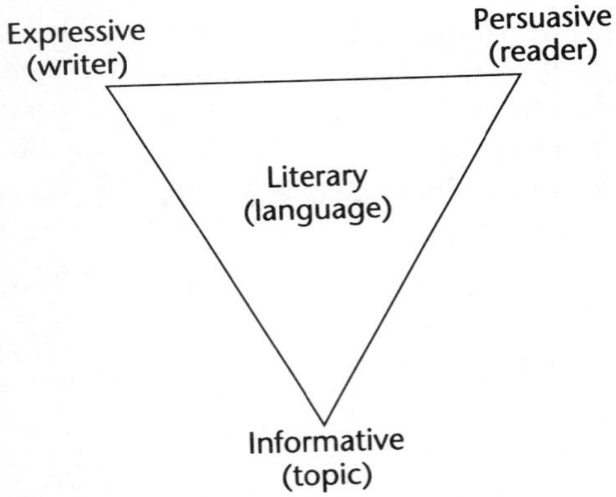

WRITING A SELF-EXPRESSIVE PARAGRAPH

Teaching Strategies

Using students' suggestions, put a sample list of responses to one of the starter sentences on the chalkboard. Then allow students to work independently to select topics and to write down ideas. Tell students that certain stylistic characteristics appear in expressive writing: the use of first person, words that express feeling, natural language, and strong connotations and associations. By having students complete the assignment in class, you can assess their effort and still allow them to write privately.

MAKING CONNECTIONS

WRITING PARAGRAPHS FOR DIFFERENT PURPOSES

In this chapter, you have studied the form and structure of paragraphs. As a result of this study, you have knowledge that you can apply by writing paragraphs for different purposes. Remember, the four basic aims or purposes of writing are to express yourself; to inform, explain, or explore; to persuade others; and to create literary works.

Writing a Self-Expressive Paragraph

If you have ever written about your thoughts and feelings in a journal, in a letter to a friend, or even in a song lyric, you've written to express yourself. Self-expressive writing is a good way to get feelings out that you might not be able to vent in any other way; and, sometimes, it can help you develop a better understanding of yourself. Self-expressive writing is often intended to be private, but not always—people write books and even movie or TV scripts about personal experiences, thoughts, and feelings.

Using one of the following "starters" or an idea of your own, write a paragraph expressing your thoughts and feelings about a subject.

A person, place, or object that's important to me is ____.
I've learned a great deal in my life about ____.
I've got to learn more about ____.
A big disappointment has been ____.
I'm very happy about ____.

Prewriting. If you're having trouble getting started, try freewriting with the starter sentence as a beginning. Don't worry about getting your ideas into any special form—just let them flow. Then use the ideas you have jotted down as the basis for a paragraph. Imagine that you're "talking" to a good friend or a special relative.

WRITING AN EXPOSITORY PARAGRAPH
OBJECTIVE

- To write an expository paragraph by using the steps of the writing process

Writing, Evaluating, and Revising. If your writing is private and you don't want to share it, write a draft of your paragraph and then leave it. Or, imagine that someone might read your paragraph many years from now, as you might read the autobiography of a movie star or famous athlete. How might you revise the paragraph so that this wider audience will understand it? What do you need to explain or clarify?

Proofreading and Publishing. If you plan to share your paragraph, proofread it carefully—you wouldn't want mistakes to prevent readers from knowing the real you. "Publish" your paragraph by sharing it with a trusted adult or friend or by putting it in your own version of a time capsule. Tuck it in the back of a drawer or closet; you might enjoy reading it a year from now.

Writing an Expository Paragraph

The purpose of many paragraphs that you write, especially those for school, is expository: You are informing, explaining, or exploring a subject. You might, for example, share information about the next Spanish Club party, explain the effects of drinking and driving, or explore possible solutions to the problems of hazardous waste disposal.

The next diagram contains some information about radio signals. Using the explanations and drawings in the diagram, write an informative paragraph. (Try the strategy of dividing to develop your paragraph; see pages 86–87.) If you need more information about radio signals, do some research in your library. In writing your paragraph, assume that your readers (classmates) know nothing about radio signals and that it is your job to give them a concise, clear, simple explanation.

GUIDELINES

Because students may choose to keep their writing private, you could assess their efforts by circulating through the room as they write. If students are willing to share their paragraphs, assess the paragraphs for central ideas and logical supporting details. In addition, check for stylistic characteristics of expressive writing.

WRITING AN EXPOSITORY PARAGRAPH
Teaching Strategies

Most writing that students do in school is expository, so it is particularly important that students master this aim. As students study the diagram of different types of radio signals, you may want to circulate throughout the room to answer questions. As students write, remind them to remain as objective as possible. Tell them to strive for precise, straightforward relaying of information.

GUIDELINES

You may want to use a focused holistic scale for assessment. Check to make sure that each paragraph contains a topic sentence, factual supporting details, an objective tone, and a clincher sentence.

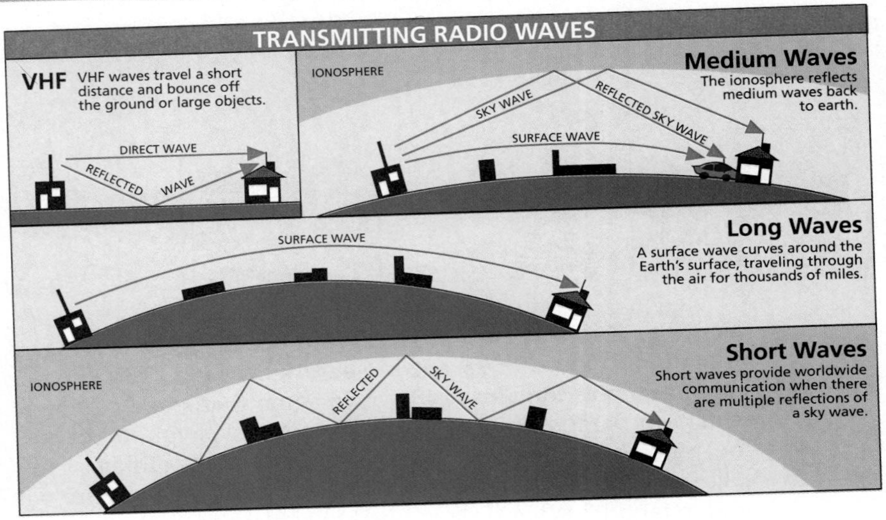

TRANSMITTING RADIO WAVES
VHF
VHF waves travel a short distance and bounce off the ground or large objects.
DIRECT WAVE
REFLECTED WAVE
IONOSPHERE
Medium Waves
The ionosphere reflects medium waves back to earth.
SKY WAVE
REFLECTED SKY WAVE
SURFACE WAVE
Long Waves
A surface wave curves around the Earth's surface, traveling through the air for thousands of miles.
SURFACE WAVE
Short Waves
Short waves provide worldwide communication when there are multiple reflections of a sky wave.
IONOSPHERE
REFLECTED
SKY WAVE

Prewriting. Study the diagram carefully to understand the different types of radio signals. Formulate your topic sentence based on the purpose of the paragraph (to inform your readers about radio signals) and the strategy of development (dividing). To divide the concept of radio signals, look at the different kinds of waves in the preceding diagram. Your supporting sentences should explain the divisions. You might try a topic sentence like this one: "Radio signals consist of VHF, medium, long, and short waves."

Writing, Evaluating, and Revising. Start with your topic sentence and then add at least three or four sentences that present information from the diagram. Remember that each supporting sentence should prove your main idea. After you've finished a first draft, take time to evaluate it. Does your topic sentence give the main idea of your paragraph and state the divisions of radio signals? Do your supporting sentences explain the divisions? Revise and rearrange any sentences that aren't clear or that break the unity of the paragraph.

Proofreading and Publishing. Review your paragraph to find and correct any errors in grammar, usage, and mechanics. (Check carefully the spellings of technical words.) Use your paragraph to inform someone, perhaps a friend or relative, about radio signals.

WRITING A PERSUASIVE PARAGRAPH
OBJECTIVE

- To write a persuasive paragraph by using the steps of the writing process

Writing a Persuasive Paragraph

When your purpose in writing is persuasive, you try to convince someone to think or act in a certain way. Persuasive writing is all around you, even though you may not realize it. Most ads, solicitation letters, and letters to the editor are persuasive writing. Entertainment reviews are persuasive writing if the reviewer's purpose is to persuade you to act or think in a certain way.

Imagine that you're trying to persuade a friend to move (or not to move) back to your area or city. What could you say that would be convincing? Write a paragraph that might persuade your friend to do what you think he or she should do.

Prewriting. Start your planning for this paragraph with what you believe about life in your area or city. You could make one list of things you think are positive and another list of things you think are negative. The list might include schools, the environment, recreational facilities, shopping, and the friendliness (or lack of it) of the residents. Then choose a position and draw your reasons and supporting information from the list.

Writing, Evaluating, and Revising. To begin your draft, write down your position statement. The remainder of your paragraph should contain the reasons and supporting information for your position. After you have written your draft, examine the reasons you've given to determine whether they sound convincing. Revise your paragraph to make it more persuasive.

Proofreading and Publishing. Correct any errors in grammar, usage, and mechanics. Then try your paragraph out by sharing it with a small group of classmates. Are they convinced?

WRITING A PERSUASIVE PARAGRAPH
Teaching Strategies

Point out to students that the key to being a successful persuasive writer is convincing readers that they will benefit from something. Persuasive writing appeals to the reader's feelings, reasoning, and sense of trust. Encourage each student to have a specific friend in mind as they prewrite and to consider that friend's interests and personality when choosing supporting details.

GUIDELINES

Each paragraph should include three or four reasons to support the stand the writer has taken. Language and supporting details should be appropriate to the audience.

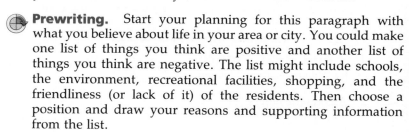

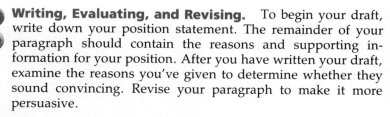

WRITING A LITERARY PARAGRAPH

OBJECTIVE

- To write a literary paragraph by using the steps of the writing process

Writing a Literary Paragraph

What is it that makes a short story different from a news story on the front page of the newspaper? Is a description of the Empire State Building in a novel different from the description of the same building in an encyclopedia article? Part of the difference is a result of imagination and creativity—the writer's urge to make a new and original statement. When you create literature, you work with language—words and groups of words—in the same way the artist uses watercolors and the composer uses musical notes.

The following poem is an example of literature; in it the poet has used his imagination and language to look at a common thing—a fire truck—in a new and unique way.

1 **The Great Figure**
by William Carlos Williams

2 Among the rain
and lights
I saw the figure 5
in gold
on a red
fire truck
moving
3 tense
unheeded
to gong clangs
siren howls
and wheels rumbling
through the dark city.

USING THE SELECTION

The Great Figure

1

From the title, what do you expect the poem to be about? [Students may be surprised that "The Great Figure" refers to a number on a fire truck. Many of Williams' poems talk about common things.]

2

Images throughout the poem recreate specific sights and sounds.

3

The fire truck is personified with the use of *tense*.

Think about the originality in the preceding poem. What words does the writer use to create images in our minds—sights and sounds? The writer creates a new impression of the fire truck; it almost seems that the truck has become a human being. How does he create this impression? Could this poem be rewritten in paragraph form and still be creative? How would you have to change it?

Paragraphs can be literary, just like poems; think of the individual paragraphs in your favorite short story or novel. To use what you know about paragraph form in a literary paragraph, borrow an idea from William Carlos Williams: Write about an ordinary object in a new and different way. Along with your imagination and language, you will use the strategy of description to point out the features or characteristics of the object you are writing about.

Prewriting. Begin by observing what is around you or brainstorming to think of an ordinary object that you find interesting, perhaps the telephone, a running shoe, a car. William Carlos Williams found the fire truck and the number on its side interesting; otherwise he wouldn't have been able to create such a delightful poem. Once you've decided what object you'll describe, think about how you might describe it in a new and different way. What could you compare it to? What features would you stress? Jot down your ideas on a piece of paper, and think about how you might organize your paragraph.

Writing, Evaluating, and Revising. Using your prewriting notes, write a draft of your descriptive paragraph. Remember that your purpose is to create literature; you want to use words imaginatively to create a new and different picture of an ordinary object. Do you want to call attention to sounds, textures, visual patterns? Let your imagination drive your ideas. After you've finished your draft, exchange paragraphs with a classmate. Does your paragraph cause your classmate to see the object you are describing in a new way? When you've decided what to add or remove, revise your paragraph.

Proofreading and Publishing. Review your paragraph to look for problems with usage and mechanics and then share it with your classmates. Are your paragraphs as imaginative as Williams' poem?

WRITING A LITERARY PARAGRAPH

Teaching Strategies

Explain to students that the emphasis of the literary aim is the arrangement of words so that attention is called not only to what is said, but also to how it is said. Literary writers often use uncommon language to create unique style.

First, you may want to discuss William Carlos Williams' unique use of words in **"The Great Figure."** As students prewrite, encourage them to work together and to incorporate unique words and figurative language—similes, metaphors, and personification. Also, suggest that students use a prewriting chart with the five senses as headings. Such a chart will help students gather images.

GUIDELINES

Because creative writing is difficult to assess, you may want to grade this assignment holistically. For example, two plus signs (+ +) indicate clear sensory details, vivid images, and a unique use of the language; one plus sign (+) indicates an occasional use of sensory details and an attempt at uniqueness; and a minus sign (−) indicates a lack of imagery and uniqueness. You might include models of each of the three levels so students can see the differences.

Chapter 3 UNDERSTANDING COMPOSITION STRUCTURE

OBJECTIVES

- To analyze and respond personally to a professional model
- To analyze and write thesis statements
- To prepare an early plan or a formal outline
- To analyze and write introductions
- To analyze the use of transitions
- To write a conclusion
- To write an informative composition

Motivation

You may want to introduce the chapter by writing *IBC* in large letters on the chalkboard. Then write *Introduction, Body,* and *Conclusion* beside the appropriate letters. Explain to students that all their compositions should have these three parts. You could ask students to state the function of each part and then to compare their responses with the **Framework for a Composition** chart on p. 121.

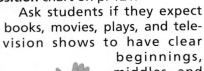

Ask students if they expect books, movies, plays, and television shows to have clear beginnings, middles, and endings. Ask students what they as readers or viewers expect of beginnings and endings. What are their responses when the plot of a book starts in the middle of a situation? What are their responses when a movie doesn't have a definite ending?

Introduction

Tell students that in this chapter they will study the basic form of a composition. A composition should be a unified piece of writing that covers one limited topic and usually has an introduction, a body, and a conclusion. You may want to write out the **Framework for a Composition** chart on the chalkboard and leave it there for reference during your presentation of the chapter.

Use the beginning of the **Looking at the Whole** segment to initiate a discussion about types of compositions. Explain to students that this chapter offers them the necessary background to write their own compositions and that in subsequent chapters they will write informative, persuasive, expressive, and creative compositions.

Integration

This chapter provides students with a strong foundation for writing activities in any course. While the chapter prepares students to write informative essays, the overall composition structure outlined in the chapter can guide students through all the aims and modes in **Chapters 4-11**. An understanding of composition structure will be helpful when students write business letters for **Chapter 38: "Letters and Forms"** and will help students organize answers to essay questions when they study **Chapter 39: "Studying and Test Taking."** The chapter can also supplement **Chapter 32: "Formal Speaking and Debate"** and **Chapter 33: "Communication Skills"** by helping students to write effective speeches and to listen for structure and organization.

The chart on the next page illustrates the strands of language arts as they are integrated into this chapter. For vocabulary study, glossary words are underlined in some writing models.

QUOTATIONS

All **Quotations for the Day** are chosen because of their relevance to instructional material presented in that segment of the chapter and for their usefulness in establishing student interest in writing.

INTEGRATING THE LANGUAGE ARTS

Selection	Reading and Literature	Writing and Critical Thinking	Language and Syntax	Speaking, Listening, and Other Expression Skills
"Learning Science" by Isaac Asimov **98-100** from **"Eliot Porter,"** *Life* **112** from **"Insert Flap 'A' and Throw Away"** by S. J. Perelman **113** from **"Geographica,"** *National Geographic* **113** **"Lax Regulation, Inadequate Laws Promote Insider-Lending Abuse"** by Mitchell Zuckoff, *The Boston Globe* **114** from **"Car-Buying: The Compleat Guide"** by Dave Barry, *The Washington Post Magazine* **114** from **"The Talk of the Town,"** *The New Yorker* **115** from **"'Dances With Garbage'"** by Mary Hager et al, *Newsweek* **115-116** from ***The Far Side Gallery*** by Gary Larson **116** from **"Emeralds"** by Fred Ward, *National Geographic* **120**	Responding personally to literature **101, 115-116** Analyzing an author's arguments **101** Finding the main idea **101** Finding details **101, 115-116** Analyzing an author's conclusion **101** Analyzing introductions **115-116** Identifying tone **115-116** Identifying direct references and transitional expressions **118**	Applying interpretive and creative thinking **101** Finding the main idea **101, 105** Evaluating a writer's arguments **101** Formulating an opinion about a subject **101** Explaining reasons for an opinion **101** Analyzing an author's conclusion **101** Analyzing thesis statements **104** Rewriting a thesis statement **104** Analyzing facts to arrive at a main idea **105, 122-123** Writing a thesis statement **105, 116, 122-123** Organizing notes to construct an early plan or a formal outline **109** Analyzing introductions **115-116** Analyzing tone **115-116** Writing an introduction to an essay **116, 122-123** Analyzing the use of transitions **118** Writing a conclusion to an essay **121, 122-123** Writing an informative composition **122-123** Creating an early plan or a formal outline **122-123** Writing body paragraphs that have unity and coherence **122-123** Proofreading and publishing a composition **123**	Identifying words and phrases that reveal tone **115** Identifying nouns, pronouns, and transitional expressions **118** Proofreading for errors in grammar, usage, and mechanics **123**	Working with a classmate to prepare an early plan or formal outline **109** Communicating ideas for effective introductions with classmates **116** Comparing introductions with those of other groups **116** Communicating ideas for effective conclusions with classmates **121** Sharing conclusions with other groups **121**

CHAPTER 3

SEGMENT PLANNING GUIDE

Whether you are planning for a quick review of a writing concept or preparing an extended lesson on composition, you can use the following Planning Guide to adapt the chapter material to the individual needs of your class.

SEGMENT	PAGES	CONTENT	RESOURCES
1 *Looking at the Whole*	*97-101*		
Literary Model **"Learning Science"**	98-100	Guided reading: a model of composition form	
Reader's Response/ Writer's Craft	101	Model evaluation: responding to literature and analyzing composition structure	
2 *The Thesis Statement*	*102-105*		The Thesis Statement 31
What Makes a Composition	102	Introduction: examining the uses of composition form	
The Thesis Statement	102-103	Explanation: writing a statement of main idea	
Hints for Writing and Using a Thesis Statement	103	Guidelines: using criteria to write a thesis statement	
Exercise 1	104	Applied practice: analyzing thesis statements	
Exercise 2	105	Applied practice: writing a thesis statement	
3 *Early Plans and Formal Outlines*	*106-111*		Early Plans 32 Formal Outlines 33
The Early Plan	106-107	Guidelines: grouping and ordering information	
The Formal Outline	107-108	Guidelines: examining a topic outline	
Exercise 3	109	Cooperative learning: making an early plan or formal outline	
Writer's Model	110-111	Guided reading: examining a composition written from a topic outline	
4 *The Introduction*	*112-116*		The Introduction 34
The Introduction	112	Introduction: examining purposes and techniques	
Techniques for Writing Introductions	112-115	Guidelines: analyzing examples of introductions in literary models	
Exercise 4	115-116	Applied practice: analyzing introductions	
Exercise 5	116	Cooperative learning: writing an introduction	

All the resources listed in this chapter are located in the *Teacher's ResourceBank*™.

SEGMENT	PAGES	CONTENT	RESOURCES
5 *The Body*	*117-118*		The Body 35
Emphasis	117	Explanation: understanding ways to emphasize ideas	
Unity	117	Explanation: relating details to main ideas	
Coherence	117-118	Guidelines: using direct references and transitions to achieve coherence	
Exercise 6	118	Applied practice: analyzing the use of transitions	
6 *The Conclusion*	*119-121*		The Conclusion 36
The Conclusion	119-120	Guidelines: analyzing techniques for writing effective conclusions	
Exercise 7	121	Cooperative learning: writing a conclusion	
Chart: Framework for a Composition	121	Guidelines: analyzing the elements of compositions	
7 *Making Connections*	*122-123*		
Writing an Informative Composition	122-123	Guidelines: writing an informative composition Applied practice: applying skills to the writing process	
WHOLE-CHAPTER RESOURCE Chapter Review			

SEGMENT 1 *(pp. 96–101)*
LOOKING AT THE WHOLE

OBJECTIVES

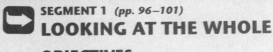

- To respond personally to a literary model
- To analyze the thesis and conclusion of a literary model

MOTIVATION

Emphasize the point of the chapter's introduction—that students encounter compositions everywhere. For example, ask students to name some reports that they've written for other classes or to name recent magazine or newspaper articles that especially caught their interest.

VISUAL CONNECTIONS
Map

About the Artist. Jasper Johns, an American artist, emphasizes everyday subjects such as maps, flags, and flashlights in his paintings and sculptures. His works give viewers the opportunity to see mundane things with a new perspective. Johns was influenced in the 1950s by the Abstract Expressionist movement, but he is also associated with the Pop art movement of the early 1960s because he was one of the first artists to explore the commonplace objects that were the main focus of Pop art.

Exploring the Subject. Discuss this painting with the class. Lead students to see that the whole map of the continental United States is actually the combination of forty-eight states. Point out that, just as each part of this map has its proper place within the whole, each part of a composition should fit with the other parts to create unity.

3 UNDERSTANDING COMPOSITION STRUCTURE

TEACHING THE LESSON

You may want to begin the study of the literary model by asking students if they are ever surprised by the accomplishments of modern science and technology. Ask them if they think the benefits of science outweigh the dangers. Then have students read the essay **"Learning Science."**

Use the **Reader's Response** questions to start students talking about the essay and about their opinions of the topic. The essay should generate a lively discussion, so allow students adequate class time to discuss the questions.

Next, direct students' attention to the form of the essay. Turn to **Looking Ahead** on p. 101 to introduce the class to the parts ☛

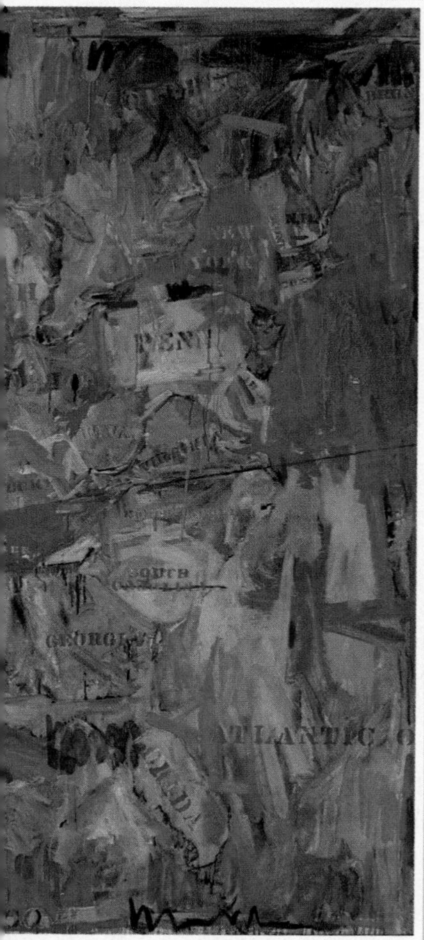

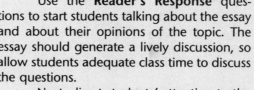

Looking at the Whole

What do you see when you look at a jazzy sports car? Do you notice the **parts**—the wheels, the sleek shape, the leather seats? Or do you notice the **whole** car—that gorgeous machine? A composition is a little like that car; taken as a whole, it's a fantastic machine.

Writing and You. What do a movie review in *People Weekly,* an article about the Buffalo Bills in *Sports Illustrated,* and an article in *PC World* have in common? They all use a standard form, the structure of a composition. You use this structure, too. Haven't you written reports in science class and essays in English class?

As You Read. As you read the following essay from a book by Isaac Asimov, think about its form. How do the words and sentences come together as a whole piece of writing?

Jasper Johns. *Map* (1961). Oil on canvas, 6′6″ × 10′3 1/8″. Collection, The Museum of Modern Art, New York. Gift of Mr. and Mrs. Robert C. Scull.

QUOTATION FOR THE DAY

"I am trying—in a good cause—to crowd people out of their own minds and occupy their space." (Robert Stone, 1937(?)– , American novelist)

The purpose of most writing is to occupy, briefly, the attention of the reader. Explain to your class that a cohesive, unified piece of writing must appeal to the reader's desire for order. As writers, students must learn to choose a topic and to develop it consistently so they can leave a single, unified impression in the reader's mind.

MEETING INDIVIDUAL NEEDS

LEP/ESL

General Strategies. ESL students should be encouraged to read through **"Learning Science"** more quickly than they might want to. You might suggest that they ignore unfamiliar words and try instead to get the general idea of each paragraph. Reading the article straight through will give students a better view of the structure of the whole composition, which is the focus of this segment.

of a composition. Point out that the essay by Asimov has a rather lengthy introduction that contains an implied thesis statement. The penultimate paragraph states the essay's thesis as part of the conclusion. Ask students to identify the article's introduction [first seven paragraphs], body [rest of article until last two paragraphs], and conclusion [last two paragraphs].

GUIDED PRACTICE

You may want the class to discuss the first **Writer's Craft** question on p. 101. You could ask volunteers to help formulate a thesis statement based on details in the introduction and body. Then write the essay's thesis statement on the chalkboard. Have the class discuss the details in the article that support the thesis statement.

USING THE SELECTION

Learning Science

1

Isaac Asimov (1920–1992) was one of the world's leading writers of science fiction and fantasy. He also was a biochemist, science professor, and author of many scientific textbooks and volumes of scientific interpretations. Asimov was born in Russia in 1920 but came to the United States with his family in 1923.

2

What do you think of the author's use of *s/he* instead of *he* or *she?* [Responses will vary. Some students may think the style looks and sounds strange but others might say the style saves space.]

3

You may want to point out Asimov's use of parallel structure here and in the next paragraph. First, he uses three infinitive phrases to express parallel ideas, and in the next paragraph, he uses a series of verbs to convey parallel ideas.

learning science

by Isaac Asimov

1

"...it is surely *fun* to know things. It brightens one's life, sharpens one's wits, reduces one's boredom, broadens one's horizon, makes one more interesting and more pleasurable to be with."

I imagine that many a young scholar has asked him- or herself, rebelliously,
2 why on Earth s/he must learn science when s/he has no intention of being a scientist.

Someone who feels that may feel that s/he need know no more than the minimum that will allow him or her to just barely get through life. Why should one know history if one is not going to be a historian? Or geography or languages if one isn't going to travel much?

But surely there is more to life than what one "does." Even if one lives quietly at home and works at some simple, routine job, there must nevertheless be
3 *some* value to understanding the world about us, to understanding events in the light of the past, to having an appreciation of other places and other cultures.

In fact, it is surely *fun* to know things. It brightens one's life, sharpens one's wits, reduces one's boredom, broadens one's horizon, makes one more interesting and more pleasurable to be with.

This is true of any sort of knowledge or skill, actually, even of those that are not strictly "school subjects." Someone who knows how to carve wood into clever little devices, or who knows all about stamp collecting, is surely more fun to be with and to watch and to listen to than someone who knows nothing at all.

INDEPENDENT PRACTICE

After the class discussion about the thesis statement and supporting details, students can answer question 4 of **Writer's Craft** independently. Tell students that their responses should explain how the author's conclusion relates to the entire composition.

ASSESSMENT

Use the evaluation of students' answers to the **Writer's Craft** questions as your assessment of students' understanding.

If, then, you know these other things, do you have to know science, *too?* Is there something special about science?

Actually, there is.

Our modern world is founded on science 4
—and on technology, which is the application of science to everyday affairs. Almost everything we do depends on our modern devices, such as automobiles, record players, and television sets, and these in turn depend on scientific principles. Our future will depend on computers, robots, nuclear power, rocket ships, all of which only make sense if we understand science.

If a person does not understand what makes these things work, they might as well be magic. People without science live in a mystery world that makes no sense to them. Even if they say, "So what? All I want to do is make a living, have a family, and look at the scenery," they may find that is not so easy. In an 5
increasingly scientific world, the good jobs, the money-making jobs, will go to those who understand science.

"Our future will depend on computers, robots, nuclear power, rocket ships, all of which only make sense if we understand science."

"In an increasingly scientific world, the good jobs, the money-making jobs, will go to those who understand science."

4
After a lengthy introduction (seven paragraphs), the body of Asimov's essay begins here.

5
What are some examples of science-based jobs today? [Responses will vary but could include those jobs associated with computer technology, space exploration, and medicine.]

CLOSURE

Ask the class to name the parts of a composition [thesis statement, introduction, body, conclusion]. You could have each student give an example of a composition that he or she has written during the last few months. ■

6
What are some examples from recent events in the news that illustrate the dangers of science? the benefits of science? [Responses will vary, but a look through several recent newspapers or news magazines should provide adequate examples.]

7
This sentence near the end of the essay is the essay's thesis.

SELECTION AMENDMENT
Description of change: excerpted
Rationale: to focus on the concept of composition structure presented in this chapter

"Surely it will be increasingly important, as the years pass, for people to understand science if they are going to be expected to help make intelligent decisions about how to use science to save the world, and not destroy it."

6 **T**hen, too, science has its dangers and its benefits. Used improperly, science can flood the Earth with pollution, with dangerous chemicals, with radiation, with devices that destroy our privacy and our freedom. Used wisely, however, science can increase our energy and food supply, improve our health, expand our joy, extend our lives, and broaden our sense of security.

Who decides how best to use science, however? In a democracy, it should be the people generally. But how can the people come to an intelligent decision if hardly any of them know much about science to begin with?

7 **S**urely it will be increasingly important, as the years pass, for people to understand science if they are going to be expected to help make intelligent decisions about how to use science to save the world, and not destroy it.

That is why it is important to study science, even if one is not going to be a professional scientist.

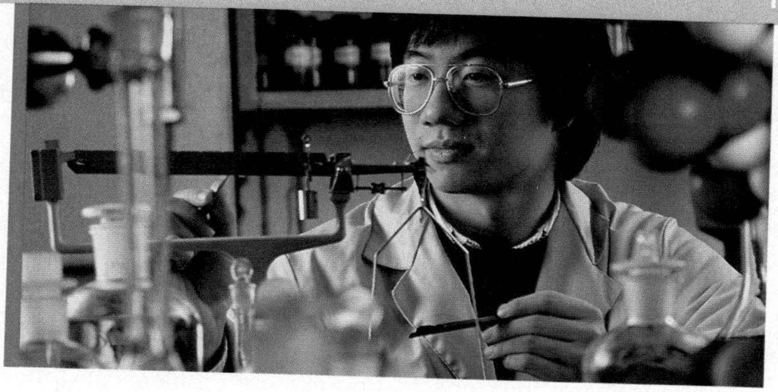

Reader's Response

1. What do you think of Asimov's arguments for studying science? Are they convincing?
2. Do you believe that everyone should study science? Why or why not?

Writer's Craft

3. What is the thesis—the main idea—of this essay? What details does the author use to support the thesis?
4. How do the last two paragraphs, the conclusion, help make this essay a "whole" piece of writing?

LOOKING AHEAD

In this chapter, you'll study the structure of a composition. You'll learn that

- most compositions have a thesis statement
- most have an introduction that catches the reader's attention
- compositions usually have a body made up of paragraphs that are unified and coherent
- most compositions have a conclusion that ties ideas together and brings the composition to a satisfying close

ANSWERS

Reader's Response

Responses will vary.

1. Have students explain why they do or do not find Asimov's arguments convincing.
2. Most students will probably agree with Asimov that everyone should study science. Students should give reasons for their answers.

Writer's Craft

3. Students' thesis statements will vary. Here is a possible answer:

   Students should study science because the science-based modern world increasingly requires scientific understanding.

   The author uses the following details to support the thesis:

   a. There is intrinsic value and pleasure in understanding the world around us.
   b. In the modern world, many things make no sense without an understanding of science.
   c. Many good jobs require an understanding of science.
   d. We need to understand science to make informed decisions about how science should be used.
4. The last two paragraphs wrap up the essay by stating the thesis and answering the question posed in the introduction.

SEGMENT 2 (pp. 102–105)
THE THESIS STATEMENT

OBJECTIVES

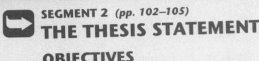

- To identify effective thesis statements and to rewrite a weak thesis statement
- To formulate a main idea from a list of details and to write a thesis statement

MOTIVATION

Write *rambling* on the chalkboard and ask students to state its meaning [wandering; moving, writing, or talking aimlessly]. Then ask what connotations the word has [connotes not having a purpose]. Point out that a composition without a clear thesis usually rambles and thus confuses the reader.

Teacher's ResourceBank™
RESOURCES

THE THESIS STATEMENT

- The Thesis Statement 31

QUOTATION FOR THE DAY

"The vitality of thought is in adventure." (Alfred North Whitehead, 1861–1947, British philosopher and mathematician)

Tell students that for their writing to have power, each of them should see his or her relationship to the topic as an adventure. If students are excited by their topics, the work of writing will be more meaningful for them and for their readers. The thesis statement allows a writer to shape and define his or her unique interest in a topic—to define the adventure. Tell students they can write out a number of thesis statements until they write one that excites them. Their excitement will motivate them to write and will also engage the reader.

VISUAL CONNECTIONS

Exploring the Subject. On July 1, 1992, New York City complied with the Federal Ocean Dumping Act of 1988, which required all municipalities to ban the practice of ocean dumping. New York City generates an estimated 35,000 tons of solid waste each workday.

What Makes a Composition

You've been writing compositions for years, but you may have called them essays or reports. You've written them for different classes as assignments and on tests, and you'll continue to write them in school and for job, college, and scholarship applications.

In other chapters in this book, you'll use the composition form when you compare and contrast subjects, write about causes and their effects, and explore problems and their solutions. You'll also use it to write about literature and to write a research paper. In this chapter, you focus on aspects of composition form itself.

The Thesis Statement

When you write a composition, you have something specific to say about your topic. This is your ***thesis,*** and the sentence that you write to express this main idea is the ***thesis statement.*** The thesis statement helps you control the direction of your composition: The entire composition will support the ideas in this statement. In the writing you do now, you might want to make the thesis statement a part of the introduction. However, experienced writers often use the thesis statement later in the composition. You'll even find compositions (articles and essays) in which the thesis statement is implied, not directly stated.

There are different kinds of thesis statements. One kind simply states the topic, as in this example: "Gotham City collects tons of garbage daily." Other thesis statements go further—they state what the writer will prove in the composition.

TEACHING THE LESSON

You may want to explain that a thesis is a position or proposition that the writer is putting forth for discussion. Tell students that the statement of that position, the thesis statement, should be clear and concise, but it must also adequately cover the topic. Have a volunteer read aloud the introductory paragraphs on pp. 102–103. Then, in a class discussion, consider each of the items in the section **Hints for Writing and Using a Thesis Statement** to be sure students understand them. Finally, analyze with the class the two thesis statements in the **Writing Note,** p. 104.

Guide students through **Exercise 1** on p. 104 by reading each thesis statement aloud. After each one, ask students to ☛

For example, "Unless some innovative solutions are found quickly, there will be no place to put the millions of tons of garbage that Gotham City collects daily."

HINTS FOR WRITING AND USING A THESIS STATEMENT

1. **Use your prewriting notes.** Before you begin to write, you'll gather a great deal of information about your topic. Look over this information carefully. What one idea is most important? What one idea unifies the facts and details you have? Answering these questions will help you to focus your thinking—an important step in developing a thesis statement.
2. **State both your topic and your main idea.** Your thesis statement needs to make clear two things: your topic and your main idea. Remember that your topic will be a limited one, and you will have a specific, unifying idea to express about it. When you first write out your thesis statement, underline your limited topic and circle your main idea to make sure you've included both.

   For example, think about this thesis statement: "If you want to be among the nearly eight million teens who are employed part time, the following tips on finding and landing a job may boost your chances of success." You can tell from this that the topic is the teen part-time job market and that the main idea is how to improve your chances of finding a part-time job.
3. **Change your thesis statement if you need to.** To begin with, reword your thesis statement until it says clearly what you want it to say. Then remember that it isn't written in concrete. If you get a different idea or decide to change the focus of your composition, just write a new thesis statement.
4. **Use your thesis statement to guide your writing.** Keep your thesis statement in front of you as you write, and be sure that all your ideas and details support it. Throw out any that don't, so that your composition will focus on your main idea.

MEETING INDIVIDUAL NEEDS

ADVANCED STUDENTS

Explain to students that often the tone of a thesis statement reveals the author's attitude about the topic. The attitude may be strong or it may be mild. Authors choose their words to reflect their attitudes (such as approval or disapproval) about their topics. Have students find five compositions from magazines and newspapers and tell them to underline the thesis statements in each article. Then ask students to circle words that they think suggest the author's attitude and to identify what that attitude is.

INTEGRATING THE LANGUAGE ARTS

Grammar Link. Remind students that complex and compound-complex sentences can help them to squeeze all the necessary information into their thesis statements.

In the example thesis statements about Gotham City garbage, the first thesis statement doesn't convey much information. In the second example, the introductory adverb clause and the adjective clause at the end of the sentence contain information that is important to the topic. The complex sentence is more concise and interesting than two simple sentences.

identify the topic and the main idea. In this way, you can help students understand what a thesis statement should do. To prepare them for **Exercise 2** on p. 105, make rewriting the ineffective thesis statement in **Exercise 1** a class project. Generate an effective thesis statement from student input and write it on the chalkboard.

Assign students **Exercise 2** as independent practice. Give students adequate class time to think about the details and then to formulate their thesis statements.

MEETING INDIVIDUAL NEEDS

LEP/ESL

General Strategies. Exercise 1 should be very beneficial to ESL students. Many of them may tend to make the kind of weak thesis statement exemplified in item 4. You might want to take extra time on this exercise to be sure students understand why item 4 is not a good thesis statement.

ANSWERS

Exercise 1

The effective thesis statements are sentences 1, 2, 3, and 5. Revisions of sentence 4 will vary. Here is an example: For members of many American families, shopping malls provide a window on the world of luxuries and a place to sample, obtain, and enjoy those luxuries.

WRITING NOTE

The first draft of your thesis statement will probably be very plain and direct. However, an indirect statement of your thesis may be more interesting to your readers. Remember that one purpose of an introduction is to capture your reader's interest, and a catchy thesis statement can help. Try rewriting your thesis statement until it sounds interesting or exciting. Notice the difference in the following preliminary thesis statement after revision.

PRELIMINARY The total solar eclipse over Hawaii on July 11, 1991, occurred under nearly ideal conditions, which resulted in some new knowledge for scientists.

REVISED When the morning sun grew dark over Hawaii on July 11, 1991, the eclipse shed light on mysteries that have baffled astronomers for centuries.

EXERCISE 1 **Analyzing Thesis Statements**

In the list below, find the four effective thesis statements: They each have a specific topic and a clear main idea. The remaining thesis statement is weak: It is missing a specific topic or a clear main idea. Rewrite it as needed to make it more effective.

1. Exciting new technology has made it possible for millions of Americans to work at home.
2. Alaska is a rugged land that is exemplified by the resourcefulness and independent spirit of its people.
3. Japanese Americans have made many important contributions to art and music in the United States.
4. Shopping malls are important to American families.
5. The citizens of Massachusetts are taking positive actions to preserve their state's natural resources.

ASSESSMENT

Use students' thesis statements from **Exercise 2** to assess their understanding of thesis statements. Have students explain why their thesis statements are adequate reflections of the details.

CLOSURE

Ask students to define *thesis statement*. Then ask students to state in their own words the four items in **Hints for Writing and Using a Thesis Statement.** ■

EXERCISE 2 **Writing a Thesis Statement**

The limited topic of the following list of details is the famous 369th Infantry Regiment. What is a specific main idea you can form from the details? Write a thesis statement for the following topic and list of details. Express both the topic and the main idea clearly and specifically in the statement.

Limited Topic: the 369th Infantry Regiment

Details

- famous African American regiment in World War I
  went from United States to France in 1918
  attended training school in France
- bravery
  received eleven citations for bravery
  entire regiment received the French *Croix de Guerre*
  not one soldier from regiment was ever captured
  never showed fear of danger
- service
  served in France more than a year
  "Battle of Henry Johnson" named for member of regiment who showed great bravery in battle
  first troop to march through Washington Square Arch in New York City after returning home

ANSWERS

Exercise 2

Responses will vary. Here is a sample thesis statement:

The 369th Infantry Regiment, the famous African American unit that fought in France in World War I, was distinguished by its exceptional bravery.

VISUAL CONNECTIONS

Exploring the Subject. Members of the 369th Infantry Regiment were among the more than 360,000 African Americans who served in World War I. About one million African Americans served in World War II.

SEGMENT 3 *(pp. 106–111)*

EARLY PLANS AND FORMAL OUTLINES

OBJECTIVE

- To organize notes into an early plan or formal outline

MOTIVATION

Have students raise their hands if they consider themselves (1) always organized, (2) sometimes organized, or (3) never organized. Then have students raise their hands if they think making outlines before writing essays is helpful. Have the class note whether or not there is a correlation between those

Teacher's ResourceBank™

RESOURCES

EARLY PLANS AND FORMAL OUTLINES

QUOTATION FOR THE DAY

"A moment's thinking is an hour in words." (Thomas Hood, 1799–1845, British poet and humorist)

Remind students that their minds generally run faster than their pencils. The shape of an entire paper may come to them in a single insight. The purpose of an outline is to sketch out what may have been glimpsed in a flash.

MEETING INDIVIDUAL NEEDS

LEP/ESL

General Strategies. To help ESL students to develop their early plans, let them use their first languages whenever they do not know an English word, and let them use doodles, abbreviations or other notations to hold onto ideas. The emphasis in this stage is on ideas, not on writing.

Early Plans and Formal Outlines

You may be a super-organized person, a super-scattered one, or sort of in-between. No matter what your organizational skills, you'll benefit from planning your writing. Before you write your composition, *group* and *order* your details. *Early plans* and *formal outlines* can help you do this.

The Early Plan

The ***early plan***—sometimes called a *rough*, or *informal, outline*—gives you a rough idea of the kinds of information you want to include in your composition. It also helps you see how to group details without the complication of arranging them into outline form with numerals and letters.

Grouping. Well-organized people often group related items in their closets. Winter clothes go in one place, summer clothes in another. School clothes have their own spot, as do clothes for after school. When you ***group*** details for a composition, you can follow these steps to put related items in one spot.

- Sort related ideas and details into separate groups.
- Make a separate list of details that don't fit into any group. (At some later stage you may find a use for them.)
- Give each group of details a separate label.

Here's an early plan for a composition on teens finding part-time jobs.

types of employer leads, types of contacts ↓ JOB LEADS
purposes, techniques ↓ APPLICATIONS
purpose, conduct, follow-up ↓ INTERVIEWS

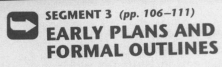

students who make outlines and those students who consider themselves organized.

TEACHING THE LESSON

Begin by stressing that most forms of writing require planning and organization. Remind students that because they want the readers to understand what they are saying, they should make their writing "reader friendly" by organizing it well. Tell students that early plans and formal outlines help organize their thoughts and notes.

Ordering. ***Ordering*** involves arranging the details within each group and the groups themselves. Your topic may suggest the best arrangement to use. For example, if you're writing about events that happen over time, you will probably use ***chronological*** (time) ***order.*** When you describe something, you often use ***spatial*** (space) ***order,*** arranging details according to their location in space. In persuasive writing, you'll probably use ***order of importance.*** If you're comparing and contrasting items, you will use ***logical order*** and group related ideas together. Often you might use a combination of two or more of these orders.

REFERENCE NOTE: For more help in arranging details, see pages 75–77.

The Formal Outline

Structured outlines sometimes grow out of early plans. A ***formal outline*** has numerals and letters to identify headings and subheadings and indentations to show levels of subordination. It may be a ***topic outline,*** which uses single words and phrases, or a ***sentence outline,*** which uses only complete sentences. Formal outlines may be used for planning, but they are more often written after the composition is complete, providing an overview or summary for the reader.

REFERENCE NOTE: For more information on formal outlines, see pages 426–427.

TIMESAVER

Through their previous studies and composition writing, students may be very familiar with grouping information and making formal outlines. If so, you may want to have students read the brief information in the chapter on early plans and formal outlines as a reminder rather than spending additional class or activity time on outlining.

In presenting the material in this segment, follow the development in the textbook of the composition on teens finding part-time jobs—from grouping to formal outline to composition.

Emphasize that all students will make early plans before they start writing because it's always necessary to group and order information. You may want to read aloud **Grouping** and **Ordering**, pp. 106–107.

Take one of the suggested main headings for **Exercise 3** such as *Income* and guide students through the process of grouping the appropriate notes under that heading. After students have completed their early plans, guide the students who want to

INTEGRATING THE LANGUAGE ARTS

Technology Link. Some students could work together on a computer to produce a color-coded formal outline for the composition on teens finding part-time jobs. Have students color-code the different parts of the outline so that all Roman-numeral headings are the same color, and so on. Then students could show their work and explain it to small groups at the computer.

MEETING INDIVIDUAL NEEDS

STUDENTS WITH SPECIAL NEEDS

Students with learning disabilities often have trouble with organizing and laboriously copying text. Therefore, they may get frustrated if they have to write the same thing over and over again. You could give students a copy of the list in **Exercise 3** and have them cut up the list so each item is on a separate slip of paper. Then they can move the slips of paper around to organize the notes. When students have the notes arranged in the order they prefer, they could tape the notes onto paper.

Here's a formal topic outline for the composition on pages 110–111 about teens finding part-time jobs. (Notice how this formal outline fleshes out the basic ideas developed in the early plan on page 106. Also notice how it follows a particular structure to show the relationships among ideas.)

Title: It Takes Work to Get Work
Thesis Statement: If you want to be among the nearly eight million teens who are employed part time, the following tips on finding and landing a job may boost your chances of success.

I. Job leads
  A. Employer leads
    1. Signs
    2. Newspaper ads
    3. Employment agencies
  B. Contacts
    1. Potential employers
    2. Friends
    3. Family members
    4. Business acquaintances
    5. School counselor

II. Job applications
  A. Purpose
  B. Techniques
    1. First impression
    2. Skills and accomplishments

III. Job interviews
  A. Purpose
  B. Conduct
    1. Grooming/dress
    2. Preparation
    3. Directness/honesty
  C. Follow-up

create formal outlines by helping them complete the title and the first main heading with its subheads.

For independent practice, have students finish the grouping of notes to complete early plans. Because **Exercise 3** may be difficult and somewhat confusing to students, you should probably allow class time during which you can be available to answer questions. Students who want to make formal outlines can complete that process as independent practice after you guide them through the title and first main heading.

EXERCISE 3 **Making an Early Plan or Formal Outline**

Do you have more week than money left at the end of a pay period? The following notes about managing money might help. Working with a partner, organize these notes into either an early plan or a formal outline. [Hint: Your main headings can be Income, Expenses, Money Management, and Savings.]

income
money management
insurance
savings bonds
investments
savings account
certificates of deposit
publications
loans
cash
options
savings
expenses
wages
college savings
living expenses
big purchases
car expenses
interest
credit cards
adult advice
unexpected expenses
charge accounts
spending
purpose
taxes
allowance
bank personnel

ANSWERS

Exercise 3

Order will vary. Here is an example of a formal outline:

I. Income
  A. Wages
  B. Interest
  C. Allowance
II. Expenses
  A. Living expenses
  B. Insurance
  C. Car expenses
  D. Taxes
  E. Charge accounts
  F. Credit cards
III. Money Management
  A. Adult advice
    1. Bank personnel
    2. Publications
  B. Cash
  C. Spending
  D. Loans
IV. Savings
  A. Savings bonds
  B. Savings account
  C. Investments
  D. Certificates of deposit
  E. Options
  F. Purpose
    1. College savings
    2. Big purchases
    3. Unexpected expenses

ASSESSMENT

Assess students' mastery of preparing early plans and formal outlines through an evaluation of their performance on **Exercise 3.**

RETEACHING

You may want to have students make an early plan of **"Learning Science."** Since the essay is short and already organized, let students identify the details themselves and label the groups. [Here is a sample early plan: understanding world, recognizing joy of knowledge—Purpose of Learning; dependence on science and technology,

MEETING INDIVIDUAL NEEDS

LEARNING STYLES

Visual Learners. As students study **A Writer's Model,** show a copy of the formal outline (p. 108) for the model on an overhead projector. Refer to words in the composition that correspond to the outline. Show students how the writer used the formal outline as a basis for the organization of the composition.

A WRITER'S MODEL

The following composition on teens getting part-time jobs includes the thesis statement on page 108 and follows the formal outline on page 108. You might want to use this composition as a model as you write your own composition.

It Takes Work to Get Work

INTRODUCTION

Thesis statement

"You're hired!" These are exciting words to any anxious teen entering the job market for the very first time. If you want to be among the nearly eight million teens who are employed part time, the following tips on finding and landing a job may boost your chances of success.

BODY
Major point: Job leads

The first step is to find out what part-time jobs are available in your area. Some job leads come directly from employers: signs in store and restaurant windows, help wanted ads in the newspaper, listings at employment agencies. Other leads can be developed by contacting potential employers yourself or by making use of contacts, such as friends, family members, business acquaintances, and your school counselor. The more leads you have, the more likely you are to find the job you want.

Major point: Job applications

Once you have a list of job leads, start applying for some jobs. In most cases, the first thing you'll be asked to do is fill out a job application. This is the way an employer decides who to interview. It's your first chance to show that you are qualified for the job.

Here are some ways to use the job application to make a good first impression. First of all, neatness counts; use a pen and write clearly. Make sure you use standard English and use no slang words. Spell words correctly and use good grammar. Finally, answer all questions honestly and clearly.

Above all, don't sell yourself short. Most job applications have a space to list special skills and accomplishments. Be honest, but don't be shy. Does the job involve selling? Maybe you've sold ads for your school annual. Do you speak a second language?

jobs, control of dangers and benefits of science, place in democratic society—Importance of Science.]

Students also could make a formal outline for the essay.

CLOSURE

Ask students to explain the differences between an early plan and a formal outline. ■

Many businesses need bilingual employees. Are you on the honor roll? Many employers know that people who work hard at school will also work hard at a job. Do you have job skills from completing courses in typing, computers, bookkeeping, shop? Let your potential employer know.

Major point: Job interviews

After reviewing all the job applications, employers will choose some candidates to interview. An interview is the employer's chance to find out more about you, and your chance to find out more about the job.

Arrive for the interview well-rested, clean, well-groomed, neatly dressed, and about five minutes early. Have your Social Security card and a pen and pad of paper with you. During the interview, look the interviewer in the eye, smile, and remember to use the interviewer's name (always Ms., Mrs., or Mr.--never first names). Be direct and honest, and be ready to answer questions. (Prepare yourself in advance by consulting employment booklets at the library that list some of the most commonly asked interview questions.) When the interview is over, express your interest in the job and thank the interviewer for his or her time.

Finally, that evening, type or neatly write a brief letter expressing your interest in the job and reminding the interviewer of the attributes that make you the perfect person for the job. Thank the interviewer for considering you. Address the envelope to the interviewer and mail the letter the next day.

CONCLUSION

It may take a little time to prepare for and follow through with your job search, but it's worth the effort. You'll be glad you did it right when you finally hear the words "You're hired!"

COOPERATIVE LEARNING

Divide the class into small groups to discuss informally the tone and structure of **A Writer's Model.** You may want to remind students that tone is the attitude a writer takes toward his or her topic and audience, and that it is conveyed through the author's choice of words and details. Specifically, ask students to talk within their groups about these questions:

1. What is the overall tone of the composition? For example, is it friendly or formal? serious or humorous?
2. How does the author's repeated use of *you* and *your* affect the tone?
3. How do the introduction and conclusion reflect a central tone?
4. How does the author's use of questions throughout the composition affect the tone?
5. Why do you think the author often begins sentences with verbs?

You may want to monitor the group discussions to keep groups on the right track and to be sure all students are contributing ideas. Then ask each group to present a brief report about its discussion. Write the groups' key findings on the chalkboard.

SEGMENT 4 *(pp. 112–116)*

THE INTRODUCTION

OBJECTIVES

- To analyze the technique and tone of two introductions by professional writers
- To write a new introduction for a professional model

TEACHING THE LESSON

You may want to stress that there are two important purposes of effective introductions—to encourage readers to read what you've written and to tell them what you're writing about.

Lead a discussion about the many competing demands for a reader's time. Point out that introductions help readers

Teacher's ResourceBank™

RESOURCES

THE INTRODUCTION

- The Introduction 34

QUOTATION FOR THE DAY

"When you write the thing through once, you find out what the end is. Then you can go back . . . and put in a lot of those foreshadowings." (Flannery O'Connor, 1925–1964, American short-story writer and novelist)

Flannery O'Connor is hinting at the fact that an introduction may be most clear when a paper is nearly finished. Advise your students to go back to the beginning of their papers to see if their introductions can be improved. Sometimes it is only at the end of a task that the beginning can be seen.

VISUAL CONNECTIONS

Exploring the Subject. Eliot Porter, born in 1901, abandoned his career as an instructor in biochemistry and bacteriology at Harvard to pursue a career in photography. He was an early master of color photography and developed his own techniques with flash illumination. Many of his color photographs communicate vividly his ideas about the environment.

SELECTION AMENDMENT
Description of change: excerpted
Rationale: to focus on the concept of composition structure presented in this chapter

The Introduction

Many writers think the ***introduction*** of an article or composition is the hardest part to write; it is the critical time to get the audience's attention and let them know what the topic is. The length of an introduction may vary a great deal—from one sentence to several paragraphs. However, there are three things an introduction needs to accomplish:

- catch the audience's attention (otherwise they may not read on)
- set the tone, or show the writer's attitude, toward the topic (humorous, serious, critical, and so forth)
- present the thesis (sometimes at the beginning, but often at the end, of the introduction)

Techniques for Writing Introductions

The following techniques represent some of the options experienced writers have for getting the reader's attention. When you're trying to decide how to start a composition, try one or two of them.

1. **Begin by addressing the reader directly.** In the writer's model on pages 110–111, the writer addresses the reader directly with "You're hired!" This also sets an informal, friendly tone and involves the reader.

2. **Begin with an interesting or dramatic quote.** A writer used this technique in a biographical sketch of American photographer Eliot Porter.

> "Color," Eliot Porter used to say when asked to reveal the secret behind his photographs. "Color is the only thing I'm really concerned about. Color and patterns. That's all."
>
> "Eliot Porter," *Life*

decide whether they want to take the time to read a piece of writing on a certain subject.

Be sure that students understand the three requirements of an effective introduction given at the beginning of this segment. They've studied the third requirement (thesis statement) and are about to study the first (catching the reader's interest), so you may want to take a few extra minutes at this point to discuss the second (setting the tone) if you haven't already done so. Define *tone* as "the attitude a writer takes toward his or her topic and audience." Tell students that a writer's choice of words and details influences the tone of his or her writing. You may want to ask students why it's important to establish tone in the introduction. [Quickly establishing tone allows the reader to have a

3. **Begin with an anecdote or example.** Starting with an anecdote, or little story, or giving an example of something can immediately involve your reader, especially if the anecdote is humorous or mysterious. This first sentence of the following introduction begins an anecdote about a discovery in an attic.

> One stifling summer afternoon last August, in the attic of a tiny stone house in Pennsylvania, I made a most interesting discovery: the shortest, cheapest method of inducing a nervous breakdown ever perfected.
>
> S. J. Perelman, "Insert Flap 'A' and Throw Away"

4. **Begin with an unusual or enlightening fact.** Some new or unusual fact will often entice your audience to read on and learn more about your topic. For example, an article about a most unusual bird begins this way:

> The hoatzin is an odd bird. Not only does it eat leaves—far more than any other bird—but it digests them like a cow or a sheep, grinding the leaves up in its specialized, muscular crop. Up close the hoatzin smells bad, and it flies poorly.
>
> "Geographica," *National Geographic*

MEETING **INDIVIDUAL** NEEDS

ADVANCED STUDENTS

You may want to let some students, either individually or in teams, present the eight techniques for writing introductions. Let each student or team be responsible for teaching one technique. They should present all the information included in the chapter for their techniques, including analyses of the models. In addition, have each find at least three other examples of the technique from magazine, newspaper, or book articles. Students should read and analyze the extra models and include them in their presentations.

A DIFFERENT APPROACH

Have students work in pairs to locate examples of the eight techniques for introductions in magazine and newspaper articles. Give students some class time to look at articles in the library. Then let students read the introductions they've found and identify the techniques used.

AMENDMENTS TO SELECTIONS

Description of change: excerpted
Rationale: to focus on the concept of composition structure presented in this chapter

clearer understanding of the writer's purpose and meaning.]

Next, use students' interests to determine how you allocate class time for covering the techniques for writing introductions. The class may want to discuss some of the techniques and examples more thoroughly than others. You may want to give other models at various stages of your presentation. You should help students realize the importance of introductions and also help them to see that creating effective introductions for their own writing can be fun and challenging.

Guide students through answering the first question in **Exercise 4** with regard to the first introduction only. Then assign the rest of **Exercise 4** as independent practice.

MEETING **INDIVIDUAL** NEEDS

LEP/ESL

General Strategies. You may want to point out to ESL students that technique 7 (on this page) is the only one that uses the first person *I* in an introduction. Because ESL writers may tend to overuse the first person, you could suggest that they try to avoid using it in their compositions and that they observe how the writers in the other examples manage to avoid using it.

COOPERATIVE LEARNING

You may want to divide the class into teams to further explore tone. You could give each team a different list of tones such as humorous, serious, formal, solemn, ironic, sarcastic, cynical, critical, friendly, personal, sincere, fearful, playful, reverent, irreverent, philosophical, mocking, admiring, amused, affectionate, angry, or loving. Ask each team to discuss the meanings of its tone words and then to write sentences or short paragraphs that convey each tone. The teams could take turns reading their examples and letting the other teams identify the tones illustrated.

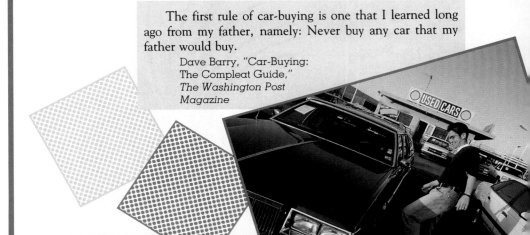

AMENDMENTS TO SELECTIONS
Description of change: excerpted
Rationale: to focus on the concept of composition structure presented in this chapter

5. **Begin with a question or a challenge.** When you start with a question or a challenge, you immediately involve your readers. Even if they know the answer, they'll want to know what you have to say about the subject.

> What do the following people have in common: Lewis Temple, inventor of a harpoon that revolutionized whaling; James Beckwourth, Western trailblazer; Benjamin Banneker, surveyor and mathematician; and Henry Blair, inventor of a corn seed planter?

6. **Take a stand on some issue.** When you are writing persuasion, you can begin with a statement that expresses a strong, even controversial, opinion. This will make your readers want to read on to see how you will support your opinion.

> Bad times don't kill banks—bad bankers do.
> When the system works, regulators protect bad bankers from their worst instincts. But the system hasn't been working.
> Mitchell Zuckoff, "Lax regulation, inadequate laws promote insider-lending abuse," *The Boston Globe*

7. **Begin with an outrageous or comical statement.** An outrageous or comical statement will let your readers know to expect a humorous or satirical composition. Most readers are attracted to humor and will want to keep reading.

> The first rule of car-buying is one that I learned long ago from my father, namely: Never buy any car that my father would buy.
> Dave Barry, "Car-Buying: The Compleat Guide," *The Washington Post Magazine*

Take advantage of the cooperative-learning aspect of **Exercise 5** on p. 116 to give students guided practice in writing effective introductions. You could have each group develop an introduction using one of the eight techniques. Circulate among the groups to offer assistance and to stimulate ideas and then have the groups read their finished introductions to the class. For independent practice, ask each group to choose a different technique and to write another introduction.

8. **Begin with a simple statement of your thesis.** Often a well-written thesis statement is all you need to catch your reader's attention.

The decision of Justice Thurgood Marshall to step down from the Supreme Court left President Bush with an unusually significant vacancy to fill.

"The Talk of the Town,"
The New Yorker

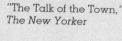

EXERCISE 4 **Analyzing Introductions**

What do the movie *Dances with Wolves* and a boy with an overactive imagination have in common? Nothing—but they help to make the following two introductions by professional writers appealing to readers. Read the introductions, and then answer the following questions about each one.

- Which of the eight techniques (on pages 112–115) does the writer use in the introduction?
- Does the technique work well enough to make you want to read the article?
- What is the tone of the introduction? What words or phrases reveal the author's attitude toward the topic?

1. *Unci Maka.* The language is Lakota, spoken by the Sioux, and the words, used in prayer, mean Grandmother Earth. Historically, Native Americans revered and defended their land, especially from the ravages of white men—a tradition portrayed in the hit movie, "Dances with Wolves." But just miles from the film's location, a civil-engineering firm is developing plans for a solid-waste landfill. Why are engineers from Connecticut on a South Dakota reservation? Leaders of the Rosebud Sioux tribe

CRITICAL THINKING
Synthesis

Have students write composition introductions that combine two or more of the techniques for writing introductions. Students could write introductions for two topics of their choice or for two topics from the following list:

1. alternative energy sources
2. latest music trends
3. students' views on some proposed or recently enacted laws

Then have students each share one introduction with the class.

ANSWERS
Exercise 4

Answers may vary.

1. The writer uses a dramatic quotation, an unusual fact, and a question. Students should explain why they do or do not want to read the article. The tone of the introduction is serious, sarcastic, and critical. Words and expressions that reveal the author's attitude are "revered," "ravaged," "outspoken opponent," and "Dances With Garbage."

SELECTION AMENDMENT

Description of change: excerpted
Rationale: to focus on the concept of composition structure presented in this chapter

ASSESSMENT

Use students' responses to **Exercises 4** and **5** to assess their mastery of analyzing and writing introductions.

CLOSURE

Ask students to name the three requirements for an effective introduction and to list the eight techniques for writing effective introductions. ■

2. The writer begins by addressing the reader directly with a comical statement and then follows with an anecdote. Students should explain why they do or do not want to read the article. The tone is informal and humorous. Words and phrases that reveal the author's attitude are "This is my brother's fault," "your standard, monster-infested basement," and "Death."

ANSWERS

Exercise 5

New introductions will vary. Each introduction should include a thesis statement and should have a clearly identifiable tone. Using one or more of the techniques for writing introductions, each student should write an attention-grabbing opening to replace the introduction of Asimov's article. The new introduction should make readers want to find out why people should study science, and it should lead gracefully to Asimov's statements about the importance of science in a democracy and in daily life.

AMENDMENTS TO SELECTIONS

Description of change: excerpted
Rationale: to focus on the concept of composition structure presented in this chapter

invited them. South Dakota Sen. Tom Daschle, an outspoken opponent, calls the plan "Dances With Garbage."

Mary Hager *et al*, "'Dances With Garbage'" *Newsweek*

2. This is my brother's fault.

As a young boy, I was plagued with an overactive imagination—compounded by the fact that we lived in a house with your standard, monster-infested basement. Occasionally, I would hear my father's command that never failed to horrify me: "Go down to the basement, Gary, and bring up some firewood." Death.

Gary Larson, *The Far Side Gallery*

"Uh-oh, Donny. Sounds like the monster in the basement has heard you crying again. ... Let's be reaaaal quiet and hope he goes away."

EXERCISE 5 **Writing an Introduction**

Get together with two or three classmates, and try writing a new introduction for "Learning Science," pages 98–100. Experiment with any of the techniques for capturing readers' interest that you've just read about, but be sure to include the thesis statement and to set the tone. When you finish, compare your introductions with those of other groups.

SEGMENT 5 *(pp. 117–118)*

THE BODY

OBJECTIVE

- To analyze the coherence of a paragraph by identifying the nouns, direct-reference pronouns, and transitional words and phrases

TEACHING THE LESSON

Tell students that an effective introduction catches the reader's attention, but the body of the composition proves whether or not that attention is deserved.

Have a volunteer read aloud the material in this segment. Discuss the concepts of emphasis, unity, coherence, direct references, and transitional words and phrases ☛

The Body

The ***body*** of a composition is the part where you develop the main idea of your thesis statement. Each paragraph expresses a major point of your thesis and supports, or proves, it with details. These paragraphs should connect with one another and relate directly to your thesis statement. You can achieve these goals if the body has *emphasis, unity,* and *coherence.*

Emphasis

To ***emphasize*** is to stress, and in most compositions you have some ideas that you want to stress because you think they are more important. The primary method for emphasizing ideas is to give them more attention, to devote more time and space to them. However, you can also emphasize an idea by discussing it first or last—the two positions that are most likely to draw the attention of the reader. The model composition on pages 110–111 places more emphasis on applications and interviews, by giving them more space and attention, than it does on leads.

Unity

Unity means "oneness." In a composition unity means that every paragraph and every detail supports a single main idea. Each topic sentence for each paragraph should relate to the thesis statement of the composition. And each sentence in a paragraph should relate to the topic sentence of the paragraph.

Coherence

Coherence means "logical connection." A composition has coherence if all the ideas are connected in a sequence that readers find easy to follow. Sentences flow smoothly, and paragraphs connect sensibly. The best way to achieve coherence is to use *direct references* and *transitional expressions.*

Direct References. One way to link ideas is to refer directly to something that came immediately before. You can achieve coherence by using the following techniques.

1. Repeat key words or phrases from the preceding paragraph, or repeat or rephrase the last idea in that paragraph.
2. Use pronouns to refer to nouns already used.
3. Use synonyms or rewordings of ideas and key words.

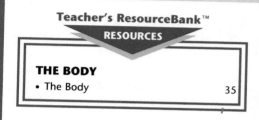

Teacher's ResourceBank™

RESOURCES

THE BODY

QUOTATION FOR THE DAY

"In making your case, you naturally use the strongest details you have, which always means the most convincing examples, and often the most colorful and intricate ones as well." (Bill Stott, 1940– , American writer and educator)

Use the quotation to initiate a discussion about the kind of information that a writer should include in the body of a composition.

MEETING INDIVIDUAL NEEDS

LEP/ESL

General Strategies. The typical body of an American composition is direct, logical, and tightly connected to the thesis statement. But composition structure is not necessarily consistent cross-culturally. Other cultures may emphasize subtlety, indirection, or sincerity. You may have to display more patience with your ESL students as they work to learn to apply new ideas about composition structure.

with the class. For guided practice, guide students through identifying the nouns, their direct-reference pronouns, and some transitional words or phrases in one or two paragraphs of **A Writer's Model**, pp. 110–111. Assign **Exercise 6** as independent practice, and evaluate students' responses to assess their mastery.

CLOSURE

Ask students to define *unity* and *coherence,* to name three ways to make direct references, and to list at least five transitional words and phrases. ■

COOPERATIVE LEARNING

Divide the class into mixed-ability groups of three or four. Give each group a composition of at least ten or twelve paragraphs in length and have groups analyze the unity and coherence of their compositions. Each group should identify the limited topic and the implicit or explicit thesis statement, number the main supporting details throughout the composition, and mark all uses of direct references and transitional words and phrases.

Ask each group to report its findings and to discuss any trouble encountered during the exercise.

INTEGRATING THE LANGUAGE ARTS

Mechanics Link. Remind students that parenthetical expressions used as transitional words and phrases are always set off by commas and that two commas are needed to set off an expression within a sentence. Have each student write five original sentences containing correctly punctuated transitional words and phrases.

ANSWERS

Exercise 6

Nouns and direct-reference pronouns: David Farragut—one, he, his, he, he, he, he, he, he, his, he; officer—who
Transitional words and phrases: when, Not long after, when, Later, and then, Although, when, Because

Transitional Expressions. ***Transitional expressions,*** words and phrases such as *for example, of course, therefore, meanwhile,* and *later,* lead your readers from one sentence or paragraph to another. They help make relationships clear and create smooth connections among ideas.

REFERENCE NOTE: For more about using direct references and transitional words and phrases, see pages 79–81.

WRITING NOTE

In a long composition or article, a short paragraph can be used to create a transition. Often such a paragraph is a single sentence acting as a bridge between the ideas in one paragraph and those in another.

EXERCISE 6 **Analyzing the Use of Transitions**

Most writers really do use the techniques you've been reading about. Identify the nouns, their direct-reference pronouns, and any transitional expressions in the following paragraph.

David Farragut, son of a Spanish naval officer who fought on the side of the American colonists during the Revolutionary War, is one of the greatest naval heroes of the United States. He made an early start on his career by joining the U.S. Navy when he was only nine years old. Not long after, when he was twelve, he became a prize master, commanding a ship captured from the British during the War of 1812. Later, he fought pirates in the Caribbean and then served in the Mexican War (1846–48). Although he was over sixty years old when the Civil War began, he took command of a Union fleet. Because of his great bravery and ability, he became the first American to be given the rank of full admiral in the U.S. Navy.

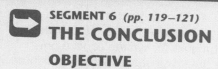

SEGMENT 6 *(pp. 119–121)*

THE CONCLUSION

OBJECTIVE

- To write an effective conclusion

TEACHING THE LESSON

You may want to caution students not to think of the conclusion as an afterthought. Explain that the writer ties the whole composition together in the conclusion.

Present the techniques for writing conclusions by having student volunteers read each one aloud. Make sure students

The Conclusion

When you read a book or see a movie, you expect it to have a definite ***conclusion,*** or ending. Compositions also need satisfying endings; readers need to feel that the ideas are tied together and are complete. The following techniques are some options that experienced writers choose from to create effective conclusions.

1. **Refer to the introduction.** The model composition on page 111 neatly wraps up ideas in the conclusion by referring to the introduction.

> You'll be glad you did it right when you finally hear the words "You're hired!"

2. **Offer a solution or make a recommendation.** When you've taken a stand on an issue, you can stress your point by offering a solution or recommending a course of action in the conclusion.

> People do get the government they deserve, and our low voter turnout shows that we deserve no better than what we have. We need a grassroots campaign nationwide to educate and convince people that voting is not only a right and a privilege but also a serious responsibility. Complaining to each other about the mess the country's in is no answer. Putting the responsibility where it belongs, on all of us, is.

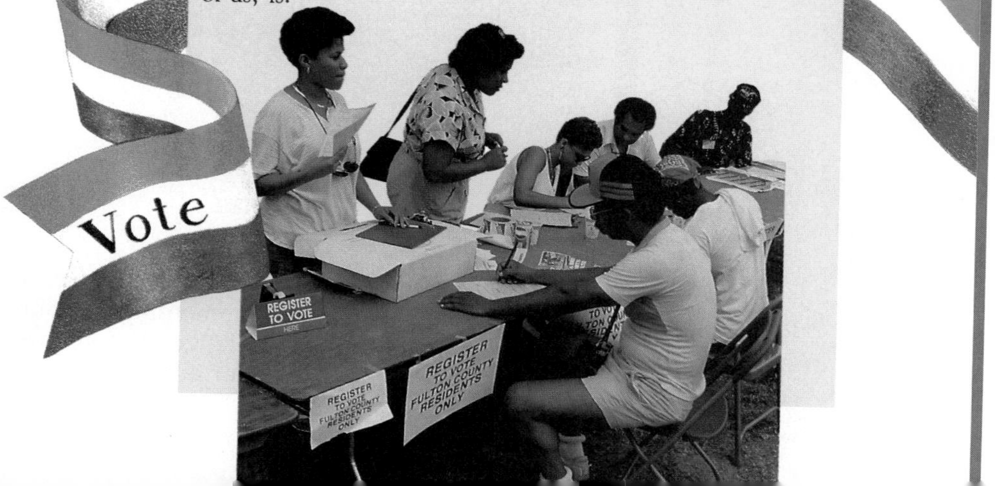

Teacher's ResourceBank™

RESOURCES

THE CONCLUSION

- The Conclusion 36

QUOTATION FOR THE DAY

"The perfect ending should take the reader slightly by surprise and yet seem exactly right to him." (William Zinsser, American scholar)

In writing a first or second draft, students may end their essays by wandering into irrelevant areas. Reassure students that this is common even for accomplished writers. Perhaps they could experiment with cutting their papers off at several different points to see which ending seems most satisfying to the reader.

MEETING INDIVIDUAL NEEDS

LEP/ESL

General Strategies. You may want to simplify the material in this segment for your ESL students. As they read each of the techniques for writing conclusions, have students read the statement in bold print and then skip the explanatory sentences and go straight to the example.

understand how each technique differs from the others.

For guided practice, choose one of the techniques for writing a conclusion and guide students through using the technique to write a new conclusion for **"Learning Science."** Have groups complete **Exercise 7** as independent practice. They could pick essays from their literature textbooks if they would prefer not to use **A Writer's Model.** Use responses to **Exercise 7** to evaluate mastery of the techniques for writing conclusions.

To close, ask students to name four techniques for writing conclusions.

INTEGRATING THE LANGUAGE ARTS

Literature Link. Have students read a modern composition such as "Circus at Dawn" by Thomas Wolfe. Then ask students to tell you which of the techniques for writing conclusions the author uses. [For example, Wolfe gives a personal comment about the effect of the memory of the morning.] You then could have students use different techniques to write different conclusions for the essay. Ask for volunteers to read their new conclusions to the class.

SELECTION AMENDMENT
Description of change: excerpted
Rationale: to focus on the concept of composition structure presented in this chapter

3. **Restate your thesis.** Another good way to wind up your composition is to restate your thesis. Use different words to say the same thing, bringing your composition to an end that echoes the beginning. For example, look at the conclusion of Isaac Asimov's essay "Learning Science" (pages 98–100).

4. **Summarize your major points.** Another satisfying ending is a summary of the major points of a composition. For instance, the main points of an article on emeralds are briefly included in this conclusion.

> Gems satisfy primal needs—the lure of instant wealth, some sort of desire, perhaps, to join with the secrets of the earth. They fulfill our longing for beauty. They are our link to mysteries we can appreciate but cannot explain. Gems are as near the eternal as anything we can ever own.
>
> Fred Ward, "Emeralds," *National Geographic*

Other ways to conclude a paragraph include closing with an example of your main idea, personally commenting on your topic, or posing a dramatic question or challenge. The important thing is that you tie your ideas together and leave your readers with the emotion you intended.

EXTENSION

Explain to students that how a conclusion is written is an important contributing factor to the tone of an essay. Conclusions tie together ideas, but they also create a final emotional effect.

Ask students to analyze the model conclusions in this segment and to identify the tone in each. [Responses will vary.

1. upbeat, cheery
2. serious, slightly angry
3. reasoned, logical
4. lyrical, philosophical] ■

EXERCISE 7 Writing a Conclusion

Try out some of your options for writing conclusions. Get together with two or three classmates. With your group members, try writing a new conclusion for "Learning Science," the essay that ends on page 100, or the Writer's Model that ends on page 111. Don't be afraid to experiment with different kinds of conclusions. When you finish, share your work with other groups.

WRITING NOTE

Often writers wait until they finish their compositions before deciding on a title. After you write your composition, try to think of a title that lets readers know what to expect in subject and tone. (Don't put a catchy, funny title on a serious essay, or vice-versa!)

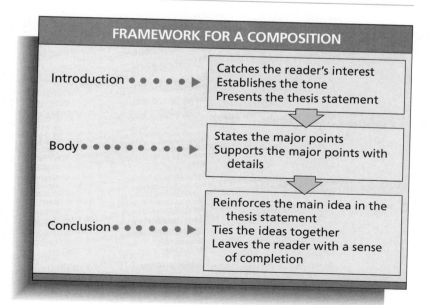

FRAMEWORK FOR A COMPOSITION

Introduction	Catches the reader's interest Establishes the tone Presents the thesis statement
Body	States the major points Supports the major points with details
Conclusion	Reinforces the main idea in the thesis statement Ties the ideas together Leaves the reader with a sense of completion

ANSWERS

Exercise 7

Answers will vary. Here is a sample conclusion for **"Learning Science"** that uses the technique of summarizing the major points:

To make sense of the modern world, to find good jobs, and to be responsible participants in deciding the future of our world—these are all reasons for everyone to study science, even those who have no desire to be scientists.

WRITING NOTE

Students could write titles for the examples for conclusion techniques 2 and 4. Tell students to come up with appropriate titles based on the content and tone of the examples. Volunteers could share their titles with the class.

MEETING INDIVIDUAL NEEDS

LEARNING STYLES

Visual Learners. You may want to display a copy of the **Framework for a Composition** chart on an overhead projector while you review the functions of a composition's introduction, body, and conclusion.

SEGMENT 7 *(pp. 122–123)*

MAKING CONNECTIONS

WRITING AN INFORMATIVE COMPOSITION

OBJECTIVE

- To prewrite, write, evaluate, revise, proofread, and publish an informative composition

TEACHING THE LESSON

Have students read over the introduction and the information listed in the section **Swimming for the Gold.** If there are any questions about the information, call on students with expertise in swimming to explain any unclear points to others.

Next, have students follow the stages of the writing process. A good way to model

QUOTATION FOR THE DAY

"Thinking means connecting things, and stops if they cannot be connected." (G. K. Chesterton, 1874–1936, British novelist and essayist)

A list is only a list until the writer connects with something on the list. In **Swimming for the Gold,** students will need to make a personal connection to several of the items on the list before they can begin to write. Suggest that they look up biographical information on Mark Spitz or have them investigate how many hours a week Olympic athletes must train. Until they find something in the list that touches them, students won't be able to touch a reader with an opening sentence.

MEETING INDIVIDUAL NEEDS

LEP/ESL

General Strategies. To help students focus on the composition task, suggest a purpose for their swimming compositions: as an article for an encyclopedia; as an article for the in-flight magazine of an airline; or as part of an information packet for the swimming announcer at the Olympic Games.

MAKING CONNECTIONS

Writing an Informative Composition

In this chapter you have reviewed the basic elements of composition form, and now you have a chance to use what you've learned in a complete piece of writing. You will be writing a composition to inform your readers about swimming as a competitive sport. The following information has already been gathered for you. Although a title is suggested, you are welcome to create a different one.

Swimming for the Gold

1. Swimming an Olympic event since 1896
2. Swimming contests believed held in Japan as early as the 1st century B.C.
3. Organized competitive swimming, beginning in England, in 1840s
4. To ancient Greeks and Romans, swimming a major part of military training programs
5. Crawl stroke often used in competition freestyle events
   —chest down, one arm extended forward out of water, arm below surface making pulling movement
   —flutter kick
6. Backstroke used in competition
   —swimmer on back, one arm out of the water to complete stroke, other arm in water for forward-pulling motion
   —flutter kick
7. Breast stroke used in competition
   —chest down in water, hands carried together forward from under the chest to full extension, then swept back in lateral plane, parallel to body
   —both legs drawn up, knees bent, each turned outward, then thrust back parallel to line of body
   —breast stroke kick

each step is to write an essay and to share each stage with the class.

Have students keep all their notes from each of the stages of the writing process. Use the notes and the completed compositions to evaluate students' mastery of the writing process.

To close, ask students to share the steps they had difficulty with in writing their compositions and to name the steps they thought were easy. ■

8. Winners of competitions determined by best elapsed time
9. Predetermined distance
10. 7 gold medals in swimming won by Mark Spitz at 1972 Olympics
11. Olympic events for both individual and team swimming, including the medley and relay

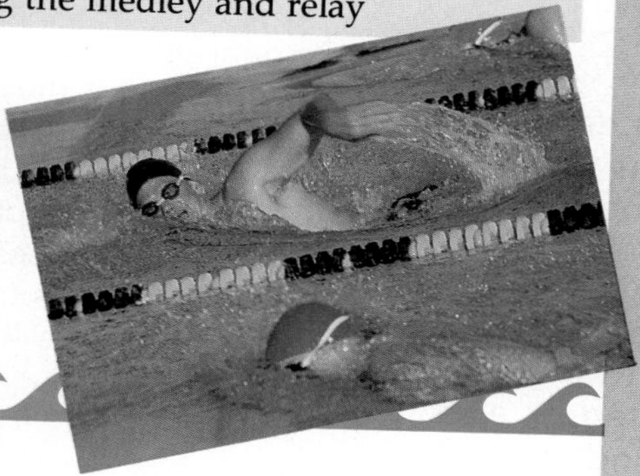

Prewriting. You may not use all the information supplied, but be sure you have enough to write a brief informative composition. If you want to add other information from personal knowledge or research, do so, but limit your topic so that it can be covered in a short paper. Then decide on a thesis statement that expresses your main idea, and create an early plan.

Writing, Evaluating, and Revising. Use your early plan to guide your writing. Start writing by using one of the introduction techniques (pages 112–115). When you write the body, be sure to emphasize the most important ideas. Keep your thesis in mind, but don't let it become a straitjacket. Write a conclusion that ties your information together (see pages 119–120). Set your paper aside and then compare it to the framework on page 121 in order to evaluate and revise it, working to achieve unity and coherence.

Proofreading and Publishing. When you've revised your paper, read it again to look for errors in grammar, usage, and mechanics. Exchange papers with a classmate and proofread each other's compositions, using the proofreading guidelines on pages 50–51. Make a clean, final copy of your paper and share it with someone interested in competitive swimming.

ADVANCED STUDENTS

You may want to have students use additional information in their essays. Give students time to use the library to locate additional and updated information about competitive swimming. They also could interview some sports experts or competitive swimmers.

AT-RISK STUDENTS

If students are not interested in the subject matter of **"Swimming for the Gold,"** you could let them get together in small groups to brainstorm lists of ideas for topics that would be more interesting for them. Allow each student to choose a topic he or she would prefer to write about. Even though using new topics will involve more work in the form of research, some students will work more effectively on topics of their choice.

Chapter 4

EXPRESSIVE WRITING

OBJECTIVES

- To respond to and analyze an expressive literary model
- To choose an experience for a personal essay
- To recall, arrange, and evaluate details for a personal essay
- To write a draft of a personal essay
- To analyze a writer's revisions
- To evaluate and revise a draft of a personal essay
- To proofread and publish a personal essay
- To plan, draft, evaluate, revise, proofread, and publish a personal anecdote
- To research and report on an instance of group self-expression in history
- To write personal goal statements

Motivation

The kind of personal essay that this chapter deals with has long been a staple on applications of many kinds. Collect as many application forms that require personal essays as you can from colleges and businesses. Bring the application forms to class and pass them around. Point out to your students that colleges and employers include personal essays for two reasons: to find out more about the applicant and to find out how well the applicant can write. Tell your students that a good personal essay has to be written in a way that shows how the writer learned from his or her experience. This chapter will take students through the complete process of writing a personal essay.

Introduction

This chapter starts with the important task of selecting a personal experience to write about. Many students feel that a good personal essay must be based on some life-or-death event, but, as the example in the **Writing Note** (p. 130) illustrates, even mundane occurrences can be significant. The rest of the chapter takes students through the writing process in an orderly and systematic manner.

Integration

Personal essays are generally written in informal language, so you may want to refer to the section on informal usage in **Chapter 13: "Style in Writing."**

The material in this chapter will be useful to students if they give expressive speeches for language arts or social studies classes.

The techniques students learn for analyzing expressive writing will be helpful when they study a literary unit that includes expressive writing such as letters, autobiographies, diaries, and journals.

The chart on the next page illustrates the strands of language arts as they are integrated into this chapter. For vocabulary study, glossary words are underlined in some writing models.

QUOTATIONS
All **Quotations for the Day** are chosen because of their relevance to instructional material presented in that segment of the chapter and for their usefulness in establishing student interest in writing.

INTEGRATING THE LANGUAGE ARTS

Selection	Reading and Literature	Writing and Critical Thinking	Language and Syntax	Speaking, Listening, and Other Expression Skills
A letter written by Major Sullivan Ballou to his wife **126-127** **"I Behold America"** by Edward Corsi **138-142** from ***I Wonder as I Wander*** by Langston Hughes **152-153**	Responding personally to literature **128, 143, 153** Analyzing an author's attitude **128, 143, 153** Identifying sensory details **143, 153** Evaluating organization in a personal essay **143** Analyzing the effectiveness of paragraphs **143** Identifying foreshadowing **153** Analyzing an anecdote **153**	Responding personally to literature **128, 143, 153** Writing a journal entry **128, 156-157** Applying interpretive and creative thinking **128, 131, 143, 150, 153, 155, 156-157** Recalling and choosing an experience for a personal essay **131** Evaluating audience response **132-133** Recalling and arranging details for a personal essay **135** Reflecting on the meaning of experience **135** Evaluating details **137, 143, 153** Evaluating organization in a personal essay **143** Analyzing the effectiveness of paragraphs **143** Writing a draft of a personal essay **147** Analyzing a writer's revisions **150** Evaluating and revising **150, 154** Proofreading and publishing **151, 154** Analyzing an anecdote **153** Writing an anecdote **154** Researching group self-expression in history **155** Writing personal goal statements **156-157**	Proofreading for errors in grammar, usage, and mechanics **151, 153, 154**	Sharing personal experiences with classmates **131** Working with classmates to evaluate audience response **132-133** Working with classmates to evaluate details in a paragraph **137** Working with a classmate to evaluate and revise a personal essay **150** Researching with classmates and reporting the results orally **155**

CHAPTER 4

SEGMENT PLANNING GUIDE

You can use the following Planning Guide to adapt the chapter material to the individual needs of your class. All the Resources listed in this chapter are located in the *Teacher's ResourceBank*™.

SEGMENT	PAGES	CONTENT	RESOURCES
1 ***Discovering Yourself***	***125-128***		
Literary Model A letter written by Major Sullivan Ballou to his wife	126-127	Guided reading: a model of expressive writing	
Reader's Response/Writer's Craft	128	Model evaluation: responding to literature and analyzing expressive writing	
2 ***Ways to Express Yourself***	***129***		
3 ***Prewriting***	***130-137***		Writing a Personal Essay Collecting Details 42
Choosing a Personal Experience	130	Guidelines: selecting an experience to write about	
Exercise 1	131	Applied practice: drawing on a personal experience	
Writing Assignment: Part 1	131	Applied practice: choosing an experience	
Thinking About Purpose, Audience, and Tone	132	Guidelines: analyzing and selecting appropriate purpose, audience, and tone	
Exercise 2	132-133	Cooperative learning: surveying reader response	
Recalling Details	133-134	Guidelines: using strategies to recall details	
Arranging Details	134-135	Guidelines: using appropriate order	
Writing Assignment: Part 2	135	Applied practice: recalling and arranging details	
Reflecting on the Meaning of the Experience	135-136	Guidelines: using criteria for reflecting	
Critical Thinking: Evaluating Details	136-137	Guielines: using criteria to evaluate details	
Critical Thinking Exercise	137	Applied practice: evaluating details	
4 ***Writing***	***138-147***		Writing a Personal Essay 43
The Structure of Your Personal Essay	138	Guidelines: writing an introduction, body, and conclusion	
Literary Model **"I Behold America"**	138-142	Guided reading: examining the structure of a personal essay	
Exercise 3	143	Cooperative learning: analyzing a personal essay	
A Basic Framework for a Personal Essay	143	Introduction: analyzing the structure of a personal essay	
A Writer's Model	143-146	Guided reading: analyzing structure in a student model	
Chart: Framework for a Personal Essay	147	Guidelines: structuring a personal essay	
Writing Assignment: Part 3	147	Applied practice: writing a first draft	

For **Portfolio Assessment** see the following pages in the *Teacher's ResourceBank*™:
Aims For Writing — pp. 41–46
Holistically Graded Composition Models — pp. 485–490
Assessment Portfolio — pp. 533–562

	SEGMENT	PAGES	CONTENT	RESOURCES
5	*Evaluating and Revising*	*148-150*		Writing a Personal Essay 44
	Evaluating and Revising	148	Introduction: evaluating and revising	
	Chart: Evaluating and Revising	149	Guidelines: applying evaluation and revision techniques	
	Exercise 4	150	Cooperative learning: analyzing a writer's revisions	
	Writing Assignment: Part 4	150	Cooperative learning: evaluating and revising	
6	*Proofreading and Publishing*	*151*		Writing a Personal Essay 45
	Publishing	151	Publishing ideas: reaching a specific audience	
	Mechanics Hint	151	Guidelines: punctuating dialogue	
	Writing Assignment: Part 5	151	Applied practice: proofreading and publishing	
7	*Writing Workshop*	*152-154*		
	Relating an Anecdote	152	Explanation: writing a personal anecdote	
	Literary Model/Questions from ***I Wonder as I Wander***	152-153	Examining techniques: analyzing a sample letter	
	Writing an Anecdote	154	Applied practice: applying skills to the writing process	
8	*Making Connections*	*155-157*		
	Writing Across the Curriculum: Group Self-Expression in History	155-156	Cooperative learning: researching and presenting a report	
	Self-Expression and the Future: Setting Goals	156-157	Applied practice: using criteria to write personal goal statements	

WHOLE-CHAPTER RESOURCES
A Writing Process Log, A Writing Prompt, Holistically Graded Models, Assessment Portfolio Materials

SEGMENT 1 *(pp. 124–128)*

DISCOVERING YOURSELF

OBJECTIVES

- To respond personally to a selection of expressive writing
- To analyze the expressive qualities of a literary model

TEACHING THE LESSON

Before you have students read the excerpt from Major Ballou's letter, ask them to imagine how they would feel approaching a piece of writing that might be their last communication with someone they love very much. Would they write about details of everyday life or about their feelings? What

VISUAL CONNECTIONS
Irises

About the Artist. Vincent van Gogh was born in the Netherlands in 1853. He did not begin painting until he was twenty-seven years old, and until then he had trouble succeeding in other occupations. Van Gogh started art studies in the Dutch city The Hague. For the next six years he painted in Holland until he moved to Paris at the age of thirty-three. Van Gogh's brother Theo directed an art gallery there that dealt in impressionist paintings; Gauguin, who influenced van Gogh greatly, was among the artists represented by Theo.

Van Gogh went to Arles in southern France in 1888. While he painted some of his most expressive and original works there, he also suffered from epileptic seizures and mental instability.

In 1889 van Gogh admitted himself to the hospital of Saint Pol at Saint-Rémy for treatment of his mental illness. There he continued to develop the imaginative, visionary style that he is noted for. After a year, van Gogh left the hospital and returned to Paris. In despair of ever being able to be cured, he committed suicide.

Although van Gogh is considered an impressionist painter, his work differs from that of other impressionists. While his contemporaries were painting realistic subjects in an expressive style, van Gogh adapted impressionist techniques to paint what he imagined, referring only indirectly to reality.

4 EXPRESSIVE WRITING

kind of impressions would they want to leave with their loved ones?

Point out that although the style of the letter beginning on p. 126 might seem rather formal and distant, during the era of the Civil War this style was considered normal and appropriate. You can also point out that students may have to reread the letter several times to get the full impact of Major Ballou's emotion.

Vincent van Gogh, *Irises,* (1889), Dutch, 1853–1890. Oil on canvas. 28" × 36 ⅝". Collection of the J. Paul Getty Museum, Malibu, CA.

Discovering Yourself

Some discoveries, like that of a planet beyond this solar system, make world news. What you **discover about yourself** through expressive writing probably won't make headlines. But it's important in its own way.

Writing and You. A man drafts a document that reflects the feelings of his fellow citizens two hundred years later. A woman, calling for the freedom of all people, writes her story. Both people expressed their thoughts and feelings in writing. When have you written to express yourself?

As You Read. In the following letter, written in 1861, a major in the Union Army during the Civil War expresses his thoughts and feelings. What are they?

QUOTATION FOR THE DAY

"So when I was a little boy, I loved listening to my old people. The other little guys would go out and play around together, but I would go sit with the old people and listen to them." (Wallace H. Black Elk, Lakota shaman)

Ask students to focus on the earliest memories they have of their "old people." Can they remember what they heard, felt, and saw? Ask students to write two or three sentences about their memories.

MEETING INDIVIDUAL NEEDS

LEP/ESL

General Strategies. In some cultures, children are taught to be close-mouthed, to keep their feelings to themselves. Students from such cultures may have difficulty sharing personal experiences with their classmates. The difficulty will probably be greater in group or class discussions than it will be in writing. To offer a possible strategy for sharing personal experiences, suggest that students relate events as if the events were from a movie or story.

GUIDED PRACTICE

To guide students through the process of personal response, you could have a class discussion of question 1 in **Reader's Response.** Then to model a response to the **Writer's Craft** questions, guide students through question 3.

INDEPENDENT PRACTICE

Assign question 2 in **Reader's Response** and question 4 in **Writer's Craft** for independent practice.

USING THE SELECTION

A letter written by Major Sullivan Ballou to his wife

1
How many times does the writer use first person pronouns, a characteristic feature of expressive writing? [He uses them more than forty times.]

2
Lest: in case

3
impelled: urged

4
The use in this paragraph and throughout the letter of words and phrases with strong connotations is characteristic of expressive writing.

5
the Revolution: American Revolutionary War

6
The writer touches on the conflict between his love for his wife and his love for his country.

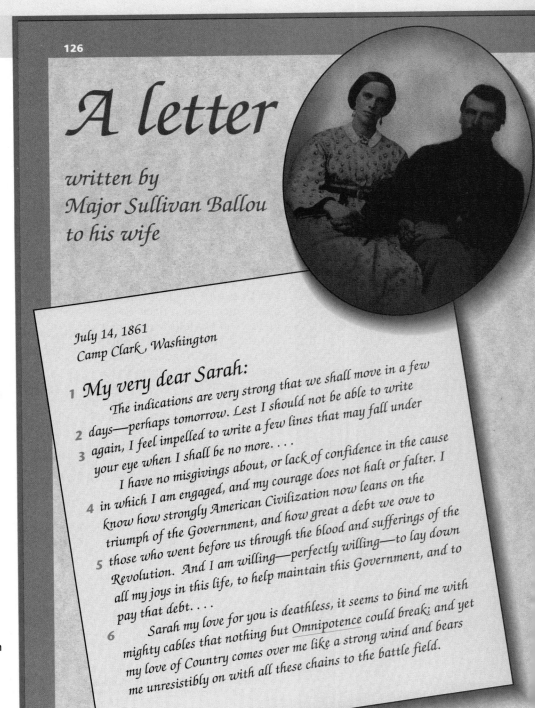

A letter

written by Major Sullivan Ballou to his wife

July 14, 1861
Camp Clark, Washington

1 *My very dear Sarah:*
The indications are very strong that we shall move in a few
2 *days—perhaps tomorrow. Lest I should not be able to write*
3 *again, I feel impelled to write a few lines that may fall under*
your eye when I shall be no more. . . .
I have no misgivings about, or lack of confidence in the cause
4 *in which I am engaged, and my courage does not halt or falter. I*
know how strongly American Civilization now leans on the
triumph of the Government, and how great a debt we owe to
5 *those who went before us through the blood and sufferings of the*
Revolution. And I am willing—perfectly willing—to lay down
all my joys in this life, to help maintain this Government, and to
pay that debt. . . .
6 *Sarah my love for you is deathless, it seems to bind me with*
mighty cables that nothing but Omnipotence could break; and yet
my love of Country comes over me like a strong wind and bears
me unresistibly on with all these chains to the battle field.

ASSESSMENT

Assess students' performance by evaluating how they answer the questions in **Reader's Response** and **Writer's Craft.**

CLOSURE

Have students help you summarize what Ballou reveals or implies concerning his feelings about the war, his chances for survival, and his relationship with his wife.

7 *The memories of the blissful moments I have spent with you come creeping over me, and I feel most gratified to God and to you that I have enjoyed them so long. And hard it is for me to give them up and burn to ashes the hopes of future years, when, God willing, we might still have lived and loved together, and*
8 *seen our sons grown up to honorable manhood, around us. I have, I know, but few and small claims upon Divine Providence, but something whispers to me—perhaps it is the wafted prayer of my little Edgar, that I shall return to my loved ones unharmed. If I do not my dear Sarah, never forget how much I love you, and when my last breath escapes me on the battle field, it will whisper your name. Forgive my many faults, and the many pains I have caused you. How thoughtless and foolish I have often times been! How gladly would I wash out with my tears every little spot upon your happiness. . . .*

But, O Sarah! if the dead can come back to this earth and flit unseen around those they loved, I shall always be near you; in the gladdest days and in the darkest nights . . . always, always, and if there be a soft breeze upon your cheek, it shall be my breath, as the cool air fans your throbbing temple, it shall be my spirit passing by. Sarah do not mourn me dead; think I am gone and wait for thee, for we shall meet again. . . .

". . . I feel impelled to write a few lines that may fall under your eye when I shall be no more. . . ."

7

The use of words that express feeling is characteristic of expressive writing.

8

Although Ballou says here that he thinks he will survive the war, the tone and purpose of his letter show that he knows his death is a strong possibility.

SELECTION AMENDMENT
Description of change: excerpted
Rationale: to focus on the concept of expressive writing presented in this chapter

ENRICHMENT

War letters are often very moving because they tell the real story of the impact of war on the lives of individuals. Ask your school librarian to help you find published collections of war letters, and read some of these to your class. ■

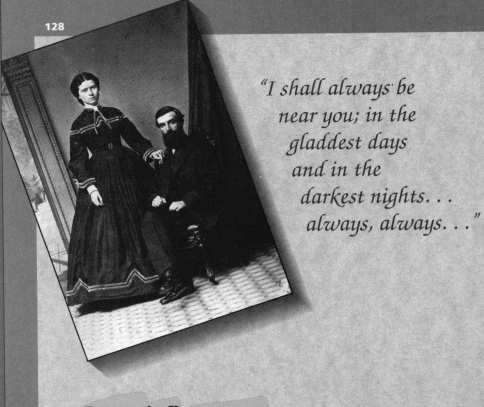

"I shall always be near you; in the gladdest days and in the darkest nights. . . always, always. . ."

READER'S RESPONSE

1. Major Ballou was killed at the first battle of Bull Run shortly after he wrote this letter. How does this knowledge affect the way you feel about the letter?
2. After reading the letter, what thoughts and feelings do you have about war? Write a short entry in your journal about Major Ballou's words.

WRITER'S CRAFT

3. Writers of personal expression may reveal their thoughts directly, or they may suggest them indirectly. How does Ballou feel about the cause for which he is fighting?
4. How does Ballou feel about his chances for survival? What direct statements does he make that reveal this feeling? What does he say that suggests the feeling?

ANSWERS

Reader's Response

1. Most students will probably feel that knowing Ballou died at Bull Run adds poignancy to his letter.
2. Journal entries should focus on personal thoughts and feelings about war, including, perhaps, the possibility that the students themselves may one day be involved in military conflict.

Writer's Craft

3. Ballou feels completely committed to the cause for which he is fighting.
4. In the fourth paragraph Ballou directly states that something "whispers" to him that he will "return . . . unharmed." However, throughout the letter, in his direct references to death and the afterlife and in the tone he uses, it is clear that he realizes there is a strong possibility he won't survive.

SEGMENT 2 *(p. 129)*

WAYS TO EXPRESS YOURSELF

TEACHING THE MODES

Have a volunteer read this page aloud. Then discuss each of the four modes and have students give additional examples of how each mode could be used with the expressive aim. ■

Ways to Express Yourself

Personal expression is all around you—in letters (like the one written by Major Ballou), poems, articles, books, and even greeting cards. There are many ways to express your thoughts and feelings in writing. Here are four ways you can express yourself.

Narration: telling a friend about a humorous incident that happened on a family trip; in your journal, recounting a disappointing experience at school.

Description: describing the unsettling chaos and unfriendliness of your new room after your family moves to a different house; in a song lyric, describing your most cherished possession and its importance to you.

Classification: in a journal entry, comparing your thoughts on starting school this year with your thoughts on starting school last year; in an informal discussion, exploring your thoughts about the advantages and disadvantages of teenagers' working part time.

Evaluation: in your journal, noting what you have learned by being on the debate team; in an essay, exploring the benefits you feel you have gained from being an only child.

LOOKING AHEAD

In the main assignment in this chapter, you'll use the strategies of evaluation and narration to develop a personal essay. As you work through the writing assignment, keep in mind that a personal essay

- tells about an important experience in your life
- uses specific narrative and descriptive details to make the experience seem real
- gradually reveals the full significance of the experience

CRITICAL THINKING

Analysis

Have students analyze the letter from Ballou to his wife to determine what mode it is written in. Have them explain the reasons for their choice. [The letter is written primarily in the descriptive mode. Ballou describes his feelings. He also uses classification when he compares and contrasts his feelings for his country with his feelings for his wife.]

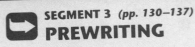

SEGMENT 3 *(pp. 130–137)*

PREWRITING

OBJECTIVES

- To draw on personal experience for ideas for a personal essay
- To choose an experience for a personal essay
- To survey reader response by speaking and listening in a group
- To recall and arrange details for a personal essay

Teacher's ResourceBank™

RESOURCES

PREWRITING

- Collecting Details 42

QUOTATION FOR THE DAY

"If every time you sat down, you expected something great, writing would always be a great disappointment." (Natalie Goldberg, American writer, poet, and teacher)

Ask students to discuss their reactions to this quotation. Remind students that even writing efforts that don't produce great literary masterpieces can give valuable practice in writing.

MEETING INDIVIDUAL NEEDS

LEP/ESL

General Strategies. For **Exercise 1** and **Writing Assignment: Part 1,** if you have students who have immigrated to the United States, suggest that they consider writing about how they have adjusted to their new country. Many things that may now seem ordinary were once new and strange to them. If you encourage them to think back to those first days and weeks, they will discover an abundance of personal experiences that will make interesting personal essays.

Writing a Personal Essay

Prewriting

Choosing a Personal Experience

Time changes you physically; experience changes you mentally and emotionally. Taking a look back over past experiences can give you fresh insights on how you've changed and developed over time. A journal or diary can be an excellent source for reviewing your important life experiences. If you don't keep a journal, use your powers of memory to call up your past. Then you can settle on an experience to explore further through your writing by asking yourself

- *What "feels important"? What experiences have played a part in forming or revealing the "real me"?* Some experiences come to mind immediately when you start reviewing what's been important in making you who you are.
- *What do I remember vividly?* If you can remember an event "like it happened yesterday," chances are it's important, even if you don't realize it—yet!
- *What's not too private to share?* Some experiences need to remain just with you, their significance explored only within your diary or journal entries. Others, however, may bloom with meaning when exposed to "the light of day."

WRITING NOTE

To qualify as "important," an experience need not be a dramatic life-and-death situation. Henry David Thoreau, for example, hoed a field of beans and discovered something about the importance of work. As Thoreau reflected on this discovery, he was able to craft some memorable writing about his experience. So don't discount your experience in art class or in sports as trivial or unimportant. Any experience—as long as it feels significant to you—can be the starting point for your personal essay. And if the experience was important to you, chances are it will be for others, too.

TEACHING THE LESSON

Explain to students that their task for this chapter will be to choose personal experiences and to plan personal essays based on those experiences. Have a volunteer read the introductory material, and then guide students through the first prompt in **Exercise 1.** Let the class finish **Exercise 1** as independent practice, and then, to give them guided practice for **Writing Assignment: Part 1,** model for them the process of exploring a list of experiences to discover aspects that could be developed into personal essays. Assign **Writing Assignment: Part 1** as independent practice.

Read aloud **Planning Your Personal Essay** on p. 132 and stress the importance of using a conversational tone and ☛

EXERCISE 1 **Drawing on Personal Experience**

What were you like last week, last month, last year, five years ago? Call up a variety of past experiences by completing each of the following sentence beginnings one or more times. How would you have finished the sentence when you were ten? Would you finish it differently today? Share your responses with a small group of classmates.

1. I never felt prouder than when . . .
2. A person who has really influenced me is . . .
3. Looking back, I wish I had . . .
4. Somehow I felt different after . . .

WRITING ASSIGNMENT PART 1: **Choosing an Experience for a Personal Essay**

What experiences made you the person you are today? Look over your collection of experiences from Exercise 1 (above) and select one to write about in your personal essay. Use the questions on page 130 as a guide in making your choice.

A DIFFERENT APPROACH

When students work **Exercise 1,** you may want to add a few more incomplete statements to stimulate their recall. You can write these on the chalkboard:

5. The funniest thing that ever happened to me was . . .
6. My most embarrassing moment was . . .
7. The happiest moment of my life was . . .
8. The most dangerous thing that ever happened to me was . . .
9. I never realized how well off I am until . . .
10. I've never been as scared as when . . .

ANSWERS

Exercise 1

Suggest to students that they read the first prompt and then close their eyes and take a couple of deep breaths and see what comes to mind. Have students quickly write anything they think of and then have them go on to the next prompt. After they have gone through all the prompts, they could repeat the process to see what further experiences they might call up.

informal language in personal essays. To guide students through **Exercise 2,** have a student share her or his experience with the class and give your responses to the three questions. Divide the class into small groups and have the groups complete **Exercise 2** as independent practice.

Have a volunteer read aloud the paragraphs on **Recalling Details.** Next, have students visualize the experiences they have chosen. After students have recalled their scenes completely and while the details are fresh in their minds, have them jot down notes on what they recalled.

Have students read the paragraphs on **Arranging Details** on pp. 134–135. Using an experience of your own, model for the class the process of arranging three or four

CRITICAL THINKING

Analysis

Unless you have a particular audience in mind for your students to write for, you may want to suggest that they assume the audience for their essays will be the other members of their class. They can use the following questions to analyze this audience with respect to their topics:

1. Will this experience interest my classmates?
2. Will I have to use technical terms the audience probably doesn't know? How can I define the terms in my essay?
3. Will my essay depend on my audience's having a detailed mental picture of a person, place, or thing?

ANSWERS

Exercise 2

You may want to have students take notes on their reactions to their fellow students' presentations. Then, as they use the notes to give their responses, have the presenters take notes so they can use the feedback in planning their essays.

Prewriting

Planning Your Personal Essay

After reading or hearing about your classmates' experiences, you may have thought *I've been in a similar situation* or *I know exactly what she means.* You'll be aiming for this type of response from your readers. However, achieving it requires careful thought and planning.

Thinking About Purpose, Audience, and Tone

Your main *purpose* for writing a personal essay is to express and explore your thoughts and feelings. You may also feel that it's important to share your experience and its meaning with others or to leave a record of your experience behind you.

Because writing a personal essay is a discovery process—you often discover the meaning of the experience as you write—your first *audience* will be yourself. Keep in mind, though, the wider audience who will read your essay. What information will they need to understand the experience? How will you reveal its importance to them?

A personal essay includes *your* thoughts and feelings, so you should write in your own natural *voice.* Write in the first person, using *I, me, our,* and *we,* and use everyday vocabulary and sentence structure to create a natural, conversational *tone.*

EXERCISE 2 **Speaking and Listening: Surveying Reader Response**

An ancient Chinese poet put his exquisite verses into a stream and watched them float away, never to be read by others. Your personal essay, however, will be read by others; and their response is important. This exercise will help you get an early response to the experience you chose to write about.

Get together with two or three classmates and take turns presenting and responding. As a "presenter," briefly review the events of your experience and your feelings about it. Then listen closely to your classmates' responses. As a "responder," events in order and of filling in the narrative and descriptive details. Then assign **Writing Assignment: Part 2** on p. 135 as independent practice. To finish the segment, read and discuss with the class **Reflecting on the Meaning of the Experience** on p. 135.

ASSESSMENT

Use students' responses to **Exercises 1** and **2** and **Writing Assignment: Parts 1** and **2** as the basis of your assessment of students' work in this segment.

listen carefully to each classmate's presentation, and ask yourself the following questions. Share your answers with each presenter in your group.

1. Have I ever had a similar experience? If so, how were my feelings similar or different?
2. What specific question(s) do I have about events in this particular experience?
3. After hearing a brief summary of the experience, what else do I want to know?

Recalling Details

By the time you have thought about purpose, audience, and tone, you probably will have remembered many things about your experience. At this point in the process, you can use your memory to "travel back in time" to recall and record details that will show readers your experience. As you do, you may gain fresh insights for yourself as well. To take yourself back in time, try these strategies:

- Close your eyes and visualize the scene, replaying the events in your mind.
- Talk with others who shared the experience with you.
- Return to the place where the experience happened.
- Use a memory prompt. You may have a particular reminder of the experience—perhaps a photograph, a ribbon, a ticket stub, or a song.

MEETING **INDIVIDUAL** NEEDS

LEARNING STYLES

Visual Learners. Some visual learners may have trouble making a presentation to a small group without using notes. You can suggest that for **Exercise 2** they write down brief outlines of their ideas to use when they tell the others in their groups about their experiences.

ADVANCED STUDENTS

Have students consult books on composition theory to find out in more detail what the characteristics of expressive writing are. Ask each student to analyze two or three selections of expressive writing for these characteristics and to take notes on how many of the characteristics occur in the selections. Then have students compare their findings in a group discussion.

CLOSURE

Have each student list the purpose, audience, and tone for his or her personal essay. Have students name three ways events can be arranged in personal essays [chronological order, spatial order, and order of importance].

ENRICHMENT

Most biographies and autobiographies contain numerous passages that are basically personal essays. One such passage in Chapter 11 of Russell Baker's autobiography *Growing Up* is about buying his first suit with long pants. You may want to read the passage aloud in class. You could ask students to locate interesting passages from

MEETING **INDIVIDUAL** NEEDS

STUDENTS WITH SPECIAL NEEDS

Because learning disabled students sometimes have problems with chronological order, you may want to pair them with other students who can prompt them as they tell their stories by asking questions such as "Then what happened?" Have students make notes as they relate their experiences to their partners.

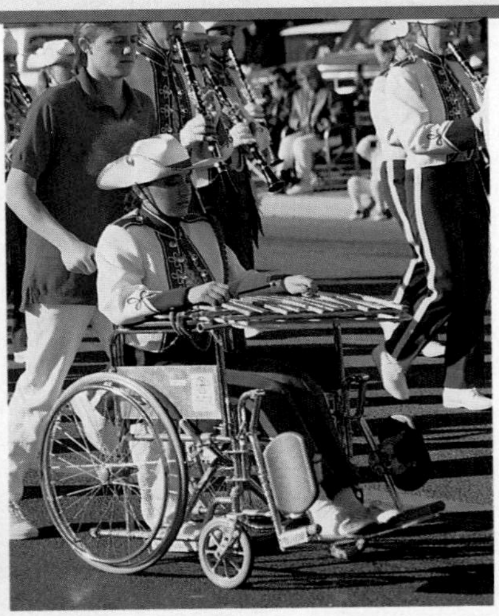

Once you're back in time, you need to record details that will help your readers understand the experience and its meaning. ***Narrative details*** tell about specific events and actions: *I stumbled clumsily into the room. There, in the glare of the spotlight, I stood on stage, absolutely alone and absolutely speechless.* They may suggest or reveal thoughts and feelings: *I stared blankly into the air, uncomfortably aware that three hundred pairs of eyes were riveted on me.* Narrative details often include ***dialogue,*** the exact words of the speaker. ***Descriptive,*** or ***sensory, details*** appeal to the five senses and describe important people, places, and objects.

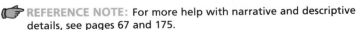

REFERENCE NOTE: For more help with narrative and descriptive details, see pages 67 and 175.

Arranging Details

Details in a personal essay are often arranged in ***chronological,*** or time, ***order.*** Sometimes, in order to heighten interest, writers begin with a particularly dramatic event and then relate earlier events that led up to it, but you may need to arrange details in other biographies and to share the passages with the class. ■

other ways as well. If you're describing a place or a person, for example, you may need to arrange details *spatially* or in *order of importance*.

The following chart shows how one writer recorded some of the details she recalled about a summer experience. Notice that the events are arranged in chronological order.

HERE'S HOW

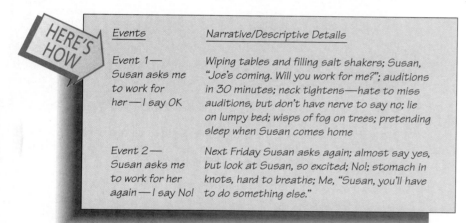

Events	*Narrative/Descriptive Details*
Event 1—Susan asks me to work for her—I say OK	*Wiping tables and filling salt shakers; Susan, "Joe's coming. Will you work for me?"; auditions in 30 minutes; neck tightens—hate to miss auditions, but don't have nerve to say no; lie on lumpy bed; wisps of fog on trees; pretending sleep when Susan comes home*
Event 2—Susan asks me to work for her again—I say No!	*Next Friday Susan asks again; almost say yes, but look at Susan, so excited; No!; stomach in knots, hard to breathe; Me, "Susan, you'll have to do something else."*

REFERENCE NOTE: For more help on arranging ideas, see pages 75–77.

WRITING ASSIGNMENT

PART 2:
Recalling and Arranging Details

In a chart like the one above, jot down the narrative and descriptive details you remember and arrange the events in the order you plan to present them. Then use at least one of the ideas on page 133 to "go back in time," reliving your experience in your memory. Add to your chart any other details you recall.

Reflecting on the Meaning of the Experience

A successful personal essay requires both the short and the long view. Recalling details has already given you the short view: an up-close examination of what happened and of the people, places, and objects that were a part of the experience.

INTEGRATING THE LANGUAGE ARTS

Study Skills Link. To help students gather more details to use in their essays, have them make charts more detailed than the one in the textbook. In one column they can list events in the order in which the events occurred. In the second column they can list the feelings each event elicited. In a third column they can list descriptive or sensory details. Point out that describing the setting in vivid detail and revealing their feelings about the experiences can also make the essays interesting and revealing.

CRITICAL THINKING
(pp. 136–137)

OBJECTIVE
- To evaluate details for a personal essay

TEACHING *EVALUATING DETAILS*
Because some students may not have a clear understanding of the meaning of *criteria,* explain that criteria are rules or standards for judging something.

The **Critical Thinking Exercise** can be used to assess students' ability to evaluate details. You may want to base your assessment on students' decisions to delete or

A DIFFERENT APPROACH
Explain to students that an additional criterion they should use to evaluate details involves length. Details should be described in an amount of space that is in proportion to their importance. In other words, lengthy or complicated details are inappropriate unless they are very important.

Now it's time to take the long view, to take a step back from the experience in order to understand its importance. Look at this experience as you are today and ask

- *What have I learned about myself or others from the experience?*
- *How did the experience cause me to change or to think differently about things?*
- *How have my goals changed as a result of this experience?*

At first, you may not fully understand what the experience has meant to you. As you plan and draft your essay, however, you will need to reflect on its meaning. Answering questions like the ones you have just read can help you do this.

CRITICAL THINKING
Evaluating Details

When you ***evaluate,*** you judge the value of something against a set of criteria. When your teacher evaluates your research paper, for example, he or she uses criteria like documentation of sources and clarity of thesis. When you're trying to decide which details to include in a personal essay, you must also use the critical-thinking skill of evaluation. You need to judge, using the following criteria, whether the details retain details and on their reasons for each decision.

Deciding to keep or cut details is closely related to the concept of unity in a composition. You may want to review the material on unity in **Chapter 2: "Understanding Paragraph Structure"** and **Chapter 3: "Understanding Composition Structure."**

- help to make the experience clear to the reader
- help make the experience seem real to the reader
- contribute to the experience's overall meaning

CRITICAL THINKING EXERCISE:
Evaluating Details for a Personal Essay

The following paragraph is part of a personal essay that tells how the writer learned to overcome his fears and trust his own instincts. As you read it, pay special attention to the four sets of underlined details. Then use the three criteria above to determine whether the underlined details are important. Identify the details that should be cut from the paragraph and those which should be kept. Share your comments with your classmates.

I had never told anyone about my secret dream to be another track and field star like Carl Lewis, not even my mom and dad. [1] <u>I thought they'd laugh at me.</u> [2] <u>My dad is a big tease and he laughs at everything I do.</u> I could hardly believe I had the nerve to think about going out for the varsity track team. But that Monday, just as I was trying to figure out what to take home out of my locker, my best friend, José, came running down the hall. [3] <u>I remember he almost ran into our science teacher.</u> It was 2:20; the team tryouts started in ten minutes, [4] <u>just time for me to change my shoes and run to the field.</u>

ANSWERS

Critical Thinking Exercise

1. Keep this detail because it meets the first and second criteria.
2. Cut this detail because it meets none of the three criteria. It distracts the reader from the topic.
3. Cut this detail because it is irrelevant to the topic.
4. Keep this detail because it meets the first and second criteria.

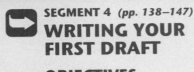

SEGMENT 4 *(pp. 138–147)*

WRITING YOUR FIRST DRAFT

OBJECTIVES

- To analyze a professional model of a personal essay
- To write a draft of a personal essay

MOTIVATION

The opening literary model of this segment deals with the arrival of a shipload of Italian immigrants at Ellis Island. You may want to discuss the role Ellis Island played in the great migration of Europeans to the United States between 1892 and 1954. It is estimated that 40 percent of the people now living in this country are descended from

Teacher's ResourceBank™

RESOURCES

WRITING YOUR FIRST DRAFT

- Writing a Personal Essay 43

QUOTATION FOR THE DAY

"A poem, a sentence, causes us to see ourselves. I be, and I see myself being, at the same time." (Ralph Waldo Emerson, 1803–1882, American poet, essayist, and philosopher)

Write the quotation on the chalkboard and ask students to freewrite about its meaning. Then have the class share its ideas on how the quotation applies to writing an expressive essay.

USING THE SELECTION

***from* I Behold America**

1

Starting with the first word, first-person pronouns are used frequently throughout this passage. This use of first-person pronouns is characteristic of expressive writing.

Writing Your First Draft

Have you ever watched a photograph slowly develop? Outlines, shapes, and highlights appear first, and then, as the process continues, images become sharper and clearer and shadows fill up until the picture is complete. Your personal essay should develop just like a photo.

The Structure of Your Personal Essay

Like other compositions, a personal essay includes an introduction, a body, and a conclusion. Unlike some other types of essays, however, its main idea—the meaning of the experience—is not directly stated in the *introduction.* Instead, the introduction only hints at the meaning. Most of these introductions do, however, give background information that readers need to understand the experience.

Each part of the *body* develops a related event and contributes to the reader's understanding of the essay's unfolding meaning. The *conclusion* may reveal the final outcome of the events, or it may include a few reflective comments. Even at the end, the essay's main idea or meaning may be implied rather than directly stated. But, whether stated or implied, it should be clearly understood.

In the following personal essay, the writer witnesses the conflicting emotions of immigrants coming to this country. As you read, notice how each event reveals feelings of wonder and hope or fear and loss. What final realization does the writer come to about these opposite feelings?

A PASSAGE FROM AN AUTOBIOGRAPHY

from I Behold America

by Edward Corsi

INTRODUCTION
Hint about meaning

1 My first impressions of the new world will always remain etched in my memory, particularly that hazy October morning when I first people who entered the country through Ellis Island.

Your school librarian may be able to supply you with books or magazines that contain photographs of Ellis Island. The buildings on the island were completely restored in the 1980s, and the island was opened as a national museum of immigration by the National Park Service in 1990.

TEACHING THE LESSON

The passage from **"I Behold America"** contains powerful pictures of the hopes and fears of the people that it's about. After you have a volunteer read the passage aloud, you may want to lead the class in a discussion of its content. Ask students to consider how they would feel about moving ☛

Background information

Feelings

2 saw Ellis Island. The steamer *Florida*, fourteen
3 days out of Naples, filled to capacity with sixteen
hundred natives of Italy, had weathered one of the
worst storms in our captain's memory; and glad we
were, both children and grown-ups, to leave the
4 open sea and come at last through the Narrows
5 into the Bay.

Background information

Feelings

BODY
Event 1

Descriptive details

My mother, my stepfather, my brother Giuseppe, and my two sisters, Liberta and Helvetia, all of us together, happy that we had come through the storm safely, clustered on the foredeck for fear of separation and looked with wonder on this miraculous land of our dreams.

Giuseppe and I held tightly to stepfather's hands, while Liberta and Helvetia clung to mother. Passengers all about us were crowding against the rail. Jabbered conversation, sharp cries, laughs and cheers—a steadily rising din filled the air. Mothers and fathers lifted up the babies so that they too could see, off to the left, the Statue of Liberty.

2
Ellis Island: an island in New York City Harbor where immigrants were processed by the U.S. Immigration Service from 1892 to 1954

3
Naples: a city in southern Italy

4
Narrows: a narrow body of water that connects Upper and Lower New York Bay between Long Island and Staten Island

5
the Bay: Upper New York Bay, where Ellis Island is located

VISUAL CONNECTIONS

Exploring the Subject. Europeans immigrated to the United States by the millions between the middle of the nineteenth century and the middle of the twentieth century, and most of them came by ship. Approximately 16 million new Americans came through the Port of New York between 1892 and 1954, the period when Ellis Island was in operation as the point of entry on the eastern seaboard. About 25 percent of the immigrants were able to afford first- or second-class passage on ships, and these people were allowed to land at the docks in Manhattan. The rest—those too poor to pay for expensive accommodations aboard ship—were processed through Ellis Island.

to a new country where they didn't know the language and where they were unsure of finding jobs. If some students are recent immigrants, they will have memories of what it was like leaving their homes and moving to the United States. If you think they might be receptive to being in the limelight, have them share their experiences with the class.

You can provide guided practice for **Exercise 3** on p. 143 by working through the first item with the class. Point out that students will have to read closely and then reread to answer the questions.

Divide the class into groups and assign the rest of **Exercise 3** as independent practice.

6
Note the use here of suggestive words and phrases such as "enormous expression" and "a thousand memories." The use of words and figures of speech with strong connotations and associations is characteristic of expressive writing.

VISUAL CONNECTIONS

Exploring the Subject. The Statue of Liberty was given to the American people by the French in 1884 and is generally considered one of the most important symbols of the United States. It is located on tiny Liberty Island in Upper New York Bay, and ships bearing immigrants had to pass the statue on their way to port at Ellis Island. Hence, the Statue of Liberty was one of the first things newcomers saw when they arrived in this country.

Narrative details—Feelings

Unfolding meaning

I looked at that statue with a sense of bewilderment, half doubting its reality. Looming shadowy through the mist, it brought silence to the decks of *6* the *Florida*. This symbol of America—this enormous expression of what we had all been taught was the inner meaning of this new country we were coming to—inspired awe in the hopeful immigrants. Many older persons among us, burdened with a thousand memories of what they were leaving behind, had been openly weeping ever since we entered the narrower waters on our final approach toward the unknown. Now somehow steadied, I suppose, by the concreteness of the symbol of America's freedom, they dried their tears.

Remember Your First Thrill of
AMERICAN LIBERTY
YOUR DUTY-Buy
United States Government Bonds
2nd Liberty Loan of 1917
The Granger Collection, New York

Event 2

Descriptive details

Dialogue

Directly in front of the *Florida*, half visible in the faintly-colored haze, rose a second and even greater challenge to the imagination.

"Mountains!" I cried to Giuseppe. "Look at them!"

"They're strange," he said, "why don't they have snow on them?" He was craning his neck

You may want to have students read silently **A Writer's Model** (pp. 143–146). Then go back and read it aloud. As you read, stop often to point out how the basic framework for a personal essay is applied in the model.

You may want to model the process of writing an introduction to an essay, and then assign **Writing Assignment: Part 3** on p. 147 as independent practice. You could let students start their drafts in class so you can answer questions and provide suggestions.

and standing on tiptoe to stare at the New York skyline.

Narrative details

Stepfather looked toward the skyscrapers, and, smiling, assured us that they were not mountains but buildings—"the highest buildings in the world."

Descriptive details

On every side the harbor offered its marvels: tugs, barges, sloops, lighters, sluggish freighters and giant ocean liners—all moving in different directions, managing, by what seemed to us a miracle, to dart in and out and up and down without colliding with one another. They spoke to us through the varied sounds of their whistles, and the *Florida* replied with a deep echoing voice. Bells
7 clanged through our ship, precipitating a new flurry among our fellow-passengers. Many of these
8 people had come from provinces far distant from ours, and were shouting to one another in dialects strange to me. Everything combined to increase our excitement, and we rushed from deck to deck, fearful lest we miss the smallest detail of the spectacle.

Narrative details—Feelings

Event 3

Finally the *Florida* veered to the left, turning northward into the Hudson River, and now the incredible buildings of lower Manhattan came very close to us.

Narrative details

The officers of the ship, mighty and unapproachable beings they seemed to me, went striding up and down the decks shouting orders and directions and driving the immigrants before them. Scowling and gesturing, they pushed and pulled the passengers, herding us into separate groups as though we were animals. A few moments later we came to our dock, and the long journey was over.

A small boat, the *General Putnam* of the Immigration Service, carried us from the pier to Ellis Island. Luckily for us, we were among the first to be transferred to the tiny vessel, and so were spared the long ordeal of waiting that occasionally stretched, for some immigrants, into several days and nights.

7 **precipitating:** causing

8 **provinces:** geographical divisions similar to states

ASSESSMENT

Base your assessment of students' abilities to analyze a personal essay on how thoroughly they answer the questions in **Exercise 3.** Base your assessment of the drafts on how well students follow the framework shown in the chart on p. 147.

RETEACHING

If students are having trouble starting on their introductions, you may want to suggest they move to the body paragraphs of their essays and return to the introductions later. You can also have them record their essays on a tape recorder and use a transcript of the tape as a first draft.

Thoughts—Unfolding meaning

During this ride across the bay, as I watched the faces of the people milling about me, I realized that Ellis Island could inspire both hope and fear. Some of the passengers were afraid and obviously dreading the events of the next few hours; others were impatient, anxious to get through the inspection and be off to their destinations. . . .

The Granger Collection, New York

CONCLUSION

Full meaning of experience

So they had shuffled aboard at the Italian port, forsaking the arduous security of their villages among the vineyards, leaving behind the friends of their youth, of their maturity, or their old age. The young accepted the challenge with the daring of youth; the old pressed forward without a hope of return. But both saw in the future, through their shadowy dreams, what they believed was an earthly paradise. They did not weigh the price of their coming against the benefits of the New World. They were convinced, long before they left Italy, that America had enough and more for all who wished to come. It was only a question of being desired by the strong and wealthy country, of being worthy to be admitted.

from *In the Shadow of Liberty*

VISUAL CONNECTIONS

Exploring the Subject. At Ellis Island many people had their names changed involuntarily by Ellis Island workers who couldn't speak the languages of the immigrants or translate the ethnic names into English. Because some immigrants were turned back as being unfit to enter the country for real or imagined medical or social problems, families were often divided. Many suffered indignities that were cruel and senseless. Ellis Island came to be known among immigrants as the Isle of Tears.

MEETING INDIVIDUAL NEEDS

LEP/ESL

General Strategies. Getting students to expand their essays to an adequate length is sometimes difficult. To remedy this potential problem, have students use the prewriting technique of clustering to develop at least three ideas or events from their clusters.

SELECTION AMENDMENT
Description of change: excerpted
Rationale: to focus on the concept of expressive writing presented in this chapter

CLOSURE

Have students supply the elements from the **Framework for a Personal Essay** chart on p. 147 as you write them on the chalkboard.

ENRICHMENT

If there are members of your community who immigrated to the United States from Europe and who passed through Ellis Island, you may want to invite one to speak to your class about his or her experiences. Local ethnic societies, such as the Sons of Italy, may be a resource to help you identify potential guest speakers. ■

EXERCISE 3 **Analyzing a Personal Essay**

After you have finished reading the excerpt from Edward Corsi's autobiography (pages 138–142), meet with two or three classmates to discuss these questions.

1. In what order does Corsi present the events in his essay?
2. What are some examples of specific sensory details, other than sight details, that Corsi includes?
3. The descriptive details in the third paragraph are arranged spatially and in order of importance. What is the effect of ending the paragraph with *the Statue of Liberty*?
4. Why do you think Corsi includes the incident in which he and Giuseppe mistake the skyscrapers for mountains?
5. What details in the body of the essay reveal or suggest the immigrants' feelings of hope or wonder? What details reveal feelings of fear or loss?
6. In your own words, explain the meaning of Corsi's experience as he explains it in the conclusion. How does this paragraph explain the immigrants' mixed feelings of hope and wonder?

A Basic Framework for a Personal Essay

In *I Behold America* Edward Corsi shows readers an experience that involves complex thoughts and feelings. The experience related in the following essay is less complex, but it has the same basic structure and purpose as Corsi's essay. As you read, notice that this writer's model includes several hints about the meaning of the experience.

A WRITER'S MODEL

An Actor Is Born

INTRODUCTION
Hint of meaning

I wish I could say that I was planning my debut on Broadway next season--or even that the experience was mildly successful. But I can't. I don't even know how I became involved in the first place. I've always known all the

ANSWERS

Exercise 3

1. Corsi presents events in chronological order.
2. Students should mention some of the many sensory images involving sound, movement, and touch.
3. Ending the paragraph with the *Statue of Liberty* places emphasis on the final and most important detail.
4. Corsi includes this incident to emphasize both his and his brother's naiveté and the strangeness of the experience for them.
5. Answers may vary. Hope and wonder are reflected in the description of seeing the Statue of Liberty, the skyscrapers, and the sights and sounds of the harbor. Fear and loss are reflected in the tears of some of the older people on the ship.
6. Responses will vary. Corsi realizes that coming to America embodied a dream the immigrants shared even though it meant tearing themselves from the security of the old country. They were all convinced that America offered them a better life than they could ever hope for at home.

CRITICAL THINKING
Analysis

Expressive writing usually contains the following four characteristics:

1. liberal use of first person pronouns
2. frequent use of words that express feelings
3. informal language that resembles everyday conversational speaking
4. use of suggestive language—words and figures of speech that have powerful connotations

Have each student choose one of the models in this chapter and have him or her analyze it for the four characteristics of expressive writing. Have students list specific examples of the characteristics they find. Divide the class into groups according to which model they analyzed and have them compare answers. Point out to students that these four characteristics should appear in the expressive essays they write for this chapter.

techniques for avoiding attention. I'm never late for class. I always sit in the back row. I keep my head down at the right times. But last year my family got involved, and life hasn't been the same since.

Background information

The yearly drama production is always a big event around school. Last year, posters with strange objects that were supposed to be windmills, but looked more like clock hands run amock, went up everywhere. They decorated every available space--over the doors, on lockers, even hanging from ceiling fixtures. One of the newspaper reporters, a real go-getter, even managed to get a write-up in the local paper: "NORTHSIDE PLAYERS PRESENT A DRAMATIZATION OF SCENES FROM DON QUIXOTE. This fall, the Northside High School drama group has scheduled a production of scenes from Cervantes' classic novel Don Quixote. . . ."

BODY
Event 1

Not long after the article appeared, my parents began one of those dinner table conversations about "Susan's Shyness and What Can Be Done About It."

Narrative details—Dialogue

"Why don't you sign up?" my father urged. "There are lots of things you can do offstage--lights, costumes, prompting. And it'll be good for you. You'll meet people and get out of yourself a little."

Sentence fragment for emphasis

Silence from me.

Sensory details

For some reason, this particular play really caught on at school. Maybe it was just the nuttiness--the strange, wonderful man who thought he was a knight and went off fighting windmills and showed people what it was like to have a dream. We had seen pictures of him in our world lit books, dressed up in his great-grandfather's old, rusty armor. Anyway, my one true friend signed up and, in a moment of misguided fervor, so did I.

Event 2 Narrative details

After that, it was all a chain of circumstances. Halfway through rehearsal, the actress playing Camilla got sick. I was learning

to work the lights, enjoying my place in the half-darkness of the back of the theater, when Mr. Guedez called my name. I don't know why he ever chose me as an understudy in the first place--probably because it was a minor role and he had to have somebody, after all. It certainly wasn't my stage presence. Anyway, no one thought for a moment that Elizabeth wouldn't be there. I don't think she'd missed a day of school since kindergarten--until opening night, that is. That's when she came down with the flu.

Event 3 Narrative details

Everything happened awfully fast that night. I was rushed into Elizabeth's costume and pushed out onstage. It took a moment for me to adjust to the bright lights (the ones I was supposed to work). Then I saw John dressed up in that crazy armor and staring at me with a strained look on his face.

Thoughts and feelings

"Oh," I thought confusedly. "I'm supposed to say something."

Event 4 Narrative details

But nothing came out. There, in the glare of the spotlight, I stood onstage, absolutely alone and absolutely speechless.

VISUAL CONNECTIONS

Exploring the Subject. The novel referred to in **A Writer's Model** is Miguel de Cervantes' seventeenth-century Spanish masterpiece *Don Quixote de la Mancha.* One of the most widely read classics of western literature, *Don Quixote* is about the adventures of an old man who has been addicted to medieval romances for years. Imagining he can recapture the ancient traditions of chivalry, he sets out to be a knight.

Cervantes intended the novel to be a satire of the ideals of chivalry, but it ended up being an enormous canvas representing a complete cross section of life in Spain in the late sixteenth and early seventeenth century.

A popular Broadway musical, *The Man of La Mancha,* which opened in 1965, was based on Cervantes' novel.

INTEGRATING THE LANGUAGE ARTS

Technology Link. Students who compose their first drafts using computers tend to produce more text than students who write by hand. In general, when they begin the revision stage, it will be better for students to have too much material in their drafts than not enough. If students have access to computers, encourage them to compose their first drafts on the computers.

Later, they told me that I seemed to be saying my lines but that nobody could hear them. It didn't get easier as the longest play in history went on. I remember stumbling onto the stage each time in a kind of merciful daze. I discovered if I didn't look at the audience, I could retrieve most of my lines from my dim memory. No one mentioned afterward that Camilla seemed fixated on the empty space above the stage.

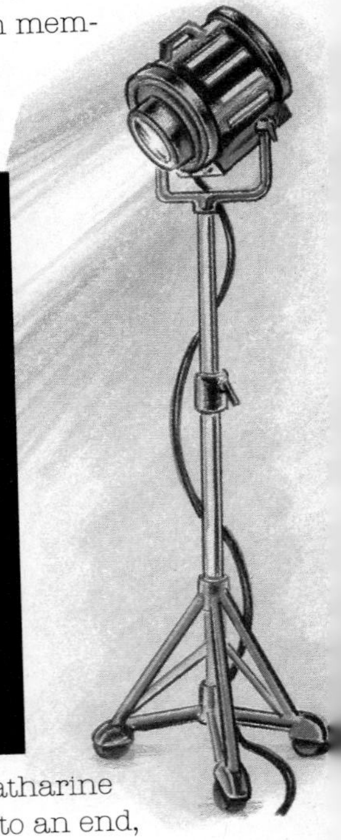

CONCLUSION
Meaning of experience

I didn't suddenly blossom into Katharine Hepburn, but the world didn't come to an end, either. You still won't find me leaping up to answer questions in class. But it was fun to go to the party with the rest of the cast, to laugh at some of the funny bloopers, and to feel good because everyone liked the play so much. For once in my life, I'd been in the limelight a little. And it didn't feel so bad, after all.

The essay you have just read is based on the following framework, which you might find helpful in developing your own personal essay.

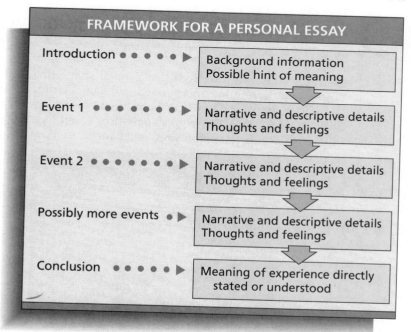

FRAMEWORK FOR A PERSONAL ESSAY

Introduction	Background information Possible hint of meaning
Event 1	Narrative and descriptive details Thoughts and feelings
Event 2	Narrative and descriptive details Thoughts and feelings
Possibly more events	Narrative and descriptive details Thoughts and feelings
Conclusion	Meaning of experience directly stated or understood

Reminder

When writing a draft of your personal essay

- introduce background information and a hint of the experience's meaning early
- use specific narrative and descriptive details
- gradually reveal more of the experience's significance
- conclude with a full recognition of significance

WRITING ASSIGNMENT PART 3:
Writing a Draft of Your Personal Essay

Now that you've gathered details and reflected on the meaning of your experience (Writing Assignment, Part 2), it's time to shape your notes and ideas into essay form. Using your prewriting notes, write a draft of your personal essay.

A DIFFERENT APPROACH

In a personal essay, the explicit statement of the meaning of the experience or of what the writer learned from the experience can come either at the beginning or at the end. For example, an essay could begin, "When I was twelve years old, I realized for the first time that other cultural traditions can really enrich my life. It all started when . . . ." Or the statement can come at the end of the essay as a conclusion arrived at from a discussion of the experience. If the meaning is stated at the beginning of the essay, it should be briefly restated or implied in the conclusion.

SEGMENT 5 *(pp. 148–150)*

EVALUATING AND REVISING

OBJECTIVES

- To analyze a writer's revisions
- To evaluate and revise a draft of a personal essay

TEACHING THE LESSON

The heart of this segment is the **Evaluating and Revising Personal Essays** chart, and most of your direct instruction will probably focus on its contents. The first item in the chart deals with tone, and some students may need help recognizing specific words and phrases that need revision to adjust the tone. In addition to replacing

Teacher's ResourceBank™

RESOURCES

EVALUATING AND REVISING

- Writing a Personal Essay 44

QUOTATION FOR THE DAY

"As to the Adjective: when in doubt, strike it out." (Mark Twain, 1835–1910, American novelist and humorist)

Too many modifiers weaken the power of nouns. Try an experiment with your class. Write a sentence from a well-written paper on the chalkboard and then insert a number of unnecessary adjectives. Show students how superfluous adjectives bleed energy from the sentence and shift the emphasis away from the original meaning.

Evaluating and Revising

Just as a sculptor "roughs out" a general shape first and then works away at refining and perfecting detail, a writer "drafts" a general shape that must later be refined. Although your first draft gives first form to your experience, careful crafting during revision may turn your final essay into a work of art!

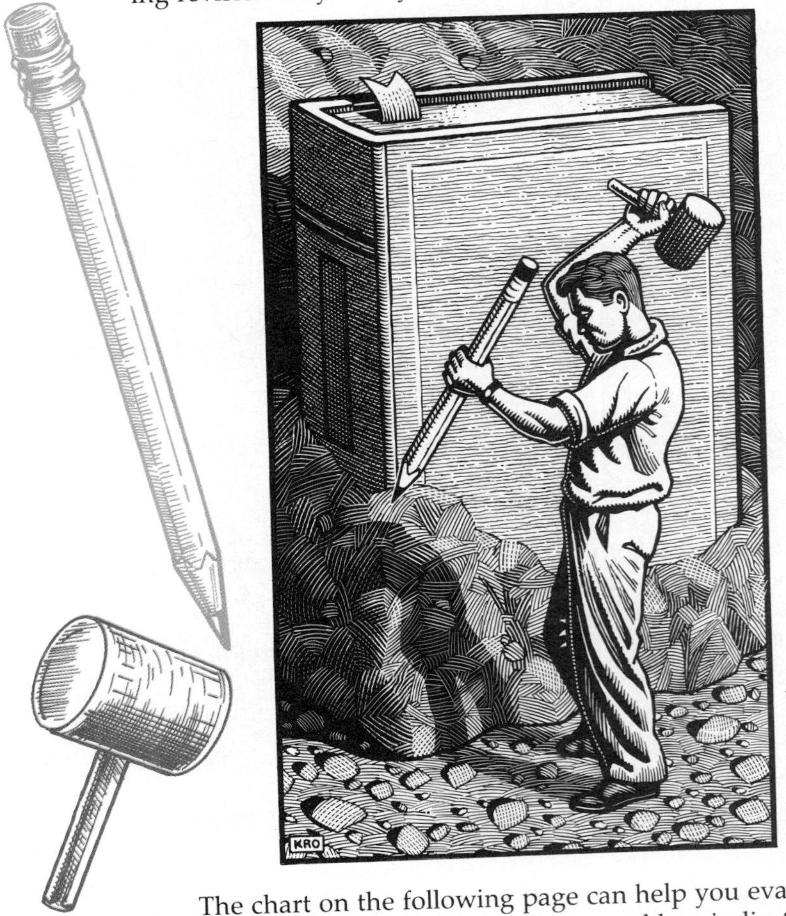

Illustrator: Dan Krovatin

The chart on the following page can help you evaluate and revise your own work. If you find a problem indicated in the left-hand column, try the revision technique suggested in the right-hand column.

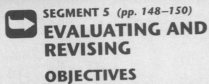

third-person pronouns with first-person pronouns, students may want to use contractions to make the tone of their essays more conversational.

To help students with the second item in the chart, suggest that every time an essay says something about how the writer feels, the writer should look closely at the passage to see if it can be revised to present an action that illustrates how the writer feels.

For **Exercise 4** on p. 150, use the first item to provide guided practice. Ask volunteers in the class to answer the question and then discuss their responses. Duplicate a paragraph from a former student's essay and guide the class through evaluating and

EVALUATING AND REVISING PERSONAL ESSAYS

	EVALUATION GUIDE	REVISION TECHNIQUE
1	Is the tone friendly and informal? Does the writer use first-person pronouns?	**Replace** stiff and formal wording with conversational language. **Replace** third-person pronouns with first-person pronouns.
2	Are events, people, and places vividly portrayed? Does the writer show, rather than tell about, the experience?	**Add** narrative details of action and speech. **Add** descriptive details appealing to the five senses.
3	Are narrative and descriptive details in an order that makes sense?	**Reorder** narrative details in the order they happened or in another order that's clear. **Reorder** descriptive details in spatial order or order of importance.
4	Does the writer give important background information?	**Add** details that help readers understand events, people, and places.
5	Does each event or section of the essay add to the meaning of the experience?	**Cut** unnecessary details that do not contribute to meaning. **Add** details that will help readers understand the meaning.
6	Is the meaning of the experience clear by the end of the essay?	**Add** (or repeat) significant details in the conclusion.

MEETING INDIVIDUAL NEEDS

LEP/ESL

General Strategies. Some students are inclined to give only positive feedback on their fellow students' work. To help them feel more comfortable as critics, give the following guidelines on how to present a particular item of criticism:

1. Begin with a positive comment.
2. Insert the criticism.
3. Ask a question. For example, "I really like the part about getting lost, but I couldn't understand how you were feeling at that point. Do you think you could add a few more details to that paragraph?"

revising it in preparation for evaluating and revising their own essays. Then assign **Exercise 4** and **Writing Assignment: Part 4** as independent practice.

Use the responses to **Exercise 4** to assess students' abilities to analyze a writer's revisions. To assess students' abilities to evaluate and revise personal essays, ask students to turn in their first drafts with revisions. Check to see whether they followed the suggestions in the **Evaluating and Revising Personal Essays** chart on p. 149.

To close, ask volunteers to share how the **Evaluating and Revising Personal Essays** chart helped them revise their essays. ■

ANSWERS

Exercise 4

1. The replacement is less formal and adds to the friendly, conversational tone.
2. The detail in the fourth sentence doesn't add anything to the meaning of the experience, nor does it make the experience clearer.
3. Both words are descriptive and make the writer's experience more immediate to the reader.
4. These superlative phrases help make the writer's predicament more vivid.

MEETING INDIVIDUAL NEEDS

ADVANCED STUDENTS

Have students revise the paragraph in **Exercise 4** even further. Encourage them to make the tone more emotional and more urgent by using stronger language, such as more vivid words with stronger connotations. For example, the second sentence could become "I was squeezed into Elizabeth's costume and catapulted onstage."

EXERCISE 4 Analyzing a Writer's Revisions

The following paragraph from the Writer's Model on page 145 shows the writer's attempts to refine the draft. With two or three classmates, try to figure out why the writer made the changes. Then answer the questions that follow.

~~Events went on at a rapid rate~~ [Everything happened awfully fast] that night.	replace
I was rushed into Elizabeth's costume and pushed out onstage. It took a moment for me to adjust to the bright lights (the ones I was supposed to work). ~~Mr. Guedez drafted Jennifer to work them in my place.~~	cut
Then I saw John dressed up in that [crazy] armor and	add
staring at me with a strained look on his face. "Oh," I thought[, confusedly]. "I'm supposed to say	add
something." But nothing came out. There, in the glare of the spotlight, I stood onstage[, absolutely alone and absolutely speechless].	add

1. In the first sentence, why did the writer replace the words *events went on at a rapid rate*? [Hint: Review page 132.]
2. Why did the writer cut the fourth sentence?
3. In the fifth and sixth sentences, why did the writer add the words *crazy* and *confusedly*? Why are these good choices?
4. Why did the writer add the words *absolutely alone and absolutely speechless* to the last sentence?

WRITING ASSIGNMENT PART 4:
Evaluating and Revising Your Personal Essay

Evaluate your finished draft overall to determine what other changes will improve it. Begin by exchanging papers with a classmate and using the questions from the chart on page 149 to evaluate each other's essays. Think about your partner's comments, and then use the chart to evaluate your own essay. Finally, make revisions to improve your essay.

SEGMENT 6 *(p. 151)*

PROOFREADING AND PUBLISHING

OBJECTIVE

- To proofread and publish a personal essay

TEACHING THE LESSON

You may want to reproduce an anonymous expressive essay on a transparency to guide students through the proofreading stage. Evaluate students' essays to assess mastery, and close by having volunteers share how they plan to publish their essays. ■

Proofreading and Publishing

Give your personal essay your personal best, including careful ***proofreading*** for mistakes in spelling, capitalization, punctuation, and usage. Then share your final copy with a larger audience. Here are two suggestions for ***publishing*** your essay.

- Send a copy (or copies) of your essay to those who shared the experience with you.
- Share your essay with a trusted adult.

MECHANICS HINT

Punctuating Dialogue

Dialogue adds a sense of immediacy to events and expresses thoughts and feelings effectively. To write dialogue, enclose a person's exact words or thoughts in quotation marks and begin a new paragraph if you switch speakers within a conversational exchange. If a dialogue tag (*he said, Joan muttered*) interrupts a sentence, the first word after the tag usually isn't capitalized.

EXAMPLE "I hate to tell you this, but you've got the measles," Dr. James observed.
"Oh, no," I groaned to myself, "a kid's disease."

REFERENCE NOTE: For more information on punctuating dialogue, see pages 878–881.

WRITING ASSIGNMENT PART 5: **Proofreading and Publishing Your Essay**

Don't let all the work you've put into your essay go unnoticed. Proofread your final draft and correct any errors. Then use one of the ideas above or one of your own to publish your essay.

Teacher's ResourceBank™

RESOURCES

PROOFREADING AND PUBLISHING

- Writing a Personal Essay 45

QUOTATION FOR THE DAY

"Every fine story must leave in the mind of the sensitive reader . . . a quality of voice that is exclusively the writer's own, individual, unique." (Willa Cather, 1873–1947, American writer, poet, and journalist)

Share the quotation with the class and explain that mechanical errors distract the reader from the story and keep the writer's individual voice from being heard.

MEETING INDIVIDUAL NEEDS

LEP/ESL

General Strategies. For these essays about personal experiences, some students will need to check their past tense verb forms. For example, in the passage "happy that we had come through the storm safely . . . [we] looked with wonder on this miraculous land of our dreams," the past perfect form is used to indicate the earlier of two events. The more recent event takes the past form.

SEGMENT 7 *(pp. 152–154)*

WRITING WORKSHOP

OBJECTIVE

- To write an anecdote

TEACHING THE LESSON

Have a volunteer read aloud the introductory paragraphs and the anecdote from ***I Wonder as I Wander*** by Langston Hughes. Guide students through the first and second questions on p. 153 and assign the third and fourth questions as independent practice.

QUOTATION FOR THE DAY

"When you tell an anecdote, tell it so your listeners can actually *see* the people you are talking about." (F. Scott Fitzgerald, 1896–1940, American novelist and short-story writer)

Suggest to your students that they become cameras when they return to the past. They should see the contents of rooms, the expressions on people's faces, and even the weather outside. Then describing what the camera sees is a simple matter.

USING THE SELECTION

from *I Wonder as I Wander*

1

Hughes introduces the central event without revealing what it is.

WRITING WORKSHOP

Relating an Anecdote

Writer Mark Twain and comedian Bill Cosby are masters of it, but so are thousands of less famous people, known only to their friends as "good company." "It" is the ability to relate an anecdote effectively.

Another form of personal expression, an ***anecdote*** is a short, entertaining account of a personal experience. Focusing on a single event, an anecdote is usually shorter than a personal essay, but it often follows a similar framework, hinting at the story's significance early but not revealing its full meaning until the end. Often humorous, an anecdote does not aim at deep meaning but may still illustrate some truth or understanding about life.

Like a personal essay, an anecdote is developed with narrative and descriptive details. In the following anecdote from his autobiographical *I Wonder As I Wander,* the poet Langston Hughes uses descriptive detail to highlight his hostess's good intentions. He uses narrative detail to underscore the humorous consequences.

from *I Wonder As I Wander*

by Langston Hughes

My name I must have written a million times that season on printed programs, in books, on scraps of paper, and even on paper
1 napkins at rural receptions. But, my most personal autograph is, I suppose, obliterated by now. I inscribed it unawares in a small town in Mississippi near the Alabama state line. I was reading my poems that evening for a colored church. I was housed with one of the pillars of the church in a tiny home, spotlessly clean and filled, when I arrived, with the fumes of wonderful cooking. Tired and dusty after a day-long drive, I wanted nothing so much as a good hot bath before dinner. My hostess in preparation for my coming had done a little painting, freshening up all the baseboards and things with white paint. At the very last moment, it seemed, in her zeal to have everything spik-and-

If any student has trouble thinking of an experience that's appropriate for an anecdote, ask the student to think back to the last time he or she told a funny story about himself or herself. Students might also think back to gifts they received that were thoughtful but useless. There may be good material for an anecdote in one of these experiences.

If students need additional models of anecdotes, a good resource is *The Little, Brown Book of Anecdotes,* edited by Clifton Fadiman, available in many libraries. This encyclopedic text contains anecdotes about many public figures.

Have the class write their anecdotes as independent practice. To assess their ☛

span, she had even freshly painted the bathtub, outside and *in,* with white enamel. Unfortunately, the enamel had not quite dried when I
2 arrived. But, unaware of this fact, I blithely ran the bath tub full of hot water and sat down therein, soaking myself happily as I lathered my hair. But ten minutes later, when I started to get up, I could not tear myself loose. I was stuck to the bottom of the tub! With great deliberateness, slowly and carefully pushing myself upward, I finally
3 managed to rise without leaving any skin behind. But I certainly left imprinted on that bath tub a most personal autograph.

That evening as I sat stiffly in the seat of honor at church, I was covered with enamel where I sat. But I didn't tell my hostess what had happened, not wishing to embarrass her. In the next town I bought a gallon of turpentine and took a bath in it.

1. What sentences near the beginning hint at the story's final outcome?
2. What are some narrative details that reveal Hughes's thoughts or feelings?
3. What are some sensory details that convey the hostess's good intentions?
4. What understanding or truth about good intentions does Hughes's anecdote illustrate?

2

blithely: in a carefree manner

3

The meaning of the anecdote is revealed completely in this statement.

VISUAL CONNECTIONS

Exploring the Subject. Langston Hughes (1902–1967) is considered a major American writer of the twentieth century. He grew up in Cleveland, Ohio, but spent most of his adult life in Harlem. Best known today for his poetry, Hughes also wrote novels, plays, essays, and short stories.

ANSWERS

Writing Workshop Questions

1. Sentences 2 and 3 hint at the final outcome.
2. Responses will vary. Two examples of details that reveal Hughes's thoughts or feelings are "wonderful cooking" and "soaking myself happily."
3. Responses will vary. Some examples of details that convey the hostess's good intentions are the cleanliness of the house, the smell of good food cooking, and the fresh paint.
4. Sometimes peoples' good intentions backfire without their realizing it.

SELECTION AMENDMENT
Description of change: excerpted
Rationale: to focus on the concept of expressive writing presented in this chapter

mastery of the material on anecdotes, evaluate their responses to questions 3 and 4 on p. 153 and their written anecdotes.

CLOSURE

As a closure activity, let your students share their anecdotes with one another. You can let them pass their papers around the class, or you can have volunteers read their papers aloud. You may even want to consider sponsoring a "Best Anecdote" contest with a prize for the winner. ■

MEETING INDIVIDUAL NEEDS

LESS-ADVANCED STUDENTS

Students may think they have to recall earth-shattering events to use as their anecdotes. Point out that relating anecdotes is a normal part of daily conversation. If there is time, give students a day to listen to their own and others' conversations and to identify anecdotes.

CRITICAL THINKING

Analysis

Much of the success of Hughes's account of his unorthodox autograph depends on his tone. Instead of seeing his experience as an uncomfortable inconvenience, he chooses to view it with humor. His respect for his hostess and his understanding of her keen desire to please her guest come through in the writing.

When students revise their anecdotes, have them analyze the tones they project. Working in small groups, students could get feedback about whether they are conveying the tones they intend. Anecdotes are supposed to be amusing, and often the humor comes from the incongruity of the situation. Students will want to use words and expressions that emphasize the humorous and incongruous aspects of the situations they write about.

Writing an Anecdote

Prewriting. Have you ever acted with the best of intentions but had something go wrong? Or, like Langston Hughes, have you ever been on the receiving end of a good-intention-gone-bad? If you haven't, brainstorm for another entertaining experience that you'd like to relate. Select one that's relatively short and amusing. Then, to recall the experience, use the techniques that you read about in this chapter.

Writing, Evaluating, and Revising. Try to follow Langston Hughes's framework in writing your anecdote:

- Introduce your anecdote with a general comment or phrase whose meaning will be completely understood at the end.
- Present your story's narrative details in chronological order and add descriptive details that reinforce your story's humor.

You may want to repeat your introductory comment or a slight variation of it at the end. Revise your draft to make the action clearer and the humor stronger.

Proofreading and Publishing. After checking for and correcting any errors, you might submit your anecdote to your school newspaper or magazine for publication. If the publication doesn't already have a humor section, you could suggest one.

"The best way to cheer yourself up is to try to cheer somebody else up."

Mark Twain

MAKING CONNECTIONS

WRITING ACROSS THE CURRICULUM

OBJECTIVE

- To research and report on an instance of group self-expression in American history

MAKING CONNECTIONS

WRITING ACROSS THE CURRICULUM

Group Self-Expression in History

In a personal essay, one person shares his or her experience with others. But groups of people can also express their shared feelings about a common experience. Group self-expression may be a public announcement, or declaration, like the Declaration of Independence, or it may take other forms, such as a myth, a creed, or a law.

With a small group of your classmates, choose one instance of group self-expression in history, such as the ones listed below and on the next page. Then do some research to find out the background and purpose of the item you select. How and why did it develop? What thoughts and feelings about the group does it express? Report to your classmates on your research.

1. the Boy Scout Oath or Girl Scout Promise
2. the Bill of Rights
3. the Equal Rights Amendment
4. the Greek myth of Persephone
5. the preamble to the charter of the United Nations

WRITING ACROSS THE CURRICULUM

Teaching Strategies

The list of topics is intended to be suggestive of the types of instances of group self-expression that students may work on. Add to the list by having the class brainstorm for additional topics.

You may want to alert the school librarian that the class is working on this assignment so that he or she can locate some resources ahead of time. If a trip to the library with the whole class is impractical, you may be able to arrange for relevant sources to be brought into the classroom.

You may want to let two or three students work independently on each topic and then pool their findings before one of them reports to the whole class.

GUIDELINES

To evaluate groups' preparations, have them show you their research notes and explain how each member participated in the process. To evaluate the actual presentations, assess thoroughness, organization, and speaking skills.

SELF-EXPRESSION AND THE FUTURE

OBJECTIVE

- To write personal short- and long-term goals

6. a Native American myth about the origin or harvesting of crops
7. your school song
8. the code of the Japanese samurai warrior
9. the Emancipation Proclamation
10. your state's laws regarding public access for people who are disabled

SELF-EXPRESSION AND THE FUTURE

Setting Goals

Do you make New Year's resolutions? Do you know other people who do? New Year's resolutions are a kind of joke because most people don't take them seriously. But resolutions in the form of goals for your future are extremely important. Without goals you don't know where you want to go or how to get there. Realistic goals are hard to set, though; to plan for the future, you have to understand your past and your present. That's where expressive writing comes in; it allows you to develop a better understanding of yourself.

Since your high school years are almost over, this is a good time to think about goals. What are you going to do with your life after high school? Are you going to a trade school or college? Are you going to look for a job right away or perhaps join the military? Where do you want to be five years from now—or even ten years from now? To begin to set goals for yourself, think through your answers to the following questions.

SELF-EXPRESSION AND THE FUTURE

Teaching Strategies

The activity in this lesson is highly personal, so you may want to proceed with caution. One way to handle the activity is to involve a guidance counselor who can offer ideas and instruction on setting personal goals. A counselor could also help students determine concrete steps they need to take to achieve their goals. You'll probably want to maintain a position of respectful assistance as your students work on this activity. The beginning of the school year or of a new grading period may be a good time to try this activity.

1. Start by looking at the expressive essay you wrote in this chapter. What did you learn about yourself? Did you discover anything that is especially important to you?
2. Think about goals you've had before. Have you achieved any of them? What have you accomplished that you set out to accomplish? How did you manage to do it?
3. Where do you want to be when you are twenty-five years old? Think about where you want to be living, what kind of work you want to be doing, whether you want to be single or married. (Your answers here are your long-range goals.)
4. What do you have to do right after you graduate from high school to ensure you can be where you want to be at the age of twenty-five? (Your answers here are your medium-range goals.)
5. What do you have to do during the next year and a half to make sure you can do what you want right after high school? (Your answers here are your immediate goals.)

After you've thought about these questions, begin to write some goals in your diary or journal. These goals aren't set in stone; you'll probably revise them from time to time. However, they will help you plan your future. If you want, share your goals with a good friend or an adult you trust. Otherwise, keep them in your journal and look back at them every few months to see if you're on your way to meeting them.

GUIDELINES

Because students may choose to keep their goals private, you could assess their efforts by circulating throughout the room as they write. If they choose to share their goals with you, you could make suggestions about how students can make their goals more specific or more realistic.

MEETING INDIVIDUAL NEEDS

AT-RISK STUDENTS

For students at risk of dropping out of school, setting goals is a good way to focus and to get a clearer picture of the benefits of finishing school. You may want to give extra encouragement and attention to at-risk students as they work on setting goals.

Chapter 5 CREATIVE WRITING

OBJECTIVES

- To respond personally to and analyze a poem
- To develop an idea, conflict, plot, characters, setting and point of view for a story
- To write a plan for a story
- To write dialogue
- To analyze a model short story
- To write a draft of a short story
- To analyze a writer's revisions
- To evaluate, revise, proofread, and publish a short story
- To analyze a scene from a play
- To write a scene for a play
- To analyze a poem
- To write a poem
- To write and present an imaginary historical dialogue
- To write a description of a fictional character

Motivation

You may increase your students' interest in writing creatively by allowing them the opportunity to use their imaginations in a non-threatening, non-evaluative manner. Allowing students to have only paper and a writing implement available, give the class five or six sentence beginnings, then allow students approximately five minutes to complete the sentences. Sample sentence beginnings include: "If I could be the school district superintendent, I would...," "I don't have my homework assignment because...," or "If I could spend next week anywhere in the world, I'd ...." Once students have completed the assignment, ask them to share some of their responses. Discuss with students how their individual creativity made the sentences unique even though all the students started with the same sentence beginnings.

Introduction

Through a discussion of the possible modes of creative writing, help students to see that creative writing should be not only entertaining, but also interesting and informative for the audience. You may want to explain to students that creative writing can have several different purposes. For example, if the student's purpose is to describe an event, the student might give a sequential listing of happenings (narrative); a portrait of the crowd attending (descriptive); a review of the event's impact on the people attending (evaluative); or a comparison with last year's event (classificatory).

With this basic introduction to creative writing, students should be prepared to appreciate the literary model **"Beware: Do Not Read This Poem"** by Ishmael Reed.

Integration

You may want to refer to this chapter when you are presenting literary selections to the class. For example, you could read Nathaniel Hawthorne's "Dr. Heidegger's Experiment" or the description of Ahab in Herman Melville's *Moby Dick* along with a discussion on the creation of characters in stories.

Emily Dickinson's poetry provides many examples of the use of figurative language. You may want to look specifically at "'Hope' Is the Thing with Feathers," "A Narrow Fellow in the Grass" or "The Soul Selects Her Own Society."

You could refer to the section in this chapter on **Purpose, Audience, and Tone** when students read Mark Twain's "Life on the Mississippi." How does Twain create a humorous, affectionate tone? Who is his audience?

The chart on the next page illustrates the strands of language arts as they are integrated into this chapter. For vocabulary study, glossary words are underlined in some writing models.

QUOTATIONS
All **Quotations for the Day** are chosen because of their relevance to instructional material presented in that segment of the chapter and for their usefulness in establishing student interest in writing.

INTEGRATING THE LANGUAGE ARTS

Selection	Reading and Literature	Writing and Critical Thinking	Language and Syntax	Speaking, Listening, and Other Expression Skills
"Beware: Do Not Read This Poem" by Ishmael Reed **160-161** ***Thousand Pieces of Gold*** by Ruthanne Lum McCunn **171** ***The Floating World*** by Cynthia Kadohata **175** **"The Gift"** by Louis Dollarhide **176-182** from **A Raisin in the Sun** by Lorraine Hansberry **194-196** **"Sunset at Twin Lake"** by Anita Endrezze **200** ***A Yellow Raft in Blue Water*** by Michael Dorris **203**	Responding personally to literature **162** Finding author's purpose **162, 200** Analyzing poetry **162, 201** Identifying conflict **162, 182, 196-197** Identifying sensory details **162, 201** Analyzing rhythm **162, 201** Analyzing point of view **171-172** Analyzing character **171-172, 182** Analyzing conflict **182, 196-197** Analyzing setting **182** Analyzing stage directions **196-197** Analyzing mood in poetry **201** Finding examples of figurative language **201**	Finding an author's purpose **162** Applying interpretive and creative thinking **162, 165, 167, 171-172, 174, 196-197, 202** Analyzing rhythm **162, 201** Using prewriting techniques **165, 169, 197, 201, 202, 203** Exploring story topics **165** Choosing a story topic **165** Developing and summarizing conflict and plot for story **167** Developing characters and setting **169, 202** Rewriting by changing point of view **171-172** Planning a story **173** Developing dialogue **174, 202** Analyzing conflict, character, and setting **182, 196-197** Writing a draft of a story **188** Analyzing a writer's revisions **189** Evaluating and revising a short story **191** Proofreading and publishing a short story **192** Analyzing stage directions for a play **196-197** Using the writing process to write a dramatic scene **197** Analyzing poetry **201** Analyzing the differences between poetry and short stories **201** Using the writing process to write a poem **201** Writing a historical dialogue **202** Writing a description **203**	Proofreading for errors in grammar, usage, and mechanics **192** Identifying alliteration and onomatopoeia **201**	Reading a poem aloud **162, 200** Working with a classmate to create dialogue for an oral presentation **174** Working with classmates to analyze a short story **182** Using feedback from classmates to revise a short story **191, 197, 201** Performing a dramatic scene **197** Working with a classmate to create and present a historical dialogue **202**

CHAPTER 5

SEGMENT PLANNING GUIDE

You can use the following Planning Guide to adapt the chapter material to the individual needs of your class. All the Resources listed in this chapter are located in the *Teacher's ResourceBank*™.

SEGMENT	PAGES	CONTENT	RESOURCES
1 ***Imagining Other Worlds***	***159-162***		
Literary Model **"Beware: Do Not Read This Poem"**	160-161	Guided reading: a model of creative writing	
Reader's Response/ Writer's Craft	162	Model evaluation: responding to literature and analyzing poetry	
2 ***Strategies for Writing Creatively***	***163***		
3 ***Prewriting***	***164-173***		Writing a Short Story Creating a Story Map 48
Exploring Story Ideas	164-165	Guidelines: developing story ideas	
Exercise 1	165	Applied practice: exploring story ideas	
Writing Assignment: Part 1	165	Applied practice: finding story ideas	
Planning Your Story	166-167	Explanation: developing conflict and plot	
Chart: Types of Conflict	166	Guidelines: analyzing external and internal conflict	
Writing Assignment: Part 2	167	Applied practice: developing conflict and plot	
Characters and Setting	168-169	Guidelines: developing characters and setting	
Writing Assignment: Part 3	169	Applied practice: imagining characters and setting	
Choosing a Point of View	169-170	Guidelines: examining narration and effects	
Critical Thinking: Analyzing Point of View	171	Guidelines: analyzing effects of point of view	
Critical Thinking Exercise	171-172	Cooperative learning: analyzing third-person limited point of view	
Literary Model/Questions from ***Thousand Pieces of Gold***	171-172	Guided reading: analyzing point of view	
Thinking About Purpose, Audience, and Tone	172	Guidelines: selecting appropriate purpose, audience, and tone	
Writing Assignment: Part 4	173	Applied practice: planning a story	
4 ***Writing***	***174-188***		Writing a Short Story 49
Combining the Basic Elements	174-176	Guidelines: using story elements	
Exercise 2	174	Cooperative learning: creating dialogue	
Literary Model from ***The Floating World***	175	Example: examining description in a model	
Literary Model **"The Gift"**	176-182	Guided reading: examining story elements in a model	
Exercise 3	182	Cooperative learning: analyzing a short story	

For **Portfolio Assessment** see the following pages in the *Teacher's ResourceBank*™:
Aims For Writing — pp. 47–52
Holistically Graded Composition Models — pp. 491–496
Assessment Portfolio — pp. 533–562

SEGMENT	PAGES	CONTENT	RESOURCES
Using a Framework	183	Guidelines: using a pattern for a short story	
A Writer's Model	183-187	Guided reading: examining a sample short story	
Chart: Framework for a Story	188	Guidelines: structuring a short story	
Writing Assignment: Part 5	188	Applied practice: writing a first draft	
5 ***Evaluating and Revising***	***189-191***		Writing a Short Story 50
Evaluating and Revising	189	Introduction: revising a story	
Exercise 4	189	Applied practice: analyzing a writer's revisions	
Chart: Evaluating/Revising	190	Guidelines: applying evaluation and revision techniques	
Writing Assignment: Part 6	191	Applied practice: evaluating and revising	
Grammar Hint	191	Writing suggestion: using precise verbs	
6 ***Proofreading and Publishing***	***192***		Writing a Short Story 51
Publishing	192	Publishing ideas: reaching a specific audience	
Writing Assignment: Part 7	192	Applied practice: proofreading and publishing	
7 ***Writing Workshop***	***193-197***		
A Scene in a Play	193	Guidelines: using story elements in play writing	
Literary Model/Questions from ***A Raisin in the Sun***	194-197	Guided reading: examining a scene from a play	
Writing a Scene	197	Applied practice: applying skills to the writing process	
8 ***Writing Workshop***	***198-201***		
Poetry	198-199	Explanation: writing poetry	
Chart: Writing Poetry	199	Examples: analyzing techniques	
Literary Model/Questions **"Sunset at Twin Lake"**	200-201	Guided reading: examining a poem	
Writing a Poem	201	Applied practice: applying skills to the writing process	
9 ***Making Connections***	***202-203***		
Speaking and Listening	202	Applied practice: writing and presenting a dialogue	
Description in Fiction	203	Applied practice: writing a description of a character	
Literary Model from ***A Yellow Raft in Blue Water***	203	Example: analyzing a written portrait	
WHOLE-CHAPTER RESOURCES A Writing Process Log, A Writing Prompt, Holistically Graded Models, Assessment Portfolio Materials			

SEGMENT 1 *(pp. 158–162)*

IMAGINING OTHER WORLDS

OBJECTIVES

- To respond personally to a poem
- To analyze the characteristics of imaginative writing in a model poem

TEACHING THE LESSON

You may want to initiate a class discussion about creative writing, especially poetry, before beginning this segment. Begin by asking students if they have favorite poems, or even favorite children's verses. If students are able, have them recite their favorite poems to the class. Ask students to explain what they like about their special

VISUAL CONNECTIONS
Last Painter on Earth

About the Artist. James Doolin, born in Connecticut in 1932 and reared in Philadelphia, became interested in visual arts when he was a young child. He was inspired by many forms of art, from cartoons and movies to paintings and photographs. He has received such awards as the Guggenheim Foundation Fellowship in Painting, and several of his paintings are included in permanent public collections. In the early 1980s Doolin spent three years living in a remote area of the Mojave Desert in California and produced a body of desert landscapes including *Last Painter on Earth.*

Exploring the Subject. It may be that when Doolin was living by himself in the desert, he had the feeling that he was the last painter on earth. Ask students if they can think of times when they used their imaginations to exaggerate or transform situations in their lives. Point out that the use of imagination is crucial to creative writing.

5 CREATIVE WRITING

poems. [Students might reply that they like the poems because of the rhythm or rhyme, the description involved, or the subject matter.]

Have a volunteer read the introductory paragraphs of the chapter. Emphasize that creative writing may use the ordinary, the unusual, or even a mix of both. Before you read Ishmael Reed's poem, explain to students that the purpose for reading poetry is for entertainment, pleasure, and whatever inspiration or meaning it may offer.

You may want to read the model poem aloud and to use your rendition as an aid in helping students interpret the poem.

Guide students through questions 1 and 4 of **Reader's Response** and **Writer's Craft** by having a class discussion. To help ☛

Imagining Other Worlds

A classroom is a natural place to talk about **imagining other worlds.** Be honest: Can't you daydream yourself right out the window?

Writing and You. When you daydream, you're just exercising your imagination, as writers do when they create places and people, settings and characters that let us—for a while—leave our ordinary worlds. Sometimes the imagined place *is* ordinary, like the hot, dusty Texas in S. E. Hinton's novels. Sometimes it's the out-of-this-world world of a science fiction movie, like *Star Wars.* Always, though, in stories, plays, and films, words and imagination create fictional worlds that seem so real we actually believe in them. Could your daydreams hold realities waiting for words?

As You Read. The poet Ishmael Reed dares you to read the following poem. What does that say about his imagination? Will you dare? What does that say about your imagination?

James Doolin, *Last Painter on Earth* (1983). Oil on canvas, 72" × 120". Courtesy of Koplin Gallery, Santa Monica, CA.

QUOTATION FOR THE DAY

"So I try to encourage them . . . to appreciate every different way of writing and to learn from what seems most alien to them." (Marvin Bell, 1937–   , American poet)

Ask students to identify parts of Ishmael Reed's poem on pp. 160–161 that seem strange to them. Do alien spelling contractions such as *abt* and *yr* add to the eerie feeling of the poem? Poets often experiment with the words' appearances to capture and guide the reader's attention.

MEETING INDIVIDUAL NEEDS

LEP/ESL

General Strategies. In **"Beware: Do Not Read This Poem,"** Reed uses some unconventional abbreviations and punctuation that may be confusing to students. You may want to interpret for them the following items: *abt, ol, w/, woman/s, yr, frm,* and *us.*

initiate discussion, share a story of your own for question 1. Assign questions 2, 3, 5, and 6 as independent practice.

ASSESSMENT

Use responses to the **Reader's Response** and **Writer's Craft** questions to assess students' abilities to respond to and analyze a poem.

USING THE SELECTION

Beware: Do Not Read This Poem

1

Ishmael Reed is an African American publisher, novelist, essayist, and poet. He was co-founder in New York City of the *East Village Other,* one of the most successful of the alternative newspapers of the 1960s.

2

thriller: a supernatural horror television show popular during the 1960s

3

Reed's odd abbreviations help set an offbeat tone.

4

This *I* in *It* is the only capital letter in the poem, and there are only a few punctuation marks in the poem. The poet uses poetic license and capitalizes, punctuates, and spells however he wants to, without regard for the rules of grammar, usage, and mechanics.

BEWARE: DO NOT READ THIS POEM

1 **by Ishmael Reed**

2 tonite, *thriller* was
3 abt an ol woman, so vain she
surrounded herself w/
many mirrors

4 It got so bad that finally she
locked herself indoors & her
whole life became the
mirrors

one day the villagers broke
into her house, but she was too
swift for them, she disappeared
into a mirror
each tenant who bought the house
after that, lost a loved one to
the ol woman in the mirror:
first a little girl
then a young woman
then the young woman/s husband

CLOSURE

Ask students to describe their emotional reactions to the model poem. What devices did the author use to evoke the reactions? How do those devices help to define the theme of the poem? ■

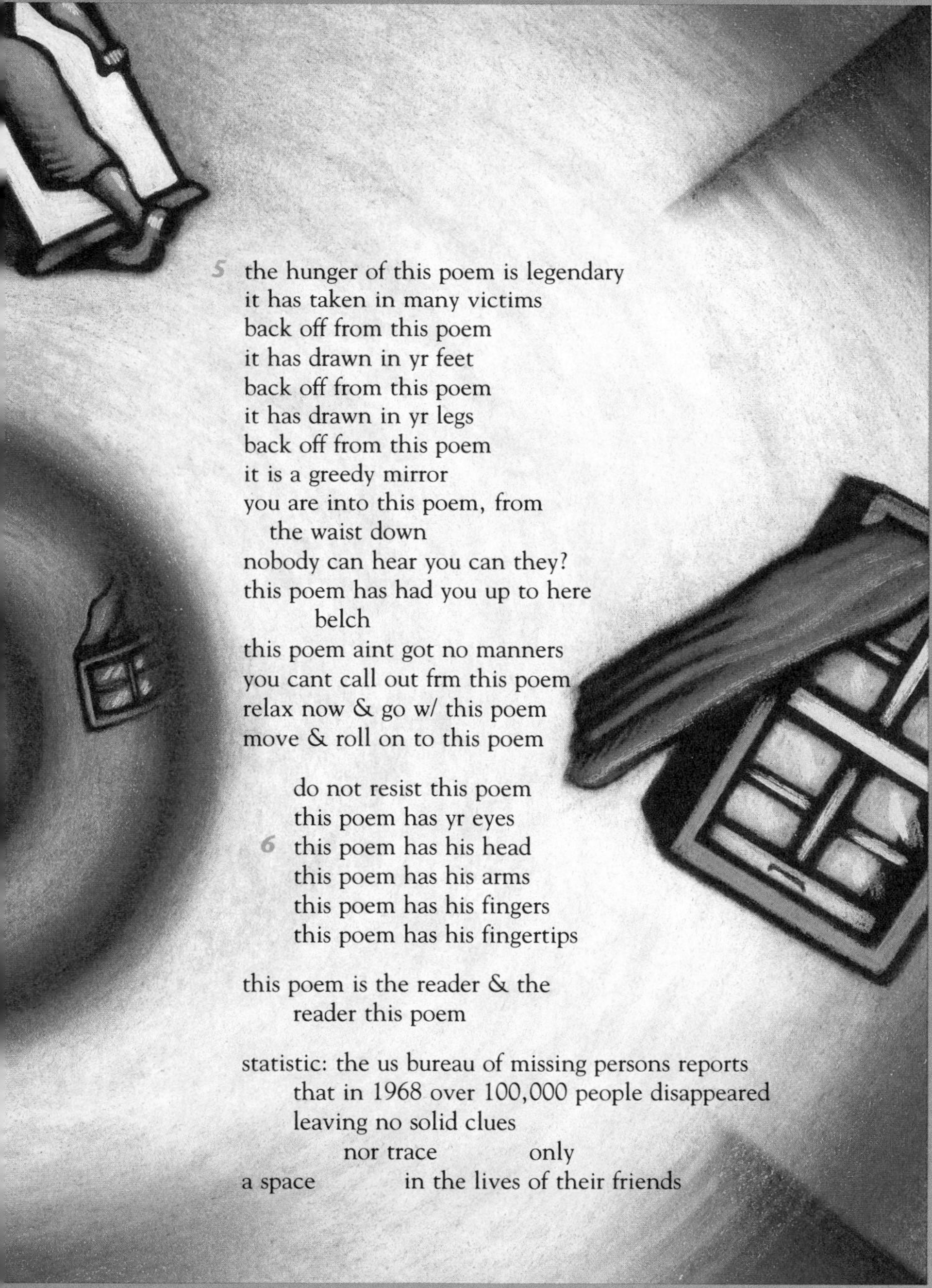

5 the hunger of this poem is legendary
it has taken in many victims
back off from this poem
it has drawn in yr feet
back off from this poem
it has drawn in yr legs
back off from this poem
it is a greedy mirror
you are into this poem, from
the waist down
nobody can hear you can they?
this poem has had you up to here
belch
this poem aint got no manners
you cant call out frm this poem
relax now & go w/ this poem
move & roll on to this poem

do not resist this poem
this poem has yr eyes
6 this poem has his head
this poem has his arms
this poem has his fingers
this poem has his fingertips

this poem is the reader & the
reader this poem

statistic: the us bureau of missing persons reports
that in 1968 over 100,000 people disappeared
leaving no solid clues
nor trace only
a space in the lives of their friends

5
Here the poet sets up the central analogy of the poem between the mirror devouring the tenants in the *thriller* episode and the poem devouring its readers.

6
Why does Reed switch from the use of second-person pronouns to the use of third-person pronouns? [This switch signifies the point at which the reader or "you" disappear and the poem and the reader merge and become one.]

ANSWERS

Reader's Response

Responses will vary.

1. Students should describe their experiences.
2. Students should explain their answers by citing relevant passages.
3. Here are some possible responses: The poem may be about responding so strongly to art that one becomes lost in it, or the poem may be about art serving as a mirror reflecting to people things about themselves.

Writer's Craft

Answers will vary.

4. Possible stories in the poem include a mirror that engulfs a vain woman and subsequent tenants of the house; the poem that slowly devours the reader until the reader and the poem merge; and the mystery suggested by the statistics on the numbers of missing persons.
5. Lines that appeal to the sense of sound are "nobody can hear you can they?"; "belch"; and "you can't call out from this poem." Lines that might appeal to the sense of taste are "the hunger of this poem is legendary"; "belch." All the lines that describe the poem devouring its victims and that mention movements or body parts appeal to the sense of touch.
6. The rhythm in the first three stanzas is relaxed, like narrative, and the second part of the poem has a stacatto, urgent rhythm, like rap music. The poem is supposedly a warning, and the sound of the poem is somewhat ominous as befits a warning.

Reader's Response

1. Being swallowed by a poem may seem like an unusual idea, but maybe Reed has just chosen an unusual way to put it. What poem, story, movie, childhood puppet show, or campfire ghost tale held your attention so completely that you were "lost"?
2. What's your reaction to this poem? Do you think it's funny? Did you have trouble following it? Any other thoughts about the poem?
3. In your opinion, what is this poem *about*? Why do you think the poet wanted to write it?

Writer's Craft

4. Poems don't have to tell stories, but this one contains several stories, or at least hints of problems or conflicts that could be stories. What are the stories or conflicts?
5. This poem gives you a series of dramatic images by appealing not just to your sense of sight, but to your other senses, too. Find lines that appeal to the senses of sound, taste, and touch.
6. Read this poem out loud if you haven't. What is the rhythm like? What does it remind you of? How does the sound of the poem relate to what it supposedly *does*?

SEGMENT 2 *(p. 163)*

STRATEGIES FOR WRITING CREATIVELY

TEACHING THE MODES

The purpose of this section is to show students how the different modes can be used to develop writing with a literary aim. Discuss the modes of writing and have students suggest additional examples for each. To help students understand the various modes, bring a picture from a magazine to class and have students work in small groups to write brief stories about the picture. Have each group try to use only one mode, and after the groups are finished, have them share their stories with the class. ■

Strategies for Writing Creatively

Writers of poems, short stories, and plays all have the same purpose—to create literary works, to use language creatively.

When people write creatively, they start with their imagination and use their craft with words to make something that has never existed before. They create not just poems and stories but novels, song lyrics, movie and television scripts—even comic strips. Here are examples of different ways in which people write creatively.

▶ **Narration:** writing a science fiction story about creatures from another galaxy who land in a huge automobile junkyard on Earth; in a mystery novel, telling about a girl detective who saves a rock star from being killed by an insane fan.

▶ **Description:** in a poem, describing a baseball field at midnight; in a story about the Civil War, describing the sounds, sights, and smells of a battlefield.

Classification: in a song, comparing the rainbow to a trail; in a poem, comparing a bird's feathers to a musical instrument.

Evaluation: in a movie script, showing how one person's honesty can teach a lesson to an entire town; in a comic strip, telling a funny story to show that men and women should share housework.

LOOKING AHEAD

In the main assignment in this chapter, you'll use the strategies of narration and description to write a story. As you work through the assignment, keep in mind that a short story

- uses imagination to entertain the reader
- has a plot built on a problem or conflict
- develops characters and settings in believable and vivid ways

INTEGRATING THE LANGUAGE ARTS

Literature Link. You may want to provide students with examples of each of the modes presented in this segment. As an example of narration, you could use Edgar Allen Poe's poem "The Raven." For description, refer to the description of setting in Washington Irving's "The Devil and Tom Walker." Irving's short story also illustrates the evaluative mode, specifically in the last few paragraphs. For an example of classification, you could show students the use of comparison in Emily Dickinson's "'Hope' Is the Thing with Feathers."

SEGMENT 3 *(pp. 164–173)*

PREWRITING

OBJECTIVES

- To explore story ideas and to develop a short-story idea
- To develop conflict and plot for a short story
- To imagine characters and setting for a story
- To decide on point of view and to make a written plan for a story

Teacher's ResourceBank™

RESOURCES

PREWRITING

- Creating a Story Map 48

QUOTATION FOR THE DAY

"Get cozy with some brown wrapping paper. Try out a felt-point italic pen. Compose with a brush. Write on the back of posters." (Toni Cade Bambara, 1939– , African American writer and lecturer)

Writers try all sorts of rituals to stimulate their imaginations. Some sharpen pencils while others imagine private gardens. Encourage students to stimulate the flow of ideas by experimenting with different writing implements and writing surfaces. Experimentation works for professional writers.

MEETING INDIVIDUAL NEEDS

LEP/ESL

General Strategies. To help students think of ideas for the central conflicts of their stories, encourage them to draw on their experiences of learning about a new culture. Explain that fiction does not have to be created only from the writer's imagination. Many stories are based on real-life incidents.

Writing a Short Story

Prewriting

Exploring Story Ideas

Any person, situation, or place can become a story, with imagination. Some of you may be thinking, "But I'm not the creative type." You're mistaken. Remember all the play stories you invented as a child—in your head or in a backyard fort with friends? One way to revive that inventiveness is by asking "What if?" questions, a technique many professional writers use.

- What if the commander of an isolated army outpost becomes a friend of the Sioux he's expected to fight?
- What if two teenagers from warring families fall in love?
- What if a race of humans is completely and totally logical—never ruled by emotions?

MOTIVATION

Writing a story may seem like a daunting task to some students. Point out to students that they probably create good story ideas every day without realizing it. Ask students if they ever imagine scenarios in which they somehow get the best of people who have just angered them—people such as parents, siblings, or friends. Do they ever fantasize about being picked up by a space ship? Do they ever imagine falling in love? Tell students that writing a story starts with an idea, and anyone who ever fantasizes has ideas.

The familiar story ideas on the previous page were once just glimmers of ideas in the writers' minds, perhaps sparked by something simple—a picture of a dusty, abandoned cabin, for example. So when you're looking for story ideas, pay attention to everything—from conversations you overhear on the bus to an article in a newspaper, to your own daydreams, nightmares, and memories—and ask "What if?" Unleash your imagination and see where it goes.

EXERCISE 1 Exploring Story Ideas

To see where your imagination leads you, start with "What if?" and freewrite about any two of the following ideas.

1. the first time you were left alone in the house
2. a dream or a nightmare
3. a stranger who made you nervous
4. a news item you couldn't believe
5. a time you were disappointed, angry, scared, happily surprised, or too excited to sleep

WRITING ASSIGNMENT
PART 1:
Finding Your Story Ideas

Did your freewriting for Exercise 1 spark a story idea? If not, keep your eyes, ears, and mind open. You could transform the familiar: *What if at breakfast your mother announces she's decided to become a country-western singer?* Or you could explore the familiar: *What if a teenager wants to drop out of school?* When you find a story idea, write it in a sentence or two.

What if

COOPERATIVE LEARNING

Having students participate in a story round is one way to stimulate students' imaginations for creative writing. Divide the class into mixed-ability groups of four or five students each. Have each group sit in a circle, and have each student start to write a short story. After five minutes, have each student pass his or her story to the person on the right. The next student must now read the story received and continue writing. Have the groups continue to pass the stories around the circles until each student has written a segment for each story in the group. Each successive round of writers will need an extra minute to read the lengthening stories. The last person to work on each story should write its conclusion. You could have each group decide on one story that a group representative will read aloud to the class.

ANSWERS
Exercise 1

Have students pick topics and then have them write for a set amount of time—perhaps three minutes. Give students a signal to start and have them keep writing until time is called. Students should then write on their second topic choice until time is called a second time. You may want to give them a moment to look over their writing to mark good ideas with an asterisk. Straying from the subject or ending with a different story should not be penalized.

TEACHING THE LESSON

Guide students in a discussion of the material on pp. 164–165 to help them begin to think about possible topics for their stories. To prepare students for **Exercise 1** and **Writing Assignment: Part 1** on p. 165, have a class brainstorming session on one of the topics in **Exercise 1.** Then assign **Exercise 1** and **Writing Assignment: Part 1** as independent practice. Be sure all students have topics in mind before moving on to the **Planning Your Story** section.

As you read over the material on planning a story with students, you may want to analyze a movie that students have seen. Discuss the movie's plot and conflict. Have students identify the movie's conflict and classify it as external, internal, or some of

INTEGRATING THE LANGUAGE ARTS

Literature Link. Have students read a short story such as Sherwood Anderson's "Sophistication" or F. Scott Fitzgerald's "Winter Dreams." Both short stories contain examples of internal and external conflicts. After students have read either story, have them identify the elements of the plot: conflict, complications, climax, and resolution. Discuss with the class how the internal conflict and the external conflict work together to make an interesting plot.

Prewriting

Planning Your Story

Now you're going to build on your idea, bringing your glimpse of a good story into full view. And you can do it. Even though there's always a touch of mystery in every creation, story writing—like any kind of writing—has basic elements that you can learn about, focus on, and make work for you.

Developing Conflict and Plot

A ***plot*** is what happens in a story, but it's not just any series of events. You may have noticed that all the examples of story ideas so far contained a problem, or at least a germ of one. That's crucial: At the heart of every plot is a ***conflict,*** a problem that the main character faces. Without conflict there's no story; and with it, there's every kind of story under the sun.

TYPES OF CONFLICT		
External Conflict	The main character is in conflict with another character, a group, or society's rules.	Alfonso's parents want him to stay in school, but he's failing computer class and English.
	The main character is in conflict with a force of nature.	A woman must survive the flood that's sweeping away her house.
Internal Conflict	The main character struggles with his or her own feelings, values, or needs.	Justine's obsession with earning money is taking over her life.

A plot also has a definite shape. It isn't as random as real life can be: The main conflict makes the characters act. Events connect to each other in a chain of cause and effect. The writer pulls readers steadily along.

To heighten interest, ***complications*** may arise: a setback for the main character or a new conflict (perhaps a wild animal threatens the flood-bound woman).

both. Using a format such as the one below in **Here's How,** map out on the chalkboard a plot plan of the movie. Have students supply the conflict, complications, climax, and resolution.

To prepare students for **Writing Assignment: Part 2,** take the same story idea from **Exercise 1** that you used for guided practice and model for students the process of developing conflict and plot for the story idea. Then assign **Writing Assignment: Part 2** as independent practice. Allow some class time for this independent work so that you can be available for students who are having difficulty.

Before reading the information on characters and setting, ask students to name favorite characters from books, movies, or ☛

But eventually comes a tense moment, the ***climax,*** when the conflict is decided, one way or another. The climax (sometimes called the "turning point") isn't always a fireworks scene; it may be a quiet decision. But it's the point in your story where your main character comes to terms with the conflict.

The complications and climax of the story eventually lead to the ***resolution:*** the aftermath, the final details that show how the conflict is resolved. The resolution should leave the reader feeling satisfied that, whether it is happy or sad, the ending is appropriate.

When you're planning your plot, keep this rising and falling shape in mind: conflict, complications, CLIMAX, resolution. Here is one writer's plan for the plot of his story.

HERE'S HOW

Conflict:	*External—Alfonso vs. computers, English, etc. He may fail.* *Internal—pride vs. feeling defeated—also wanting to succeed for parents*
Plot Events:	*Alfonso struggles with his computer assignment. Getting mad. Thinks about parents, past. Elvira comes in, offers to teach Alfonso. He tries, it's worse, gets madder, pops off at Elvira. She starts to leave.*
Climax:	*Alfonso swallows his pride and apologizes. Elvira stays.*
Resolution:	*Alfonso's doing better in school. He's dating Elvira.*

WRITING ASSIGNMENT

PART 2:
Developing Your Conflict and Plot

Now, start to shape your story idea from Writing Assignment, Part 1. What conflict will be the heart of your plot? How will it be solved? What events will lead to the climactic moment? What complications could create suspense? After you know what's going to happen in your story, summarize the plot in a few sentences. You might follow the format in the Here's How.

MEETING **INDIVIDUAL** NEEDS

AT-RISK STUDENTS

For students facing serious problems in their lives, creative writing offers the opportunity for transformation. Through the creative process, students can sometimes gain a new perspective and learn a coping or healing strategy. Remind students that they can write about their own experiences and that as writers, they are the masters of all the elements in their stories.

television shows. Have students analyze how the characters are presented and why the characters are effective. Then have a student volunteer read aloud **Exploring Characters and Setting.**

To prepare students for **Writing Assignment: Part 3,** again use the story idea from guided practice for **Exercise 1.** Guide the class through the questions on pp. 168–169 to develop one character and three or four details of setting for the model story. Then allow students to work independently on **Writing Assignment: Part 3.**

As you discuss point of view, ask students to identify books, movies, or television shows that illustrate each of the three types of point of view discussed. After students

INTEGRATING THE LANGUAGE ARTS

Technology Link. If students are composing on computers, they might use a painting or drawing program to illustrate their stories. At the prewriting stage, student art will help them to picture the setting and characters for themselves. At the final stage, the pictures will serve as illustrations for the reader.

Exploring Characters and Setting

Characters. *Characters* are fun to dream up. You can make them be anything and do anything, but you can also borrow bits and pieces from real-life people. You might, for instance, create a woman space explorer who looks a little like your cousin Deanna but has the brains of your math teacher. Even if your main character is a horse (why not?), that horse has to be a solid, distinctive individual. Here are some questions to help you create your characters.

- What's the character's name?
- How does the character look, dress, and talk?
- What does the character like to do and think about?
- What words best describe the character's personality?
- What do other characters think about this character?

Setting. If the time or place of your story, its ***setting,*** is unusual—frontier days, for example, or another galaxy—you've probably already imagined some details. Remember, though, that any setting—a mall, a car—can tell readers about your characters and their world.

Setting can even be central to a conflict, like a flood, and it can definitely set a mood (create a general feeling). Just think of stories set in a scorching, breathless desert or at a sad, cheap carnival. Use the following questions to explore how setting can work for your story.

have completed the **Critical Thinking Exercise** on pp. 171–172, have a volunteer read aloud **Thinking About Purpose, Audience, and Tone,** p. 172. Using the same story idea you used for the earlier **Writing Assignment Parts,** model for students the process of choosing a point of view and drawing up a plan for a story. Explain to students that they can make outlines of their plans or they may prefer to use clustering or webbing. Assign **Writing Assignment: Part 4** on p. 173 as independent practice.

- Exactly when and where does the story take place?
- What objects, weather, buildings, or details of everyday life could be important?
- Could setting add to mood? Could it convey a particular emotion or atmosphere?
- What sounds, smells, sights, tastes, and textures should be described?
- What details of setting could convey information about the plot or the characters in your story?

WRITING NOTE

You will probably come up with many more details about characters and setting than you'll actually use when you write your story, but the details you jot down now will make your characters and their background more real to you. It's like putting money into savings. Once it is there, you can take out what you need when you need it. So feel free to explore your characters and setting fully.

WRITING ASSIGNMENT

PART 3:

Imagining Your Characters and Setting

Can you imagine your setting and characters so vividly that you can see yourself standing there with them? To make your readers see your characters and setting, you must first be able to see them clearly yourself. Use the questions on page 168 and above to give flesh to your creations. You may want to use freewriting or brainstorming to keep ideas flowing. Save your notes to use later.

Choosing a Point of View

When you choose a ***point of view*** for your story, you are deciding the vantage point from which readers will see events. Remember, though, it is not your personal viewpoint; it is the viewpoint of the narrator. As the following chart shows, you have three basic points of view to choose from: first-person, third-person omniscient, and third-person limited. Each point of view has its own set of advantages and disadvantages.

INTEGRATING THE LANGUAGE ARTS

Vocabulary Link. To give students practice in writing descriptions, write the following paragraph on the chalkboard:

The man drove down the street in his car. He waved to the people he saw on the porch of the house. A girl and her two dogs crossed the street behind his car.

Ask students to copy the paragraph and to add at least ten vivid adjectives, adverbs, or verbs.

Before having students share their paragraphs with the class, remind them that they all began with the same sentences. As students share their revisions, discuss with them how different images of the man, house, girl, and dogs are created through different choices of words.

ASSESSMENT

To assess students' mastery of the material on prewriting, evaluate the work from **Exercise 1** and **Writing Assignment: Parts 1–4.** It is important that students complete all the prewriting stages before they move on to the next segment on writing drafts.

RETEACHING

Students who have difficulty developing a story plan might benefit from first completing a story plan for a familiar story such as Poe's "The Tell-Tale Heart." Have students analyze the familiar story for each of the story elements. This process may help students feel more able to develop their own story plans. ***Cont. on p. 172***

INTEGRATING THE LANGUAGE ARTS

Literature Link. Explain to students that although shifts in point of view can be confusing for the reader, writers do sometimes use such a shift as an effective literary device.

Have students read Ambrose Bierce's short story "An Occurrence at Owl Creek Bridge." Ask them to identify two points at which shifts in point of view occur and to identify the shifts. [At the beginning of the third part of the story, there is a shift from third-person omniscient to third-person limited; in the final paragraph there is a shift back to third-person omniscient.] Ask students why they think Bierce shifted to third-person limited point of view for the third part of the story. [Answers may vary. Since this part of the story is a fantasy from Farquhar's imagination, he is the only one who witnessed it. The shift in point of view sets the fantasy apart from the rest of the story.]

POINT OF VIEW

NARRATOR	EFFECTS
First-person: The narrator is a character in the story and uses the first-person pronouns *I, me, our,* and so on.	This point of view is personal and immediate but can only tell what one person sees, hears, feels, and believes.
Third-person omniscient: The narrator is outside of the story and can enter any character's mind. (*Omniscient* means "all-knowing." *Third-person* means using the pronouns *he, them,* and so on.)	This narration is more impersonal but has unlimited freedom—showing the past or future, speaking to the reader, telling (or withholding) any detail.
Third-person limited: The narrator is outside the story but enters the mind of *one* character.	This point of view gives one character's perspective without being restricted to that person's actions or location. It combines the personal with a storyteller's distance.

Once you have decided on the point of view you want to use, you must stick to it. Shifts in point of view can be very confusing to your readers.

IN OR OUT (DEPENDING ON YOUR POINT OF VIEW)
THAVES 9-6
FRANK & ERNEST reprinted by permission of N

CRITICAL THINKING
(pp. 171–172)

OBJECTIVES
- To analyze point of view in a passage
- To rewrite a passage to change its point of view

TEACHING *ANALYZING POINT OF VIEW*

Before reading the introductory text, ask students if they have ever been in a situation where their perception of an event differs from someone else's. You may want to use the perception of fault in a traffic accident as an example. After this discussion,

CRITICAL THINKING

Analyzing Point of View

When you use the critical thinking skill of *analysis*, you examine something closely, studying its parts in order to understand how they function or how they relate to each other. To understand point of view, it is essential to analyze, or examine closely, its effects on the telling of a story. Here are some questions you can use to analyze point of view:

- What is the effect if the narrator stands back in the distance, knowing everything that is going on, including what all of the characters are thinking?
- What is the effect if the narrator is a minor character in the story—perhaps the friend or younger brother of the hero or heroine? What can this narrator know about what the main character thinks and feels?
- What is the effect if the narrator is the main character in the story? How objective is this narrator?

CRITICAL THINKING EXERCISE:
Analyzing Point of View

The following passage uses third-person limited point of view. Working with two or three classmates, read it and use the questions for discussion and analysis.

> Lalu felt herself shoved in front of the customs officer. She had never been close to a white man before and she stared amazed at the one that towered above her. His skin was chalk white, like the face of an actor painted to play a villain, only it was not smooth but covered with wiry golden hair, and when his mouth opened and closed, there were no words to make an audience shake with anger or fear, only a senseless roaring. Beside him, a Chinese man spoke.
>
> Ruthanne Lum McCunn, *Thousand Pieces of Gold*

MEETING **INDIVIDUAL** NEEDS

LEP/ESL

General Strategies. In the passage from *Thousand Pieces of Gold,* there are four personal pronouns and one proper noun that refer to the central character. Each of these pronouns or nouns will have to be changed to a first-person pronoun for question 2. You could have students highlight all the pronouns that denote point of view in their rewrites to make sure each pronoun in their rewrites maintains a consistent point of view. Refer students to the lists of first- and third-person pronouns on p. 675.

SELECTION AMENDMENT
Description of change: excerpted
Rationale: to focus on the concept of creative writing presented in this chapter

students should be better prepared to analyze point of view.

After students have completed the **Critical Thinking Exercise,** ask volunteers to share their rewrites. Discuss with the class the effects of changing the point of view in the passage.

Cont. from p. 170

CLOSURE

Have students name the steps involved in planning a story. [Find an idea, develop conflict and plot, imagine characters and setting, choose a point of view, and put a story plan on paper.] ■

ANSWERS

Critical Thinking Exercise

1. Lalu's mind is entered in the narration. The character is female and probably not white. Most of Lalu's personal perceptions are amazement at the white man: noticing the whiteness of his face, noticing the hair on his face, comparing him to an actor in a play, and being unable to make any sense of his roaring.
2. Narrations will vary, but all should use first-person point of view and should contain personal impressions.
3. Rewrites will vary. For first-person point of view, students can write from the point of view of either the customs officer or the Chinese man. If students choose third-person omniscient point of view, they should demonstrate that they know what all the characters are thinking.

1. Which character's mind is "entered" in the narration? What are you told about the character? What are some of the character's personal perceptions?
2. How would the narration change if the central character were telling about this incident? To explore, rewrite the passage in the first person. Be sure to use *I* and *me* and to think about the character's personality.
3. Choose one of the other characters (there are two others: did you find both?), and rewrite the passage, using *either* first-person or third-person omniscient point of view. You may add details, but don't change events.

Thinking About Purpose, Audience, and Tone

Purpose and Audience. Your main *purpose* in writing your story is to be creative and to entertain your *audience,* which will probably be your classmates. That's why it is important to think ahead about the effect you want to have on your readers. Do you want to scare them or give them the creeps? Would you love for them to cry buckets of tears? Remember that entertaining people doesn't always mean making them laugh, but it does mean keeping them interested and involved.

Sometimes you may want to plant in your readers' minds the seed of an idea—about pride or gangs or even dieting. A message like this is called a ***theme,*** and although you don't usually state messages outright in a story (*our society's obsession with thinness often hurts people*), you can often show them through characters and plot.

Tone. *Tone,* of course, is tied up with purpose because it's the attitude you take toward the characters and events. Your story's tone may be mysterious, affectionate, joking, angry, matter-of-fact—you name it. It's any feeling that fits your tale.

The point of view you choose contributes to tone. A depressed character, for instance, won't make a cheerful first-person narrator. You also create tone through descriptive details (perhaps flying clouds and warm sun), type of language (perhaps blunt words and slang), and rhythm of sentences (perhaps short, simple ones). In a story, everything adds up.

Reminder

To plan your story

- start with a main character facing a definite conflict, and decide how you'll solve it
- give the plot a shape—a chain of events with complications, climax, and resolution
- imagine characters and setting in solid detail
- choose a point of view and stick with it
- think ahead about the effects and ideas you want to create for readers

WRITING ASSIGNMENT

PART 4:
Planning Your Story

Now it's time to gather together the notes you have made about plot, character, and setting (from Parts 2 and 3 of your Writing Assignment). Also decide on your point of view. Remember that you are drawing a blueprint, not building a final house with solid walls and locked doors. You're very likely to make some changes—dropping events, even adding a character—when you draft, but put your plan on paper first.

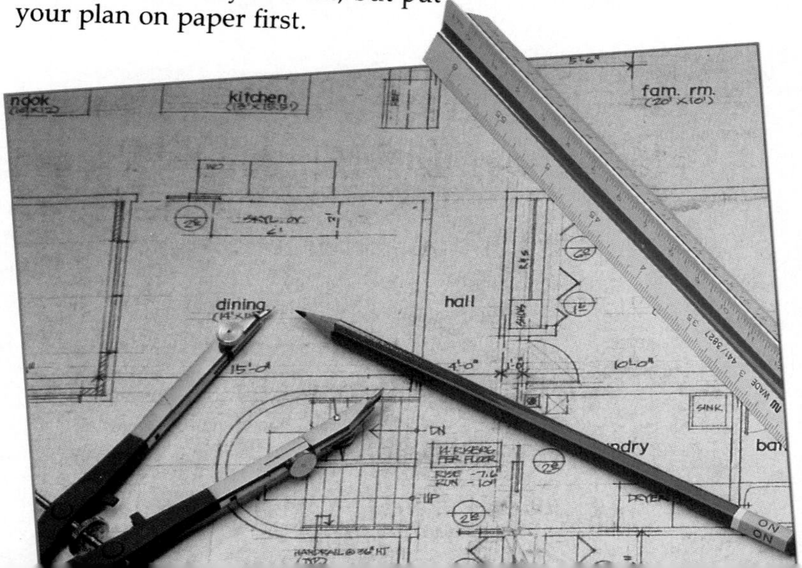

MEETING INDIVIDUAL NEEDS

AT-RISK STUDENTS

Most likely, some of your students work at jobs after school, are responsible for the care of younger siblings, or have other duties that severely cut into homework time. Because it is difficult to write imaginatively or creatively when one is tired, you may need to provide class time for prewriting activities or allow some of your students extra time to complete their writing assignments.

SEGMENT 4 *(pp. 174–188)*

WRITING YOUR FIRST DRAFT

OBJECTIVES

- To write and present dialogue
- To analyze a professional model of a short story
- To write a draft of a short story

MOTIVATION

Writing the first part of the story is often a major stumbling block for students. They believe that if they can figure out how to begin, the rest of the story will fall more naturally into place. To inspire students, share with them the beginnings of some stories. For example, you might share the first few sentences of an Edgar Allen Poe short

Teacher's ResourceBank™

RESOURCES

WRITING YOUR FIRST DRAFT

- Writing a Short Story 49

QUOTATION FOR THE DAY

"Never go inside a character's head until you know what he looks like." (Flannery O'Connor, 1925–1964, American short-story writer and novelist)

A technique commonly employed by impressionists on the stage is to use a hat, facial tic, or mannerism that identifies the public figure they are portraying. These props help the impressionist locate the heart of the person he or she is mimicking. A similar technique is useful to a writer of dialogue who needs to see the jaw line, eyes, or gait of the character he or she is describing before writing realistic dialogue.

ANSWERS

Exercise 2

Dialogues should contribute to character development. In addition to evaluating the presentations, you may want to assess the written versions of the dialogues, since the written form of the dialogues is what students will have to concentrate on when they write their first drafts. Peer evaluation of dialogues should be specific.

Writing Your First Draft

You know what it's like to lose yourself in a story. You are so drawn into the story that you seem to be living alongside the characters. That's the kind of reality you need to aim for in your first draft, and here are some tips that will help.

Combining the Basic Elements of Stories

Believable Characters. It's tempting to tell your readers about a character: *Aisha was a vain girl who spent a lot of time working on how she looked.* However, it is better to stand back and let your characters create themselves.

- **Show the character in action.** *Aisha stepped in front of the mirror to check her hair for the third time.*
- **Let readers hear the character's thoughts.** *Aisha thought her new lipstick looked extremely cool with her golden skin.*
- **Show how other characters react.** *"Aisha," Kim said, "like, you're the fairest, OK? Give me my compact and let's go."*

Notice that ***dialogue*** really adds to believability. It must sound natural, though, so give each speaker words that fit the character's age, personality, and background. You can use contractions, slang, fragments—whatever sounds right.

EXERCISE 2 **Speaking and Listening: Creating Dialogue**

Get together with a partner to make up a dialogue for the characters in one of the following situations. First, spend some time imagining details of character and setting. When you're happy with your dialogue, set the scene for the class and present the dialogue. Ask for some feedback on why you sounded natural—or why you didn't quite make it.

1. A teenager tells a parent that he or she wants to get married right after graduation from high school.
2. A police officer talks to a young boy he has found out on the street after midnight.
3. A woman tells her boss she has won the lottery and is quitting her job.

story. His stories usually begin with a dramatic description or action. The opening of Katherine Anne Porter's "The Jilting of Granny Weatherall" provides a good character description.

TEACHING THE LESSON

Have a volunteer read the introductory paragraphs aloud before working on **Exercise 2** with the class. To prepare students for **Exercise 2**, model the process of creating a dialogue by using the characters in the following situation: The star player of the basketball team has just gotten her report card and has to tell her coach that ☛

Vivid Descriptions. A good story is a sensory experience. You can create such a story by using ***images***—sensory details that let readers see, hear, smell, taste, and touch what's happening. This doesn't mean describing every object, person, and event in microscopic detail, but it does mean using imagery to bring important elements into sharp focus. Notice how every descriptive detail in the following passage makes the setting concrete, moves the action forward, reveals character, or creates mood.

> We hurried along. The white daytime moon showed on a patch of turquoise sky between clouds. The rain was fine, like sifted flour. My mother was in a good mood but seemed aware this could easily pass. She looked at the rain and the sky as if they were possessions someone might take from her at any moment. The clouds suddenly seemed to be turning over themselves, and in a second they broke. We got drenched.
>
> Cynthia Kadohata, *The Floating World*

The passage also shows how ***figurative language*** such as ***metaphors*** and ***similes***—comparisons of two unlike things—can enrich description. Rain "like sifted flour" is a swift, clear word picture far more vivid than "fine rain."

☛ REFERENCE NOTE: For more about figurative language, see pages 373 and 495–497.

MEETING **INDIVIDUAL** NEEDS

LEP/ESL

General Strategies. You may want to assure students that their first drafts will not be graded on grammar, usage, and mechanics. Tell them not to focus too much on spelling, punctuation, and grammar, but rather to concentrate on the development of their ideas.

SELECTION AMENDMENT
Description of change: excerpted
Rationale: to focus on the concept of creative writing presented in this chapter

her low grades make her ineligible to play. After creating dialogue for the model situation, assign the completion of **Exercise 2** as independent practice.

When discussing vivid description, you may want to share other examples with your students. For example, you could analyze the description of the bear in William Faulkner's short story "The Bear." The bear is characterized both by his physical appearance and by his relationship to nature and the wilderness. Emphasize that description need not include every minute detail to etch a picture and create a scene for the reader.

To analyze how plot and conflict work in a short story, refer to the material on plot on pp. 166–167 after reading Louis Dollarhide's **"The Gift."** Discuss with students how each

CRITICAL THINKING
Analysis

Louis Dollarhide clearly establishes the mood in the first few paragraphs of **"The Gift."** Lead students in a discussion of how the mood is created. What words create a specific mood? [Students might suggest words such as "cold brown water" or "claimed . . . and surrounded."] How does the rhythm of the words and sentences establish the mood? [Students might suggest mood is established by the repetition of words (such as "From hour to hour") and the parallel use of verbs (such as "watching . . . dissolving . . . driving . . . beating" or "slithered . . . poured . . . claimed . . . surrounded.")]

USING THE SELECTION
The Gift

1
drift: something moved by water currents

2
Tar is used to seal and preserve wood, especially in wet environments.

A Tight Plot. If an action or a detail doesn't advance your story, don't let it in. In other words, keep your plot lean and mean. The best way to hook your readers is to get to the conflict and main character as soon as possible. And remember the "chain-link" plot: One event clearly leads to another. Keep readers guessing about what a scene will hold, not how they got there!

Another way to make events clear for your readers is to maintain chronological order (see page 75), except when you must give a ***flashback,*** a passage that supplies important past events. Use a flashback only if it is really needed—to help readers understand a conflict, for example.

Looking at a Short Story

Although the following story, by a professional writer, is a real knuckle-whitener, it has a simple plot, just one human character, and almost no dialogue. As you read, notice how the writer gets your attention and keeps it. What makes the characters believable and the plot a tight chain?

A SHORT STORY

The Gift
by Louis Dollarhide

Setting/Suspense

Flashback

Setting/Mood

How many days, she wondered, had she sat like this, watching the cold brown water inch up the dissolving <u>bluff</u>. She could just faintly remember the beginning of the rain, driving in across the swamp from the south and beating against the shell of her house. Then the river itself started rising, slowly at first until at last it paused as if to turn back. From hour to hour it slithered up creeks and ditches and poured over low places. In the night, while she slept, it claimed the road and surrounded her so that she sat alone, her boat gone, the house
1 like a piece of drift lodged on its bluff. Now even
2 against the tarred planks of the supports the waters
touched. And still they rose.

event in the story leads to future events and how all of the action is interconnected.

As guided practice for **Exercise 3** on p. 182, pick one of the questions and lead the class in a discussion in which you demonstrate how to find details in the story to answer the question. Then assign the rest of the questions in **Exercise 3** as independent practice.

The two short-story models presented in this segment are very different from each other. As students read or listen to **"The Gift,"** they should pay close attention to the descriptions and the character portrayals. Use the side glosses and the annotations to analyze the way in which short-story elements are employed.

Third-person limited point of view

Conflict established

Character developed

Mood heightened/ Sight and sound images

Figurative language and sensory images

As far as she could see, to the treetops where the opposite banks had been, the swamp was an empty sea, awash with sheets of rain, the river lost somewhere in its vastness. Her house with its boat bottom had been built to ride just such a flood, if one ever came, but now it was old. Maybe the boards underneath were partly rotted away. Maybe the cable mooring the house to the great live oak would snap loose and let her go turning downstream, the way her boat had gone.

No one could come now. She could cry out but it would be no use, no one would hear. Down the length and breadth of the swamp others were fighting to save what little they could, maybe even their lives. She had seen a whole house go floating by, so quiet she was reminded of sitting at a funeral. She thought when she saw it she knew whose house it was. It had been bad seeing it drift by, but the owners must have escaped to higher ground. Later, with the rain and darkness pressing

3 in, she had heard a panther scream upriver.

Now the house seemed to shudder around her like something alive. She reached out to catch a lamp as it tilted off the table by her bed and put it between her feet to hold it steady. Then creaking and groaning with effort the house struggled up from the clay, floated free, bobbing like a cork, and

3

The appearance of the panther is here foreshadowed.

When reading or listening to **A Writer's Model** on pp. 183–187, students should pay close attention to the plot development and the use of dialogue. The side glosses will be useful for identifying story elements and details. After students have read both stories, lead the class in a discussion of the differences and similarities in the elements of the two stories.

When students have practiced writing dialogue and have analyzed two short stories, they should be prepared to complete **Writing Assignment: Part 5** on p. 188 as independent practice.

Suspense

Complication

Suspense
Descriptive details

Suspense

swung out slowly with the pull of the river. She gripped the edge of the bed. Swaying from side to side, the house moved to the length of its mooring. There was a jolt and a complaining of old timbers and then a pause. Slowly the current released it and let it swing back, rasping across its resting place. She caught her breath and sat for a long time feeling the slow pendulous sweeps. The dark sifted down through the incessant rain, and, head on arm, she slept holding on to the bed.

Sometime in the night the cry awoke her, a
4 sound so anguished she was on her feet before she was awake. In the dark she stumbled against the bed. It came from out there, from the river. She could hear something moving, something large
5 that made a dredging, sweeping sound. It could be another house. Then it hit, not head on but glancing and sliding down the length of her house. It was a tree. She listened as the branches and leaves cleared themselves and went on downstream, leaving only the rain and the lappings of the flood, sounds so constant now that they seemed a part of the silence. Huddled on the bed, she was almost asleep again when another cry sounded, this time

4
anguished: full of great pain and suffering

5
dredging: scraping along a river bottom

ASSESSMENT

You can assess students' mastery of the segment concepts through an evaluation of responses to **Exercises 2** and **3** and **Writing Assignment: Part 5.** Conferences will provide the opportunity to assess students' progress in the writing of their drafts.

RETEACHING

If students are still having difficulty creating a tight plot after reading **"The Gift"** and **A Writer's Model,** you may want to bring a video of a television program to class and have students analyze its story elements.

so close it could have been in the room. Staring into the dark, she eased back on the bed until her hand caught the cold shape of the rifle. Then crouched on the pillow, she cradled the gun across her knees. "Who's there?" she called.

Dialogue

The answer was a repeated cry, but less shrill, tired sounding, then the empty silence closing in. She drew back against the bed. Whatever was there she could hear it moving about on the porch. Planks creaked and she could distinguish the sounds of objects being knocked over. There was a scratching on the wall as if it would tear its way in. She knew now what it was, a big cat, deposited by the uprooted tree that had passed her. It had come with the flood, a gift.

Suspense

Unconsciously she pressed her hand against her face and along her tightened throat. The rifle rocked across her knees. She had never seen a panther in her life. She had heard about them from others and had heard their cries, like suffering, in the distance. The cat was scratching on the wall again, rattling the window by the door. As long as she guarded the window and kept the cat hemmed in by the wall and water, caged, she would be all right. Outside, the animal paused to rake his claws across the rusted outer screen. Now and then, it whined and growled.

Character developed/ Actions

Setting and plot details

When the light filtered down through the rain at last, coming like another kind of dark, she was still sitting on the bed, stiff and cold. Her arms, used to rowing on the river, ached from the stillness of holding the rifle. She had hardly allowed herself to move for fear any sound might give strength to the cat. Rigid, she swayed with the movement of the house. The rain still fell as if it would never stop. Through the gray light, finally, she could see the rain-pitted flood and far away the cloudy shape of drowned treetops. The cat was not moving now. Maybe he had gone away. Laying the gun aside she slipped off the bed and moved without a sound to the window. It was still there, crouched at the edge of the porch, staring up at the

Character developed

CLOSURE

Have students share portions of their drafts with the class. Ask for examples of a vivid description, a segment of dialogue, or a transition from one bit of action to the next.

ENRICHMENT

You may want to refer to Ishmael Reed's poem **"Beware: Do Not Read This Poem"** on pp. 160–161. Discuss the ways in which the poem shares many of the characteristics of short stories such as use of description, plot development, and a changing point of view. ■

6
napped: raised up by brushing

Character developed/ Thoughts

Conflict

live oak, the mooring of her house, as if gauging its chances of leaping to an overhanging branch. It did not seem so frightening now that she could see
6 it, its coarse fur napped into twigs, its sides pinched and ribs showing. It would be easy to shoot it where it sat, its long tail whipping back and forth. She was moving back to get the gun when it turned around. With no warning, no crouch or tensing of muscles, it sprang at the window, shattering a pane of glass. She fell back, stifling a scream, and taking up the rifle, she fired through the window. She could not see the panther now, but she had missed. It began to pace again. She could glimpse its head and the arch of its back as it passed the window.

Setting/Sensory images/Mood

7
lulling: smoothly, gently calming

Shivering, she pulled back on the bed and lay
7 down. The lulling constant sound of the river and the rain, the penetrating chill, drained away her purpose. She watched the window and kept the gun ready. After waiting a long while she moved again to look. The panther had fallen asleep, its head on its paws, like a housecat. For the first time

Character developed/ Thoughts and actions

Sensory images

Character and suspense developed/ Dialogue and actions

Climax

since the rains began she wanted to cry, for herself, for all the people, for everything in the flood. Sliding down on the bed, she pulled the quilt around her shoulders. She should have got out when she could, while the roads were still open or before her boat was washed away. As she rocked back and forth with the sway of the house a deep ache in her stomach reminded her she hadn't eaten. She couldn't remember for how long. Like the cat, she was starving. Easing into the kitchen, she made a fire with the few remaining sticks of wood. If the flood lasted she would have to burn the chair, maybe even the table itself. Taking down the remains of a smoked ham from the ceiling, she cut thick slices of the brownish red meat and placed them in a skillet. The smell of the frying meat made her dizzy. There were stale biscuits from the last time she had cooked and she could make some coffee. There was plenty of water.

While she was cooking her food, she almost forgot about the cat until it whined. It was hungry too. "Let me eat," she called to it, "and then I'll see to *you*." And she laughed under her breath. As she hung the rest of the ham back on its nail the cat growled a deep throaty rumble that made her hand shake.

After she had eaten, she went to the bed again and took up the rifle. The house had risen so high now it no longer scraped across the bluff when it swung back from the river. The food had warmed her. She could get rid of the cat while light still hung in the rain. She crept slowly to the window. It was still there, mewing, beginning again to move about the porch. She stared at it a long time, unafraid. Then without thinking what she was doing, she laid the gun aside and started around the edge of the bed to the kitchen. Behind her the cat was moving, fretting. She took down what was left of the ham and making her way back across the swaying floor to the window she shoved it through the broken pane. On the other side there was a

ANSWERS

Exercise 3

Answers may vary.

1. The conflict that sets the story in motion is the flood that maroons the main character and threatens her house. The second conflict begins when the panther is deposited on the main character's porch.
2. The main character is reflective, brave, independent, and compassionate. Here are a few examples of details that reveal her character and personality: her sitting and musing over the progress of the flood; her concern over the occupants of the house that drifted by; her wanting to cry for victims of the flood; the fact that she lives alone; her ability to protect herself from the cat; and her sharing the ham with the cat. The main character apparently had an internal conflict over whether or not to evacuate earlier. She has an internal conflict over whether or not to kill the panther.
3. The cat's personality is drawn through description of its physical characteristics, by tracking its movements, and through the main character's reactions.
4. In this story, the setting is pivotal. The flood provides the central conflict (the issue of survival for the main character) and the second conflict (the arrival of the panther). Some examples of passages that illustrate this point are the first three paragraphs, the passage where the main character discovers the cat, and any passages where the water or rain are mentioned.

hungry snarl and something like a shock passed from the animal to her. Stunned by what she had done, she drew back to the bed. She heard the sounds of the panther tearing at the meat. The house rocked around her.

Resolution

The next time she awoke she knew at once that everything had changed. The rain had stopped. She felt for the movement of the house but it no longer swayed on the flood. Drawing her door open, she saw through the torn screen a different world. The house was resting on the bluff where it always had. A few feet down, the river still raced on in a torrent, but it no longer covered the few feet between the house and the live oak. And the cat was gone. Leading from the porch to the live oak and doubtless on into the swamp were tracks, indistinct and already disappearing in the soft mud. And there on the porch, gnawed to whiteness, was what was left of the ham.

Setting

Descriptive details

EXERCISE 3 Analyzing a Short Story

After you read "The Gift," meet with a small group of classmates to discuss the story. See if you can agree on the answers to the following questions.

1. The main conflict in this story is external: a character versus nature. Survival is at stake. What conflict sets the story in motion? What second conflict arises in a complication?
2. What kind of person is the main character? What details reveal her character and personality? Do you see any internal conflicts in her? Explain.
3. The big cat is also a character. How does the writer give it "personality"?
4. What role does setting play in this story? Point out passages to show what you mean.
5. The climax of this story is a decision and an action. What is it? How is it related to the character's main conflict?

Using a Framework for a Short Story

"The Gift" is a very successful story, but in a way the writer set himself quite a task: using a single human character, closed up in a house, with two "opponents" who can't talk (the flood and the cat). Most writers, like the one whose story follows, are easier on themselves and use a more common pattern. You may want to follow this pattern when you write your own story.

A WRITER'S MODEL

A Little Help

Character introduced
Dialogue and action

Alfonso Moreno stared at the computer screen and wished he had a shovel to hit it with.

"Don't go blinking BAD COMMAND at me," he ordered. "Just tell me what to do!" Like a caged animal he glared around the lab but saw no one who could free him from the machine. Row after row of bright blue monitors shone coldly back at him.

Hint of conflict

Desperate to finish his computer assignment, Alfonso began to press buttons. He hit escape and enter, then help, end, and exit, pausing to groan at questions the computer demanded answers to--like SAVE DOCUMENT?

5. The climax comes when the main character feeds her last food to the panther. The woman's main conflict revolves around whether or not she can survive the forces of nature. The cat is a force of nature that threatens her, but it is also threatened by the flood, so the cat is both fellow victim and adversary. By sharing her food with the cat, the main character chooses to focus on the cat as fellow victim.

INTEGRATING THE LANGUAGE ARTS

Vocabulary Link. The first few paragraphs of **A Writer's Model** serve to establish the conflict between Alfonso and the computers. What words are important in establishing this conflict? [Students might suggest *wished, hit, caged, glared,* or *fury.*]

INTEGRATING THE LANGUAGE ARTS

Literature Link. Many of the short stories in literature textbooks contain good examples of the use of dialogue to present characters and actions. You may want to use an excerpt from Mark Twain's *Adventures of Huckleberry Finn* as an example. Discuss with students how Twain is able to use dialect and dialogue to show characterization and to set the tone of the story.

Character developed/ Dialogue and action	"What document?" he demanded in a fury. "There isn't any document, dummy. You won't let me make a document!"
Setting/ Background	Alfonso smacked the side of his computer terminal with the flat of his hand and jumped out of his seat. At the window he stared out at the empty tennis courts and the deserted baseball field behind them. He had never been to a school like this. A lawn and covered walks. A sports program. He still felt like a stranger.
Conflict	"I'll never make it," he muttered to himself. "I'm failing English. I'm failing this stupid computer class. I'm already seventeen and still in tenth grade. What's the use?"
Character's thoughts (third-person) **Background** **Flashback** **Sensory images** **Figurative language**	Education had never been his dream, anyway, he thought angrily. It was his parents' dream for him, and it wasn't coming true. His father had made it as far as the sixth grade. His mother had an eighth-grade education. They were traveling south now, looking for work. Alfonso had traveled with them and worked in the fields for much of each school year until this past September. When he thought of the fields, he remembered how the odor of garlic never left his hands. He remembered the ache in his knees and back, like the bite of a snake, the sweat streaming down his face and neck. His parents had taken him to stay with his godfather, a mechanic who had steady work in a garage.
	"You stay in school, now," his father said. "You can do better than us. We want you to make something of yourself."
	Alfonso turned quickly as the door to the computer lab opened, and Elvira Valdez walked in. "Hi," she said. "¿Qué pasa?"
Dialogue	Alfonso just stared. She spoke again. "I'm Elvira Valdez."
Character developed/ Actions	Alfonso glanced around to make sure no one else was in the lab. Was Elvira talking to him? "Oh. Sure. ¿Qué pasa?" Well, that was a cool response. He turned back to his computer, feeling like an idiot. He tried not to look at her, but it wasn't

Descriptive details

easy. She didn't have to introduce herself. He knew who she was. One of just a handful of Hispanic girls in the school, Elvira was beautiful, with long, dark brown hair, and deep eyes that had never looked at him before. At least not on purpose. Elvira was a senior, and Alfonso had heard that next year she was going to a big-name college on a full scholarship.

Sensory images

Alfonso began punching keys again. A clean, flowery smell, right at his elbow, suddenly awakened all of his senses. She was right there beside him! "Isn't your name Alfonso Moreno?" she asked.

"Yeah, that's me," Alfonso mumbled. She must think he was stupid!

Characters developed/ Dialogue

"You're working late," Elvira said. "You like computers?"

"Oh, yes," he answered, starting to get worked up again, Elvira beside him or not. "I love computers, but they hate my guts. The truth is I never saw a computer before this year, and I wish it'd stayed that way." He pulled out his last test paper. "See, I don't even know what the words mean. What's scroll? What's default? What kind of crazy English is this anyway?"

"Oh, that's just word-processing stuff. Let's see." Elvira tapped a couple of keys. "Computers are easy when you know what the commands mean. You want me to show you?"

A DIFFERENT APPROACH

Encourage students who speak in dialects other than standard English to use dialect in the dialogue for the first drafts of their stories. Have them experiment with how they might spell words to show the dialect in writing.

Character's thoughts

Plot developed

Alfonso started to say, "Yeah, help the dumb kid," but he hesitated. She seemed OK.

He pulled a chair over for her. She told him to do this and that, he did it. So far so good. He tried something on his own, he got lost. Every time. As he grew more and more nervous, he slouched farther and farther in his seat. He couldn't look at her.

They both turned sharply when the lab door opened and three girls stepped in, looking surprised.

Complication/ Suspense

"Elvira," said the little blond one, "we thought you were coming." They stared at Alfonso.

"I am. This won't take long. I'll see you at Shelley's." And she waved them off.

Character's thoughts

Alfonso wanted to be invisible. The dumb garlic picker. He won't take long.

"OK," said Elvira. "Let's try that part again. You remember the symbols for 'all files'?"

He touched * *.

"No, but almost--"

Conflict heightened

Alfonso shoved his chair back so hard it almost tipped. "Well, hey. I'm real sorry I didn't get it all right so you could leave faster. Go on. Catch up with your friends. I didn't ask you anyway and this is getting boring, man."

Elvira gathered her books in a very dignified way and stood up. "All right," she said. "Hasta la vista."

Climax

Alfonso reached back to the computer and hit exit. Hard. Then he turned away, pretending to look out the window, but a very small voice struggled out: "Sorry."

Characters developed/ Dialogue and action

Elvira paused with her hand on the door.

"It's my problem, not yours," he said. "Computers are too complicated for me. A lot of things are complicated."

"Yeah," said Elvira. "Yeah. But not computers."

To his surprise she was sitting back down beside him.

"Do you want to get simple?" she asked.

He had to laugh. "As simple as you can get."

"All right," said Elvira, "get some paper. When I wanted to kill my computer, I once made a list of Computer Steps for Any Idiot. Number one . . ."

Resolution

That afternoon Alfonso learned enough to get a C on Friday's quiz. By the end of the month he had the top grade in his computer class. And somehow figuring out crazy computer English made regular English not so scary. He wasn't failing any more.

"How did you do it?" his bewildered computer instructor, Mr. Washington, asked when Alfonso first aced a computer quiz. He shook his gray head. "You were the worst student I ever had--not because you were dumb, but because you had such a bad attitude. I knew you could make it, but you didn't know. Now you're acting like college material. What happened?"

"Oh, a lot of long hours in the lab. Dedication." Alfonso could have stopped, but he didn't. "Really, I had a tutor, a very patient one. She's waiting for me now."

"In the lab?" Mr. Washington asked. He held up the quiz. "But you have a perfect score."

"No," said Alfonso, "she's not in the lab. Uh, it's complicated, Mr. Washington. Hasta la vista."

INTEGRATING THE LANGUAGE ARTS

Mechanics Link. Many students avoid using dialogue because of their uncertainty about how to punctuate it. To remind students of how to punctuate dialogue correctly, write this group of words on the chalkboard: Bill said Mary Sue is here.

Ask students to punctuate the group of words in as many ways as they can and to use quotation marks in each sentence created. Students might come up with these possibilities:

1. Bill said, "Mary Sue is here."
2. "Bill," said Mary, "Sue is here."
3. "Bill," said Mary Sue, "is here!"

Discuss with students how changing the punctuation changes the sentence's meaning.

The Writer's Model follows the framework below, which you may also want to use for your story. As you can see, the framework includes the basic parts of the plot identified on pages 166–167.

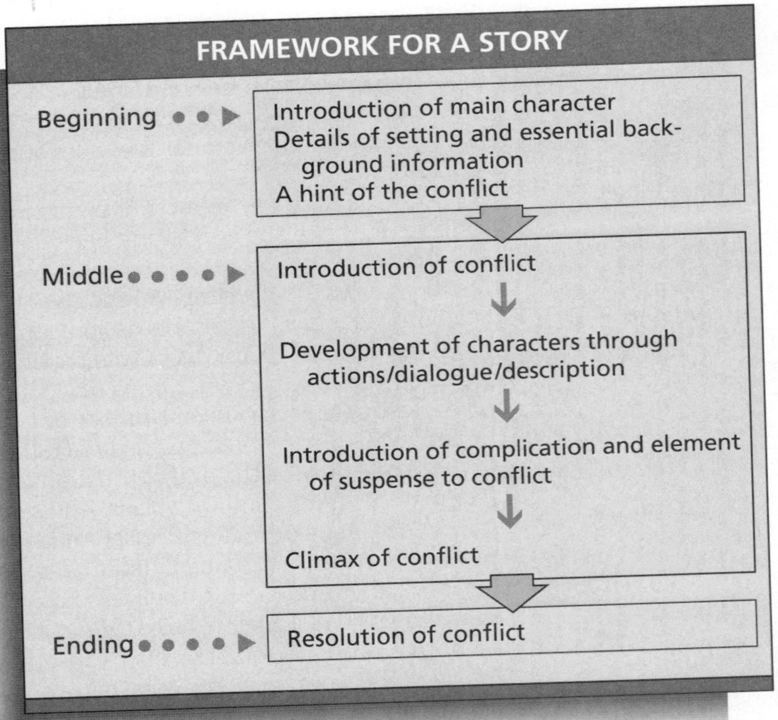
FRAMEWORK FOR A STORY
Beginning
Introduction of main character
Details of setting and essential background information
A hint of the conflict
Middle
Introduction of conflict
Development of characters through actions/dialogue/description
Introduction of complication and element of suspense to conflict
Climax of conflict
Ending
Resolution of conflict

WRITING ASSIGNMENT PART 5:
Writing a Draft of Your Story

By now you have done so much thinking about your story that it is ready to take on a life of its own. Let your story write itself: *Record* what your characters say and do, the events they cause and confront. And if you do get stuck, use your prewriting notes to get your creative juices flowing again.

A DIFFERENT APPROACH

When students begin writing their first drafts for **Writing Assignment: Part 5,** you may want to allow them to get comfortable in the classroom by letting them sit wherever they feel most at home. Some students find it difficult to write creatively while sitting in desks. They may be more comfortable sitting on the floor, leaning against a wall, or turned away from the other students.

SEGMENT 5 *(pp. 189–191)*

EVALUATING AND REVISING

OBJECTIVES

- To analyze a writer's revisions
- To evaluate and revise a short story

TEACHING THE LESSON

Remind students that the process of evaluation and revision can easily take as long as, or even longer than, the process of writing their first drafts. Have a volunteer read aloud the introductory paragraphs, and then lead students in answering question 1 in **Exercise 4.** In a class discussion, help students analyze the reason for the change and ☛

Evaluating and Revising

Even the best writers revise their stories. It's only after getting a fictional world down on paper that they can judge whether words have made their imaginings real. And with all the words available, and all the ways you can connect them, it would be very surprising if a first creation were a final one.

Trying your world out on other readers is also a good idea. Since it will be completely new to them, they can tell you how they find "living" there. The chart on page 190 gives you and peer reviewers specific elements to check in a story as well as ways to attack problems.

EXERCISE 4 **Analyzing a Writer's Revisions**

The writer of "A Little Help" made the following changes in one paragraph of his story (page 183). Use the evaluation and revising chart on page 190 to help you answer the questions after the paragraph.

"Don't go blinking BAD COMMAND at me," he ordered. ~~He didn't know why the computer was blinking BAD COMMAND and said,~~ "Just tell me what to do!" Like a caged animal he glared ~~looked~~ around the lab but saw no one who could free him from the machine. ~~And he dreaded the rest of the day. He still had to help Juan with a transmission and write a paper.~~ Row after row of bright blue monitors shone coldly back at him. ~~He hated looking at all these computers.~~

replace

replace/add

cut

replace

1. Why did the writer make the replacement in the first sentence? What's its effect?
2. How do the words *glared* and *the lab* help the paragraph?
3. Why did the writer cut two sentences?
4. What do you think the writer was aiming for by replacing the last sentence?

Teacher's ResourceBank™

RESOURCES

EVALUATING AND REVISING

- Writing a Short Story 50

QUOTATION FOR THE DAY

"No tears in the writer, no tears in the reader." (Robert Frost, 1874–1963, American poet)

Remind your students that the cardinal rule in creative writing is not to say that a character is lonely or frightened but to show the loneliness or fear. To do this, creative writers must call up emotions from their own lives. If no emotion is put into a story, no emotion will be evoked by a story.

ANSWERS

Exercise 4

Answers may vary.

1. The writer replaces description with dialogue to achieve a more dramatic opening.
2. *Glared* conveys more emotion than *looked,* and *lab* depicts the setting more clearly.
3. The writer cut two sentences to get rid of unnecessary, cumbersome details.
4. The replacement emphasizes the loneliness of Alfonso's situation, the word *coldly* helps set a tone of antagonism, and the description of the rows of monitors makes the setting more vivid.

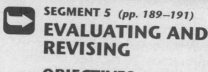

the effect of change. Assign the rest of **Exercise 4** as independent practice.

To further model the process of evaluation and revision, you could guide the class through applying the questions from the chart **Evaluating and Revising Short Stories** to **A Writer's Model**, pp. 183–187. To teach the material in **Grammar Hint**, have volunteers share a sentence or two from their stories, and have the class brainstorm for precise verbs. Students should then be prepared to complete **Writing Assignment: Part 6** as independent practice. To evaluate students' work, have them show you their original drafts with their revisions written in. To close, have students discuss what they found especially satisfying or especially difficult in revising their stories. ■

MEETING INDIVIDUAL NEEDS

LEP/ESL

General Strategies. The revision stage is a good place for ESL students to expand the number of verbs they know and use, but they will need assistance. Pair them with native English-speaking students who can suggest colorful and accurate verb replacements for more ordinary verbs. Let ESL students use their bilingual dictionaries to verify meanings and to agree or disagree with their partners' choices for revision.

LEARNING STYLES

Auditory Learners. Auditory learners might benefit from being allowed to read their stories aloud. You may want to provide a location in the classroom where students can read aloud to themselves or where they can have another student read to them without disturbing other students. By hearing their stories as opposed to reading them, students may notice problems or difficulties that they might not catch in a visual reading.

EVALUATING AND REVISING SHORT STORIES

	EVALUATION GUIDE	REVISION TECHNIQUE
1	Does a conflict set a chain of events in motion?	**Add** an external or internal conflict that the main character faces.
2	Is the order of events clear?	**Reorder** events in chronological order, or **add** a flashback.
3	Do the events create curiosity or suspense?	**Cut** events that slow the story, and **add** details that create uncertainty.
4	Do the events build to a climax and satisfying resolution?	**Add** a scene that clearly solves the conflict. **Add** details to tie up events.
5	Are the characters believable?	**Add** details showing what your characters do, say, and feel.
6	Does the setting establish a mood or help readers understand events?	**Add** details of time, place, and weather. **Add** sensory details to create the mood.
7	Is description vivid?	**Add** sensory images.
8	Is the point of view consistently first person or third person?	**Cut** details that make the point of view inconsistent.

WRITING ASSIGNMENT

PART 6:
Evaluating and Revising Your Story

Use feedback from your classmates and the chart on page 190 as a guide to revising your story. Don't be afraid to change things. As a "world-maker," you have a chance to get one particular slice of life just right. Go for it.

GRAMMAR HINT

Using Precise Verbs

Many beginning story writers pile up adverbs to be descriptive about actions. Here's a hint from professional writers: The right verb can often paint a word picture more vividly than a vague verb plus an adverb. Look for action verbs that will create precise, accurate pictures in your reader's mind.

EXAMPLES

Vague Verbs with Adverbs	Precise Verbs
She **entered** the room **happily.**	She **bounced** into the room.
She **took** his hand **fearfully.**	She **gripped** his hand.
The smoke trail **blew lightly** toward them.	The smoke trail **floated** toward them.

REFERENCE NOTE: For more information on verbs and adverbs, see pages 565–569.

GRAMMAR HINT

Ask students to list as many precise verbs as possible for the list of common words below:

1. run [speed, dart, sprint, trot, dash]
2. say [utter, yell, mutter, whisper]
3. eat [gulp, gobble, nibble, devour, consume]
4. write [scribble, scrawl, copy, jot down]

Next, ask students to look up the common words in thesauruses and to add any synonyms not already listed. Remind students that all words listed as synonyms in the thesaurus are not interchangeable. The meanings may be similar, but the different words have different connotations that could make one of the words more appropriate in a given situation.

SEGMENT 6 *(p. 192)*

PROOFREADING AND PUBLISHING

OBJECTIVE

- To proofread and publish a short story

TEACHING THE LESSON

Write on the chalkboard a paragraph containing several errors in grammar, usage, and mechanics. Guide students through the process of proofreading the paragraph, and then have them proofread their stories. To close, have students share ideas for publishing their stories. ■

Teacher's ResourceBank™
RESOURCES

PROOFREADING AND PUBLISHING
- Writing a Short Story 51

QUOTATION FOR THE DAY

"There are probably no words to describe the joy you feel when you see your first words in print." (Nikki Giovanni, 1943– , African American writer)

It is not always easy to get a short story published or to accept the rejection that comes with being turned down. Encourage your students to be brave and to persevere. Often the only difference between a published and an unpublished writer is that the published writer never gave up.

MEETING INDIVIDUAL NEEDS

LEP/ESL

General Strategies. You could suggest that ESL students send copies of their stories to friends and family in their native countries who are studying English. They could add glossaries of words that they think their friends might not have learned yet.

Proofreading and Publishing

Proofreading. You are probably prone to making certain errors in writing (everyone is), and you probably know to look carefully for them—perhaps misspelling words or confusing pronouns like *I* and *me.* In addition to looking for these kinds of problems, you can proofread your story for errors that are common in stories.

For example, be sure you have included both beginning and ending quotation marks for dialogue and have begun a new paragraph when speakers change. Pronoun antecedents are another checkpoint. When you say "she" jumped out of the car, do readers know who "she" is? It can make quite a difference.

Publishing. Besides turning your story in to your teacher or sending it to magazines (see your library's copy of *Writer's Digest* for markets), you could try these publishing ideas:

- Divide your story into parts and serialize it in the school newspaper (you might revise a bit to create cliffhanger scenes).
- Give your story to an art class for practice in illustration.

WRITING ASSIGNMENT

PART 7:
Proofreading and Publishing Your Story

It is time to give your story one final polish before letting your audience read it. Proofread your work carefully before sharing it with others. People like stories, so don't just hide yours in a folder. Why not read it to your younger brother or sister at bedtime or use one of the publishing choices listed above?

SEGMENT 7 *(pp. 193–197)*

WRITING WORKSHOP

OBJECTIVES

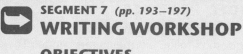

- To read and analyze a scene from a professional model of a play
- To write a scene for a play

TEACHING THE LESSON

Before beginning this segment, you may want to ask students how they think a story is different from a play. Then read aloud the introductory paragraphs and discuss the differences with the class. You could have three volunteers read aloud the excerpt from Lorraine Hansberry's ***A Raisin in the Sun.*** One could read the stage directions

WRITING WORKSHOP

A Scene in a Play

In many ways plays are like short stories. Both are written for the purpose of creating literature; and both have characters, settings, and a central conflict.

Stories and plays, though, have one major difference. A story is written to be read, but a play is written to be acted out in front of a live audience or a movie camera. This means that the writer of a play can show character and conflict only through dialogue, action, and a kind of description called stage directions that appears only in the written script. ***Stage directions*** tell how the actors should move and speak and can also describe setting, mood, costumes, props, and lighting. A ***scene*** is a portion of a play. Most scenes have a continuous action, with no break in time and no change of place.

As you read the following scene from an award-winning stage play, think about how you find out about the characters. What do you learn about them from what they say and do? What do the stage directions tell you about them?

QUOTATION FOR THE DAY

"I don't have to tell you that speech on the stage is not the speech of life, not even the written speech." (Lillian Hellman, 1905–1984, American playwright)

Playwrights have long been mystified by the fact that dialogue that looks good on the page often sounds stilted from the stage. They try to correct for this conflict between eye and ear by shifting words about, by experimenting with punctuation, and by rewriting the dialogue during rehearsal readings.

MEETING INDIVIDUAL NEEDS

LEP/ESL

General Strategies. ESL students may not know all of the verbs and adverbs used in the stage directions for ***A Raisin in the Sun.*** Have native English-speaking students act out these descriptions. For example, the direction "Travis jabs his spoon into his cereal bowl viciously" could more easily be demonstrated than paraphrased.

and the other two could read the parts of Travis and Ruth.

Because students write at different paces, you may need to be very specific about any requirements in length or number of pages when assigning the writing of the scene.

GUIDED PRACTICE

You could guide students through the first question following the literary model. To prepare students for writing their scenes, model writing a few lines of dialogue and stage directions.

USING THE SELECTION

from A Raisin in the Sun

1

Lorraine Hansberry was born in Chicago in 1930. Before succeeding as a playwright with ***A Raisin in the Sun,*** which ran for 530 performances after it opened in 1959, Hansberry worked as a clerk in a department store; a tag girl in a fur shop; an aide to a theatrical producer; and a waitress, hostess, and cashier in a Greenwich Village restaurant.

2

The central conflict of Travis's wanting money is introduced at the beginning of the scene.

from A Raisin in the Sun

1 *by Lorraine Hansberry*

RUTH Sit down and have your breakfast, Travis.
2 TRAVIS Mama, this is Friday. (*Gleefully*) Check coming tomorrow, huh?
RUTH You get your mind off money and eat your breakfast.
TRAVIS (*Eating*) This is the morning we supposed to bring the fifty cents to school.
RUTH Well, I ain't got no fifty cents this morning.
TRAVIS Teacher say we have to.
RUTH I don't care what teacher say. I ain't got it. Eat your breakfast, Travis.
TRAVIS I *am* eating.
RUTH Hush up now and just eat!
(*The boy gives her an exasperated look for her lack of understanding, and eats grudgingly.*)
TRAVIS You think Grandmama would have it?
RUTH No! And I want you to stop asking your grandmother for money, you hear me?
TRAVIS (*Outraged*) Gaaaleee! I don't ask her, she just gimme it sometimes!
RUTH Travis Willard Younger—I got too much on me this morning to be—
TRAVIS Maybe Daddy—
RUTH *Travis!*
(*The boy hushes abruptly. They are both quiet and tense for several seconds.*)

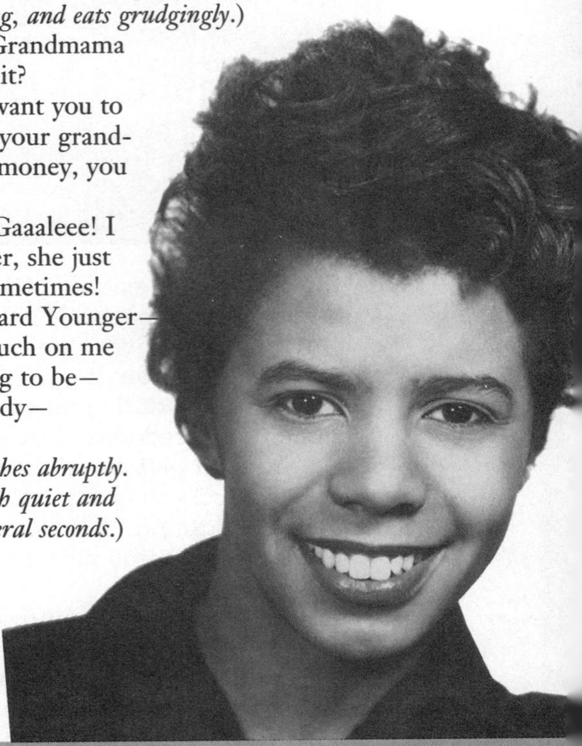

Lorraine Hansberry

INDEPENDENT PRACTICE

Assign the rest of the questions following the literary model along with the writing of a scene as independent practice.

ASSESSMENT

To assess students' scenes, divide the class into groups of three or four. Ask members of the groups to read their scenes aloud and to give each other feedback as you monitor the process.

☛

TRAVIS (*Presently*) Could I maybe go carry some groceries in front of the supermarket for a little while after school then?

RUTH Just hush, I said. (*Travis jabs his spoon into his cereal bowl viciously, and rests his head in anger upon his fists.*) If you through eating, you can get over there and make up your bed.

(*The boy obeys stiffly and crosses the room, almost mechanically, to the bed and more or less carefully folds the covering. He carries the bedding into his mother's room and returns with his books and cap.*)

TRAVIS (*Sulking and standing apart from her unnaturally*) I'm gone.

RUTH (*Looking up from the stove to inspect him automatically*) Come here. (*He crosses to her and she studies his head.*) If you don't take this comb and fix this here head, you better! (TRAVIS *puts down his books with a great sigh of oppression, and crosses to the mirror. His mother mutters*
3 *under her breath about his "slubbornness."*) 'Bout to march out of here with that head looking just like chickens slept in it! I just don't know where you get your slubborn ways . . . And get your jacket, too. Looks chilly out this morning.

TRAVIS (*With conspicuously brushed hair and jacket*) I'm gone.

RUTH Get carfare and milk money—(*Waving one finger*)—and not a single penny for no caps, you hear me?

TRAVIS (*With sullen politeness*) Yes'm.

(*He turns in outrage to leave. His mother watches after him as in his frustration he approaches the door almost comically. When she speaks to him, her voice has become a very gentle tease.*)

RUTH (*Mocking; as she thinks he would say it*) Oh, Mama makes me so mad sometimes, I don't know what to do! (*She waits and continues to his back as he stands stock-still in front of the door.*) I wouldn't kiss that woman good-bye
4 for nothing in this world this morning! (*The boy finally turns around and rolls his eyes at her, knowing the mood has changed and he is vindicated; he does not, however, move toward her yet.*) Not for nothing in this world! (*She finally laughs aloud at him and holds out her arms to him and we see that it is a way between them, very old and*

3
slubbornness: a made-up word, probably a combination of *sloppy* and *stubborn*

4
The climax of the scene comes here when Travis turns to his mother.

CLOSURE

Have students discuss how the process of writing a scene for a play differs from the process of writing a short story. ■

practiced. He crosses to her and allows her to embrace him warmly but keeps his face fixed with masculine rigidity. She holds him back from her presently and looks at him and runs her fingers over the features of his face. With utter gentleness—) Now—whose little old angry man are you?

TRAVIS (*The masculinity and gruffness start to fade at last.*) Aw gaalee—Mama . . .

RUTH (*Mimicking*) Aw—gaaaaalleeeee, Mama! (*She pushes him, with rough playfulness and finality, toward the door.*) Get on out of here or you going to be late.

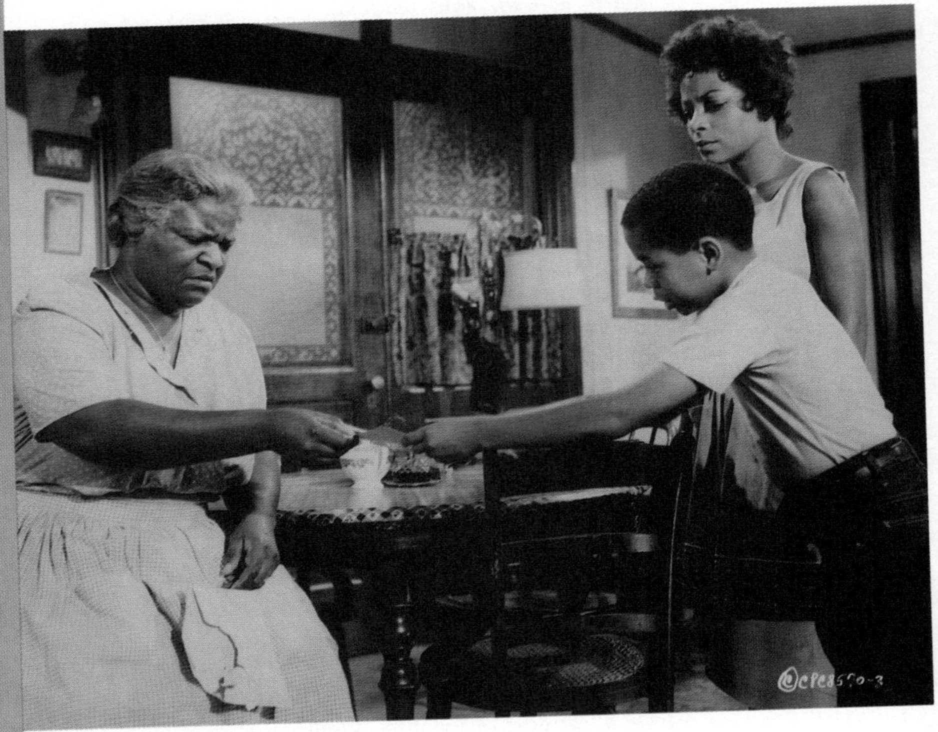

1. Most scenes center on a minor conflict within the larger conflict of the play. What is the conflict between Travis and Ruth? How is it resolved?
2. What kind of person is Ruth? How do you know?

ANSWERS
Writing Workshop Questions

Answers may vary.

1. The conflict between Travis and Ruth revolves around his wanting money for school and Ruth's not giving it to him. The conflict is resolved when Ruth teases Travis and he gives up his resentment.
2. Ruth seems to be bossy, impatient, and somewhat angry, but also loving and playful. She argues with Travis, directs his every action, and talks to him and about him with irritation and anger. Then, because she doesn't want him to leave angry, she lovingly teases him until they make up.

SELECTION AMENDMENT
Description of change: excerpted
Rationale: to focus on the concept of creative writing presented in this chapter

3. What words would you use to describe Travis? What dialogue and actions cause you to describe him in this way?
4. What role do stage directions play in the scene? Give examples to support your ideas.

Writing a Scene

Prewriting. To find an idea for your scene, you might think about conflicts that come up in a family, at school, or in a community. By asking "What if?" you can imagine your way to specific characters and conflict details. Since you won't have much time to develop actions in a single scene, keep the conflict simple. Flesh out your characters' attitudes and personalities, as well as their physical characteristics. And don't forget that you're writing for a stage—keep your setting simple.

Writing, Evaluating, and Revising. As you write, remember that you have two means to reveal your characters to the audience: dialogue and action. Make sure the language you use in the dialogue reflects the characters' personalities and backgrounds. And in your stage directions be as thorough and clear as possible. If you "see" a character constantly cracking his knuckles, write it down so the actor will know. Describe what the characters will be wearing as well as where and how they will move.

After drafting, get some friends to read your scene aloud as actors. Are they—in the flesh—accomplishing what you intended? Ask them, too, to make suggestions and to point out places where they weren't sure what to do or felt uncomfortable with dialogue. Then revise.

Proofreading and Publishing. Notice the way the script from *A Raisin in the Sun* is set up, and use the same form for your scene. After you've proofread your script, you can make copies and hold an audition or ask particular people to take parts. You'll need a director (maybe not yourself) and possibly someone in charge of props. Be sure to allow time for at least three rehearsals before a performance. How about videotaping the performance so both you and the actors can see it?

3. In the beginning Travis is enthusiastic and persistent; then he becomes frustrated, sullen, and angry. Finally he softens and forgives his mother, and at the end he is perhaps even embarrassed.
4. The stage directions indicate Travis's moods (for example, he is "exasperated," "outraged," and "he jabs . . . viciously") and direct the physical interaction between the two characters (for example, "He . . . allows her to embrace him . . . .").

COOPERATIVE LEARNING

Rather than have students write individual scenes to different plays, have the class develop one play plot. Then groups of four to five students could each write one scene of the class play. One student in each group should be designated as the group's coordinator. This student will meet with the other groups' coordinators to make certain that the scenes will smoothly complete a single play.

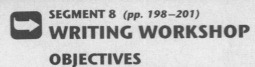

SEGMENT 8 *(pp. 198–201)*

WRITING WORKSHOP

OBJECTIVES

- To analyze a professional model of a poem
- To write a poem

TEACHING THE LESSON

You may want to introduce this segment by reading aloud Anita Endrezze's **"Sunset at Twin Lake"** on p. 200.

As you read about and discuss the poetic techniques on p. 199, you could refer to the poem and point out the poet's use of these techniques to create the mood and tone of the poem.

QUOTATION FOR THE DAY

"A house can be as apt a metaphor for life as a ship." (Diane Johnson, 1934– , American novelist)

Everyone has seen a house or a ship in all sorts of conditions: lavish, modest, or in sad disrepair. Ask your students to imagine a house or a ship and to describe in poems of ten or twelve lines how it appears. They should describe either object in sharp detail and describe to some extent the object's surroundings. After they finish, ask them if their poems are about more than a ship or a house. Might they also be metaphorically about time, nature, or change?

MEETING INDIVIDUAL NEEDS

LEP/ESL

General Strategies. An auditory strategy can help ESL students to understand **"Sunset at Twin Lake"** (p. 200). Have a native English-speaking student read the poem aloud—more than once, if possible.

WRITING WORKSHOP

Poetry

Poems are another form of literary, or creative, writing. Like fiction (the story and play you wrote earlier in this chapter), poems are ways for you to create something new from your imagination; and also like fiction, poems can tell stories. But not all, or even most, poems do that. Instead of capturing a period of time, they capture a moment. Like a flash camera, the poet's imagination illuminates an experience, emotion, object, or person and holds it still for you.

GUIDED PRACTICE

You may want to complete one or two of the questions following the literary model in a class discussion. To prepare students for the writing assignment, you could work with the class to create a few lines of poetry.

INDEPENDENT PRACTICE

Ask students to complete the rest of the questions following the model poem and to write their original poems as independent practice.

Description is a large part of the poet's magic, just as it is in stories; but poems are also musical. They use the sounds and rhythm of language very deliberately to communicate emotion and meaning. Here are some specific techniques that you can use in writing poetry.

WRITING POETRY

TECHNIQUE	EXAMPLE
Imagery: Concrete details that appeal to the senses of sight, sound, touch, taste, or smell.	"water lilies as they float / in the cooling air" (Anita Endrezze)
Simile: A comparison of unlike things using *like* or *as.*	"And eyes, like sparks of frost" (Walter de la Mare)
Metaphor: A comparison that equates two unlike things.	"Juliet is the sun!" (Shakespeare)
Personification: Human qualities given to something nonhuman.	"belch / this poem aint got no manners" (Ishmael Reed)
Rhyme: Repetition of words in which accented vowel sounds and all following sounds are the same.	"No time to see, in broad daylight, / Streams full of stars, like skies at night." (W. H. Davies)
Alliteration: Repetition of the same consonant sounds in words close together.	"still seeking / the last light" (Anita Endrezze)
Rhythm: The beat made by accented and unaccented syllables. **Metrical verse** has meter: a regular, recurring pattern of beats. **Free verse** has no pattern. Language's natural beats, repetition, and pauses create rhythm.	**Metrical:** "The Grass divides as with a Comb— /A spotted shaft is seen—" (Emily Dickinson) **Free:** "one day the villagers broke / into her house, but she was too / swift for them, she disappeared" (Ishmael Reed)

INTEGRATING THE LANGUAGE ARTS

Literature Link. Poets use different types of meter and rhythm to create different effects in their poetry. One common rhythm is the iambic couplet. Have students read a poem (such as one of Anne Bradstreet's poems) written in this rhythm. Discuss with students how the established, definite rhythm affects the poetry. You may want to have students compare this rhythm with an example of free verse such as Walt Whitman's "Song of Myself."

TIMESAVER

To allow students time to write privately and to save on grading time, use this segment and assignment as a freewriting opportunity for students. You could require that students write poems and then evaluate their performance by their participation, but you may not want to grade individual poems.

AMENDMENTS TO SELECTIONS
Description of change: excerpted
Rationale: to focus on the concept of creative writing presented in this chapter

ASSESSMENT

To assess students' mastery of the segment concepts, evaluate responses to the questions following **"Sunset at Twin Lake."** When assessing student poems, evaluate the use of description and specific poetic techniques.

CLOSURE

Ask students what they liked and disliked about writing poetry, especially as compared to the other types of creative writing they have done. Some students may be willing to share their poems with their classmates. ■

USING THE SELECTION

Sunset At Twin Lake

1
Anita Endrezze is an artist, poet, and short-story writer. She is of mixed Yaqui and European ancestry.

2
Colville Indian Reservation is a reservation for several different Salish-speaking tribes in northeastern Washington.

3
The idea that the waterlilies, the heron, and the mountains have messages may be related to the idea in Native American spirituality that everything is alive—that all of creation is imbued with spirit.

Read the following poem, aloud if you can, listening to its music and letting its images unfold. What experience does the poet want to give to you?

Sunset at Twin Lake

1 *by Anita Endrezze*

2 *Colville Indian Reservation*

The heron stalks
the webbed water,
its feathers made of mirrors.

We hear the white breath
of water lilies as they float
in the cooling air.

The heron is a bringer
of reed music:
legs, beak, feathers—
all are godly instruments
in the evening wind.

3 Even the mountains
have a distant message
although we are more concerned
with things closer:
our hands still seeking
the last light
as we cast our lines
and the trout jumping
into the net
of the low-rising moon.

1. How would you describe the mood of this poem? Point out one line or phrase that you think helps create the mood.
2. Often a poem is called a "word picture," but many senses, not just sight, can be involved. Find images of sound, touch, and sight.
3. What examples of figurative language do you see in the poem?
4. Is this poem metrical, or is it free verse? Where has the poet used alliteration or onomatopoeia to create musical effects?
5. What if the poet had used this experience to create a short story? Discuss how the story would be different from the poem.

Writing a Poem

Prewriting. Does the model poem remind you of an experience you have had? Think about something that's important to you, something you love, hate, or will always remember. You could write about a food, an animal, a person, a place (mall, cafeteria); a time (an early memory, vacation); an object (clothing, camera, car). Write your subject on a sheet of paper and cluster phrases, images, and comparisons around it, or try freewriting about it.

Writing, Evaluating, and Revising. If you write free verse, the form of your poem is up to you. You can arrange the lines any way that makes sense to you. However, if you would rather try another form, you can experiment with regular meter and rhyming lines. After you've written a draft, evaluate your use of sound effects and sensory images. Be a stern judge: Have you used rhyme, alliteration, or rhythm to heighten the effect you want to create? Are your visual images concrete? Ask a classmate for reactions and then revise.

Proofreading and Publishing. After you have checked your poem carefully to make sure it looks the way you want, recopy it. You may want to give your poem to someone you care about. Do keep it for yourself: It will be a record of something you felt strongly about at an important time in your life.

ANSWERS

Writing Workshop Questions

Answers may vary.

1. The mood is peaceful. Many lines and phrases help create the mood. One example is "distant message."
2. Images of sound include the "white breath of water lilies," the "reed music," the "godly instruments," and the "trout jumping." Images of touch include "the heron stalks the webbed water," the "cooling air," the "hands seeking . . . light," and "we cast our lines." Images of sight include "webbed water," "feathers made of mirrors," "waterlilies as they float," "mountains," "last light," "lines," "trout jumping," and "low-rising moon."
3. Examples of personification include the waterlilies' "breath," the mountains' "distant message," and the hands "still seeking." Depicting the moon as a net is an example of metaphor.
4. The poem is free verse. Examples of alliteration in the poem include "webbed water," "made of mirrors," "still seeking," and "last light." There are no examples of onomatapoeia in the poem.
5. A short story based on this experience would have characters, a central conflict, a plot, a climax, and a resolution. The only real similarities between the short story and the poem would probably be mood and setting.

SEGMENT 9 *(pp. 202–203)*

MAKING CONNECTIONS

IMAGINING A HISTORICAL DIALOGUE

OBJECTIVE

- To write and present orally a historical dialogue

IMAGINING A HISTORICAL DIALOGUE

Teaching Strategies

Have a volunteer read aloud the assignment in the textbook. Suggest to students that they choose historical figures about whom they have some strong feelings, either negative or positive. Allow students to form pairs according to their shared interests. If students choose obscure historical figures for their dialogues, have them present brief biographies before going into their dialogues.

GUIDELINES

Dialogues will vary. Each dialogue should present consistent character development for the historical figure, and the historical figure's point of view in each dialogue should be consistent with historical fact.

MAKING CONNECTIONS

SPEAKING AND LISTENING

Imagining a Historical Dialogue

Have you ever thought about what might happen if historical figures from different times could meet? For example, what might Abraham Lincoln and Martin Luther King, Jr., say to each other? With a partner, create a scene in which two historical figures talk about a social or political topic. Do you want to use people whose lives had common aspects or people from wildly different backgrounds—say St. Francis and Albert Einstein? Try to come up with a pair whose lives are important to you or who will generate an unusual exchange.

Do some basic research if you need to about the people and their times, and then brainstorm for comments each historical figure might say about the topic. Write the dialogue, at least in rough form, decide which role each of you will assume, and practice the conversation before presenting it to your class. You might even take questions and improvise answers. Here are some suggestions of figures to start your thinking: Eleanor Roosevelt and Harriet Tubman; Hernando Cortés and Adolf Hitler; Cleopatra and Queen Victoria.

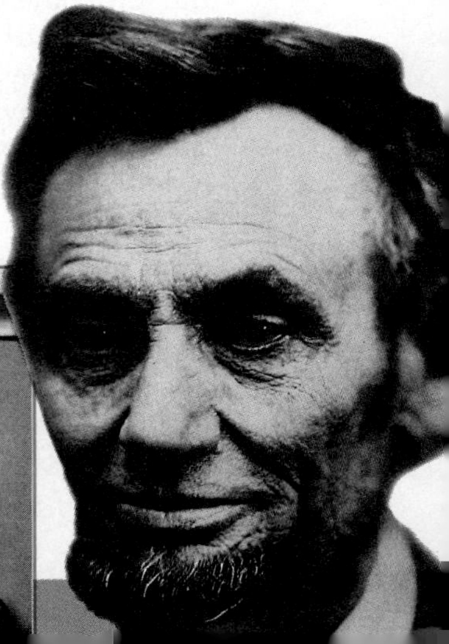

DESCRIPTION IN FICTION
OBJECTIVE

- To use sensory words and figurative language to write a character description

DESCRIPTION IN FICTION

Sensory words and figurative language are as basic to fiction as to poetry, especially as writers try to create living pictures of people and places. In the following portrait of "Aunt Ida," notice not only the wealth of detail but its wonderful sharpness. Read it once—as a whole piece—and then read it again, taking time with each word. Which part of the description (even a word) do you wish you had thought of? Which of your senses does the description tap? Where is metaphor or simile used?

> I heard a swishing sound like knives being sharpened on stones, and Aunt Ida appeared from where the building had concealed her. Her size amazed me, the breadth of her brown shoulders, the columns of her arms as they stretched before her, pushing a lawnmower, plowing through the grass. At first I thought she had dyed her hair, but then I saw it was a wig, the kind of thing advertised on the back pages of comic books, "$11.95 and natural-looking." She wore overalls and sunglasses and had false teeth. She sang like Stevie Wonder, tilting her neck as she moved, bellowing a Johnny Lee song in English to an invisible audience. . . .
>
> Michael Dorris, *A Yellow Raft in Blue Water*

Now, bring your own character to life in a description for a short story. You can start with an image of someone real, but transform the person imaginatively into a new character. If you would like, you may rewrite a description from the story you wrote earlier. Perhaps you'll be able to improve your story. Let Michael Dorris's description be your inspiration:

use details that appeal to all senses, not just sight
create swift, surprising pictures with figurative language like "the columns of her arms"

DESCRIPTION IN FICTION
Teaching Strategies

After reading over the introductory material, present a character description in an anonymous short story from a previous year. Read the description and then have students add as many powerful details as possible. Before they begin writing their own character descriptions, have students brainstorm about possible people and characters they could describe.

GUIDELINES

Descriptions will vary. If students use characters from the stories they wrote for this chapter, you could compare the new descriptions with the old ones. Evaluate descriptions for amount of detail, sensory words, and figurative language.

SELECTION AMENDMENT
Description of change: excerpted
Rationale: to focus on the concept of creative writing presented in this chapter

Chapter 6

WRITING TO INFORM

OBJECTIVES

- To analyze and respond personally to a professional model
- To choose a subject for a comparison/contrast essay
- To gather and arrange information for a comparison/contrast essay
- To write a draft of a comparison/contrast essay
- To evaluate and revise a comparison/contrast essay
- To proofread and publish a comparison/contrast essay
- To plan, draft, evaluate, revise, proofread, and publish an extended definition
- To locate and discuss a poem containing situational irony
- To write a classification paragraph about science

Motivation

To begin this chapter, show a videotape of a TV commercial that uses contrast. Ask your students to pay close attention to how the product being sold is contrasted with similar products. Ask why the similarities between the products aren't emphasized. [The advertisers want to show how their product is different and, by implication, better than similar products.] Next, show a commercial that emphasizes similarities between two products. Why do the advertisers emphasize the similarities? [Probably because the product being advertised is less well-known or less popular than the product it's compared to.]

Explain to students that comparing and contrasting are organizational strategies used to develop the main idea.

Introduction

Using a system of classification to organize a paper is an effective method for achieving clarity. This chapter focuses on the comparison/contrast method and covers both the block and point-by-point methods of organization. The chapter emphasizes using classification to inform, but the comparison/contrast strategy of development can also be used with the expressive, literary, and persuasive aims of writing.

Integration

The study of the comparison/contrast strategy can be easily integrated with many aspects of language arts. For example, students might compare and contrast characters in a story or play or they might compare and contrast the styles or works of two writers.

You may want to do some joint planning with other teachers in your school who assign comparison/contrast writing. Determine how you can work with these teachers to enhance your students' writing in all classes. You may even want to consider working with other teachers to develop school-wide standards for evaluating comparison/contrast writing.

The chart on the next page illustrates the strands of language arts as they are integrated into this chapter. For vocabulary study, glossary words are underlined in some writing models.

QUOTATIONS

All **Quotations for the Day** are chosen because of their relevance to instructional material presented in that segment of the chapter and for their usefulness in establishing student interest in writing.

INTEGRATING THE LANGUAGE ARTS

Selection	Reading and Literature	Writing and Critical Thinking	Language and Syntax	Speaking, Listening, and Other Expression Skills
from ***The Joy Luck Club*** by Amy Tan **206-207** from **"What's That Pig Outdoors?"** by Henry Kisor **220-223** **"One Perfect Rose"** by Dorothy Parker **237**	Responding personally to literature **208, 234-235** Identifying details **208, 224** Identifying comparisons and contrasts **208, 224** Analyzing the introduction of an article **224** Identifying techniques used in an extended definition **234-235** Identifying situational irony in a poem **237-238**	Responding personally to literature **208** Drawing conclusions and making inferences **208, 214-215, 229-230, 234-235, 238-239** Identifying details **208, 224** Identifying comparison and contrast **208, 224** Choosing appropriate subjects for an informative paper **212, 236** Analyzing subjects for their relevant features **214-215** Brainstorming and researching **218** Gathering and arranging information **218, 236, 238-239** Developing a thesis statement **218, 236** Writing a first draft **226** Analyzing a writer's revisions **229-230** Evaluating and revising **230, 236** Proofreading and publishing **232, 236** Identifying techniques used in an extended definition **234-235** Writing an extended definition **236** Using classification in a scientific writing assignment **238-239**	Proofreading for errors in grammar, usage, and mechanics **232, 236**	Telling classmates about an experience **208** Listening for subjects for an informative paper **212** Working with classmates to analyze subjects for their relevant features **214-215** Working with classmates to evaluate and analyze an essay **224, 230, 236** Working with classmates to analyze a writer's revisions **229-230** Reading an extended definition aloud to classmates **236** Reading a poem aloud and discussing its irony with the class **238**

CHAPTER 6

SEGMENT PLANNING GUIDE

You can use the following Planning Guide to adapt the chapter material to the individual needs of your class. All the Resources listed in this chapter are located in the *Teacher's ResourceBank*™.

	SEGMENT	PAGES	CONTENT	RESOURCES
1	***Seeing Patterns and Relationships***	***205-208***		
	Literary Model from ***The Joy Luck Club***	206-207	Guided reading: a model of informative writing	
	Reader's Response/ Writer's Craft	208	Model evaluation: responding to literature and analyzing informative writing	
2	***Strategies for Writing to Inform***	***209***		
3	***Prewriting***	***210-218***		Writing a Comparison / Contrast Essay Developing a Venn Diagram 54
	Considering Subjects, Purpose, and Audience	210-211	Guidelines: using criteria to select appropriate subjects	
	Writing Assignment: Part 1	212	Applied practice: choosing subjects to compare and contrast	
	Exercise 1	212	Applied practice: listening for subjects	
	Planning a Comparison/ Contrast Essay	213	Introduction: gathering and arranging information	
	Gathering Information	213-214	Guidelines: gathering and evaluating information	
	Critical Thinking: Analyzing Subjects	214	Guidelines: analyzing subjects for their relevant features	
	Critical Thinking Exercise	214-215	Cooperative learning: identifying relevant features	
	Developing a Thesis Statement	216	Guidelines: analyzing examples of thesis statements	
	Arranging Information	217-218	Guidelines: organizing information in a comparison/contrast essay	
	Chart: Block/Point-by-Point Method	218	Example: analyzing methods of organization	
	Writing Assignment: Part 2	218	Applied practice: gathering and arranging information	
4	***Writing***	***219-226***		Writing a Comparison/ Contrast Essay 55
	The Structure of a Comparison/Contrast Essay	219	Guidelines: using criteria to structure an essay	
	Literary Model from **"What's That Pig Outdoors?"**	220-223	Guided reading: examining structure in a model	
	Exercise 2	224	Cooperative learning: analyzing a comparison/ contrast article	

For **Portfolio Assessment** see the following pages in the *Teacher's ResourceBank*™:

Aims For Writing — pp. 53–58
Holistically Graded Composition Models — pp. 497–502
Assessment Portfolio — pp. 533–562

SEGMENT	PAGES	CONTENT	RESOURCES
A Basic Framework	224	Introduction: analyzing an article	
A Writer's Model	224-226	Guided reading: examining organizational method in an essay	
Writing Assignment: Part 3	226	Applied practice: writing a first draft	
5 *Evaluating and Revising*	*227-230*		Writing a Comparison/ Contrast Essay 56
Evaluating and Revising	227	Introduction: using a chart	
Chart: Evaluating and Revising	228	Guidelines: applying evaluation and revision techniques	
Exercise 3	229-230	Applied practice: analyzing a writer's revisions	
Writing Assignment: Part 4	230	Applied practice: evaluating and revising	
6 *Proofreading and Publishing*	*231-233*		Writing a Comparison/ Contrast Essay 57
Usage Hint	231	Writing suggestion: using degrees of comparison	
Publishing	232	Publishing ideas: reaching a specific audience	
Writing Assignment: Part 5	232	Applied practice: proofreading and publishing	
A Student Model	232-233	Sample: examining a student essay	
7 *Writing Workshop*	*234-236*		
An Extended Definition	234-235	Guidelines: writing an extended definition	
Writing an Extended Definition	236	Applied practice: applying skills to the writing process	
8 *Making Connections*	*237-239*		
Writing Across the Curriculum: Comparison/ Contrast in Literature	237-238	Guidelines: identifying situational irony in a poem	
Literary Model **"One Perfect Rose"**	237	Guided reading: examining irony in a poem	
Writing Across the Curriculum: Classification in Science	238-239	Guidelines: using classification in writing Applied practice: writing a paragraph that classifies and describes blood cells	

WHOLE-CHAPTER RESOURCES
A Writing Process Log, A Writing Prompt, Holistically Graded Models, Assessment Portfolio Materials

SEGMENT 1 *(pp. 204–208)*

SEEING PATTERNS AND RELATIONSHIPS

OBJECTIVES

- To read and respond personally to a professional model
- To locate information and to identify comparisons in a professional model

TEACHING THE LESSON

Begin by having a volunteer read aloud the introductory paragraphs about patterns and relationships. The literary model from Amy Tan's ***The Joy Luck Club*** is about a boy trying to teach his younger sister how to play chess. The children are members of a family of Chinese immigrants who settled in San Francisco after World War II. The girl in

VISUAL CONNECTIONS
Ethel Scull Thirty-six Times

About the Artist. Andy Warhol, a leader of the Pop Art movement that started in the early 1960s, used images from advertising and the mass media to show how he saw the consumer culture of the United States. Warhol's portrayal of commercial America, focusing on household goods, comic strip characters, and movie stars, was somewhat controversial. Although some critics felt the subjects were too mundane for great art, others admired Warhol's ability to convey a sense of his society through everyday objects.

About the Artwork. Warhol often did portraits of movie stars, rock stars, and other famous people. One notable feature of many of these paintings, including *Ethel Scull Thirty-six Times,* is repetition. Some people believe that this treatment of the subject is a statement about how even the public images of famous people are packaged and advertised in the media.

6 WRITING TO INFORM

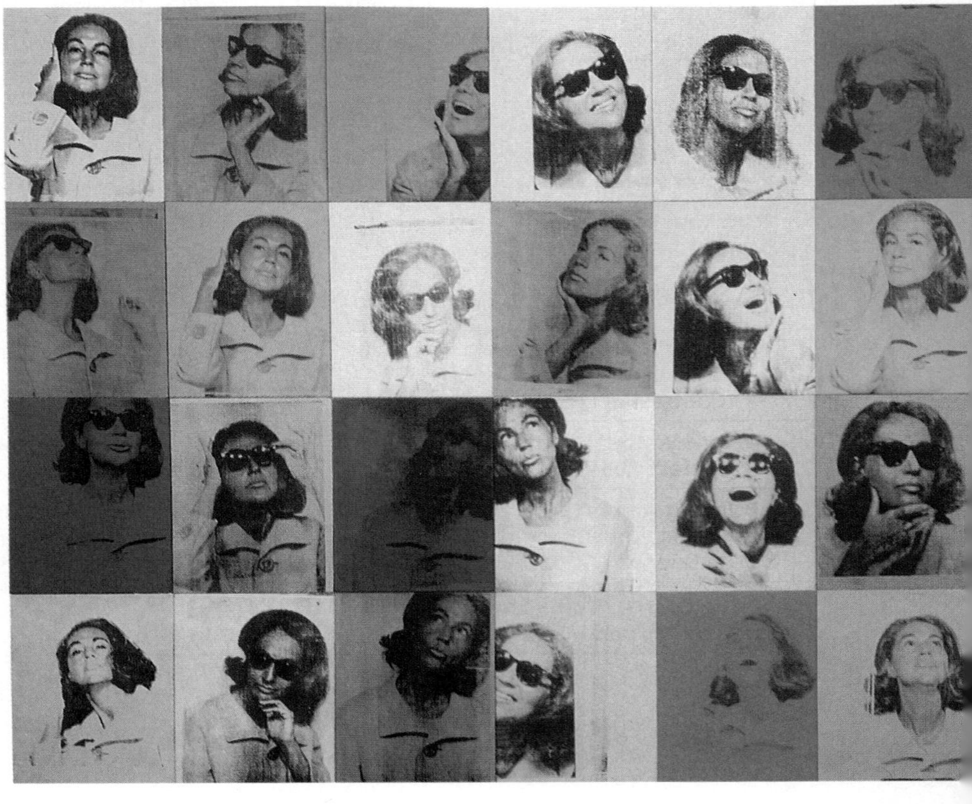

the passage is Waverly Jong, and after this episode with her brother Vincent, Waverly goes on to become a national chess champion.

The comparison in the passage is between the rules of chess and the rules of life in America. Waverly's mother, Lindo, attempts to teach her daughter that chess is a metaphor for life: One must learn to play the game of life by the rules and later learn the meaning of the rules—and of life—for oneself. Thus, the information given in the passage is a rather subtle lesson on an important part of the process of growing up.

After students have read the passage, you could use the **Reader's Response** and **Writer's Craft** questions as a basis for discussion.

Seeing Patterns and Relationships

What's the most economical car on the road today? Which had the more advanced civilization—the Aztecs or the Incas? It is natural to want information and to want to share what you know with others. One common way of gaining and sharing information is by looking at **patterns and relationships.**

Writing and You. People share information by showing patterns or relationships in several ways. For example, a movie critic gives information about a movie by comparing the sequel to the original. A politician defines *liberty* by saying what it is and what it is not. When you're deciding which sound system to buy, you might put them in categories—by price or speaker size. When was the last time you noticed patterns or relationships in something?

As You Read. In the following passage, a character sees a relationship between two things. What are they? What is the relationship?

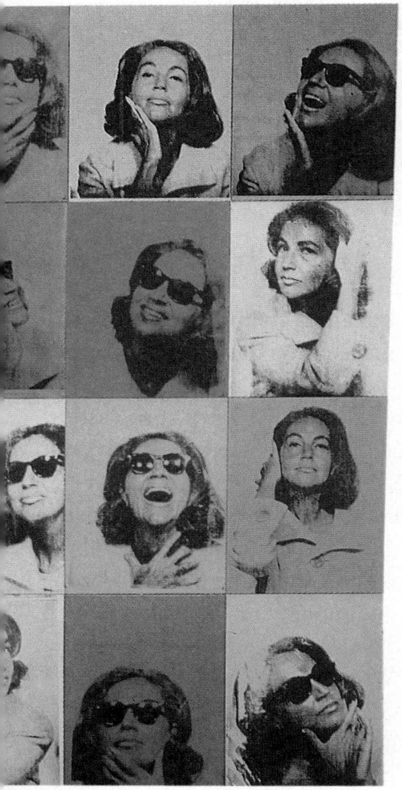

Andy Warhol, *Ethel Scull Thirty-six Times* (1963). Silkscreen ink on synthetic polymer paint on canvas. 36 Panels, each 19 7/8" × 15 7/8"; overall, 6'7 3/4" × 11'11". © 1993 The Andy Warhol Foundation for the Visual Arts, Inc./ARS, N.Y.

QUOTATION FOR THE DAY

"Nothing is good or bad but by comparison." (Thomas Fuller, M.D., 1654–1734, English physician, writer and compiler)

Ask students to freewrite briefly about what the quotation means to them. Then discuss with students how the strategy of comparison can lead to discovery and can make one realize the value of something.

MEETING INDIVIDUAL NEEDS

LEP/ESL

General Strategies. The two experiences that Amy Tan relates in the excerpt from ***The Joy Luck Club*** are playing chess and immigrating to the United States. Possibly, some students have had no exposure to the game of chess and, therefore, will find it difficult to establish a connection between the two experiences. You could bring a chess set to class and show students each piece mentioned in the story. In addition, be aware that although some of your ESL students may be immigrants and may be willing to discuss their experiences, others will find self-disclosure embarrassing or even intimidating. Remain sensitive to this possibility when discussing the second **Reader's Response** question.

ASSESSMENT

You can base your assessment of students' understanding of the passage on their answers to the second **Writer's Craft** question. You may need to encourage students to reread the passage. You can point out that the shift in focus from the children to the mother signals the comparison.

CLOSURE

Ask students to think about how they've recently used comparisons and contrasts to inform someone about something. Encourage volunteers to share examples.

USING THE SELECTION

from *The Joy Luck Club*

1

The speaker is Waverly Place Jong, a girl seven years old (eight by Chinese reckoning). She was named for the street her family lived on in San Francisco's Chinatown neighborhood, but her family name is *Meimei,* which means "little sister."

2

Vincent, Waverly's older brother, had received the used chess set as a gift at a Christmas party at the First Chinese Baptist Church, and two of the pieces were missing.

3

relented: gave in

4

Pawns are chess pieces of the lowest rank. Other meanings of the word are "hostage" and "something given to secure a loan."

5

crossways: diagonally

from

**by
Amy Tan**

1 "Let me! Let me!" I begged between games when one brother or the other would sit back with a deep sigh of relief and victory, the other annoyed, unable to let go of the out-
2 come. Vincent at first refused to let me play, but when I offered my Life Savers as replacements for the buttons that filled in for the missing
3 pieces, he relented. He chose the flavors: wild cherry for the black pawn and peppermint for the white knight. Winner could eat both.

As our mother sprinkled flour and rolled out small doughy circles for the steamed dumplings that would be our dinner that night, Vincent explained the rules, pointing to each piece. "You have sixteen pieces and so do I. One king and queen, two bishops, two knights, two castles,
4 and eight pawns. The pawns can only move forward one step, except on the first move. Then they can move two. But they can only take men by
5 moving crossways like this, except in the beginning, when you can move ahead and take another pawn."

"Why?" I asked as I moved my pawn. "Why can't they move more steps?"

"Because they're pawns," he said.

"But why do they go crossways to take other men. Why aren't there any women and children?"

ENRICHMENT

You may want to bring to class copies of *The Joy Luck Club* and *The Kitchen God's Wife,* Tan's second novel. Pass the books around and let students flip through them. Some students may become interested enough to want to read the novels. ■

"Why is the sky blue? Why must you always ask stupid questions?" asked Vincent. "This is a game. These are the rules. I didn't make them up. See. Here. In the book." He jabbed a page with a pawn in his hand. "Pawn. P-A-W-N. Pawn. Read it yourself."

My mother patted the flour off her hands. "Let me see book," she said quietly. She scanned the pages quickly, not reading the foreign English symbols, seeming to search deliberately for nothing in particular.

6 "This American rules," she concluded at last. "Every time people come out from foreign country, must know rules. You not know, judge say, Too bad, go back. They not telling you why so you can use their way go forward. They say, Don't know why, you find out yourself. But they knowing all the time. Better you take it, find out why yourself." She tossed her head back with a satisfied smile.

"I studied each chess piece, trying to absorb the power each contained."

I found out about all the whys later. I read the rules and looked up all the big words in a dictionary. I borrowed books from the Chinatown library. I studied each chess piece, trying to absorb the power each contained.

6

The mother, Lindo Jong, compares the rules of chess to the "rules" of her new country, the United States.

SELECTION AMENDMENT

Description of change: excerpted

Rationale: to focus on the concept of comparison presented in this chapter

ANSWERS

Reader's Response

Responses will vary.

1. Each answer should include a description of an experience involving a rule the student didn't understand, as well as a description of the student's feelings about the experience.
2. If some students don't know of any problems that immigrants face, ask the students to imagine what it would be like to move to a country where they didn't know the language and where customs and traditions were different from the ones they're used to. What's the first thing they would do upon arrival? How would they survive until they could learn the language and find work?

Writer's Craft

3. The passage gives minimal information about the playing pieces and the rules of chess. On a more subtle level, the passage contains the information that learning the rules of chess can serve as a metaphor for learning the rules of a new country and of life.
4. The less familiar subject is the rules of life in the United States, which differ from the rules of life in China. Metaphorically, the rules of chess illuminate the rules of life: one has to learn the rules of life and follow them, even if one doesn't understand them.

Reader's Response

1. Think of a time you had to follow rules you didn't understand, perhaps at school, in your driving, or at a part-time job. Tell your classmates about the experience. How did it make you feel?
2. Perhaps your forebears came to this country from another country, or perhaps you know someone from another country. If so, explain what problems immigrants to this country face with "rules." Are there problems getting jobs, succeeding in schools, finding a place to live? Explain.

Writer's Craft

3. *The Joy Luck Club* is a work of fiction; Amy Tan's primary purpose is to create a literary work, not to inform. Yet, there is information in this passage. What information does she share?
4. Writers often explain an unfamiliar subject by showing how it relates to a more familiar subject; they *compare* the two subjects. If the chess game is the more familiar subject, what is the less familiar one it is compared with?

Author Amy Tan

SEGMENT 2 *(p. 209)*

STRATEGIES FOR WRITING TO INFORM

TEACHING THE MODES

This segment gives an overview of the four basic strategies (modes) of writing. Have students read about the four strategies and then explain to students that this chapter will instruct them in using the mode of classification to develop an informative essay.

You may want to have students find examples of informative writing that illustrate each of the strategies. Suggest that students use textbooks from other classes to find their examples. ■

Strategies for Writing to Inform

Looking at patterns and relationships is one strategy writers use to inform; it's the strategy of *classification*. Following are examples of how you might use the four basic strategies of writing—narration, description, classification, and evaluation—to inform.

Narration: writing a biographical sketch of a famous movie star or sports figure; reporting what happened at a four-alarm fire in your neighborhood.

Description: in a travel essay, describing the view from the Sears Tower in Chicago; in a report for your art appreciation class, describing one of the paintings of Winslow Homer.

Classification: in an essay for history class, comparing Presidents George Bush and Ronald Reagan; explaining *loyalty* to your younger brother.

Evaluation: explaining to your best friend why you don't want to go back to the new sandwich shop on the corner; in English class, writing a review of a movie you saw last weekend.

LOOKING AHEAD

In the main assignment in this chapter, you'll learn how to write a comparison/contrast essay. You will be using the strategy of classification to share information. As you work through the writing assignment, keep in mind that a comparison/contrast essay

- looks at relationships or patterns
- looks at two or more subjects
- focuses on similarities or differences or both

MEETING INDIVIDUAL NEEDS

ADVANCED STUDENTS

You may want to explore with your advanced students how the evaluation mode can be used to inform readers. Point out that evaluation assumes a set of criteria for judging what's good and what isn't. Essentially, an evaluation informs readers of how well a particular object, place, event, and so on, meets the criteria. Sometimes the criteria are stated, but often they are implied.

CRITICAL THINKING

Synthesis

Have students create another type of comparison, an analogy. Explain that in an analogy two objects (or ideas) are not compared; instead, their relationship is compared.

Writers commonly use analogies to simplify complex relationships, such as equating the scattering of billiard balls on a pool table with what happens to atomic particles during nuclear bombardment.

Ask students to write their own analogies to show comparisons between relationships. For example, they might compare the process of writing an essay to the process of building a house.

SEGMENT 3 *(pp. 210–218)*

PREWRITING

OBJECTIVES

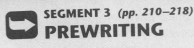

- To choose a subject for a comparison/contrast essay
- To write a thesis statement
- To gather and arrange information for a comparison/contrast essay

MOTIVATION

Ask your students to identify the courses they're taking that require them to write comparison/contrast essays and write the list on the chalkboard. (If you're using this chapter early in the school year, check with colleagues in other departments to find out which of them will require this kind of writing at some point in their courses.) Most

Teacher's ResourceBank™

RESOURCES

PREWRITING

- Developing a Venn Diagram 54

QUOTATION FOR THE DAY

"So before writing, learn to think." (Nicolas Boileau-Despréaux, 1636–1711, French critic and poet)

You could use this quotation as a basis for a discussion about prewriting. Reassure students that thinking through a topic and formulating a plan will facilitate writing.

MEETING INDIVIDUAL NEEDS

LESS-ADVANCED STUDENTS

Some of your students will shy away from essay topics that require research, simply because their research skills are poorly developed. Pairing students with peer tutors and sending them together to the school library (or public library, if necessary) may be an effective strategy for developing their skills in using the card catalog, accessing magazine and newspaper articles, and finding their way through the stacks.

Writing a Comparison/Contrast Essay

Prewriting

Considering Subjects, Purpose, and Audience

You're starving for a taco. Which fast-food joint will you visit to satisfy your craving? You quickly narrow it to two choices: Tons of Tacos and Tacos R Us. Tons of Tacos is closer and cheaper, while Tacos R Us is farther and more expensive. That thought process is an example of how you apply the strategy of comparison/contrast to common decisions in your everyday life, but comparison/contrast is equally important as a writing strategy you can use to develop many kinds of topics.

Subjects. In school, you have probably found that many test questions and essay writing assignments ask you to compare and contrast—two short stories, two countries, two animals. Later in your life, you may find yourself writing to compare and contrast on your job—perhaps you need to compare two possible locations for a new shoe store or two candidates for a clerk in your office. In many of these situations, you don't have to decide what two *subjects* to compare or contrast. The pairing of the two subjects is a natural part of the writing situation.

When you do need to identify subjects (people, places, or things) to compare and contrast, however, what do you look for? Following are some suggestions to get you started.

- *Subjects with something in common.* For example, during World War II, both General George Patton of the U.S. Army and German Field Marshal Erwin Rommel commanded tank forces in the desert of North Africa.
- *Subjects that have some significant differences.* The most obvious difference between Patton and Rommel is that they fought on opposite sides during the war.
- *Subjects about which information is fairly accessible.* You would have no trouble finding information about Patton and Rommel, but you might have difficulty if you chose lesser-known military leaders.

students will list English, social studies, and science, at the minimum. You can point out that this segment will show students how to plan and organize information for writing assignments they will be doing during the year in many of their school subjects.

TEACHING THE LESSON

This segment covers the entire prewriting phase of the writing process, and you may need to spend two or more days on it. The segment deals first with analyzing purpose and audience for the assignment. The purpose is to inform, but the audience may not be so clear. Unless you have a specific audience in mind, you may want to ☛

Purpose and Audience. The strategy of comparison/contrast can be used for all of the basic *purposes* of writing—to express yourself, to inform, to persuade, or to create literary works. In the main part of this chapter, however, you're going to concentrate on using comparison/contrast to inform. Within the overall purpose of informing, you may have a more specific purpose:

- to show similarities between the subjects
- to show differences between the subjects
- to show both similarities and differences between the subjects

Since you are attempting to inform (part of the expository aim), you will be concerned about your *audience's* knowledge. What do they already know? What information will be new to them? Informative writing is interesting only if it presents new information, or old information in a new way. Perhaps by comparing two subjects no one else has compared, you can help your audience see one or both of them in a new way.

WRITING NOTE Comparison points out the similarities between things, people, or ideas, while contrast points out the differences. However, the word *comparison* is often used to mean both comparing and contrasting. For example, when your United States history teacher asks you to "compare" Abraham Lincoln and Robert E. Lee, you probably need to point out differences as well as similarities.

CRITICAL THINKING
Analysis

Although the general purpose of the essays students will write is to inform through comparison and contrast, each student should analyze his or her specific purpose. For example, a general purpose may be to show how movies made for TV differ from those made for theater viewing, but the writer's specific purpose may be to show how movies made for theaters have better special effects, actors with better draw, and more diversity in subject matter.

Ask your students to analyze their subjects to discover the specific purposes they want to achieve. The purpose can be stated in a clause or phrase that can later be used as part of the thesis statement of the essay.

suggest that your students assume their audience will be the members of their class. By making the audience limited and specific, you can encourage students to analyze what subjects might interest the audience and what the audience might already know about the subjects. After students have selected subjects in **Writing Assignment: Part 1** or in **Exercise 1**, you may want to spend some time discussing some of these in class to help students evaluate their choices in terms of appropriateness for their purposes and audiences. You can then let students revise their choices if they need to. After students read **Planning a Comparison/Contrast Essay**, remind students that informative writing doesn't include opinions—only facts. As some students may not be

A DIFFERENT APPROACH

People seem to learn best when they apply something they know to something they don't know. This principle of learning can help students choose subjects for the comparison/contrast essays. For example, if students want to inform their readers about the zydeco music of southern Louisiana, they may find it useful to compare and contrast this music to more familiar genres.

MEETING INDIVIDUAL NEEDS

AT-RISK STUDENTS

Some at-risk students may be able to draw on personal experiences as sources of subjects. For example, children of migrant workers may be able to compare and contrast their itinerant lifestyle to other lifestyles that don't involve moving around. Students who are parents may be able to compare and contrast their attitudes toward maintaining personal schedules and routines to their attitudes before their children were born. In any case, you can help at-risk students see their particular situations as potential assets, instead of as liabilities, to their academic work.

WRITING ASSIGNMENT

PART 1:
Choosing Subjects to Compare/Contrast

For this assignment, you have a chance to choose your own subjects, so think about what interests you. Is it pro basketball, music of the 1960s, or Chinese food? Start with that area of interest, and then choose two subjects to explain through the strategy of comparison/contrast. Just be sure your subjects have some basic similarity and enough differences to be interesting. Also, remember that explanations aren't interesting unless they give readers some new information.

EXERCISE 1 **Speaking and Listening: Listening for Subjects** Have students share their findings with the rest of the class.

If you're stuck for subjects, try listening to radio or TV with paper and pencil in hand. What do you see or hear that bothers you or makes you curious? Are you upset that your favorite team is in the doldrums? Maybe you can explain its losing streak by comparing and contrasting this season's coaching staff and players with last year's coaching staff and players. Are you puzzled when the announcer says that a typhoon has hit Japan? Perhaps you can explain the storm by comparing and contrasting it with a more familiar storm, the tornado.

familiar with a Venn diagram, you may want to explain the one on p. 214.

After students have written thesis statements, you can discuss a few in class to make sure students' statements are appropriate for comparison/contrast writing. You may want to conference briefly with each student to discuss the type of organization — block or point-by-point — that will be best for each thesis statement.

Cont. on p. 215

Prewriting

Planning a Comparison/Contrast Essay

Here's a comparison for you. Your comparison/contrast essay is like a building, and you have just laid the foundation by choosing two subjects. The next step is to gather the main building blocks—information about the two subjects—and start to arrange them as you'll need them later.

Gathering Information

Sources of Information. When you are writing to inform, you need to share accurate information. If you're writing about two subjects you know well, you may be able to pull most of the information out of your own memory and knowledge. For example, if you're a great baseball fan and you want to compare the Cincinnati Reds and the Boston Red Sox, you may know enough to write the essay. However, if you're writing about Patton and Rommel, you will probably have to do some research. In your research, remember that you're not just looking for *enough* information; you need *all* the important information. For example, you would not want to leave out the fact that Patton was American and Rommel was German. Refer to Chapter 11 (pages 413–417 and 437–446), if you need help with identifying and documenting sources.

Relevance of Information. As you are gathering information, you may come up with all kinds of similarities and differences; but they aren't all equally useful. The Cincinnati Reds and the Boston Red Sox are both located in cities that are north of the Mason-Dixon line, but that's of no importance when you are comparing and contrasting their World Series records. What you're looking for are ***relevant*** (related and important) ***features*** or points that both subjects have in common.

The following example shows how one writer gathered information on the relevant features of schools in Colonial America and schools in the year 2150. Notice that this writer used a Venn diagram to sort differences and similarities. In a Venn diagram, you place any points the subjects have in common in the overlapping segments of the circles.

COOPERATIVE LEARNING

One way to gather relevant similarities and differences between two subjects is to use the *5W-How?* questions. The questions *Who? What? When? Where? Why?* and *How?* can be applied to a wide variety of subjects to focus on the most important points of comparison and contrast. Some subjects may allow students to use all six questions, while others may require only one or two questions. Have students work in pairs to take turns asking and answering questions about their subjects. Partners could offer additional information and suggestions.

CRITICAL THINKING
(pp. 214–215)

OBJECTIVE

- To analyze related subjects to identify their differences

TEACHING *ANALYZING SUBJECTS*

Ask a volunteer to read aloud the introductory information. Then discuss with students the example in the **Critical Thinking Exercise;** focus on explaining the concepts of *common group* and *relevant features.* Use the first item in the exercise to guide students through the analysis process. Then assign the remaining items for

MEETING INDIVIDUAL NEEDS

LEARNING STYLES

Visual Learners. You may want to show students how to use graphic organizers to analyze a subject for relevant features. Display and discuss the following cluster that uses familiar subjects:

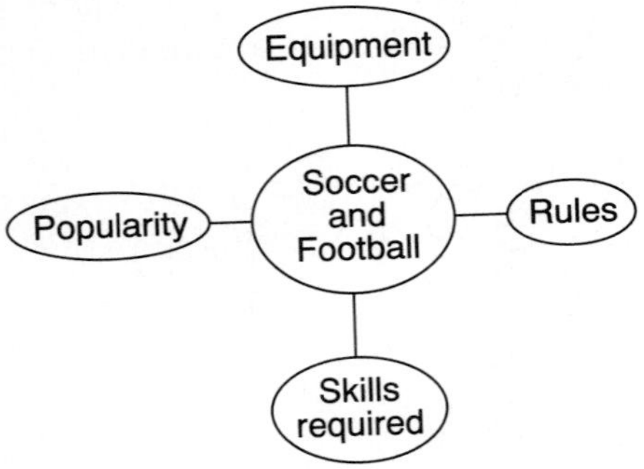

INTEGRATING THE LANGUAGE ARTS

Library Link. You may want to consider making the **Critical Thinking Exercise** a library activity because students might have to research how the two subjects in each item differ from one another. If either time or library facilities are limited, let students work in pairs on only one of the items (but make sure that all items are covered). After students

HERE'S HOW

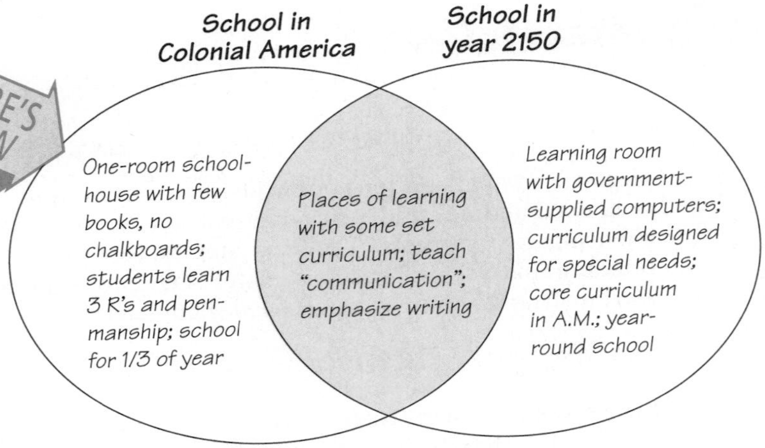

CRITICAL THINKING

Analyzing Subjects for Their Relevant Features

When you ***analyze*** something, you try to understand it by looking at its parts. Before you can compare or contrast two subjects, you have to analyze them to find their relevant (related and important) features or points.

To identify relevant features, think about the basis for comparison—the common groups your subjects belong to. Red Cloud and Sitting Bull, for example, were two great Sioux leaders. Features that would help you show this basic similarity include their leadership in war, spiritual matters ("medicine"), and politics.

CRITICAL THINKING EXERCISE:
Analyzing Subjects for Their Relevant Features

Working with a partner or small group, try out your analyzing skills. For each set of subjects in the list on the next page, first independent practice. Despite their familiarity with the subjects, students may need to do research to find out about differences between them. You can minimize the need for research by discussing the subjects before students do the exercise. When students finish, have the pairs or small groups share their answers.

Cont. from p. 213

GUIDED PRACTICE

Students may need guided practice in choosing subjects. Using a major headline from a current newspaper or news magazine, write a suggested subject on the chalkboard. For example, if the headline deals with Haitian immigration to the United States, ask students to suggest possible subjects to finish the exercise, each pair of students can share its findings with the whole class.

decide what group both subjects belong to. (You may need to do some research on subjects you're not familiar with.) Then, for each set of subjects, identify at least three or four relevant features. Remember that the relevant features are the important characteristics the two subjects have in common.

EXAMPLE

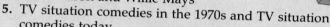

Subjects: pyramids in Mexico, pyramids in Egypt
Common group: huge structures with similar shapes
Relevant features: size, religious uses, astronomical uses

1. tepees and igloos
2. tornadoes and hurricanes
3. jazz and blues
4. Hank Aaron and Willie Mays
5. TV situation comedies in the 1970s and TV situation comedies today

ANSWERS

Critical Thinking Exercise

Answers will vary. Here are some possibilities:

1. Common group: types of dwellings
   Relevant features: climate where each is used, materials used in construction, portability
2. Common group: types of storms
   Relevant features: locations where each type occurs, precautions taken to prepare for each type, cause(s) of each type
3. Common group: styles of music
   Relevant features: origins, emotional content, instrumentation
4. Common group: African American baseball players
   Relevant features: positions, career achievements, length of career
5. Common group: television situation comedies
   Relevant features: subjects, popularity, frequency

compare or to contrast with this one. Such subjects might include "the first immigration to the New World" or "the immigration of Cuban refugees to the United States."

Then you can help students compose thesis statements for the chosen subjects and discuss how the essays could be organized.

INDEPENDENT PRACTICE

The two parts of the **Writing Assignment** in this segment should provide ample opportunity for independent practice.

DEVELOPING A THESIS STATEMENT

Explain to students that when they develop their thesis statements, they can decide whether or not they want to list the relevant features they will compare or contrast in their essays. For example, instead of writing "Dogs and wolves are close relatives, but dogs relate to human beings in ways wolves don't," a student may write "Dogs and wolves are close relatives, but dogs assist human beings more than wolves do by serving as pets, as work animals, and as protectors." The second version can guide the writer in selecting and arranging details, and it can also help the reader follow the organization of the essay. However, remind students that listing the relevant features they've covered in their essays is also a good concluding technique; encourage students not to repeat the technique if they've used it in their thesis statements.

Developing a Thesis Statement

At some point during the planning of your essay, you have to think about your *thesis*, the main idea you will be sharing. You have two subjects. Are you going to stress how much they are alike, or are you going to stress how different they are? Perhaps you don't want to do either; you just want to share information about their similarities as well as their differences. Once you have made that decision, you know the main idea of your essay. Then you can write a thesis statement to guide your planning and writing. (For more information about developing thesis statements, see pages 102–104.) Here are some examples of thesis statements for comparison/contrast essays.

EXAMPLES The Sioux chiefs Red Cloud and Sitting Bull differed in their attitudes toward the government but were similar in their approaches to war, spiritual matters ("medicine"), and politics. [This essay will look at both differences and similarities.]

The effects of migrating west during the nineteenth century were much different for American women than for American men. [This essay will stress the differences, even though the two subjects obviously had the migration itself in common.]

General George Patton of the U.S. Army and German Field Marshal Erwin Rommel had similar leadership styles. [This essay will stress similarities, even though there are many differences between the two men.]

WRITING NOTE

The fact that you are comparing two subjects does not mean you should ignore their differences. Essays that explore similarities often begin with one or two differences and then focus primarily on the similarities. And the reverse is true with essays that contrast two subjects. You might begin with a similarity or two and then devote the rest of the essay to information related to the differences between the subjects. In fact, by acknowledging both similarities and differences, you show your audience that you are aware of various aspects of your topic. This can make your readers more likely to take your ideas seriously.

ASSESSMENT

Assess students' subjects by determining whether they are similar enough to warrant comparison, yet different enough to allow for interesting contrasts. You can also determine whether the subjects will enable students to write informative essays that are appropriate for their intended audiences.

The thesis statements should clearly indicate whether the subjects are going to be compared, contrasted, or both, and they should also briefly sketch the similarities and differences the essays will deal with. The organizational plans can use either the block or the point-by-point method.

Sitting Bull

Red Cloud

Arranging Information

Once you have identified relevant features and thought about your thesis, you need to turn your thoughts back to your readers. You can make it easy for them to understand the relationships between your subjects by using one of the following methods of organization.

- **Block method:** It is possible to discuss each subject separately—in a "block." First you discuss all the relevant features of one subject; then you discuss all the relevant features of the second subject.
- **Point-by-point method:** Instead of focusing on the subject, you focus on the features. You discuss one feature at a time, as it relates to both subjects; then you go on to the next feature.

No matter which method you use, be consistent about the order in which you present information. In the block method, if you're discussing the size, subject, and material of Chinese sculpture, follow that same order (size, subject, material) in discussing Japanese sculpture. And in the point-by-point

ARRANGING INFORMATION

Although both organizational methods are good ways to structure comparison/contrast essays, each method seems to suit slightly different situations. The block method may work best when the audience is familiar with one of the two subjects under discussion. In this case, the more familiar subject can be dealt with first, and the relevant points of comparison or contrast can be mentioned without a great deal of explanation. When both subjects are relatively unfamiliar to the audience, the point-by-point method (which doesn't require readers to remember new information for longer periods of time, as the block method does) may be easier for readers to follow.

CLOSURE

Ask students to share their work with the other members of the class. You can do this by having each student read his or her thesis statement to the class or by having students circulate their thesis statements and organizational plans so that others in the class may read them. ■

MEETING INDIVIDUAL NEEDS

STUDENTS WITH SPECIAL NEEDS

Students with learning disabilities generally have difficulty organizing information. You may want to conference with each student to help him or her decide which organizational method to use—block or point-by-point. Then provide copies of a blank chart like the one on this page with the **Block Method** and **Point-by-Point Method** columns. Students can fill in either column of the charts with their topic-specific information.

TIMESAVER

When students work on **Writing Assignment: Part 2,** you may want to require them to submit tentative outlines of their essays along with the thesis statements they're asked to write in the assignment. By having students write outlines, you can quickly tell the method of organization they plan to use, whether the order of details is logical, and whether they have chosen relevant similarities or differences to write about.

method, keep the same order of subjects (Chinese first and then Japanese) when discussing each feature. The following chart shows how the two methods work.

BLOCK METHOD	POINT-BY-POINT METHOD
Subject 1: Red Cloud Feature 1: war leadership Feature 2: spiritual leadership Feature 3: politics Subject 2: Sitting Bull Feature 1: war leadership Feature 2: spiritual leadership Feature 3: politics	Feature 1: war leadership Subject 1: Red Cloud Subject 2: Sitting Bull Feature 2: spiritual leadership Subject 1: Red Cloud Subject 2: Sitting Bull Feature 3: politics Subject 1: Red Cloud Subject 2: Sitting Bull

Reminder

To plan a comparison/contrast essay

- analyze your subjects to find relevant features
- gather specific information about the features
- develop a thesis statement that identifies the subjects and the main idea
- decide on the block or point-by-point method of organization

WRITING ASSIGNMENT PART 2:

Gathering and Arranging Information

Get down to the building blocks of your essay by gathering information about your subjects. Brainstorm or research each subject you identified in Writing Assignment, Part 1; then choose the relevant features you'll focus on. If you want, use a Venn diagram like the one on page 214 to jot down information. Write a thesis statement to guide your thinking as you plan and draft your essay. Then decide whether to use the block or point-by-point method to arrange your information and use that method to organize your notes.

SEGMENT 4 *(pp. 219–226)*

WRITING YOUR FIRST DRAFT

OBJECTIVES

- To analyze a comparison/contrast article from a newspaper
- To write the first draft of a comparison/contrast essay

MOTIVATION

Bring to class a copy of the Sunday edition of the *New York Times* or some other newspaper from a large city. Divide the class into groups of four and give one section of the newspaper to each group. Ask each group to read the first three or four paragraphs of the major articles in the section and to identify articles developed by comparison and ☛

Writing Your First Draft

Once you have gathered and arranged the building blocks of your essay, you can start bringing it all together. At this stage, you begin to think about the structure of the essay itself.

The Structure of a Comparison/Contrast Essay

Like most other essays, a comparison/contrast essay usually has three main parts: an introduction, a body, and a conclusion. These suggestions can help you structure your essay.

1. Begin your *introduction* with an anecdote, a quotation, a question, or specific details to grab your reader's attention. To help readers follow your main points, include a statement of your thesis near the end of the introduction.
2. Use the block or point-by-point method to present information in the *body* of the essay. Use facts, statistics, examples, and other kinds of information to develop each of the features you discuss here. (If you need more information, use the prewriting techniques on pages 22–31 to help you find it.)
3. Bring the paper to a satisfying close by summarizing or restating the main idea. Often, the *conclusion* adds a question or final comment, ending with a new thought.

This basic essay structure was used by Henry Kisor in the following article. He wrote the article after an interview with Ved Mehta, a journalist who is blind. In this article, Kisor, who is deaf, compares his own disability with that of Mehta.

Henry Kisor, author of *What's That Pig Outdoors?*

Teacher's ResourceBank™

RESOURCES

WRITING YOUR FIRST DRAFT
- Writing a Comparison/Contrast Essay 55

QUOTATION FOR THE DAY

"The perfect presence of mind, unconfused, unhurried by emotion, that any artistic performance requires . . ." (Henry James, 1843–1916, American author)

Ask each student to complete the quotation to make a statement about informative writing. Then have students share their responses.

MEETING INDIVIDUAL NEEDS

LEP/ESL

General Strategies. Many students know how to use their native languages to get the attention of readers. However, due to cultural and linguistic differences, students might be uncertain about how to catch the attention of native speakers of English. Offer examples of attention-grabbing introductions and explain why they are effective. You may want to work individually with students to offer specific suggestions.

contrast. Let each group share with the class the number of articles they were able to find and the subjects that the articles dealt with. Point out that comparison/contrast writing is an important tool of journalists, whose job is to inform their readers.

TEACHING THE LESSON

The information on the structure of a comparison/contrast essay at the beginning of the segment should refresh students' memories about the three basic divisions of an essay. You might want to remind students that the three divisions have nothing to do with the number of paragraphs an essay has, nor does the structure imply that each

USING THE SELECTION

from *What's That Pig Outdoors?*

1
Often, journalistic writers don't include thesis statements. However, the reader could infer a thesis statement from the first two sentences.

2
Kisor uses the word *resonates* figuratively to mean the work contains experiences and emotions shared by all human beings.

3
candid: honest, frank

4
meningitis: an inflammation of the membranes surrounding the brain, caused by a bacterial infection; can cause brain damage and loss of vision or hearing

5
The writer uses transitions such as *both* and *likewise* to signal comparisons.

A NEWSPAPER ARTICLE

from What's That Pig Outdoors?

by Henry Kisor

INTRODUCTION Attention grabber

1 NEW YORK—It is not often that a deaf person learns something from a blind one. But I did from Ved Mehta, a celebrated writer for *The New Yorker*.

His fifth volume of autobiography— *Sound-Shadows of the New World*—is to be published next month. It is the fascinating story of Mehta's adolescence at the Arkansas School for the Blind in Little Rock after arriving from his native India at age 15 in 1949.

Background

As are all his other memoirs, this one is much more than the history of a person who happens to be physically handicapped. It is also about what it was like for a youngster from another culture to grow up in the United States in a certain
2 time and place, and it resonates with universal experience and shared emotion.

Best of all, it is written in prose as clear and musical as a mountain brook, with a wealth of
3 candid detail only a prodigious memory could provide.

Similarities

Some particulars of *Sound-Shadows* spoke to me in a way they may not to other readers: they made me relive many special events of my childhood and youth, for Mehta and I have a good deal
4 in common. We share a profession. And meningitis robbed him of his sight at age 4; the same disease took my hearing at age 3.

Relevant feature 1: Henry Kisor

5 We both learned to make our other senses compensate for the loss. Early on I developed an acute sensitivity to vibrations and the movement of air. A creak of floorboards and a puff of wind from an opened door often will announce that someone has entered the room behind me.

division should be of equal length. Point out to students that many writers find it easier to write introductions after they've written the bodies of the papers. Basically, the introduction should create a context for the essay by providing background information that leads up to the thesis statement. If students use anecdotes, quotations, questions, or specific details to grab their readers' attention, they should provide background information to connect the attention grabber to the thesis.

Before students read the literary model by Henry Kisor, you can ask if any of them know people who are deaf or blind. If some students do know deaf or blind people, ask the students to relate how deaf people communicate or how blind people are able to get around.

Relevant feature 1: Ved Mehta

6 Likewise, Mehta sharpened his "facial vision," a kind of blind person's radar. Its precise nature is elusive, but it helps those lucky enough to have it to detect the presence of obstacles without needing artificial aids, such as canes and seeing-eye dogs.

Relevant feature 2: Ved Mehta

Most important, however, we both learned to be independent. As a young student at an impecunious state school, Mehta may not have received much of an academic education—that would come later, at Pomona College, Oxford and Harvard—but he shunned canes and did everything he could to get rid of "blindisms," physical idiosyncrasies that signaled sightlessness.

Relevant feature 2: Henry Kisor

7 So, also, did I avoid "deafisms" such as sign language. Whether it was by chance or my parents' design, I grew up entirely among hearing people, speaking and lipreading well enough, however imperfectly, to consider myself a normal person. Sign language was for those unlucky enough to be born deaf or lose their hearing before they had developed speech. Those who needed sign, I thought, were condemned to a narrow, limited world, and I felt sorry for them.

Background about interview

When I met Mehta early one morning in New York, I half-expected an intense fellow, perhaps one constantly on edge, always out to prove himself. But the slim 51-year-old man who greeted me gravely in his living room was relaxed and dignified, with a gentle smile. He gave a fatherly

Ved Mehta

6

elusive: difficult to grasp

7

People who are born deaf aren't able to acquire language in the ordinary way—by hearing it used. Some deaf people, including those who are born deaf, can learn to speak quite well, but many of them use American Sign Language to communicate.

As students read the article, ask them to note the comments in the left-hand margin. You may want to point out that Kisor compares Ved Mehta's facial vision with his own awareness of acoustic vibrations, but Kisor says relatively little about vibrations under the assumption that his audience is much more familiar with this skill than with facial vision.

Then ask students to read **A Writer's Model** on pp. 224–226 and to evaluate it by using the criteria listed on p. 219.

peck and a pat to his 14-month-old daughter, Sage, before sending her off with his wife of three years, Linn.

Development through interview

He hesitated before passing through the doorway to the library where we would talk, as if he knew he was off center, then adjusted his step to enter straight through the middle. "Were you using facial vision for that?" I asked. "What is facial vision, anyway?"

Details—Relevant feature 1: Ved Mehta

"Sometimes my mind isn't on what I'm doing," he said with a chuckle. "I tend to be a dreamy person, like most writers. If I'm not concentrating, it's quite likely that I'd go off center. Also, you got me in the morning before I had my first cup of coffee.

"As for facial vision, it's not clear that scientists know what it is. There's much misunderstanding about it. I go by sound, echoes, the air pressure around the ears. When I'm in a familiar place, I know where the door is and, as I poetically call it, 'where the sound-shadows change.' That's an open, more airy place."

"Can you always depend on facial vision?" I asked, thinking about how my knack for lipreading can desert me at the worst possible moments. The compensations handicapped people can make are remarkable, but they're by no means foolproof.

"It lets me down when there's a pneumatic drill or terrific wind, or at the airport with a lot of planes," he said. "If there are a lot of blanketing sounds, then my facial vision suffers. A jackhammer almost completely paralyzes me; I can't tell where I am or what I'm doing."

8 Ironically, another situation in which Mehta's facial vision falters is in "an absolutely open field without trees. For facial vision to be most effective, there has to be an object to which I can establish some kind of relationship—and also there has to be a fair degree of quiet so that I can discriminate between different kinds of sound-shadows."

8
The writer uses *another* as a transition to show the relationship between two situations.

GUIDED PRACTICE

Use the first question in **Exercise 2** on p. 224 to guide students through the process of analyzing Kisor's article. Before students write the first drafts of their essays, you may want to model the process. As a model for a first draft, you could use one of the subjects suggested in the **Critical Thinking Exercise** on p. 215, or you could ask a volunteer to share his or her thesis statement and organizational plan.

Facial vision serves Mehta well enough so that he can stand at a busy Manhattan intersection, listening for changes in the thrum of traffic and for the click of crossing signals, and make his
way across the street as agilely as any other New 9
Yorker—and without a cane or a guide dog. 10
Facial vision does not, however, guard him from such hazards as two-foot-long standpipes jutting at waist level from the side of a building.

"Do you think a seeing-eye dog could be of some help?" I asked.

"Not to me," he replied. "As with people who have all their faculties, the abilities of the blind and perhaps the deaf vary a lot. Certain blind people, especially those who lose their eyesight late in life, find a seeing-eye dog very useful. But when I was growing up I didn't even know there was such a thing."

"Do you use any kind of device to aid you?" I asked. "Not at the moment," Mehta said, "but as I grow older and injuries take longer to heal, I might well start using a cane. There's a real shift in the way I think about some of these problems. When I was younger, perhaps I had contempt for people who had to rely on the cane. But now I will use whatever helps me to function. If a time should come that I lose my hearing as well, I might use a seeing-eye dog, too.

CONCLUSION

"But there are so many ways in which you can be independent. Independence is a matter of the spirit."

9
agilely: easily

10
cane: a special cane used by visually impaired people to assist them in detecting obstacles in their paths as they walk; not used for physical support

SELECTION AMENDMENT
Description of change: excerpted
Rationale: to focus on the concept of structure in a comparison/contrast essay presented in this chapter

INDEPENDENT PRACTICE

Exercise 2 should provide students sufficient independent practice in analyzing a comparison/contrast essay. Writing the first drafts of their own essays is necessarily an independent activity, although some students may have difficulties and need your suggestions about how to proceed.

ASSESSMENT

Students' analytical abilities can be evaluated with **Exercise 2.** To assess the drafts of students' essays, use the following questions:

1. Is the thesis a clear statement of comparison or contrast between two appropriate subjects?

ANSWERS

Exercise 2

Answers may vary. Here are some possibilities:

1. Kisor grabs attention in the first two sentences by telling of his and Mehta's disabilities.
2. He describes Mehta's facial vision.
3. Kisor expects Mehta to be intense, on edge, and always out to prove himself. Instead, Kisor found him to be relaxed and dignified, with a gentle smile.
4. Kisor establishes his credentials for evaluating Mehta's book by showing that his own life is similar in some ways to Mehta's.
5. Students may have learned about facial vision and the problems visually impaired people have with mobility.

INTEGRATING THE LANGUAGE ARTS

Usage Link. Remind students that using transitional words and phrases will help their writing flow more smoothly and clearly. You may want to list on the chalkboard the following transitions that show comparison or contrast:

Comparison	Contrast
like	unlike
similarly	on the other hand
both	in contrast
the same as	but
just as	on the contrary
likewise	

EXERCISE 2 Analyzing a Comparison/Contrast Article

What was your reaction to this article? Meet with two or three classmates to discuss these questions about the Kisor piece.

1. What does the writer do to grab the reader's attention in the introduction?
2. Kisor briefly compares several features of his and Ved Mehta's lives. What is the feature that he devotes most of the article to?
3. At one point, Kisor contrasts his expectations of Ved Mehta with his experience on meeting him. How does the expectation differ from the reality?
4. Kisor's main purpose is to share information about Ved Mehta and his book. How does his comparison of his own life to Mehta's help him accomplish that purpose?
5. What new information did you learn about people with disabilities from this article?

A Framework for a Comparison/Contrast Essay

Kisor uses comparison/contrast as a part of a longer article focused on one of his two subjects, Ved Mehta. You might find it easier to organize your essay like the following writer's model. See if you think the block method of organization makes the essay easy to follow.

A WRITER'S MODEL

INTRODUCTION
Attention grabber

Imagine you could travel back in time to Colonial America and then zip forward to the year 2150. Probably the last place you'd choose to be is in school, but imagine that's where you find yourself. What was school like then, and what will it be like in the future? You would probably find some amazing differences in classroom equipment, curriculum, and length of school year.

Thesis statement

BODY
SUBJECT 1: School in 1720

In 1720 in a small Connecticut town, you would find yourself in a one-room schoolhouse made of logs. The dozen or so girls and boys--with no slates,

2. Has the student employed one of the two basic organizational methods?
3. Does the essay have an obvious introduction, body, and conclusion?

At this point there is no need to be concerned with errors in grammar, usage, and mechanics, but you may want to point out areas that need fuller development.

CLOSURE

Ask students to discuss what they found easiest about writing their drafts. What did they find most difficult? List responses in two columns on the chalkboard. Have volunteers suggest strategies for overcoming their difficulties.

Feature 1: classroom equipment

chalkboards, or maps--sit on benches. You use a goose-quill pen and homemade ink to write in a copybook you've made by carefully sewing together several sheets of folded coarse, dark paper. The few books in your classroom are filled with proverbs, fables, and stories to improve your character.

Feature 2: curriculum

Reading, writing, penmanship, and ciphering (that's arithmetic) are what you study. To learn arithmetic, you listen to your teacher read from a sum book. Then you copy the rules and problems he reads aloud into your own sum book. You're in a "moving school"--one that sets up in three different parts of a region during a year. You only go to school a third of the year, but you like seeing your friends every day. Your neighbor has written in his copybook: "School is better than doing chores sunup to sundown, everyday, everyday, everyday. School has friends and recess."

Feature 3: length of school year

SUBJECT 2: School of 2150

Feature 1: classroom equipment

Zapped into the future, in 2150 in the very same Connecticut town, you can't find a school anywhere. You've landed inside a dwelling unit (home) inside a housing unit next to a girl your age. She explains that students are instructed by government-supplied computers in the Learning Room inside each dwelling unit. There are no pencils, pens, or textbooks. Everything is done by a voice-activated computer. From the beginning, the curriculum is specially designed to meet each student's special

INTEGRATING THE LANGUAGE ARTS

Literature Link. If they are interested by the subject matter of **A Writer's Model,** students might also enjoy Mark Twain's account of the school Tom Sawyer attends in *The Adventures of Tom Sawyer.* You may want to locate a copy of the book and read aloud the relevant passage that begins about halfway through chapter six and concludes with the first several pages of chapter seven. Ask students how they would react to a school where corporal punishment was the order of the day. They can compare Twain's school with the schools of colonial times and with their school.

ENRICHMENT

If your school has classes for the visually impaired or the hearing impaired, you may want to invite some of these students to your class to share their experiences with your students. If visually or hearing impaired students aren't available to come to your class, you may be able to recruit a speaker from the community who is visually or auditorily impaired or who has worked with people who are. If speakers are unavailable, you could read excerpts from Helen Keller's autobiography *The Story of My Life,* in which she discusses her deafness and blindness. ■

INTEGRATING THE LANGUAGE ARTS

Technology Link. If students have access to computers, you might have them build bibliography or reference files for any of the research they do on their topics. Suggest that students use the hanging-indent (block indent) format for each entry and then add entries periodically. Finally, students should sort the files to obtain alphabetically arranged bibliographies.

abilities and interests. Three morning hours cover required curriculum: earth science, communication (including foreign languages), and social sciences. The three afternoon hours are reserved for exploring any subject that interests the students, with heavy emphasis on writing. Every student has a Visiting Tutor, who checks progress once a week and suggests creative projects. From age one, children learn to use their computers. And the school year runs year-round, six hours a day. It's lonesome, you complain--you miss your friends.

Feature 2: curriculum

Feature 3: length of school year

CONCLUSION Final comment

Your journey is finished. Which school did you enjoy more--the primitive school in a one-room log cabin or the high-tech, but lonely, school of the future? Maybe you prefer your familiar school of the present. After looking back and ahead, it might seem like a good choice.

WRITING ASSIGNMENT

PART 3:
Writing a First Draft

You have focused your creativity on planning your essay; now it's time to unleash it! Using your prewriting diagrams and notes and your thesis statement, write a first draft of your essay. Remember to develop your comparison/contrast with specific examples and details that the reader can understand.

SEGMENT 5 *(pp. 227–230)*

EVALUATING AND REVISING

OBJECTIVES

- To analyze a writer's revisions
- To evaluate and revise the first draft of a comparison/contrast essay

TEACHING THE LESSON

You can demonstrate how to evaluate and revise an essay by duplicating a draft (your own or, with permission, one written by a student) and working through the process with the class. You can use the questions in the **Evaluating and Revising Comparison/Contrast Essays chart** on the next page to guide your discussion.

Evaluating and Revising

Sometimes, years after they've published books, writers become dissatisfied with the books—and revise and publish them again. The evaluation and revision process won't take that long for you. In fact, you may have to begin shortly after completing your first draft. However, the following chart can help you to get the objective view of your paper that time might otherwise give you. Begin by asking yourself each question in the left-hand column, and if your answer reveals a weakness, use the revision technique in the right-hand column.

"I like to tinker. Every sentence is potentially revisable in 30 directions, and it's tough to stop doing that, to know when you've ended."

Jay McInerney

Teacher's ResourceBank™

RESOURCES

EVALUATING AND REVISING

- Writing a Comparison/Contrast Essay 56

QUOTATION FOR THE DAY

"I have made this letter longer than usual, only because I have not had the time to make it shorter." (Blaise Pascal, 1623–1662, French philosopher and mathematician)

Have students freewrite about how the quotation applies to the process of evaluating and revising.

MEETING INDIVIDUAL NEEDS

LEP/ESL

General Strategies. Getting an objective view of one's paper is a difficult task for many students. They might need help from you or from peer tutors to analyze their compositions with the chart on p. 228. This process requires continual encouragement with an emphasis on those parts of the paper that are exact and well done, as well as those that require further work.

SELECTION AMENDMENT
Description of change: excerpted
Rationale: to focus on the concept of evaluating and revising presented in this chapter

As students work together on **Exercise 3** and on **Writing Assignment: Part 4,** you can take the opportunity to circulate in the classroom to answer questions and to discuss aspects of students' papers that need to be changed. If students have trouble evaluating their work objectively, you may want to try having them write answers to the questions in the **Evaluating and Revising Comparison/Contrast Essays** chart with respect to their own papers or the papers of other students. If the answer to a question in the chart is yes, have students explain why. If the answer is no, have them explain how they'll revise their essays to yield a positive answer.

COOPERATIVE LEARNING

As an alternative evaluation technique, divide the class into groups of seven. First, have each group member choose one of the **Evaluation Guide** questions from the chart. Then regroup students so that all who have the first question are together, all who have the second question are together, and so forth. Ask the group members to discuss their question; their purpose is to become experts on that one aspect of evaluation.

Then have students return to their original groups to complete peer evaluations. As the members' papers are passed among the group, each expert should evaluate the paper for his or her area of expertise. You may want to allow class time for the groups to compare findings.

EVALUATING AND REVISING COMPARISON/CONTRAST ESSAYS

	EVALUATION GUIDE	REVISION TECHNIQUE
1	Does the introduction grab the reader's attention?	**Add** an anecdote, quotation, question, or specific detail.
2	Is the main idea clear?	**Add** a thesis statement that identifies the subjects and states the main idea of the essay.
3	Is the essay organized clearly?	**Reorder** the essay by moving sentences to follow the block or the point-by-point organization.
4	Are the relevant features handled in the same order for both topics?	**Reorder** sentences so the relevant features are discussed in the same order for both subjects.
5	Does the essay contain information that will interest the reader?	**Add** details or information that will be new to your readers. **Add** details that show your subjects in a new way.
6	Does the essay include all important information?	**Add** facts or details that are essential to an understanding of the significant similarities and differences.
7	Is the essay brought to a satisfying end?	**Cut** the ineffective sentences. **Add** statements that summarize or restate the main idea.

ASSESSMENT

You can have your students write their revisions on their first drafts in a different color ink than they used originally. You may want to use the questions in the **Evaluating and Revising Comparison/Contrast Essays** chart to help guide your assessment of students' revisions.

CLOSURE

After students have finished evaluating and revising their drafts, lead the class in a discussion of the most common kinds of revisions students made.

EXERCISE 3 Analyzing a Writer's Revisions

Before you begin to attempt to evaluate and revise your own essay, it's helpful to study some other writer's work. The following paragraphs show a writer's work in progress—a portion of the first draft of the model on pages 224–226. This sample shows some revisions the writer made after evaluating the essay. To analyze the writer's revisions, get together with two or three other students and discuss the questions on the next page. Were the writer's revisions effective?

you could travel back in time to / *then zip forward to*

Imagine Colonial America and the year 2150. Probably the last place you'd choose to be is in school, but imagine that's where you find yourself. What was school like then, and what will it be like in the future? You would probably find some amazing differences *in classroom equipment, curriculum, and length of school year.* — **add** (twice)

In 1720 in a small Connecticut town, you would find yourself in a one-room schoolhouse made of logs. The dozen or so girls and boys--with no slates, chalkboards, or maps--sit on benches. Reading, writing, penmanship, and ciphering (that's arithmetic) are what you study. You use a goose-quill pen and homemade ink to write in a copybook *you've made by carefully sewing together several sheets of folded coarse, dark paper.* The few books in your classroom are filled with proverbs, fables, and stories to improve your character. To learn arithmetic, you listen to your teacher read from a sum book. Then you copy the rules and problems he reads aloud into your own sum book.

reorder **add**

CRITICAL THINKING
Analysis

You may want to stress the importance of using transitions and transitional phrases to create coherence. Have students use the following questions to analyze **A Writer's Model** on pp. 224–226 and **A Student Model** on pp. 232–233. Then ask students to apply the questions to their own first drafts.

1. What does the author do to make the paragraph transitions?
2. Does the author repeat an idea, or does the author actually repeat a word or phrase?
3. Does the author make a reference to the thesis statement to maintain continuity?

EXTENSION

Besides evaluating and revising the content of their essays, students might also evaluate and revise the stylistic aspects of their papers. You could have students employ the following revision strategies to guide them as they assess their writing:

1. Bracket the first words of all sentences to check for sentence variety.
2. Highlight all verbs to check for active voice and vivid verbs.
3. Circle all *who, which,* and *that* constructions to check for possible ways to reduce wordiness. ■

ANSWERS

Exercise 3

Answers will vary. Here are some possibilities:

1. The writer added the words to the first sentence to grab the reader's attention. The changes improve the essay by making it a kind of science-fiction fantasy that involves time travel.
2. These three points are the areas that will be contrasted. Stating them in the thesis helps guide the reader.
3. The sentence that was moved deals with curriculum, and it was originally in the middle of the section of the paragraph that deals with equipment. Moving the sentence strengthens the coherence of the paragraph by adhering to the order set up in the thesis statement.
4. The addition is an interesting detail that is probably new information for most readers.

TIMESAVER

Ask your students to code their revisions by writing the number of the question in the **Evaluating and Revising Comparison/Contrast Essays** chart next to the revision that is related to it. This coding will save you time in trying to figure out why the student thought each revision was necessary.

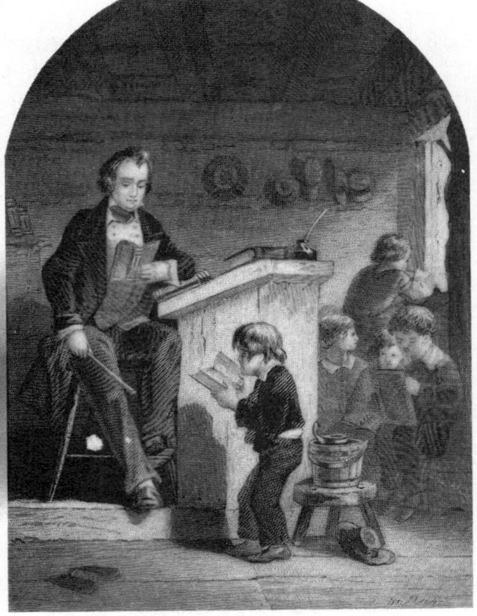

1. Why did the writer add the words *you could travel back in time to* and *then zip forward to* to the first sentence? How do these changes improve the essay?
2. Why did the writer add *in classroom equipment, curriculum, and length of school year* to the last sentence of the first paragraph?
3. Why did the writer move the third sentence of the second paragraph? [Hint: Review pages 217–218.]
4. Why did the writer add the information about hand-sewn sheets of dark paper? Is this information new to you?

***WRITING* ASSIGNMENT** PART 4:

Evaluating and Revising Your Comparison/Contrast Paper

Now you be the judge—of both your essay and a partner's essay. First, use the chart on page 228 to evaluate your own essay, and then exchange papers with a classmate and evaluate each other's papers. Try to be as objective as a real judge (or literary critic) might be. Finally, use your partner's comments and your own evaluations to revise your essay.

SEGMENT 6 *(pp. 231–233)*

PROOFREADING AND PUBLISHING

OBJECTIVE

- To proofread and publish a comparison/contrast essay

TEACHING THE LESSON

Proofreading involves two discrete activities. First, students should read the revised drafts of their essays before they put the drafts in final form to detect and correct errors in grammar, usage, and mechanics. They can make these corrections on the revised drafts without worrying about neatness. Second, after students have recopied

Proofreading and Publishing

Proofreading. Once you have evaluated and revised your essay, it is ready for its final inspection, a search for any mistakes in spelling, capitalization, punctuation, and usage. (See pages 50–51 for **Guidelines for Proofreading.**)

USAGE HINT

Degrees of Comparison

When you compare and contrast, you often use adjectives and adverbs, the forms of which change according to the number of subjects being compared. Most adjectives and adverbs have three degrees of comparison. You add *–er* and *–est* to words of one syllable and *more* and *most* to words of two or more syllables. A few words, like *good,* have irregular forms to show comparison.

POSITIVE	COMPARATIVE	SUPERLATIVE
thin	thinner	thinnest
carefully	more carefully	most carefully
good	better	best

When comparing two subjects, use the comparative degree.

Going to school is **easier** than doing chores from sunup to sundown.

When comparing three or more subjects, use the superlative degree.

Of all the things I can think of doing, lying in front of the TV is the **easiest.**

REFERENCE NOTE: For more information about degrees of comparison, see pages 770–774.

Teacher's ResourceBank™

RESOURCES

PROOFREADING AND PUBLISHING

- Writing a Comparison/Contrast Essay 57

QUOTATION FOR THE DAY

"Sloppily prepared pieces, peppered with mechanical glitches that could easily have been caught and corrected by the writer, are rarely going to sell—and the few that do are bound to be heavily edited." (David Petersen, American author and editor)

Write this quotation on the chalkboard and ask students to discuss why they think writing that has good content but poor grammar might not sell.

their essays in final form, they should proofread the essays a second time to make sure they have copied accurately. You may need to remind your students to perform both readings before they turn in their essays.

You could use a sample paragraph you have created to model proofreading. Then have students complete **Writing Assignment: Part 5.**

Publishing can be as simple a matter as letting students pass their papers around the classroom for others to read.

MEETING INDIVIDUAL NEEDS

LEP/ESL

Spanish. Call students' attention to the **Usage Hint** on p. 231. In Spanish the comparative is formed by using the word *más* (translated as *more* or *most*) in front of the adjective or adverb. Your students might, therefore, use the expressions *more thin* or *more smart* instead of *thinner* or *smarter.* In addition, because of the Spanish use of the word *que* (translated as *than* or *that*) with comparisons, some students might substitute *that* for *than* resulting in sentences such as "My brother is more thoughtful that my sister." You may want to help students proofread their papers for the correct use of comparisons.

ADVANCED STUDENTS

Have students work in pairs or in small groups to devise step-by-step proofreading systems that the rest of the class can use. Each pair or group can present a plan and the class can vote to decide which one to use.

Publishing. Try one of these ideas for publishing your finished paper.

- Use your comparison/contrast essay as the basis for a game. Choose three items of information about each subject, and read them to a partner or small group of classmates. Jot down pieces of information that are new to listeners. When everyone has finished, determine the total amount of new information in your group.
- Compile your essays into a booklet and send it to your local middle school. Younger students might find your information very interesting.

WRITING ASSIGNMENT

PART 5:
Proofreading and Publishing Your Essay

Is your essay ready for final inspection? Proofread it carefully to correct all errors. Write your final version, and then decide how you will publish or share it with others.

A STUDENT MODEL

Kelli Mulholland, a student at Carrick High School in Pittsburgh, Pennsylvania, compares two part-time jobs for students. Kelli offers this advice about how to write this kind of essay: "Ask several friends or fellow students about their part-time jobs. After some research, compare two jobs that sound interesting and put it together in essay form." As you read Kelli's essay, ask yourself which job sounds more appealing.

CLOSURE

Errors in grammar, usage, and mechanics sometimes end up in print. As a closure activity, bring to class copies of a local newspaper. Give students five minutes to proofread for errors. The student who finds the most can be proclaimed Ace Proofreader or be given some suitable prize. ■

Choosing a Part-Time Job

by Kelli Mulholland

Working a part-time job after school can be a fun and educating experience. By working after school, a young person can gain knowledge in the working field and make some extra money. There are many jobs out there for high school students. Two of the most popular jobs are telemarketing and working at fast-food restaurants. These two fields are worlds apart, but they also have a great deal in common.

Telemarketing, selling goods or services over the telephone, has been around for many years. Telemarketing offices are always looking for outgoing, enthusiastic people to fill telemarketing positions. It doesn't take much experience to be a telemarketer, just a good disposition. There are many advantages to telemarketing. You only have to work about four hours a day. Most telemarketing places pay their employees an hourly wage, although some places pay both an hourly wage and a commission. Another advantage is that some telemarketing places let employees work out of their homes. Imagine not even leaving the house and getting paid for it. Telemarketing is also good experience in sales. Unlike delivering papers or baby-sitting, telemarketing is a very pleasant and easy part-time job for those who enjoy talking with other people.

Another very popular and exciting job is working at a fast-food place. Fast-food places are always hiring high school students. The benefits of this kind of job are great. Meeting people and making money while doing it is one advantage. An employee will learn how to cook and how to use a cash register and may even become manager of the whole store. Also, when young people apply for a job after high school, employers want to see that prospective workers have worked with other people and are able to be productive under a little pressure. Working at a fast-food restaurant will show that.

Both jobs are very appealing in many ways. They will both look good on a résumé after high school and show that you do have some work experience. Baby-sitting and delivering papers show responsibility, but they don't show punctuality and compatibility. Consider your options in choosing a part-time job. Find a job that fits your personality, and one that interests you most.

A STUDENT MODEL

Evaluation

1. To grab the reader's attention, Kelli lists some advantages of having a part-time job.
2. The thesis statement clearly states the main idea that telemarketing and working at fast food restaurants are two of the most popular jobs for young people.
3. Kelli used the block method to organize her essay.
4. Most high school students will be interested in the subject of choosing a part-time job.

SEGMENT 7 *(pp. 234–236)*

WRITING WORKSHOP

OBJECTIVES

- To analyze an extended definition
- To write an extended definition

TEACHING THE LESSON

The extended definition can be taught alone or in conjunction with a concept in literature. If you decide to use this segment as a separate composition lesson, your students can choose subjects from those suggested in the text, or they can select subjects of their own. In either case, it's usually easier to write extended definitions of

QUOTATION FOR THE DAY

"A definition is the enclosing a wilderness of idea within a wall of words." (Samuel Butler, 1835–1902, English novelist, scholar, and translator)

Ask students to freewrite about what they think Butler's quotation means. [Some students might say that once something is defined, imaginative powers are no longer necessary.]

MEETING INDIVIDUAL NEEDS

LEP/ESL

General Strategies. For the writing assignment on p. 236, create groups of two or three students based on topic preferences. Make sure the LEP/ESL students are well integrated with their native English-speaking classmates. Have students work together to arrive at an extended definition. This collaborative situation should be more productive for LEP/ESL students than working alone would be.

WRITING WORKSHOP

An Extended Definition

When you organized and wrote your comparison/contrast essay for this chapter, you were using the strategy of *classification*. You had to be sure that the two subjects you chose to write about belonged to the same class or group of things before you examined them in terms of their relationship to each other. You also use the strategy of classification when you define a subject. First, you identify the general category your subject belongs to. Then, you describe the characteristics that distinguish it from (show its relationship to) other items in its category. Here's a one-sentence definition of *independence*.

> Independence is a character trait that enables an individual to make decisions and act upon them without placing too much emphasis on the opinions of others.

The first part of the definition shows that *independence* belongs to the general category "character traits." The second part distinguishes *independence* from other character traits.

An ***extended definition*** also puts the subject into a category and shows how it is different from other subjects in the category. But then it goes further: It extends the basic definition with details such as examples, descriptions, explanations, and opinions. For example, following is an extended definition of *independence*. As you read, notice the many techniques the writer uses to extend the definition of this character trait.

> When teenagers think about what independence means, we often think of it as something someone else gives us. But independence is not something that comes from outside ourselves. We may also think of independence as the freedom to do anything we want. But that is probably not the real meaning of the word. Independence is a character trait that enables an individual to make decisions and act upon them

concrete objects than of abstractions. If you use a subject in literature, such as Romanticism or realism, you may want to let the extended definition essay come at the end of a unit of study, after students have been exposed to several literary works that are appropriate as examples of the term being defined.

You may want to guide students through the questions following the model before you ask students to write their extended definitions.

without placing too much emphasis on the opinions of others.

A very young girl may think of herself as achieving independence the first time her parents let her go to the mall unsupervised. That, of course, can be a step toward independence. But if the girl is concerned the whole time she's there with doing what other kids consider cool, then she's really not independent at all. She is only trading dependence on her parents for dependence on her friends. Her parents have given her the opportunity to be independent. She is the one who has to become independent, who has to develop the character trait.

Some kids say that they are really independent because they don't care what anyone else says or thinks. But that attitude stretches or distorts the meaning of independence. There's a difference between refusing to slavishly follow what other people do and being absolutely indifferent to what others think. Total indifference to others is selfishness, not independence. And even the founding fathers who declared this nation independent were concerned with having "a decent respect to the opinions of mankind."

To develop into independent people, we have to learn to think for ourselves, but we don't have to act as if we are the only ones who can think or the only ones whose opinions matter. Only then can we learn to act independently in the best interests of ourselves and others.

1. **What techniques does the writer use to extend the definition?**
2. **Do you think the writer clearly explains the meaning of *independence*? What other examples or descriptions could you add to this definition?**

CRITICAL THINKING
Evaluation

The model essay uses both positive and negative examples to support its points. A negative example is an example of what something isn't. Ask students to evaluate the writer's use of negative examples. Would the extended definition of *independence* be clearer if the negative examples had not been used? [Answers may vary, but most students will probably feel that the negative examples help clarify the concept of independence because they help clear up misconceptions that many people have on the subject.]

ANSWERS
Writing Workshop Questions

1. The writer uses examples, negative examples, and quotations.
2. Answers will vary. Students may mention resisting peer pressure, earning spending money, and being able to handle freedom as examples of independence.

ASSESSMENT

You can base your assessment of students' extended definitions on how fully they explain the object or idea. An extended definition of an object should include its appearance and uses, and an extended definition of an idea should include its origins and implications.

CLOSURE

Ask volunteers to announce their subjects to the class, and let the other students jot down questions about the subjects. Then let the volunteers read their extended definitions to the class as the others listen for answers to their questions. Discuss any unanswered questions. ■

A DIFFERENT APPROACH

Your students can publish their extended definitions by compiling a kind of dictionary. Instead of putting the entries in alphabetical order, though, they can group them by subject matter. If you have several classes that work on this activity, you can create a booklet of interesting articles that should have wide appeal.

Writing an Extended Definition

Prewriting. Think of a subject that interests you and that can't be adequately defined in just one or two sentences. Here are some possibilities:

longtime friend	dream car
country music	bad date
loyalty	bravery

Think of examples, details, comparisons, contrasts, facts, or quotes to extend your definition. Consult a dictionary, encyclopedias, magazines, or friends for ideas. List any background information your audience will need.

Writing, Evaluating, and Revising. As you begin your extended definition, try to sum up your subject in one or two sentences. Start by identifying the class to which it belongs, and then extend your definition by showing how it is similar to or different from others in its class. Let another student read your definition and make suggestions for improving it. Does your definition have enough specific details? Would your definition help someone unfamiliar with your subject to understand it fully? Keep revising until you're satisfied with your definition.

Proofreading and Publishing. Be sure to proofread your definition carefully before sharing it with others. (For help with proofreading, see pages 50–51.) Then read your definition to a small group of classmates or to the whole class. See if they can guess the subject.

SEGMENT 8 *(pp. 237–239)*

MAKING CONNECTIONS

COMPARISON/CONTRAST IN LITERATURE

OBJECTIVES

- To discuss situational irony in a poem
- To find or write a poem containing situational irony

MAKING CONNECTIONS

WRITING ACROSS THE CURRICULUM

Comparison/Contrast in Literature

Situational irony is a literary device that relies on indirect comparison/contrast; the writer shows a discrepancy between the outcome of a situation and what was expected. When it is humorous, irony creates a delicious pleasure for the reader. It's fun to have expectations turned upside down in fiction—as they often are in real life. For example, the poet Dorothy Parker creates situational irony in the following poem about a rose.

One Perfect Rose

by Dorothy Parker

1 A single flow'r he sent me, since we met.
All tenderly his messenger he chose;
Deep-hearted, pure, with scented dew still wet—
One perfect rose.

2 I knew the language of the floweret;
"My fragile leaves," it said, "his heart enclose."
3 Love long has taken for his amulet
One perfect rose.

Why is it no one ever sent me yet
One perfect limousine, do you suppose?
Ah no, it's always just my luck to get
One perfect rose.

COMPARISON/CONTRAST IN LITERATURE

Teaching Strategies

After students read the introductory paragraph, give some examples of situational irony in real life, such as a fire station that catches fire or a driver education teacher who causes an automobile accident.

Use the annotations to discuss with students **"One Perfect Rose."** If students have trouble finding another poem containing situational irony, you could suggest "Richard Cory" by Edwin Arlington Robinson.

USING THE SELECTION

One Perfect Rose

1

Parker uses *flow'r* as a contracted form of *flower.* The first three lines of each stanza are written in iambic pentameter (ten syllables that alternate between unstressed and stressed syllables), and the word *flow'r* has to be pronounced as one syllable to fit the iambic pattern.

2

Floweret refers to a small flower. The poet needed a three-syllable word that has the stressed-unstressed-stressed pattern to fit the meter.

3

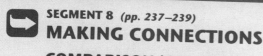

amulet: a charm worn to protect the wearer from an evil power

CLASSIFICATION IN SCIENCE
OBJECTIVE

- To write a paragraph that classifies and describes blood cells

GUIDELINES

The poems students select should contain obvious examples of situational irony. If students write poems, each poem should contain an ironic twist.

CLASSIFICATION IN SCIENCE
Teaching Strategies

As with comparison/contrast writing, students can organize their classification paragraphs by either the block method or the point-by-point method. In the paragraph about types of blood cells, for example, students can treat red blood cells, platelets, and white blood cells as three blocks and discuss the aspects of one type of cell within each block. Or they can use the point-by-point method and consider individually certain aspects of each of the three types of blood cells.

Think about the irony in "One Perfect Rose." How does the ending of the poem contrast with what you expected? Find another poem that contains situational irony (or you may write your own). Bring the poem to class and read it aloud, asking everyone to describe the irony. Discuss how the situation leads you to expect one thing and then how the poet creates a different (contrasting) outcome.

WRITING ACROSS THE CURRICULUM

Classification in Science

Classifying, looking at subjects in terms of their relationships to other subjects, is an extremely useful tool for making sense of the world. A large part of science consists of attempts to classify things. Plants, animals, clouds, rocks, bodies of water, and weather systems are just a few examples of things that are classified into categories.

On science tests or reports, you are often asked to classify items. The first step is to identify the principle of classification. For example, if you are to classify viruses, you must decide how. Will it be by genetic material (RNA or DNA) or by disease (like influenza, hepatitis, or rhinovirus)? Next, be sure to divide the whole subject. For example, if you are classifying burns, you don't want to leave out any of the three degrees of burns: first degree, second degree, and third degree. As you describe each category, use enough details to show the reader the differences among the categories. You might even decide which main characteristics you will describe for each category. As in your comparison/contrast essay, you'll want to present the same characteristics in the same order for each category.

Following is a jumbled list of facts about the three types of blood cells. First, identify the three categories (for help you might consult an encyclopedia or science text). Then organize the facts for each category in the same general order. Write a paragraph that classifies and describes the blood cells.

Red blood cells carry oxygen to body tissues.
Platelets measure 150,000–500,000 per microliter of blood ($\frac{1}{30,000}$ of an ounce).

Red blood cells live approximately 120 days.
Life span of a platelet is 8–10 days.
White blood cells fight disease and invading substances.
Platelets formed in the bone marrow.
5,000–10,000 white blood cells per microliter of blood.
Platelets essential for clotting blood.
Four to six million red blood cells per microliter.
White blood cells formed in the bone marrow; some mature in tissues like lymph nodes and spleen.
Red blood cells formed in the bone marrow.
Life span of white blood cell varies from a few hours to many years.

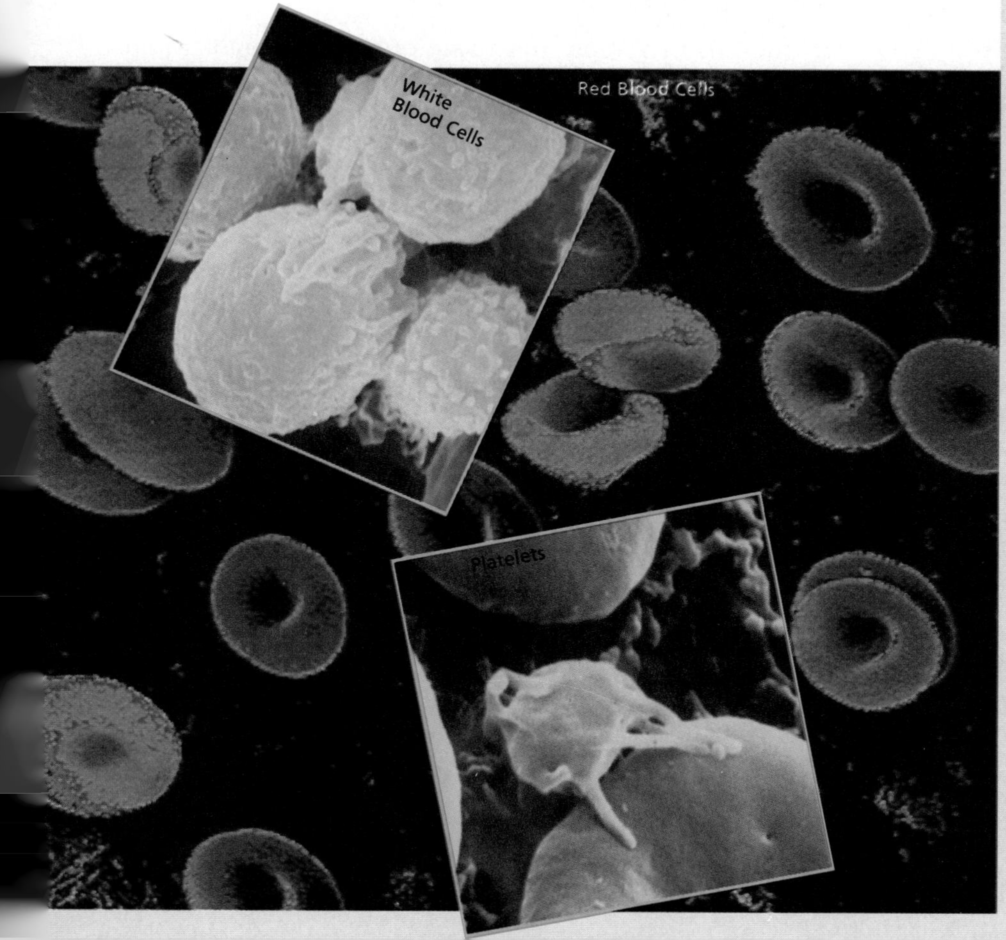

GUIDELINES

Students' paragraphs should have obvious organizational patterns and cover all of the facts in the list.

Chapter 7

WRITING TO EXPLAIN

OBJECTIVES

- To choose a workable, limited topic for a cause-and-effect essay
- To identify causes and effects about a topic and to gather supporting information and evidence
- To formulate a thesis statement, to create an organizational map, and to write a first draft of a cause-and-effect essay
- To evaluate and revise the content and organization of a cause-and-effect essay
- To proofread a cause-and-effect essay and prepare it for publication
- To write a process explanation, an answer to a cause-and-effect essay question, and a descriptive explanation

Motivation

You may wish to tell students that writing to explain means exploring cause-and-effect situations. Read the three questions at the beginning of the chapter and point out how each one involves causes and effects. Then ask students to give you two questions beginning with "What causes...?", two beginning with "What are the effects of...?", and two beginning "How will I...?" You could then ask students to list some causes and effects for a few of these questions. Tell students that in thinking of topics and identifying causes and effects, they have begun the writing process for a cause-and-effect explanation.

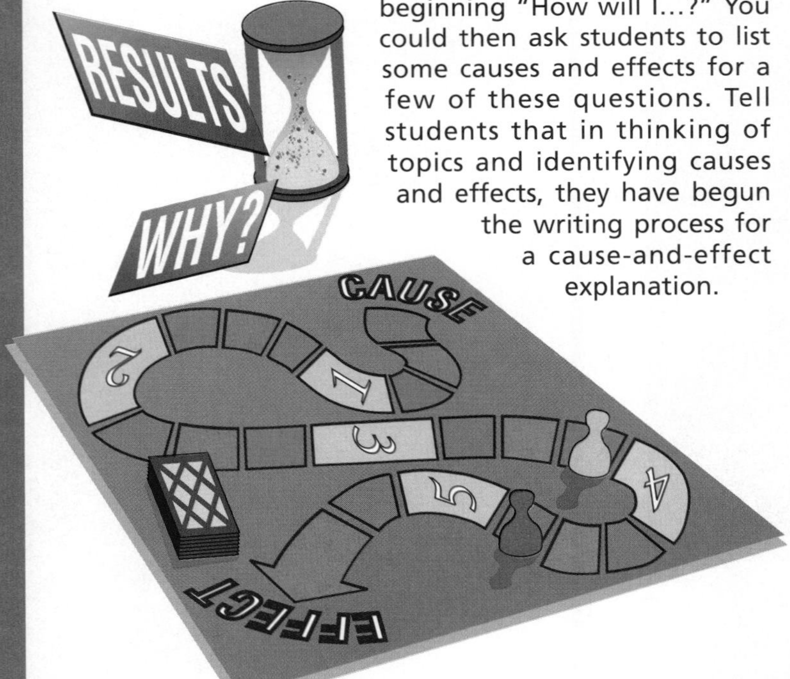

Introduction

Tell students that the chapter guides their writing of a cause-and-effect explanation by taking them through the stages of the writing process. To help students distinguish the informative aim from the other aims of discourse, have the class discuss the purposes suggested by these (or similar) titles: "Why I Love School" (expressive), "Why the School Counselor Is Always Busy" (informative: cause-and-effect explanation), "Ode to My Classmates" (literary), and "Why You Should Go to College" (persuasive). However, you should also remind students that there is some overlap of these aims. For example, the persuasive essay "Why You Should Go to College" may also exhibit expressive and informative characteristics.

Integration

Students can apply the techniques and organization for writing a cause-and-effect explanation to any academic subject. Writing models and special features in the chapter are designed to give students insight into preparing explanations across the curriculum. Cause-and-effect explanations also are crucial to language arts. For example, you could ask students to explain the causes of the American Renaissance in literature in the 1800s or the effects of transcendental philosophy on the writings of Thoreau.

In a broader sense, training in identifying and analyzing cause-and-effect situations is a valuable tool in writing, reading, and living.

The chart on the next page illustrates the strands of language arts as they are integrated into this chapter. For vocabulary study, glossary words are underlined in some writing models.

QUOTATIONS
All **Quotations for the Day** are chosen because of their relevance to instructional material presented in that segment of the chapter and for their usefulness in establishing student interest in writing.

INTEGRATING THE LANGUAGE ARTS

Selection	Reading and Literature	Writing and Critical Thinking	Language and Syntax	Speaking, Listening, and Other Expression Skills
from ***Kaffir Boy in America*** by Mark Mathabane **242-245** from ***Nation of Nations*** by James West Davidson, et. al. **256-259** **"Once Is Not Enough"** by Jane O'Connor and Katy Hall **270-271** from ***The Birder's Handbook*** by Paul R. Ehrlich, David S. Dobkin, and Darryl Wheye **275**	Responding personally to literature **245, 260, 271** Applying interpretive and creative thinking **245, 260, 271** Identifying causes and effects **245, 249, 260** Analyzing an introduction **260, 271** Identifying evidence **260** Analyzing details **260, 271** Identifying a topic **271** Examining organization in an essay **271** Evaluating an essay for clarity **271** Examining the use of description in an explanation **274-275**	Identifying causes and effects **245, 249, 252, 260** Choosing a topic **249, 272, 275** Identifying a thesis **252** Using brainstorming, research, observation, and interviewing to gather information and supporting evidence **252, 272** Organizing information **254, 272, 273-274** Analyzing an introduction **260, 271** Analyzing details **260, 271, 273-274** Analyzing the validity of generalizations **265** Writing a first draft **265, 272** Analyzing a writer's revisions **266** Evaluating and revising a first draft **268, 272** Proofreading and publishing **269, 272** Evaluating an essay for clarity **271** Answering a cause-and-effect essay question **273-274** Writing an explanation using description **275**	Proofreading for errors in grammar, usage, and mechanics **269, 272** Using transitional expressions **272**	Exploring causes and effects in nonprint sources **249, 252** Presenting an oral report **249** Brainstorming topics with classmates **249** Interviewing for information **252** Creating a map to organize information **254** Discussing a cause-and-effect essay with classmates **260** Discussing with classmates the validity of generalizations **265** Working with a classmate to evaluate and revise an essay **268, 272**

CHAPTER 7

SEGMENT PLANNING GUIDE

You can use the following Planning Guide to adapt the chapter material to the individual needs of your class. All the Resources listed in this chapter are located in the *Teacher's ResourceBank*™.

SEGMENT	PAGES	CONTENT	RESOURCES
1 ***Making Things Clear***	***241-245***		
Literary Model from ***Kaffir Boy in America***	242-245	Guided reading: a model of explanatory writing	
Reader's Response/ Writer's Craft	245	Model evaluation: responding to literature and analyzing explanatory writing	
2 ***Strategies for Writing***	***246***		
3 ***Prewriting***	***247-254***		Writing a Cause-and-Effect Essay Listing Causes and Effects 60
Considering Topic, Purpose, and Audience	247-249	Guidelines: selecting suitable topics and examining purpose and audience	
Exercise 1	249	Cooperative learning: exploring causes and effects	
Writing Assignment: Part 1	249	Applied practice: choosing a topic	
Planning a Cause-and-Effect Explanation	250	Introduction: identifying the main idea and gathering information	
Identifying Your Thesis	250	Guidelines: formulating a main idea	
Gathering Information	251	Guidelines: understanding sources and types of information	
Chart: Questions for Gathering Information	251	Guidelines: examining questions to ask about causes, effects, and evidence	
Writing Assignment: Part 2	252	Applied practice: identifying a thesis and gathering information	
Organizing Information	252-254	Guidelines: examining cluster maps to focus on causes and effects	
Writing Assignment: Part 3	254	Applied practice: creating an organizational map	
4 ***Writing***	***255-265***		Writing a Cause-and-Effect Essay 61
The Structure of a Cause-and-Effect Explanation	255	Guidelines: writing an introduction, body, and conclusion	
Literary Model from ***Nation of Nations***	256-259	Guided reading: examining structure in a model	
Exercise 2	260	Cooperative learning: analyzing a cause-and-effect essay	
A Basic Framework	260	Guidelines: structuring an essay	
A Writer's Model	260-262	Guided reading: analyzing cause-and-effect in an essay	
Chart: Framework for a Cause-and-Effect Explanation	262	Guidelines: structuring a cause-and-effect essay	

For **Portfolio Assessment** see the following pages in the *Teacher's ResourceBank™*:

Aims For Writing — pp. 59–64
Holistically Graded Composition Models — pp. 503–508
Assessment Portfolio — pp. 533–562

SEGMENT	PAGES	CONTENT	RESOURCES
Critical Thinking: Using Induction	263-265	Guidelines: examining a reasoning process	
Critical Thinking Exercise	265	Cooperative learning: analyzing the validity of a generalization	
Writing Assignment: Part 4	265	Applied practice: writing a first draft	
5 *Evaluating and Revising*	*266-268*		Writing a Cause-and-Effect Essay 62
Exercise 3	266	Applied practice: analyzing a writer's revisions	
Chart: Evaluating and Revising	267	Guidelines: applying evaluation and revision techniques	
Grammar Hint	268	Writing suggestion: using subordinate clauses	
Writing Assignment: Part 5	268	Applied practice: evaluating and revising	
6 *Proofreading and Publishing*	*269*		Writing a Cause-and-Effect Essay 63
Publishing	269	Publishing ideas: reaching a specific audience	
Writing Assignment: Part 6	269	Applied practice: proofreading and publishing	
7 *Writing Workshop*	*270-272*		
A Process Explanation	270	Explanation: learning about explaining a process	
Literary Model/Questions **"Once Is Not Enough"**	270-271	Guided reading: examining a model of process writing	
Writing a Process Analysis	272	Applied practice: applying skills to the writing process	
8 *Making Connections*	*273-275*		
Test Taking: Cause-and-Effect Essay Questions	273-274	Applied practice: writing the answer to a given essay question	
Explaining Through Description	274-275	Explanation: using description to explain Applied practice: writing paragraphs that explain by description	
Literary Model from ***The Birder's Handbook***	275	Guided reading: analyzing a model of descriptive writing	
WHOLE-CHAPTER RESOURCES A Writing Process Log, A Writing Prompt, Holistically Graded Models, Assessment Portfolio Materials			

SEGMENT 1 *(pp. 240–245)*
MAKING THINGS CLEAR

OBJECTIVES

- To respond personally to a literary model and to analyze its effectiveness
- To identify causes and effects in a literary model

MOTIVATION

You may want to begin the lesson by having students think about how many times a day they ask someone—a teacher, a friend, a parent, a boss—to explain something. Point out that giving and receiving explanations is a necessary, important part of everyday life.

VISUAL CONNECTIONS
Milk-Drop Splash Series

About the Artist. Dr. Harold Edgerton, an American scientist and an assistant professor at M. I. T., invented the stroboscopic flash in the early 1930s. His invention revolutionized photography, making possible not only stop-motion photographs but also candid snapshots.

Dr. Edgerton has used the techniques he invented to produce many educational photographs. These pictures blend science and art. Edgerton is mainly interested in objectively showing the unseen aspects of events, but many viewers are also impressed by the beauty of these images.

Exploring the Subject. This series of images, taken from a sequence of thiry-six frames, represents a time period of less than half a second. You might discuss the sequence with the class as an example of the many causes and effects that are usually unnoticed.

7 WRITING TO EXPLAIN

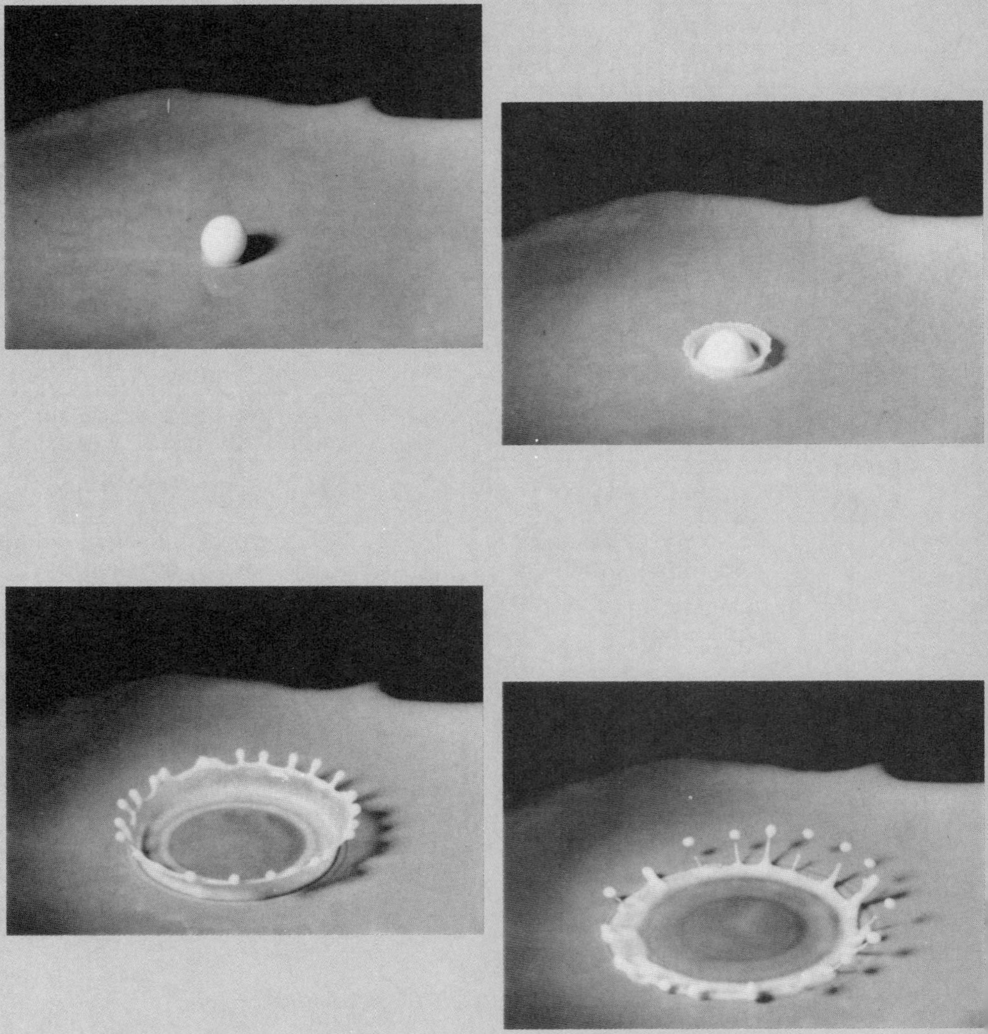

TEACHING THE LESSON

Before considering the literary selection with students, you may want to explain and discuss the title and the connotations of the word *Kaffir.* (*Kaffir* is of Arabic origin and means "infidel." In South Africa it is used derogatorily by whites to refer to blacks.) Point out that the book's subtitle is *An Encounter with Apartheid* and ask students if the whole title suggests positive or negative experiences. [Negative experiences could be suggested by the negative connotation of the word *Kaffir* in South Africa and the negative connotations of the word *boy* in African American history. Because apartheid is a policy of strict racial segregation, the subtitle also suggests negative experiences.]

Making Things Clear

What causes recessions? What are the effects of the loss of the ozone layer? How will I have time to finish my homework if I get a job after school? These questions show that we live in a world in which we are constantly looking for explanations, explanations that will **make things clear.**

Writing and You. Writers often attempt to explain something in the world around them. A scientist tells how a new medication combats a form of cancer. A biographer examines the effects of a backwoods childhood on Abraham Lincoln. A reporter for a school newspaper writes about the causes of the football team's winning season. What explanations could you give that would help make the world a little clearer to other people?

As You Read. In the following selection, Mark Mathabane tells how he explained the benefits of knowledge and education to the young people of Harlem. How did he make the benefits clear?

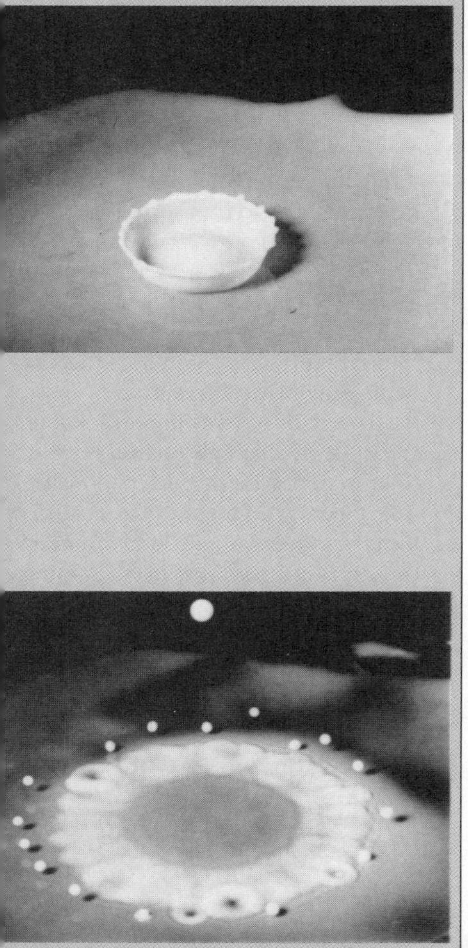

Dr. Harold E. Edgerton, *Milk-Drop Splash Series* (1935). Photograph. © The Harold E. Edgerton 1992 Trust. Courtesy of Palm Press, Inc., Concord, MA.

QUOTATION FOR THE DAY

"As I see it, writing is applied psychology because it is the art of creating desired effects. It follows from this that our chief need is to know *what* effects are desirable and *how* to create them." (John R. Trimble, American writer and teacher)

Ask students to freewrite about the quotation. Encourage them to make connections between the quotation and the title of the segment, **"Making Things Clear."**

MEETING INDIVIDUAL NEEDS

AFRICAN AMERICAN

The excerpt from ***Kaffir Boy in America*** explores sensitive issues. The references to drugs and gangs, crime and teenage motherhood, and the disintegration of family life (all set within an African American framework) may create a sense of uneasiness among some students. The challenge in presenting this lesson is to shift the focus to the universal issue of education as the key that unlocks human potential.

As students read the literary selection, alert them to look for cause-and-effect relationships. To help students find such relationships, you could write the following guidelines on the chalkboard:

1. To identify causes, ask "Why did it happen? What made it happen?"
2. To identify effects, ask "What is the result?"

After students have finished reading the selection, you could use the annotations as a basis for discussion. To model the process of responding personally to literature, share your response to the first **Reader's Response** question. To prepare students for the **Writer's Craft** questions, use the annotations to help them identify some of the cause-and-effect relationships

USING THE SELECTION
***from* Kaffir Boy in America**

1
What experiences in Harlem and in South Africa's ghettos might Mathabane have found to compare? [Comparisons could have been drawn about conditions such as housing, population, income, race relations, quality of life, education, and opportunity for improvement or change.]

2
Malcolm X (1925–1965) was a radical African American Civil Rights leader of the 1960s. James Baldwin and Langston Hughes were famous twentieth century African American writers.

3
The use of *because* indicates that the effect (being able to reach youngsters) precedes the cause (trust) in the sentence.

4
The Wimbledon men's singles champion in 1972 was Stan Smith and in 1975 was Arthur Ashe.

from Kaffir Boy in America

by Mark Mathabane

I was at this time writing more commentary articles for the *St. Petersburg Times* on events in South Africa than learning the basics of objective journalism. I poured my time into completing
1 *Kaffir Boy*; wandered about Harlem comparing the black experience there with that in South Africa's
2 ghettos; read the speeches of Malcolm X, the essays of James Baldwin, and the poetry of Langston Hughes; and taught tennis to black youngsters who were part of the I-House tutorial program. I shared with them my experiences growing up in Alexandra, and the important role education had played in my life. I encouraged them never to give up the fight to escape from the ghetto; it could be done, I said, provided they believed in themselves, kept away from drugs and gangs, and never allowed villains to become their role models and peer pressure to force them to do bad things.

I was able to reach many of 3 these youngsters because they trusted me, and considered me a celebrity because I was friends with 4 Stan Smith and Arthur Ashe. It wrung my heart to realize that most of these kids were as impressionable and talented as kids anywhere, but that in their case the lack of positive role models and support systems, the deadly influence and lure of street life, the disintegration of black fam-

Arthur Ashe

in the selection. Then assign the **Reader's Response** and the **Writer's Craft** questions for independent practice. You may want to have students answer the second **Reader's Response** question in their journals.

Students' answers to the **Reader's Response** and **Writer's Craft** questions can be used to assess understanding.

RETEACHING

If students are having difficulty understanding cause and effect, try diagraming on the chalkboard some of the cause-and-effect relationships from the literary model. For example, the last sentence in the first paragraph on p. 242 could be illustrated as follows:

☛

Clockwise from lower left: Marian Anderson, Ralph Bunche, Maya Angelou, James Baldwin; Center: Paul Robeson.

ily life and the attendant loss of positive values, and the inhumanity of life in New York City for the powerless and the have-nots would eventually <u>derail</u> them into the dead-end life of crime and drugs and teenage motherhood.

The only way I could fight their struggle, I clearly saw, was to become a role model to them, in much the same way as Arthur Ashe had been one to me. But I was quick to warn them that they could not all hope to become professional athletes; that they could not all be Diana Ross or Michael Jackson; but that they could all become proud and productive human beings by becoming educated. Many wondered why I made such a big deal about an education, and challenged me to show them blacks who, because of an education, were as famous or as rich as the athletes and entertainers or the drug dealers with the fancy cars, expensive jewelry, flashy clothes, and Rolex watches.

"These men and women have more power than most of your athletes and entertainers and all of the drug dealers you know."

VISUAL CONNECTIONS

Exploring the Subject. You may want to ask students how many of these famous African American achievers they can identify without referring to the caption [Anderson—singer; Bunche—diplomat; Angelou—author; Baldwin—novelist and essayist; Robeson—actor and singer]

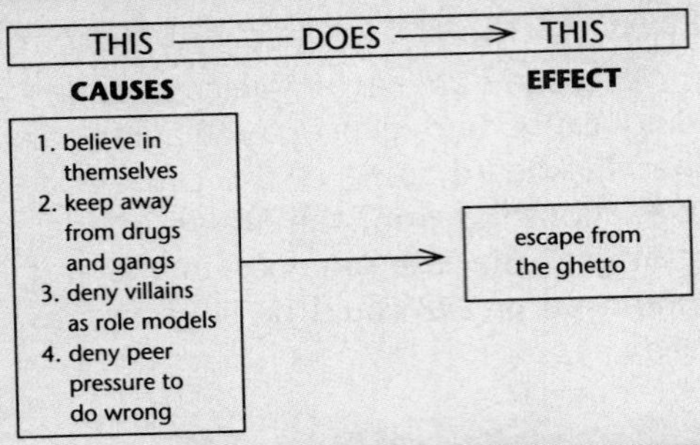

CLOSURE

Ask students to identify the primary ways explanations are presented in the literary model by showing causes and effects.

I brought up the names of famous black achievers, including Jesse Jackson, A. Philip Randolph, Harriet Tubman, Paul Robeson, Ralph Bunche, Marian Anderson, Maya Angelou, and George Washington Carver. Except for Jackson, they hardly recognized any of the names.

5 "These men and women have more power than most of your athletes and entertainers and all of the drug dealers you know."

"What you mean? Do they have a lot of money?" asked a thirteen-year-old boy.

"Many don't. But they have something more valuable than money."

"What could be more valuable than money?" asked a twelve-year-old boy.

Bob Marley

"An educated mind."

"What's that?" a fifteen-year-old girl asked facetiously.

"You see, money, fancy clothes, Rolexes, chains, all that can be lost, can be taken away from you. But the treasures in your mind, those no one can ever take away from you. And by the treasures of the mind I mean
6 knowledge. Knowledge of what freedom means. Knowledge of what you can do despite what others may say. Knowledge of what your rights and responsibilities are as an American citizen. Knowledge of how computers work. Knowledge of how to read
7 and write. Knowledge of your true heritage as a black person. And through knowledge one can overcome the greatest oppression of all: mental slavery. Any of you heard of Bob Marley?"

A few had heard the legend's music.

"Well, Bob Marley once wrote a song called 'Redemption Song,' in which he said that to be truly free black people must liberate themselves from mental slavery, and that none but ourselves can free our
8 minds. So instead of getting high on drugs why don't we get high on knowledge? You know, a free mind is a most powerful weapon. Armed with it you'll be able to fight for what is yours, to define who you are, rather than have others do things for you, set limits to your aspirations, and end up running your life."

5
The use of dialogue gives immediacy and relevance to the explanation; it shows how much the students need such an explanation.

6
What is the effect of Mathabane's use of parallelism? [The use of parallelism stresses the importance and scope of knowledge.]

7
Why is knowledge of "true heritage" important? [A knowledge of heritage can give a person a sense of belonging and pride in historical accomplishments.]

8
What does Mathabane imply is the state of a mind "high on drugs"? [It is a trapped state; the mind is a slave and is not free.]

ENRICHMENT

Students could provide additional support for Mathabane's views by writing and presenting short reports on the famous African American achievers listed on p. 243. Have students include information about the individuals' education and about any hardships the individuals had to overcome. ■

Some of the youngsters seemed unable to grasp the full meaning of my words; but there was no doubt that I had made some impression on all of them. I hoped that in time, 9 whatever seeds I had planted in their young minds would blossom into a determination to be educated, to realize their potential as human beings, no matter what the obstacles.

Mark Mathabane

Reader's Response

1. Mark Mathabane writes about the importance of role models. Do you have a role model or a hero? What do you think are the characteristics of a good role model?
2. By explaining the effects of an education, Mathabane attempted to inspire the young people he worked with in Harlem. Do you think this kind of explanation can change people's lives? Can you think of a time when learning about the possible effects of something made you think or act differently?

Writer's Craft

3. In this passage from his book, Mathabane explains some of the causes for lives of "crime and drugs and teenage motherhood." What causes does he identify?
4. According to Mathabane, what are the effects of an educated mind?

9

Mathabane ends on an optimistic but a realistic note. He recognizes that not all students understood his explanations, that not all students will follow his advice, and that students face many obstacles.

ANSWERS

Reader's Response

Responses will vary.

1. Responses should be serious and thoughtful. Accept all logical role models and characteristics.
2. Personal experiences will greatly affect students' answers. Students might share what makes them change: finding role models, seeing described effects in friends, or fearing consequences.

Writer's Craft

3. He identifies poor role models and support systems, the influence and allure of street life, the disintegration of black family life, the loss of positive values, and the inhumanity of New York City life.
4. The effects of an educated mind include gaining knowledge that can't be taken away; overcoming mental slavery; and acquiring the ability to fight for what is yours, to define who you are, to set limits to your aspirations, and to run your own life.

SELECTION AMENDMENT
Description of change: excerpted
Rationale: to focus on the concept of cause-and-effect explanations presented in this chapter

SEGMENT 2 *(p. 246)*

STRATEGIES FOR WRITING TO EXPLAIN

TEACHING THE MODES

Use this section to give students a structured overview of the strategies or modes that can be used to develop an explanatory composition. Discuss the examples with students and make sure they understand that the two narrative examples involve cause-and-effect explanations. Then ask students to give further examples of how each mode might be used in developing an explanatory composition. You may want to bring to class some other examples of explanations and to work with students to identify the modes that the explanations use. ■

COOPERATIVE LEARNING

Divide the class into four groups, one representing each of the strategies. Instruct each group to use its assigned strategy to select a topic that could be developed in a composition. Then have group members work together to list at least five details that could be included in a composition on the chosen topic. Close by involving all groups in a discussion about the appropriateness and workability of the topics and details they developed.

A DIFFERENT APPROACH

After students have studied and discussed the strategies for writing to explain, put the following information in two columns on the chalkboard and tell students to match the numbered items with the lettered items that best describe them:

1. narration	a. divide; define; compare and contrast
2. description	b. look at the value of a subject or make a judgment
3. classification	c. use sensory details; look at individual features
4. evaluation	d. tell a story; explain a process or causes and effects

[**1**–d, **2**–c, **3**–a, **4**–b]

Strategies for Writing to Explain

In explaining the effects of an education, Mathabane used the strategy of narration. Narration always involves things happening, or changing, over the course of time; an effect is always a change, and it always happens later than the cause. Darkness (the effect) occurs *after* the sun goes down (the cause). Of course, writers can use other strategies to explain. Here are some examples that show how the four basic writing strategies can be used to explain.

Narration: in a history paper, looking at the causes of the War of 1812; explaining to the principal how the elimination of a third level of Spanish would affect students in your school.

Description: describing a rock cliff and giving evidence to illustrate the different strata (layers) of rock; describing the structure of your city's government and showing that your description is accurate.

Classification: explaining and giving evidence to show the differences between the rock music of today and of the 1950s; defining the word *brave* and supporting your definition.

Evaluation: taking a stand on the value of a poem and attempting to prove to your English teacher that your evaluation is sound; evaluating a new hair dryer on the basis of performance and identifying evidence to support your evaluation.

LOOKING AHEAD

In the main assignment in this chapter, you'll use the strategy of narration to explain causes and/or effects. As you work through the chapter, keep in mind that a cause-and-effect explanation

- identifies a situation or condition
- answers one or both of these questions: Why did it happen (what caused it)? What were the effects?
- attempts to prove that the explanation is sound

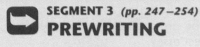

SEGMENT 3 *(pp. 247–254)*
PREWRITING

OBJECTIVES

- To give a brief oral report about the causes and/or effects of a current issue
- To choose a workable, limited topic for a cause-and-effect essay
- To formulate a thesis statement for a cause-and-effect essay
- To use brainstorming and researching to gather information and evidence to support a cause-and-effect explanation
- To create a map to organize information for a cause-and-effect essay

Writing a Cause-and-Effect Explanation

Prewriting

Considering Topic, Purpose, and Audience

An Appropriate Topic. A topic for a cause-and-effect explanation starts with a situation or condition. Then it asks *Why?* or *What's the result?*

EXAMPLE	*Situation*:	A new law
	Why?	Why was this law passed?
	What's the result?	What will be the effects of this new law?

As with all writing, a good topic is one that you find interesting. If you couldn't care less about the reasons for the soccer team's recent loss, don't write about it. If you're worried about what will happen if car insurance rates are raised in your state, you may have found yourself a topic.

How do you begin finding a topic? One good way is to call to mind any recent changes that have affected your life. They could be problems, trends, or inventions.

Problem: Our high school band is losing members. What are the causes?
Trend: Some teenagers are spending $100 for athletic shoes. What are the causes? the effects?
Invention: More and more people are getting telephone answering machines. What are the effects, good and bad?

Another approach is to focus on a particular subject that interests you—science, law, history, sports—and look for interesting situations. What will be the effects of artificial blood

Teacher's ResourceBank™
RESOURCES

PREWRITING
- Listing Causes and Effects 60

QUOTATION FOR THE DAY

"Shallow men believe in luck . . . . Strong men believe in cause and effect." (Ralph Waldo Emerson, 1803–1882, American poet, essayist, philosopher)

Ask students if they believe in luck. Do things happen randomly, or is there a cause for every situation? Have volunteers explain what they think Emerson meant by this statement.

MEETING INDIVIDUAL NEEDS

AT-RISK STUDENTS

You may want to focus students' attention on goals and aspirations as they are exploring topics for cause-and-effect essays. Tell students to think about the decisions they might have to make in their own lives. For example, what careers will they choose? Will they want to get married? Where do they see themselves five years from now?

MOTIVATION

Involve students by asking them to name situations or events—international, national, or local—that are of interest to them. Write their responses on the chalkboard and have students ask "Why did it happen?" or "What is the result?" with respect to the situations or events they named. Explain that if it is possible to ask one or both of these questions, the situation or event could be an appropriate topic for a cause-and-effect essay.

INTEGRATING THE LANGUAGE ARTS

Literature Link. You may want to point out to students that often they can discover good topic ideas for essays by reading literature. Refer students to a short story that they have read and ask them to think about the story in terms of possible topic ideas for cause-and-effect essays. For example, here are two possible topic ideas inspired by Jack London's short story "To Build a Fire":

1. Jack London's own experiences in the Yukon had a tremendous effect on his writing.
2. There are many reasons for the Yukon's popularity and growth since the late 1800s.

Library Link. Provide time for your students to make use of the library's resources for topic ideas. You could divide the class into groups and ask each group to explore a particular source, such as magazines, newspapers, nonfiction books, or reference books. Let each group report its findings of topic ideas to the whole class.

on medicine? Why did the Chicago Cubs break a 72-year tradition and finally install lights for night games at Wrigley Field?

Of course, there are many times when you don't have to look for a topic for a cause-and-effect essay. The topic "comes to you." Your history teacher may ask you to write an essay explaining the causes of the decline of communism in the Soviet Union. Or perhaps you have a job in the mayor's office in your town. Someone has proposed adding a stoplight at an intersection near the high school, and the mayor asks you to investigate and explain the possible effects. The ability to look at and explain causes and effects will be useful throughout your school and work life.

Purpose and Audience. Although you could look at causes and effects in order to persuade, to express yourself, or to create a literary work, in this chapter your basic *purpose* is to explain. That purpose will affect how you present the causes or effects.

In an explanation, you are attempting to clarify something, to make it clear. You want your *audience* to understand your explanation and to accept it as reasonable and thoughtful. For that reason, you can't just say one thing caused another and be done with it. You have to give some evidence that will lead your audience to accept your explanation. For example, you might want to explain to your audience that the band doesn't play well because the members don't take the band seriously. What if your audience says, "How do you know that?" Then you need to provide evidence. "Our band comes in last in the county band contest every year." "Attendance at band practice is lower than it has been in the past ten years."

TEACHING THE LESSON

Before students read the information in the **Prewriting** section, emphasize that their essays will be easier to write (and to read) if they follow the prescribed prewriting steps: choose a workable topic, develop a clear thesis statement, gather appropriate information, and organize the information effectively. You may want to write the following definitions on the chalkboard for students to refer to as they read:

1. topic—a limited, specific subject
2. thesis statement—a statement of the main idea and purpose of the essay
3. cause—an event or situation that produces a result
4. effect—anything brought about by a cause

WRITING NOTE

The expository purpose (or aim) for writing includes three categories: informing, explaining, and exploring. When you inform (see Chapter 6), you share facts. When you explain, you use facts to prove that your explanation is accurate or sound. When you explore (see Chapter 9), you attempt to discover facts and/or other evidence.

Reminder

To find a topic for a cause-and-effect essay

- brainstorm, read, or observe to find a situation that intrigues you
- look for situations created by problems, trends, or inventions
- be sure you can ask *Why?* or *What's the result?* about your topic

EXERCISE 1 Speaking and Listening: Exploring Causes and Effects

Increase your awareness of causes and effects by reviewing your local newspaper, watching a television news program, or looking through a current issue of a news magazine such as *Time* or *Newsweek*. Look for stories or issues that interest you, and then select one for which the reporter or writer identifies some causes and/or effects. In a brief oral report to your class, identify the story or issue, the causes and/or effects mentioned by the reporter or writer, and any additional causes or effects you may think of.

WRITING ASSIGNMENT PART 1: Choosing a Topic

Select a topic that interests you. You might use one you discovered in your research for Exercise 1 or you might brainstorm alone or in a small group for other ideas. Be careful that your topic is not too broad. In a brief essay, you can't cover all the effects of the Civil War, but you can discuss the military equipment invented as a result of that conflict.

A DIFFERENT APPROACH

Tell students that many TV commercials present short, fast-paced, attention-grabbing cause-and-effect situations. For example, an ad for a laundry detergent shows dirty clothes (effect) unaffected by an inferior detergent brand (cause), and then the ad states that Brand X (cause) will produce cleaner clothes (effect).

Several students may want to work together to videotape some commercials that present cause-and-effect situations. Then they could show the tapes to the class and let students identify the causes and effects.

ANSWERS

Exercise 1

You may want to help students develop a set of criteria by which the members of the audience can evaluate the oral reports. For example, students can use a rating scale of 1–5 in such areas as delivery and clarity of causes and effects.

TIMESAVER

After students complete **Writing Assignment: Part 1,** pass around a sheet of paper and have students write their names and the topics they've chosen. The list should provide a quick and easy way for you to detect inappropriate topics.

5. evidence—factual information used to support a reason

The **Prewriting** segment is divided into two sections: **Considering Topic, Purpose, and Audience** and **Planning a Cause-and-Effect Explanation.** Because most eleventh-grade students will have encountered this information previously, you may want to assign these headings for individual reading and then lead a class discussion of the prewriting steps.

COOPERATIVE LEARNING

You may want to give students practice in developing thesis statements for different focuses of a subject. Divide the class into groups of three. One member of the group will focus on causes, another on effects, and the third on causes and effects. Give each group a subject and instruct each member to write a thesis statement on his or her assigned focus. Tell students to use the textbook examples on teenage car ownership as a guide. You may want to give each group more than one subject and to switch the members' focus assignments. The groups should present their thesis statements to the whole class for discussion and evaluation. Ask students to comment on difficulties they experienced in writing their thesis statements to reflect a certain focus.

VISUAL CONNECTIONS

Related Expression Skills. Have students create cartoons or illustrations based on their own experiences of car ownership or driving. Then have students discuss possible cause-and-effect situations suggested by the artwork.

Prewriting

Planning a Cause-and-Effect Explanation

Remember that your purpose is to explain clearly the causes and/or effects of a situation. To do this, you'll need to identify your main idea and gather information about your topic, including facts, statistics, and examples to back up your statements.

Identifying Your Thesis

Between the time you identify the situation, or topic, and the time you begin to organize your ideas, you need to identify your main idea, or ***thesis.*** There's nothing wrong with identifying your thesis before you gather information, but you may find you change your mind as you look into the situation. For example, you may be concerned about the effects of "increased student activity fees." While you're gathering your information, however, you decide that you also need to look at the causes—low funding from the state, an economic recession, and so forth.

The focus of a cause-and-effect explanation may be the causes of a situation, the effects, or both causes and effects. That focus will determine your main idea, or thesis. Here are examples of thesis statements with the three different focuses.

Causes: There are three basic reasons most teenagers feel they need to buy a car.

Effects: While buying a car seems like a liberation, it may bring consequences that are not so pleasant.

Causes and Effects: Many teenagers have good reasons for buying a car, but some effects may be negative.

GUIDED PRACTICE

Guide students through the steps of **Exercise 1** on p. 249 by choosing an appropriate news article and presenting a brief oral report. To prepare students for **Writing Assignment: Parts 1–3**, you could model on the chalkboard the prewriting process. Choose a sample topic (perhaps one that was generated in **Exercise 1**) that is familiar to your class and enlist their participation. List cause-and-effect relationships and evidence to support them. Develop a thesis statement. Finally, create a map of your information that is logically organized.

Gathering Information

Sources of Information. For some topics, you will be able to analyze both causes and effects from your own knowledge. For example, if you're writing about a local school issue, like the effects of starting school an hour earlier, you can probably rely on your own experience and understanding of the situation. However, for many topics your critical thinking will have to include some research. If you were writing about the causes and effects of brain injuries, for example, you might need to consult a number of different sources—magazine or newspaper articles, books, experts on the subject, and so forth. (For more help with research, see Chapter 11.)

Types of Information. A cause-and-effect explanation has two types of information: (1) the causes and/or effects of the situation and (2) the evidence to show that the causes and/or effects are accurate. Here are some questions you can use to guide your search for causes, effects, and evidence:

QUESTIONS FOR GATHERING INFORMATION

Causes

- What are the obvious causes?
- Are there any hidden causes? What are they?
- Is there a main, or most important, cause? What is it?
- What is the most recent cause?
- Did any of the causes occur in the distant past?

Effects

- What are the obvious effects?
- Are there any hidden effects? What are they?
- What was (or will be) the first effect?
- What effect(s) might occur in the distant future?

Evidence

- What facts or statistics show that this cause (or effect) exists?
- What expert(s) acknowledges that this cause (or effect) exists?
- What is enough evidence?

MEETING INDIVIDUAL NEEDS

LEP/ESL

General Strategies. The textbook suggests that interviewing experts is a good way to gather information. The interview process is a particularly useful strategy for students because it offers them invaluable practice in the four basic skill areas of speaking, listening, writing, and reading. You might consider requiring students to conduct an interview as part of their prewriting process.

INDEPENDENT PRACTICE

Students should be ready to do **Exercise 1** and **Writing Assignment: Parts 1–3** independently. If you allow students to work in groups to explore topics as suggested in **Writing Assignment: Part 1**, circulate from group to group to answer questions and to check their progress. A good grouping strategy for this exercise would be to put creative and analytical students together. The creative students might be better at generating ideas, while the more analytical students might be better at evaluating them.

Because an appropriate topic and a clear, effective thesis statement are so important to the success of a cause-and-effect explanation, you will probably want to monitor students as they complete **Writing**

INTEGRATING THE LANGUAGE ARTS

Listening Link. To help students develop their skills in gathering information from interviews or other oral sources, read aloud a short article from a newspaper or magazine and have students write down the most important facts as you read. You also could assume the role of an expert on the subject of the article and field questions from students, who would write down important information. Afterward, call on students to state the most important facts gained from the reading and questioning.

This activity also would be effective if a student volunteer reads an article and fields questions. Another approach would be to divide the class into groups of interviewers and experts.

MEETING INDIVIDUAL NEEDS

ADVANCED STUDENTS

While gathering information, students might find that there are often differences of opinion about the causes and effects of significant historical or current events. Encourage students to present these differing opinions in their cause-and-effect essays and then draw their own conclusions based on the evidence.

WRITING ASSIGNMENT

PART 2:
Identifying a Thesis and Gathering Information

Ask the two big questions about your topic: *Why?* and *What's the effect?* Brainstorm for as many causes and effects as you can think of; then research others in books or tapes, or do on-site observation and interviewing. Write down all the causes and effects you come up with, as well as evidence to back them up. Stop at some point to identify your focus and write your thesis statement.

Organizing Information

Occasionally a single cause produces a single effect, but not often: Most interesting situations or trends have multiple causes and/or effects. Depending upon the focus of your essay—causes only, effects only, or both causes and effects—the organization may vary a great deal. One helpful way to organize your information is to "map" it. The following example shows how one writer mapped an essay that focused on the effects of buying a car.

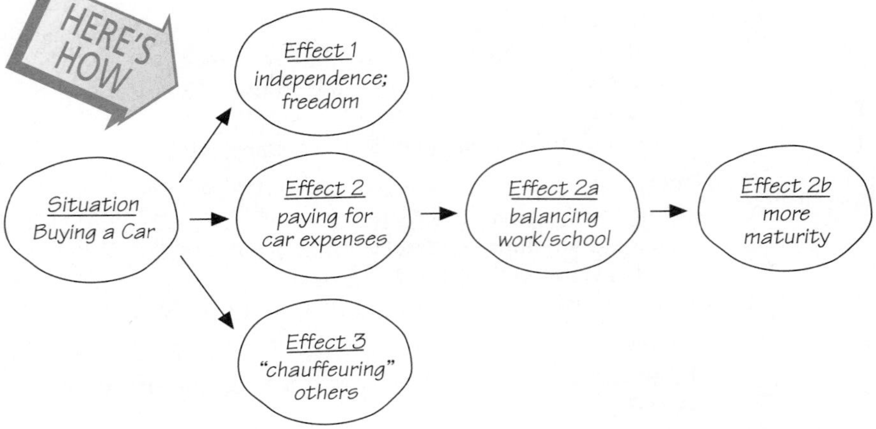

The following examples illustrate how mapping works with other focuses.

Assignment: Parts 1 and **2.** Students might need time for research, either to go to the library or to interview an expert. You may want to make yourself accessible during this process to answer any questions students might have.

ASSESSMENT

Students' oral reports in **Exercise 1** should help you assess students' understanding of causes and effects. You can use students' responses to **Writing Assignment: Parts 1–3** to evaluate their understanding and application of the prewriting steps: choosing a topic, identifying a thesis, gathering information, and organizing information.

Focusing on Causes

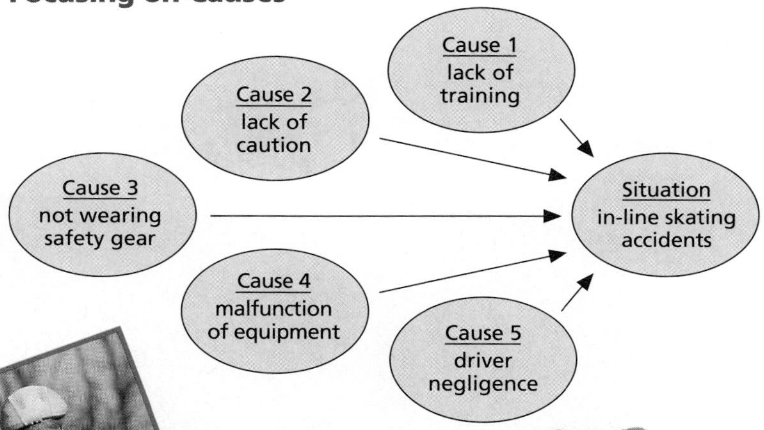

Focusing on Causes and Effects

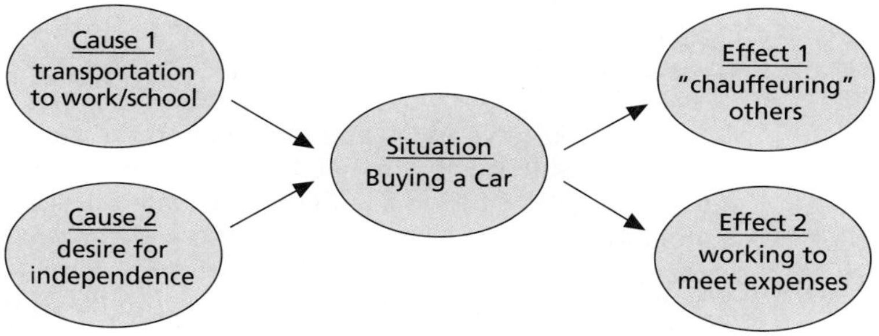

CRITICAL THINKING
Analysis

Lead a class discussion in which students analyze the examples of mapping in the textbook. Read through the numbered causes and effects for each example and ask volunteers to explain the relationships presented.

CLOSURE

Ask students to state the basic steps in the prewriting stage of the writing process [choosing a topic, identifying a thesis, gathering information, organizing information]. Then ask students why these steps are important. [They provide a foundation and a framework for writing.] ■

MEETING **INDIVIDUAL** NEEDS

LEARNING STYLES

Kinetic Learners. You may want to offer students an alternative organizational strategy. Suggest that students write each cause and/or effect on a separate index card. Remind them to include supporting facts or evidence on each card. Then students can lay the index cards out on their desks and rearrange the cards until they find the most effective order.

Focusing on a Chain of Causes and Effects

Cause: Marsh filled for home construction → Effect/Cause: Loss of wildlife habitat → Effect/Cause: Alligators enter yards and pools → Effect: Alligators moved to wildlife preserve

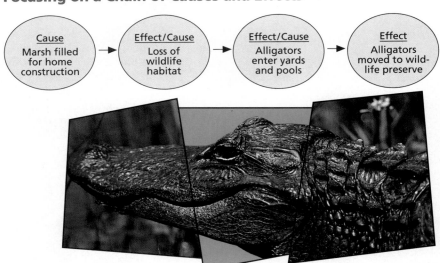

You'll notice that in the Here's How section and in two of the other maps, the causes and effects are numbered. That means the writer will discuss the first cause and related evidence, then the second cause and related evidence, and so forth. But how do you know which cause or effect to list first or last? Most of the time you would use *order of importance* and list the most important cause or effect last, where it will have the most impact. However, with some topics it would make sense to list the causes and effects in *chronological order*.

REFERENCE NOTE: See pages 38–39 and 75–76 for more information on order of importance and chronological order.

WRITING ASSIGNMENT

PART 3:
Organizing Your Information

Now that you have ideas and information, as well as a focus and a thesis statement, you need to think about how to put this material together for your audience. Create an organizational map of your information that you can use later as a guide for writing. Remember that the shape of your map (see pages 252–254) is determined by your focus and your thesis statement.

SEGMENT 4 *(pp. 255–265)*

WRITING YOUR FIRST DRAFT

OBJECTIVES

- To analyze a model cause-and-effect essay
- To identify the causes and effects, evidence, and unrelated details in a model essay
- To write a first draft of a cause-and-effect explanation that contains an introduction, a body, and a conclusion

Writing Your First Draft

The Structure of a Cause-and-Effect Explanation

When you are ready to write, the usual question is *Where do I begin?* Actually, it doesn't matter. The important thing is to start. This is the structure you will use in your draft.

1. In your *introduction*
   - grab the readers' attention
   - identify the situation or condition you are explaining
   - let your reader know what your main idea (thesis) is
2. In the *body*
   - explain the causes and/or the effects of the situation
   - use facts, statistics, and examples to illustrate and clarify each cause or effect
3. In your *conclusion*
   - sum up the explanation
   - possibly, predict future changes or effects

In the following essay about frontier life, the writers explain *effects.* As you read, notice how the authors establish an interesting situation in the introduction. In the body of the essay they lead you into a discussion of several effects, each one supported with specific, colorful details. In the conclusion the writers provide a historical perspective by summarizing how the overall situation changed over the course of time.

urtesy Museum of New Mexico, #14659

Teacher's ResourceBank™

RESOURCES

WRITING YOUR FIRST DRAFT

- Writing a Cause-and-Effect Essay 61

QUOTATION FOR THE DAY

"An idle reason lessens the weight of the good ones you gave before." (Jonathan Swift, 1667–1745, English satirist)

You could use this quotation to emphasize the importance of using valid reasons as supporting details. As students write their first drafts, they should be reminded that each cause and/or effect needs supporting reasons or evidence to prove its accuracy.

MEETING INDIVIDUAL NEEDS

LEP/ESL

General Strategies. ESL students are not only acquiring language but also culture, which means learning about attitudes, humor, and values. Therefore, ESL students may find it helpful to be paired with native speakers of English for the stage of writing a first draft.

MOTIVATION

Tell your students that a first draft is like a base coat of paint: It should cover the subject, but it doesn't have to be perfect. And just as each painter has his or her own procedure to get the base coat of paint applied, so does each writer have a plan that works best for him or her. Some writers prefer to spend time on just the right introduction as the first step, while others prefer to skip the introduction and begin writing the body. This discussion should help students understand that writing is an individualized process.

USING THE SELECTION
from Nation of Nations

1
The book is subtitled *A Narrative History of the American Republic.*

2
The Plains Indians included the Comanches, Osages, Pawnees, Sioux, and Kiowas.

3
Do you think the introduction is effective? Do you think the author should have opened with information about the Indians if the rest of the article is about white settlement? [Opinions will vary. The introduction does serve as a contrast of two cultures that existed simultaneously on the plains.]

4
The result of this "rooting" was the eventual establishment of communities, cities, and states.

5
What other transportation links existed? [Responses will vary, but students may mention stagecoach lines and covered wagon caravans.]

6
The quotation adds a personal, real feeling to the explanation. It provides details with the regional flavor of vivid verbs and descriptive adjectives.

A PASSAGE FROM A BOOK

1 # *from* Nation of Nations
by James West Davidson et al.

The Frontier Kitchen of the Plains

INTRODUCTION
Attention grabber
Background information

2 Out on the treeless plains the Indians had adjusted to scarcity of food, water, and other necessities by adopting a nomadic way of life. Their small kinship groups moved each season to wherever nature supplied the food they needed. Such mobility discouraged families from acquiring extensive material possessions. Tools and housing had to be light and portable. Even tribes that raised crops as part of their subsistence cycle often moved with the seasons.

Situation

Thesis statement

3 White settlement was different. Farmers,
4 ranchers, and townspeople rooted themselves to a single place. What the surrounding countryside could not supply had to be brought from afar, generally at great effort and expense. In areas distant
5 from the railroad or other transportation links, families generally had to learn either to do without or to improvise from materials at hand.

Effect 1
Evidence for effect 1

Keeping food on the table was nearly impossible some seasons of the year. Coffee and sugar were staples in such short supply that resourceful
6 women invented a variety of substitutes. "Take a gallon of bran, two tablespoonsful of molasses, scald and parch in an oven until it is somewhat browned and charred," one woman suggested. Something as simple as finding water suitable for drinking or cooking became a problem in many western areas, where the choice might be between "the strong alkaline water of the Rio Grande or the purchase of melted manufactured ice (shipped by rail) at its great cost." To prepare for the lean winter months, women stocked their cellars and made wild fruits into leathery cakes, eaten to

TEACHING THE LESSON

This segment concentrates on the separate components that constitute a basic expository essay: the introductory paragraph, the paragraphs that compose the body, and the concluding paragraph. Use the model essay from ***Nation of Nations*** and the essay in **A Writer's Model** on pp. 260–262 to show the structure of a cause-and-effect essay. Ask students if they think the models meet all the criteria established in the section **The Structure of a Cause-and-Effect Explanation** on p. 255. [Most students will probably agree that the models meet the criteria.] To emphasize the importance of evidence to support each cause or effect, have volunteers point out the evidence that supports the topic sentence of each body paragraph of ☛

ward off the scurvy that resulted from vitamin deficiency.

Effect 2

Evidence for effect 2

Gardening, generally a woman's responsibility, brought variety to the diet and color to the yard. The legume family of peas and beans, in particular, provided needed protein. Superstition had it that plants which grew above ground, like peas, beans, and squash, should be planted in the new moon, whereas root plants such as carrots, potatoes, radishes, and turnips went in as the moon waned. As the moon rose, the theory went, plants rose; as it dropped, so did the root plants. Flowers
7 were much prized but seldom survived the winds, heat, and dry periods. Dishwater and laundry water helped keep them alive. One woman was so excited by the discovery of a hardy dandelion that she cultivated it with care and planted its seeds each spring.

Montana Historical Society, Helena

8 Until rail lines made shipment of goods cheap and Sears, Roebuck "wishbooks" brought mail order to the frontier, a woman's kitchen was fairly modest. A cast iron stove, which sold for $25 in the East, was in such demand and so expensive to ship that it fetched $200 in some areas of the West.

Effect 3
Evidence for effect 3

7
Why would flowers have been prized on the plains? [They added color to the dull, treeless landscape.]

VISUAL CONNECTIONS

Exploring the Subject. Ask students what they can infer about the woman in the picture based on her clothes, her expression, and the surroundings. You could ask students if there are any gardeners—women or men—in their families. If so, do the gardeners plant according to any superstitions or folk methods?

8
Mail-order catalogs were often called "wishbooks" at this time. What is implied by the term? [The wisher often didn't have money to buy the longed-for items.]

A Writer's Model. You'll probably want to emphasize, as the textbook does, that the model provides a simplified organizational structure that students can follow when they write their first drafts.

GUIDED PRACTICE

Use the questions in **Exercise 2** on p. 260 as a basis for a class discussion about the structure and content of a cause-and-effect explanation. Then help students compare **A Writer's Model** with the **Framework for a Cause-and-Effect Explanation** chart on p. 262.

9

The contrast between a plains kitchen of the 1870s and one of today is amazing. What are considered necessities in many modest kitchens today? [Responses will vary, but students will probably mention ranges, sinks, and various utensils.]

10

patent medicines: nonprescription drugs with a trademark

11

What do these folk remedies show about the character of the plains women? [Responses will vary, but a possible answer is that the remedies showed that the women were resourceful, practical, and imaginative.]

9 One miner's wife in Montana during the 1870s considered her kitchen "well-furnished" with two kettles, a cast iron skillet, and a coffeepot. A kitchen cupboard might be little more than a box nailed to a log. In sod houses cooking could be difficult after a cloudburst. One "soddie" recalled that her kitchen remained snug and dry during a rainstorm, but she discovered that the downpour had taken its toll as the water seeped slowly through the thick roof. After the sun came out, the still-waterlogged roof began to leak. She ended up frying pancakes on her stove under the protection of an umbrella while the sun shone brightly outside.

Montana Historical Society, Helena

Effect 4
Evidence for effect 4

Without doctors, circumstances forced women to learn the <u>rudiments</u> of caring for the hurt and sick. Most folk remedies did little more
10 than ease pain. Whiskey and patent medicines, often more dangerous than the disease, were used to treat a range of ills from frostbite to snake bite and from sore throats to burns and rheumatism.
11 Settlers believed that onions and gunpowder had valuable medicinal properties. Cobwebs could bandage small wounds; turpentine served as a disinfectant. Mosquitoes were repelled with a paste of vinegar and salt. One woman in Wyoming prevented winter snow blindness by burning pitch pine until it was black and smudging the skin below the eyes with it to cut glare.

INDEPENDENT PRACTICE

As students write the first drafts of their essays in **Writing Assignment: Part 4** on p. 265, suggest that they use the **Framework for a Cause-and-Effect Explanation** chart in conjunction with the organizational maps they developed in **Writing Assignment: Part 3** on p. 254. You may want to schedule individual conferences to be sure that students have adequately developed their thesis statements.

Most parents thought the laxative castor oil could cure any childhood malady. And if a family member had a fever, one treatment was to bind the head with a cold rag, wrap the feet in cabbage leaves, and then force down large doses of sage tea, rhubarb, and soda. Some women adapted remedies used on their farm animals. Sarah Olds, a Nevada homesteader whose family was plagued by fleas and lice, recalled that "we all took baths with plenty of sheep dip in the water. . . . I had no disinfectant . . . so I boiled all our clothing in sheep dip and kerosene."

CONCLUSION
Statement about later changes

Gradually, as the market system penetrated the West, families had less need to improvise in matters of diet and medicine. Through catalogs one might order spices like white pepper or poultry seasoning and appliances such as grinders for real coffee. If a local stagecoach passed by the house, a woman might send her eggs and butter to town to be exchanged for needed store-bought goods like threads and needles. It took a complex commercial network to bring all that the good life required to a land that produced few foods and necessities in abundance.

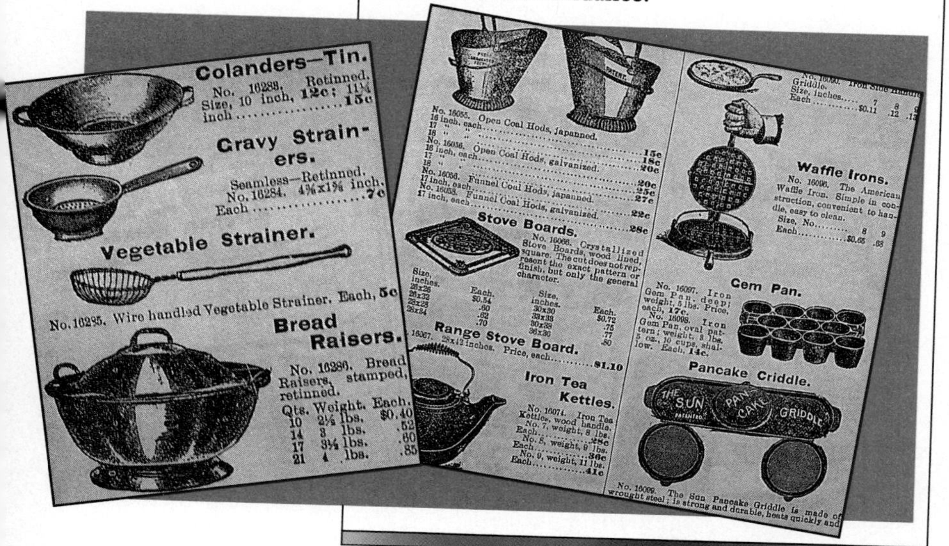

SELECTION AMENDMENT

Description of change: excerpted and modified
Rationale: to focus on the concept of cause-and-effect explanations presented in this chapter

ASSESSMENT

Use the first drafts of students' essays to evaluate their understanding of the structure and content of a cause-effect explanation and to assess their ability to arrange and convey ideas and information.

RETEACHING

To help students see how a prewriting map can be converted into a first draft, create a prewriting map that the author of **A Writer's Model** might have used. You may want to have a volunteer draw the map on the chalkboard as you and other class members offer suggestions.

ANSWERS

Exercise 2

Answers may vary.

1. Some students may suggest that the author begins with Plains Indians to grab the reader's attention and to offer a vivid, interesting contrast.
2. Frontier families did not adapt a nomadic way of life to follow food and water as the seasons changed. They had to find ways to make the surrounding countryside produce life's necessities because transporting goods was difficult and expensive.
3. Four effects are that keeping food on the table was difficult; gardening provided food and aesthetics; kitchens were modest; and women cared for the hurt and sick. Additional responses will vary, but they should include other aspects of domestic life.
4. The authors use quotations to back up effects 1 (about making coffee and finding water) and 4 (remedies); various examples for each effect; and incidents to illustrate effects 2 (dandelion discovery), 3 (woman cooking pancakes), and 4 (use of sheep dip and kerosene).
5. Some students may suggest that superstitions about planting do not strictly illustrate the main idea.

EXERCISE 2 **Analyzing a Cause-and-Effect Essay**

Now that you have read the essay on the frontier kitchen (pages 256–259), meet with two or three classmates to discuss the following questions.

1. The authors' subject is white settlers, yet they begin with the Plains Indians. Why do you think they do this?
2. The essay focuses on the *effects* of this situation: frontier families had to improvise or do without. Some *causes* of this situation are briefly presented as background in the introduction. What are the causes?
3. A map of this essay would show four main effects. What are they? Can you think of others to add to the essay—anything you're curious about when you think of frontier survival?
4. The authors use evidence to back up their main points. Find examples of the types of support they use—such as quotations, examples, or anecdotes.
5. Do you find details that don't strictly illustrate the essay's main idea about improvising on the frontier? If so, discuss them, and explain why you would keep them or cut them.

A Basic Framework for a Cause-and-Effect Essay

The following essay on buying a car gives you another example of cause-and-effect writing. Like "The Frontier Kitchen of the Plains," it presents a series of effects. However, you'll notice that the writing here is not as detailed, and its organizational structure is more straightforward. You may wish to follow this model when you write your own essay.

A WRITER'S MODEL

Owning a Car: The Pros and Cons

INTRODUCTION
Attention grabber

What one object do most teenagers want to own? A car. Why? Freedom. Buying a car seems like liberation: You can go where you want when you

CLOSURE

Ask volunteers to state the three purposes of an introduction [to grab readers' attention, to identify situation or condition, to present thesis]; to list the roles of the body paragraphs [to explain causes and/or effects and to give facts, statistics, and examples]; and to give two purposes of a conclusion [to sum up explanations and to predict future changes or effects].

Thesis statement

want. And that's true--up to a point. Putting yourself in the driver's seat can also have consequences that aren't so cool. I am speaking from experience.

Effect 1
Evidence for effect 1

One benefit of buying a car is definitely independence. You don't have to count on parents, friends, bus schedules, or good weather (waterlogged biking is no fun). You are not always asking favors, making last-minute arrangements, and following other people's schedules. You can accept a good job that's on the other side of town, and you won't miss parties because you're stranded at home without a ride.

Effect 2
Evidence for effect 2

But an unexpected part of not needing a chauffeur is that you can become one. With another car in the household, I'm now the one who takes my sister to Little League and goes to the store for milk. And I'm now the one who gives rides to my carless friends. Because I know what they're up against, I don't want to refuse them, but after a while I need money for expenses, and having to ask for it is no fun.

Effect 3
Evidence for effect 3

Owning a car costs money--in ways you don't appreciate as a passenger. Gasoline isn't free, insurance for teenagers is expensive, and maintenance (not to mention repairs) drains finances. To meet car expenses, I had to work more hours, which meant less free time. Unfortunately, I responded to that situation by studying less, which caused one term of very bad grades, which in turn put my car keys in my parents' pockets for six weeks.

ENRICHMENT

Explain to students that advertisements frequently use false cause and effect to promote products. For example, an ad might imply that you will have more dates if you use a certain product. Advertisements also use oversimplification of cause and effect. For example, an ad might promise that you will be healthy if you take a certain vitamin. (Vitamins alone cannot ensure good health.)

Have students compile a scrapbook of such advertisements from newspapers and magazines, or you may prefer to have students make a collage or poster. ■

MEETING INDIVIDUAL NEEDS

STUDENTS WITH SPECIAL NEEDS

Extra structure is often helpful for students with learning disabilities. Therefore, you could extend the **Framework for a Cause-and-Effect Explanation** chart to create an outline form on which students could write complete sentences. For the introduction, provide separate blank lines for each student to write an attention grabber, a situation, and a thesis statement. For each body paragraph, provide lines for students to write the causes and effects and three examples of evidence. For the conclusion, provide a blank line for students to write a summarizing statement.

Effect 4 **Evidence for effect 4** **Summary of effects** **CONCLUSION**	So, a final effect of car ownership can be growing up. You have to balance freedom with responsibility, learn how to afford your dream of driving without shortchanging something else. Car keys really are the key to a lot of fun and to being on your own, but you have to be ready to pay the price.

This essay follows a standard, easy-to-follow framework for any cause-and-effect essay. Basically, it follows this pattern.

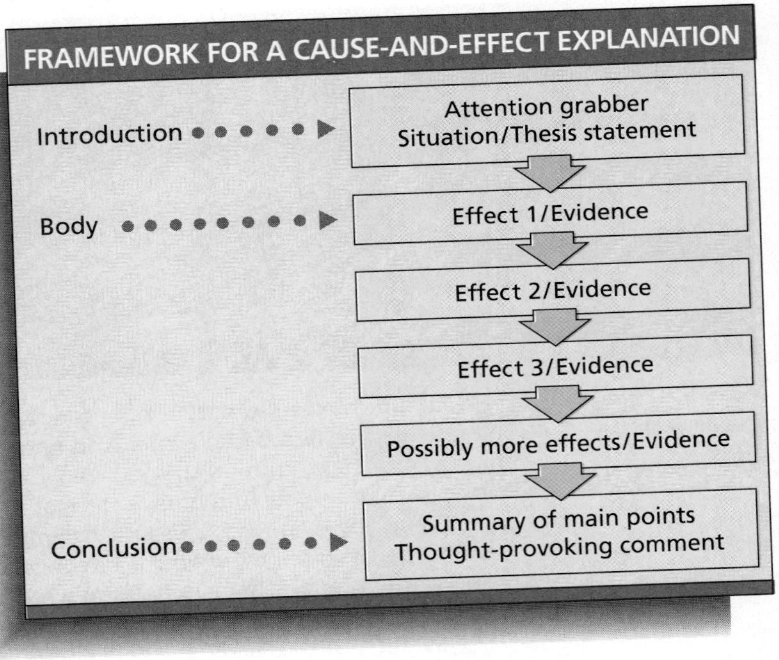

If your essay focuses on causes only, you can follow this same framework, simply substituting causes for effects. Or, you might describe both causes and effects—for example, in an essay that treats the causes and effects of the Vietnam War. And, if your essay focuses on both causes and effects, you can still use this framework: First you treat the causes, and then the effects.

CRITICAL THINKING

(pp. 263–265)

OBJECTIVE

- To identify kinds of research and sources needed to make generalizations valid

TEACHING *USING INDUCTION*

Begin by giving students a clear, concise definition of *induction:* "the act of inferring or deducing generalized conclusions from specific facts or observations." Tell students that inductive reasoning depends on ample evidence. Then have students read the first two paragraphs and the first example in the **Critical Thinking** section. At this

CRITICAL THINKING

Using Induction

As you plan and write, you're in a continual process of drawing conclusions and making judgments about causes and effects. How can you tell if the conclusions you reach are ***valid,*** or grounded in evidence? One good way is to think about how you think! Examine your reasoning process.

Induction is one basic and sound reasoning process. When you use induction, you begin with a set of specific facts or observations. By studying this evidence, you reach a general conclusion, or generalization. Induction always goes from the *specific* to the *general.* Here's an example.

The first time I went to Bessy's room, it was a mess.
The second time, her room was a disaster.
I've never been to Bessy's room when it was neat.
Generalization: Bessy is not a tidy housekeeper.

Calvin & Hobbes, copyright 1990 Universal Press Syndicate. Reprinted with permission of Universal Press Syndicate. All rights reserved.

Chances are, you'll find yourself using induction in your cause-and-effect essay, especially if you're examining a new trend or a social situation. Suppose, for example, you want to explore how high school students' studies are affected when they take outside jobs with long hours. You might begin by interviewing students who have held jobs for at least twenty

MEETING **INDIVIDUAL** NEEDS

ADVANCED STUDENTS

Ask students to contrast induction with deduction. Have students look up explanations of deduction in the textbook, a dictionary, or handbook of critical thinking and reading terms. Then have them write brief definitions of deduction and provide at least two original examples of deductive reasoning. Ask students to state the main difference between deduction and induction. [Deduction begins with a generalization while induction ends with a generalization.]

point, you may want to point out that students have used the reasoning process of induction since they were children and that everyone makes generalizations based on what he or she has observed or experienced.

Next, read through the remainder of the section and guide students through the first topic in the **Critical Thinking Exercise.** Divide students into small groups and assign the second topic as independent practice. You can use students' responses to assess their understanding of induction. You may want to require that each group turn in a list of kinds of research and sources, or you may want to have each group present its suggestions during a class discussion. At the conclusion of the exercise, ask students to write, in

INTEGRATING THE LANGUAGE ARTS

Literature Link. You may want to tell students that induction is often used in studying and analyzing works of literature. By using induction, readers may be able to make generalizations about an author or about a period, for example. To give students practice in using induction to study literature, assign several poems by the same author, such as Carl Sandburg or Robert Frost. Then ask students what generalizations they can make about the author based on the style or content of the poems. Tell students that they could read other poems by the same author to see if the generalizations continue to apply.

hours or more per week. The data you gather and your subsequent generalization could look something like this.

> Marna's grade average dropped from A– to B–.
> Joe's grade average dropped in everything but math.
> Lucy's grade average went from B to C; her grades rose again when she quit the job.
> *Generalization:* Students' taking jobs of twenty hours or more per week causes grades to drop.

How can you tell if the generalization you make (your conclusion) is valid? The validity depends partly on the population you are generalizing about. If you're generalizing about everyone in the United States, you obviously need to do more research than interview a few friends. A *mixture* of research is usually best: personal observations, published statistics, and opinions of authorities. To reach a sound conclusion for the example you've just read, you would need to interview a large sampling of students, interview teachers and counselors, and read magazine articles about national trends.

their own words, one-paragraph explanations of induction.

Here are three key questions to ask yourself when you want to test the validity of your conclusion.

How much evidence supports my generalization?
Is the source of the evidence trustworthy?
Does all the evidence lead to the same generalization?

CRITICAL THINKING EXERCISE:
Analyzing the Validity of a Generalization

Read the inductions below with two or three classmates. Determine together what kind of research is needed to make each generalization valid. Suggest sources for gathering the necessary data.

1. *Topic: The effects of a high-sugar breakfast*
   When I have only a doughnut for breakfast, I feel a "letdown" by 10 A.M. It's hard for me to concentrate on my school work. Tina says she feels the same way.
   Generalization: A sugary breakfast interferes with learning.
2. *Topic: The effects of dropping out of high school on a person's earning ability*
   David dropped out of high school and got a low-paying job. Margie dropped out and went on welfare.
   Generalization: Dropping out of high school lessens the chance of making a good income.

REFERENCE NOTE: For information about deduction, see page 401.

WRITING ASSIGNMENT

PART 4:
Writing a Draft of Your Explanation

Finally, with much good work behind you, it's time to write a rough draft of your cause-and-effect explanation. Start wherever you want; but before you finish your draft, write an introduction, the body, and a conclusion. Then put your draft aside so you can come back to it later.

ANSWERS
Critical Thinking Exercise

Responses will vary. Here are some possible responses:

1. Research: personal observations, published statistics, opinions of authorities. Sources: friends and relatives, scientific journals, newspaper and magazine reports, interviews with health professionals
2. Research: personal observations, published statistics, opinions of authorities. Sources: friends, relatives, workers in the community, government wage and earnings reports, interviews with job counselors

SEGMENT 5 *(pp. 266–268)*

EVALUATING AND REVISING

OBJECTIVES

- To analyze the revision of a paragraph from a model essay
- To evaluate and revise a cause-and-effect essay

TEACHING THE LESSON

Ask students what any reputable craftsperson or artist does after completing a project. [He or she checks over the project to see if any changes need to be made that would make the project better.] Similarly, students should check over their first drafts to see if they can make their drafts better.

Teacher's ResourceBank™

RESOURCES

EVALUATING AND REVISING

- Writing a Cause-and-Effect Essay 62

QUOTATION FOR THE DAY

"To be more objective as I reread, I have to let some time pass, so that I won't anticipate what the next sentence is going to be." (Colleen McElroy, 1935– , African American poet)

Ask students to discuss the quotation in terms of their personal writing habits. Is such a waiting period helpful to them?

ANSWERS

Exercise 3

1. The addition is more specific and more clearly supports the thesis.
2. The addition provides more evidence for the position taken in the first sentence—it is another expense.
3. The change puts the information in chronological order and clarifies the cause-and-effect sequence.
4. The writer deleted the last sentence because evidence in the paragraph doesn't support the generalization.

Evaluating and Revising

After you finish drafting your essay, push it from your mind for a while. Then when you've cleared your mind a bit, you can use the chart on the following page to pinpoint the strengths and weaknesses in your first draft. Ask yourself each question in the left-hand column, and use the revision techniques in the right-hand column to solve any problems you discover.

EXERCISE 3 **Analyzing a Writer's Revisions**

Before you revise your own essay, take time to study another writer's revision efforts. Here's the revision of the fourth paragraph in the essay on pages 260–262. Use the questions that follow to help you analyze the changes that were made.

Owning a car costs money—in ways
~~There are things~~ you don't appreciate as a passenger. — **replace**
insurance for teenagers is expensive,
Gasoline isn't free, and maintenance (not to mention repairs) drains finances. — **add**
To meet car expenses, I had to work more hours, which meant less free time. Unfortunately, I responded to that situation by studying less, which in turn put my car keys in my parents' pockets for six weeks.
which caused
~~I had~~ one term of very bad grades. — **replace/reorder**
~~No teenager can afford a car.~~ — **cut**

1. Why did the writer replace *There are things* with *Owning a car costs money—in ways* in the first sentence?
2. Why did the writer add the additional information to the second sentence? What does it tell the reader?
3. Why did the writer move the information about bad grades to the previous sentence?
4. Why did the writer delete the last sentence? [Hint: See the information on inductive thinking, pages 263–265.]

Review carefully the **Evaluating and Revising Cause-and-Effect Explanations** chart. Explain to students that the information in the **Grammar Hint** on p. 268 could be used as a revision technique for the sixth evaluation question in the chart.

Guide students in the analysis of the revisions in **Exercise 3** and then assign **Writing Assignment: Part 5** on p. 268 as independent practice. If your circumstances permit, provide ample time for peer evaluation. Positive criticisms, encouragement, and other responses from peers may be helpful and instructive for student writers.

EVALUATING AND REVISING CAUSE-AND-EFFECT EXPLANATIONS

	EVALUATION GUIDE	REVISION TECHNIQUE
1	Does the introduction capture the reader's attention?	**Add** an anecdote or interesting details.
2	Does the introduction clearly present the event or situation to be discussed?	**Add** information (or **replace** an existing sentence) that clearly indicates the topic.
3	Does the introduction establish the focus of the essay: causes, effects, or both?	**Add** a sentence that states the thesis of the essay.
4	Does the essay provide a sufficiently complete answer to at least one of these questions: What are the causes? What are the effects?	Do more research to find additional causes or effects. **Add** them to the essay.
5	Is evidence given to show that the explanation is sound?	**Add** examples, statistics, and quotes that support the explanation.
6	Is the essay organized in a clear, easy-to-read way?	**Rearrange** causes or effects in order of importance or chronological order. Present causes before effects.
7	Does the conclusion bring the essay to a satisfying end?	**Add** a brief summary of the explanation. **Add** a thought-provoking comment about the future.

MEETING **INDIVIDUAL** NEEDS

ADVANCED STUDENTS

Students might be interested in learning how professional writers revise their works. Many libraries carry biographies of famous authors that show writers' works in various stages. Ask students to write informative paragraphs on their findings and to present them to the class.

A DIFFERENT APPROACH

To give students practice in adding anecdotes or interesting details to introductions, give them copies of brief newspaper or magazine articles with informative but ordinary introductions. Ask students to add attention-grabbing details based on the information given in the articles. Students could read their introductions to the class. After all introductions have been presented, students could vote on the best ones.

ASSESSMENT

Use students' responses to **Exercise 3** and the revisions of their first drafts to assess their understanding and application of the evaluation and revision stage of the writing process.

CLOSURE

Ask students to share some of the revisions they made to their cause-and-effect explanations. ■

GRAMMAR HINT

Subordinate Clauses

In a cause-and-effect essay, you want to show clearly the relationships between ideas. What's the cause? What's the effect? Subordinate conjunctions, which introduce subordinate clauses, can help you do this if you are careful to choose conjunctions that make relationships clear. Examples of conjunctions that show *cause* are *because, as, since, whereas*. Conjunctions that show *effects*, or results, include *that, in order that, so that*.

You may find yourself using the word *and* to connect clauses, when more specific conjunctions would work better. If so, replace *and* (or other unclear conjunctions) with words or phrases that clarify the causes and effects.

CONFUSING The crop failed and there was a drought.
CLEAR The crop failed **because** there was a drought.

CONFUSING Owning a car costs so much money, and I had to work.
CLEAR Owning a car costs so much money **that** I had to work.

REFERENCE NOTE: For more information about subordinate clauses, see pages 629–637.

WRITING ASSIGNMENT

PART 5:
Evaluating and Revising Your Cause-and-Effect Essay

Put your essay aside for at least a day. Next, reread your paper and use the evaluating and revising chart on page 267 to decide what changes will improve it. Mark passages that seem thin, and jot down ideas you would like to add. Then, exchange papers with another student and use the chart to evaluate each other's essays. Carefully consider your partner's comments as well as your own evaluation. Finally, make the changes on either your hard copy or your word processor.

TIMESAVER

Encourage competent student writers to help students who need guidance in revising their first drafts. You could check the completed revisions.

SEGMENT 6 *(p. 269)*

PROOFREADING AND PUBLISHING

OBJECTIVES

- To use proofreading strategies to prepare a cause-and-effect essay for publication
- To share an essay with an audience

TEACHING THE LESSON

You may want to make copies of an anonymous cause-and-effect explanation and to use it to guide students through the proofreading stage. If peer proofreading seems appropriate, students could share their essays before making final copies. ■

Proofreading and Publishing

Proofreading. Most cause-and-effect essays have technical or difficult words you don't often use. Check your sources again to make sure you spelled all these words correctly, including the names of people you have quoted. Then proofread your entire essay once again, making a final check for spelling, grammar, and punctuation. Use any proofing method that works for you—one that helps you slow down and concentrate in order to find errors. Some writers proofread one line at a time, keeping other lines covered.

Publishing. You wrote with real readers in mind, and now is the time to send your work out to them. Try to share your essay with at least two people other than your teacher, perhaps using one of the following suggestions.

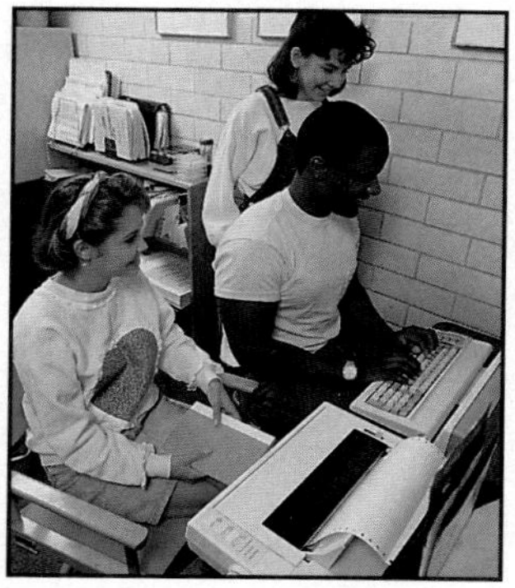

- Send your essay to people who are personally involved or interested in your topic. If your essay deals with a community event, send it to the newspaper as a letter to the editor. If it deals with a school event, submit it as an article for your school newspaper. If you wrote about a subject such as history or science, share it with a teacher who specializes in that subject.
- Have a class-wide essay swap. Post a sheet in the classroom that lists the titles of all the essays. Each classmate can find the topic that interests him or her most and sign up to read it.

WRITING ASSIGNMENT

PART 6:
Proofreading and Publishing Your Essay

Proofread your paper with care, and correct any errors you find. Then let others read your work.

Teacher's ResourceBank™

RESOURCES

PROOFREADING AND PUBLISHING

- Writing a Cause-and-Effect Essay 63

QUOTATION FOR THE DAY

"Proofreading is like the quality-control stage at the end of an assembly line." (John R. Trimble, American writer and teacher)

Write this quotation on the chalkboard and ask students to freewrite about its meaning.

MEETING INDIVIDUAL NEEDS

LEP/ESL

General Strategies. You may want to have peer tutors help LEP/ESL students with proofreading. As students proofread together, ask them to note the areas in which most errors occur. If at all possible, provide students with further explanation and extra practice in those particular areas. After the proofreading process is completed, have students answer the following question: What are three things I really like about my essay? This exercise leaves them with a positive view of their writing efforts.

SEGMENT 7 *(pp. 270–272)*

WRITING WORKSHOP

OBJECTIVES

- To analyze the content and organization of a model process explanation essay
- To critique the clarity of a model process explanation essay
- To write a process analysis

TEACHING THE LESSON

Begin by showing students some intriguing and perhaps amusing headlines for "how" and "how-to" articles from newspapers and magazines. Include a variety of publications, from sensational tabloids to literary magazines. Students may want to tell about other "how" and "how-to" articles that they've read. Lead the class in a

QUOTATION FOR THE DAY

"In a very real sense, the writer writes in order to teach himself." (Alfred Kazin, 1915–   , literary critic)

Tell students that as they explain a process, they will probably learn more about it. Explain that in teaching others, one also makes discoveries.

USING THE SELECTION

Once Is Not Enough

1

How does the introduction grab the reader's attention? [It gives descriptive details of an interesting subject.]

2

frame: a single photograph from a strip of film

WRITING WORKSHOP

A Process Explanation

While the cause-and-effect essay that you wrote earlier in this chapter explains *why*, writing that examines a process explains *how* or *how to*. You don't have to look far to find examples of process explanations. Just take a glance at any magazine stand and you'll see titles like these: "How Your VCR Works," "How Ad Agents Find New Talent," "How to Lose Weight Quickly and Forever," "What to Do When Your Friends Give You the Silent Treatment," and "How to Be Your Own Car Mechanic."

Each of these articles is an example of a process analysis. As the term implies, this type of writing breaks down a process and explains each step. Process analyses fall into two basic types: the "how," which simply tells how the process works or happens; and the "how-to," which tells how *you* can make the process work or happen.

This essay explains the process of one special effect used in the movies. To most people it's a "how-it-works" essay, but if you are an amateur filmmaker, it could be a "how-to" guide.

Once Is Not Enough

by Jane O'Connor and Katy Hall

1 Late-night TV movies abound with ghosts—those semitransparent figures that may appear out of nowhere (thanks to stop-motion photography), walk through a few closed doors, and then, just as suddenly, disappear. Often these spirits are the result of an optical trick called *double exposure.*

To make a ghost walk right through a cemetery wall, from one side to the other, a camera is set up so that both sides of the wall are visible. The cameraman then exposes, say, twenty feet of film of just
2 this wall. (Film is talked about in *feet* rather than frames when so much film is used that it would be awkward to talk about a huge number of frames. There are 16 frames to one foot of movie film.)

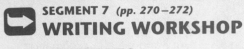

discussion of the widespread appeal of "how" and "how-to" articles.

Next, introduce the model essay as an example of a process explanation. You may want to read the essay aloud or to ask a student interested in movies to read the essay aloud. Then use the questions as a basis for discussion. As you give students the assignment to write their own process explanations, stress that their topics should be ones about which they are enthusiastic.

Bob Hope in *The Ghost Breaker.* (1940)

3 Now the cameraman winds the twenty feet of film *backward* in the camera. There is a footage counter on the camera so that he knows just how far to rewind the film. The same twenty feet of film are now ready to be exposed *again.* The camera is taken to another set at this point and the actor playing the ghost is filmed—on the same twenty feet of film—simply walking across the set. Now the twenty feet of film has been exposed to light two different times. It has been *double exposed.*

The scene that was filmed first—the cemetery wall—"burned" its image onto the film and, on screen, it will appear as a solid image. The scene that was filmed second—the walking ghost—was photographed with
4 the camera's iris closed down, letting less light into the camera, and so the image is fainter,
5 and appears translucent on the screen—just the way a ghost should look.

from *Magic in the Movies*

1. What optical trick are the authors explaining? How do they catch your interest and make you curious to read on?
2. The basic organization for a process essay is chronological order, giving the steps in the order of occurrence. Why do you suppose the "closing the iris" event is explained at the end of the essay, not when it happens?
3. Could you now explain this special effect to someone else, or do you still have questions? "Grade" this essay on its clarity, giving specific examples.

3

Note the use of transitions such as *now, again, at this point, first,* and *second.*

4

How is a camera's iris like the iris of a human eye? [The iris is in front of the pupil. The size of its opening changes, thus controlling the amount of light to the pupil.] What does the iris do in bright light? [It closes down to let in less light.] In dim light? [It widens to let in more light.]

5

translucent: partially transparent, as frosted glass

ANSWERS

Writing Workshop Questions

Responses may vary.

1. They are explaining double exposure. The subject of ghosts is attention-getting.
2. The second paragraph gives a chronological explanation of what a cameraman and an actor do to create the appearance of a ghost walking through a wall. Defining "iris" in this paragraph probably would have interrupted the flow.
3. "Grades" and examples will vary. Some students might ask for a definition of stop-motion photography and an explanation of how other things on the set fail to show up on film.

SELECTION AMENDMENT

Description of change: excerpted
Rationale: to focus on the concept of a process explanation presented in this chapter

ASSESSMENT

Use students' completed essays to assess their understanding of writing "how-to" explanations.

CLOSURE

Ask volunteers to identify and explain the two basic types of process explanations ["how," which tells how a process works or happens; "how-to," which tells how to make a process work or happen]. ■

MEETING **INDIVIDUAL** NEEDS

LEARNING STYLES

Visual and Kinetic Learners. An organizational strategy that may be helpful to some students is to make charts and drawings as they think through the steps of the processes they will be explaining. Then students can use these drawings to help them make their prewriting notes and lists.

Auditory Learners. Before students begin writing, you may want to pair them and let them discuss their topics with partners. Instruct the partners to take turns briefly explaining their chosen processes and outlining the steps in the processes. After these oral reviews, students should begin writing their essays.

INTEGRATING THE LANGUAGE ARTS

Technology Link. As pictures and diagrams generally help clarify "how-to" explanations, suggest that students develop graphics to enhance their essays.

Writing a Process Analysis

Prewriting. What process are you curious about or expert in? Would you like to know how to copyright a song or how a facsimile (fax) machine works? Can you explain how to format columns on a computer (better than your badly written manual) or how a bill becomes a law? Choose a process that you can explain with enthusiasm, and start analyzing it. Make notes on terms, equipment, or materials that readers will need to know or have; and then list the steps of the process.

Writing, Evaluating, and Revising. As always, draft an attention-grabbing opening, and then be sure to give readers any "advance" information they need—ingredients, tools, technical definitions, scientific principles—before launching into steps. Generally, a process essay is organized chronologically. Use transitional expressions to keep order clear: *first, now, next, at the same time,* and so on.

When you've finished, have others read your essay and mark any passage that "lost" them or seemed out of place. You or others can test a "how-to" essay by performing the process (or pretending to). Make any revisions that will make the process clearer.

Proofreading and Publishing. It's important to proofread carefully because errors in punctuation or grammar can confuse or frustrate readers who are trying to understand the process you are explaining. After you have finished proofreading and correcting errors, you should be able to find a real audience—a receptive one—for your essay. Practical how-to explanations and clear breakdowns of intriguing processes attract readers. For example, you might send instructions for making tortillas to the newspaper's food editor or give a speech to a local nature club explaining how certain species of hummingbirds "hibernate."

SEGMENT 8 *(pp. 273–275)*

MAKING CONNECTIONS

TEST TAKING OBJECTIVE

- To write an answer for an essay question by describing causes of a historical event

MAKING CONNECTIONS

TEST TAKING

Cause-and-Effect Essay Questions

When taking history or social studies tests, you will often face essay questions that ask you to explain causes and effects. The skills you have learned in this chapter will help you when that kind of question appears. Just write a shorter version of what you did in your essay—a clear, logical explanation of causes, effects, or both. Back up your main ideas with evidence—specific facts or examples.

Below is a typical essay question that might appear on a social studies test. Answer it in a paragraph or two by using the information that's provided. Simply describe the causes, and provide any backup data that you think is necessary.

Question: How were only 1,000 Spanish troops able to overthrow millions of Aztecs in Mexico in 1521? Describe the causes.

CAUSES

- The Spanish had superior weapons the Aztecs had not seen.
- Aztecs, unprepared for threat, welcomed Spanish at first.
- The Spanish attacked the Aztecs' capital city.
- Smallpox brought by the Spanish caused many deaths the Aztecs could not explain or prevent.
- Enemies of the Aztecs aided the Spanish.

EVIDENCE

- Spanish battle equipment: guns, cannons, horses, armor. Aztecs: none of these.
- Aztec's capital city, Tenochtitlan (now Mexico City). Population: 100,000. Center of Aztec civilization and government. A strategic target.

(continued)

TEST TAKING

Teaching Strategies

Point out to students that most of them undoubtedly have encountered cause-and-effect essay questions on tests in a variety of subjects, including science and literature. Have students name some cause-and-effect essays they've written.

You may want to remind students to begin their essays by turning the question into a statement to use as a thesis statement. They could also add a summation of causes to the statement. The body of the essays should describe the causes.

EXPLAINING THROUGH DESCRIPTION
OBJECTIVE

- To write one or two paragraphs explaining a topic by describing it in detail

GUIDELINES

You may want to replicate a testing situation by using the activity as a timed assignment. Essays will vary, but each should have an introduction that restates the question; all causes should have appropriate backup evidence; and the conclusion should comment on the significance of the event.

EXPLAINING THROUGH DESCRIPTION
Teaching Strategies

You may want to read the model essay aloud and then discuss its visual details. Point out to students that the expository writer aims for objectivity.

Before students write their paragraphs, give them time to brainstorm some topics, either as a class, in groups, or individually. You could suggest that students make lists of some details about their topics before beginning to write.

EVIDENCE *(continued)*

- After Montezuma II, supreme ruler of Aztecs, was killed, his replacement died of smallpox.
- Thousands of people whom the Aztecs had previously conquered joined the Spanish and actually saved their lives in an important battle, *la noche triste* (the sad night).

The Bettmann Archive

EXPLAINING THROUGH DESCRIPTION

Causal and process analyses are narrative strategies, but you can also use the strategy of description to explain. In descriptive writing, you explain a topic by describing its physical qualities—how it looks, feels, sounds, moves, smells, or tastes. Because your purpose is *to explain,* you need to supply accurate information. Since you're using the strategy of *description,* you need images that appeal to the senses.

The following essay describes the courtship rituals of various birds. Notice how the writer *explains* what's involved in the rituals by *describing* in detail what goes on. While other descriptions may use a variety of sensory details, this essay focuses on visual and sound details.

from The Birder's Handbook
by Paul R. Ehrlich, David S. Dobkin, and Darryl Wheye

1 Often courtship displays accent a striking feature of the bird's plumage. The conspicuous, labored flight displays of the male Red-winged Blackbird exaggerate its red shoulder patches. The display flight of the male Yellow-headed Blackbird is performed with the body cocked upward so that its prominent yellow head is held high.

On the other hand, some male birds do not advertise with physical attributes; they demonstrate skills. Male terns court females by displaying a fresh-caught fish. Courting male European Gray Herons perform ritualized hunting movements, erecting head feathers,
2 pointing their bills downward and clashing their mandibles together. Many male passerines [birds that perch], when courting, also lower
3 their bills as if pecking at something below them. Perhaps, next to singing, the most common component of courtship displays in male songbirds is vibration of the wings; other components include fluffing of the body feathers, bill raising, thrusting the head forward, and running using short steps.

Write one or two paragraphs of your own that explain something by describing it in accurate detail. Pick any topic that you know well. You could explain the characteristics of a kind of flower or fish, the features of an electric guitar, the movements of an aerobics class, a performance you've seen of your favorite musician, or a custom or lifestyle difference you noticed while traveling. Remember that your purpose is to explain through the use of description.

USING THE SELECTION
from The Birder's Handbook

1

The first sentence states the topic—a description of birds' courtship displays.

2

mandibles: jaws

3

Most descriptions include the unique aspects of the things being described, as well as the aspects that are common to many other things.

GUIDELINES

Students should focus on limited topics, appropriate for one or two paragraphs. You may want to evaluate students' objectivity and use of specific details.

SELECTION AMENDMENT

Description of change: excerpted and modified
Rationale: to focus on the concept of description presented in this chapter

Chapter 8

WRITING TO PERSUADE

OBJECTIVES

- To analyze the characteristics of persuasion
- To choose a topic for a persuasive essay and to write a statement of opinion about the topic
- To analyze the audience of a persuasive essay
- To develop support for an opinion statement
- To organize and draft a persuasive essay
- To evaluate and revise a draft of a persuasive essay
- To proofread and publish a persuasive essay
- To compose a persuasive speech
- To analyze and create political cartoons
- To present a media analysis of an advertisement
- To write a letter to the editor

Motivation

To interest students in the chapter, bring several examples of persuasion to class: advertisements from newspapers or magazines; cartoons, columns, and letters to the editor from publications; or handbills from local businesses. You might include a plea for a favor from one friend to another or from a child to a parent. Have students decide what the examples have in common.

Introduction

Allow students to discuss their experiences in being persuaded and in persuading others and help students understand that persuasion is the art of convincing others. Lead students to understand that persuasion involves an appeal to the emotions of the audience, an appeal to the rational nature of the audience, or an appeal based on the personality of the persuader.

To distinguish the persuasive aim from other aims of discourse, the class might discuss how a writer would treat topics such as high school football, landfills, elephants, and situation comedies if the writer's purpose were persuasive. Then students could compare these treatments to informative, expressive, or creative methods. Ask students to list reasons that understanding the persuasive aim could be important in daily living. With this introduction, students should be prepared to begin the chapter.

Integration

This chapter can serve as a resource for other activities in your classroom. For example, if your class is studying persuasive speeches and essays of historical figures such as Patrick Henry, Thomas Paine, or Thomas Jefferson you could use the chapter opener and **Evaluating and Revising Persuasive Essays** to assist students in analyzing these discourses. If you are teaching a critical-thinking unit, you may want to incorporate the **Critical Thinking Exercise** to help students better understand the nature of fallacies.

If you assign persuasive speeches, you might use the prewriting exercises to assist students in finding appropriate topics. The **Writing Workshop** provides students with information about writing a speech. The **Framework for a Persuasive Essay** can be used as a guide for almost any writing or speaking assignment that requires persuasion, and the questions in the **Evaluating and Revising Persuasive Essays** may be adapted for use in evaluating speeches.

The chart on the next page illustrates the strands of the language arts curriculum as they are integrated into this chapter. For vocabulary study, glossary words are underlined in some of the writing models.

QUOTATIONS
All **Quotations for the Day** are chosen because of their relevance to instructional material presented in that segment of the chapter and for their usefulness in establishing student interest in writing.

INTEGRATING THE LANGUAGE ARTS

Selection	Reading and Literature	Writing and Critical Thinking	Language and Syntax	Speaking, Listening, and Other Expression Skills
from **"An Indian's View of Indian Affairs"** by Chief Joseph **278-280** **"Keep 'The Star-Spangled Banner'"** by Vicki Williams **294-295** **"Replace 'The Star-Spangled Banner'"** by Andy Jacobs, Jr. **295-297** **"Keep Your Eyes on the Prize"** by Jesse Jackson **311-312**	Responding personally to literature **281, 297-298, 312** Identifying supporting evidence **281, 297-298, 312** Understanding opposing positions **281, 297-298** Analyzing emotional appeal **281, 312** Evaluating persuasive appeal **297-298, 312** Analyzing style **312**	Applying interpretive and creative thinking **281, 285, 297-298, 301, 312-313, 315, 316** Identifying supporting evidence **281, 292, 297-298, 312** Brainstorming **285, 286, 292, 298** Stating a position **286, 297-298, 312-313** Evaluating position statements **286, 292, 297-298, 312** Choosing a topic **286, 312-313** Identifying an audience **287** Making inferences and drawing conclusions **287, 292, 297-298, 305, 312, 316** Supporting an opinion **292, 305, 312-313** Analyzing the organization of a persuasive essay **297-298, 311-312** Writing a draft of a persuasive essay **301** Evaluating reasoning **305, 312, 316** Analyzing a writer's revisions **307** Evaluating and revising **307, 309, 313** Proofreading and publishing **310, 313** Writing a persuasive speech by using the writing process **312-313** Analyzing advertisements for logical and emotional appeals **316** Writing a letter to the editor **317**	Identifying loaded words and contrasting them with neutral words **281** Proofreading for errors in grammar, usage, and mechanics **310, 312-313** Varying sentence patterns **312-313**	Working with classmates to explore issues **285, 286, 292** Making a chart to organize information **287, 292** Working with classmates to analyze rebuttals **292** Working with classmates to evaluate a persuasive essay **297-298, 309** Creating a political cartoon **315** Working with classmates to analyze political cartoons **315** Giving a persuasive speech **316**

CHAPTER 8

SEGMENT PLANNING GUIDE

You can use the following Planning Guide to adapt the chapter material to the individual needs of your class. All the Resources listed in this chapter are located in the *Teacher's ResourceBank*™.

SEGMENT	PAGES	CONTENT	RESOURCES
1 *Taking a Stand*	*277-281*		
Literary Model **"An Indian's View of Indian Affairs"**	278-280	Guided reading: a literary model of persuasive writing	
Reader's Response/ Writer's Craft	281	Model evaluation: responding to literature and analyzing persuasive writing	
2 *Ways to Persuade*	*282*		
3 *Prewriting*	*283-292*		Writing a Persuasive Essay Listing Reasons and Evidence 66
Focusing on an Issue	283-285	Guidelines: selecting a suitable topic and developing a position statement	
Exercise 1	285	Cooperative learning: brainstorming ideas	
Exercise 2	286	Cooperative learning: evaluating position statements	
Writing Assignment: Part 1	286	Applied practice: choosing an issue to write about	
Thinking About Purpose, Audience, and Tone	286-287	Guidelines: analyzing and selecting appropriate purpose, audience, and tone	
Writing Assignment: Part 2	287	Applied practice: identifying an audience	
Supporting Your Opinion	288-290	Guidelines: using logical, emotional, and ethical appeals	
Identifying Opposing Positions	290-292	Guidelines: designing a rebuttal	
Writing Assignment: Part 3	292	Applied practice: gathering and organizing support	
Exercise 3	292	Cooperative learning: refining a rebuttal	
4 *Writing*	*293-301*		Writing a Persuasive Essay 67
Writing Your First Draft	293	Guidelines: combining basic elements effectively	
Literary Models **"Keep 'The Star-Spangled Banner'"** and **"Replace 'The Star-Spangled Banner'"**	294-297	Guided reading: examining evidence and appeals in models	
Exercise 4	297-298	Cooperative learning: analyzing persuasive elements	
A Writer's Model	298-300	Guided reading: examining a sample persuasive essay	
Chart: A Basic Framework	301	Guidelines: structuring a persuasive essay	
Writing Assignment: Part 4	301	Applied practice: writing a first draft	

For **Portfolio Assessment** see the following pages in the *Teacher's ResourceBank*™:
Aims For Writing — pp. 65–70
Holistically Graded Composition Models — pp. 509–514
Assessment Portfolio — pp. 533–562

	SEGMENT	PAGES	CONTENT	RESOURCES
5	*Evaluating and Revising*	*302-309*		Writing a Persuasive Essay 68
	Evaluating and Revising	302	Explanation: evaluating the logic of a persuasive essay	
	Critical Thinking: Evaluating Your Reasoning	302-305	Guidelines: analyzing examples of fallacies	
	Critical Thinking Exercise	305	Applied practice: identifying and replacing fallacies	
	Chart: Evaluating and Revising	306	Guidelines: applying evaluation and revision techniques	
	Exercise 5	307	Applied practice: analyzing a writer's revisions	
	Exercise 6	307-308	Cooperative learning: evaluating and revising	
	Grammar Hint	308-309	Writing suggestion: varying sentence structure	
	Writing Assignment: Part 5	309	Applied practice: evaluating and revising	
6	*Proofreading and Publishing*	*310*		Writing a Persuasive Essay 69
	Publishing	310	Publishing ideas: reaching a specific audience	
	Writing Assignment: Part 6	310	Applied practice: proofreading and publishing	
7	*Writing Workshop*	*311-313*		
	A Persuasive Speech	311	Explanation: understanding oral persuasion	
	Literary Model/Questions **"Keep Your Eyes on the Prize"**	311-312	Guided reading: analyzing persuasive techniques	
	Writing a Speech	312-313	Applied practice: applying skills to the writing process	
8	*Making Connections*	*314-317*		
	Persuasion Across the Curriculum: Political Cartoons	314-315	Guidelines: making a cartoon Applied practice: expressing an opinion in a cartoon	
	Speaking and Listening: Persuasion in the Media	315-316	Guidelines: analyzing persuasive techniques Applied practice: reporting on media appeals	
	Persuasion in Action: Letters to the Editor	317	Guidelines: writing a letter to the editor Applied practice: writing a letter to the editor	

WHOLE-CHAPTER RESOURCES
A Writing Process Log, A Writing Prompt, Holistically Graded Models, Assessment Portfolio Materials

SEGMENT 1 *(pp. 276–281)*

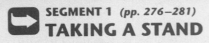

TAKING A STAND

OBJECTIVES

- To respond personally to literature
- To identify and analyze the characteristics of a persuasive essay
- To evaluate the persuasive qualities of an essay

MOTIVATION

You might begin this chapter by having students research the derivation of the word *persuasion* in an etymological dictionary. Students could discover that *suave* and *persuade* have similar word roots. Then have students discuss how it is suave to sway someone to your way of thinking.

VISUAL CONNECTIONS

Exploring the Subject. You might want to discuss this poster, an admonition against driving while intoxicated, with the class. You could point out that the message it expresses is conveyed not only through a direct statement, "Don't mix 'em," but also through the use of images that imply messages. Have students give a one-sentence summary of the poster's message. Then have students determine what elements of the poster make it effective and contribute to the message.

Explain that in this chapter students will learn how writers can also present images with implied messages by skillfully manipulating words.

8 Writing to Persuade

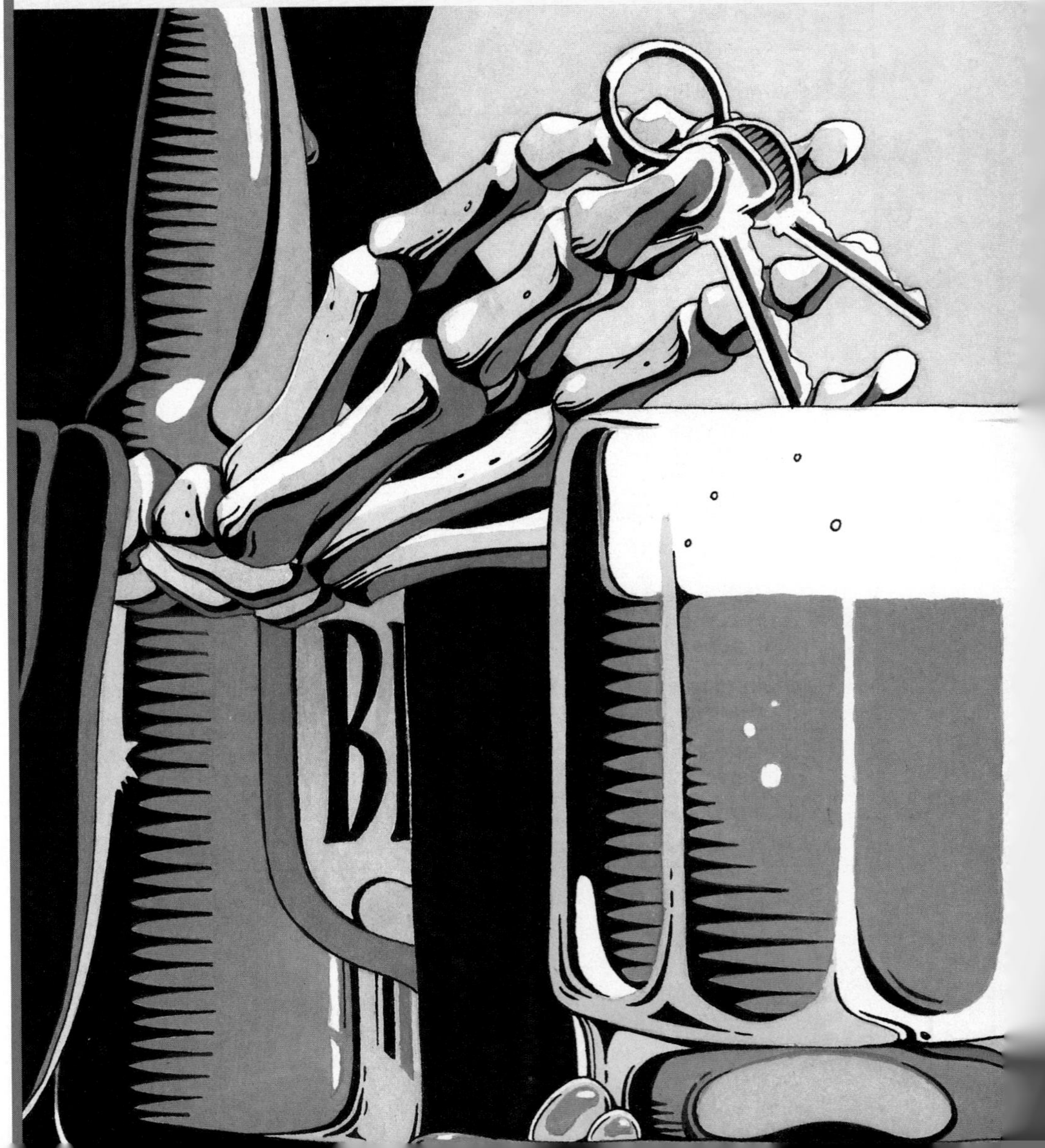

TEACHING THE LESSON

Begin the lesson by reading aloud the first paragraph of **Taking a Stand.** Give students opportunities to respond to the questions either by freewriting or discussion. Then have a volunteer read the remainder of the introduction.

Students will probably benefit from hearing Chief Joseph's speech read aloud. Refer to the history of the speech in **As You Read** before you begin, and have a student volunteer read the speech with the audience Chief Joseph intended in mind. Use the annotations to guide your discussion of the selection and to point out the persuasive qualities of the speech.

Before you assign the **Reader's Response** and **Writer's Craft** questions, ☛

Taking a Stand

Wouldn't life be boring if everybody agreed on everything all the time? Where would new ideas come from? What incentive would we have to take risks? How would we ever make progress if everyone was afraid to **take a stand**?

Writing and You. When we want to change someone's mind about something or convince others to take action, we have to take a stand. Advertisers take a stand when they persuade you to buy CDs, jeans, and cereal. You take a stand for your own qualifications when you apply for a job. Politicians take a stand when they want a new law passed or defeated. Have you ever admired someone who took a stand—and won?

As You Read. Two years after the 1877 surrender of the Nez Perce to the United States Army, Chief Joseph's views of Native American life were published in a magazine. As you read the following selection, notice how he combines reason with emotional appeal to persuade whites to view Native Americans differently.

QUOTATION FOR THE DAY

"The beginning of thought is in disagreement—not only with others but also with ourselves." (Eric Hoffer, 1902–1983, American longshoreman and philosopher)

Remind students that it is easy to find opinions—they come from parents, school, and society. But Hoffer suggests that real thought begins when people sift through information and experiences and change their opinions. Ask students to freewrite about times when they have changed their minds about something.

MEETING INDIVIDUAL NEEDS

LEP/ESL

General Strategies. Students who are new to the United States may be unfamiliar with how westward movement of European settlers affected Native Americans. Some may have stereotypical views of the early West from movies or TV. You might explain the background of the Nez Perce War and how Chief Joseph's persuasive writing came to be published. Two excellent references are *"I Will Fight No More Forever": Chief Joseph and the Nez Perce War* by Merrill D. Beal and *Chief Joseph Country: Land of the Nez Perce* by Bill Gullick.

review some of the characteristics of persuasive writing and have students analyze the model for persuasive qualities. Help the class discover what makes the arguments convincing.

You might also go through a few paragraphs of the essay and list on the chalkboard things that Chief Joseph mentions that you also believe are important, such as good health and a peaceful home.

Use the **Reader's Response** and **Writer's Craft** questions for independent practice. Responses to the questions should help you to assess students' understanding of persuasive writing.

USING THE SELECTION

***from* "An Indian's View of Indian Affairs"**

1
Chief Joseph of the Nez Perce was the son of a chief who converted to Christianity. Educated in mission schools, Chief Joseph wrote this appeal for an audience of white settlers. He appeals for justice because his people have been forced to relocate to Fort Leavenworth, Kansas, where many of his people have died without food or blankets.

2
Even though Chief Joseph is tired of talk and good words that do not amount to anything, he chooses his own words carefully. The "words do not pay for . . ." statements compare words to the death of his people, the loss of a homeland, and the desecration of the land; he carefully blends logical and emotional appeals.

3
To escape military hostilities Chief Joseph, along with two hundred warriors and three times as many women and children, attempted a retreat to Canada. The retreat was halted by General Nelson Miles.

4
Chief Joseph restates his proposition that the talk is nothing but broken promises.

5
What documents that play a major role in United States history express ideas similar to the ones Chief Joseph expresses here? [Answers should include the Declaration of Independence and the Constitution.]

FROM

"An Indian's View of Indian Affairs"

1 **BY CHIEF JOSEPH (IN-MUT-TOO-YAH-LAT-LAT) OF THE NEZ PERCE**

. . . I have heard talk and talk, but nothing is done. Good words do
2 not last long unless they amount to something. Words do not pay for my dead people. They do not pay for my country, now overrun by white men. They do not protect my father's grave. They do not pay for all my horses and cattle. Good words will not give me back my children. Good words will not make good the promise of your War chief
3 General Miles. Good words will not give my people good health and stop them from dying. Good words will not get my people a home where they can live in peace and take care of themselves.

I am tired of talk that comes to nothing. It makes my heart sick
4 when I remember all the good words and all the broken promises. There has been too much talking by men who had no right to talk. Too many misrepresentations have been made, too many misunderstandings have come up between the white men about the Indians.

If the white man wants to live in peace with the Indian he can live
5 in peace. There need be no trouble. Treat all men alike. Give them the same law. Give them an even chance to live and grow. All men were made by the same Great Spirit Chief. They are all brothers. The earth is the mother of all people, and all people should have equal rights upon it.

RETEACHING

Explain to students that because persuasion plays such an important role in life, it is often used by characters in literature, film, and television. Encourage students to identify examples of persuasion they have encountered in reading fiction or watching films or television.

CLOSURE

Discuss the characteristics of persuasion. Then ask students to name occasions when persuasion is useful. You might also have students think of occupations in which persuasive abilities are required.

6 You might as well expect the rivers to run backward as that any man who was born a free man should be contented when penned up and denied liberty to go where he pleases. If you tie a horse to a stake, do you expect he will grow fat? If you pen an Indian up on a small spot of earth, and compel him to stay there, he will not be contented, nor
7 will he grow and prosper. I have asked some of the great white chiefs where they get their authority to say to the Indian that he shall stay in one place, while he sees white men going where they please. They cannot tell me.

"IT MAKES MY HEART SICK WHEN I REMEMBER ALL THE GOOD WORDS AND ALL THE BROKEN PROMISES."

I only ask of the government to be treated as all other men are treated. If I cannot go to my own home, let me have a home in some country where my people will not die so fast. . . .

When I think of our condition my heart is heavy. I see men of my race treated as outlaws and driven from country to country or shot down like animals.

VISUAL CONNECTIONS
Chief Joseph of the Nez Perce

Exploring the Subject. Chief Joseph's pleas were officially ignored, and he was returned to the Oklahoma Indian Territory where he remained for the next six years. Eventually a handful of the Nez Perce were allowed to return to their original reservation in Idaho, but Chief Joseph and most of the rest of his people were moved to the Colville Reservation in Washington, where Chief Joseph eventually died.

6

Chief Joseph uses vivid comparisons from nature to emphasize the unhappiness and unnatural state of his tribe.

7

Chief Joseph uses logical appeal. He argues that the government leaders do not have the right to imprison his people while white men are free and that the leaders must know this is true because they do not respond to his questions.

EXTENSION

Ask students to keep persuasion logs for a day or two. Students could record in their logs examples of persuasion they hear in ordinary conversations in the classroom, the home, the workplace, and so on. Then they could use the logs to evaluate the importance of persuasion in daily life. ■

I know that my race must change. We cannot hold our own with white men as we are. We ask only an even chance to live as other men live. We ask to be recognized as men. We ask that the same law shall work alike on all men. If the Indian breaks the law, punish him by the law. If the white man breaks the law, punish him also.

8 Let me be a free man—free to travel, free to stop, free to work, free to trade where I choose, free to choose my own teachers, free to follow the religion of my fathers, free to think and talk and act for myself—and I will obey every law, or submit to the penalty.

Whenever the white man treats an Indian as they treat each other, then we will have no more wars. We shall all be alike—brothers of one father and one mother, with one mother, with one sky above us and one country around us, and one government for all.
9 Then the Great Spirit Chief who rules above will smile upon this land, and send rain to wash out the bloody spots made by brothers' hands from the face of the earth.

For this time the Indian race are waiting and praying. I hope that no more groans of wounded men and women will ever go to the ear of the Great Spirit Chief above, and that all people may be one people.

"YOU MIGHT AS WELL EXPECT THE RIVERS TO RUN BACKWARD AS THAT ANY MAN WHO WAS BORN A FREE MAN SHOULD BE CONTENTED WHEN PENNED UP AND DENIED LIBERTY TO GO WHERE HE PLEASES."

8

Why might these three paragraphs be considered an emotional appeal? [Answers will vary. Certainly the plight of the Nez Percés would touch all but the hardest hearts.]

9

Chief Joseph uses poignant imagery that seems to indicate the possibility of forgiveness for all who have fought. He points out to readers the benefits of a changed viewpoint.

SELECTION AMENDMENT

Description of change: excerpted and adapted

Rationale: to focus on the concept of persuasion presented in this chapter

Reader's Response

1. Does Chief Joseph convince you that the government had treated the Nez Perce unfairly? If you were a government official listening to this speech, how would you answer Chief Joseph?
2. What values do you share with Chief Joseph? Which of his ideas do you think are still important today?

Writer's Craft

3. What specific support—reasons, facts, and examples—does Chief Joseph give for the idea that his people should be free to go wherever they choose?
4. Find some words and phrases that carry a definite emotional charge. Contrast them with more neutral words that would carry the same basic meaning.
5. Which groups might most strongly object to what Chief Joseph says? What might be their reasons? Has Chief Joseph considered and answered these reasons? Explain.

ANSWERS

Reader's Response

Answers will vary.

1. Many students will find that Chief Joseph presents very convincing proof of unfair treatment of the Nez Percés. Some students will recognize that officials of the time were bound by the policies of the U. S. government operating at the time.
2. Freedom and equality are valued by most students. Most students place strong value on good health, fellowship, a peaceful existence, and respect for the land.

Writer's Craft

3. Chief Joseph relies primarily on two reasons: Human beings should be equal in the eyes of the law, and government does not have the right to determine where people live. His facts include the broken promises and the high mortality rate among his people. The examples he gives of what happens when a free person is penned up are very effective, as are the examples of kinds of freedoms.
4. Students may suggest synonyms for emotionally charged words such as *overrun, brothers,* and *pen* or reword phrases such as "live in peace," "an even chance to live and grow," and "rain to wash out the bloody spots."
5. Settlers interested in claiming Indian lands would probably object to Chief Joseph's words, as would politicians elected by those settlers. However, Chief Joseph only wants the white man to treat the Indian as they treat each other, with no special consideration.

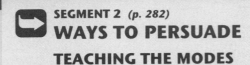

SEGMENT 2 *(p. 282)*

WAYS TO PERSUADE

TEACHING THE MODES

This segment can be used to increase students' awareness of the development options available to them in writing persuasive papers. Have students read **Ways to Persuade** and discuss the differences between the various modes. You might want to include in your discussion several television commercials or magazine advertisements that use different modes to present their sales pitches.

To assess understanding, ask volunteers to suggest other ways that each method might be used in persuasive writing. ■

COOPERATIVE LEARNING

Choose several products or services that you think your class might be interested in, such as portable radios, sneakers, jeans, or fruit juice. Tell the class to imagine that the manufacturers are looking for new advertising campaigns for their products, campaigns that involve four different magazine ads — each emphasizing a different mode.

Ask students to form teams of four and commission each team to come up with a portfolio of four ads to present to one of the manufacturers. You might even consider having teachers or students from another class judge the portfolios.

Ways to Persuade

Like Chief Joseph, writers who persuade want people to change their minds or take action about something. Persuasive writing shows up in speeches, of course, but you also see it in advice columns, advertisements, editorials, sermons, magazine and newspaper articles, and business proposals. Here are some examples showing the basic ways you can develop a persuasive message.

Narration: telling about a narrow escape from a hurricane to convince others to follow evacuation directions; telling about having to help your uncle fix his car to persuade your teacher to let you take the exam later.

Description: describing the dance competitions at a powwow to get some friends to go with you; describing your old watch to persuade a friend to buy it from you.

Classification: comparing two used cars to convince your parents that one of them is a better buy; defining the word *democracy* to convince your audience to vote in the student council election.

Evaluation: evaluating a rap group you heard on the radio to convince your friends that their concert ticket is worth the price; forming an opinion about gun control and writing to the head of the National Rifle Association attacking or supporting its position on the subject.

LOOKING AHEAD

In this chapter, your main writing assignment will be to develop a persuasive essay. Your primary writing and thinking strategy will be evaluation. Keep in mind that persuasive essays

- state the writer's point of view, or opinion, about an important issue
- provide convincing support for the writer's stand, or position
- answer the main opposing positions

SEGMENT 3 *(pp. 283–292)*
PREWRITING

OBJECTIVES

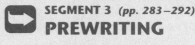

- To generate a list of issues for persuasive essays with a group
- To evaluate position statements with a group
- To choose a topic for a persuasive essay
- To write a position statement
- To identify an audience for a persuasive essay
- To develop and organize support for a position
- To propose opposing arguments and rebuttals for position statements

Writing a Persuasive Essay

Prewriting

Focusing on an Issue

You have strong feelings about many ***issues,*** topics about which people have opposing opinions. Many of these issues would make good topics for a persuasive essay.

Choosing a Specific Issue

Should the same amount of money be spent for boys' and girls' athletic teams in high school? Does the government have the right to censor artists that it helps support? If you ask around, you'll find people who will say yes, as well as people who will say no, to both of these questions. Clearly, these issues spark disagreement; but if they don't spark your interest, they aren't the best choice for you to write about. To find a good topic for your own essay, use these criteria:

- The issue is important to you. You have an opinion about it, or at least a strong interest and curiosity.
- It is a real issue, not just a matter of personal taste. (You may be a football fanatic, but you'll never be able to persuade die-hard baseball fans that football is a better sport.)
- The issue is arguable. People have different opinions about it, and it matters to them.
- There is an audience out there that you would really like to convince.

When you find an issue that meets all of these criteria, you've got a winner.

WRITING NOTE

It's possible to choose an issue because you feel it is important and you want to know more about it. Sometimes you have an opinion that leans to one side of an issue, but you don't yet feel qualified to draw a final conclusion. Gathering information and writing the essay will

Teacher's ResourceBank™
RESOURCES

PREWRITING

QUOTATION FOR THE DAY

"Every man has a right to his opinion, but no man has a right to be wrong in his facts." (Bernard Baruch, 1870–1965, American financier)

Have a few volunteers respond to the quotation and ask students how they can be sure they are right in their facts. Lead the class in discovering that the facts used in persuasive papers must be verifiable through respected sources. Discuss how even the most noble opinion can collapse if an opponent can prove that the facts presented are wrong.

MEETING INDIVIDUAL NEEDS

LEP/ESL

General Strategies. Exploring issues for a persuasive essay may be difficult for ESL students because the process requires language fluency and specific vocabulary. Allow students to brainstorm for ideas and possibly to write their position statements in their native languages. When their ideas and positions are clear, they can carry out **Writing Assignment: Part 1** in English.

MOTIVATION

Have students suggest topics they've heard people argue about recently as you list the topics on the chalkboard. Ask students what topics would make good persuasive essays and place stars by the ones students agree upon. Check the list again after students have read the first page of the segment.

TEACHING THE LESSON

This segment of the chapter engages students in choosing topics and developing position statements. Students will learn to consider tone and purpose in persuading their audiences. Next, they will explore ways to support their position statements. You may want to cover this segment

VISUAL CONNECTIONS

Exploring the Subject. Cubism is an artistic movement popularized in Paris shortly after the turn of the century and associated with Pablo Picasso and Georges Braque. Cubist artists reduce their subject matter to basic geometric forms, ignoring the traditional concerns with perspective and light.

MEETING INDIVIDUAL NEEDS

STUDENTS WITH SPECIAL NEEDS

Pairing one student with a student on the opposing side of a controversial issue may help many students with learning problems. The partnership could help students to verbalize their opposing positions and to develop strategies for organizing their papers logically. In addition, students will be able to assist each other in the research process.

For students with severe difficulties in writing skills, a debate between teams of students may be an alternative method for them to demonstrate an understanding of the art of persuasion.

help you explore your own opinion. By the time you finish, you may have strengthened your original belief or even have changed your opinion. (For more on writing to explore, see Chapter 9, pages 318–357.)

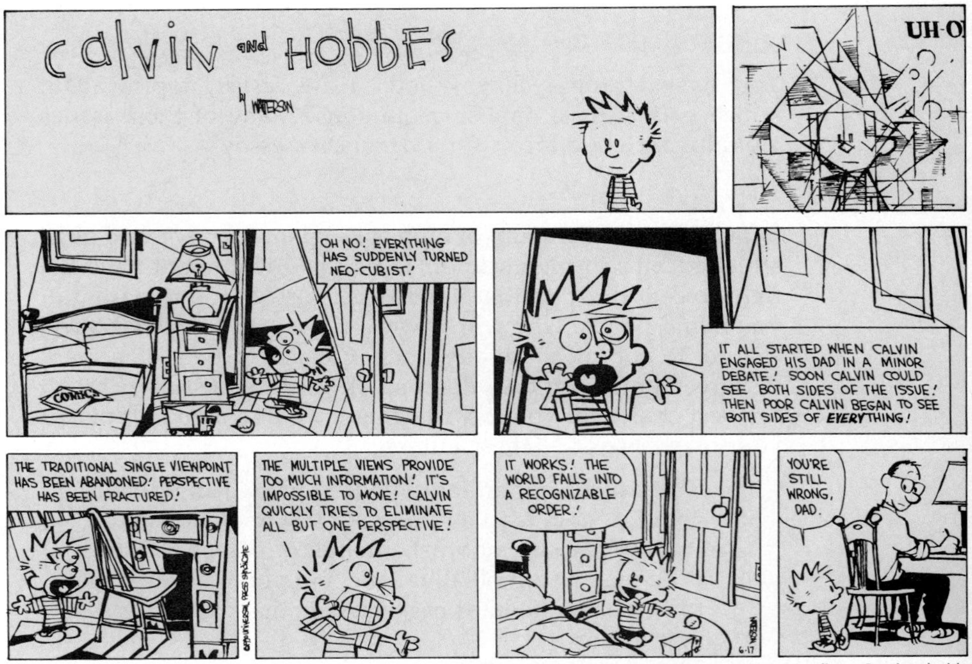

Developing a Position Statement

When you select an issue to write about, you usually know your opinion, or position, on it. For example, you have chosen the issue of the amount of money spent on girls' and boys' sports, and you know which side you are on: You think the amount spent should be equal. In a persuasive essay, this is your position on the issue. As you begin to plan your essay, it's good to state your position, or opinion, in a sentence. This statement of position, often called a ***proposition,*** will help you focus your ideas as you gather support and draft your paper.

over several days so that students will have ample opportunities to internalize the concepts.

As students read and discuss **Focusing on an Issue** on p. 283, have a topic in mind, such as those mentioned in **Choosing a Specific Issue** on the same page. Discuss with students how this topic may or may not be an appropriate issue for a writer by checking it against the bulleted criteria on p. 283. You might use the brainstorming activity in **Exercise 1** as an additional opportunity to work with students in exploring ideas. Let students work in groups to complete the remainder of the activities.

Have students work in small groups on **Exercise 2** on p. 285. When they complete their discussions, have each group report

EXAMPLE POSITION STATEMENTS

Girls should pay their own expenses when they're out with boys on dates.

Serving in the armed forces builds character.

Children up to age ten and pregnant women should receive free medical care.

Foreign language classes in high school should be abolished.

EXERCISE 1 **Exploring Issues**

With a group, use the following idea starters to generate a list of possible issues for a persuasive essay. Don't be shy about expressing opinions when good ideas surface: That's part of your exploration.

- Brainstorm about any of these subjects: dating, schools, taxes, violence, rip-offs, discrimination, food, imports, pollution.
- Complete each of these sentences:
  If I could get rid of anything, I'd abolish ____.
  There ought to be a law against ____.
  We should have the right to ____.
- Skim the articles, pictures, and advertisements in a school, local, or national newspaper. What issues do they raise or suggest?

POLLUTION ORDINANCE PASSES
Protesters Challenge New Taxes
VOTERS APPROVE SCHOOL FUNDING

ANSWERS

Exercise 1

Ideas generated will vary. You might divide the class into three groups and allow each group to work on one of the activities. Or have students take turns rotating through activity stations. Make sure students focus on specific issues that they can take positions on but that are not too emotionally charged.

VISUAL CONNECTIONS

Related Expression Skills. Students might discuss the headlines and photos that would be included in a collage if it focused on the events of last week. You might use the discussion as a springboard for generating additional topics for essays.

how they could rework the unsuitable statements into suitable position statements.

Students should now have sufficient practice in thinking about issues to select issues and to draft position statements independently in **Writing Assignment: Part 1.** Assess students' ability to write position statements by using the criteria for selecting an issue. Help students make minor adjustments as needed.

Read **Thinking About Purpose, Audience, and Tone** with students and go through the process of identifying an audience for the issue you've worked with or for other issues students suggest. Then have students work independently on **Writing**

ANSWERS

Exercise 2

2. Virtually everyone would agree that children should be protected from abuse. Therefore, there is no one to convince. Students might take a stand on how children should be protected or how those guilty of child abuse should be treated.
3. Few would disagree that disabled people can perform well on many jobs. To make the statement debatable, students might propose that hiring quotas for people with disabilities be required or that work environments for workers with handicaps be redesigned.

MEETING INDIVIDUAL NEEDS

ADVANCED STUDENTS

Allow students to explore those factors that help determine how audiences react. Challenge them to make a list of possible audience variables, such as age, sex, occupation, religious or political affiliations, educational background, and other personal beliefs and interests. Then have each student select a persuasive issue to analyze in terms of audience variables. Students might share their analyses with the class.

EXERCISE 2 Evaluating Position Statements

Working with a small group, use the criteria for choosing an issue (page 283) to decide which of the following positions is suitable for a persuasive essay. Explain why any statement isn't appropriate, and try to rework it so it could be used.

EXAMPLE Cars with front-wheel drive are better than cars with rear-wheel drive.
Unsuitable: Personal taste, not an issue
Suitable rewrite: Smaller cars are better for the environment.

1. U.S. consumers should buy only products made in the United States. **1. suitable**
2. Children must be protected from abuse. **2. unsuitable**
3. Disabled people can perform well in many jobs. **3. unsuitable**
4. Smoking should be banned in all restaurants. **4. suitable**

WRITING ASSIGNMENT — PART 1: Choosing an Issue to Write About

Did you find your issue in Exercise 1? If not, listen to yourself carefully for a day or so. When do you say (or *want* to say), "Well, **I** think . . ."? You could also do some brainstorming or look in your writer's journal for issues you think are important. When you have an issue you care about, write your position statement. Check it carefully. Is it an arguable opinion—not a matter of personal taste or a belief that most people share?

Thinking About Purpose, Audience, and Tone

Your *purpose* in writing a persuasive essay is (1) to make your readers think as you do about an issue and sometimes (2) to move them to do what you suggest.

It isn't easy to get people to change their minds, adopt a new idea, or act on their beliefs. That's why in a persuasive essay you pay very close attention to *audience*. And as you think about your audience, don't be surprised if you find that it's made up of different groups. To target each group, you need to explore their interests and concerns by looking for answers to crucial questions. How much do they know about this issue?

Assignment: Part 2. Look for the range of identified concerns when you evaluate students' work on this assignment.

To help students understand **Supporting Your Opinion** on p. 288, direct their attention to the presence of the elements for building support (reasons, evidence, facts, expert opinion, examples, details, and connotative language) in some of the literary selections they have read—in a Jonathan Edwards sermon or in a Patrick Henry speech or in the Declaration of Independence, for example. Encourage students to develop adequate support for their essays and to recognize the validity of opposing arguments.

What points do you and your audience agree on? Why is their opinion different from yours? What arguments will they use to oppose you?

Purpose and audience are also linked to the *tone* and *style* of persuasion. General persuasion is often informal and may use everyday speech. When the purpose is purely to convince the audience, a direct, personal—sometimes even humorous—tone can be very persuasive. Most speeches, letters to the editor, and advertising fall into this category.

However, the persuasive essay is sometimes more formal and serious. In school, for example, you may be asked to develop a logical, reasoned argument. In that case, your tone and language should be formal and serious. For more information on formal and informal language, see pages 484–488.

***WRITING* ASSIGNMENT**

PART 2:
Identifying the Audience for Your Essay

There is little point in aiming persuasion at people who already agree with you. In school you're often writing for your teacher and class, but a persuasive paper is a real chance to target an audience. Look closely at the issue you identified in Writing Assignment, Part 1 (page 286). Exactly who is it that needs to be convinced on the issue? Who actively disagrees with your opinion? Who is neutral but important to sway? Make a chart listing real readers for your essay, and identify which ones are neutral, which ones actively disagree, and which ones already agree with you.

VISUAL CONNECTIONS

Ideas for Writing. Ask students to respond orally to what is happening in the picture. Then have them freewrite in response to one or more of the following prompts:

1. Describe a demonstration that you have seen, either in person or on television, and explain how you reacted to the demonstrators.
2. Discuss a cause you strongly believe in and tell why you would or would not participate in a public demonstration in support of that cause.
3. Invent a past for one of the people in the picture and tell what you think led that person to participate in the demonstration.

You may want to allow some library time for students to work on **Writing Assignment: Part 3** on p. 292. You could have students consider the kinds of connotative language that might be appropriate for their audiences. Students might consult with one another or with you. Evaluate their charts for the range of support they develop.

To prepare students for improving their rebuttal arguments in **Exercise 3,** guide them through the rebuttal plan using Chief Joseph's speech on p. 278. Who is Chief Joseph's audience? What arguments against his opinions would his audience have? As you identify concerns, list them on the chalkboard and find reasons to counter the

INTEGRATING THE LANGUAGE ARTS

Literature Link. Ask students to evaluate the logical and emotional appeals used in a selection from Michel Guillaume Jean de Crèvecoeur's "Letters from an American Farmer" or in Patrick Henry's "Speech to the Virginia Convention." Encourage the class to pay particular attention to the writer's main points (reasons).

MEETING INDIVIDUAL NEEDS

LEP/ESL

General Strategies. A direct, well-reasoned, and logical approach is the standard of good persuasive writing in American culture. But not all cultures share this approach. Some cultures prefer indirect persuasion; others use passionate emotion; and many place much less importance on logic.

Many of your students may have already received instruction in persuasive writing in their native countries. When critiquing students' papers, acknowledge that other approaches are useful, but that mastering this method will help students to persuade others in American society.

Prewriting

Supporting Your Opinion

To win others to your opinion, you could try shouting louder than your opponents, but why waste your time and lungs on something that won't work? To be successful at persuading, you need to develop support that will convince your readers that your opinion is right.

Using Logical Appeals

Logical appeals are appeals to reason, not emotion. Because most people like to think that they are rational, thoughtful citizens, you need to show that your opinions are based on clear thinking and solid evidence.

Reasons. ***Reasons*** are the main points you use to support your opinion. They are often the answer to the audience's question "Why should I accept your opinion?"

Position Statement: A class in multicultural history and literature should be required for graduation from our high school.

Reasons: An understanding of cultures other than European and Anglo-Saxon will benefit all of our students.

A narrow cultural focus is unfair to our diverse student body.

Evidence. Most audiences, however, aren't satisfied if you just give them reasons. They also want ***evidence,*** that is, proof that your reasons are sound. Two basic kinds of evidence are

- **facts**—statements that can be checked by testing, by reading a reliable reference source, or by observing firsthand. Facts may be statistics, examples, and anecdotes (brief stories, often based on personal experiences).

The student body is now 25 percent Hispanic, 25 percent African American, 7 percent Native American, and 9 percent Asian American.

Our school offers only one year of U.S. history and one year of European history.

opposing arguments. Use **Exercise 3,** a small group activity, to help assess students' rebuttal planning.

RETEACHING

Ask the class to decide on two or three topics. After listing the topics on the chalkboard, discuss the suitability of each topic for a persuasive essay. Choose an appropriate topic and ask the class to formulate three possible position statements. Write the statements on the chalkboard and ask the class to evaluate them.

For the past two years, groups of students taking U.S. history have asked to give special reports to their classes on African American and Native American roles in the nation's history.

- **expert opinions**—statements by people who are considered authorities on the subject.

Patricia Ann Romero and Don Zancanella, who teach Hispanic American literature in Albuquerque, New Mexico, recently wrote in the *English Journal* that American students are lucky to have so many cultures around them and should explore different literatures to "better understand the diversity of American society."

For some issues, your own knowledge and experience will provide all the support any audience could ask for. For other issues, you will need to do some research. Although a persuasive essay is not a research paper, you might refer to Chapter 11 for help with identifying sources. As you collect information, make sure it's objective and reliable. Inconsistent sources—or just one biased source—can wreck your audience's trust in you.

Using Emotional Appeals

When you take a stand on something important to you, you often want to appeal to readers' hearts as well as their minds. In analyzing your audience and collecting evidence, you may already have seen ways to use emotional appeals in your essay.

Examples and Details. Suppose that you want to persuade your audience to contribute money for the homeless. To show that the homeless need help, you present the evidence that

SELECTION AMENDMENT
Description of change: excerpted
Rationale: to focus on the concept of persuasion presented in this chapter

After selecting the best statement, ask the class to help you design a chart on the chalkboard modeled after the example in **Here's How** on p. 291. Finally, discuss with the class how emotional language might be used in the essay.

CLOSURE

Conclude the lesson by asking students to list what they have learned about planning a persuasive essay. Students might do this individually, in small groups, or as a class.

COOPERATIVE LEARNING

To reinforce students' understanding of connotative and denotative language, have them work in groups of four or five and have each group use a dictionary to look up the denotative meaning of the terms *elderly, thin,* and *friendly.* Then have each group decide on positive and negative synonyms for each term. Students should write sentences to demonstrate their findings.

INTEGRATING THE LANGUAGE ARTS

Speaking and Listening Link. Have pairs of students select controversial topics, gather information about the topics, and then present the data to the class. One student from each pair could argue for a position and the other could argue against it. The primary purpose would not be for students to argue the issues but for them to listen closely to decide what points each side has to concede.

many have no jobs or are unable to work and therefore cannot pay for housing. But then you add an emotional appeal by telling the story of how one woman froze to death on a cold night. Numerical facts may be impressive, but they're impersonal. The specific example and vivid details make the suffering real.

Language. You also use emotional appeals when you pick words with strong connotative meanings. ***Denotative*** meanings are the ones that the dictionary gives you, but ***connotative*** meanings are the feelings or attitudes that a word suggests. For example, Chief Joseph (pages 278–280) chose strongly connotative words. Some of the words with negative connotations he used are *bloody, wounded, outlaws, die,* and *punish.* But he repeated words with positive connotations more often: *smile, earth, mother, brothers, peace, law,* and *free.*

Choose emotional appeals carefully, and recognize their power. They're best used to focus attention on important arguments because using them too often may make your audience feel that you are exaggerating the situation and misleading them.

Using Ethical Appeals

Do you know someone whom you think is intelligent, responsible, and sincere? Would you accept that person's opinion more quickly than the opinion of someone you think is unintelligent, irresponsible, and insincere? That's the way ***ethical appeals*** work. They suggest to the audience that the writer is of good character—someone sincere who speaks with some knowledge and authority.

When you write your essay, you can show that you can be trusted (that you are fair) by showing both sides of the issue. If you have experience with the issue, you can also discuss it in personal terms, as Chief Joseph did in "An Indian's View of Indian Affairs."

Identifying Opposing Positions

Effective persuasion doesn't *ignore* strong opposing positions: It counters them. Your audience analysis may yield some good reasons against your position, and you should also be on the alert for opposing reasons and evidence while doing research. Plan your answer to these objections— your ***rebuttal.***

ENRICHMENT

Ask students if they have ever heard the expression, "One picture is worth a thousand words." Ask students to apply that expression to persuasion, particularly to persuasive advertising. Have them look through magazines for ads that use pictures especially well—better than a thousand words. You might display their ads as wordless persuasion. ■

In collecting support, you may come across an opposing position you should mention but can't answer. Don't worry. Admitting this, called ***conceding a point,*** shows your audience that you've considered all sides of the issue and are fair. The chart below shows how one writer organized her support.

HERE'S HOW

Position statement: Drivers younger than twenty-one who have a blood alcohol content over the legal limit should lose their licenses for two years.	
Audience: Teenagers and adults who read the local newspaper	
Logical Appeal:	
Reasons	*Evidence*
• will save lives of both drivers and victims	*quotation from Cohens—more accidents than other age groups*
	quotation from Golden—25,000 killed each year by drunk drivers
• stop dangerous behavior before it happens	*teens not addicted, respond to peer pressure*
Emotional Appeal: loss of freedom	
Ethical Appeal:	
Opposing Positions	*Rebuttals*
• unfair to treat teens differently	*teens don't know limits; judgment clouded by alcohol*
• teens are better drivers than older people	*teens have less experience and are less cautious*

WRITING NOTE

Sometimes your purpose may be to develop a ***formal argument,*** a line of reasoning that proves your proposition (opinion) is true. A formal argument relies strictly on logic and looks at all available evidence, both favorable ***(pro)*** and unfavorable ***(con).*** Some school essays and business proposals require formal arguments, but if your purpose is to persuade (not prove), you don't have to follow this strict procedure. To convince your audience, you can select the evidence that is favorable and appeal to your audience's emotions and biases. Most of the examples of persuasion you find in magazines, newspapers, and popular books do not present formal arguments.

CRITICAL THINKING
Analysis

Persuasion can appeal to many emotions. Have students make a list of emotions that persuasive writing arouses. Start the class off by beginning a list on the chalkboard with pity, the fear of rejection, the need to feel important, and nostalgia for the past. Give students time to think of four or five other emotions on their own, and then ask students to compile a group list. Ask students to analyze several magazine and television ads to determine the emotional appeals that are present.

Reminder

In planning your support

- identify logical appeals (reasons and evidence) to support your position statement
- identify emotional and ethical appeals appropriate for your audience
- plan your rebuttal by considering audience objections, looking for opposing reasons and evidence in your research, and deciding how to answer the objections

WRITING ASSIGNMENT

PART 3:
Supporting Your Opinion

You are now ready to gather support for your position statement (Writing Assignment, Part 1, page 286). Start by listing the information you already have about the issue or by brainstorming ideas—alone or with someone else. Then decide whether you need to refer to outside sources. Remember to look for logical appeals and to consider possible emotional and ethical appeals. After you take notes, organize your information in a chart like the one in the Here's How on page 291.

EXERCISE 3 **Speaking and Listening: Refining Your Rebuttal**

Work with a partner or small group to find out if the rebuttal you plan is strong and realistic. Begin by identifying your audience and asking your listeners to play their role. Using your chart of support, read your position statement and your supporting reasons and evidence (*not* your rebuttal). Your classmates should listen carefully, take notes, and then get together to propose objections. As they present opposing arguments, you must think on your feet—draw on your planning to answer as persuasively as possible. Afterward, discuss how your written plan compared to the actual exchange, and make revision notes. Then change roles.

ANSWERS

Exercise 3

Responses will vary. Encourage students to listen carefully and to present objections that have been planned carefully. You may also want to encourage students to think about the emotional reaction of the argument. For example, listeners might be encouraged to tell speakers how they think the intended audience would react emotionally to certain portions of the argument. If the reaction is not what the speaker intends, classmates could work together to find the best way to achieve the intended effect.

SEGMENT 4 *(pp. 293–301)*

WRITING YOUR FIRST DRAFT

OBJECTIVES

- To analyze the principles of organization and the basic elements in persuasive essays
- To write a draft of a persuasive essay

MOTIVATION

Begin the lesson by asking students to list the advantages that people who are able to persuade others have. What benefits might they reap at home, at school, in the work place, and in public life? Give each student a chance to share an answer with the class.

Writing Your First Draft

The Basic Elements of Persuasion

The basic elements of persuasion fit clearly into composition form (pages 112–121). In the *introduction* you present your opinion, or position, and give any background readers will need to understand the issue. It is especially important in persuasion to get the audience's attention right away and make them care about your issue.

In the *body* you develop all of the support for your position—logical and emotional appeals—and present opposing positions with your rebuttal.

In the *conclusion* you return with force to your position and possibly give a ***call to action,*** something you want readers to do.

The Organization of a Persuasive Essay

Persuasive essays can be organized in varied ways, but a simple, effective plan is to present your logical and emotional appeals first, followed by opposing positions and rebuttals.

- **Order of Importance.** You may want to arrange your appeals by ***order of importance,*** beginning or ending with your most irresistible appeal. Remember to think about their importance *to your audience.*
- **Chronological Order.** For other topics, though, ***chronological order*** may be natural. For example, if you were attempting to persuade your readers to stop smoking, you might present the effects in the order they would occur.
- **Logical Order.** A comparison and contrast strategy works well in presenting opposing positions and rebuttals. You may present all the objections at once, followed by all your answers, or you may go back and forth from each objection to its answer (a good plan if you're covering several opposing positions).

The writers of the following persuasive essays combine the elements of persuasion in two different ways. As you read, notice the kinds of evidence and appeals each uses.

Teacher's ResourceBank™

RESOURCES

WRITING YOUR FIRST DRAFT

QUOTATION FOR THE DAY

"We want the facts to fit the preconceptions. When they don't, it is easier to ignore the facts than to change the preconceptions." (Jessamyn West, 1907–1984, American writer)

Make sure that students understand that a preconception is a prejudice or an opinion formed in advance of actual knowledge. Ask students if they have ever researched something to bolster their opinions and discovered facts that would undermine their arguments.

MEETING INDIVIDUAL NEEDS

LEP/ESL

General Strategies. The editorials on pp. 294–297 present opposing views. This debate over "The Star-Spangled Banner" and its proposed replacement, "America the Beautiful," will have more meaning for ESL students if they hear the songs. Look in a public library for recordings of these anthems. If recordings are not available, you might copy the words to both songs for students to compare.

TEACHING THE LESSON

Before students read the two newspaper editorials, discuss **The Basic Elements of Persuasion** on p. 293 with the class. Students should need only a cursory review of the concepts of introduction, body, and conclusion.

You may want to spend more time presenting **The Organization of a Persuasive Essay** on p. 293. Explain to students that the topics and the information gathered influence the organizational order of essays. Some students may not understand why order of importance and chronological order are not considered logical order. You may want to point out that logical order involves organizing the essay by means of classification or comparison and contrast.

USING THE SELECTION

Keep "The Star-Spangled Banner"

1
Why does the writer begin by announcing that she can't sing the national anthem? [Answers will vary. Many readers will identify with her situation and listen sympathetically to her argument. Also, the introduction acts as a rebuttal to an opposing argument.]

2
What parts of the anthem does she refer to? [Answers will vary. "The rockets' red glare" gives many people trouble.]

3
Many people mistakenly believe "The Star-Spangled Banner" has been our national anthem since the Revolutionary War or at least since the War of 1812.

4
Do you agree that both freedom and brotherhood are achieved through struggle? [Responses will vary. The idea that freedom requires struggle is not strange to most students, but some students may insist that brotherhood should come naturally.]

TWO NEWSPAPER EDITORIALS

Opinion

Keep "The Star-Spangled Banner"

by Vicki Williams

Attention grabber

1 I've never been able to sing *The Star-Spangled Banner.* But, then, there are lots of songs I've never been able to sing.

Ethical appeal

I have a musical range of exactly one octave.

When a song rises above or falls below it, I simply drop out and resume when my personal octave returns.

Opposing position

Most people are more capable musically than I am, but they still can't pull off the entire *Star-Spangled Banner.* In any audience of 10,000, there will generally be only 1,000 or so who can stretch their lungs to the full capacity demanded

2 by the most difficult parts of this song.

Rebuttal

Facts

3 But still, we've been struggling to sing *The Star-Spangled Banner* since Congress adopted it in 1931 as our national anthem. In fact, Americans have been working at singing it since 1814, when Francis Scott Key wrote the words and set them to the music of an old English tune.

Reason

Emotional appeal

And perhaps there should be some effort to singing our national anthem, just as there must be effort in keeping the United States the kind of country it is.

Opposing position

America the Beautiful is a lovely song, but it is too easy, with its pleasant talk of purple mountain majesties and amber waves of grain. There is

Rebuttal

Emotional appeal

4 no sense of struggle here. It just flows along as if freedom and brotherhood came naturally, without hardship.

Emotional appeal

By contrast, in *The Star-Spangled Banner,* we can almost feel the imprisoned patriot's anguish as he wondered during that long night in Baltimore Harbor if the flag would continue to wave. And his heartfelt gratitude when the rockets' red glare and the bombs bursting in air revealed that

Ask students to keep in mind the basic methods of organization as they read the models. The newspaper editorials might be read independently, or you or one of the students might read them aloud as the class follows in the textbook. Use the annotations and the side glosses to guide your class discussion. Be sure to discuss the kinds of emotional appeals used as well as the facts and reasons presented. Have students discuss the effectiveness of each kind of appeal used in the essays. Use **Exercise 4** on p. 297 as independent practice and evaluate students' analysis skills by reviewing their answers to this exercise.

After they have read and discussed the editorials, students should be ready to read and discuss **A Basic Framework for a**

it was still proudly flying over Fort McHenry.

There are many songs about America, and we should sing them wholeheartedly, for they all illustrate elements of what this country represents.

It is "America the beautiful" and "this land is your land and my land." And it is "a sweet land of liberty."

Reason

Emotional appeal

But I don't believe our national song should change with the passing whim of popularity.

Restatement: main reason

Emotional appeal

The Star-Spangled Banner deserves to be our anthem because it reminds us that patriotism sometimes requires sacrifice, and that, in order to continue to be the land of the free, we must also remain the home of the brave.

USA TODAY

Replace "The Star-Spangled Banner"

by Andy Jacobs, Jr.

Attention grabber *1*

"I have two favorite songs. One of them is *Yankee Doodle* and the other one ain't." The words are those of our 18th president, Ulysses Grant.

Background *2*

On March 4, 1931, when he signed it into law, *The Star-Spangled Banner* was one of the favorite songs of our 31st president, Herbert Hoover.

VISUAL CONNECTIONS

Ideas for Writing. Ask students to freewrite for three to five minutes about how they would react to hearing another song replace "The Star-Spangled Banner" at a sporting event.

USING THE SELECTION

Replace "The Star-Spangled Banner"

1

The writer piques the reader's interest by using an amusing quotation, ". . . and the other one ain't." Readers are curious about what Grant's other favorite song is or whether "Yankee Doodle" is his only real choice.

2

In addition to adding historical background, the writer shows that presidential song favorites are personal choices that change from president to president. He implies personal prejudice influenced the choice of our anthem.

Persuasive Essay on p. 298. To help students analyze the essay, you might have them generate questions about the essay for their classmates to answer by working in small groups. Allow some class time to discuss the questions and answers.

Both **Exercise 4** and **Writing Assignment: Part 4** on p. 301 give students opportunities for independent practice. You might have students begin work on their essays during class even if you plan for them to write their drafts as homework. You could circulate through the room to check that students are keeping their audiences in mind.

3
Do you agree with the writer that a distinction can be made between a song about our flag and a song about our country? [Answers will vary. Students should explain their responses.]

4
Do you agree with the writer's assessment of "America the Beautiful"? [Answers will vary. Many students who can recall the words to the song will agree.]

5
tribute: declaration of respect

Reason / **Emotional appeal**

As time becomes history, what we favor musically to express our love of country may change. The love itself, like the love of family, remains pretty much the same.

Facts

But listen: *Their blood has washed out their/ foul footsteps' pollution . . .* The third verse of *The Star-Spangled Banner* does not speak well of our friends, the British.

Reason / **Opposing position/ Ethical appeal** / **Emotional appeal**

America the Beautiful is not about hatred for
3 long-ago enemies. It is not about a war nor about the flag. It is about America. Yes, an instrumental presentation of *The Star-Spangled Banner* does wondrously chilling things to our feelings. As a former Marine, I snap to attention and present arms. *The land of the free and the home of the brave.* I love that line, even if I can't sing it.

Reason repeated / **Emotional appeal/ Fact**

But the thrust of our anthem is war. Martial matters do not measure the length and breadth
4 of our national being. *America the Beautiful* sends a more positive message at a time when enlightenment seems to be showering peaceful and liberating dividends around the globe.

Facts / **Emotional appeal**

The Star-Spangled Banner would endure as a suitable and stirring sound for military occasions. But not all of them. At the memorial for our Challenger astronauts, *The Star-Spangled Banner* was not heard. It was *America the Beautiful* which splendidly stated our pride and sorrow. At the Statue of Liberty rededication, *The Star-Spangled Banner* was initially and perfunctorily played. But the ceremony itself was laced and graced by *America the Beautiful,* which suggests the inner strength of a self-confident people.

Reason / **Fact**

This all-American song does not lack suitable
5 tribute to those who have given their lives in uniform: *Oh beautiful for heroes proved/in liberating strife. Who more/than self their country loved/and mercy more than life.*

Emotional appeal

Those words are calm yet strong, like heroism itself, which is *proved* not so much by politically histrionic demands for inflicting pain as by enduring it.

ASSESSMENT

As students work on their drafts, check each draft for clear patterns of organization. You may also want to gauge how well students are using logical appeals in their essays.

RETEACHING

Choose an essay topic with students and then have them generate a list of reasons and appeals for the essay. Ask them to visualize the paragraphs of the essay as boxes stacked atop one another. Ask students what sequence the reader should find for the boxes. [The introduction should be first, followed by an ordered presentation of

Summarizing statement/ Emotional appeals

America the Beautiful is not boisterous; neither is true patriotism—an abiding thing, calm and steady in storm as well as in the safety of the harbor. Vicarious violence may fire the passions of some, but, as in marriage, passion isn't much upon which to build a lifetime of loyalty.

USA TODAY

EXERCISE 4 **Analyzing the Elements of Persuasive Essays**

You can't agree with both of the writers taking a stand on the national anthem, but you can learn something about persuasion from both of them. After you've read the essays, meet with two or three classmates to discuss the answers to the following questions.

1. The opinions of both writers are in their titles, but their positions are actually more specific than just "keeping" or "replacing" the current national anthem. Give a full position statement for each.
2. Which reason do you think is strongest in each essay? Where in the essay does it appear? Why do you think it was placed there?

VISUAL CONNECTIONS

Related Expression Skills. Ask students to create a monologue in which the Statue of Liberty explains which song she would prefer as the national anthem.

ANSWERS

Exercise 4

Answers will vary.

1. The first writer believes that "The Star-Spangled Banner" is the best choice for an anthem because it accurately reflects the country's patriotic struggles. The second writer argues that the tone of the anthem is inappropriate to the real spirit of the United States.
2. Most students will agree that both writers have saved their strongest points for last. The placement in both essays bolsters the writers' arguments and leaves readers with memorable phrases to recall.

SELECTION AMENDMENT

Description of change: excerpted and adapted
Rationale: to focus on the concept of persuasion presented in this chapter

reasons and appeals.] What will encourage a reluctant reader to keep opening boxes? [Logical reasoning, verifiable evidence, and moving emotional appeals that are organized and presented well should keep a reader interested.]

If you think students require additional practice, you might provide students with jumbled sentences from a persuasive essay and ask them to arrange the sentences in the most functional order.

3. Both writers make strong cases, but many students may be emotionally attached to the anthem. Others will recognize the strong reasons of the second argument.
4. Examples of effective details include the description of the night Keyes wrote the song in the first essay and the quotation from a verse of the song in the second essay. Examples of connotative language include "imprisoned patriot's anguish" in the first essay and "showering peaceful and liberating dividends" in the second.
5. The first writer refutes the idea that "America the Beautiful" would make a better anthem with the claim that it has no sense of struggle. The second writer refutes the idea that "America the Beautiful" does not pay tribute to military heroes by quoting from the song. The first writer may have missed the opposing position that war and "bombs bursting in air" are seen as detriments to achieving world peace. The second writer may have missed the opposing argument that an anthem, like the flag, should not be changed capriciously.

COOPERATIVE LEARNING

Ask students to work in small groups to determine what points in this model would have to be conceded to an opposing argument.

3. In your opinion, which essay has stronger reasons and evidence? Explain your judgment.
4. Both essays employ many emotional appeals. In each one, point out effective details and connotative language.
5. Find an opposing position in each essay. Exactly how does the writer rebut it? Brainstorm to think of any opposing positions each writer may have missed.

A Basic Framework for a Persuasive Essay

The two essays you've just read are by professional writers, tackling an issue that is inescapably emotional. Your essay will be more heavily based on logic and facts and will use a more conventional organization. You may want to follow the basic framework in the following writer's model.

A WRITER'S MODEL

A Chance for Life

INTRODUCTION
Attention grabber

Last week eight teenagers on their way home from a party were killed when their truck crashed into a tree. The autopsy on the seventeen-year-old driver showed that his blood alcohol level was more than twice the legal limit.

Background
Emotional appeal
Position statement

The leading cause of death for youths sixteen to nineteen years old is not cancer or heart disease or any other illness that may strike without warning. It is driving while under the influence of alcohol. We must do something to stop this slaughter, and we can: Drivers under the age of twenty-one who have a blood alcohol level over the legal limit should immediately lose their licenses, and they should not be allowed to drive again for at least two years.

BODY
Reason
Evidence/ Expert opinion and facts

The most important reason for my proposal is that it will save lives of both drivers and innocent victims. Drunk driving is a tragic mistake at any age, but as Susan and Daniel Cohen write in their book A Six-Pack and a Fake I.D., "Drivers under twenty-one are involved in much more than their

CLOSURE

Ask students to discuss their reactions to persuasive writing and to writing their drafts. What did they most enjoy? What did they find easiest? Most difficult? You might want to list the responses on the chalkboard and to use them to discuss writing strategies. ■

share of serious traffic accidents." According to Sandy Golden, author of Driving the Drunk off the Road, of the 25,000 people who are killed every year in drunk driving accidents, one fifth are teenagers.

Reason
Explanation
Evidence/Fact

Another reason is that the penalty can stop dangerous behavior before it happens. Teenagers are not like adults, who may have hardened, hard-to-change habits. Most teens drink, not because they're addicted to alcohol, but because of peer pressure. With the freedom that a driver's license brings, they can go to unchaperoned parties where they drink to prove their new adult status. But if teens knew they could lose this glorious freedom, they would be less likely to take the risk.

Emotional appeal

Opposing position/ Ethical appeal

Some people claim that it's unfair to treat teens differently from others. If eighteen-year-olds are old enough to vote and fight in a war, they argue, then eighteen-year-olds are adults and should have the same rights as adults.

Rebuttal
Evidence/Facts

Emotional appeal

I believe teenagers should be treated differently. As new drinkers, teens don't fully understand the effects of alcohol. They don't know their limits, and they don't realize how alcohol clouds their judgment. To make this shaky condition worse, teens have curfews. Often they rush home, without giving themselves time to sober up.

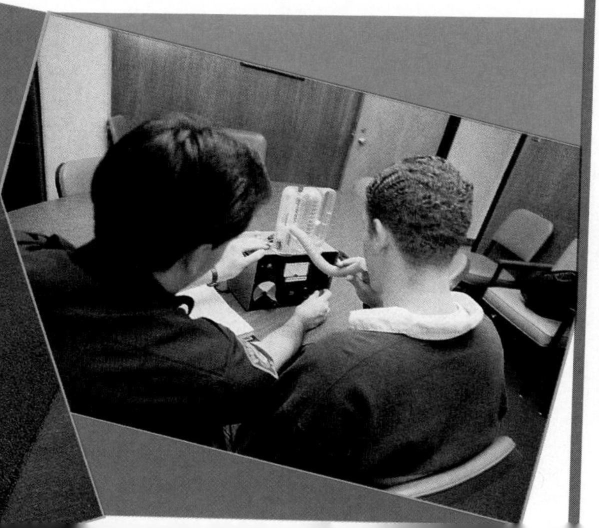

MEETING INDIVIDUAL NEEDS

LEARNING STYLES

Visual Learners. Visual learners understand, perhaps better than others, that a picture can be worth a thousand words. You might ask a group of students to talk about how to turn this model into a picture essay. Have them discuss what visual images they would choose to represent emotions and reasons.

AT-RISK STUDENTS

Some students, particularly those anxious to enjoy adult privileges, may have difficulty with the concept that teenagers should be treated differently than adults. You may want to give them the opportunity to discuss the circumstances that would warrant different treatment of teenagers.

VISUAL CONNECTIONS

Exploring the Subject. Have students discuss what the tests for sobriety are in the community. What are the penalties for driving under the influence of alcohol? What do students believe the penalties ought to be?

CRITICAL THINKING
Analysis

Ask students to compare the structure suggested in the **Framework for a Persuasive Essay** chart with the structure of each of the two editorials they read earlier. What similarities do they find? What differences?

Fact

Moreover, teenagers are breaking the law just by buying and drinking alcohol. They are already different from adults under the law, and they compound their crime when they drink and drive.

Opposing position

Rebuttal

Facts

Some people argue that teenagers are better drivers than older people. It's generally true that young people have faster reflexes than middle-aged and elderly drivers, but they also have less experience on the road. Some older drivers who are under the influence of alcohol drive slowly; but teenagers, confident in their abilities, tend to be less cautious even when sober. In fact, most alcohol-related collisions involving teens are caused by reckless driving and speeding.

CONCLUSION

Repeat of opinion and call to action

Emotional appeal

We must keep all drunk drivers off the road, and tough penalties for teenagers are a firm step toward that goal. Support a law that gives teenagers a clear message: If you drink, your license is gone. Give them this chance to learn. It may be their last chance at life.

WRITING NOTE You may have noticed that both of the professional models and the writer's model use contractions. In persuasion, the language of everyday communication helps create a personal appeal. If you were writing a formal argument in school or at work, you might need to use formal language, avoiding contractions and colloquial words.

REFERENCE NOTE: For more information on colloquial language, see pages 486–487.

The author of "A Chance for Life" presented two main reasons and rebutted two opposing positions, but your essay may be different. The issue you've picked will shape your line of reasoning, rebuttal, and organization: Persuasion (like deeply felt opinions) takes many forms. You can, though, use a framework like the following one to put your thoughts in order.

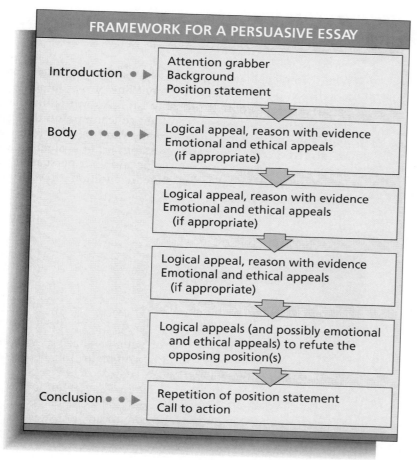

FRAMEWORK FOR A PERSUASIVE ESSAY

Introduction ▶
- Attention grabber
- Background
- Position statement

Body ▶
- Logical appeal, reason with evidence
  Emotional and ethical appeals (if appropriate)
- Logical appeal, reason with evidence
  Emotional and ethical appeals (if appropriate)
- Logical appeal, reason with evidence
  Emotional and ethical appeals (if appropriate)
- Logical appeals (and possibly emotional and ethical appeals) to refute the opposing position(s)

Conclusion ▶
- Repetition of position statement
- Call to action

***WRITING* ASSIGNMENT**

PART 4:
Writing a Draft of Your Persuasive Essay

Now's the time to go back to your chart of support and put your ideas in order. What details can you add to create emotional appeals? How will you order your logical appeals and rebuttal? Make a final plan now. Then, before you write, think of your audience one more time. Picture them. Step into their shoes. What will get them walking in the direction of your ideas? Keep these readers vividly in your mind as you draft.

TIMESAVER

Ask students to code their drafts for you before they turn the drafts in. Have them underline the position statements, circle the logical appeals, bracket the emotional appeals, and underline twice the calls to action. Reading these sentences and scanning for development should help you quickly evaluate students' organizational skills. (It should also increase students' awareness of the strengths and weaknesses of their papers.)

SEGMENT 5 *(pp. 302–309)*

EVALUATING AND REVISING

OBJECTIVES

- To analyze a writer's revision of a persuasive essay
- To evaluate and revise a persuasive essay

Cont. on p. 304

CRITICAL THINKING

(pp. 302–305)

OBJECTIVE

- To distinguish illogical or faulty reasoning from valid reasoning

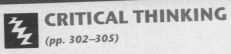

Teacher's ResourceBank™

RESOURCES

EVALUATING AND REVISING

- Writing a Persuasive Essay 68

QUOTATION FOR THE DAY

"By persuading others, we convince ourselves." (Junius, a pseudonym of an unidentified author of a series of letters contributed to a popular eighteenth-century British newspaper)

As you discuss this quotation with your class, remind students that when they evaluate their persuasive essays, they must convince not only the audience but also themselves. If the arguments do not seem strong enough, they must be rewritten more convincingly to persuade not only the reader but also the writer.

Evaluating and Revising

When you evaluate a persuasive essay, you check to see whether you have laid out a potent line of reasoning. Is your persuasion foolproof? It probably isn't: A draft is the place to get something *said* so you can then concentrate on the *saying*. Even though your persuasion really can't be foolproof (there are no "true" opinions), an important part of evaluating a persuasive essay is checking your logic and your persuasive powers. You need to take this step in addition to your usual evaluation and revision.

CRITICAL THINKING

Evaluating Your Reasoning

An extremely important part of your persuasive essay is the logical support for your position statement. But here's something to watch out for: ***fallacies.*** They look like reasons; they sound like reasons. But they're fakes: They're not logical.

These fallacies sometimes work, of course. People who aren't thinking clearly may be convinced, but at least some members of your audience will be reading your essay critically. If critical readers find any of these fallacies, they may decide that you are a sloppy thinker—or a sneaky one. And neither idea will help your case. In your review, be tough on your reasoning, and watch for these fallacies.

1. **Begging the Question.** When you beg a question, you assume something is true that you really need to prove.

Begging the Question:	Our local newspaper's bias against nuclear energy is responsible for public opposition to the proposed plant.
Assumption to Be Proved:	Local newspaper coverage is biased against nuclear energy.

TEACHING *EVALUATING YOUR REASONING*

Begin by pointing out that students encounter fallacies all the time, especially if they watch television. Television commercials, political speeches, and other popular propaganda are all filled with fallacies. Go over the five kinds of fallacies listed under **Evaluating Your Reasoning,** and ask students to suggest more examples of each kind of fallacy. You may want to write some of the examples on the chalkboard. Ask for students' help in suggesting ways a critical thinker might deal with each kind of fallacy.

After this guided practice, students should be ready to do the **Critical Thinking Exercise** independently. As closure for the lesson, have students list additional examples

The Granger Collection, New York

1960 debate between presidential candidates John F. Kennedy and Richard M. Nixon.

2. **Attacking the Person.** The formal name of this fallacy is the *ad hominem* fallacy (literally, "to the person"); informally, it's known as name-calling. You may notice examples of this type of illogical argument during political campaigns when candidates attack their opponents instead of facing issues.

Attacking the Person:	People who oppose capital punishment are soft on crime.
Facing the Issue:	Some people oppose capital punishment because they think it's an act of vengeance, not punishment.

3. **Hasty Generalization.** A hasty generalization is a conclusion based on insufficient evidence or one that ignores exceptions. Sometimes broad generalizations can be made acceptable by using qualifying words like *most, generally,* and *some.*

Hasty Generalization:	Network television focuses on violence, crime, and abnormality.
Acceptable Generalization:	Many prime-time network programs focus on violence, crime, and abnormality.

MEETING **INDIVIDUAL** NEEDS

ADVANCED STUDENTS

Students who are successful in understanding the fallacies of logic presented in this lesson might want to research other fallacies, such as denying the antecedent, biased or insufficient statistics, or the genetic fallacy. After students have had time to get familiar with the vocabulary and reasoning used in logic syllogisms, have them present their fallacies to the class in a forum as Greek philosophers might have done. Pairs of students could present short discussions using fallacious thinking.

LESS-ADVANCED STUDENTS

Before you assign the **Critical Thinking Exercise** on p. 305, you may want to reinforce students' understanding of fallacies by providing them with some real-life examples clipped from magazine advertisements. You might clearly identify the fallacies in some ads, provide strong hints as to what the fallacies are in others, and let the students work independently to identify other fallacies.

of the five fallacies. To extend the lesson, have students discuss other types of faulty reasoning.

Cont. from p. 302

TEACHING THE LESSON

Remind students that revising (improving the content and organization of an essay) and proofreading (checking spelling, punctuation, and usage) are different activities.

Explain to students that they should think of their drafts as trial runs in which they

A DIFFERENT APPROACH

Ask students to engage in a twenty-four hour search for fallacies. Students should not only examine magazines, newspapers, and television, but they should also pay close attention to conversations they overhear and conversations with peers. You may want students to record their findings in list form and to indicate the source of each fallacy on the list.

COOPERATIVE LEARNING

Provide several additional examples of each of the fallacies mixed in with examples of sound reasoning and ask that students work in small groups to identify the fallacies.

MEETING INDIVIDUAL NEEDS

LEP/ESL

General Strategies. Nonnative speakers may have difficulty with the **Critical Thinking Exercise,** not because their reasoning is flawed, but because detecting a fallacy requires a language facility that they may not have acquired yet.

Pair students with peer tutors to work on the exercise and allow class time so they can discuss the fallacies and write new reasons to replace them.

4. **Either-Or Reasoning.** This fallacy assumes that only two extreme alternatives exist for a question or course of action. In most situations, several choices or positions are possible between the extremes.

Either-Or Reasoning: If funding for the space program is cut, the United States will destroy its own future.

Realistic Reasoning: If funding for the space program is cut, it will eliminate research now dedicated to solving problems Earth will face in the future.

5. **False Analogy.** Comparing two things that are alike in important ways is an analogy, and it's a good way to make a point swiftly and vividly. A false analogy makes an illogical and misleading link: The similarities are false or trivial.

False Analogy: Putting Native Americans on reservations is like sentencing them to death row.

Effective Analogy: A Native American confined to a reservation is like a free horse suddenly tied to a stake.

have discovered what they have to say and how to make the ideas sensible to an audience. Now they must make sure that the ideas are clear and presented in the best way. They must decide whether the drafts say what the students want them to say.

Remind students that few pieces of writing are ever perfect—even after several drafts—and that it is unlikely that they have written drafts that cannot be improved.

You may wish to use **Exercise 5** on p. 307 as guided practice for **Writing Assignment: Part 5** on p. 309 by leading the class through the revision process before they revise their papers independently. Allow students to work in small groups on **Exercise 6** on p. 307 for independent practice.

CRITICAL THINKING EXERCISE:
Evaluating Reasons

See how good you are at catching sloppy, or sneaky, thinking. First, identify which of the five kinds of fallacies each statement is. Then, write a logical reason to replace each fallacy. Write your reasons either in favor of the opinion or against it.

Opinion: Tipping in restaurants should be prohibited.

1. Tipping is so established that all waiters and waitresses expect tips, no matter what service they provide.
2. If tipping continues, employers will never pay waiters and waitresses decent salaries.
3. People who tip simply like to show off how much money they have.
4. We should follow the example of the thrifty people who don't tip.
5. Tipping is like giving a handout to a beggar.

Shoe, by Jeff MacNelly, reprinted by permission: Tribune Media Services.

The following chart will help you evaluate and revise other elements in your essay. Begin by asking yourself a question in the left-hand column. If you find that weakness in your essay, strengthen your paper by using the revision technique suggested in the right-hand column.

ANSWERS
Critical Thinking Exercise

Reasons may vary.

1. Hasty generalization. *Possible rewrite:* Some waiters and waitresses seem to expect tips regardless of the quality of the service.
2. Either-or reasoning. *Possible rewrite:* Employers sometimes use tipping to justify keeping salaries low for waiters and waitresses.
3. Attacking the person. *Possible rewrite:* People who are financially well off usually find tipping less burdensome.
4. Begging the question. *Possible rewrite:* One sensible approach to tipping is to follow the example of those who decide how much to tip based on the quality of the service rather than the size of the bill.
5. False analogy. *Possible rewrite:* To give a tip to a waiter who has given little or no service is rather like paying a repairman not to fix your television set.

Before you begin **Writing Assignment: Part 5,** you might use the **Grammar Hint** on pp. 308–309 to suggest techniques students might use in revising their own drafts. If students need more examples of techniques to vary sentence structure, refer to excerpts from literature and use the reference note information for additional practice.

As suggested in **Writing Assignment: Part 5,** students should be able to use the **Evaluating and Revising Persuasive Essays** chart and the suggestions of their peers to guide them in revising their essays independently.

MEETING **INDIVIDUAL** NEEDS

LESS-ADVANCED STUDENTS

Even with the help of the chart, students may have difficulty evaluating not only their drafts but also the drafts of other students. They may fail to recognize weaknesses when they agree with another writer's opinion, and they may fail to identify strengths when they disagree. You may want to work closely with students to help them distinguish between emotional responses and valid critiques.

EVALUATING AND REVISING PERSUASIVE ESSAYS

	EVALUATION GUIDE	REVISION TECHNIQUE
1	Does the first paragraph grab the reader's attention?	**Add** an interesting fact, anecdote, or quotation, or **replace** existing sentences with one.
2	Does a clear statement of the writer's position appear early in the essay?	**Add** a sentence (or **replace** an existing sentence) that clearly states the issue and your position on it.
3	Would background information help clarify the issue?	**Add** facts or examples to help your audience grasp the issue.
4	Are logical appeals (reasons and evidence) provided to convince the audience?	Do further research, and **add** more reasons, facts, or expert opinions.
5	Is the reasoning sound?	**Cut** or **replace** fallacies in logic.
6	Does the essay contain appropriate emotional or ethical appeals?	**Add** words or examples with emotional content. **Add** references to your experience or concede a point to the opposition.
7	Does the essay present and respond to opposing positions?	**Add** the strongest positions on the opposing side, and refute them with reasons and evidence.
8	Is the line of reasoning clear and easy for readers to follow?	**Reorder** information to present your reasons first (using order of importance or cause-and-effect order), followed by objections and rebuttal.
9	Is the conclusion effective?	**Add** a strong restatement of opinion, a summary of reasons, or a call to action.

ASSESSMENT

Each student might revise at least one paragraph of his or her essay during class. You could have partners write answers to the **Evaluation Guide** questions in the **Evaluating and Revising Persuasive Essays** chart and make comments for revision. By doing this you could assess both evaluation and revision skills. As students work, you could circulate through the classroom to note the kinds of comments and changes that students make.

EXERCISE 5 Analyzing a Writer's Revisions

Examine the writer's revision of one paragraph of "A Chance for Life" (pages 298–300). Working with a partner or a small group, answer the questions that follow the paragraph to analyze the writer's changes.

Another reason is that the penalty can stop dangerous behavior <u>before</u> it happens. Teenagers are not like adults, who (may have hardened, hard-to-change habits.) ~~just can't change.~~ ~~But some people say punishment has to be the same for teens and adults.~~ Most teens (drink, not because they're) ~~aren't~~ addicted to alcohol (but because of peer pressure). With the freedom that a driver's license brings, they (can go to unchaperoned parties where they drink) ~~start drinking~~ to prove their new adult status. But if teens (knew they could lose this glorious freedom) ~~stand to lose their licenses~~, they would be less likely to take the risk.

Teenagers are not like adults, who just can't	replace
change. But some people say punishment	cut
has to be the same for teens and adults.	cut
Most teens aren't addicted to alcohol. With	replace/add
they start drinking to prove their new adult	replace
status. But if teens stand to lose their	replace

1. What logical fallacy does the writer avoid by replacing *just can't change* in the second sentence?
2. Why did the writer cut the entire third sentence?
3. Where has the writer strengthened evidence in the paragraph?
4. What's the reason for the replacement in the final sentence?
5. Who do you think is one audience for this writer's essay? Why do you think so?

EXERCISE 6 Evaluating and Revising a Persuasive Essay

Working with one or two classmates, evaluate the beginning of the following persuasive essay. Figure out what changes might improve it. Remember to use the suggestions in the evaluating and revising chart on page 306. You might enjoy discussing your suggestions with another group.

ANSWERS

Exercise 5

Responses will vary.

1. The writer avoids the fallacy of hasty generalization.
2. The sentence interferes with the logical flow of the argument.
3. The writer adds additional information about why teens drink.
4. The change adds emotional appeal.
5. One audience is the state legislature. It has the power to pass laws governing drinking and driving.

RETEACHING

After you have evaluated students' draft revisions, select an essay from another class and guide students through the steps of the **Evaluating and Revising Persuasive Essays** chart. Ask students to suggest other improvements using the techniques mentioned in the **Grammar Hint** or to find flaws in the logic if any fallacies are present.

CLOSURE

Ask students to name and describe the five kinds of fallacies presented in this segment [begging the question, attacking the person, hasty generalization, either-or reasoning, and false analogy]. Then have students recall ways to vary sentence structure. [Change standard structure by starting

ANSWERS

Exercise 6

Answers will vary. The writer might provide more specific evidence about the distances between classrooms and lockers to avoid begging the question. The writer also might consider whether "late to class all the time" is a hasty generalization. The analogy between sprinting and jet planes is a false one. In general, the logic is weak and the tone is overly emotional.

VISUAL CONNECTIONS

Related Expression Skills. Ask students to pretend that this scene is taken from a television situation comedy set in a high school. The plot for this week's episode revolves around whether or not students have enough time between classes. Ask students to put the scene in motion by using dialogue and action to show that students either do or do not need more time.

GRAMMAR HINT

Remind students that while it is a good idea to vary sentence structure to avoid monotony, it isn't necessary to do so with every sentence. Beginning each sentence with something other than the subject can also make sentence structure monotonous. Encourage students to read their sentences out loud to decide what patterns sound best.

Three minutes between classes isn't enough. If you're not a winner of the 100-yard dash, you're late to class all the time. I know I am. We don't even have time to get to our lockers between classes. I'm tired of dragging all my stuff from one class to the next. We just sprint from one class to the next like jet planes. It's little wonder we sometimes crash in the halls. But don't worry. Your friendly hall supervisor is sure to be sympathetic and give you a nice restful detention-- after school. Stressed-out students, we need to revolt.

GRAMMAR HINT

Varying Sentence Structure

In persuasive writing, the last thing you want to do is bore your readers. But even with an enticing issue and convincing logical, emotional, and ethical appeals, you risk that effect if your sentences are monotonous. The standard English sentence begins with a subject that is closely followed by a verb. To avoid being monotonous, use the following techniques to vary sentence structure.

sentences with prepositional phrases, verbal phrases, or dependent clauses.] ■

- Start with a prepositional phrase.

  As new drinkers, teens don't fully understand the effects of alcohol.

- Start with a verbal phrase.

  To make this shaky condition worse, teens have curfews.

- Start with a dependent clause.

  If eighteen-year-olds are old enough to vote and fight in a war, they argue, eighteen-year-olds are adults and should have the same rights as adults.

REFERENCE NOTE: For more on prepositional phrases, verbal phrases, and dependent clauses, see pages 605–620 and 629–637; for more on improving sentence style, see pages 541–548.

WRITING ASSIGNMENT

PART 5:
Evaluating and Revising Your Persuasive Essay

You are no doubt thoroughly convinced by your paper, but then you're a pushover audience! Try out your logic and emotional appeals on someone else. Exchange essays with a classmate, and use the chart on page 306 to evaluate each other's essays and suggest improvements. After hearing what your partner says, evaluate and revise your own writing.

MEETING INDIVIDUAL NEEDS

ADVANCED STUDENTS

Encourage students to write new drafts that argue the issues clearly and cogently from the opposing point of view. Ask them to discuss what they have learned from the experience.

TIMESAVER

If you prefer to read students' drafts before evaluating their final essays, you may find it helpful to make copies of the **Evaluating and Revising Persuasive Essays** chart on p. 306 and to attach a copy to each draft as you work. You can then read the drafts quickly and respond to the questions in the chart with *yes* or *no.*

SEGMENT 6 *(p. 310)*

PROOFREADING AND PUBLISHING

OBJECTIVES

- To use proofreading strategies to prepare an essay for an audience
- To share an essay with an audience

TEACHING THE LESSON

Focus on several punctuation errors that students tend to make. Then have students proofread their essays for those errors. After students proofread, help them decide where they might publish the essays. As you evaluate, keep in mind the audience and publishing plans students selected.

Teacher's ResourceBank™

RESOURCES

PROOFREADING AND PUBLISHING

- Writing a Persuasive Essay 69

QUOTATION FOR THE DAY

"Cut out all those exclamation marks. An exclamation mark is like laughing at your own joke." (F. Scott Fitzgerald, 1896–1940, American writer of novels and short stories)

Remind students that when they write to persuade, they may be tempted to use exclamation marks after emotional statements, but exclamation points are lazy writers' trumpets. Jazzy punctuation cannot take the place of strong, persuasive prose. Explain that there are more forceful ways to persuade a reader. Vivid language and well-reasoned logic is its own fanfare.

MEETING INDIVIDUAL NEEDS

LEP/ESL

General Strategies. When an ESL student prepares a paper for publication, it is often difficult for both the teacher and the student to know when to stop making corrections. You might want to start with a small checklist and as students become more proficient, add more items to the list.

Proofreading and Publishing

Proofreading. Evidence of thoroughness and care is important in persuasion, because an error-free paper may make your readers accept your ideas more easily. People who don't agree with your opinion will be looking for all kinds of mistakes in your paper, so don't let them find mistakes in usage, punctuation, and spelling.

Publishing. Because you can't convince someone who hasn't heard or read what you have to say, publishing is an essential step in persuasive writing. If you didn't have a specific publishing plan as you developed your essay, you need to think of one, perhaps with your teacher's help or the help of an expert you consulted. Also consider these ideas:

- Send a copy of your essay to a national magazine that covers the kind of issue you wrote about.
- Get permission to set up a table outside a supermarket or mall, and hand out copies of your class's essays.
- Present or mail your paper to a local group concerned with the issue.

WRITING ASSIGNMENT

PART 6:
Proofreading and Publishing Your Essay

Don't let all your exploration and thinking remain a private accomplishment. Now is the time to share with others the essay you have created: They'll admire your effort even if you make them mad! Proofread, correct, and publish.

WRITING WORKSHOP

OBJECTIVES

- To analyze techniques used in a persuasive speech
- To use the writing process to compose a persuasive speech

TEACHING THE LESSON

To interest students in this segment, play recordings of one or two particularly famous or moving speeches. Engage students in a discussion of speakers that they consider to be particularly persuasive.

Ask a volunteer to read **"Keep Your Eyes on the Prize"** aloud. Then use the questions that follow to guide your

WRITING WORKSHOP

A Persuasive Speech

Another way to take a stand on an issue is to give a speech about it: to persuade both with words and voice. Exactly the same elements occur in a persuasive essay and a persuasive speech, but in a speech you must make a swift connection with your audience—command their interest in some way and make your argument clear on one hearing.

Jesse Jackson, an outstanding speaker of our time, gave the following persuasive speech to a group of young people in 1978. As you read, imagine how Jackson delivered this speech, and notice how he combines logical and emotional appeals.

Keep Your Eyes on the Prize

by Jesse Jackson

Every now and then I hear young people brag about the new generation. It's not really anything to brag about because you didn't do anything to become the new generation. Your parents did something to make the new generation. You are the new generation without effort. So why brag about being *new* when it's not the result of your work? Why brag about being black or white? It's not the result of your work. Your challenge is to become a greater generation. And you become a greater generation because you
1 serve. If you feed more hungry people, you are a greater generation. If more people of this generation are educated, it's a greater generation. If the racial lines that separate us are overcome, you are a greater generation. And so our challenge is to be not just a new generation, based on birth, but to be a greater generation based upon work and effort.

There's always the challenge of concentration. We used to have a saying some years ago in the freedom struggle, "Keep your eyes on the prize." If your prize is to develop your mind; if your prize is to develop your body; if your prize is to develop spiritual depth; if

QUOTATION FOR THE DAY

"The most precious things in speech are pauses." (Sir Ralph Richardson, 1902–1983, British actor)

You might use this quotation before you read Jesse Jackson's speech. Point out that Jackson understands the power of repetition. But he also understands the power of a slower, more deliberate beat. By balancing the cadence, Jackson keeps his speech from becoming monotonous.

USING THE SELECTION
Keep Your Eyes on the Prize

1
Jackson uses *if* statements to explain to young people what challenges they must take up if they are to become a greater generation.

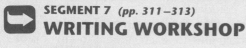

discussion. You may want to allow time for students to answer those questions in small groups before directing a full class discussion.

After a thorough analysis of Jackson's speech, have students use the writing process to generate their own speeches, either as homework or as an in-class assignment.

Students may present their speeches to the class for assessment, or you may schedule time for each student to tape his or her speech and for you to provide feedback after listening to the tapes.

2
The travel analogy is applied to the task to show that no road to success is easy.

VISUAL CONNECTIONS

Exploring the Subject. Jesse Jackson became a political activist during the civil rights movement of the late 1950s and early 1960s. When Jackson first began his campaign for equal opportunities, African Americans had not made any serious bids for the U.S. presidency.

ANSWERS

Writing Workshop Questions

1. Jackson reacts to the opinion that the new generation can be proud of being new. His position is that people should not take credit for what they have not personally achieved.
2. The last three sentences express those difficulties in figurative language. He speaks of *bumps, potholes, nails,* and *broken glass.*
3. Students will select different words and phrases with strong personal connotations. References to feeding the hungry, to educating more people, and to the freedom struggle may be among the emotional appeals cited.
4. Examples might include the repetition and variety of the *If . . .* clauses in both the first and second paragraphs. The analogies of travel and life are examples of subtle variations.

SELECTION AMENDMENT
Description of change: excerpted
Rationale: to focus on the concept of persuasion presented in this chapter

your prize is to grow up healthy, marry, and develop a family—if that is your prize, then don't let any activity divert you from your
2 prize. When we are traveling, sometimes there are bumps in the road. Sometimes there are potholes in the road. Sometimes nails and broken glass may puncture our tire and delay us and divert us from the prize. Keep your eyes on the prize.

from *Jesse Jackson: Still Fighting for the Dream*

1. To what opinion is Jesse Jackson reacting in this speech? Put his position statement into one sentence.
2. Jackson admits that what he is arguing for isn't easy. Where and how does he express the difficulties that his audience may face?
3. What words and phrases have the strongest connotations, positive or negative, for you? What other emotional appeals does Jackson use?
4. Jackson skillfully uses both repetition and subtle variety to emphasize important points. Find some examples of each technique in his speech.

Writing a Speech

Prewriting. What issue can automatically put energy or an edge into your voice? What worries you or makes you angry? Try to find something that stirs your feelings. You

CLOSURE

Ask students to discuss the similarities and differences between writing a persuasive essay and giving a persuasive speech. ■

may want to look through your writing journal or think about the last time you had an argument. You can also use a current magazine or newspaper for ideas.

After you have your topic, write a sentence that states your position on it. Do some research if you need to find reasons and evidence to back up your opinion. To get an expert opinion, you may want to talk to a teacher or to another person who is knowledgeable about this issue.

Writing, Evaluating, and Revising. People usually speak from notes. But you need to write out your speech first. Seeing your ideas on paper will help you build a sound argument. When you do your first draft, don't worry about choosing each word carefully. Just get your reasons and evidence down on paper.

When you are ready to evaluate and revise your speech, say it aloud. Listen not just to the ideas, but to how they sound. Vary your sentence structure and use repetition to emphasize important ideas.

Proofreading and Publishing. To get permission to give a speech, you sometimes have to show a group what you're going to say. Proofread your speech carefully, looking for errors in spelling, capitalization, and usage, before you show it to anyone. Since TV and radio stations often provide free time for speeches and announcements in the public interest, consider sending a copy of your speech to the closest television or radio station. If your topic is related to school, you might want to deliver your speech before the student council, school board, or parents and teachers association.

"IF MY MIND
CAN CONCEIVE IT,
AND MY HEART
CAN BELIEVE IT,
I KNOW I CAN ACHIEVE IT."

JESSE JACKSON

MEETING INDIVIDUAL NEEDS

LEP/ESL

General Strategies. When faced with making speeches, many ESL students become concerned with pronouncing words correctly—an area of potential embarrassment. You might want to pair students with native speakers who can coach them on difficult pronunciations.

SELECTION AMENDMENT
Description of change: excerpted
Rationale: to focus on the concept of persuasion presented in this chapter

SEGMENT 8 *(pp. 314–317)*

MAKING CONNECTIONS

PERSUASION ACROSS THE CURRICULUM

OBJECTIVES

- To analyze political cartoons
- To create an original political cartoon

PERSUASION ACROSS THE CURRICULUM

Teaching Strategies

To prepare students for this activity, you might collect several political cartoons and make copies for the class. For each political cartoon, have students determine what the cartoonist's opinion is. Then discuss how the cartoonist conveys that opinion. What images and language are used? Have each student highlight parts of the cartoons that are most effective and then discuss what makes these parts effective.

Select an issue to work on as a class—such as cafeteria food or lockers—and brainstorm a list of words or images that could be used. Have a volunteer sketch a drawing and have another decide upon the text. Have students use the same process when they plan their own political cartoons. Students might work in pairs with one planning the drawing and another planning the text.

MAKING CONNECTIONS

PERSUASION ACROSS THE CURRICULUM

Political Cartoons

No one in modern America could doubt the power of visual images to sway our feelings and ideas: We're practically under attack through our eyeballs. But getting a message across with pictures is nothing new. As just one example, political cartoons (or *editorial cartoons*) go back to colonial times. They're still a prominent feature of editorial pages and give us the artists' concise, witty, pointed opinions about breaking events.

Here is a political cartoon by Ben Sargent. What is his opinion about the status of free speech in 1991 America?

To create your own political cartoon, first find some examples in newspapers or magazines. Study them carefully to see how they create their effects. The cartoons with most impact

SPEAKING AND LISTENING OBJECTIVES

- To analyze advertisements
- To present an oral media analysis to the class

tend to be simple and direct. Notice that there's a reason for every single detail in a cartoon. Especially notice how the cartoonist draws people. Features are exaggerated to create the personality or feeling that the cartoonist wants to convey. You may find some cartoons with no words at all. Bring your cartoons to class and discuss which ones are most effective. How do the artists make an *idea* clear?

Next, watch or listen to the news for a day or two to find an issue about which you have strong feelings. Write a sentence that expresses your opinion about the issue, and then draw a political cartoon that puts your opinion into pictures.

SPEAKING AND LISTENING

Persuasion in the Media

If there were competitions in the art of persuading, advertisers would probably walk off with most of the prizes. That's because millions of dollars depend on their ability to convince you that you won't be happy until you buy whatever they are selling. Unfortunately for the consumer, advertisers rely more on emotional appeals than on logical appeals. Here are some of the emotional appeals they use:

- The ***bandwagon appeal*** tries to make you think that you should "jump on the bandwagon," that is, not be left out of what everybody else is doing. Advertisers know that most people don't want to be oddballs. What is an example? *Put on Sound Barrier Blades for your next roll down the street. You don't want to be out of formation when everybody else takes off.*

GUIDELINES

Combining the skills required to create a political cartoon is difficult; therefore, you might want to evaluate students' work by using a three-part check—clarity of opinion, choice of language, and presentation of images. That way students who are weak in one area might score well in another area.

SPEAKING AND LISTENING

Teaching Strategies

To provide students with models and guidelines for this activity, show the class some videotaped television commercials and allow students to listen to several radio commercials in class. You might also have them examine some magazine and newspaper ads. Assist students in identifying the emotional appeals used in the ads.

With the class, devise a rating scale to use to evaluate the various media presentations. You might include emotional appeals, logical appeals, choice of language, and presentation of images. You might also include negative points for emotional appeals that could backfire.

You may want to have students refer to the **Evaluating and Revising Persuasive Essays** chart on p. 306 to help devise the rating scale.

GUIDELINES

You could divide the class into three "Media Watchers" groups, one for each medium. Have groups use the rating scale the class devised, and evaluate their progress by how well they assessed each ad on the rating scale.

- ***Snob appeal*** uses words that appeal to your desire to be famous, wealthy, brainy, witty, and, *especially*, better than other people: *Elegante Inn is the perfect setting for a magnificent vacation. The only kind you deserve.* The opposite of snob appeal is called ***plain folks,*** and it reinforces down-to-earth values: *For value, versatility, and comfort you can't beat a Bumpo flannel shirt. The design hasn't changed for fifty years, because if it was good enough for our grandfathers, it's best for us.*

- A ***veiled threat*** cleverly suggests that something bad may happen if you don't buy the product: *If you use Denta-well, you'll know you've done as much as you can to make your teeth last as long as you do.*

Form a "Media Watchers" group, and look for radio, television, and print ads that use one or more of these emotional appeals. Find examples in each medium, and take notes on them or cut them out. Analyze the ads, paying attention to the roles of words, sounds, and images, and rating each ad's persuasiveness. Then give a talk about their logical and emotional appeals.

PERSUASION IN ACTION
OBJECTIVES
- To read letters to the editor
- To write a letter to the editor

PERSUASION IN ACTION

Letters to the Editor

Letters to the editor are a form of persuasion that countless people use every day. In fact, many readers turn immediately to the editorial page of a newspaper or the "sound off" page of a magazine: Gripes, outrages, and passions make for lively reading.

Usually, the audience for letters to the editor isn't really the editor; it is the publication's readers, some of whom are bound to care about the same issue that the writer cares about. The writer may be responding to an article or an earlier letter or introducing a totally new issue. Letters to the editor are a great way to express your opinions.

To see what these letters are like, read the ones printed in a local newspaper for several days, or read the ones in several recent issues of a favorite magazine. What ideas do you want to challenge? What issue do you want to bring into the forum?

In writing your letter, apply everything you've learned about persuasion in this chapter, but *be brief.* Publications usually reserve the right to edit, so be your own editor first. Also be sure to read any requirements about form and submission. Mail your letter, and look for it in print. If it's published, bring a copy to class. Check, too, for responses. Other readers may give you a pat on the back or an argument.

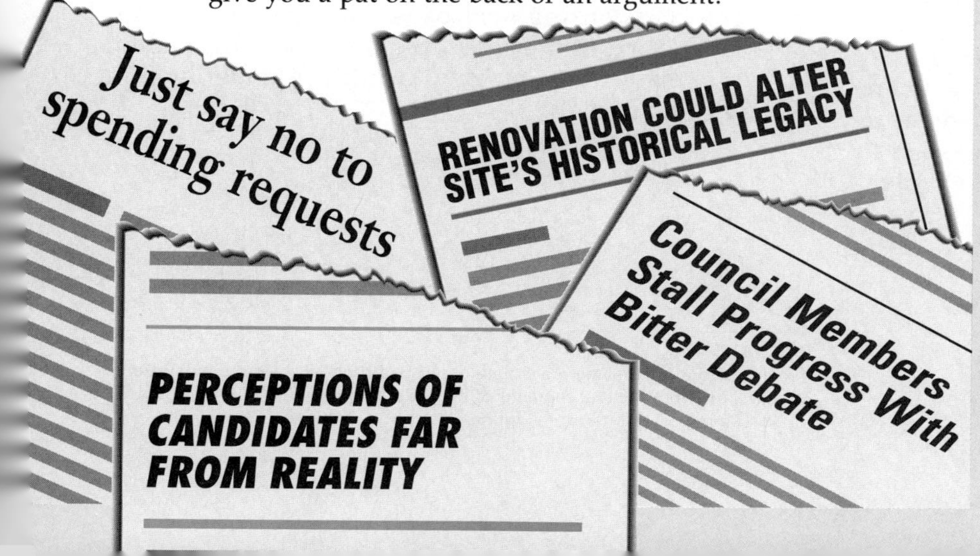

Just say no to spending requests
RENOVATION COULD ALTER SITE'S HISTORICAL LEGACY
Council Members Stall Progress With Bitter Debate
PERCEPTIONS OF CANDIDATES FAR FROM REALITY

PERSUASION IN ACTION
Teaching Strategies

You may want to use letters from magazines that your students read as models for this activity. Have students work in groups to evaluate the models before they begin writing their own letters.

To help students shorten lengthy letters, give them the following checklist:

1. Are there any wordy phrases that can be revised?
2. Are there any long words that might be replaced with shorter but equally effective synonyms?
3. Is there any unnecessary repetition in the letter?

You may want to work with students who need help with revision techniques.

GUIDELINES

Use the guidelines in the **Evaluating and Revising Persuasive Essays** chart on p. 306 to judge students' letters to the editor. Encourage students to submit their letters to publications.

Chapter 9

WRITING TO EXPLORE

OBJECTIVES

- To critically assess an essay on a personal level
- To analyze the use of exploration in an essay and to assess critically an exploratory essay on a personal level
- To identify anomalies in an essay
- To identify and investigate community problems and their possible solutions
- To plan a problem-solution essay
- To evaluate evidence in terms of trustworthiness, accuracy, and usefulness
- To analyze a problem-solution essay
- To write a draft of a problem-solution essay by using a basic framework
- To analyze a writer's revisions
- To evaluate and revise an essay
- To proofread and publish an essay
- To engage in group problem solving
- To participate in a group presentation
- To explore and express ideas in a journal entry
- To analyze the Declaration of Independence as a problem-solution essay

Motivation

Motivate the class for this lesson by asking them to write a paragraph describing their vision of an ideal school. Ask students to explain why they would change their current school and how they would implement the changes to solve problems. Explain that because this writing activity explores a subject and proposes solutions to problems, it is called exploratory writing. Explain that they will be writing problem-solution essays in this chapter.

Introduction

Students should understand that exploration is part of the expository writing aim achieved through narration, description, classification, and evaluation. Explain to students that they will focus on narration and classification to write essays in this chapter. Explain objective tone to students to let them know the most effective problem-solution essays present problems and solutions with documented, trustworthy, accurate, and useful facts and reasons.

Integration

Students can use this chapter to analyze the Declaration of Independence as a problem-solution essay in history classes. Students can apply these analysis techniques to other historical documents to explore why the documents were necessary and what solutions were presented.

Students can use this chapter to integrate the study of grammar by reviewing the use and definitions of *affect* and *effect*.

Students can apply the basic elements of a problem-solution essay to other papers they write and to essay answers for tests. Explain to students that this chapter will show them how to write problem-solution essays logically and convincingly.

After they have written their essays, students should be familiar enough with problem-solution essays to identify, evaluate, and analyze problem-solution essays in literature.

The chart on the next page illustrates the strands of language arts as they are integrated into this chapter. For vocabulary study, glossary words are underlined in some writing models.

QUOTATIONS

All **Quotations for the Day** are chosen because of their relevance to instructional material presented in that segment of the chapter and for their usefulness in establishing student interest in writing.

INTEGRATING THE LANGUAGE ARTS

Selection	Reading and Literature	Writing and Critical Thinking	Language and Syntax	Speaking, Listening, and Other Expression Skills
from **"Pilgrim at Tinker Creek"** by Annie Dillard **320-321** **"Wheelchair Hell: A Look at Campus Accessibility"** by Shannon Long **338-342**	Responding personally to literature **321** Analyzing exploration in literature **321** Reading for specific details **321, 342** Determining intended audience for an essay **342** Identifying an author's techniques **342**	Relating literature to personal experience **321** Finding the main idea **321, 342** Making inferences and drawing conclusions **325, 326, 329 331, 335-336, 342, 351, 357** Choosing a topic **326, 355** Brainstorming **326, 329** Analyzing and freewriting possible solutions **329, 331** Evaluating evidence **331, 335-336** Listing steps **332** Planning a problem-solution essay **336** Analyzing a problem-solution essay **342** Writing a first draft **347** Analyzing a writer's revisions **349-351** Evaluating and revising **351, 355** Proofreading and publishing **353, 355** Writing a group presentation **355** Writing a journal entry to explore and express feelings **357** Analyzing exploratory writing in history **357**	Proofreading for errors in grammar, usage, and mechanics **353**	Speaking and listening to identify problems **325** Working with classmates to evaluate evidence **335-336** Talking with classmates to analyze a problem-solution essay **351, 357** Working with classmates to explore a problem **355** Giving an oral presentation **355**

CHAPTER 9

SEGMENT PLANNING GUIDE

You can use the following Planning Guide to adapt the chapter material to the individual needs of your class. All the Resources listed in this chapter are located in the *Teacher's ResourceBank*™.

SEGMENT	PAGES	CONTENT	RESOURCES
1 ***Asking Questions, Seeking Answers***	***319-321***		
Literary Model from ***Pilgrim at Tinker Creek***	320-321	Guided reading: a model of an exploratory essay	
Reader's Response/ Writer's Craft	321	Model evaluation: responding to literature and analyzing an exploratory essay	
2 ***Ways to Explore***	***322-323***		
3 ***Prewriting***	***324-336***		Writing a Problem-Solution Essay Listing and Evaluating Solutions 72
Exploring Problems	324-326	Guidelines: identifying and investigating a problem	
Exercise 1	325	Cooperative learning: identifying problems	
Writing Assignment: Part 1	326	Applied practice: identifying and investigating a problem	
Exploring Solutions	327-328	Guidelines: indentifying possible solutions and finding the best one	
Writing Assignment: Part 2	329	Applied practice: identifying possible solutions	
Finding the Best Solution	329-331	Guidelines: using questions to find the best solution	
Exercise 2	331	Applied practice: evaluating possible solutions	
Listing Necessary Steps	332	Guidelines: using criteria to list steps	
Writing Assignment: Part 3	332	Applied practice: identifying the best solution and listing steps	
Planning Your Essay	333-334	Guidelines: considering purpose, audience, and tone and providing support	
Critical Thinking: Evaluating Evidence	335	Guidelines: using criteria to evaluate support	
Critical Thinking Exercise	335-336	Cooperative learning: evaluating evidence	
Writing Assignment: Part 4	336	Applied practice: reseaching and listing solutions	
4 ***Writing***	***337-347***		Writing a Problem-Solution Essay 73
The Basic Elements	337	Guidelines: analyzing basic elements of an essay	
Literary Model **"Wheelchair Hell: A Look at Campus Accessibiity"**	338-342	Guided reading: examining basic elements in a model	
Exercise 3	342	Cooperative learning: analyzing a problem-solution essay	

For **Portfolio Assessment** see the following pages in the *Teacher's ResourceBank*™:
Aims For Writing — pp. 71–76
Holistically Graded Composition Models — pp. 515–520
Assessment Portfolio — pp. 533–562

SEGMENT	PAGES	CONTENT	RESOURCES
A Basic Framework	343	Introduction: following a framework	
A Writer's Model	343-346	Guided reading: examining structure in a model	
Chart: Framework for an Essay	346	Guidelines: structuring an essay	
Writing Assignment: Part 5	347	Applied practice: writing a first draft	
5 *Evaluating and Revising*	*348-351*		Writing a Problem-Solution Essay 74
Evaluating and Revising	348	Introduction: editing a first draft	
Chart: Evaluating and Revising	349	Guidelines: applying evaluation and revision techniques	
Exercise 4	349-351	Cooperative learning: analyzing a writer's revisions	
Writing Assignment: Part 6	351	Applied practice: evaluating and revising	
6 *Proofreading and Publishing*	*352-353*		Writing a Problem-Solution Essay 75
Publishing	352	Publishing ideas: reaching a specific audience	
Grammar Hint	353	Writing suggestion: using *affect* and *effect* correctly	
Writing Assignment: Part 7	353	Applied practice: proofreading and publishing	
7 *Writing Workshop*	*354-355*		
Group Problem Solving	354-355	Guidelines: exploring a problem Cooperative learning: exploring a problem and writing a group presentation	
8 *Making Connections*	*356-357*		
Writing to Explore and to Express Yourself: A Journal Entry	356-357	Guidelines: writing a journal entry Applied Practice: writing to explore and express feelings	
Exploratory Writing Across the Curriculum: History	357	Cooperative learning: exploring the Declaration of Independence	

WHOLE-CHAPTER RESOURCES
A Writing Process Log, A Writing Prompt, Holistically Graded Models, Assessment Portfolio Materials

SEGMENT 1 *(pp. 318–321)*

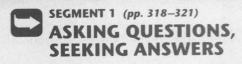

ASKING QUESTIONS, SEEKING ANSWERS

OBJECTIVES

- To respond personally to exploratory literature
- To identify and analyze the use of exploration in an essay

VISUAL CONNECTIONS
Inner Outer Space

About the Artist. Isadore Seltzer is a freelance illustrator who has created artwork for several national publishing and advertising companies. Seltzer's work includes magazine covers, book jackets, and graphics for movies. The artist teaches illustration and painting at Parsons School of Design in Manhattan. A versatile artist, Seltzer writes and illustrates children's books and is also a sculptor, furniture maker, and photographer. Seltzer has exhibited work around the world and has won awards at the major graphic art exhibitions.

Exploring the Subject. Ask students if they have ever stared at the clouds and discovered familiar forms among them. Have the class free associate with this illustration of clouds, lines, and shapes. What does the title *Inner Outer Space* suggest? What do the contrasting elements—the soft, fluffy, white clouds juxtaposed with the dark, angular, square shapes—suggest?

9 WRITING TO EXPLORE

TEACHING THE LESSON

Have students imagine that they have the opportunity to explore anything that they are curious about—a free trip to investigate a lifelong interest. Have a few volunteers suggest what they would be interested in and why. Explain that exploratory writing is the result of people's curiosities about the world and the questions people ask.

You might want to show how exploratory writing is part of the expository aim by comparing exploratory writing to exploratory science. Scientists must observe and classify facts; they inform others of their results. But some scientists go a step further. They plan and conduct research when they have questions about what they observe. Exploratory writers are informative writers ☛

Asking Questions, Seeking Answers

Out in the dark, silent expanse of outer space, the U.S. spaceship *Voyager 2* travels, sending messages back to earth, shedding light on mysteries of the universe. Human beings have always **asked questions** and **sought answers** for mysteries or problems. As they do, they constantly develop new ideas.

Writing and You. Explorations may start in the mind, but often they turn into an article, an essay, or a book. Thor Heyerdahl asked questions about the seafaring abilities of ancient people and wrote *Kon-Tiki.* A reporter explores problems in education and writes an editorial outlining possible solutions. What about your own explorations—questions you've asked, answers you've found?

As You Read. In the following selection, Annie Dillard wonders about the weather and its effects. Does her exploration lead to answers, or just to more questions?

Isadore Seltzer, *Inner Outer Space* (1984). Acrylic on canvas. 20″ × 30″.

QUOTATION FOR THE DAY

"To write is to put the seeming insignificance of human existence into a different perspective." (Alfred Kazin, 1915–   , American literary critic)

Ask students if they've ever read about something very trivial, yet been intrigued by what the writer said. Lewis Thomas, a medical doctor, wrote several biology books about his observations and questions. One of these was certainly about small things, *The Lives of a Cell,* yet the book had a unique perspective. Have students freewrite for a few minutes about something simple that they don't understand and have questions about.

MEETING INDIVIDUAL NEEDS

LEP/ESL

General Strategies. ESL students spend time learning about the American experience but may have few opportunities to discuss their own cultures. If you have students from other countries in your classroom, you might have native students explore topics they've wondered about by asking ESL students questions about their countries, languages, and cultures. In turn, ESL students might quiz native students about customs in the United States they are curious about.

who go one step further; their emphasis is on discovery.

Have a volunteer read **Asking Questions, Seeking Answers** as an introduction to the selection by Annie Dillard. Ask students to think about the questions the writer explores as they read the selection. After they have had time to read, have students name several curiosities about everyday things that Dillard addresses in her essay, and list their responses on the chalkboard. Use the annotations and the **Reader's Response** questions to guide your class discussion.

Students should be prepared to write responses to the **Writer's Craft** questions independently. Suggest that they refer to the essay for specific details. Assess students'

USING THE SELECTION
from Pilgrim at Tinker Creek

1
Most of the time when people say they talked about the weather, they mean they talked about nothing of significance. But weather and people's thoughts about it can be very extraordinary. What kinds of weather can be phenomenal?
[tornadoes, hurricanes, hail storms, thunder and lightning, sunrises, sunsets, and whatever people view with imagination]

2
tailwind: a wind blowing in the same direction as the course of a ship or aircraft

3
iceboat: a vehicle for rapid movement on ice, with a T-shaped frame on three runners

4
sonant: having sound; sounding

5
surd: a voiceless sound

from Pilgrim at Tinker Creek
by Annie Dillard

There are seven or eight
categories of phenomena in the world
that are worth talking about, and one of
them is the weather. Any time you care
to get in your car and drive across the country
and over the mountains, come into our valley, cross
Tinker Creek, drive up the road to the house, walk across the
1 yard, knock on the door and ask to come in and talk about
the weather, you'd be welcome. If you came tonight from up
2 north, you'd have a terrific tailwind; between Tinker and Dead
3 Man you'd chute through the orchardy pass like an iceboat.
When I let you in, we might not be able to close the door. The
4 wind shrieks and hisses down the valley, sonant and surd, drying
5 the puddles and dismantling the nests from the trees.

understanding by having volunteers discuss their answers to the **Writer's Craft** questions.

To reteach, have students watch a news commentary to determine what issue or problem was addressed and what solutions were suggested.

To close, have students discuss the following questions:

1. Where do explorations begin? [in the minds of the explorers]
2. What are the results of explorations? [solutions to problems] ■

6 Inside the house, my single goldfish, Ellery Channing, whips around and around the sides of his bowl. Can he feel a glassy vibration, a ripple out of the north that urges him to swim for deeper,
7 warmer waters? Saint-Exupéry says that when flocks of wild geese migrate high over a barnyard, the cocks and even the dim, fatted chickens fling themselves a foot or so into the air and flap for the south. Eskimo sled dogs feed all summer on famished salmon flung to them from creeks. I have often wondered if those dogs feel a wistful downhill drift in the fall, or an upstream yank, an urge to leap ladders, in the spring. To what hail do you hark, Ellery?—what sunny bottom under chill waters, what Chinese emperor's petaled pond? Even the spiders are restless under this wind, roving about alert-eyed over their fluff in every corner.

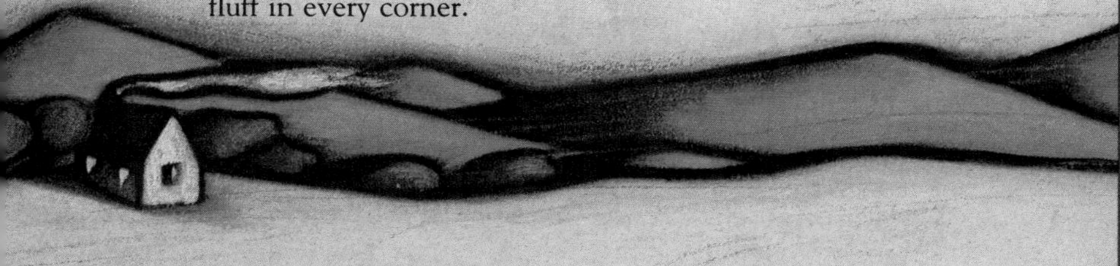

Reader's Response

1. Have you ever noticed how often people talk about the weather? Why is it so important to people? Can you remember a time when the weather created a problem, or perhaps solved one, in your life? Explain.
2. Many people like to read Annie Dillard's observations of nature because of her curiosity and her sense of wonder. Did you enjoy reading this piece? Why or why not?
3. Why do you think the goldfish "whips around and around the side of his bowl"? What unexplained animal, bird, or fish behavior have you noted and wondered about?

Writer's Craft

4. When you write to explore, you may do it to raise questions or to find a new answer. What kind of exploration does Annie Dillard write about?
5. Part of exploring a subject is noticing anomalies, things that are unusual or different. What anomalies does Dillard think might be caused by the wind?

6
What idea about her fish Ellery Channing is Dillard exploring? [the idea that Ellery Channing may have instincts that urge him to swim to deeper, warmer waters]

7
Saint-Exupéry (1900–1944) was a French aviator and writer.

ANSWERS

Reader's Response

Responses will vary.

1. Students might say that weather is important because weather has a daily effect on people's lives — their choice of clothing, their outdoor activities, and their plans for travel. Students should explain how weather created or solved a problem.
2. Urge students to explain what they like or dislike about Dillard's writing.
3. Perhaps the goldfish is responding to the chilly north wind. Encourage varied responses about the goldfish and other unexplained animal behavior.

Writer's Craft

4. She raises questions about animals' reactions to impending weather changes.
5. Dillard mentions that her goldfish's whipping around his bowl might be related to the wind. Then she questions how chickens flying into the air and flapping for the south and Eskimo dogs rejoicing are related to the seasonal changes manifest by the wind.

SELECTION AMENDMENT
Description of change: excerpted
Rationale: to focus on exploratory writing presented in this chapter

SEGMENT 2 *(pp. 322–323)*

WAYS TO EXPLORE

TEACHING THE MODES

Explain to students that like the other aims of writing, exploratory writing can be accomplished by using several strategies. Have a volunteer read the introduction in **Ways to Explore** and then read the examples of modes. After you or a student has read the examples, ask students to brainstorm and suggest other examples of the methods used for exploring.

Have a student read the information in the **Looking Ahead** box and note that the bulleted information identifies the hallmarks of exploratory writing. To help students distinguish exploratory writing from informative

MEETING INDIVIDUAL NEEDS

LESS-ADVANCED STUDENTS

Because many students will be unfamiliar with exploratory writing, you may want to expand upon the meaning of the word *explore.* Have students suggest ways people explore in daily life [exploring a cave, an underwater reef, an art museum, a wilderness area, a computer program, the night sky through a telescope, or a new relationship].

Next ask why people explore [curiosity and the need to confirm, negate, or expand ideas]. Then have students suggest how they could turn each of the exploring ideas into something to write about and have them explain which strategy might work best.

INTEGRATING THE LANGUAGE ARTS

Test-taking Link. Point out to students that essay tests in literature, social studies, and other subjects often encourage exploratory responses that use one or more of the development strategies. Tell students that as they progress through the chapter, they should look for ways to apply the strategies presented here to test-taking situations.

Ways to Explore

Annie Dillard's writing is an example of open-ended exploration: She lets her own curiosity and wonder take over and explores for the sake of exploring. Other writers are often more focused and deliberate; they want to solve a problem or discover a new idea. The explorations may be in writing, or they may take place entirely in the writers' minds. Once the writers find solutions or new ideas, however, they want to inform other people and sometimes even to convince others to do something. Exploratory writing, combined with informative or persuasive writing, may appear in newspapers, magazines, speeches and sermons, business proposals, and books.

There is more than one way that exploratory writing can be developed. Here are some examples of how you might use the four strategies to develop your own explorations.

Narration: tracing the history of your family to discover and explain where your favorite family heirloom came from; studying the events that preceded the Persian Gulf Conflict of 1990–1991 to discover how future international conflicts might be avoided.

Description: describing the symptoms of a sick person over the phone so that a doctor can make a diagnosis; describing the sound your car transmission makes to help your mechanic identify the problem.

Classification: comparing and contrasting two possible solutions to school overcrowding; looking at three classes of cafeteria lunches—salad bar, hot-food bar, and sandwich bar—as you explore solutions to the problem of low student interest in cafeteria food.

Evaluation: asking questions about three recent presidents of the United States and identifying what personal and professional characteristics to look for in our next president; explaining why your football team did so poorly (or so well) last season and explaining how the team might improve (or maintain excellence).

and explanatory writing, refer them to the **Writing Note** on p. 249. ■

LOOKING AHEAD

In this chapter, you'll learn the process of exploration and discovery. The main writing assignment takes the form of a problem-solution essay. You'll use the strategies of narration and classification to explore the problem. Later, as you discuss possible solutions to the problem, you'll use mostly the strategy of narration. As you work through the main writing assignment, keep in mind that in a problem-solution essay, the writer

- identifies and explores a problem
- proposes and evaluates solutions to the problem
- explains (and proves) the best solution to the problem

"Problems are only opportunities in work clothes."

Henry J. Kaiser

CRITICAL THINKING
Application

To help students learn to think in terms of problems and solutions, brainstorm with students to list problems in your school on the chalkboard. Then have the class think of solutions to the problems. After students have listed all the solutions they can dream up, have them read over the solutions and eliminate weak or unrealistic ones.

SELECTION AMENDMENT
Description of change: excerpted
Rationale: to focus on exploratory writing presented in this chapter

SEGMENT 3 *(pp. 324–336)*

PREWRITING

OBJECTIVES

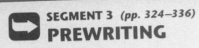

- To identify community problems
- To identify and investigate a problem
- To evaluate possible solutions and select the best solution
- To identify the best solution and list the steps necessary to solve a problem
- To plan a problem-solution essay

Teacher's ResourceBank™

RESOURCES

PREWRITING

- Listing and Evaluating Solutions 72

QUOTATION FOR THE DAY

". . . writing helped me face myself, helped me tell myself things." (Sherwood Anderson, 1876–1941, American novelist and short-story writer)

Ask students if they can remember how they have made important decisions or have solved difficult problems. Discuss how personal writing can provide written records of the routes leading to valuable insights or to solving problems. Explain that writing to explore can also go beyond personal problems to encompass universal problems.

MEETING INDIVIDUAL NEEDS

AT-RISK STUDENTS

Help students see that exploring solutions to problems has many everyday applications. Have students brainstorm and list commonplace matters that writing to explore might influence. Students might suggest exploring problems with parents, employers, or business and community leaders.

Writing a Problem-Solution Essay

Prewriting

Exploring Problems

When you use writing to explore, you often do so for personal reasons. Maybe you've used your diary or journal to explore the solutions to a personal problem—a disagreement with a friend, for example. You probably don't share that kind of personal exploration with an audience. Instead, you consider what you've learned and act on it.

At times, however, you may be called upon to explore a problem and present your findings to an audience. When that happens, you're usually expected to think through the problem and its possible solutions carefully. And you are expected to explain clearly to your audience why the solution you propose is an effective one. In school, this kind of audience-directed exploratory writing is often called a ***problem-solution essay.*** It has two basic aims. The first aim is to explore the problem and all its possible solutions in order to identify the best one. Then, as you write the essay, your aim shifts to one of explaining, and proving, the advantages of the solution (or solutions) you decide is best.

Identifying a Problem

The personal problems you explore may have meaning only to you: *How am I ever going to get money together for gas this week?* The problem you write about for an audience, however, should be significant not only to you but to others. "My split ends and what to do about them" is not an appropriate topic for a serious problem-solution essay, except, perhaps, for a hairstylist. On the other hand, you don't want to choose a problem that even the best minds have been unable to solve satisfactorily. "Achieving world peace in our time" is probably too tough to handle.

If you're concerned about a national or international issue, you may want to follow the advice "Think globally; act locally." For example, if you're concerned about world hunger, focus

TEACHING THE LESSON

Have students imagine that they have been hired to propose solutions to a challenging problem in the school. When they have selected a problem, have them suggest solutions. Then with students' assistance list the strengths and weaknesses of each solution on the chalkboard. Explain that this is the process involved in writing a problem-solution essay.

Begin this prewriting segment by having students read **Exploring Problems.** As you discuss **Identifying a Problem,** emphasize the way to focus large problems locally by using the information in the box to stimulate discussion. You might help students get ☛

your attention on the problem of hunger in your community. Many writers find it rewarding to work with problems that directly affect them or people they know well.

> *Perhaps you're concerned about something at school:* Does the band need new uniforms? Are there too many students in classes at your school?
> *You may be concerned about something that's happening in your community:* Do the parks need cleaning up? Are there enough street lights?

As you brainstorm for problems, consider the significance of each one by asking

- Does it affect a number of people?
- Is it important to the people that it affects?

EXERCISE 1 **Speaking and Listening: Identifying Problems**

One way to learn about problems of local concern is to tune in to local news and commentary on radio and TV. If a local station has a listener or viewer call-in show, you may want to make a point to watch or listen during those hours—perhaps even call in with your own views. Follow the news for an evening or two to identify problems in your community. Make a list of three or four problems and share them in class discussion. Which ones are important to a number of people?

MEETING INDIVIDUAL NEEDS

ADVANCED STUDENTS

Challenge advanced students to tackle and explore difficult community problems. Encourage students not only to write about their community problems but also to become involved in solving the problems. Encourage students to make a difference in their community by becoming active, involved citizens. Suggest that they attend public forums, city council meetings, public debates, or community awareness meetings and that they write letters to people who have the power to make changes.

ANSWERS

Exercise 1

Each student should identify three or four problems that affect the community. Encourage students to narrow their focus to specific rather than general problems and to determine which problems seem to affect the largest number of people in the community.

started with **Exercise 1** by taping a news commentary to share with the class and by brainstorming with the class before they work on their own.

Make sure students understand how to identify a problem before you assign **Exercise 1** as independent practice. You might have students work in pairs on the assignment. After the class has had time to follow the news at home, initiate a discussion in class.

Using the problems that the class generated earlier (either from brainstorming or tuning in to news commentaries), model the skills necessary for completion of **Writing Assignment: Part 1.**

Begin **Exploring Solutions** by having a volunteer read the introduction.

INTEGRATING THE LANGUAGE ARTS

Literature Link. Help students identify exploratory writing in the literature they read. For example, in Ernesto Galarza's short story "Barrio Boy," the narrator tells about his first days in an American school and the special problems he encountered. Ask students to identify at least three problems Galarza encountered and to describe Galarza's solutions.

MEETING INDIVIDUAL NEEDS

STUDENTS WITH SPECIAL NEEDS

Learning disabled students often have difficulty organizing their ideas so they can complete assignments. Therefore, choosing a topic can be crucial for learning disabled students to write a successful exploration paper. Topics must be narrow enough so that students don't get bogged down in research. If topics are familiar ones, students may feel comfortable with the information and already have strong research questions about their topics. Some students may find it helpful to choose topics that can be researched through recorded interviews or surveys.

Investigating a Problem

You can't begin to solve a problem that you don't understand. The following questions will help you investigate the problem you've chosen.

- Who or what is directly affected by this problem?
- How does this problem affect them?
- What causes the problem? Is there more than one cause?
- Is this problem like any other problem? Is it related to another problem?

Usually you won't have the answers to all of these questions—you'll need to do some research. You can use the library to find out how widespread the problem is or do some personal or telephone interviewing with people who have expert knowledge about the problem. For example, if you think there aren't enough street lights in your neighborhood, check out other neighborhoods. Or, ask a local police officer if poor lighting contributes to the crime or accident rate in the community.

WRITING ASSIGNMENT

PART 1:
Identifying and Investigating a Problem

What's bothering you? Start with your list from Exercise 1, and brainstorm a list of problems that affect your school and community, as well as some national and international problems. Then evaluate the problems to decide which one would make the best topic and find out as much as you can about it. Use the list of questions above to guide your search for information.

Emphasize the suggestions under **Strategies for Analyzing Possible Solutions** as ways to discover new, more creative solutions than those that have already been proposed.

You might want to model possible solutions to another of the problems students have suggested in the same way as the **Here's How** example on p. 328 before they begin **Writing Assignment: Part 2** on p. 329, which requires students to identify possible solutions independently. You could limit the number of solutions each student considers to five so that students can be more thorough.

Have students read **Finding the Best Solution** on p. 329 and carefully go over the **Here's How** chart on p. 330. Have students help you generate and analyze some ☛

Prewriting

Exploring Solutions

How much information do you have about your problem? Could you talk about it for ten or fifteen minutes? Would you be able to answer someone's questions about the background to the problem? If you've thoroughly investigated your problem, you're ready to move on to the answers.

Identifying Possible Solutions

Most problems have more than one possible solution, and many of these solutions may have already been tried. Still, it is always possible to devise creative solutions to problems that seem to defy solution. Continue your exploration by finding out how others have tried to solve the problem and how effective these solutions have been. To find information, you may again have to do some interviewing, viewing, listening, or reading. A questioning strategy can help you analyze possible solutions.

STRATEGIES FOR ANALYZING POSSIBLE SOLUTIONS

Ideas of Others

1. What solutions to the problem have already been tried?
2. How effective have these solutions been?
3. What solutions are currently being proposed?

Your Own Ideas

1. Can some of the problem's causes be eliminated? How?
2. What can be done about the effects of the problem?
3. Is there any part of the problem that seems especially difficult to solve?
4. Which part of the problem is easiest to solve? Why?
5. What is the most unusual way you can think of to solve the problem? the easiest way? the most popular way?

As you answer some of these questions, you may discover your own solutions. For example, one writer used two of the

MEETING INDIVIDUAL NEEDS

LESS-ADVANCED STUDENTS

Give students guidelines for interviewing. Many students will not have experience interviewing and may need some tips, such as these:

1. Introduce yourself to the person you wish to interview and tell him or her why you want an interview.
2. Ask when a phone or personal interview would be convenient.
3. Ask if you can record the interview.
4. If the person you wish to interview declines, ask if he or she knows someone else with knowledge of the problem who is available for an interview.

You might also refer students to **Chapter 33: "Communication Skills."** Information on conducting interviews begins on p. 950.

compromise solutions and discuss whether different parts of the problem might warrant different solutions. The chart illustrates the organization necessary to plan and arrange solutions to problems. Before students begin **Exercise 2** on p. 331, which requires students to add solutions to a list, you might want to model how you would select one other possible solution. Emphasize that carrying out the solutions must be possible.

Model how to list the necessary steps by using one of the problems the class has discussed. Explain that part of the process involves arranging the steps in order. Then assign **Writing Assignment: Part 3** on p. 332 as independent practice.

INTEGRATING THE LANGUAGE ARTS

Literature Link. Show students how they can use literature to locate problems in their community. For example, Langston Hughes's poem "Harlem" is a commentary on society. Point out that Hughes wonders how society offers hope to those who must wait for their dreams to become a reality. Connect this to local circumstances by asking students to identify those people in their community who must wait to turn their dreams into realities.

questions as prompts for focused freewriting about the problem of homelessness. Notice that the writer isn't evaluating the solutions yet, just trying to come up with ideas.

HERE'S HOW

Can some of the causes of homelessness be eliminated? How?

One cause of homelessness is a lack of low-cost housing. We could eliminate this lack by building more low-cost housing, but where would the money come from? Maybe there could be a special tax on every real estate transaction. Maybe we wouldn't even need to build more low-cost housing if we just fixed up what we already have. Maybe a program like Habitat for Humanity to help rehab existing properties as well as build new ones?

What is the strangest way you can think of to solve the problem?

Maybe the local government could pay people to take homeless families into their homes. This might help some marginal families earn more money so they wouldn't become homeless, too. This could provide a role model for the homeless, too. But could complete strangers get along?

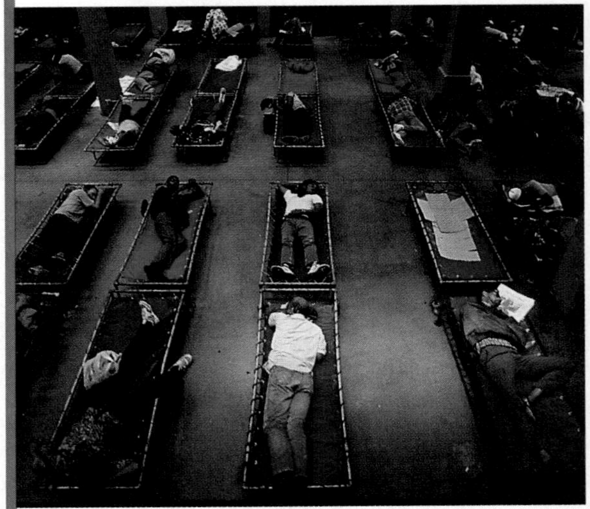

Students might have difficulty differentiating between the purpose of their exploratory essays and the purpose of persuasive essays. Explain that although they are recommending a particular solution to a problem, the recommendation is based on facts, and the language used should be neutral and tentative. Remind students that persuasive essays, on the other hand, can be based on opinions and often include emotional appeals.

Before students begin reading **Planning Your Problem-Solution Essay** on p. 333, point out that although the next step is still prewriting, the planning switches to the essay itself. Emphasize that as in persuasive writing, the audience and what the audience already knows about the ☛

WRITING ASSIGNMENT

PART 2:
Identifying Possible Solutions

Find out how many minds have tried to solve your problem and how effective they have been. Using the strategies on page 327, analyze the solutions other people have proposed—and remember that this process of analysis may require some further research on your part. Then search for your own solutions, using brainstorming or freewriting to come up with as many solutions as possible. Save your list for later use.

Finding the Best Solution

In the search for possible solutions to a problem, you may find several. But all solutions (just like all apples in the barrel) are not created equal. Which is the best one? How do you begin to decide which solutions to discard when there is no single solution that is CLEARLY THE BEST? Following are three questions you can ask yourself to try to sort through the solutions you are considering:

1. **What are the strengths and weaknesses (or advantages and disadvantages) of each solution?** To find the answer to this question, list all the possible solutions you've identified. Then create a chart in which you list the strengths and weaknesses of each solution. Which solutions start to look better than others?
2. **Which solution is the most practical?** Often, the best solution is the most practical one: It can be put into effect easily, and it doesn't create more problems than it solves. If you have several solutions that look equally strong or equally weak, look to see which one is the most practical.
3. **Does any solution have a comparative advantage?** Sometimes one solution appears to be the fairest one: It will actually do the most good for the most people. In that case it has a comparative advantage. If an analysis of strengths and weaknesses and practicality doesn't identify a single "best" solution, look at the solution that does the most good for the most people.

The following chart shows how one writer found the best solution to the pet overpopulation problem.

MEETING INDIVIDUAL NEEDS

LEARNING STYLES

Auditory Learners. Ask auditory learners to record the weaknesses and strengths of their solutions on tape recorders and then have the students listen to their responses to determine which are the best. Students might need to take notes as they listen to help them make their choices.

problem are very important in problem-solution essays.

Before students begin planning their essays in **Writing Assignment: Part 4** on p. 336, you might want to suggest how an essay could be adapted according to the proposed audience by modeling one of the problems you have already discussed.

Because students may need to do some research for support for their solutions, you might want to point out that sources like *Time* and *Newsweek* are good places to start, but that highly technical problems might need data from other sources. If students are going to use references in their papers, show the class how to list and cite sources.

MEETING **INDIVIDUAL** NEEDS

LEARNING STYLES

Kinetic Learners. Some students may prefer writing the strengths and weaknesses for each solution on separate note cards. Then students can arrange the cards on tables or desktops to determine which solutions seem more practical than the others.

Visual Learners. Visual learners might benefit from reproducing their charts on large posterboard or paper and filling in the charts as they gather information. To help students get a visual image of the process, have them color-code their charts in a way that is meaningful for them.

HERE'S HOW

Problem: Many animals are killed at the local animal shelter every week because nobody wants them.

Possible Solutions	*Strengths*	*Weaknesses*
educate public	*increases public awareness*	*doesn't target pet owners; facts impersonal and abstract*
encourage adoption from animal shelters	*fewer animals must be killed*	*too many animals; each family of four would need to adopt 28 dogs and cats*
encourage pet owners to spay and neuter animals	*gets at pet owners; works in communities with active Humane Society programs—they report 30–60% fewer euthanized animals*	*cost of operation; 6 to 7 million animals still put to death each year*
provide low-cost spay/neuter programs	*lower cost $50–$100; 15 yrs. after first spay/neuter clinic in Los Angeles, shelter animals decrease from 150,000 to 80,000*	*some people still don't spay and neuter pets; still 60,000 animals killed per yr. in Los Angeles*
pass a law requiring pet owners to spay/neuter pets	*covers all pets; makes owners responsible; makes noncompliance more costly than compliance; San Mateo, Calif., passed a similar law*	*drastic action that infringes on personal freedom*

Practicality

The solution of only encouraging adoptions from the shelters is not practical; number of abandoned animals too high. That eliminates that solution.

Comparative Advantage

Law requiring pet owners to spay and neuter their pets seems to be the fairest solution; also seems to do the most good for the most animals—seems to be the best solution, because it's the only way to counteract irresponsible behavior of some pet owners.

You might refer students to **Chapter 11: "Writing a Research Paper."**

ASSESSMENT

Assess students' progress by evaluating **Writing Assignment: Parts 3** and **4.** Checking the chart in **Writing Assignment: Part 3** will allow you to see quickly whether students have chosen appropriate problems, proposed valid solutions, and completed lists of strengths and weaknesses.

Notice that the strengths and weaknesses listed by the chart's writer include solid facts and sound reasons that are as specific as possible. Because two solutions may be inexpensive, listing *it won't cost much* as an advantage for each won't help you to decide between the two. But listing *the cost to the average taxpayer would be only about fifty-five cents per year* for one and *the cost to the average taxpayer would be only about a dollar per year* for the other would help. Again, finding this information may require that you do outside research.

EXERCISE 2 Evaluating Possible Solutions

You are the director of youth services in your community, and this problem has come to your attention: Teenagers don't have very many places to go at night.

In the following chart, several possible solutions and some of their strengths and weaknesses are listed. Think of at least one other possible solution and add it to the list. And, if you see strengths or weaknesses in addition to those already listed, make a note of these as well. Use the criteria of *practicality* and *most good for the most people* to evaluate all possible solutions and then select the one that you feel is best. Be prepared to explain your decision to others in your class.

Possible Solutions	Strengths	Weaknesses
open the community center in the evening	programs and facilities already in place	additional staff and operating expenses for extended hours; not just for teens
recruit teen-oriented businesses like a "juice bar" for the community	new, different types of activities; might increase commercial revenues	recruiting may take a long time; costs may keep some teens from using
encourage existing programs (Scouts; church, synagogue, and school groups; YMCA; Rec. Dept.) to offer more teen programming	programs already in existence; variety of groups meets a variety of needs	need added commitment from adult volunteers; limited outreach to those not already involved

ANSWERS

Exercise 2

Each student should add at least one solution to the list shown, list other strengths or weaknesses, and determine which solution is best. Encourage students to tell what they found practical and useful to the largest number of people when they explain their decisions to the class.

INTEGRATING THE LANGUAGE ARTS

Technology Link. When students have to categorize and manipulate large amounts of information like the data in the solutions chart, a database can be a convenient way to store the details. Having a database also gives students the advantage of being able to reshape their material quickly and easily—to add, delete, change, or reorganize new information as it is received.

RETEACHING

Ask a local journalist to visit your classroom and have students prepare questions concerning problems in the community for the interview. After students have recorded their interview notes, discuss the problems that are relevant to the most people, the solutions that are most practical, and the strengths and weaknesses of the solutions.

CLOSURE

Close the lesson by discussing the following questions:

1. How can problems for exploration be identified? [by thinking about how to solve global problems locally]
2. How can the best solutions be determined? [by investigating and researching solutions]

CRITICAL THINKING

Analysis

Explain to students that because many solutions to problems involve money, lack of funds often prevents a problem from receiving attention. Ask students to find out or estimate how much money their solutions would require. Students should break down the amounts and prepare to justify how the money would be spent. Then students should think of realistic proposals to generate money. Students should find out what community funds are available by checking local finance records housed in public libraries.

Listing Necessary Steps

Don't put away your thinking cap just because you've identified the best solution. You still have to think through the steps that will be needed to put your idea into action. Think in specific, practical terms. "First, get a million dollars" is not very helpful advice. You must decide exactly what has to be done, how it is to be done, and in what order it is to be done. For example, getting a spay/neuter law passed might involve these steps:

1. Propose a law that (a) requires all pet owners to have their dogs and cats spayed or neutered, (b) makes an exception for professional breeders but requires them to purchase a special breeding license, and (c) imposes stiff fines for those who break the law.
2. Make people aware of the need for spaying and neutering, and gather support for such a law.
3. Convince officials that most citizens support such a law.

Reminder

To explore a problem and find a solution

- choose a problem that is significant but solvable
- investigate the problem to see what its causes and effects are
- identify a number of possible solutions, including both your own ideas and the ideas of others
- identify the best solution by looking at strengths and weaknesses, practicality, and comparative advantages

WRITING ASSIGNMENT

PART 3:
Identifying Your Best Solution and Listing Necessary Steps

So, what's your answer? Take time to evaluate all your possible solutions carefully and identify the best solution to your problem. Use a chart like the one in the Here's How on page 330 to identify strengths and weaknesses, practicality, and comparative value. Then make a list of the steps necessary to carry out this solution. Try to arrange these steps in the order they'll need to be done.

EXTENSION

To help students detect flaws in their solutions, have them work in pairs to read each other's problems and solutions. Suggest that as one student reads, the other acts as a representative of the community at large. The representative could then think of reasonable questions the community would have about the proposed solutions. If solutions seem impractical, students should help their partners rewrite the solutions or propose more feasible ones. ■

Prewriting

Planning Your Problem-Solution Essay

Up to this point you have been exploring the problem and its possible solutions. Now your attention will shift to the planning of your paper.

Considering Your Purpose, Audience, and Tone

Purpose. You have gone through the stages in which your purpose is to explore the problem. Now, as you get ready to write your essay, your purpose shifts to explaining the problem and its solution(s) to your readers. You've been asking *What is the solution to this problem?* Now your question is *How can I prove to my audience that this solution is the best?*

Audience. Your audience becomes really important at this point, and answering these questions will help you address their concerns:

- *Who is the audience?* It may be your teacher and other students in your class, but there are other possible audiences as well. Who would have a vested interest in solving this problem? Who would have the power to solve this problem?
- *What do your readers already know about this problem? How do they react to it?* If your audience isn't personally affected by the problem, you may have to spend more time showing them that the problem really exists and that it's important to solve it.
- *What solutions might your audience favor?* Some readers may favor a solution you've rejected. In this case, you'll need to explain the disadvantages of your rejected solutions carefully.
- *What objections might your audience have to your solution?* Some readers may be quick to point out the flaws in your solution, so you'll need to explain its value thoroughly and attempt to answer their objections.

A DIFFERENT APPROACH

Have students record their ideas about the purpose, audience, and tone for their essays to refer to when they are writing. Suggest that they include the information in notes at the top of the prewriting chart. Students can use this information as an aid to keep their focus in mind as they write.

INTEGRATING THE LANGUAGE ARTS

Library Link. Students may need guidance in locating information in the library. You may want to introduce students to the library's microfilm to help them investigate local issues. Also, you might show students where the microfilm indexes are located.

SELECTION AMENDMENT
Description of change: excerpted
Rationale: to focus on exploratory writing presented in this chapter

Tone. Your exploration has been thorough and objective, and you want your essay to reflect that attitude, so use objective language as you write. Stay away from words that carry emotional overtones. But since you're recounting a personal exploration (your own investigation), put yourself into your writing by using the first person pronoun *I*. This will make your exploration and explanation seem credible to your audience. It will also make your problem-solution essay sound more informal than some other types of expository essays.

"Will the reader turn the page?"

Catherine Drinker Bowen

Providing Support

When you present the problem you have identified and the solution you think is best in your essay, you have two tasks:

- explain the problem and solution to your audience
- prove to your audience that the problem is serious and that your solution will work

Your audience won't automatically accept the seriousness of the problem or the solution you propose. They may say, "Why should I worry about how to solve this problem? How do you know this is the best solution?" To convince your audience, you need to provide reasons and evidence, or proof, that you are right. Reasons, facts, statistics, and examples will help you build a solid case for the seriousness of the problem and the desirability of your solution.

Where do you find reasons and evidence to support the solution you have chosen? When you are investigating the problem and exploring possible solutions—looking at strengths and weaknesses, practicality, and comparative advantage—you are (whether you realize it or not) identifying bits and pieces of evidence. As you plan your essay, you can go back and look at those reasons and pieces of evidence and write down the ones that would be convincing to your audience. You may also need to do some research to identify additional reasons, examples, or facts and statistics that show the seriousness of the problem and that support the solution you have identified.

CRITICAL THINKING

(pp. 335–336)

OBJECTIVE

- To evaluate evidence for trustworthiness, accuracy, and usefulness

TEACHING *EVALUATING EVIDENCE*

Begin **Critical Thinking** by reading **Evaluating Evidence** with the class. As you read, write the criteria for evaluating evidence on the chalkboard and leave spaces for examples.

You might mention some sources that would not be trustworthy or reliable and discuss why. Then list trustworthy ones on the

CRITICAL THINKING

Evaluating Evidence

When you ***evaluate*** something, you judge whether it measures up to a set of criteria or standards. For example, to evaluate a TV, you might measure it against these criteria: price, length of warranty, quality of color, and repair record. When you are looking for support for a problem-solution essay, you may also need to evaluate your evidence (your facts, statistics, and examples). To be acceptable, your evidence must meet these criteria:

1. The evidence should be **trustworthy.** It should be from sources that are reliable, sources with reputations for integrity such as *The New York Times, Time, Newsweek,* the Gallup Poll, and many individual "experts."
2. The evidence should be **accurate.** Even the best sources sometimes make errors, so learn to question the information you find. If a fact or statistic seems unlikely, check its accuracy in a second source. Also, be certain that you copy facts and statistics correctly.
3. The evidence should be **useful,** or relevant. Evidence that is both trustworthy and accurate may not be useful. Useful evidence has a logical connection to your problem or solution. It helps to prove your point.

CRITICAL THINKING EXERCISE:
Evaluating Evidence

A writer is exploring the problem of teachers' lack of time for class preparation. The solution that has been proposed is "Use parent volunteers to serve as class sponsors, reading tutors, and library aides, thus freeing teachers from these responsibilities." Following is the evidence gathered by the writer to support this solution. Based on the information you've just read, how acceptable is the evidence? Get together with a partner and weigh each piece of evidence against the three criteria—trustworthiness, accuracy, and usefulness.

MEETING **INDIVIDUAL** NEEDS

LEP/ESL

General Strategies. The textbook suggests pairing students to complete the **Critical Thinking Exercise.** It may be more advantageous to create groups of three when ESL students are involved. This grouping might give ESL students more opportunities to practice English and to listen to groups of native English speakers.

INTEGRATING THE LANGUAGE ARTS

Listening Link. Help students to listen critically and to use reasoning skills to determine if evidence they hear is accurate. Read to students evidence you have gathered about a certain problem. Include information that is acceptable and information that is unacceptable. Have students listen to each fact or statistic to determine which ones they would question and why. Have them explain which criteria for evaluation apply.

chalkboard. Point out that if students use experts to provide information, they may need to tell the experts' credentials.

To discuss factors that affect accuracy, explain that one factor affecting accuracy is timeliness; information that is dated is often inaccurate because the statistics and facts are no longer correct. You could use an old science journal or news magazine to show how accuracy can be affected.

Point out that inappropriate information is not useful in exploratory papers. As an example, add a superfluous statement to an analytical article and ask students to identify the irrelevant data.

ANSWERS

Critical Thinking Exercise

Answers will vary. Encourage students to explain their decisions and to tell how one criteria relates to another.

1. Although this statement is relevant to the solution, its accuracy cannot be determined. The source is not given so it cannot be considered trustworthy.
2. This statement comes from a trustworthy source. However, it may be anecdotal rather than factual so it may not be accurate. It is relevant to the proposal of using volunteers to assist teachers.
3. The source for this statement is not given so its trustworthiness can't be assured. If it is accurate, it is a useful adjunct to the solution.
4. The federal study is probably a trustworthy source. The statement may be accurate but no statistics are given. It supports the problem and is relevant in a problem-solution essay, but it is not useful in proposing a solution.
5. The statement is probably from a trustworthy source and the statistics tend to lend credence to its accuracy. It is relevant to the proposed solution.

1. Parent volunteers would save teachers more than forty-four hours per week.
2. An article in *The Washington Post* says that volunteerism is up all over the country.
3. One parent has donated money for an informational mailing to all parents.
4. A federally funded study of education says that teachers have too many nonclassroom duties to perform.
5. A survey of teachers in the school indicates that 88 percent of them support the plan.

WRITING ASSIGNMENT

PART 4:
Planning Your Problem-Solution Essay

Now take the time to pull together the results of your own exploration and create a plan for your essay. First, list the problem, your solution, and the steps needed to implement it. Then, look at your evaluation of possible solutions (Writing Assignment, Part 3) and list any evidence that would support your solution. If necessary, do some additional research to identify more reasons, examples, facts, and statistics. Add those to your list of support. Don't forget to include information that will help you respond to any objections your audience might have. Finally, list the possible solutions you have rejected and the major disadvantage of each.

SEGMENT 4 *(pp. 337–347)*

WRITING YOUR FIRST DRAFT

OBJECTIVES

- To analyze a problem-solution essay
- To write a draft of a problem-solution essay

TEACHING THE LESSON

To grab students' attention and to demonstrate a compelling way to introduce an essay, read aloud a few unusual facts. You could include information such as the length of the Wright brothers' maiden flight (twelve seconds) or the weight and number of stones in the Great Pyramid of Giza (two million weighing as much as two and a half ☛

Writing Your First Draft

The Basic Elements of a Problem-Solution Essay

Like many other essays, a problem-solution paper can follow several different patterns. However, most problem-solution essays contain the following elements:

- an explanation of the problem
- evidence of the problem's seriousness
- a description of the proposed solution
- a list of steps to implement the solution
- evidence to support the solution and counter possible objections
- discussion of the advantages and disadvantages of other solutions

Like other types of essays, the problem-solution essay often begins with some sort of attention grabber. This may be especially important to do if your audience isn't really convinced that a problem even exists. The problem-solution essay may end with a call to action—telling readers what they can do to help—or it may end with a simple restatement of the proposed solution and its advantages.

In the following essay, Shannon Long discusses the problem that she and other students faced on her college campus. The problem is not a unique one. It is faced by many students and workers on campuses and in office buildings across the country. What solution to the problem does Long propose?

Teacher's ResourceBank™
RESOURCES

WRITING YOUR FIRST DRAFT
- Writing a Problem-Solution Essay 73

QUOTATION FOR THE DAY

"I don't want to read a book that simply reinforces all my prejudices and ignorances and things I half-know." (Toni Morrison, 1931– , American novelist)

Discuss Morrison's quotation with students and ask them what they think she means by *half-know*. Explain that when people explore, their knowledge expands and they leave behind their half-known ideas and beliefs. Remind students that they will know when they have reached a new solution to a problem when they feel the surprise of discovery.

MEETING INDIVIDUAL NEEDS

LESS-ADVANCED STUDENTS

Some students may be overwhelmed by the length of the models in this segment. Explain to students that the length of a problem-solution essay often depends upon the number of solutions. Explain that each student may choose to focus on two well-written solutions rather than cover them all.

tons each). Explain that attention grabbers like this engage readers and help to interest them in what is to follow.

Have volunteers read **The Basic Elements of a Problem-Solution Essay** on p. 337. Have students pay particular attention to the elements contained in an essay before they read the professional model. Tell students to look for each element as they read.

Have students read the professional essay first, and then discuss the side glosses and annotations with the class. Guide students in understanding the framework of this essay by analyzing the elements of an exploratory essay. Make sure students are

USING THE SELECTION

Wheelchair Hell: A Look at Campus Accessibility

1
Shannon Long writes this essay in first-person point of view to describe a problem personally encountered. The writer describes problems in a way to engage the reader's attention.

2
The author emphasizes the problem's seriousness by offering examples.

3
Is the evidence presented acceptable?
[The federal law is both accurate and trustworthy as well as relevant to the topic of accessibility for the handicapped.]

A PROBLEM-SOLUTION ESSAY

Wheelchair Hell: A Look at Campus Accessibility

by Shannon Long

INTRODUCTION Personal anecdote

Attention grabber

1 It was my first week of college, and I was going to the library to meet someone on the third floor and study. After entering the library, I went to the elevator and hit the button calling it. A few seconds later the doors opened, I rolled inside, and the doors closed behind me. Expecting the buttons to be down in front, I suddenly noticed that they were behind me—and too high to reach. There I was stuck in the elevator with no way to get help. Finally, someone got on at the fourth floor. I'd been waiting fifteen minutes.

BODY Statement of problem

2 I'm not the only one who has been a victim of inaccessibility. The University of Kentucky currently has twelve buildings that are inaccessible to students in wheelchairs (Karnes). Many other buildings, like the library, are accessible, but have elevators that are inoperable by handicapped students.
3 Yet, Section 504 of the Rehabilitation Act of 1973 states that

> No qualified handicap person shall, because a recipient's facilities are inaccessible to or unusable by handicapped persons, be denied the benefits of, be excluded from participation in, or otherwise be subjected to discrimination under any program or activity receiving Federal financial assistance (Federal 22681).

When this law went into effect in 1977, the University of Kentucky started a renovation process in which close to a million dollars was spent on handicap modifications (Karnes). But even though that much money has been spent, there are still able to differentiate this kind of essay from an informative or a persuasive one by having volunteers restate the characteristics of an exploratory essay [identify and explore a problem, propose and evaluate solutions, and explain the best solution] and by discussing how the characteristics differ from those of the other aims of writing.

Divide the class into groups of two or three and have the groups complete **Exercise 3** on p. 342 independently.

You might use a similar procedure for reading and discussing **A Writer's Model** on pp. 343–346. Because the nature of an exploratory essay may be new to students, you could outline on the chalkboard the

Examples/ seriousness of problem

many more modifications needed. Buildings still inaccessible to wheelchair students are the Administration Building, Alumni House, Barker Hall, Bowman Hall, Bradley Hall, Engineering Quadrangle, Gillis Building, Kinkead Hall, Miller Hall, Safety and Security Building, and Scovell Hall (Transition).

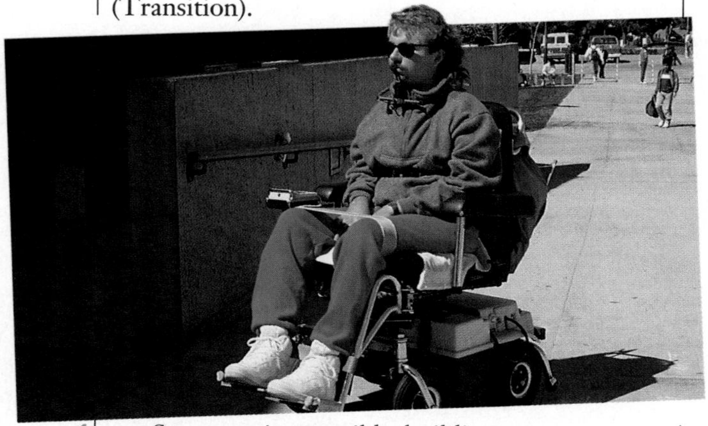

4 So many inaccessible buildings creates many unnecessary problems. For example, if a handicapped student wants to meet an administrator, he or she must make an appointment to meet somewhere more accessible than the Administration Building. Making appointments is usually not a problem, but there is still the fact that able-bodied students have no problem entering the Administration Building while handicapped students cannot. Though handicapped students can enter the Gillis Building, they cannot go above the ground floor and even have to push a button to get someone to come downstairs to help them. Finally, for handicapped students to get counseling from the Career Planning Center, they must set up an appointment to meet with someone at another place. In this case, some students might not use the Center's services because of the extra effort involved (Croucher).

Examples/Extent of problem

Even many of the accessible buildings have elevators, water fountains, and door handles that are inoperable by handicapped students (Karnes).

4

The writer cites several examples of the problems handicapped students may experience on campus. Are the examples adequate to show the extent of the problem? [The article covers having to make appointments outside facilities that are not equipped for the handicapped; difficulties in moving from floor to floor; hardships arranging to use campus services; inaccessibility of water fountains, elevators, and bathrooms; and problems in residence halls.]

steps involved in developing a framework after you have discussed both essays. Or refer students to the **Framework for a Problem-Solution Essay** on p. 346. Show how in a well-planned essay one step leads to the next.

The **Writing Note** on p. 347 explains how the writer of the wheelchair essay uses citations to credit sources. You might want to mention any requirements that you have before students draft their essays. Give the students sample citation information for reference.

Before students begin their essays, you may want to guide students in writing by modeling a short essay for them. Show how you could turn one of the unusual facts you brought up earlier into a

Elevators in the Library and Whitehall Classroom Building, for instance, have buttons too high for wheelchair students, forcing them to ask somebody else to hit the button. If there is nobody around to ask, the handicapped person simply has to wait. In the Chemistry and Physics Building, a key is needed to operate the elevator, forcing wheelchair students to ride up and down the hall to find somebody to help. Many water fountains are inaccessible to people in wheelchairs. Some buildings have only *one* accessible water fountain. Finally, hardly any buildings have doorknobs that students with hand and arm impairments can operate.

Many residence halls, such as Boyd Hall, Donovan Hall, Patterson Hall, and Keenland Hall, are also completely inaccessible. If a handicapped student wanted to drop by and see a friend or attend a party in one of these dorms, he or she would have to be carried up steps. Kirivan and Blanding Towers have bathrooms that are inaccessible. Also, in Kirivan Tower the elevator is so small that someone has to lift the back of the chair into the elevator. The complex lowrises—Shawneetown, Commonwealth Village, and Cooperstown Apartments—are also inaccessible. Cooperstown has some first floor apartments that are accessible, but a handicapped student couldn't very well live there because the bathrooms are inaccessible. All eleven sororities are inaccessible, and only five of the sixteen fraternities are accessible. Since the land sororities and fraternities are on is owned by U.K., Section 504 does require that houses be accessible (Transition 14, 15).

With so many U.K. places still inaccessible, it is obvious that hundreds of modifications need to be done. According to Jake Karnes, the Assistant Dean of Students and the Director of handicap Student Services, "It will probably take close to a million dollars to make U.K. totally accessible."
Current solution 5 U.K.'s current budget allows for just $10,000 per year to go toward handicap modification (Karnes).

5
Long suggests that before additional campus modifications can be made, more money will need to be budgeted.

problem-solution essay. For example, the length of the Wright brothers' flight could introduce problems in urban transportation; stones for the Pyramid could begin an essay on mobilizing people to build homes for the homeless.

Have students begin their essays in class so that you can monitor their progress.

ASSESSMENT

Evaluate students' progress in understanding problem-solution essays by assessing their answers to **Exercise 3.** Evaluate students' first drafts to see that they have followed a framework similar to the one suggested on p. 346. Look to see if they are citing sources correctly.

Disadvantage

If no other money source is sought, the renovation process could be strung out for many years.

Proposed solution
Advantage

6 A possible solution could be the use of the tuition. If only $2 could be taken from each student's tuition, there would be almost $50,000 extra per semester for handicap modification. Tuition is already used to pay for things ranging from teacher salaries to the funding of the campus radio station. This plan could be started with the beginning of the 1990 Fall semester. The money could be taken from each of the existing programs the tuition now pays for, so there would be no need for an increase in tuition. Also, this would not be a permanent expense because with an extra $50,000 a semester, all of the needed modifications could be finished in ten years. After that, the amount taken from the tuition could be lowered to fifty cents to help cover upkeep of campus accessibility. This plan is practical—but more important, it is ethical. Surely if part of our tuition goes to fund a radio station, some of it can be used to make U.K. a more accessible place. Which is more important, having a radio station to play alternative music or having a campus that is accessible to all students?

Steps necessary for implementation

Answer to possible objections

6
Is Long's suggestion for allocating two dollars from each student's tuition reasonable? Has the writer anticipated what the objections might be and countered the arguments? [Answers will vary.]

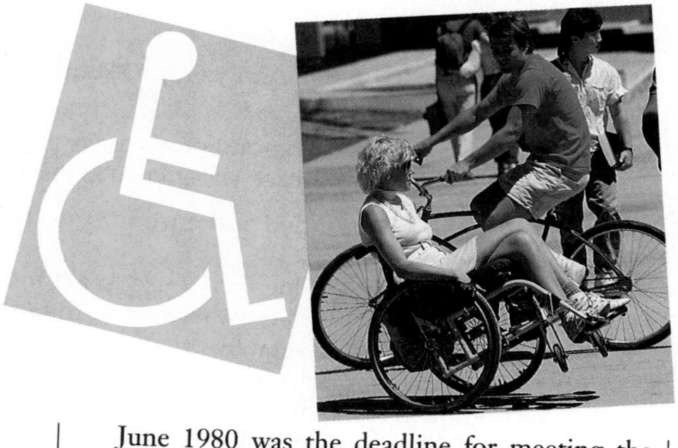

CONCLUSION

June 1980 was the deadline for meeting the requirements of Section 504 (Robinson 28). In compliance with the law, the University of Kentucky has spent close to a million dollars making

RETEACHING

Reteach this lesson by writing on a transparency a problem-solution essay from a former student or from a magazine. Working with the class, read the essay and determine how closely the essay follows the **Framework for a Problem-Solution Essay** on p. 346. Discuss with the class how the essay could be improved and what its strengths are.

7
The writer uses a combination of articles, interviews, and legal records to document the essay.

ANSWERS

Exercise 3

1. Long's intended audience is anyone responsible for allotting money to make campus adaptations for handicapped students at the University of Kentucky. The audience may also be the student body, and the intent is to rally their support.
2. Long makes the reader aware of campus accessibility problems for those in wheelchairs by using a personal anecdote to describe being trapped in an elevator unable to reach the buttons.
3. Shannon describes the buildings on the University of Kentucky campus that are still inaccessible to wheelchairs, even after a million dollars has been spent on handicap modifications.
4. The solution's comparative advantage is that implementation money would come from already existing tuition money, so there would be no need to increase tuition. Also, the renovations would be in place in ten years, and then only a nominal fee for upkeep would be necessary.
5. The disadvantages are the cost and the source of funding. The writer addresses these concerns by stating that tuition would not increase and by pointing out that handicap modifications are as important to students as a campus radio station and other programs already funded by tuition fees.

Restatement of proposed solution

its campus more accessible. But there are still many more changes needed. These changes will take a lot of money, but if two dollars could be used out of each student's tuition, the money would be there. Handicapped students often work to overachieve to prove their abilities. All they ask for is a chance, and that chance should not be blocked by high buttons, heavy doors, or steps.

7

Works Cited

Croucher, Lisa. "Accessibility at U.K. for Handicapped Still Can Be Better." *Kentucky Kernal.* Date unknown.

Federal Register. Volume 42 (4 May 1977):22681.

Karnes, Jake. Personal Interview. 17 Oct. 1989.

Robinson, Rita. "For the Handicapped: Renovation Report Card." *American School & University* (Apr. 1980):28.

University of Kentucky – Transition Plan. [report]. Date unknown.

EXERCISE 3 Analyzing a Problem-Solution Essay

Read and review Shannon Long's essay (pages 338–342) before meeting with two or three classmates to discuss these questions.

1. Who is the intended audience for the essay? Explain your answer.
2. What technique does Long use to get her readers' attention and to increase their awareness of the problem?
3. How does Long establish that the problem is a serious one?
4. What comparative advantage does Long's proposed solution have over the current solution? What other strengths does Long's proposed solution have?
5. What are the disadvantages of Long's solution? How does she address possible objections on the basis of those disadvantages?

CLOSURE

Close the lesson by discussing the following questions as a group:

1. How might a problem-solution essay begin? [with an attention grabber]
2. Why does a discussion of the solutions rejected by the writer strengthen an essay? [It helps show the advantages of the proposed solution.]

EXTENSION

After the class begins investigating problems, you may discover that some students have become experts because of their interests, research work, or problem-solving capabilities. Suggest that students interview one another to find out who is becoming knowledgeable and what their fields of expertise are. Post students' interests

A Basic Framework for a Problem-Solution Essay

Although the problem-solution essay can follow several different patterns, the following Writer's Model illustrates one basic pattern. You might want to follow this pattern when you write your own essay.

A WRITER'S MODEL

Pet Overpopulation in Cranford County

INTRODUCTION
Attention-grabbing facts

I had heard the statistics. I knew, for example, that only one out of four puppies born in the United States actually finds a home. I knew that about fifteen million pet animals are brought to municipal and private animal shelters each year. I knew it, but these statistics didn't really make an impact on me until I went to the county animal shelter last Thursday to adopt a cat. There I was faced with how serious the pet overpopulation problem really is.

Statement of the problem

Anecdote illustrating problem

In the shelter that day, there were eighteen adult dogs, twenty-seven puppies, thirteen adult cats, and twenty-nine kittens. By Saturday morning, most of them would be gone, but they would not be missing because someone adopted them. They would be gassed because no one wanted them. By the next Friday, the shelter would be full again. On Saturday, the gas chamber would be full again, too.

MEETING INDIVIDUAL NEEDS

LEP/ESL

General Strategies. You may want to search for a problem-solution essay that is relevant to ESL students' concerns, such as problems of learning a new language or adapting to a new culture. Students may be more encouraged to understand the form for this kind of essay if they are interested in the material. For an example, see "Breaking the Bonds of Hate" in *Newsweek,* April 27, 1992, for an essay by a young Cambodian immigrant.

in the classroom so that they can share their problems and solutions with one another. ■

COOPERATIVE LEARNING

Have students work in groups to collect information for directories of sources to use in exploratory writing. Ask each student to select an area of interest such as adult literacy, homelessness, or the environment. Then have students with similar interests work together to scan telephone directories, collect community brochures, or speak to experts.

With the information they collect, they could organize a directory of organizations working to solve problems. Students could include the solutions the organizations have proposed and the success of each solution.

I was horrified. I had always assumed that animals taken to the local shelter were adopted. I think most people assume that. But that's not the case. According to its director, Madge Simmons, our local shelter takes in from fifty to eighty animals in any given week. A small percentage of those animals--on the average three or four per week--turn out to be lost, and their owners claim them. Sometimes as many as five animals are adopted in a week. The rest are kept from seven to ten days and then destroyed.

BODY
Evidence of seriousness and extent of problem

But this is just one of the awful consequences of the pet overpopulation problem. Many unwanted animals never make it to the relatively humane conditions in the shelter. They are dumped along the highways in rural areas and left to starve. The people who dump them may believe they are giving the dogs or cats a chance at survival. But the animals' chances may be much better at the shelter. Local veterinarian Dr. Kanzer estimates that fewer than one in fifty abandoned dogs survives longer than six months. The odds are not much better for cats. And death for an abandoned animal is often prolonged and painful.

Possible solution

In the past, various solutions have been tried to solve the pet overpopulation problem. Groups such as the American Humane Association have tried to educate the public about pet overpopulation through pamphlets and news releases.

Disadvantage

Unfortunately, many people, like me, hear the numbers but the problem remains abstract to them.

Possible solution

These groups have also promoted adoption programs for abandoned animals. But according to a pamphlet from our local shelter, to give every cat and dog alive in our country at this moment a home, every individual in the United States would have to adopt at least seven animals. That's twenty-eight animals for a typical family of four.

Disadvantage

Clearly, this is not a practical solution.

Possible solution

Encouraging the voluntary spaying and neutering of pets is another possible solution. Educating pet owners targets those with the ability and responsibility to act. If pet owners understand that unrestricted breeding is a kind of animal murder, then they will see the importance of spaying and neutering their pets. Many people, however, who intend to have their cats or dogs spayed will put off the operation when they discover the cost at the local veterinarian's office. For these people, programs such as our own shelter's low-cost spay and neuter program are a solution. But in cities with low-cost spay and neuter programs such as Los Angeles, even this solution doesn't go far enough. Some people simply refuse to cooperate. They think of their animals as property that they have a right to control. Or they want their pets to experience the "miracle of birth." Or they just procrastinate.

Disadvantage

Possible solution

Disadvantage

Explanation of comparative advantage

Only one solution can meet the magnitude of the pet overpopulation problem and counteract the irresponsible behavior of some pet owners. The solution is a law that takes the good, but inadequate, voluntary solutions of the past a step further by making them mandatory. Under this law, owners, except licensed breeders, must have their pets spayed or neutered or face a stiff fine if they do not. A recent survey by the Cranford County Gazette indicates that almost 65 percent of the county's pet owners support such a law. And the current participation of veterinarians in our low-cost spay/neuter clinics suggests that they, too, are in favor of the law. Also, the mechanism for carrying it out--the clinics--is already in place.

Evidence/ Statistic

Evidence/Fact

A DIFFERENT APPROACH

Have students prepare to defend their solutions before classmates representing the city council or a similar governing group. Students should anticipate possible counter-arguments when they plan their defenses. Students could also prepare summaries of their proposals for the council. The council members should be given time to read the proposals before the presentations. Then the council could vote on the proposals and explain their decisions.

CONCLUSION
Answers possible objections
Necessary steps
Restatement of proposed solution

Although this solution may seem a bit drastic, it is not as drastic as sending hundreds of unwanted animals to the gas chamber each year. The major hurdle is convincing our local officials to pass such a law. First, we have to propose the law in a public forum and convince the general public that it will help solve our pet overpopulation problem. Once we can demonstrate public support for the law, our local officials will also see the benefits and move ahead to pass the ordinance.The animals who suffer and die daily can't speak for themselves. A spay and neuter ordinance would let the law speak for them.

"Pet Overpopulation in Cranford County" uses the following framework. You might follow it as you write your first draft.

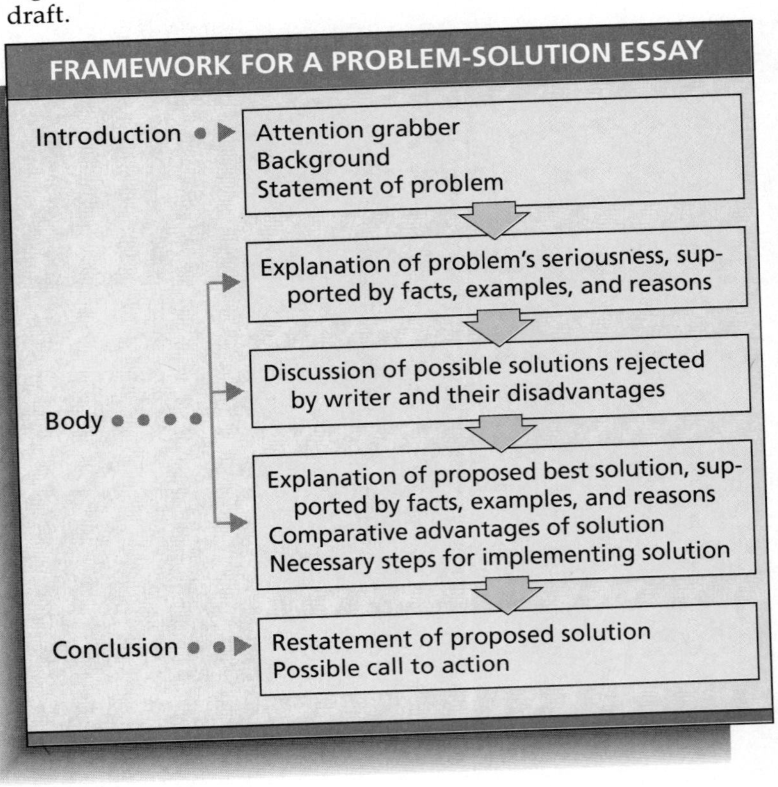
FRAMEWORK FOR A PROBLEM-SOLUTION ESSAY
Introduction
Attention grabber
Background
Statement of problem
Explanation of problem's seriousness, supported by facts, examples, and reasons
Body
Discussion of possible solutions rejected by writer and their disadvantages
Explanation of proposed best solution, supported by facts, examples, and reasons
Comparative advantages of solution
Necessary steps for implementing solution
Conclusion
Restatement of proposed solution
Possible call to action

WRITING NOTE

In "Wheelchair Hell," Shannon Long uses parenthetical citations and a list of Works Cited to tell readers where she got her information. The Writer's Model, "Pet Overpopulation in Cranford County," credits its information sources more informally by naming the sources within the paper. Either form is acceptable as long as you acknowledge your sources. (For more help with crediting sources, see Chapter 11, Writing a Research Paper.)

WRITING ASSIGNMENT

PART 5:
Writing a Draft of Your Essay

Now you can put your exploration to good use as you attempt to explain why your solution is a good one. As you write your first draft, remember to use solid evidence to back up your explanation. Also, think about how you can best show that the problem is serious and that your proposed solution is both good and workable.

WRITING NOTE

After students read the **Writing Note,** have them refer to the different essays in the chapter. Although one essay includes a Works Cited section, others do not. Have students suggest circumstances that would call for a Works Cited list; then have them suggest situations in which no references would be needed.

TIMESAVER

Save time checking over first drafts by asking students to include the framework sequence in the left column and to follow the models as guides. You can quickly assess whether or not students have included necessary steps.

SEGMENT 5 *(pp. 348–351)*

EVALUATING AND REVISING

OBJECTIVES

- To analyze a writer's revisions
- To evaluate and revise a problem-solution essay

TEACHING THE LESSON

Have a volunteer read the introductory material to the class. Then have students independently examine the **Evaluating and Revising Problem-Solution Essays** chart. After students review the chart, discuss questions they may have and compare the evaluation chart to the framework on p. 346.

Teacher's ResourceBank™

RESOURCES

EVALUATING AND REVISING

- Writing a Problem-Solution Essay 74

QUOTATION FOR THE DAY

"The discipline of the writer is to learn to be still and listen to what his subject has to tell him." (Rachel Carson, 1907–1964, American writer and marine biologist)

Writing to explore gives students opportunities to listen to what their subjects have to tell them. Have students discuss whether the ideas they discovered in writing caused them to revise some of their earlier proposed solutions.

Evaluating and Revising

Any first draft is just a starting point. You always need to evaluate the strengths and weaknesses in what you've written. Even if you do find problems, however, your revision solutions needn't be as drastic as those suggested in the following cartoon. Consider *adding, cutting, replacing,* and *reordering* before exploding. (And remember: It's usually very helpful to have someone else read your writing and offer suggestions for improvement. Many professional writers would be lost without their editors!)

The following chart can be used to evaluate and revise problem-solution essays. Start by asking yourself the question in the left-hand column. If the answer is no, you can use the revision technique suggested in the right-hand column.

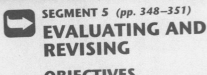

Before students begin **Exercise 4,** you might consider modeling a few revisions on the chalkboard. You could use an introduction from a previously written paper that begins without much interest. Suggest a new introduction using an amusing anecdote or a little-known fact. You might also want to include a body paragraph to revise.

Then have students work independently in small groups on **Exercise 4.** Before you assign **Writing Assignment: Part 6** on p. 351, remind students to use the chart to evaluate what they have written and to add details or rewrite what doesn't follow a good problem-solution arrangement.

To assess the lesson, evaluate how well the groups have been able to analyze ☛

EVALUATING AND REVISING PROBLEM-SOLUTION ESSAYS

	EVALUATION GUIDE	REVISION TECHNIQUE
1	Does the introduction grab the readers' attention?	**Add** an interesting anecdote or facts. **Replace** dull material.
2	Is the problem clearly stated and its seriousness established?	Rewrite the explanation. **Add** examples, facts, and reasons that establish the seriousness of the problem.
3	Are other possible solutions and their disadvantages discussed?	**Add** details concerning other solutions and their weaknesses, practicality, and comparative advantages.
4	Is the proposed solution clearly stated and supported?	**Add** sound reasons. **Add** trustworthy, accurate, and useful evidence.
5	Are answers provided to possible objections to the proposed solution?	**Add** several sentences that answer possible objections to your solution.
6	Is the process for implementing the proposed solution clearly presented?	**Add** details to identify the steps in the process. **Reorder** steps in the order they're to be done.

EXERCISE 4 **Analyzing a Writer's Revisions**

Following is a revised draft of the last two paragraphs of "Pet Overpopulation in Cranford County" (pages 345–346). Working with some classmates, figure out how the revisions improve the paragraphs. Then answer the questions that follow.

MEETING INDIVIDUAL NEEDS

LEP/ESL

General Strategies. Writing attention-grabbing introductions requires practice as well as familiarity with language. You might want to gather some essays with interesting beginnings to examine with students. You might include personal anecdotes, thought-provoking questions, humorous tales, bizarre statistics, or unusual historical events. The more examples students can review, the more they will understand and be able to use interesting introductions.

the writer's revisions. To evaluate students' revised drafts, ask student readers to evaluate revised drafts and to write in the margin which revision techniques were used or which evaluation number applies. You could then cursorily evaluate the drafts and delay assessment until the proofreading stage.

RETEACHING

Select another passage from **"Pet Overpopulation in Cranford County"** and make suggestions for revisions. Then have students offer other revisions and explain why they would make the changes.

INTEGRATING THE LANGUAGE ARTS

Speaking Link. Ask students to prepare public service announcements to present their problems and solutions. Students could write clear, concise messages for their audiences. Suggest that students conform to a sixty-second format. Students could then present their announcements to the class so that fellow classmates can hear the problems others are trying to solve.

Only one solution can meet the magnitude of the pet overpopulation problem and ~~To~~ counteract the irresponsible behavior of some pet owners. ~~we need~~ The solution is a law that takes the good, but inadequate, voluntary solutions of the past a step further by making them mandatory. Under this law, owners, except licensed breeders, must have their pets spayed or neutered or face a stiff fine if they do not. A recent survey by the Cranford County Gazette indicates that almost ~~90~~ 65 percent of ~~registered voters own pets~~ the county's pet owners support such a law. And the current participation of veterinarians in our low-cost spay/neuter clinics suggests that they, too, are in favor of the law. Also, the mechanism for carrying it out--the clinics--is already in place.

replace
add/replace
replace
replace

Although this solution may seem a bit drastic ~~to some people, it is not~~ it is not as drastic as sending hundreds of unwanted animals to the gas chamber each year. The major hurdle is convincing our local officials to pass such a law. First, we have to propose the law in a public forum and convince the general public that it will help solve our pet overpopulation problem. Once we can demonstrate public support for the law, our local officials will also see the benefits and move ahead to pass the ordinance. The animals who suffer and die daily can't speak for themselves. A spay and neuter ordinance would let the law speak for them.

replace
add/reorder

CLOSURE

Close the lesson by asking the following questions:

1. Which revision technique did you use the most? Which was the most helpful? Why?
2. Which technique do you need more experience mastering? What makes it difficult for you? ■

1. Why did the writer add the new information and create a new sentence at the beginning of the first paragraph? How does this sentence make a connection to other possible solutions?
2. In the third sentence, why did the writer replace the words *90 percent of registered voters own pets* with the words *65 percent of the county's pet owners support such a law*? (How did the change strengthen the evidence?)
3. Why did the writer revise the sentence at the beginning of the second paragraph? How is this a better answer to possible objections?
4. Why did the writer reorder the two sentences in the second paragraph?

WRITING ASSIGNMENT

PART 6:
Evaluating and Revising Your Essay

You may, of course, use the Evaluating and Revising Chart (page 349) as a guide to revise the draft of your essay. However, after you have made those changes, you might still benefit from feedback. Why not ask at least one classmate who is interested in the problem you've explored to read your draft and make suggestions? Based on your reader's responses, make any changes that you feel are necessary.

ANSWERS

Exercise 4

1. The writer added new information to stress that there is only one reasonable solution to the problem. The sentence shows that no other solution will be adequate.
2. The writer replaced the evidence presented with facts that are more relevant to the problem.
3. The writer rewrote the sentence to show that the alternative is much more drastic than the measure suggested. This is a better counter to possible objections because specific results are given.
4. The writer reordered to put information in sequential order.

TIMESAVER

Save time grading essays by making copies of the **Evaluating and Revising Problem-Solution Essays** chart and attaching them to students' essays. You could refer to the revised areas and write comments on the attached cover sheets.

SEGMENT 6 *(pp. 352–353)*

PROOFREADING AND PUBLISHING

OBJECTIVE

- To proofread and publish a problem-solution essay

TEACHING THE LESSON

Have a volunteer read the introduction. Then initiate a discussion of additional places students can publish their work.

Point out that the **Usage Hint** is useful for the problem-solution essay because the noun *effect* is often used when writing about problems. If students need more

Teacher's ResourceBank™

RESOURCES

PROOFREADING AND PUBLISHING

- Writing a Problem-Solution Essay 75

QUOTATION FOR THE DAY

"Every reform was once a private opinion, . . . "(Ralph Waldo Emerson, 1803–1882, American essayist, poet, and philosopher)

Remind students that although everyone won't have as many opportunities as Emerson to solve the problems of life in prose and poetry, each person can present his or her own private opinion and help initiate reform, if only in people's thinking, with polished writing. Remind students that the proofreading stage is the time to perfect their work so that reform-minded readers can read it and be inspired.

Proofreading and Publishing

Proofreading. By now you know the importance of proofreading your final draft to find and correct careless mistakes in grammar, usage, or mechanics. Most writers feel about their manuscripts the way parents do about their children. They don't want to send them out into the world without their hair combed and their teeth brushed.

Publishing. But where can you send your essay? You might want to consider how you can best reach the people with the power to solve the problem. Perhaps you can do that in one of these ways:

- ask the editor of the school newspaper or the local newspaper to publish your essay as a column on the Op-Ed page
- rewrite your essay in the form of a business letter and mail it to the chairperson of an organization that can work to solve the problem
- send a copy of your essay to a local TV or radio talk show host and volunteer to talk with the host and answer questions about the problem and your proposed solution

examples using *effect,* refer them to **Chapter 27: "A Glossary of Usage."**

As students proofread their essays, have them exchange papers for a second check. Ask students to create catchy titles for their works that reflect the content and interest the reader. Guide students in determining the best places for them to publish their essays.

To interest students in their classmates' ideas, close the lesson by having students share the titles of their essays. ■

USAGE HINT

Affect and *Effect*

When you explored your problem, you asked yourself about the causes and effects of the problem. When you write your essay, you'll be using the words *affect* and *effect* to explain the causes and effects to readers. If you're like most people, you probably find these words confusing. One way to keep them straight is to remember that *affect* is almost always used as a verb:

How did that decision *affect* the people of Detroit?
Charissa was *affected* by her parents' decision to move.

Effect, on the other hand, is almost always a noun.

The *effect* of the decision was a decline in population.
The move had a good *effect* on Charissa.

Of course, just to complicate things, *effect* can also be a verb that means "to bring about."

How will we ever *effect* change in that policy?

You can test to see whether your are using *effect* correctly as a verb by substituting "bring about." If "bring about" sounds awkward or wrong, use *affect*.

REFERENCE NOTE: For more help with *affect* and *effect,* see page 793.

WRITING ASSIGNMENT

PART 7:
Proofreading and Publishing Your Essay

You've done a great deal of thinking, planning, rethinking, and rewriting for your essay—and one last push will help ensure that your efforts will be noticed. Proofread your essay and make any necessary corrections. Then share it with an audience.

MEETING INDIVIDUAL NEEDS

LESS-ADVANCED

If students use typewriters for their work, provide printed templates for students to place under the typing paper. A heavily bordered template showing top, bottom, and side margins that can be seen through typing paper will help ensure that each student has an attractive essay with consistent margins.

COOPERATIVE LEARNING

Working in mixed-ability groups of four, students might prepare a time capsule for next year's students. Students could include the following items:

1. newspaper articles relating to their topics
2. copies of their essays

CRITICAL THINKING
Synthesis

Have students create leaflets or handouts to present their problems and solutions to the school or community as another method of publishing. Students might want to incorporate artwork into their leaflets. Remind students that their problems and solutions must be summarized but still describe the problems and possible solutions adequately.

SEGMENT 7 *(pp. 354–355)*

WRITING WORKSHOP

OBJECTIVE

- To engage in group problem solving and to prepare a group report to present orally

TEACHING THE LESSON

Encourage all students to participate in this activity by making sure they each have a role. You could document their time and activities on a time card, or ask a group member to write an overview of each member's contributions.

When students present their reports to the class, you might impose time limits so

QUOTATION FOR THE DAY

"All human beings have this burden in life to constantly figure out what's true, what's authentic, what's meaningful, what's dross, what's a hallucination, what's a figment, what's madness." (Maxine Hong Kingston, 1940– , Chinese American writer)

You might want to use this quotation after students have worked together to solve problems. Remind students that as they work together in groups, they will frequently disagree. Assure them that by working together they will probably arrive at more imaginative solutions.

MEETING INDIVIDUAL NEEDS

ADVANCED STUDENTS

Ask advanced students to present their papers in oratory style with few or no notes to prompt them. Ask students to work on developing public-speaking skills by speaking without the use of prompts.

WRITING WORKSHOP

Group Problem Solving

You've probably heard the old saying "Two heads are better than one." That's often the case when it comes to exploring problems and their solutions. In that case, three—four—even five or six heads are usually better than one.

To be most effective, group exploration needs to be a bit more systematic than many typical brainstorming sessions. One way to begin is by assigning specific roles to the members of the group.

ROLE	DUTY
Facilitator	Keeps discussion focused on the subject. Monitors the noise level of the group. Watches the time.
Questioner	Attempts to keep the group open to possibilities. Asks the questions necessary to keep ideas flowing. Asks group members to explain or elaborate upon answers. Asks members who haven't spoken for their ideas.
Clarifier	Paraphrases and sums up what others have said. Often acts as the recorder.

For the group to function well, it's important that everyone speak. But it's equally important that everyone *listen* carefully. The group can arrive at the best solution only if members really hear one another.

Why not put these ideas into practice? With four or five classmates, select a problem to explore. You can explore the problem of homelessness in your community by beginning with some of the ideas you read about in the Here's How (page 328), or you can explore a problem from the list you developed in Writing Assignment, Part 1 (page 326).

students know how much information they need to present. Students could practice their presentations with the facilitators judging their speaking rate and determining the information that can be covered in the allotted time.

Before students present their reports, discuss public-speaking skills with students. Remind students to speak clearly and loudly enough for everyone to hear. Students should not fidget or stand too rigid. Encourage students to stand and gesture naturally. You might suggest a prop related to the problem or the solution. ■

Exploring a Problem and Writing a Group Presentation

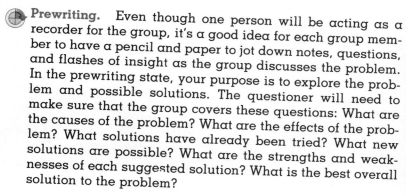

Prewriting. Even though one person will be acting as a recorder for the group, it's a good idea for each group member to have a pencil and paper to jot down notes, questions, and flashes of insight as the group discusses the problem. In the prewriting state, your purpose is to explore the problem and possible solutions. The questioner will need to make sure that the group covers these questions: What are the causes of the problem? What are the effects of the problem? What solutions have already been tried? What new solutions are possible? What are the strengths and weaknesses of each suggested solution? What is the best overall solution to the problem?

Writing, Evaluating, and Revising. For this project, you'll prepare a report to present orally to the rest of the class. The report need not be as carefully structured as an essay—it should, however, serve as a guide to the presenters. If your group couldn't agree on a proposed solution, your report should explain the solutions you considered and the reasons that you couldn't agree. Your purpose in making the presentation is to explain the problem and solutions to your audience, so be certain that you have evidence—facts, examples, and reasons—to support your explanation.

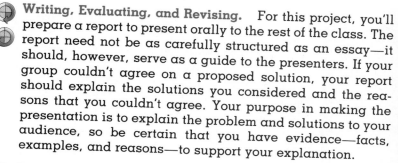

Proofreading and Publishing. Although you can't literally proofread it, an oral report can still be polished. Before presenting the group's analysis of the problem and its solutions, ask the person who will be speaking for the group to practice before the group. Listen carefully and offer positive suggestions for improvements.

MEETING INDIVIDUAL NEEDS

LEARNING STYLES

Auditory Learners. Encourage students to practice presenting their speeches into tape recorders and to listen to their own voices. This process should help students evaluate their speaking skills and make improvements where necessary.

INTEGRATING THE LANGUAGE ARTS

Speaking Link. To help students prepare for their oral presentations, remind students of the following speaking guidelines:

1. Look at the audience. Eye contact holds the audience's attention and helps the speaker identify the audience's reaction.
2. Keep gestures to a minimum.
3. Pronounce words correctly and refer to a dictionary for guidance.
4. Enunciate words correctly by not omitting essential sounds or syllables.

SEGMENT 8 *(pp. 356–357)*

MAKING CONNECTIONS

WRITING TO EXPLORE AND TO EXPRESS YOURSELF

OBJECTIVE

- To explore and express a problem in a journal entry

WRITING TO EXPLORE AND TO EXPRESS YOURSELF

Teaching Strategies

Explain to students that many times they can explore and express themselves in writing to help them make important decisions. Suggest that students use pros and cons to help them establish the advantages and disadvantages of major decisions.

Remind students that they are the only audience, so they can write openly and honestly about any issue. Suggest to students that they try this technique the next time they are angry or disappointed to help them sort out their feelings and to find solutions to their problems.

GUIDELINES

Rather than evaluate journal entries, check to see that students have completed the assignment.

MAKING CONNECTIONS

WRITING TO EXPLORE AND TO EXPRESS YOURSELF

A Journal Entry

In the main writing assignment of this chapter, you combined the aim of writing to explore with writing to explain. It's also useful to combine writing to explore with writing to express yourself—especially when you're faced with a personal problem. One way to sort out the thoughts and issues that sometimes bombard your brain is to put them down on paper. Following is a sample journal entry in which one writer explores her need to convince her parents to allow her to get a job.

I'm supposed to be studying for my chemistry test, but all I can think about is that job at Peterson's that my parents won't even let me apply for. They say it'll hurt my studying, but their refusal to listen is hurting it right now! I want a job! I don't want to ask them for money for everything. Since they won't discuss it, maybe I should write them a letter. Maybe I should make it a formal proposal. Maybe even a contract—"I'll work and keep my grades up, or at the end of the semester, I'll quit my job."

EXPLORATORY WRITING ACROSS THE CURRICULUM OBJECTIVE

- To analyze the Declaration of Independence as a problem-solution essay

If you've had a falling-out with your best friend or you're thinking about dropping out of school or you're bothered by something else, you might try exploring the causes of your problem or possible solutions to it in a journal entry. Although you'll be writing for an audience of one (yourself), don't skimp on details. You may be surprised at the understandings you uncover with a little exploration.

EXPLORATORY WRITING ACROSS THE CURRICULUM

History

One way to think of history is as a study of problems faced by people, both collectively and individually, and their solutions to them. In this light, you can think of the Declaration of Independence as a problem-solution essay.

Find a copy of the Declaration of Independence and read it over carefully. Then get together with several classmates and answer these questions:

1. What problem did the colonists face?
2. What part of the Declaration discusses the extent and seriousness of the colonists' problem? Name three specific examples from the Declaration that illustrate the extent and seriousness of the problem.
3. What solution does the Declaration propose?
4. What other solutions are mentioned within the Declaration? What are their disadvantages?

EXPLORATORY WRITING ACROSS THE CURRICULUM

Teaching Strategies

Introduce students to the Declaration of Independence by reading part of it to orient students to the language.

Ask volunteers to share information about the lives of some of the writers of the document and to present their findings to the class. Have students discuss why the writers might have had a personal interest in the document and the contributions that the writers made to history.

After students have completed the activity, recommend that students apply these analysis skills to a historical document of their own choosing in a cooperative-learning activity.

Then discuss with the class recent historical documents that are posing solutions to problems.

GUIDELINES

Evaluate how well students integrate their knowledge of history with their ability to propose solutions.

Chapter

10 WRITING ABOUT LITERATURE

OBJECTIVES

- To analyze different types of writing about literature—personal responses, literary analyses, movie reviews, music reviews, and book advertisements
- To respond personally to literature
- To read a poem critically
- To identify literary elements of poetry and fiction
- To evaluate and incorporate supporting evidence
- To identify focus and thesis
- To organize and outline ideas for a literary analysis
- To write, evaluate, and revise a literary analysis
- To proofread and publish a literary analysis
- To write a movie review
- To write a musical performance review
- To write a book advertisement

Motivation

Ask students to imagine an invention that can influence their emotions—one that can make them laugh or cry or become depressed, happy, or angry against their will.

Tell students that such an invention does exist—literature. Ask them to name stories or movies that have recently manipulated their emotions and to recall specific scenes. Point out that because of literature and media's power, it is important that students learn to analyze in what ways and by what methods movies and stories affect them. This chapter provides the tools to aid in that analysis.

Introduction

After students discuss the importance of analyzing literature, have them discuss the different purposes for writing about stories, poems, and movies. Ask students to identify the purposes suggested by the following titles: "Why *The Deerslayer* Is My Favorite Book" [expressive], "Every Eleventh Grader Should Read *The Deerslayer*" [persuasive], "The Life of James Fenimore Cooper" [informative], "The Hero Natty Bumpo: A Poem" [literary]. Explain to students that the main purpose of the literary analysis they will write in this chapter is to inform.

To prepare students for the review by Mark Twain, tell them that critics analyze a literary work much as people choose a new car. First, they respond emotionally, either liking or disliking it. Then they analyze how well it has been put together. Finally, they decide whether it is a good value. This explanation should prepare students to read Mark Twain's literary criticism.

Integration

Students will practice the skills learned in this chapter whenever they read literature or enjoy a movie or musical performance. When they are studying literature, you will probably want to refer to this chapter often: to the charts of **The Elements of Poetry** (p. 372-373) or **The Elements of Fiction** (p. 374) as well as to the instruction in the process of writing a literary analysis of any kind.

Students can also be quite effective teachers of literature once they understand how to analyze a piece of writing. Before a poetry unit, for example, you could assign each student a different poem to teach to the class, requiring each student to go through the analytic process of this chapter up to writing. Then the literary analyses can be presented orally to the entire class. (There is the added incentive that everyone will be aware of the results, not just the teacher.)

The chart on the next page illustrates the strands of language arts as they are integrated into this chapter. For vocabulary study, glossary words are underlined in some writing models.

QUOTATIONS
All **Quotations for the Day** are chosen because of their relevance to instructional material presented in that segment of the chapter and for their usefulness in establishing student interest in writing.

INTEGRATING THE LANGUAGE ARTS

Selection	Reading and Literature	Writing and Critical Thinking	Language and Syntax	Speaking, Listening, and Other Expression Skills
from *The Deerslayer* by James Fenimore Cooper **360** **"Fenimore Cooper's Literary Offences"** by Mark Twain **361-365** **"Ex-Basketball Player"** by John Updike **369-370** **"an ordinary woman"** by Lucile Clifton **375-376** **"Star Wars"** by Roger Ebert **395-396** **"Típica Sound of Cuba"** by Peter Watrous **399** ***Riding the Iron Rooster*** by Paul Theroux **400**	Responding personally to writing **365, 371, 396-397** Analyzing humor **365** Analyzing persuasive strategy **365** Analyzing supporting details **365, 382** Using critical reading strategies **377** Examining literary elements of poetry and fiction **377** Identifying sensory images **377** Identifying central theme of a poem **377** Analyzing tone **396**	Responding personally to literature **365, 371** Applying interpretive and creative thinking **365, 377, 382, 396-397** Analyzing supporting details **365, 382** Recording responses in a journal **371** Responding creatively to a poem or short story **371** Reading and responding critically to a poem **371, 377** Finding a focus **379** Developing a thesis statement **379** Gathering and organizing ideas **383, 397** Writing a first draft **388, 397** Analyzing a writer's revisions **391** Evaluating and revising **391, 397** Proofreading and publishing **392, 397** Analyzing a critical analysis **396-397** Writing a movie review using the writing process **397** Using criteria to evaluate a musical performance **398-399** Writing a musical performance review **399** Analyzing a musical performance review **399** Writing a book advertisement **401** Identifying and evaluating deductive reasoning **401**	Proofreading for errors in grammar, usage, and mechanics **392, 397**	Sharing responses to a poem **371** Presenting a scene to the class **371** Working cooperatively to evaluate supporting evidence **382** Evaluating first drafts in small groups **391** Working cooperatively to revise a movie review **397** Listening to a musical performance and using criteria to evaluate it **398-399** Reading a critical review of a musical performance to classmates **399** Discussing examples of deductive reasoning **401**

CHAPTER 10

SEGMENT PLANNING GUIDE

You can use the following Planning Guide to adapt the chapter material to the individual needs of your class. All the Resources listed in this chapter are located in the *Teacher's ResourceBank*™.

SEGMENT	PAGES	CONTENT	RESOURCES
1 ***Reading and Responding***	***358-365***		
Literary Model from ***The Deerslayer***	360	Guided reading: a model of creative writing	
Literary Model from **"Fenimore Cooper's Literary Offences"**	361-365	Guided reading: a model of literary analysis	
Reader's Response/ Writer's Craft	365	Model evaluation: responding to literature and analyzing creative writing/literary analysis	
2 ***Purposes for Writing***	***366-367***		
3 ***Prewriting***	***368-383***		Writing a Critical Analysis Analyzing a Poem 78-79 Analyzing a Short Story 80-81
Chart: Strategies for Responding to Literature	369	Guidelines: using criteria to respond to literature	
Literary Model **"Ex-Basketball Player"**	369-370	Guided reading: responding to a poem	
Exercise 1	371	Applied practice: responding to a poem	
Exercise 2	371	Cooperative learning: giving an oral response	
Reading Literature Critically	371-372	Explanation: understanding critical reading	
Chart: Strategies	372	Guidelines: using criteria for critical reading	
Charts: The Elements of Poetry and Fiction	372-374	Guidelines: identifying and examining literary elements	
Literary Model **"an ordinary woman"**	375-376	Guided reading: examining critical comments on a poem	
Exercise 3	377	Applied practice: reading critically	
Writing Assignment: Part 1	377	Applied practice: responding critically	
Thinking About Purpose, Audience, and Tone	378	Guidelines: analyzing and selecting appropriate purpose, audience, and tone	
Finding a Focus	378	Guidelines: using criteria for focusing on a poem	
Developing a Statement	379	Guidelines: writing a thesis statement	
Writing Assignment: Part 2	379	Applied practice: identifying a focus and writing a thesis statement	
Gathering Evidence	379-380	Guidelines: finding evidence in sources	
Critical Thinking: Evaluating Supporting Evidence	381	Guidelines: using criteria to evaluate evidence	
Critical Thinking Exercise	382-383	Cooperative learning: evaluating evidence	
Deciding on an Order	383	Guidelines: arranging ideas	
Writing Assignment: Part 3	383	Applied practice: gathering and organizing ideas	

For **Portfolio Assessment** see the following pages in the *Teacher's ResourceBank*™:
Aims For Writing — pp. 77–85
Holistically Graded Composition Models — pp. 521–526
Assessment Portfolio — pp. 533–562

SEGMENT	PAGES	CONTENT	RESOURCES
4 ***Writing***	***384-389***		Writing a Critical Analysis 82
Structure	384	Explanation: structuring a literary analysis	
Mechanics Hint	385	Writing suggestion: incorporating supporting evidence	
A Writer's Model	386-387	Guided reading: examining structure	
Chart: Framework	388	Guidelines: structuring a literary analysis	
Writing Assignment: Part 4	388	Applied practice: writing a first draft	
5 ***Evaluating and Revising***	***390-391***		Writing a Critical Analysis 83
Chart: Evaluating and Revising	390	Guidelines: applying evaluation and revision techniques	
Exercise 4	391	Applied practice: analyzing a writer's revisions	
Writing Assignment: Part 5	391	Cooperative learning: evaluating and revising	
6 ***Proofreading and Publishing***	***392-394***		Writing a Critical Analysis 84
Publishing	392	Publishing ideas: reaching a specific audience	
Writing Assignment: Part 6	392	Applied practice: proofreading and publishing	
A Student Model	393-394	Sample: examining an analysis of a short story	
7 ***Writing Workshop***	***395-397***		
A Movie Review	395	Introduction: identifying elements	
Literary Model/Questions **"Star Wars"**	395-397	Examining technique: analyzing a movie review	
Writing a Movie-Review	397	Applied practice: applying skills to the writing process	
8 ***Making Connections***	***398-401***		
Evaluation Across the Curriculum	398-399	Applied practice: using criteria to evaluate a musical performance and writing a critical analysis	
Literary Model **"Típica Sound of Cuba"**	399	Guided reading: identifying elements in a model	
Literature and Persuasion	400	Applied practice: writing an ad for a book	
Literary Model from ***Riding the Iron Rooster***	400	Guided reading: evaluating a book cover	
Literature and Evaluation	401	Cooperative learning: finding deductive reasoning	
WHOLE-CHAPTER RESOURCES A Writing Process Log, A Writing Prompt, Holistically Graded Models, Assessment Portfolio Materials			

SEGMENT 1 *(pp. 358–365)*

READING AND RESPONDING

OBJECTIVES

- To read and respond to a critical review
- To evaluate critical assertions
- To analyze the techniques used in a critical review

MOTIVATION

Read aloud the reviews of several current movies and ask students who have seen the movies if they agree with the reviews. The discussion will probably result in a demonstration of how widely several critics' opinions can differ. Explain to students that a reviewer must first analyze the movie and

VISUAL CONNECTIONS

Three Literary Gentlemen

About the Artwork. This painting shows the influence of cubism—a style of painting that employs multiple perspectives, geometrical shapes, and bold colors. Max Weber adapted cubism and also incorporated the impressionistic influences of other artists, such as Cézanne and Matisse, to create his own unique style. In *Three Literary Gentlemen,* the cubist technique of multiple perspectives is evident in the faces of the men.

10 WRITING ABOUT LITERATURE

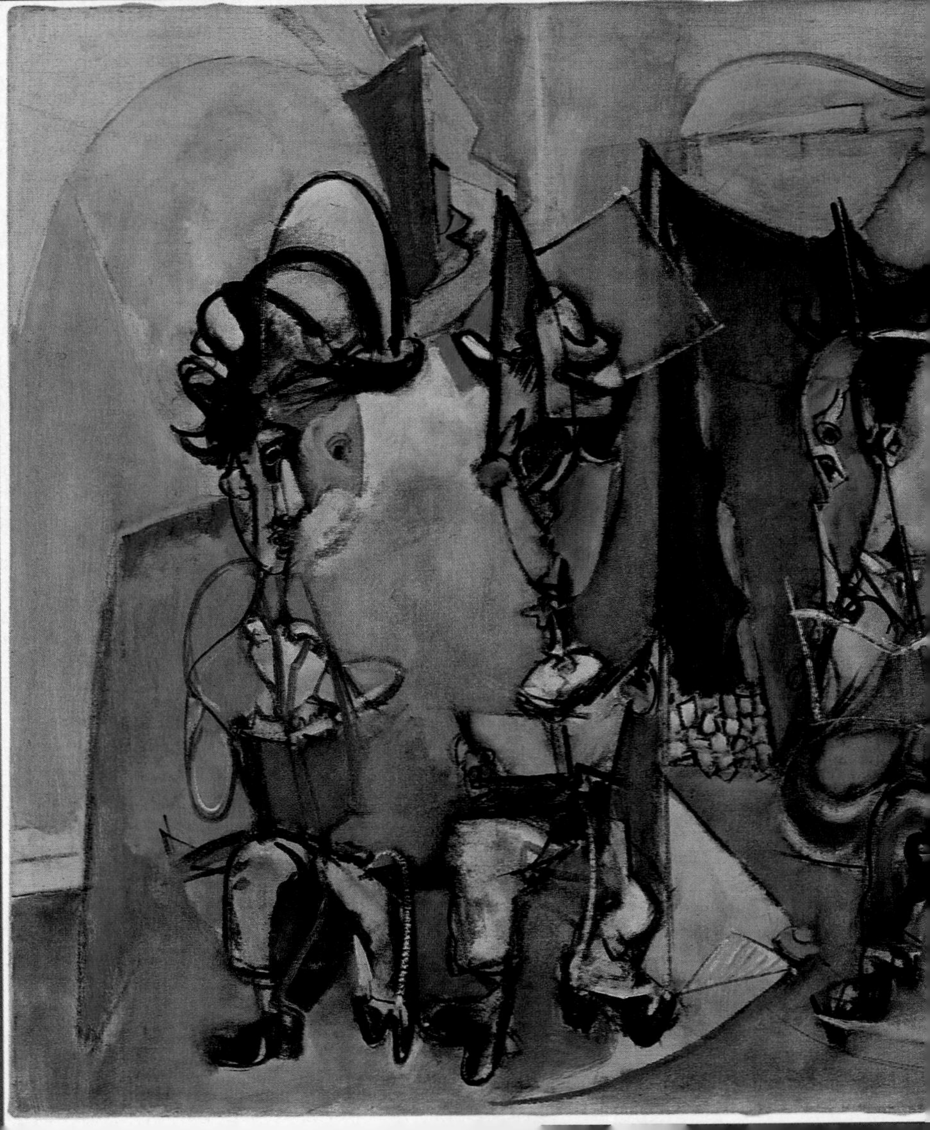

find support for his or her opinions before he or she evaluates it.

TEACHING THE LESSON

Before students read Mark Twain's critical analysis, you may want to give the class some background information about the works of James Fenimore Cooper. Explain that Cooper wrote a series of novels, *The Leatherstocking Tales,* that romanticized the American frontier. *The Deerslayer* belongs to that series. The central figure of the series is ☛

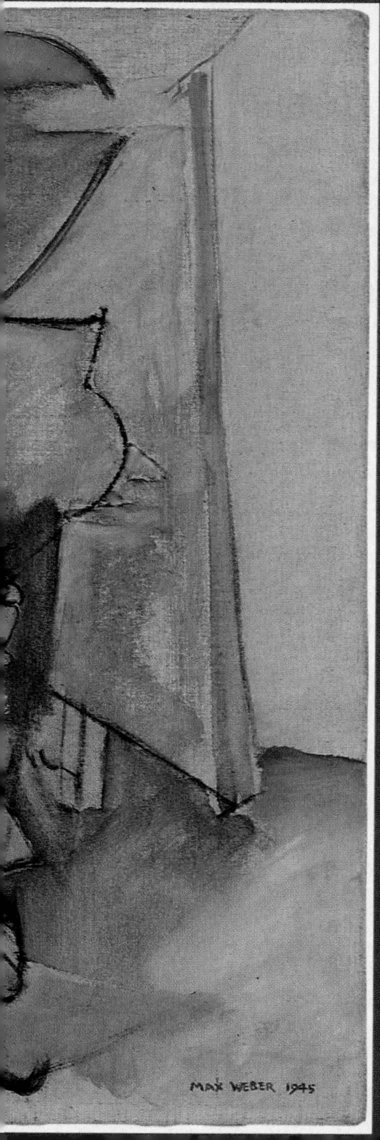

Reading and Responding

Have you ever read a story that was so exciting you passed it on to a friend as soon as you finished it? We all **respond to literature as we read** it, just as we respond to movies we see or music we listen to.

Writing and You. Sometimes our responses are as simple as "It's terrible!" or "It's terrific!" At other times we look at the book (or movie or concert) more critically and write about it. In English class, you write an essay about a story you just read. A book reviewer reads a book that has just been published and writes a review that is printed in a national magazine. Have you ever decided whether or not to read a book (or see a movie or concert) on the basis of a review you read?

As You Read. In the following essay, one writer, Mark Twain, takes a critical look at the work of another writer, James Fenimore Cooper. On the basis of Twain's comments, would you want to read Cooper's novel *The Deerslayer*?

Max Weber, U.S., 1881–1961. *Three Literary Gentlemen* (1945). Oil on canvas, 29 1/4″ × 36″. Gift of the William H. Lane Foundation. Courtesy of Museum of Fine Arts, Boston.

QUOTATION FOR THE DAY

"You may scold a carpenter who has made you a bad table, though you cannot make a table." (Samuel Johnson, 1709–1784, English lexicographer and conversationalist)

Some students may feel reluctant to criticize published writing. Assure them that they can respond critically to a story or a poem, even if they are unable to write such a story or poem.

MEETING INDIVIDUAL NEEDS

ADVANCED STUDENTS

Suggest that students explore what other literary critics say about *The Deerslayer.* Refer students to reference works such as *Nineteenth-Century Literature Criticism.* Varying opinions might motivate students to read at least one of Cooper's books and to reach their own conclusions. Students could report orally to the class and read examples of Cooper's writing to support their opinions.

359

loyal, courageous Natty Bumppo, a frontiersman who prefers the moral code of the Native Americans to the exploitation of nature by the white settlers.

Ask students to look at the title of Twain's essay and to predict whether the analysis will be positive or negative. [*Offences* has negative connotations.] You may want to read aloud the essay to help students appreciate Twain's humor. Then you can go back over the essay in more detail and use the annotations as a basis for discussion. Students may be interested to know that although Twain found fault with Cooper's style, James Fenimore Cooper was highly thought of by other writers such as Balzac, Victor Hugo, Joseph Conrad, Herman Melville, and D. H. Lawrence.

THE DEERSLAYER

The excerpt from *The Deerslayer* that appears here is the beginning of Chapter 1. Because Mark Twain's criticism refers to adventure scenes and dialogue in Cooper's book, you may want to read aloud an additional excerpt that reflects more of the action.

SELECTION AMENDMENT

Description of change: excerpted
Rationale: to focus on the concept of literary criticism presented in this chapter

The Deerslayer

by James Fenimore Cooper

CHAPTER I.

On the human imagination, events produce the effects of time. Thus, he who has travelled far and seen much, is apt to fancy that he has lived long; and the history that most abounds in important incidents, soonest assumes the aspect of antiquity. In no other way can we account for the venerable air that is already gathering around American annals. When the mind reverts to the earliest days of colonial history, the period seems remote and obscure, the thousand changes that thicken along the links of recollections, throwing back the origin of the nation to a day so distant as seemingly to reach the mists of time; and yet four lives of ordinary duration would suffice to transmit, from mouth to mouth, in the form of tradition, all that civilized man has achieved within the limits of the republic. Although New York, alone, possesses a population materially exceeding that of either of the four smallest kingdoms of Europe, or materially exceeding that of the entire Swiss Confederation, it is little more than two centuries since the Dutch commenced their settlement, rescuing the region from the savage state. Thus, what seems venerable by an accumulation of changes, is reduced to familiarity when we come seriously to consider it solely in connection with time.

This glance into the perspective of the past, will prepare the reader to look at the pictures we are about to sketch, with less surprise than he might otherwise feel; and a few additional explanations may carry him back in imagination, to the precise condition of society that we desire to delineate. It is matter of history that the settlements on the eastern shores of the Hudson, such as Claverack, Kinderhook, and even Poughkeepsie, were not regarded as safe from Indian incursions a century since; and there is still standing on the banks of the same river, and within musket-shot of the wharves of Albany, a residence of a younger branch of the Van Rensselaers, that has loop-holes constructed for defence against the same crafty enemy, although it dates from a period scarcely so distant.

GUIDED PRACTICE

Guide students through the **Reader's Response** and **Writer's Craft** questions. The first **Reader's Response** question, which asks for students to give their opinions about Twain's style, gives you the opportunity to reinforce that opinions about literature will vary because individuals' likes and dislikes vary; however, emphasize to students that opinions in a piece of critical writing require valid support.

Explain to students that the two sets of questions in the textbook model the steps they will follow when they write their own critical analyses: students will respond personally to a piece of literature (as they did for the **Reader's Response** questions), and they

Fenimore Cooper's Literary Offences

by Mark Twain

1 *The Pathfinder* and *The Deerslayer* stand at the head of Cooper's novels as artistic creations. There are others of his works which contain parts as perfect as are to be found in these, and scenes even more thrilling. Not one can be compared with either of them as a finished whole.

The defects in both of these tales are comparatively slight. They were pure works of art.—*Prof. Lounsbury.*

The five tales reveal an extraordinary fulness of invention. . . . One of the very greatest characters in fiction, Natty Bumppo. . . .

The craft of the woodsman, the tricks of the trapper, all the delicate art of the forest, were familiar to Cooper from his youth up.—*Prof. Brander Matthews.*

Cooper is the greatest artist in the domain of romantic fiction yet produced by America.—*Wilkie Collins.*

2 It seems to me that it was far from right for the Professor of English Literature in Yale, the Professor of English Literature in Columbia, and Wilkie Collins to deliver opinions on Cooper's literature without having read some of it. It would have been much more decorous to keep silent and let persons talk who have read Cooper.

3 Cooper's art has some defects. In one place in *Deerslayer,* and in the restricted space of two-thirds of a page, Cooper has scored 114 offences against literary art out of a possible 115. It breaks the record.

4 There are nineteen rules governing literary art in the domain of romantic fiction—some say twenty-two. In *Deerslayer* Cooper violated eighteen of them. These eighteen require:

USING THE SELECTION

Fenimore Cooper's Literary Offences

1

What kind of writing would you expect from Cooper after reading these statements by "experts"? [A reader would probably expect appealing writing of the highest quality.]

2

Twain sets the tongue-in-cheek tone immediately.

3

This understatement precedes a passage of hyperbole.

4

Twain's rules are themselves criticisms; the rules hardly need to be stated because they are so obvious, and that's Twain's point.

will analyze a piece of literature (as they did for the **Writer's Craft** questions).

ASSESSMENT

You can use students' responses to the **Reader's Response** and **Writer's Craft** questions to assess students' understanding.

VISUAL CONNECTIONS

Exploring the Subject. Mark Twain is the pen name of Samuel Langhorne Clemens, born November 30, 1835. Twain's origins as a writer began when he was apprenticed to a printer and later began assisting his brother in the production of a newspaper. Twain contributed reports, poems, and humorous sketches to the newspaper for several years. He continued to write during his travels and during his experiences with different vocations until his reputation grew to the point where he could make a living from his writing.

Twain was a versatile writer. He is known as one of the most famous of U.S. humorists. His masterpiece *The Adventures of Huckleberry Finn* is seen by some critics as the first truly American novel.

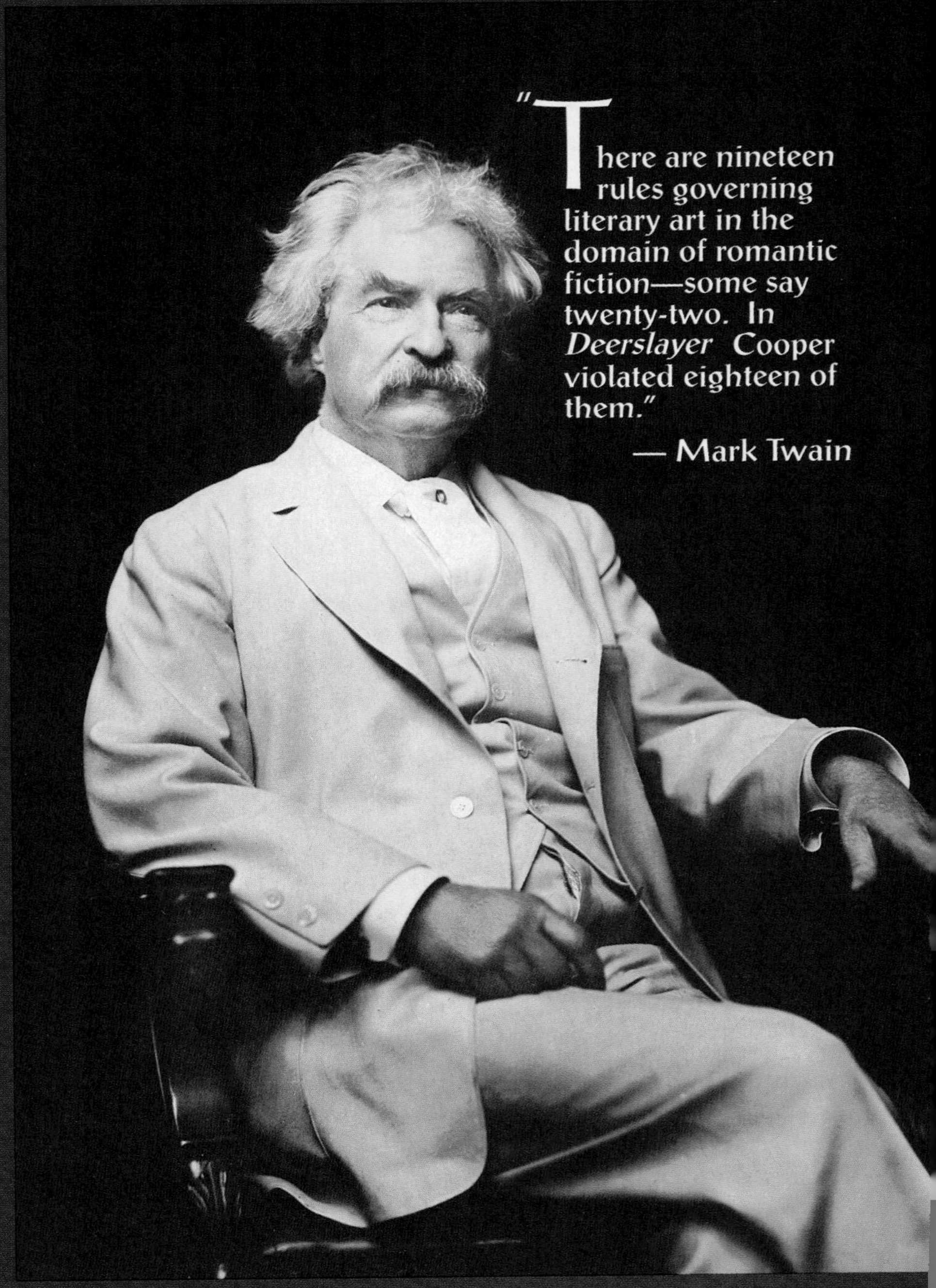
"There are nineteen rules governing literary art in the domain of romantic fiction—some say twenty-two. In *Deerslayer* Cooper violated eighteen of them."
— Mark Twain

RETEACHING

Students who have difficulty reading and analyzing Twain's essay will probably benefit from working in small groups. The groups could read one short part at a time and discuss Twain's use of details and examples to support his opinions. Circulate throughout the groups to offer assistance as needed.

CLOSURE

Write on the chalkboard the phrases *personal response* and *critical analysis.* Ask students to explain the difference between the two processes. Then remind students that they can react to a work of literature through both personal response and critical analysis.

5 1. That a tale shall accomplish something and arrive somewhere. But the *Deerslayer* tale accomplishes nothing and arrives in the air.

2. They require that the episodes of a tale shall be necessary parts of the tale, and shall help to develop it. But as the *Deerslayer* tale is not a tale, and accomplishes nothing and arrives nowhere, the episodes have no rightful place in the work, since there was nothing for them to develop.

3. They require that the personages in a tale shall be alive, except in the case of corpses, and that always the reader shall be able to tell the corpses from the others. But this detail has often been overlooked in the *Deerslayer* tale.

4. They require that the personages in a tale, both dead and alive, shall exhibit a sufficient excuse for being there. But this detail also has been overlooked in the *Deerslayer* tale.

5. They require that when the personages of a tale deal in conversation, the talk shall sound like human talk, and be talk such as human beings would be likely to talk in the given circumstances, and have a
6 discoverable meaning, also a discoverable purpose, and a show of relevancy, and remain in the neighborhood of the subject in hand, and be interesting to the reader, and help out the tale, and stop when the
7 people cannot think of anything more to say. But this requirement has been ignored from the beginning of the *Deerslayer* tale to the end of it.

6. They require that when the author describes the character of a personage in his tale, the conduct and conversation of that personage shall justify said description. But this law gets little or no attention in
8 the *Deerslayer* tale, as Natty Bumppo's case will amply prove.

7. They require that when a personage talks like an illustrated, gilt-edged, tree-calf, hand-tooled, seven-dollar Friendship's Offering in the beginning of a paragraph, he shall not talk like a negro minstrel in the end of it. But this rule is flung down and danced upon in the *Deerslayer* tale.

8. They require that crass stupidities shall not be played upon the reader as "the craft of the woodsman, the delicate art of the forest," by either the author or the people in the tale. But this rule is persistently violated in the *Deerslayer* tale.

9. They require that the personages of a tale shall confine themselves to possibilities and let miracles alone; or, if they venture a miracle, the author must so plausibly set it forth as to make it look possible and reasonable. But these rules are not respected in the *Deerslayer* tale.

5

Twain's rules are valid points for literary criticism although their humorous phrasing may camouflage their truth. For example, Rule 1 deals with plot structure; Rule 2 deals with coherence; and Rule 3 deals with characterization.

6

relevancy: having a connection with the matter in hand

7

Twain could have included dialogue from the story to support his fifth rule. He gives little evidence to support his opinions.

8

amply: more than enough

EXTENSION

You could ask students to bring to class reviews of books, television programs, or movies. Then ask students to analyze the reviews in the same way that they have been analyzing the essay by Mark Twain. Remind them to support each comment with specific examples.

ENRICHMENT

You may want to let students give Twain a dose of his own medicine. Ask students to choose one of Twain's short stories (or a novel such as *The Adventures of Huckleberry Finn,* if they have all read it) and apply to it the "rules governing literary art" Twain describes in his essay. ■

9
Twain assumes that his reactions will be felt by all readers. Is this a fair assumption?

10
vacated: abandoned

11
Why does Twain use words here that are so different from the diction of the rest of the essay? [*Eschew* means "to avoid" and *surplusage* means "superfluous words." He is humorously illustrating what an author should not do.]

12
What tone does the word *sweet* impart? [ironic]

10. They require that the author shall make the reader feel a deep interest in the personages of his tale and in their fate; and that he shall make the reader love the good people in the tale and hate the bad
9 ones. But the reader of the *Deerslayer* tale dislikes the good people in it, is indifferent to the others, and wishes they would all get drowned together.
11. They require that the characters in a tale shall be so clearly defined that the reader can tell beforehand what each will do in a
10 given emergency. But in the *Deerslayer* tale this rule is vacated.

In addition to these large rules there are some little ones. These require that the author shall

12. *Say* what he is proposing to say, not merely come near it.
13. Use the right word, not its second cousin.
11 14. Eschew surplusage.
15. Not omit necessary details.
16. Avoid slovenliness of form.
17. Use good grammar.
18. Employ a simple and straightforward style.

Even these seven are coldly and persistently violated in the *Deerslayer* tale.

Cooper's gift in the way of invention was not a rich endowment; but such as it was he liked to work it, he was pleased with the effects,
12 and indeed he did some quite sweet things with it. In his little box of stage properties he kept six or eight cunning devices, tricks, artifices for his savages and woodsmen to deceive and circumvent each other with, and he was never so happy as when he was working these innocent things and seeing them go. A favorite one was to make a moccasined person tread in the tracks of the moccasined enemy, and thus hide his own trail. Cooper wore out barrels and barrels of moccasins in working that trick. Another stage-property that he pulled out of his box pretty frequently was his broken twig. He prized his broken twig above all the rest of his effects, and worked it the hardest. It is a restful chapter in any book of his when somebody doesn't step on a dry twig and alarm all the reds and whites for two hundred yards around. Every time a Cooper person is in peril, and absolute silence is worth four dol-

lars a minute, he is sure to step on a dry twig.

There may be a hundred handier things to step on, but that wouldn't satisfy Cooper. Cooper requires him to turn out and find a dry twig; and if he can't do it, go and borrow one. In fact, the Leather Stocking Series ought to have been called the Broken Twig Series.

James Fenimore Cooper

Reader's Response

1. Did you enjoy this review of *The Deerslayer*? What did you like or dislike about Twain's style?
2. It's fairly obvious that Twain thinks Cooper's novels are not very good. If you haven't read any of Cooper's novels, how can you tell if Twain's criticisms are valid? Try reading the first paragraph from *The Deerslayer,* printed on page 360; or see if you can find a copy of the book and sample a few pages. What do you think?

Writer's Craft

3. You've probably read some other things written by Mark Twain and know that much of his writing is humorous. How does Twain create humor with his third point—the point about corpses? What other examples of humor can you find?
4. Twain begins his essay by quoting three people who think highly of Cooper's work. Why do you think he includes these quotes? How does he counteract their comments?
5. Twain says there are at least nineteen rules governing the literary art of "romantic fiction," and he claims that Cooper broke eighteen of those rules. Which of these rules do you think you could apply to writing today? Why?
6. How does Twain use details and examples to support his opinions? Why do you suppose he doesn't develop rules 12–18 at all?

ANSWERS

Reader's Response

Responses will vary.

1. Responses should be supported with specific references.
2. Students will probably say that valid judgments cannot be made without reading the work being criticized.

Writer's Craft

Responses will vary.

3. Twain creates humor by making the ridiculously obvious statement that characters need to be alive. There is also the implied criticism that many of Cooper's readers don't seem to notice Cooper's obvious shortcomings.
   The last paragraph about Cooper's limited imagination makes fun of his repeated use of certain effects.
4. Twain may have wanted to indicate his awareness that many "experts" disagreed with his response to Cooper's writing. He counters the quotations by declaring in the first paragraph that people who claim to like the book must not have read it.
5. Students should offer reasons to support their opinions.
6. Twain doesn't try to prove each rule by offering specific examples from the story. However, he does use specific examples in the last paragraph to support his opinion.
   Developing rules 12–18 might have made the essay too tedious.

SELECTION AMENDMENT

Description of change: excerpted
Rationale: to focus on the concept of literary criticism presented in this chapter

SEGMENT 2 *(pp. 366–367)*

PURPOSES FOR WRITING ABOUT LITERATURE

TEACHING THE AIMS

Explain to students that although a writer has a main purpose in mind when he or she begins writing, very seldom does the writer adhere exclusively to that aim. Generally, the writer has one or several secondary aims. For example, Mark Twain's main purpose in writing *Fenimore Cooper's Literary Offences* is to persuade; however, he also incorporates the other aims. Ask students to identify excerpts from Twain's essay that are self-expressive, persuasive, expository, and literary. [Here are some possibilities: The introduction following the quotations is

COOPERATIVE LEARNING

Focusing on movies might help to make the aims of writing more relevant for students. Divide the class into groups of three and have each group choose a movie that all of its members have seen. Each group's assignment is to use all four of the aims to write a movie review. Some groups may need help getting started. If so, you can suggest that they express their personal opinions about the movie (self-expressive), convince their readers to see the movie or not to see it (persuasive), give a brief plot summary (expository), and rewrite the movie's ending (literary). Allow time for the groups to share their completed movie reviews.

Purposes for Writing About Literature

Even though he's funny about it, Mark Twain despises *The Deerslayer* and Cooper's fiction in general, and he gives eighteen reasons why. His purpose is to persuade his audience to accept his opinion about Cooper's novels. (His essay, by the way, became quite famous—or infamous.)

But there are other purposes for writing about literature (or for writing about any of the other arts—music, dance, film, photography, painting, sculpture). In school your purpose for writing about literature may be to show your teacher that you understand the poem or the story you've read in class. Another purpose might be just to share information—what you've learned by looking closely at the poem or story—with your teacher and your classmates. Here are some examples of the purposes you might have when you write about literature.

Self-Expressive: writing an entry in your response journal about a novel, a story, or a poem that has special meaning for you; starting a reading list—with comments—of your favorite novels (perhaps in your response journal).

Persuasive: for a column in your school newspaper, writing a review of the drama club's production of Cole Porter's *Anything Goes* to encourage readers to buy tickets and see the play; writing a letter to the editor of your local newspaper explaining why a particular novel shouldn't be banned from the library.

Expository: in your school literary magazine, writing about the latest winner of the Nobel Prize for literature and discussing some of the writer's works that are in your school library; writing a critical analysis explaining the use of symbolism in a poem you read for English class.

Literary: writing a poem in which you respond to a poem that is one of your favorites; writing a skit that is a *parody* (a "mocking imitation") of a television soap opera.

self-expressive; the first eleven rules include reasons to help persuade the reader that *The Deerslayer* commits literary offenses; the list of eighteen rules governing literary art in the domain of romantic fiction is expository; and the last paragraph of the excerpt contains literary satire.] ■

LOOKING AHEAD

In this chapter, you'll explore several purposes and ways of writing about literature, but you'll concentrate most of your attention on the critical analysis. In the critical analysis you write, your purpose will be to inform and explain. As you work through the assignments in this chapter, keep in mind that an effective critical analysis

- starts with a careful reading of the work
- identifies the writer's main idea, or thesis, about the work
- provides examples from the work that support, or prove, the main idea

"Some books are to be tasted, others to be swallowed, and some few to be chewed and digested."

Sir Francis Bacon

SELECTION AMENDMENT

Description of change: excerpted

Rationale: to focus on the concept of literary criticism presented in this chapter

SEGMENT 3 *(pp. 368–383)*

PREWRITING

OBJECTIVES

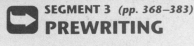

- To respond personally to a poem
- To write a script cooperatively and to perform the scene
- To read a poem critically
- To write a personal response to a poem
- To identify a focus and a thesis for a critical analysis of a poem
- To collect evidence and make an early plan for a critical analysis of a poem

Teacher's ResourceBank™

RESOURCES

PREWRITING

• Analyzing a Poem	78–79
• Analyzing a Short Story	80–81

QUOTATION FOR THE DAY

"The good critic is he who narrates the adventures of his soul among masterpieces." (Anatole France, 1844–1924, French novelist and essayist)

Tell students that being critics does not necessarily mean that they have to evaluate literature for others. Criticism also entails the solitary reader's investigation of how and why he or she is affected by what is read. In the prewriting stage of the writing process, this investigation involves recording responses and determining aspects of the literature that are responsible for the responses.

MEETING INDIVIDUAL NEEDS

LEP/ESL

General Strategies. Some ESL students may have difficulty responding to the unusual uses of poetic language in English. You may want to allow them to work with native speakers who can help them with vocabulary or idiomatic phrasing.

Writing a Literary Analysis

Prewriting

Reading and Responding to Literature

When you read a poem or story, your first thought may be *I like this* or *I don't like this.* But to really enjoy or understand what you read, you need to go beyond this first thought. You start with the poem or story itself and your personal responses to it, but then you look at it critically to understand it more fully.

Starting with Personal Response

Trace a writer's words. They go from the writer's brain onto the printed page, then from the printed page into the reader's brain—an amazing journey. But once in the reader's brain another amazing thing happens. Each reader responds—feels and reacts—differently.

Twenty different readers respond to a poem or story in twenty different ways because every reader is unique. Since there is no one exactly like you, no one who's led your life and thought your thoughts, your responses to a poem or any work of literature may be different from those of your friends, your classmates, and your teacher.

MOTIVATION

You may want to begin by reading aloud a personal poem from your literature textbook, such as "Elegy for Jane" by Theodore Roethke. Ask students to share their thoughts or feelings in response to the reading. [Roethke's poem will probably make students think of friends who have been injured or killed or about how people seldom realize how many others care about them. Be sure to emphasize the differences in students' responses.] Lead students to see that each reader makes his or her own connection with the poem based on prior knowledge and experience.

STRATEGIES FOR RESPONDING TO LITERATURE

1. **Listen to your inner voice.** Let yourself respond without worrying about what other people would think.
2. **Write your responses in your journal.** Allow the poem or story to trigger your thoughts and then freewrite in any direction. Does a character in the story remind you of anyone you know? Have you had a similar experience? How did you feel when you finished reading?
3. **Get together with a friend or a group of classmates and share your responses.** Remember that your responses will be different but equally valid.
4. **Respond creatively.** Write another poem or story based on something you felt or thought when you were reading. Write a new ending or beginning to a story. Convert the ideas in a poem to a play or story.

The following poem is about a man who lived his greatest moments in his youth. What would that be like?

A POEM

Ex-Basketball Player

by John Updike

1 **Pearl Avenue runs past the high-school lot,**
Bends with the trolley tracks, and stops, cut off
Before it has a chance to go two blocks,
At Colonel McComsky Plaza. Berth's Garage
Is on the corner facing west, and there,
Most days, you'll find Flick Webb, who helps Berth out.

2 **Flick stands tall among the idiot pumps—**
Five on a side, the old bubble-head style,
Their rubber elbows hanging loose and low.
3 **One's nostrils are two S's, and his eyes**
An E and O. And one is squat, without
A head at all—more of a football type.

INTEGRATING THE LANGUAGE ARTS

Listening Link. To make students more comfortable with poetry, you may want to begin or end each class period during this lesson by asking a volunteer to read a poem or by listening to a recording of an oral reading of a poem. Then briefly discuss the poem and encourage students to share their personal responses and observations about its literary elements.

USING THE SELECTION

Ex-Basketball Player

1

How could the description of Pearl Avenue be seen as a metaphor for Flick's life? [The street is cut off just past the high school by a plaza, just as Flick's stardom was cut off after his graduation from high school.]

2

Updike personifies the gas pumps by calling them idiots and giving them heads, elbows, nostrils, and eyes.

3

The letters refer to the brand name *Esso*, the former name of the Exxon gasoline company.

TEACHING THE LESSON

To give students a brief overview of the writing assignment, list the following steps on the chalkboard:

1. Choose a poem.
2. Read for a personal response.
3. Read again critically.
4. Determine audience, purpose, and tone for a literary analysis of the poem.
5. Find a focus for the literary analysis and write a thesis statement.
6. Gather and evaluate evidence.
7. Develop an early plan.

Learning how to respond to literature and to read critically won't mean much to students until the skills are applied to a poem or story. Because students' responses and interpretations will vary, working in groups

4
Basketball jargon includes *bucketed, rack up,* and *dribbles.*

5
The poet uses personification and a simile to describe Flick's basketball skills.

6
The present contrasts starkly with Flick's famous past.

7
The image of Flick's hands is repeated, but the context has changed.

8
How does the final use of personification create irony? [The "applauding tiers" are rows of candy, not cheering fans.]

Once Flick played for the high-school team, the Wizards.
He was good: in fact, the best. In '46
4 He bucketed three hundred ninety points,
5 A county record still. The ball loved Flick.
I saw him rack up thirty-eight or forty
In one home game. His hands were like wild birds.

6 He never learned a trade, he just sells gas,
Checks oil, and changes flats. Once in a while,
As a gag, he dribbles an inner tube,
But most of us remember anyway.
7 His hands are fine and nervous on the lug wrench.
It makes no difference to the lug wrench, though.

Off work, he hangs around Mae's Luncheonette,
Grease-grey and kind of coiled, he plays pinball,
Sips lemon cokes, and smokes those thin cigars;
Flick seldom speaks to Mae, just sits and nods
8 Beyond her face towards bright applauding tiers
Of Necco Wafers, Nibs, and Juju Beads.

can allow students to share their ideas as well as hear the ideas of others.

Explain to students that the information in **Reading Literature Critically** will help them to become active readers. Active reading is like a lively conversation between the reader and the printed material, and the process involves a mixture of emotional and analytical responses. Readers should question anything that confuses, puzzles, or provokes them, and they should respond to anything that pleases, annoys, or interests them. You will probably want to review the terminology in **The Elements of Poetry** chart on pp. 372–373, as students will need to be familiar with the terms to write their critical analyses.

EXERCISE 1 **Responding to a Poem**

What did your inner voice tell you about this poem? Respond in writing in one of the following ways.

1. Write your response in your journal. Start with the title of the poem or the line or image that you reacted to most strongly. Follow where your own thoughts and feelings lead you. Or start with what you think Updike means by the poem and your own reaction to that meaning.
2. Write another poem, one that reflects the feelings or thoughts "Ex-Basketball Player" triggered in your mind.
3. Write a short story with Flick as the main character. Set the story in the past, when he played basketball, or in his future.

EXERCISE 2 **Speaking and Listening: Giving an Oral Response**

With a partner, develop one of the following ideas in response to "Ex-Basketball Player." Write a script, decide which role each of you will take, and present the scene to your class.

A local news reporter is interviewing the ex-basketball player on the occasion of the twentieth anniversary of the state championship game.

The ex-class nerd and the ex-basketball player meet at their twenty-year class reunion.

Reading Literature Critically

Think about your personal response to a car. It's fun to drive; the seats are comfortable; you'd like to drive it again. But what if you had to prepare an analysis of that car for a consumer-awareness report? You would certainly have to look at the car more closely and more critically. You might have to know something about different types of brakes or transmissions, as well as how well they work on this particular car. And just as you would need to look more critically at a car to write a consumer report, you have to look more closely at a poem or story to write a literary analysis. An analysis of literature, unlike a personal response, uses objective standards that many people agree upon to examine a piece of writing.

ANSWERS
Exercise 1

Responses will vary. If students choose item 1, they can freewrite in class. However, students may need extra time to complete items 2 or 3.

ANSWERS
Exercise 2

If videotaping equipment is available, students could record their presentations. You may want to require that students turn in their scripts.

GUIDED PRACTICE

You may want to model the prewriting steps with one of your favorite poems. Make a transparency of the poem or reproduce it on paper so you can annotate it for the class. Have the class help you to create a thesis statement, gather evidence to support the thesis statement, and to create an early plan.

In **Exercise 1** on p. 371 students will practice responding personally and creatively to poems, and in **Exercise 3** on p. 377 students will practice reading a poem critically. In each case, allow students to work in groups first. Then all groups can contribute to a class discussion. As students work with partners to complete **Exercise 2** on p. 371, you will probably want to circulate

INTEGRATING THE LANGUAGE ARTS

Reading Link. Emphasize to students that reading is a process, just as writing is a process. A writer cannot expect to create his or her best work with just one draft; similarly, a reader cannot expect to fully appreciate a piece of literature with just one reading.

Give students copies of a poem with which they are unfamiliar. Ask them to read the poem silently and to rate their understanding on a scale of 1–5, with 5 indicating complete understanding. Ask students to read the poem again, this time more carefully, and to annotate as they read. Have them rate their understanding again on a scale of 1–5. Then divide the class into small groups to discuss the poem. After five minutes, have each student again rate his or her understanding.

Complete the activity by asking students to share their ratings and to explain why their ratings might have changed with each reading. Lead students to see that the reading process does not focus on arriving at a right answer; instead, it focuses on an increased awareness through rereading and hearing the interpretations of others.

Using Critical Reading Strategies. You may read many things carefully—the instruction manual for a new camera, a chapter in your history book, and so on. But reading carefully is not quite the same thing as reading critically. Here are some strategies that will help you read literature critically.

STRATEGIES FOR READING CRITICALLY

1. **Read the work again.** Once isn't enough. Each time you reread a poem or a story, you'll discover something new. Read a poem aloud to hear the sound effects.
2. **Look for the elements.** Find examples of the elements (see this page and pages 373–374), and take notes. If you can, make a copy of the work so you can underline, circle, and write marginal notes.
3. **Be prepared for puzzles.** Don't give up if you don't understand something. Do what you can (reread, use context clues, try a dictionary, ask someone) and go on.
4. **Compare your findings.** Talk about the work with classmates who have read it, too.

Examining Literary Elements. An automobile expert talks about transmissions and disc brakes and mph; a critical reader of literature talks about imagery and plot and symbols. To analyze and describe a work of literature, you need a special vocabulary, as well as an understanding of what the terms mean. The following charts define some of the basic terms, or elements, and provide some questions for use in analyzing a poem or story.

THE ELEMENTS OF POETRY	
Speaker—the voice that talks to the reader, that tells the poem	Who is the speaker? How does the speaker affect the mood and theme of the poem?
Imagery—words or phrases that appeal to the senses	What images are contained in the poem? How do they affect the poem's meaning?

(continued)

throughout the room to offer assistance and answer questions.

INDEPENDENT PRACTICE

In **Writing Assignment: Part 1** on p. 377, students will begin work on a critical analysis by selecting a poem and reading it personally and critically. You may want to divide the class into groups and to have each group select one poem so that students can work together on this writing project.

THE ELEMENTS OF POETRY *(continued)*	
Diction—the writer's choice of words	What kind of language does the poet use—formal or informal? concrete or abstract? unusual words or phrases?
Figurative Language—a word or phrase that is not meant to be taken literally	Does the poet use personification—giving human qualities to an object or animal? Does the poet use similes or metaphors to compare two unlike things? What feelings or ideas does this language suggest?
Symbol—a person, place, thing, or event that stands for something else	Does any person, place, thing, or event seem to have symbolic value? If so, what?
Sound Effects—use of sounds of words to create certain effects	What sound effects are used? How do they contribute to meaning or suggest images?
Rhyme—repetition of vowel sounds in accented syllables and all succeeding syllables	Does the poem contain rhyme? If so, what is the pattern, and how does it affect the meaning of the poem?
Rhythm—pattern of stressed and unstressed syllables	Is the rhythm regular or like the natural pattern of speech? How does it reflect the mood and theme of the poem?
Repetition—repeated consonant sounds, vowel sounds, words, or phrases	What words, phrases, or sounds are repeated? What impression do they create? What effect do they have on the meaning of the poem?
Theme—the meaning, or main idea, the poem reveals or suggests	Does the poem examine any common problem or life experience? What message or theme does it suggest?

MEETING INDIVIDUAL NEEDS

STUDENTS WITH SPECIAL NEEDS

Figurative language and symbolism may be difficult concepts for learning disabled students who generally rely heavily on literal comprehension. You may want to work one-on-one with some students to annotate the poems they choose and to help explain the poetic elements.

Students will continue planning their critical analyses of selected poems in **Writing Assignment: Part 2** on p. 379. Each student will be required to write an appropriate focus and a thesis. Sharing plans with their groups will help students to evaluate their work up to this point. Group members can respond to each other's work on the importance of the focus and the clarity of the thesis. Encourage students to use the two questions in the **Critical Thinking** section on p. 381 to evaluate their supporting evidence. You will probably want to monitor individual progress with student-teacher conferences.

INTEGRATING THE LANGUAGE ARTS

Literature Link. You may prefer to use a short story for the literary analyses students will write in this lesson. If so, you could review **The Elements of Fiction** chart and lead a class discussion of one short story before students begin projects of their own. A good choice for class discussion is "The Leader of the People" by John Steinbeck. Then have students write a critical analysis of that story or of another short story of their choice.

THE ELEMENTS OF FICTION	
Setting—the time and place of the story	Does the setting suggest a tone or a mood? How does the setting affect the development of the plot?
Character—a person (sometimes an animal or thing) in a story or novel	What is the role of the characters in the development of the plot? Are any meanings suggested by their names or their physical descriptions? How do they talk? act? think?
Plot—the events that follow each other and cause other events to happen	Are the events predictable? What is the central problem or conflict in the story? How does the outcome of the story relate to theme or meaning?
Point of View—the perspective or vantage point from which a story is told	Is the story told by a first-person or a third-person narrator? How much does the narrator know? How does the narrator seem to feel about the characters and events in the story?
Theme—an underlying idea or insight that the work reveals about life and people	Does this work reveal any underlying idea or insight about human experiences and problems? Does it attempt to teach any lessons about human nature or relationships? What details and passages reflect the theme?

ASSESSMENT

You may want to create and reproduce for your students a checklist that includes all of the prewriting steps. When students turn in their prewriting, have them attach the checklist. Then either you or your students can check off each step as it is completed.

RETEACHING

You may want to provide detailed study questions for students who have difficulty with this lesson. For example, as the class reads **"Ex-Basketball Player"** on pp. 369–370, provide at least one question for each line of the poem to direct students in a close reading of the poem. Students will probably benefit from working in pairs. (You ☛

Some people make notes as they are reading critically. Here is an example of one person's critical comments as she read Lucille Clifton's poem "an ordinary woman."

HERE'S HOW

	an ordinary woman
	by Lucille Clifton
Speaker	the thirty eighth year
	of my life,
Simile	plain as bread
	round as a cake
Repetition for emphasis and sound	an ordinary woman.
	an ordinary woman.
Difference in expectation and reality	i had expected to be
	smaller than this,
	more beautiful,
	wiser in Afrikan ways,
	more confident,
Meaning?	i had expected
	more than this.
	i will be forty soon.
	my mother once was forty.
	my mother died at forty four,
Diction—only hard word	a woman of sad countenance
	leaving behind a girl
Simile	awkward as a stork.
	my mother was thick,
Metaphor	her hair was a jungle and
	she was very wise
	and beautiful
	and sad.

A DIFFERENT APPROACH

Suggest that to make notes for literary analyses students use a two-column chart with the headings **Reader's Response** and **Critical Reading.** Under the first heading, students could list emotional responses, and under the second heading they could list analytical responses.

You may want to model using this chart by annotating the first stanza of **"an ordinary woman."** The demonstration should help students understand the differences between the two kinds of responses.

might also want to review the elements of poetry before students begin their work.) Then ask each pair of students to read **"an ordinary woman"** and to write at least one question about each line. Have each pair then exchange questions with another pair of students and answer the other pair's questions.

CLOSURE

You may want to plan a quick check of students' progress by asking each student to present his or her focus and thesis to the rest of the class. Through this activity, students will hear a variety of approaches to the critical analysis, and they may get ideas for improving the work they have done so far.

Repetition of consonant	i have dreamed dreams
sounds	for you mama
	more than once.
Meaning?	i have wrapped me
	in your skin
	and made you live again
Repetition	more than once.
	i have taken the bones you hardened
	and built daughters
Symbol	and they blossom and promise fruit
Simile	like Afrikan trees.
	i am a woman now.
Repetition of phrase	an ordinary woman.
	in the thirty eighth
	year of my life,
	surrounded by life,
Repetition of consonant	a perfect picture of
sounds	blackness blessed,
Why isn't she happy?	i had not expected this
Emphasizes loneliness	loneliness.
Metaphor	if it is western,
Repetition of long "i"	if it is the final
sounds	Europe in my mind,
	if in the middle of my life
	i am turning the final turn
Symbol of death?	into the shining dark
Diction—pun on "whole"	let me come to it whole
and "holy"	and holy
Wish to end her life	not afraid
unafraid, no longer lonely	not lonely
	out of my mother's life
Theme—acceptance of	into my own.
her own identity	into my own.
Repetition of earlier lines	i had expected more than this.
	i had not expected to be
	an ordinary woman.

TIMESAVER

A checklist could save you time in tracking your students' prewriting progress. Either you or your students can check off each step as it is completed. You may want to use the following design:

	DUE DATE	EVALUATION
1. Choose a poem.		
2. Respond personally and critically.		
3. Write a thesis statement.		
4. Collect evidence.		
5. Make an early plan.		

EXTENSION

To extend students' understanding of poetry and literary analysis, have students look for "found" poetry, the hidden poetry inside everyday language. Such a search will show students that the elements of poetry—metaphor, emotional language, vivid imagery, irony, rhythm—can apply to literary prose as well as to poetry. First, show your students some examples of "found" poetry; then have them look for more examples in various sources such as newspapers, textbooks, magazines, and reference books. Ask students to choose some of the best examples to illustrate on posters for the classroom.

☛

EXERCISE 3 **Reading Critically**

You had a chance to respond personally to "Ex-Basketball Player" (pages 369–370); now take another look at it. Use the strategies for critical reading (page 372) and what you know about the elements of poetry to study the poem and answer these questions.

1. Who is the speaker in the poem? How does the speaker feel about the subject of the poem?
2. What sensory images occur in the poem? How do they affect the poem's meaning?
3. What figures of speech are used in the poem? What feelings do they suggest?
4. What kind of language does the poet use? How does it affect the meaning of the poem?
5. What is the central theme or meaning of the poem?

***WRITING* ASSIGNMENT** PART 1: **Responding and Reading Critically**

In this chapter, you'll write an analysis of a poem. Choose a poem, either one you would like to read or one your teacher recommends. You can always skim through your literature book or a book of poetry until you find something you like. First, read the poem and respond to it naturally. How do you feel about it? Then, read it critically, using the strategies on page 372. It might also help to refer to the definitions of the elements and related questions on pages 372–374.

ANSWERS

Exercise 3

Responses will vary.

1. The speaker is someone who has known the ex-basketball player for some time. The speaker seems to appreciate and respect Flick's past but seems saddened by Flick's present condition.
2. Sensory images include the personification of the gas pumps and Flick's being described as tall and "grease-grey and kind of coiled." The sensory images serve to give the poem an ironic depth.
3. The figures of speech include personification of the gas pumps, the basketball, the lug wrench, and the rows of candy at Mae's; synecdoche in which Flick's hands are symbols of himself; and similes in which Flick's hands are compared to wild birds. The figures of speech suggest sadness.
4. The poet uses common, everyday language punctuated with basketball jargon such as *bucketed* instead of *made* or *scored.* The language reinforces the poet's stance as someone who has known Flick for a long time.
5. The theme of the poem is one man's fall from fame. His life seems meaningless because his days of glory are past.

ENRICHMENT

Introducing to students the idea of personal responses to literature opens doors for them to respond personally to other artistic forms. Ask your students to respond to each of two or three varied aesthetic experiences that you present. You might show copies or slides of a work of art; play part of a symphony; or show a video recording of part of a ballet, an opera, or a play. The activity will enrich students' aesthetic experiences and will provide students with an opportunity to respond to and discuss these experiences. ■

MEETING INDIVIDUAL NEEDS

ADVANCED STUDENTS

You may want to ask students to study professional literary critiques about the poems they have chosen and to include information from the critiques in the literary analyses that they will write. Good sources are *Twentieth Century Literary Criticisms* and *Contemporary Literary Criticisms.* Refer students to the information about documenting sources and creating a Works Cited in **Chapter 11: "Writing a Research Paper."**

Prewriting

Planning a Literary Analysis

It is possible to read a poem or story critically and stop there. You have developed a better understanding of the work, and that's enough. But when you are going to write a literary analysis, you need to think about what you want to accomplish in the paper. Then you need to plan how you will bring your information and ideas together.

Thinking About Purpose, Audience, and Tone

The *purpose* of a literary analysis is expository. The writer wants to share information, explain how the piece of literature works, and convince readers that his or her information and explanation are sound.

When you write a literary analysis for your English class, you have two *audiences*—your classmates and your teacher. You need to explain the poem or story in a way that will be clear and interesting to your classmates, and you need to demonstrate to your teacher that you have a clear understanding of the poem or story and its elements.

Most literary analyses are formal papers with a formal, businesslike *tone.* Unlike the book and movie reviews you may read, the typical literary analysis avoids the first-person point of view, contractions, and colloquial language.

Finding a Focus for Your Analysis

What part of the poem do you think is the most interesting? the most challenging? You probably can't write an analysis of all the elements in any poem; you have to focus on some aspect of the poem or the writer's style. For example, you might

- analyze the images and figures of speech and explain why they're unusual or particularly effective
- analyze the use of sound effects (rhyme, rhythm, and so on) and explain how sound contributes to meaning
- explain the poem's theme and show how the poet develops it through images and figures of speech

Developing a Thesis Statement

Once you have identified the focus for your analysis, you are very close to having a preliminary *thesis statement*. The ***thesis statement*** identifies the thesis, or main idea, that you will attempt to explain and prove in your paper. You can use a preliminary thesis statement as a guide for your planning and writing, but you should feel free to revise it at any time. As you collect evidence and start to write, you may find that your thesis is too broad or too narrow and needs to be revised. Thesis statements may be more than one sentence, as the following example shows.

> In "an ordinary woman," Lucille Clifton uses figurative language, diction, and sound patterns to reveal her theme. This theme is a woman's discovery that, although she is a simple woman, she has an important identity of her own.

WRITING ASSIGNMENT PART 2:

Identifying a Focus and a Thesis

Trying to analyze all of the literary elements in a poem would be overwhelming to both you and your audience. Target the two or three elements you've decided to focus on and ignore the others. Then think about what thesis, or main idea, you want to try to prove in your analysis and write a thesis statement.

Gathering Evidence to Support Your Thesis

In a literary analysis you can't just state your thesis and forget it. For example, someone who read the thesis statement given above might ask, "How do you know Lucille Clifton uses figurative language to reveal her theme?" You need to back up your statements with specific evidence.

Where does the evidence come from? Most evidence comes from the *primary source*, the work itself. However, a *secondary source* such as an encyclopedia or literary reference work can provide helpful information about the writer and his or her work. (See pages 416–417 for more information on secondary sources.)

DEVELOPING A THESIS STATEMENT

Tell students that a good formula for a thesis statement is THESIS STATEMENT = A SUBJECT + YOUR IDEAS OR OPINIONS ABOUT THE SUBJECT. Write the following thesis statement on the chalkboard and have students compare it with the one in the textbook: "Lucille Clifton uses figurative language, interesting diction, and sensory detail in her poem 'an ordinary woman'."

Lead students to see that the thesis statement on the chalkboard lacks an opinion and would result in an essay that simply lists facts. On the other hand, the thesis statement in the textbook contains an opinion and will result in a true literary analysis.

MEETING INDIVIDUAL NEEDS

AT-RISK STUDENTS

Students who have trouble concentrating in class probably will have similar problems at home; therefore, giving such students analysis assignments that require considerable work at home may guarantee their failure. To offset this difficulty, help students schedule their tasks in small increments.

STRATEGIES FOR GATHERING EVIDENCE

1. Review the work of literature, looking for details and quotations you can use to support your thesis.
2. As you read, make notes on note cards or sheets of paper.
3. Identify the line (for poetry) or page (for fiction) where you found the detail or quotation.
4. Avoid plagiarism by giving credit to your sources for ideas as well as quoted material.

The following example shows how one writer used a chart to compile her notes for an analysis of "an ordinary woman."

HERE'S HOW

ELEMENT	EXAMPLES	SUPPORT FOR THESIS
SIMILES	"plain as bread," l. 3 "round as cake," l. 4	Very plain household images show ordinary woman—not glamorous
	"awkward as a stork," l. 19	awkward, ungraceful woman—like ugly duckling
	"promise fruit/like Afrikan trees," ll. 34–35	trees of Africa (woman) bring life
METAPHORS	the speaker's mother had hair that was "a jungle," l. 21	jungle—something that grows wild—not shaped
REPETITION	"an ordinary woman," ll. 5, 6, 37, 60—used 4 times	ll. 5, 6, speaker "ordinary woman" at 38 l. 37, speaker "ordinary woman" has "dreamed dreams" and has daughters l. 60, speaker "ordinary woman" but "into my own"
DICTION	ll. 51–52, "whole"/"holy" mostly small words	"whole" suggests whole person, not lonely "holy" suggests sacred quality of identity
	"countenance," l. 17, only big word	small, everyday words fit theme of "ordinary"

CRITICAL THINKING

(pp. 381–383)

OBJECTIVE

- To evaluate supporting evidence

TEACHING *EVALUATING SUPPORTING EVIDENCE*

After students read the introductory paragraph, you could discuss the thesis statement and the two examples of supporting evidence for an essay on **"an ordinary woman."** Ask volunteers to explain why some of the evidence given is acceptable and some is not. Then guide students through

CRITICAL THINKING

Evaluating Supporting Evidence

When you ***evaluate,*** you judge the value or worth of something. This thinking skill comes into play when you are gathering evidence for a literary analysis. During that process you need to evaluate the evidence to determine whether or not it will help you prove your thesis. For example, the person writing an essay about "an ordinary woman" wrote the thesis statement you read on page 379:

> In "an ordinary woman," Lucille Clifton uses figurative language, diction, and sound patterns to reveal her theme. This theme is a woman's discovery that, although she is a simple woman, she has an important identity of her own.

How will the person evaluate the evidence she gathers to determine whether it is valid? She can judge it by applying two standards or criteria: (1) Is it specific information that goes beyond the thesis statement and does not merely repeat it? and (2) Is it relevant to the main idea in the thesis?

EXAMPLES

- Specific information rather than a restatement of the thesis.

UNACCEPTABLE In "an ordinary woman," Lucille Clifton uses language and sound to show how a simple woman discovers she has an identity of her own. [Repeats the thesis statement.]

ACCEPTABLE Clifton's simple vocabulary (the only difficult word is *countenance* in line 17) highlights the "ordinary" quality of the speaker.

- Information that is relevant (related) to the main idea.

UNACCEPTABLE Many women feel that their lives are ordinary. [This has nothing to do with the thesis statement.]

ACCEPTABLE The simple words "an ordinary woman" used four times in the poem indicate that the speaker accepts her identity as an ordinary woman.

MEETING INDIVIDUAL NEEDS

LESS-ADVANCED STUDENTS

You may want to make this critical thinking process more visual by asking students to identify and write down the parts of the thesis statement from the textbook that require evidence. With your help, they should find three categories of evidence needed: figurative language, diction, and sound patterns. In addition, point out they must also be able to relate an example from any category to the theme expressed in the second sentence of the thesis statement. Then go over examples to discuss the reasons why the information in each is acceptable or not acceptable as supporting evidence.

You could continue this process to help students with the **Critical Thinking Exercise.**

the first item in the **Critical Thinking Exercise** and assign the remaining items for independent practice. Assess students' understanding by having them share their answers.

MEETING **INDIVIDUAL** NEEDS

LEP/ESL

General Strategies. Before students can evaluate supporting evidence (even in a collaborative setting), they must have a sound grasp of the basic elements of poetry listed on pp. 372–373. Pair students and give them study sheets of short, simple literary excerpts that contain multiple examples of basic poetic elements. Have students work together to identify the elements. If possible, include literature that has already been introduced in class. ESL students may need extra guidance with diction, rhythm, and tone because determining these elements is usually dependent on an awareness of subtle nuances in the language.

ANSWERS

Critical Thinking Exercise

1. not valid — repeats thesis
2. valid — can be used to contrast the player's days of glory with his present meaningless life
3. not valid — irrelevant to main idea
4. valid — supports main idea

CRITICAL THINKING EXERCISE:
Evaluating Supporting Evidence

Before you attempt to evaluate the evidence you are using for your own literary analysis, take this opportunity to practice the skill. Get together with two or three of your classmates and review the following thesis statement and list of supporting evidence from Updike's poem "Ex-Basketball Player" (pages 369–370). Decide which evidence is valid support for the thesis and which is not. Apply these criteria as you evaluate: (1) The evidence provides new information and does not merely repeat the thesis. (2) The evidence is relevant to the main idea.

Thesis Statement: The imagery in John Updike's poem "Ex-Basketball Player" depicts the meaningless life of an athlete when the days of glory are past.

Evidence:

1. In John Updike's poem "Ex-Basketball Player," an ex-athlete's life has little meaning.
2. Images such as "He bucketed three hundred ninety points" (line 15) and "His hands were like wild birds" (line 18) show the glory of Flick's basketball days.
3. Many basketball players don't do as well as Flick, who is the subject of John Updike's poem "Ex-Basketball Player."
4. The fact that Flick looks "towards bright applauding tiers/Of Necco Wafers, Nibs, and Juju Beads" (lines 29–30) is an ironic reminder of the days when he faced cheering crowds.

5. Today, Flick's hands "are fine and nervous on the lug wrench" (line 23), but "It makes no difference to the lug wrench" (line 24).

5. valid—supports main idea

Deciding on an Order of Ideas

How you organize your ideas depends partly on the direction you are taking in your analysis. If you're analyzing the imagery and figures of speech in "Ex-Basketball Player" (pages 369–370), for instance, you might arrange your ideas in the ***order of importance.*** That is, if you decided the most important element is imagery, you would discuss it first and then go on to discuss figures of speech. If you intended to focus your essay on imagery alone, you'd probably arrange your details (including quotations and line references) in ***chronological order,*** the order in which the images occur in the poem.

Reminder

As you gather and organize your evidence

- remember your focus and stick to it
- find examples of each element you plan to discuss
- if necessary, consult secondary sources for background information on the poet and/or the poem
- evaluate your evidence to make sure it's specific and relevant
- arrange your ideas in an order that will make sense to your reader

WRITING ASSIGNMENT

PART 3:

Gathering and Organizing Your Ideas

It's time to pick up where you left off in Writing Assignment, Part 2 (page 379). Collect evidence to support your thesis and then make an early plan for your essay. Jot down each main idea and its supporting evidence, perhaps using a chart like the one on page 380. Then decide on an order for presenting your ideas.

COOPERATIVE LEARNING

Have students record their evaluations on critique sheets when they check each other's prewriting. The critique sheet might include the following questions:

1. Is the thesis clear? If not, what is unclear?
2. Is the thesis interesting? Will it add to your understanding of the poem?
3. Is the supporting evidence relevant?
4. Is the supporting evidence clearly organized? In what order are the ideas arranged?

You may want to require that at least three other students evaluate each student's paper. Then ask students to respond to the critiques of their papers. You will probably want to emphasize that students must analyze all evaluations to make the final judgment about whether or not changes are needed.

SEGMENT 4 *(pp. 384–389)*

WRITING YOUR FIRST DRAFT

OBJECTIVE

- To write a first draft of a critical analysis

TEACHING THE LESSON

Because students' work up to now has dealt primarily with the thesis statement and the body of the essay, you may want to spend some time discussing the introduction and the conclusion of a literary analysis.

As students read **A Writer's Model** on pp. 386–387, have them refer to the **Here's How** chart on p. 380 that outlines the

Teacher's ResourceBank™

RESOURCES

WRITING YOUR FIRST DRAFT

- Writing a Critical Analysis 82

QUOTATION FOR THE DAY

"How do I know what I think until I see what I say?" (E. M. Forster, 1879–1970, British novelist)

You may want to use the quotation as the basis for a discussion on writing a first draft. Reassure students that their prewriting plans may take a different turn once students start writing their drafts.

SELECTION AMENDMENT

Description of change: excerpted

Rationale: to focus on the concept of writing presented in this chapter

Writing Your First Draft

You have decided on a focus and a main idea for your literary analysis, turned your main idea into a thesis statement, and gathered supporting evidence. Now it's time to turn your plan into a first draft. When you are writing your draft, remember that an essay of literary analysis is objective. The word *I*, referring to your personal thoughts and feelings, is not appropriate.

The Structure of a Literary Analysis

Like other expository compositions (see pages 112–120, 204–275, and 318–357), a literary analysis often has three parts.

- The ***introduction*** states the poem's title and author and may give some background information. The thesis statement expresses the main idea of your paper and mentions the literary elements of the poem in the order you will discuss them.
- The ***body*** presents a major point about each of the elements (one element at a time) in a separate paragraph. Specific examples from the poem support each major point.
- The ***conclusion*** brings the essay to an end, summarizing its major points.

"When you consider that there are a thousand ways to express even the simplest idea, it is no wonder writers are under a great strain."

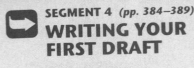

E. B. White

basis for the essay. Emphasize the structure of a literary analysis by discussing the **Framework For a Literary Analysis Essay** chart on p. 388. Before students write their first drafts, ask them to read **A Writer's Model** again to get a feel for a good, finished essay.

GUIDED PRACTICE

To reinforce the structure of a literary analysis, help students to fill in the **Framework for a Literary Analysis Essay** chart with information from **A Writer's Model.**

MECHANICS HINT

Incorporating Supporting Evidence

As you write your draft, you'll use supporting evidence—direct quotations and paraphrases—from the literary work to support your main ideas. Follow these conventions for using direct quotations and paraphrases:

1. Incorporate the quotation into your own sentence structure (it shouldn't sound as though it has just been plunked down into your paper).
2. Enclose the direct quotation in quotation marks. Double-check to be sure you've copied the quote exactly as it appears in the original work.
3. Use a slash (/), with a space before and after it, to indicate the end of a line of poetry.
4. Use ellipsis points (. . .) to indicate an omission.
5. For both direct quotations and paraphrases, cite the line numbers (page numbers, for fiction) or secondary source in parentheses at the end of a sentence.

QUOTATION The speaker in "an ordinary woman" wants to be different from her mother: "not afraid / not lonely / out of my mother's life / into my own. / into my own." (lines 53–57).

PARAPHRASE The speaker in "an ordinary woman" expresses a wish to be different from her mother, to be unafraid, and to live her own life (lines 53–57).

REFERENCE NOTE: For more help with using quotation marks and ellipses, see pages 878–883 and 885–886.

MEETING INDIVIDUAL NEEDS

LEP/ESL

Spanish. Some of the punctuation rules in Spanish differ from those stated in the **Mechanics Hint.** For example, dashes are used in Spanish to indicate quotations, and ellipses are used to indicate incomplete thoughts. You may wish to work individually with Spanish-speaking students to help them incorporate punctuation in their first drafts.

CRITICAL THINKING
Synthesis

The process of paraphrasing information requires students to use the critical thinking skills of summarizing and formulating ideas in their own words. To give students practice using these skills, select several quotations from short stories and from literary criticism and ask students to paraphrase the information. Be sure to emphasize that the material must be fully paraphrased to avoid plagiarism. Encourage students to change not only vocabulary but also sentence structure and, where possible, the arrangement of ideas.

INDEPENDENT PRACTICE

Have students complete **Writing Assignment: Part 4** on p. 388. Remind students that they can deviate from their prewriting plans as long as their topic sentences and details support their thesis statements.

ASSESSMENT

Because students' drafts are not final, you will not want to grade them, although you may want to award credit for completion. Schedule student-teacher conferences if students need individual evaluation and help.

MEETING **INDIVIDUAL** NEEDS

LESS-ADVANCED STUDENTS

You may want to use **A Writer's Model** extensively with students who still don't feel confident about the structure of a literary analysis. To approach the assignment in a different way, you could provide students with copies of **A Writer's Model** and ask students to use colored pens to underline the annotated parts. For each annotation, students should underline the corresponding part of the essay. For example, if the annotation is *major point,* students should underline the major point in the paragraph to the right. Similarly, if the annotation is *figures of speech,* students should underline the figures of speech in the paragraph to the right. In this way, students' understanding of terms is reinforced when they are able to find the corresponding example in the essay.

A Basic Framework for a Literary Analysis

Here's an essay of literary analysis based on Lucille Clifton's poem "an ordinary woman" (pages 375–376). As you read, notice the writer's use of evidence from the poem to support the thesis statement.

A WRITER'S MODEL

No "Ordinary Woman"

INTRODUCTION
Poet/Title
Background

In contrast to the title of her poem, Lucille Clifton is no "ordinary woman." She is an award-winning African American poet whose memoirs and four volumes of poetry are widely read. All these works celebrate African American men and women who have a strong sense of their own identities.

Thesis statement
Theme of poem

In "an ordinary woman," Clifton uses figurative language, diction, and sound effects to reveal her theme. This theme is a woman's discovery that, although she is a simple woman, she has an important identity of her own.

BODY
Major point: Figures of speech
Quotations from work
Quotations from work

Clifton carefully chooses figures of speech that support the image of an "ordinary" woman. For example, the speaker uses two similes to compare herself to common foods. She says that she is "plain as bread" and "round as a cake" (lines 3-4). She also uses metaphors, saying her daughters are her "fruit," who "blossom and promise fruit / like Afrikan trees" (lines 34-35). These metaphors show that the woman has also given the gift of life that promises to grow and develop.

Major point: Diction
Examples of diction

Diction--the choice of words--also contributes to the poem's meaning. Clifton's simple vocabulary (the only difficult word is countenance in line 17) highlights the "ordinary" quality of the speaker. A play on the words whole and holy (lines 51-52) shows the speaker's growing awareness of her identity as she prepares to die. She is no longer

RETEACHING

Possibly the most difficult task students have in writing a literary analysis is starting and ending their papers without being too abrupt. One way to help students is by giving them specific strategies to follow. Refer students to pp. 112–115 and pp. 119–120 in **Chapter 3: "Understanding Composition Structure"** for information on introductions and conclusions. Then work one-on-one with students to help them decide which strategies would work best for their particular topics.

lonely because she knows herself as a "whole" woman. The simple words "an ordinary woman" used four times in the poem indicate that the speaker accepts her identity as an ordinary woman.

Major point: Sound effects

Examples of repetition

Repetition of vowel sounds

The poem has no regular rhythm or rhyme, but there are many sound effects. Repetition is important. The repetition of "not afraid" and "not lonely" (lines 53-54) suggests a new spirit of life. Moreover, the repetition of "into my own. / into my own." (lines 56-57) shows that the speaker accepts her identity as an African American woman. Assonance (repetition of the long i sound in final, mind, life, shining, my, i) is also important. Here the speaker emphasizes her growing sense of I--her own identity.

CONCLUSION Restatement of theme

Restatement of thesis

The speaker "had not expected to be / an ordinary woman" (lines 59-60), but she has come to realize that being an ordinary woman is a triumph. It is ordinary women, after all, who care for their families and help their children to a more promising future than their own. Throughout the poem, Clifton effectively develops this theme through figures of speech, diction, and sound effects.

MEETING **INDIVIDUAL** NEEDS

LEARNING STYLES

Visual Learners. You may want to create on the chalkboard a formal outline for **A Writer's Model** so students can see the supporting details as subheads. If this visual presentation seems to help students understand the writer's organization, you could help them organize their early plans into formal outlines before they write their first drafts.

CLOSURE

Ask students to list the parts of a literary analysis and to explain what each part contains [introduction—poem's title and author, background information, thesis statement; body—major points and supporting information; conclusion—restatement of thesis or summary of major points]. ■

MEETING **INDIVIDUAL** NEEDS

LEARNING STYLES

Auditory Learners. Some students might benefit from verbally organizing their drafts. You may want to pair each student with another who will ask questions and record responses. Have one student question the other about his or her paper's major points, supporting quotations, and details.

ADVANCED STUDENTS

Encourage advanced students to concentrate on writing style: maintaining a strong voice, varying sentence beginnings and lengths, using active verbs to avoid wordiness, and being careful about word choice. Because they have probably mastered the organization and content of an essay, they can deal with higher level concerns even in their first drafts.

You may find it helpful to model your own composition on the preceding literary analysis. It follows this framework.

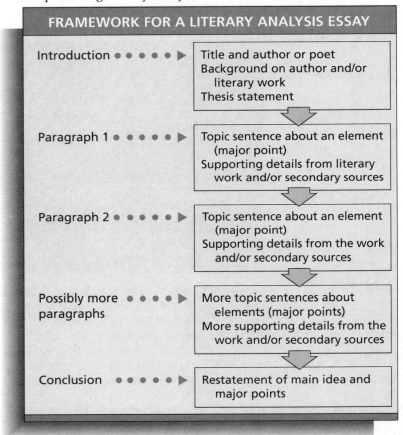

FRAMEWORK FOR A LITERARY ANALYSIS ESSAY

Introduction	Title and author or poet Background on author and/or literary work Thesis statement
Paragraph 1	Topic sentence about an element (major point) Supporting details from literary work and/or secondary sources
Paragraph 2	Topic sentence about an element (major point) Supporting details from the work and/or secondary sources
Possibly more paragraphs	More topic sentences about elements (major points) More supporting details from the work and/or secondary sources
Conclusion	Restatement of main idea and major points

WRITING ASSIGNMENT PART 4:

Writing a Draft of Your Essay of Literary Analysis

Michelangelo wrote this note to his young assistant: "Draw, Antonio, draw, Antonio, draw and do not waste time." So follow the advice of Michelangelo. Gather what you need: paper, pen, or pencil (or even a word processor), your prewriting notes, the poem itself, and the framework. Now write. Unless there's a fire or other emergency, don't stop until you've finished your draft.

WRITING NOTE

When you draft your essay, use the *literary* (or *historical*) *present* tense. This means that you refer to most events in the poem in the present tense.

> The speaker **uses** two similes to compare herself with common foods.
> She **is** no longer lonely because she **knows** herself as a "whole" woman.

Use other tenses, such as past or past perfect, when characters themselves speak in those tenses.

> The speaker says that her mother **died** at age forty-four.
> The speaker says that she **had thought** she **would be** different.

REFERENCE NOTE: For more help on verb tenses, see pages 736–747.

COOPERATIVE LEARNING

After the first drafts are completed, students working in pairs can annotate each other's essays by identifying the parts of the introduction, the main ideas, the supporting evidence, and the conclusion. If the reader has any questions about the paper, he or she can ask the writer for clarification. You may want to help students with their annotations as you monitor their work.

SEGMENT 5 *(pp. 390–391)*

EVALUATING AND REVISING

OBJECTIVES

- To analyze a writer's revisions
- To evaluate and revise a literary analysis

TEACHING THE LESSON

After students have read the **Evaluating and Revising Essays of Literary Analysis** chart, you may want to help them apply the questions in the left-hand column to **A Writer's Model** on pp. 386–387 and to **A Student Model** on pp. 393–394. If students answer no to any of the questions, help them to use the prescribed revision techniques.

Teacher's ResourceBank™

RESOURCES

EVALUATING AND REVISING

- Writing a Critical Analysis 83

QUOTATION FOR THE DAY

"... how hard it is to make your thoughts look anything but imbecile fools when you paint them with ink on paper." (Olive Schreiner, 1855–1920, South African writer, feminist, and social critic)

Even experienced, professional writers find writing a difficult process, so students should not become discouraged if they have trouble evaluating and revising. Explain that it's a time-consuming process and that it often takes longer than writing the first draft.

MEETING INDIVIDUAL NEEDS

LESS-ADVANCED STUDENTS

To lead a group revision, have students look at their first drafts while you go over each question in the **Evaluating and Revising Essays of Literary Analysis** chart. For example, you can explain the chart's first point about the introduction and ask students to check their papers. If they need to add anything, they should do so at that time. Before discussing the next point, check

Evaluating and Revising

The following chart can help you step back and take an objective look at your paper. Ask yourself the questions in the left-hand column. If you find a problem, use the revision technique suggested in the right-hand column.

EVALUATING AND REVISING ESSAYS OF LITERARY ANALYSIS

	EVALUATION GUIDE	REVISION TECHNIQUE
1	Does the introduction give the title and author and provide necessary background information?	**Add** the title and author; **add** interesting, relevant information about the author and the work.
2	Does the thesis statement appear in the introduction? Does it clearly state the main idea and the elements to be discussed in the essay?	**Add** a thesis statement or **replace** the existing one. In your statement, identify the elements you will discuss in the same order you will cover them in the essay.
3	Does the essay include enough supporting evidence? Is the evidence relevant and specific?	**Add** additional evidence from the work or from secondary sources. **Cut** irrelevant, general, or repetitious evidence.
4	Is the essay's organization clear and consistent?	**Reorder** the ideas and evidence in an order that makes sense, such as chronological order or order of importance.
5	Does the conclusion bring the essay to a definite close?	**Add** a sentence that restates your thesis and/or summarizes the major points.

Guide students through the analysis questions in **Exercise 4** and then have them complete **Writing Assignment: Part 5** as independent practice. Use students' responses to **Exercise 4** and their revisions of their drafts to assess their understanding of evaluating and revising.

As closure, ask students to answer in their journals the following questions:

1. What is my essay's greatest strength?
2. What is my essay's greatest weakness? ■

EXERCISE 4 **Analyzing a Writer's Revisions**

Here's the writer's draft of the third paragraph on pages 386–387. (As you can see, it wasn't perfect the first time.) See if you can figure out why the writer made these changes.

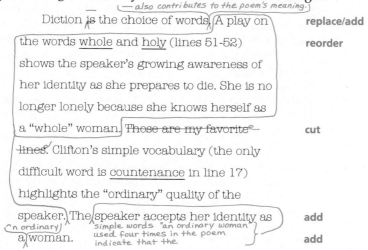

Diction ~~is~~ [insert: — also contributes to the poem's meaning.] the choice of words. A play on	replace/add
the words whole and holy (lines 51-52)	reorder
shows the speaker's growing awareness of her identity as she prepares to die. She is no longer lonely because she knows herself as	
a "whole" woman. ~~These are my favorite~~	cut
~~lines.~~ Clifton's simple vocabulary (the only difficult word is countenance in line 17) highlights the "ordinary" quality of the	
speaker. The [insert: simple words "an ordinary woman" used four times in the poem indicate that the] speaker accepts her identity as	add
a [insert: n ordinary] woman.	add

1. Why did the writer add the information about diction contributing to the poem's meaning? What is the function of this sentence in the paragraph?
2. Why did the writer change the order of the second and third sentences? By moving these sentences, what order does the writer follow?
3. Why did the writer delete the fourth sentence?
4. Why did the writer add the information in the last sentence? [Hint: What does the reader need in order to accept the writer's thesis?]

***WRITING* ASSIGNMENT**

PART 5:

Evaluating and Revising Your Literary Analysis

Work with some classmates in a small group to evaluate each other's first drafts. Then, read over your own essay, deciding for yourself what changes need to be made. Finally, evaluate your own and your classmates' suggestions and make changes that will improve your essay.

to see that students who are not finished feel confident enough to complete the task on their own. You can circulate among students to help as needed.

INTEGRATING THE LANGUAGE ARTS

Library Link. You may want to have students research professional writers' comments and beliefs about revision. Some suggested writers are Ernest Hemingway, James Michener, John Updike, and Emily Dickinson.

ANSWERS

Exercise 4

1. The added information relates the paragraph to the thesis statement. This sentence is the topic sentence of the paragraph.
2. The change in order follows the order in which the examples appear in the poem. The writer follows chronological order.
3. It is irrelevant to the thesis.
4. The reader needs evidence to prove that the statement is true.

SEGMENT 6 *(pp. 392–394)*

PROOFREADING AND PUBLISHING

OBJECTIVES

- To proofread a final draft
- To publish a critical analysis of a poem

TEACHING THE LESSON

Have a volunteer read aloud the material that deals with proofreading and publishing. Emphasize the importance of turning in error-free analyses.

Using unidentified students' papers, show examples of common weaknesses in such areas as comma usage, quotation marks, and consistency of tense. Then ask

Teacher's ResourceBank™

RESOURCES

PROOFREADING AND PUBLISHING

- Writing a Critical Analysis 84

QUOTATION FOR THE DAY

"If you do not write for publication, there is little point in writing at all." (Bernard Shaw, 1856–1950, British playwright, critic, and social reformer)

Have students write brief journal entries recording their reactions to this quotation. Then have students share their opinions in a class discussion.

MEETING INDIVIDUAL NEEDS

LEP/ESL

General Strategies. Requiring students to adhere strictly to standard English in the proofreading stage of their papers may discourage students. You may want to select one or two areas for students to concentrate on, such as spelling and the use of quotation marks, and to defer work in other areas for later attention.

Proofreading and Publishing

Proofreading. Your final draft should be as free as possible from any errors. If you suspect a mistake, look up the appropriate section in the grammar, usage, and mechanics chapters of this textbook. Use a college dictionary to check spellings. Also, check carefully to see that you've spelled the author's name and the title of the work correctly.

Publishing. With your teacher's help, plan some special class time for sharing papers. Here are two ways to find an audience beyond your classroom:

- Start a literary magazine or journal, if one doesn't exist already. Encourage everyone in school to submit original poems and stories, as well as essays of literary analysis.
- Organize a literary conference. Volunteers should read their papers to a group of teachers and students from other classes. Plan a question-and-answer period after each reading.

Shoe, by Jeff MacNelly, reprinted by permission: Tribune Media Services.

WRITING ASSIGNMENT

PART 6:
Proofreading and Publishing

This is the time to catch and correct every error. Read your essay aloud—or have someone read it to you—to spot mistakes. When you're sure your essay is the best you can make it, use the suggestions you've just read—or use some ideas of your own—to share it with a wider audience.

students to complete **Writing Assignment: Part 6** as independent practice. You could reproduce a limited list of criteria for students to focus on as they proofread. Continue with impromptu teacher-student conferences to deal with any questions that arise.

You may want to give both a grade on the process and a grade on the final copy to motivate students to work through the complete writing process.

As closure, you may want to do a quick oral survey to define the kinds of errors that students corrected in the proofreading stage.

A STUDENT MODEL

In her essay of literary analysis, Niaima Turner writes about L. Woiwode's short story "The Beginning of Grief." Niaima, who attends Woodrow Wilson High School in Camden, New Jersey, analyzes how the author uses point of view to reveal the father's character to the reader. As you read her essay, notice how Niaima uses evidence from the story to support her ideas.

A Father's Trial by Grief and Parenthood
by Niaima Turner

In his short story "The Beginning of Grief," L. Woiwode uses the limited third-person point of view to help the reader understand the main character's responses to his sorrows and difficulties. William Stanion is a bereaved husband who lost his wife one year earlier. Now in his role as a single parent he undergoes additional stress as he attempts to raise his five children alone.

At home Stanion thinks constantly about his performance as a responsible father while he tries to keep his sanity. He is tormented by his memories of his wife who was "the periphery of everything" (84). At one point Stanion even thinks he might take "his life just to end the torment, just to be at peace, and maybe to be with her" (84). Yet, he doesn't commit suicide because he loves his children and recognizes his obligations to them. Bothered by feelings of helplessness, he worries about disciplining his children and rearing them properly.

Stanion is very conscious of what is going on with his children. At supper time, he travels through the events of their day, "prying his way into them, find out what the trouble was, find out who had caused it, and set right the one who

A STUDENT MODEL

Evaluation

1. In the introduction Niaima gives the title and author of the story and provides interesting background.
2. Niaima's thesis statement is the first sentence of the introduction.
3. Niaima uses specific examples from the story to support her topic sentences.

EXTENSION

Ask students to freewrite about the following questions and to attach their freewriting to their final copies. Their answers will provide you with valuable information about individual students' needs.

1. Is the process you just used effective for writing a literary analysis? Why or why not?
2. What was the most difficult part of the process?
3. What ideas do you have for the next time you write a literary analysis? ■

TIMESAVER

Here is a suggested analytical scale that could ease the grading process. You could attach a complete copy of the scale to the front of each student's paper to give students clear feedback on their work.

Analytical Scale					
Introduction (title, author, background)	1	2	3	4	5
Thesis (in introduction, clear)	2	4	6	8	10
Organization (clear, consistent)	5	10	15	20	25
Evidence (enough, relevant)	5	10	15	20	25
Conclusion (definite close)	1	2	3	4	5
Writing Style (voice, diction, rhythm)	2	4	6	8	10
Mechanics	1	2	3	4	5
Grammar	1	2	3	4	5
Spelling	1	2	3	4	5
Manuscript Form	1	2	3	4	5
Total					

was at fault, or, if there had been fighting, punish him" (83). A gentle man, he hates to punish the children. Stanion had left the discipline up to his wife which she had done prudently and judiciously. Now "it was difficult for him to pass judgment on anyone, much less his own children, and even harder for him to see them hurt" (83).

A turning point for Stanion comes during an incident with Kevin, his ten-year-old son. A practiced liar with a strong temper, Kevin is difficult to handle. Stanion resents the fact that Kevin is always in trouble. After discovering that Kevin has kicked a child in his most recent encounter, Stanion realizes punishment is in order. But when he becomes angry, he accidentally slaps his youngest daughter and out of frustration he kicks Kevin in the rump. Following the chaos, Stanion "realized what he had done" (87) and he knows he must bring calm to the family.

As Stanion works through the crisis with Kevin, he examines himself and achieves a greater understanding of his role as a single parent. He realizes his behavior must change. He needs to alter the way he communicates. After their conversation, Stanion and Kevin start to understand each other's point of view. Stanion has begun to question Kevin's behavior in his mind: "what led the boy to do this? what did this hark back to?" (88-89). Both want to be closer to each other and they start to reach out to one another. Though he still feels helpless, Stanion has begun to seek solutions.

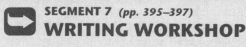

SEGMENT 7 *(pp. 395–397)*

WRITING WORKSHOP

OBJECTIVES

- To analyze a movie review
- To write a movie review

TEACHING THE LESSON

To interest your students in writing a movie review, you may want to bring to class several reviews of popular movies from magazines or local newspapers. Encourage students who have seen the movies to discuss whether or not they agree with the reviews.

WRITING WORKSHOP

A Movie Review

In Shakespeare's day, audiences went to the theater for a rollicking good time; today, you go to the movies. As expensive as movies are today, you can be sure you're getting your money's worth by checking out the review first. In many ways, a movie review is similar to the essay of literary analysis you wrote about a poem. A movie review analyzes the elements of a movie—script, acting, special effects, and so on. However, a review combines analysis with evaluation; the writer judges the worth of the work. As you read this excerpt from Roger Ebert's review of the classic film *Star Wars,* think about its content and its tone. Notice that the tone is less formal than that of a literary analysis.

Star Wars

by Roger Ebert

1 *Star Wars* is a fairy tale, a fantasy, a legend, finding its roots in
2 some of our most popular fictions. The golden robot, lion-faced space pilot, and insecure little computer on wheels must have been suggested by the Tin Man, the Cowardly Lion, and the Scarecrow in *The Wizard of Oz.* The journey from one end of the galaxy to another is out of countless thousands of space operas. The hardware is from *Flash Gordon* out of *2001,* the chivalry is from *Robin Hood,* the heroes are from Westerns and the villains
3 are a cross between Nazis and sorcerers. *Star Wars* taps the pulp
4 fantasies buried in our memories, and because it's done so brilliantly, it reactivates old thrills, fears, and exhilarations we thought we'd abandoned when we read our last copy of *Amazing Stories.*

The movie works so well for several reasons, and they don't all have to do with the spectacular special effects. The effects *are* good, yes, but great effects have been used in such movies as *Silent Running* and *Logan's Run* without setting all-time box-office records. No, I think the key to *Star Wars* is more basic than that.

QUOTATION FOR THE DAY

"Movies can overwhelm us, as no other art form." (Pauline Kael, 1919–   , American film critic)

Remind students that writing a movie review is trickier than it seems because film is such an extraordinarily powerful medium that frequently sweeps aside all reasoning. Ask students to ponder the following questions: Is a film good simply because it creates powerful emotions? Can a film have wonderful special effects and yet be empty of meaning?

USING THE SELECTION

Star Wars

1
Title and genre are identified.

2
The background indicates sources of elements of the movie.

3
The purpose/theme is entertainment.

4
The "pulp" in "pulp fantasies" refers to a magazine printed on cheap paper, featuring articles of a cheap, sensational nature.

Then ask students to read Roger Ebert's review of *Star Wars*. Discuss with students the questions that follow the review and call students' attention to the six features of movie reviews listed in **Prewriting.** As guided practice, help students identify the six features in the review of *Star Wars*.

To help with the prewriting stage, you may want to let the class compile a brainstorming list of possible movies for review; ask a volunteer to record the list on the chalkboard as students think of titles. As students write their reviews, you will probably want to make yourself available to answer questions and offer guidance.

5
The short plot summary doesn't give away any surprises.

6
foibles: weaknesses

7
hyperspace: speed faster than light

8
intergalactic: taking place between galaxies

ANSWERS
Writing Workshop Questions

1. He tells us there is a journey into hyperspace by unusual characters, but he doesn't ruin the movie for us by telling us what happens.
2. Answers will vary. The tone is informal, a bit chatty, including the reader with the pronoun *we.* It is fun to read because it appeals to our fond memories of other good adventure stories.

SELECTION AMENDMENT
Description of change: excerpted
Rationale: to focus on the concept of movie reviews presented in this chapter

5 The movie relies on the strength of pure narrative, in the most
basic storytelling form known to man, the Journey. All of the best
tales we remember from our childhoods had to do with heroes
setting out to travel down roads filled with danger, and hoping to
find treasure or heroism at the journey's end. In *Star Wars,*
George Lucas takes this simple and powerful framework into
outer space, and that is an inspired thing to do, because we no
longer have maps on Earth that warn, "Here there be dragons."
We can't fall off the edge of the map, as Columbus could, and we
can't hope to find new continents of prehistoric monsters or lost
tribes ruled by immortal goddesses. Not on Earth, anyway, but
anything is possible in space, and Lucas goes right ahead and
shows us very nearly everything. We get involved quickly,
because the characters in *Star Wars* are so strongly and simply
6 drawn and have so many small foibles and large, futile hopes for
us to identify with. And then Lucas does an interesting thing. As
he sends his heroes off to cross the universe and do battle with
the Forces of Darth Vader, the evil Empire, and the awesome
Death Star, he gives us lots of special effects, yes—ships passing
7 into hyperspace, alien planets, an infinity of stars—but we also
get a wealth of strange living creatures, and Lucas correctly
guesses that they'll be more interesting for us than all the
8 intergalactic hardware.

1. How much does the writer tell you about the plot of *Star Wars*? What *doesn't* he tell you?
2. Describe the review's tone. What makes it fun to read?

ASSESSMENT

To evaluate students' movie reviews, use the list of features in the **Prewriting** section. You could limit your grading to these few criteria that stress only the content of the students' papers.

CLOSURE

Ask students to explain the difference between a literary analysis and a movie review. [A review combines analysis with evaluation; the film reviewer judges the worth of the movie.]

3. This is only part of Ebert's review of *Star Wars*. What do you think is Ebert's overall evaluation of the film?
4. Have you seen *Star Wars*, either in a theater or on videotape? Do you agree with Ebert's evaluation?

Writing a Movie Review

Prewriting. Make a list of movies you've seen recently, and decide which movie you'd like to review for an audience of your friends and classmates. You may want to choose one that's available on videotape so you can see it again.

These features are usually found in movie reviews.

1. The title and genre (horror, comedy, romance, science fiction, adventure, and so on).
2. Some background information about the movie's subject.
3. The purpose and/or theme. Is the purpose of the work simply to entertain (a scary adventure thriller), or does it reveal some truth about life and people?
4. A very short summary of the plot. (Don't give away any surprises, including the movie's ending.)
5. An evaluation of the main characters' performances.
6. An overall evaluation, backed up with solid reasons.

Writing, Evaluating, and Revising. Keep your tone light, and find a way to capture your reader's interest. The introduction might cover features 1–3 on the list above. Features 4 and 5 and whatever else you would like to say about the movie could be discussed in the body of the review. Your conclusion should cover feature 6, your overall evaluation.

In a group of three or four classmates, comment on each other's first drafts. Does the review give the reader enough information to decide whether to see the movie? Is the review concise? Is it fun to read?

Proofreading and Publishing. If you are writing about a first-run movie or a video available at local stores, submit your review to your school newspaper. Consider compiling a special edition of movie reviews to share with friends and other classes. (It's especially interesting to compare several students' reviews of the same movie.) Before you publish, proofread the final draft carefully.

3. He likes it. It "reactivates old thrills, fears, and exhilarations" and "works so well" with special effects and "the strength of pure narrative." Twice Ebert explicitly states that he finds aspects of the movie "interesting."
4. Answers will vary.

MEETING INDIVIDUAL NEEDS

LEP/ESL

General Strategies. Students are asked to use a light tone in their movie reviews; however, establishing tone is an element of style that could prove especially difficult for students who lack familiarity with English. You could suggest that students write their first drafts with attention to including the necessary information. Then either work individually with ESL students or pair ESL students with native English-speakers to lighten the tone of ESL students' movie reviews.

SEGMENT 8 *(pp. 398–401)*
MAKING CONNECTIONS
EVALUATION ACROSS THE CURRICULUM
OBJECTIVES
- To evaluate a musical performance
- To analyze a critical review of a musical performance

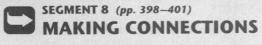

EVALUATION ACROSS THE CURRICULUM
Teaching Strategies

You may want to begin by asking students about favorite musical performances they have either seen live or on videotape or heard on the radio. After students have decided on the subject for their reviews, you might want to allow students who have selected the same musical performance to work together in a group.

Before the groups begin writing their reviews, you could ask them to read the review of **"Tipica Sound of Cuba"** by Peter Watrous and to list the elements Watrous evaluates.

Discussing this review should help the groups to have a better idea of what their final products should be like.

GUIDELINES
Ask students to help you compile a checklist that you will use to grade the reviews. You might include the following questions:

1. Is the review interesting?
2. Is the review written in a three-part format—introduction, body, and conclusion?
3. Does the review cover most of the questions in the list on pp. 398–399?
4. Are opinions supported with examples?
5. Are the usage, mechanics, and spelling correct?

MAKING CONNECTIONS

EVALUATION ACROSS THE CURRICULUM

A Musical Performance Review

Literary performances share certain elements with musical performances: Both communicate feelings about events and people. Likewise, a critical evaluation of a musical performance resembles a critical review of a movie in many ways.

Think of a musical performance that you've heard or seen lately, or think of one you would like to hear or see in the next few days. The performance could be a live or taped musical drama; a video performance of a single rock, pop, or country song; or an audiotape, record, or compact disc recording of a song. After you have selected the performance, use the following questions to evaluate it.

1. What kind of music is being performed, and who are the performers?
2. What type of musical performance (for example, musical drama, video recording, or audio recording) is it? What style (rock, pop, country, classical, dramatic) is it?
3. What is the quality of the performance? How good is the music itself? How good are the lyrics?

4. How effective are individual performers? How good is the lead singer or musician? How good is the backup?
5. If the performance is visual, how effective are the costumes, props, and lighting?

As you read the following review of a performance, identify the elements the reviewer has chosen to evaluate.

Típica Sound of Cuba

by Peter Watrous

1 The band was playing the típica style of Cuban music, a form that mixes strings with flute and heavy percussion and that is rarely heard anymore.

2 Formed four months ago by Rene Lorente, who arrived in the United States from Cuba some eight months ago, the group is meant to be an American version of Cuba's great Orquesta Aragon, in which Mr. Lorente played the flute.

The flute in the típica style plays the role of the lead singer,
3 and Mr. Lorente didn't fool around: he's an exciting improviser, almost vicious with his use of rhythms. When the band moved into the improvisatory montuno section of a piece, he kept an
4 endless flow of ideas rolling, starting a solo with a short riff or two, playing some long and gently floating lines, then jumping back into a sharp riff.

The rhythms, meant to give dancers accents to play with, snapped and exploded and made themselves feel inevitable.

5 The singers, Pepe Mora and Jorge Castillo, offered words of advice to the audience on how to enjoy themselves, throwing up a choir of voices to counter Mr. Lorente's improvising. The
6 audience, taking the verbal and rhythmic suggestions, did just that.

Write a brief critical review of a musical performance, and share it with your classmates. Follow the three-part format (introduction, body, conclusion) of your movie review (page 397). Your musical performance review should cover some—though not necessarily all—of the questions above and on page 398. If you write about tapes or compact discs, you might play an excerpt before you read your review aloud to the class.

USING THE SELECTION

Tipica Sound of Cuba

1

The writer describes the kind of music and type of performance (live band).

2

The main performer is identified.

3

The writer assesses quality of performance by Lorente.

4

Details describe the music.

5

Other performers are described.

6

The effects on the audience are noted.

SELECTION AMENDMENT

Description of change: excerpted

Rationale: to focus on the concept of a musical performance review presented in this chapter

LITERATURE AND PERSUASION
OBJECTIVE

- To write an advertisement for a book

LITERATURE AND PERSUASION

Teaching Strategies

You could begin by reading several book advertisements (from book jackets) to familiarize students with this type of essay. Then ask them to read the advertisement for Paul Theroux's book *Riding the Iron Rooster.* Point out the basic features of the piece—especially the title and author, the interesting opening, and the information about the type of book and its content designed to make the reader want to read the book.

You could suggest that students write their advertisements about a selection from their literature books.

GUIDELINES

Giving students a checklist of items to be considered when evaluating will probably help them design and evaluate their advertisements. Here are some possibilities:

1. Are the names of the title and author included?
2. Does the opening catch the reader's interest?
3. Does the ad give enough information to get the reader interested?
4. Is the ad written clearly?
5. Is it well organized?

LITERATURE AND PERSUASION

A Book Advertisement

Books, like movies, are often advertised in newspapers, magazines, and book club flyers, and on the covers of the books themselves. A book advertisement has a different purpose than a literary analysis. The purpose of the advertisement is to persuade the reader to buy a particular book; the purpose of a literary analysis is to inform and explain.

Book advertisements differ greatly, but most ads have these basic features:

- title and author
- an interest-catching opening
- information about the type of book and its content that will be appealing to the reader

The following advertisement is the back-cover text of Paul Theroux's *Riding the Iron Rooster,* the author's account of train travel through China. Does reading the ad make you want to read the book?

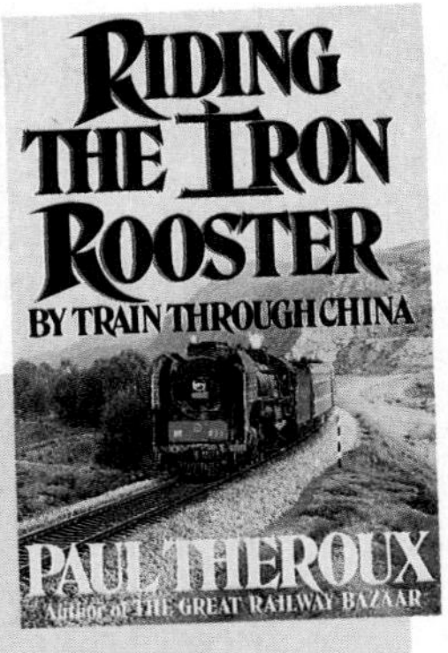

The world seems to grow smaller every day. Travelers cross oceans and continents in the blink of an eye. But the world is not so small that there is no room left for adventure and discovery. In RIDING THE IRON ROOSTER, Paul Theroux invites you to join him on the journey of a lifetime—a journey in the grand romantic tradition. Vowing to reach the other side of the world without jet lag, Theroux began his odyssey in London. He traveled by train across Europe, through the vast underbelly of Asia, and into the heart of Russia. But the crown jewel of his journey was China itself. Here is a magnificent land and an extraordinary people as you have never before known them: China by rail, as seen and heard through the eyes and ears of one of the most intrepid and insightful travel writers of our time.

LITERATURE AND EVALUATION OBJECTIVE

- To identify deductive reasoning in reviews

Try writing an advertisement for a book you have read recently or for one of your all-time favorites. Do you own some books—perhaps paperbacks—that you would like to sell or swap? Your class might start a Book Swap Shop. You can "publish" ads on the bulletin board, or you can start a small weekly or monthly flyer advertising books you and your classmates would like to sell or swap. You can even illustrate your ads. The final step is to enjoy your ads and the new books you'll get from the Swap Shop.

LITERATURE AND EVALUATION

Understanding Deductive Reasoning

When you reason *inductively* (Chapter 7, pages 263–265), you observe a number of particulars or specific instances and draw a conclusion about them. The opposite kind of reasoning is called ***deductive:*** You start with a general rule or general knowledge and apply it to a specific instance in order to draw a conclusion about that instance.

You use deductive reasoning when you evaluate something, whether it is a movie, a pair of shoes, or a poem. If you wrote a movie or music review earlier in this chapter, part of your task was to evaluate. For example, the *Star Wars* review (page 395) uses deductive reasoning to evaluate the movie.

General rule (Major premise): A strong narrative, strongly drawn characters, and good special effects create a good movie.
Specific instance (Minor premise): *Star Wars* has a strong narrative, strongly drawn characters, and good special effects.
Conclusion: *Star Wars* is a good movie.

Get together with a partner and reread the reviews you wrote earlier in this chapter as well as four or five movie, book, or music reviews in newspapers or magazines. Look for deductive reasoning. What general rule does the writer state? How is it applied to the work being reviewed? What is the writer's conclusion?

LITERATURE AND EVALUATION

Teaching Strategies

Have students read the information about deductive reasoning and discuss the example with them. Before students look for deductive reasoning in other reviews, you may want to have the class work together to evaluate **"Tipica Sound of Cuba"** on p. 399. The class may decide upon a general rule such as "Skillful musicians, a variety of musical selections, and positive audience response create a good musical performance." Then help students to arrive at a specific instance such as "Rene Lorente's band skillfully performed a variety of musical selections, and the audience obviously enjoyed the performance." Using deductive reasoning, students would probably conclude that "Rene Lorente's band gave a good performance."

GUIDELINES

Because the reviewers' general rules will vary, you may want to have students include copies of the reviews they are using to locate deductive reasoning.

Chapter 11 WRITING A RESEARCH PAPER

OBJECTIVES

- To analyze the ideas and details in an informative essay
- To write about a personal observation
- To evaluate and choose topics for a research report
- To formulate preliminary research questions and use reference works to acquire an overview of a topic
- To locate and evaluate sources for a research report
- To make source cards and note cards for a research report
- To write a thesis statement for a research report
- To group and order information and write a working outline
- To write a first draft of a research report, including citations and a Works Cited list
- To evaluate and revise the contents and organizations of research reports
- To proofread a research report and prepare it for publication
- To write an informative article about a community person
- To research a place and write a brief travel article

Motivation

Initiate a class discussion about research reports that students in your class or other students have written. Make a list on the chalkboard of the topics. You could add to the list with topics that previous students have selected. Point out to students the variety of subjects and interests represented. Emphasize that exploring subjects through research can be interesting and challenging. Explain that increasingly in school, and later in their college courses and careers, they will be required to conduct research, write reports, and accurately document their sources. Tell students that it is time for them to master these skills in writing formal research reports.

Introduction

Help students understand that when they write their research reports, they will not simply be copying the research of others; they also will be organizing others' information to show their own unique views of particular topics. Tell students that the chapter takes them step by step through the writing process to help them produce interesting, well organized, and accurately documented reports.

Your students should understand that the basic purpose of a formal research report is informative, as distinguished from other writing aims (expressive, literary, and persuasive). Help them see that they can use the strategies of narration, description, classification, or evaluation to achieve the informative aim.

Integration

This chapter can be a resource for research writing in your classroom and in other subjects. You could assign research reports about particular genres of writing, historical and literary periods, or individual writers. Social studies and science teachers frequently require students to write research reports; students who are comfortable with their skill can write research reports in any area. The **Making Connections** feature gives students an example of research in the science field. You might emphasize the value of research abilities in different careers, perhaps using the **Writing Workshop** activity on travel writing as an example.

The chart on the next page illustrates the strands of language arts as they are integrated into this chapter. For vocabulary study, glossary words are underlined in some writing models.

QUOTATIONS
All **Quotations for the Day** are chosen because of their relevance to instructional material presented in that segment of the chapter and for their usefulness in establishing student interest in writing.

INTEGRATING THE LANGUAGE ARTS

Selection	Reading and Literature	Writing and Critical Thinking	Language and Syntax	Speaking, Listening, and Other Expression Skills
from **"Making Time Portable"** by Daniel J. Boorstin **404-406** from **"The Last Days of Eden"** by Spencer Reiss **422-423** **"Education: A Sit-Down Tour"** by Matt Tomlinson **455** from **"Sands of Time"** by James Kotsilibas-Davis **457** from ***What Do You Care What Other People Think?*** by Richard Feynman **459**	Responding personally to literature **406, 459** Identifying reference sources **406, 455-456** Analyzing explanations **406** Identifying explanatory details and illustrations **406** Identifying details **406, 422, 455-456** Reading for specific information **422, 424** Analyzing an introduction **455-456** Analyzing the content and organization of a report **455-456** Analyzing an author's use of quotations **455-456** Analyzing research for a travel article **457** Analyzing a passage from an autobiography **459** Researching and reading about a scientist **459**	Writing a journal entry **406** Forming an opinion on a topic **406** Making inferences and drawing conclusions **406, 411, 418, 424, 437-438, 449, 455-456, 459** Evaluating topics for research **411, 424** Choosing a limited topic **411, 456** Evaluating sources **418, 419** Forming preliminary research questions **419, 422, 456** Using reference works to get an overview of a topic **419, 456** Locating sources for a research paper **419, 456** Making source cards **419, 422** Reading or viewing sources **422, 424, 456** Taking notes from sources **422, 424, 456** Writing questions for an interview or a survey **424, 436** Taking notes during an interview **424** Writing a follow-up note to an interviewee **424** Organizing information and developing an outline **427, 456** Judging what information to document **437-438** Writing a first draft of a report, including parenthetical citations **446** Preparing a Works Cited list **446** Analyzing a writer's revisions **447** Evaluating and revising a report **449, 456** Proofreading and publishing a report **451, 456** Writing an article based on an interview **456** Researching and writing a brief travel article **458**	Proofreading for errors in grammar, usage, and mechanics **451, 456**	Discussing and evaluating sources **418** Working with a classmate to develop research questions **422** Working with a classmate to plan an interview and discussing the results of the interview **424** Conducting an interview **424, 456** Finding information in nonprint sources **424** Working with others to plan and conduct a survey **436** Creating a table to display survey findings **436** Discussing documentation **437** Discussing a writer's revisions **447** Working with a classmate to evaluate reports **449** Reporting on a scientist **459**

SEGMENT PLANNING GUIDE

You can use the following Planning Guide to adapt the chapter material to the individual needs of your class. All the Resources listed in this chapter are located in the *Teacher's ResourceBank*™.

SEGMENT	PAGES	CONTENT	RESOURCES
1 *Exploring Your World*	*403-406*		
Literary Model from **"Making Time Portable"**	404-406	Guided reading: a model of a research report	
Reader's Response/ Writer's Craft	406	Model evaluation: responding to literature and analyzing a research article	
2 *Ways to Develop a Report*	*407-408*		
3 *Prewriting*	*409-427*		Writing a Research Paper Developing an Early Plan 88 Focusing Your Research 89
Discovering Subjects	409-411	Guidelines: selecting suitable subjects	
Exercise 1	411	Applied practice: evaluating topics for research	
Writing Assignment: Part 1	411	Applied practice: choosing a limited topic	
Considering Purpose, Audience, and Tone	412	Guidelines: analyzing and selecting appropriate purpose, audience, and tone	
Asking Research Questions	413	Guidelines: posing general questions about topic	
Getting an Overview	413-417	Guidelines: finding and evaluating sources	
Chart: Information Resources	414	Guidelines: finding sources	
Chart: Source Cards	415	Guidelines: using criteria for source cards	
Evaluating Sources	416-417	Guidelines: using the "4R" test	
Critical Thinking: Evaluating Sources	417	Guidelines: using the "4R" test to evaluate sources	
Critical Thinking Exercise	418	Cooperative learning: evaluating and selecting sources	
Writing Assignment: Part 2	419	Applied practice: beginning research	
Taking Notes	420-421	Guidelines: writing direct quotations and paraphrases	
Chart: Taking Notes	420	Guidelines: using criteria to make note cards	
Exercise 2	422-423	Cooperative learning: taking notes from a model	
Exercise 3	424	Cooperative learning: planning/conducting an interview	
Writing Assignment: Part 3	424	Applied practice: taking notes	
Writing a Thesis Statement	425	Guidelines: writing a thesis statement	
Developing an Outline	426-427	Guidelines: examining a formal outline	
Writing Assignment: Part 4	427	Applied practice: writing a working outline	

For **Portfolio Assessment** see the following pages in the *Teacher's ResourceBank™*:
Aims For Writing — pp. 87–93
Holistically Graded Composition Models — pp. 527–532
Assessment Portfolio — pp. 533–562

SEGMENT	PAGES	CONTENT	RESOURCES
4 ***Writing***	***428-446***		Writing a Research Paper 90
Chart: Elements of a Research Report	428	Guidelines: examining a report's main parts	
A Writer's Model	429-434	Guided reading: examining a report	
Chart: Using Quotations	435	Guidelines: analyzing rules for using quotations	
Exercise 4	436	Cooperative learning: creating visuals	
Documenting Sources	437	Guidelines: using criteria for documenting sources	
Exercise 5	437-438	Cooperative learning: judging what to document	
Parenthetical Citations/Chart	438-440	Guidelines: identifying content and correct form	
List of Works Cited	441	Introduction: preparing a Works Cited list	
Chart: A Works Cited list	442	Guidelines: using correct form	
Chart: Sample Entries	442-446	Examples: analyzing entries from a Works Cited list	
Writing Assignment: Part 5	446	Applied practice: writing a first draft	
5 ***Evaluating and Revising***	***447-449***		Writing a Research Paper 91
Exercise 6	447	Cooperative learning: analyzing a writer's revisions	
Chart: Evaluating and Revising	448	Guidelines: applying evaluation and revision techniques	
Writing Assignment: Part 6	449	Applied practice: evaluating and revising	
6 ***Proofreading and Publishing***	***450-453***		Writing a Research Paper 92
Grammar Hint	450	Guidelines: using a quotation as part of a sentence	
Writing Assignment: Part 7	451	Applied practice: proofreading and publishing	
A Student Model	452-453	Guided reading: examining a sample report	
7 ***Writing Workshop***	***454-456***		
A Research Article	454	Guidelines: using criteria for interviewing	
Writing an Article Based on an Interview	456	Applied practice: applying skills to the writing process	
8 ***Making Connections***	***457-459***		
Travel Writing	457-458	Applied practice: writing a travel article	
Research Across the Curriculum: Science	458-459	Applied practice: researching and reporting information on a scientist	
WHOLE-CHAPTER RESOURCES	A Writing Process Log, A Writing Prompt, Holistically Graded Models, Assessment Portfolio Materials		

SEGMENT 1 *(pp. 402–406)*

EXPLORING YOUR WORLD

OBJECTIVES

- To write a journal entry about a personal impression
- To formulate an opinion about a topic in response to a literary model
- To identify possible reference sources for locating information
- To analyze and evaluate how an author explains concepts and uses details

VISUAL CONNECTIONS

Exploring the Subject. This photograph shows a gateway to Banteay Kdei, one of the first temples built by Jayavarman VII, Angkor's last great king. Located in present-day Cambodia, Angkor was the capital of the ancient Khmer empire from the ninth to the fifteenth century A.D. The Khmer empire covered all of Cambodia and much of present-day Vietnam, Laos, and Thailand. The Angkor kings built many Hindu and Buddhist temples like Banteay Kdei; the grandeur of these buildings is evidence of the prosperity of the Khmer empire and its capital, Angkor.

Related Expression Skills. Have students research other monuments created by ancient peoples. You might suggest topics such as the Nazca lines in Peru or the giant stone sculptures on Easter Island. Students can report their findings to the class.

11 WRITING A RESEARCH PAPER

MOTIVATION

Write the words *listen, observe, experiment,* and *read* on the chalkboard. Have students name interesting or important discoveries they've made about the world by using these methods. Point out that people constantly learn about the world as they assimilate information from many sources.

TEACHING THE LESSON

As you start students on the path to writing their research papers, encourage them to appreciate others' research efforts and to enjoy their own investigations. You may want to lead a discussion about various kinds of research reports that students encounter every day (such as those in school classes, periodicals, and even advertisements). Help ☛

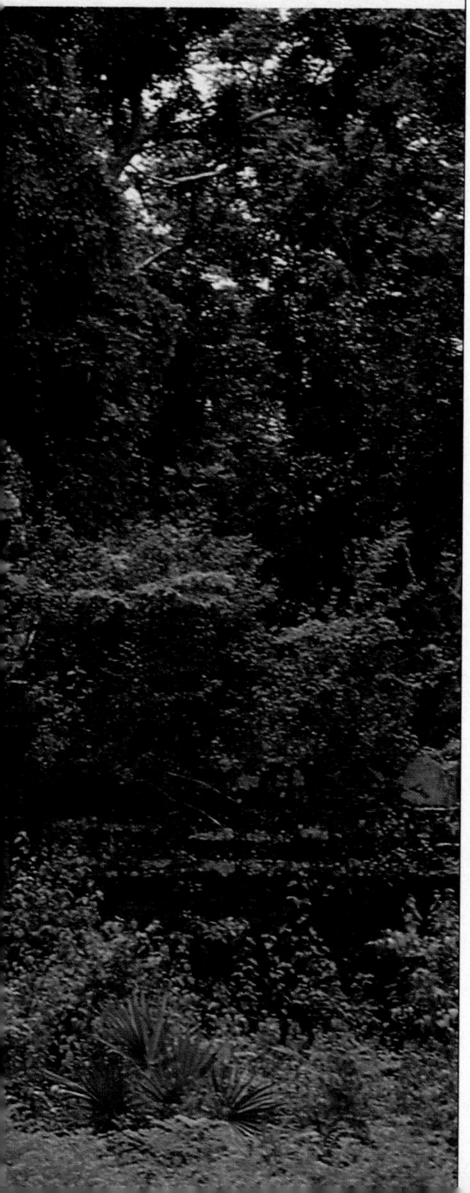

Exploring Your World

When you think of someone exploring the world, you may think of expeditions to the South Pole or to the top of Mount Everest. But there are other ways to **explore your world:** you can listen, observe, experiment, and read.

Writing and You. Reports of research and explorations come in many forms. A corporate executive puts her findings about a new management technique in a memo; a football scout takes notes on a rival team's strategies and presents the coach with a written or oral report; and a reporter researches the state's court system and prepares a documentary for a local television station. How do you think these people found their information?

As You Read. The following selection explains how the young Galileo discovered a principle that changed timekeeping significantly. What way did Galileo use to explore his world?

QUOTATION FOR THE DAY

"People do not have words to fit ideas that have never occurred to them." (Robert H. Jackson, 1892–1954, United States Supreme Court Justice)

Remind your students that as they explore new subjects, they may discover new, specialized vocabularies. As they write, this new vocabulary will become increasingly familiar, but they must remember that the vocabulary may be bewildering to readers. New words must be presented simply and explained carefully to keep readers involved.

MEETING INDIVIDUAL NEEDS

LEP/ESL

General Strategies. Methods of exploration and sources of materials may be vague concepts to some students. Complement the information in the model with other resources and media to stimulate their interest and broaden their exposure to the world.

You might bring reference material to class on Galileo or timekeeping to discuss how to obtain these materials. Include almanac, encyclopedia, biographical dictionary, magazine, and newspaper references, as well as audiovisual material. (The video from the PBS series *The Ascent of Man* discusses Galileo's life.) Exposure can give students a model to follow as they engage in research.

students to see how much they depend on other people's research for valuable information. Then, by again equating research with exploration, impress upon students how interesting it can be for them to do their own research and to share their findings with others.

In presenting the literary model, tell students to be aware of three avenues of discovery to explore in the article: Galileo's, the author's, and students' own. Have volunteers read the excerpt from **"Making Time Portable"** and use the annotations to guide the class discussion. During the discussion, have students answer the question posed in the introduction: "What method did Galileo use to explore his world?" [He observed.] You could use question 3 of **Writer's Craft**

USING THE SELECTION
from "Making Time Portable"

1
The baptistery and cathedral are located in Pisa's Piazza (plaza) del Duomo along with one of the world's most famous structures—the Leaning Tower of Pisa. The tower is actually the cathedral's bell tower. The baptistery is a huge, circular structure that is famous for its impressive echoes.

2
Each heart contraction is followed by a contraction of the arteries. This pulsation (pulse rate) occurs about seventy-two times per minute in a healthy person.

3
pendulum: a weight hung from a fixed point so that it can swing back and forth; the movement of clock parts is sometimes regulated by a pendulum

VISUAL CONNECTIONS
Exploring the Subject. In addition to his work in mathematics and physics, Galileo made important discoveries in astronomy. Galileo built and improved telescopes and used them to study the heavens. He discovered that the moon was mountainous and discovered four moons circling Jupiter. Galileo supported the Copernican theory of the solar system, which holds that the earth revolves around the sun.

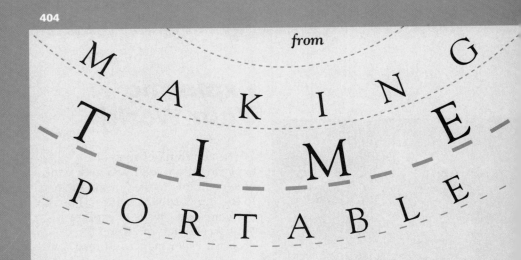

from
MAKING TIME PORTABLE

In 1583 Galileo Galilei (1564–1642), a youth of nineteen attending prayers in the
1 baptistery of the Cathedral of Pisa, was, according to tradition, distracted by the swinging of the altar lamp. No matter how wide the swing of the lamp, it seemed that the time it took the lamp to move from one end to the other was the same. Of course Galileo had no watch, but he checked the intervals
2 of the swing by his own pulse. This curious everyday puzzle, he said, enticed him away from the study of medicine, to which his father had committed him, to the study of mathematics and physics. In the baptistery he had discovered what physicists would call the isochro-
3 nism, or equal time of the pendulum—that the time of a pendulum's swing varies not with the width of the swing but with the length of the pendulum.

The Bettman Archive

"...Galileo's own way of learning, from observing and measuring what he saw, expressed the science of the future."

to consider how the author explored the subject. And you could point out that the class explored the subject by reading the article and then responding to it. You could use question 4 in **Writer's Craft** as a class discussion to guide students' understanding of the content and techniques of Boorstin's research.

After you and your students have discussed the article and various research sources, students can answer **Reader's Response** questions 1 and 2 on their own. You might present these two assignments as brief explorations of the students' thoughts involving observation. Evaluate answers to the **Writer's Craft** questions ☛

This simple discovery symbolized the new age. Astronomy and physics at the University of Pisa, where Galileo was enrolled, had consisted of lectures on the texts of Aristotle. But Galileo's own way of learning, from observing and measuring what he saw, expressed the science of the future. His discovery, although never fully exploited by Galileo himself, opened a new era in timekeeping. Within three decades after Galileo's death the average error of the best timepieces was reduced from fifteen minutes to only ten seconds per day.

A clock that kept perfect step with countless other clocks elsewhere made time a measure transcending space. Citizens of Pisa could know what time it was in Florence or in Rome at that very moment. Once such clocks were synchronized they would stay synchronized. No longer a mere local convenience for measuring the craftsman's hours or fixing the time for worship or the town council's meeting, henceforth the clock was a universal yardstick. Just as the equal hour standardized the units of day and night, summer and winter, in any particular town, so now the precision clock standardized the units of time all over the planet.

Certain peculiarities of our planet made this magic possible. Because the earth turns on its axis, every place on earth experiences a 24-hour day with each full 360-degree turn. The
7 meridians of longitude mark off these degrees. As the earth turns, it brings noon successively to different places. When it is noon in Istanbul, it is still only 10 A.M. westward at London. In one hour the earth turns 15 degrees. Therefore we can say that London is 30 degrees longitude, or two hours, west of Istanbul, which makes those degrees of longitude measures of both space and time. If

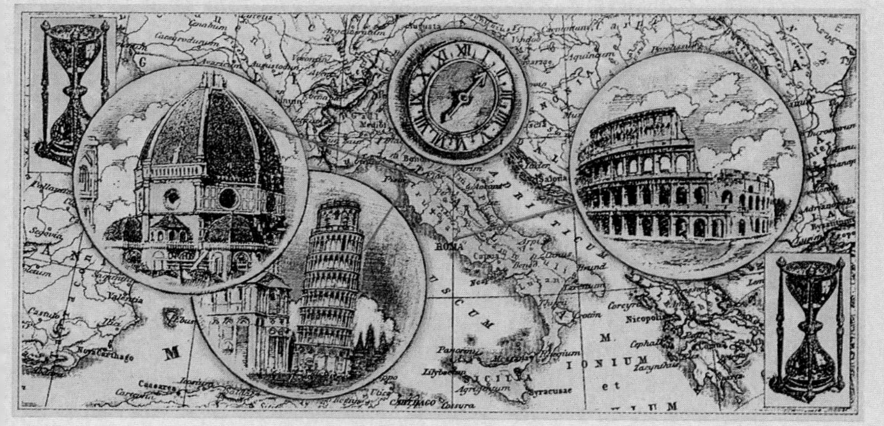

4

The time period from the era of Aristotle (384–322 B.C.) to the era of Galileo (1564–1642) is more than 1900 years. What discoveries have been made since the time of Galileo? [In the 350 years since Galileo's time, discoveries have multiplied tremendously and include explorations from atomic to celestial.]

5

Stephen W. Hawking, one of the twentieth century's greatest physicists, says in his book *A Brief History of Time* that Galileo is one of the people most responsible for the beginning of modern science.

6

In 1656 Dutch scientist Christiaan Huygens (1629–1695), applying Galileo's discovery, designed a clock that used a pendulum and revolutionized timekeeping.

7

Meridians are marked off east and west of the prime meridian, which is numbered 0 and runs through Greenwich, England.

discussed in class to assess students' understanding.

Have students identify the main ideas that they learned from Boorstin's research and discuss what they found interesting.

ENRICHMENT

Students might be interested in learning about other discoveries in the measurement of time. Small groups could research subjects such as sundials or star dials, water clocks, sandglasses, modern electric clocks, atomic clocks, or geographical time lines to add to the discussion of **"Making Time Portable."** ■

ANSWERS

Reader's Response

Responses will vary.

1. Each student should include a clear topic and reasons for the lasting impression.
2. All students should clearly address each of the three questions with personal opinions.

Writer's Craft

Answers may vary.

3. Here are some sample responses: encyclopedias, biographies, nonfiction books about timekeeping, scientific journals and magazines, history and science books, and books and articles about Pisa.
4. Boorstin explains isochronism by giving a short, clear, interesting narrative account of what Galileo observed in the baptistery; he makes meridians of longitude and degrees of rotation understandable by comparing the time in Istanbul and London.

SELECTION AMENDMENT

Description of change: excerpted

Rationale: to focus on the concept of research reports presented in this chapter

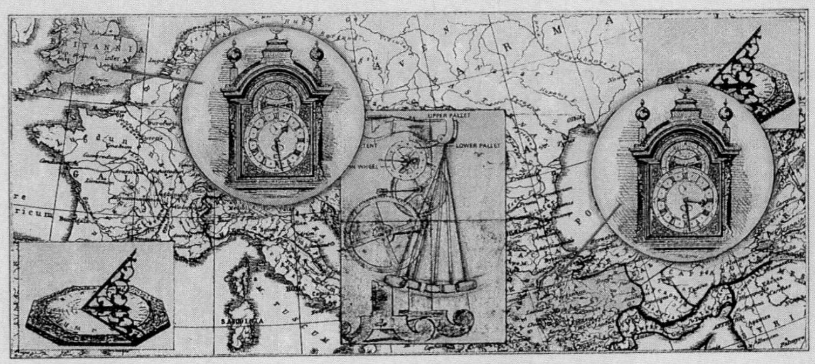

you have an accurate clock set to the time at London and carry it to Istanbul, by comparing the time on the clock you have carried with the local time in Istanbul, you will also know precisely how far you have traveled eastward, or how far east Istanbul is from London.

The Discoverers

Reader's Response

1. Few people make the world-shaking discoveries that Galileo did. Yet most people, at one time or another, notice some of the oddities of the physical world—a chameleon changing colors, water disappearing into steam, the optical illusion of a mirage. In a brief journal entry, explore one such oddity that made an impression on you.
2. Some people argue that we would be better off *without* timepieces accurate to the microsecond and life geared to the clock. What do you think? What would it be like if every town in America just kept time for itself? More personally, what do you notice about your life when you don't wear a watch?

Writer's Craft

3. Daniel Boorstin gives no source notes for his information because it has been known and handed down for centuries. In what books or reference works might you find information about Galileo or timekeeping?
4. Boorstin explains some potentially difficult concepts—isochronism, meridians of longitude, degrees of rotation as measures of space and time—clearly and simply. How does he do it? Point out some good explanatory details and illustrations.

SEGMENT 2 *(pp. 407–408)*

WAYS TO DEVELOP RESEARCH

TEACHING THE MODES

You may want to use this section as a brief overview of the kinds of written research that students encounter. Begin by discussing informal and formal reports. You could point out that most research articles in periodicals for the general public are informal. Ask students why it's important that a scientific research article include a detailed list of sources. [The sources validate the author's work and aid other scientists who are doing additional work in the same area.]

Next, discuss the four modes as they apply to research writing. To assess students'

Ways to Develop Research

In our age, every day seems to bring an amazing advance in the communication of information: encyclopedias on diskettes, research data and pictures from spacecraft, computer networks for everything from disease control to sports statistics. You have available to you a multitude of research reports from a multitude of sources: businesses, government, "think tanks," and marketers.

Some of these reports are ***informal;*** that is, they don't contain footnotes or a detailed list of the sources of the report's information. The preceding selection by Daniel J. Boorstin is an example of this kind of informal report. A ***formal report,*** on the other hand, like the one you'll be writing in this chapter or the ones in scholarly journals, always documents the sources used. Formal reports not only cover a topic in depth, but also tell readers where the writer obtained the information, so that readers can consult the writer's sources if they wish.

Reports on research, whether they give information informally or formally, can be developed in various ways. Here are some examples.

Narration: producing a documentary videotape about how volunteers in your community helped citizens build new houses; reporting on events leading up to the Persian Gulf Conflict (1990–1991) in the Middle East.

Description: describing the camouflage markings of rain forest moths; describing the Mayan artifacts discovered in an archaeological dig in Yucatán.

Classification: reporting on specific genes that produce hereditary diseases; comparing and contrasting the military achievements of American Civil War generals Ulysses S. Grant and Robert E. Lee.

Evaluation: reporting scientific findings about the effects of pollutants dispersed from a paper mill into a local river; reporting the results of tests to determine which brand of television set has the best performance record.

INTEGRATING THE LANGUAGE ARTS

Library Link. Give students practice in identifying and locating sources to use for research papers. Divide the class into eight groups, with each group taking one of the development examples listed under each mode. Instruct each group to cite at least three details that might be explored for each topic. Then give the groups library time for each to find at least five sources for information to develop the topic (if your library is well equipped). Ask a representative from each group to give an oral report about the group's findings.

Literature Link. Students should understand that all writers—those of fiction as well as nonfiction—use research in their writing. To show students research in a fictional work, assign a story such as "The Devil and Tom Walker" by Washington Irving. Tell students that the story is written in the narrative mode and its primary aim is literary. However, like many creative writers, Irving probably did some research before writing the story.

After they read the story, ask students what the author may have researched to develop a vivid setting and characters. [Irving could have read about historical figures and events of the time; he could have explored German folk tales; he could have observed or talked to people about the features of the setting.]

understanding of the modes, ask each student to write an example other than the ones in the textbook for each mode. You could point out that the basic aim of these modes for a research paper is informative, but that some research also has other aims (persuasive, expressive, and literary).

Use the **Looking Ahead** section to give students a concise idea of what they will be expected to accomplish in this chapter and to give them the basic criteria for writing a formal report. ■

MEETING INDIVIDUAL NEEDS

LESS-ADVANCED STUDENTS

Some students may find the terms *narration, description,* and *evaluation* confusing because they don't sound like terms associated with research. Help students see that the terms represent ways authors use their research. You could give this example: An article describing an archaeological dig in Egypt may not at first seem like a research article, but an author who did not witness the dig or had never seen a dig would have to rely strictly on research in writing the article. Even an author who had witnessed a dig probably would want to research technical information about archaeology. And, of course, witnessing the dig itself is first-hand research.

SELECTION AMENDMENT
Description of change: excerpted
Rationale: to focus on the concept of research reports presented in this chapter

LOOKING AHEAD

In this chapter, you will work step by step in planning, organizing, gathering data for, and writing a formal research report. You'll also work on informal reports about travel and about a newsmaker in your community. In your formal report, you will use the strategy of either narration or classification. As you work, keep in mind that a formal report

- presents factual information about a specific topic
- presents information from a number of sources
- documents its sources of information

"RESEARCH is formalized curiosity. It is poking and prying with purpose."

Zora Neale Hurston

SEGMENT 3 *(pp. 409–427)*

PREWRITING

OBJECTIVES

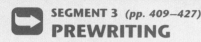

- To evaluate the suitability of topics for research reports and to suggest more limited, workable topics
- To choose a limited topic for a research paper and to consider the requirements of sufficient sources, objectivity, and reader interest
- To formulate preliminary research questions
- To use general reference works to acquire an overview of a topic
- To use library and community resources to find possible sources

Writing a Research Paper

Prewriting

Finding a Research Topic

When the Library of Congress purchased the six thousand books in Thomas Jefferson's library, those books formed the basis of its entire collection. The world was a simpler place then. Today if you walk into a public library in any city, you are likely to find many times that number of books. Some are fiction, of course, but many represent a whole world of research: results of research, reports on research studies, and springboards for additional research.

Discovering Subjects

Any library, bookstore, or video store provides evidence of the inexhaustible list of subjects people find fascinating. But what fascinates *you*? To write an effective research report, investigate your own interests first. Here are some ways to get started.

SOURCES FOR RESEARCH SUBJECTS

- **Family and friends:** Does someone you know have an interesting job or hobby—a legislator? a spelunker?
- **Heroes:** Whom do you admire and wish you knew more about—an inventor? a film director? a president?
- **Places near and far:** What trip was a highlight of your life? What place have you always wanted to see—a city? a landmark? a landform? a country?
- **Current events:** When you turn on television news or open a newspaper, which events and subjects grab your attention—environmental disasters? civil rights?
- **Library and media:** What subjects arouse your curiosity if you browse through books, magazines, and the card catalog; turn the pages of the *Readers' Guide to Periodical Literature;* or check out television listings and videotapes—modern warfare? opera? American pioneers?

Teacher's ResourceBank™

RESOURCES

PREWRITING

QUOTATION FOR THE DAY

"I take notes on four-by-six index cards, reminding myself about once an hour of a rule I read long ago in a research manual, 'Never write on the back of anything.'" (Barbara Tuchman, 1912–1989, American historian)

Even professional writers like Tuchman abide by rules when they do research. Explain Tuchman's rule to students this way: If a researcher takes notes on several articles but writes essential information on the back of just one card, the stack has doubled. Every time the writer searches for information, he or she will have to flip every card.

MEETING INDIVIDUAL NEEDS

LEP/ESL

General Strategies. ESL students may be anxious about writing research papers. Meet with them individually to talk about their topics and discuss their strengths and weaknesses to help them arrive at suitable topics and to develop effective research plans.

- To evaluate sources as to whether they are relevant, reliable, recent, and representative
- To make source cards for possible sources
- To apply guidelines for taking notes and making note cards
- To follow the steps for conducting an interview
- To write a thesis statement for a research report
- To group and order information and to write a working outline for a research report

Selecting a Specific Topic

Your first idea may be a very broad subject, such as "great scientists" or "the American Civil War" or "African American literature." However, you have to narrow the focus of that broad idea: to find a specific aspect of the subject that intrigues you and that can be covered in a composition. (Your teacher may specify a length for the paper; a usual range is five to ten pages.)

One way to narrow the focus is to look for subtopics in the card catalog, the *Readers' Guide,* encyclopedias, and specialized dictionaries. And sometimes you can narrow a topic just by closer scrutiny. Whatever your process, your constant challenge to yourself is this: *Be more specific.*

HERE'S HOW

Subject:	*I'm interested in African American literature.*
Be more specific:	*Zora Neale Hurston is great.*
Be more specific:	*She was an anthropologist and a novelist.*
Be more specific:	*I could research her work as an anthropologist and her fiction.*
Limited topic:	*How Zora Neale Hurston's study of anthropology and her fiction are related*

Finally, your choice of topic must be suitable for a research paper. Besides personal interest and scope, keep the following requirements in mind.

MEETING INDIVIDUAL NEEDS

LESS-ADVANCED STUDENTS

If students have difficulty selecting appropriate subjects, you could review sources for subjects and offer examples. For example, a relative who works in construction might suggest trends in housing designs; a TV documentary on Africa today might suggest a paper on the beginnings of apartheid; a news report on flooding in Texas might suggest a paper on modern flood control; a Native American folk tale might suggest a study of modern reservation life; an interest in ancient Egypt might lead to a paper on recent archeological finds.

VISUAL CONNECTIONS

Exploring the Subject. Zora Neale Hurston was a southern writer who lived from 1891 to 1960. She was born in Eatonville, Florida. She was a folklorist, and her novels are noted for their accurate depiction of African American culture, dialect, and idiom.

MOTIVATION

Select an interesting, full-page color photograph of a person, an animal, a faraway locale, or a natural event from a magazine or a book and display it for the class. After you give a brief explanation of the picture, direct students to write down several questions that come to mind about the subject. Call on students to read some of their questions and ask students how they might go about answering their questions. [Responses might include books, periodicals, interviews, or videotapes.] Tell students that asking questions and forming ideas as they have done is the beginning of writing research papers.

CHECKLIST FOR A SUITABLE TOPIC

1. **Available sources of information.** Since your purpose is to report information, be sure you can *find* five or six good sources. You may not be able to find enough sources for very new or technical topics.
2. **Objectivity and facts.** Your interest leads to a topic, but your experience isn't the basis of a report. You could write about how sonar detection of fish works, but not about your fishing trips using the equipment.
3. **Audience interest.** Almost any topic can be interesting, but think ahead. If your topic isn't automatically appealing ("the Hawley-Smoot Tariff of 1930") or is so appealing it's widely known ("the disappearance of dinosaurs"), what unusual approach can you take? What could intrigue your readers?

EXERCISE 1 **Evaluating Topics for Research**

Which of the following topics are suitable for a seven- to ten-page research report? Some may be too broad, too narrow, or too personal. For each topic that seems unsuitable, first tell what's wrong with it; then suggest a more workable topic.

1. how the War of Jenkins' Ear got its name
2. a television program worth watching
3. daily life of women in the Iroquois Nation
4. John Bardeen's contributions to developing the transistor
5. the American space-exploration program

***WRITING* ASSIGNMENT** PART 1: **Choosing a Limited Topic**

What topic can hold your attention? What do you wish you knew more about? Use the idea starters on page 409; if your idea is too broad, *be more specific.* Narrow your topic, and make sure it meets checklist requirements given above.

A DIFFERENT APPROACH

Let students find out for themselves what current topics seem to interest people. Have students go to a library, a bookstore, or a video store to ask what books or videos are most popular. What current topics are big sellers? Have each student make a brief oral report about his or her findings. Ask students if they discovered any topics that they would like to write about while investigating current interests.

ANSWERS

Exercise 1

1. suitable
2. This topic is too personal. Possible limited topic: why television network news shows are changing
3. This topic is too narrow and there may be a possible lack of information. Possible workable topic: role of women in the Iroquois Nation
4. suitable
5. This topic is too broad. Possible limited topic: the accomplishments of America's space shuttle program

TEACHING THE LESSON

This segment not only provides information about the first stage of the writing process but also begins students on writing assignments that lead to their own finished research reports. The prewriting stage of the writing process is divided into several steps, which makes it convenient for you to divide your teaching into those steps. Allow plenty of time to discuss and direct students through each step and gear your time to students' comprehension of the process. Be sure that students understand how to apply each step to the preparation of their research reports before proceeding to the next step. Failures in completing steps in the early stages can lead to flawed research and difficulty in preparing a paper.

COOPERATIVE LEARNING

To explore purpose, audience, and tone, divide the class into two groups. Have one group find articles from popular magazines such as *People,* whose purpose is to entertain, whose audience is general, and whose tone tends to be light, informal, and chatty. Have the other group obtain articles from magazines such as *Smithsonian, National Geographic,* or *Psychology Today*. These magazines are designed to inform educated adults, and the tone tends to be formal and more scholarly.

Have students identify details that illustrate the tone of the publications and have each group share its findings.

INTEGRATING THE LANGUAGE ARTS

Literature Link. Tell students that tone is achieved through choice of words and details. Have students read an essay with a serious tone, such as *The Way to Rainy Mountain* by N. Scott Momaday. Then ask students to identify specific words and details that contribute to the tone.

You also could have students speculate about the sources of the author's details. What printed research sources might he have used? Finally, ask students if the author sounds like an authority on the topic. Why or why not?

Prewriting

Beginning Your Research

In a real way, you're a hunter on the eve of a wide-open hunt. You don't know exactly what you are going to find or where you will find it. A hunter in this position could be excited, apprehensive—or both, although a research hunt doesn't have to be aimless or its trail filled with obstacles. There's a well-established method that will help you in your search.

Considering Purpose, Audience, and Tone

Start with first things first: Why are you setting out, and what are you supposed to bring back?

Purpose. Your *purpose* is to inform readers through research; but you're not just compiling a list of facts and expert opinions, and you're not writing only for others. Your research paper will be an original ***synthesis*** (combination) of information, and it will widen your own experience and knowledge. To write, you'll have to *think about* what you discover, and you'll pass along your insights.

Audience. Usually you are writing for your classmates and teacher and have a good idea of what background explanations you must give and how technical you can be. Don't lose readers by being either too elementary or too complex. If you plan your report for another specific *audience,* then tailor your approach and content to them.

Tone. Anyone who bothers to thoroughly investigate a topic takes that topic seriously; but the *tone* of the report, although a serious one, may vary from somewhat informal to very formal. Research reports that are included in popular periodicals or in mass market nonfiction may be relatively informal. However, the typical academic report, like the ones that are required in school, and the typical professional report, like the ones you may do on your job someday, are formal in tone. In this chapter, you are writing an academic report, and your audience will probably expect a formal tone. A formal tone usually has the following characteristics:

You might begin by telling students not to panic—they aren't required to write research papers overnight. Tell them that the chapter provides step-by-step guidelines. You might want to prepare your lessons according to the prewriting steps. Here are three divisions with textbook headings that you will want to use when teaching this segment:

1. Finding a Research Topic. This section involves choosing a subject and limiting it to a specific topic. You might use the questions in **Sources for Research Subjects** (p. 409) to brainstorm with the class. As they mention additional ideas, have recorders write ideas on the chalkboard as quickly as students generate them. To explain how to narrow a focus, select one of ☛

- *Third-person point of view.* You do not use the word *I.*
- *Relatively formal language.* You don't want to sound stuffy, but you should not be too casual and colloquial. Formal language usually does not include slang, colloquial expressions, or contractions.

REFERENCE NOTE: To review the use of formal and informal language, see pages 484–488.

Asking Research Questions

A first step toward your research is posing general questions that you want to answer. At this early stage, you can't come up with *all* the important questions about your topic, but you can establish guides for exploration. The following example shows how one writer developed questions to focus the research about Zora Neale Hurston's anthropology and fiction.

HERE'S HOW

> *Did Zora Neale Hurston write any fiction before becoming an anthropologist? If so, did it differ from her fiction written afterward?*
>
> *What did Hurston focus on as an anthropologist?*
>
> *Do elements of her studies appear in her fiction, and how? folk tales? characters?*
>
> *Did Hurston herself ever suggest links between her academic studies and her fiction?*

Getting an Overview and Finding Sources

You can use general reference works like encyclopedias and biographical dictionaries to get an overview of your topic. In the process, you may get ideas for other research questions, and you may find helpful references to other information sources.

If your topic is narrowly focused ("weather forecasting by supercomputer"), you may not find an encyclopedia entry for it, but you can look for related or larger topics ("meteorology," "supercomputers"). If you already have a solid background in your topic, you can eliminate general reference works and go directly to the types of sources listed in the chart on the next page. As you look for information, remember both print and nonprint sources, library and community resources.

A DIFFERENT APPROACH

Brainstorming and clustering are often useful methods for developing limited topics. You may want to give students class time to use brainstorming and clustering with their general subjects. To review clustering, refer to **Chapter 1: "Writing and Thinking."**

INTEGRATING THE LANGUAGE ARTS

Library Link. At this point in the beginning research process, students might benefit from an overview of your library's reference section. You may want to discuss various kinds of specialized reference books and dictionaries that students can find there, such as those on specific subjects like theater and medicine. You might also plan trips to the school library's reference section with small groups of students.

the brainstorming subjects and show how questioning can lead to subtopics. Then have a few volunteers pick topics and suggest questions that might lead to subtopics. Be sure students are familiar with the **Checklist for a Suitable Topic** (p. 411) before they work on **Exercise 1.** When you're satisfied that students understand how to find and limit a subject, assign **Writing Assignment: Part 1** on p. 411. You will want students to select subjects that have sufficient current information in the school and local libraries.

2. Beginning Your Research. This section includes considering purpose, audience, and tone; asking research questions; getting an overview and finding sources; making source cards; and evaluating sources (a **Critical Thinking** feature). Present the information as

INTEGRATING THE LANGUAGE ARTS

Technology Link. Students may need to review how to use microfilm or microfiche to find desired newspapers or magazines in a library. If possible, plan a library trip to explain and demonstrate the use of microfilm or microfiche.

MEETING INDIVIDUAL NEEDS

LESS-ADVANCED STUDENTS

Give students the following brief quiz as a review of the segment so far:

1. What are five possible sources for research subjects? [family and friends, heroes, places, current events, library and media]
2. What are three factors to keep in mind when deciding whether a topic is suitable for a research paper? [Answers may include personal interest, scope, available sources of information, objectivity and facts, and audience interest.]
3. What is the purpose of writing a research paper? [to inform]
4. What is the best tone for your research paper? [serious]
5. What viewpoint should be used in your research paper? [third-person point of view]

INFORMATION RESOURCES	
LIBRARY	
RESOURCE	SOURCE OR INFORMATION
Card catalog or on-line catalog	Books, audiovisuals (separate catalogs in some libraries)
Readers' Guide to Periodical Literature or on-line periodical indexes	Magazines and some journal articles
Newspaper indexes, specialized reference books	Newspapers (often on microfilm); dictionaries, encyclopedias, bibliographies on particular topics
Microfilm or microfiche	Indexes to major newspapers; back issues of some newspapers and magazines
COMMUNITY	
RESOURCE	SOURCE OR INFORMATION
Museums, historical societies, government offices	Exhibits, records, experts
Schools and colleges	Libraries, experts
Television and radio, video stores	Documentary and instructional programs and videotapes

REFERENCE NOTE: For more help on using the library, see pages 959–965.

Making Source Cards. When you find possible sources, it's important to keep accurate and complete information on them. ~~Your~~ ***Works Cited list***—the list of sources at the end of your report—must contain specific information because some of your readers may want to consult your sources.

The best method of collecting accurate information is to put each source on a 3″ x 5″ card. Sample ***source cards*** (sometimes called *bibliography cards*) are shown on page 415. In the long run you'll save time by doing your source cards in final format, prepared in the exact style required for the Works Cited list. (Many more examples of proper style are shown in **Sample Entries for the List of Works Cited,** pages 442–446.)

a set of understandings about research and as a series of steps to be accomplished. Have volunteers read the material aloud, but stop to provide clarification when needed. When discussing **Getting an Overview and Finding Sources** (p. 413), you might have a few information resources available and look up one of the topics you have brainstormed. You might draw a note card on the chalkboard and use one of the references to demonstrate **Guidelines for Source Cards.** Although students can refer to the chapter as they begin research, it is important for them to get a feel for research techniques before they work independently. Tell students that these are important considerations in the early ☛

GUIDELINES FOR SOURCE CARDS

1. **Assign each source a number.** Later, when you're taking notes, it will save time to write a number instead of the author and title.
2. **Record full publishing information.** Record everything you might need: subtitles, translators, and volume and edition numbers. It's better to have too much than to be missing information for your Works Cited list and have to backtrack. (For examples of the types of information you will need, see the sample Works Cited entries on pages 442–446.)
3. **Note the call number or location.** This information will help you relocate the source quickly if you need to.

Sample Source Cards

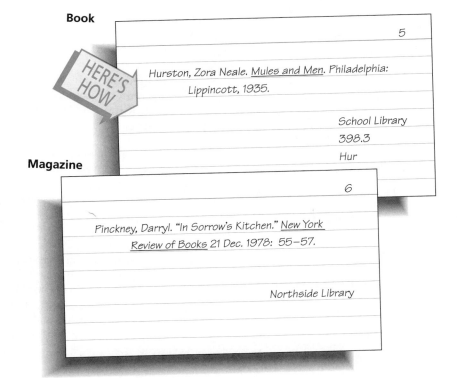

HERE'S HOW

Book

5

Hurston, Zora Neale. Mules and Men. Philadelphia: Lippincott, 1935.

School Library
398.3
Hur

Magazine

6

Pinckney, Darryl. "In Sorrow's Kitchen." New York Review of Books 21 Dec. 1978: 55–57.

Northside Library

A DIFFERENT APPROACH

Students often don't know how to use community resources because they don't know about the sources. Have students look through local telephone books to make lists of museums, historical societies, and government offices.

During class, have students name some of the resources as you write the suggestions on the chalkboard. Have volunteers suggest at least one topic for which each resource might be consulted.

stages of prewriting. After you've presented these steps, assign **Writing Assignment: Part 2** on p. 419.

Cont. on p. 419

TIMESAVER

You could make the most recent edition of the *MLA Handbook for Writers of Research Papers* available to students. Keep a copy on your desk or at a central location in the classroom. Instruct students to look in the handbook for particular style situations, such as books with editors or translators, rather than have students ask you.

A DIFFERENT APPROACH

Ask students to imagine this situation: They are receiving awards for career-achievement years from now. For the awards program, friends have written about the students' lives. They are reading the list of sources for the article.

Have students create that list by using five primary sources and five secondary sources. Students should make up these sources to reflect their imagined accomplishments and activities. For example, a student who imagines herself to be a famous ballet star might cite her autobiography, with an appropriate title, as a primary source, and a feature article in *Time* magazine as a secondary source. Students could volunteer to read their lists aloud to the class.

WRITING NOTE

Although the style for documenting sources shown in this chapter is the one recommended by the Modern Language Association of America (MLA), an organization of language scholars, your teacher may ask you to use a different style. Whatever style you use, it is important to be consistent and to include all the information required.

Evaluating Sources. Just as you can't judge a book by its cover, you can't always judge your sources by their titles. Before using a source, you need to evaluate its usefulness to you. A good way is to see if it meets the "4R" test.

1. *Relevant*. Does the source's information relate directly to your limited topic? For a book, check the table of contents and index. Skim magazine articles. Some nonprint sources include summaries and you may also find reviews.
2. *Reliable*. Can you trust it? A respected scholar, or a respected magazine such as *The Atlantic* or *Scientific American*, can usually be relied on for accuracy. Look for authors who are quoted frequently or appear in most bibliographies on your topic.
3. *Recent*. Be sure you aren't using outdated information, especially for rapidly changing topics. For any topic, look for the most recent work about it. If the author is thorough, you'll learn which older sources of information are still being consulted.
4. *Representative*. If you are working on a controversial topic, you'll need to show different points of view. You don't want a list of sources that are all pro or all con. Your task as a researcher is to study, balance, and interpret the views on all sides.

Using Primary and Secondary Sources. A ***primary source*** is firsthand, original information: a letter, an autobiography, an interview with a person who participated in the experience being researched, a work of literature, historical documents. A ***secondary source*** is information derived from, or about, primary sources and even from other secondary sources: an encyclopedia, a documentary film, a biography, history books, or an interview with a historian.

CRITICAL THINKING

(pp. 417–418)

OBJECTIVES

- To evaluate sources using the "4R" (relevant, reliable, recent, and representative) test
- To explain what information would make sources useful

TEACHING *EVALUATING SOURCES*

You may want to emphasize that a careful evaluation of sources should be done prior to research, not afterward. Ask students to explain why this is necessary [so as not to waste time on a source that is not relevant, reliable, recent, or representative].

Tell students that their evaluations of the sources presented in the **Critical**

For example, if you are writing about post-Revolutionary America, the Articles of Confederation and Thomas Jefferson's letters are primary sources. A biography of Jefferson is a secondary source (as your completed paper will be).

Although secondary sources are plentiful and essential to your paper and usually provide excerpts from primary sources, don't use them exclusively when primary sources are available. At the same time, don't assume that all primary sources are exempt from evaluation. Memory may be faulty or selective in an autobiography, and emotions may override facts in a letter. Read and research as widely as possible, so that you have a good basis for deciding what's accurate and what's slanted or biased.

CRITICAL THINKING

Evaluating Sources

Sometimes it isn't possible to know whether a book, an article, or a tape contains material useful to your research until you examine it. But you can evaluate, or judge, some sources even during your initial search by taking careful note of authors, titles, the reputation of magazines and journals, and dates. Remember *relevant, reliable, recent,* and *representative,* the "4R" test (discussed on page 416) that gives you particular qualities to look for in your sources.

MEETING INDIVIDUAL NEEDS

ADVANCED STUDENTS

You may want to require that students use a certain number of primary sources (such as journals, letters, works of literature, or historical documents) as appropriate for their topics.

LEP/ESL

General Strategies. Because they may not share the same backgrounds and experiences as their mainstream counterparts, ESL students may have difficulty evaluating sources on their own. You might assign small mixed-ability groups of students to work together on this activity. Suggest that students look for several clues in the sources listed:

1. What kind of publication (magazine, book, or quarterly bulletin) is it? How extensive will the information be?
2. What is the year of publication?
3. Is the publication written by or about Ms. Hurston?
4. Is the publication about the life of Ms. Hurston (biographical) or about a more general topic?

Students can benefit from learning what their peers have to say in analyzing the material.

Thinking Exercise should be based on the criteria listed under discussion of relevant, reliable, and recent in the textbook. Explain that the fourth of the "4Rs," *representative,* can't really be determined from a partial listing of sources being considered without a closer knowledge of the sources' contents.

If you feel your students haven't had much practice in evaluating sources, you'll probably want to use the exercise as a whole-class activity and lead the discussion yourself. If you feel your students are fairly proficient in evaluation skills, you'll probably want to let students discuss the sources in small groups.

CRITICAL THINKING EXERCISE: Evaluating Sources

Assume that you are working on this topic: "how Zora Neale Hurston's study of anthropology relates to her fiction." From your overview, you know that Hurston lived from either 1891 or 1901 (her birth records aren't certain) to 1960. She studied in the 1930s with Franz Boas, a distinguished anthropologist at Columbia University, and her best novel is generally considered *Their Eyes Were Watching God,* published in 1937.

Discuss the following possible sources in class or in smaller groups. Which ones would probably be helpful? Which ones would not? Why? If you feel uncertain about a source, explain what further information you would like to have about it.

1. Wilson, Margaret F. "Zora Neale Hurston: Author and Folklorist." Negro History Bulletin Oct.-Nov.-Dec. 1982: 109-10.
2. Walker, Alice. "In Search of Zora Neale Hurston." Ms. Mar. 1975: 74+.
3. Fisher, Maxine. Recent Revolutions in Anthropology. New York: Franklin Watts, 1986.
4. Hemenway, Robert E. Zora Neale Hurston: A Literary Biography. Urbana: U of Illinois P, 1977.
5. Boas, Franz. Anthropology and Modern Life. Rev. ed. [revised edition]. New York: Norton, 1932.
6. Hurston, Zora Neale. Jonah's Gourd Vine [a novel]. Philadelphia: Lippincott, 1934, 1971.
7. Bone, Robert. The Negro Novel in America. New Haven: Yale UP, 1958.

ANSWERS

Critical Thinking Exercise

Answers may vary. Discussion should include the reasons each source is considered relevant, reliable, and recent.

1. helpful (assuming author and publication reliable; relevant, recent)
2. helpful (relevant, reliable, recent)
3. not helpful (not relevant as it does not relate to Hurston or Hurston's time)
4. helpful (assuming author reliable; relevant, recent)
5. possibly helpful (author is reliable; relevant because Hurston studied with the author during the time period)
6. helpful (Hurston's novel)
7. helpful (assuming author is reliable; relevant; contemporary to Hurston)

Use students' responses to the exercise to judge their skill in evaluating sources.

Cont. from p. 416

3. Recording and Organizing Information. This section includes guidelines for taking notes, writing a thesis statement, and developing an outline. Draw another note card on the chalkboard or on a piece of poster board and use the **Guidelines for Note Cards** on p. 420 to show how information should be recorded. Explain how

Reminder

To begin your research

- identify preliminary research questions
- using general reference works, develop an overview of your topic
- use library and community resources to find possible sources, recording full publishing information for each one on a source card
- evaluate each source according to the "4R" test (page 416)

WRITING ASSIGNMENT

PART 2:

Beginning Your Research

Follow the steps in the Reminder above to start your research, but remember that every research project is unique. Perhaps an instructional videotape, rather than an encyclopedia, could provide an overview of your topic. You may find all the sources you need in a library, or your topic may lead you first to a museum. Whatever path you follow, find at least five or six sources for your paper, each one carefully evaluated and then accurately recorded on a source card.

A DIFFERENT APPROACH

You may want to have students tell about their experiences in trying to evaluate books, magazines, audio tapes, CDs, or movie videos from their covers. Ask if anyone has ever rented a movie based strictly on how it looked on the box cover and then discovered the movie was horrible. At the conclusion of the discussion, point out that it's always best to make evaluations on criteria other than looks or first impressions.

quotations, summaries, and paraphrases should be handled. **Exercise 2** on p. 422 gives students practice in taking notes and **Exercise 3** on p. 424 covers conducting interviews. In **Writing Assignment: Part 3** (p. 424), students begin taking notes for their reports.

When you discuss **Writing a Thesis Statement** (p. 425), you might want to refer to the **Here's How** on p. 410, which shows how the topic on Zora Neale Hurston was selected. Compare that to the first sample thesis statement shown on p. 425. How has the topic been treated in the thesis statement? Help students realize the importance of a clear and concise yet thorough thesis statement to guide their writing.

In **Developing an Outline** (p. 426), rough and formal methods are discussed. If

TIMESAVER

If you've already covered the material on summarizing and paraphrasing in **Chapter 39: "Studying and Test Taking,"** you may want to bypass this **Taking Notes** section except for the **Guidelines for Note Cards.**

INTEGRATING THE LANGUAGE ARTS

Mechanics Link. To give students practice in using quotation marks to enclose a person's exact words, have students read about the use of quotation marks in **Chapter 30: "Punctuation,"** (pp. 878–885) and assign one or two exercises in using quotation marks for drill.

Prewriting

Recording and Organizing Information

Your source cards list promising sources of information. Your preliminary questions show some of the specific paths your research will take. Now it's time to collect the information you'll need and to find a way of organizing it.

Taking Notes

Before you begin to take notes, read through the material and think about its full meaning. Then go back over the material, using 4″ x 6″ cards to record your notes. Later, when you're organizing your report, cards make it easy to arrange and rearrange information. Here are more specific tips about note cards. A sample note card is shown on page 421.

GUIDELINES FOR NOTE CARDS

1. **Use a separate card or a half-sheet of paper for each source and item of information.** Again, this will pay off in ease of organizing.
2. **Record the source number.** In the upper right-hand corner of each note card, write the number you have assigned each source. This is important; it's a shorthand system to show exactly where you got the information.
3. **Write a label, or heading.** In the upper left-hand corner of the card, identify the main idea of your note so that you don't later have to reread each note card to discover its basic content.
4. **Write the page number(s).** At the end of your note, write the page numbers from which the information comes. Page references are required for the documentation in your paper.

There are two main kinds of notes you'll take: *direct quotations* and *summaries or paraphrases.*

you have any special requirements for outlining, explain to students what you would like. You might let students choose the form of outlining that works best for them. Analyze and discuss the outline on Hurston on p. 427 before having students do **Writing Assignment: Part 4** on p. 427.

GUIDED PRACTICE

You may want to guide students through **Exercises 1–3** and the **Critical Thinking Exercise.** You'll probably want to approve topics and interviewees for **Exercise 3** before students begin conducting their interviews.

Direct Quotations. Resist the urge to quote too much. Quote an author directly only when you want to be sure of technical accuracy or when the author's words are especially interesting or well phrased. Copy the statement exactly (including punctuation, capitalization, and spelling) and enclose it in quotation marks.

Summaries and Paraphrases. In most of your notes, you will record the author's ideas and facts *in your own words.* A ***summary*** is highly condensed—typically one fourth to one third the length of the original. A ***paraphrase*** is a restatement in your own words that allows for more detail.

Whether you summarize or paraphrase, you must use your own words and sentence structure. Try setting the passage aside and writing ideas from memory. Also, use lists and phrases—not complete sentences. (See pages 1018–1024 for information on more formal uses of summaries and paraphrases.)

Mules and Men by Zora Neale Hurston. Cover design by Suzanne Noli, Cover Illustration © 1990 by David Diaz. Courtesy of Harper Perennial, a Division of HarperCollins Publishers. All rights reserved.

SAMPLE NOTE CARD

early use of folk tales 5

Arna Bontemps (a black writer and Hurston's friend) says many of folk tales in Mules and Men were part of Hurston's storytelling before anthropology at Barnard. Some early short stories confirm his memory of hearing the tales when she first came to NY.

pp. 166–67

INTEGRATING THE LANGUAGE ARTS

Literature Link. To illustrate the difference between a summary and a paraphrase, have students summarize a poem, such as Emily Dickinson's "'Hope' Is the Thing with Feathers." Then have students paraphrase the poem, line by line. [Possible summary: Hope continues to comfort despite circumstances. Paraphrases should include an explanation of the metaphor of the bird that keeps singing.]

Speaking Link. You may want to have a few students research plagiarism—the meaning of the word, its history, and recent examples of plagiarism in the news—and have students give brief oral reports on their findings.

MEETING INDIVIDUAL NEEDS

LEARNING STYLES

Auditory Learners. Before students begin **Exercise 2** on p. 422, read aloud the excerpt on the Yanomama Indians and discuss any unfamiliar words, such as these:

1. *juggernaut*: big force that destroys all in its path
2. *obliteration*: total destruction
3. *plantains*: banana-like fruits
4. *unacculturated*: having a culture not merged with other cultures

INDEPENDENT PRACTICE

After you've discussed the prewriting stage and have guided students through the exercises, give students **Writing Assignment: Parts 1–4** as independent practice. Because prewriting is so critical to shaping a well-crafted research paper, you might want to give students a checklist of dates for completion of each task.

Assignment	Due Date	✓
Topic Selected		
Research Questions Posed		
Sources Located		
Notes Taken		
Thesis Statement Written		
Outline Developed		

ANSWERS

Exercise 2

Questions may vary. Here are some possibilities:

1. Who are the Yanomama and where do they live?
2. What is their culture and everyday life like?
3. How are they threatened? What may happen to them?
4. Why does this matter?

Source Card:

9

Reiss, Spender, "The Last Days of Eden," *Newsweek* 3 Dec. 1990: 48

writing textbook

Note Cards:

who & where are Yanomama 9

- world's largest remaining group of unacculturated tribal people
- live in Amazonian rain forest just north of the equator
- inhabit 60,000 square miles on Venezuelan-Brazilian border
- 9,000 Yanomama men, women, and children live in Brazil

WRITING NOTE

Remember that you must give the writer credit when you use an author's *words or ideas* in your paper. Not to do so is ***plagiarism,*** an extremely serious offense. Even a summary or paraphrase—if it is someone else's original idea—must be credited.

REFERENCE NOTE: For more help with summarizing and paraphrasing, see pages 1018–1024.

EXERCISE 2 **Taking Notes**

The following excerpt is from an article about the Yanomama Indians that appeared in *Newsweek,* December 3, 1990, on page 48. Assume that you're researching a paper on the world's ancient peoples (those most untouched by civilization) who are threatened by modern life. You've given the article the source number 9. Working with a partner, develop a list of questions using the *5W-How?* questions (page 27). Then prepare a source card and take notes on note cards to answer the questions you have written.

from The Last Days of Eden
by Spencer Reiss

Doshamosha-teri sits on a little hill near a bend in the clear black Siapa River, just north of the equator, in one of the least traveled regions of the Amazonian rain forest. Two dozen extended families of Yanomama Indians—149 broad-chested men, painted women and their children—live there, in one roughly circular thatch-roofed dwelling furnished only with bark hammocks. They cultivate small plots of plantains, gourds and bananas on the hillside. Beyond that the great wall of the emerald rain forest rises, enclosing a dazzling bazaar of wild pigs, monkeys and plumed birds. Most people in Doshamosha-teri ("Maggot-of-the-Gumba-Tree Place") have never heard of Venezuela, though they happen to live there. They have yet to invent the wheel. Their entire number system consists of "one," "two" and "many." Ask about abstractions such as work and

ASSESSMENT

The four writing assignments in this segment, which cover choosing a topic, researching, taking notes, and outlining, give you a good opportunity to measure students' understanding of the prewriting stage.

RETEACHING

Select a short, interesting video to show to students. Then ask students to discuss the following points about the video:

1. its broad subject
2. its limited topic and main idea (thesis statement)
3. its purpose and intended audience

leisure, poverty or wealth, and you get a blank stare. Life consists of survival. . . .

Until recently, the Yanomama had the good fortune to live their Stone Age lives on land that no one else wanted. Today their world, 60,000 square miles of rain forest straddling the Venezuelan-Brazilian border, sits in the path of the onrushing juggernaut of development. The 9,000 Yanomama in Brazil have dwindled by one sixth since the gold rush began three years ago, luring tens of thousands of prospectors—and the malaria and other diseases they carry. The dazed survivors are scattered among 19 reserves, gold-hungry miners pressing in from all sides. "The dangers to the Yanomama 20 years ago were minuscule compared to what they are now," anthropologist Napoleon Chagnon said during a recent three-day visit to Doshamosha-teri and other Yanomama settlements in Venezuela's remote Siapa River Valley. "The best we can hope for is a respite, long enough for them to consider their choices."

As the world's largest remaining group of unacculturated tribal people, the Yanomama represent a last chance for the modern world to atone for the savage obliteration of so many of the original Americans, North and South alike. Without fast action, the Yanomama will suffer the same fate—or, perhaps worse, give up their independent ways and join the modern world's long list of pathetic misfits. Governments, Indian activists and scientists agree on the need to save them. The question is, how?

culture & everyday life 9

- live in circular thatch-roofed homes, furnished with bark hammocks
- grow plantains, gourds, and bananas
- little understanding of the world (don't know they live in Venezuela)
- limited counting system ("one," "two," and "many")

threats to Yanomama 9

- their land lies in the path of development
- thousands of gold prospectors bring malaria and other diseases (Yanomama dwindled by 1/6 since gold rush began 3 years ago)
- Yanomama may be obliterated or become misfits in the modern world

last tribal people? 9

- Yanomama survivors scattered among 19 reserves
- represent last chance for modern world to atone for obliteration of Native Americans
- government, Indian activists, and scientists agree something should be done, but they don't know what

SELECTION AMENDMENT

Description of change: excerpted
Rationale: to focus on the concept of research reports presented in this chapter

4. its tone
5. possible sources used in researching the video (video credits should indicate some of these)

You also could require students to take notes while the video is being shown and then have each student make an outline of information contained in the video.

You may want to have students imagine that their research papers are to be turned into videos. Summarize the steps that they will follow in producing a research paper/video—selecting a specific topic; considering purpose, audience, and tone; getting an overview and finding sources; researching and taking notes; and preparing an outline.

ANSWERS

Exercise 3

Responses will vary. To help students generate subject ideas and names of knowledgeable people in the community, give them time to brainstorm together in class. You may want to give students the following checklist so that they can be sure they have covered all sections of the exercise:

1. Choose a subject.
2. Identify and contact a person knowledgeable about the subject.
3. Prepare a list of eight to ten questions.
4. Conduct the interview.
5. Write a follow-up note.
6. Compare interview notes with a partner's.

Be sure that students complete each section of the exercise. You may want to look over the students' questions and interview notes.

EXERCISE 3 Speaking and Listening: Conducting an Interview

It's one thing to take notes from a written passage; it's quite another to take notes while you are interviewing someone. To practice your interviewing techniques, get together with a partner and identify someone in your community who is knowledgeable about one of the following subjects or another subject of your choice:

emerging technologies
a local historical figure or building
high school or college athletics
domestic animals or wildlife

After you've chosen a subject and identified a person you could interview, contact that person and request an interview. Then, follow these steps:

- Using the *5W-How?* questioning strategy (page 27), prepare a list of eight to ten questions to ask. You may have to do a little background reading to prepare the questions.
- Limit the interview to twenty or thirty minutes, even if you don't finish all your questions. During the interview, one of you should ask the first four or five questions, and the other should ask the remaining four or five questions. Both of you should take notes related to all questions. Be sure to thank the interviewee orally.
- After you've finished the interview, write a follow-up note thanking the interviewee for his or her time. Then compare your interview notes with those of your partner. What are the differences? What do you think caused those differences?

WRITING ASSIGNMENT

PART 3:
Taking Notes

Look back at your preliminary research questions (from Writing Assignment, Part 2, page 419) to identify ideas you intend to explore further. Then start reading or viewing your sources and taking notes. Really think about which information you'll

CLOSURE

Ask students to briefly summarize the most important steps in the prewriting stage of the writing process and to tell the main purpose of each part of the writing assignment in the segment.

EXTENSION

Give students copies of a short research article from a popular magazine or a newspaper. After students have read the article, ask them to analyze the article and to discuss the following questions:

1. What is the subject of the article?
2. Why might the author have selected the subject?

need to remember and use when you write. If you aren't selective in your note taking, you will soon be buried in 4″ × 6″ note cards.

Writing a Thesis Statement

You may sit at your desk staring at a stack of notes without knowing what to do next. Read them—again. While you are recording information, you can't see your information as a whole. Once you have gathered your information, you need to review and reflect.

After rereading your notes, you should have a fairly clear picture of your report's main ideas, and you should be able to write a preliminary, or working, thesis statement. The ***thesis statement*** is a sentence or two stating both your topic and what you will say about it. It's an aid that will help keep you on track as you write your report. Still, your thesis may change as your writing progresses, and often you'll word it differently when drafting. Consider the thesis statement to be a guidepost, not a one-way road. Following are some examples of thesis statements for research papers.

SAMPLE THESIS STATEMENTS

Zora Neale Hurston's work in anthropology affected her fiction--its events, characters, and language.

In the 1960s, Senator Margaret Chase Smith of Maine had the qualifications to be president, but a woman was considered unelectable at the time.

The great Apache chief Cochise was quite different in real life from the Cochise shown in the movies.

COOPERATIVE LEARNING

Pair students and have them plan and conduct interviews with each other. Pairs could switch roles so that each student can be the interviewer and the interviewee. Have students decide upon their subjects and make up at least four questions for each interview. After practicing, have students discuss problems or questions about conducting interviews.

Give students these pointers for conducting interviews:

1. Be courteous and respectful during the interview.
2. Listen carefully.
3. Be mindful of your nonverbal signals.
4. Keep good eye contact with the interviewee.
5. Nod to show that you understand what is being said.
6. Smile occasionally so that the interview keeps a friendly tone.

3. What is the specific topic?
4. Why do you think the author limited the subject to this topic?
5. What is the purpose of the article?
6. Who is the audience?
7. What is the tone of the article?
8. What are three general research questions that the author may have asked about the topic?
9. Can you tell from the article what sources the author used?
10. Are these sources reliable?
11. What other sources might the author have used?
12. What is the article's thesis statement?
13. What are three details that support that thesis statement?

MEETING **INDIVIDUAL** NEEDS

LESS-ADVANCED STUDENTS

You may want to give students a review of important terms by using the following matching quiz:

1. primary source
2. paraphrase
3. plagiarism
4. thesis statement
5. formal outline
a. literary theft
b. gives main idea about topic
c. original information
d. prepared after report
e. restatement with more detail

[Answers: 1–c, 2–e, 3–a, 4–b, 5–d]

STUDENTS WITH SPECIAL NEEDS

Some learning disabled students have problems with classification, the underlying critical-thinking skill required for developing outlines. You may want to have students sort their note cards in class so that you or peer tutors can help them classify and label their cards.

Show students the value of outlines for guiding writing by having students write several paragraphs of their reports in class as they refer to their outlines. Suggest changes in outlines as needed or use peer tutors for guidance.

Zora Neale Hurston

Margaret Chase Smith

Cochise

REFERENCE NOTE: See pages 102–104 for more help with writing thesis statements.

Developing an Outline

After you have identified your thesis, you are ready to give order to your wealth of information. Start by sorting your note cards into stacks according to their labels. These stacks may immediately suggest the main sections or ideas of your report, as well as the ideas you will emphasize (the larger the stack of note cards, the more attention you will probably give to that idea in your report). Then you can decide how best to order the ideas and which supporting details to use, in which sequence.

Your working outline can be rough or more formal—whatever will give shape and direction to your drafting. But for your completed paper, your teacher may request a final, ***formal outline.*** This serves basically as a table of contents and is prepared *after* you've finished the report. Following is a portion of a final outline that a writer prepared for a report on Zora Neale Hurston. (Formal outlines often omit the introduction and conclusion.)

You may want to use this activity for whole-class discussion or for cooperative learning in small groups. ■

Folklore into Fiction:
The Writings of Zora Neale Hurston

I. Childhood in Eatonville
   A. Incorporated black town
   B. Early exposure to folklore
II. College years
   A. Morgan College and Howard University
   B. Early stories using folk tales and Eatonville
   C. Study of anthropology
      1. Ruth Benedict at Barnard College
      2. Franz Boas at Columbia University
         a. Decision to become social scientist
         b. Grant to collect southern folklore
III. Connections between anthropology and fiction
   A. Plots and characters
   B. Dialect and idiom
   C. Portrayal of black life

REFERENCE NOTE: See pages 107–108, 1018 for more on outlining.

WRITING ASSIGNMENT

PART 4:
Organizing Your Information

Doing a research paper doesn't have to be like entering a maze. To start organizing your information, remember your research questions and thesis statement, as well as the labels on your note cards. Develop a sense of your main ideas first. Then group your note cards and arrange them in a sensible order, and write a working outline for your draft.

MEETING INDIVIDUAL NEEDS

AT-RISK STUDENTS

Giving at-risk students more opportunity to discuss their progress on the reports every step of the way with classmates may help them through the stages of the writing process. You may want to pair students or to have students work in small groups throughout this chapter. Student pairs or groups could have regular meetings to talk about their progress and problems. Circulate during these meeting times to answer questions and to be sure students are following the writing stages.

SEGMENT 4 *(pp. 428–446)*

WRITING YOUR FIRST DRAFT

OBJECTIVES

- To plan and conduct a survey and to record findings in a table
- To determine whether or not information for a research paper should be documented
- To write a first draft of a research report, including citations
- To prepare a list of Works Cited from source cards

Teacher's ResourceBank™

RESOURCES

WRITING YOUR FIRST DRAFT
- Writing a Research Paper 90

QUOTATION FOR THE DAY

"Quotations are illustrations, not proofs." (Jacques Barzun, 1907– , author and literary consultant)

Explain to your students that their own thoughts must dominate their essays. Quotations are merely welcome guests, throwing light on a subject but in the end representing only other people's ideas.

MEETING INDIVIDUAL NEEDS

LEP/ESL

General Strategies. To give students needed extra practice with the Works Cited format, pair students needing practice. Create several versions of the Works Cited page following the model. One version could have the entries scrambled alphabetically. Another could have neither book titles nor journals underlined while a third could omit dates or punctuation. To focus students on details of the bibliographical form, tell them to correct the three versions and to compare them to the original on p. 434.

Writing Your First Draft

Structuring the Report

The research report is longer than most papers you write, with several special elements. Use the chart below to get an overview of a report's main parts.

ELEMENTS OF A RESEARCH REPORT	
Formal outline (optional)	Your teacher may ask you to include a final outline of the content of your report.
Title	Your title, often on a separate title page, should be both attention-catching and informative. Ask your teacher about format.
Introduction	Your introduction should draw readers into your report with interesting details or a striking quotation.
Thesis statement	The statement of your thesis should appear early, usually in or at the end of the introduction. It might be more than one sentence.
Body	Paragraphs in the body of your report should develop the main ideas that support the thesis statement.
Conclusion	The conclusion should briefly restate your thesis in different words, summarize your main points, or both.
Citations	Throughout the paper, you should include brief references in parentheses (or footnotes if your teacher recommends them) to credit sources for specific information.
Works Cited list	In a list at the end of the report, you should include all the sources you have cited.

The following writer's model, which shows how one writer used research findings to develop an original paper, can be a guide for writing your first draft. Notice how facts, quotations, and summaries of ideas are worked in. You will see source information in parentheses throughout the paper; these *citations* are fully explained on pages 438–441.

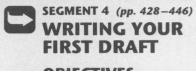

MOTIVATION

Remind students that painters frequently make preliminary sketches of their ideas before transferring the ideas to the final canvases. Tell students that they will be painting with words and that their rough drafts will be their preliminary sketches. Be sure students know that they don't have to get everything organized and correct at this point. Encourage students to enjoy using the information they've collected and putting it all together in ways that are uniquely their own. Stress the creativity involved in choosing facts and in finding relationships.

A WRITER'S MODEL

Folklore into Fiction:
The Writings of Zora Neale Hurston

INTRODUCTION
Interesting anecdote/ Summary of article, author named

In 1973, Alice Walker, the author of The Color Purple, made a sentimental visit to the all-black city of Eatonville, Florida. Her goal was to find the grave of a writer she greatly admired, Zora Neale Hurston. Hurston, a major figure of the Harlem Renaissance, died in poverty in 1960. Walker found no grave or marker in Eatonville, Hurston's hometown. Instead, she learned that her literary idol had been buried in an unmarked grave in a segregated cemetery in Fort Pierce, Florida. She commissioned a headstone, which now stands at the site:

ZORA NEALE HURSTON
"A GENIUS OF THE SOUTH"
NOVELIST FOLKLORIST
ANTHROPOLOGIST
1901 1960

Background information

It is significant that Alice Walker, poet, novelist, and winner of the Pulitzer Prize for fiction, would add "folklorist" and "anthropologist" to her description of the neglected author. For Zora Neale Hurston was more than a gifted novelist. She was also a perceptive student of her own culture, an author of two notable books of folklore, a member of the American FolkLore Society, the American Ethnological Society, and the American Anthropological Society (Hurston, Dust Tracks 171).

Thesis statement

Hurston's work as an anthropologist is, in fact, directly related to her creative writing. The connection is clear in many elements of her fiction.

BODY
Eatonville childhood

Hurston's life story begins in Eatonville, Florida, not far from Orlando. Eatonville was originally incorporated as an all-black town--a unique situation that had an impact throughout Hurston's life. Her

Important details

hometown was also her earliest training ground

TIMESAVER

Instead of discussing the basic elements of a research paper, the use of quotations, and documenting sources individually, you may want to combine these elements when you discuss the model research paper. You could then teach these items as you read through the paper. You may find this an especially good alternative method if your class is an advanced one.

MEETING INDIVIDUAL NEEDS

AT-RISK STUDENTS

Stagger the deadlines for completed first drafts to give more time to students who need it. You may need to compensate for home environments that would make writing especially difficult. If your schedule allows, you could set up additional first-draft meetings before or after school or during free periods to give at-risk students extra time to discuss their problems and to write their reports. You could also encourage students to discuss their writings with each other.

TEACHING THE LESSON

You'll probably want to begin this section with an overview of a report's main parts, which are covered in the **Elements of a Research Report** chart on p. 428. You may want to point out that a research paper includes the basic elements of any informative composition.

It might be useful when you discuss the chart to demonstrate how the elements fit together by passing around old research reports from other students. Make sure everyone has a chance to examine a report as you locate the elements.

Next, have students read **A Writer's Model** beginning on p. 429. Then use the

MEETING INDIVIDUAL NEEDS

LEARNING STYLES

Visual Learners. You may want to make a chart by copying the **Elements of a Research Report** chart on p. 428 onto poster board. This chart could be displayed in a prominent place in the classroom so that students can refer to it as needed.

Auditory Learners. Repetition aids memory, so make it a point to repeat the basic elements of a research report several times aloud during class. You may want to make the repetition into a quick, verbal fill-in-the-blank game or a question-and-answer game. For example, "A conclusion restates . . . ." or "What does a conclusion restate?" Repeat these several times until students know the answers quickly.

Direct quotation

(although she could hardly have realized it at the time) in black southern folklore, the place where she heard the local storytellers tell their big "lies" (Hurston, Dust Tracks 197).

Young Zora, whose father was a Baptist preacher, received little formal education and worked at menial jobs. However, she read whenever and whatever she could, and her great goal was education.

College years

Paying her own way, Hurston was able to study at Morgan College and Howard University. By that time she was already a writer, using folk tales and her hometown in her fiction. At Howard she wrote "John Redding Goes to Sea," which had "black folk beliefs" about witches' curses and screech owls (Ikonné 185-186). Another early short story, "Spunk," was set in "an unnamed village that is obviously Eatonville" (Hemenway 41, 77-78).

Specific examples

Authors and pages cited

Then came a turning point in her life. In 1925 she was admitted to prestigious Barnard College in New York City--its first black student (Howard, "Being Herself" 101-02). At Barnard, Hurston studied anthropology under Ruth Benedict. Just before she graduated, Franz Boas of Columbia University, another eminent anthropologist, read one of her term papers. Boas invited Hurston to study with him and gave her another way to look at the Eatonville tales she loved to tell. According to Lillie Howard, "She learned to view the good old lies and racy, sidesplitting anecdotes . . . as invaluable folklore, creative material that continued the African oral tradition . . ." ("Hurston" 135). Hurston decided then to become a serious social scientist. In 1927 Boas recommended her for the first of several grants she was to receive, and she headed south to gather folklore.

Study of anthropology

Author named in text, more than one title in Works Cited

Clearly, Hurston's attraction to her culture's stories and to writing fiction were always intertwined. Anthropology simply made her natural attention to black folklore and culture more systematic and intensive; as she said, "research is formalized curiosity" (qtd. in Chamberlain).

Writer's conclusion/ transitional statement

Direct quotation within a sentence

side glosses to focus a discussion on the organization and form of the paper.

Be sure that students understand the basic elements of an informative composition before they start writing their first drafts. You might want to have students locate the citations in **A Writer's Model** and discuss how they are presented. If you want students to use footnotes instead of citations, demonstrate how the footnotes should be handled. Tell students to refer to the form and organization of the model as they write their papers.

Discuss the Works Cited page to show how references should be organized and placed on the page. Make sure students ☛

Connections between anthropology and fiction

After she began doing fieldwork, she alternated between anthropological and creative writing. Her study of Eatonville folk tales and New Orleans hoodoo (voodoo) in 1927 and 1928 resulted in the book of folk tales Mules and Men, and she wrote her first novel, Jonah's Gourd Vine, soon after. Many critics have noted that all of Hurston's novels showed the effects of her study of anthropology, and one of the most obvious connections between the two appears in her fiction's plots and characters.

Plots and characters

Examples

Just one example of how Hurston's research worked into the plot of Jonah's Gourd Vine is the "bitter bone" that An' Dangie uses in a ritual to make Hattie invisible (200). In Mules and Men, Hurston reported how she underwent a whole ceremony to get the "Black Cat Bone," or bitter bone, of invisibility (272).

In later books, too, these connections occur. A field trip to Haiti and Jamaica in 1936 produced Tell My Horse, another study of voodoo. A year after its appearance she published the novel Moses, Man of the Mountain, which has been described as a blend of "fiction, folklore, religion, and comedy" (Howard, "Hurston" 140). In it, Moses is a "hoodoo man," an idea that also appears in Jonah's Gourd Vine (231).

Dialect and black idiom

Dialect and black idiom are also important parts of both Hurston's scientific work and her creative writing. She worked into her fiction the words she heard and researched in the field. According to her biographer, Robert Hemenway, the long sermon that is the climax of Jonah's Gourd Vine "was taken almost verbatim from Hurston's field notes" (197). The novel, in fact, contains so many folk sayings that Robert Bone has claimed ". . . they are too nonfunctional, too anthropological . . . " (127).

Most critics have agreed with Darryl Pinckney that Hurston's "ear for the vernacular of folk speech is impeccable" (56). Even a critic in 1937 who found Hurston's dialect "less convincing" than another writer's suggested that Hurston's dialect might be more realistic (Thompson). Her excellent

INTEGRATING THE LANGUAGE ARTS

Vocabulary Link. As students read the model, see if they can determine the meanings of the words below from the context. Write the terms on the chalkboard before students begin reading.

anthropology: science of human beings
menial: lowly
prestigious: honored
eminent: prominent, famous
intertwined: united
voodoo: an African religion
verbatim: word for word
vernacular: regional language or dialect
minstrel: performer of traditional folk melodies
patronizing: condescending, assuming a superior attitude

understand that it is an alphabetical list of the research references used in writing a paper. You might want to discuss how unusual sources should be handled and explain any additional requirements you may have for citing references.

Before students begin writing, you could review **Using Quotations** on p. 435. Use the examples in **Guidelines for Using Quotations** to demonstrate how quotations can be varied for interest.

You might review methods to create tables, charts, and graphs before students begin **Exercise 4** on p. 436. If you have computers available, seize the opportunity to use spreadsheet programs to experiment with graphs. It also may be helpful to display a variety of creative graphs or charts from

MEETING **INDIVIDUAL** NEEDS

ADVANCED STUDENTS

You may want to ask some students to make brief oral reports on Alice Walker and the Harlem Renaissance. Give students library time to research these topics. Have them write brief informal reports (two to three pages) to read to the class.

Other students may enjoy reading one or more of Hurston's novels mentioned in the report and then telling the class about the books and their opinions of the books.

These book reports could be written and read or could be presented informally from notes. You may want to encourage students to read a few excerpts from the books.

ear and her "skill at transcribing" (Young 220) made the language in her first novel something new and therefore somewhat hard to read:

Long quotation, indented; quotation marks for dialogue

> "Iss uh shame, Sister. Ah'd cut down dat Jonah's gourd vine in uh minute, if Ah had all de say-so. You know Ah would, but de majority of 'em don't keer whut he do, some uh dese people stands in wid it. De man mus' is got roots uh got piece uh dey tails buried by his door-step. . . ." (230)

However, some black writers of Hurston's time disapproved of her "playing the minstrel" in her fiction's use of southern black dialect--and in other ways as well. Zora Neale Hurston was in fact a controversial figure within the Harlem Renaissance. She was attacked for her novels' picture of black life, and this portrayal is another connection between her anthropology and her fiction (Howard, "Being Herself" 156).

Portrayal of black life

Background: *Harlem Renaissance*

Hurston came to New York when the Harlem Renaissance was in full bloom. This literary movement of the 1920s included such noted writers as Langston Hughes, Countee Cullen, Jean Toomer, and Arna Bontemps. They, too, were celebrating blackness and bringing it to the public, but they saw their mission as "a guiding elite" for other blacks who were not as liberated (Pinckney 55). They didn't want to support a stereotyped image in art. Sterling Brown even attacked Hurston's nonfiction. He said that "Mules and Men should be more bitter" (qtd. in Howard, "Hurston" 139).

Paraphrase

Hurston, on the other hand, believed she was serving an unmet need. Negro folklore had always fascinated the American public; but it had been presented mostly by white writers (such as Joel Chandler Harris), and to her it seemed either patronizing or inadequate (Wilson 109). She wanted to put it in its true social context.

Moreover, Hurston felt her picture of blacks in Jonah's Gourd Vine and in Their Eyes Were Watching God, generally regarded as her finest magazines to demonstrate how numerical data can be made interesting.

Read the **What to Document** chart on p. 437 and use **A Writer's Model** as a reference to guide students. Assign **Exercise 5** on p. 437 to give students practice in deciding what material needs to be documented.

You might use the **Parenthetical Citations** and **List of Works Cited** sections on pp. 438–446 as demonstrations or as references, depending upon the needs of your class. Stress that all the guidelines are to be understood and referred to rather than memorized. The guidelines should be helpful to students in organizing their papers.

You may want to devise a time-table for writing the first draft. Depending on the nature and capabilities of your class, give

novel, was thoroughly realistic. She felt that the Harlem Renaissance writers were unfairly criticizing her fiction because it didn't have a political message. She said they believed ". . . Negroes were supposed to write about the Race Problem," while her intent in Jonah's Gourd Vine was "to tell . . . a story about a man" (Dust Tracks 214).

Several sources used as support

Hurston did not intend to be a reformer if it meant falsifying what she saw as a scientist and wanted to achieve as an artist. Through her fieldwork she knew intimately the everyday, "normal life of Negroes in the South," and that's what she focused on in much of her fiction (Thompson). Also, her study of many cultures showed her that folk tales functioned, in part, the same way all over the world, as "communal tradition in which distinctive ways of behaving and coping with life were orally transmitted" (Pinckney 56). Hurston thought the tales were sophisticated and important and should be shown as they were. Margaret Wilson sums up Hurston's anthropological and fictional beliefs this way: "She saw people as people" (110).

Writer's addition in brackets

Two sources cited at once

So even though critics like Richard Wright, Alain Locke, and Sterling Brown objected to the "minstrel image" of blacks in a novel such as Their Eyes Were Watching God, other critics saw both a realistic, vibrant main character (Janie) and Hurston's "fullest description of the mores [customs and values] in Eatonville" (Hemenway 241-42; Pinckney 56). Perhaps Hurston would have been more "race conscious" if she had not grown up in and studied Eatonville, a wholly self-governing black town; but that does not negate the reality of what she observed and transformed into fiction (Wilson 109; Pinckney 56).

CONCLUSION

Restatement of thesis

Clincher statement

For better or worse, Hurston's fictional world-- its plots, characters, language, and picture of life-- grew out of the folklore she had heard as a child and then studied as a professional. Like the fine anthropologist she was, Zora Neale Hurston intended to get that world down on paper, and to get it down right.

INTEGRATING THE LANGUAGE ARTS

Literature Link. To take a closer look at Zora Neale Hurston the person and writer, students could read an excerpt from one of her books. For example, if your literature book contains *Dust Tracks on a Road,* you could assign the story about two women visiting Hurston's school. Then have students discuss what the excerpt reveals about Hurston's personality and her writing style. In that excerpt, for example, readers learn that Hurston was very perceptive as a child and that her writing was filled with lively images and descriptions.

Vocabulary Link. You may want to point out the effective use of transitional expressions in the model. Ask students to read the model and to identify words and phrases that indicate the relationships between ideas. For example, *instead* is used in the first paragraph, and *for, also,* and *in fact* are used in the second paragraph.

Encourage students to use transitional expressions to make their own writing clearer.

students a definite length requirement for their first drafts. You might want to include this on any checklist for prewriting that you use.

INDEPENDENT PRACTICE

You could give students time in class (perhaps one or two days) to start writing their first drafts (**Writing Assignment: Part 5** on p. 446) so that you can assist them with any initial problems. Be sure that students have interesting introductions and clear thesis statements.

MEETING INDIVIDUAL NEEDS

LEARNING STYLES

Kinetic Learners. You may want to have students write or type the Works Cited for **A Writer's Model** before they study the **Guidelines for Preparing the List of Works Cited** on p. 442. For a kinetic learner the action of writing itself rather than analyzing something visually is the best way to imprint what he or she needs to learn.

TIMESAVER

You may want to appoint a student or a student team to be in charge of checking Works Cited forms for all reports and helping other students with problems in preparing their Works Cited pages. Such a technical task might appeal to some students, greatly help others (especially at-risk and less-advanced students), and save you time.

MLA NOTE

The MLA calls for a five-space indent. For the typeface used in this book, the five-space indent translates into a printer's measure which is slightly different.

Works Cited

Bone, Robert. The Negro Novel in America. New Haven: Yale UP, 1958.

Chamberlain, John. "Books of the Times." New York Times 7 Nov. 1942: 13.

Hemenway, Robert E. Zora Neale Hurston: A Literary Biography. Urbana: U of Illinois P, 1977.

Howard, Lillie P. "Zora Neale Hurston." Dictionary of Literary Biography. 1987 ed.

---. "Zora Neale Hurston: Just Being Herself." Essence Nov. 1980: 100+.

Hurston, Zora Neale. Dust Tracks on a Road: An Autobiography. Philadelphia: Lippincott, 1942.

---. Jonah's Gourd Vine. Philadelphia: Lippincott, 1934, 1971.

---. Moses, Man of the Mountain. Philadelphia: Lippincott, 1939.

---. Mules and Men. Philadelphia: Lippincott, 1935.

---. Tell My Horse: Voodoo and Life in Haiti and Jamaica. Philadelphia: Lippincott, 1938.

Ikonné, Chidi. From Du Bois to Van Vechten: The Early New Negro Literature, 1903-1926. Westport: Greenwood, 1981.

Pinckney, Darryl. "In Sorrow's Kitchen." New York Review of Books 21 Dec. 1978: 55-57.

Thompson, Ralph. "Books of the Times." New York Times 6 Oct. 1937: 23.

Walker, Alice. "In Search of Zora Neale Hurston." Ms. Mar. 1975: 74+.

Wilson, Margaret F. "Zora Neale Hurston: Author and Folklorist." Negro History Bulletin Oct.-Nov.-Dec. 1982: 109-10.

Young, James O. Black Writers of the Thirties. Baton Rouge: Louisiana State UP, 1973.

You could suggest that each student freewrite various ideas for interesting introductions and select the best one for the first draft. Also, check to be sure that students are properly citing their sources and correctly using quotations.

Have students write the remainder of their first drafts on their own after you think students have a good understanding of the basic elements of an informative composition and know how to document sources correctly.

Using Quotations

Even though much of what you put in your report will be summarized or paraphrased, you'll find that good quotations, especially short ones, can add interest and authority to your writing. You can work quotations smoothly into your paper in several ways.

GUIDELINES FOR USING QUOTATIONS

1. ***Quote a whole sentence, introducing it in your own words.***

   EXAMPLE Margaret Wilson sums up Hurston's belief this way: "She saw people as people" (110).

2. ***Quote part of a sentence within a sentence of your own.***

   EXAMPLE The long sermon "was taken almost verbatim from Hurston's field notes" (Hemenway 197).

3. ***Quote just one or a few words within a sentence of your own.***

   EXAMPLE Eatonville was where she heard the local storytellers tell their "lies" (Hurston, Dust Tracks 197).

4. ***Use ellipses (three spaced dots) to indicate omissions from quotations.*** Sometimes you need only a part of a quotation to make your point. Use ellipses to indicate words deleted within a quotation or any deletion that leaves a quotation that appears to be a complete sentence but is only part of the original.

   EXAMPLE According to Lillie Howard, "She learned to view the good old lies . . . as invaluable folklore . . . " ("Hurston" 136).

5. ***Set off longer quotations as "blocks."*** If a quotation will be more than four typed lines, start a new line, indent the entire quotation ten spaces from the left, and do not use quotation marks. Double-space a long quotation just like the rest of your report. For an example, see the blocked quotation on page 432. [Note: The example uses quotation marks because it is *dialogue* in the source.]

MEETING INDIVIDUAL NEEDS

LESS-ADVANCED STUDENTS

Have each student work with a partner to find two examples from printed sources (newspapers, magazines, books) that illustrate the five guidelines for using and punctuating direct quotations. Have students underline the examples. Then have students exchange examples and tell the guideline numbers for each example.

A DIFFERENT APPROACH

Students could engage their imaginations and practice using quotations at the same time. Have students imagine that they are each writing an article for a community magazine about school life. Have them base their articles on facts or made-up material. They should include quotation from real or made-up sources. Have them include quotation lead-ins such as the following ones:

1. "As ____ stated, . . .,"
2. "According to ____ . . .,"
3. "____ reports that . . . ."

ASSESSMENT

Use the students' first drafts to assess their comprehension of the techniques involved in writing research reports. Be sure to check the documentation of sources and use of quotations.

RETEACHING

If some students are still having difficulty mastering the basics of writing a research report, you could let them analyze the form and organization of three or four magazine or newspaper articles of their own choosing. You might transfer an article to a transparency and guide them through the process first.

ANSWERS

Exercise 4

Answers may vary. You may want to approve the wording and content of students' surveys. Surveys should cover only student finances and spending habits to arrive at data for the table. Students' surveys should be given to representative groups so that the data has some validity.

INTEGRATING THE LANGUAGE ARTS

Technology Link. Computer programs that set up tables, charts, and graphs, such as those in spreadsheet programs, can be useful for research papers. When you assign **Exercise 4,** you may want to ask one or two students who are adept at various programs to demonstrate some software for these purposes.

You may also want to point out the footnoting capabilities of modern word-processing programs, which can save time and reduce frustrations.

EXERCISE 4 Creating Tables, Charts, and Graphs

Sometimes neither summary nor quotation is the best method of presenting source information to readers. For numerical data or other detailed facts, a table, chart, or graph can show a great deal of information clearly and compactly. You can use a chart you find during research or create your own. (For more information on creating charts, see pages 39–41 and 1017.)

Suppose you're writing a paper about the role teenagers play in the national economy. To practice putting research findings into graphic form, work with others to conduct a survey of students about finances and spending habits. Use an anonymous questionnaire, and survey representative groups, perhaps all members of one homeroom at each grade level. Find out the facts indicated in the sample table, and follow its form to display your findings. [Note: *Discretionary spending* is spending for personal, nonessential purposes—a student's "free" money.] The sample table follows the MLA style.

Table 1

Average Weekly Income and Discretionary Spending of Students at [High School Name, Year][a]

	Allowance	Earnings	Discretionary Spending	% of Total Income
Seniors	$ —	$ —	$ —	—
Juniors	$ —	$ —	$ —	—
Sophomores	$ —	$ —	$ —	—
Freshmen	$ —	$ —	$ —	—

[a] Figures based on a survey of [Report the number of students surveyed and the groups they represent]

Tell students to identify the introduction, thesis statement, body, and conclusion of each article. You also could have each student make a rough outline of the content of at least one article. If time permits, have students discuss whether or not they think the articles are well organized and interesting.

CLOSURE

Ask students to list the basic elements of an informative composition that are to be included in a research report.

Documenting Sources

Deciding which information you must ***document,*** or give credit for, in a research paper sometimes requires thought. That thought process can start with noticing what is or is not documented when you read reports of research. The following guidelines will also help you stay clear of documentation pitfalls.

WHAT TO DOCUMENT

1. In general, don't document information that appears in several sources or facts that appear in standard reference books. For example, a statement like "*Their Eyes Were Watching God* is generally considered Hurston's finest novel" needs no documentation because it clearly relies on several sources. The main facts of her life that are available in encyclopedias and other standard references also do not need to be credited.
2. Document the source of each direct quotation (unless it's very widely known, such as Patrick Henry's "Give me liberty or give me death!").
3. Document any original theory or opinion other than your own. Since ideas belong to their authors, you must not present the ideas of other people as your own.
4. Document the source of data or other information from surveys, scientific experiments, and research studies.
5. Document unusual, little known, or questionable facts and statistics.

EXERCISE 5 **Judging What to Document**

If each of the following items were to appear in a research paper on the baseball player Christy Mathewson, which ones would you need to document? Discuss your responses in class.

1. Christy Mathewson, a right-handed pitcher, played for the New York Giants from 1900 to 1916.
2. A little-known Chicago Cub first baseman, Vic Saier, hit five career home runs off Mathewson—more than any other player. 2. document

COOPERATIVE LEARNING

Deciding when to give credit can be difficult even for your best writers. To help students see the difference between general information and information that needs to be documented, divide the class into four groups and assign each group a different author about whom information is widely and easily available.

Each group member should consult reference books and write down one fact about the assigned author that should be documented and one fact that would not need to be documented, according to the guidelines. Group members should discuss the information and make decisions about documenting.

ENRICHMENT

By adapting the material in **A Writer's Model,** students could prepare a reader's theater presentation about the life and writings of Zora Neale Hurston. You could assign a group of interested students to write the script. Tell them to use the information in the research paper but to emphasize the dramatic aspects of the author's life.

You could suggest that the writers turn some parts of the essay into dialogue for Alice Walker, Hurston herself, or other people mentioned in the paper. Then the writers should divide the script into sections to be read by students (perhaps around six students). The students will read their parts of the scripts, but they should use dramatic

VISUAL CONNECTIONS

Exploring the Subject. Christopher Mathewson was born in 1880 in Factoryville, Pennsylvania. His nicknames were Christy and Big Six. Noted for his number of strikeouts, Mathewson became famous for developing a reverse curve pitch called a "fadeaway." He died in 1925 and was elected to the National Baseball Hall of Fame in 1936, the very first year of balloting.

SELECTION AMENDMENT

Description of change: excerpted
Rationale: to focus on the concept of research reports presented in this chapter

3. About Mathewson's early death, Kenesaw Mountain Landis said, "Why should God wish to take a thoroughbred like Matty so soon, and leave some others down here that could well be spared?" **3. document**
4. The grave of Christy Mathewson is in City Cemetery, Lewisburg, Pennsylvania.
5. Luke Salisbury, commenting on Eric Rolfe Greenberg's novel *The Celebrant*, said that Mathewson embodied baseball. **5. document**

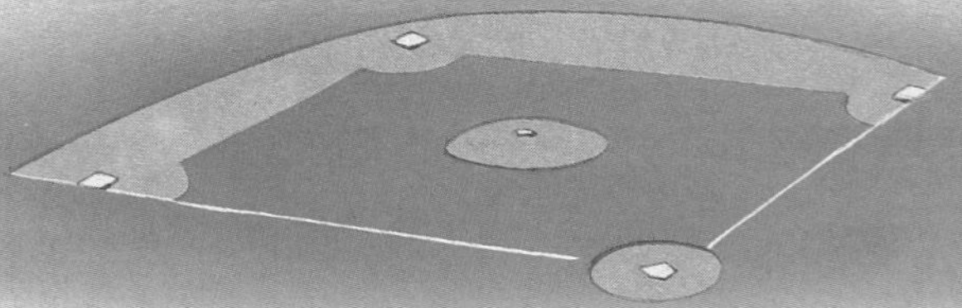

Parenthetical Citations. A ***parenthetical citation*** gives source information in parentheses in the body of a research paper. There are two main issues concerning the handling of these citations: (1) Exactly where does the citation go? (2) What are the content and correct form of the citation?

To determine where to place a citation, you can follow the general rules given below. You'll also find it helpful to look at the Writer's Model to see how citations appear there.

PLACEMENT OF CITATIONS

1. Place the citation as close as possible to the material it documents, if possible at the end of a sentence or at another point of punctuation.
2. Place the citation *before* the punctuation mark of the sentence, clause, or phrase you are documenting.

   EXAMPLE Her best work appeared after she had abandoned the narrow academic approach (Hemenway 215).

(continued)

inflections and gestures as appropriate for their characters or material. ■

PLACEMENT OF CITATIONS *(continued)*

3. **For a quotation that ends a sentence, put the citation *after* the quotation mark but *before* the end punctuation mark.**

   EXAMPLE As Lillie P. Howard points out, "She wasn't but had sense enough to say that she was" ("Being Herself" 160).

4. **For an indented quotation, put the citation *two spaces after* the final punctuation mark.**

   EXAMPLE **(See page 432.)**

The content and form of parenthetical citations are fairly easy once you understand the basic principle, which is this: *The citation should provide just enough information to lead the reader to the full source listing in Works Cited.*

Since the Works Cited list is alphabetized by authors' last names, an author's last name and the page numbers are usually enough. There are some exceptions of course; information about some of them is given below.

- A nonprint source such as an interview or audiotape will not have a page number.
- A print source of fewer than two pages (such as a one-page letter) will not require a page number.
- If you name the author in your sentence, you need give only the page number (for print sources of more than one page) in parentheses:

  According to her biographer, Robert Hemenway, the long sermon that is the climax of Jonah's Gourd Vine "was taken almost verbatim from Hurston's field notes" (197).

- If the author has more than one work in the Works Cited list, you will also have to give a short form of the title so readers will know which work you are citing:

  (Hurston, Dust Tracks 171).

Sources do vary, of course, and you'll sometimes have to refer to guidelines for correct form. The chart that follows shows the form for seven kinds of sources.

MEETING INDIVIDUAL NEEDS

LESS-ADVANCED STUDENTS

You may want to help students, either individually or in groups, complete the outline of **A Writer's Model.** Creating an outline may help them to visualize the concise and logical overall organization of the report. First, refer them to the formal outline on p. 427, which begins outlining the model. Tell students that the side glosses in the model indicate the Roman numerals for the outline and the location of details. Refer them to the first two Roman numerals in the outline and to the side glosses. [Students' suggestions for other Roman numerals may vary. Other Roman numerals may include Study of Anthropology, Connections Between Anthropology and Fiction, and Portrayal of Black Life.]

COOPERATIVE LEARNING

After students have read the report about Zora Neale Hurston, you may want to divide the class into three or four groups to consider the existing title and alternative titles for the report. Instruct group members to discuss whether or not the model's title is both attention-catching and informative. Then instruct each student in the group to suggest at least one other title for the paper. Group members should vote on the best title suggested and report that title to the rest of the class. The class then could choose the best one of the suggested titles (or decide the existing title is the best one). You could emphasize the importance of titles to attract readers.

BASIC CONTENT AND FORM FOR PARENTHETICAL CITATIONS

These examples assume that the author or work has not already been named in a sentence introducing the source's information.

Works by One Author

Author's last name and a page reference	(Hemenway 197)

Separate Passages in a Single Work

Author's last name and multiple page references	(Hemenway 41, 77-78)

Works by More than One Author

All authors' last names or *et al.* ("and others") if over three	(Brooks and Warren 24) (Anderson et al. 313)

Multivolume Works

Author's last name plus volume and page	(Cattell 2: 214-15)

Works with a Title Only

Full title (if short) or a shortened version	("Old Eatonville" 2) (<u>World Almanac</u> 809)

Literary Works Published in Many Editions

As above, but with other identifying information after a semicolon (for example, act and scene numbers)	(Shakespeare, <u>Hamlet</u> III. 4. 107–08)

Indirect Sources

Abbreviation *qtd. in* [quoted in] before the source	(qtd. in Howard 161)

More than One Work in the Same Citation

Citations separated with semicolons	(Bone 127; Pinckney 56)

[Note: One-page articles do not require a page number.]

WRITING NOTE

Your teacher may want you to use a documentation style different from the parenthetical citation system just discussed. The other common system uses footnotes or endnotes. Footnotes and endnotes are identical except that a footnote is placed at the bottom of the page where you use the source information, while endnotes are listed all together at the end of the report.

Each note is numbered, and a number also appears in the body of your report. The first note for a source gives full information; following notes are shortened. You will need guidelines to prepare notes. One example follows.

EXAMPLE

Note number in body of report	The long sermon "was taken almost verbatim from Hurston's field notes."[3]
Note (full form)	[3] Robert E. Hemenway, Zora Neale Hurston: A Literary Biography (Urbana: U of Illinois P, 1977) 197.

"Writing is the only thing that, when I do it, I don't feel I should be doing something else."

Gloria Steinem

List of Works Cited. As its name tells you, the Works Cited list contains all the sources, print and nonprint, that you credit in your report. (The term *Works Cited* is a broader title than *Bibliography,* which refers to print sources only.) You may have used other sources, such as general reference works, but if you didn't need to name them, you don't include them in a Works Cited list. (However, some teachers want a list of Works Consulted—all the sources you examined, whether cited or not, instead of, or in addition to, the Works Cited list. Ask to be sure.)

LIST OF WORKS CITED

Another type of source list used either to describe or to evaluate the contents of sources is an annotated bibliography. Students may need to produce an annotated bibliography to summarize what they have examined or researched about a given subject.

The form of an annotated bibliography is very similar to that of a Works Cited, except that after each entry, the writer includes either descriptive or evaluative notes on the source. Also, some annotated bibliographies are arranged in chronological order rather than in alphabetical order. The following entry is an example from an annotated bibliography:

Parrott, Thomas M. *William Shakespeare: A Handbook.* New York: Charles Scribner's Sons, 1955. A narration and interpretation of Shakespeare's life and works.

SELECTION AMENDMENT

Description of change: excerpted

Rationale: to focus on the concept of research reports presented in this chapter

CRITICAL THINKING
Analysis

Tell students that after reading **A Writer's Model,** some of them may have the opinion that Zora Neale Hurston was one of America's most important writers during the 1930s. Then explain that an opinion is a statement that can be supported by facts but that is not itself a fact. Tell the class that an opinion should be supported with facts and with reasoned arguments.

Instruct students to use information in **A Writer's Model** to give you two reasons why they might consider Hurston to be one of America's most important writers during the 1930s. [Responses will vary. Possible answers are her use and preservation of dialect and her realistic portrayal of black life.]

GUIDELINES FOR PREPARING THE LIST OF WORKS CITED

1. Center the words *Works Cited* on a new sheet of paper.
2. Begin each entry on a separate line. Position the first line of the entry even with the left margin and indent the second and all other lines five spaces. Double-space all entries.
3. Alphabetize the sources by the author's last name. If there is no author, alphabetize by title, ignoring *A, An,* and *The* and using the first letter of the next word.
4. If you use two or more sources by the same author, include the author's name only in the first entry. For all other entries, write three hyphens where the author's name would normally be, followed by a period (---.).

You can use the following sample entries, which use MLA style, as a reference for preparing your Works Cited list. All of the information you need to prepare your list is already on your source cards. Notice that you supply page numbers only for articles or other works that are one part of a whole work, such as one essay in a collection of essays.

SAMPLE ENTRIES FOR THE LIST OF WORKS CITED

Standard Reference Works

When an author of an entry is given in a standard reference work, that person's name is written first. Otherwise, the title of the book or article appears first. Page and volume numbers aren't needed if the work alphabetizes entries. For common reference works, only the edition year is needed.

ENCYCLOPEDIA ARTICLE

"Hurston, Zora Neale." Encyclopedia Americana. 1991 ed.

ARTICLE IN A BIOGRAPHICAL REFERENCE BOOK

Howard, Lillie P. "Zora Neale Hurston." Dictionary of Literary Biography. 1987 ed.

(continued)

SAMPLE ENTRIES FOR THE LIST OF WORKS CITED *(continued)*

Books

ONE AUTHOR

Huggins, Nathan Irvin. Harlem Renaissance. New York: Oxford UP, 1971.

TWO AUTHORS

Logan, Rayford W., and Irving S. Cohen. The American Negro: Old World Background and New World Experience. Boston: Houghton, 1970.

THREE AUTHORS

Bell, Roseann, Bettye Parker, and Beverly Gwy-Sheftall. Sturdy Black Bridges: Visions of Black Women in Literature. Garden City: Anchor, 1979.

FOUR OR MORE AUTHORS

Anderson, Robert, et al. Elements of Literature: Fifth Course. Austin: Holt, 1989.

NO AUTHOR SHOWN

American Statistics Index. Washington: Congressional Information Service, 1992.

EDITOR OF A COLLECTION OF WRITINGS

Locke, Alain, ed. The New Negro: An Interpretation. New York: Boni, 1925.

TWO OR THREE EDITORS

Meier, August, and Elliott Rudwick, eds. The Making of Black America: Essays in Negro Life and History. New York: Atheneum, 1969.

TRANSLATION

Niane, D. T. Sundiata: An Epic of Old Mali. Trans. G. D. Pickett. London: Longman, 1965.

Selections Within Books

FROM A BOOK OF WORKS BY ONE AUTHOR

Hughes, Langston. "April Rain Song." The Dream Keeper and Other Poems. New York: Knopf, 1932. 8.

(continued)

INTEGRATING THE LANGUAGE ARTS

Vocabulary Link. You may want to refer students to the section in **Chapter 2: "Understanding Paragraph Structure"** on connecting ideas within and between sentences in a paragraph. Explain that direct references and transitional expressions are also used to connect ideas between paragraphs in longer compositions. You could display an article from a newspaper or a magazine on the overhead projector and ask students to find the direct references and transitional expressions that help link ideas between paragraphs.

A DIFFERENT APPROACH

Encourage interested students to provide visuals for their research reports. They should be thinking of ideas for illustrations as they write and complete their first drafts. You could help students select appropriate visual categories based on their topics. For example, some topics may lend themselves to paintings or drawings, while others may be best illustrated with models or maps. Students could provide original visuals or find appropriate existing visuals. Students can be creative in designing their artwork, but they can also be creative in selecting visuals.

SAMPLE ENTRIES FOR THE LIST OF WORKS CITED *(continued)*

FROM A BOOK OF WORKS BY SEVERAL AUTHORS

Hemenway, Robert. "Zora Neale Hurston and the Eatonville Anthropology." The Harlem Renaissance Remembered: Essays Edited with a Memoir. Ed. Arna Bontemps. New York: Dodd, 1972. 190-214.

FROM A COLLECTION OF LONGER WORKS (NOVELS, PLAYS)

Edmonds, Randolph. Bad Man. The Negro Caravan. Ed. Sterling A. Brown, Arthur P. Davis, and Ulysses Lee. New York: Arno, 1969. 507-34. [Bad Man is a play. The Negro Caravan is a collection.]

Articles from Magazines, Newspapers, and Journals

FROM A WEEKLY MAGAZINE

Huggins, Nathan Irvin. "The Negro Artist and the Racial Mountain." Nation 23 June 1926: 692-94.

FROM A MONTHLY OR QUARTERLY MAGAZINE

Howard, Lillie P. "Zora Neale Hurston: Just Being Herself." Essence Nov. 1980: 100+. [The + sign indicates that the article isn't printed on consecutive pages.]

WITH NO AUTHOR SHOWN

"The Battle for Malcolm X." Newsweek 26 Aug. 1991: 52-54.

FROM A DAILY NEWSPAPER, WITH A BYLINE

Chamberlain, John. "Books of the Times." New York Times 7 Nov. 1942: 13.

FROM A DAILY NEWSPAPER, WITHOUT A BYLINE

"Zora Hurston, 57, Writer, Is Dead." New York Times 5 Feb. 1960: 27.

UNSIGNED EDITORIAL FROM A DAILY NEWSPAPER, NO CITY IN TITLE

"The Last Hurrah." Editorial. Star-Ledger [Newark, NJ] 29 Aug. 1991: 30.

(continued)

SAMPLE ENTRIES FOR THE LIST OF WORKS CITED *(continued)*

FROM A SCHOLARLY JOURNAL

Beal, Frances. "Slave of a Slave No More." Black Scholar 6 (1975): 2-10.

Other Sources

PERSONAL INTERVIEW

Wilson, August. Personal interview. 27 Aug. 1990.

TELEPHONE INTERVIEW

Brooks, Gwendolyn. Telephone interview. 3 Nov. 1991.

PUBLISHED INTERVIEW

Walker, Alice. Interview. Interviews with Black Writers. Ed. John O'Brien. New York: Liveright, 1973. 185-211.

RADIO OR TELEVISION INTERVIEW

Morrison, Toni. All Things Considered. Natl. Public Radio. WNYC, New York. 16 Feb. 1986.

UNPUBLISHED LETTER

Hurston, Zora Neale. Letter to Mary Holland. 13 June 1955. Historical Collection. U of Florida, Gainesville.

UNPUBLISHED THESIS OR DISSERTATION

Ward, Hazel Mae. "The Black Woman as Character: Images in the American Novel, 1852-1953." Diss. U of Texas, Austin, 1977.

CARTOON

Frascino, Edward. Cartoon. New Yorker 2 Sep. 1991: 46.

SPEECH OR LECTURE

King, Rev. Martin Luther, Jr. "I Have A Dream." Lincoln Memorial. Washington, 28 Aug. 1963.

RECORDING

Robeson, Paul. "Going Home." Rec. 9 May 1958. Paul Robeson at Carnegie Hall. Vanguard, VCD-72020, 1986.

(continued)

MEETING **INDIVIDUAL** NEEDS

LESS-ADVANCED STUDENTS

As a review, you may want to give students the following true-or-false test:

1. A Works Cited contains only print material. [false]
2. A parenthetical citation is placed at the bottom of a page. [false]
3. In general, facts that appear in standard reference books are not documented. [true]
4. Use dashes to indicate omissions from quotations. [false]
5. A thesis statement should appear early in the paper. [true]

SAMPLE ENTRIES FOR THE LIST OF WORKS CITED *(continued)*

FILM, FILMSTRIP, OR VIDEOTAPE

<u>The Color Purple</u>. Dir. Steven Spielberg. With Danny Glover, Whoopi Goldberg, Margaret Avery, and Oprah Winfrey. Warner Bros., 1985. [The title, director, distributor, and year are standard information. You may add other information, such as performers.]

Shoe, by Jeff MacNelly, reprinted by permission: Tribune Media Services.

WRITING ASSIGNMENT

PART 5:
Writing Your First Draft

Using your outline, note cards, and any other prewriting notes, write the first draft of your research report. As with any draft, focus on getting your ideas down, not writing with a final polish. Also, don't worry unnecessarily about the mechanics of your parenthetical documentation. While drafting, just insert a citation with basic information wherever you *think* one may be needed; you can check and correct the form later (see pages 439–440) and delete any unnecessary citations. When you have finished writing, prepare your list of Works Cited from your source cards, using the sample entries as guides (pages 442–446). Include only the sources you credited in the text.

SEGMENT 5 *(pp. 447–449)*

EVALUATING AND REVISING

OBJECTIVES

- To analyze a writer's revisions
- To apply evaluating and revising guidelines to one's own and another's research reports

TEACHING THE LESSON

Tell students that they need to stand back and look at their writing objectively and to think about what needs to be improved. Remind students that their goals are to turn rough drafts into polished papers.

The **Evaluating and Revising Research Reports** chart on p. 448 provides a focal point for teaching this section. Be ☛

Evaluating and Revising

You've put a great deal of work into your paper so far. Take some time to assess the content, organization, and presentation of your material, using the chart on page 448.

EXERCISE 6 **Analyzing a Writer's Revisions**

In a small group, discuss the following revised paragraph from the Writer's Model (page 431). Use the questions below and the guidelines on page 448 to explore the writer's changes.

In later books, too, these connections occur. *A field trip to Haiti and Jamaica in 1936 produced* Tell My Horse, *another story of voodoo.* ~~"By 14 April 1936 she was in the Caribbean, collecting material for her second book of folklore, Tell My Horse (1938)" (Howard, Hurston 139).~~ — replace

~~Hurston had been working for the WPA Federal Theater Project before that.~~ — cut

A year after ~~Tell My Horse~~ *its appearance* she published the novel Moses, Man of the Mountain, which has been described as a blend of "fiction, folklore, religion, and comedy" (Howard, *"Hurston"* 140). — replace, add

In it, Moses is a "hoodoo man," ~~a pretty wild~~ *an* idea *that also appears in* Jonah's Gourd Vine *(231)*. — replace, add

1. Why did the writer replace the second sentence, which is a direct quotation?
2. Why was the third sentence deleted? How is the change in the following sentence related to this deletion?
3. Why did the writer add a shortened title to the parenthetical citation? [Hint: See the Works Cited list.]
4. Why did the writer replace *pretty wild* in the final sentence?
5. Why did the writer add information to the last sentence? How does it help the paper?

Teacher's ResourceBank™

RESOURCES

EVALUATING AND REVISING

- Writing a Research Paper 91

QUOTATION FOR THE DAY

". . . if I type out a poem, I immediately see defects which I missed when I looked through it in manuscript." (W. H. Auden, 1907–1973, British poet)

Suggest that students input their nearly completed essays on computers or type them on typewriters to see how they look in print. When sentences are set in cold type, they often reveal structural and stylistic flaws that are easy to spot and correct.

ANSWERS

Exercise 6

1. The second sentence contains facts about Hurston's life that can be found in many sources and does not need to be quoted.
2. It does not relate directly to the topic of the paragraph. With the sentence deleted, the writer can use *its* to refer to the book *Tell My Horse* and does not need to repeat the title.
3. The title is needed because the author has two works in the Works Cited.
4. The writer cut a personal opinion.
5. The added information is relevant and gives another example of how the author's research worked into her novels.

sure that students understand how to use the chart and call attention to the three techniques emphasized under **Revision Technique** (add, replace, and cut). To show students how to use the chart, you could go over **Exercise 6** on p. 447 with them in class as guided practice. Then you could let students work together on **Writing Assignment: Part 6** as independent practice. Encourage students to be supportive and positive as they offer constructive criticism.

Use students' revisions of their research papers as your assessment of their understanding of the evaluating and revising stage. If time permits, compare each student's first draft and revision. Or you could look over one or two pages of each student's first draft and revision.

MEETING INDIVIDUAL NEEDS

LEARNING STYLES

Visual Learners. Another way to present the information in the chart is to write on the chalkboard *Add, Replace,* and *Cut.* Pull basic information from the chart to put under each heading. For example, under *Cut,* write "unnecessary quotations" and "unnecessary material."

TIMESAVER

Instruct students to mark additions, cuttings, and replacements on their rough drafts so that you can easily identify intended changes. If they are writing on word processors, have students make printouts of the rough drafts and mark revisions.

EVALUATING AND REVISING RESEARCH REPORTS

	EVALUATION GUIDE	REVISION TECHNIQUE
1	Is the report developed with sufficient primary and secondary sources that meet the "4R" test (page 416)?	**Add** facts, examples, opinions of experts, and primary sources if possible. **Cut** outdated or questionable information.
2	Is a thesis statement included early in the report?	**Add** a sentence or two stating your main idea to the introduction of your report.
3	Is the report suitable for and appealing to its audience?	**Add** needed definitions, background information, and explanations. **Add** interesting, unusual, or surprising details.
4	Is the tone of the report appropriate?	**Replace** words or phrases that are too informal for a research report.
5	Are facts and ideas stated mostly in the writer's own words?	**Cut** unnecessary quotations. **Replace** words, phrases, and sentences that do not use your own wording.
6	Is all information in the report related directly to the topic and thesis?	**Cut** unnecessary material.
7	Is every source of information credited when necessary?	**Add** documentation for any direct quotations and facts or ideas that aren't common knowledge.
8	Does all documentation follow the format recommended by your teacher?	**Replace** as necessary to follow the MLA format or another format recommended by your teacher.

You may want to tell students to read through the first drafts of their research papers to check for the "4R" test (shown on p. 416) for primary and secondary sources, placement of thesis statement, suitability of report for audience, appropriateness of report's tone, use of own words, relevancy of all information to topic, and documentation of sources.

Ask students to discuss some aspects of their research reports that they evaluated and decided to revise. ■

Reminder

When you evaluate and revise your report, remember to

- include every element of the report that your teacher has specified
- develop ideas with enough details to make them clear and convincing
- indicate differing viewpoints when they exist and are important to the topic

WRITING ASSIGNMENT

PART 6:
Evaluating and Revising Your Report

Exchange reports with a classmate. Read each other's reports and, using the guidelines on page 448, offer advice and criticism. Think about your classmate's suggestions carefully, and accept any recommended changes that seem valid. Then evaluate your own report and make any additional changes you think will make it more effective.

"I had written a few short stories, but the idea of attempting a book seemed so big, that I gazed at it in the quiet of the night, but hid it away from even myself in the daylight."

Zora Neale Hurston,
on writing Jonah's Gourd Vine

INTEGRATING THE LANGUAGE ARTS

Technology Link. Students who are writing their papers on word processors could use the boldfacing capability to highlight all quotations they have used. By seeing all the quotations in boldface, students could easily determine if they have used too many or too few quotations and, if too many, they could paraphrase the information.

Vocabulary Link. You may want to discuss *colloquialisms* (words or expressions used in informal conversations but not accepted as good usage in formal written English) and give students a list of words that you consider too informal for a research report. Examples are *got, a lot of,* and *kind of.*

SELECTION AMENDMENT
Description of change: excerpted
Rationale: to focus on the concept of research reports presented in this chapter

SEGMENT 6 *(pp. 450–453)*

PROOFREADING AND PUBLISHING

OBJECTIVES

- To proofread a research paper, including the documentation in the body and the Works Cited
- To publish a research report

TEACHING THE LESSON

You may want to instruct students to divide the proofreading stage of the writing process into three parts. First, refer students to standard guidelines for proofreading. Tell students to check grammar, usage, and mechanics in the bodies of their papers. Then have students check the mechanics of their documentation by referring to the

Teacher's ResourceBank™

RESOURCES

PROOFREADING AND PUBLISHING

- Writing a Research Paper 92

QUOTATION FOR THE DAY

"Trifles make perfection, and perfection is no trifle." (Michelangelo Buonarroti, 1475–1564, Italian sculptor and painter of the Sistine Chapel)

Tell students that checking punctuation and verifying spelling seem like minor tasks after the time-consuming job of putting together a research paper, but they are indispensable. Explain that they are the polish on the piece of sculpture, the final touch that puts a smooth finish on the work.

MEETING INDIVIDUAL NEEDS

LEP/ESL

General Strategies. As part of the proofreading process, students might be instructed to focus on only one element of the language at a time. Pair students with peer tutors. Ask LEP/ESL students to underline all verbs in the report and, with the peer tutor's assistance, to check only for correct tense and agreement. Using this diagnostic process, students can more easily identify problem areas.

Proofreading and Publishing

Proofreading. Checking the mechanics of your documentation (parenthetical citations and list of Works Cited) is a very important part of proofreading a research paper. Remember that your documentation is there for readers' use and accuracy is required because they may want to find one of your sources. Also be sure to check capitalization, spelling, punctuation, grammar, and usage—your accomplishment is significant and you don't want errors to detract from your efforts.

GRAMMAR HINT

Using a Quotation as Part of a Sentence

When you use a direct quotation within your own sentence, you must incorporate the quote so that the entire sentence is grammatically correct. Always check the sentence to be sure the quotation serves properly as a grammatical part and is not merely "hanging" within the sentence or stuck onto it.

EXAMPLES

Quotation as part of a subordinate clause	The novel was even criticized because the "folk sayings may become the main point of the novel" (Bone 127).
Quotation as a subject	Her "skill at transcribing" made the language in <u>Jonah's Gourd Vine</u> somewhat hard to read (Young 220).
Quotation as a direct object of the verb	She knew intimately the everyday, "normal life of Negroes in the South" (Thompson).

REFERENCE NOTE: For more information on using quotations within sentences, see page 879.

guidelines in this chapter. Finally, tell students to check the mechanics of their Works Cited against the guidelines in the chapter.

Some class time may be needed to give students special instructions in any areas of grammar, usage, and mechanics in which they are generally weak. You also may want to require students to read **A Student Model** on pp. 452–453 for another example of a polished paper.

After students have proofread their papers, you may want to give them directions about how their papers should be handed in (directions about cover sheets, folders, and so on). Then join students in brainstorming ways to publish the reports.

Publishing. A research report is a substantial piece of work, a paper to be proud of and *use.* Since using implies sharing your research with others, you might try one of the following suggestions for publishing your paper.

- During your research, you may have discovered persons or groups that are especially interested in your subject. For example, the researcher who did the Zora Neale Hurston report learned of an organization called Preserve Eatonville Community, Inc., which might appreciate a copy of the Hurston report for its files. If you came across anyone or any group similarly involved with your subject, consider sending them a copy of your report.
- Make an audiotape of your report, adding sound effects or background music, if appropriate. Play the tape for your family, for your class, or for a club or other organization. You might also use your report for a videotape documentary.
- Since schools and employers frequently request writing samples, save your report as an example of your writing and research skills for a college or job application.

***WRITING* ASSIGNMENT**

PART 7:
Proofreading and Publishing Your Report

Proofread your research paper, paying special attention to documentation in the body of the paper and in your list of Works Cited. Be sure to refer to the chart on pages 442–446 for help with the correct format for various kinds of sources. Then use one of the suggestions given above for publishing your paper.

INTEGRATING THE LANGUAGE ARTS

Grammar Link. You may want to remind students to use verbals to add variety to their sentence structures. Ask students to define *participle* [a verbal used as an adjective], *gerund* [a word ending in *–ing* formed from a verb and used as a noun], and *infinitive* [a verb form, usually preceded by *to,* used as a noun or a modifier]. Write a few examples such as these on the chalkboard:

1. Drawing upon her anthropology research, Zora Neale Hurston wrote many books. [participial phrase]
2. Using folklore in stories was a distinctive characteristic of Zora Neale Hurston's writings. [gerund phrase]
3. Zora Neale Hurston liked to research [infinitive phrase]

CLOSURE

Ask students to discuss briefly what they found most challenging, difficult, interesting, and enjoyable about writing their research papers. ■

INTEGRATING THE LANGUAGE ARTS

Usage Link. *Which* and *that* are frequently used in informative papers. Be sure students understand when to use the two words. Tell students *which* is used to refer to things only, while *that* may be used to refer to either people or things.

Discuss the use of *that* and *which* in introducing subordinate clauses. Remind students *that* is a restrictive pronoun and *which* is nonrestrictive. Write some clauses on the chalkboard and ask students whether *that* or *which* should be used and why.

A STUDENT MODEL
Evaluation

1. The thesis statement introduces the main idea early in Bill's report—Lopez shows animals' lives from a scientific and naturalistic point of view.
2. Bill is able to keep the tone of the report appropriate by avoiding contractions and by using formal words and phrases.
3. Bill balances quotations with his own ideas and words. His quotations are from the naturalist his report explores.
4. Bill's paragraphs support his main idea by expounding upon the theme while keeping to the topic.

A STUDENT MODEL

Bill Langhofer, a student at Washington High School in South Bend, Indiana, readily acknowledges that a well-written research paper results from good writing skills, research, and hard work. As you read each of the following excerpts from Bill's research paper, notice how he develops his thesis: from the introduction, to a paragraph in the body, to his paper's conclusion.

from Barry Holstun Lopez--The Naturalist
by Bill Langhofer

Barry Lopez began his life as the Modern Age drew to a close, making way for contemporary writing. The change from modern to contemporary literature resulted in little variety from the previous period. One of the few fluctuations was that authors expanded the ideas from the past. Unlike previous authors, who gave wild animals the appearance of being ravenous beasts, Barry Lopez shows us animals' lives from a scientific and naturalistic point of view. He broadens the insight of the reader by producing a realistic concept of nature. . . .

Barry Lopez's greatest books are Of Wolves and Men and Arctic Dreams. In Of Wolves and Men he appeals to the reader's senses and gets him to think about the future of animals by showing how badly the wolf has been treated in the past. Lopez says

> . . . if I focused on this one animal, I might be able to say something sharp and clear about the way we treat all animals, and about how we relate to the natural world in the latter part of the twentieth century. (Goldsworthy 250)

In discussing Arctic Dreams, Lopez tells about two incidents that inspired him to write this book:

> One was the sight, in the midnight light of the northern summer, of a flight of birds and a small herd of

caribou crossing a river. The other took place not in the Arctic but in rural Michigan, where he came across the grave of a sailor who had died in an Arctic expedition in 1884. (Goldsworthy 250)

From these inspirations Lopez produced a book that contained many different themes, including Arctic exploration, geography, weather, and animal migration and behavior. . . .

Barry Lopez uses powerful imagery to show us our forefathers' mistakes. As the settlers fought for a living in this rugged wilderness, they ruined the natives' lifestyles, wreaked havoc on the environment, and eliminated many animal populations. His book Of Wolves and Men centers on one animal, the wolf. He hopes that people will see the destruction they have brought on themselves in their desire to overcome the forces of nature, and he hopes that they will change their ways. "What is in my gut as a writer is a concern with the fate of the country I live in and the dignity and morality of the people I live with" (Colby 550). In his other book, Arctic Dreams, Lopez covers the geography, the history, and the bird and animal life in the Arctic. He realizes that technology has radically altered the landscape and the animals living on the land. As a superb naturalist, he has helped all of us realize that we have squandered valuable resources. It is now our choice to make a difference.

INTEGRATING THE LANGUAGE ARTS

Speaking Link. You may want to encourage students to present their reports aloud to the class or to other classes or clubs. Tell students to rehearse their presentations on their own. If possible, schedule some time when you can give them pointers on eye contact, facial expressions, gestures, posture, and pronunciation.

TEACHING NOTE

You will want to explain to students that although a Works Cited has not been included for **A Student Model,** one was produced. It does not appear in the students' textbook because of space constraints.

SEGMENT 7 *(pp. 454–456)*

WRITING WORKSHOP

OBJECTIVES

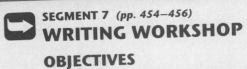

- To analyze informative research
- To plan and conduct an interview of a person in the community
- To write an informative research article about a person

TEACHING THE LESSON

Start by telling students that one great value of research for reports and articles is that it puts the researcher in contact with new and interesting ideas, situations, and people. Emphasize that the **Writing Workshop** will give them opportunities to meet interesting people and to learn about these people's activities.

QUOTATION FOR THE DAY

"Knowledge is of two kinds. We know a subject ourselves, or we know where we can find information upon it." (Samuel Johnson, 1709–1784, British critic, lecturer, lexicographer, and writer)

Use Johnson's quotation as a springboard for teaching the lesson. Besides the library, where else can a researcher go to get information?

MEETING INDIVIDUAL NEEDS

LEP/ESL

General Strategies. Suggest that students write about an unsung hero in the community who devotes time to helping others or who is passionate about a career. Students could consult newspaper lifestyle sections for ideas and models. Positive role models from their own cultural communities not only give students someone to write about but also someone to emulate.

WRITING WORKSHOP

An Informative Research Article

The articles that you read in newspapers and magazines almost always involve research, frequently a personal interview. These articles cover all types of topics, but some of the more interesting ones focus on one person's unique experiences or interests. From the smallest hamlet to the largest city, creative people can be found doing interesting things, and reporters make a point of finding them. For this workshop, you'll identify one such person in your community and write a 200-word report on what he or she is doing. Before you do your interview, use the guidelines that follow to plan what you'll ask and record. (See also the steps listed in Exercise 3, page 424.)

GUIDELINES FOR A REPORT OF AN INTERVIEW

1. Identify clearly the person you're writing about: Give his or her name and position or job title. Make absolutely certain that the spelling and wording in your identifications are correct.
2. Show what is especially intriguing about the person you've chosen—what it is that sets him or her apart.
3. Include enough details so that the reader gets a good idea of what the person does.
4. Use at least one quotation from the person you've interviewed plus any other quotes that add substance and appeal to your report.

Following is a brief report that appeared in *New Jersey Monthly* magazine. Study it to determine whether the writer's published article, based in part on an interview, adheres to the guidelines given above.

Let students familiarize themselves with **Guidelines for a Report of an Interview** and then have them read the sample article. You may want to discuss the topic of the article and the accompanying questions about the article during class.

Point out that students will be following the stages of the writing process as they plan and write their research articles. Tell them that although the interviews are the primary parts of their prewriting research, they may not be the only parts. Be sure students understand that they can consult sources both before and after the interviews to find out about the persons they will interview and the persons' interests.

You may want to approve the subjects of the articles before allowing students ☛

Education: A Sit-Down Tour

by Matt Tomlinson

For high school students who are eyeing Stanford University
1 instead of Stockton State College, the all-important trip to visit the campus can carry a steep price tag.

Cliff Kramon has a solution. As vice president of Tenafly's Collegiate Choice Inc.—professional guidance counselors for college-bound kids—Kramon spent the last three and a half years videotaping more than 300 U.S. colleges. Students interested in faraway schools can now pop one of Kramon's tapes into the VCR and evaluate their choices.

Collegiate Choice counsels mostly Bergen County and New York City students, but orders for the videotapes come from all over the country. Twelve New Jersey schools are in the catalog,
2 and the videotapes are more helpful than any sanitized pamphlet. While a Drew University brochure says that the school offers "an impressive array of unusual opportunities in the context of an education rooted in the liberal arts," the onscreen guide covers everything from graduation to the university's resident ghosts. The Rutgers video is wonderfully cacophonous, full of the trains and traffic that provide the school's urban background music.

3 Still, Kramon has the heart of a guidance counselor, not a salesman: He tries to convince students to skip the video tours when campuses are close by. The tapes are the second best way to see a school, he says: "The best way is going yourself."

USING THE SELECTION

Education: A Sit-Down Tour

1

What are some specific words in the first two paragraphs that reflect a lively, nonscholarly style? [Examples include *eyeing, steep price tag, kids,* and *pop.*] What words might be used in a scholarly report? [Responses may vary but could include *considering, expensive, students,* and *insert.*]

2

How does the reader know what the author means by "sanitized pamphlet"? [The author gives an example, the Drew University brochure.]

3

Ask students to respond to Kramon's remarks in the last paragraph and to discuss their own experiences in looking at colleges.

VISUAL CONNECTIONS

Ideas for Writing. Have students write brief journal entries about what types of colleges most interest them. Students could consider such features as courses, facilities, location, and size.

SELECTION AMENDMENT

Description of change: excerpted
Rationale: to focus on the concept of research reports presented in this chapter

to begin research. Before students begin writing, remind them to use a lively, nonscholarly tone and style and to try to capture the personalities of their subjects. How well students plan and conduct their interviews and package their findings will give you further indication of students' mastery of the writing process. After students have completed their articles, you may want to ask students to compare the **Writing Workshop** assignment with the writing of their research reports. ■

ANSWERS

Writing Workshop Questions

1. The writer interviewed Kramon, looked through the catalog of Tenafly's Collegiate Choice Inc., watched some of the company's videotapes, and looked at some college brochures.
2. Stockton State College is in New Jersey. The writer could have used names of other well-known colleges throughout the country.
3. The second paragraph clearly identifies the person being written about (name and position) and what is interesting about the person.
4. Details include information about the varied content of the videos (graduation, ghosts) and sounds of the videos (such as trains and traffic).
5. The author uses quotations when quoting from the Drew University brochure in the third paragraph and when quoting Kramon directly in the last paragraph.

MEETING **INDIVIDUAL** NEEDS

AT-RISK STUDENTS

You may want to let pairs of students plan and conduct interviews. That way students who are unsure of themselves and their abilities will have help in arranging the interviews and in thinking up questions. They will also have support during the actual interviews.

1. What kinds of research evidently went into the writing of this report? How can you tell?
2. The first paragraph shows that the focus of the article is local, not national. In what way? How might the writer have changed the first sentence if the article were aimed at a national audience?
3. What two purposes do you think the second paragraph accomplishes?
4. What kinds of specific details are used in the third paragraph to illustrate the nature of the videotapes?
5. Where and why does the writer use quotations?

Writing an Article Based on an Interview

Prewriting. For your interview, you might consider people you already know—a friend who's won a prize, a relative with an intriguing job, a neighbor who's gained community attention. Or check the local newspaper for people in the news. When you've found your person, set up a personal or a telephone interview. Do some background research in the library or by talking to other people to learn whatever else you can about the person and his or her featured activity, and plan questions in advance. Take careful notes—even if you use a tape recorder. (For more information on interviewing, see pages 424 and 950–952.)

Writing, Evaluating, and Revising. Since this is a brief report, you can easily plan its paragraphing. You may want to follow the four-paragraph "Sit-Down Tour" model—introduction, identification, support, conclusion—or you may prefer a plan of your own. In evaluating and revising your first draft, use the guidelines on page 448. Also compare your article with others in the newspaper. Does yours have a similar lively, nonscholarly tone and style?

Proofreading and Publishing. Go over your final draft, correcting any errors in spelling, capitalization, punctuation, and usage. Then see if the local paper or a city magazine will publish your report. Your school paper could also run a "Newsmaker" series to publish all the class articles. Finally, be *sure* to give a copy to the person you interviewed.

SEGMENT 8 *(pp. 457–459)*

MAKING CONNECTIONS

TRAVEL WRITING OBJECTIVES

- To analyze the research involved in a travel article
- To research information about an interesting place
- To write a brief travel article about an interesting place

MAKING CONNECTIONS

TRAVEL WRITING

From one-line postcards to full-length books, records of travel are being written and read by millions every day. People seem to have as great a need to tell and read about new places and events as they do to experience them. And all writing about travel involves research in some way, from firsthand observation to reading a map to browsing through a brochure. What research might have gone into this introduction to an article on the Painted Desert?

from Sands of Time

by James Kotsilibas-Davis

They resemble sailing frigates and fairytale castles, gigantic mushrooms or abstract forms that might be found in a Soho art gallery. But these random sculptures, such as the geological flukes in Blue Canyon, are not man-made. They were shaped by the erosional action of the Little Colorado River as it wound its prehistoric way through what is now the American West. The color-stroked mounds that form the Painted Desert were deposited some 225 million years ago, toward the end of the Triassic Period of the Mesozoic Era. Protected in Petrified Forest National Park, this sequence of rocks is part of the meandering Chinle Formation, which sweeps majestically across Arizona, Utah and New Mexico like a land-bound rainbow.

Petrified logs in the Blue Mesa section of the Petrified Forest fell like fragments of ancient pillars after their 150-million-year-old coating eroded. The once-verdant forest, which flourished here 200 million years ago, was buried, then preserved, when rainwater seeped through deep layers of volcanic ash, dissolving silica from it. As the water penetrated, silica replaced the logs' organic materials with glasslike deposits of silicon dioxide. Paiutes believed these gleaming formations were the arrow shafts of their thunder god. To Navajos, they were bones of a mythic giant.

Travel-Holiday

TRAVEL WRITING

Teaching Strategies

Have volunteers suggest places that they would like to visit but have never visited. List their selections on the chalkboard. Ask them what intrigues them about the places they have mentioned. Since they have no personal knowledge on these sites, suggest that many of their ideas about faraway places come from reading what writers have to say about their travels.

Have volunteers read the introduction and the excerpts from **"Sands of Time."** Discuss the factual data included in the information and probable sources for the information.

GUIDELINES

Students' own brief travel articles should include interesting and vivid details to entice readers to visit the places described. You may want to have students make informal lists of their resources, including times that they may have visited the locations about which they are writing.

SELECTION AMENDMENT

Description of change: excerpted

Rationale: to focus on the concept of research reports presented in this chapter

RESEARCH ACROSS THE CURRICULUM OBJECTIVES

- To identify a research technique described in a book excerpt
- To respond personally to literature
- To read about a scientist and to make a report to the class

RESEARCH ACROSS THE CURRICULUM

Teaching Strategies

After reading the passage from Richard P. Feynman's autobiography, students should state that Feynman's father was teaching him the research technique of investigation and personal observation. Students then should suggest that Feynman applied that technique in his scientific investigations of the *Challenger* disaster.

Where have you been that you'd like to tell other people about? You may not live in—or have visited—a landscape as spectacular as the Painted Desert, but the places you have traveled to or your own community are sure to contain some attraction for armchair travelers. Do some research, and write a few paragraphs to entice someone to visit a new place. It could be a park, a local museum, an old farmers' market, a turn-of-the-century house, or a modern factory.

Your information may come from interviews, visits, newspaper clippings, books, videotapes, or brochures. Just be sure to provide important and interesting facts about the place and to arouse curiosity with vivid description. And since the rules against plagiarism apply in travel writing, too, be sure to use your own words and give credit for ideas you have borrowed from someone else.

RESEARCH ACROSS THE CURRICULUM

Science

Richard P. Feynman, one of the most accomplished physicists of this century, worked on the Manhattan Project, won the Nobel Prize, and played in a samba band. When the nation mourned the explosion of the space shuttle *Challenger* in 1986, he was asked to sit on the president's commission to determine the cause of the disaster. It was he who uncovered the problem with the faulty O-rings. What produces a creative scientist like

Feynman? In his autobiography, *What Do You Care What Other People Think?*, he explains how his father taught him to think. In the passage below, Feynman's father is speaking to his son.

> "See that bird?" he says. "It's a Spencer's warbler." (I knew he didn't know the real name.) "Well, in Italian, it's a *Chutto Lapittida.* In Portuguese, it's a *Bom da Peida.* In Chinese, it's a *Chung-long-tah,* and in Japanese, it's a *Katano Tekeda.* You can know the name of that bird in all the languages of the world, but when you're finished, you'll know absolutely nothing whatever about the bird. You'll only know about humans in different places, and what they call the bird. So let's look at the bird and see what it's *doing*—that's what counts." (I learned very early the difference between knowing the name of something and knowing something.)
>
> Richard Feynman, *What Do You Care What Other People Think?*

1. What research technique was Feynman's father teaching him?
2. How do you think Feynman might have applied this technique in his later life?

You might want to read more about this unusual scientist or about one of these other remarkable scientists: Albert Einstein, Robert H. Goddard, Irène Joliot-Curie, George Washington Carver, Nikola Tesla, Maria Mitchell. Check your library's card catalog, on-line catalog, or *Readers' Guide to Periodical Literature* for information on these scientists; then report back to your classmates on your findings.

GUIDELINES

Students' reports should include interesting and important details about the scientists' lives and accomplishments.

ANSWERS

1. He uses a combination of critical thinking and observation.
2. Answers will vary. Be sure students support their responses with reasons.

SELECTION AMENDMENT

Description of change: excerpted

Rationale: to focus on the concept of research reports presented in this chapter

Chapter 12

English: History and Development

OBJECTIVES

- To use a dictionary to check the origins of words
- To use a dictionary to identify Americanisms
- To translate British expressions
- To identify differences among regional and ethnic dialects
- To research borrowed words in the area of food and cooking

Motivation

Write these two sentences on the chalkboard:
1. According to my devyse, we begynne here.
2. Let us commence at this juncture.

Ask students which sentence is more modern. Ask students to explain what factors influenced their decision. [Students will probably mention spelling and word choice.] Point out that throughout the history of English there have been enormous changes in vocabulary and spelling.

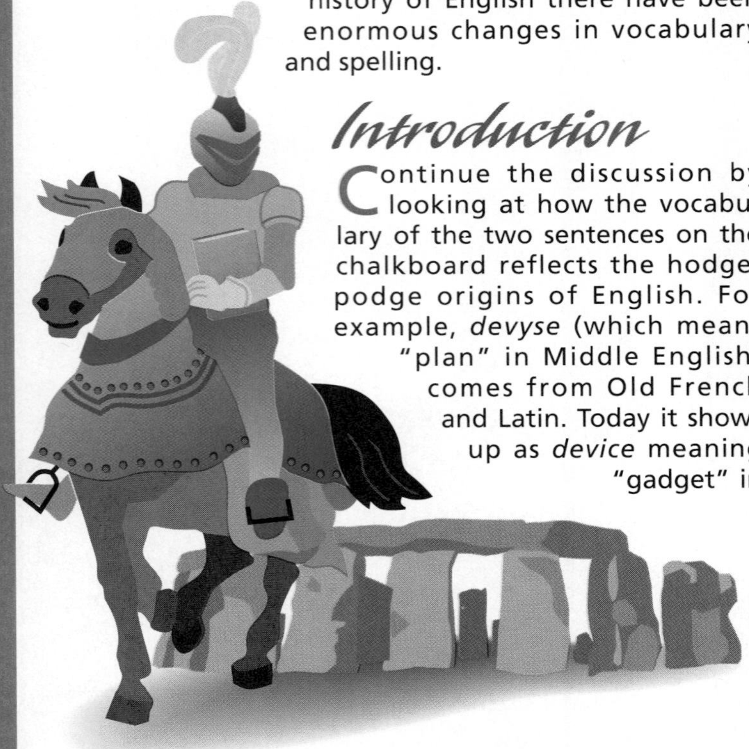

Introduction

Continue the discussion by looking at how the vocabulary of the two sentences on the chalkboard reflects the hodgepodge origins of English. For example, *devyse* (which means "plan" in Middle English) comes from Old French and Latin. Today it shows up as *device* meaning "gadget" in Modern English while *begynne*—now *begin*—has Germanic roots. The Latinate expressions *commence* and *juncture* were quite common terms for *begin* and *point* one hundred years ago, but today the terms are seen primarily in formal usage. Explain that in this chapter, students will study the development of the English language as well as the evolution of American English.

Integration

The material in this chapter will be especially appealing to students who enjoy words, but it should increase everyone's appreciation and understanding of language as a living, evolving tool. It also provides valuable background for **Chapter 13: "Style in Writing."** You may want to refer to this chapter as you discuss usage issues treated in **Chapter 27: "A Glossary of Usage."** The varied origins of English words may help some students understand and deal with the many peculiarities in the spelling of English, treated in **Chapter 31: "Spelling."** Students may need to review **Chapter 36: "The Dictionary"** before completing the etymology activities in **Exercises 1-5.**

The introduction of Germanic, French, and Scandinavian terms into English and the differences between American and British English all reflect sociopolitical changes that allow the chapter to integrate very well with any English or American history class students might be taking.

The chart on the next page illustrates the strands of language arts as they are integrated into this chapter. For vocabulary study, glossary words are underlined in some writing models.

QUOTATIONS
All **Quotations for the Day** are chosen because of their relevance to instructional material presented in that segment of the chapter and for their usefulness in establishing student interest in writing.

INTEGRATING THE LANGUAGE ARTS

Selection	Reading and Literature	Writing and Critical Thinking	Language and Syntax	Speaking, Listening, and Other Expression Skills
	Reading critically for specific information **464, 467, 471, 473, 479**	Applying interpretive and creative thinking **467, 479** Taking notes **479** Planning and writing a menu for a "word meal" **479** Using descriptive writing **479**	Using dictionaries to research word origins **464, 467, 471, 479** Identifying the origins of loan-words **467, 479** Researching words derived from names **467** Translating British expressions into American English **472** Analyzing differences in ethnic and regional dialects **478**	Interviewing others to identify dialect differences **478** Working with classmates to arrange a "word meal" **479**

CHAPTER 12

SEGMENT PLANNING GUIDE

Whether you are planning for a quick review of a writing concept or preparing an extended lesson on composition, you can use the following Planning Guide to adapt the chapter material to the individual needs of your class.

SEGMENT	PAGES	CONTENT	RESOURCES
1 *A Various Language*	*460-467*		Old, Middle, and Modern English 95
A Various Language	460-461	Introduction: understanding how language changes	
Origins of English: Pre-English	461-462	Explanation: examining Indo-European roots of English	
Old English	462-464	Explanation: examining Anglo-Saxon roots of English	
Exercise 1	464	Applied practice: identifying original forms of words	
Middle English	465	Explanation: examining the evolution of Middle English	
Modern English	465-466	Explanation: examining the evolution of Modern English	
Exercise 2	467	Applied practice: identifying the origins of loanwords	
Exercise 3	467	Applied practice: identifying word origins	
2 *American English*	*467-474*		American and British English 96 Borrowings from Other Languages 97
American English	467	Introduction: examining the Americanization of English	
The Colonial Period	468-469	Explanation: examining the evolution of American English before 1776	
The National Period	469-470	Explanation: examining the evolution of American English from 1776-1900	
Looking at Language	470	Example: learning the origin of the expression "OK"	
Exercise 4	470-471	Applied practice: identifying Americanisms	
The International Period	471-472	Explanation: examining borrowed words	
American and British English	472	Explanation: examining differences between American and British English	
Exercise 5	473	Applied practice: translating British expressions	
The Future of English	473-474	Explanation: considering how international use may affect English	
Looking at Language	474	Example: examining body language	

All the resources listed in this chapter are located in the *Teacher's ResourceBank*™.

SEGMENT	PAGES	CONTENT	RESOURCES
3 *Varieties of American English*	*474-478*		Varieties of American English 98
Varieties of American English	474	Introduction: examining dialects and standard English	
Dialect	475	Introduction: learning about the main dialects used in the United States	
Regional Dialects	475-476	Explanation: examining the four main regional dialects of American English	
Chart: Features of Regional Dialects	476	Guidelines: analyzing features that distinguish regional dialects	
Ethnic Dialects	476-477	Explanation: examining major ethnic dialects in America	
Exercise 6	478	Cooperative learning: identifying dialect differences	
Standard English	478	Explanation: examining the nature of standard English and its appropriate use	
4 *Making Connections*	*479*		
The Foreign Gourmet	479	Guidelines: using criteria for writing an international menu Applied practice: researching the origins of food-related expressions Cooperative learning: planning a meal of international foods and writing a descriptive menu	
WHOLE-CHAPTER RESOURCES Review Form A, Review Form B			

SEGMENT 1 *(pp. 460–467)*
A VARIOUS LANGUAGE

OBJECTIVES

- To identify original forms and meanings of words
- To discover the origins of borrowed words
- To research words from names

MOTIVATION

Show students pictures of a warrior from the time of Beowulf, a medieval craftsperson, a Victorian woman, and a modern teenager. Discuss what each one's dress indicates about the historical period. Explain that just as clothing has changed throughout history as a result of cultural, political, and technological developments, language has also

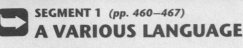

Teacher's ResourceBank™
RESOURCES

A VARIOUS LANGUAGE

QUOTATION FOR THE DAY

"Words truly are little windows through which we can look into the past." (Wilfred Funk, 1883–1965, American publisher)

Ask the class to share stories they know of any words that have colorful and interesting pasts. Remind students that knowing the origin of a word helps make its meaning clearer and more memorable. The study of word origins often leads to fascinating information about political and sociological factors in history.

MEETING INDIVIDUAL NEEDS

LEP/ESL

General Strategies. The English names for places such as Europe, Germany, and the British Isles may sound nothing like the names for those places in students' native languages. You might want to make a map available to students as you teach this segment.

12 ENGLISH: HISTORY AND DEVELOPMENT

LOOKING AHEAD

The English language is as lively and varied as the people who use it. Over thousands of years, it's grown and changed to become the most expressive and the most widely used language in the world. In this chapter, you will learn

- where English comes from
- how English has grown and developed
- what varieties of English are used in the United States and throughout the world

A Various Language

What would you think if someone came up to you and said, "Hæl, god freond! Hwæt destu?" Among other things, you would probably think you were hearing a foreign language. That, however, is the way an English speaker a thousand years ago might have said, "Hey, good buddy, what's up?" (or, more literally, "Hail, good friend! What dost thou?").

evolved and adjusted to reflect those same influences.

TEACHING THE LESSON

To present the material on the four main periods in the history of English, write the headings "Period," "Dates," "Precipitating Events," and "Linguistic Ingredients" on the chalkboard. For each period, have a volunteer read the textbook material aloud and then have students supply you with the ☛

The English of today has come to us from ancient times. During the past seven thousand years, our language has changed so much that now we cannot easily recognize its earlier forms. Even the English of one thousand years ago is so different from the language we speak that it seems like a foreign tongue. Yet there is continuity across the ages.

A language changes gradually as it is passed on from one generation to the next. New words are added, and old ones are lost. The way we pronounce and spell words changes, and so does the way we put them together to make sentences. We imitate speakers of other languages and change our own language in the process. The result is a wonderfully various language, containing within itself the fruits of its long and varied past.

The history of our language can be divided into four main periods: *Pre-English, Old English, Middle English,* and *Modern English.* The following time line shows approximately when English moved from one period to the next. It also shows which languages had the most influence on the early development of English.

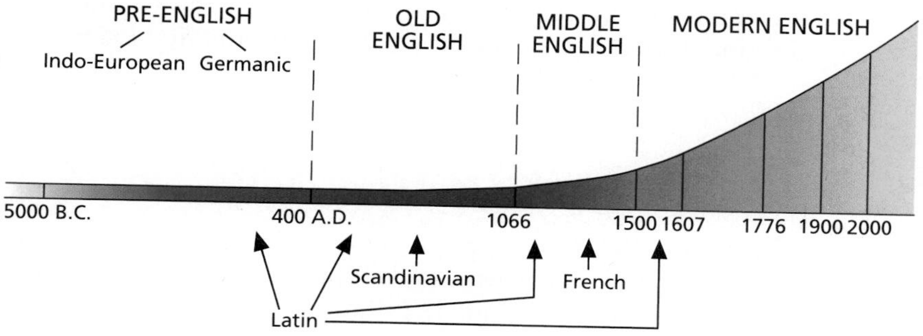

The Origins of English: Pre-English

Seven thousand or more years ago, a language that was the ancestor of English (and of many other languages, too) was spoken in Asia Minor or southeast Europe—we are not sure exactly where. We call that language ***Proto-Indo-European*** because most of the languages of Europe and many of those of north India and Iran developed from it. (*Proto–* means "first or earliest.")

MEETING **INDIVIDUAL** NEEDS

LEARNING STYLES

Visual Learners. The time line may make it easier for visually oriented students to understand that English has developed over a very long period of time and has absorbed new words from many different languages. You may want to have students make their own time lines that expand on the one in the textbook. Each student could list at least three words that have been assimilated into English from each of the languages shown.

VISUAL CONNECTIONS

Related Expression Skills. If possible, bring in the *Oxford English Dictionary* or copies of several of its entries. Discuss how this dictionary provides not only etymological information but also an indication of when the word first entered English. Call on students to read entries. Then have students show where each word would belong on the time line and have them identify the country of origin for each on a map.

information to go under each of the four headings.

Each of the three exercises in this segment consists of looking up etymologies of words. To prepare students for all three exercises, guide them through the first item in **Exercise 1** on p. 464. Write out the dictionary entry for *earth* and display it on an overhead projector. Call on individuals to identify and explain abbreviations and symbols such as < (from) or *OE* (Old English). Show students the key to abbreviations and symbols in a classroom dictionary. You may want to have students review the material on etymologies in **Chapter 36: "The Dictionary."**

Assign the rest of **Exercise 1** and **Exercises 2** and **3** on p. 467 as independent practice.

A DIFFERENT APPROACH

Divide the class into mixed-ability groups of three or four. Provide each group with ten lines from *Beowulf.* Have each group translate the lines into modern English. Discuss as a class which words, if any, have so completely disappeared from English that they could not be identified.

MEETING INDIVIDUAL NEEDS

LEARNING STYLES

Visual and Kinetic Learners. Provide each student with a large map of Europe and the British Isles that is simple and easy to read. Also provide each student a sheet with dates on it that are relevant to this segment. As you present the material in this segment, have students find on the map the places being discussed and then have them paste each date on the area it matches. You could also have students draw arrows on their maps to illustrate the migrations and invasions.

The people who spoke Proto-Indo-European migrated all around Europe and south central Asia. One group of those migrants settled in what is today northern Germany and along the coast of the North Sea. They were organized into several tribes—the Angles, the Saxons, and the Jutes. Their version of the Indo-European language, called ***Germanic,*** is the ancestor of present-day English.

While living in northern Europe, the Anglo-Saxons (as the tribes are collectively called) got to know another Indo-European people to their south, the Romans. They learned from the Romans—among other things—about streets, dishes, miles, and walls. At the same time, the Anglo-Saxons learned the Latin words for these things. *Street* is from the Latin words *strata via,* "paved road." *Dish* is from *discus* (which later was also borrowed in that form, as well as the shorter *disk* and *disc*). *Mile* is from *milia passuum,* "a thousand paces." And *wall* is from *vallum,* "a rampart."

Words that people borrow from other languages are called ***loanwords.*** Early English speakers certainly borrowed from other languages before they came into contact with the Romans. But the Latin words borrowed on the continent of Europe nearly two thousand years ago are the first loanwords we can be sure about.

Old English

Eventually, the Romans hired some of the Angles and Saxons to serve in the Roman army and shipped them off to the British Isles. The Romans had made Britain and its native population of Celts into a province of the Roman Empire. The Romans needed help in defending the southern part of the main island and the Celts who lived there against some fierce northern neighbors called Picts.

Although the Romans eventually gave up ruling Britain, the Anglo-Saxons stayed on after their job was done. Soon kin of theirs from the Continent arrived to join them. Eventually these Germanic peoples took over the south of the main island from the native Celts. The Anglo-Saxons called the island after themselves, *Engla land*—the land of the Angles—or, as we know it today, England. They called their language *Englisc;* we call it ***Old English.***

ASSESSMENT

Use students' performances on **Exercises 1–3** to assess each individual's ability to identify word origins by using a dictionary.

CLOSURE

Have students name the four historical stages in the development of the English language [Pre-English, Old English, Middle English, and Modern English].

The English the Anglo-Saxons spoke was very different from the English we know today. They had sounds we have lost, as in their word *hnutu,* which became our *nut.* At first they wrote with an angular-looking alphabet called runes—when they wrote at all, which wasn't often.

The Anglo-Saxons had some words we don't, such as *guma* for "man" or *boda* for "messenger," and they lacked a great many words we have, such as *message.* Some words have changed meaning. For example, *wif* meant "woman" rather than "wife," as it now does; and *gift* referred to a kind of wedding present rather than to any sort of gift.

Their words also had endings or alternative forms to show how they fit together in a sentence. The order of most words in the sentence could stay the same, while the form of the words changed to express different meanings.

MODERN ENGLISH	The man gave the messenger an answer. The messenger gave the man an answer.
OLD ENGLISH	**Se guma** geaf **thæm bodan** andsware. **Thæm guman** geaf **se boda** andsware.

Although English has changed over the centuries, many of our most familiar, everyday words are still native English. That is, they have been used by English speakers as far back in the past as we can see or imagine. Most of these words have changed their pronunciation and spelling, and many have changed their meanings, too. Yet the old forms of the words are still recognizable from the modern ones. The following lists show the Old English and Modern English forms of several everyday words.

VISUAL CONNECTIONS

Exploring the Subject. Let students know that the Old English Runic alphabet does not match modern English letter for letter; several runes represent sounds that are spelled with two letters today. For example, the *ng* sound is represented by a single rune. There is also a rune for each of the two *th* sounds (in *them* and *thick*). *The Cambridge Encyclopedia of Language* by David Crystal shows the runic alphabet and its modern English equivalents.

INTEGRATING THE LANGUAGE ARTS

Dictionary Link. Divide the class into an even number of mixed-ability groups of three or four students. Have each team of students use a dictionary to create a list of ten etymologies for fairly common words. Students should not give the word but only the original spelling and meaning. Then ask sets of two teams to exchange lists to identify the contemporary English words and their meanings.

EXTENSION

Students might work in small groups to make up five new words based on the names of local, national, or international figures. Have groups write out a dictionary entry for each new word by including the word, its part of speech, its definition, its etymology, and a sample sentence. Have groups share their entries, perhaps in a classroom dictionary. [Example: *oprah*—verb; to bring attention through interviews to someone with an unusual claim to fame (from *Oprah Winfrey*). "Channel 6's Reggie Roper plans to oprah an eighty-seven-year-old woman who sells coffee tables made from recycled coffee cans."]

ANSWERS

Exercise 1

Answers may vary according to the dictionary used. These are taken from *Webster's New World Dictionary,* Third College Edition:

1. eorthe; no change in meaning
2. lufu; no change in meaning
3. strutian; to stand rigid
4. meledeaw; nectar
5. waden; to go

VISUAL CONNECTIONS

Ideas for Writing. Let students know that many English words beginning with *sk* or *sc* have Scandinavian origins. Challenge students to work independently or with partners to write alliterative sentences that use all or almost all *sk* or *sc* words. Have students use a dictionary to check that all their words really are of Scandinavian or Old Icelandic origin. Arrange for students to share their creations.

OLD ENGLISH	MODERN ENGLISH
cnif	knife
hus	house
modor	mother
æppel, "fruit"	apple
wyrm, "serpent"	worm

EXERCISE 1 **Identifying Original Forms of Words**

Look up each of the following words in a dictionary that gives ***etymologies*** (word origins). What did the word look like in Old English? What did it mean in Old English?

1. earth
2. love
3. strut
4. mildew
5. wade

After they had settled in the British Isles, the English were converted to Christianity and borrowed many more Latin words. Many of these words were for religious matters, such as *church* and *bishop,* but some were for other subjects, such as *school* and *butter.*

In a series of raids during the ninth to eleventh centuries, the Norse from Scandinavia invaded England and settled there, introducing Scandinavian words such as *sky, skirt,* and the pronouns *they, them,* and *their.* The corresponding Anglo-Saxon forms were *heofon* (which survives as *heaven*), *scyrte* (which survives as *shirt*), and the pronouns *hie, hem, heora.*

ENRICHMENT

Ask students to check in the library for one of the many books about word origins and have each student report on the origin of one word or expression. The reports might be done on index cards that could be collected in a file. Possible resources include *All Those Wonderful Names* by J. N. Hook or any one of Willard Espy's books, such as *O Thou Improper, Thou Uncommon Noun.* ■

Middle English

In 1066, another group of Norse conquered England. Called the Normans (or "north men"), these people had earlier settled in France and learned French. The Normans began the process of introducing French words into the English language. *Castle, chair, table, pen, judge,* and *library* are a few of those words.

During much of the ***Middle English*** period, English was displaced by French and Latin as the important language of the country. Government, education, religion, law, and literature were in those foreign languages rather than in English.

English wasn't used for important purposes again until around the fourteenth century. By that time, English speakers had forgotten the native English words for many technical and specialized subjects. They found it easiest to borrow large numbers of French and Latin words to use in talking about these matters. For example, the native English word *leorningcild* ("learning-child") was replaced by a word from Latin, *studiante,* which became our word *student.*

Following are some more examples of French and Latin loanwords from the Middle English period:

FRENCH	armee	lettre	palais	preiere
MODERN ENGLISH	army	letter	palace	prayer

LATIN	alphabetum	ecclesiasticus
MODERN ENGLISH	alphabet	ecclesiastical

Modern English

After moving to Britain, the Anglo-Saxons lived there fairly comfortably and as quietly as they could, considering that their neighbors in Scandinavia and France kept moving in with them without waiting for an invitation. Despite the Scandinavian and Norman French invasions of England, the English were relatively isolated and protected for nearly 1,200 years. Most of them were illiterate, with no need to write or read because handwritten manuscripts were too expensive for ordinary people. When the English did write, they spelled (and used) words in many different ways.

Near the end of the fifteenth century, however, William Caxton introduced the printing press to England, and cheap books soon became readily available. Mass publication and the

CRITICAL THINKING
Analysis

Students may be interested in exploring how sociopolitical factors sometimes affected which words from other languages were adopted into English to replace Old English terms. Ask students to name as many kinds of meat as they can think of and also to name the animal from which each kind of meat comes. For each meat and animal, ask students to predict whether the word comes from Old English or from French and to use a dictionary to verify the etymology. When the list is done, challenge the class to group the animal and meat terms according to origins. Then have them analyze how the pattern reflects historical factors in English between 1066 and 1500. [Almost all meat names have French origins (pork, beef, mutton, veal). In contrast, most animal names are Anglo-Saxon (pig, cow, sheep). The pattern makes sense given that for several hundred years after the Norman Conquest in 1066, the upper classes in England were French. These were the people who could feast on prepared meats. In contrast, the peasants who had to take care of the animals were Anglo-Saxons.]

COOPERATIVE LEARNING

Divide the class into small groups of mixed abilities and ask each group to choose a non-English-speaking culture and to see how many borrowed words in English they can list as coming from that culture's language. To foster ethnic pride, suggest that students look for words that reflect their own ethnic backgrounds. Some students might need to use the library to draw up their lists. Results might be used to create a bulletin-board display listing all the words and their origins.

resulting increase in literacy helped to standardize the English language.

Around the sixteenth century, some English people got the itch to travel and see whether they could make their fortunes in foreign lands. A little more than one hundred years after Columbus had stumbled upon the Western Hemisphere, the English decided they would try to plant some colonies there, too. The first successful English settlement in the New World was at Jamestown, Virginia, in 1607; the next was at Plymouth, Massachusetts, in 1620. Later, English settlers and traders ventured to Canada, the Caribbean, India, Australia, New Zealand, South Africa, and many other places, taking the English language with them wherever they went.

"Look! Look, gentlemen! . . . Purple mountains! Spacious skies! Fruited plains! . . . Is someone writing this down?"

Meanwhile, back in England, the Industrial Revolution of the late eighteenth and early nineteenth centuries introduced more efficient methods of manufacturing. The combination of abundant goods and worldwide commerce helped spread the English language all over the globe and make it into an important international tongue. At the same time, English people's interaction with other cultures brought many new loanwords into English.

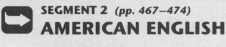

SEGMENT 2 *(pp. 467–474)*

AMERICAN ENGLISH

OBJECTIVES

- To identify Americanisms
- To translate British expressions into American English

MOTIVATION

Write the following sentence on the chalkboard and challenge students to explain what it says and to identify the nationality of the speaker:

I would be honoured if you would join me for dinner at my flat.

Discuss how the sentence demonstrates the differences in spelling and

EXERCISE 2 **Discovering the Origins of Borrowed Words** Answers may vary according to the dictionary used. These are from *Webster's New World Dictionary,* Third College Edition.

What language was each of the following words borrowed from? Make a guess first, and then check the etymology of each word in the dictionary.

1. anchovy **1.** Portugese
2. bluff ("to mislead") **2.** Dutch
3. cosmonaut **3.** Russian
4. kimono **4.** Japanese
5. kindergarten **5.** German
6. lacrosse **6.** French
7. luau **7.** Hawaiian
8. moccasin **8.** Algonquian
9. piano **9.** Italian
10. tamale **10.** Spanish

EXERCISE 3 **Researching Words from Names**

Many words in English come from the names of people. Who was the person commemorated in each of the following words? To find the answers, look up the etymology of each word in a dictionary.

1. Braille
2. levis
3. maverick
4. sequoia
5. cardigan

American English

When people are in close contact with one another and talk together often, their language will change in the same way for all of them. For example, most people will talk alike in a small town where everybody knows everybody else. But if half the townspeople move to the other side of a mountain and lose touch with their old neighbors, within a few generations the two groups will be talking very differently from each other. They will have developed two distinct varieties of the language.

That is what happened to the English settlers in the New World and the English who stayed home. The language went on changing on both sides of the Atlantic Ocean, but it changed in different ways on the two sides. In time, *American English* and *British English* drifted apart and became two recognizably different varieties.

The history of American English is divided into three periods: *Colonial, National,* and *International.*

ANSWERS

Exercise 3

1. Louis Braille invented raised dot writing for the blind.
2. Levi Strauss developed denim jeans during the California Gold Rush.
3. Texas rancher Samuel Maverick did not brand his cattle.
4. Sequoya was a Cherokee chief who created a written version of his people's language.
5. The seventh Earl of Cardigan was a nineteenth-century English general.

Teacher's ResourceBank™

RESOURCES

AMERICAN ENGLISH

QUOTATION FOR THE DAY

". . . worldwide the number of people who now learn English as an additional language surpasses those who learn it as a mother tongue." (Richard W. Bailey, American scholar and author)

Have students freewrite in their journals a response to the quotation. Ask students where they think this trend is leading. Will English fragment into a number of separate languages? Will other languages die out as more people use English?

vocabulary that have developed between British and American English.

TEACHING THE LESSON

To present the material on the development of American English in this segment, write the headings "Period," "Dates," and "Linguistic Developments" on the chalkboard. Have a volunteer read aloud the text for the colonial, national, and international periods. Then have the class supply the

MEETING INDIVIDUAL NEEDS

LEARNING STYLES

Visual and Auditory Learners. Show a brief videotaped segment from a British television program such as *East-Enders* or *Monty Python's Flying Circus.* Have students identify specific examples of accent, vocabulary, or grammar that they find difficult to understand. Use these examples to discuss how American and British English have diverged.

VISUAL CONNECTIONS

Related Expression Skills. Have students imagine that, by accident, a Pilgrim boarded a time machine instead of the *Mayflower* and landed in a typical American living room. Working individually or in cooperative groups, students should prepare a vocabulary list (including definitions) so that the time-traveler will know how to refer to the items in the room. Have students underline terms that they feel would be totally unfamiliar to the stranger because the terms had not yet come into use in England in the 1600s.

The Colonial Period (1607–1776)

When the first English speakers set foot in the New World, they talked just the way the people back home did. But they had to start adapting their language to new conditions almost as soon as they arrived.

The early settlers had to borrow and invent words for some animals they had never known before. For example, they encountered a bushy-tailed, black animal that had a white streak down its back and that sprayed a foul-smelling liquid when it was frightened. They imitated the Algonquian name for this creature as best they could, calling it a *skunk.* Another unfamiliar animal they met lived in the water and had a long tail and webbed hind feet. Because it was a rodent and because it had a musky smell about it, the settlers called it a *muskrat.*

In other cases, the settlers adapted old words to new uses. In England the streams that flowed through the countryside were for the most part nearly level with the surrounding land. In America, however, many of the rivers had worn a deep channel down through the earth. To get to those streams, the settlers had to climb down an incline. The settlers needed a name for these inclines for which there was no distinctive English term. They took the English word for a mound or ridge or slope of a hill—*bank*—and applied it to the slope leading down to a stream. And so a new use was born, which became the normal American meaning of the word.

information under each heading. You could combine **The Future of English** (p. 473) with **The International Period** (p. 471).

Have a volunteer read aloud **American and British English** on p. 472 and ask students if they know any other examples of differences between American and British syntax, spelling, or vocabulary.

You may want to have students read the two **Looking at Language** sections (p. 470 and p. 474) independently.

Use **Exercise 4** on pp. 470–471 as a class activity by asking students to scan the list for items that they think originated in the United States or that reflect some aspect of American culture. Have the class predict

The early English colonists in the New World had some language changes forced on them almost immediately because of the new conditions under which they lived. However, all languages are constantly changing from one generation to the next. If a language is alive, it changes.

The National Period (1776–1898)

At first, English was spoken in the New World only in the colonies along the eastern seaboard of the continent. But as settlers moved westward, English gradually began to spread. More and more new words entered the language, and American English became increasingly different from British.

The year 1776, when the thirteen original colonies declared their independence from England, was the beginning of ***American English*** as a separate national standard. A number of the nation's founders—including Thomas Jefferson, John Adams, and Benjamin Franklin—recognized that the new nation had to be independent not only in government but also in literature, language, and thought. The person who did the most toward establishing American English as a separate national standard was Noah Webster.

Webster wrote a spelling book, popularly known as the "Blue-Backed Speller," that was very widely used in the United States. It popularized certain spellings in this country that still distinguish American English from British English. In the eighteenth century, many words were spelled in more than one way: *center* or *centre, humor* or *humour, realize* or *realise.* Webster settled in each case on one spelling that he thought was simpler, better historically, or more like other English spellings.

The spellings Webster chose were learned by generations of schoolchildren and were used in the dictionaries he wrote. Thus they became the normal American forms of the words. However, Webster also proposed some simplified reform spellings, like *tung* for *tongue* and *fether* for *feather.* Though these spellings were sensible, they never caught on and so did not survive.

Today, many dictionaries have the name "Webster" in their titles, yet present-day dictionaries are considerably larger and more complete than Webster's early books. The name "Webster" has simply become associated with dictionaries the way "Roget" has with thesauruses.

which six of the ten items are Americanisms. Assign individuals to verify their predictions with a dictionary.

Guide students through the first item in **Exercise 5** on p. 473. You could reproduce the dictionary entry on a transparency.

Have students work independently on the rest of **Exercise 5** and then have them check results with partners.

ASSESSMENT

Responses to **Exercises 4** and **5** will give you an opportunity to assess students' abilities in using standard reference tools such as dictionaries to identify word origins.

CRITICAL THINKING
Evaluation

If a copy of Cecil Adams' book *More of the Straight Dope* is available, students might enjoy comparing Adams' explanation of the origins of *okay* with the explanation given in **Looking at Language.** Adams accepts Allen Walker Read's explanation as one possibility but also gives other possible origins. Ask students to evaluate which explanations they find most plausible and to give reasons for their choices.

By the end of the nineteenth century, American English was a distinct national variety, with its own words, pronunciations, spellings, and grammar. The American variety of the language was recorded in its own dictionaries and grammars, with its own literature and outlook on life.

LOOKING AT Language

I'm OK—You're OK

The most successful of all American words is *OK,* now used by speakers of languages all over the globe. Its origin was a puzzle until solved by the linguist Allen Walker Read. He discovered that *OK* stands for "oll korrect," a comic misspelling (among others like *OW* for "oll wright" and *KG* for "know go") used in Boston newspapers of 1838–1839.

In 1840, a political organization called the "O.K. Club" was formed to support Martin Van Buren's reelection as President of the United States. Van Buren was nicknamed "Old Kinderhook" after his hometown of Kinderhook, New York. The O.K. Club's name referred to that nickname but also punned on the humorous misspelling: Old Kinderhook was "oll korrect." During the election campaign of 1840, the expression *OK* was spread all over the country. Van Buren lost the election, but *OK* went on to win a permanent place in American English—and in other languages all over the world.

EXERCISE 4 **Identifying Americanisms**

Which of the following words are Americanisms—words that entered the English language in the United States? To find out, look up each word in a dictionary that identifies Americanisms.

CLOSURE

Have students identify the three main periods in the development of American English.

EXTENSION

Challenge students to bring the lyrics of songs from British music groups and to identify Briticisms in the vocabulary. The class might work on translating these expressions into Americanisms.

(A good one is *Webster's New World Dictionary,* which labels each Americanism with a star.)

1. A-OK
2. clipboard
3. cocoa
4. dogfight
5. electrician
6. foxhole
7. hologram
8. kerosene
9. locker room
10. sloppy

The International Period (1898 to the Present)

Near the end of the nineteenth century, America became increasingly involved with foreign affairs. As a result of the Spanish-American War in 1898, the United States brought Puerto Rico and the Philippines within its sphere of influence. Nineteen years later (in 1917), America entered World War I; and twenty-three years after the conclusion of that war, our country entered World War II (in 1941).

The continued presence of U.S. military bases in Europe, the location of the United Nations headquarters in New York, and our embroilments in Korea, Vietnam, and Kuwait have kept the United States involved in international matters. Those wars and political affairs, as well as commercial activities around the globe, have helped spread the influence of American English to other lands. They have also promoted the influence of other languages on English.

Following are some of the words English has borrowed from other languages in the twentieth century.

Afrikaans: apartheid
Arabic: falafel
Chinese: chow mein
Czech: robot
French: discothèque
German: moped
Greek (Classical): cybernetics
Greek (Modern): pita (bread)
Hawaiian: ukulele
Italian: pepperoni
Japanese: honcho
Latin: spelunking
Mexican Spanish: bronco
Norwegian: slalom
Pennsylvania German: spritz
Portuguese: bossa nova
Russian: sputnik
Spanish: rumba
Swedish: smorgasbord
Swiss German: muesli
Tagalog: boondocks
Yiddish: schmaltz

MEETING INDIVIDUAL NEEDS

LEP/ESL

General Strategies. You might want to invite your ESL students to add to the list of borrowed words on this page. Ask students if they have discovered words from their first languages being used in American English.

ENRICHMENT

Have students work in pairs or small groups to develop lists of plants, animals, or other items that were not in England but would have been found in America when British settlers came during the colonial period. Students can use prior knowledge or reference books to develop the lists. Have students use dictionaries to find out whether the names of these items were borrowed from Native American languages (as *moccasin* was). Groups might compete to see who can generate the longest list or the most unusual entries. ■

A DIFFERENT APPROACH

Encourage students to look up and to share especially interesting and amusing entries in reference works such as *British English, A to Zed* by Norman Schur or *British-American Language Dictionary* by Norman Moss.

COOPERATIVE LEARNING

Obtain copies of a current British magazine or newspaper. Give small groups of students passages to edit and rewrite as they think the passages might appear in a mainstream American publication. Have each group list the changes they make. Have them categorize the changes to differentiate among vocabulary, spelling, and grammatical constructions.

In turn, English has been influencing other languages around the world. Nowadays the French may *golfer* on *le weekend* (play golf on the weekend), while the Dutch who are not worried about their *fitness* spend the time watching a *videofilm*. When Danes decide not to *zappe* from one television channel to another, they may go for a real *workout* in a *triatlon* (triathlon). The well-dressed German may wear a *Pullover* (nicknamed a *Pulli*) at a *Fussball* (football) game. And a Japanese person may eat a *hotto doggu* (hot dog) while watching *futtobooru* (football) on *terebi* (television).

American and British English

In some respects, American English has changed less than British English. Those who traveled to the new land were more conservative in the way they talked than the homebodies were. For example, most Americans pronounce *r* where it is spelled, as in *roar* and *card*. But many English people do not pronounce *r* unless it is immediately followed by a vowel, so their *roar* sounds like *raw*, and their *card* sounds like *cod*. The American pronunciation is older, as the spelling suggests.

So, too, Americans say both "She's got an idea" and "She's gotten an idea" but mean different things by them. "She's got an idea" is equivalent to "She has an idea," whereas "She's gotten an idea" means "An idea has occurred to her" or "She's thought up an idea." *Got* and *gotten* are both past participles of the verb *get*, but *gotten* is the older form. In England today, people do not generally use *gotten* anymore. They have lost one of the forms of the verb, while Americans have kept it.

On the other hand, Americans have added many words to the English language, perhaps more than the British have. Here is a sample of words—both older and newer ones—that Americans have contributed to English.

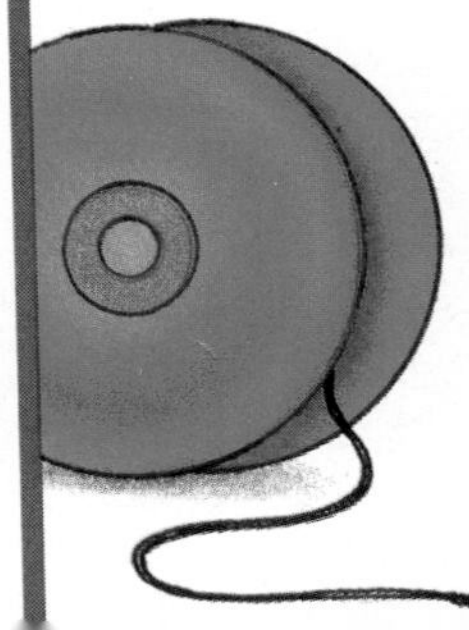

avocado
belittle
cedar chest
day-glo
eggbeater
finger painting
glitzy
hamburger
inchworm

jampacked
kerosene
lipstick
mileage
nifty
ouch!
parking lot
quarterback
road hog

shack
T-shirt
upside-down cake
volleyball
waffle
xerox
yo-yo
zipper

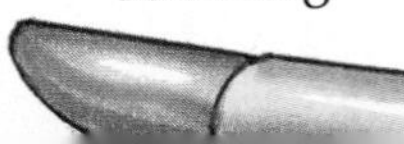

EXERCISE 5 **Translating British Expressions**

Look up each of the following expressions in a dictionary to find out what meaning it has in British English. What word or words do you use to mean the same thing?

1. bed-sitting room
2. biscuit
3. convenience
4. pram
5. tube

The Future of English

Today the English language is spread all over the world. It is the world's most important language for international communication in business, diplomacy, science, technology, and entertainment. Several countries, such as India, that have more than one native language use English as a second language for government and education. Some people in most nations of the world use English at least occasionally for a number of special purposes.

For a long while, the British variety of English was the one most widely studied and used by speakers of other languages. But movies, television, popular music, and technology have helped to spread American English outside the United States. Now both major national varieties—those of the United States and of the United Kingdom—are widely used, and some newer ones, such as Australian English, are also becoming influential.

On a popular level, English is becoming more diversified around the world as it is being used by many peoples for their own purposes. Japanese conducting business with Arabs are likely to do so in English—but an English rather different from what a native English speaker would use. International use exposes standard English to increased influence from many other languages.

Some people fear that as English is used in different regions around the world, it will break up into many local languages—just as Latin developed into Italian, French, Spanish, Portuguese, and Romanian at the end of the Roman Empire. Local varieties of English are developing, but so is an international standard of English usage. Airplane travel, television, movies, computers, and other forms of mass communication promote uniformity in our language.

ANSWERS

Exercise 5

1. The British bed-sitting room (or bed-sitter) is an American studio apartment—that is, a single multiple-purpose room used as a residence.
2. A British biscuit is a cracker or cookie.
3. *Convenience* is the discreet British way of referring to restrooms or lavatories.
4. An English pram (or *perambulator*) is a baby carriage or stroller.
5. The English word *tube* means the same thing as the American word *subway*.

CRITICAL THINKING

Analysis

The incorporation of English words into French has become so common that there is a term for it—*franglais* (from *français* for *French* and *anglais* for *English*). There is a movement by some French people to take official steps to impose fines on publications that use franglais because these people feel that French language and culture are being corrupted. Have students debate whether or not they think such concerns are legitimate and whether or not they think it is possible to prevent a language from changing.

SEGMENT 3 *(pp. 474–478)*

VARIETIES OF AMERICAN ENGLISH

OBJECTIVE

- To identify dialect differences

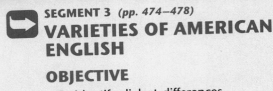

TEACHING THE LESSON

To introduce this segment, call on volunteers to read aloud the entries in the **Features of Regional Dialects** chart on p. 476. Whenever possible, draw on the dialectical differences within the class to examine the nature of dialect.

Have student volunteers read aloud the introductory material in the textbook and

COOPERATIVE LEARNING

Have students work in small groups to develop several entries for a "body language" dictionary. Each entry should include a description of the gesture—its meaning, the context in which it is commonly used, and indications of whether or not it is language-specific. Gestures must be appropriate for the classroom. Students from ethnic backgrounds should be able to make valuable contributions in this regard. While entries may be written, it would also be appropriate to have demonstrations of the gestures and perhaps even to record them on video.

Some students may be interested in doing a special presentation on American Sign Language, for which gesture is the primary component.

Teacher's ResourceBank™

RESOURCES

VARIETIES OF AMERICAN ENGLISH

- Varieties of American English 98

Today we are well on the way toward an international variety of English combining American, British, and many other influences. It will still be a various language, but following the motto of the United States, *e pluribus unum*, the English of the future will be one language joining many varieties.

LOOKING AT Language

What's Your Body Language?

The language we speak is accompanied by hundreds of gestures that reinforce what we are saying—or sometimes contradict it. Many gestures are universal—that is, people all over the world, whatever language they speak, use similar gestures in similar ways. For example, when people are puzzled and want an answer to some question, they tend to lift their eyebrows and open their eyes wide. That gesture seems to say, "I need to see more, so I am looking with wide-open eyes."

Other gestures are language-specific—that is, different cultures and languages may use quite different gestures for the same thing, just as they use different words for the same thing (like English *goodbye*, Spanish *adiós*, and Hebrew *shalom*). When English speakers want to say goodbye with a gesture, they raise a hand with the palm away from them and hold the fingers together while moving them repeatedly down to a horizontal position and back up to a vertical one. We call that "waving goodbye." In some other countries the corresponding gesture is made by holding the hand with the palm facing the gesturer. The result is similar to the gesture we use to signal "Come here," just the opposite of "Goodbye."

Varieties of American English

From the time when English speakers first came to America, they have varied in the way they spoke and wrote the language. The most widely used variety of English is *standard English*. In addition, American English includes many subvarieties called *dialects*.

the sections titled **Regional Dialects, Ethnic Dialects,** and **Standard English.** At the end of each section, discuss the material with the class. Ask students to share experiences they have had involving dialect differences and to identify features of their own or other dialects they have noticed. Emphasize that dialects are a fundamental feature of language and language development. What is called standard English is merely the dialect that has become dominant.

For guided practice for **Exercise 6** on p. 478, conduct an initial survey of the class. Then assign students to interview a specified number of individuals outside of class as independent practice.

To assess their performance on **Exercise 6,** have students show written notes ☛

Dialect

The language we use tells much about us—our home locality, ethnic background, education, gender, and age. Language variation that tells such things about us, thus helping to identify who we are and where we come from, is called ***dialect.*** The two main types of dialect used in the United States are *regional dialects* and *ethnic dialects.*

Regional Dialects

The earliest settlement of America by English colonists set a pattern for geographical differences, or ***regional dialects,*** in the United States. The colonists settled in four main cultural areas: (1) New England, (2) the Middle Atlantic area centered on Philadelphia, (3) the Southern Mountains, and (4) the Coastal South. From those areas, the early population moved westward, taking their dialects with them.

Today there are four main regional dialects spoken in the eastern and midwestern United States. However, it's important to remember that not everyone in a region speaks that region's dialect.

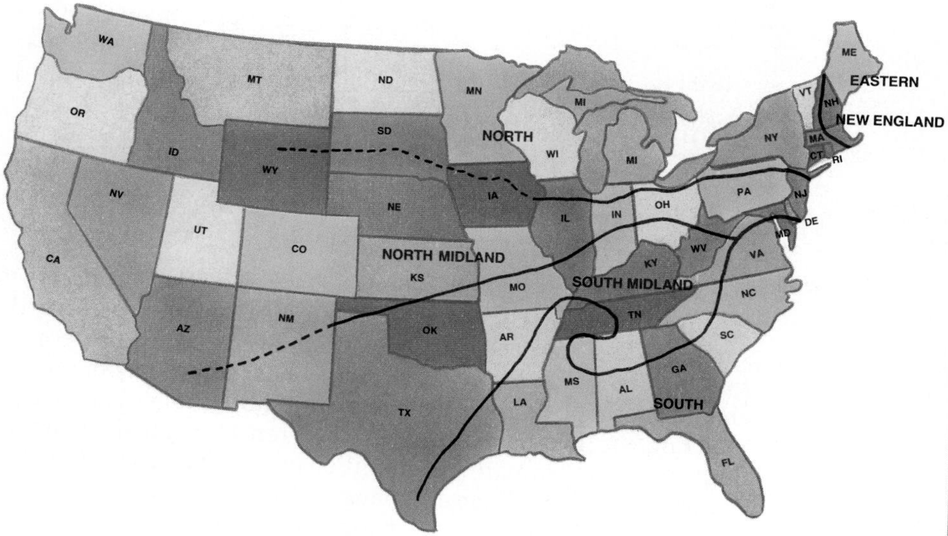

QUOTATION FOR THE DAY

"There is no one in America who does not speak Black English; there is no one in America who does not speak Yiddish. There is no one in America who does not sigh with the sigh of Mexican grandmothers." (Richard Rodriquez, 1944– , American writer)

Television takes viewers everywhere in America—to the Southwest, the Great Lakes, the Cajun country around New Orleans. Ask your class to make a list of all of the American places and speech patterns they have experienced through television. Remarkably, despite the diversity of regional and ethnic dialects, Americans have little difficulty in understanding each other's use of English.

MEETING **INDIVIDUAL** NEEDS

LEP/ESL

General Strategies. To demonstrate how English varies across the United States, play the record *Our Changing Language* (available from the National Council of Teachers of English) for the class. One side is a recording of students from different cities in the United States reading a story.

on the interviews they did. To close, call on students to define *regional dialect, ethnic dialect,* and *standard English.*

EXTENSION

Have the class conduct a survey of dialects on network television. Students might go through a weekly program guide to analyze which programs use predominantly standard English and which programs feature performers or speakers with identifiable regional or ethnic dialects. Ask students to categorize the shows and to draw conclusions

INTEGRATING THE LANGUAGE ARTS

Research Link. Have the class do a local dialect census. Assign students to keep notebooks in which they list each person with whom they have verbal communication during a specified day, including casual acquaintances such as store clerks. The purpose is to record whether the person used standard English or a regional or ethnic dialect. Have students tally results for the whole class and then calculate what proportion of the interactions included some use of dialect.

This chart shows some of the features of pronunciation, vocabulary, and grammar that distinguish one regional dialect from another.

FEATURES OF REGIONAL DIALECTS

	NORTHERN	NORTH MIDLAND	SOUTH MIDLAND	SOUTHERN
PRONUNCIATION	"greassy"	"greassy"	"greazy"	"greazy"
	"hahg"	"hahg" or hog	hog	"hawg"
	"pahked cah"	parked car	parked car	"pawked caw"
WORD CHOICE	burlap bag or gunny sack	burlap bag	burlap bag	burlap bag or croker sack
	pail	bucket	bucket	bucket
	devil's darning needle	snake feeder	snake doctor	skeeter hawk
GRAMMAR	quarter of/to	quarter to	quarter till	quarter till/to
	you, youse	you	you, you'uns	you, y'all

Ethnic Dialects

In addition to regional dialects, there are also ***ethnic dialects***—the speech patterns of special communities that have preserved some of their heritage from the past. Every group of people that has come to the United States has brought something characteristic of its original homeland and culture. For example, English, Scottish, Irish, Welsh, French, Spanish, Dutch, Scandinavian, German, Yiddish, Polish, Czech, Italian, Greek, Armenian, Indic, Chinese, Japanese, Korean, and Vietnamese people have all influenced American English.

The most prominent ethnic dialect in the United States is that of African Americans. It unites some features of West about the kinds of programming in which dialect is found [situation comedies and some dramas] and the areas in which it is unacceptable [news and news-type shows].

ENRICHMENT

Some students have little patience for or see little need for adapting language styles to different circumstances. Get them to examine the grounds for that opinion by staging a debate on the textbook's assertion: "Standard English is the most useful and the most widely used of all functional varieties (of English)" (p. 478). ■

African languages with some features of early Southern speech and yet other usages developed by the African American community itself. Some features are *aunt* pronounced "ahnt," *He be sick* meaning a continuing rather than temporary illness, and *tote* meaning "carry" (of African origin but now common in all Southern use).

The boundaries of ethnic dialects, like those of regional dialects, are fluid. For example, not all African Americans use the ethnic dialect associated with their group, and some features of African American dialect turn up in other speech communities, too.

The second most prominent ethnic dialect is Hispanic English, which has three subvarieties: Mexican-influenced English in the Southwest, Cuban-influenced English in Florida, and Puerto-Rican-influenced English in New York City and, of course, in Puerto Rico.

Early Hispanic influence in the West introduced such words as *vamoose* (from Spanish *vamos*, "let's go"), *hoosegow* (from *juzgado*, "courtroom"), *lariat* (from *la reata*, "the lasso"), and *mesa* ("table"). Today, Spanish-influenced English uses English words with the meanings of similar Spanish words. For example, *apple* is often used with the meaning of *manzana*, "city block" (*manzana* also means "apple"); *conference* with the meaning of *conferencia*, "lecture"; and *direction* with the meaning of *dirección*, "address." The number of speakers of Hispanic English has been growing in recent years and so, consequently, has the importance of their dialect.

CRITICAL THINKING
Analysis

Give each student a copy of a poem written in a regional or ethnic dialect. Possibilities include "Mother to Son" by Langston Hughes, "Little Boy Blue" by James Whitcomb Riley, or a poem by T. A. Daly that imitates the Italian and Irish accents heard in New York City. After you read the poem aloud, have students analyze it linguistically to identify features of grammar, spelling, and vocabulary that are dialectical. Then discuss the impact the dialect has on their responses to the poem. Explore how much of the poetic quality would be lost if the work were translated into standard English.

INTEGRATING THE LANGUAGE ARTS

Listening Link. Have students test their ear for regional and ethnic accents. Have a small group of students prepare a tape of people speaking a variety of regional and ethnic dialects. If students cannot find enough people who speak different dialects, they could use a record such as *Our Changing Language*, available from the National Council of Teachers of English. Play the tape for the class and have students write down the specific dialect they think each speaker is using. Have students exchange and correct the papers as the answers are read aloud.

ANSWERS

Exercise 6

Answers may vary. Here are some possibilities:

1. elastic, elastic band, rubber band, gumband
2. soft drink, soda, soda water, soda pop, pop, tonic, coke
3. faucet, spiggot, tap
4. grinder, dogwood, hoagie, hero, submarine, poor boy, torpedo, cheese steak
5. flapjack, hot cake, griddle cake, pancake

INTEGRATING THE LANGUAGE ARTS

Usage Link. Refer students to **Chapter 27: "A Glossary of Usage"** for further discussion of standard English expressions and constructions that are commonly misused.

EXERCISE 6 **Identifying Dialect Differences**

What word do you use for each of the following items? Do you know any other words for the same thing? Read each description to a friend, relative, or neighbor who grew up in a different region (or a different country) than you did. Note any differences between that person's word choices and your own.

1. a thin, circular band of elastic material put around things to hold them together
2. a flavored, sweet, carbonated beverage sold in capped bottles or in cans
3. a fixture over a sink for turning the water on and off
4. a sandwich made on a long roll sliced lengthwise and filled with meats, cheeses, and vegetables
5. a round, flat piece of fried batter, usually eaten with syrup

Standard English

Standard English is a variety of language that is not limited to a particular place or ethnic group. It is used all over the country (and even all over the world) by people of all backgrounds without indicating what place or group they belong to. It is the one variety of English that belongs to everybody.

Standard English is more a matter of writing than of speech, especially in the United States. It is used for treating important matters seriously, and it is especially appropriate for talking with or writing to people we don't know well. It is the language of public affairs and education, of publications and television, of science and technology, of business and government. It is the variety of English recorded in dictionaries and grammar books.

You can find some of the rules and guidelines for using standard English in the **Handbook** in this textbook. To identify the differences between standard English and other varieties of English, the **Handbook** uses the labels *standard* and *nonstandard*. *Nonstandard* doesn't mean wrong language. It means language that is inappropriate where standard English is expected.

Standard English is the most useful and the most widely used of all functional varieties. Nobody needs to use it all the time, but everybody should be able to use it when it is the right variety to use.

SEGMENT 4 *(p. 479)*

MAKING CONNECTIONS

THE FOREIGN GOURMET

OBJECTIVES

- To use a dictionary to discover the origins of ethnic food terms
- To write an international menu and to give etymological information on the food items listed

MAKING CONNECTIONS

The Foreign Gourmet

An area that is especially productive of words borrowed from other languages is food and cooking. Many terms come from abroad along with the items of food or the style of cooking that they name. Here are two activities to make you a gourmet linguist.

1. Make a list of ten foods you particularly like. Look up the names of those foods in a dictionary to find out where the words come from. How many of these names came into English from other languages?

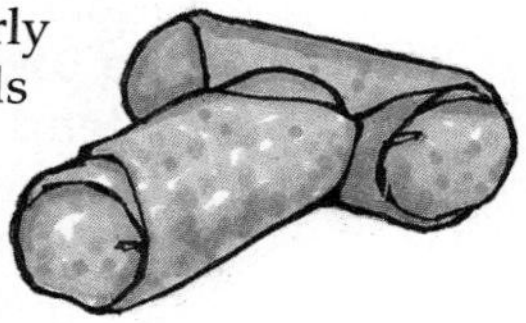

2. Do you ever eat in ethnic restaurants? Many communities have Italian, Chinese, Mexican, Indian, Greek, Japanese, and other ethnic restaurants. Do some fieldwork by going to an ethnic restaurant and reading its menu. Jot down any food terms that seem to be special to the ethnic style of cooking of that restaurant.

Then, using an unabridged dictionary, look up the terms you have gathered from the menu to see what they mean and where they come from. If any of the words are not in the dictionary, they may be new words for English. See whether you can find out what they mean.

As a group project, join with four or five other members of your class to arrange a "word-meal." Plan an imaginary dinner consisting of international foods from the menus people in your group have read. Write your own menu of various dishes. For each item on the menu, give its name, describe the dish, and identify the ethnic origin of both the dish and the name.

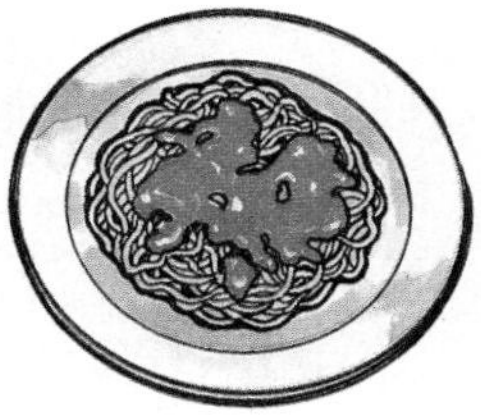

THE FOREIGN GOURMET

Teaching Strategies

This assignment provides an opportunity for multisensory and experiential learning. To get students' mouths watering and ideas ticking, put out menus from ethnic restaurants, food sections from the newspapers, gourmet magazines, and recipe cards or illustrated cookbooks. You can provide some of these items and invite students to bring in others. Let students browse through the materials as they prepare their ten-item lists of favorite foods.

Encourage the groups to illustrate the word-meals they have planned. If your school has an international club, you may want to arrange coordinating an International Foods Fair, during which different ethnic dishes could be prepared and available for sampling.

GUIDELINES

In evaluating students' responses, check that each entry includes the designated information—especially the etymology. You might offer extra credit for more inclusive research that gives the origins of all food-related words.

Chapter 13

STYLE IN WRITING

OBJECTIVES

- To experiment with tone
- To classify language as formal or informal
- To write an informal dialogue
- To replace general words in sentences with synonyms
- To analyze connotations
- To identify jargon and to replace it with everyday language
- To revise a review to eliminate tired words and clichés
- To revise sentences containing mixed figures of speech
- To revise a paragraph to eliminate euphemisms and gobbledygook
- To write a persuasive letter to the editor
- To write an informative, expressive letter to a friend

Motivation

To interest students in the material in this chapter, begin by presenting them with a style sampler. A style sampler is a series of paragraphs by different authors, each with a distinctive style. (Suggested authors and sources include Ernest Hemingway, William Faulkner, Bobbie Ann Mason, Annie Dillard, N. Scott Momaday, Joan Didion, a government document, ad copy, and a contract.) Ask students to describe each of the authors' styles and to consider what makes these styles different. Ask students to describe their own writing styles and to offer examples.

Introduction

You might begin by pointing out to students that all good writers employ a variety of styles. For example, the style that Faulkner uses in his stream-of-consciousness novels is not the same style he uses to write letters to his publisher.

Explain that everyone needs to develop stylistic flexibility because people must write in a variety of aims, for a variety of audiences, and in a variety of situations.

You may want to relate styles of writing to styles in clothing by asking students to discuss what styles are appropriate for the beach, for the high school prom, for a job interview, and so on. Students may also enjoy identifying stylistic mistakes in both writing and fashion.

Integration

This chapter may be taught independently or in conjunction with one or more writing assignments. It is also a useful reference chapter for students with stylistic problems.

The section on denotation and connotation should prove helpful in conjunction with the study of poetry, while the section on informal English will help students understand the role that language plays in characterization in literature. The material on informal English will also be useful if students write plays or short stories containing dialogue.

The chart on the next page illustrates the strands of language arts as they are integrated into this chapter. For vocabulary study, glossary words are underlined in some writing models.

QUOTATIONS
All **Quotations for the Day** are chosen because of their relevance to instructional material presented in that segment of the chapter and for their usefulness in establishing student interest in writing.

INTEGRATING THE LANGUAGE ARTS

Selection	Reading and Literature	Writing and Critical Thinking	Language and Syntax	Speaking, Listening, and Other Expression Skills
from **"My Wonder Horse"** by Sabine Ulibarri **483** from ***Roughing It*** by Mark Twain **483** from ***Please Don't Eat the Daisies*** by Jean Kerr **486** from ***Through the Looking Glass*** by Lewis Carroll **488**	Classifying language as formal or informal **486** Finding evidence to support an opinion **486**	Writing a descriptive piece **484** Experimenting with and analyzing tone **484, 493** Applying interpretive and creative thinking **486, 491, 493, 496-497, 500, 501-502** Classifying language as formal or informal **486** Writing an informal dialogue **488** Using synonyms **491** Revising a paragraph to create clear, vivid images **491** Analyzing connotations **493** Writing sentences using similar words **493** Replacing jargon with everyday language **494** Revising to eliminate tired words and clichés **496-497** Identifying tired words and clichés **496-497** Revising mixed figures of speech **498** Revising to eliminate euphemisms and gobbledygook **500** Writing a letter to the editor of a newspaper **501-502** Writing a letter to a friend **502**	Using a thesaurus to find synonyms **491** Analyzing connotations **493** Using a dictionary for technical translations **494** Identifying tired words and clichés **496** Identifying mixed figures of speech **498** Analyzing euphemisms and gobbledygook **500**	Working with classmates to analyze tone **484, 493** Discussing responses to connotations **493**

CHAPTER 13

SEGMENT PLANNING GUIDE

Whether you are planning for a quick review of a writing concept or preparing an extended lesson on composition, you can use the following Planning Guide to adapt the chapter material to the individual needs of your class.

SEGMENT	PAGES	CONTENT	RESOURCES
1 *What Is Style?*	*480-488*		Voice and Tone 103 Formal and Informal English 104
What Is Style?	480-481	Guidelines: learning the definition of style	
Adapting Your Style	481	Guidelines: examining the four aims of writing	
Voice and Tone	482-483	Guidelines: using appropriate voice and tone	
Literary Model from **"My Wonder Horse"**	483	Guided reading: analyzing tone in a model	
Literary Model from ***Roughing It***	483	Guided reading: analyzing tone in a model	
Exercise 1	484	Applied practice: writing a description using different tones	
Formal to Informal	484	Guidelines: defining levels of usage	
Chart: Writing/Speaking Formal and Informal English	484	Guidelines: analyzing appropriate usage of formal and informal English	
Chart: Features of Formal an Informal English	485	Guidelines: examining features of formal and informal English	
Exercise 2	486	Applied practice: classifying language as formal or informal	
Literary Model from ***Please Don't Eat the Daisies***	486	Guided reading: examining tone in a model	
Informal English Usage	486-488	Guidelines: analyzing examples of slang and colloquialisms	
Style Note	488	Writing suggestion: using slang words appropriately	
Exercise 3	488	Applied practice: writing an informal dialogue	
2 *Levels of Meaning*	*488-495*		Synonyms 105 Nonsexist Language 106 Denotation and Connotation 107
Levels of Meaning	488-489	Guidelines: using the right word	
Literary Model from ***Through the Looking Glass***	488	Guided reading: examining meaning in a model	
Synonyms	489	Guidelines: using exact words	
Looking at Language	490	Example: avoiding malapropisms	
Nonsexist Language	491-492	Guidelines: examining nonsexist terms	
Exercise 4	491	Applied practice: using synonyms	

All the resources listed in this chapter are located in the *Teacher's ResourceBank*™.

SEGMENT	PAGES	CONTENT	RESOURCES
Denotation and Connotation	492	Guidelines: distinguishing between denotation and connotation	
Loaded Words	492	Guidelines: understanding loaded words	
Exercise 5	493	Applied practice: responding to connotations	
Exercise 6	493	Applied practice: analyzing connotations	
Jargon	493-494	Guidelines: using jargon appropriately	
Exercise 7	494-495	Applied practice: replacing jargon with everyday language	
3 *Don't Cramp Your Style*	*495-500*		
Tired Words	495	Guidelines: identifying tired words	Jargon, Tired Words, and Clichés 108 Mixed Figures of Speech 109 Euphemism and Gobbledygook 110
Clichés	495	Guidelines: identifying clichés	
Style Note	496	Writing suggestion: experimenting with clichés	
Exercise 8	496-497	Applied practice: revising to eliminate tired words and clichés	
Mixed Figures of Speech	497	Guidelines: identifying mixed figures of speech	
Exercise 9	498	Applied practice: revising mixed figures of speech	
Euphemisms	498-499	Guidelines: using euphemisms appropriately	
Chart: Euphemism/More Direct Term	499	Example: examining common euphemisms	
Gobbledygook	499	Guidelines: identifying gobbledygook	
Exercise 10	500	Applied practice: revising to eliminate euphemisms and gobbledygook	
4 *Making Connections*	*501-502*		
Write with Different Aims	501-502	Guidelines: using criteria to write a persuasive letter and an expressive letter Applied practice: writing in the persuasive and expressive aims	
WHOLE-CHAPTER RESOURCES Review Form A, Review Form B			

SEGMENT 1 *(pp. 480–488)*

WHAT IS STYLE?

OBJECTIVES

- To experiment with tone in writing descriptions
- To classify language as formal or informal
- To write an informal dialogue

TEACHING THE LESSON

Begin by reading aloud the chapter opener. Before students address the material in the next two paragraphs, you may want to have them arrive at their own definitions of style in language. Students may then compare their definitions with the definition in the text.

Teacher's ResourceBank™

RESOURCES

WHAT IS STYLE?

- Voice and Tone 103
- Formal and Informal English 104

QUOTATION FOR THE DAY

"A change of style is a change of subject." (Wallace Stevens, 1879–1955, American poet)

In his poetic way, Stevens might be saying that a change in words signals a change in how a subject is presented. In the examples describing the rescue of the four-year-old girl (p. 481), have students notice how the style in **Informative** is distant and coolly factual. In **Expressive** the subject switches to the rescuer's thoughts and the style becomes human and immediate. In **Literary** the rescue is described as if from above by a caring and compassionate eyewitness. In each case the event is the same, but the subject of the writer's concern shifts with subtle changes in writing style.

13 Style in Writing

LOOKING AHEAD

Skillful writing can seem like magic. But behind every compelling story, article, poem, letter, and advertisement is a real-life writer who chose words with care. With practice, you can develop your own style to bring life to your writing. In this chapter, you will work on your style by

- adapting your writing to audience, situation, and aim
- experimenting with voice and tone
- choosing livelier, clearer words
- sidestepping some common obstacles to style

What Is Style?

How many ways can you think of to explain how to ride a bike? to thank someone for a gift? to describe a rainy day? The English language offers you many different ways to express your thoughts and ideas. Every time you talk and write, you make your own choices about what words to use and how to use them. The kinds of choices you make add up to your *style*.

Have a volunteer read aloud the material under **Adapting Your Style** and ask students how they would explain why different aims seem to require different styles.

To teach **Voice and Tone** on pp. 482–484, read through the material paragraph by paragraph. Pause after each paragraph to give students a minute or two to write any responses they may have. Then ask each student to write a two- or three-sentence response to the whole reading and to share the response with the class.

After reading the literary models on p. 483, ask students for their impressions of voice and tone in each passage.

To prepare students for **Exercise 1** on p. 484, model a sample response on the chalkboard

☛

Style is your unique way of adapting your language to suit different occasions. When you develop a style, you make your words your own. You craft your writing to put something of yourself—your own personality—into it.

Adapting Your Style

Having a style doesn't mean writing in the same way all the time. When you speak and write, your language changes depending on

- your ***audience***—who you are writing for
- your ***situation***—when and where you are writing
- your ***aim***—why you are writing

Audience and situation are the circumstances of your writing. They help determine whether your language should be formal or informal, serious or playful. Aim is what gives your words a purpose. Your aim may be to persuade, to give information, to express your thoughts and feelings, or to create literature. Each of these four aims of writing has distinctive features of style.

Read the following four sentences about the same event. Notice how in each case, a change in aim brings a change in language.

INFORMATIVE — At a banquet held in her honor on Saturday evening, ten-year-old Raven Carmichael was named Hero of the Year for her rescue of a four-year-old child trapped in a drainage pipe.

PERSUASIVE — I urge you to name Raven Carmichael Hero of the Year because of her bravery, her quick thinking, her composure in the face of danger, and her disregard for her personal safety during the rescue of a child not much younger than she.

EXPRESSIVE — When I saw Tommy's head go under, I figured he was stuck, so I jumped in and kept feeling around until I could tear him loose from the branches and stuff that were washing down the ditch.

LITERARY — Scurrying down the muddy embankment into the flooding ditch, Raven groped for the child's head and arms, yanking him above water and then tearing at the sodden debris that entangled his legs.

MEETING INDIVIDUAL NEEDS

LEP/ESL

General Strategies. Although students may have command of several speaking and writing styles in their first languages, they may have command of only one style in English. They will probably grasp the concept of style variation but will have trouble recognizing different styles in English. Before they can produce variations in style, students may need extra practice reading and identifying English style types. You could substitute style identification tasks whenever the writing tasks in this chapter seem too challenging for students.

ADVANCED STUDENTS

Have each student find works by an author that exhibit different aims. For example, a writer of fiction may also have published literary criticism, personal essays, or informative magazine articles.

Ask students to determine the aims of the works they have chosen and to identify the characteristics that define the purposes. Then have each student compare and contrast the works he or she has chosen. How do the works differ from one another? How are they similar? Have students share their observations with the class.

for them. Then assign **Exercise 1** as independent practice. Encourage students to be as specific as possible when they compare paragraphs with classmates.

To begin the **Formal to Informal** section on p. 484, draw a line on the chalkboard and label one end *Very Formal* and the other *Very Informal*. Ask students to provide examples of formal writing and speaking and examples of informal writing and speaking. Then compare students' responses with the chart on p. 484. You may want to go over the **Features of Formal and Informal English** chart on p. 485 and have students suggest additional examples.

For guided practice, work through **Exercise 2** on p. 486 with the class. Point out the informal phrases in the passage.

MEETING INDIVIDUAL NEEDS

LESS-ADVANCED STUDENTS

Some students may have difficulty grasping the idea that it is possible for an individual to have more than one true voice. You may need to help them relate this concept to everyday life. For example, you might ask them to describe how they interact with grandparents, small children, friends of the same sex, friends of the opposite sex, and so on.

Voice and Tone

People have distinctive voices in writing just as they do in speaking. ***Voice*** in writing is the unique sound and rhythm of the writer's language. You can recognize voice by the ring of authenticity it brings to writing. When you read a letter from a friend and can imagine the person standing right there talking to you, you know your friend has written in a true voice.

Voice is an important part of your style. It gives your writing a sound of honesty and authority. Your voice can shine through in any kind of writing—not just in letters and journal entries but also in research papers and poems. Most often, you will want to write in a voice that sounds like you. Sometimes, though, you will want to write in a voice that sounds like someone else—for example, when you imitate another writer's style or when you write dialogue for a character in a story.

Like your speaking voice, your writing voice has a wide range. When you speak, your tone of voice helps express how you feel—happy, sad, angry, afraid, serious, offhand, sarcastic. It even tells people how you want *them* to feel about your subject. But when you write, your words have to do all the work, putting across feelings as well as meanings.

Tone in writing is the attitude or feeling that the writer's words express. If you're writing a newspaper editorial to protest the killing of dolphins in commercial fishing nets, your tone might be angry. But if you're writing a report on marine mammals for biology class, your tone will probably be neutral and objective.

Sometimes you can create a tone with just a few words. If you describe rain on a window as looking "like a string of diamonds," your tone is positive, even romantic. If you describe the rain as looking "like tears streaking a face," your tone is sad and mournful.

For independent practice have each student analyze one of his or her short writing assignments.

Have a volunteer read the material in the section **Informal English Usage** (pp. 486–488), and encourage students to give further examples of colloquialisms, idioms, and slang. To prepare students for **Exercise 3** on p. 488, have students supply you with a few sentences of informal dialogue and write the sentences on the chalkboard. Then assign the writing for **Exercise 3** as independent practice.

As you read the following passages, listen to each writer's voice. How do each writer's words and sentences help create the sound and rhythm of the writing? How do they help set the tone?

> He was white. White as memories lost. He was free. Free as happiness is. He was fantasy, liberty, and excitement. He filled and dominated the mountain valleys and surrounding plains. He was a white horse that flooded my youth with dreams and poetry.
>
> Around the campfires of the country and in the sunny patios of the town, the ranch hands talked about him with enthusiasm and admiration. But gradually their eyes would become hazy and blurred with dreaming. The lively talk would die down. All thoughts fixed on the vision evoked by the horse. Myth of the animal kingdom. Poem of the world of men.
>
> Sabine Ulibarrí, "My Wonder Horse"

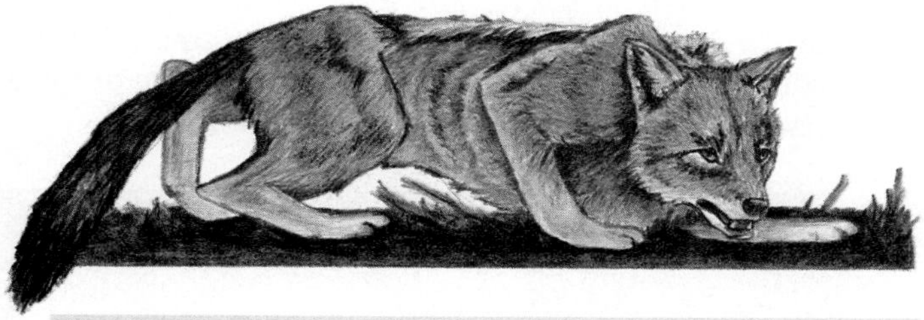

> The coyote is a long, slim, sick, and sorry-looking skeleton, with a gray wolf-skin stretched over it, a tolerably bushy tail that forever sags down with a despairing expression of forsakenness and misery, a furtive and evil eye, and a long, sharp face, with slightly lifted lip and exposed teeth. He has a general slinking expression all over. The coyote is a living, breathing allegory of Want. He is *always* hungry. He is always poor, out of luck, and friendless. The meanest creatures despise him, and even the fleas would desert him for a velocipede. He is so spiritless and cowardly that even while his exposed teeth are pretending a threat, the rest of his face is apologizing for it.
>
> Mark Twain, *Roughing It*

MEETING **INDIVIDUAL** NEEDS

LEARNING STYLES

Auditory Learners. Reinforce the concept of tone by having students identify your tone as you speak. You might try repeating a sentence such as "Soon Crentha will be leaving town," in a variety of tones. For example, you could portray sadness, excitement, and anger. Then explain that writers can't use voice inflection; instead, they must choose specific words and phrases to convey tone. Ask the class what word or words could be added to the sentence to make different tones clear to someone reading the sentence.

AMENDMENTS TO SELECTIONS

Description of change: excerpted
Rationale: to focus on the concept of style presented in this chapter

ASSESSMENT

To determine whether your students have a basic understanding of the concepts in this segment, assess their responses to each of the three exercises.

RETEACHING

Present students with reviews of a recent film taken from distinctly different sources—*New Yorker, People,* and *Seventeen,* for example. Guide students through analyzing the voice and tone of each selection. Help students identify the levels of usage and any examples of slang or colloquialisms.

ANSWERS

Exercise 1

Descriptions will vary. Here is an example of a neutral, objective description followed by a description with a distinctive voice and tone:

My cat Snowball is a long-haired white cat. She is a large female cat weighing about fourteen pounds. Her eyes are blue. Snowball has a rough, pink tongue and sharp claws.

My cat Snowball has long, white, silky, beautiful hair. She's very large for a cat—she weighs almost fourteen pounds. She has azure-blue eyes the color of the sea. Her pink tongue is rough and raspy like sandpaper. Snowball's claws are so sharp they could be considered deadly weapons, but no matter how rough our playing gets, she never scratches me.

EXERCISE 1 **Experimenting with Tone**

Write two descriptions of an animal, a place, or a thing that's familiar to you. In the first version, give a neutral, objective description of your subject. In the second version, use words that reveal your attitude toward your subject—affection, disgust, fear, humor, or whatever.

Compare your paragraphs with those of a classmate. How are your word choices different from one another's? What distinguishes your voice from your classmate's?

Formal to Informal

Audience, situation, and aim help determine whether your language is *formal* or *informal*. In many cases, you change the formality of your language automatically. For example, your language is naturally more formal in a graduation speech or a research paper than it is in a journal entry or a note to a friend.

The kinds of language you use in different situations are called ***levels of usage.*** The levels of usage in standard English range from very formal to very informal. Most usage falls somewhere in between. Following are some of the appropriate uses of ***formal English*** and ***informal English.***

WRITING	
Formal	**Informal**
serious essays, official reports, research papers, some literary criticism, and speeches on serious or solemn occasions	personal letters, journal entries, newspaper and magazine articles, nonfiction books, novels, short stories, and plays
SPEAKING	
Formal	**Informal**
formal occasions, banquets, dedication ceremonies, addresses, presentation ceremonies	everyday conversation at home, school, work, and recreation

CLOSURE

As you write their responses on the chalkboard, have students verbally list the aims of writing, the definitions of *voice* and *tone,* three features of formal and informal writing, respectively, and three types of informal usage.

EXTENSION

Choose a short piece written in formal English and have students rewrite it in informal English. Then chose a piece written in informal English and have students rewrite it in formal English. You may also want to allow students to experiment with rewriting short pieces to change tone. ■

The following chart lists some of the features of formal and informal English in both speaking and writing.

FEATURES OF FORMAL AND INFORMAL ENGLISH			
WORDS			
FORMAL	EXAMPLE	INFORMAL	EXAMPLE
longer	*angry*	**shorter**	*mad*
technical	*accelerate*	**everyday**	*speed up*
rare	*funambulist*	**common**	*tightrope walker*
precise	*helpful, friendly*	**fuzzy**	*nice*
specialized	*allegro*	**general**	*lively*
serious	*distasteful*	**offhand**	*icky*
restrained	*very enjoyable*	**exaggerated**	*absolutely incredible*
PRONUNCIATION			
FORMAL	EXAMPLE	INFORMAL	EXAMPLE
slower	*Stand up quickly.*	**faster**	*Standupquick!*
precise	*What do you say?*	**relaxed**	*Whatcha say?*
SPELLING			
FORMAL	EXAMPLE	INFORMAL	EXAMPLE
in full	*will not*	**contractions**	*won't*
conventional	*through*	**unconventional**	*thru*
GRAMMAR			
FORMAL	EXAMPLE	INFORMAL	EXAMPLE
complex	*The band that played today was from Milwaukee.*	**compound**	*The band was from Milwaukee, and it played today.*
complete	*It is hot today.*	**fragmentary**	*Hot today.*
explicit	*What you just said is surprising.*	**implied**	*Wow!*

A DIFFERENT APPROACH

Before going over the **Features of Formal and Informal English** chart, give students copies of the chart with some of the examples missing. Ask students to provide the examples and then to compare their responses with the information in the textbook.

ENRICHMENT

Have students make dictionaries of slang terms, colloquialisms, or idioms that are unique to their region or age group. Have them guess at the origins of the terms. They might even invent a history for each term. Then have students check their guesses in reference books on word origins. ■

ANSWERS

Exercise 2

The passage is informal. Supporting examples will vary. Here are some possibilities:

the use of contractions (*didn't* and *wouldn't*), the use of everyday language (You take Kelly, for instance), and the use of compound sentences (He's a wire-haired fox terrier and he's had us for three years now)

MEETING INDIVIDUAL NEEDS

STUDENTS WITH SPECIAL NEEDS

Because personal involvement with the lesson is an effective motivator for students with attention-deficit disorders, call on them frequently while you are teaching **Informal English Usage.** Give students opportunities to share examples of slang and colloquialisms they use in their speaking and writing.

SELECTION AMENDMENT
Description of change: excerpted
Rationale: to focus on the concept of style presented in this chapter

EXERCISE 2 **Classifying Language as Formal or Informal**

How would you classify the following passage—formal or informal? Give specific examples to support your answer.

> I never meant to say anything about this, but the fact is that I have never met a dog that didn't have it in for me. You take Kelly, for instance. He's a wire-haired fox terrier and he's had us for three years now. I wouldn't say that he was terribly handsome but he does have a very nice smile. What he *doesn't* have is any sense of fitness. All the other dogs in the neighborhood spend their afternoons yapping at each other's heels or chasing cats. Kelly spends his whole day, every day, chasing swans on the millpond. I don't actually worry because he will never catch one. For one thing, he can't swim. Instead of settling for a simple paddle like everybody else, he has to show off and try some complicated overhand stroke, with the result that he always sinks and has to be fished out. Naturally, people talk, and I never take him for a walk that somebody doesn't point him out and say, "There's that crazy dog that chases swans."
>
> Jean Kerr, *Please Don't Eat the Daisies*

Informal English Usage

Because informal English is flexible, its style is loose and free. Out of this freedom come two types of expressions: *colloquialisms* and *slang*.

Colloquialisms are words and phrases of conversational language. In fact, the word *colloquial* derives from a Latin word meaning "conversation." Used appropriately, colloquialisms can give your writing a lively, personal tone.

EXAMPLES Gene **took a notion** to wash the car in the rain.
I think I'll **put in for** that delivery job.
Colloquialisms can **put across** a point **pretty** fast.
We're all **pulling** for Ramona to win the race tonight.

Many colloquialisms are *idioms*. ***Idioms*** are words and phrases that mean something different from the literal meanings of the words. For example, if a friend says it's time to "hit the road," that doesn't mean you should run outside and slap the pavement. It means it's time to leave. Always use idioms with care. In many idioms, the change of a word or two can alter the whole meaning of the expression.

CLEAR **We're up a creek.** [The idiom *up a creek* means "in deep trouble."]

UNCLEAR **We're down a creek.** [The use of *down* makes the reader unsure whether the writer misused the expression *up a creek* or intended a completely different meaning.]

Slang is highly informal language that consists of made-up words or of words used in new ways. It is often lively, imaginative, and entertaining. Almost any group of closely associated people creates slang. Teenagers, musicians, sailors, cooks, truck drivers, and fashion models all build a slang vocabulary that's unique to each group.

The following words and phrases are considered slang when used with the given meanings.

bad: good, excellent	*stupid fresh:* very good
dudette: woman or girl	*yup yup:* yes
par: good	*gear:* clothing
rad or *radical:* good	*frontin':* not being honest

Don't be surprised if many of these slang words seem outdated. Most slang rides a crest of popularity and then dies out quickly. For instance, for some young people in the 1950s, the slang word *shoe* briefly replaced the slang words *neat* and *cool*.

Other slang words have been around for centuries. The word *duds*, meaning "clothing," dates back to the sixteenth century. Occasionally, slang words are used so widely that they stop being slang and become part of general English usage. The words *nice, pants,* and *nickel* were once slang.

INTEGRATING THE LANGUAGE ARTS

Research Link. Give students the following list of words and phrases:

attractive female	clothing
attractive male	crazy
good or pleasing	home
strange or unusual	car
undesirable	money

Have students list their slang words for each of these things. Then have them interview people of different ages and list the equivalent slang terms from earlier times.

Use the lists as the basis for a discussion on how language changes. Then ask students if they can name any examples of slang terms they have used that have gone out of style.

MEETING INDIVIDUAL NEEDS

LEP/ESL

General Strategies. It is useful for teenage newcomers to American schools to learn the slang expressions of their classmates as soon as possible. Rather than have ESL students write out the dialogue assignment for **Exercise 3** on p. 488, let them listen while native speakers read their dialogues aloud. You could also ask ESL students to share slang expressions from their first languages and to explain the expressions to the class.

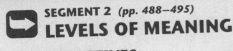

SEGMENT 2 *(pp. 488–495)*

LEVELS OF MEANING

OBJECTIVES

- To find synonyms to replace bland words in a paragraph
- To respond to connotations of words
- To analyze connotations and to write pairs of sentences containing synonyms
- To replace jargon with everyday language in sentences

ANSWERS

Exercise 3

Dialogues will vary. Encourage students to have specific adventure movies in mind as they write their dialogues.

Teacher's ResourceBank™

RESOURCES

LEVELS OF MEANING

SELECTION AMENDMENT

Description of change: excerpted
Rationale: to focus on the concept of style presented in this chapter

STYLE NOTE

A few slang words can instantly set a story in time and make characters seem real. For example, if a character uses the expression "the cat's pajamas," a slang expression from the 1920s, this tells you that the story probably isn't set in the present day.

When you write a story, make sure that any slang expressions you use are from the right time period. Otherwise your characters' dialogue may sound inauthentic.

EXERCISE 3 **Writing an Informal Dialogue**

Write an informal dialogue in which two teenagers talk about an adventure movie they've just seen. One character is very impressed with the movie; the other thinks it is awful. Have each character talk in the informal, everyday language that you and your friends use. Give "translations" for any slang words that readers from another generation may not understand.

Levels of Meaning

In the following passage, Lewis Carroll's Humpty Dumpty presents his solution to the task of choosing the right word.

> "When *I* use a word," Humpty Dumpty said, in rather a scornful tone, "it means just what I choose it to mean—neither more nor less."
> "The question is," said Alice, "whether you *can* make words mean so many different things."
> "The question is," said Humpty Dumpty, "which is to be master—that's all."
> Lewis Carroll, *Through the Looking-Glass*

Humpty Dumpty may think he is "master" of his words, but he really isn't. Having mastery of language doesn't mean using words any way you want. It means being able to express

MOTIVATION

To interest students in this segment, list two or three words on the chalkboard that have synonyms with distinctly different connotations—*thin* (skinny), and *economical* (stingy), for example. Ask students to list four or five synonyms for each word and to discuss the similarities and differences in meanings.

TEACHING THE LESSON

Begin this segment by asking a volunteer to read aloud the excerpt from ***Through the Looking Glass.*** Invite students to respond to Humpty Dumpty's claim, and then have the volunteer read the next two paragraphs aloud.

Write on the chalkboard the following headings: *Synonyms, Malapropisms,* ☛

your ideas with clarity and style. To make words work for you, you need to know what meanings they will communicate to your readers.

Dictionaries help you choose words that have the right literal meanings. But words are much more than their dictionary definitions. A word can mean different things depending on how, when, why, and even by whom it is used. And two words that mean basically the same thing can have very different effects on people.

Synonyms

Using ***synonyms***—different words with similar meanings—is an excellent way to add zest to your writing. Instead of using the word *said* over and over, why not opt for some livelier, more specific words—*blurted, growled, muttered, shrieked?* Instead of writing that someone *laughed,* why not have the person *giggle, hoot, snicker,* or *snort?*

You can use a *thesaurus,* a book of synonyms, to find different ways of saying the same thing. But remember that no two words have exactly the same meaning. Be sure to look up an unfamiliar synonym in a dictionary before you use it as a replacement. Otherwise you may write something you did not intend. Notice how the replacement of one word changes the meaning in the following sentences.

The young man **walked** toward the crowd in the street.
The young man **strolled** toward the crowd in the street.
The young man **strutted** toward the crowd in the street.

Strolled and *strutted* are both synonyms for *walked.* But while *walked* is a general word, *strolled* and *strutted* describe specific ways of walking. *Strolled* suggests the man is casual and relaxed, while *strutted* suggests he is proud and swaggering.

QUOTATION FOR THE DAY

"A good stylist should have narcissistic enjoyment as he works." (Karl Kraus, 1874–1936, Austrian satirist)

Ask students to freewrite short journal entries about what they think Kraus might mean. Then discuss the quotation with the class. Encourage students to develop the feeling that they are playing with words when they write. Ideally, writers—even young writers—take pleasure in the process of choosing words as they write and revise, and they feel a sense of personal pride in their work.

MEETING INDIVIDUAL NEEDS

LEP/ESL

General Strategies. You may want to spend some time teaching students how to use a thesaurus to find synonyms. You could choose two sentences from **Exercise 4** on p. 491 and then guide students through the process of finding synonyms for the underscored words.

Nonsexist Terms, Denotative and Connotative Pairs, and *Loaded Words.* Have volunteers read aloud the definitions and examples of each category. After each section, challenge the class to think of further examples as you write their offerings on the chalkboard under the appropriate headings.

GUIDED PRACTICE

To prepare students for **Exercise 4,** guide them through the first two or three substitutions in the paragraph. For **Exercise 5** on p. 493, you could model responses to one or two of the words. Then model possible responses to the first item in **Exercise 6** on p. 493 and the first item in **Exercise 7** on pp. 494–495.

A DIFFERENT APPROACH

To give interested students more exposure to the humor of malapropisms, you could have them read Mrs. Malaprop's lines in the play *The Rivals* by Richard Sheridan. A more recent source of malapropisms is Archie Bunker, the main character of the television shows *All in the Family* and *Archie's Place.* If reruns or videotapes of these shows are available, students could watch them. Have students share with the rest of the class some of the malapropisms they find.

MEETING INDIVIDUAL NEEDS

ADVANCED STUDENTS

Divide the class into groups of three or four to write dialogues containing malapropisms. The groups could use a combination of brainstorming, looking through dictionaries, and doing library research to create their malapropisms. Have groups share their dialogues with the class, perhaps by performing or reading them aloud.

SELECTION AMENDMENT
Description of change: excerpted
Rationale: to focus on the concept of style presented in this chapter

LOOKING AT Language

Malapropisms

When Richard Sheridan wrote his play *The Rivals,* he created the now-famous character Mrs. Malaprop. Mrs. Malaprop is the sort of person who pretends to know more than she does. Her misuse of words is so strikingly humorous that similar blunders are now called *malapropisms.* (*Malaprop* comes from the French phrase *mal à propos,* meaning "not appropriate.")

Mistaking the word *pineapple* for *pinnacle,* Mrs. Malaprop exclaims, "He is the very pineapple of politeness!" When her niece becomes interested in a man Mrs. Malaprop finds unsuitable, she advises the girl to "Illiterate him, I say, quite from your memory." Of course, the word Mrs. Malaprop was looking for was *obliterate,* not *illiterate.*

Seen from afar, Mrs. Malaprop's bloopers are humorous. However, mistakes like hers are all too easy to make because many words sound alike or have similar meanings. For example, which of the following sentences is correct?

The perfect anecdote for a broken heart is a new romance.
The perfect antidote for a broken heart is a new romance.

The second sentence uses the correct word. An *antidote* counteracts poison or relieves pain. An *anecdote* is something else entirely—a very brief story. Familiarize yourself with the precise meanings of easily confused words, such as *effect* and *affect, imply* and *infer.* With careful word choice, you'll be a *prodigy* of learning rather than, as Mrs. Malaprop would say, "A *progeny* of learning."

Nonsexist Language

Nonsexist language is language that applies to people in general, both male and female. For example, *humanity* and *humankind* are nonsexist replacements for the gender-specific word *mankind.* If you are referring to humanity as a whole, it's preferable to replace gender-specific expressions with nonsexist synonyms. Otherwise, your words may distract your audience and interfere with your aim.

INDEPENDENT PRACTICE

Assign the remainder of **Exercises 4–7** as independent practice.

ASSESSMENT

To assess how well your students have understood the concepts in this segment, evaluate their responses to **Exercises 4–7.**

In the past, many occupations were open only to men or only to women. Job titles such as *policeman* and *stewardess* reflect those limitations. Now that most jobs are held by both men and women, our language is adjusting to reflect this change in our society.

Following are some widely used nonsexist terms that you can use to replace the older, gender-specific ones.

Gender-specific	Nonsexist
chairman	chairperson
deliveryman	delivery person
fireman	firefighter
mailman	mail carrier
manmade	synthetic
may the best man win	may the best person win
policeman	police officer
salesman	salesperson
steward, stewardess	flight attendant
watchman	security guard

EXERCISE 4 Using Synonyms

Use a thesaurus and your imagination to rewrite the following paragraph. Replace the underlined general words with specific synonyms. To create clear, vivid images, you may need to replace one word with several words. You may also replace or rearrange other words and add details. Make sure your synonyms are appropriate in the context of the paragraph.

We went up the mountain path early on a Saturday morning. Everywhere we looked, colorful leaves were falling from tree branches and moving in the air. As we struggled up the steep trail, the cold October wind went through our jackets as if they were paper. We climbed steadily for almost an hour. By the time we reached the top of the ridge, we were all tired and sore. But the difficult climb was worth it. As we rested against a rock, the first light of the sun began to show above the trees. Colors fanned out across the sky. It was the nicest sunrise I had ever seen.

CRITICAL THINKING
Evaluation

To sharpen students' abilities to recognize sexist language, have them compare magazine articles from the fifties or the sixties with current articles on similar topics. Have the students analyze the articles to identify specific sexist and nonsexist language and then have them evaluate the effects of the two types of usage. Lead a class discussion in which students share some of their findings and discuss their reactions.

ANSWERS
Exercise 4

Synonyms will vary. Here are some possibilities:

went—hiked
colorful—golden
falling—tumbling
moving—flying
went—cut
tired—exhausted
difficult—strenuous
show—glow
Colors—Warm reds and oranges
nicest—most dramatic

RETEACHING

If students have trouble with synonyms or denotation and connotation, work with them to create a neutral description of a place or thing. Next, guide them through the process of replacing neutral words with positive ones. Finally, show them how to replace positive terms with negative ones.

CLOSURE

Have students give examples of synonyms, malapropisms, nonsexist terms, denotative and connotative pairs, and jargon.

A DIFFERENT APPROACH

Students will probably be familiar with the concepts of denotation and connotation, but they may be confused about the terminology. The following mnemonic device can help: *Denotation* and *dictionary definition* both begin with *d*.

INTEGRATING THE LANGUAGE ARTS

Research Link. Have students function as a media watch group for several days in an effort to discover examples of loaded words in print and television advertisements and in news broadcasts. Have students record the specific examples they find. In a class discussion, they could share their findings and evaluate the effects of the uses of loaded words they discovered.

Denotation and Connotation

Before you use a word, you need to know both its *denotation* and its *connotations*. ***Denotation*** is the literal meaning given in a dictionary's definition of a word. ***Connotations*** are the emotional meanings and associations that people may connect with the word.

Some words tend to evoke positive emotions in the people who hear or read the words. For instance, people often have positive responses to the words *new*, *vacation*, and *victory* because they connect these words with pleasant experiences. Other words bring out negative emotions. For example, the words *pollute*, *exploitation*, and *defeat* have negative connotations for almost everyone. Many words, such as *paper*, *cloth*, and *table*, are emotionally neutral because they don't have strong associations for most people.

Be aware of connotations when you write. Keep in mind that emotionally charged words affect the tone of writing. If you use a word without considering its connotations, you may send an emotional message you do not intend.

Loaded Words

A word that has very strong connotations, either positive or negative, is said to be a ***loaded word.*** Loaded words affect the tone of your writing because they appeal to your readers' emotions. For example, in the following sentence pairs, notice how the tone changes when a neutral word is replaced with a loaded one.

EXAMPLES She is an **easygoing** person who rarely argues.
She is a **wishy-washy** person who rarely argues.

Advertisers want to **influence** your opinion.
Advertisers want to **prejudice** your opinion.

Politicians, advertisers, lobbyists, and writers of newspaper editorials know and use the power of loaded words. You might use loaded words in persuasive writing to influence your audience. However, keep in mind that loaded language can't take the place of clear reasons and evidence in a persuasive essay. Support your opinions with facts and examples, not with appeals to emotion.

ENRICHMENT

Have students collaborate in groups of three or four to create skits involving characters who speak in the jargon of a particular field. ■

EXERCISE 5 **Responding to Connotations**

What feelings do you associate with each of the following words? Which words remind you of pleasant experiences? Which words have negative associations? Which words don't stir any feeling at all? Compare your reactions with those of your classmates.

1. sit
2. sunny
3. worn-out
4. compete
5. free
6. flow
7. musical
8. gossip
9. genuine
10. arrogant

EXERCISE 6 **Analyzing Connotations**

The words in each of the following pairs have similar meanings but different connotations. For each word pair, write a sentence using the first word to describe an imaginary person. Then rewrite the sentence using the second word in place of the first. (You may have to rearrange the sentence slightly.) How is the tone of the second version different? Which description is more flattering?

EXAMPLE **1.** fastidious, fussy
1. *Nathan is a fastidious dresser; his shirts never have a wrinkle.*
Nathan is a fussy dresser; his shirts never have a wrinkle.

1. determined, stubborn
2. sly, cunning
3. blunt, frank
4. slender, skinny
5. weak, delicate

Jargon

People who share the same profession, occupation, hobby, or field of study often use a specialized or technical vocabulary called *jargon*. ***Jargon*** is language that has a special meaning for a particular group of people.

ANSWERS

Exercise 5

Responses will vary widely. Encourage students to discuss reactions that differ, as they may not be aware that words have different connotations for different individuals.

MEETING INDIVIDUAL NEEDS

LEP/ESL

General Strategies. To help ESL students complete **Exercise 6,** arrange the word pairs so that it is clear to them which words have positive connotations and which have negative connotations. Next, let the students read several sample sentences from your native students' papers that highlight the connotative differences between pairs. Finally, challenge ESL students to fill in the blanks of additional sentences.

ANSWERS

Exercise 6

Sentences and answers to the questions will vary. You may want to lead a discussion after students complete this exercise so the class can compare their responses.

CRITICAL THINKING

Analysis

Point out to students that some terms used in teaching constitute educational jargon. For example, in **Chapter 39: "Studying and Test Taking,"** in the chart on key verbs and tasks for answering essay questions (pp. 1036–1037), the task listed for the verb *compare* is "point out likenesses." This is a specialized usage, as the word *compare* actually means "to mark or point out the similarities and differences of," according to *The Compact Edition of the Oxford English Dictionary.*

Have students spend a week analyzing the terminology used in all their classes to see if they can identify any other examples of educational jargon. Then have them share their findings in a class discussion.

ANSWERS

Exercise 7

Responses will vary. Here are some possibilities:

1. The lawyer consulted his record of the facts in the case before answering the question.
2. Printed in thick, dark type, the newspaper headline practically jumped off the page.
3. The entire staff worked all night to fix the problems in the new computer program.

Informative writing or speaking often employs jargon. Used appropriately, jargon is a practical way of compressing technical information into a precise word or two. For example, when a doctor writes in a medical report that a patient has a "circumorbital hematoma," he or she is using medical jargon in a perfectly acceptable way. But if the doctor writes about that patient for a magazine of general interest, the ordinary, less precise term *black eye* is a more appropriate choice.

Similarly, if you write a sports article with the headline "Islanders Snap Sabers' Winning Streak," you are using sports jargon appropriately. But you would be misusing jargon if you wrote in an English essay that Edgar Allan Poe "had a short winning streak and then struck out."

EXERCISE 7 **Replacing Jargon with Everyday Language**

Each of the following five sentences contains jargon. First, decide which word or words are being used in a technical sense. Then, rewrite the sentence and replace the jargon with plain, ordinary words. Use a dictionary if necessary.

1. The lawyer consulted his briefs before answering the question.
2. Printed in boldface type, the newspaper headline practically jumped off the page.
3. The entire staff worked all night to get the bugs out of the new computer program.

SEGMENT 3 *(pp. 495–500)*

DON'T CRAMP YOUR STYLE

OBJECTIVES

- To revise to eliminate tired words and clichés
- To revise mixed figures of speech
- To revise to eliminate euphemisms and gobbledygook

MOTIVATION

Before students begin the lesson, you might write the following constructions on the chalkboard:

as black as ____, as white as ____, as high as ____, and as quiet as ____

Ask students to fill in the blanks with the expressions they have most often heard

4. In the opening scene of the film, the camera panned the corral and then zoomed in on the cowhand.
5. The relief pitchers warmed up in the bullpen before the game.

Don't Cramp Your Style

Some kinds of words and expressions get in the way of style. They weaken your writing by boring or confusing your reader. When you eliminate these stumbling blocks to style, you bring clarity and interest to your writing.

Tired Words

A ***tired word*** is one that has been used so much that it has become worn out and weak. Most tired words were clear and forceful when they were first used. For example, the word *fabulous* originally referred to something so striking that it might be legendary—worthy of a position in a fable. But today, *fabulous* is used to refer to anything very pleasant. When we say that a book or a film or a meal is "fabulous," we aren't saying much at all. The adjectives *good, nice, great,* and *wonderful* are also tired words.

Tired words most often appear in everyday conversation. They may be acceptable when you talk to friends or family, but they are not precise enough to be effective in writing. Each tired word is a lost opportunity to develop an exact, vivid description of your subject.

Clichés

A tired expression is called a ***cliché.*** Some clichés began as apt quotations that became fashionable sayings. For instance, vivid phrases like "Footprints on the sands of time" helped make Henry Wadsworth Longfellow a popular poet. But overuse has killed the freshness of the expression and made it trite.

Many clichés are figurative comparisons, such as *quick as a flash, hungry as a horse,* and *light as a feather.* Other clichés are simply common phrases like *last but not least, I for one,* and *with all due respect.*

4. In the opening scene of the film, the camera moved across the whole length of the corral and then quickly focused on the cowhand.
5. The players who might substitute for the pitcher warmed up in a special area before the game.

Teacher's ResourceBank™

RESOURCES

DON'T CRAMP YOUR STYLE

QUOTATION FOR THE DAY

". . . translate what you write into the words you would use to express the thought in conversation." (Bill Stott, 1940– , American writer and educator)

Many young writers form the mistaken impression that they need to use big words to make their writing seem impressive. Assure students that a natural, conversational style is always more readable than artificial, overblown prose.

in those phrases. Next, ask that they create some fresher images. Tell students they are going to learn how to bring freshness to their own writing.

TEACHING THE LESSON

Have a volunteer read aloud the material on tired words and clichés and then ask the class to provide further examples of each category. Encourage students to discuss why people often rely heavily on such language in ordinary conversation.

Guide students through the revision of the first two sentences of **Exercise 8**

MEETING **INDIVIDUAL** NEEDS

LEP/ESL

General Strategies. It is likely that ESL students will not at first be able to identify tired words, mixed figures of speech, euphemisms, and gobbledygook. However, understanding a few examples of each category can lead them to the ideas behind these terms. Take some extra time to present two or three examples in each category and to analyze the examples in detail. When students work **Exercises 8–10,** you could shorten the exercise and have students do an accurate job on a smaller number of items.

SELECTION AMENDMENT

Description of change: excerpted
Rationale: to focus on the concept of style presented in this chapter

STYLE NOTE

Clichés are so familiar to us that we rarely think about what they really mean or whether they're actually true. Oscar Wilde, who was famous for his wit, liked to contradict the stock expressions that were popular in his time. Through humor, he helped readers see such expressions in a new light.

On what clichés did Wilde base the following statements?

> Truth is rarely pure, and never simple.
> *The Importance of Being Earnest*

> A man cannot be too careful in the choice of his enemies.
> *The Picture of Dorian Gray*

Experiment with rearranging clichés to create lively, meaningful expressions. For example, instead of saying someone is *busy as a bee,* why not say the person is *busy as the freeway at rush hour* or *busy as the hallway between classes?* Instead of offering *a word to the wise,* why not offer *a word to the unwise* (those who could use the advice!)?

EXERCISE 8 Revising to Eliminate Tired Words and Clichés

A student has drafted the following review for publication in the school newspaper. Because tired words and clichés distract from the writer's message, the review isn't as convincing as it could be. Help the writer out by suggesting changes to improve the style. First, identify any tired words and clichés in the review. (You should be able to find at least five.) Then, write down livelier, more specific words and phrases to replace the dull, vague ones. You may also see other ways to improve the style of the review. **Answers may vary. Students should replace at least five of the underscored words and phrases.**

Star Trek: The Next Generation is a far cry from the original Star Trek series, but it's good in its own way. Viewers notice the change as soon as they hear the voice-over at the opening of each episode. The Enterprise is still on its "continuing mission," but its captain, Jean-Luc Picard, has learned about nonsexist language: the crew now ventures "where no one has gone before."

before assigning the rest of the exercise as independent practice.

Read aloud the definition of a *figure of speech* and ask students to give some examples. Then read the definitions and examples of *mixed figures of speech* and have students discuss how some of their examples might be misused. Guide students through the first revision in **Exercise 9** on p. 498 and assign the remainder for independent practice.

Have a student volunteer read aloud the material on euphemisms. Initiate a discussion of who would use the euphemisms cited in the text and for what reason.

Have students read the material on gobbledygook and ask them to consider who would use this kind of language and ☛

On the Enterprise of the '90s, women play more important roles: navigating the ship, running Sick Bay, and counseling the crew. In addition, the next-generation crew is more diverse than the old one. Not all of the main characters are human or humanlike. There's even a Klingon security officer--a fact that might cause Captain James T. Kirk to turn over in his grave.

The Klingon crew member Worf represents another nice thing about the series: a generation later, the Federation has made peace with some of its fiercest enemies, including the Klingons. In fact, the new Enterprise crew engages in more peacekeeping than fighting--though when they do launch into battle, the special effects are great.

Some viewers may complain that the new show isn't as good as the old one because it has more dialogue and less action. But if the characters do tend to beat around the bush sometimes, that's just because they're confronting real-life moral dilemmas--a rare thing in this day and age of prime-time television. When all is said and done, Star Trek: The Next Generation is worth taking a chance on.

Mixed Figures of Speech

A ***figure of speech*** is an expression that describes one thing by comparing it to something else. Figures of speech aren't meant to be taken literally. For example, the expression "it's a jungle out there" doesn't mean that lions and tigers actually prowl the streets. It means that, like a jungle, the world can be a savage and dangerous place.

When you use figurative language, be sure to stay consistent. If you begin by comparing a man's voice to a horn and then compare his eyes to a dog's, you create a ***mixed figure of speech.***

MIXED The burning question of how to rescue those still at sea drowned all other discussion. ["Burning question" suggests fire, which would hardly have "drowned" anything.]

BETTER The burning question of how to rescue those still at sea swept away all other discussion.

COOPERATIVE LEARNING

Divide the class into mixed-ability groups of three or four students. Have each group collaborate to write a short composition incorporating as many tired words and clichés as possible. Each group should choose a student to read its composition aloud. Initiate a class discussion on these compositions to lead students to see that their writing is more powerful if they avoid using tired words and clichés.

why they would use it. Encourage students to consider whether they have used gobbledygook in an attempt to impress someone else. Did it work? Why or why not?

Guide students through the revision of the first two sentences in **Exercise 10** on p. 500 and assign the remainder as independent practice.

ASSESSMENT

Responses to **Exercises 8–10** may be used to assess students' understanding of the concepts presented in the lesson. You may want to simply spot-check the work of each student to see if he or she has a basic understanding of the concepts.

ANSWERS

Exercise 9

Answers may vary.

1. Like a mother hen, the young woman clucked at her child as she guided her through the park.
2. In the heat of anger, he scorched us with his stare.
3. Our inflated hopes collapsed at the sad news.
4. Like summer dew, tears of joy moistened her eyes.
5. A flock of reporters swooped down on the woman as she emerged from the courthouse.

EXERCISE 9 Revising Mixed Figures of Speech

Each of the following sentences contains a mixed figure of speech. Revise each sentence to make the figure of speech consistent throughout.

1. Like a mother hen, the young woman shepherded her child through the park.
2. In the heat of anger, he froze us with his stare.
3. Our inflated hopes were dampened by the sad news.
4. Like summer dew, tears of joy crept from her eyes.
5. A flock of reporters pounced on the woman as she emerged from the courthouse.

Shoe, by Jeff MacNelly, reprinted by permission: Tribune Media Services.

Euphemisms

Euphemisms are indirect, agreeable words and phrases that replace more direct, less appealing ones. We often use euphemisms to avoid offending people or hurting their feelings. For instance, few people would tell a woman that her child is a *brat;* instead, they might say the child is *high-spirited.* Similarly, you might call someone *cautious* rather than labeling him or her a *coward*.

Euphemisms help eliminate negative connotations that could interfere with a writer's aim. For example, a writer's job may be to persuade people to accept a garbage dump in their

CLOSURE

Ask students to explain why people use tired language, clichés, euphemisms, and gobbledygook. Have each student identify a tired word, cliché, or euphemism that he or she tends to rely on. ■

neighborhood. Very likely, the writer will avoid the negative connotations associated with the word *garbage*. Instead, he or she may say *waste disposal plant* or *refuse management facility*.

Some of the euphemisms you might hear or read on almost any day are included in the following chart.

EUPHEMISM	MORE DIRECT TERM
casualties	dead
correctional institution	prison
offender	criminal
faux	imitation
memorial garden	cemetery
misrepresentation	lie
additional revenues	higher taxes
socially maladjusted	rude

Euphemisms are appropriate when they are used as a courtesy. However, too many euphemisms can weaken your writing and obscure your meaning. Use direct language whenever possible. When you must use euphemisms, use them sparingly and purposefully.

Gobbledygook

Gobbledygook is wordy, puffed-up language. You can recognize gobbledygook by its long, confusing sentences filled with long, difficult words. For example, read the following sentence:

> Experience indicates that timely measures of effective implementation may consequently result in a ninefold savings in labor expenditures.

If the same statement were written in clear and simple language, it might read like the following proverb:

> A stitch in time saves nine.

Don't bury your own natural voice in gobbledygook. Few readers are impressed by confusing, empty language. In fact, gobbledygook leaves most people wondering what the writer is trying to hide. Show that you respect the intelligence of your readers by writing in a clear, straightforward manner.

INTEGRATING THE LANGUAGE ARTS

Library Link. Point out to students that euphemisms and gobbledygook are sometimes used to obscure something or to make it seem different than it really is, particularly in politics and government. Have students find examples of euphemisms and gobbledygook being used to obscure the real meanings of events and things. A good resource to start with is the *Quarterly Review of Doublespeak*. Have students share some of their findings with the rest of the class.

MEETING INDIVIDUAL NEEDS

ADVANCED STUDENTS

Encourage some of your students to read George Orwell's novels *1984* and *Animal Farm* and his essay "Politics and the English Language" and to report on his concerns about the misuse of English.

ANSWERS
Exercise 10

Responses will vary. A thorough revision should resemble the following example:

Employees should follow these guidelines in case of fire. Use the stairs to exit the building. Allow people on the lower floors of the building to exit first. Move quickly, cautiously, and courteously to a site at least one thousand yards from the fire. Don't talk.

EXERCISE 10 Revising to Eliminate Euphemisms and Gobbledygook

The following paragraph is written in wordy, indirect, confusing language. First, figure out what the writer is really saying. (You may need to look up some words in a dictionary.) Then, rewrite the paragraph in simple, straightforward language.

In the event that a conflagration is being experienced, personnel are advised to modify their deportment in accord with the implementation of the following prescribed series of actions. All personnel within ambulatory distance of a nonelectric device for descent to lower levels shall avail themselves of the opportunity to vacate the area. In order to ensure an orderly procession to a secure area, personnel deployed in lower levels shall have priority in evasion of any possible exposure to unacceptable levels of heat. All personnel are summarily advised to maintain a cautious deportment as well as to practice courtesy as they proceed at minimum speed to an area not less than one thousand yards from the site of the problematic situation. Additionally, due to the fact that communication between members of staffing pools is sometimes counterproductive, supervisors are advised to direct subordinates to limit verbalization at all times during any circumstances that may tend to warrant such a precautionary measure.

SEGMENT 4 *(pp. 501–502)*

MAKING CONNECTIONS

WRITE WITH DIFFERENT AIMS
OBJECTIVES

- To write a persuasive letter to the editor
- To write an expressive/informative letter to a friend

MAKING CONNECTIONS

Write with Different Aims

You're glancing through the newspaper one morning when you see the following article.

Teenagers Find and Return Stolen Money

On Friday evening, local police were surprised to see two juveniles carrying a large, battered suitcase into the 5th Street station house. Dwight E. Jones, 16, and Yolanda Mae McClaren, 17, reported that they spotted the suitcase in an alley near the Hollendale-Branchwater Bank on their way home from school. The suitcase contained over $100,000 in unmarked currency. Detectives have confirmed that the same amount of money was stolen from the bank in an armed robbery Friday afternoon. The alleged perpetrators, who were apprehended minutes after the robbery occurred, apparently abandoned the heavy suitcase as they fled the scene. Bank officials expressed their thanks to the teenagers but said that they have no plans for issuing a reward.

Writing to Persuade

Do you think that Dwight and Yolanda should receive a reward for returning the money? Write a letter to the editor expressing

WRITE WITH DIFFERENT AIMS
Teaching Strategies

Have volunteers read aloud both parts of the writing assignment. Then have students write drafts of their letters and have them work with partners to polish their drafts by using the revision checklists.

GUIDELINES

Letters should meet the criteria in the revision checklists. You may want to have students identify in margin notes specific examples of ways in which they have met the criteria.

your opinion. If you think a reward is due, try to persuade readers that they should write letters of protest asking the bank officials to reconsider. If you think the bank officials made the right decision, give reasons to support your opinion.

Remember that your aim is to persuade readers to think or act in a certain way. Choose your words carefully to make your letter convincing. The following checklist will help you revise your letter for style.

Revision Checklist

- Is your tone appropriate for your aim and your audience?
- Have you used any highly informal expressions, such as slang, that may distract readers from your message?
- Are your words clear and straightforward?
- Have you avoided tired words and clichés?
- Have you weighed words for their connotations—their likely effect on readers?

Writing to Express Yourself

How would it feel to be a hero for the day? Put yourself in the place of Dwight or Yolanda, and write a letter to a friend describing your experience. Explain how it felt to discover the money, to turn it over to the authorities, and to read about yourself in the newspaper the next day.

You want to share your experience with your friend in every detail. The following checklist will help you make your letter more expressive.

Revision Checklist

- Does your letter have an authentic voice? That is, does it sound like a real person talking?
- Have you used lively, vivid words to describe your experience?
- Have you used figures of speech in a consistent way?

Chapter 14

WRITING CLEAR SENTENCES

OBJECTIVES

- To select subordinating conjunctions that show specific relationships
- To use adjective clauses to subordinate ideas
- To identify faulty coordination and faulty parallelism and to revise sentences in paragraphs for clarity
- To revise paragraphs to eliminate sentence fragments and run-on sentences
- To write a descriptive paragraph using parallel structures that add rhythm and emphasis

Motivation

To begin this chapter on sentence structure, you may want to initiate a discussion about how children learn to talk. Ask students to recall and analyze the stages they have observed in young children's language acquisition. [They will probably suggest stages such as babbling, practicing sounds, saying individual words, putting words together in sentences without prepositions and conjunctions, making incorrect sentences, and putting words together correctly in sentences.] Have students point out similarities between this process and the process of learning to write.

Emphasize the importance of correctness in written sentence structure, perhaps pointing out similarities and differences between baby talk and incorrect sentence structure. [Baby talk indicates a need to learn through practice as does incorrect sentence structure. Baby talk sometimes makes a favorable impression; incorrect sentence structure does not. Babies' sentences are incomplete because they have not yet learned the language; written sentence structure may be incomplete because of carelessness or laziness.]

Introduction

This chapter covers sentence clarity and effectiveness. It presents important foundations for composition: coordinating and subordinating ideas, using parallel structure, correcting sentence fragments and run-on sentences, and improving sentence style. The goals of the chapter are to review correct sentence structure and to teach refinements such as parallelism and subordination.

Integration

Because the chapter deals with how to write rather than what to write, it can be a valuable resource for teaching the various aims for writing presented in other composition chapters. The **Ways to Achieve Clarity** segment, pp. 503-515, can be used during the revision stage of the writing process.

The **Obstacles to Clarity** segment, pp. 515-523, can be especially helpful as a reference tool. **Chapter 20: "The Clause"** will be a helpful resource for some students in overcoming obstacles to clarity.

The concept of parallel structure will integrate well with the study of literature. Students may have been moved by a particular poem or speech without knowing exactly why it was so effective. The study of parallel structure will give them a possible explanation and a new tool for literary analysis.

The chart on the next page illustrates the strands of language arts as they are integrated into this chapter. For vocabulary study, glossary words are underlined in some writing models.

QUOTATIONS

All **Quotations for the Day** are chosen because of their relevance to instructional material presented in that segment of the chapter and for their usefulness in establishing student interest in writing.

INTEGRATING THE LANGUAGE ARTS

Selection	Reading and Literature	Writing and Critical Thinking	Language and Syntax	Speaking, Listening, and Other Expression Skills
from **"A Flight of Geese"** by Leslie Norris **516** from ***"The Jilting of Granny Weatherall"*** by Katherine Ann Porter **522** from **"The Toynbee Convector"** by Ray Bradbury **524**	Evaluating the effects of changing emphasis in sentences **510-511** Evaluating sentences to identify faulty parallelism **513-514, 514-515** Evaluating sentences to identify faulty coordination **514-515** Evaluating and identifying sentence fragments or run-ons **516-517, 519-520, 522-523** Finding parallel structures **524**	Selecting subordinating conjunctions **508-509** Subordinating ideas by using adjective clauses **510-511** Using parallel structures **513-514, 514-515, 524-525** Revising a paragraph for clarity **514-515** Revising to eliminate sentence fragments **516-517, 519-520, 523** Revising run-on sentences **522-523** Gathering ideas for writing **524-525** Categorizing ideas for writing to identify parallel ideas **524-525** Writing a paragraph using parallel structures **524-525**	Selecting appropriate subordinating conjunctions **508-509** Using adjective clauses to show relationships between ideas **510-511** Using parallel structure to express parallel ideas **513-514, 524** Identifying correct placement of correlative conjunctions **514-515** Correcting faulty coordination and faulty parallelism **514-515** Revising to eliminate sentence fragments **516-517, 519-520, 523** Revising to eliminate run-on sentences **522-523** Proofreading for correct capitalization and punctuation **523**	Reading a passage aloud to understand parallel structure **524**

SEGMENT PLANNING GUIDE

Whether you are planning for a quick review of a writing concept or preparing an extended lesson on composition, you can use the following Planning Guide to adapt the chapter material to the individual needs of your class.

	SEGMENT	PAGES	CONTENT	RESOURCES
1	*Ways to Achieve Clarity*	*503-515*		Coordinating Ideas 117; Subordinating Ideas in Adverb Clauses 118; Subordinating Ideas in Adjective Clauses 119; Faulty Coordination and Parallel Structure 120
	Ways to Achieve Clarity	503-504	Introduction: showing appropriate relationships between ideas	
	Coordinating Ideas	504-505	Guidelines: analyzing examples relating independent clauses	
	Mechanics Hint	505	Writing suggestion: punctuating compound sentences	
	Subordinating Ideas	506	Guidelines: elaborating on a main idea	
	Adverb Clauses	506-507	Guidelines: examining models using subordinating conjunctions	
	Chart: Subordinating Conjunctions	507	Guidelines: expressing time or place, cause or reason, purpose or result, or condition	
	Writing Note	508	Writing suggestion: positioning an adverb clause clearly	
	Exercise 1	508-509	Applied practice: selecting subordinating conjunctions	
	Adjective Clauses	509-510	Guidelines: analyzing adjective clauses	
	Exercise 2	510-511	Applied practice: reversing emphasis by using adjective clauses	
	Correcting Faulty Coordination	511	Guidelines: making writing smoother and clearer by correcting faulty coordination	
	Using Parallel Structure	512-513	Guidelines: analyzing sentences comparing parallel and non-parallel structure	
	Exercise 3	513-514	Applied practice: revising sentences by using parallel structure	
	Review A	514-515	Applied practice: revising paragraphs for clarity	
2	*Obstacles to Clarity*	*515-523*		Sentence Fragments and Run-on Sentences 121
	Obstacles to Clarity	515	Introduction: avoiding sentence fragments and run-on sentences	
	Sentence Fragments	515-516	comparing examples of complete sentences and sentence fragments	
	Style Note	516	Writing suggestion: using sentence fragments for effect	

All the resources listed in this chapter are located in the *Teacher's ResourceBank*™.

SEGMENT	PAGES	CONTENT	RESOURCES
Literary Model from "A Flight of Geese"	516	Guided reading: examining sentence fragments in a model	
Exercise 4	516-517	Guided practice: revising to eliminate sentence fragments	
Phrase Fragments	518	Guidelines: comparing examples of phrase fragments and complete sentences	
Subordinate Clause Fragments	518-519	Guidelines: comparing examples of clause fragments and complete sentences	
Exercise 5	519-520	Applied practice: revising to eliminate sentence fragments	
Run-on Sentences	521-522	Guidelines: examining different ways to correct run-on sentences	
Style Note	522	Writing suggestion: using run-on sentences for effect	
Literary Model from **"The Jilting of Granny Weatherall"**	522	Guided reading: examining a run-on sentence in a model	
Exercise 6	522-523	Applied practice: revising run-on sentences	
Review B	523	Applied practice: revising paragraphs to eliminate fragments and run-on sentences	
3 ***Making Connections***	***524-525***		
Use Parallel Structure for Rhythm and Emphasis	524-525	Guidelines: identifying parallel structures Applied practice: writing a paragraph using parallel structures	
Literary Model from **"The Toynbee Convector"**	524	Guided reading: examining the effects of parallel structure in a model	
WHOLE-CHAPTER RESOURCES Review Form A, Review Form B			

SEGMENT 1 *(pp. 503–515)*
WAYS TO ACHIEVE CLARITY

OBJECTIVES
- To select subordinating conjunctions that show specific relationships
- To subordinate with adjective clauses
- To revise sentences by using parallel structure

MOTIVATION
Initiate a class discussion by asking students if they have ever tried to assemble something and then discovered that the directions were unclear or incomplete. Explain that any kind of writing can be confusing if the relationship among the writer's ideas is unclear.

14 WRITING CLEAR SENTENCES

LOOKING AHEAD

Clarity is important for the style as well as the sense of what you write. In this chapter, you will learn how to make your sentences clearer and smoother by

- structuring sentences to show the relationships between ideas
- checking sentences for completeness and correct punctuation

Ways to Achieve Clarity

Have you ever adjusted a camera lens to bring an image into focus? Just as you can sharpen the focus of a camera to take a clearer picture, you can sharpen the focus of your writing to better express your meaning. One of the best ways to achieve

Teacher's ResourceBank™
RESOURCES

WAYS TO ACHIEVE CLARITY

QUOTATION FOR THE DAY
"The order of ideas in a sentence or paragraph should be such that the reader need not rearrange them in his mind." (Robert Graves, 1895–1985, British poet and novelist; and Alan Hodge, 1915–1979, British journalist and writer)

Write the quotation on the chalkboard and ask students to freewrite about how the statement relates to clarity in writing.

TEACHING THE LESSON

As students study the section on coordinating ideas, have volunteers read the examples aloud. Then discuss as a class the relationships shown by the various conjunctions and the semicolon. Because the text includes only compound sentences with *and* and *but,* you may want to provide additional examples in which the independent clauses are connected by *or, for, nor, so,* and *yet.*

Students might benefit from a review of the material in **Chapter 20: "The Clause"** as preparation for the section on subordination. To emphasize the importance of subordinating conjunctions in showing relationships between ideas, read aloud the

MEETING **INDIVIDUAL** NEEDS

STUDENTS WITH SPECIAL NEEDS

Because students with language disabilities often use run-on sentences and stringy sentences, you may want to downplay sentence combining. Instead, have students focus on including one complete thought in each sentence.

LESS-ADVANCED STUDENTS

Some students may gain more from concentrating on the examples and exercise sentences than on the grammatical explanations. With practice students can learn to write good compound and complex sentences even when they do not understand the technical terms that describe what is being done.

AMENDMENTS TO SELECTIONS
Description of change: excerpted
Rationale: to focus on the concept of coordinating ideas presented in this chapter

clarity is to write sentences that show the appropriate relationships between ideas. You show these relationships by adapting the structure of your sentences.

Coordinating Ideas

Equally important ideas in a sentence are called ***coordinate*** ideas. To show that ideas are coordinate, you join them with a coordinating conjunction (*and, but, or, for, nor, so, yet*) or another connective. The connective tells your reader how the ideas are related. For example, *and* links equal and similar ideas, while *but* links equal and contrasting ideas.

In each of the following sentences, notice how the writer uses a coordinating conjunction to join two complete thoughts, or *independent clauses.* When you use coordination to link two independent clauses, the result is a ***compound sentence***.

EXAMPLES The watch was ended at last**, and** we took our supper and went to bed.
Mark Twain, *Life on the Mississippi*

In the fall the war was always there**, but** we did not go to it any more.
Ernest Hemingway, "In Another Country"

You can also form a compound sentence with a semicolon and a conjunctive adverb or just a semicolon.

EXAMPLE But that L-shaped rip on the left sleeve got bigger**;** bits of stuffing coughed out from its wound after a hard day of play.
Gary Soto, "The Jacket"

Subordinating Conjunctions chart on p. 507 and have volunteers suggest example sentences in which the conjunctions given introduce adverb clauses.

As the class reads and discusses **Adjective Clauses** on p. 509, emphasize the analytical process a writer goes through in deciding which ideas to subordinate. **Exercise 2** will give students practice in making such decisions.

When teaching parallel construction, make sure that students concentrate on recognizing parallel structure and not on memorizing the grammatical labels. If students find a sentence such as "The band director likes practicing and to perform,"

MECHANICS HINT

Punctuating Compound Sentences

When you join two independent clauses with a coordinating conjunction, you usually put a comma before the conjunction.

> We walked along the shore for a while, and then we dove into the ice-cold water.

However, a comma isn't necessary if the clauses are very short and clear.

> Shawna swam and I sunbathed.

REFERENCE NOTE: For more about using commas with coordinating conjunctions, see pages 848–849.

Sometimes you may have several equal, related ideas within a single independent clause. In addition to linking coordinate independent clauses, you can also link coordinate words and phrases in a sentence.

EXAMPLES Some **distant lamp or lighted window** gleamed below me. [compound subject]

James Joyce, "Araby"

I cleared my throat and coughed tentatively. [compound predicate]

Robert Cormier, "The Moustache"

Anyone who had passed the day with **him and his dog** refused to share a bench with them again. [compound object of a preposition]

Kurt Vonnegut, "Tom Edison's Shaggy Dog"

For three days the fire had been burning and Evans, **red-armed in his shirt sleeves and sweating along the seams of his brow,** was prodding it with a garden fork. [coordinate verbal phrases]

V. S. Pritchett, "The Wheelbarrow"

CRITICAL THINKING

Synthesis

To prompt further student discussion of coordinate ideas, write the following sentences on the chalkboard:

1. The troops were hungry, and their morale was low.
2. The troops were hungry, but their morale remained high.
3. The troops must have supplies, or they will have to withdraw.
4. The colonel was concerned for the soldiers; therefore, he sent an urgent dispatch to headquarters.

Through questions and discussions, bring out the following points about the sentences:

1. In all four sentences, the two ideas receive equal emphasis and are of equal importance.
2. The relationship between coordinate ideas is usually expressed by the connective that joins them.
3. Four kinds of relationship are illustrated: addition, contrast, choice, and result.

For further practice, ask students to write compound sentences and to identify the kinds of relationships between the clauses.

AMENDMENTS TO SELECTIONS
Description of change: excerpted
Rationale: to focus on the concept of coordinating ideas presented in this chapter

they should be able to realize that the sentence is unclear and correct it even if they don't know that the problem is a gerund paired with an infinitive.

GUIDED PRACTICE

To guide students through the process of selecting subordinating conjunctions in **Exercise 1** (p. 508), complete the first sentence orally. Refer students to the chart on p. 507 to find conjunctions that show condition. The clearest answer is *although,* but you may want to point out that *even*

COOPERATIVE LEARNING

This activity uses the jigsaw puzzle approach to review subordinating conjunctions. Organize students into groups of four. From the **Subordinating Conjunctions** chart, assign one of the four types of relationships to each student in each group. Then have students who have the same relationship assignment, for example *time or place,* form a new group. Each newly formed group should then discuss and master their type of relationship using different conjunctions to express the relationships in three example sentences.

Have the original groups reassemble and have each member present his or her relationship to the group by discussing the example sentences.

Subordinating Ideas

Look at the money in this picture.

Just as some of this money has greater value than the rest, some of your ideas in writing are more important than others. However, the importance of an idea isn't always as obvious as the worth of a coin. To make the main ideas stand out in your writing, you need to downplay, or ***subordinate,*** the less important ones.

You can subordinate an idea in a sentence by putting the idea in a subordinate clause. The subordinate clause elaborates on the thought expressed in the independent clause.

EXAMPLES Maria, **who likes Kevin Costner,** saw the movie *Dances with Wolves* three times.

Dances with Wolves is a rare moviegoing experience **because it uses Native American dialogue with English subtitles.**

Adverb Clauses

An ***adverb clause*** modifies a verb, an adjective, or an adverb in a sentence. You introduce an adverb clause with a subordinating conjunction (*although, after, because, if, since, when, whenever, where, while*).

though and *while* could also be used to express condition in the sentence. Point out that some sentences could be answered with more than one conjunction but that students need only select the one that is clearest.

To demonstrate for students how to change emphasis in sentences by using subordinating adjective clauses, work through the first sentence in **Exercise 2** (p. 510) on the chalkboard. Ask students to decide which version of the sentence sounds better and to give reasons for their responses. If you feel students need more guidance in analyzing and changing the emphasis in sentences containing adjective clauses, work through the second sentence on the chalkboard and discuss it as well.

EXAMPLES **Whenever the memory of those marigolds flashes across my mind,** a strange nostalgia comes with it and remains long after the picture has faded.

Eugenia Collier, "Marigolds"

This confession he spoke harshly **because its unexpectedness shook him.**

Bernard Malamud, "The Magic Barrel"

She held back her skirts and turned her feet one way and her head another **as she glanced down at the polished, pointed-tipped boots.**

Kate Chopin, "A Pair of Silk Stockings"

"If there'd been any farther west to go, he'd have gone."

John Steinbeck, *The Red Pony*

The subordinating conjunction you use is important. It shows your reader the relationship between the ideas in the adverb clause and the independent clause. This chart lists the subordinating conjunctions you can use to express the following relationships of *time or place, cause or reason, purpose or result,* or *condition.*

SUBORDINATING CONJUNCTIONS				
TIME OR PLACE				
after	before	until	whenever	wherever
as	since	when	where	while
CAUSE OR REASON				
as	because		since	whereas
PURPOSE OR RESULT				
that		in order that		so that
CONDITION				
although		even though		unless
if		provided that		while

MEETING **INDIVIDUAL** NEEDS

ADVANCED STUDENTS

Have students select from their literature textbooks a few particularly well-written sentences that illustrate coordination of ideas and subordination of ideas. You may want to have students explain why they consider the selections to be well written. You could have students share their examples with the rest of the class.

AMENDMENTS TO SELECTIONS

Description of change: excerpted
Rationale: to focus on the concept of subordinating ideas presented in this chapter

Before students begin **Exercise 3** on pp. 513–514, you may want to have volunteers read aloud the examples on pp. 512–513. Then you could work through the first sentence of the exercise on the chalkboard. Students will discover that there are two ways of revising the sentence (using two gerunds or two infinitives). Write both possibilities on the chalkboard. Have the class and discuss which response is clearer and sounds better.

WRITING NOTE

As you can see from the examples on page 507, an adverb clause can make sense at either the beginning or the end of a sentence. Try a clause in both positions to see which sounds better to you. When you place an adverb clause at the beginning of a sentence, remember to separate it from the independent clause with a comma. Otherwise, you may confuse your reader.

EXAMPLE A space shuttle must have a foolproof thermal protection system **because friction with the earth's atmosphere creates intense heat.**

or

Because friction with the earth's atmosphere creates intense heat, a space shuttle must have a foolproof thermal protection system.

EXERCISE 1 **Selecting Appropriate Subordinating Conjunctions**

For each of the following sentences, choose an appropriate subordinating conjunction to fill in the blank. The hint in parentheses tells you what kind of relationship the conjunction should express. Answers may vary.

1. ____ it is called a lake, Moraine is really a three-acre pond located beneath a high majestic ridge on Grapetree Mountain. (condition) **1.** Although
2. ____ we visited Lake Moraine, we heard wild geese and saw beavers building dams. (time) **2.** Whenever
3. ____ we were sitting by the tent one summer evening, a snowshoe hare crept from behind the pine trees to eat lettuce from our hands. (time) **3.** As
4. Lake Moraine, a wonderful, peaceful place, is now threatened ____ acid rains are destroying the brook trout that swim in its waters. (cause or reason) **4.** because
5. ____ acid pollutants from factory fumes enter the atmosphere, they fall to the earth in rain and snow. (time) **5.** After
6. High-altitude ponds such as Lake Moraine get a heavy dose of acid rains ____ the mountains trap moisture-bearing air masses. (cause or reason) **6.** because

INDEPENDENT PRACTICE

You may wish to have students complete the remaining sentences in **Exercises 1–3** as independent practice. Then ask students to discuss their analyses of the sentences in **Exercise 2** and to give reasons for their choices.

As further independent practice you could have students revise papers they have already written. Students should focus on clarifying the relationships between their ideas by combining sentences and by using parallel structures.

7. ____ the acid pollutants end up in the mountain ponds, fish, especially trout, suffer and die in great numbers. (time) **7. When**
8. Many remote trout ponds are encased in granite ____ little soil or organic matter exists to trap or buffer the acid rain. (purpose or result) **8. so that**
9. ____ it is possible to develop acid-tolerant strains of trout, such a program of selective breeding will likely take many years. (condition) **9. Although**
10. More and more isolated ponds like Lake Moraine will become trout graveyards ____ we don't find a way to combat the effects of acid rain. (condition) **10. if**

Adjective Clauses

An ***adjective clause*** modifies a noun or pronoun in a sentence. It usually begins with *who, whom, whose, which, that,* or *where.*

EXAMPLES Stashed somewhere in the larder there was always a jar of raisins and some vanilla pods **which appeared in the kitchen only on special occasions.**

Ernesto Galarza, *Barrio Boy*

Chicago seemed an unreal city **whose mythical houses were built of slabs of black coal wreathed in palls of gray smoke,** houses **whose foundations were sinking slowly into the dank prairie.**

Richard Wright, *American Hunger*

CRITICAL THINKING
Analysis

The effect of subordination is more obvious in the case of adjective clauses than in that of adverb clauses, so the section on adjective clauses may more directly benefit students when they are revising their own work. Have each student bring a copy of a paragraph, an essay, or perhaps an answer to an essay question that he or she has written. Ask students to analyze the sentence structure and to combine sentences using adjective clauses to add subordinate ideas to the main clauses.

INTEGRATING THE LANGUAGE ARTS

Usage Link. Students might be confused about which word they should use to introduce an adjective clause. Tell them that *who* and *whom* refer to people, *which* refers to things, and *that* may refer to either people or things.

AMENDMENTS TO SELECTIONS
Description of change: excerpted
Rationale: to focus on the concept of subordinating ideas presented in this chapter

ASSESSMENT

You can use **Exercise 1** to judge students' comprehension of the material on subordinating conjunctions. Students' performance on **Exercise 2** should indicate their level of mastery in subordinating ideas in complex sentences, and **Exercise 3** will test students' understanding of the use of parallel structures. The true test, however, is an evaluation of the application of these skills in students' writing.

Before you use an adjective clause in a sentence, you need to decide which idea you want to emphasize and which you want to subordinate. For example, suppose you want to combine these two ideas in one sentence:

> *Award-winning novelist Rolando Hinojosa-Smith writes in both Spanish and English. He was raised in a bilingual family.*

If you want to emphasize that Hinojosa-Smith writes in Spanish and English, put the information in the second sentence into an adjective clause.

> Award-winning novelist Rolando Hinojosa-Smith, **who was raised in a bilingual family,** writes in both Spanish and English.

But if you want to emphasize that Hinojosa-Smith was raised in a bilingual family, put that information in an independent clause and the other information in an adjective clause. You may need to change the word order to make the sentence work. For clarity, be sure that you place the adjective clause next to the word it modifies.

> Award-winning novelist Rolando Hinojosa-Smith, **who writes in both Spanish and English,** was raised in a bilingual family.

REFERENCE NOTE: For more about combining sentences by subordinating ideas, see pages 536–538.

EXERCISE 2 Subordinating Ideas by Using Adjective Clauses

Change the emphasis in each of the following sentences. Emphasize the idea that is now in the subordinate clause, and subordinate the idea that is now in the independent clause. You may have to delete some words, change the word order, or use a different word to begin the new subordinate clause. Which version of the sentence sounds better to you? Why?

1. N. Scott Momaday, who writes eloquently about Native American culture, won a Pulitzer Prize for the novel *House Made of Dawn*.
2. *House Made of Dawn*, which was published in 1968, focuses on a Native American man's struggle to reconcile traditional tribal values with modern-day American life.

ANSWERS

Exercise 2

Revisions will vary.

1. N. Scott Momaday, who won a Pulitzer Prize for the novel *House Made of Dawn,* writes eloquently about Native American culture.
2. *House Made of Dawn,* which focuses on a Native American man's struggle to reconcile traditional tribal values with modern-day American life, was published in 1968.

CLOSURE

Ask a volunteer to explain the difference between coordinating ideas and subordinating ideas.

EXTENSION

Have students bring to class examples of unclear directions, or have them create examples. Then ask students to use subordinating clauses and parallel structure to rewrite and clarify the directions.

3. Momaday spent his boyhood on several different reservations, where he acquired extensive knowledge of Native American history and culture.
4. Momaday's book *The Way to Rainy Mountain,* which gives a perceptive account of Native American life, focuses on the history and culture of the Kiowa tribe.
5. Momaday, who has also published two collections of poems, considers himself primarily a poet.

Correcting Faulty Coordination

Before you join ideas with a coordinating conjunction, it's important to make sure the ideas are of equal importance. Otherwise you may end up with ***faulty coordination,*** unequal ideas presented as if they were coordinate. Faulty coordination blurs the focus of your writing because it doesn't show the relationships between ideas. You can correct faulty subordination by putting the less-important ideas into phrases or subordinate clauses.

FAULTY My aunt is one of the performers in the musical, and she was able to get us tickets, and the tickets were for opening night.

REVISED **Because she is one of the performers in the musical,** my aunt was able to get us tickets **for opening night.**

or

My aunt, **who is one of the performers in the musical,** was able to get us tickets **for opening night.**

3. Momaday, who spent his boyhood on several different reservations, acquired extensive knowledge of Native American history and culture.
4. Momaday's book *The Way to Rainy Mountain,* which focuses on the history and culture of the Kiowa tribe, gives a perceptive account of Native American life.
5. Momaday, who considers himself primarily a poet, has also published two collections of poems.

VISUAL CONNECTIONS

Exploring the Subject. N. Scott Momaday's Native American ancestry is Kiowa on his father's side and Cherokee on his mother's side. The Kiowa tribe migrated southward from Montana to Oklahoma by crossing the rugged Great Plains. They benefited from the migration, accumulated wealth, and became skillful horsemen. However, due to the influx of many white settlers, their tribe dispersed in the late 1800s.

ENRICHMENT

Have students find children's stories that consist of simple sentences. Ask students to rewrite the stories for an audience of their peers. In the revisions, students should coordinate ideas, subordinate ideas, and use parallel structure. Encourage students to adapt the language of the stories, as well as their sentence structure, to their audience. Allow students to share the original stories and their rewritten versions. ■

INTEGRATING THE LANGUAGE ARTS

Literature Link. Parallelism is a device much employed by great writers and speakers. To impress students with its use, read aloud the famous "I went to the woods . . ." paragraph from Henry Thoreau's *Walden* (chapter 2, paragraph 16). Thoreau uses many parallel structures in this paragraph; in particular, he repeats infinitive phrases that boldly declare how he chooses to live.

Tell students that parallelism is also frequently used by poets for its rhythm, emphasis, and beauty. Ask students to find examples of parallelism in Walt Whitman's "Song of Myself" and in Carl Sandburg's "Chicago" and to discuss the effect.

Great orators also use parallelism for its elegance and beauty, but more practically for its clarity and memorability. Have students study Abraham Lincoln's "Gettysburg Address" to identify parallel structures and to analyze their effect.

Using Parallel Structure

If you've ever ridden a bicycle on a rocky road, you know the difference between the smooth feel of gliding over concrete and the jolting sensations of a bumpy ride on gravel. Like a comfortable bicycle ride, writing should have smooth movement and not be a journey over mental potholes and gravel.

You can make your writing smoother and clearer by checking your sentences for ***parallel structure.*** You create parallel structure in a sentence by using the same grammatical form to express equal, or parallel, ideas. For example, you pair a noun with a noun, a phrase with a phrase, a clause with a clause, and an infinitive with an infinitive.

Use parallel structure when you link coordinate ideas.

NOT PARALLEL In winter I usually like skiing and to skate. [gerund paired with infinitive]

PARALLEL In winter I usually like **to ski** and **to skate**. [infinitive paired with infinitive]

NOT PARALLEL The company guaranteed that salaries would be increased and shorter working days. [noun clause paired with a noun]

PARALLEL The company guaranteed **that salaries would be increased** and **that working days would be shorter.** [noun clause paired with noun clause]

Use parallel structure when you compare or contrast ideas.

NOT PARALLEL To think logically is as important as calculating accurately. [infinitive compared with a gerund]

PARALLEL **Thinking** logically is as important as **calculating** accurately. [gerund compared with a gerund]

NOT PARALLEL Einstein liked mathematical research more than to supervise a large laboratory. [noun contrasted with an infinitive]

PARALLEL Einstein liked mathematical **research** more than **supervision** of a large laboratory. [noun contrasted with a noun]

Use parallel structure when you link ideas with the conjunctions *both . . . and, either . . . or, neither . . . nor,* or *not only . . . but also.* These pairs are called ***correlative conjunctions.***

NOT PARALLEL With *Ship of Fools,* Katherine Anne Porter proved she was talented not only as a short-story writer but also in writing novels.

PARALLEL With *Ship of Fools,* Katherine Anne Porter proved she was talented not only **as a short-story writer** but also **as a novelist.**

When you use correlative conjunctions, be sure to place the conjunctions directly before the parallel terms. Otherwise the relationship between the ideas won't be clear.

UNCLEAR A President of the United States must not only represent his own political party but also the entire American people.

CLEAR A President of the United States must represent **not only** his own political party **but also** the entire American people.

EXERCISE 3 **Revising Sentences by Using Parallel Structure**

Some of the following sentences are out of balance. Bring balance to them by putting the ideas in parallel form. You may need to delete, add, or move some words. If a sentence is already correct, write *C.* Answers may vary.

1. Sports fans may disagree over whether going to baseball games or ~~to watch~~ football is more fun, but few people can ignore the importance of sports in America. 1. watching

MEETING **INDIVIDUAL** NEEDS

LEARNING STYLES

Auditory Learners. Some students will more easily identify a sentence that needs revision if they hear it read aloud in addition to reading it themselves. Have volunteers read aloud the textbook's examples of nonparallel structures. Also read aloud the revised versions and discuss the differences between them and the original flawed sentences. If some students find it helpful to read the sentences aloud, encourage them to do so as they complete **Exercise 3.**

Visual Learners. Some students will learn to identify problems with parallel structure more quickly if sentences are presented graphically. Placing in columns the parts of a sentence that need parallel structure may help students better understand the concept. For example, "I'm not a great athlete, but I like softball, soccer, and to play hockey" could be presented as follows:

I'm not a great athlete, but I like
softball (noun)
soccer (noun)
to play hockey (infinitive phrase)

REVIEW A

OBJECTIVE

- To identify faulty coordination and faulty parallelism and to revise sentences in paragraphs for clarity

MEETING INDIVIDUAL NEEDS

LESS-ADVANCED STUDENTS

Remind students that parallel structure is used with coordinate ideas; therefore, the placement of coordinating conjunctions in a sentence can offer clues about the sentence's parallelism. Suggest that students first locate the coordinating conjunctions in each sentence of **Exercise 3.** Then students can determine what is linked by the conjunctions and decide if the structures are parallel.

Revising the paragraph in **Review A** may prove difficult for some students. You could pair less-advanced students with classmates who could offer assistance.

ANSWERS

Review A

Revisions will vary. Here is a possibility:

For most writers, the road to fame is long and difficult, but Amy Tan published *The Joy Luck Club* in 1989 and became an instant celebrity. *The Joy Luck Club,* which was Tan's first novel, topped the bestseller list soon after its publication.

Tan is a Chinese American writer who writes skillfully about the lives of second-generation Chinese Americans. In *The Joy Luck Club* and in *The Kitchen God's Wife,* her second novel, she portrays family relationships with both humor and insight.

2. Sports has always been a topic for friendly and not-so-friendly arguments. 2. C
3. Some sports fans argue endlessly and ~~with anger~~ [3. angrily] about whether football or baseball is truly the American pastime.
4. Baseball backers may insist that baseball is the more important game because it requires skill, dexterity, and ~~to be fast~~. 4. speed
5. On the other hand, football fans may praise a quarterback's speed, skill, and ~~how agile he is~~. 5. agility

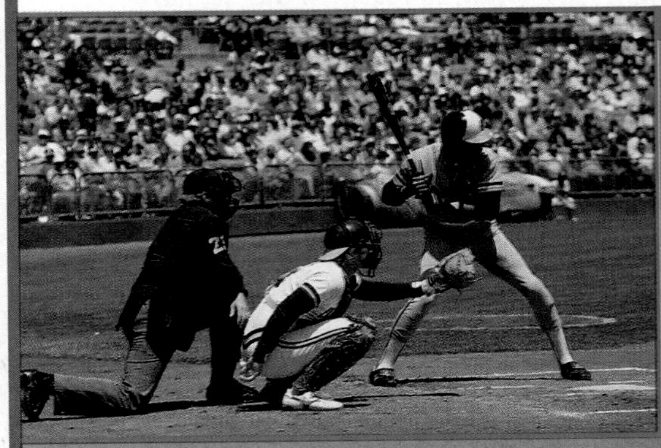

REVIEW A **Revising a Paragraph for Clarity**

Faulty coordination and faulty parallelism make the following paragraphs confusing. Using the methods you've learned in this chapter, revise each faulty sentence to make it clear and smooth. You may need to add, delete, or rearrange some words in the sentences. Remember to check the placement of correlative conjunctions.

For most writers, the road to fame is long and with difficulty. But Amy Tan published The Joy Luck Club in 1989, and she became an instant celebrity. The Joy Luck Club topped the bestseller list soon after its publication, and it was Tan's first novel.

Tan is a Chinese American writer, and she writes skillfully about the lives of second-generation Chinese Americans. In The Joy Luck Club and her second novel, The Kitchen God's Wife, she also portrays family relationships both with humor and insightful.

SEGMENT 2 *(pp. 515–523)*

OBSTACLES TO CLARITY

OBJECTIVES

- To revise sentences to eliminate sentence fragments
- To revise and correct run-on sentences

MOTIVATION

To help students see that fragments and run-on sentences create confusion, write the following directions on the chalkboard:

If you are sitting in the first row. Students in the second row are on another team the remaining students will judge. Might win concert tickets.

Tan seems like a natural-born storyteller, but she didn't always plan to write fiction. In fact, her parents hoped she would become a neurosurgeon. Tan was working as a freelance business writer, and she decided to try her hand at writing short stories. She joined a writing workshop and submitted her first story. She was revising it, and the story grew, changed, and eventually to become the basis for The Joy Luck Club.

Tan seems like a natural-born storyteller, but she didn't always plan to write fiction. In fact, her parents hoped she would become a neurosurgeon. Tan was working as a freelance business writer when she decided to try her hand at writing short stories. She joined a writing workshop and submitted her first story. When she was revising it, the story grew, changed, and eventually became the basis for *The Joy Luck Club.*

Obstacles to Clarity

In the first part of this chapter, you had some practice at putting your ideas in proper relationship to one another. The next important step toward clarity is to check your sentences for completeness. As you revise, you need to be on the alert for two obstacles to clarity, *sentence fragments* and *run-on sentences.*

Sentence Fragments

A sentence should express a complete thought. If you punctuate a part of a sentence as if it were a complete sentence, you create a ***sentence fragment.***

FRAGMENT Has large horns shaped like corkscrews. [The subject is missing. *What* has large horns shaped like corkscrews?]

SENTENCE **A male kudu** has large horns shaped like corkscrews.

FRAGMENT The kudu, a type of antelope, in Africa. [The verb is missing.]

SENTENCE The kudu, a type of antelope, **lives** in Africa.

FRAGMENT The kudu, a type of antelope, found in Africa. [The helping verb is missing.]

SENTENCE The kudu, a type of antelope, **is** found in Africa.

FRAGMENT While the kudu stands 5 feet high at the shoulder. [This has a subject and a verb, but it doesn't express a complete thought.]

SENTENCE While the kudu stands 5 feet high at the shoulder, **with its long horns its total height can reach past 10 feet.**

Teacher's ResourceBank™

RESOURCES

OBSTACLES TO CLARITY

- Sentence Fragments and Run-On Sentences 121

QUOTATION FOR THE DAY

"Written sentences should sound like natural speech, but they can't be natural speech." (Lucile Vaughan Payne, American teacher and writer)

Ask students what they think the quotation means. Why can't written sentences be natural speech? [In natural speech, tone of voice, inflection, facial expressions, and gestures all contribute to an understanding of what is being said. However, written sentences must depend upon word choice and punctuation to make their messages clear.]

Ask students if they would know exactly what to do, based on the directions. Point out how the use of the two sentence fragments and the run-on sentence leads to confusion.

TEACHING THE LESSON

After students have read **Sentence Fragments,** you may want to introduce a three-step check to help students identify fragments:

1. Does the group of words have a subject?
2. Does it have a verb?
3. Does it express a complete thought?

MEETING **INDIVIDUAL** NEEDS

LEP/ESL

General Strategies. Sentences without stated subjects may seem perfectly acceptable to students. They might be accustomed to conversations that use sentences such as "Had to wake up too early this morning" or "Could talk to my sister about it." Such sentences imply the subject *I* but don't directly state it. You may want to have students read aloud a number of complete sentences, including some that begin with *I,* so students can become more familiar with the concept of sentence completeness.

SELECTION AMENDMENT
Description of change: excerpted
Rationale: to focus on the concept of sentence fragments presented in this chapter

The meaning of a fragment you have written may seem clear to you because you know the information you have left out. Try looking at what you have written as though the information is all new to you. Ask what else a reader might need to know.

STYLE NOTE

Experienced writers sometimes use fragments deliberately for effect. For example, in the following excerpt, Leslie Norris uses fragments to imitate the sounds of natural speech. Notice that the meaning of the fragments is made clear by the sentences that come before and after them.

> "This was an unusual goose," my uncle said. "Called at the back door every morning for its food, answered to its name. An intelligent creature. Eddie's sisters tied a blue silk ribbon around its neck and made a pet of it. It displayed more personality and understanding than you'd believe possible in a bird. Came Christmas, of course, and they couldn't kill it."
>
> Leslie Norris, "A Flight of Geese"

Fragments can be effective when they are used as a stylistic technique. You may want to experiment with using them in expressive and creative writing such as journals, poems, and short stories. You can also use fragments when an informal, shorthand style is appropriate—for example, in classified ads.

However, don't use fragments if they might interfere with your aim or confuse your audience. For example, you wouldn't use fragments in a research paper or a book report, since your readers expect formal, straightforward language in these kinds of informative writing.

EXERCISE 4 **Revising to Eliminate Sentence Fragments** Revisions will vary.

Decide which of these word groups are sentences and which are fragments. If an item contains only complete sentences, write *C.* If it contains a fragment, revise the fragment.

Another way that students can identify sentence fragments in their compositions is to read the last sentence of their compositions first and then work backward to the first sentence. Breaking up the narrative flow should make sentence fragments easier to recognize.

You may want to call students' attention to the **Style Note** about the intentional use of fragments by experienced writers. Encourage students to experiment but to consider their audience and purpose.

After the class reads **Run-on Sentences** on p. 521, you may want to suggest that students practice reading their writing aloud. A natural, distinct pause usually marks the end of one thought and the beginning of another. If students pause at a place where ☛

Susan B. Anthony — Willa Cather — Booker T. Washington

1. Many great Americans had little or no formal education. Among these are political leaders, writers, artists, scientists, and business executives. 1. C
2. Eleanor Roosevelt had little formal education. Susan B. Anthony^ the equivalent of a high-school education. 2. had
3. When Abraham Lincoln was a young man, he worked in a general store. ~~And~~ at the same time^ studied books on law. 3. , he
4. Although Carl Sandburg left school when he was thirteen years old^, ~~H~~e later went on to Lombard College after serving in the army during the Spanish-American War.
5. Andrew Carnegie, who gave away many millions to charity, started to work at the age of thirteen. He did not go to high school. 5. C
6. Gordon Parks, who had a high-school education,^ named photographer of the year by a major magazine. 6. was
7. Booker T. Washington walked five hundred miles to attend school at Hampton Institute.^ ~~L~~ater founded Tuskegee Institute. 7. He
8. One of the great letter writers of all time, Abigail Adams, had no formal schooling. 8. C
9. Our first president, George Washington, was a slow reader and a poor speller~~.~~ ~~W~~ho struggled in later life to overcome his educational deficiencies.
10. On the other hand, many famous Americans had excellent educations. As a child, Willa Cather, for instance, was taught Greek and Latin by a Nebraska shopkeeper. 10. C

CRITICAL THINKING
Application and Analysis

To prepare for this assignment, have students gather examples of sentence fragments in published writing—newspapers, magazines, short stories, plays, and novels.

Organize the class into cooperative learning groups of five or six students. Have the group members share the examples they have found. Ask them to analyze each example by asking the following questions:

1. Does the fragment seem to have been intentional?
2. Is the meaning clear?
3. Does the fragment make the passage more or less effective?
4. If the fragment interferes, how can it be corrected?

Then have students draw conclusions based on their analyses. [They may conclude that fragments sound natural in dialogue and informal, creative writing but that they interfere with clarity in more formal writing.]

they don't have any end punctuation, they may have found a run-on sentence.

The **Style Note** on p. 522 encourages students to experiment with run-ons, but it also reminds students to consider their audience.

GUIDED PRACTICE

Use **Exercise 4** (pp. 516–517) as guided practice for identifying and revising sentence fragments. If you find that some students are unable to recognize fragments, you could give independent or small-group instruction. Then guide students through the first item in **Exercise 6** on p. 522 to model the procedure for revising run-on sentences.

INTEGRATING THE LANGUAGE ARTS

Speaking Link. Ask volunteers to read the example sentence fragments in such a way as to make it clear the fragments aren't complete sentences. Explain that at the end of the fragment the speaker's voice should clearly indicate that a continuation of the sentence is expected. For example, in the phrase fragment "During her long and productive life . . . ," the last syllable should remain at a high pitch so that a listener's mental response will be something like "Well, what happened?"

Then have the volunteers form sentences from the fragments to illustrate how voice inflection changes at the end of a sentence.

Phrase Fragments

One type of sentence fragment is a phrase fragment. A ***phrase*** is a group of related words that doesn't contain a subject and a verb. Because a phrase doesn't express a complete thought, it can't stand on its own as a sentence.

REFERENCE NOTE: The types of phrases include prepositional, appositive, and verbal phrases. For explanations of these types of phrases, see pages 605–621.

Often, you can correct a phrase fragment by attaching it to the sentence that comes before or after it.

FRAGMENT	**During her long and productive life.** Nina Otero excelled as an educator, writer, and public official. [prepositional phrase]
SENTENCE	During her long and productive life, Nina Otero excelled as an educator, writer, and public official.
FRAGMENT	**Descended from a long line of political leaders.** Otero became active in politics soon after she graduated from college. [verbal phrase—participial]
SENTENCE	Descended from a long line of political leaders, Otero became active in politics soon after she graduated from college.
FRAGMENT	She was one of the first Mexican American women. **To hold important public posts in New Mexico.** [verbal phrase—infinitive]
SENTENCE	She was one of the first Mexican American women to hold important public posts in New Mexico.
FRAGMENT	In 1917, she became superintendent of schools in Santa Fe County. **An unusual position for a woman at that time.** [appositive phrase]
SENTENCE	In 1917, she became superintendent of schools in Santa Fe County, an unusual position for a woman at that time.

Subordinate Clause Fragments

A ***clause*** is a group of words that contains a subject and a verb. An ***independent clause*** expresses a complete thought and can stand alone as a sentence. But a ***subordinate clause*** doesn't express a complete thought and can't stand alone as a sentence. It is another type of sentence fragment.

INDEPENDENT PRACTICE

Once students can recognize fragments, they should be ready to complete **Exercise 5** as independent practice. After you have guided students through the first item in **Exercise 6,** assign the remainder for independent practice.

ASSESSMENT

You can use **Exercise 5** to judge students' ability to identify and correct sentence fragments. Students' performance on **Exercise 6** should indicate their ability to identify and correct run-on sentences. The true test of mastery, however, is correct sentence structure in students' writing.

FRAGMENT Michael Jackson made his film debut as the Scarecrow in *The Wiz.* **Which was based on *The Wizard of Oz.***

CORRECT Michael Jackson made his film debut as the Scarecrow in *The Wiz,* which was based on *The Wizard of Oz.*

FRAGMENT Jackson topped his earlier popularity. **When he performed in his first music video.**

CORRECT Jackson topped his earlier popularity when he performed in his first music video.

REFERENCE NOTE: If you have any questions about the difference between independent clauses and subordinate clauses, see pages 628–637.

While checking over your work, you may find that two other constructions cause you trouble. They are items in a series and compound verbs.

FRAGMENT I packed only casual clothes. **A pair of jeans, two T-shirts, and a sweater.** [items in a series]

CORRECT I packed only casual clothes. **I packed** a pair of jeans, two T-shirts, and a sweater.

or

I packed only casual clothes**:** a pair of jeans, two T-shirts, and a sweater.

FRAGMENT Jay went sightseeing on his own. **But caught up with the group later.** [compound verb]

CORRECT Jay went sightseeing on his own but caught up with the group later.

EXERCISE 5 **Revising to Eliminate Fragments**

Some of the following items are sets of complete sentences, while others contain fragments. If an item has only complete sentences, write *C*. If it contains a fragment, revise it to include the fragment in a complete sentence. Revisions will vary.

1. Nat Love, who was born a slave in Tennessee, became a cowboy. When he was just fifteen years old.
2. An expert horseman, Love traveled throughout the West. ~~Driving~~ cattle on the open range. 2. and drove
3. After taking first prize in a riding, roping, and shooting contest in Deadwood, South Dakota, became known as "Deadwood Dick." 3. Love

RETEACHING

Reversing the process—having students remove words from sentences to form fragments—might help to illustrate the concept of sentence completeness. Write the following sentences on the chalkboard:

1. Hilda bought a new word processing program for her computer.

2. The program is supposed to be more versatile.

3. Since she bought the program, Hilda has not had time to install it.

Have students remove words from the first sentence to create a fragment with no verb. Have them use the second sentence to create a fragment with no subject. For the third sentence, have students

4. In 1907, Love published his autobiography, *The Life and Adventures of Nat Love, Better Known in Cattle Country as Deadwood Dick*. 4. C
5. The book both true stories and "tall tales" about Love and other famous characters of the Old West. Because Love did have many real-life adventures, it's difficult to tell which stories are fact and which are fiction. 5. has

Montana Historical Society, Helena.

6. Another figure of the Old West, Andrew García, tells of similar exploits in his autobiography *Tough Trip Through Paradise*.
7. García describes some of the tough characters he met when he traveled with an outlaw band. One of the most notorious characters was the horse thief George Reynolds, better known as "Big Nose George." 7. C
8. Like many of the outlaws García knew, Reynolds died a violent death.
9. Although tempted to become an outlaw himself, García eventually settled down. And began writing his exciting account of his life.
10. García didn't live to see his memoirs published. The manuscripts, which he had packed away in dynamite boxes, Were discovered years after his death.

create a fragment that does not express a complete thought but that does contain a subject and verb.

You could use a similar tactic by having students incorrectly combine two sentences to form a run-on sentence.

CLOSURE

Ask a volunteer to explain how to identify sentence fragments and how to correct them. Then have students review aloud the methods of identifying and correcting run-on sentences.

Run-on Sentences

When you're writing a draft, you may like to race full-speed ahead to get your thoughts down on paper. But when you revise, it's important to know when to put on the brakes. Each complete thought should come to a full stop or be linked correctly to the next thought. If you run together two sentences as if they were a single thought, you create a ***run-on sentence.***

There are two kinds of run-on sentences. A ***fused sentence*** has no punctuation at all between the two complete thoughts. A ***comma splice*** has just a comma between them.

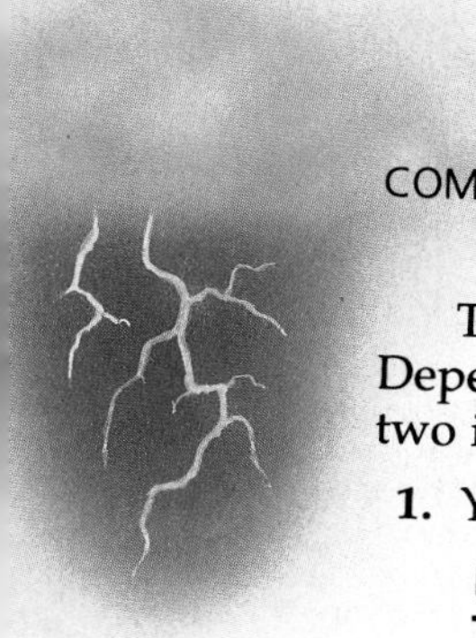

FUSED Lightning speeds to our eyes at 186,000 miles per second thunder creeps to our ears at 1,087 feet per second.

COMMA SPLICE We can't hear and see the event at the same time, we sense it twice in different ways.

There are many different ways to correct a run-on sentence. Depending on the relationship you want to show between the two ideas, one method may be better than another.

1. You can make two sentences.

Lightning speeds to our eyes at 186,000 miles per second**.** Thunder creeps to our ears at 1,087 feet per second.

2. You can use a comma and a coordinating conjunction.

Lightning speeds to our eyes at 186,000 miles per second**, but** thunder creeps to our ears at 1,087 feet per second.

3. You can change one of the independent clauses to a subordinate clause.

While lightning speeds to our eyes at 186,000 miles per second, thunder creeps to our ears at 1,087 feet per second.

4. You can use a semicolon.

Lightning speeds to our eyes at 186,000 miles per second**;** thunder creeps to our ears at 1,087 feet per second.

5. You can use a semicolon and a conjunctive adverb.

Lightning speeds to our eyes at 186,000 miles per second**; however,** thunder creeps to our ears at 1,087 feet per second.

MEETING INDIVIDUAL NEEDS

LEARNING STYLES

Auditory Learners. Ask students to read aloud a selection with syntactically mature sentence structure, such as Katherine Anne Porter's "The Grave," and to omit pauses indicated by punctuation. When students hear the confusion created by the run-on constructions, they may become more sensitive to the importance of clear, correct sentence structure.

EXTENSION

You could make copies of several anonymous compositions that contain fragments and run-ons and have students evaluate and revise them. Students could then work in pairs to check each other's revisions. ■

INTEGRATING THE LANGUAGE ARTS

Literature Link. As is mentioned in the **Style Notes** in this segment, experienced writers sometimes intentionally use sentence fragments and run-on sentences for effect. If your literature book contains William Faulkner's "Spotted Horses," have students discuss the effects of the writer's use of sentence fragments and run-on sentences. [Many writers include fragments in dialogue to reflect natural speech. Faulkner's additional use of fragments in the narrative makes the story seem more like an oral narrative. The fragments and run-on sentences, along with the dialect, add to the believability of the Southern characters.]

SELECTION AMENDMENT
Description of change: excerpted
Rationale: to focus on the concept of run-on sentences presented in this chapter

STYLE NOTE

You've probably noticed that well-known writers sometimes use run-ons in their works. You might wonder: If an expert writer uses run-ons, why can't I use them, too?

You *can* use run-ons occasionally in short stories, journal entries, and other kinds of expressive and creative writing. Run-ons can be especially effective in *stream of consciousness writing*, a style that imitates the natural flow of a character's thoughts, feelings, and perceptions. What is the effect of the run-on sentence below?

> The blue light from Cornelia's lampshade drew into a tiny point at the center of her brain, it flickered and winked like an eye, quietly it fluttered and dwindled.
>
> Katherine Anne Porter,
> "The Jilting of Granny Weatherall"

Always check your writing for unintentional run-ons. If you use run-ons for effect, make sure that your meaning will be clear to your reader.

EXERCISE 6 **Revising Run-on Sentences**

The following items are confusing because they're run-on sentences. Revise each run-on by using the method given in parentheses. (The examples on page 521 will help you.) If you have to choose a connecting word or subordinate an idea, make sure your revised version shows the appropriate relationship between the ideas.

1. The Victorian Era was a time of extreme delicacy and tact in language, direct references to the body were considered offensive in polite society. (two sentences)
2. The word *limb* had to be used instead of *leg* or *arm* even a reference to the "leg" of a chair was considered impolite. (semicolon)
3. In reference to poultry, the thigh was called the second joint the leg was called the first joint or the drumstick. (comma and coordinating conjunction) **3.** , and

REVIEW B

OBJECTIVE

- To revise paragraphs to eliminate sentence fragments and run-on sentences

4. Delicate language was carried to an even greater extreme by some people; they referred to a bull as a "gentleman cow." (subordinate clause) **4.** who
5. This kind of prissy language seems funny to us now, even today we use indirect language to replace words and phrases that might be considered offensive. (semicolon and conjunctive adverb) **5.** ; however,

REVIEW B **Revising Paragraphs to Eliminate Fragments and Run-Ons**

Revise the following paragraphs to eliminate the fragments and run-ons. Add or delete words wherever necessary. Be sure to check your revised version for correct capitalization and punctuation.

Revisions will vary.

War reports--both fact and fiction--have fascinated people since the first warriors and bards sat around campfires. Not all war literature is based on firsthand experience; some comes out of imagination. One of America's most prominent war novelists, Stephen Crane, wrote about war before he ever saw a battle. Crane's short novel The Red Badge of Courage, about a young soldier's reactions to fear during a major Civil War battle, Was written almost thirty years after the battle took place. , which was

On the other hand, many of Ernest Hemingway's novels and stories were based on his own experiences during World War I. Before the United States entered the war, Hemingway worked as an ambulance driver for the Italian army. His novel A Farewell to Arms, Which is often called the most important novel about World War I, follows the experiences of a young ambulance driver.

After World War II, Writer John Hersey introduced a journalistic technique to war fiction. His book Hiroshima, Which describes the effect of the dropping of the A-bomb, Combines the literary techniques of fiction with the factual style of journalism. The Vietnam era produced several notable works of nonfiction, Including Ron Kovic's Born on the Fourth of July, which became an Academy-Award-winning movie. A Vietnam veteran, Kovic describes how his feelings about war changed after he lost the use of his legs.

INTEGRATING THE LANGUAGE ARTS

Test-Taking Link. Remind students of the importance of using correct sentence structure when answering essay questions on tests. Incorrect sentence structure distracts the reader and weakens the essay. Tell students that a quick way to check to be sure they have no run-on sentences or sentence fragments is to analyze each sentence by lightly drawing one line under each subject and two lines under each verb. This procedure will also allow students to check their sentences for subject-verb agreement.

SEGMENT 3 *(pp. 524–525)*

MAKING CONNECTIONS

USE PARALLEL STRUCTURE FOR RHYTHM AND EMPHASIS

OBJECTIVE

- To write a descriptive paragraph by using parallel structures that add rhythm and emphasis

USE PARALLEL STRUCTURE FOR RHYTHM AND EMPHASIS

Teaching Strategies

You may want to read aloud the excerpt from "The Toynbee Convector." Point out to students that much of the paragraph's enthusiastic tone is a result of parallel structure. The repeated pattern of verbs and direct objects with the subject *we* emphasizes the number and grandeur of the subject's achievements, as well as the speaker's wonderment. The parallel use of *oh* also expresses the speaker's excitement, but its repetition emphasizes the paragraph's final note of hopefulness as well.

Before students start writing, have them review the information about parallel structure on pp. 512–513. Examine with students the use of many parallel structures in the student model—parallel hyphenated adjectives, adjectives paired to correspond with a pair of nouns, dual prepositional phrases, and a repetition of gerund phrases. While students are writing, you may want to circulate throughout the room and offer suggestions of ways to incorporate parallel structures.

SELECTION AMENDMENT

Description of change: excerpted
Rationale: to focus on the concept of parallel structure presented in this chapter

MAKING CONNECTIONS

Use Parallel Structure for Rhythm and Emphasis

Parallel structure can add more than clarity to language. It can also add rhythm and emphasis. The best way to appreciate the effect of parallelism is to hear it. Read aloud the following passage, listening to the rhythm and emphasis that parallel structure creates. How does parallel structure affect the tone of the passage? How does it help you hear the similarities between the parallel ideas?

from "The Toynbee Convector"

by Ray Bradbury

"We made it!" he said. "We did it! The future is ours. We rebuilt the cities, freshened the small towns, cleaned the lakes and rivers, washed the air, saved the dolphins, increased the whales, stopped the wars, tossed solar stations across space to light the world, colonized the moon, moved on to Mars, then Alpha Centauri. We cured cancer and stopped death. We did it—Oh Lord, much thanks—we did it. Oh, future's bright and beauteous spires, arise!"

Write a paragraph about a familiar object—something that you see every day at home or at school. Use parallel structure to create rhythm in your paragraph and to show similarities between ideas.

Before you start writing, jot down words and phrases that come to mind when you think of the object. List as many details as you can think of. Then, read through your list to see which details express similar, equal ideas. Write a second list in which you pair the equal ideas and put them in parallel form.

Finally, draw on these parallel ideas to write your paragraph. As you write, you may want to add, discard, or rearrange some details. When you've finished your paragraph, check to make sure you've presented each set of parallel ideas in the same grammatical form.

Here are one writer's sample lists and final paragraph.

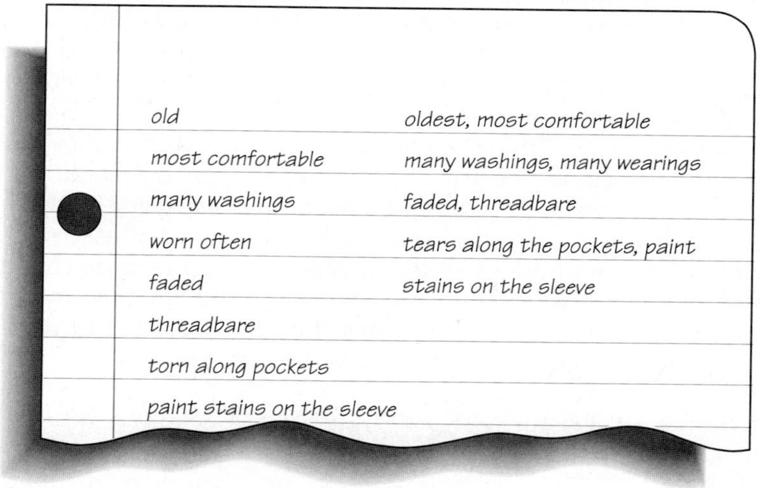

old
most comfortable
many washings
worn often
faded
threadbare
torn along pockets
paint stains on the sleeve
oldest, most comfortable
many washings, many wearings
faded, threadbare
tears along the pockets, paint
stains on the sleeve

My oldest, most comfortable shirt is a sorry-looking blue button-down that I've had since I was twelve. It's faded and threadbare from many washings and wearings. With tears along the pockets and paint stains on the sleeve, it looks like a perfect candidate for someone's rag collection. But it's still my favorite shirt for mowing the lawn, washing the dog, or just hanging around the house.

TIMESAVER

To make your evaluation of students' paragraphs easier, have students underline or highlight the parallel structures they use in their paragraphs.

GUIDELINES

You may want to have each student analyze his or her writing for the effects of the parallel structures. Does the parallelism add rhythm, emphasis, and show similarities between ideas? Check to see that students have presented each set of ideas in the same grammatical form.

Chapter
15 COMBINING SENTENCES

OBJECTIVES

- To use sentence combining to add detail and variety to writing
- To combine sentences by inserting details from one sentence into another
- To combine sentences by coordinating equally important ideas
- To combine sentences by subordinating less-important ideas
- To revise a paragraph by using sentence combining techniques
- To write a fictional passage by expanding on given details
- To revise a passage by using sentence combining techniques

Motivation

Initiate a discussion about the rhythm and balance of sentence structure by comparing language to musical performances. Ask students to think about the order in which songs are performed in concerts, at dances, and on tapes and radio. Try to elicit the idea that there is usually a discernible pattern. Two fast songs may be followed by a slow one. A long song may be followed by a short one. Bands often end concerts with fast, upbeat numbers that put the audience in happy, cheering moods as the events end. Dances often end with slow, romantic songs that evoke memories of the dance theme. Explain that writers try to achieve the same kinds of effects. In this chapter, students will learn how they can add rhythm and balance to their writing.

Introduction

List and define the aims of composition on the chalkboard (expressive, literary, informative, persuasive). Then guide the class in reviewing examples of each. You might comment that writers, like musicians, tailor their performances to suit their purposes.

Then list and explain the modes or strategies writers use to achieve their aims (narration, description, classification, evaluation). Use the examples of writing purposes that students have suggested to guide students in deciding which methods writers could use to achieve their aims.

Then have volunteers suggest topics they have interest in and the aims and strategies that could be used to develop each topic. Encourage variety in the suggestions.

Finally, point out that, regardless of purpose, method, or style, writers try to achieve rhythm and balance in compositions. Stress that in this unit students will learn techniques they can use to add rhythm and balance to their own writing styles.

Integration

This chapter can serve as a resource for many of the writing activities in your classroom. Students can use their knowledge of sentence combining to discuss poetry that effectively combines and powerfully concentrates language. Students can analyze narrative paragraphs or dialogue in short stories to see how writers balance short sentences with longer, detailed ones.

You may also find the material in this chapter helpful to students who are preparing papers for other classes. Writing assignments for social studies and science, as well as for other courses, can benefit from the concepts and strategies presented in this chapter.

The chart on the next page illustrates the strands of language arts as they are integrated into this chapter. For vocabulary study, glossary words are underlined in some writing models.

QUOTATIONS
All **Quotations for the Day** are chosen because of their relevance to instructional material presented in that segment of the chapter and for their usefulness in establishing student interest in writing.

INTEGRATING THE LANGUAGE ARTS

Selection	Reading and Literature	Writing and Critical Thinking	Language and Syntax	Speaking, Listening, and Other Expression Skills
FROM *Life, the Universe and Everything* by Douglas Adams **527** **"To Da-duh, in Memoriam"** by Paule Marshall **531** ***Blue Highways*** by William Least Heat-Moon **532** ***Yeager: An Autobiography*** by Chuck Yeager **534** **"New African"** by Andrea Lee **536** **"A Wagner Matinée"** by Willa Cather **536** **"Gentlemen of Río en Medio"** by Juan Sedillo **536**	Reading pairs of sentences to determine relationships between ideas **535, 538** Reading a paragraph to decide which sentences need revision **539**	Combining sentences by inserting single-word modifiers and prepositional phrases **529-531** Combining sentences by inserting participial phrases **532** Combining sentences by inserting appositive phrases **533-534** Combining sentences by coordinating ideas **535** Combining sentences by subordinating ideas **538-539** Revising a paragraph by combining sentences **539, 540** Choosing details for the opening of a story **540** Writing the opening of a story **540**	Using commas correctly **529-531, 538-539** Changing the forms of words while combining sentences **529-531, 538-539** Using a variety of sentence lengths and structures **529-531, 532, 533-534, 535, 538-539, 540** Correctly placing participial phrases in sentences **532** Using correct punctuation **533-534, 535** Choosing conjunctions that express relationships clearly **535**	

CHAPTER 15

SEGMENT PLANNING GUIDE

Whether you are planning for a quick review of a writing concept or preparing an extended lesson on composition, you can use the following Planning Guide to adapt the chapter material to the individual needs of your class.

SEGMENT	PAGES	CONTENT	RESOURCES
1 *Combining Sentences*	*526-534*		Combining by Inserting Words and Phrases 131
Combining Sentences for Style	526-527	Guidelines: combining sentences for smoother writing	
Literary Model from ***Life, the Universe and Everything***	527	Guided reading: examining a model of rhythmic, balanced writing	
Inserting Words and Phrases	528	Guidelines: inserting key words and phrases	
Single Word Modifiers	528-529	Guidelines: analyzing examples of adjectives and adverbs	
Prepositional Phrases	529	Guidelines: analyzing examples that use prepositional phrases	
Exercise 1	529-531	Applied practice: combining by inserting single-word modifiers and prepositional phrases	
Participial Phrases	531	Guidelines: analyzing examples that use participial phrases	
Literary Model from **"To Da-duh, in Memoriam"**	531	Guided reading: examining a model that uses participial phrases	
Writing Note	531	Writing suggestion: avoiding misplaced participles	
Exercise 2	532	Applied practice: combining by inserting participial phrases	
Appositive Phrases	532-533	Guidelines: analyzing examples that use appositive phrases	
Literary Model from ***Blue Highways***	532	Guided reading: examining the use of appositive phrases in a model	
Exercise 3	533-534	Applied practice: inserting appositive phrases	
2 *Combining by Coordinating and Subordinating Ideas*	*534-539*		Combining by Coordinating Ideas 132 Combining by Subordinating Ideas 133
Combining by Coordinating Ideas	534	Guidelines: analyzing examples that use conjunctions to coordinate words, phrases, and clauses	
Literary Model from ***Yeager: An Autobiography***	534	Example: using a semicolon to link independent clauses	
Exercise 4	535	Applied practice: combining by coordinating ideas	

All the resources listed in this chapter are located in the *Teacher's ResourceBank*™.

SEGMENT	PAGES	CONTENT	RESOURCES
Combining by Subordinating Ideas	536	Guidelines: analyzing examples that use subordinate clauses	
Literary Model from **"New African"**	536	Example: examining an adjective clause	
Literary Model from **"A Wagner Matinée"**	536	Example: examining an adverb clause	
Literary Model from **"Gentlemen of Río en Medio"**	536	Example: examining a noun clause	
Adjective Clauses	536	Guidelines: analyzing examples that use adjective clauses	
Mechanics Hint	537	Writing suggestion: punctuating adjective clauses	
Adverb Clauses	537	Guidelines: analyzing examples that use adverb clauses	
Mechanics Hint	538	Writing suggestion: punctuating adverb clauses	
Noun Clauses	538	Guidelines: analyzing examples that use noun clauses	
Exercise 5	538-539	Applied practice: combining by subordinating ideas	
Review	539	Applied practice: revising a paragraph by combining sentences	
3 *Making Connections*	*540*		
Writing the Opening of a Mystery Story	540	Applied practice: using given details to write and revise the opening paragraph of a mystery story	
WHOLE-CHAPTER RESOURCES Review Form A, Review Form B			

SEGMENT 1 *(pp. 526–534)*

COMBINING SENTENCES FOR STYLE and COMBINING BY INSERTING WORDS AND PHRASES

OBJECTIVES

- To combine sentences by inserting single-word modifiers and prepositional phrases
- To combine sentences by inserting participial phrases
- To combine sentence by inserting appositive phrases

Teacher's ResourceBank™

RESOURCES

COMBINING SENTENCES FOR STYLE and COMBINING BY INSERTING WORDS AND PHRASES

- Combining by Inserting Words and Phrases 131

QUOTATION FOR THE DAY

"Whate'er is well conceived is clearly said, /And the words to say it flow with ease." (Nicolas Boileau-Despréaux, 1636–1711, French critic and poet)

Remind students that sentences are the building blocks of writing. A string of poorly written sentences cannot build a thought-provoking composition. You might discuss how a string of short, choppy sentences discourages the reader from becoming engaged in thought, just as a series of long, drawn-out sentences also distracts the reader.

15 COMBINING SENTENCES

LOOKING AHEAD

Sentence-combining techniques are handy tools for improving your style. They can help you add detail to your sentences and variety to your writing. In this chapter, you will learn how to combine sentences by

- inserting words and phrases
- coordinating ideas
- subordinating ideas

Combining Sentences for Style

Revising isn't just a matter of checking your writing for completeness and correctness. When you revise, you also look at your writing with an eye for style. It's important to notice how

TEACHING THE LESSON

To help students understand how varied sentence lengths can help keep an audience's attention, compare planning a composition to staging a track meet. Discuss the sequences of events at track meets and elicit the idea that meet officials alternate long and short races to keep the audience interested, just as writers must alternate sentence lengths to keep the audience interested. Tell students that this segment will show them ways to combine sentences so that their writing is balanced and their readers read on.

Have a student read aloud **Combining Sentences for Style**. Discuss with students how the choppy sentence style in the example is improved in the model by ☛

your sentences work together to shape each of your paragraphs. A short sentence may be fine by itself, but a long series of short sentences can make writing sound choppy and dull.

Read the following sentences. Does the writing style help hold your interest, or does it distract you from the meaning of the paragraph?

> He was stranded. He was on prehistoric Earth. He was stranded as the result of a sequence of events. The sequence was complex. It involved his being blown up. It involved his being insulted. These things had happened in bizarre regions of the galaxy. There were more of these bizarre regions than he had ever dreamed existed. Life had now turned quiet. It was very, very, very quiet. He was still feeling jumpy.
>
> He hadn't been blown up now for a while. It had been five years.

The choppy sentences you just read are based on the following well-crafted sentences by science fiction writer Douglas Adams. Notice how much better Adams's sentences sound. Also notice how his smooth, lively style helps create a humorous tone.

> He was stranded on prehistoric Earth as the result of a complex sequence of events that had involved his being alternately blown up and insulted in more bizarre regions of the Galaxy than he had ever dreamed existed, and though life had now turned very, very, very quiet, he was still feeling jumpy.
>
> He hadn't been blown up now for five years.
>
> Douglas Adams,
> *Life, the Universe and Everything*

Perhaps you have your own sentence style, one that's unique to your writing. But no matter what your style, you can add a smooth rhythm to your writing by balancing short sentences with longer, more detailed ones. Sentence combining helps you create this balance. It also helps make your sentences more precise by eliminating repeated words and ideas. In this chapter, you'll learn several different ways to combine sentences for style.

MEETING INDIVIDUAL NEEDS

LEP/ESL

General Strategies. Students who lack facility with English may have difficulty with many of the exercises in the segment. You might duplicate the exercises and leave enough space between each numbered question for students to rewrite sentences.

Help students to locate key words and phrases in each question and to highlight them. Then have students select and underline the most important idea as the main sentence. Next have them circle the words to be inserted and draw arrows to the best place to insert the words. Students could rewrite their sentences using the preliminary work as a guide.

ADVANCED STUDENTS

Students who demonstrate a flair for combining sentences might create posters for a bulletin-board display. Have students select their themes, write original simple sentences, and revise their writing by using sentence-combining techniques. Remind students to label the combination techniques. Students might use colored printing for emphasis and original art or magazine pictures to illustrate their themes.

SELECTION AMENDMENT
Description of change: excerpted
Rationale: to focus on the concept of sentence combining presented in this chapter

Douglas Adams. Then have a student read **Combining by Inserting Words and Phrases.** Emphasize finding key words and phrases when you guide students in analyzing the sample sentences.

When discussing awkward-sounding combinations, tell students that a good rule is to place a modifier as close as possible to the word it modifies. Remind students that adverbs modify adjectives and other adverbs, as well as verbs.

When covering **Single-Word Modifiers,** you might have students copy the original sentences and cross out redundant words. Then have students circle the words to be inserted and draw arrows to the points of insertion.

INTEGRATING THE LANGUAGE ARTS

Literature Link. If your literature book contains "Ain't I a Woman?" by Sojourner Truth, you might want to discuss the writer's style and note how she uses sentence combining and repetition for dramatic effect. Point out how the short title question "Ain't I a Woman?" is preceded by longer exclamatory sentences to balance the writing.

The composition has several passages that combine pleas for the abolitionist movement and for women's rights in one sentence. To illustrate this technique, use the chalkboard to convert each of these sentences into a pair of sentences (one about African Americans, the other about women).

Combining by Inserting Words and Phrases

Often, you can combine related sentences by taking a key word or phrase from one sentence and inserting it into another sentence. The word or phrase adds detail to the other sentence, and repeated words are eliminated.

THREE SENTENCES	This flight simulator gives a realistic experience of flight. It uses computer graphics to do this. The experience is so real it's amazing.
ONE SENTENCE	Using computer graphics, this flight simulator gives an amazingly realistic experience of flight.
	or
	With computer graphics, this flight simulator gives an amazingly realistic experience of flight.

Usually you will have some choice in where you insert a word or phrase. Just watch out for awkward-sounding combinations and ones that confuse the meaning of the original sentences. For example, avoid combinations like this one: *Amazingly, using computer graphics, this flight simulator gives a realistic experience of flight.*

Single-Word Modifiers

Sometimes you can take a word from one sentence and insert it directly into another sentence as a modifier. Other times you will need to change the word into an adjective or adverb before you can insert it.

To discuss **Prepositional Phrases,** remind students that prepositional phrases always include noun or pronoun objects. You might model the example sentence on the chalkboard and review the use of commas before students complete **Exercise 1.** For independent practice, have students write the combined sentences in **Exercise 1** on their own.

Before students read **Participial Phrases** on p. 531, remind them that a participle is a verb form ending in *–ed* or in *–ing* that can be used as an adjective. Discuss the example sentences and call students' attention to the **Writing Note.** Explain that misplaced participles can be revised by moving them as shown or by changing the sentence construction.

USING THE SAME FORM

ORIGINAL Timing is essential for performing magic tricks. The magician's timing must be excellent.

COMBINED **Excellent** timing is essential for performing magic tricks.

ORIGINAL Magicians guard the secrets of their tricks. They guard them carefully.

COMBINED Magicians **carefully** guard the secrets of their tricks.

CHANGING THE FORM

ORIGINAL The famous magician Harry Houdini performed impossible escapes. The escapes only seemed impossible.

COMBINED The famous magician Harry Houdini performed **seemingly** impossible escapes.

ORIGINAL He escaped from a sealed crate that had been lowered into a river. He had handcuffs on.

COMBINED **Handcuffed,** he escaped from a sealed crate that had been lowered into a river.

Prepositional Phrases

You can usually take a prepositional phrase from one sentence and insert it into another without any change in form.

ORIGINAL Our English class is reading "Everyday Use." It is by Alice Walker.

COMBINED Our English class is reading "Everyday Use" **by Alice Walker.**

You can also combine sentences by changing part of a sentence into a prepositional phrase.

ORIGINAL A female narrator tells the story. Her tone is conversational.

COMBINED A female narrator tells the story **in a conversational tone.**

EXERCISE 1 **Combining by Inserting Single-Word Modifiers and Prepositional Phrases**

Combine each group of short, related sentences by inserting adjectives, adverbs, or prepositional phrases into the first sen-

MEETING **INDIVIDUAL** NEEDS

STUDENTS WITH SPECIAL NEEDS

Some learning disabled students may find it frustrating to write sentences over and over as they rearrange the phrases and combine sentences. To help make the activity more interesting, have students write their sentences on sentence strips or construction paper and cut the words or phrases apart as needed. Students can rearrange as much as they want and then paste the new combined sentences in place. This concrete illustration may help students become aware of how efficient and concise writing can be.

COOPERATIVE LEARNING

A collaborative approach to completing **Exercise 1** could prove beneficial to many students. After guiding students through the example, divide the class into groups of five. Explain that each member will complete two items independently. Then students will read their sentence combinations to the group. Members should offer suggestions for improvements and write the final sentences on their own papers. Have students initial their personal contributions.

Use the example in **Exercise 2** on p. 532 to guide students in understanding how to insert participial phrases. Students should complete the exercise independently.

Begin the study of appositives by explaining that *appositive* comes from a French word meaning "to place near to." Tell the class that an appositive must have the same grammatical construction as the word it explains. An appositive phrase consists of a noun and its modifiers, and it is always in apposition to a noun or a pronoun.

Explain that television commercials frequently make use of appositives to create audience identification with their products. You might make up an example such as

tence. You may need to change the forms of some words before you insert them. Add commas where they are necessary.

EXAMPLE **1. The Iroquois moved to the Northeast. They moved during the thirteenth century. They moved from the Mississippi region.**
1. ***During the thirteenth century, the Iroquois moved from the Mississippi region to the Northeast.***

1. The Iroquois formed a confederation. The confederation was powerful. The Iroquois formed the confederation in the Northeast region.
2. A central council of the confederation made decisions. The council made decisions unanimously.
3. Women nominated delegates. They were women from the confederation. They nominated delegates to the central council.
4. The Iroquois confederation subdued other groups of people. These people were Native American. Their subduing of the groups was systematic.
5. The groups exchanged belts to ratify treaties. Their belts were of wampum. The treaties were important.
6. The Iroquois developed trade routes. The trade routes were extensive. The trade routes were along waterways and trails.
7. Hunting was an important element. It was an element in Iroquois society. It was always an important element.
8. The Iroquois also depended on farming. They depended heavily on farming. They depended on farming for food.

ANSWERS

Exercise 1

Sentences may vary. Here are some possibilities:

1. The Iroquois formed a powerful confederation in the Northeast region.
2. A central council of the confederation made decisions unanimously.
3. Women from the confederation nominated delegates to the central council.
4. The Iroquois confederation systematically subdued other groups of Native American people.
5. Tribes exchanged belts of wampum to ratify important treaties.
6. The Iroquois developed extensive trade routes along waterways and trails.
7. Hunting was always an important element in Iroquois society.
8. The Iroquois also depended heavily on farming for their food.

"Olympiads, the shoes of champions." Brainstorm with the class for appositive phrases they associate with brand name items such as food, footwear, or games. Write several good examples on the chalkboard. Then discuss the two-sentence and one-sentence examples on pp. 532–533 and show how the emphasis can be changed.

Use the example in **Exercise 3** on p. 533 for additional guided practice and use the exercise for independent practice. Assess the completed exercises and students' own writing to evaluate their sentence-combining abilities.

9. Entire villages moved in search of soil. They were searching for soil that was richer. They needed the rich soil for farming.

10. The structure of Iroquoian life changed. The structure was complex. The change was considerable. The structure changed during the late seventeenth century.

Participial Phrases

A ***participial phrase*** contains a participle and words related to it. The whole phrase acts as an adjective. Like other modifiers, participial phrases add concrete details to sentences.

EXAMPLE Da-duh, **holding fast to my hand,** became my anchor as they circled around us like a nervous sea, exclaiming, **touching us with calloused hands, embracing us shyly.**

Paule Marshall, "To Da-duh, in Memoriam"

REFERENCE NOTE: For more about participles and participial phrases, see pages 611–612.

Sometimes you can lift a participial phrase directly from one sentence and insert it into another sentence. Other times you will need to change a verb into a participle before you can insert the idea into another sentence.

ORIGINAL Ants smell, taste, touch, and hear with antennae. The antennae are attached to their heads.

COMBINED Ants smell, taste, touch, and hear with antennae **attached to their heads.**

ORIGINAL Weaver ants bind leaves together to make nests. They use the silk from their silk-spinning larvae.

COMBINED **Using the silk from their silk-spinning larvae,** weaver ants bind leaves together to make nests.

WRITING NOTE

Be sure to place a participial phrase close to the noun or pronoun you want it to modify. Otherwise, your sentence may end up with a meaning you did not intend.

MISPLACED Hidden under the bench, we found the kitten.

IMPROVED We found the kitten **hidden under the bench.**

9. Entire villages moved in search of richer soil for farming.

10. The complex structure of Iroquoian life changed considerably during the late seventeenth century.

INTEGRATING THE LANGUAGE ARTS

Technology Link. To teach students computer skills as well as composition methods, enter **Exercise 2** on p. 532 as a file on your school computers. Have students work in pairs with one partner calling up the files and using the computer functions to boldface the sentence that will be converted into a participial phrase. Then have the partners enter their revisions and underline any verb endings they have changed.

TIMESAVER

Use the printouts from the **Technology Link** activity to facilitate your assessment of students' abilities.

SELECTION AMENDMENT

Description of change: excerpted

Rationale: to focus on the concept of sentence combining presented in this chapter

RETEACHING

If students have difficulty with insertion of words and phrases, extract from each sentence its most basic parts: subject, predicate, and (in most cases) object. List these on the chalkboard in diagram form. Next, show how single-word and phrase modifiers are inserted in building the sentences. Use the same technique for reteaching participles and appositives.

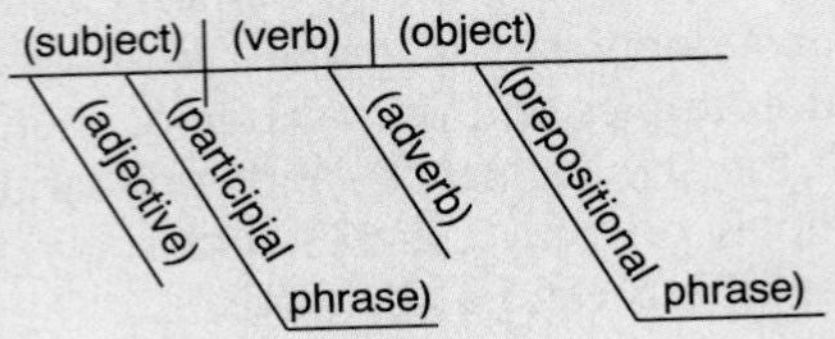

ANSWERS

Exercise 2

Answers may vary. Here are some possibilities:

1. Waste paper, processed through a container called a pulper, becomes wet, soft pulp.
2. Next, a spinning cylinder, removing paper clips, staples, and other trash, helps clean the pulp.
3. Squeezing out chemicals, ink, and other liquid, a water removal machine further processes the pulp.
4. Mixed with clean water, the pulp forms a thick substance.
5. Rolled in layers, the material dries to form clean, white sheets of paper.

CRITICAL THINKING
Application

After the initial discussion of appositive phrases and correct punctuation, ask each student to write an original sentence using an appositive about a favorite place and another sentence describing an admired person. After students complete the assignment, select several students to read their work to the class before you collect and evaluate the papers.

SELECTION AMENDMENT

Description of change: excerpted
Rationale: to focus on the concept of sentence combining presented in this chapter

EXERCISE 2 **Combining by Inserting Participial Phrases**

Combine each of the following sentence pairs. First, reduce the second sentence to a participial phrase, changing the form of the verb if necessary. Then, insert the phrase into the first sentence. Be sure to place the participial phrase next to the noun or pronoun it modifies.

EXAMPLE
1. Recycling helps reduce pollution. It transforms useless trash into new materials.
1. *Transforming useless trash into new materials, recyling helps reduce pollution.*

1. Waste paper becomes wet, soft pulp. It becomes pulp when it is processed through a container called a pulper.
2. Next, a spinning cylinder helps clean the pulp. The cylinder removes paper clips, staples, and other trash.
3. A water removal machine further processes the pulp. It squeezes out chemicals, ink, and other liquid.
4. The pulp forms a thick substance. It becomes thick as it is mixed with clean water.
5. The material dries to form clean, white sheets of paper. It dries as it is rolled in layers.

Appositive Phrases

Appositive phrases can also add detail to your sentences. An ***appositive phrase*** is made up of an appositive and its modifiers. (An appositive identifies or explains a noun or pronoun in a sentence.) Like a participial phrase, an appositive phrase should be placed directly before or after the noun or pronoun it modifies. It should be set off by a comma (or two commas if you place the phrase in the middle of the sentence).

EXAMPLE In Gainesboro, **a hill town with a square of businesses around the Jackson County Courthouse,** I stopped for directions and breakfast.

William Least Heat-Moon, *Blue Highways*

You can also combine two sentences by placing one of the ideas in an appositive phrase.

TWO SENTENCES Arna Bontemps wrote for the magazine *Opportunity.* Arna Bontemps was a major figure in the Harlem Renaissance.

CLOSURE

Select volunteers to define key terms, such as *single-word modifiers, prepositional phrases, participial phrases,* and *appositive phrases* and have them provide examples. Allow students to use examples from the text, but encourage original composition. ■

ONE SENTENCE Arna Bontemps, **a major figure in the Harlem Renaissance,** wrote for the magazine *Opportunity.*

or

A major figure in the Harlem Renaissance, Arna Bontemps wrote for the magazine *Opportunity.*

or

Arna Bontemps, **a writer for the magazine *Opportunity,*** was a major figure in the Harlem Renaissance.

Notice that the last combination emphasizes Bontemps' role in the Harlem Renaissance, while the first two combinations emphasize his work for *Opportunity.* In the last example, the ideas have been rearranged to change the emphasis, and the verb *wrote* has been changed to a noun, *writer,* to form the appositive.

EXERCISE 3 **Combining by Inserting Appositive Phrases**

Combine each pair of sentences by turning one of the sentences into an appositive phrase. You may see several ways to create the appositive; choose the combination that sounds best to you. Be sure to set off the appositive phrase with commas.

EXAMPLE
1. Calligraphy is an elegant form of handwriting. It requires a special pen or brush.
1. *Calligraphy, an elegant form of handwriting, requires a special pen or brush.*

1. Calligraphy has been used for over two thousand years to decorate books and paintings. It is an ancient art form.
2. Chinese calligraphy is done with a paint brush. Chinese calligraphy is the oldest form of calligraphy.
3. In the 600s, Japanese artists learned calligraphy from the Chinese. The Chinese were the first masters of the art.

MEETING **INDIVIDUAL** NEEDS

AT-RISK STUDENTS

As the class progresses through this chapter, identify the strengths and weaknesses of any at-risk students. Hold individual conferences to praise strong writing skills and to suggest ways students might improve weak sentence combinations. If students have sporadic periods of absence, you might assign student partners to relay assignments and to explain missed classwork. Gear assignments toward the goal of developing successful writing skills, not completing a given number of exercises.

ANSWERS

Exercise 3

Answers may vary. Here are some possibilities:

1. Calligraphy, an ancient art form, has been used for over two thousand years to decorate books and paintings.
2. Chinese calligraphy, the oldest form of calligraphy, is done with a paint brush.
3. In the 600s, Japanese artists learned calligraphy from the Chinese, the first masters of the art.

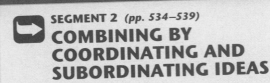

SEGMENT 2 *(pp. 534–539)*

COMBINING BY COORDINATING AND SUBORDINATING IDEAS

OBJECTIVES

- To combine sentences by using conjunctions to coordinate equally important ideas
- To combine sentences by using noun, adjective, and adverb clauses to subordinate less important ideas

4. Islamic artists developed Kufic writing, one of the most graceful styles of calligraphy.
5. In Islamic countries, you can see sentences from the Koran, the Islamic holy book, inscribed in beautiful calligraphy on buildings.

Teacher's ResourceBank™

RESOURCES

COMBINING BY COORDINATING AND SUBORDINATING IDEAS

QUOTATION FOR THE DAY

"Word-carpentry is like any other kind of carpentry: you must join your sentences smoothly." (Anatole France, 1844–1924, French novelist and essayist)

Using Anatole France's carpentry metaphor, discuss with your class how one tests for the smoothness of joined sentences. [The parts of a sentence must flow logically together and the sentence must sound smooth when read aloud. There should be no jagged edges, no splinters that catch and interrupt the reader's thoughts.]

SELECTION AMENDMENT
Description of change: excerpted
Rationale: to focus on the concept of sentence combining presented in this chapter

4. Islamic artists developed Kufic writing. Kufic writing is one of the most graceful styles of calligraphy.
5. In Islamic countries, you can see sentences from the Koran inscribed in beautiful calligraphy on buildings. The Koran is the Islamic holy book.

Combining by Coordinating Ideas

Sometimes you will want to combine sentences that contain *coordinate,* or equally important, ideas. You can join coordinate words, phrases, or clauses with coordinating conjunctions (*and, but, or, for, yet*) or correlative conjunctions (*both—and, either—or, neither—nor*). The relationship of the ideas determines which connective works best. When they are joined in one sentence, the coordinate ideas form compound elements.

ORIGINAL Richard will lend you the album. Mark will lend you the album.
COMBINED **Either Richard or Mark** will lend you the album. [compound subject]

ORIGINAL We could drive across country. We could take the train.
COMBINED We could **drive across country or take the train.** [compound predicate]

ORIGINAL The baseball player argued forcefully. The umpire refused to listen.
COMBINED The baseball player argued forcefully, **but** the umpire refused to listen. [compound sentence]

You can also form a compound sentence by linking independent clauses with a semicolon and a conjunctive adverb (*however, likewise, therefore*) or just a semicolon.

EXAMPLE You accept risk as part of every new challenge**;** it comes with the territory.
Chuck Yeager, *Yeager: An Autobiography*

TEACHING THE LESSON

Begin by having a volunteer read the opening paragraph of **Combining by Coordinating Ideas.** Write on the chalkboard the coordinating conjunctions and give a short clarification of how each is used. For example, *and* shows agreement; *but,* opposition; *or,* an alternative; and *yet,* contradiction.

Then list the correlative conjunctions and explain that each member of the pair shows the same relationship. Use the combined sentences shown as examples. You might explain that a semicolon can be useful when coordinating ideas. List the conjunctive adverbs on the chalkboard and ask students to define their usage.

REFERENCE NOTE: For more about coordination, see pages 504–505.

EXERCISE 4 **Combining by Coordinating Ideas**

Combine each of the following sets of sentences by forming a compound element. Be sure to choose a connective that expresses the correct relationship between the ideas. You may need to add punctuation, too.

EXAMPLE
1. **William Least Heat-Moon traveled across America. He wrote about his trip.**
1. ***William Least Heat-Moon traveled across America and wrote about his trip.***

1. William Least Heat-Moon's first name comes from an English ancestor. His last name was given to him by his Sioux father.
2. In 1977, Least Heat-Moon left his Missouri home. He began traveling across the country on back roads.
3. The title of his book *Blue Highways* doesn't refer to the actual color of roads. It refers to the blue lines that marked the back roads on his highway map.
4. Least Heat-Moon's trip began in the middle of the nation. His route was shaped like a jagged sideways heart.
5. Small, oddly named towns made his journey memorable. Friendly, helpful people made his journey memorable.

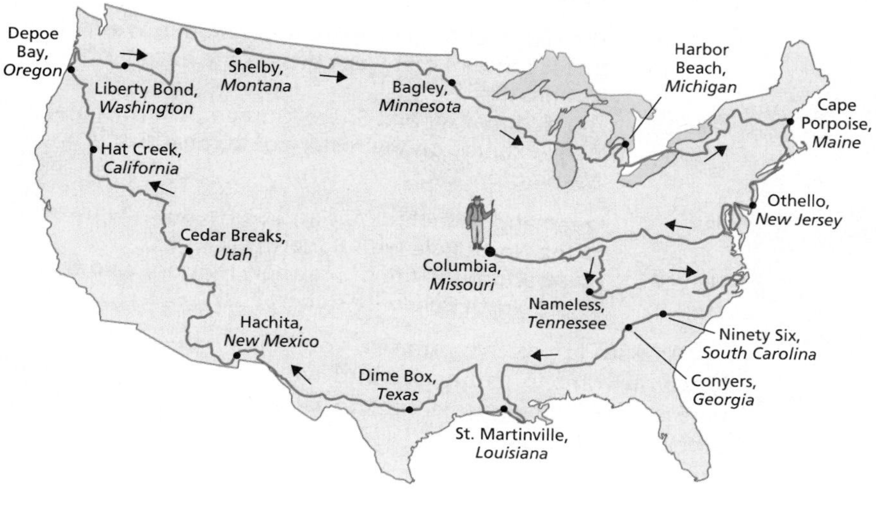

ANSWERS

Exercise 4

Answers may vary. Here are some possibilities:

1. William Least Heat-Moon's first name comes from an English ancestor, but his last name was given to him by his Sioux father.
2. In 1977, Least Heat-Moon left his Missouri home and began traveling across the country on back roads.
3. The title of his book *Blue Highways* doesn't refer to the actual color of the roads; it refers to the blue lines that marked the back roads on his highway map.
4. Least Heat-Moon's trip began in the middle of the nation, and his route was shaped like a jagged sideways heart.
5. Small, oddly named towns and friendly, helpful people made his trip memorable.

MEETING INDIVIDUAL NEEDS

LEARNING STYLES

Auditory Learners. Because speaking and listening are essential for auditory learners to comprehend how sentences can be combined, you might provide oral practice. If possible, provide a section of the classroom where auditory learners can talk softly to themselves as they independently work on the exercises.

To begin **Combining by Subordinating Ideas,** have volunteers read the professional examples to show how subordinating can enrich language. To illustrate the difference between coordinating clauses and subordinating clauses of unequal importance, you might show a diagram of the two.

As you discuss each type of subordinate clause, list the words that introduce the types of clauses in columns on the chalkboard. Use the original and revised samples to guide students' understanding.

Remind students that subordinate clauses serve the same function as the parts of speech they are named for. You might want to note that adjective clauses are placed as close as possible to the nouns or pronouns modified and that questions

MEETING INDIVIDUAL NEEDS

LEP/ESL

General Strategies. Languages vary in how adjective clauses are formed. In English, the adjective clause follows the noun that it modifies. (The team that scored the most points received T-shirts.) In other languages, such as Japanese, Chinese, and Korean, the adjective clause comes before the noun that it modifies. (That scored the most points the team received T-shirts.)

In Arabic, Hebrew, and Persian, an object pronoun in an adjective clause is retained. (We rebuilt the house that the storm destroyed it.)

Language arrangements such as these often carry over into a second language. Have your ESL students explain other differences of placement to the class as they learn more about English.

AMENDMENTS TO SELECTIONS
Description of change: excerpted
Rationale: to focus on the concept of sentence combining presented in this chapter

Combining by Subordinating Ideas

If two sentences are unequal in importance, you can combine them by placing the less-important idea in a subordinate clause.

EXAMPLES He had a habit of pausing to fix his gaze on part of the congregation as he read, and that Sunday he seemed to be talking to a small group of strangers **who sat in the front row.** [adjective clause]
Andrea Lee, "New African"

My aunt Giorgiana regarded them **as though they had been so many daubs of tube-paint on a palette.** [adverb clause]
Willa Cather, "A Wagner Matinée"

What he had the most of was time. [noun clause]
Juan Sedillo, "Gentleman of Río en Medio"

REFERENCE NOTE: For more about subordinating ideas, see pages 506–510. For more about the different types of subordinate clauses, see pages 629–637.

Adjective Clauses

You can change a sentence into an adjective clause by replacing its subject with *who, whose, which,* or *that.* Then you can use the adjective clause to give information about a noun or pronoun in another sentence.

ORIGINAL The National Air and Space Museum is in Washington, D.C. It contains many exhibits on the history of aeronautics.
REVISED The National Air and Space Museum, **which contains many exhibits on the history of aeronautics,** is in Washington, D.C.

ORIGINAL I read about the life of Matthew Henson. He traveled to the North Pole with Robert Peary.
REVISED I read about the life of Matthew Henson, **who traveled to the North Pole with Robert Peary.**

As with appositive phrases, you need to decide first which idea you want to emphasize and which you want to subordinate in the sentence. Be sure to keep your main idea in the independent clause.

like *What kind?* and *Which?* help identify them.

To demonstrate the use of commas in the **Mechanics Hint,** omit the adjective clause from both of the examples shown. Then discuss the effect on the meaning of the sentences.

Remind students that adverb clauses can be identified by asking questions like *When?* and *Where?* When they are placed after the main clause, they are usually not set off by commas.

Explain to students that noun clauses can usually be identified by asking questions like *Who?* or *What?* Note that when noun clauses are inserted, they become the subjects or objects in the revised sentences and are essential to the meaning of the sentence. ☛

MECHANICS HINT

Punctuating Adjective Clauses

How you punctuate an adjective clause depends on whether the clause is essential to the meaning of the sentence. If the clause is not essential, you need to set it off from the rest of the sentence with a comma or commas. If the clause is essential, no commas are necessary.

NONESSENTIAL	The baseball game**, which was the first of the season,** was played in the park on Saturday.
ESSENTIAL	The coach postponed the game **that was scheduled for Saturday.**

☞ REFERENCE NOTE: For more information on punctuating adjective clauses, see page 632.

Adverb Clauses

An adverb clause modifies a verb, an adjective, or another adverb in the sentence it is attached to. To make a sentence into an adverb clause, add a subordinating conjunction like *although, after, because, if, when, where,* or *while* at the beginning. The conjunction shows the relationship between the ideas in the adverb clause and the independent clause. It can show a relationship of time, place, cause or reason, purpose or result, or condition.

ORIGINAL	The British general Burgoyne attacked a second time. The Americans won a decisive victory.
REVISED	**When the British general Burgoyne attacked a second time,** the Americans won a decisive victory. [time]
ORIGINAL	Yukio and Julia both receive high grades. They work hard.
REVISED	Yukio and Julia both receive high grades **because they work hard.** [cause]

☞ REFERENCE NOTE: For more about using adverb clauses to subordinate ideas, see pages 506–508.

MECHANICS HINT

Ask each student to write one original sentence that contains a nonessential adjective clause and another with an essential clause. Select volunteers to write examples on the chalkboard. Have the class discuss the sentences and offer any suggestions for comma corrections. You might follow a similar procedure for commas used in adverbial clauses. Collect students' work for evaluation of strengths and weaknesses.

MEETING INDIVIDUAL NEEDS

LESS-ADVANCED STUDENTS

To aid students who are having difficulty writing and punctuating sentences that contain adjective, adverb, and noun clauses, review the related grammar and mechanics rules in small groups. Then ask each group to write several original sentences using each clause type. You might want to be available for help as students write. Cooperative, mixed-ability group experiences may also help improve writing skills and give more confidence to students.

Therefore, noun clauses are never set off by commas. When you discuss the example, review direct and indirect objects.

Before students complete **Exercises 4** and **5** as independent practice, model the example sentences on the chalkboard to guide students. Assess students' progress by evaluating their answers. If students have difficulty, review the parts of speech. Include diagramming if it seems helpful. ■

A DIFFERENT APPROACH

You may find that your students are competent in combining sentences when instructions are clear as to what technique to use, but are unable to evaluate their own work for the best revision techniques to try.

You might want to use more exercises like the **Review** on p. 539, which requires a combined approach. Also, when students need to revise their compositions, they might work in pairs on computers with one partner highlighting or boldfacing sentences that could be changed and the other responding to the clues. (See **Technology Link** on p. 531.)

ANSWERS

Exercise 5

Answers may vary. Here are some possibilities:

1. Space medicine, which deals with the physical effects of space travel, is one of the most important areas of space study.
2. Doctors learned more about the human body's reactions to space travel as they collected medical data during early space missions.

MECHANICS HINT

Punctuating Adverb Clauses

When you place an adverb clause at the beginning of a sentence, separate it from the independent clause with a comma.

EXAMPLE **Although the shar-pei was first bred as a guard dog,** it was later used for fighting.

REFERENCE NOTE: For more about the use of commas with subordinate clauses, see pages 632, 851–852, and 854.

Noun Clauses

You can make a sentence into a noun clause by adding a word like *that, how, what, whatever, who,* or *whoever* at the beginning. You may also have to delete or move some words. Then, insert the clause into another sentence just like an ordinary noun.

ORIGINAL Ramón is going to the carnival tonight. Eliza told me this.

REVISED Eliza told me **that Ramón is going to the carnival tonight.**

EXERCISE 5 **Combining by Subordinating Ideas**

Combine each of the following pairs of sentences by turning one sentence into a subordinate clause. [Hint: You may have to add, delete, or change some words in the sentences. Add commas where necessary.]

1. Space medicine is one of the most important areas of space study. Space medicine deals with the physical effects of space travel.
2. Doctors learned more about the human body's reactions to space travel. They collected medical data during early space missions.

REVIEW

OBJECTIVE

- To revise a paragraph by inserting words and phrases, coordinating ideas, and subordinating ideas

3. Engineers must consider the effects of acceleration. They must consider how the spacecraft's acceleration will affect the astronauts' bodies.
4. A space shuttle is designed to protect the astronauts against the high-intensity radiation. They encounter this radiation in space.
5. Astronauts must exercise regularly in space. A person's heart and muscles weaken in a weightless condition.

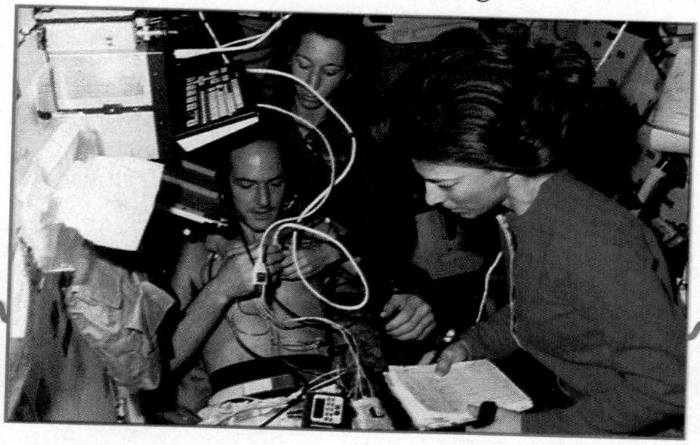

REVIEW **Revising a Paragraph by Combining Sentences**

Using all the sentence-combining skills you have learned, revise the following paragraph for style. Use your judgment about which sentences to combine and how to combine them. Don't change the meaning of the original paragraph.

Mildred ("Babe") Didrikson Zaharias was born in Port Arthur, Texas, around 1911. She was considered one of the finest track-and-field performers of all time. Babe gained national attention in 1930. She competed in a track-and-field meet in Dallas. She won two events. She broke the world record in a third event. The event was the long jump. Babe competed in the Olympic games in 1932. She entered the high jump, the javelin throw, and the hurdles. She set records in all of these events. They were world records. Only two of these records were made official. Babe's high-jump performance was disqualified. It was disqualified over a technicality. Babe was a champion in women's track and field for more than a decade. She was a world champion in track and field. Babe later became a world champion golfer.

3. Engineers must consider how the spacecraft's acceleration will affect the astronauts' bodies.
4. A space shuttle is designed to protect the astronauts against the high-intensity radiation that they encounter in space.
5. Because a person's heart and muscles weaken in a weightless condition, astronauts must exercise regularly in space.

ANSWERS

Review

Paragraphs will vary. Here is a possibility:

Mildred ("Babe") Didrickson Zaharias, considered one of the finest track-and-field performers of all time, was born in Port Arthur, Texas, around 1911. Babe gained national attention in 1930 when she competed in a track-and-field meet in Dallas. She won two events and broke the world record in a third event, the long jump. Entering the high jump, the javelin throw, and the hurdles, Babe competed in the Olympic games in 1932. Although she set world records in all of these events, only two of these records were made official. Babe's high-jump performance was disqualified because of a technicality. Babe was a world champion in women's track and field for over a decade and later became a world

SEGMENT 3 *(p. 540)*

MAKING CONNECTIONS

WRITE THE OPENING OF A MYSTERY STORY

OBJECTIVES

- To write the opening of a mystery story by expanding on details
- To combine sentences to improve a draft

WRITE THE OPENING OF A MYSTERY STORY

Teaching Strategies

Discuss with the class several of their favorite mysteries and ask why these stories are appealing. Then tell students to freewrite any ideas the list of details brings to mind. Have students use their freewriting notes as the bases for their first drafts. As students write and revise their mysteries, offer assistance to any student having difficulty. After students have completed their revisions, ask volunteers to read their final paragraphs before you collect the paragraphs for assessment.

GUIDELINES

Students' paragraphs will vary. You may want to have students work in pairs to revise their writing. Students should read each other's first drafts and make suggestions for combining sentences and adding details. Revised paragraphs should include proper punctuation.

MAKING CONNECTIONS

Write the Opening of a Mystery Story

By day, you're an ordinary teenager. But by night, you're the Masked Mystery Writer, penning thrillers under a pseudonym. You're hard at work on your next gripping story. To help set the mood for the opening, you've jotted down these details.

Write the first paragraph or two of your story, using at least five of the words, phrases, and clauses in your list. To hook your reader's attention, you'll want to craft interesting, varied sentences that work together smoothly.

After you've written your paragraph, check to see if you can improve any of your sentences by combining them.

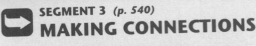

Chapter 16 IMPROVING SENTENCE STYLE

OBJECTIVES

- To revise sentences to vary sentence beginnings
- To revise a paragraph to vary sentence structure
- To revise sentences to reduce wordiness
- To write a short story and to focus on style while revising

Motivation

You could introduce this chapter with a class discussion on the meaning of *style*. List on the chalkboard the names of athletes, television personalities, movie stars, or politicians that students think have style. Then have students volunteer the names of famous people that they think do not have style. Ask students to analyze the difference between those who have style and those who do not. Point out that less heralded basketball players (for example, Scottie Pippen of the Chicago Bulls) sometimes score as many points as Michael Jordan. If the results are the same, why would most fans rather watch Jordan? Help students see that style depends less on what a person does than on how he or she does it.

Introduction

After discussing style, explain to students that a good writing style, like style in other endeavors, is entertaining, graceful, clear, concise, and effective. Writing style depends not so much on what a person writes, but on how the person writes it.

This chapter covers three methods of improving sentence style. First, the chapter presents three ways of varying sentence beginnings—using single-word modifiers, phrase modifiers, and clause modifiers. The second section of the chapter discusses varying sentence structure by using a mix of simple, compound, complex, and compound-complex sentences. Finally, students are given guidelines for avoiding wordiness in their writing.

Integration

Because the chapter deals with how to write rather than what to write, it can be a valuable resource for teaching the various aims for writing presented in other composition chapters. The skills can be used during the revision stage of the writing process, and the concepts can serve as goals during the drafting stage.

The chapter also integrates well with the study of literature. It will provide students with keys for analyzing strengths of fine writing.

The chart on the next page illustrates the strands of language arts as they are integrated into this chapter. For vocabulary study, glossary words are underlined in some writing models.

QUOTATIONS

All **Quotations for the Day** are chosen because of their relevance to instructional material presented in that segment of the chapter and for their usefulness in establishing student interest in writing.

INTEGRATING THE LANGUAGE ARTS

Selection	Reading and Literature	Writing and Critical Thinking	Language and Syntax	Speaking, Listening, and Other Expression Skills
from ***All Creatures Great and Small*** by Daniel Mannix **542** from ***Pilgrim at Tinker Creek*** by Annie Dillard **546**	Reading a paragraph to decide which sentences need revision **546** Reading sentences to determine wordiness **548**	Revising sentence beginnings **544** Revising a paragraph to vary sentence structures **546** Revising sentences to reduce wordiness **548** Imagining details for a short story **549** Writing a short story **549** Revising a short story to vary sentence beginnings and sentence structures **549**	Analyzing sentence beginnings **544** Evaluating sentence structures in a paragraph **546** Combining sentences to vary sentence structures **546**	Looking at a picture to get ideas for writing **549**

CHAPTER 16

SEGMENT PLANNING GUIDE

Whether you are planning for a quick review of a writing concept or preparing an extended lesson on composition, you can use the following Planning Guide to adapt the chapter material to the individual needs of your class.

SEGMENT	PAGES	CONTENT	RESOURCES
1 *Revising for Variety and Revising to Reduce Wordiness*	*541-548*		Varying Sentence Beginnings 143 Varying Sentence Structure 144 Revising to Reduce Wordiness 145
Revising for Variety	541-542	Introduction: using a variety of sentence patterns to enrich writing	
Literary Model from ***All Creatures Great and Small***	542	Guided reading: examining a model of sentence variety to see how sentences work together to form an effective paragraph	
Varying Sentence Beginnings	542	Guidelines: writing attention-grabbing sentenes by beginning sentences with single-words, phrases, and clause modifiers	
Chart: Sentence Connectives	543-544	Examples: analyzing sentences with subject first revised to sentences opening with introductory words, phrases, and clauses	
Exercise 1	544	Applied practice: revising sentences by varying their beginnings	
Varying Sentence Structure	545	Guidelines: comparing a paragraph made up of only simple sentences to a paragraph with varying sentence structure	
Writing Note	545	Writing suggestion: using simple sentences effectively	

All the resources listed in this chapter are located in the *Teacher's ResourceBank*™.

SEGMENT	PAGES	CONTENT	RESOURCES
Exercise 2	546	Applied practice: using sentence-combining techniques to revise a paragraph	
Revising to Reduce Wordiness	546-548	Guidelines: using criteria to compare examples of clear, concise sentences to wordy sentences	
Literary Model from ***Pilgrim at Tinker Creek***	546	Guided reading: examining conciseness in a model	
Chart: Wordy Phrases and Simpler Replacements	548	Guidelines: examining replacements for wordy phrases	
Exercise 3	548	Applied practice: reducing wordiness	
2 ***Making Connections***	***549***		
Craft a Short Story	549	Guidelines: writing a short story	
		Applied practice: writing a short story and revising for style	
WHOLE-CHAPTER RESOURCES Review Form A, Review Form B			

SEGMENT 1 *(pp. 541–548)*

REVISING FOR VARIETY AND REVISING TO REDUCE WORDINESS

OBJECTIVES

- To revise sentences to vary sentence beginnings
- To revise a paragraph to vary sentence structure
- To revise sentences to reduce wordiness

16 IMPROVING SENTENCE STYLE

LOOKING AHEAD

Chapter 15 explained some methods of combining short sentences into longer ones. Now you can use these and other revision techniques to improve your style. As you work through this chapter, you will learn how to

- vary the beginnings of your sentences
- vary the structure of your sentences
- pare down wordy sentences

Revising for Variety

Look closely at this woven tapestry. What makes it interesting?

Teacher's ResourceBank™

RESOURCES

REVISING FOR VARIETY AND REVISING TO REDUCE WORDINESS

QUOTATION FOR THE DAY

"To understand why anyone—including ourselves—writes badly, we have to be able to look at a sentence and understand how it works, how the ideas have been distributed through its different parts, and then decide how to write it better." (Joseph M. Williams, American writer and teacher)

You may want to use Williams' quotation to help students examine their own revision processes. Do they revise for clarity, for variety, or for both?

MOTIVATION

You may want to write the following sentence beginnings on the chalkboard and have students brainstorm possible ways to complete the sentences:

1. Surprised and pleased, . . .
2. In spite of a long delay, . . .
3. The team . . .
4. Having finally decided what to do, . . .
5. With noisy anticipation, . . .
6. Six hikers . . .

Ask students to compare the effects of beginning sentences with subjects to beginning sentences with descriptive words and phrases.

MEETING INDIVIDUAL NEEDS

STUDENTS WITH SPECIAL NEEDS

The exercises in this chapter require extensive writing and revision, which can be extremely tedious and frustrating for students who have trouble writing or transferring written material from one place to another. Word processors are valuable tools for these students. For students who are not yet skilled with the keyboard, revision exercises could be entered by the teacher and then revised by the students. Students need to be familiar with basic word-processing skills, including inserting, deleting, and rearranging blocks of text.

LESS-ADVANCED STUDENTS

Students who have not mastered the concept of sentence parts might have problems with the revision techniques in this chapter. You may want to review subjects and verbs to help students identify the sentence base in some of the example sentences. Explain the importance of first locating the sentence base of each clause when attempting to add variety to sentences.

SELECTION AMENDMENT
Description of change: excerpted
Rationale: to focus on the concept of sentence variety presented in this chapter

Just as artists can use a variety of colors and textures to enrich their art, you can use a variety of sentence patterns to enrich your writing.

As you read the following passage, notice how the sentences work together to form a smooth, effective paragraph.

> Grace advanced her hand toward the nearest cobra. The snake swayed like a reed in the wind, feinting for the strike. Grace raised her hand above the snake's head, the reptile twisting around to watch her. As the woman slowly lowered her hand, the snake gave that most terrible of all animal noises—the unearthly hiss of a deadly snake. I have seen children laugh with excitement at the roar of a lion, but I have never seen anyone who did not cringe at that cold, uncanny sound. Grace deliberately tried to touch the rigid, quivering hood. The cobra struck at her hand. He missed. Quietly, Grace presented her open palm. The cobra hesitated a split second, his reared body quivering like a plucked banjo string. Then he struck.
>
> *Daniel Mannix, All Creatures Great and Small*

Mannix's carefully crafted sentences add syle and interest to his writing. You can improve your own writing style by revising your sentences for variety.

Varying Sentence Beginnings

Have you ever heard or read a story that kept you on the edge of your seat? Chances are the sentence openings helped hold your attention. Instead of beginning every sentence with a subject and a verb, the storyteller probably began some sentences with attention-grabbing words, phrases, and clauses: "Suddenly . . ."; "At the bottom of the cliff . . ."; "When she opened the door . . .".

Varied sentence beginnings do more than hold a reader's attention. They also improve the overall style of writing. The following examples show how you can revise your sentences to open them with introductory words, phrases, and clauses. Note that when you vary sentence beginnings, you sometimes must reword the sentences for clarity. Be sure to place phrase modifiers close to the words they modify.

TEACHING THE LESSON

Begin by listing on the chalkboard the two ways of revising for variety that students will study: varying sentence beginnings and varying sentence structure within paragraphs. Have a volunteer read aloud the excerpt from ***All Creatures Great and Small,*** but reserve discussion of the mechanics of the excerpt until after you have discussed the information about varying sentence beginnings and varying sentence structure.

In **Varying Sentence Beginnings,** you may want to have volunteers read aloud the examples and changes to emphasize the improvements. Before students read **Varying Sentence Structure** on p. 545, review simple, compound, complex, and compound-complex sentences. Emphasize that students

SENTENCE CONNECTIVES	
SUBJECT FIRST	The seal has a few natural enemies, including sharks, polar bears, and killer whales. The seal's most dangerous enemies are human beings, though.
COORDINATING CONJUNCTION FIRST	The seal has a few natural enemies, including sharks, polar bears, and killer whales. **But** the seal's most dangerous enemies are humans.
SUBJECT FIRST	Animal protection laws forbid commercial harvesting of seals in the United States. Seals are still hunted in many parts of the world.
CONJUNCTIVE ADVERB FIRST	Animal protection laws forbid commercial harvesting of seals in the United States. **However,** seals are still hunted in many parts of the world.
SINGLE-WORD MODIFIERS	
SUBJECT FIRST	The octopus is shy and intelligent and rarely harms people.
SINGLE-WORD MODIFIERS FIRST	**Shy and intelligent,** the octopus rarely harms people.
SUBJECT FIRST	Octopi usually keep their distance from humans.
SINGLE-WORD MODIFIER FIRST	**Usually,** octopi keep their distance from humans.
SUBJECT FIRST	An octopus may bite a person with its sharp beak if provoked.
SINGLE-WORD MODIFIER FIRST	**Provoked,** an octopus may bite a person with its sharp beak.
PHRASE MODIFIERS	
SUBJECT FIRST	A team of determined Norwegian skiers began a 413-mile trek to the North Pole in March 1990.
PREPOSITIONAL PHRASE FIRST	**In March 1990,** a team of determined Norwegian skiers began a 413-mile trek to the North Pole.
SUBJECT FIRST	They used only skis and manually drawn sledges and set a record for reaching the Pole unassisted.
PARTICIPIAL PHRASE FIRST	**Using only skis and manually drawn sledges,** they set a record for reaching the Pole unassisted.

(continued)

INTEGRATING THE LANGUAGE ARTS

Listening Link. You may want to point out one of the main differences between the sentence styles of spoken and written language. Written language is more likely to include long introductory phrases and clauses before the main verb of a sentence. For example, the following sentences are characteristic of written and spoken language respectively:

1. Crossing the street at the corner, she then hurriedly walked down the hill.
2. She crossed the street at the corner, and then she walked quickly down the hill.

Write the two sentences on the chalkboard and ask students to determine which one they might read and which one they might hear. Explain that in first drafts writers often write material that mirrors speech. When revising, however, writers can change and combine sentences to create an effective and interesting style.

should not turn simple sentences into unnatural sounding compound or complex sentences; they should only consider sentence structure during revision if a draft sounds dull or flat.

After students read **Varying Sentence Structure,** ask them to go back to the excerpt on p. 542 and to analyze it for variety of sentence beginnings and sentence structure.

Students may be familiar with wordiness in writing, as wordiness is often the result of padding word or page counts. After students have read **Revising to Reduce Wordiness** (pp. 546–547), discuss the examples on pp. 547–548. You may want to have students look over their past writing assignments to find examples of wordiness

G6 **A DIFFERENT APPROACH**
Hand out copies of paragraphs written primarily in simple sentences. (You might use papers from previous years to avoid embarrassing any of your current students.) Have students revise the paragraphs by varying sentence beginnings and sentence structure. You may want to have students work in groups to evaluate their revisions and to discuss specific strengths.

ANSWERS
Exercise 1

Revisions will vary. Here are some possibilities:

1. Since prehistoric times, people have used signs and gestures to communicate their thoughts.
2. Often, a system of commonly understood gestures helped Native American nations communicate with each other.
3. Because nations in the Plains area spoke many different languages, a well-developed sign language was essential for trading.
4. As more groups settled on the Plains, the scope of the sign language grew.
5. Known by many nations, the gesture shown at right was used to mean "peace."

PHRASE MODIFIERS *(continued)*	
SUBJECT FIRST	They wanted to keep their sledges light, so they brought only enough fuel to melt ice for water.
INFINITIVE PHRASE FIRST	**To keep their sledges light,** they brought only enough fuel to melt ice for water.
CLAUSE MODIFIERS	
SUBJECT FIRST	Over one million species of plants, animals, and insects may be wiped out if burning of the Brazilian rain forest continues.
ADVERB CLAUSE FIRST	**If burning of the Brazilian rain forest continues,** over one million species of plants, animals, and insects may be wiped out.
SUBJECT FIRST	Parts of the rain forest are now protected, but about 10 percent of the forest has already been destroyed.
ADVERB CLAUSE FIRST	**Although parts of the rain forest are now protected,** about 10 percent of the forest has already been destroyed.

EXERCISE 1 Varying Sentence Beginnings

Revise each of the following sentences by varying their beginnings. The hint in parentheses will tell you which type of beginning to use.

1. People have used signs and gestures to communicate their thoughts since prehistoric times. (phrase)
2. A system of commonly understood gestures often helped Native American nations communicate with each other. (single-word modifier)
3. Nations in the Plains area spoke many different languages, so a well-developed sign language was essential for trading. (clause)
4. The scope of the sign language grew as more groups settled on the Plains. (clause)
5. The gesture shown at right was used to mean "peace" and was known by many nations. (phrase)

GUIDED PRACTICE

To prepare students for **Exercise 1** on p. 544 and **Exercise 3** on p. 548, guide them through the first few sentences in each exercise. To prepare students for **Exercise 2** on p. 546, discuss the revisions of the paragraph on this page about San Francisco.

INDEPENDENT PRACTICE

Have students complete the remaining sentences in **Exercises 1** and **3,** and have them revise the paragraph in **Exercise 2.**

Varying Sentence Structure

You can also improve your style by varying the structure of your sentences. That means using a mix of simple, compound, and complex (and sometimes even compound-complex) sentences in your writing.

REFERENCE NOTE: For information about the four types of sentence structure, see pages 640–641.

Read the following short paragraph, which is made up of only simple sentences.

> San Francisco is famous for its scenic views. The city sprawls over more than forty hills. Driving through San Francisco is like riding a roller coaster. Atop one of San Francisco's hills is Chinatown, a thriving ethnic neighborhood. Atop another is Coit Tower, a great lookout point. The most popular place to visit is the San Francisco Bay area. There the stately Golden Gate Bridge and the picturesque Fisherman's Wharf attract a steady stream of tourists.

Now read the revised version of the paragraph. Notice how the writer has used sentence-combining techniques to vary the structure of the sentences.

> San Francisco is famous for its scenic views. Because the city sprawls over forty-two hills, driving through San Francisco is like riding a roller coaster. Atop one of San Francisco's hills is Chinatown, a thriving ethnic neighborhood; and atop another is Coit Tower, a great lookout point. The most popular place to visit is the San Francisco Bay area, where the stately Golden Gate Bridge and the picturesque Fisherman's Wharf attract a steady stream of tourists.

WRITING NOTE

You may find that simple sentences work best in some of your paragraphs. Don't try to force sentences into compound or complex structures if a simple structure sounds better. But if a paragraph sounds flat and dull, varied sentence structure may help improve it.

INTEGRATING THE LANGUAGE ARTS

Literature Link. Katherine Anne Porter is known for her clarity of style. Have students read and discuss one of her stories such as "The Grave," and then have the class analyze several paragraphs for style. Ask students to identify the types of sentence structures and the varied sentence beginnings she uses. Students may be interested to know that Porter's graceful, flowing style resulted from painstaking care in writing and revising.

ASSESSMENT

Exercises 1–3 should be helpful in determining whether or not students have a sufficient grasp of the material. However, evaluating students' writing samples should give a clearer picture of individual sentence style.

RETEACHING

You may want to schedule individual conferences with students who are having difficulty improving sentence style. Have each student bring a multiple-paragraph writing sample to the conference. Help students revise their samples by suggesting ways to vary sentence beginnings, vary sentence structure, and reduce wordiness.

COOPERATIVE LEARNING

Organize the class into groups of four to six students and have them participate in a contest. Have each group use their literature textbooks to find an excellent example in each of the following categories: varying sentence beginnings; varying sentence structure; and avoiding wordiness. Students should analyze entire works and then select individual paragraphs that provide effective examples. Have volunteers share their findings by reading and discussing example paragraphs. The class can vote to determine which selection in each category is most effective.

MEETING INDIVIDUAL NEEDS

ADVANCED STUDENTS

As most legal documents are purposefully wordy, you might want to bring in contracts (lease agreements or contracts for hire) and have students revise the contracts to eliminate wordiness. Encourage students to use dictionaries to help them understand legal terminology.

SELECTION AMENDMENT
Description of change: excerpted
Rationale: to focus on the concept of conciseness presented in this chapter

EXERCISE 2 **Revising a Paragraph to Vary Sentence Structures**

Decide which sentences in the following paragraph will sound better with compound, complex, or compound-complex structures. Then use sentence-combining techniques to vary the sentence structures. Work for clear sentences that fit together smoothly. **Revisions will vary.**

These people may look like villains from a science fiction movie, but they're actually kendo players. Kendo is an ancient Japanese martial art ~~. It requires~~ requiring skill, concentration, and agility. The contestants fight with long bamboo swords called shinai. Because kendo can be dangerous, the players must wear protective gear that includes a mask, a breastplate, and thick gloves. Each match lasts three to five minutes, and the first contestant to score two points wins. Kendo is a graceful, dignified sport. Respectfulness toward one's opponent is important, and a contestant can even be disqualified for rudeness.

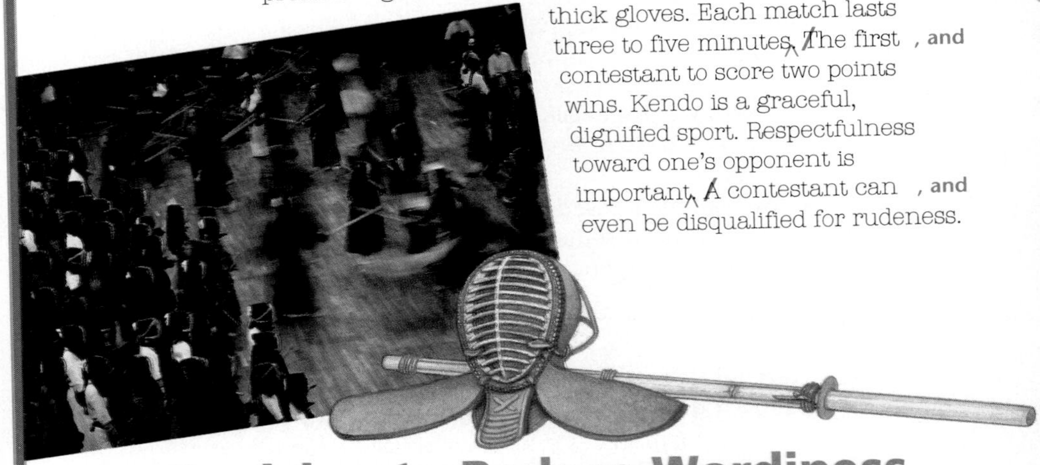

Revising to Reduce Wordiness

Read the following sentence. Could you remove a single word from it without changing its meaning or lessening its impact?

> At last I knelt on the island's winter-killed grass, lost, dumbstruck, staring at the frog in the creek just four feet away.
>
> Annie Dillard, *Pilgrim at Tinker Creek*

Skilled writers make every word count. They know that conciseness is essential for style. You can make your own writing more concise by eliminating the clutter of extra words.

Emphasize that there is often more than one way to revise and that the result should be clear, concise, and interesting writing.

CLOSURE

Ask students to help you list on the chalkboard the three techniques presented in this chapter for improving sentence style. Have students give examples of each. [Vary sentence beginnings, vary sentence structure, and eliminate wordiness.]

To avoid wordiness in your writing, keep these three points in mind:

- Use only as many words as you need to make your point.
- Choose simple, clear words and expressions over pretentious, complicated ones.
- Don't repeat words or ideas unless it's absolutely necessary.

The following examples show some ways to revise wordy sentences.

1. Take out a whole group of unnecessary words.

WORDY After descending to the edge of the river, we boarded a small boat that was floating there on the surface of the water.

BETTER After descending to the edge of the river, we boarded a small boat.

2. Replace pretentious words and expressions with straightforward ones.

WORDY The young woman, who was at an indeterminate point in her teenage years, wore in her hair a streak of pink dye that could be considered garish.

BETTER The **teenager** wore a streak of **bright** pink dye in her hair.

3. Reduce a clause to a phrase.

WORDY Su Li, who lives in Washington, D.C., can conveniently visit the Smithsonian.

BETTER **Living in Washington, D.C.,** Su Li can conveniently visit the Smithsonian.

WORDY George, who is my childhood friend, lives in Baltimore.

BETTER George, **my childhood friend,** lives in Baltimore.

CRITICAL THINKING
Synthesis

Because models might help students see the folly of inflated diction, have students read Russell Baker's "Little Red Riding Hood Revisited" or a similar spoof from your literature textbook. Then challenge your students to write their own satires. They could rewrite a folk tale, an article from the school paper, or any other work by using jargon and inflated language.

EXTENSION

Have students analyze their abilities as writers by focusing on two or three specific strengths and two or three weaknesses. Then have students write paragraphs of self-evaluation. When revising their paragraphs, students should focus on varying sentence beginnings, varying sentence structure, and avoiding wordiness. ■

INTEGRATING THE LANGUAGE ARTS

Literature Link. While most professional writers follow the guidelines for avoiding wordiness in writing, the range of writing styles varies widely. You may want to have students compare writers of nonfiction from various centuries. Possible writers are Benjamin Franklin, Henry Thoreau, and E. B. White. Franklin's writing requires careful concentration for students because of his diction and his use of complex sentence structures. Thoreau's writing is more easily understood despite complex ideas conveyed in complex sentence structures. E. B. White is known for his clarity.

COOPERATIVE LEARNING

This activity shows students that there is more than one correct way to revise. Have students work in groups of three to revise a paragraph. Their goals should be to vary sentence beginnings, to vary sentence structure, and to eliminate wordiness. Each group should have the same paragraph to revise. After groups have completed their revisions, have a representative from each group write its revised paragraph on the chalkboard. Then have the class compare and discuss the revisions.

4. Reduce a phrase or a clause to one word.

WORDY Angelo likes cooking from the South.
BETTER Angelo likes **Southern** cooking.

WORDY The dance class that has been canceled will be rescheduled.
BETTER The **canceled** dance class will be rescheduled.

Here is a list of wordy phrases and their simpler replacements. Watch out for these wordy phrases in your writing.

Wordy	Simpler
at this point in time	now
at which time	when
by means of	by
due to the fact that	because, since
in spite of the fact that	although
in the event that	if
the fact is that	actually

EXERCISE 3 **Reducing Wordiness**

Some of the following sentences are wordy. Revise each wordy sentence to make it straightforward and concise. If a sentence doesn't need improving, write *C*. Revisions will vary.

1. Good writing is precise and straightforward. 1. C
2. Have you ever read sentences that ~~seem to~~ ramble? ~~on and keep going forever?~~
3. Annie Dillard, who is a careful writer, revises heavily.
4. Redundant sentences are boring. ~~and repetitive.~~
5. Sentences that are longer than ~~it is~~ necessary ~~for them to be~~ may confuse your reader.
6. A sentence with too many subordinate clauses ~~that are subordinate~~ becomes a mental maze for the unsuspecting reader. 6. subordinate
7. Think of the sounds and rhythms of the writing you like best. 7. C
8. Sentences stuffed with extra ~~unneeded~~ words resemble Saint Bernards squeezed into Chihuahua-size sweaters.
9. Carefully crafted sentences are like well-tailored suits. 9. C
10. William Strunk, Jr., said "Vigorous writing is concise." 10. C

SEGMENT 2 *(p. 549)*

MAKING CONNECTIONS

CRAFT A SHORT STORY
OBJECTIVE

- To write a short story and to revise it by focusing on sentence style

MAKING CONNECTIONS

Craft a Short Story

Walking down the street, you catch sight of the people in this picture. You wonder: *Who are they? Where are they going? What's their story?* Use your imagination to come up with some answers to these questions. Then write a short story (two or three paragraphs) about the people. Invent as many details as you wish.

After you've completed a draft or two, read your story slowly, sentence by sentence. Are the sentences lively and varied? Are they concise? Do they fit together smoothly? Using the methods you've learned, revise your sentences for style.

CRAFT A SHORT STORY
Teaching Strategies

You may want to remind students of short-story elements: setting, plot, character, point of view, and conflict. Suggest that students formulate a story plan based on the italicized questions in the text. Because two or three paragraphs will not accommodate an entire story, have students think of the assignment as a tableau, or dramatic scene, excerpted from the story plan. You may want to have students work together to revise their first drafts.

GUIDELINES

Have students turn in both story drafts—the first and the revised—so you can assess their understanding of revising for style.

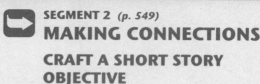

PART TWO

HANDBOOK

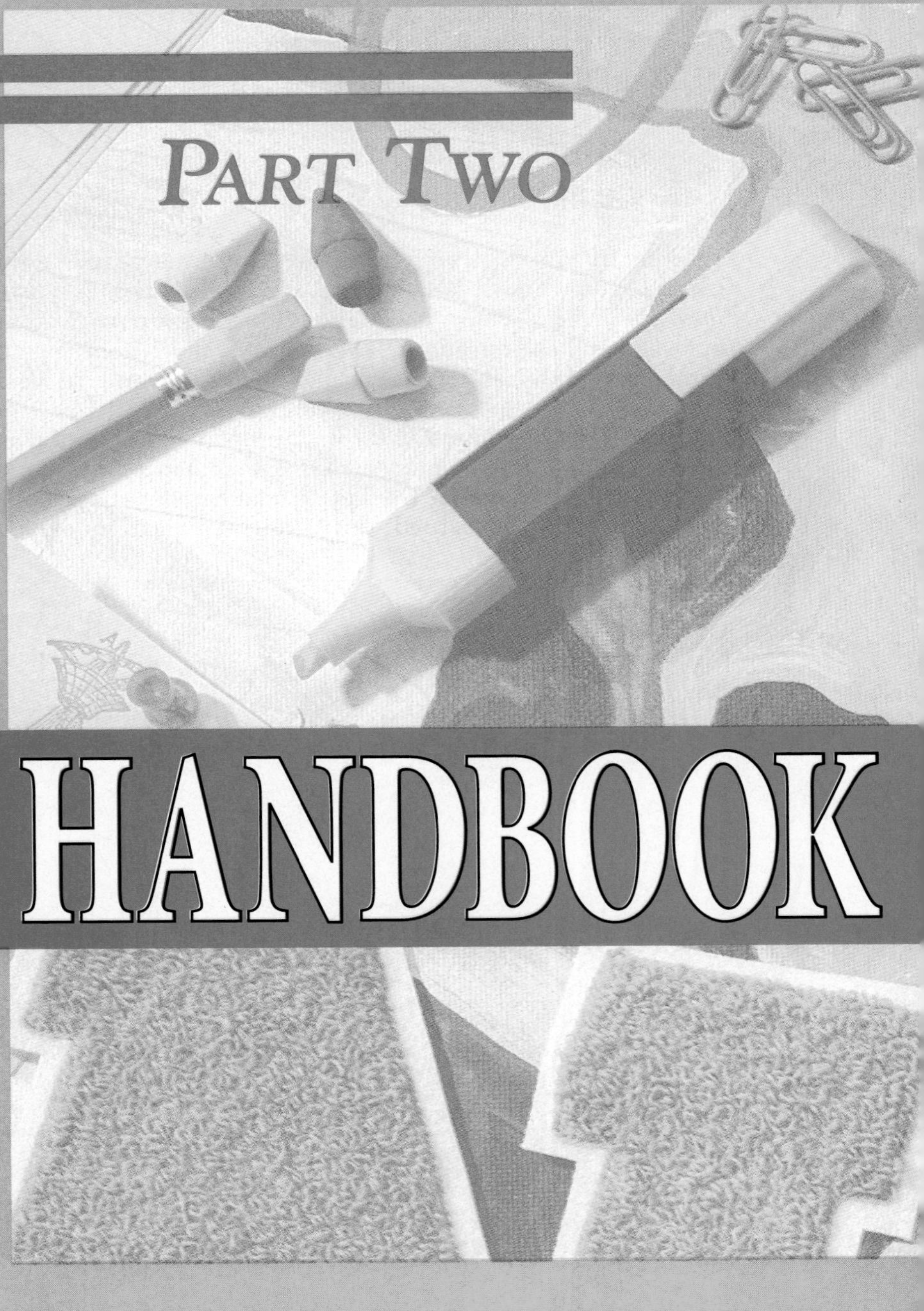

Grammar

Usage

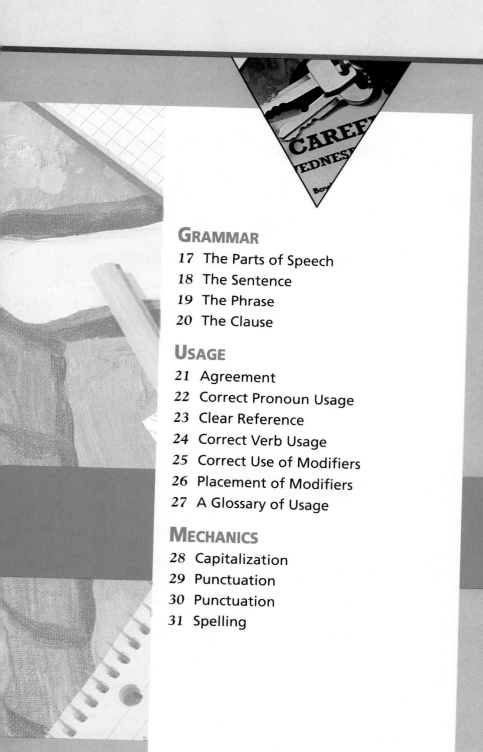

Mechanics

SEGMENT 1 *(pp. 552–553)*

DIAGNOSTIC TEST

OBJECTIVE

- To determine the parts of speech of selected words by analyzing the use of those words in sentences

Teacher's ResourceBank™

RESOURCES

FOR THE WHOLE CHAPTER

• Chapter Review Form A	163–164
• Chapter Review Form B	165–166
• Assessment Portfolio	
Grammar Pretests	563–570
Grammar Mastery Tests	587–595

GRAMMAR

CHAPTER OVERVIEW

This chapter classifies words in the English language by defining the eight parts of speech according to function. In the **Writing Application,** students practice using specific adjectives in descriptions. Because usage rules, punctuation rules, and revision suggestions often mention parts of speech, you may want to refer students to this chapter throughout the year.

USING THE DIAGNOSTIC TEST

The **Diagnostic Test** requires students to identify the parts of speech of twenty italicized words in a paragraph. The results of the test will help you to determine the needs of individual students and the areas that require teaching or review.

GRAMMAR

17 THE PARTS OF SPEECH

Their Identification and Function

Diagnostic Test

Identifying Parts of Speech

Identify the part of speech of each italicized word in the following paragraph. n. = noun v. = verb pro. = pronoun adv. = adverb adj. = adjective prep. = preposition conj. = conjunction itj. = interjection

1. v.
2. adv.
3. n.
4. prep.
5. adj.
6. adj.
7. pro.
8. adv.
9. itj.
10. adj.

Thursday, April 4, 1974, **[1]** *was* a day that will **[2]** *always* be remembered in the history of **[3]** *baseball*. At 2:40 P.M. in Riverfront Stadium in Cincinnati, Henry Aaron **[4]** *of* the Atlanta Braves tied Babe Ruth's **[5]** *unbroken* record of 714 home runs during a major league baseball career. Aaron was at bat for the first time in the **[6]** *baseball* season. It was the first inning. He hit a 3–1 pitch **[7]** *that* sailed 400 feet, zooming **[8]** *neatly* over the fence in left center field and driving in the first runs of the 1974 baseball season. Jumping to their feet, Braves fans yelled **[9]** *"Bravo!"* from the packed stands. The **[10]** *horsehide* ball was

SEGMENT 2 *(pp. 553–555)*

THE NOUN Rule 17a

OBJECTIVE

- To distinguish between concrete and abstract nouns

11. n. **12.** prep.
caught on the first bounce by Clarence Williams, a Cincinnati **[11]** *police officer,* standing **[12]** *behind* the fence. "I couldn't see what was going on," said Williams, **[13]** *one* of Aaron's fans, **[14]** "*but* I knew he was up when I saw 44 on the scoreboard under the 'at bat' sign." While being interviewed by the press after the game, Aaron smiled in his usual gracious **[15]** *way* **[16]** *and* said he was **[17]** *positively* delighted to have tied the Babe's **[18]** *longstanding* record. Later that month, on April 8, Aaron **[19]** *broke* Babe Ruth's record, a feat that **[20]** *many* had thought they would never see.

13. pro. **14.** conj. **15.** n. **16.** conj. **17.** adv. **18.** adj. **19.** v. **20.** pro.

GRAMMAR

THE EIGHT PARTS OF SPEECH

noun	verb	conjunction
pronoun	adverb	interjection
adjective	preposition	

The Noun

17a. A ***noun*** is a word used to name a person, a place, a thing, or an idea.

PERSONS	architect	travelers	family	Kira Alvarez
PLACES	restaurant	islands	wilderness	Salt Lake City
THINGS	computer	sailboats	insects	Brooklyn Bridge
IDEAS	education	beliefs	ambition	Utopianism

Common and Proper Nouns

A ***common noun*** names any one of a group of persons, places, or things. A ***proper noun*** names a particular person, place, or thing. Common nouns are not capitalized; proper nouns are.

GRAMMAR

Teacher's ResourceBank™

RESOURCES

THE NOUN

QUICK REMINDER

Write the following sentences on the chalkboard and have students fill in the blanks with nouns:

1. On the weekends (person) and (person) like to go to the (place).
2. The music of (person) fills me with (idea).
3. (Person) gave his best friend a (thing) for his birthday.

MEETING INDIVIDUAL NEEDS

LEP/ESL

General Strategies. Students might better understand the concept of a noun if they associate the term with familiar words. You could have the students fill in the following chart with names of persons, places, things, and ideas by using nouns that have personal significance. Students might need help filling the *Idea* column.

Person	Place	Thing	Idea

LEARNING STYLES

Visual Learners. To help students distinguish between abstract and concrete nouns, have them make some drawings of the meanings of words you dictate. Ask them to do pencil drawings or sketches of the following nouns: *award, courage, rose, beauty, sailboat, adventure,* and *monkey.* Then discuss with students how concrete nouns should result in somewhat similar drawings, while abstract nouns will not.

GRAMMAR

COMMON NOUNS	PROPER NOUNS
woman	Sylvia Bryan, Eda Seasongood, Queen of England
nation	Switzerland, Canada, Mexico
event	World Series, Mardi Gras, Fall of Rome
holiday	Memorial Day, Thanksgiving Day, Fourth of July
language	English, Spanish, Japanese

Concrete and Abstract Nouns

A ***concrete noun*** names an object that can be perceived by the senses. An ***abstract noun*** names a quality, a characteristic, or an idea.

CONCRETE NOUNS	fire, garlic, cotton, horses, Liberty Bell
ABSTRACT NOUNS	confidence, strength, charm, ability, Zen

Collective Nouns

A ***collective noun*** names a group.

COLLECTIVE NOUNS	swarm, team, herd, crew, committee, fleet, family, class, group

Compound Nouns

A ***compound noun*** consists of two or more words used together as a single noun. Some compound nouns are written as one word, some as separate words, and others as hyphenated words.

ONE WORD	sidewalk, tablecloth, Greenland
SEPARATE WORDS	attorney general, telephone pole, Empire State Building
HYPHENATED WORDS	daughter-in-law, great-grandfather, jack-o'-lantern

SEGMENT 3 *(pp. 555–559)*

THE PRONOUN Rule 17b

OBJECTIVE

- To identify pronouns in sentences

NOTE: When you are not sure about the form of a compound noun, look it up in a dictionary.

EXERCISE 1 Classifying Nouns

Classify each of the following nouns as either *concrete* or *abstract*.

1. tradition
2. flower
3. courage
4. cafeteria
5. dancers
6. honor
7. security
8. lake
9. happiness
10. bench

The Pronoun

17b. A ***pronoun*** is a word used in place of a noun or of more than one noun.

EXAMPLE **Angelo borrowed a hammer and some nails. He will return them tomorrow.** [The pronoun *he* takes the place of the noun *Angelo.* The pronoun *them* takes the place of the nouns *hammer* and *nails.*]

The word that a pronoun stands for is called the ***antecedent*** of the pronoun. In the preceding example, *Angelo* is the antecedent of *he,* and *hammer* and *nails* are the antecedents of *them.*

A pronoun may also take the place of another pronoun.

Several of the students have entered the essay contest because **they** are extremely interested in the topic. [The pronoun *they* takes the place of the pronoun *several.*]

REFERENCE NOTE: For more information about antecedents, see pages 664–666 and 701–707.

Personal Pronouns

A ***personal pronoun*** refers to the one speaking (first person), the one spoken to (second person), or the one spoken about (third person).

ANSWERS

Exercise 1

1. abstract
2. concrete
3. abstract
4. concrete
5. concrete
6. abstract
7. abstract
8. concrete
9. abstract
10. concrete

Teacher's ResourceBank™

RESOURCES

QUICK REMINDER

Write the following sentences on the chalkboard. Ask students to improve each sentence by finding substitutes for any overused words or groups of words. Remind students that a word that takes the place of a noun is a pronoun.

1. Chuck opened Chuck's locker, got out Chuck's comb, and used Chuck's comb to comb Chuck's hair. [Chuck opened his locker, got out his comb, and used it to comb his hair.]
2. Lola found the clean towels and took a towel with Lola when Lola left for the pool. [Lola found the clean towels and took one with her when she left for the pool.]

MEETING INDIVIDUAL NEEDS

LEP/ESL

Asian Languages. In English, the second-person pronoun *you* suffices when addressing any person or persons, a deity, or an animal. However, many Asian languages such as Indonesian, Japanese, and Vietnamese have a variety of nouns and pronouns meaning "you." Some of your Asian students might avoid using *you* because it may seem impolite or awkward to use the same word to address elders, peers, both men and women, and animals. Remind students that in English, it is acceptable to use *you* in nearly all situations.

CRITICAL THINKING

Analysis

Some people consider the English language deficient for not having a separate, distinguishable, second-person plural, personal pronoun form. Ask students to consider this deficiency, to list slang or colloquial expressions commonly used as second-person plural forms, and to propose a solution. [Students may mention *you guys, y'all,* or *you all.*]

GRAMMAR

First person	I, me, my, mine, we, us, our, ours
Second person	you, your, yours
Third person	he, him, his, she, her, hers, it, its, they, them, their, theirs

EXAMPLES **I** hope that **you** can help **me** with **my** homework.
He said that **they** would meet **us** outside the theater.

NOTE: This textbook refers to the words *my, your, his, her, its, our,* and *their* as possessive pronouns. However, because they come before nouns and tell *which one* or *whose,* many authorities prefer to call these words adjectives. Follow your teacher's instructions regarding these possessive forms.

Reflexive and Intensive Pronouns

A ***reflexive pronoun*** refers to the subject of a sentence and directs the action of the verb back to the subject. An ***intensive pronoun*** emphasizes a noun or another pronoun.

First person	myself, ourselves
Second person	yourself, yourselves
Third person	himself, herself, itself, themselves

EXAMPLES Kimiko wrote **herself** a note. [reflexive]
Leonora **herself** organized the school's recycling program. [intensive]

Demonstrative Pronouns

A ***demonstrative pronoun*** points out a person, a place, a thing, or an idea.

this that these those

EXAMPLES **This** is our favorite song by Ella Fitzgerald.
The apples I picked today taste better than **these**.

Interrogative Pronouns

An ***interrogative pronoun*** introduces a question.

who	whom	which	what	whose

EXAMPLES **What** is the answer to the last algebra problem?
Whose car is parked outside?

Relative Pronouns

A ***relative pronoun*** introduces a subordinate clause.

that	which	who	whom	whose

EXAMPLES The house **that** you saw is a historical landmark.
She is the woman **who** is running for mayor.

REFERENCE NOTE: For more information about relative pronouns and subordinate clauses, see pages 631–632.

Indefinite Pronouns

An ***indefinite pronoun*** refers to a person, place, or thing that is not specifically named.

all	either	much	other
another	everybody	neither	several
any	everyone	nobody	some
anybody	everything	none	somebody
anyone	few	no one	someone
anything	many	nothing	something
both	more	one	such
each	most		

EXAMPLES I have packed **everything** we will need for the trip.
Has **anyone** seen my binoculars?

GRAMMAR

INTEGRATING THE LANGUAGE ARTS

Grammar, Speaking, and Writing. Have students formulate some interview questions that use interrogative pronouns. Ask students to use the questions to survey a group of friends about music groups, food choices in the cafeteria, clothing styles, or another topic of interest.

When students have completed the surveys, have them write their results in informative paragraphs. Require the use of at least five indefinite pronouns. [For example: No one in my survey liked squash, but everyone liked pizza.]

Literature Link. Walt Whitman's "Song of Myself" provides an excellent model for studying the relationship between form and content. His poem is packed with pronouns and gives a sense of intimacy similar to that of conversation. Whitman considered himself a poet "for the masses," and he uses familiar conversational forms to highlight his accessibility.

GRAMMAR

REVIEW A

OBJECTIVE

- To distinguish between nouns and pronouns used in a paragraph

MEETING INDIVIDUAL NEEDS

ADVANCED STUDENTS

Students might not realize that English is more closely related in structure to German than to Latin-based (Romance) languages such as French or Spanish. During the Middle Ages, when French was the official language of the English court (from 1066 to about 1400), English lost its Germanic case endings on nouns and adjectives. The only place in English where the Germanic inflectional, or case, endings can still be found is on personal pronouns.

Students who are interested in exploring this subject might research and report on the original Old English forms of personal pronouns and compare them to Middle English forms and to those in modern English. Ask students to make a chart that groups the pronouns according to nominative, objective, and possessive cases.

GRAMMAR

GRAMMAR

EXERCISE 2 Identifying Pronouns

Identify the pronouns in the following sentences.

EXAMPLE **1. Someone told me they had moved to Iowa.**
1. *Someone; me; they*

1. Deven himself knew everyone who either had a ticket or could get one for him at a low price.
2. Nobody has bought more than one of the records on sale at the discount store.
3. A friend of mine said that you won several of the events at the 4-H competition.
4. Those are photographs of some of the many contemporary politicians who are women.
5. What is the large body of water that borders Ethiopia called?

REVIEW A Identifying Nouns and Pronouns

Tell whether each italicized word in the following paragraph is a noun or a pronoun.

EXAMPLE Tessellation is the filling of a plane with shapes so that [1] *each* of the [2] *shapes* touches the others without any space between them.
1. *pronoun*
2. *noun*

For centuries, cultures all over the world have used tessellated [1] *designs* to decorate fabrics, walls, floors, pottery, and many other [2] *things* used in daily life. The [3] *Moors*, for example, were masters at creating intricate tiled walls and floors. Because their religion did not allow [4] *them* to make images of any animals or [5] *people*, they worked with geometric shapes. Notice also that [6] *all* of the Moorish designs shown on the next page are symmetrical. One twentieth-century Dutch artist [7] *who* was inspired by designs like [8] *these* from Moorish buildings was [9] *M. C. Escher*. [10] *Many* of Escher's designs, however, feature birds, lizards, and other natural [11] *forms*. In addition, he often used asymmetrical [12] *shapes* in [13] *his* interlocking designs. Of the Escher designs on the next page, the [14] *first* is the only [15] *one* that uses a symmetrical shape to fill the plane. The [16] *others* all consist of asymmetrical shapes. For example, in the second design, one [17] *kind* of creature interlocks with

SEGMENT 4 *(pp. 559–564)*

THE ADJECTIVE Rule 17c

OBJECTIVE

- To identify adjectives and the words they modify in sentences

[18] <u>another</u>. In the third—an amazing [19] <u>achievement</u>—a single, complicated shape interlocks in two ways with [20] <u>itself</u>.

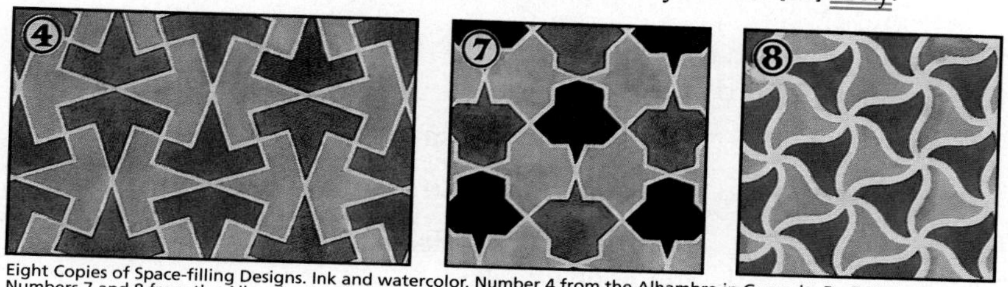

Eight Copies of Space-filling Designs. Ink and watercolor. Number 4 from the Alhambra in Granada, 5 x 7 3/4 inches. Numbers 7 and 8 from the Alhambra in Granada, 5 x 5 inches. ©M.C. Escher/Cordon Art—Baarn—Holland.

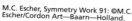

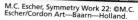

M.C. Escher, Symmetry Work 91: ©M.C. Escher/Cordon Art—Baarn—Holland.

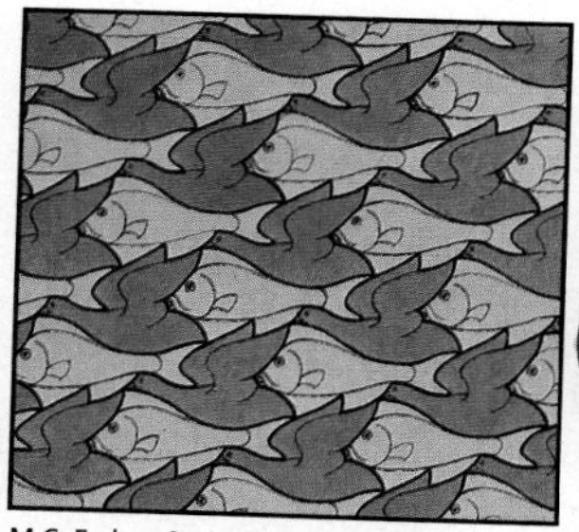

M.C. Escher, Symmetry Work 22: ©M.C. Escher/Cordon Art—Baarn—Holland.

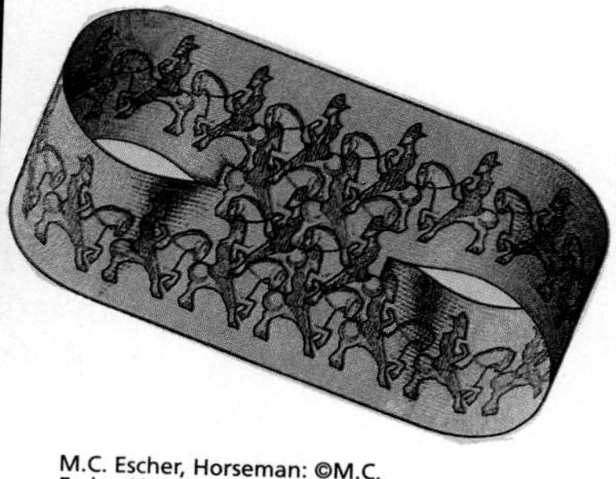

M.C. Escher, Horseman: ©M.C. Escher/Cordon Art—Baarn—Holland.

The Adjective

17c. An ***adjective*** is a word used to modify a noun or a pronoun.

To modify means "to describe or to make more definite" the meaning of a word. Adjectives modify nouns or pronouns by telling *what kind, which one,* or *how many (how much).*

WHAT KIND?	WHICH ONE?	HOW MANY?	HOW MUCH?
brown shoes	**those** cars	**ten** boxes	**some** water
large animal	**this** street	**several** books	**less** time
narrow road	**first** step	**fewer** mistakes	**more** space
nice person	**last** one	**many** students	**enough** money

VISUAL CONNECTIONS

About the Artist. The Dutch artist Mauritis Cornelis Escher was born in Holland in 1898. A poor student, he finished high school only because of his art classes. His engineer father sent him to architectural school, but Escher quickly transferred to the study of graphic arts. After visiting the Alhambra (a Moorish castle) in Spain in 1936, Escher began to incorporate the patterns and complexity of Moorish mosaics into his work.

Teacher's ResourceBank™

RESOURCES

THE ADJECTIVE

QUICK REMINDER

Tell each student to think of a visible object in the room and to write five adjectives that describe the object. Remind students that adjectives can tell *what kind, which one, how many,* or *how much.*

Then ask volunteers to read their descriptive words aloud; have other students guess the objects being described.

MEETING **INDIVIDUAL** NEEDS

LEP/ESL

General Strategies. In English, descriptive adjectives usually precede the nouns they modify, as in *messy locker*. In languages such as Portugese, Spanish, and Vietnamese, adjectives usually follow the noun, as in *locker messy*. Speakers of these languages may try to identify adjectives in English by their position, so they may think *messy* is the noun and *locker* is the adjective. Stress the adjective-noun order of English—perhaps by writing several adjective-noun pairs on the chalkboard and by having students correctly label the parts of speech.

Adjectives usually precede the words they modify.

EXAMPLE **The wild** and **graceful** deer ran through the forest.

For emphasis, however, adjectives are sometimes placed after the words they modify.

EXAMPLE The deer, **wild** and **graceful,** ran through the forest.

Adjectives may be separated from the words they modify.

EXAMPLES The casserole was **delicious.**
Luís appeared **ill.**

The adjectives in these two examples are called *predicate adjectives*.

REFERENCE NOTE: For more information about predicate adjectives, see page 595.

Articles

The most frequently used adjectives are *a, an,* and *the*. These words are called ***articles.***

A and *an* are ***indefinite articles,*** which refer to one of a general group. *A* is used before a word beginning with a consonant sound. *An* is used before a word beginning with a vowel sound.

EXAMPLES Jorge drew pictures of **a** pelican and **an** albatross.
For **an** hour I rode through the park in **a** horsedrawn carriage.

Notice in the second example above that *an* is used before a noun beginning with the consonant *h,* because the *h* in *hour* is not pronounced. *Hour* is pronounced as if it began with a vowel (like *our*).

The is the ***definite article.*** It indicates someone or something in particular and can precede any word, regardless of the initial sound.

EXAMPLES **The** lion is often called **the** "king of **the** beasts."

Adjective or Pronoun?

A word may be used as one part of speech in one context and as a different part of speech in another context. For example, the following words may be used as *adjectives* or *pronouns*.

all	each	more	one	that	what
another	either	most	other	these	which
any	few	much	several	this	whose
both	many	neither	some	those	

Remember that an adjective *modifies* a noun and that a pronoun *takes the place* of a noun.

ADJECTIVE **Which museum did you visit?** [*Which* modifies the noun *museum.*]

PRONOUN **Which did you visit?** [*Which* takes the place of the noun *museum.*]

ADJECTIVE **Leslie Marmon Silko wrote these stories.** [*These* modifies *stories.*]

PRONOUN **Leslie Marmon Silko wrote these.** [*These* takes the place of the noun *stories.*]

REFERENCE NOTE: Possessive pronouns may also be classified as adjectives. See the note on page 683.

Nouns Used as Adjectives

Sometimes nouns are used as adjectives.

NOUNS	NOUNS USED AS ADJECTIVES
business	business letter
saxophone	saxophone player
tuna fish	tuna fish salad
United States	United States government

NOTE: Some pairs or groups of nouns are considered *compound nouns* (see pages 554–555).

EXAMPLES road map, blood bank, soap opera, country club, United States of America

By checking an up-to-date dictionary, you can avoid confusing a noun that is used as an adjective with a noun that is part of a compound noun.

GRAMMAR

INTEGRATING THE LANGUAGE ARTS

Grammar and Vocabulary. Remind students that well-chosen adjectives can make writing more colorful and descriptive.

Write the following sentences on the chalkboard. Have students replace the underlined adjectives with vivid, descriptive adjectives without changing the meanings of the sentences.

1. The terrible storm caught the town by surprise.
2. That group makes great music.
3. His nice smile makes everyone feel better.
4. They have a cute kitchen.
5. I wouldn't mind having an old car.

Technology Link. Many software programs, in addition to spell-check features, have thesauruses. If your school has the facilities and the appropriate software for computer-assisted instruction, encourage students to use the thesaurus to find synonyms for stale, overused adjectives. Caution students to check the meanings of words in a dictionary, so as not to use a word with an inappropriate connotation.

GRAMMAR

REVIEW B

OBJECTIVE

- To identify words in sentences as nouns, pronouns, or adjectives

EXERCISE 3

Teaching Note. After students read the **Note** on p. 556, you probably told them whether you wanted possessive pronouns to be called pronouns or adjectives. Your decision will affect the answer to the third sentence: *Your* could be called either a pronoun or an adjective.

GRAMMAR

GRAMMAR

EXERCISE 3 **Identifying Adjectives and the Words They Modify**

Identify the adjectives and the words they modify in each of the following sentences. [Note: Do not include the articles *a*, *an*, and *the*.]

EXAMPLE **1. Put those aluminum cans in that empty box in the hall closet.**

1. *those, aluminum—cans; that, empty—box; hall—closet*

1. John lives on this street.
2. You need four cups of flour for this recipe.
3. Your new apartment, so spacious and sunny, certainly seems ideal for you.
4. The image of the eagle is quite powerful in many Native American cultures.
5. Which bookstore did you go to today?
6. All of the books on these shelves were written by Mark Twain.
7. Neither film was enjoyable.
8. The local stores open at 9:00 A.M.
9. Speaking of the space program, which astronaut do you admire more—Lt. Colonel Bluford or Dr. Jemison?
10. Tomás bought a new tie for the dance.

REVIEW B **Identifying Nouns, Pronouns, and Adjectives**

Identify each italicized word in the following sentences as a *noun*, a *pronoun*, or an *adjective*. If the word is an adjective, give the word it modifies.

EXAMPLE **1.** ***Most*** **people do not realize the *tremendous* number of books the library has available for *them*.**

1. *Most—adjective—people; tremendous—adjective—number; them—pronoun*

1. Many *shop* owners decided to close *their* shops early on Halloween. 1. adj./pro. [*or* adj.—shops]
2. *What* are the *other* choices on the menu? 2. pro./adj.
3. The manuscript for Andrew García's autobiography was found packed in dynamite *boxes* under his bed five years after *he* had died. 3. n./pro.

WRITING APPLICATION

OBJECTIVE

- To use specific adjectives to make descriptive writing vivid

4. We had a *family* reunion at my grandparent's house *last* summer.
5. As people encounter different *ways* of life, *they* gradually alter their *speech* patterns.
6. Thanks to the development of *digital* recording, symphony *performances* can now be recorded with higher fidelity.
7. *Oboe* players carry *extra* reeds with *them* because of the *possibility* that a reed might split during a performance.
8. *Alonzo* had never bought *that* brand before.
9. *Some* of the players felt nervous about the *athletic* contests.
10. *They* were penalized *fifteen* yards for holding.

4. adj./adj. **5.** n./pro./adj. **6.** adj./n. **7.** adj./adj./pro./n. **8.** n./adj. **9.** pro./adj. **10.** pro./adj.

GRAMMAR

WRITING APPLICATION

Using Specific Adjectives to Make Descriptions Vivid

When you want to describe something—for example, a concert, a painting, or a sports car—the more precisely you choose your words, the more successful you'll be. In choosing your words, try to avoid inexact adjectives such as *great, awesome, amazing, gross, terrible,* and *awful*. These words tell only that your response was positive or negative. Instead, make your description compelling by saying exactly what you like or dislike about your subject.

TIRESOME The concert was totally great! The band was excellent.

INTERESTING The **wild, insistent** beat kept us rocking in our seats. The lead singer's **intense** gaze and **husky** voice sent **personal** messages to each of us.

Which description would be more likely to make you want to buy concert tickets?

WRITING ACTIVITY

Your class is having *Share the Music* week. Each person will bring in a tape of a favorite piece of music and a paragraph

GRAMMAR

WRITING APPLICATION

The writing assignment asks students to write descriptive paragraphs about pieces of music they choose (and you approve). You may want to have students bring tapes and small cassette players with headphones to class. You may be able to provide equipment from the library for students who don't have players of their own.

CRITICAL THINKING

Application

Students might find it difficult to avoid inexact adjectives in their descriptions of music. Some adjectives seem almost automatic: *steady* beat, *great* lyrics, *good* voice.

To have students think critically and apply learned material to new situations, suggest that they work in pairs to think of other aspects of music that might help develop their descriptions. For example, a beat could seem *hypnotic, irresistible,* or *compelling.* Lyrics might be *baffling, disturbing, uplifting,* or *brilliant.* A voice might be *inspiring, thrilling, whispery, unsettling, screaming,* or *soothing.*

A DIFFERENT APPROACH

You may want to encourage students to bring to class teen magazines from various cultures. Make sure the magazines include music reviews. Have students list on the chalkboard the effective adjectives they find as they read the reviews. This word bank should be helpful to the class members as they write about the musical pieces they chose.

GRAMMAR

GRAMMAR

describing it. The paragraphs will be displayed, and the tapes will be placed nearby with tape players and headphones. Write a paragraph describing any piece of music that you like. (You don't have to own the tape.) You can choose from rap, rock, country, classical, or another type of music. In your paragraph, use at least ten adjectives. Make each adjective as specific as you can.

Prewriting Write down the names of five pieces of music that you enjoy. Then decide which piece will make the most interesting topic for your paragraph. (Be sure to get your teacher's approval of your selection.) Listen to your selection several times. Sit quietly with your eyes closed, and think about how the piece sounds and makes you feel. While you are thinking, jot down any adjectives that occur to you.

Writing As you write your first draft, include the adjectives that you jotted down. Try to give a clear description of the music. At the same time, imagine what specific details might persuade your classmates to listen to this piece of music. Think of your paragraph as an advertisement for the music.

Evaluating and Revising Reread your paragraph, replacing vague, inexact adjectives with words that are more descriptive. Ask yourself, *What exactly makes this music great* or *awesome* or *amazing*? Be sure you have included at least ten adjectives.

Proofreading and Publishing Check your spelling, especially of compound nouns. Use a dictionary to find out whether a compound noun is spelled as one word, as separate words, or as a hyphenated word. (See pages 554–555 for more about compound nouns.) You might wish to gather the class's music descriptions and arrange them on a bulletin board titled *Share the Music!* You could also take a survey to find out which three pieces of music sound the most interesting from the descriptions. Then, with your teacher's approval, you might borrow a tape player from the school library and obtain tapes of those pieces to play in class.

SEGMENT 5 *(pp. 565–568)*

THE VERB Rule 17d

OBJECTIVES

- To identify verbs and verb phrases in sentences
- To classify verbs as *transitive, intransitive,* or *linking*

The Verb

17d. A ***verb*** is a word used to express action or a state of being.

Action Verbs

An ***action verb*** expresses physical or mental activity.

PHYSICAL	write	sit	arise	describe	receive
MENTAL	remember	think	believe	consider	understand

(1) A ***transitive verb*** is an action verb that takes an ***object***—a word that tells who or what receives the action.

EXAMPLES Everyone in the school **cheered** the football team. [*Team* receives the action of *cheered.*]
Nikki Giovanni **writes** poetry. [*Poetry* receives the action of *writes.*]

(2) An ***intransitive verb*** is an action verb that does not take an object.

EXAMPLES The gorilla **smiled.**
Suddenly, the child next to the door **screamed.**

A verb can be transitive in one sentence and intransitive in another.

EXAMPLES We **ate** our lunch quickly. [transitive]
We **ate** quickly. [intransitive]

Ms. Marino **measured** the boards carefully. [transitive]
Ms. Marino **measured** carefully. [intransitive]

REFERENCE NOTE: For more on objects of verbs, see pages 592–593.

Linking Verbs

A ***linking verb*** connects the subject with a word that identifies or describes it. Linking verbs are sometimes called *state-of-being*

Teacher's ResourceBank™

RESOURCES

THE VERB

QUICK REMINDER

Write the following verbs and verb phrase on the chalkboard and have students use them in sentences. Ask students to identify whether they have used each as an action verb or as a linking verb.

1. will arrive [The pizza will arrive in fifteen minutes. (action)]
2. looks [Sy looks exhausted. (linking)] [The examiner looks carefully at your parallel parking skills. (action)]
3. is [The microwave recipe is easy. (linking)]
4. understand [He always understands what I mean. (action)]

MEETING INDIVIDUAL NEEDS

LEP/ESL

General Strategies. Verbs that express action are the most easily learned part of speech for many students. Therefore, you may want to use activities such as pantomime and charades as a way of involving all students in the lesson.

MEETING INDIVIDUAL NEEDS

GRAMMAR

LEARNING STYLES

Auditory Learners. Some students will have an easier time identifying linking verbs if they hear them read aloud from the **Commonly Used Linking Verbs** list. Afterward, have students close their books and call out linking verbs for you to write on the chalkboard. You could extend the activity by reading aloud an interesting excerpt and asking students to identify the linking verbs they hear.

COMMON ERROR

Problem. Students often overuse forms of the verb *be* in their writing. Instead of searching for precisely the right action verb to describe a situation, they too often settle for *is*.

Solution. Tell students to read through their papers and to circle the forms of the verbs *be* and *have*. Point out that these verbs are not incorrect, but that students can add more vigor to their writing by showing, rather than telling, what they mean. Have students revise their work; then have volunteers read their "before" and "after" papers aloud.

GRAMMAR

verbs because they help describe the condition or state of being of a person or thing.

EXAMPLES **Patience is the best remedy for many troubles.** [*Remedy* identifies the subject *Patience.*]
Edmonia Lewis became a highly respected sculptor in America. [*Sculptor* identifies the subject *Edmonia Lewis.*]
The dessert looks delicious. [*Delicious* describes the subject *dessert.*]

COMMONLY USED LINKING VERBS			
Forms of *Be*			
am	be	will be	had been
is	can be	could be	shall have been
are	may be	should be	will have been
was	might be	would be	could have been
were	must be	has been	should have been
being	shall be	have been	would have been
Others			
appear	grow	seem	stay
become	look	smell	taste
feel	remain	sound	turn

Some linking verbs may be used as action verbs.

LINKING The soup **tasted** spicy.
ACTION We **tasted** the soup.

LINKING She **felt** good about her presentation.
ACTION The explorers **felt** rain on their faces.

NOTE: To determine whether a verb in a sentence is a linking verb, substitute a form of the verb *be.* If the sentence makes sense, the verb is probably a linking verb.

LINKING The milk **smelled** sour. [The verb *was* can replace *smelled: The milk was sour.*]
ACTION I **smelled** the milk to see whether it was fresh. [The verb *was* cannot sensibly replace *smelled.*]

The forms of the verb *be* are not always used as linking verbs. They may be followed by words that tell *where* or *when.*

EXAMPLE **My relatives from Ohio will be here tomorrow.** [The verb *will be* is followed by *here,* which tells *where,* and *tomorrow,* which tells *when.*]

The Verb Phrase

A ***verb phrase*** consists of a main verb and at least one ***helping verb*** (also called an ***auxiliary verb***). Notice in these examples that as many as three helping verbs may precede the main verb.

EXAMPLES **has** spoken **will be** arriving **should have been** told

COMMONLY USED HELPING VERBS				
Forms of *Be*	am were	is be	are being	was been
Forms of *Have*	has	have	having	had
Forms of *Do*	do	does	doing	did
Others	may might must	can shall will		could should would

The helping verb may be separated from the main verb by another word.

EXAMPLES **Should** we **leave** immediately?
I **have** not **read** Alice Walker's latest novel.

REFERENCE NOTE: The word *not* and its contraction, *–n't,* are never part of a verb phrase. Instead, they are adverbs telling *to what extent.* For more information about adverbs, see pages 568–569.

EXERCISE 4 **Identifying and Classifying Verbs**

Identify the verbs and verb phrases in the following sentences. Then classify each verb or verb phrase as *transitive, intransitive,* or *linking.* Be prepared to give the object(s) of each transitive verb and the complement(s) of each linking verb.

GRAMMAR

INTEGRATING THE LANGUAGE ARTS

Literature Link. If your literature textbook contains William Carlos Williams's poem "Spring and All," read the poem aloud to the class. Then read it again and ask students to listen for verbs and to analyze how the verbs affect the poem.

[A major part of the deadness of the opening winter/spring scene is that Williams doesn't use a verb until line 15. The scene is static and barren until the first hint of change as spring *approaches.* The budding plants *enter* and *are defined;* the scene gradually *quickens.* The last line surprises with the first real action, as the roots *grip* and start to *awaken.*]

MEETING INDIVIDUAL NEEDS

ADVANCED STUDENTS

Point out to students that words such as *across, away, down, in, for, up,* and *out* can be combined with verbs to form idiomatic usages in which the combination acts as a single-word verb. For example, in "We ran up the hill," *up* is a preposition; however, in "We ran up a big phone bill last month," *up* is idiomatically tied to the verb *ran.* Such idiomatic constructions are sometimes called phrasal verbs. Ask advanced students to compile lists of phrasal verbs with example sentences. In addition, have the students explore how various dictionaries list phrasal verbs. Then have the students present their lists, examples, and explanations to the rest of the class.

GRAMMAR

SEGMENT 6 *(pp. 568–571)*

THE ADVERB **Rule 17e**

OBJECTIVE

- To identify adverbs and the words they modify in sentences

GRAMMAR

1. Throughout its history English has borrowed many words from other languages. **1.** tr.
2. Because a newly borrowed word often sounds unfamiliar, people sometimes do not hear it correctly. **2.** link./tr.
3. They will pronounce the word and will spell it as if it had come from other, more familiar English words. **3.** tr./tr./itr.
4. The wrong spelling hides the true origin of the word and gives the false impression that its source is contemporary English. **4.** tr./tr./link.
5. The word *woodchuck*, for example, might have come from two English words, *wood* and *chuck*. **5.** itr.
6. Actually, *woodchuck* came from the Cree *otchek*. **6.** itr.
7. Another word of Native American origin is the Algonquian word *musquash*. **7.** link.
8. When English-speaking settlers adopted the word, it became *muskrat*. **8.** tr./link.
9. In a similar way, the Dutch word for cabbage salad, *koolsla*, became the English word *coleslaw*, and the French word for a kind of cart, *cariole*, is now the English word *carryall*. **9.** link./link.
10. Linguists generally call this kind of word history "folk etymology." **10.** tr.

The Adverb

17e. An ***adverb*** is a word used to modify a verb, an adjective, or another adverb.

Adverbs modify by telling *how, when, where,* or *to what extent* (*how much* or *how often*).

Adverbs Modifying Verbs

EXAMPLES Marian Anderson sang **magnificently.** [*how*]
Marian Anderson sang **earlier.** [*when*]
Marian Anderson sang **there.** [*where*]
Marian Anderson sang **frequently.** [*to what extent*]

GRAMMAR

Teacher's ResourceBank™

RESOURCES

THE ADVERB

- The Adverb 160

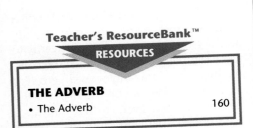

QUICK REMINDER

Write the following sentences on the chalkboard and have students identify the adverbs:

1. The parrot talked loudly. [loudly]
2. We quickly left the theater. [quickly]
3. I type very carefully. [very carefully]
4. The team looks rather tired. [rather]
5. Let's go tomorrow. [morrow]

17e

GRAMMAR

Adverbs Modifying Adjectives

EXAMPLES The players are **exceptionally** skillful. [The adverb *exceptionally* modifies the adjective *skillful,* telling *to what extent.*]

The documentary about global warming was **quite** interesting. [The adverb *quite* modifies the adjective *interesting,* telling *to what extent.*]

Adverbs Modifying Other Adverbs

EXAMPLES Cheetahs can run **extremely** fast. [The adverb *extremely* modifies the adverb *fast,* telling *to what extent.*]

André reacted to the news **rather** calmly. [The adverb *rather* modifies the adverb *calmly,* telling *to what extent.*]

Nouns Used as Adverbs

Some nouns may be used as adverbs.

EXAMPLES They were happy to return **home.**

The teacher reviewed what had been covered **yesterday.**

In identifying parts of speech, label nouns used in this way as adverbs.

EXERCISE 5 **Identifying Adverbs and the Words They Modify**

Identify the adverbs and the words they modify in the following sentences. Be prepared to state whether the adverb tells *how, when, where,* or *to what extent.*

1. Her calm, friendly manner always inspired confidence. 1. when
2. I understand now what he was saying. 2. when
3. The index lists all the book's topics alphabetically. 3. how
4. The guests have already left. 4. when
5. They thought that the decorations would be too expensive. 5. extent
6. Maurice and Gregory Hines tap-danced professionally when they were very young children. 6. how/extent

MEETING INDIVIDUAL NEEDS

LEP/ESL

Spanish. The Spanish suffix *–mente* sometimes corresponds to the English suffix *–ly* (*immediatamente* = *immediately; terriblemente* = *terribly*). Have students work in pairs to identify other Spanish words that end in *–mente* and to translate those words into English. This procedure might help students to recognize and use adverbs.

INTEGRATING THE LANGUAGE ARTS

Grammar and Writing. When students are writing dialogue, remind them that adverbs can be used to indicate the manner in which a speaker says something. To show students the effect of such adverb use, you could refer them to a piece of writing by John Steinbeck, such as "The Leader of the People." Steinbeck's characters might speak *excitedly, lamely, quietly,* or *irritably.* In contrast, Ernest Hemingway rarely supplies such tag lines; you may want to refer students to one of Hemingway's stories, such as "The End of Something," so that they can see the different writing styles.

GRAMMAR

REVIEWS C and D

OBJECTIVES

- To identify the parts of speech of words used in sentences and in a paragraph
- To identify words modified by adverbs and adjectives

COOPERATIVE LEARNING

Pair students to play a game that focuses on adverbs and vocabulary development. The object of the game is for each pair to come up with an adverb and a word for it to modify (a verb, an adjective, or another adverb), both beginning with the same letter of the alphabet. Each pair should work through the alphabet as quickly as possible. Some examples are *always authentic, bravely brings, casually cuts,* and *dangerously dependent.*

Give students ten minutes to work on their combinations. Encourage them to use dictionaries. When time is up, determine which pair has the most combinations.

ANSWERS

Review C

1. verb; pronoun; noun
2. verb; noun
3. adjective — Rome; verb; adjective — month
4. adjective — transportation; adjective — caravan; pronoun; adjective — miles
5. noun; adverb — excellent; adjective — critics; adverb — dull; adjective — costumes
6. pronoun; adjective — houses; adjective — hillsides
7. verb; pronoun; noun
8. adjective — readers; adverb — complained; pronoun; pronoun; pronoun
9. adverb — blanketed; noun; verb; adjective — road
10. pronoun; adverb — recall; adjective — part; noun

GRAMMAR

7. The messenger said that she felt rather uncertain about the quickest route. **7.** extent
8. "Are you quite sure that this is the person you saw?" the detective asked. **8.** extent
9. The teacher told the students, "Take your essays home for revision and return them to me tomorrow." **9.** where/when
10. Visitors to China often bring back small figures that are delicately carved from solid blocks of jade. **10.** when/where/how

REVIEW C Identifying Parts of Speech

Identify the part of speech of each italicized word in the following sentences. If the word is an adjective or an adverb, give the word or words it modifies.

1. He *announced* the names of *everybody* who had contributed *time* or money.
2. Jesse Owens *won* four gold medals in the 1936 *Olympics.*
3. In *ancient* Rome the new year began on March 1, and September *was* the *seventh* month of the year.
4. In 6000 B.C. the *usual* transportation for long distance was the *camel* caravan, *which* averaged *eight* miles per hour.
5. The *play* received *generally* excellent reviews, but *several* critics were disappointed with the *rather dull* costumes.
6. As *we* approached Santorini, I saw sparkling *white* houses along the *steep* hillsides.
7. The teacher *posted* a list of students *who* would give *reports* about Sacagawea.
8. *Many* readers complained *angrily* about the editorial *that* appeared in yesterday's newspaper, but *others* found *it* amusing.
9. *Silently,* the drifting *snow blanketed* the *narrow* road.
10. *I* recall *vividly* that small town in the *southern part* of Texas.

REVIEW D Identifying Parts of Speech

Identify the part of speech of each italicized word in the following paragraph. If the word is an adjective or an adverb, give the word or words it modifies. n. = noun pro. = pronoun v. = verb adj. = adjective adv. = adverb

1. n. **2.** pro. **3.** adv. **4.** adv. **5.** v. **6.** adv.

My Aunt Laurette is just about the nicest [1] *grown-up* [2] *that* I know. I do [3] *not* get to see her [4] *very* often because she [5] *works* in Chicago, but when she comes [6] *home* to visit, I'm in

SEGMENT 7 *(pp. 571–573)*

THE PREPOSITION Rule 17f

OBJECTIVE

- To use prepositions and compound prepositions in original sentences

heaven. [7] *What* do I like about her? For one thing, we share [8] *many* of the same interests—both of us play the piano, [9] *sew* our own clothes, and love to make [10] *puns*. She is also a sympathetic listener and lets me tell about [11] *myself* without interrupting or criticizing me. Laurette shares [12] *her* own [13] *career* stories with me, and sometimes she even asks me for [14] *some* advice. A day with Laurette [15] *is* sometimes silly and sometimes [16] *serious,* but it's always a delight. As you can see in [17] *this* picture of the two of us at the park, I always feel relaxed with Laurette. She's living proof that a person [18] *can* go through adolescence and [19] *still* emerge as a happy, [20] *highly* competent adult!

7. pro. **8.** pro. **9.** v. **10.** n. **11.** pro. **12.** pro. [*or* adj.] **13.** adj. **14.** adj. **15.** v. **16.** adj. **17.** adj. **18.** v. **19.** adv. **20.** adv.

The Preposition

17f. A ***preposition*** is a word used to show the relationship of a noun or pronoun to some other word in the sentence.

Notice how the prepositions in the following examples show different relationships between the words *ran* and *me.*

EXAMPLES
The playful puppy ran **beside** me.
The playful puppy ran **toward** me.
The playful puppy ran **around** me.
The playful puppy ran **past** me.
The playful puppy ran **after** me.
The playful puppy ran **behind** me.
The playful puppy ran **in front of** me.

Teacher's ResourceBank™

RESOURCES

THE PREPOSITION

- The Preposition 161

QUICK REMINDER

Write the following prepositions on the chalkboard: *beside, around, past, over, in front of, down, beyond, in, inside, near, into, out, over, through,* and *up.*

Have students use prepositions from the list to write directions to the gymnasium (or other appropriate locations).

GRAMMAR

MEETING INDIVIDUAL NEEDS

LEP/ESL

General Strategies. To many students, knowing which preposition to use (*on* or *in*) is not an obvious matter. "We got *in* the train." "We got *on* the train." Here are guidelines that might help: With vehicles that carry just one person, use *on: get on a motorcycle, on a bicycle,* or *on a skateboard.* For vehicles that carry about five people, use *in: get in a car, in a truck,* or *in a van.* For vehicles that carry about twenty or more passengers, switch back to *on: get on a train, on a bus,* or *on a plane.*

LEARNING STYLES

Auditory Learners. You may want to read aloud the **Commonly Used Prepositions** and **Commonly Used Compound Prepositions** lists and have students take turns saying sentences with each preposition.

GRAMMAR

A preposition always introduces a phrase. The noun or pronoun that ends a prepositional phrase is called the ***object of the preposition***. In each of the preceding examples, the object of the preposition is *me*.

REFERENCE NOTE: For more information about prepositional phrases, see pages 605–607.

Commonly Used Prepositions

about	beneath	in	through
above	beside	inside	throughout
across	besides	into	to
after	between	like	toward
against	beyond	near	under
along	but (meaning "except")	of	underneath
among	by	off	until
around	down	on	unto
as	during	out	up
at	except	outside	upon
before	for	over	with
behind	from	past	within
below		since	without

NOTE: Some words in this list may also be used as adverbs. Remember that an adverb is a modifier and does not take an object.

PREPOSITION We drove **around** the parking lot. [*Parking lot* is the object of *around.*]

ADVERB We drove **around** for a while. [*Around* modifies *drove.*]

A preposition that consists of more than one word is called a ***compound preposition.***

Commonly Used Compound Prepositions

according to	because of	in spite of
along with	by means of	instead of
apart from	in addition to	next to
aside from	in front of	on account of
as of	in place of	out of

EXAMPLES The young sculptor made a scale model of Mount Rushmore **out of** clay.
She placed a photograph of Mount Rushmore **next to** her clay model.

EXERCISE 6 **Writing Sentences Using Prepositions and Compound Prepositions**

The celebrities shown below are noted for their high-energy performances. Imagine that you are watching one of them (or another energetic performer), and write five sentences about the experience. Use at least ten different prepositions in your sentences, including at least three compound prepositions. Underline the prepositions you use. Be prepared to identify the object of each preposition.

EXAMPLE **1.** ***As Robin Williams walked out of the wings and onto the stage, everyone in the audience began to laugh and applaud.***

Gabriela Sabatini

Arantxa Sanchez Vicario

n Williams

Bruce Lee

ANSWERS

Exercise 6

Responses will vary. Before students write, you may want to have a brief class discussion about the four celebrities — Gabriella Sabatini, Arantxa Sanchez Vicario, Robin Williams, and Bruce Lee — to ensure that students are familiar with them.

SEGMENT 8 *(pp. 574–578)*

THE CONJUNCTION and THE INTERJECTION Rules 17g–17i

OBJECTIVE

- To write a paragraph using interjections correctly

Teacher's ResourceBank™

RESOURCES

THE CONJUNCTION and THE INTERJECTION

GRAMMAR

QUICK REMINDER

Ask students to write original sentences with the following conjunctions: *for, yet, not only . . . but (also), although,* and *because.* You may want to have students exchange papers to check for the correct use of the conjunctions.

MEETING INDIVIDUAL NEEDS

LEP/ESL

Spanish. Some students might find *either . . . or* and *neither . . . nor* confusing because the pairs look so much alike. Remind students that the *n* (as in *neither . . . nor*) often marks negative words in both English and Spanish. Explain that *neither . . . nor* implies a negative meaning, while *either . . . or* indicates a choice between two possibilities.

GRAMMAR

The Conjunction

17g. A ***conjunction*** is a word used to join words or groups of words.

Coordinating Conjunctions

A ***coordinating conjunction*** connects words or groups of words used in the same way.

Coordinating Conjunctions						
and	but	for	nor	or	so	yet

EXAMPLES We found a bat **and** a glove. [connects two words]
Will Rogers said, "My forefathers didn't come over on the *Mayflower,* **but** they were there to meet the boat." [connects two clauses]

Correlative Conjunctions

Correlative conjunctions are pairs of conjunctions that connect words or groups of words used in the same way.

Correlative Conjunctions	
both . . . and	not only . . . but (also)
either . . . or	whether . . . or
neither . . . nor	

EXAMPLES **Both** athletes **and** singers must train for long hours. [connects two words]
Either your fuel line is clogged, **or** your carburetor needs adjusting. [connects two clauses]

Subordinating Conjunctions

A ***subordinating conjunction*** begins a subordinate clause and connects it to an independent clause.

REVIEW E

OBJECTIVE

- To identify and classify conjunctions and to identify prepositions

17g

GRAMMAR

Commonly Used Subordinating Conjunctions

after	because	since	when
although	before	so that	whenever
as	even though	than	where
as if	how	that	wherever
as much as	if	though	whether
as though	in order that	unless	while
as well as	provided	until	why

EXAMPLES We arrived late **because** our train was delayed.
Sherlock Holmes listened quietly **while** Dr. Watson explained his theory.

A subordinating conjunction does not always come between the groups of words it joins. It may come at the beginning of a sentence.

EXAMPLE **While** Dr. Watson explained his theory, Sherlock Holmes listened quietly.

REFERENCE NOTE: For more information about subordinate clauses, see pages 629–637.

REVIEW E **Identifying Prepositions and Conjunctions; Classifying Conjunctions**

For each of the following sentences, identify every word or word group that is the part of speech indicated in parentheses. Classify each conjunction as *coordinating*, *correlative*, or *subordinating*.

EXAMPLE 1. Seeds were removed from cotton bolls by hand until Eli Whitney invented the cotton gin. (*conjunction*)
1. *until—subordinating*

1. Eli Whitney not only invented the cotton gin but also manufactured muskets and other weapons. (*conjunction*) 1. corr.
2. Nowadays we take the idea of interchangeable parts for granted, but it was a revolutionary concept at that time. (*conjunction*) 2. coor.
3. For example, when a rifle is constructed with interchangeable parts, a defective part can be replaced quickly and easily with an identically made piece. (*preposition*)

MEETING INDIVIDUAL NEEDS

ADVANCED STUDENTS

Ask students to identify the error pattern in the following sentences and to rewrite them correctly. [The structures of the elements connected by the correlative conjunctions are not parallel.]

1. Both running and a bicycle ride are good aerobic exercises. [Both running and cycling. . . .]
2. Barbara's report was both interesting and we got good information. [. . . both interesting and informative.]
3. The airline flies not only to United States cities but also foreign countries. [. . . not only to United States cities but also to foreign countries.]
4. Neither money nor being famous is my uncle's ambition. [Neither money nor fame. . . .]

GRAMMAR

COOPERATIVE LEARNING
Organize the class into small groups and have the groups create comic strips in which the characters use interjections. Students can create their own characters or use existing comic-strip characters. As most languages include interjections, you could ask students who speak other languages to share appropriate interjections from those languages; therefore, the comic strips could reflect various cultures.

MEETING INDIVIDUAL NEEDS

LEARNING STYLES

Visual and Kinetic Learners. Diagram on the chalkboard the following sentence to help students to see the relationships of the words within the sentence:

Wow! The boisterous laughter and the loud noise of the crowd really disoriented me.

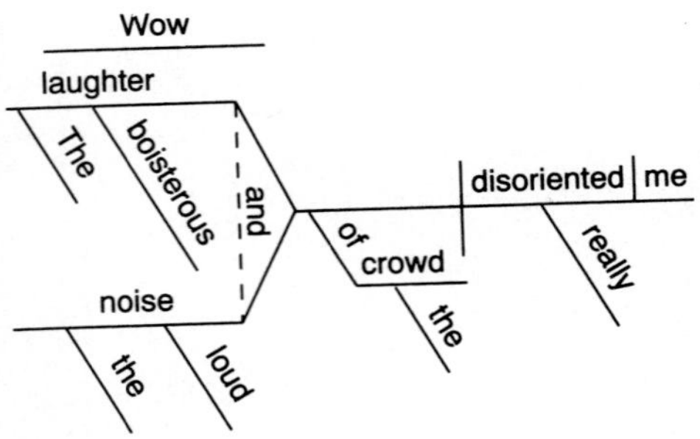

4. Before Eli Whitney introduced the idea of interchangeable parts, manufacturers had to employ many skilled workers. (*preposition*)
5. Although the new technology benefited manufacturers, it cost many workers their jobs, and this has been the case with most technological advances. (*conjunction*) **5. sub./coor.**

The Interjection

17h. An ***interjection*** is a word used to express emotion. It has no grammatical relation to other words in the sentence.

EXAMPLES	Ah	Hey	Ouch	Whew
	Gosh	Oh	Well	Wow

An interjection is set off from the rest of the sentence by an exclamation point or a comma. An exclamation point indicates strong emotion. A comma indicates mild emotion.

EXAMPLES **Ouch!** That hurts!
Well, I think you should apologize to her.

Determining Parts of Speech

17i. The part of speech of a word is determined by the way the word is used in a sentence.

EXAMPLES The coach decided that the team needed more **practice.** [noun]
The girls **practice** every Saturday afternoon. [verb]
They will have a **practice** session after school on Wednesday. [adjective]

Winston-Salem, North Carolina, is the **home** of the talented writer Maya Angelou. [noun]
The last **home** game will be played tomorrow night. [adjective]
We decided to stay **home.** [adverb]

REVIEW F

OBJECTIVE

- To identify the parts of speech of words in a paragraph

Celine has won the citizenship award **before.** [adverb]
The two candidates debated each other **before** the election. [preposition]
Read the directions **before** you begin answering the questions. [conjunction]

n. = noun v. = verb pro. = pronoun adj. = adjective
adv. = adverb prep. = preposition conj. = conjunction itj. = interjection

REVIEW F **Identifying the Parts of Speech**

Identify the part of speech of each italicized word or word group in the following paragraphs.

Suddenly the radio announcer broke in on the [1] *musical* selection. "A [2] *funnel* cloud [3] *has been sighted.* [4] *All* people should take immediate [5] *precautions!*" [6] *Those* were the [7] *last* words Denise Moore heard [8] *before* the electricity went off and the [9] *terrible* roar came closer. [10] *She* and her two children [11] *ran* to the basement [12] *quickly.*

When they [13] *emerged* forty-five minutes later, [14] *they* weren't sure what they might see. [15] *Oh,* the terrible wind had [16] *truly* performed freakish tricks! It had driven a fork [17] *into* a brick up to the handle. It had sucked the [18] *wallpaper* from a living room wall [19] *but* had left the picture hanging [20] *there* intact. It [21] *had driven* a blade of grass into the [22] *back* of Denise Moore's neighbor. Nevertheless, the citizens of the [23] *town* considered [24] *themselves* lucky because [25] *no one* had been killed.

1. adj. 2. adj. 3. v. 4. adj. 5. n. 6. pro. 7. adj. 8. conj. 9. adj. 10. pro. 11. v. 12. adv. 13. v. 14. pro. 15. itj. 16. adv. 17. prep. 18. n. 19. conj. 20. adv. 21. v. 22. n. 23. n. 24. pro. 25. pro.

GRAMMAR

PICTURE THIS

You're backpacking through a Florida forest. In a stand of huge live-oak trees, you sit down to rest and enjoy the scenery. After a short time, you glance up and see the magnificent Florida panther shown on the next page. As you watch, it strides along a tree limb—not twenty yards from where you are sitting!—then the big cat leaps easily to another tree and travels on without noticing you. Thrilled at seeing the big cat, you realize that it's one of only about fifty of these endangered creatures left in the wild. When you get home, you write a one-paragraph article for your school newspaper. Tell what it was like to see the

INTEGRATING THE LANGUAGE ARTS

Grammar and the Dictionary. As students work to master the parts of speech, they will find it helpful to use dictionaries to check whether words in question can be used as certain parts of speech. Encourage this use of dictionaries.

You may want to challenge students to spend fifteen minutes finding the word that can be used in the greatest variety of ways as a part of speech. Afterward, you could have the class compose sentences that contain the winning word as each part of speech.

GRAMMAR

PICTURE THIS

As a prewriting strategy, you could suggest that students use the reporter's *5W–How?* questions: *Who? What? When? Where? Why?* and *How?*

SEGMENT 9 *(pp. 578–580)*

REVIEW: POSTTESTS 1 and 2

OBJECTIVES

- To identify the parts of speech of words used in sentences
- To use words as designated parts of speech in sentences

MEETING INDIVIDUAL NEEDS

STUDENTS WITH SPECIAL NEEDS

When you grade students' articles, you may want to give one grade for content and the use of interjections and another grade for mechanics. This will reinforce students' good ideas and divorce content from mechanical shortcomings.

GRAMMAR

panther and what you learned from the experience. Use at least three interjections to express how you felt. Punctuate the interjections correctly.

Subject: seeing a Florida panther in the wild
Audience: students at your school
Purpose: to inform

Review: Posttest 1

n. = noun pro. = pronoun v. = verb adj. = adjective adv. = adverb prep. = preposition conj. = conjunction itj. = interjection

Identifying Parts of Speech

For each sentence in the following paragraph, write each underlined item and identify its part of speech.

EXAMPLE **[1]** In the past few years, African American film directors have suddenly begun to flourish.
1. *few—adjective; suddenly—adverb*

1. int./pro./adv./adj.
2. adj./prep./v.
3. conj./conj./conj./adj.
4. pro./pro. [*or* adj.]/prep.

[1] Hey, nobody who goes to the movies fairly often can fail to notice this exciting trend! **[2]** In 1991 alone, nineteen feature films directed by African Americans were released. **[3]** Whether you know it or not, that's more than there were in the whole previous decade. **[4]** The success of Spike Lee's films, which include the blockbuster *Do the Right Thing*, inspired other young black directors to create their own movies about the black experience. **[5]** The absorbing stories and real-life settings

of these films attract many thousands of moviegoers, not just **5.** v./n.
African Americans. **[6]** Who are some of the black directors **6.** pro./adj./adv.
building their careers in Hollywood nowadays? **[7]** Rising stars **7.** n./v./n.
include Charles Lane, Mario Van Peebles, John Singleton, Bill
Duke, and Matty Rich. **[8]** Their success helps create job oppor- **8.** adj./adj./n.
tunities for all types of black film workers, including hairdress-
ers, actors, stuntpersons, cinematographers, and sound
technicians. **[9]** For example, the crew that worked along with **9.** pro./prep./adj.
John Singleton on his 1991 hit film *Boyz N the Hood* was 90 per-
cent black! **[10]** After you've read these facts, maybe you'll
watch the movie listings in your local newspaper for some
upcoming films from young black directors. **10.** conj./v./adj./adj.

GRAMMAR

Review: Posttest 2

Writing Sentences with Words Used as Specific Parts of Speech

Write twenty sentences according to the following guidelines.

1. Use *ride* as a verb.
2. Use *hammer* as a noun.
3. Use *sink* as a transitive verb.
4. Use *whose* as an adjective.
5. Use *some* as a pronoun.
6. Use *fast* as an adverb.
7. Use *paper* as an adjective.
8. Use *inside* as a preposition.
9. Use *well* as an interjection.
10. Use *yet* as a conjunction.
11. Use *country* as an adjective.
12. Use *that* as a demonstrative pronoun.
13. Use *which* as an interrogative pronoun.
14. Use *both . . . and* as a correlative conjunction.
15. Use *smell* as a noun.
16. Use *have* as a helping verb.
17. Use *tomorrow* as a noun.
18. Use *down* as an adverb.
19. Use *before* as a subordinating conjunction.
20. Use *as* as a subordinating conjunction.

GRAMMAR

ANSWERS

Posttest 2

You may want to suggest that students vary their sentence structure and vary their sentence beginnings.

TIMESAVER

To decrease your time spent on grading papers and to give students a review of the parts of speech, have them exchange papers to check each other's sentences in **Posttest 2.** They may need to use their textbooks as references as they check the work.

MEETING INDIVIDUAL NEEDS

LEARNING STYLES

Visual Learners. If you are covering more than one part of speech at a time, a permanent classroom display or poster will probably help students to remember the names of those parts of speech. Also include lists of examples from the textbook. You may even want to include model sentences. The chart on this page could be enlarged and displayed in the classroom.

GRAMMAR

GRAMMAR

SUMMARY OF PARTS OF SPEECH

Rule	Part of Speech	Use	Examples
17a	noun	names	**Shane** is playing **soccer** in the **park**.
17b	pronoun	takes the place of a noun	**She herself** said **that all** of **us** have been invited.
17c	adjective	modifies a noun or a pronoun	**This rare** coin is a **valuable** one.
17d	verb	shows action or a state of being	Shelby **is** the candidate who I **believe will win**.
17e	adverb	modifies a verb, an adjective, or another adverb	I jogged **nearly** five miles **today**, but I think I ran **too fast**.
17f	preposition	relates a noun or a pronoun to another word	Some **of** the streets will be closed **on** Friday afternoon **because of** the homecoming parade.
17g	conjunction	joins words or groups of words	**Either** Brandon **or** I will meet you **and** Darla at the airport **so that** you won't have to take a taxi.
17h	interjection	shows emotion	**Hooray!** We're home! **Well,** we'll see.

SEGMENT 1 *(pp. 581–582)*

DIAGNOSTIC TEST

OBJECTIVES

- To identify subjects, verbs, and complements in sentences
- To classify sentences as declarative, interrogative, imperative, or exclamatory

18 THE SENTENCE

GRAMMAR

Subjects, Predicates, Complements

Diagnostic Test

A. Identifying Subjects, Verbs, and Complements

Identify the italicized word or word group in each of the following sentences as a *subject*, a *verb*, a *direct object*, an *indirect object*, a *predicate nominative*, or a *predicate adjective*.

Answers for Part A are in the right margin; answers for Part B are in the left.

EXAMPLE 1. Computers *have provided* work and play in today's world.

1. *verb*

1. decl. 1. Frances Perkins, the first woman in the history of the United States to hold a Cabinet post, was *secretary of labor* during Franklin Roosevelt's administration. 1. p.n.

2. excl. 2. Thanks to my "green thumb," these squash *plants* are spreading vines and fruits all over the garden! 2. s.

3. int. 3. Did Kimi write *you* a letter about her trip to Norway? 3. i.o.

4. decl. 4. Since the ballots have not yet been counted, the names of next year's class representatives are not *available* yet. 4. p.a.

5. decl. 5. At the end of World War I, the United States signed separate peace *treaties* with Germany, Austria, and Hungary. 5. d.o.

Teacher's ResourceBank™

RESOURCES

FOR THE WHOLE CHAPTER

GRAMMAR

CHAPTER OVERVIEW

This chapter discusses aspects of the sentence and begins with definitions of complete sentences and sentence fragments. Students are then taught how to identify subjects and predicates (simple and compound) and how to find the subject of a sentence. In the **Writing Application,** students are asked to combine sentences by using compound subjects and compound verbs. Finally, the chapter covers how to classify sentences by purpose and how to use appropriate punctuation.

USING THE DIAGNOSTIC TEST

Evaluate students' abilities by using the **Diagnostic Test** to pinpoint the areas in which students show weaknesses.

Students who have problems with **Part A** of the **Diagnostic Test** may need to spend more time with the examples and exercises and to pay particular attention to instruction on specific sentence parts.

Students having difficulty with **Part B** of the **Diagnostic Test** can review **Classification of Sentences,** pp. 597–598, which explains the different sentence classifications and provides a useful reference for students when they write and edit compositions.

SEGMENT 2 *(pp. 582–583)*

SENTENCE OR FRAGMENT? Rule 18a

OBJECTIVE

- To write complete sentences from notes

6. imp. **6.** Please bring *me* the hacksaw and two pipe wrenches from the garage. 6. i.o.

7. decl. **7.** Edward MacDowell's orchestral work based on Iroquois, Dakota, Chippewa, and Kiowa melodies *was performed* for the first time in 1895. 7. v.

8. decl. **8.** Martin Luther King, Jr., a nonviolent activist and civil rights leader, was a *recipient* of the Nobel Prize for peace. 8. p.n.

9. int. **9.** Do *you* know that the difference between wasps and bees is that wasps have long, narrow bodies and slim waists? 9. s.

10. excl. **10.** How stirringly *Sidney Poitier* portrayed Justice Thurgood Marshall! 10. s.

GRAMMAR

B. Classifying Sentences

Classify each sentence in Part A as *declarative*, *interrogative*, *imperative*, or *exclamatory*. See left margin of Part A for answers.

EXAMPLE **1.** Computers have provided work and play in today's world.
1. *declarative*

Sentence or Fragment?

18a. A ***sentence*** is a group of words that expresses a complete thought.

A thought is complete when it makes sense by itself.

EXAMPLES The weary executive had left her briefcase on the commuter train.
For how many years was Winston Churchill the prime minister of England?
What extraordinary courage the early settlers must have had!

As you can see, a sentence begins with a capital letter and ends with a period, a question mark, or an exclamation point. Do not be misled, however, by a group of words that looks like a sentence but does not make sense by itself. Such a word group is called a ***sentence fragment.***

GRAMMAR

Teacher's ResourceBank™

RESOURCES

SENTENCE OR FRAGMENT?

- The Sentence 171

QUICK REMINDER

Focus students' attention on sentences and sentence fragments by having each student write two sentences and two fragments on a sheet of paper. Call on volunteers to write their sentences and fragments on the chalkboard and to explain why some groups of words are sentences while others are fragments.

SENTENCE FRAGMENT	Athletes representing 160 nations.
SENTENCE	Athletes representing 160 nations will compete in the Summer Olympics.
SENTENCE FRAGMENT	The offices designed for high efficiency.
SENTENCE	The offices have been designed for high efficiency.
SENTENCE FRAGMENT	Plans every month for future growth.
SENTENCE	The board of directors plans every month for future growth.

REFERENCE NOTE: For more about sentence fragments, see pages 515–519.

EXERCISE 1 **Writing Complete Sentences from Notes**

When making notes, writers often jot down information rapidly, using sentence fragments. Later, when drawing on their notes to write reports or articles, these writers expand the fragments into complete sentences. Read the set of notes below and look at the picture. Then write a paragraph using the information given. Your paragraph should have at least ten complete sentences.

Nat Love
("Deadwood Dick")

fifteen-year-old Tennessee
  sharecropper in 1869
  won raffle--prize was horse
  sold horse, split money with mother
  took his share, headed west to become a cowboy
got to Dodge City, Kansas
  already knew how to train horses (was hired for this)
  fast learner--soon could herd, brand, use gun
  good all-around cowboy, scout, range boss, rodeo rider
Deadwood, South Dakota, 1876
  big Fourth of July celebration
  Love--twenty-two years old
  won marksmanship matches: rifle, handgun
  set records: roping, bronco-riding
  "Deadwood Dick" (nicknamed by admiring townspeople)

MEETING INDIVIDUAL NEEDS

LEARNING STYLES

Auditory Learners. If students are having trouble in recognizing differences between complete sentences and sentence fragments, you could give more oral examples. Some students are better at hearing differences than at recognizing them in print. For example, give pairs of word groups such as "the girl with the red shoes" and "I saw the girl with the red shoes." After students read aloud several such pairs, give students written pairs and have the students decide which word groups are fragments and which are sentences.

ANSWERS

Exercise 1

Paragraphs will vary. Here is one possibility:

In 1869, when Nat Love was a fifteen-year-old sharecropper living in Tennessee, he won a horse as a prize in a raffle. Nat sold the horse and split the money with his mother. He took his share of the money and headed west to become a cowboy. When he got to Dodge City, Kansas, a rancher hired him to train horses (which he already knew how to do). He was a fast learner, and before long he could also herd and brand cattle and use a gun. He went on to become a good all-around cowboy, scout, range boss, and rodeo rider. Nat went to a big Fourth of July celebration in Deadwood, South Dakota, in 1876, when he was twenty-two years old. He won marksmanship matches with a rifle and a handgun. He set records for roping and bronco-riding. To honor these achievements, the admiring townspeople nicknamed Nat Love "Deadwood Dick."

GRAMMAR

SEGMENT 3 *(pp. 584–590)*

THE SUBJECT AND THE PREDICATE

Rules 18b–18f

OBJECTIVE

- To identify subjects and verbs in sentences

Teacher's ResourceBank™

RESOURCES

THE SUBJECT AND THE PREDICATE

QUICK REMINDER

Write the following sentences on the chalkboard and have students identify the simple subject and simple predicate in each sentence. Subjects are underlined once. Verbs are underlined twice.

1. My gold chain is lost.
2. I was looking for it yesterday.
3. Marty saw it yesterday.
4. Did I lose it at school?
5. Javier thinks I'll find it.

GRAMMAR

The Subject and the Predicate

18b. A sentence consists of two parts: a *subject* and a *predicate.* A ***subject*** tells *whom* or *what* the sentence is about. A ***predicate*** tells something about the subject.

Subject | Predicate
Lightning | struck.

Subject | Predicate
Everyone | enjoyed reading *The Piano Lesson.*

Subject | Predicate
All of the seeds | sprouted.

Predicate | Subject
Into the sky soared | the young eagle.

Predicate | Subject | Predicate
Where did | your family | go on vacation?

As you can see, a subject or a predicate may consist of one word or more than one word. In these examples, all the words labeled subject make up the ***complete subject,*** and all the words labeled predicate make up the ***complete predicate.***

The Simple Subject

18c. A ***simple subject*** is the main word or group of words that tells *whom* or *what* the sentence is about.

EXAMPLES Who was the **coach** of the hockey team in 1988? [The complete subject is *the coach of the hockey team.*]

Supported by grants, **scientists** constantly search for a cure for cancer. [The complete subject is *Supported by grants, scientists.*]

The **scenes** that you see in these tapestries show the beauty of Pennsylvania in the 1700s. [The complete subject is *The scenes that you see in these tapestries.*]

The **Corn Palace** in Mitchell, South Dakota, is quite a popular tourist attraction. [The complete subject is *The Corn Palace in Mitchell, South Dakota.*]

REFERENCE NOTE: A compound noun, such as *Corn Palace,* is considered one noun and may therefore be used as a simple subject. For more about compound nouns, see pages 554–555.

NOTE: In this book, the term *subject* refers to the simple subject unless otherwise indicated.

The Simple Predicate

18d. A ***simple predicate*** is a verb or verb phrase that tells something about the subject.

EXAMPLES
Catalina **ran** swiftly and gracefully. [The complete predicate is *ran swiftly and gracefully.*]
The puppy **chased** its tail frantically. [The complete predicate is *chased its tail frantically.*]
Another space probe **was** successfully **launched** today. [The complete predicate is *was successfully launched today.*]
Did Ethan ever **find** his history book? [The complete predicate is *did ever find his history book.*]

NOTE: In this book, the term *verb* refers to the simple predicate (a one-word verb or a verb phrase) unless otherwise indicated.

The Compound Subject and the Compound Verb

18e. A ***compound subject*** consists of two or more subjects that are joined by a conjunction and have the same verb.

Compound subjects are usually joined by the conjunction *and* or *or*.

EXAMPLES
The **ship** and its **cargo** had been lost.
Marva or **Antonio** will drive us to the track meet.
Athens, Delphi, and **Nauplia** are on the mainland of Greece.

18f. A ***compound verb*** consists of two or more verbs that are joined by a conjunction and have the same subject.

MEETING INDIVIDUAL NEEDS

LEP/ESL

Asian Languages. In some Asian languages, verbs always appear at the ends of the sentences. Consequently, speakers of such languages might have difficulty locating subjects and verbs in English, especially in sentences that begin with verbs.

Make sure students are aware that verbs in English can appear at the beginning, middle, or end of a sentence. Give students examples of the possibilities and then ask the students to create similar sentences.

Spanish. Point out to Spanish-speaking students that when three or more verbs make up a compound verb, the verbs should be separated by commas, as in the sentence "Purple clouds billowed, rolled, and swirled across the darkening sky." In Spanish, commas are not necessary in such a situation.

COMMON ERROR

Problem. Prepositional phrases in even the shortest sentences can create problems because students might mistake the object of the preposition for the simple subject of the sentence.

Solution. Suggest to students that the first step in analyzing a sentence should be to put brackets around all of the prepositional phrases. The brackets indicate that the phrases are modifiers and don't contain essential parts of the sentence. This process should remind students to look outside the brackets for the subject of the sentence. You may want to refer students to the list of prepositions on p. 572.

GRAMMAR

GRAMMAR

Compound verbs are usually joined by the conjunction *and*, *but*, or *or*.

EXAMPLES We **chose** a seat near the door and quietly **sat** down.
Kendra **recognized** the song but **could** not **remember** its title.
For exercise I **swim** or **play** racquetball nearly every day.
Truth **enlightens** the mind, **frees** the spirit, and **strengthens** the soul.

How to Find the Subject of a Sentence

A simple way to find the subject of a sentence is to ask *Who?* or *What?* before the verb.

EXAMPLES The **crew** of the whaling ship had worked hard. [Who worked? Crew worked.]
On the quarterdeck stood **Captain Ahab.** [Who stood? Captain Ahab stood.]
Swimming fast toward the ship was the great white **whale.** [What was swimming? Whale was swimming.]

Remembering the following guidelines will also help you locate the subject of a sentence.

(1) The subject of a sentence expressing a command or a request is always understood to be *you*, although *you* may not appear in the sentence.

COMMAND Turn left at the next intersection. [Who is being told to turn? *You* is understood.]

REQUEST Please tell me the story again. [Who is being asked to tell? *You* is understood.]

The subject of a command or a request is *you* even when the sentence contains a ***noun of direct address***—a word naming the one or ones spoken to.

EXAMPLE Jordan, (you) close the window.

(2) The subject of a sentence is never in a prepositional phrase.

EXAMPLES A **group** of students gathered near the library. [Who gathered? Group gathered. *Students* is the object of the preposition *of*.]

One of the paintings by Vincent van Gogh sold for $82.5 million. [What sold? One sold. *Paintings* is the object of the preposition *of. Vincent van Gogh* is the object of the preposition *by.*]
Out of the stillness came the loud **sound** of laughter. [What came? Sound came. *Stillness* is the object of the preposition *out of. Laughter* is the object of the preposition *of.*]

REFERENCE NOTE: For a discussion of prepositional phrases, see pages 605–607 and 853–854.

(3) The subject of a sentence expressing a question usually follows the verb or a part of the verb phrase.

EXAMPLES Is the **dog** in the house? [What is in the house? Dog is.]
When was **Katherine Ortega** appointed the Treasurer of the United States? [Who was appointed? Katherine Ortega was appointed.]

Turning the question into a statement will often help you find the subject.

QUESTION Have you read Ernesto Galarza's *Barrio Boy?*
STATEMENT **You** have read Ernesto Galarza's *Barrio Boy.* [Who has read? You have read.]

QUESTION Were Shakespeare's plays popular during his own lifetime?
STATEMENT Shakespeare's **plays** were popular during his own lifetime. [What were popular? Plays were popular.]

(4) The word *there* or *here* is never the subject of a sentence.

EXAMPLES There is the famous ***Mona Lisa.*** [What is there? *Mona Lisa* is there.]
Here are your **gloves.** [What are here? Gloves are here.]

In these two examples, the words *there* and *here* are used as adverbs telling *where.* The word *there* may also be used as an ***expletive***—a word that fills out the structure of a sentence but does not add to the meaning. In the following example, *there* does not tell *where* but serves only to make the structure of the sentence complete.

EXAMPLE There is a soccer **game** after school this Friday. [What is? Game is. The subject is *game.*]

GRAMMAR

COOPERATIVE LEARNING

Divide the class into groups of three students each and set a time limit in which each group must compose the longest complete simple sentence they can possibly create. Tell students to add modifiers and prepositional phrases but to include only one subject and one verb.

When the time is up, have someone from each group write the sentence on the chalkboard. Have other members of the class identify the simple subject and the verb.

GRAMMAR

TIMESAVER

To save time, go over the odd-numbered items in **Exercise 2** orally. Students who need additional practice can do the even-numbered items for homework.

GRAMMAR

GRAMMAR

EXERCISE 2 **Identifying Subjects and Verbs**

For each of the following sentences, identify the simple subject and the verb. Be sure to include all parts of a compound subject or a compound verb and all words in a verb phrase.

EXAMPLE **1.** In ancient Japan, the fierce-looking samurai shown below and others like him ruled society with an iron hand.

1. *samurai, others—subject; ruled—verb*

1. The men, women, and children of the peasant class lived in terror of these landlord-warriors.
2. A samurai's powerful position gave him the right to kill any disobedient or disrespectful peasant.
3. Did anyone in Japan refuse to serve the samurai?
4. There was one dedicated group of rebels, called ninja, meaning "stealers in."
5. Off to the barren mountain regions of Iga and Koga fled the ninja people with their families.
6. There they could train their children in the martial arts of ninjutsu.
7. Lessons in camouflage, escape, and evasion were taught to children as young as one or two years of age.
8. Childhood games also provided practice in both armed and unarmed combat.
9. The ninja sneaked down into the settled areas and struck at the samurai in any way possible.
10. In time, the ninja warriors gained a reputation all over Japan and were feared by the mighty samurai.

WRITING APPLICATION

OBJECTIVE

- To write a letter containing sentences with compound subjects and compound verbs

WRITING APPLICATION

Using Compound Subjects and Compound Verbs to Combine Sentences

Writing is like planning a menu. Just as chefs choose foods to create a meal, writers choose words and sentences to create compositions. Like a good meal, an effective piece of writing has variety. Writers achieve such variety in several ways. They may vary the placement or the kinds of phrases and clauses they use, or they may invert the subject and predicate of a sentence. Another excellent way to add variety to writing is to use a mix of longer and shorter sentences. Often, writers combine short sentences into longer ones by using compound subjects and compound verbs.

TWO SENTENCES	After school yesterday, Suzanne showed me how to rotate the tires on my car. Ron showed me how to rotate the tires, too.
ONE SENTENCE WITH A COMPOUND SUBJECT	After school yesterday, **Suzanne** and **Ron** showed me how to rotate the tires on my car.
THREE SENTENCES	Later that afternoon, I checked the fluid levels. Then I vacuumed the carpeting and the seats. Finally, I washed the car.
ONE SENTENCE WITH A COMPOUND VERB	Later that afternoon, I **checked** the fluid levels, **vacuumed** the carpeting and the seats, and finally **washed** the car.

WRITING ACTIVITY

You've just won the new car of your choice! All you need to do now is to decide what model and options you want. The car will be shipped to your local dealership. Write a letter to the sponsors of the contest thanking them for the prize and telling them what kind of car you want. Name six or more options that you've chosen for your car. Money is no object! For ideas, consult the list of options on the next page. You may also request other options that are not listed. In your letter, use at least three sentences with compound subjects and two sentences with compound verbs.

GRAMMAR

WRITING APPLICATION

If the topic of this assignment doesn't appear to be appropriate for some students, you can let them write letters describing new wardrobes, personal libraries, stereos, computers, or something else they are interested in. You may want to take a few minutes to discuss the forms of business letters in **Chapter 38: "Letters and Forms."**

GRAMMAR

GRAMMAR

CRITICAL THINKING
Synthesis

After students have chosen the options they want, they will have to synthesize information to write their letters. Students will need to organize the options in a logical order and then write descriptions that comprise coherent wholes.

PREWRITING

Some of your students may not be familiar with all of the options listed in the chart, so you may want to conduct a discussion with the class to clarify what the terms refer to.

PROOFREADING

After students have written drafts of their letters, review the parts of business letters and the tone and style that are appropriate for a letter of this type.

INTEGRATING THE LANGUAGE ARTS

Technology Link. If students have access to a desktop publishing program, ask them to create letterheads that they can use for their letters.

GRAMMAR

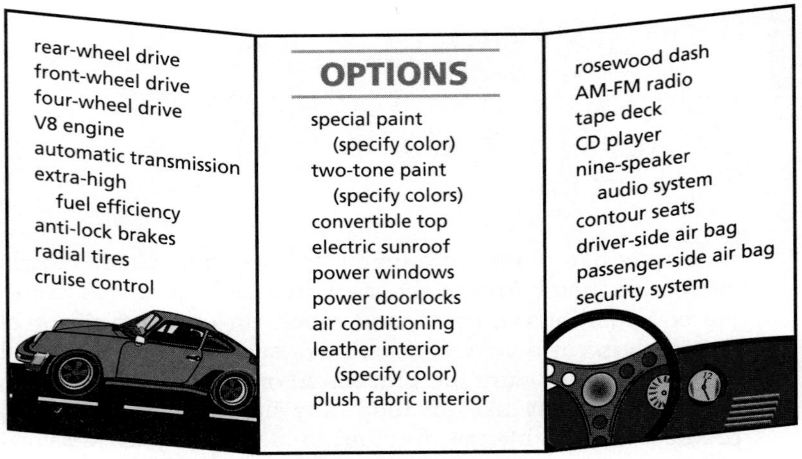

Prewriting First, you'll need to decide what kind of car you'd like to have. List the options that interest you the most. Choose as many options as you like. Choose wisely, though—don't pick options that you really wouldn't use.

Writing As you write your draft, you may wish to review the information on pages 994–999 regarding business-letter style. Address your letter to an imaginary contest sponsor. Begin by thanking the sponsor for your prize. Then describe your "dream" car as clearly and specifically as possible. Include your telephone number so that the person ordering your car can call you with any questions about your choices.

Evaluating and Revising As you evaluate and revise your letter, you may think of more options you'd like to include. Check to see that your letter includes at least three sentences with compound subjects and two sentences with compound verbs. If it doesn't, you'll need to combine or rewrite some sentences in the letter. (See pages 526–538 for more on combining sentences.)

Proofreading Check over the grammar, spelling, and punctuation of your letter. Be sure that your letter follows one of the standard business-letter forms.

SEGMENT 4 *(pp. 591–597)*

COMPLEMENTS Rules 18g–18l

OBJECTIVES

- To identify direct objects, indirect objects, and objective complements in sentences
- To identify linking verbs, predicate nominatives, and predicate adjectives in sentences

Complements

18g. A ***complement*** is a word or a group of words that completes the meaning of a verb.

A sentence may contain only a subject and a verb. The subject may be expressed or understood.

EXAMPLES
S V
Everyone participated.

V
Stop! [The subject *you* is understood.]

Generally, however, a sentence also includes at least one complement. Without the complement or complements in the sentence, the subject and the verb may not express a complete thought.

INCOMPLETE
S V
José Canseco caught

COMPLETE
S V C
José Canseco caught the **ball**.

INCOMPLETE
S V
They sent

COMPLETE
S V C C
They sent **us** an **invitation**.

INCOMPLETE
S V
The judges named

COMPLETE
S V C C
The judges named **Consuelo** the **winner**.

INCOMPLETE
S V
The ancient Picts dyed

COMPLETE
S V C C
The ancient Picts dyed their **skin blue**.

INCOMPLETE
S V
Denzel Washington became

COMPLETE
S V C
Denzel Washington became a versatile **actor**.

INCOMPLETE
S V
The players seem

COMPLETE
S V C
The players seem **weary**.

Teacher's ResourceBank™

RESOURCES

COMPLEMENTS

• Direct and Indirect Objects	175
• Objective Complements	176
• Subject Complements	177

GRAMMAR

QUICK REMINDER

Define for students the five complements that most often complete verbs. Write on the chalkboard the names of these complements (direct object, indirect object, predicate nominative, predicate adjective, and objective complement). Also write the following sentences on the chalkboard and ask students to identify the kind of complement each of the italicized words represents:

1. Mary Ellen is a *veterinarian.* [pred-
2. She is *ambitious.*
3. She opened a *clinic* for small animals.
4. She gave *us* a tour of her animal hospital yesterday.
5. Carla dyed her hair *purple.*

MEETING INDIVIDUAL NEEDS

LEP/ESL

Spanish. In Spanish the direct-object pronoun generally precedes the verb. You may want to illustrate for students the differences between the positions of a direct-object pronoun in English and in Spanish.

GRAMMAR

As you can see in the examples on the previous page, a complement may be a noun, a pronoun, or an adjective. Do not mistake an adverb for a complement.

ADVERB **Janna writes well.** [The adverb *well* tells *how* Janna writes.]

COMPLEMENT **Janna writes adventure stories.** [The noun *stories* completes the meaning of *writes.*]

Also, do not confuse a word in a prepositional phrase with a complement.

PREPOSITIONAL PHRASE Janna also writes **for the school newspaper.** [The noun *newspaper* is the object of the preposition *for.*]

REFERENCE NOTE: For more about prepositional phrases, see pages 605–607.

The Direct Object and the Indirect Object

18h. A ***direct object*** is a word or word group that receives the action of a verb or shows the result of the action. A direct object tells *whom* or *what* after a transitive verb.

EXAMPLES Drought destroyed the **crops.** [Destroyed what? Crops.]
The journalist interviewed the **astronauts** before and after their flight. [Interviewed whom? Astronauts.]
Kerry called **me** at noon. [Called whom? Me.]

A direct object may be compound.

EXAMPLES The dog chased **Eli** and **me** through the park.
Beethoven composed **sonatas** and **symphonies.**

NOTE: For emphasis, the direct object may come before the subject and the verb.

EXAMPLE What a compelling **speech** the senator gave! [Gave what? Speech.]

18i. An ***indirect object*** is a word or word group that comes between a transitive verb and a direct object and tells *to whom* or *to what* or *for whom* or *for what* the action of the verb is done.

GRAMMAR

EXAMPLES **Ms. Cruz showed our class a video about Moorish architecture.** [Showed to whom? Class.]
The animal trainer fed the **bears** fish. [Fed to what? Bears.]
Their artistic skill won **them** many honors. [Won for whom? them.]

Do not confuse an indirect object with an object of the preposition *to* or *for*.

INDIRECT OBJECT The principal gave **her** the award.
OBJECT OF THE PREPOSITION The principal gave the award to **her.** [*Her* is the object of the preposition *to.*]

An indirect object may be compound.

EXAMPLES The architect showed **Mom** and **Dad** the plans for the new family room.
Uncle Eugene built my **cousin** and **me** a tent in the back yard.

The Objective Complement

18j. An ***objective complement*** is a word or word group that helps complete the meaning of a transitive verb by identifying or modifying the direct object.

An objective complement may be a noun or an adjective.

EXAMPLES The members elected Carlotta **secretary.** [The noun *secretary* identifies the direct object *Carlotta.*]
Everyone considered her **dependable.** [The adjective *dependable* modifies the direct object *her.*]

Only a few verbs take an objective complement: *consider, make,* and verbs that can be replaced by *consider* or *make,* such as *appoint, call, choose, elect, name, cut, paint,* and *sweep.*

EXAMPLES Many literary historians call Shakespeare the greatest **dramatist** of all time. [or *consider* Shakespeare the greatest dramatist]
The flood had swept the valley **clean.** [or *had made* the valley clean]

An objective complement may be compound.

EXAMPLES The Gibsons named their two cats **Bruno** and **Waldo.**
Charlena painted her old bicycle **black** and **silver.**

GRAMMAR

EXERCISE 3 Identifying Direct Objects, Indirect Objects, and Objective Complements

Identify each complement in the following sentences as a *direct object*, an *indirect object*, or an *objective complement*.

1. Candles have tremendous appeal as decorative, religious, and utilitarian objects.
2. Every year the United States consumes many tons of paraffin for candle making.
3. Tutankhamen's tomb contained a candleholder.
4. Before the invention of electricity, many people lit their homes with candles.
5. Candles on the dinner table can make even an average meal special.
6. Many of the colonists made their own candles at home.
7. Nowadays, candle making offers hobbyists a relaxing and rewarding pastime.
8. These pictures show you the steps in candle making.
9. Incense mixed into the melted wax will give your candles a pleasant scent.
10. You can also dye candle wax various colors.

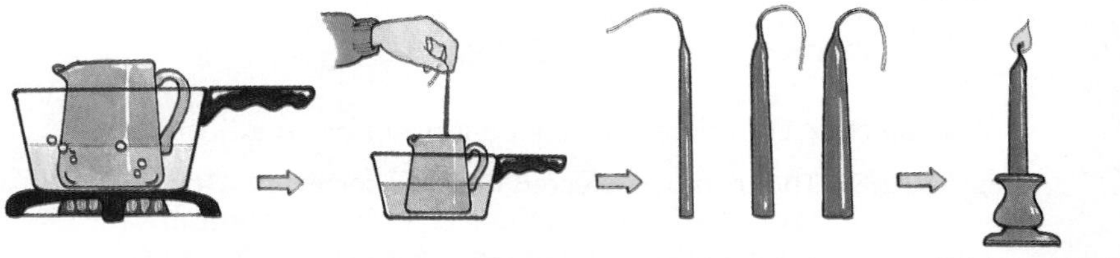

Melt wax in a double boiler or something similar.

Dip wick into wax, remove, and let cool.

Repeat this procedure until the candle is the thickness you want.

Finished product

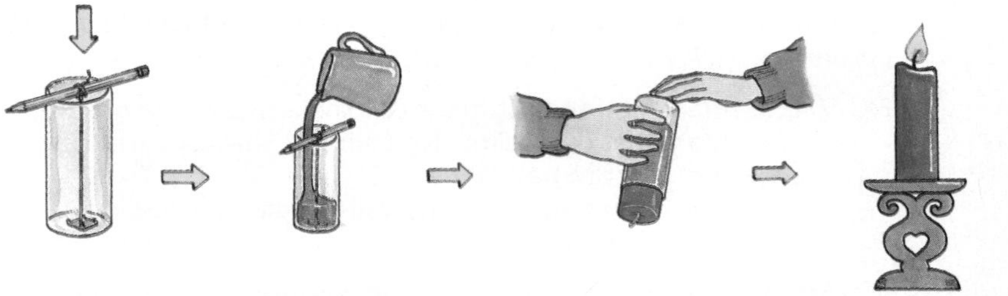

Insert wick into mold as shown.

Carefully pour wax into mold and let cool.

Run mold under hot water, turn upside down, and tap on bottom to remove candle.

Finished product

GRAMMAR

18 k–l

GRAMMAR

The Subject Complement

A ***subject complement*** is a word or word group that completes the meaning of a linking verb and identifies or modifies the subject.

REFERENCE NOTE: For a list of linking verbs, see page 566.

There are two kinds of subject complements: the *predicate nominative* and the *predicate adjective.*

18k. A ***predicate nominative*** is the word or group of words that follows a linking verb and refers to the same person or thing as the subject of the verb.

EXAMPLES Adela Rogers St. Johns was a famous **journalist.** [The noun *journalist* refers to the subject *Adela Rogers St. Johns.*]
The white bird with the long, slender neck is a **heron.** [The noun *heron* refers to the subject *bird.*]
Of the three applicants, Carlos is the most competent **one.** [The pronoun *one* refers to the subject *Carlos.*]

A predicate nominative may be compound.

EXAMPLES The two candidates for class treasurer are **Marco** and **I.**
South Dakota's chief crops are **corn, wheat,** and **oats.**

18l. A ***predicate adjective*** is an adjective that follows a linking verb and modifies the subject of the verb.

EXAMPLES The ocean is **calm.** [The adjective *calm* modifies the subject *ocean.*]
Does that orange taste **bitter?** [The adjective *bitter* modifies the subject *orange.*]
All of the astronauts look **confident.** [The adjective *confident* modifies the subject *All.*]

A predicate adjective may be compound.

EXAMPLES Illuminated manuscripts are **rare** and **valuable.**
Eben Flood felt **old, lonely,** and **sad.**

NOTE: For emphasis, the subject complement may come before the subject and the verb.

PREDICATE NOMINATIVE What an outstanding basketball **player** Michael Jordan is! [The noun *player* refers to the subject *Michael Jordan.*]

MEETING INDIVIDUAL NEEDS

LEP/ESL

General Strategies. Students must be able to identify linking verbs in order to find subject complements. Many linking verbs are easy to spot, but some, such as *taste, feel, smell,* and *grow,* which can also be action verbs, are more difficult to identify.

Tell students that when they encounter a verb that can be used either as a linking verb or as an action verb, they should put the verb to the following test: If the verb can be replaced by some form of the verb *to be,* as in the sentence "The stew smells (is) delicious," the verb is a linking verb.

GRAMMAR

REVIEW

OBJECTIVE

- To identify the parts of sentences

GRAMMAR

GRAMMAR

EXERCISE 4 **Identifying Linking Verbs and Subject Complements**

Identify the linking verb and the subject complement in each of the following sentences. Indicate whether the complement is a *predicate nominative* or a *predicate adjective.*

1. The most common deer in India is a species of axis deer. **1.** p.n.
2. Icy is the stare of the glacier. **2.** p.a.
3. Was Jane Austen the author of *Pride and Prejudice*? **3.** p.n.
4. Wilhelm Roentgen was the discoverer of the X-ray. **4.** p.n.
5. The violin solo sounded beautiful. **5.** p.a.
6. The animals grew restless at the sound of the crackling flames. **6.** p.a.
7. Harriet Tubman was active in the Underground Railroad. **7.** p.a.
8. Many people feel concerned about the spread of AIDS not just in the United States but throughout the world. **8.** p.a.
9. Why does the spaghetti sauce taste too spicy? **9.** p.a.
10. A massive work of carved stone is the Great Sphinx. **10.** p.n.

REVIEW **Identifying the Parts of Sentences**

For each of the following sentences, identify the sentence part or parts indicated in parentheses. Be sure to include all parts of a compound subject or a compound verb.

EXAMPLE **1.** (*complete subject*) The people of New Orleans are famous for their creativity with food as well as with music.
1. *The people of New Orleans*

1. (*simple subject*) Both Creole cooking and Cajun cooking flourish in the kitchens of the city's French Quarter.
2. (*complete predicate*) Some visitors to New Orleans have trouble telling the difference between these two similar styles of food preparation.
3. (*indirect object, direct object*) My aunt, a restaurant critic, showed me the differences between Creole cooking and Cajun cooking.
4. (*verb, direct object*) The French founders of New Orleans developed the savory Creole style of cooking.
5. (*predicate nominative*) The *beignet* (a square doughnut) and *boudin* (a spicy, savory sausage) are tasty local favorites from French cuisine.

SEGMENT 5 *(pp. 597–599)*

CLASSIFICATION OF SENTENCES Rule 18m

OBJECTIVES

- To identify the four kinds of sentences
- To use the four kinds of sentences in notes for an interview

6. (*simple subject*) In Creole dishes, there are also tangy traces of Spanish, African, and Caribbean cooking.
7. (*verb*) Cajun cooking is Creole's peppery country cousin and was born in the rural bayou areas surrounding New Orleans.
8. (*predicate adjective*) My aunt's favorite Cajun treat, alligator gumbo, is wonderfully thick and spicy.
9. (*subject, direct object*) Don't the little red shellfish on this platter resemble tiny lobsters?
10. (*objective complement*) They're New Orleans crawfish, and I declare them the tastiest morsels I've ever eaten!

Classification of Sentences

18m. Sentences may be classified according to purpose.

(1) A ***declarative sentence*** makes a statement. It is followed by a period.

EXAMPLES The lock on the front door is broken.
Jorge Farragut led naval forces against the British in both the Revolutionary War and the War of 1812.

(2) An ***interrogative sentence*** asks a question. It is followed by a question mark.

EXAMPLES Have you seen a sculpture by Augusta Savage?
Is Santa Fe the capital of New Mexico?

VISUAL CONNECTIONS

Exploring the Subject. Crawfish (also known as crayfish in some parts of the United States) fixed Cajun or Creole style are boiled in a spicy and very salty brew. Crawfish live in wetlands all over the United States, but in Louisiana they are harvested and processed with something approaching fanatical zeal. The crawfish season is from November to early July, and many restaurants that specialize in crawfish dishes simply shut down when the mud bugs, as they're called, aren't available.

Teacher's ResourceBank™

RESOURCES

CLASSIFICATION OF SENTENCES

QUICK REMINDER

Write the names of the four types of sentences—*declarative, imperative, interrogative,* and *exclamatory*—on the chalkboard and have each student write one of each type of sentence. Ask a few volunteers to read their sentences to the class.

MEETING INDIVIDUAL NEEDS

LEP/ESL

Spanish. In written Spanish, interrogative and exclamatory sentences are introduced by inverted question marks and inverted exclamation points, respectively. Consequently, Spanish speakers might have trouble recognizing these types of sentences without the introductory marks. Point out to students that in English, such marks are found only at the ends of sentences.

GRAMMAR

GRAMMAR

(3) An ***imperative sentence*** makes a request or gives a command. It is usually followed by a period. A very strong command, however, is followed by an exclamation point.

EXAMPLES Please give me the dates for the class meetings. [request]
Call this number in case of an emergency. [mild command]
Help me! [strong command]

(4) An ***exclamatory sentence*** expresses strong feeling or shows excitement. It is followed by an exclamation point.

EXAMPLES What a noble leader he was!
Ah, you have discovered the secret!

EXERCISE 5 **Identifying the Four Kinds of Sentences**

Identify each of the following sentences as *declarative, interrogative, imperative,* or *exclamatory.* Also supply the appropriate end mark after the last word in the sentence.

1. Anyone with a little free time and a generous heart can help make the world of books available to people with visual impairments. 1. decl.
2. For example, have you ever wondered how Braille schoolbooks for sight-impaired students are created? 2. int.
3. Imagine dozens and dozens of volunteers, all with their fingers flying across the keys of machines that look much like miniature typewriters. 3. imp.
4. Different combinations of six keys on the machines make the raised-dot patterns that represent letters and numbers in Braille. 4. decl.
5. First, Braille typists take a course to learn how to use the machines. 5. decl.
6. Once you learn how, typing in Braille isn't difficult at all. 6. decl.
7. If I participate, can I work at home in my spare time? 7. int.
8. What rewarding volunteer work this is! 8. excl.
9. When I considered how much time I waste every week, I decided to use that time constructively by volunteering to help create Braille textbooks. 9. decl.
10. If you know someone who might be interested in participating, help him or her find out how to get in touch with the Braille Association in your community. 10. imp.

PICTURE THIS

What makes people want to run in a long, grueling marathon like this one? As a newspaper reporter covering the marathon, it's your job to find out. You are conducting brief interviews with runners at the finish line. Jot down notes on one of the interviews, writing down at least four of your questions or comments along with the interviewee's responses. In your notes, use at least one of each of the four kinds of sentences—declarative, interrogative, imperative, and exclamatory.

Subject: a marathon
Audience: you; readers of your article
Purpose: to record information; to inform

GRAMMAR

PICTURE THIS

Some students might never have seen marathon runners at the finish line, so you may want to spend a few minutes brainstorming with the class about what someone might feel like after running more than twenty-six miles. Have the class also brainstorm possible questions they would like to ask in their interviews.

Tell students that their notes need to be written in complete sentences with appropriate punctuation.

VISUAL CONNECTIONS

Exploring the Subject. The long-distance footrace known as the marathon was created for the first modern Olympic Games in 1896. The race commemorates the legendary run of a Greek soldier from the plain of Marathon to Athens in 490 B.C. to bring news that the Athenians had defeated the Persians.

The distance of that original run was about twenty-five miles. The distance of the modern marathon, standardized in 1924, is twenty-six miles plus 385 yards. Marathon races are held all over the world with thousands of participants, and the marathon remains an important event in the Olympic Games.

GRAMMAR

SEGMENT 6 *(pp. 600–602)*
REVIEW: POSTTESTS 1 and 2

OBJECTIVES

- To identify subjects, verbs, and complements in the sentences of a paragraph
- To classify sentences as declarative, interrogative, imperative, or exclamatory and to supply the appropriate end marks
- To write sentences according to specific criteria

GRAMMAR

SHOE by Jeff MacNelly, reprinted by permission: Tribune Media Services.

GRAMMAR

Review: Posttest 1

A. Identifying Subjects, Verbs, and Complements in the Sentences of a Paragraph

Identify the italicized word or word group in each sentence in the following paragraph as a *subject*, a *verb*, or a *complement*. If it is a complement, identify it as a *direct object*, an *indirect object*, a *predicate nominative*, a *predicate adjective*, or an *objective complement*.

EXAMPLE **[1]** The National Science Foundation (NSF) is undergoing a great *surge* of growth.
1. *complement (direct object)*

1. p.a. **[1]** The NSF is relatively *small* compared with other government agencies like the National Institutes of Health and the National Aeronautics and Space Administration. **[2]** Recently, however, it *has accepted* more and more challenges. **[3]** In 1991, with funding of only $2.3 billion, the *foundation* participated heavily in several big government programs. **[4]** *One* of these important programs investigates global climate change. **[5]** There is another *program* for which the NSF is developing sophisticated computer technology. **[6]** In a third project, the foundation boosts science and mathematics *education* and *literacy*. **[7]** How important this project *must be* to the foundation's enthusiastic director, physicist Walter E. Massey! **[8]** Throughout his career, Dr. Massey has shown *hundreds* of students the excitement of physics, chemistry, biology, and the other sciences. **[9]** Dr. Massey is especially sensitive to the needs of minority students because he is an *African American* himself. **[10]** Perhaps through the programs of the National Science Foundation, many more students will now make themselves *candidates* for rewarding careers in science.

6. d.o./d.o.
8. i.o.
9. p.n.
10. o.c.

B. Classifying Sentences

Classify each of the following sentences as declarative, interrogative, imperative, or exclamatory. Then supply the appropriate end mark after the last word in the sentence.

EXAMPLE **1. The school is five blocks from here**
1. *declarative—here.*

11. The umpire called a strike. **11.** decl.
12. The pear tree grew well in our back yard. **12.** decl.
13. His hard work earned him a promotion. **13.** decl.
14. Anita ran errands during most of the day. **14.** decl.
15. Why did Earl leave the party so early? **15.** int.
16. Debbie Allen is a choreographer. **16.** decl.
17. What a wonderful day we had yesterday! **17.** excl.
18. Please hold my umbrella for a minute. **18.** imp.
19. Where did you park the car? **19.** int.
20. Leave your classrooms quickly. **20.** imp.

GRAMMAR

Review: Posttest 2

Writing Sentences

Write your own sentences according to the following guidelines. In your sentences, underline the words that indicate the italicized sentence parts. Also, use a variety of subjects, verbs, and complements in your sentences.

1. a declarative sentence with a *compound subject*
2. an interrogative sentence with a *compound verb*
3. an exclamatory sentence with a *direct object*
4. an imperative sentence with a *compound direct object*
5. a declarative sentence with an *indirect object*
6. a declarative sentence with a *predicate nominative*
7. an interrogative sentence with a *compound predicate adjective*
8. a declarative sentence with an *objective complement*
9. an imperative sentence with an *indirect object*
10. a declarative sentence with a *predicate adjective*

GRAMMAR

ANSWERS

Review: Posttest 2

Sentences will vary. The following sentences are examples of the kinds of sentences students might write. The underlined words are the sentence parts specified for each item.

1. The superintendent and the principal are visiting English classes today.
2. Have you seen or talked to either of them?
3. What a nice time we will have when they visit!
4. Give them your attention and respect when they come to our class.
5. I'll give you a quiz when they leave the room.
6. The superintendent is the head of our school system.
7. Is she intelligent and decisive in her decisions about the school system?
8. The governor named her Superintendent of the Year.
9. Tell me the secret of her success.
10. She was kind to take an interest in me.

GRAMMAR

SUMMARY OF COMMON SENTENCE PATTERNS

Together the subject and the verb produce the most basic sentence pattern. All other sentence patterns are combinations of the subject, the verb, and various complements.

S V
Emilia sang.

S V D.O.
Emilia sang a solo.

S V I.O. D.O.
The audience gave Emilia a standing ovation.

S V D.O. O.C. (N)
Some people called her an inspired performer.

S V D.O. O.C. (Adj)
Everyone considered her performance outstanding.

S V P.N.
Emilia was the star of the show.

S V P.A.
Her performance was flawless.

SEGMENT 1 *(pp. 603–604)*
DIAGNOSTIC TEST

OBJECTIVE

- To distinguish and identify prepositional, appositive, and verbal phrases

19 THE PHRASE

Kinds of Phrases and Their Functions

Diagnostic Test

A. Identifying Phrases

In each of the following sentences, identify the italicized phrase as a *prepositional phrase,* a *gerund phrase,* a *participial phrase,* an *infinitive phrase,* or an *appositive phrase.* Do not separately identify a prepositional phrase that is part of a larger phrase.

EXAMPLE **1.** ***Smiling warmly,*** **they greeted us on our arrival.**
1. ***participial phrase***

1. In Israel, farmers use innovative agricultural methods to meet the difficulties of *growing food in a desert country*. 1. ger.
2. Harriet Beecher Stowe wrote that famous novel *to awaken the country's consciousness to the evils of slavery*. 2. inf.
3. Woodrow Wilson, *the U.S. President during World War I*, tried with his Fourteen Points to prevent another world war. 3. app.
4. *In the Roaring Twenties* the Teapot Dome scandal contributed to American dissatisfaction with the presidency of Warren Harding. 4. prep.
5. During our vacation in Hawaii, we saw Mauna Loa, a volcano *rising six miles from the floor of the ocean*. 5. part.

GRAMMAR

Teacher's ResourceBank™
RESOURCES

FOR THE WHOLE CHAPTER

CHAPTER OVERVIEW

This chapter begins with a review of prepositional phrases used to modify nouns and verbs. Exercises give students practice in identifying adjective and adverb phrases and the words they modify. A **Writing Application** asks students to use prepositional phrases to add clarity and interesting detail to descriptive paragraphs.

Next, the chapter examines the three types of verbal phrases—participial, gerund, and infinitive—and their uses. Exercises give students practice in identifying and distinguishing each type of phrase. Then the chapter discusses appositives and appositive phrases. Finally, a review measures students' progress in distinguishing types of phrases and in using phrases appropriately in sentences.

Because the reason for using phrases is to present information clearly, concisely, and vividly, the discussion of phrases fits well with the objectives of writing clear sentences and of developing variety and interest when combining sentences. Especially during revision, an awareness of phrases can help students eliminate wordiness, focus interest, and control emphasis in their writings.

GRAMMAR

USING THE DIAGNOSTIC TEST

The **Diagnostic Test** measures students' abilities to distinguish and identify prepositional, appositive, participial, gerund, and infinitive phrases in both sentences and paragraphs. Many eleventh-graders will have acquired a good sense of how to use phrases, but even advanced students will likely benefit from learning more about the reasons and rules behind using phrases. The results of the **Diagnostic Test** should tell you how well students understand the use of phrases and should help focus your instruction.

GRAMMAR

GRAMMAR

6. Thomas Nast, *a nineteenth-century illustrator and political cartoonist*, is famous for his numerous drawings of Santa Claus. 6. app.
7. Withdrawing from the race, the candidate cited personal reasons for her unexpected decision *to return to private life*. 7. inf.
8. To conserve water, farmers water only the roots of plants, using a series *of underground irrigation pipes*. 8. prep.
9. In a speech *delivered to the graduating class*, the principal encouraged the graduates to improve the quality of life in our world. 9. part.
10. *Using an opponent's strength against himself or herself* is the basis of the martial art jujitsu. 10. ger.

B. Identifying Phrases

Identify each italicized phrase in the following paragraph as a *prepositional phrase*, a *gerund phrase*, a *participial phrase*, an *infinitive phrase*, or an *appositive phrase*. Do not separately identify a prepositional phrase that is part of the larger phrase.

EXAMPLE **[1]** Have you heard of Susan Butcher, *the four-time winner of the grueling Iditarod Sled Dog Race*?
1. *appositive phrase*

11. app.
12. part.
13. ger.
14. prep.
15. inf.
16. prep.
17. part.
18. inf.
19. ger.
20. app.

[11] *A woman of rare determination*, Butcher raises her own dogs. **[12]** *Tucked away in the Alaskan wilderness not far from the Arctic Circle*, her kennel is a four-hour drive from the nearest grocery store. **[13]** Butcher believes that only when she is this isolated from society can she concentrate on *creating a tight bond with her 150 dogs*. **[14]** *For more than ten years*, she has raised huskies in her own unique way. **[15]** From the moment each puppy is born, she spends plenty of time with it *to get it used to her voice and her touch*. **[16]** She handles and talks *to the newborn puppy* frequently, breathing on it so that it can also learn her scent. **[17]** *Growing closer and closer to Butcher*, the puppy is personally fed, trained, and even sung to and massaged by her. **[18]** When the puppy is four and one-half months old, Butcher begins *to train it in harness*. **[19]** By *showing the dogs her love for them*, Butcher gains the devotion needed to create championship teams. **[20]** The Iditarod, *1,130 miles of mountains, frozen seas, and snowy wilderness between Anchorage and Nome*, is the ultimate test of a dog team's devotion.

SEGMENT 2 *(pp. 605–610)*

THE PREPOSITIONAL PHRASE Rules 19a–19d

OBJECTIVES

- To identify adjective phrases and the words they modify
- To identify adverb phrases and the words they modify

19a. A ***phrase*** is a group of related words that is used as a single part of speech and does not contain a verb and its subject.

VERB PHRASE	**has been canceled** [no subject]
PREPOSITIONAL PHRASE	**before the party** [no subject or verb]

REFERENCE NOTE: A group of words that has a subject and a verb is called a ***clause.*** For more about independent and subordinate clauses, see pages 628–637.

GRAMMAR

The Prepositional Phrase

19b. A ***prepositional phrase*** begins with a preposition and ends with a noun or a pronoun, called the ***object of the preposition.***

EXAMPLES The tall building **with the red roof** is our new library. [The noun *roof* is the object of the preposition *with.*]
Next to it is the old library, which is now being used **for storage.** [The pronoun *it* is the object of the compound preposition *Next to.* The noun *storage* is the object of the preposition *for.*]

An object of a preposition may be compound.

EXAMPLE *Brian's Song* is an inspiring story **about friendship and courage.** [Both *friendship* and *courage* are objects of the preposition *about.*]

REFERENCE NOTE: For lists of prepositions, see page 572.

The Adjective Phrase

19c. An ***adjective phrase*** is a prepositional phrase that modifies a noun or a pronoun.

An adjective phrase tells *what kind* or *which one.*

EXAMPLES Cassie Soldierwolf made a batch **of fry bread,** using a recipe very similar to that **of her ancestors.** [*Of fry bread* modifies the noun *batch,* telling *what kind. Of her ancestors* modifies the pronoun *that,* telling *which one.*]

Teacher's ResourceBank™

RESOURCES

THE PREPOSITIONAL PHRASE

QUICK REMINDER

Ask students to suggest some common prepositions and write a few of the prepositions on the chalkboard. You can then remind students that a preposition requires a noun or a pronoun to complete its meaning. Then ask students to suggest some imaginative nouns to serve as objects of the prepositions. Have each student jot down a brief sentence that incorporates each prepositional phrase on the chalkboard. Then ask a few students to share some of their sentences with the class.

GRAMMAR

MEETING INDIVIDUAL NEEDS

LEP/ESL

General Strategies. Nonnative speakers may have trouble in telling prepositional phrases from idiomatic or phrasal verbs in sentences such as "We dropped in on the people in the apartment below," "I bumped into my old boyfriend at the dance," and "Quite by accident, scientists have hit upon a solution to the problem of global warming."

Because the meaning of such sentences is idiomatic, attempts to translate them literally may yield surprising (and humorous) results. You can capitalize on this humor by having students visualize (even draw) the literal situations portrayed by such phrasal verbs.

GRAMMAR

VISUAL CONNECTIONS

Exploring the Subject. Lemmings are rodents related to mice and are found primarily in north temperate and polar regions of North America and Eurasia. Lemmings have long been the subject of folklore because of the effect their seemingly suicidal drives have had on the human imagination.

Ideas for Writing. Students might like to find out more about the relationships between overpopulation, food supply, and behavior in the human world. You could have students read *Beyond the Limits* by Donella H. Meadows and then have them write brief reports on the book's content.

GRAMMAR

An adjective phrase always follows the word it modifies. That word may be the object of another preposition.

EXAMPLE Sarah Kemble Knight kept a journal **of her trip to New York.** [*Of her trip* modifies the direct object *journal. To New York* modifies *trip,* which serves as the object of the preposition *of.*]

More than one adjective phrase may modify the same word.

EXAMPLE Sarah Knight's journey **on horseback from Boston to New York** was long and difficult. [The three phrases *on horseback, from Boston,* and *to New York* modify the noun *journey.*]

EXERCISE 1 Identifying Adjective Phrases and the Words They Modify

The following sentences contain ten adjective phrases. Identify each adjective phrase and the word it modifies.

1. The instinct for self-preservation is a basic drive in nearly all living things.
2. Yet these small Scandinavian animals, called lemmings, occasionally follow a pattern of self-destruction.
3. Ordinarily, lemmings lead peaceful, quiet lives, eating a diet of moss and roots.
4. Every few years, however, their population exceeds their food supply, and they ford streams and lakes, devouring everything in their path and leaving no trace of vegetation.

5. When they reach the cliffs along the sea, they leap into the water and swim until they drown.
6. Explanations of their rush to the sea are only guesses, and the lemming remains a mystery to those who study animal behavior.

The Adverb Phrase

19d. An ***adverb phrase*** is a prepositional phrase that modifies a verb, an adjective, or an adverb.

An adverb phrase tells *how, when, where, why,* or *to what extent* (*how long* or *how far*).

An adverb phrase may modify a verb.

EXAMPLE **During the Civil War,** Louisa May Alcott worked **in a hospital as a nurse for six weeks.** [Each phrase modifies the verb *worked. During the Civil War* tells *when, in a hospital* tells *where, as a nurse* tells *how,* and *for six weeks* tells *how long.*]

As you can see in this example, more than one adverb phrase can modify the same word. The example also shows that an adverb phrase, unlike an adjective phrase, can precede the word it modifies.

An adverb phrase may modify an adjective.

EXAMPLE Louisa May Alcott wrote *Little Women,* a novel rich **in New England traditions.** [*In New England traditions* modifies the adjective *rich,* telling *how* rich.]

An adverb phrase may modify an adverb.

EXAMPLE Too late **for Alcott and other early suffragists,** U.S. voting laws were changed. [*For Alcott and other early suffragists* modifies the adverb *late.*]

EXERCISE 2 **Identifying Adverb Phrases and the Words They Modify**

The following sentences contain ten adverb phrases. Identify each adverb phrase and the word or words it modifies.

1. Duncan is sitting in his chair, eating a bowl of oatmeal.
2. I got the twins ready for bed.

COMMON ERROR

Problem. When a preposition takes a compound object, students may supply the nominative case instead of the objective case for pronouns, as in "Joey said he would come by for Sandy and I."

Solution. Write the sample sentence above on the chalkboard, and ask students whether it is correct. If it sounds right to many of them, cross out the words *Sandy and* so students can see immediately that the *I* needs to be changed to the objective case *me.* You can also suggest that students review **Chapter 22: "Correct Pronoun Usage."**

WRITING APPLICATION

OBJECTIVE

- To use prepositional phrases to add detail, clarity, and vividness to a descriptive paragraph

GRAMMAR

3. In the classic Japanese movie *The Seven Samurai*, fierce professional warriors save a village from bandits.
4. Every rumor in the world has been started by somebody.
5. They were assembled on benches for the presentation.
6. Especially for the children, the mariachi band played "The Mexican Hat Dance."
7. Fear sometimes springs from ignorance.
8. Is this outfit appropriate for a job interview?

WRITING APPLICATION

Using Prepositional Phrases to Add Information to Sentences

If you heard that a friend was "modifying" her stereo, you'd probably assume she was adding features or components to improve its sound. Just as an extra set of speakers can make a stereo sound better, a modifying phrase can make a sentence sound clearer and more interesting. Like all modifiers, prepositional phrases help you include more information when you express your ideas. For example, compare the following two sentences. What does the second sentence tell you that the first one doesn't? Without prepositional phrases, could you express the complete idea as clearly or as simply?

> Sean Harrigan hopes to have his own riding stable.
> Sean Harrigan hopes to have his own riding stable with the name Harrigan's Happy Trails in huge letters over the entrance.

WRITING ACTIVITY

There's going to be a special Careers issue of your school newspaper. For a feature page, the editor has invited students to name and describe businesses they'd like to own ten years from now. You've decided to contribute a description of your business-to-be. Think of your business, invent a name for it, and write a paragraph describing it. Use at least five prepositional phrases in your sentences.

GRAMMAR

WRITING APPLICATION

Successful description depends on specific detail and coherent order. This assignment allows students to create vivid depictions of their potential work environments, and it gives students practice in organizing their business ideas coherently by arranging details in a meaningful sequence, such as in a spatial or logical order.

CRITICAL THINKING

Analysis

As students generate details, ask them to think about arranging the details according to spatial, chronological, or logical order or order of importance. You might suggest some typical prepositions, such as *above, underneath, across from, next to, on the right, beside, until, in the first place, after,* and *above all,* that students can use to guide their thinking. You may want to ask students to think of details for more than one type of arrangement. Students can then determine which type of order their readers would find most effective.

REVIEW A

OBJECTIVES

- To locate all prepositional phrases in a paragraph
- To classify prepositional phrases as adjective phrases or adverb phrases
- To classify words modified by prepositional phrases as nouns, pronouns, verbs, adjectives, or adverbs

Prewriting Brainstorm ideas for three or four kinds of businesses you'd enjoy owning and running ten years from now. List several catchy names for each one. Choose the business and name you like best. Then jot down details about your product or service, your location, your equipment, and your customers.

Writing As you write your first draft, think about the students who will be your audience. What details about your business would interest your readers? Make sure that you include plenty of these specific details in your paragraph. You may choose to use formal or informal language in your paragraph, and your tone may be either humorous or serious.

Evaluating and Revising Ask a friend to read your paragraph before you revise it. Can your friend clearly imagine your business? If not, add, cut, or rearrange details to make your paragraph clearer and more interesting. Then reread your paragraph for sentence style. If your sentences sound choppy, combine them into longer, smoother sentences. (For more about sentence combining, see pages 526–538.) Be sure that you've used at least five prepositional phrases in your paragraph.

Proofreading and Publishing Check over the grammar, spelling, and punctuation of your paragraph. Mentally identify the subject and verb of each sentence to make sure all your sentences are complete. (See the discussion of sentence fragments on pages 515–519.) You and your classmates may want to gather your paragraphs into a booklet to include in a class time capsule. At the tenth reunion of your class, you can open the time capsule to see how your career goals have (or haven't) changed.

REVIEW A **Identifying Prepositional Phrases**

For each sentence in the following paragraph, list all the prepositional phrases. Be sure to include any prepositional phrase that modifies the object of another preposition. Then tell whether each prepositional phrase is an *adjective phrase* or an

GRAMMAR

PREWRITING

Students may find it easier to provide vivid detail by imagining the kinds of details that appeal directly to the senses. For example, instead of selling oriental rugs, students might imagine "springy carpets that people can dig their toes into, that hold the scents of exotic spices from the markets where these carpets are traded."

INTEGRATING THE LANGUAGE ARTS

Technology Link. If students have access to word processors, assign pairs of students to prepare the **Writing Application** on diskettes. Have the students trade diskettes.

Ask each student to boldface or underline the adjective and adverb prepositional phrases in his or her partner's paragraph, to write a brief assessment of the effectiveness of the details and their arrangement in the paragraph, and to print out the results.

GRAMMAR

ANSWERS

Review A

1. from Africa — adverb phrase (come — verb); from the family — adverb phrase (are — verb); of musical instruments called *mbira* — adjective phrase (family — noun)
2. About the size — adjective phrase (*mbiras* — noun); of a paperback book — adjective phrase (size — noun); from smooth, warm-colored wood — adverb phrase (made — adjective)
3. with your thumbs — adverb phrase (pluck — verb); by some people — adverb phrase (is called — verb)
4. Below the keys — adverb phrase (is — verb); like the one — adjective phrase (hole — noun); on a guitar — adjective phrase (one — pronoun)
5. inside the box — adverb phrase (resonate — verb)
6. like a cross — adverb phrase (sounds — verb); between a small xylophone, a music box, and a set — adjective phrase (cross — noun); of wind chimes — adjective phrase (set — noun)
7. in size — adverb phrase (small — adjective); in a pocket or backpack — adverb phrase (to carry — adverb)
8. with both thumbs — adverb phrase (hit — verb)
9. to the kalimba — adverb phrase (similar — adjective); by Portuguese explorers — adverb phrase (were noted — verb); in the sixteenth century — adverb phrase (were noted — verb); along the East African coast — adverb phrase (were noted — verb)
10. In 1586 — adverb phrase (wrote — verb); of a harpsichord — adjective phrase (those — pronoun); of accordant sounds — adjective phrase (harmony — noun)

GRAMMAR

GRAMMAR

adverb phrase. Be prepared to give the word each prepositional phrase modifies and to identify the word as a *noun*, a *pronoun*, a *verb*, an *adjective*, or an *adverb*.

EXAMPLE [1] From what part of the world do these strange-looking items come?
1. *from what part—adverb phrase; of the world—adjective phrase*

[1] They come from Africa, and they are from the family of musical instruments called *mbira*. [2] About the size of a paperback book, these small *mbiras*, called *kalimbas*, are boxes made from smooth, warm-colored wood. [3] You pluck the steel keys with your thumbs to play melodies, which explains why the instrument is called a thumb box by some people. [4] Below the keys, there is a sound hole like the one on a guitar. [5] When one or more keys are plucked, the notes resonate inside the box. [6] The *kalimba* sounds like a cross between a small xylophone, a music box, and a set of wind chimes. [7] Small in size, it's easily carried in a pocket or backpack, and it is simple to play. [8] Nearly everybody enjoys the soft, light sound, even if you hit a wrong note with both thumbs! [9] Instruments similar to the *kalimba* were noted by Portuguese explorers in the sixteenth century along the East African coast. [10] In 1586, Father Dos Santos, a Portuguese traveler, wrote that native *mbira* players pluck the keys lightly, "as a good player strikes those of a harpsichord," producing "a sweet and gentle harmony of accordant sounds."

SEGMENT 3 *(pp. 611–614)*

THE PARTICIPLE and THE PARTICIPIAL PHRASE Rules 19e, 19f

OBJECTIVE

- To identify participial phrases and the words they modify

Verbals and Verbal Phrases

A ***verbal*** is a form of a verb used as a noun, an adjective, or an adverb. The three kinds of verbals are the *participle,* the *gerund,* and the *infinitive.*

A ***verbal phrase*** consists of a verbal and its modifiers and complements. The three kinds of verbal phrases are the *participial phrase,* the *gerund phrase,* and the *infinitive phrase.*

The Participle

19e. A ***participle*** is a verb form that is used as an adjective.

There are two kinds of participles—the *present participle* and the *past participle.*

Present participles end in *-ing.*

EXAMPLES Esperanza has taken **singing** lessons for several years. [*Singing,* a form of the verb *sing,* modifies the noun *lessons.*]

Waving, the campers boarded the bus. [*Waving,* a form of the verb *wave,* modifies the noun *campers.*]

We could hear something **moving** in the underbrush. [*Moving,* a form of the verb *move,* modifies the pronoun *something.*]

Most past participles end in *–d* or *–ed.* Others are irregularly formed.

EXAMPLES The **baked** chicken with yellow rice tasted delicious. [*Baked,* a form of the verb *bake,* modifies the noun *chicken.*]

In your own words, define each term **given** in the first column. [*Given,* a form of the verb *give,* modifies the noun *term.*]

Confused and **frightened,** they fled into the jungle. [*Confused,* a form of the verb *confuse,* and *frightened,* a form of the verb *frighten,* modify the pronoun *they.*]

The perfect tense of a participle is formed with the helping verb *having,* as in *having worked* and *having been washed.*

EXAMPLES **Having worked** all day, Abe was ready for a rest.

Having been washed, the car gleamed in the sun.

Teacher's ResourceBank™

RESOURCES

THE PARTICIPLE AND THE PARTICIPIAL PHRASE

QUICK REMINDER

Write the following verb forms randomly on the chalkboard: *fly, flew, flown, flying; miss, missed, missed, missing; burst, burst, burst, bursting;* and *lie, lay, lain, lying.* Ask the class to help you arrange the verbs into four columns according to the usual order of principal parts: infinitive (present), present participle, past, and past participle. Have students supply helping verbs that belong with past participles. Then ask students to explain the difference between using the present participles and past participles on the chalkboard as verbs and using them as participles.

MEETING INDIVIDUAL NEEDS

LEP/ESL

Asian Languages. Some Asian languages such as Vietnamese do not have participles, so students may interchange participles ending in *–ing* and participles ending in *–ed,* or they may even omit the endings entirely, such as "In the movie *Wild at Heart,* Sailor and Lula appear to be very confuse."

You might demonstrate the differences in meaning in the easily confused participles by drawing simple pictures to illustrate the phrases. You could have students work with word pairs such as *amused/amusing* person, *bored/boring* student, *trusted/trusting* friend, and *confused/confusing* writer.

COMMON ERROR

Problem. When opening a sentence with a participial phrase, students often misplace the phrase, as in "Mewing and clawing frantically, Sally eventually subdued the wild kitten."

Solution. Remind students that a participial phrase should be placed as close as possible to the word it modifies. Students should first determine what word the phrase modifies and then revise the sentence so that the phrase is close to the word. You might also refer students to **Chapter 25: "Correct Use of Modifiers."**

GRAMMAR

Do not confuse a participle used as an adjective with a participle used as part of a verb phrase.

ADJECTIVE The Vietnam Veterans Memorial, **designed** by Maya Ying Lin, was completed in 1982.

VERB PHRASE The Vietnam Veterans Memorial, which **had been designed** by Maya Ying Lin, was completed in 1982.

The Participial Phrase

19f. A ***participial phrase*** consists of a participle and all of the words related to the participle.

Participles may be modified by adverbs and may also have complements.

EXAMPLES ***Speaking eloquently,*** Barbara Jordan enthralled the audience. [The participial phrase modifies the noun *Barbara Jordan.* The adverb *eloquently* modifies the present participle *speaking.*]

Nodding his head, the defendant admitted his guilt. [The participial phrase modifies the noun *defendant.* The noun *head* is the direct object of the present participle *nodding.*]

Encouraged by his family, he submitted his book of poems for publication. [The participial phrase modifies the pronoun *he.* The adverb phrase *by his family* modifies the past participle *Encouraged.*]

Florence Griffith Joyner, **often called Flo Jo,** holds the U.S. national record for the women's 100-meter dash. [The participial phrase modifies the noun *Florence Griffith Joyner.* The adverb *often* modifies the past participle *called.* The noun *Flo Jo* is the direct object of *called.*]

When writing a sentence with a participial phrase, be sure to place the phrase as close as possible to the word it modifies.

MISPLACED **Singing in the trees,** the explorers heard the birds **walking along the path.**

IMPROVED **Walking along the path,** the explorers heard the birds **singing in the trees.**

REFERENCE NOTE: For more information about misplaced participial phrases, see pages 782–786.

REVIEW B

OBJECTIVE

- To classify phrases as prepositional or participial and to identify the word or words each phrase modifies

GRAMMAR

EXERCISE 3 Identifying Participial Phrases and the Words They Modify

Each of the following sentences contains at least one participial phrase. Identify each participial phrase and the word or words it modifies.

1. Known as Johnny Appleseed, John Chapman distributed apple seeds and saplings to families headed West.
2. Needing a sustained wind for flight, the albatross rarely crosses the equator.
3. Forty adders coiled together can prevent heat loss.
4. The salmon, deriving the pink color of its flesh from its diet, feeds on shrimp-like crustaceans.
5. Having been aided by good weather and clear skies, the sailors rejoiced as they sailed into port.
6. Smiling broadly, our champion entered the hall.
7. Searching through old clothes in a trunk, John found a map showing the location of a treasure buried on the shore.
8. Sparta and Athens, putting aside their own rivalry, joined forces to fight the Persians.
9. Trained on an overhead trellis, a white rosebush growing in Tombstone, Arizona, covers some 8,000 square feet of aerial space.
10. I would love to see it bursting into bloom in the spring; it must be quite a sight!

REVIEW B Identifying Prepositional and Participial Phrases and the Words They Modify

Identify each italicized phrase in the following sentences as a *prepositional phrase* or a *participial phrase*. Then give the word or words each phrase modifies. Do not separately identify a prepositional phrase that is part of a participial phrase.

EXAMPLE 1. *Delighted by the play,* the critic applauded *with great enthusiasm.*
1. *Delighted by the play—participial phrase—critic; with great enthusiasm—prepositional phrase—applauded*

1. Mahalia Jackson, *called the greatest potential blues singer since Bessie Smith,* would sing only religious songs.
2. Her version of "Silent Night" was one *of the all-time best-selling records* in Denmark.

MEETING INDIVIDUAL NEEDS

LESS-ADVANCED STUDENTS

Some students may have trouble in distinguishing the main verb in a sentence and a participle being used as an adjective. You might want to have students work in small groups to identify all the main verbs in **Exercise 3** before they try locating the participles that begin participial phrases.

GRAMMAR

SEGMENT 4 *(pp. 614–616)*

THE GERUND AND THE GERUND PHRASE Rules 19g, 19h

OBJECTIVE

- To identify gerunds and gerund phrases and indicate how they are used in sentences

Teacher's ResourceBank™

RESOURCES

THE GERUND AND THE GERUND PHRASE

- Gerunds and Gerund Phrases 189

GRAMMAR

QUICK REMINDER

Write the following sentences on the chalkboard:

1. Winning isn't everything.
2. At least it isn't losing.
3. I practice my singing daily.
4. Now I give listening a chance.
5. I'm thinking about studying.

Ask students to identify how the verbal forms ending in *–ing* are used in each sentence. [(1) subject, (2) subject complement, (predicate nominative), (3) direct object, (4) indirect object, (5) verb/object of a preposition]. Remind students that gerunds are used as nouns.

GRAMMAR

3. *Setting out in a thirty-one-foot ketch*, Sharon Sites Adams, a woman *from California*, sailed *across the Pacific* alone.
4. *Having been rejected by six publishers*, the story *of Peter Rabbit* was finally published privately *by Beatrix Potter*.
5. *Known for his imaginative style*, architect Minoru Yamasaki designed the World Trade Center, *located in New York City*.
6. *In 1932*, Amelia Earhart, *trying for a new record*, began her solo flight *over the Atlantic*.
7. Maria Tallchief, an Osage Indian, was the prima ballerina *of the New York Ballet Company*.
8. *Dancing to unanimous acclaim in both the United States and Europe*, she was known *for her brilliant interpretation* of Stravinsky's *Firebird*.
9. *Continuing her research on radium after her husband's death*, Marie Curie received the Nobel Prize *in chemistry*.
10. *First elected to the House of Representatives in 1968*, Shirley Chisholm was the first black female member *of Congress*.

The Gerund

19g. A ***gerund*** is a verb form ending in *–ing* that is used as a noun.

SUBJECT	**Swimming** is excellent exercise.
PREDICATE NOMINATIVE	Janetta's hobby is **knitting.**
DIRECT OBJECT	She has always loved **dancing.**
INDIRECT OBJECT	He gave **studying** all his attention.
OBJECT OF PREPOSITION	In **cooking,** use salt sparingly.

Do not confuse a gerund with a present participle used as an adjective or as part of a verb phrase.

GERUND	I enjoy **reading** late at night. [direct object of the verb *enjoy*]
PRESENT PARTICIPLE	I sometimes fall asleep **reading** late at night. [adjective modifying the pronoun *I*]
PRESENT PARTICIPLE	Sometimes, I listen to classical music while I am **reading** late at night. [part of the verb phrase *am reading*]

NOTE: When writing a noun or a pronoun directly before a gerund, use the possessive form of the noun or pronoun.

EXAMPLES **Rodrigo's** winning the contest surprised no one.
Mom was upset about **our** being late.

EXERCISE 4 **Identifying Gerunds and Their Functions**

Find the gerunds in the following sentences. Then identify each gerund as a *subject*, a *direct object*, an *indirect object*, a *predicate nominative*, or an *object of a preposition*.

EXAMPLE 1. By reading the newspaper daily, you will become an informed citizen.
1. *reading—object of a preposition*

1. Judging should be an exercise in objectivity. 1. s.
2. Do you enjoy skiing? 2. d.o.
3. I sometimes dream about flying. 3. o.p.
4. My Navajo grandmother thinks that weaving would be a good hobby for me. 4. s.
5. I have given camping a fair try, but I still do not like it. 5. i.o.
6. Some of my friends earn extra money by baby-sitting. 6. o.p.
7. My exercise schedule includes jogging. 7. d.o.
8. My favorite pastime is snorkeling. 8. p.n.
9. Typing is a useful skill. 9. s.
10. Have you ever wished for a career in acting? 10. o.p.

The Gerund Phrase

19h. A ***gerund phrase*** consists of a gerund and all of the words related to the gerund.

Like participles, gerunds may have modifiers and complements.

EXAMPLES **Exercising regularly** is important to your health. [The gerund phrase is the subject of the verb *is.* The adverb *regularly* modifies the gerund *Exercising.*]

My brother likes **working at the travel agency.** [The gerund phrase is the direct object of the verb *likes.* The adverb phrase *at the travel agency* modifies the gerund *working.*]

Walter Mitty daydreamed of **being a courageous pilot.** [The gerund phrase is the object of the preposition *of.* The noun *pilot* is a predicate nominative completing the meaning of the gerund *being.*]

An excellent way to build your vocabulary is **reading good literature.** [The gerund phrase is a predicate nominative explaining the subject *way.* The noun *literature* is the direct object of the gerund *reading.*]

COMMON ERROR

Problem. Students frequently forget to use the possessive case with gerunds.

Solution. Remind students that they know to use possessives with nouns. Students simply need to remember that gerunds always function as nouns. You might illustrate this by substituting a noun for a gerund in a sentence. For example, write the following sentence on the chalkboard:

"We worried about my sister's driving Dad's car."

Then have students replace the gerund phrase with the word *journey.* Remind them that both sentences require the possessive form of *sister.*

REVIEW C

OBJECTIVE

- To distinguish between participial and gerund phrases

Teacher's ResourceBank™

RESOURCES

THE INFINITIVE AND THE INFINITIVE PHRASE

- Infinitives and Infinitive Phrases 190

GRAMMAR

QUICK REMINDER

To reinforce the distinction between infinitives and prepositional phrases, write the following infinitives in columns on the chalkboard:

to	plan
to	place
to	show

In each space between the columns, have students supply an article (*a, the*), adjective (*some, any, no*), or possessive noun or pronoun (*Harry's, nobody's, my, their*). After students experiment with several such phrases, point out that students are converting the words in the right-hand column from verbs to nouns and converting the infinitives to prepositional phrases.

GRAMMAR

REVIEW C **Identifying Participial Phrases and Gerund Phrases**

Identify the verbal phrase in each of the following sentences as a participial phrase or a gerund phrase.

1. Mary Shelley wrote *Frankenstein* after having a nightmare about a scientist and his strange experiments.
2. Dr. Mae Jemison became an astronaut by placing among the best fifteen candidates out of two thousand applicants.
3. Beginning with *Pippi Longstocking*, Astrid Lindgren has written a whole series of stories for children.
4. Marian Anderson was the first African American employed as a member of the Metropolitan Opera.
5. Fighting for women's suffrage was Carrie Chapman Catt's mission in life.
6. Appointed principal of the Mason City Iowa High School in 1881, Catt became the city's first female superintendent.
7. The Nineteenth Amendment to the Constitution, adopted in 1920, was largely the result of Catt's efforts.
8. Mildred "Babe" Didrikson, entering the 1932 Olympics as a relatively obscure athlete, won gold and silver medals.
9. Working for *Life* throughout her long career, Margaret Bourke-White was the first female war photographer.
10. Phyllis McGinley, a famous writer of light verse, began publishing her work while she was still in college.

The Infinitive

19i. An ***infinitive*** is a verb form that can be used as a noun, an adjective, or an adverb. An infinitive usually begins with *to.*

INFINITIVES

USED AS	EXAMPLES
Nouns	**To fly** was an ambition of humans for many centuries. [subject of *was*] Some fishes must swim constantly, or they start **to sink.** [direct object of *start*] Darius Freeman's dream is **to act.** [predicate nominative identifying the subject *dream*]

SEGMENT 5 (pp. 616–620)

THE INFINITIVE and THE INFINITIVE PHRASE Rules 19i, 19j

OBJECTIVE

- To identify infinitives and infinitive phrases and to indicate how they are used in sentences

INFINITIVES *(continued)*	
USED AS	EXAMPLES
Adjectives	His attempt **to fly** was a failure. [adjective modifying the noun *attempt*] The one **to ask** is your guidance counselor. [adjective modifying the pronoun *one*]
Adverbs	With his dog Wolf, Rip van Winkle went into the woods **to hunt.** [adverb modifying the verb *went*] Everyone in the neighborhood was willing **to help.** [adverb modifying the adjective *willing*]

NOTE: Do not confuse an infinitive with a prepositional phrase that begins with *to.* An infinitive is a verb form. A prepositional phrase begins with *to* and ends with a noun or a pronoun.

INFINITIVES	to write	to forgive	to visit
PREPOSITIONAL PHRASES	to the game	to someone	to them

The word *to,* the sign of the infinitive, is sometimes omitted.

EXAMPLES Let us [to] **sit** down.
Please make him [to] **stop** that noise.
We wouldn't dare [to] **disobey.**
Will you help me [to] **finish**?

EXERCISE 5 **Identifying Infinitives and Their Functions**

Identify the infinitive in each of the following sentences. Then tell whether it is used as a *noun*, an *adjective*, or an *adverb*. If the infinitive is used as a noun, indicate whether it is a *subject*, a *direct object*, or a *predicate nominative*. If the infinitive is used as a modifier, give the word it modifies.

EXAMPLE **1.** Swans and geese are fascinating to watch.
1. *to watch—adverb—fascinating*

1. To land an American on the moon became the national goal of the United States during the 1960s. **1.** s.
2. For me, one of the worst chores is to clean my room. **2.** p.n.
3. Karl "The Mailman" Malone slam-dunked the ball with one second to go in the game!

REVIEW D

OBJECTIVE

- To identify participles, gerunds, and infinitives and to indicate how they are used in sentences

COMMON ERROR

Problem. Students often use nominative case pronouns as compound subjects with infinitives and infinitive phrases, as in "They wanted he and I to run track."

Solution. Tell students that if they omit one of the subjects in such a sentence, the omission will reveal the need for the objective case. ("They wanted him to run track" or "They wanted me to run track.") You can refer students to **Chapter 22: "Correct Pronoun Usage"** for help.

GRAMMAR

ANSWERS

Review D

1. honored — participle — modifies symbol
2. watching/bringing — gerunds (objects of a preposition); to make — infinitive (adjective); (to) grow — infinitive (adjective)
3. to dance — infinitive (adverb)
4. to chase/to bring — infinitives (predicate nominatives)
5. holding — participle — modifies dancer; charging — participle (figure)
6. valued — participle — modifies pearl
7. beating/clashing/popping — gerunds (objects of a preposition)
8. amazing — participle — modifies dragon)
9. covering — gerund (subject); hand-cut — participle — modifies mirrors; multicolored — participle — modifies scales
10. working — participle — modifies people; to carry — infinitive (adverb)

GRAMMAR

4. Since I have taken up track in addition to my other extracurricular activities, it seems I haven't a [moment] to spare.
5. Did you find that book [difficult] (to understand)?
6. According to our judicial system, the state makes the [decision] to prosecute the defendant in criminal cases.
7. Mom made me finish the dishes before I could go to the movies. 7. d.o.
8. Anita's job was to interview all qualified applicants who had applied for the position. 8. p.n.
9. I did not have the [time] to watch the football game on television. 10. d.o.
10. In my spare time I like to read stories by Laurence Yep.

REVIEW D **Identifying Participles, Gerunds, and Infinitives**

Identify the participles, gerunds, and infinitives in the sentences in the following paragraph. For each participle, give the word it modifies. For each gerund, tell what part of a sentence it is used as. For each infinitive, indicate what part of speech it is used as.

EXAMPLE [1] In Chinese communities all over the world, parading a huge paper dragon is an exciting part of the New Year celebration.

1. *parading—gerund (subject); exciting—participle—modifies* part

[1] Dragons are an honored symbol of happiness to many Chinese people. [2] According to ancient Chinese mythology, dragons are responsible for watching over people and bringing rain to make the crops grow. [3] There are five different types of dragons, but it is the imperial dragon that is chosen to dance through the streets in traditional New Year celebrations. [4] The dragon's role is to chase away bad luck and to bring good fortune for the new year. [5] Holding a stick with a white ball on the top, one dancer runs ahead of the charging dragon figure. [6] The ball symbolizes the highly valued pearl of wisdom, which the dragon chases. [7] The dragon's dance is accompanied by the beating of drums and gongs, the clashing of cymbals, and the popping of firecrackers. [8] The amazing dragon in the photograph on the next page, the largest dragon figure in the world, is three meters tall and nearly 100 meters long. [9] Its

19j

covering is decorated with 84,000 hand-cut mirrors and 6,000 multicolored silk "scales." [10] Because of its great weight and size, this dragon takes two hundred people, working in shifts, to carry it.

GRAMMAR

The Infinitive Phrase

19j. An ***infinitive phrase*** consists of an infinitive and all of the words related to the infinitive.

Like other verbals, infinitives may have modifiers and complements.

EXAMPLES **To finish early** is our plan. [The infinitive phrase is the subject of the verb *is.* The adverb *early* modifies the infinitive *to finish.*]

Julia wants **to go to the beach with us on Saturday.** [The infinitive phrase is the direct object of the verb *wants.* The adverb phrases *to the beach, with us,* and *on Saturday* modify the infinitive *to go.*]

Napoleon's plan **to conquer the world** failed. [The infinitive phrase modifies the noun *plan.* The noun *world* is the direct object of the infinitive *to conquer.*]

Because of his sprained ankle, Chico was unable **to play in the football game.** [The infinitive phrase modifies the adjective *unable.* The adverb phrase *in the football game* modifies the infinitive *to play.*]

INTEGRATING THE LANGUAGE ARTS

Literature Link. The poetry of Robert Frost is rich with lyrical phrases that are uncomplicated enough to parse easily. You might want to have students identify prepositional phrases, verbals, and infinitives in some of Frost's poems such as "Design," "Birches," or "The Death of the Hired Man." You might want to duplicate copies of the poem so that students can mark phrases and visually analyze the contributions phrases make to the poetry.

GRAMMAR

REVIEW E

OBJECTIVE

- To identify prepositional, participial, gerund, and infinitive phrases in sentences

GRAMMAR

NOTE: Unlike other verbals, an infinitive may have a subject. Such a construction is called an ***infinitive clause.*** Notice in the second example below that the subject in the infinitive clause *(them)* is in the objective case.

EXAMPLES The director has asked **Rebecca to star in the play.** [*Rebecca* is the subject of the infinitive *to star.* The entire infinitive clause is the direct object of the verb *has asked.*]

The sergeant commanded **them to march faster.** [*Them* is the subject of the infinitive *to march.* The entire infinitive clause is the direct object of the verb *commanded.*]

REFERENCE NOTE: For more information about clauses, see pages 628–637.

REVIEW E Identifying Prepositional, Participial, Gerund, and Infinitive Phrases

Identify each italicized phrase in the following sentences as a *prepositional phrase*, a *participial phrase*, a *gerund phrase*, or an *infinitive phrase*. Do not separately identify a prepositional phrase that is part of a larger phrase.

EXAMPLE
1. *Celebrating the strength of the human spirit,* Christy Brown's book My Left Foot tells the story *of his life.*
1. *Celebrating the strength of the human spirit—participial phrase; of his life—prepositional phrase*

1. Christy Brown, *born with cerebral palsy*, was unable *to speak a single word*.
2. Everyone *including his family* assumed he had very little intelligence, because he could not express himself *to them*.
3. Christy's left foot was the only limb he could control, and one day he succeeded in *grabbing a piece of chalk with it* and began *to write the word MOTHER on the wooden floor*.
4. Christy's family, *amazed at this remarkable achievement*, suddenly realized that *his leading a full, rewarding life* was not an impossible dream.
5. *Typing the entire manuscript with his left foot*, Christy Brown was eventually able *to tell his story in this inspiring book about his life*.

GRAMMAR

SEGMENT 6 *(pp. 621–623)*

THE APPOSITIVE Rules 19k, 19l

OBJECTIVE

- To use verbal and appositive phrases to provide vivid detail in paragraphs

Appositives and Appositive Phrases

19k. An ***appositive*** is a noun or a pronoun placed beside another noun or pronoun to identify or explain it.

An appositive usually follows the word it identifies or explains.

EXAMPLES We went to the Navajo Gallery in Taos, New Mexico, to see R. C. Gorman's painting ***Freeform Lady.*** [The noun *Freeform Lady* identifies the noun *painting.*]

Did Dan Namhinga complete *Red Desert,* **one** of his colorful acrylic paintings, in 1980? [The pronoun *one* refers to the noun *Red Desert.*]

Namhinga, a Hopi-Tewa **artist,** often paints abstract images of Hopi pueblos. [The noun *artist* explains the noun *Namhinga.*]

For emphasis, however, an appositive may come at the beginning of a sentence.

EXAMPLE A younger **painter,** Jaune Quick-to-See Smith shows a deep awareness of her French, Cree, and Shoshone heritage. [The noun *painter* refers to the noun *Jaune Quick-to-See Smith.*]

19l. An ***appositive phrase*** consists of an appositive and its modifiers.

EXAMPLES We visited Boston Harbor, **the site of the Boston Tea Party.** [The adjective *the* and the adjective phrase *of the Boston Tea Party* modify the appositive *site.*]

The Kenai Peninsula is the home of the Alaska moose, **the largest deer in the world.** [The adjectives *the* and *largest* and the adjective phrase *in the world* modify the appositive *deer.*]

Our graduating class is planning to hold a reunion on Monday, January 1, 2001, **the first day of the twenty-first century.** [The adjectives *the* and *first* and the adjective phrase *of the twenty-first century* all modify the appositive *day.*]

Teacher's ResourceBank™

RESOURCES

THE APPOSITIVE

- Appositives and Appositive Phrases 191

QUICK REMINDER

Write these sentences on the chalkboard, and ask students to find nouns that identify or explain other nouns:

1. *Middlemarch,* a nineteenth-century novel, was written by George Eliot, a woman.
2. A nineteenth-century female author, Marian Evans had to publish her book *Middlemarch* under a male pseudonym, George Eliot.

Explain that these identifying or explaining nouns are called appositives. *Appositive* has a Latin root meaning "to place near." The adjacent terms in an appositive construction have the same function in the sentence and can be substituted for each other.

MEETING INDIVIDUAL NEEDS

LESS-ADVANCED STUDENTS

Brief appositives are easy for most students to recognize; but as appositive phrases become more complex, students may mistake them for sentences and create fragments. (Ann was surprised to find herds of elk and huge flocks of pelicans. The largest congregation of wildlife she had seen so near the city.)

When revising their written work, have students check carefully for proper placement of appositive phrases.

REVIEW F

OBJECTIVE

- To distinguish and identify prepositional, verbal, and appositive phrases in a paragraph

COMMON ERROR

Problem. Students may often misuse commas when punctuating appositives, especially in a sentence such as "I remember the Beatles' songs 'She Loves You' and 'She Was Just Seventeen.' "

Solution. Remind students that appositive phrases can be restrictive or nonrestrictive. In the example above, the appositive provides information essential to the meaning of the sentence. The appositive is therefore restrictive, and it requires no commas. In the sentence "I remember when the Beatles' first two American hit songs, 'She Loves You' and 'She Was Just Seventeen,' appeared in record stores," the appositive provides information that is not essential to the meaning; thus, the appositive phrase is set off with commas.

PICTURE THIS

Before students begin to write, remind them of the importance of deciding on a type of order in which to present their material. You might want to discuss the merits of using chronological order to describe the events as they take place or spatial order to describe the journey's route for a travelogue. Or students might use logical order to compare Australia with another travel spot.

GRAMMAR

REVIEW F Identifying Prepositional, Verbal, and Appositive Phrases

Identify each italicized phrase in the following paragraph as a *prepositional phrase,* a *participial phrase,* a *gerund phrase,* an *infinitive phrase,* or an *appositive phrase.* Do not separately identify a prepositional phrase that is part of a larger phrase.

1. prep. Each year, thousands of Americans travel [1] *to hundreds of*
2. part. *vacation spots in the United States and other countries.* [2] *Anticipating all kinds of weather and activities,* many eager travelers pack far too much clothing and equipment. The most effective way
3. inf. to pack is [3] *to set out clothes for the trip* and then to put half of
4. prep. them back [4] *in the closet.* Of course, travelers should give par-
5. app. ticularly careful thought to walking shoes, [5] *the most important item of apparel on any sightseeing trip.* Experienced travelers pack only two or three changes of casual clothing, even if they plan
6. inf. [6] *to be away for some time.* [7] *Taking out the smallest piece of luggage*
7. part. *they own,* they study its capacity. It is possible to pack enough
8. app. clothes for three weeks in small luggage, [8] *perhaps a duffel bag or shoulder bag.* Passengers can carry such bags onto an airliner
9. ger. and avoid [9] *waiting at the baggage claim area.* For most people,
10. ger. [10] *doing a bit of hand laundry every few days* is preferable to spending their vacation burdened with heavy suitcases.

PICTURE THIS

You always knew you'd find a way to travel around the world and satisfy your longing for adventure. As a successful travel writer, you've managed to make your dreams come true. This month you are traveling aboard a schooner along the Great Barrier Reef off the coast of Australia, where fantastic sights like the ones on the next page give you plenty to write about. Write one or two paragraphs to include in your next article. Use at least three verbal phrases and two appositive phrases to add vivid detail to your writing.

Subject: sailing along the northwestern coast of Australia
Audience: readers of a travel magazine
Purpose: to record events of your journey; to describe exotic sights for your readers

SEGMENT 7 *(pp. 623–625)*

REVIEW: POSTTESTS 1 and 2

OBJECTIVES

- To identify prepositional, participial, gerund, infinitive, and appositive phrases in sentences and paragraphs
- To understand the function of participial, verbal, and appositive phrases and to use them appropriately in sentences

GRAMMAR

Review: Posttest 1

A. Identifying Phrases

Identify the italicized phrase in each of the following sentences as a *prepositional phrase,* a *participial phrase,* a *gerund phrase,* an *infinitive phrase,* or an *appositive phrase.* Do not separately identify a prepositional phrase that is part of a larger phrase.

EXAMPLE **1.** ***Talking after the bell rings*** **is strictly forbidden.**
1. ***gerund phrase***

1. ger.

1. *Working on the school newspaper* has taught me responsibility.
2. *Delayed by the snowstorm,* the flight from Chicago to Seattle was finally cleared for takeoff. 2. part.

GRAMMAR

GRAMMAR

3. inf.

3. Today's crossword puzzle is difficult *to complete correctly*.
4. If you want *to go to the concert tonight*, give me a call after school. 4. inf.
5. At the beginning of class today, we sang "La Marseillaise," *the French national anthem*. 5. app.
6. Preserving rare and valuable books and documents is one of the challenges *facing the Library of Congress*. 6. part.
7. The emu, *a flightless bird from Australia*, is similar to the ostrich. 7. app.
8. Franklin's history report was on Booker T. Washington, founder *of Tuskegee Institute*. 8. prep.
9. Refreshed by the cool breeze, I didn't object to *going back to work*. 9. ger.
10. The United States, a true "melting pot," has been greatly enriched *by many diverse cultures*. 10. prep.

B. Identifying Phrases

Identify each italicized phrase in the following paragraph as a *prepositional phrase*, a *participial phrase*, a *gerund phrase*, an *infinitive phrase*, or an *appositive phrase*. Do not separately identify a prepositional phrase that is part of a larger phrase.

11. ger. By **[11]** *being elected to the Baseball Hall of Fame in 1953*, Charles
Albert Bender became a symbol of pride for all Native Ameri-
12. part. cans. Bender, **[12]** *born in 1884 in Crow Wing County, Minnesota*,
13. app. was half Chippewa. "Chief," **[13]** *the nickname given to him by his*
14. ger. *teammates*, stuck with him throughout his career. **[14]** *Pitching*
for the Philadelphia Athletics was his first job in baseball.
15. prep. Although he never played **[15]** *on a minor league team*, he pitched
a four-hit victory in his first game. He won twenty-three games
16. app. and lost only five during the 1910 season, **[16]** *the best season of*
17. prep. *his career*. **[17]** *During that same year*, he had an earned-run aver-
18. inf. age of 1.58. If it was crucial **[18]** *to win a game*, Connie Mack, the
Athletics' manager, would always send Bender to the mound.
19. part. **[19]** *Finishing with a lifetime total of 212 wins and only 128 losses*,
Bender led the American League three times in winning per-
centage. His last full active year as a pitcher was 1917, but he
20. inf. returned to the mound **[20]** *to pitch one inning for the White Sox in*
1925.

Review: Posttest 2

GRAMMAR

Writing Sentences with Phrases

Write ten sentences according to the following guidelines. In each of your sentences, underline the italicized phrase given, and tell what kind of phrase it is.

1. Use *whistling softly* as a participial phrase.
2. Use *to go* as an infinitive used as a modifier.
3. Use *with the green shirt* as an adjective phrase.
4. Use *with kindness* as an adverb phrase modifying an adjective.
5. Use *for me* as an adverb phrase modifying a verb.
6. Use *of fruits and vegetables* as an adjective phrase.
7. Use *buying a gift for Jane* as a participial phrase.
8. Use *diving into the pool* as a gerund phrase.
9. Use *to be happy* as an infinitive phrase used as a noun.
10. Use *a city in Mexico* as an appositive phrase.

ANSWERS

Review: Posttest 2

Responses will vary. Here are some possibilities:

1. Whistling softly to himself, he entered the dark woods.
2. Annabelle was ready to go to the lake.
3. The red-haired boy with the green shirt spoke to her cordially.
4. A wild animal treated with kindness will soon be tamed.
5. My mom did all this for me.
6. Red Riding Hood took her granny a basket of fruits and vegetables.
7. Buying a gift for Jane and several for himself, Tom whipped out his credit card.
8. His mistake was diving into the pool.
9. Who wants to be happy?
10. Guanajuato, a city in Mexico, is a delightful place to visit.

GRAMMAR

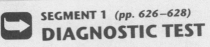

SEGMENT 1 *(pp. 626–628)*
DIAGNOSTIC TEST

OBJECTIVES
- To identify independent and subordinate clauses and to classify them according to use
- To classify sentences according to structure

Teacher's ResourceBank™
RESOURCES

FOR THE WHOLE CHAPTER

• Chapter Review Form A	206–207
• Chapter Review Form B	208–209
• Assessment Portfolio	
Grammar Pretests	563–570
Grammar Mastery Tests	587–595

GRAMMAR

CHAPTER OVERVIEW

This chapter discusses independent clauses, the three types of subordinate clauses (noun, adjective, and adverb), and related concepts. The chapter also covers the classification of sentences according to structure, and the **Writing Application** requires students to use a variety of sentence structures in their writing.

Learning about clauses should help students to subordinate ideas and to add variety to their writing. Therefore, the information presented in this chapter could be integrated with any of the composition chapters.

GRAMMAR

20 The Clause

Adjective, Noun, Adverb Clauses

Diagnostic Test

A. Identifying Independent and Subordinate Clauses

Identify the italicized word group in each of the following sentences as an *independent clause* or a *subordinate clause*. Then classify each italicized subordinate clause as an *adjective clause*, an *adverb clause*, or a *noun clause*.

EXAMPLE **1.** This novel, *which is the latest best-seller,* will be the perfect birthday gift for my mother.
1. *subordinate clause; adjective clause*

1. *If there is an increase in the amount of carbon dioxide present in the atmosphere*, plant growth also will increase. **1.** adv. cl.
2. *Many Americans believed in and voted for the New Deal*, which was the political philosophy of Franklin D. Roosevelt.
3. *When you travel abroad*, you gain greater perspective on being American. **3.** adv. cl.

4. Amy thought *that "The Rockpile" was the best short story in our literature book,* and she asked the librarian to help her find other stories by James Baldwin. 4. n. cl.
5. *Since both of Len's parents are short,* Len doesn't expect to be tall. 5. adv. cl.
6. The governor had to answer several questions about the budget *after he addressed the legislature.* 6. adv. cl.
7. Please turn down that stereo *so that I can do my homework.* 7. adv. cl.
8. In 1981 Sandra Day O'Connor, *who had been an Arizona judge,* became the first female Supreme Court Justice. 8. adj. cl.
9. Scientists are carefully monitoring *how much carbon dioxide is present in the atmosphere.* 9. n. cl.
10. *The Civil War, often called the War Between the States, resulted in the deaths of more than 600,000 Americans;* it devastated the nation socially, politically, and economically.

B. Classifying Sentences According to Structure

Classify each of the following sentences as *simple, compound, complex,* or *compound-complex.*

11. A familiar proverb states that the longest journey begins with a single step; another tells us that little strokes fell great oaks. 11. cd.-cx.
12. Many people have heard these wise sayings but haven't applied them to their own lives. 12. simp.
13. For example, suppose you are required to read a 400-page novel before a test at the end of the school year. 13. cx.
14. If you don't start reading the book until the last possible weekend, you will probably not read it well; furthermore, you may not have time to finish the book, and you will almost certainly not enjoy it! 14. cd.-cx.
15. Instead, if you start now and read just ten pages a day, you'll be finished within six weeks. 15. cx.
16. The championship golfer Chi Chi Rodriguez knows this technique for completing a large project in small sections. 16. simp.
17. When Rodriguez was a child in Puerto Rico, he learned this approach from his father, who wanted to plant corn in a small field that was thickly overgrown with bamboo. 17. cx.
18. Mr. Rodriguez could not afford to take several weeks off from his job to clear the whole field, so every evening after work, he would cut down a single bamboo plant. 18. cd.

USING THE DIAGNOSTIC TEST

In evaluating students' writing, you may discover that some students are unaware of how to achieve interesting and varied syntax. You could use the **Diagnostic Test** to assess students' understanding of independent and subordinate clauses. Then have students work individually or in small groups on activities and exercises designed for their particular needs.

SEGMENT 2 *(pp. 628–630)*

THE INDEPENDENT CLAUSE AND THE SUBORDINATE CLAUSE Rules 20b, 20c

OBJECTIVE

- To identify independent and subordinate clauses

Teacher's ResourceBank™

RESOURCES

THE INDEPENDENT CLAUSE AND THE SUBORDINATE CLAUSE

- Independent and Subordinate Clauses 201

QUICK REMINDER

Write the following sentences on the chalkboard and have students identify the underlined clauses as independent or subordinate:

1. When she answered correctly, the teacher nodded. [independent]
2. The story that he is writing is almost finished. [subordinate]
3. Could someone who lives nearby drive me home? [subordinate]

Remind students that a subordinate clause cannot stand alone as a sentence.

19. cd.

19. Gradually, the field was cleared, and by the following spring, the Rodriguez family was eating corn for dinner.
20. Today, Chi Chi Rodriguez and his dedicated staff at the Chi Chi Rodriguez Youth Foundation help hundreds and hundreds of disadvantaged youngsters—one child at a time. **20.** simp.

20a. A ***clause*** is a group of words that contains a verb and its subject and is used as part of a sentence.

Every clause has a subject and a verb. Not every clause, however, expresses a complete thought.

SENTENCE **Lichens are small plants that are composed of both fungi and algae.**

CLAUSE **Lichens are small plants.** [complete thought]

CLAUSE **that are composed of both fungi and algae** [incomplete thought]

There are two kinds of clauses: the *independent clause* and the *subordinate clause.* When an independent clause stands alone, it is generally called a simple sentence. Like a word or a phrase, a subordinate clause functions as a single part of speech in a sentence.

The Independent Clause

20b. An ***independent*** (or ***main***) ***clause*** expresses a complete thought and can stand by itself as a sentence.

EXAMPLES **Ms. Martin** (S) **explained** (V) **the binary number system.** [one independent clause]

In the binary system, each number (S) **is expressed** (V) **in powers of two,** and **only the digits** (S) ***0* and *1* are used** (V)**.** [two independent clauses joined by *and*]

The binary number system is important to know because it is used by computers. [an independent clause combined with a subordinate clause] (S and V are marked above *system*/*is* and *it*/*is used*.)

The Subordinate Clause

20c. A ***subordinate*** (or ***dependent***) ***clause*** does not express a complete thought and cannot stand alone as a sentence.

EXAMPLES that we collected
what Hui Su named her pet beagle
when Rudy proofread his essay

The thought expressed by a subordinate clause becomes complete when the clause is combined with an independent clause.

EXAMPLES Mr. Platero took the aluminum cans **that we collected** to the recycling center.
Do you know **what Hui Su named her pet beagle**?
When Rudy proofread his essay, he found several typographical errors.

EXERCISE 1 Identifying Independent and Subordinate Clauses

Identify each italicized word group in the following paragraph as an independent clause or a subordinate clause.

EXAMPLE [1] The photographs on the next page show *how eggs are processed in a large processing plant.*
1. *subordinate clause*

[1] Large plants like the one in the photographs are *where most eggs are processed today.* [2] After an egg is laid, *it gently rolls along the slanted floor of the cage to a narrow conveyor belt.* [3] These narrow conveyor belts converge into one wide belt *that runs directly into the processing plant.* [4] *As soon as the eggs reach the processing plant,* they are automatically sprayed with detergent and

MEETING INDIVIDUAL NEEDS

LEP/ESL

Spanish. Because some Spanish-speaking students might invert subjects and verbs in subordinate clauses, reinforce that in English the subject generally precedes the verb. You could help students to locate the subject and verb in each subordinate clause in **Exercise 1.**

LEARNING STYLES

Auditory Learners. Some students may find it easier to hear the difference between a complete and an incomplete thought than to recognize the difference visually. You could read aloud the examples in this segment and the italicized clauses in **Exercise 1.** Have volunteers explain why each example is either a complete sentence or a sentence fragment.

TIMESAVER

To simplify the evaluation of **Exercise 1,** you could have students list the numbers of the sentences with subordinate clauses. The numbers [1, 3, 4, 5, 7, 8, and 10] are easy to check by scanning.

SEGMENT 3 *(pp. 630–633)*

THE ADJECTIVE CLAUSE Rule 20d

OBJECTIVES

- To identify adjective clauses and the words they modify
- To write a journal entry that contains adjective clauses

GRAMMAR

Teacher's ResourceBank™

RESOURCES

THE ADJECTIVE CLAUSE

QUICK REMINDER

Write the following sentences on the chalkboard and have students combine them by using the relative pronoun or relative adverb in parentheses. Ask students to underline the adjective clauses in their sentences.

1. The tree must be cut down and cleared away. The tree was struck by lightning. (that) [The tree that was struck by lightning must be cut down and cleared away.]
2. I interviewed a man. His daughter is an astronaut. (whose) [I interviewed a man whose daughter is an astronaut.]
3. Do you remember the night? We first met on that night. (when) [Do you remember the night when we first met?]

GRAMMAR

water. [5] The eggs then pass through a specially lit inspection area, *where defective eggs can be detected and removed.* [6] After the eggs are weighed, *they are separated by weight into groups*. [7] Each group of eggs goes onto a separate conveyor belt, *which leads to a forklike lifting device.* [8] This device lifts six eggs at a time *while the empty egg cartons wait two feet below it*. [9] *The eggs are gently lowered into the cartons*, which are then shipped to grocery stores and supermarkets. [10] *What is truly amazing* is that no human hands ever touch the eggs during the entire process.

The Adjective Clause

20d. An ***adjective clause*** is a subordinate clause that modifies a noun or a pronoun.

An adjective clause always follows the word or words that it modifies.

EXAMPLES

In the 1930s, Dr. Charles Richter devised a scale **that is used to measure the magnitude of earthquakes.** [The adjective clause modifies the noun *scale.*]

Ferdinand Magellan, **who was the commander of the first expedition around the world,** was killed before the end of the journey. [The adjective clause modifies the noun *Ferdinand Magellan.*]

Didn't John Kieran once say, "I am a part of all **that I have read"**? [The adjective clause modifies the pronoun *all.*]

20d

GRAMMAR

Relative Pronouns

Usually, an adjective clause begins with a ***relative pronoun***—a word that not only relates an adjective clause to the word or words the clause modifies but also serves a function within the clause.

Relative Pronouns				
that	which	who	whom	whose

EXAMPLES I have read nearly every novel **that Shirley Ann Grau has written.** [The relative pronoun *that* relates the adjective clause to the noun *novel* and serves as the direct object of the verb *has written.*]

The treasure **for which they are searching** belonged to the Aztec emperor Montezuma II. [The relative pronoun *which* relates the adjective clause to the noun *treasure* and serves as the object of the preposition *for.*]

Grandma Moses, **who began painting at the age of seventy-six,** became famous for her primitive style of art. [The relative pronoun *who* relates the adjective clause to the noun *Grandma Moses* and also serves as the subject of the verb *began.*]

An adjective clause may begin with a relative adverb, such as *when* or *where.*

EXAMPLES Uncle Chim told Lori and me about the time **when he backpacked across the island of Luzon.** [The adjective clause modifies the noun *time.*]

From 1914 to 1931, Isak Dinesen lived in Kenya, **where she operated a coffee plantation.** [The adjective clause modifies the noun *Kenya.*]

Sometimes the relative pronoun or relative adverb is not expressed, but its meaning is understood.

EXAMPLES The book [that] I am reading is a biography of Harriet Tubman.

We will never forget the wonderful summer [when] we stayed with our grandparents in Mayaguez, Puerto Rico.

MEETING INDIVIDUAL NEEDS

LEARNING STYLES

Visual Learners. You could display a chart listing the functions and characteristics of adjective clauses. Use the following four headings: *Kind of Clause, Function, Words That Introduce the Clause,* and *Examples.* Students can refer to the chart as they work through the exercises in this segment. As noun clauses and adverb clauses are introduced, add them to the chart.

GRAMMAR

COOPERATIVE LEARNING

You may wish to integrate this activity with a study of the library. Divide the class into pairs of students. Have each student use various resources (encyclopedias, biographies, the *Readers' Guide,* or *Who's Who*) to make a list of five names with which his or her partner may be unfamiliar. Students should list on a separate sheet of paper the sources of the listed names and then exchange their lists with their partners. Next, each student must use his or her partner's list to write an informative sentence containing an adjective clause that modifies each name. The more obscure the name, the more the partner must search for information. Only as a last resort should partners share their sources.

When students have finished writing their sentences, have partners check to see that adjective clauses have been used correctly.

A DIFFERENT APPROACH

Remind students that a limerick is a five-line comical poem that uses the rhyme scheme *aabba*. Ask each student to write the first two lines of a limerick and to make the second line an adjective clause. You may wish to provide the following example:

"There once was a lady from Maine
Who was walking two dogs on a chain"

Then have students pass their limericks to the persons behind them, who will add third and fourth lines such as these:

"A man tried to flirt
And nearly got hurt"

Have students pass the limericks one more time to the persons behind them, who will finish the limericks:

"Seeking love is a dangerous game."

The result will be "chain-reaction" limericks that can each be read aloud by whoever writes the last line.

GRAMMAR

GRAMMAR

Depending on how it is used, an adjective clause is either essential or nonessential. An ***essential clause*** provides information that is necessary to the meaning of a sentence. A ***nonessential clause*** provides additional information that can be omitted without changing the meaning of a sentence. A nonessential clause is always set off by commas.

ESSENTIAL Students **who are going to the track meet** can take the bus at 7:45 A.M. [Omitting the adjective clause would change the meaning of the sentence.]

NONESSENTIAL Nancy Stevens, **whose father is a pediatrician,** plans to study medicine. [The adjective clause gives extra information. Omitting the clause would not affect the meaning of the sentence.]

REFERENCE NOTE: For more about punctuating nonessential clauses, see pages 851–852.

EXERCISE 2 Identifying Adjective Clauses and the Words They Modify

Identify the adjective clause in each of the following sentences, and give the noun or pronoun that it modifies. Then tell whether the relative pronoun is used as the *subject*, *direct object*, or *object of a preposition* in the adjective clause.

EXAMPLE
1. Theo, who is the editor of the school newspaper, wrote an article about the inhumane treatment of laboratory animals.
1. *who is the editor of the school newspaper; Theo; subject*

1. Some of us have read *Native Son*, which was written by Richard Wright. 1. s. 2. o.p.
2. The book to which he referred was ordered yesterday.
3. In March many countries have festivals that can be traced back to ancient celebrations of spring. 3. s. 4. d.o. 5. d.o.
4. The fish that I caught yesterday weighed three pounds.
5. The nominee was a statesman whom everyone admired.
6. It's not easy to understand someone who mumbles. 6. s.
7. They finally found my briefcase, which had been missing for weeks. 7. s. 8. o.p.
8. Please indicate the people to whom we should go for help.
9. The guide advised those who enjoy Native American art to visit the new exhibit of Hopi weaving and pottery. 9. s.
10. Everyone cheered for the player that had the better serve. 10. s.

PICTURE THIS

You've been fascinated by archaeology ever since you saw *Raiders of the Lost Ark.* This summer, you're working as a volunteer on this large excavation in Mexico. After a day of digging in the hot sun, you realize that archaeology isn't nearly as glamorous as it looks in the movies. But you're learning many things, and you've experienced the excitement of finding your first artifact—a large shard of Mayan pottery. After the day's work is done, you head back to your tent and begin writing in your journal. Write a journal entry telling about your first day at the excavation site. Tell how you feel about making your first archaeological find. In your journal entry, use at least five adjective clauses to add descriptive details to your sentences.

Subject: archaeological dig in Mexico
Audience: yourself
Purpose: to record the day's events and to express your feelings about them

GRAMMAR

PICTURE THIS

Before students begin writing, brainstorm with the class to list on the chalkboard sensory details one might experience on an archaeological dig. Remind students that expressive writing includes thoughts and feelings and is written from the first-person point of view.

GRAMMAR

SEGMENT 4 *(pp. 634–636)*

THE NOUN CLAUSE Rule 20e

OBJECTIVE

- To identify and classify noun clauses

Teacher's ResourceBank™

RESOURCES

THE NOUN CLAUSE	
• The Noun Clause	203

QUICK REMINDER

Write the following noun clauses on the chalkboard. Ask students to write sentences using the noun clauses as specified in parentheses.

1. what we plan to do (subject) [What we plan to do will surprise you.]
2. where the money is hidden (predicate nominative) [My bottom drawer is where the money is hidden.]
3. that the bus was late (direct object) [The coach announced that the bus was late.]
4. whoever wins (indirect object) [We will give whoever wins a prize.]
5. whomever I choose (object of a preposition) [I can give a ticket to whomever I choose.]

GRAMMAR

The Noun Clause

20e. A ***noun clause*** is a subordinate clause used as a noun.

A noun clause may be used as a subject, a predicate nominative, a direct object, an indirect object, or an object of a preposition.

Subject	**That Ntozake Shange is a talented writer** is an understatement.
Predicate Nominative	A catchy slogan is **what we need for this campaign.**
Direct Object	The Greek astonomer Ptolemy believed **that the sun orbited the earth.**
Indirect Object	The choreographer will give **whoever can dance the best** the role of Snow Princess.
Object of a Preposition	Grandmother Gutiérrez has a kind word for **whomever she meets.**

Common Introductory Words for Noun Clauses

what	whatever	whichever	whoever	whomever
that	which	who	whom	whose
how	whether	when	where	why

The word that introduces a noun clause may or may not have another function in the clause.

EXAMPLES Do you know **who painted *Washington Crossing the Delaware?*** [The word *who* introduces the noun clause and serves as the subject of the verb *painted.*]
Ms. Picard, an environmentalist, will explain **what the greenhouse effect is.** [The word *what* introduces the noun clause and serves as the predicate nominative to complete the meaning of the verb *is.*]
She said **that she would be late.** [The word *that* introduces the noun clause but does not have any function within the noun clause.]

EXERCISE 3 **Identifying Noun Clauses**

Identify the noun clause in each of the following sentences. Tell whether the noun clause is a *subject*, a *direct object*, an *indirect object*, a *predicate nominative*, or an *object of a preposition*.

REVIEW A

OBJECTIVES

- To identify adjective and noun clauses in sentences
- To identify in sentences the words that adjective clauses modify
- To classify noun clauses according to usage

20e

GRAMMAR

EXAMPLES **1.** Please address your letter to whoever manages the store.

1. *whoever manages the store; object of a preposition*

2. Do you know where the new municipal center is?

2. *where the new municipal center is; direct object*

1. Would you please tell me what the past tense of the verb *swing* is? **1.** d.o.
2. I will listen carefully to whatever you say. **2.** o.p.
3. Whatever you decide will be fine with me. **3.** s.
4. Give whoever wants one a free pass. **4.** i.o.
5. That Jill was worried seemed obvious to us all. **5.** s.
6. Do you know why Eduardo missed the Cinco de Mayo celebration? **6.** d.o.
7. The teacher said that we could leave now. **7.** d.o. **8.** d.o.
8. In biology class we learned how hornets build their nests.
9. You can appoint whomever you like. **9.** d.o.
10. A remote desert island was where the pirates buried their treasure. **10.** p.n.

REVIEW A **Distinguishing Between Adjective and Noun Clauses**

Identify the subordinate clause in each of the following sentences. Tell whether the subordinate clause is used as an *adjective* or a *noun*. Then give the word that each adjective clause modifies, and state whether each noun clause is used as a *subject*, a *direct object*, an *object of a preposition*, or a *predicate nominative*.

EXAMPLE **1.** Until recently, most scientists believed that the giant sequoias of California were the oldest living trees on earth.

1. *that the giant sequoias of California were the oldest living trees on earth—noun; direct object*

1. Now, however, that honor is given to the bristlecone pine, a small, gnarled tree that few people have ever heard of.
2. Botanists estimate that some bristlecone pines are more than six thousand years old. **2.** d.o.
3. The oldest sequoias are only 2,200 years old, according to those who know. **4.** s.
4. Whoever respects hardiness has to respect the bristlecone.
5. The high altitude of the Rocky Mountains, the bristlecone's natural habitat, is what makes the tree grow so slowly. **5.** p.n.

MEETING **INDIVIDUAL** NEEDS

LESS-ADVANCED STUDENTS

That *who, whom,* and *that* introduce both adjective and noun clauses might confuse students. You may want to write the following examples on the chalkboard. Using arrows should help to illustrate that an adjective clause modifies a noun or pronoun in the sentence.

1. Gina, who wore the bizarre mask, won first prize.
2. We didn't know who wore the bizarre mask.

GRAMMAR

CRITICAL THINKING
Analysis

When a noun clause is removed from a complex sentence, the remaining words do not stand alone as an independent clause. However, when either an adjective clause or an adverb clause is removed from a complex sentence, a complete thought remains.

Ask students to think of an explanation for this seeming contradiction. [Adjective and adverb clauses function as adjectives and adverbs in sentences; a modifier can be removed, and the sentence will still convey a complete thought. A clause functioning as a noun, however, is needed to complete the structure of a sentence—as a subject, an object, or a predicate nominative.]

GRAMMAR

SEGMENT 5 *(pp. 636–639)*

THE ADVERB CLAUSE Rules 20f, 20g

OBJECTIVES

- To identify adverb clauses and the words they modify
- To determine whether an adverb clause tells *how, when, where, why, to what extent,* or *under what condition*

Teacher's ResourceBank™

RESOURCES

THE ADVERB CLAUSE

- The Adverb Clause 204

QUICK REMINDER

Write the following sentences on the chalkboard. Ask students to rewrite each sentence and to switch the positions of the adverb clause and the main clause. Remind students to use a comma after an introductory adverb clause.

1. I feverishly practiced my lines until it was my turn to speak.
2. I looked for a place to hide when my name was called.
3. Unless a miracle occurs, I have no way out!

Encourage students to vary sentence beginnings in their own writing by using adverb clauses.

GRAMMAR

6. Do you think that the bristlecone pine will win any beauty contests?
7. Judge by what you can see in this photograph. **6.** d.o. **7.** o.p.

8. The bristlecone's needles last on the branches for twelve to fifteen years, a length of time that is extraordinary.
9. Botanists tell us that the bristlecone is a member of the foxtail family. **9.** d.o.
10. Like all members of this family, the bristlecone has needle clusters that resemble a fox's tail.

The Adverb Clause

20f. An ***adverb clause*** is a subordinate clause that modifies a verb, an adjective, or an adverb.

An adverb clause tells *how, when, where, why, to what extent,* or *under what condition.*

EXAMPLES The pitcher felt **as though all eyes were on her.** [The adverb clause modifies the verb *felt,* telling *how* the pitcher felt.]

Frédéric Chopin made his debut as a concert pianist **when he was eight years old.** [The adverb clause modifies the verb *made,* telling *when* Chopin made his debut.]

Ariel takes his new camera **wherever he goes.** [The adverb clause modifies the verb *takes,* telling *where* Ariel takes his new camera.]

At first, communicating with my deaf friend was difficult **because I did not know how to sign.** [The adverb clause modifies the adjective *difficult,* telling *why* communicating was difficult.]
Zoe can explain the theory of relativity to you better **than I can.** [The adverb clause modifies the adverb **better,** telling *to what extent* Zoe can better explain the theory of relativity.]
If we leave now, we will avoid the rush-hour traffic. [The adverb clause modifies the verb *will avoid,* telling *under what condition* we will avoid the traffic.]

Subordinating Conjunctions

An adverb clause is introduced by a ***subordinating conjunction***—a word or word group that relates the adverb clause to the word or words the clause modifies.

Common Subordinating Conjunctions

after	as though	provided that	until
although	as well as	since	when
as	because	so that	whenever
as if	before	than	where
as long as	if	through	wherever
as soon as	in order that	unless	while

REFERENCE NOTE: The words *after, as, before, since,* and *until* may also be used as prepositions. See pages 571–572.

The Elliptical Clause

20g. Part of a clause may be left out when the meaning can be understood from the context of the sentence. Such a clause is called an ***elliptical clause.***

Most elliptical clauses are adverb clauses. In each of the adverb clauses in the following examples, the part given in brackets may be omitted because its meaning is clearly understood.

EXAMPLES Roger knew the rules better **than Elgin [did].**
While [he was] painting, Rembrandt concentrated completely on his work.

MEETING **INDIVIDUAL** NEEDS

LEP/ESL

General Strategies. Most languages have constructions similar to adverb clauses; however, often the order of the subject and the verb is inverted. You may want to have students use the **Common Subordinating Conjunctions** list to practice saying and writing sentences with adverb clauses. Emphasize the subject-verb pattern that is most common in English by having students identify the subject and the verb of each clause they write.

COMMON ERROR

Problem. Students often misuse commas with adverb clauses.

Solution. Explain that a comma is used if an adverb clause introduces a sentence. A familiarity with subordinating conjunctions will help students locate the position of an adverb clause in a sentence. You could display a chart of the subordinating conjunctions or refer students to the list on this page. Suggest that during the proofreading stage of the writing process, students circle subordinating conjunctions and check the position of the adverb clauses in their sentences.

REVIEW B

OBJECTIVES

- To identify independent and subordinate clauses in sentences
- To classify subordinate clauses according to their function as adverbs, adjectives, or nouns

COOPERATIVE LEARNING

This activity will give students practice in using adverb clauses to subordinate ideas. Divide the class into small groups and have each group write a short skit about two friends discussing an exciting event. One friend tries to tell about the experience, but the other keeps interrupting with adverb questions. (*How? When? Where? Why? To what extent? Under what condition?*) The person answering the questions should answer with some adverb clauses and some complete sentences containing adverb clauses.

Have each group perform its skit for the rest of the class. Encourage the audience to listen for adverb clauses.

GRAMMAR

GRAMMAR

EXERCISE 4 Identifying Adverb Clauses and the Words They Modify

Identify the adverb clause in each of the following sentences, and give the word or words that the clause modifies. Then state whether the clause tells *how, when, where, why, to what extent*, or *under what condition*. [Note: If a clause is elliptical, be prepared to supply the omitted word or words.]

EXAMPLE 1. If we stop by the mall, we might be late for the movie.
1. *If we stop by the mall; might be; under what condition*

1. When our school has a fire drill, everyone must go outside. 1. when
2. Your trip to New York will not be complete unless you see the Alvin Ailey American Dance Theater. 2. condition
3. She walked until she was too tired to take another step. 3. extent
4. Because he was late so often, he bought a watch. 4. why
5. Gazelles need to be able to run fast so that they can escape their enemies. 5. why
6. Return this revolutionary, new sonic potato peeler for a full refund if not completely satisfied. 6. (you are)/condition
7. As soon as you're ready, we'll leave. 7. when
8. You can help by setting the table while I prepare the salad. 8. when
9. I visited the collection of Aztec artifacts because I wanted to see the religious and solar calendars. 9. why
10. You understand the situation much better than I. 10. (do)/extent

REVIEW B Identifying Independent and Subordinate Clauses

In the following paragraph, identify each italicized clause as *independent* or *subordinate*. If the italicized clause is subordinate, tell whether it is used as an *adverb*, an *adjective*, or a *noun*.

EXAMPLE [1] *When thinking of Native Americans,* many people immediately picture the Dakota Sioux.
1. *subordinate—adverb*

1. n. 2. adv. 3. adv.

Do you know [1] *why the Dakota spring to mind?* I think it is [2] *because they are known for their impressive eagle-feather headdresses.* Until recently, [3] *if an artist painted or drew Native Americans of any region,* the people were usually shown wearing

Dakota headdresses, fringed buckskin shirts, and elaborately beaded moccasins. Even paintings of the Pemaquid people receiving the Pilgrims [4] *as they landed on Cape Cod* show the Pemaquid dressed in the style of the Dakota, [5] *who lived far away in the northern plains region.* Artists apparently did not recognize [6] *that there are many different groups of Native Americans*. Each group has its own traditional clothing, and [7] *the variety of Native American dress is truly amazing*. For example, [8] *compare the turbans and bearclaw necklaces of these Fox men with the headband and turquoise jewelry of this Navajo boy*. [9] *While these images may not be familiar to you,* they are just as authentic as the image of the Dakota. To see other colorful and unique styles of dress, you might want to research the clothing worn by Native Americans [10] *that live in different regions of the United States.*

4. adv.
5. adj.
6. n.
9. adv.
10. adj.

GRAMMAR

Charles Milton Bell (1890)/From the Collection of Kurt Koegler

Carl Moon (1905)/From the Collection of Kurt Koegler

A DIFFERENT APPROACH

This activity will help familiarize students with subordinating conjunctions, but it could also be integrated with the study of a piece of literature. Write the subordinating conjunctions from p. 637 on two identical sets of index cards, with one conjunction on each card. Divide the class into two teams and give each team a set of cards. Each team's object is to write on each card at least one sentence about a particular piece of literature or its author. Each sentence must contain an adverb clause introduced by the conjunction on the card. The time limit is ten minutes.

At the end of ten minutes, have each team read its sentences aloud. Award a point for each correct sentence.

GRAMMAR

SEGMENT 6 *(pp. 640–644)*

SENTENCES CLASSIFIED ACCORDING TO STRUCTURE Rule 20h

OBJECTIVE

- To classify sentences as simple, compound, complex, or compound-complex

Teacher's ResourceBank™

RESOURCES

SENTENCES CLASSIFIED ACCORDING TO STRUCTURE

- Classifying Sentences by Structure 205

GRAMMAR

QUICK REMINDER

Have students use the words in parentheses to combine the following sets of sentences. Then ask students to classify the resulting sentences according to structure.

1. Juan read an article about book groups. He started a science fiction club. (after) [After Juan read an article about book groups, he started a science fiction club. complex]
2. The members choose a book. The book appeals to everyone. A local bookstore orders multiple copies. (that; and) [The members choose a book that appeals to everyone, and a local bookstore orders multiple copies. compound-complex]
3. The members prefer science fiction. Sometimes they read mysteries. (but) [The members prefer science fiction, but sometimes they read mysteries. compound]

GRAMMAR

Sentences Classified According to Structure

20h. According to their structure, sentences are classified as *simple, compound, complex,* and *compound-complex.*

(1) A ***simple sentence*** has one independent clause and no subordinate clauses.

EXAMPLES Uncle Alan taught me how to play the mandolin.
The spotted owl is an endangered species.
Covered with dust and cobwebs, the old bicycle looked terrible but worked just fine.

(2) A ***compound sentence*** has two or more independent clauses but no subordinate clauses.

Independent clauses may be joined together by a comma and a coordinating conjunction (*and, but, for, nor, or, so,* or *yet*), by a semicolon, or by a semicolon and a conjunctive adverb or a transitional expression.

EXAMPLES Lorenzo's story sounded incredible, but it was true. [two independent clauses joined by a comma and the coordinating conjunction *but*]

Agatha Christie was a prolific writer; she wrote more than eighty books in less than sixty years. [two independent clauses joined by a semicolon]

The defeat of Napoleon at Waterloo was a victory for England; however, it brought to an end an era of French grandeur. [two independent clauses joined by a semicolon and the conjunctive adverb *however*]

Common Conjunctive Adverbs

also	however	nevertheless
anyway	instead	otherwise
besides	likewise	still
consequently	meanwhile	then
furthermore	moreover	therefore

20h

GRAMMAR

Common Transitional Expressions

as a result	for example	in other words
at any rate	in addition	on the contrary
by the way	in fact	on the other hand

NOTE: Do not confuse a simple sentence that has a compound subject or a compound predicate with a compound sentence.

EXAMPLES The archaeological discovery was made in the fall and was widely acclaimed the following spring. [simple sentence with compound predicate]

The archaeological discovery was made in the fall, and it was widely acclaimed the following spring. [compound sentence]

(3) A ***complex sentence*** has one independent clause and at least one subordinate clause.

EXAMPLES Thurgood Marshall, who served on the United States Supreme Court for twenty-four years, retired in 1991. [The independent clause is *Thurgood Marshall retired in 1991.* The subordinate clause is *who served on the United States Supreme Court for twenty-four years.*]

While we were on our vacation in Washington, D.C., we visited the Folger Shakespeare Library. [The independent clause is *we visited the Folger Shakespeare Library.* The subordinate clause is *While we were on vacation in Washington, D.C.*]

(4) A ***compound-complex sentence*** has two or more independent clauses and at least one subordinate clause.

EXAMPLES The two eyewitnesses told the police officer what they saw, but their accounts of the accident were quite different. [The two independent clauses are *The two eyewitnesses told the police officer* and *their accounts of the accident were quite different.* The subordinate clause is *what they saw.*]

Chelsea is only seven years old, but she can already play the violin better than her tutor can. [The two independent clauses are *Chelsea is only seven years old* and *she can already play the violin better.* The subordinate clause is *than her tutor can.*]

MEETING INDIVIDUAL NEEDS

LEP/ESL

General Strategies. In some languages, such as Spanish, clauses do not always require subjects. You might remind students that a clause in English contains both a subject and a verb. As practice, have students locate the subject/verb combinations in the example sentences on pp. 640–641.

GRAMMAR

INTEGRATING THE LANGUAGE ARTS

Literature Link. Show students the effect of sentence structure on style by having them compare passages from the works of both Ernest Hemingway and F. Scott Fitzgerald. If the stories are in your literature textbook, you may want to use Hemingway's "In Another Country" and Fitzgerald's "Winter Dreams." Ask students to comment on how each writer's use of sentence structure contributes to his style. [Hemingway's repetitive, rhythmic use of simple and compound sentences produces a matter-of-fact, plain style. Fitzgerald characteristically uses complex sentence structures and lyrical, evocative words and phrases, which together create a poetic style.]

WRITING APPLICATION

OBJECTIVE

- To use a variety of sentence structures in writing an entry for a guidebook

INTEGRATING THE LANGUAGE ARTS

Grammar and Listening. Read aloud several paragraphs from an interesting article or story. As you read, have students tally the number of sentences they hear. The more familiar students are with the various sentence structures, the easier it will be for them to identify sentence completeness. You may want to provide students with copies of the paragraphs so that they can visually check their tallies.

WRITING APPLICATION

The writing assignment gives students practice in varying sentence structure. You may want to encourage students to concentrate first on including all necessary information in their descriptions. Then they can focus on varying the structure of their sentences.

GRAMMAR

GRAMMAR

EXERCISE 5 Classifying Sentences According to Structure

Classify each of the following sentences as *simple*, *compound*, *complex*, or *compound-complex*.

EXAMPLE **1. Using the pith of the papyrus plant, ancient Egyptians made the first paper.**
1. *simple*

1. Charles Drew did research on blood plasma and helped develop blood banks. **1.** simp.
2. Supposedly, if the month of March comes in like a lion, it goes out like a lamb. **2.** cx.
3. The Malayans believe that sickness will follow the eating of stolen foods. **3.** cx.
4. When World War I ended in 1918, many people thought that there would be no more wars; but twenty-one years later, World War II began. **4.** cd.-cx.
5. In his letter to Mrs. Bixby, Abraham Lincoln consoled her for the loss of several sons and hoped that time would ease her sorrow. **5.** cx.
6. After the announcement of the final score, all of us fans cheered the team and clapped enthusiastically. **6.** simp.
7. In England and Wales, salmon was once king, yet few salmon rivers remain. **7.** cd. **8.** cd.
8. The English philosopher Thomas Hobbes once aspired to be a mathematician, but he never fulfilled this ambition.
9. As an older woman, Queen Elizabeth I always wore a dark-red wig, so no one knew whether her own hair had grayed or not. **9.** cd.-cx. **10.** simp.
10. Professional tennis star Zina Garrison devotes time to training and encouraging young inner-city tennis players.

WRITING APPLICATION

Using a Variety of Sentence Structures

Style and sense go hand in hand in writing. You may have the most interesting topic in the world, but if your writing style isn't smooth and appealing, you may not hold your reader's interest. One of the best ways to improve your style is to vary the length and structure of your sentences.

As you read the following passage, notice how the writer has used a variety of sentence structures to create an engaging style.

> It was a popular exhibit, and sometimes, when there were too many children about, the entrance had to be roped off, as the children loved to race up and down the blood vessels and match their cries to the heart's beating. I could see that the heart had already been punished for the day—the floor of the blood vessel was worn and dusty, the chamber walls were covered with marks, and the notice "You Are Now Taking the Path of a Blood Cell Through the Human Heart" hung askew. I wanted to see more of the Franklin Institute and the Natural Science Museum across the street, but a journey through the human heart would be fascinating. Did I have time?
>
> Janet Frame, "You Are Now Entering the Human Heart"

GRAMMAR

WRITING ACTIVITY

The student council has asked your class to write a guidebook, describing popular attractions in your area. The purpose of the guidebook is to inform new students and their families about the area. Write an entry for the guidebook, telling about a local attraction that people might enjoy visiting. Use a variety of sentence structures to add variety and interest to your writing.

Prewriting If you were a newcomer to your area, what exhibits, landmarks, historical sites, and other attractions would you find interesting? Brainstorm a list of points of interest in your city or area. Then choose one attraction that you are familiar with. If possible, visit the attraction and take notes for your description. Be sure to note down specific details, such as when the place is open to the public, how much admission is, and why it's worth a visit.

Writing Begin your guidebook entry by identifying the name, location, and significance of the attraction. Then capture your reader's interest with a clear, vivid description

CRITICAL THINKING

Analysis

Depending on their familiarity with local points of interest, students might create extensive lists in the prewriting stage. Limiting a broad subject to find a narrow topic requires analysis. Remind students that they must keep their audience and purpose in mind when narrowing their topic.

GRAMMAR

SELECTION AMENDMENT

Description of change: excerpted

Rationale: to focus on the concept of sentence variety presented in this chapter

SEGMENT 7 *(pp. 644–646)*

REVIEW: POSTTESTS 1 and 2

OBJECTIVES

- To identify independent and subordinate clauses in sentences
- To classify subordinate clauses according to usage
- To classify sentences according to structure
- To write sentences with a variety of structures

INTEGRATING THE LANGUAGE ARTS

Technology Link. Encourage students with expertise in graphic design to create maps, illustrations, and other graphic aids for the class guidebook.

GRAMMAR

of the place. Since your paragraph will appear in a guidebook, be sure to use formal English. (For more about formal English, see pages 484–485.)

Evaluating and Revising Ask a friend to read your paragraph. Does your description give a clear, accurate picture of the attraction? Does it convince your reader that the attraction is worth visiting? Does it give exact information about how to get there and when to go? If not, add, cut, and rearrange details to include all important information. After you've revised the content of your paragraph, read it with an eye for style. Use sentence-combining techniques to vary the structure of your sentences. (For more about sentence combining, see pages 526–538.

Proofreading and Publishing Proofread your paragraph for any errors in grammar, usage, or mechanics. Watch out for subordinate clauses punctuated as if they were complete sentences. (For more about sentence fragments, see pages 515–519.) Your class may want to compile a guidebook for your area. Double-check all the information included in your paragraphs. Then type the paragraphs neatly and collect them in a binder. Place your guidebook in a central location in your school so that anyone can read it, or make photocopies to give to new students.

Review: Posttest 1

A. Identifying Independent and Subordinate Clauses

Identify the italicized clause in each of the following sentences as <u>*independent*</u> or <u>*subordinate*</u>. If the italicized clause is subordinate, tell whether it is used as an <u>*adverb*</u>, an <u>*adjective*</u>, or a <u>*noun*</u>.

EXAMPLE **1.** Miguel and Bette, *who were visiting us over the weekend,* have returned to Rhode Island.
1. *subordinate; adjective*

1. *Whenever Jorge practices the clarinet*, his neighbor's beagle howls. 1. adv.
2. Advertisements encourage people to want products, and *many people cannot distinguish between their wants and their needs*.
3. In science class we learned *that chalk is made up mostly of calcium carbonate*. 3. n.
4. Liliuokalani, *who was the last queen of Hawaii*, was an accomplished songwriter. 4. adj.
5. Does each of you know *how you can protect yourself* if a tornado strikes? 5. n.
6. *If there is a tornado warning*, go quickly to the lowest level in your house, cover your head with your hands, and lie flat or crouch low until the danger is past. 6. adv.
7. The Native Americans *who inhabited the area of Connecticut around the Naugatuck River* were called the Pequots. 7. adj.
8. *When you enter the school*, the principal's office is the third room on your right. 8. adv.
9. *That the girls' volleyball team was well coached* was clearly demonstrated last night when the team won the state championship. 9. n.
10. *American music has been enriched by Ella Fitzgerald, Leslie Uggams, and Lena Horne*, who are all contemporary black vocalists.

GRAMMAR

B. Classifying Sentences According to Structure

Classify each sentence in the following paragraph as *simple*, *compound*, *complex*, or *compound-complex*.

[11] Just who is Phoebe Jeter from Sharon, South Carolina? **[12]** Phoebe Jeter, officially known as Lieutenant Jeter, led an army platoon during the Persian Gulf Conflict in 1991. **[13]** Jeter will always remember the tense January night when she heard the words "Scud alert!" **[14]** On her orders, thirteen Patriot missiles were fired, and at least two Scud missiles were destroyed. **[15]** When the Conflict was over, Jeter was the only woman who had shot down a Scud! **[16]** That 40 percent of the women who served in the Gulf were African Americans may be an understatement. **[17]** Figures have not been released by the Pentagon, but some say the actual number may have been closer to 50 percent. **[18]** The Persian Gulf Conflict tested the mettle of all

11. simp.
12. simp.
13. cx.
14. cd.
15. cx.
16. cx.
17. cd.-cx.
18. cd.

GRAMMAR

MEETING INDIVIDUAL NEEDS

STUDENTS WITH SPECIAL NEEDS

Because of the format of **Review: Posttest 1 Part B,** students with learning disabilities might easily lose their places. You could adapt the activity by providing index cards or rulers for students to use as horizontal guides. The guides will help students concentrate on one line at a time.

GRAMMAR

ANSWERS

Review: Posttest 2

Sentences will vary. Here are some possibilities:

1. Celise and Maria reported on James Weldon Johnson, a poet of the Harlem Renaissance.
2. Our class had read some of Johnson's poetry, but we knew little about his life.
3. Celise or Maria can explain the poet's background better than I can.
4. I found James Weldon Johnson so fascinating that I want to read his autobiography, *Along This Way*.
5. Johnson, who was an exponent of civil rights, sought recognition for the contributions of African Americans to culture in the United States.
6. "Fifty Years" and "O Black and Unknown Bards" are two poems that were written by James Weldon Johnson.
7. What prompted him to write his autobiography makes an interesting story.
8. Many of his readers had thought that the fictional *The Autobiography of an Ex-Colored Man* was true.
9. Celise has read more of Johnson's poems than I.
10. After I heard Celise's report, I wanted to learn about other poets of the Harlem Renaissance, and I will start with Countee Cullen.

GRAMMAR

female military personnel; throughout the conflict, women shared hazardous assignments, primitive living conditions, and various battle responsibilities with men. **[19]** Their professionalism and courage earned the women who served in the Gulf considerable respect. **[20]** Perhaps now, because of soldiers like Phoebe Jeter, people will think differently about the role of women in the United States armed forces. **19.** cx. **20.** simp.

Review: Posttest 2

Writing a Variety of Sentence Structures

Write ten sentences according to the following guidelines:

1. a simple sentence with a compound subject
2. a compound sentence with the conjunction *but*
3. a complex sentence with an adverb clause modifying an adverb
4. a complex sentence with an adverb clause modifying an adjective
5. a complex sentence with an adjective clause introduced by the relative pronoun *who*
6. a complex sentence with an adjective clause introduced by the relative pronoun *that*
7. a complex sentence with a noun clause used as the subject of the sentence
8. a complex sentence with a noun clause used as the direct object of the sentence
9. a complex sentence with an elliptical adverb clause
10. a compound-complex sentence

SEGMENT 1 *(pp. 647–648)*

DIAGNOSTIC TEST

OBJECTIVE

- To choose correct forms for subject-verb and pronoun-antecedent agreement

Teacher's ResourceBank™

RESOURCES

FOR THE WHOLE CHAPTER

- Chapter Review Form A 236–237
- Chapter Review Form B 238–239
- Assessment Portfolio
  - Usage Pretests 571–578
  - Usage Mastery Tests 597–604

21 AGREEMENT

Subject and Verb, Pronoun and Antecedent

USAGE

Diagnostic Test

A. Choosing Correct Forms for Subject-Verb and Pronoun-Antecedent Agreement

For each of the following sentences, choose the word in parentheses that completes the sentence correctly.

EXAMPLE 1. Both Arapaho and Cheyenne (*is, are*) part of the Algonquian language group of Native Americans.
1. *are*

1. When I begin cutting out this skirt pattern, I know I'll discover that my scissors (*need, needs*) sharpening.
2. British sailors are frequently called "limeys" because the British navy (*was, were*) responsible for supplying them with limes to prevent scurvy during long sea voyages.
3. Either Dad or my brother (*go, goes*) down to the store to buy a newspaper each morning.
4. In the San Ildefonso Village, two days (*is, are*) not considered a long time to spend polishing one piece of black pottery.

CHAPTER OVERVIEW

This chapter deals with agreement of subjects and verbs and of pronouns and antecedents. After a brief review of number, the textbook takes up the idea of subject-verb agreement and addresses situations involving intervening phrases and clauses, indefinite pronouns, compound subjects, and a number of special problems in subject-verb agreement. The last part of the chapter is concerned with agreement of pronouns and antecedents. The **Writing Application** focuses on using pronoun-antecedent agreement for clear meaning.

Students can use the rules and examples to solve specific problems they encounter when proofreading their writing. You can also use the chapter for introducing the concepts to nonnative speakers of English and for general review for the whole class.

USAGE

USING THE DIAGNOSTIC TEST

If you notice that some students are having problems with agreement in their compositions, you can use the **Diagnostic Test** to pinpoint error patterns as well as specific strengths and weaknesses. Assessing students' responses will help you to determine which rules of agreement they need to review.

USAGE

5. A small number of adults (*is, are*) coming along on our trip to Washington, D.C.
6. When Suzanne and Anita arrive, would you please help (*her, them*) find some good seats?
7. (*Here's, Here are*) those extra two tickets for tonight's rap concert at the arena.
8. Exactly one third of the students in my American history class (*is, are*) African American.
9. In-line skates (*is, are*) the fastest way of getting to my best friend's house.
10. *The Borrowers*, a fantasy story about some tiny people, (*was, were*) my favorite book when I was ten years old.

B. Choosing Correct Forms for Subject-Verb and Pronoun-Antecedent Agreement

For each sentence in the following paragraph, choose the word in parentheses that will complete the sentence correctly.

EXAMPLE **Kenny Walker is the only player in the NFL who [1] (*has, have*) a hearing impairment.**
1. *has*

The Denver Broncos, my favorite team, **[11]** (*was, were*) smart to choose Walker in the 1990 football draft. Walker certainly **[12]** (*don't, doesn't*) let his deafness keep him from being a great linebacker. Passed over by many a coach because **[13]** (*he, they*) thought a player who was deaf would be a problem, Walker was finally picked 228th by Denver. Even today, not everyone **[14]** (*know, knows*) that spinal meningitis cost Kenny Walker his hearing when he was two years old. Sign language and lip reading **[15]** (*was, were*) taught to him at a special school, beginning when he was four. Because of his hearing impairment, most of the neighborhood boys **[16]** (*was, were*) unwilling to choose Walker to be on a team. But after they saw him play, everyone wanted him on **[17]** (*their, his*) team! Now that Walker is a professional football player, neither he nor his coaches **[18]** (*has, have*) much difficulty with his deafness. One of the accommodations the Broncos made **[19]** (*was, were*) to hire a full-time interpreter to sign plays to Walker. Although he can't hear a sound, Walker feels the vibrations in his shoulder pads when the crowd **[20]** (*cheers, cheer*) him.

SEGMENT 2 *(pp. 649–655)*

AGREEMENT OF SUBJECT AND VERB

Rules 21a–21i

OBJECTIVES

- To identify in sentences subjects and verbs that agree in number
- To correct errors in subject-verb agreement

Number

Number is the form of a word that indicates whether the word is singular or plural.

21a. A word that refers to one person or thing is ***singular*** in number. A word that refers to more than one is ***plural*** in number.

SINGULAR	computer	brush	story	woman	this	it
PLURAL	computers	brushes	stories	women	these	they

Agreement of Subject and Verb

21b. A verb should agree with its subject in number.

(1) Singular subjects take singular verbs.

EXAMPLES My **grandfather trains** dogs.
The **senator is** in favor of the bill.
She owns and **operates** a video store.

(2) Plural subjects take plural verbs.

EXAMPLES My **grandparents train** dogs.
Many **senators are** in favor of the bill.
They own and **operate** a video store.

Like the one-word verb in each of the preceding examples, a verb phrase must also agree in number with its subject. The number of a verb phrase is indicated by the form of its first auxiliary (helping) verb.

EXAMPLES This **song was performed** by Bonnie Raitt. [singular subject and verb phrase]
These **songs were performed** by Bonnie Raitt. [plural subject and verb phrase]

The dancer **has been rehearsing** since noon. [singular subject and verb phrase]
The dancers **have been rehearsing** since noon. [plural subject and verb phrase]

Teacher's ResourceBank™

RESOURCES

AGREEMENT OF SUBJECT AND VERB

QUICK REMINDER

Write these two nonsense sentences on the chalkboard (correct "verbs" are underscored.):

1. The shink (*grimp, grimps*) the vork.
2. The shinks (*grimp, grimps*) the vork.

Ask students to select the correct "verbs." Then ask how they were able to make the correct choices. [Answers will vary, but the basic idea is that students recognized the subject-verb-object pattern of the sentences and knew how to make the verbs agree in number with the subjects.] Point out that not all sentences are as obvious as these, but the same rule applies in all sentences.

MEETING INDIVIDUAL NEEDS

LEP/ESL

General Strategies. Some students may be confused by the meaning of the word *agreement.* They might expect this to mean that when the subject ends in –*s,* the verb must also end in –*s.* Emphasize that *agreement* means that a singular subject requires a singular verb, often one ending in –*s.* It may be helpful to point out that *singular* starts with *s*– and singular verbs with a third-person subject usually end in –*s.*

MEETING INDIVIDUAL NEEDS

LEP/ESL

General Strategies. To demonstrate how subject-verb agreement is determined in English, write the following sentences on the chalkboard:

1. Maria dances.
2. Susan and Juan dance.
3. They dance.
4. You dance.
5. I dance.

You may want to reinforce ESL students' understanding of singular and plural verb endings by having them write sentences in their native languages. Have them compare verb endings in their native languages with the English verb endings. Their native languages may have more or fewer possible endings for present tense verbs. (Spanish, for instance, has a different ending for each of the verbs in the five example sentences.)

USAGE

Intervening Phrases and Clauses

21c. The number of the subject is not changed by a phrase or a clause following the subject.

EXAMPLES This **tape is** by the Boston Pops Orchestra.
This **tape** of songs **is** by the Boston Pops Orchestra. [The prepositional phrase *of songs* does not affect the number of the subject *tape.*]

The **characters represent** abstract ideas.
The **characters** in an allegory **represent** abstract ideas. [The prepositional phrase *in an allegory* does not affect the number of the subject *characters.*]

Langston Hughes was a major influence in the Harlem Renaissance.
Langston Hughes, who wrote *The Weary Blues* and other books of poems, **was** a major influence in the Harlem Renaissance. [The adjective clause *who wrote The Weary Blues and other books of poems* does not affect the number of the subject *Langston Hughes.*]

The number of the subject is also not affected when the subject is followed by a phrase that begins with an expression such as *along with, as well as, in addition to,* and *together with.*

EXAMPLES The history **teacher,** as well as her students, **was fascinated** by the exhibit of artifacts at the DuSable Museum of African American History. [singular subject and verb]
The history **students,** as well as their teacher, **were fascinated** by the exhibit of artifacts at the DuSable Museum of African American History. [plural subject and verb]

USAGE

EXERCISE 1 Identifying Subjects and Verbs That Agree in Number

For each of the following sentences, identify the subject of the verb in parentheses. Then choose the verb form that agrees in number with the subject.

EXAMPLE 1. The many varieties of American quilts (*reflect, reflects*) the spirit of the people who developed them.
1. *varieties—reflect*

1. During the Colonial Period, only women of means made quilts; however, by the mid-nineteenth century, women throughout the United States (*was making, were making*) quilts.
2. The abilities that someone needs to make a quilt (*include, includes*) patience, coordination, and a good sense of color and design.
3. A scrap-bag full of colorful bits of cotton and wool fabrics (*was put, were put*) to good use in a quilt.
4. Usable fabric from worn-out shirts, as well as from other articles of clothing, (*was cut, were cut*) into pieces of various shapes and sizes.
5. The Amish people, known for their beautiful quilting, (*live, lives*) very simply.
6. Amish quilts, which are often brightly colored, (*seem, seems*) to convey the joyous spirits of their makers.
7. Several quilters, gathering at one person's home for a quilting bee, often (*work, works*) on a quilt together.
8. Quilts designed by the Amish usually (*include, includes*) only solid-color fabrics, not patterned ones.
9. This quilt, which features colors typical to Amish quilts, (*glow, glows*) with red, purple, blue, pink, and green.
10. In contrast, the clothing worn by Amish women (*is, are*) more subdued in color.

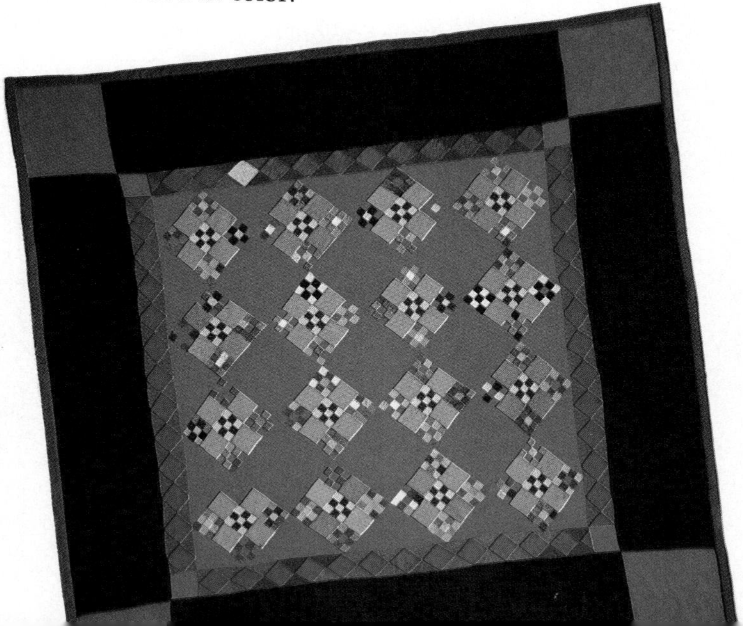

Double Ninepatch © 1930 made by Dorothy Bieler, Lancaster Co., PA/Courtesy Esprit Quilt Collection, San Francisco.

USAGE

COMMON ERROR

Problem. The list of singular indefinite pronouns given in **Rule 21d** might be difficult for students to remember.

Solution. You can simplify the rule by emphasizing that all indefinite pronouns that are compound words are singular and require singular verbs.

USAGE

MEETING INDIVIDUAL NEEDS

LEARNING STYLES

Auditory Learners. Have students practice saying these additional examples to use with **Rule 21f:** Is any of the watermelon gone? Are any of the watermelons gone? Most of the watermelons are gone. None of the watermelon is gone. None of the watermelons are gone.

Indefinite Pronouns

21d. The following indefinite pronouns are singular: *one, anybody, anyone, each, either, everybody, everyone, neither, nobody, no one, somebody,* and *someone.*

EXAMPLES **Neither** of the books **contains** any illustrations.
Everyone in the Pep Club **is wearing** the school colors.
One of the most beautiful places in North Carolina **is** the Joyce Kilmer Memorial Forest.

21e. The following indefinite pronouns are plural: *both, few, many,* and *several.*

EXAMPLES **Both** of the poems **were written** by Claude McKay.
Many of our words **are derived** from Latin.
Several of the juniors **have volunteered.**

21f. The following indefinite pronouns may be singular or plural: *all, any, most, none,* and *some.*

These pronouns are singular when they refer to singular words and are plural when they refer to plural words.

EXAMPLES **Some** of her artwork **is** beautiful. [*Some* refers to the singular noun *artwork.*]
Some of her paintings **are** beautiful. [*Some* refers to the plural noun *paintings.*]

None of the equipment **was damaged.** [*None* refers to the singular noun *equipment.*]
None of the machines **were damaged.** [*None* refers to the plural noun *machines.*]

Most of the food **has been eaten.** [*Most* refers to the singular noun *food.*]
Most of the sandwiches **have been eaten.** [*Most* refers to the plural noun *sandwiches.*]

NOTE: The word *none* is singular when it means "not one" and plural when it means "not any."

EXAMPLES **None** of the hats **fits.** [*Not one* fits.]
None of the hats **fit.** [*Not any* fit.]

USAGE

21 d–g

EXERCISE 2 **Identifying Subjects and Verbs That Agree in Number**

For each of the following sentences, identify the subject of the verb in parentheses. Then choose the verb form that agrees in number with the subject.

EXAMPLE **1. Not one of the pears (*look, looks*) ripe.**
1. *one—looks*

1. Many of the recipes in this cookbook (*is, are*) adaptable to microwave cooking.
2. Neither of my parents (*has, have*) any trouble using the metric system.
3. I know that all the workers (*is, are*) proud to help restore the Statue of Liberty.
4. Most of the English classes in my school (*stresses, stress*) composition skills.
5. Few of the students (*was, were*) able to spell *bureaucracy* correctly.
6. (*Do, Does*) each of you know what you're supposed to bring tomorrow?
7. None of the written language from the Inca civilization (*remain, remains*), but scholars have learned about these people through oral communication.
8. Some of the word-processing software for our computer (*has, have*) arrived late.
9. Both of the paintings (*shows, show*) the influence of the work of Emilio Sánchez.
10. Others besides you and me (*advocates, advocate*) a town cleanup day.

USAGE

Compound Subjects

A ***compound subject*** is two or more subjects that have the same verb.

21g. Subjects joined by *and* usually take a plural verb.

EXAMPLES **Basil** and **thyme are** plants of the mint family.
Following Julius Caesar's death, **Antony, Octavian,** and **Lepidus become** the rulers of Rome.

MEETING INDIVIDUAL NEEDS

LEARNING STYLES

Visual Learners. You may want to have students write the sentences in **Exercise 2** and highlight the indefinite pronoun and the verb in each sentence. You could model the process on the chalkboard by using colored chalk to underscore subjects and verbs in sample sentences.

USAGE

MEETING **INDIVIDUAL** NEEDS

LEP/ESL

General Strategies. Certain agreement rules for compound subjects depend on an understanding of the constructions *either . . . or* and *neither . . . nor.* Students often have trouble with the meanings of these constructions. You can help by substituting more familiar forms. For example, *Neither Daytona Beach nor Panama City Beach* could be paraphrased as *Not Daytona Beach and not Panama City Beach. Either Mrs. Gomez or Mr. Tompkins* could be rewritten as *Mrs. Gomez or Mr. Thompkins.* Point out that *neither* and *either* add emphasis.

USAGE

A compound subject may name a single person or thing. Such a compound subject takes a singular verb.

EXAMPLES **The secretary** and **treasurer is** Gretchen. [one person]
Grilled chicken and **rice is** the restaurant's specialty. [one dish]

21h. Singular subjects joined by *or* or *nor* take a singular verb.

EXAMPLES **Neither Juan nor Jeff wants** to see the movie.
Either Felita or Terry plans to report on Lao Tzu.
Has your **mother or** your **father met** your teacher?

21i. When a singular subject and a plural subject are joined by *or* or *nor,* the verb agrees with the subject nearer the verb.

EXAMPLES Neither the **performers** nor the **director was** eager to rehearse the scene again. [The singular subject *director* is nearer the verb.]
Neither the **director** nor the **performers were** eager to rehearse the scene again. [The plural subject *performers* is nearer the verb.]

NOTE: Whenever possible, avoid this awkward construction.

EXAMPLE The **director was** not eager to rehearse the scene again, and neither **were** the **performers.**

USAGE

EXERCISE 3 **Correcting Errors in Subject-Verb Agreement**

Most of the following sentences contain verbs that do not agree with their subjects. If the verb does not agree, give the correct form of the verb. If the verb agrees with its subject, write *C.*

EXAMPLE **1.** Each of the issues were resolved.
1. *was*

1. Emily Dickinson's imagery and verse structure have been analyzed and praised by many critics. 1. C
2. One or both of the Shakespearean plays about Henry IV are likely to be performed this summer. 2. C
3. The effective date of the new regulations for nuclear power plants ~~have~~ not yet been determined. 3. has

SEGMENT 3 *(pp. 655–664)*

SPECIAL PROBLEMS IN SUBJECT-VERB AGREEMENT Rules 21j–21s

OBJECTIVES

- To select verbs that agree with their subjects in sentences
- To read sentences aloud and stress subject-verb agreement
- To write an informative speech

4. Each of the region's environmental groups ~~have~~ already presented its recommendations to the governor. 4. has
5. My hero, Spike Lee, has made a great contribution to the film industry. 5. C
6. The fact that compact discs do not wear out and do not have to be flipped over ~~make~~ them attractive. 6. makes
7. The sales representative, with the help of her assistant, ~~are~~ making plans to expand her territory. 7. is
8. Not one of the speakers in the debate on South America ~~were~~ eager to suggest a solution to the problem. 8. was
9. Neither the proposals of the air traffic controllers nor the report of the FAA's committee ~~have~~ been heeded. 9. has
10. James Baldwin, along with Richard Wright and Ralph Ellison, ~~rank~~ as one of the major African American writers of the twentieth century. 10. ranks

USAGE

Special Problems in Subject-Verb Agreement

21j. The verb agrees with its subject, even when the verb precedes the subject.

The verb usually comes before its subject in sentences beginning with *Here* or *There* and in questions.

EXAMPLES Here **is** a **copy** of my report.
Here **are** two **copies** of my report.

There **was** a **message** on her answering machine.
There **were** no **messages** on her answering machine.

Where **is Arsenio**?
Where **are Arsenio** and his **brother**?

NOTE: Contractions such as *here's, there's,* and *where's* contain the verb *is* (*here is, there is,* and *where is*). Use these contractions only with subjects that are singular in meaning.

NONSTANDARD	Here's your keys.
STANDARD	Here **are** your **keys**.
STANDARD	Here**'s** your **set** of keys.
NONSTANDARD	Where's the islands located?
STANDARD	Where **are** the **islands** located?
STANDARD	Where**'s each** of the islands located?

Teacher's ResourceBank™

RESOURCES

AGREEMENT OF SUBJECT AND VERB

QUICK REMINDER

Write the following sentences on the chalkboard and ask students to correct errors in subject-verb agreement:

1. Here's my pants. [Here are]
2. The band are playing Saturday afternoon. [is]
3. Fifty dollars are a lot to pay for one record album. [is]
4. "Roses" are my favorite poem. [is]
5. The National Council of Teachers of English meet every November. [meets]

USAGE

MEETING INDIVIDUAL NEEDS

LESS-ADVANCED STUDENTS

In sentences that follow a verb-subject pattern, students can learn to identify the subject by inverting the order of the subject and verb and substituting the word *someplace* for the words *here, there,* or *where.* For example, "Where is my seat?" becomes "My seat is someplace."

MEETING INDIVIDUAL NEEDS

LEP/ESL

General Strategies. In British English, which is taught in many African and Asian countries, the rules governing agreement between collective-noun subjects and their verbs differ from the rules of American English. In British English, the plural verb is used more frequently than in American English, as in "The government have decided to. . . ." If you have students who were taught British English, you could provide additional examples of sentences containing collective nouns from the list on this page.

USAGE

USAGE

21k. Collective nouns may be either singular or plural.

A ***collective noun*** is singular in form but names a group of persons or things.

Common Collective Nouns

army	club	family	squadron
assembly	crowd	group	swarm
audience	fleet	herd	team
class	flock	public	troop

A collective noun takes a singular verb when the noun refers to the group as a unit and takes a plural verb when the noun refers to the parts or members of the group.

SINGULAR The **band practices** every day. [The band practices as a unit.]
PLURAL The **band buy** their own uniforms. [The members of the band buy separate uniforms.]

SINGULAR The tour **group is** on the bus. [The group as a unit is on the bus.]
PLURAL The tour **group are talking** about what they expect to see. [The members of the group are talking to one another.]

SINGULAR A **flock** of geese **is** flying over. [The flock is flying as a unit.]
PLURAL The **flock** of geese **are** joining together in a V-shaped formation. [The members of the flock are joining together.]

21l. An expression of an amount may be singular or plural.

An expression of an amount is singular when the amount is thought of as a unit and is plural when the amount is thought of as many parts.

EXAMPLES **Five thousand bricks is** a heavy load for this truck. [The bricks are thought of as a unit.]
Five thousand bricks are what we need. [The bricks are thought of separately.]

Two days is the amount of time we will spend visiting each college campus. [one unit]
Two **days** of this month **are** school holidays. [separate days]

A fraction or a percentage is singular when it refers to a singular word and is plural when it refers to a plural word.

EXAMPLES **One fourth** of the student body **is employed** part-time after school. [The fraction refers to the singular noun *student body.*]
One fourth of the students **are employed** after school. [The fraction refers to the plural noun *students.*]

Seventy-five percent of the junior class **is** sixteen years old. [The percentage refers to the singular noun *class.*]
Seventy-five percent of the juniors **are** sixteen years old. [The percentage refers to the plural noun *juniors.*]

Expressions of measurement (length, weight, capacity, area) are usually singular.

EXAMPLES **Four and seven-tenths inches is** the diameter of a CD.
Eight fluid ounces equals one cup.
Two hundred kilometers was the distance we flew in the hot-air balloon.

NOTE: In the expression *number of,* the word *number* is singular when preceded by *the* and is plural when preceded by *a.*

EXAMPLES The **number** of students taking computer courses **has increased.**
A **number** of students taking computer courses **belong** to the Computer Club.

EXERCISE 4 Selecting Verbs That Agree with Their Subjects

For each of the following sentences, identify the subject of each verb in parentheses. Then choose the verb form that agrees in number with the subject.

EXAMPLE 1. The band (*is, are*) tuning their instruments.
1. *band—are*

1. The gigantic Colossus of Rhodes (*was, were*) one of the Seven Wonders of the Ancient World.
2. The stage crew (*is, are*) working together to make a rapid scene change for Rita Moreno's entrance.

USAGE

3. Where (*is, are*) the other flight of stairs that go up to the roof?
4. On display in the entrance to the library, there (*is, are*) several oil paintings of famous local people.
5. The Hispanic population (*is, are*) one of the two fastest growing ethnic groups in the United States.
6. On our block alone, over two hundred dollars (*was, were*) collected for the American Cancer Society.
7. Of the world's petroleum, approximately one third (*was, were*) produced by the United States at that time.
8. Red beans and rice (*is, are*) often served as a side dish at Cajun meals.
9. Either brisk walks or jogging (*serves, serve*) as a healthful way to get daily exercise.
10. A number of the seeds (*has, have*) failed to sprout.

USAGE

21m. The title of a creative work (such as a book, song, film, or painting) or the name of a country (even if it is plural in form) takes a singular verb.

EXAMPLES ***Those Who Ride the Night Winds* was written** by the poet Nikki Giovanni.
"Tales from the Vienna Woods" is only one of Johann Strauss's most popular waltzes.
The **United States calls** its flag "Old Glory."
The **Philippines comprises** more than 7,000 islands.

21n. The name of an organization, though plural in form, usually takes a singular verb.

EXAMPLES The **United Nations was formed** in 1945.
Avalon Textiles is located on King Street.

The names of some organizations, however, may take singular or plural verbs. When the name refers to the organization as a unit, it takes a singular verb. When the name refers to the members of the organization, it takes a plural verb.

EXAMPLES The **New York Yankees has won** the World Series twenty-two times. [The New York Yankees has won as a unit.]
The **New York Yankees are signing** autographs. [The players are signing autographs.]

21o. Many nouns that are plural in form are singular in meaning.

(1) The following nouns always take singular verbs.

civics	genetics	mumps
economics	mathematics	news
electronics	measles	physics

EXAMPLES **Measles is** a contagious disease.
The **news was** disappointing.

(2) The following nouns always take plural verbs.

binoculars	pliers	shears
eyeglasses	scissors	trousers

EXAMPLES The **scissors are** in the sewing basket.
The first modern **Olympics were held** in Athens.

NOTE: Many nouns ending in *–ics,* such as *acoustics, athletics, ethics, politics, statistics,* and *tactics,* may be singular or plural.

EXAMPLES **Statistics is** a collection of mathematical data.
The **statistics are** misleading.

If you do not know whether a noun that is plural in form is singular or plural in meaning, look in a dictionary.

21p. A verb agrees with its subject, not with its predicate nominative.

EXAMPLES Sore **muscles are** one symptom of flu.
One **symptom** of flu **is** sore muscles.

Perhaps the greatest **contribution** of ancient African scholars **was** many of the concepts used in higher mathematics.
Many of the concepts used in higher mathematics **were** perhaps the greatest contribution of ancient African scholars.

21q. Subjects preceded by *every* or *many a* take singular verbs.

EXAMPLES **Every sophomore** and **junior is participating.**
Many a person supports the cause.

USAGE

CRITICAL THINKING
Analysis

To determine whether a word ending in *–ics* is singular or plural, students can apply a simple test. A word that ends in *–ics* is singular if it means the science or the study of something. For example, *acoustics* means "the science that deals with the way sound behaves in an enclosed area." The same word is used in a plural sense to refer to the individual kinds of sound behavior within an area.

In the sentence "The acoustics in the new auditorium are excellent," it is not the science or the study of sound that is being referred to, so *acoustics* is plural.

USAGE

INTEGRATING THE LANGUAGE ARTS

Usage and Style. Most people use contractions frequently in speech, but in writing, contractions are usually reserved for an informal style. Contractions can weaken and detract from some expressions. For example, President Kennedy's famous "Ask not what your country can do for you . . ." seems much more powerful than "Don't ask what your country can do for you. . . ." You may want to point this out to your students and encourage them to choose words, including contractions, carefully to achieve the exact effect they want to create in their writing.

USAGE

21r. *Doesn't*, not *don't*, is used with singular subjects except *I* and *you*.

Remembering that *doesn't* is the contraction for *does not* and that *don't* is the contraction for *do not* may help you avoid using *don't* incorrectly.

NONSTANDARD **She don't** [do not] **know what the word means.**
STANDARD **She doesn't** [does not] **know what the word means.**

NONSTANDARD **It don't** [do not] **belong to me.**
STANDARD **It doesn't** [does not] **belong to me.**

NONSTANDARD **Don't** [do not] that **boy** understand the rules?
STANDARD **Doesn't** [does not] that **boy** understand the rules?

USAGE

EXERCISE 5 Selecting the Correct Verb

For each of the following sentences, choose the correct verb form in parentheses.

1. The Girl Guides (*is*, *are*) a scouting organization that began in Great Britain.
2. (*Does*, *Do*) every boy and girl in the city schools vote in the student council elections?
3. Two teaspoonfuls of cornstarch combined with a small amount of cold water (*makes*, *make*) an ideal thickener for many sauces.
4. One indication of African Americans' influence on our culture (*is*, *are*) the use of many black-originated slang expressions by people of other ethnic backgrounds.
5. "Seventeen Syllables" (*recounts*, *recount*) the story of a Japanese American family.
6. This (*doesn't*, *don't*) make sense to me.
7. Microelectronics, the area of electronics dealing with the design and application of microcircuits, (*has*, *have*) made possible many of the tremendous advances in computers and robotics in recent years.
8. There (*is*, *are*) many a slip between the cup and the lip, as my grandpa says.
9. When she is doing needlepoint, Aunt Ching's scissors always (*hang*, *hangs*) around her neck on a red ribbon.
10. The majority of high school juniors (*think*, *thinks*) that computer literacy is important.

EXERCISE 6 Choosing the Correct Verb

For each of the following sentences, choose the correct verb form in parentheses.

EXAMPLE 1. How many of the foods shown below (*is, are*) native to Central America and North America?
1. *are*

1. Almost every one of the following sentences (*give, gives*) you a clue to the answer.
2. Peanuts, as well as popcorn, (*was, were*) introduced to European settlers by Native Americans.
3. No one in Europe (*was, were*) familiar with the taste of pumpkins, blueberries, or maple syrup until explorers brought these foods back from the Americas.
4. One American food that helped reduce famine in Europe (*was, were*) potatoes.
5. A field planted in potatoes (*produce, produces*) almost twice as much food in about half as much growing time as the same field planted in wheat.
6. News of tomatoes, sweet peppers, beans, and zucchini (*was, were*) received warmly in Europe, and now these foods are the heart and soul of southern Italian cooking.
7. At our school, the Original American Chefs (*is, are*) a club that prepares and serves such Native American foods as baked sweet potatoes and steamed corn pudding.
8. Statistics (*shows, show*) that three fifths of all crops now in cultivation originated in the Americas.
9. (*Doesn't, Don't*) it seem obvious by now that every one of the foods shown here was first eaten by Native Americans?
10. *Indian Givers* (*is, are*) a wonderful book about all kinds of contributions that Native Americans have made to the world.

REVIEW A

OBJECTIVE

- To identify subjects and select verbs that agree with their subjects

21s. When a relative pronoun (*that, which*, or *who*) is the subject of an adjective clause, the verb in the clause agrees with the word to which the relative pronoun refers.

EXAMPLES Ganymede, **which is** one of Jupiter's satellites, is the largest satellite in our solar system. [*Which* refers to the singular noun *Ganymede*.]
I have neighbors **who raise** tropical fish. [*Who* refers to the plural noun *neighbors*.]

NOTE: When preceded by *one of [plural word]*, the relative pronoun takes a plural verb. When preceded by *the only one of [plural word]*, the relative pronoun takes a singular verb.

EXAMPLES The dodo is **one of the birds that are** extinct.
Pluto is **the only one of the planets that crosses** the orbit of another planet.

USAGE

USAGE

ORAL PRACTICE **Using Subject-Verb Agreement**

Read each of the following sentences aloud, stressing the italicized words.

1. *Has either* of the essays been graded?
2. *Both* green beans and broccoli *are* nourishing vegetables.
3. Here *are* the *minutes* I took at the meeting.
4. The *salary is* the minimum wage.
5. Not *one* of the driver's education students *forgets* to fasten the seat belt.
6. Where *are* her *mother and father?*
7. The *coach doesn't* want us to eat sweets.
8. *Several* of the research papers *were* read aloud.

REVIEW A **Selecting Verbs That Agree with Their Subjects**

For each of the following sentences, identify the subject of the verb in parentheses. Then choose the verb form that agrees in number with the subject.

EXAMPLE 1. Both of the brothers (*play, plays*) in the zydeco band at the Cajun Cafe.
1. *Both—play*

1. Neither the Litchfield nor the Torrington exit (*is, are*) the one you should take.
2. The president, after meeting with several of his advisers, (*has, have*) promised to veto the proposed tax bill.
3. A medical study of World War II veterans (*has, have*) concluded that the veterans have the same health prospects as nonveterans.
4. The list of the greatest baseball players of all time (*is, are*) dominated by outfielders.
5. Babe Ruth, Hank Aaron, Willie Mays, and Joe DiMaggio (*is, are*) all outfielders on the list.
6. The Mariana Trench, located in the Pacific Ocean near the Mariana Islands, (*is, are*) the deepest known ocean area in the world.
7. Styles in clothing (*seems, seem*) to change as often as the weather.
8. (*Do, Does*) the New York City Triborough Bridge and Tunnel Authority, which oversees the collection of bridge tolls, have a major problem with a small Mexican coin?
9. Yes, the Mexican peso, worth a fraction of a cent, (*is, are*) easily accepted by the present toll machines.
10. These vegetables (*doesn't, don't*) look fresh.

PICTURE THIS

In your daydreams, you've pictured this event a thousand times—delivering a speech in front of the assembled delegates to the U.S. House of Representatives. Write out the speech that

USAGE

PICTURE THIS

Encourage students to do a careful audience analysis. They can consider the following questions:

1. Is the subject of the speech appropriate for the House of Representatives?
2. How much information do the members of the House already have on the subject? How much more do they want or need?
3. How should I present myself—as an expert on the subject or as somebody who wants to provide a high school student's perspective on the subject?
4. What can I say that will get the Representatives' attention?

In addition to following the conventions of standard written English, the speech should be clear and direct. It should include concrete examples that clearly illustrate the writer's points.

SEGMENT 4 *(pp. 664–669)*

AGREEMENT OF PRONOUN AND ANTECEDENT Rules 21t–21w

OBJECTIVE

- To supply pronouns that agree with their antecedents in sentences

Teacher's ResourceBank™

RESOURCES

AGREEMENT OF PRONOUN AND ANTECEDENT

- Agreement of Pronoun and Antecedent 235

QUICK REMINDER

Write the words *he, she, it,* and *they* in one column on the chalkboard. In a second column write *Maria, book, babies,* and *Patrick.* Ask students to copy the lists and to label each column according to the part of speech it contains [first column, *pronoun;* second column, *noun*]. Then ask students to draw lines to connect each pronoun to the noun that agrees with it [he—Patrick, she—Maria, it—book, they—babies].

you would deliver. It can be on any topic that's important to you and can be humorous or serious. Your speech will be printed in the *Congressional Record,* the daily publication of the proceedings of Congress, so be sure to check your writing carefully for subject-verb agreement.

Subject: an issue that's important to you
Audience: U.S. House of Representatives
Purpose: to inform the other delegates about an issue

Agreement of Pronoun and Antecedent

A pronoun usually refers to a noun or another pronoun. The word to which a pronoun refers is called its ***antecedent.***

REFERENCE NOTE: For more on antecedents, see pages 555 and 701–707.

21t. A pronoun agrees with its antecedent in number and in gender.

(1) Singular pronouns refer to singular antecedents. Plural pronouns refer to plural antecedents.

EXAMPLES **Sammy Davis, Jr.,** made **his** movie debut in 1931.
The **joggers** took **their** canteens with **them.**

(2) A few singular pronouns indicate gender (*masculine, feminine, neuter*). The singular pronouns *he, him, his,* and *himself* refer to masculine antecedents. The singular pronouns *she, her, hers,* and *herself* refer to feminine antecedents. The singular pronouns *it, its,* and *itself* refer to antecedents that are neuter (neither masculine nor feminine).

EXAMPLES **Shay** has more credits than **he** needs.
Maria has misplaced **her** class ring.
A **snake** swallows **its** prey whole.

21 t–u

21u. Singular pronouns are used to refer to the following antecedents: *anybody, anyone, each, either, everybody, everyone, neither, nobody, no one, one, somebody,* and *someone.*

These words do not indicate gender. To determine their gender, look in phrases following them.

EXAMPLES **Each** of the **girls** has already memorized **her** part.
One of the **boys** left **his** helmet on the bus.

If the antecedent may be either masculine or feminine, use both the masculine and feminine pronouns to refer to it.

EXAMPLES **Anyone** who is going on the field trip needs to bring **his or her** lunch.
Any qualified **person** may submit **his or her** application.

You can often avoid the awkward *his or her* construction by substituting an article (*a, an,* or *the*) for the construction or by rephrasing the sentence, using the plural forms of both the pronoun and its antecedent.

EXAMPLES Any interested **person** may submit **an** application.
All interested **persons** may submit **their** applications.

NOTE: In conversation, plural pronouns are often used to refer to singular antecedents that can be either masculine or feminine.

EXAMPLES **Everybody** wanted Ms. Hirakawa to sign **their** yearbooks.
Each of the employees will receive **their** new ID cards tomorrow.

This usage is becoming increasingly popular in writing. In fact, using a singular pronoun to refer to a singular antecedent that is clearly plural in meaning may be misleading.

MISLEADING **Nobody** left the prom early, because **he or she** was enjoying **himself or herself.** [Since *nobody* is clearly plural in meaning, the singular pronouns *he or she* and *himself or herself,* though grammatically correct, are confusing.]

IMPROVED **Nobody** left the prom early, because **they** were enjoying **themselves.**

MISLEADING **Everyone** in the audience had enjoyed the performance so much that **he or she** called for an encore.

IMPROVED **Everyone** in the audience had enjoyed the performance so much that **they** called for an encore.

USAGE

MEETING INDIVIDUAL NEEDS

LEARNING STYLES

Visual Learners. To help students see the relationship of pronouns to antecedents, write on the chalkboard some of the examples under **Rule 21t.** Then draw an arrow from the pronoun in each sentence to the antecedent of the pronoun.

INTEGRATING THE LANGUAGE ARTS

Usage and Writing. Students may be unfamiliar with certain pronoun constructions in situations when the gender of the antecedent isn't clear. For example, they may see *he/she, (s)he* or *s/he* used in some publications. You can explain to them that gender-neutral constructions are a relatively recent development in the history of the English language.

Usage hasn't fully been settled, but the prevailing trend seems to be the one described in the textbook.

USAGE

21v. A plural pronoun is used to refer to two or more singular antecedents joined by *and.*

EXAMPLES If **Jerry and Francesca** call, tell **them** that I will not be home until this evening.
Pilar, Kimberly, and Laura have donated **their** time to the hospital.

21w. A singular pronoun is used to refer to two or more singular antecedents joined by *or* or *nor.*

EXAMPLES **Either Rinaldo or Philip** always finishes **his** geometry homework in class.
Neither Cindy nor Carla thinks **she** is ready to write the final draft.

NOTE: Revise awkward constructions caused by antecedents of different genders.

AWKWARD Either Leo or Rose will give her report.
REVISED Either **Leo** will give **his** report, or **Rose** will give **hers.**

USAGE

EXERCISE 7 Supplying Pronouns That Agree with Their Antecedents

Complete each of the following sentences by supplying at least one pronoun that agrees with its antecedent. Use standard formal English.

EXAMPLE **1.** Each of the girls took ____ turn at bat.
1. *her*

1. Each student prepares ____ own outline. 1. his or her
2. One of the birds built ____ nest in our chimney. 2. its
3. Both Jane and Ruth wrote ____ essays about ecology. 3. their
4. If anyone else wants to drive, ____ should tell Mrs. Cruz. 4. he or she
5. Many of the students in our class have turned in ____ reports on the Frida Kahlo exhibit. 5. their
6. Not one of the students typed ____ research paper. 6. his or her
7. Neither Angela nor Carrie has given ____ dues to me. 7. her
8. Either Mark or David must hand in a slip to take ____ car on the field trip. 8. his
9. Each of the visitors filled ____ own plate with tacos, fajitas, and guacamole at the cookout. 9. his or her
10. Everyone in the class has paid ____ lab fees. 10. his or her

USAGE

WRITING APPLICATION

OBJECTIVE

- To conduct a poll and write a report of the findings

WRITING APPLICATION

Using Pronoun-Antecedent Agreement for Clear Meaning

Like many rules in English, the rules of pronoun-antecedent agreement have some exceptions. Checking for agreement can be tricky when an antecedent is an indefinite pronoun like *anyone, either, no one, everyone, neither, nobody,* or *somebody*. In formal writing, a singular pronoun is generally used to refer to one of these antecedents. However, a plural pronoun should be used if a singular one would be awkward or misleading. How might the following sentence cause confusion?

Everyone believes that he or she will cut back on spending during this recession.

WRITING ACTIVITY

For your term project in history class, you've decided to poll people about what current events they think will be the most important events of the decade. Take a poll of at least ten people and write a brief report discussing your findings. Wherever appropriate, use pronouns to avoid repeating nouns. Be sure that the pronouns you use agree with their antecedents.

Prewriting First, write down several specific questions that you will ask in your poll. Group your questions in categories, such as political events, environmental issues, sports, medicine, and entertainment. Your poll can cover global events or events just in the United States or in your local community. Be sure to ask "open-ended" questions, which prompt people to explain their answers. Next, make a list of people to poll. You can include friends, relatives, and neighbors. Then, poll your subjects, either tape-recording or noting down their answers. If you are using a tape recorder, get your respondent's permission before you begin recording. Be sure to record the answers clearly and accurately and to identify each source by his or her full name. After you

USAGE

WRITING APPLICATION

The writing assignment in this feature is rather involved, and you may want to plan to spend several days on it in class. If your students are taking history, government, or some other social studies class, you may want to team up with their social studies teacher to make this a lesson in writing across the curriculum. Encourage your students to select a variety of respondents, including adults and students, men and women.

CRITICAL THINKING

Synthesis

Once students have interviewed their respondents, they will have to study the responses. Since it's unlikely the responses will be identical, students may have to identify trends. For example, several respondents may indicate that an oil spill, a nuclear accident, and problems with the ozone layer are the most important events. These events can be grouped under the general heading of environmental disasters. Remind your students that they'll have to find common elements in answers that may appear to differ greatly.

USAGE

REVIEW B

OBJECTIVE

- To proofread a paragraph for subject-verb and pronoun-antecedent agreement

COOPERATIVE LEARNING

Once students have developed questions for their surveys, you may want them to do a pilot study by trying out some of the questions on each other. You can let them work in groups of three. One student in the group asks the questions, one answers them, and the third notes potential problems with the questions.

TIMESAVER

You can save time in grading papers if you have students do **Review B** orally. This will give you a chance to reteach if students seem to need it.

USAGE

USAGE

take your poll, compile lists of the responses. Finally, note the answers given most often to each question and the reasons why people consider these events the most important.

Writing As you write your report, identify the answers people gave most frequently to each of your questions. Clearly identify your sources as well as the events you're discussing. For each event, sum up the reasons people gave for their choices. You might wrap up your report with a paragraph telling what conclusions you've drawn from the results of the poll.

Evaluating and Revising Check the organization of your report. Make sure your discussion follows a clear, logical order. Also be sure you've accurately represented the responses to your poll. If you find that you've repeated the names of people and events too often, use pronouns for variety. Check for pronoun-antecedent agreement, paying special attention to antecedents that are singular indefinite pronouns. You may need to reword some sentences to avoid awkward or unclear constructions.

Proofreading Proofread your paper for any errors in grammar, spelling, or punctuation. Check again for errors in agreement of pronouns and antecedents.

REVIEW B

Proofreading a Paragraph for Subject-Verb and Pronoun-Antecedent Agreement

Most of the sentences in the following paragraph contain errors in agreement. If the sentence contains an error in agreement, identify the incorrect verb or pronoun, and supply the correct form. If the sentence is correct, write *C*.

EXAMPLE [1] Don't the concept of child prodigies fascinate you?
1. *Don't—Doesn't*

1. are

[1] Prodigies, people who have immense talent, ~~is~~ born very infrequently. [2] One of the most interesting child prodigies of

this century ~~are~~ young Wang Yani of China. [3] Two and a half years ~~were~~ the age at which Wang began painting. [4] How old do you think she was when this wonderful painting of frolicking monkeys ~~were~~ completed? [5] Neither of us ~~were~~ able to guess correctly that she was only five. [6] It shouldn't surprise you to learn that *Little Monkeys and Mummy* ~~are~~ the painting's title. [7] The people of China ~~has~~ recognized Wang as a prodigy since she was four years old. [8] By the time she was six, she had already painted four thousand pictures. [9] As you can see, wet ink and paint ~~is~~ freely mixed in Wang's pictures, producing interesting puddles and fuzzy edges. [10] Honored at home and abroad, Wang Yani is the youngest painter ever to have ~~their~~ works displayed in a one-person show at the Smithsonian Institution.

2. is
3. was
4. was
5. was
6. is
7. have
8. C
9. are
10. his or her

USAGE

Wang Yani, "Little Monkeys and Mummy",

USAGE

SEGMENT 5 *(pp. 670–671)*

REVIEW: POSTTEST

OBJECTIVE

- To proofread sentences for subject-verb and pronoun-antecedent agreement

A DIFFERENT APPROACH

To evaluate the nature of the difficulties students may still be having with agreement, have students bracket the subject of each sentence and tell whether the subject is singular or plural. You can also have students bracket antecedents of pronouns and tell whether the antecedents are singular or plural.

USAGE

Review: Posttest

A. Proofreading Sentences for Subject-Verb and Pronoun-Antecedent Agreement

Most of the following sentences contain errors in agreement. If the sentence is correct, write C. If it contains an error in agreement, identify the incorrect verb or pronoun, and supply the correct form.

EXAMPLE **1. Each of the members of the school board are hoping to be reelected this fall.**
1. *are hoping—is hoping*

1. Half the members of my history class this year ~~is~~ in the National Honor Society. **1. are**
2. Over one thousand miles of tunnels ~~travels~~ through El Teniente, the largest copper mine in the world. **2. travel**
3. If she already has needle-nose pliers, she can exchange them for something else at the hardware store. **3. C**
4. The etchings of Mary Cassatt, one of America's leading impressionist painters, ~~was~~ definitely influenced by the style used in Japanese prints. **4. were**
5. Either drizzle or heavy rainfall is supposed to be headed this way. **5. C**
6. If you see either Veronica or Sabrena in the cafeteria, will you please tell ~~them~~ that I won't be able to go with ~~them~~ after school today? **6. her/her**
7. Neither Adrianne nor Lillian ~~expect~~ to make the varsity softball team this year; nevertheless, both girls are trying out for it. **7. expects**
8. To learn more about our municipal government, our civics class is planning to invite a number of guest speakers to school. **8. C**
9. Unfortunately, neither Mayor Ella Hanson nor Mrs. Mary Ann Powell, the assistant mayor, ~~have~~ responded to our invitations yet. **9. has**
10. *Blue Highways* by William Least Heat-Moon ~~tell~~ about the fascinating people he met on a trip through small-town America. **10. tells**

USAGE

B. Proofreading a Paragraph for Subject-Verb and Pronoun-Antecedent Agreement

Most of the sentences in the following paragraph contain errors in agreement. If a sentence contains an error in agreement, identify the incorrect verb or pronoun, and supply the correct form. If a sentence is correct, write *C.*

EXAMPLE **[1] My friends and I have stopped buying records in favor of its more modern competitor, the compact disc.**

1. *its—their*

[11] Do you know what the differences between records and compact discs ~~is~~? **[12]** One of the differences ~~are~~ that the music is encoded onto a compact disc by a computer, not pressed into the disc mechanically. **[13]** Another difference is that a CD recording is played back with a laser beam instead of a needle. **[14]** ~~There's~~ several built-in advantages to this technology; for example, because a needle never touches the disc's surface, a CD never wears out. **[15]** And although a CD is usually more expensive than a record album or cassette tape, ~~they~~ can hold over seventy minutes of music on each side. **[16]** You may ask, "~~Doesn't~~ a record and a compact disc yield the same high-fidelity sound?" **[17]** Yes, both kinds of technology ~~does~~ play the same music, but the compact disc also offers total freedom from unwanted noise and distortion. **[18]** My aunt recently told me that a CD of mine has a brighter treble and a truer bass than ~~their~~ record of the same album. **[19]** This great sound quality is obvious even when you play a compact disc on one of the tiny, inexpensive portable players. **[20]** Because virtually all CD players ~~offers~~ the same excellent performance, you should choose the lowest-priced player that has the features you want.

11. are
12. is
13. C
14. There are
15. it
16. Don't
17. do
18. her
19. C
20. offer

USAGE

USAGE

SEGMENT 1 *(pp. 672–673)*
DIAGNOSTIC TEST
OBJECTIVE
- To select correct forms of pronouns

Teacher's ResourceBank™
RESOURCES

FOR THE WHOLE CHAPTER
- Chapter Review Form A 253–254
- Chapter Review Form B 255–256
- Assessment Portfolio
  - Usage Pretests 571–578
  - Usage Mastery Tests 597–604

CHAPTER OVERVIEW
This chapter opens with a discussion of case as it applies to pronoun use. This discussion is followed by a section on nominative case use, one on objective case, one on possessive case, and one on special pronoun problems such as appositives, elliptical constructions, reflexive and intensive pronouns, and the use of *who* and *whom.* A **Writing Application** feature asks students to use *who* and *whom* correctly in letters to a school newspaper's editor. The chapter closes with a **Review: Posttest** designed to check students' mastery of pronoun use.

USAGE

USAGE

22 CORRECT PRONOUN USAGE

Case Forms of Pronouns

Diagnostic Test

A. Selecting Correct Forms of Pronouns

For each of the following sentences, choose the correct form of the pronoun in parentheses.

EXAMPLE 1. Since (*he, him*) and I now have our licenses, Aunt Arabella allowed us to drive her car to the lake.
1. *he*

1. This afternoon the talent committee will audition Tina and (*myself, me*).
2. As I waited for the elevator, I heard the receptionist say, "(*Who, Whom*) shall I say is calling?"
3. The best tennis players in school are my cousin Adele and (*he, him*).
4. I helped Two Bear and (*she, her*) take down the tepee and load it onto the travois.
5. (*Who, Whom*) did you talk to at the information desk?

6. Because Alberto and (*they*, *them*) have taken dancing lessons, they were chosen to be in the chorus line.
7. My math teacher objects to (*me*, *my*) yelling out answers before I have been called on.
8. I learned about life in post-World War II Cuba from my great-grandmother and (*he*, *him*).
9. Between you and (*I*, *me*), I'm glad it's almost lunchtime.
10. When we were small, Ellie always got into more trouble than (*I*, *me*).

B. Selecting Correct Forms of Pronouns

For each sentence in the following paragraph, choose the correct form of the pronoun in parentheses.

EXAMPLE [1] As teenagers, my mother and my uncle decided between (*them*, *themselves*) to enlist in the Army.
1. *themselves*

[11] Years later, in 1991, Mom served in the Persian Gulf Conflict; in fact, both Uncle Tony and (*she*, *her*) did. **[12]** When Mom told my brother Pete and (*me*, *myself*) that she was going to the Persian Gulf, we were worried. **[13]** However, Pete and (*I*, *me*) knew that she was well prepared for the job she had to do. **[14]** Mom is a fine officer, and the troops she commands respect no one else as much as (*she*, *her*). **[15]** Before Mom left for the Gulf, she, Pete, and (*I*, *myself*) had several interesting discussions about the U.S. military. **[16]** Mom thought that (*us*, *our*) knowing some statistics about the fighting forces might make us feel better about her safety. **[17]** For one thing, (*we*, *us*) boys learned that the average age of the enlisted troops being sent to the Persian Gulf was twenty-eight years, whereas those who fought in Vietnam had a median age of only twenty-one years. **[18]** Between you and (*I*, *me*), both my brother and I were glad to hear that Mom would be serving with older troops who had that extra seven years of maturity and experience. **[19]** Mom also told Pete and (*I*, *me*) that, for the first time in U.S. history, a major war was being fought entirely by volunteer troops. **[20]** I will debate (*anyone*, *anyone's*) saying that having a volunteer army didn't improve morale. **20.** both are correct

USAGE

USING THE DIAGNOSTIC TEST

If you notice problems with pronoun usage in students' writing, you can use the **Diagnostic Test** to determine which students need review in particular areas. **Part A** of the **Diagnostic Test** asks students to use pronouns correctly in sentences, and **Part B** asks students to identify correct pronoun forms in a paragraph. Test results will tell you how much your students know about the nominative, objective, and possessive cases of pronouns.

USAGE

SEGMENT 2 *(pp. 674–675)*
CASE

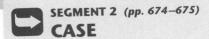

Teacher's ResourceBank™

RESOURCES

CASE

- Pronoun Case 245

QUICK REMINDER

Tell your students that the pronoun forms *you, it,* and *her* are each used for more than one case. To determine the case of these pronouns, students must analyze the pronouns' use in sentences. Write the following sentences on the chalkboard and ask students to identify the case of the pronouns:

1. You already have a book. [nominative]
2. Inez gave you the book. [objective]
3. Pierre sent it yesterday. [objective]
4. Here is her blue scarf. [possessive]

USAGE

MEETING INDIVIDUAL NEEDS

LEP/ESL

General Strategies. Ask students to create a chart of pronouns found in their native languages. Then have them write the English equivalents beside the words from their first language. Since you may have a difficult time checking these (unless you are multilingual), you could try extending this assignment beyond the classroom. Offer students extra credit, perhaps, if they can have some adult who speaks their first language verify their work.

Case

Case is the form that a noun or a pronoun takes to indicate its use in a sentence. In English, there are three cases: *nominative, objective*, and *possessive*.

The form of a noun is the same for both the nominative case and the objective case. For example, a noun used as a subject (nominative case) will have the same form if used as an object (objective case).

NOMINATIVE CASE	The **general** explained the strategy. [subject]
OBJECTIVE CASE	The strategy was explained by the **general.** [object of the preposition]

USAGE

A noun changes its form for the possessive case, usually by adding an apostrophe and an *s* to most singular nouns and only the apostrophe to most plural nouns.

POSSESSIVE CASE	The **general's** explanation was clear and concise. [singular modifier]
	The **generals'** explanations were clear and concise. [plural modifier]

REFERENCE NOTE: For more information about forming possessive nouns, see pages 887–890.

Unlike nouns, most personal pronouns have three forms, one for each case. The form a pronoun takes depends on its function in a sentence.

NOMINATIVE CASE	**We** listened closely to the teacher's directions. [subject]
OBJECTIVE CASE	The teacher gave **us** a vocabulary quiz. [indirect object]
POSSESSIVE CASE	The teacher collected **our** papers. [modifier]

Within each case, the forms of the personal pronouns indicate *number, person*, and *gender*.

- ***Number*** is the form of a pronoun that indicates whether it is *singular* or *plural*.
- ***Person*** is the form of a pronoun that indicates the one(s) speaking (*first person*), the one(s) spoken to (*second person*), or the one(s) spoken of (*third person*).
- ***Gender*** is the form of a pronoun that establishes it as *masculine, feminine*, or *neuter* (neither masculine nor feminine).

SEGMENT 3 *(pp. 675–678)*

THE NOMINATIVE CASE Rules 22a, 22b

OBJECTIVES

- To read sentences aloud, stressing pronouns
- To use pronouns in the nominative case in sentences

PERSONAL PRONOUNS			
SINGULAR			
	NOMINATIVE CASE	OBJECTIVE CASE	POSSESSIVE CASE
FIRST PERSON	I	me	my, mine
SECOND PERSON	you	you	your, yours
THIRD PERSON	he, she, it	him, her, it	his, her, hers, its
PLURAL			
	NOMINATIVE CASE	OBJECTIVE CASE	POSSESSIVE CASE
FIRST PERSON	we	us	our, ours
SECOND PERSON	you	you	your, yours
THIRD PERSON	they	them	their, theirs

Notice in the chart that *you* and *it* have the same forms for the nominative and the objective cases. All other personal pronouns have different forms for each case. Notice also that only third person singular pronouns indicate gender.

The Nominative Case

Personal pronouns in the nominative case—*I, you, he, she, it, we,* and *they*—are used as subjects of verbs and as predicate nominatives.

REFERENCE NOTE: Personal pronouns in the nominative case may also be used as appositives. See page 621.

22a. A subject of a verb is in the nominative case.

EXAMPLES **We** ordered the concert tickets. [*We* is the subject of the verb *ordered.*]
Why does she think that they are too expensive? [*She* is the subject of the verb *does think. They* is the subject of the verb *are.*]

A subject may be compound, with a pronoun appearing in combination with a noun or another pronoun. To help you

USAGE

USAGE

Teacher's ResourceBank™

RESOURCES

THE NOMINATIVE CASE

QUICK REMINDER

Write the following sentences on the chalkboard and have students choose the correct pronouns. (Correct answers are underscored.)

1. (He, him) and (I, me) arrived early for the test Saturday morning.
2. (He, him) said that (we, us) could go.
3. The person who called you is (her, she).
4. The winners of the raffle are (her, she) and (I, me).

MEETING INDIVIDUAL NEEDS

LEP/ESL

Spanish. Because most Spanish personal pronouns have the same form for the nominative and objective cases ("She spoke to she"), Spanish speakers usually do not have to distinguish between nominative and objective cases when they speak their native language. Extra oral practice can help students establish a correct nominative/objective system for English personal pronouns. You could have students practice saying aloud the sentences in the exercises as well as those in the oral practices.

COOPERATIVE LEARNING

As students study the material on **Rule 22b** regarding the use of the nominative case for predicate nominatives, you may want to point out that this construction is rare in casual speaking or writing. To demonstrate this, have students bring in newspaper articles or sports magazines. Have students work in groups of four or five to scan articles for the use of pronouns as predicate nominatives. A spokesperson from each group could report the group's findings.

USAGE

choose the correct pronoun form in a compound subject, try each form as the simple subject of the verb.

EXAMPLE: Onawa and (*he, him*) counted the votes.
CHOICES: *he counted* or *him counted*
ANSWER: Onawa and **he** counted the votes.

EXAMPLE: (*She, Her*) and (*I, me*) will make the piñata.
CHOICES: *She will make* or *Her will make*
I will make or *me will make*
ANSWER: **She** and **I** will make the piñata.

ORAL PRACTICE 1

Using Pronouns as Subjects

Read each of the following sentences aloud, stressing the italicized pronoun(s).

1. You and *I* will go to the library this afternoon.
2. *We* and *they* have some research to do on the Kiowa people.
3. Either Terrell or *he* will select a topic about the environment.
4. Neither *they* nor *we* should use periodicals older than three months.
5. Both *she* and *I* will write about modern art.
6. Risa, Irena, and *I* might write about Georgia O'Keeffe.
7. Which playwright did Kaye and *she* select?
8. She said that you and *they* decided to do a production of August Wilson's award-winning play *The Piano Lesson*.

22b. A predicate nominative is in the nominative case.

A ***predicate nominative*** follows a linking verb and explains or identifies the subject of the verb.

A pronoun used as a predicate nominative always follows a form of the verb *be: am, is, are, was, were, be,* or *been.*

EXAMPLES The chairperson of the prom committee is **she.** [*She* follows *is* and identifies the subject *chairperson.*]
The one who made the comment was **I.** [*I* follows *was* and identifies the subject *one.*]
The lucky winners may have been **they.** [*They* follows *may have been* and identifies the subject *winners.*]

As you can see, the predicate nominative and the subject of the verb both indicate the same individual(s). To identify the correct pronoun form to use as a predicate nominative, try each form as the subject of the verb.

EXAMPLE: The only applicant for the job was (*he, him*).
CHOICES: *he was* or *him was*
ANSWER: The only applicant for the job was **he.**

Like a subject, a predicate nominative may be compound.

EXAMPLES The only students who auditioned for the part of King Arthur were **he** and **Carlos.** [*He* and *Carlos* identify the subject *students.*]
The two debaters are **she** and **I.** [*She* and *I* identify the subject *debaters.*]

NOTE: Expressions such as *It's me, This is her,* and *It was them* are examples of informal usage. Though acceptable in everyday situations, such expressions should be avoided in formal speaking and writing.

REFERENCE NOTE: For more about predicate nominatives, see page 595.

USAGE

EXERCISE 1 Using Pronouns in the Nominative Case

Complete the following sentences by supplying personal pronouns in the nominative case. For each pronoun you add, tell whether it is used as a *subject* or a *predicate nominative.* Use a variety of pronouns, but do not use *you* or *it.*

Pronouns will vary.

EXAMPLE 1. When the man shown on the next page, Charles L. Blockson, was a child, ____ was eager to learn about African American heroes.
1. *he—subject*

1. When he told his teachers of his interest, it was ____ who said that there had been very few black heroes. 1. they—p.n.
2. Sure that ____ must be wrong, Blockson started looking for African Americans in the history books. 2. they—s.
3. He began to collect books, and ____ showed him plenty of heroic black Americans. 3. they—s.
4. Blacks had not been inactive in shaping American history, he learned; and in fact, ____ had played important roles in most of its key events! 4. they—s.
5. When Blockson's great-grandfather was a teenager, ____ and many other slaves had escaped with the help of the Underground Railroad. 5. he—s.

USAGE

TIMESAVER
To save paper-grading time and to give students additional oral practice, have students do **Exercise 1** orally. Ask them to read the sentences aloud and to supply the correct answers.

6. It was ____ who inspired Blockson's lifelong study of the Underground Railroad. 6. he—p.n.
7. It may have been my friends Latisha and ____ who read about Blockson's studies in a magazine article and then gave a report in history class. 7. they—p.n.
8. Using Blockson's map as a source, ____ and ____ made this simplified map of the main Underground Railroad routes to freedom. 8. she—s./they—s.

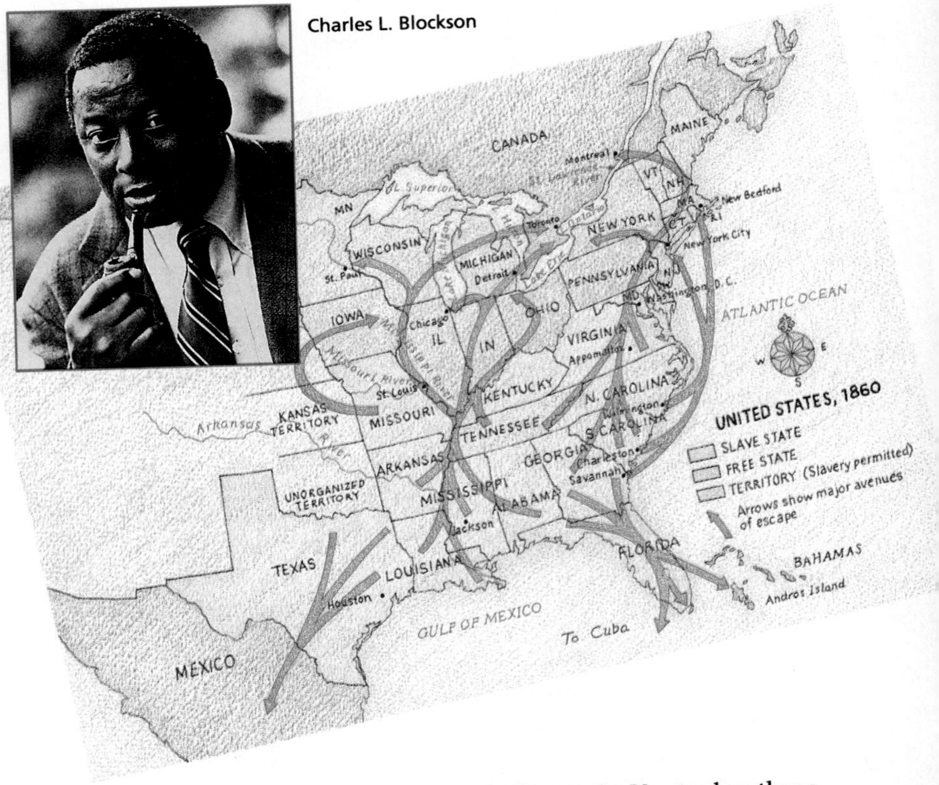

Charles L. Blockson

9. My ancestors escaped from slavery in Kentucky; therefore as you can see, ____ must have followed one of the main routes to arrive in Detroit. 9. they—s.
10. Latisha's great-great-great-grandmother traveled with her younger brother on the Underground Railroad from Virginia to Toronto, and later both ____ and ____ moved here to Detroit to find work. 10. she—s./he—s.

USAGE

VISUAL CONNECTIONS

Exploring the Subject. For more than fifty years, Charles L. Blockson has traced the history of African Americans in the United States, Canada, and Europe through the books, sheet music, and art objects he has collected. His collection is now housed at Temple University in Philadelphia, where Blockson is curator of the African American Collection.

Blockson's career has included lecturing in colleges and universities, writing books on the history of African Americans, and serving as a guidance counselor.

SEGMENT 4 *(pp. 679–682)*

THE OBJECTIVE CASE Rules 22c, 22d

OBJECTIVES

- To read sentences aloud, stressing pronouns in the objective case
- To use pronouns in the objective case in sentences
- To select pronouns used as objects of prepositions

22c

The Objective Case

Personal pronouns in the objective case—*me, you, him, her, it, us,* and *them*—are used as objects of verbs and as objects of prepositions.

REFERENCE NOTE: Personal pronouns in the objective case may also be used as appositives. See page 621.

22c. An object of a verb is in the objective case.

The object of a verb may be a *direct object* or an *indirect object*. A ***direct object*** follows an action verb and tells *whom* or *what*.

EXAMPLES My pen pal from Manila visited **me** last summer.
The car stalled, and we couldn't restart **it**.

An ***indirect object*** comes between an action verb and a direct object and tells *to whom or what* or *for whom or what*.

EXAMPLES The coach awarded **her** a varsity letter.
We gathered the chickens and gave **them** some feed.

An object of a verb may be compound. To help you choose the correct pronoun form in a compound object, try each form as the object of the verb.

EXAMPLE: The new student asked Kelly and (*I, me*) for directions.
CHOICES: *asked I* or *asked me*
ANSWER: The new student asked Kelly and **me** for directions.

EXAMPLE: The editor in chief gave (*he, him*) and (*she, her*) an interesting assignment.
CHOICES: *gave he* or *gave him* and *gave she* or *gave her*
ANSWER: The editor in chief gave **him** and **her** an interesting assignment.

REFERENCE NOTE: For more information about objects of verbs, see pages 592–593.

ORAL PRACTICE 2 **Using Pronouns in the Objective Case**

Read each of the following sentences aloud, stressing the italicized words.

1. The judges chose Carmen and *me*.
2. Do you think that they *will provide us* with what we need?

USAGE

Teacher's ResourceBank™

RESOURCES

THE OBJECTIVE CASE

QUICK REMINDER

Remind students that pronouns in the objective case receive the action of verbs or are objects of prepositions. Write the following sentences on the chalkboard. Then have students identify the objective-case pronouns and ask students to tell how the pronouns are used in the sentences.

1. Cecilia left me there for two hours. [me—direct object]
2. Raphael gave her his jacket. [her—indirect object]
3. As soon as we got the package, we passed it on to them. [it—direct object; them—object of preposition]

USAGE

3. *Call* either *her* or Rhea about the yearbook deadline.
4. *Him* I *like*, but don't *ask me* about the others.
5. These instructions *confuse* my brother and *me*.
6. *Give* the other girls and *her* the chemistry assignment.
7. *Were* they *accusing them* or *us*?
8. The success of the carwash *surprised* Mr. Kahn and *him*.

EXERCISE 2 **Using Pronouns in the Objective Case**

Complete the following sentences by using personal pronouns in the objective case. For each pronoun you add, tell whether it is used as a *direct object* or an *indirect object*. Use a variety of pronouns, but do not use *you* or *it*. Pronouns will vary.

EXAMPLE **1. Marcia drove ____ to the civic center.**
1. *us—direct object*

1. Have you given Nick and ____ the outside reading list? 1. them—i.o.
2. Did Bob show ____ his autographed copy of Amy Tan's latest book? 2. her—i.o.
3. With a smile Mrs. Martin handed Lena, Chris, and ____ their notebooks. 3. him—i.o.
4. Our teacher has already graded Latoya and ____ on our oral reports to the class. 4. me—d.o.
5. Ms. Gutiérrez has invited both ____ and ____ to the Diez y Seis Festival. 5. him—d.o./me—d.o.
6. Would you please lend ____ and her the manual for the fax machine? 6. him—i.o.
7. During practice today, the coach taught Patricia and ____ the proper form for the inward dive. 7. him—i.o.
8. The play gave ____ some ideas for a skit. 8. her—i.o.
9. My mother is picking up both you and ____. 9. him—d.o.
10. Please tell ____ the plans for the prom. 10. them—i.o.

22d. An object of a preposition is in the objective case.

An ***object of a preposition*** comes at the end of a phrase that begins with a preposition.

EXAMPLES	for **me**	after **her**	next to **them**
	with **us**	beside **him**	between **you** and **me**

REFERENCE NOTE: For lists of common prepositions, see page 572. For more discussion of prepositional phrases, see pages 605–607.

USAGE

MEETING **INDIVIDUAL** NEEDS

LEP/ESL

General Strategies. To help students perform well on **Exercise 2,** allow them to make small pronoun charts like the one on p. 675 that they can refer to as they work. If some students feel ready to sort the forms in their heads without using a chart, encourage them to do so.

USAGE

REVIEW A

OBJECTIVE

- To select correct forms of personal pronouns

An object of a preposition may be compound, such as in the phrase *between you and me.* To help you determine which pronoun form to use, read each form separately with the preposition.

EXAMPLE: **Esteban wants to go camping with you and (*I, me*).**
CHOICES: ***with I* or *with me***
ANSWER: **Esteban wants to go camping with you and me.**

EXAMPLE: **Please return these videotapes to Ms. Chang and (*he, him*).**
CHOICES: ***to he* or *to him***
ANSWER: **Please return these videotapes to Ms. Chang and him.**

EXERCISE 3 Selecting Pronouns Used as Objects of Prepositions

For each of the following sentences, choose the correct form of the pronoun in parentheses.

EXAMPLE **1. The Irish terrier belongs to (*she, her*).**
1. *her*

1. Would you like to play baseball with Eugenio and (*I, me*)?
2. These photographs were taken by Dwight and (*she, her*).
3. We can rely on Theresa and (*he, him*) for their help.
4. Would you like to sit next to Elaine and (*I, me*)?
5. There has been much cooperation between the Hispanic Chamber of Commerce and (*we, us*).
6. Teammates like Dave and (*he, him*) can almost read each other's minds on the basketball court.
7. The closing lines of the play will be spoken by you and (*she, her*).
8. We have been studying the early settlers from England and learning about the help that Native American peoples gave to (*they, them*).
9. Most of the credit belongs to (*we, us*).
10. The captain tried to steer the ship between the lighthouse and (*they, them*).

REVIEW A Selecting Correct Forms of Personal Pronouns

For each sentence in the following paragraph, choose the correct form of the pronoun in parentheses. Then identify its use

USAGE

USAGE

INTEGRATING THE LANGUAGE ARTS

Literature Link. Have each student find in his or her literature textbook a poem in which the poet has used first-person pronouns. Ask students to rewrite the poems by substituting third-person singular forms for the first-person pronouns. Have volunteers read the old versions and the new versions aloud. Discuss how the effects of the message are altered when feelings and impressions are presented as a report about someone who has them rather than spoken as if coming directly from the heart and mind of the speaker.

USAGE

MEETING INDIVIDUAL NEEDS

STUDENTS WITH SPECIAL NEEDS

The dense paragraph format of **Review A** might be difficult for learning disabled students to read. To simplify the task, you could list the sentences in sequence without putting them into paragraph form. Other possibilities would be to enlarge the exercise or to have students use horizontal rules as they read through the paragraph.

VISUAL CONNECTIONS

Exploring the Subject. Oaxaca (wa 'ha ka), one of the thirty-one states of Mexico, is located on the Pacific Ocean in the southwest corner of the country. Oaxaca was originally inhabited by the Aztecs, and its people carry on traditional crafts that predate the Spaniards' arrival in the 1500s. The carvings pictured represent only one of the region's many types of folk art.

in the sentence—as a *subject*, a *predicate nominative*, a *direct object*, an *indirect object*, or an *object of a preposition*.

EXAMPLE **During our vacation in Mexico, my grandmother, her brother Luís, and [1] (*I*, *me*) visited the Oaxaca Valley.**
1. *I—subject*

USAGE

1. s. The state of Oaxaca is where [1] (*they*, *them*) and their two older brothers were born. As we drove through Arrazola, their village, Uncle Luís was amazed to find well-built brick homes
2. o.p. where all of [2] (*we*, *us*) had expected to see bamboo houses.
3. s. Turning to Grandma, [3] (*he*, *him*) exclaimed, "Something good has happened here, Nita!" After visiting Arrazola, my relatives
4. s. and [4] (*I*, *me*) drove to the city of Oaxaca, which is the state capital, and strolled along its main street. I pointed out some
5. i.o. painted woodcarvings to Grandma and showed [5] (*she*, *her*) and Uncle Luís the ones I liked best. I took this picture of a pair
6. p.n. of dancing chickens and decided it would be either [6] (*they*, *them*), this alligator playing a horn, or the striped cat on the right that I'd buy for a souvenir. While I was making up my mind, Uncle Luís spoke to the shopkeeper, asking questions of
7. o.p. [7] (*he*, *him*) and his wife. It seems that not long before, a local man named Manuel Jiménez had started making colorful
8. d.o. wooden figures and since then had been selling [8] (*they*, *them*) to American visitors. Seeing his success, others in the Oaxaca
9. s. Valley began carving too, and within a few years [9] (*they*, *them*) and their fanciful woodcarvings had become famous. These people's imagination, skill, and hard work have rapidly
10. d.o. brought [10] (*they*, *them*) and their communities out of poverty.

SEGMENT 5 *(pp. 683–685)*

THE POSSESSIVE CASE Rules 22e–22g

OBJECTIVES

- To identify gerunds and present participles and to choose the correct noun and pronoun forms to be used with them in sentences
- To write a persuasive letter containing pronouns

The Possessive Case

The personal pronouns in the possessive case—*my, mine, your, yours, his, her, hers, its, our, ours, their, theirs*—are used to show ownership or relationship.

NOTE: Many authorities prefer to call these words adjectives. Follow your teacher's instructions regarding these possessive forms.

22e. The possessive pronouns *mine, yours, his, hers, its, ours,* and *theirs* are used in the same ways that the pronouns in the nominative and the objective cases are used.

SUBJECT	Your car and **mine** need a tune up.
PREDICATE NOMINATIVE	This yearbook is **hers.**
DIRECT OBJECT	We ordered **ours** yesterday.
INDIRECT OBJECT	Ms. Kwan gave **theirs** a quick look.
OBJECT OF PREPOSITION	Next to **yours,** my Siamese cat looks puny.

22f. The possessive pronouns *my, your, his, her, its, our,* and *their* are used as adjectives before nouns.

EXAMPLES **My** watch is broken.
His first public performance as a concert pianist was in 1968.
Do you know **their** address?

22g. A noun or a pronoun preceding a gerund is in the possessive case.

A ***gerund*** is a verb form that ends in *–ing* and functions as a noun. Since a gerund acts as a noun, the noun or pronoun that comes before it must be in the possessive case in order to modify the gerund.

EXAMPLES We were all thrilled by **Joetta's** scoring in the top 5 percent. [*Joetta's* modifies the gerund *scoring.* Whose scoring? Joetta's scoring.]
His parents objected to **his** working late on school nights. [*His* modifies the gerund *working.* Whose working? His working.]

Do not confuse a gerund with a present participle, which is also a verb form that ends in *–ing*. A gerund acts as a noun,

USAGE

Teacher's ResourceBank™
RESOURCES

THE POSSESSIVE CASE
- The Possessive Case 248

QUICK REMINDER

Write the following sentences on the chalkboard and ask your students to choose the correct pronoun for each. (Correct answers are underscored.)

1. Peter lost his book, but this one is (my, mine).
2. Do you have (your, yours) book?
3. Oh! Stephanie has (your, yours).
4. Well, what happened to (her, hers) book?

USAGE

![MEETING INDIVIDUAL NEEDS]

MEETING INDIVIDUAL NEEDS

LEARNING STYLES

Visual Learners. Students who are visually oriented may benefit from diagraming a sentence in which the *-ing* word can be either a participle or a gerund, depending on the emphasis desired. If the technique is helpful, students could also diagram the sentences in **Exercise 4.**

Here are diagrams of the first two example sentences in the middle of this page:

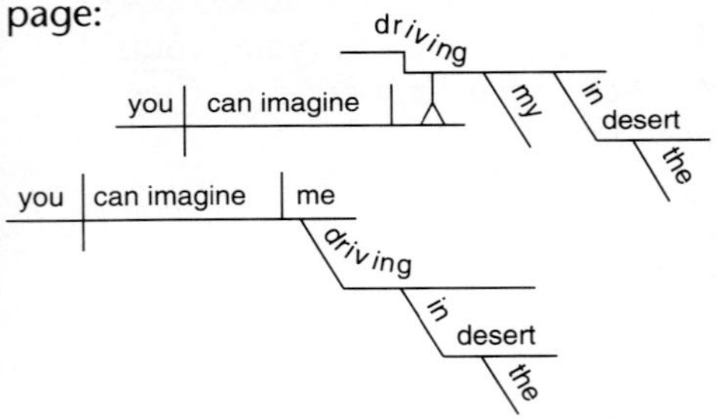

A DIFFERENT APPROACH

Point out to your students that spelling is a clue to the grammatical function of most of the possessive pronouns. If a possessive pronoun ends in *–s,* it's usually used as a subject, predicate nominative, or object. ("Hers is the red one.") Without the *–s* the pronoun is usually used as a possessive adjective. ("I found her red purse.") The only exceptions are *his* and *its.*

TIMESAVER

You can save time grading papers for **Exercise 4** by having your students do the exercise orally. This approach will also give you an opportunity to discuss the items that can be correctly completed in more than one way.

whereas a present participle serves as an adjective. A noun or pronoun that is modified by a present participle should not be in the possessive case.

EXAMPLES **She nearly stepped on the puppy frolicking around her.** [*Puppy* is modified by the participial phrase *frolicking around her.*]
We found him sitting on a bench in the park. [*Him* is modified by the participial phrase *sitting on a bench in the park.*]

The form of a noun or pronoun before an *–ing* word often depends on the meaning you want to express. If you want to emphasize the *–ing* word, use the possessive form. If you want to emphasize the noun or pronoun preceding the *–ing* word, avoid the possessive form. Notice the difference in meaning between the two sentences in each of the following pairs.

EXAMPLES **Can you imagine my driving in the desert?** [emphasis on the gerund *driving*]
Can you imagine me driving in the desert? [emphasis on *me,* not on the participial phrase *driving in the desert*]

The Glee Club's singing of "Hail, Columbia!" got the most applause. [emphasis on the gerund *singing*]
The Glee Club singing "Hail, Columbia!" got the most applause. [emphasis on *Glee Club,* not on the participial phrase *singing "Hail, Columbia!"*]

EXERCISE 4 Using Pronouns with Gerunds and Present Participles

For each of the following sentences, identify the *–ing* word as either a *gerund* or a *present participle,* and then choose the correct noun or pronoun in parentheses. Be prepared to explain your choices. [Note: A sentence may be correctly completed in more than one way.]

EXAMPLE **1. Jody saw (*us, our*) standing on the corner and waved.**
1. *present participle—us*

1. Hao didn't see the huge green wave until she felt (*it, its*) crashing over her shoulders. **1. pres. part.**
2. I like my stepfather, but I just can't get used to (*him, his*) cooking. **2. ger.—his [*or* pres. part.—him]**

3. The baby reached out to touch the shiny (*ribbons*, *ribbon's*) decorating the gift. **3. pres. part.**
4. (*Him*, *His*) being sarcastic has ruined our chance to win the debate. **4. ger.**
5. Did you mind (*me*, *my*) telling Denzel that you entered the essay contest? **5. ger.**

PICTURE THIS

Along with these other volunteers, you and some friends have spent the weekend gathering up the trash that had been spoiling the beauty of this lake. You worked hard, and you feel good knowing you've helped clean up your community. Now, you want to persuade other people to take part in the clean-up effort. Write a letter to your local newspaper, telling how your group of volunteers cleaned up the shoreline and describing the results of your work. Convince your readers that volunteer "trash detail" is well worth the effort for a cleaner community. In your letter, use at least ten pronouns. Be able to tell whether each pronoun you use is in the nominative, objective, or possessive case.

Subject: cleaning up trash in your community
Audience: readers of the local newspaper
Purpose: to persuade readers to volunteer their time

USAGE

PICTURE THIS

Remind students that persuasive writing can employ both emotional and rational arguments to enlist support from readers. The assigned topic and audience for this activity seem well suited to both types of arguments. Encourage students to deal with counter arguments. For example, one argument holds that local citizens pay taxes for services, one of which should be lake shore cleanup.

USAGE

Teacher's ResourceBank™

RESOURCES

SPECIAL PRONOUN PROBLEMS

USAGE

QUICK REMINDER

Write the following sentences on the chalkboard and ask your students to select the correct pronouns. (Correct answers are underscored.)

1. My grandfather told (us, we) boys stories about pioneer days.
2. I'm much taller than (she, her).
3. Mr. Riera ate lunch with his daughter Judy and (me, myself).
4. He gave it to (who, whom)?

MEETING INDIVIDUAL NEEDS

LEP/ESL

Spanish. In Spanish, *who* does not change form when used as an object, so Spanish-speaking students do not have a first-language context for this concept. You may want to have students practice reading aloud sentences in which *who* and *whom* are used correctly. You could also have students work in pairs to create original sentences containing *who* and *whom.* After you check for correct usage, suggest that students read the sentences aloud for reinforcement.

SEGMENT 6 *(pp. 686–697)*

SPECIAL PRONOUN PROBLEMS Rules 22h–22l

OBJECTIVES

- To use the appropriate pronoun appositives in phrases and to write sentences containing the phrases
- To complete elliptical clauses with the appropriate pronouns and to identify the pronouns as subjects or objects

Special Pronoun Problems

Appositives

An ***appositive*** is a noun or a pronoun placed next to another noun or pronoun to explain or identify it.

REFERENCE NOTE: For more information about appositives, see page 621.

22h. An appositive is in the same case as the noun or pronoun to which it refers.

USAGE

EXAMPLES My best friends, **Raúl** and **she,** have been nominated for class treasurer. [*Raúl* and *she* are in apposition with the subject *friends.* Since a subject is always in the nominative case, an appositive to a subject is in the nominative case.]

My grandfather paid the two boys, **Mario** and **him,** for raking leaves. [*Mario* and *him* are in apposition with the direct object *boys.* Since a direct object is always in the objective case, an appositive to a direct object is in the objective case.]

To identify which pronoun form to use as an appositive, try each form in the position of the word it refers to.

EXAMPLE: Two juniors, Erin and (*she, her*), conducted the survey.
CHOICES: *she conducted* or *her conducted*
ANSWER: Two juniors, Erin and **she,** conducted the survey.

EXAMPLE: The survey was conducted by two juniors, Erin and (*she, her*).
CHOICES: *by she* or *by her*
ANSWER: The survey was conducted by two juniors, Erin and **her.**

NOTE: Sometimes the pronoun *we* or *us* is followed by a noun appositive. To determine which pronoun form to use, try each form without the noun appositive.

EXAMPLE: On our field trip to the planetarium, (*we, us*) students learned many interesting facts about our solar system.
CHOICES: *we learned* or *us learned*
ANSWER: On our field trip to the planetarium, **we** students learned many interesting facts about our solar system.

- To identify pronouns as reflexive or intensive and to identify the words the pronouns refer to or emphasize
- To use *who* and *whom* correctly and to identify their uses in sentences

EXAMPLE: The guidance counselor talked to (*we, us*) students about the requirements for graduation.
CHOICES: *to we* or *to us*
ANSWER: The guidance counselor talked to **us** students about the requirements for graduation.

EXERCISE 5 **Using Appositives in Sentences**

Supply an appropriate pronoun for each blank in the following groups of words. Then write a sentence using each group of words in the way specified in parentheses.

EXAMPLE 1. my neighbors, ____ and Steven (*indirect object*)
1. *We gave my neighbors, her and Steven, a ride to the basketball game.*

1. the two star players, ____ and Kelly (*direct object*)
2. ____ and ____, the loudest fans (*subject*)
3. ____ Tigers boosters (*object of a preposition*)
4. ____ juniors (*predicate nominative*)
5. the world's best coaches, ____ and Mr. Gresham (*indirect object*)

USAGE

Pronouns in Elliptical Constructions

An ***elliptical construction*** is a clause from which words have been omitted. The word *than* or *as* often begins an elliptical construction.

22i. A pronoun following *than* or *as* in an elliptical construction is in the same case as it would be if the construction were completed.

ELLIPTICAL Keiko was more frustrated by the assignment **than he.**
COMPLETED Keiko was more frustrated by the assignment **than he was frustrated.**

ELLIPTICAL The assignment frustrated me as much **as him.**
COMPLETED The assignment frustrated me as much **as it frustrated him.**

The pronoun form in an elliptical construction determines the meaning of the elliptical clause. Be sure to use the pronoun

ANSWERS
Exercise 5

Answers will vary. Here are some possibilities:

1. The coach sent the two star players, her and Kelly, to the bench to allow others a chance to play.
2. He and she, the loudest fans, were called onto the stage.
3. We appreciated the complimentary tickets the team sent to us Tigers boosters.
4. It could be we juniors the principal was talking about.
5. The Coaches Association gave the world's best coaches, her and Mr. Gresham, a special award last year.

USAGE

pronoun form that expresses the meaning you intend. Notice how the meaning of each of the following sentences depends on the pronoun form in the elliptical construction.

EXAMPLES **I have known Leigh longer than she.** [I have known Leigh longer *than she has known Leigh.*]
I have known Leigh longer than her. [I have known Leigh longer *than I have known her.*]

Did Mr. Matsuda pay you as much as I? [Did Mr. Matsuda pay you as much *as I paid you*?]
Did Mr. Matsuda pay you as much as me? [Did Mr. Matsuda pay you as much *as he paid me*?]

USAGE

EXERCISE 6 **Selecting Pronouns for Incomplete Constructions**

For each of the following sentences, add words to complete the elliptical clause. Include in the clause the appropriate pronoun form. Then tell whether the pronoun is a *subject* or an *object*. [Note: Some of the elliptical clauses may be corrected in more than one way; you need to give only one correction.]

EXAMPLE **1. Jo works longer hours than (*I, me*).**
1. *than I work—subject*

1. No one else in my class is as shy as (*I, me*).
2. Judges in the salsa dance contest presented Estella with a larger trophy than (*I, me*).
3. Can you whistle as loudly as (*he, him*)?
4. If you want to sell more raffle tickets than Bradley, you should call on more people than (*he, him*).
5. My coach told me that I had more agility than (*he, him*).
6. We were all more eager than (*he, him*).
7. I am more interested in Spike Lee's films than (*she, her*).
8. The editors of our newspaper have written as much as (*they, them*).
9. They sent Lois as many get-well cards as (*I, me*).
10. No one gave more time to good causes than (*she, her*).

Reflexive and Intensive Pronouns

Reflexive and intensive pronouns (sometimes called *compound personal pronouns*) have the same forms.

USAGE

ANSWERS
Exercise 6

1. I am shy—subject
2. they presented to me—object
3. he can whistle—subject
4. he calls on—subject
5. he has agility—subject
6. he was eager—subject
7. she is interested in them—subject; than I am interested in her—object
8. they have written—subject
9. I sent Lois—subject; they sent me—object
10. she gave to good causes—subject

REFLEXIVE AND INTENSIVE PRONOUNS		
	SINGULAR	PLURAL
FIRST PERSON	myself	ourselves
SECOND PERSON	yourself	yourselves
THIRD PERSON	himself, herself, itself	themselves

A ***reflexive pronoun*** refers to another word that indicates the same individual(s) or thing(s).

EXAMPLES I hurt **myself.** [*Myself* refers to *I*.]
These computers can repair **themselves.** [*Themselves* refers to *computers*.]

An ***intensive pronoun*** emphasizes another word that indicates the same individual(s) or thing(s).

EXAMPLES My grandfather and I restored the car **ourselves.** [*Ourselves* emphasizes *grandfather* and *I*.]
The weather **itself** seemed to be our enemy. [*Itself* emphasizes *weather*.]

NOTE: Unlike a reflexive pronoun, an intensive pronoun can be omitted from a sentence without changing its meaning.

EXAMPLE The children decorated the gym themselves.
The children decorated the gym.

22j. A pronoun ending in *–self* or *–selves* should not be used in place of a simple personal pronoun.

NONSTANDARD Lupe and **myself** went to the ballet.
STANDARD Lupe and **I** went to the ballet.

NONSTANDARD Did Rosa make lunch for herself and **yourself**?
STANDARD Did Rosa make lunch for herself and **you**?

EXERCISE 7 **Using Reflexive and Intensive Pronouns Correctly**

For each of the following sentences, identify the italicized pronoun as *intensive* or *reflexive*. Then, give the word or words that

USAGE

the pronoun refers to or emphasizes. [Note: If the sentence is imperative, the word may be understood.]

EXAMPLE **1. To get the special beads she wanted for her bead work, Ruthie taught *herself* how to make them.**
1. *reflexive—Ruthie*

1. Long before the tiny glass "seed beads" and the larger china "pony beads" were brought from Europe, Native Americans made different kinds of beads *themselves*. **1. its.**
2. Imagine *yourself* laboriously using a hand drill to bore a tiny hole through the center of hundreds of small cylinders of bone, shell, or stone! **2. refl.—(You)**
3. All by *itself*, an individual bead doesn't look particularly impressive, does it? **3. refl.**
4. I asked Ruthie to give me some beads so that I can make *myself* a necklace. **4. refl.**
5. The librarian found the address of a bead distributor for us, but Ruthie and I had to order the materials *ourselves*. **5. its.**

USAGE

Who and *Whom*

Like most personal pronouns, the pronoun *who* (*whoever*) has three case forms.

NOMINATIVE CASE	**who**	**whoever**
OBJECTIVE CASE	**whom**	**whomever**
POSSESSIVE CASE	**whose**	**whosever**

These pronouns may be used in two ways: to form questions and to introduce subordinate clauses. When they are used to form questions, they are called ***interrogative pronouns.*** When they are used to introduce subordinate clauses, they are called ***relative pronouns.***

22k. The form an interrogative pronoun takes depends on its use in the question.

Who is used as a subject or as a predicate nominative. *Whom* is used as an object of a verb or as an object of a preposition.

NOMINATIVE **Who played this role on Broadway?** [*Who* is the subject of the verb *played.*]
Who could it have been? [*Who* is the predicate nominative identifying the subject *it.*]

OBJECTIVE **Whom** did the president recommend? [*Whom* is the direct object of the verb *did recommend.*]
With **whom** did Moss Hart write the play? [*Whom* is the object of the preposition *with.*]

NOTE: In spoken English, the use of *whom* is gradually disappearing. Nowadays it's acceptable to begin a spoken question with *who* regardless of whether the nominative or objective form is grammatically correct. In writing, though, it's still important to distinguish between *who* and *whom.*

22l. The form a relative pronoun takes depends on its use in the subordinate clause.

When choosing between *who* and *whom* in a subordinate clause, follow these steps:

STEP 1: Find the subordinate clause.
STEP 2: Decide how the relative pronoun is used in the clause—*subject, predicate nominative, direct object, indirect object,* or *object of a preposition.*
STEP 3: Determine the case for this use of the relative pronoun.
STEP 4: Select the correct case form of the relative pronoun.

EXAMPLE: Ms. Gonzalez, (*who, whom*) I greatly admire, operates a shelter for homeless people in our community.
STEP 1: The subordinate clause is *(who, whom) I greatly admire.*
STEP 2: The relative pronoun serves as the direct object of the verb *admire.*
STEP 3: A direct object is in the objective case.
STEP 4: The objective form of the relative pronoun is *whom.*
ANSWER: Ms. Gonzalez, **whom** I greatly admire, operates a shelter for homeless people in our community.

The case of the relative pronoun in a subordinate clause is not affected by any word outside the subordinate clause.

EXAMPLE: The prize goes to (*whoever, whomever*) is the first to solve the riddles.
STEP 1: The subordinate clause is *(whoever, whomever) is the first to solve the riddles.*
STEP 2: The relative pronoun serves as the subject of the verb *is,* not the object of the preposition *to.* (The entire clause is the object of the preposition *to.*)
STEP 3: A subject of a verb is in the nominative case.
STEP 4: The nominative form of the relative pronoun is *whoever.*
ANSWER: The prize goes to **whoever** is the first to solve the riddles.

USAGE

COOPERATIVE LEARNING

A team race will help students become more familiar with the correct use of *who* and *whom* in sentences. Divide the class into an even number of teams of three or four students each. Put the following clauses on the chalkboard:

1. whom we adore
2. who believed in us
3. who wandered by
4. who asked directions
5. whom we helped

Ask each team to write as many sentences as possible in five minutes and to use each clause at least once. Award a point for each correct sentence.

You may continue the game by having each team write clauses beginning with *who* and *whom* and then having them exchange clauses with another team. Again, give the teams a time limit for writing sentences.

USAGE

A DIFFERENT APPROACH

Challenge students to find and evaluate uses of *who* and *whom* in book and poem titles and in song lyrics. Ask students to list the titles, to write one or two lines of each song, and to identify the usage as standard or nonstandard. Have students work in groups of four or five and have them share their findings with the class. (Nonstandard use occurs frequently in popular song lyrics.) Point out that language is always changing. What is considered nonstandard today may come to be considered standard at some future time.

USAGE

NOTE: When choosing between *who* and *whom* to begin a question or a subordinate clause, do not be misled by a parenthetical expression consisting of a subject and a verb, such as ***I think, do you suppose, he feels,*** or ***they believe.*** Select the pronoun form you would use if the expression were not in the clause.

EXAMPLES **Who** do you think will win the Super Bowl? [*Who* is the subject of the verb *will win.*]
She is the one **who** we believe was named Teacher of the Year. [*Who* is the subject of the verb *was named.*]

REFERENCE NOTE: For more information about parenthetical expressions, see pages 872–874.

USAGE

EXERCISE 8 Using *Who* and *Whom* Correctly

For each of the following sentences, choose the correct form of the pronoun in parentheses. Then identify its use in the sentence—as a *subject*, a *predicate nominative*, a *direct object*, an *indirect object*, or an *object of the preposition*.

EXAMPLE **1. Here are the names of some of the authors (*who, whom*) we will study this semester.**
1. *whom—direct object*

1. Betty Smith, the author of *A Tree Grows in Brooklyn*, was an obscure writer (*who, whom*) became a celebrity overnight. 1. s.
2. Her novel is an American classic about a young girl (*who, whom*) she called Francie Nolan. 2. d.o.
3. Francie, (*who, whom*) we follow through girlhood to adulthood, had only one tree in her city back yard. 3. d.o.
4. Carson McCullers, (*who, whom*) critics describe as a major American writer, also wrote a novel about a young girl's coming of age. 4. d.o.
5. (*Who, Whom*) could not be moved by *The Member of the Wedding*? 5. s.
6. Do you know (*who, whom*) it was that played Frankie in the Broadway production of *The Member of the Wedding*? 6. p.n.
7. Pearl Buck is a novelist (*who, whom*) most Americans are familiar with. 7. o.p.
8. Pulitzer Prizes are awarded to (*whoever, whomever*) is selected by the panel of judges. 8. s.
9. Gwendolyn Brooks, (*who, whom*) you told me won the Pulitzer Prize for poetry, also wrote a book called *Maud Martha*. 9. s.
10. Guess (*who, whom*) Maud Martha really is. 10. p.n.

REVIEWS B–D

OBJECTIVES

- To select correct forms of pronouns in sentences
- To proofread sentences for correct pronoun forms

REVIEW B Selecting Correct Forms of Pronouns

For each sentence in the following paragraph, choose the correct form of the pronoun in parentheses.

Jordan and [1] (*I*, *me*) had thought of Impressionism as a French style of painting, and for the most part, we were right. But every artist is exposed to other artists' ideas, and often it is [2] (*they*, *them*) that inspire changes of style. If you have heard of Edgar Degas, you might know that both [3] (*he*, *him*) and the American Impressionist Mary Cassatt were very much influenced by exhibitions of Japanese prints that came to Paris. At first glance, Impressionist paintings don't appear very Japanese, but just look at [4] (*they*, *them*) and Japanese prints placed side by side, and you can see strong parallels. This morning, Ms. Kent pointed out some of those stylistic similarities to Jordan and [5] (*me*, *myself*), using the paintings shown here. Neither of [6] (*we*, *us*) two art lovers could possibly mistake the resemblance. "Just between you and [7] (*I*, *me*)," said

Henri Toulouse-Lautrec, "Jane Avril" (color lithograph), 1893. Albi, Musee Toulouse-Lautrec/ Giraudon/Art Resource, New York

Andro Hiroshige, "Branch of a Flowering Apple Tree (color woodcut)". Paris, Galerie Janette Ostier/ Giraudon/ Art Resource, New York (PEC5667/ AR5018)

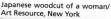

Mary Cassatt (1845–1926), "The Letter". Drypoint, soft-ground etching and aquatint, printed in color Third state. From a series of ten. H 13 5/8" W 8 15/16" /The Metropolitan Museum of Art, Gift of Paul J. Sachs, 1916 (16.2.9)

Japanese woodcut of a woman/ Art Resource, New York

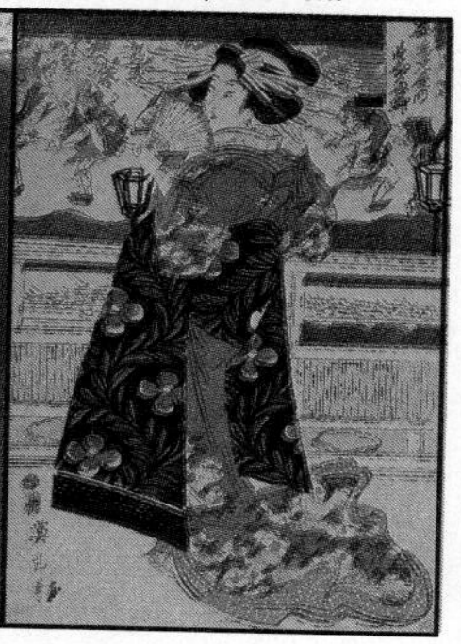

Ms. Kent, "almost all of the Impressionists openly copied ideas from the Japanese." One of my favorite painters is Toulouse-Lautrec, [8] (*who*, *whom*) often used the Japanese technique of including a large object in the extreme foreground to lend a

USAGE

VISUAL CONNECTIONS

Exploring the Subject. The French school of painting that came to be known as Impressionism began about 1874 when a group of young painters, whose works had been rejected by the highly traditional and academic Salon in Paris, mounted their own exhibition. A journalist called the group "Impressionists" based on Monet's painting *Impression: Sunrise.*

The Impressionist Movement didn't last long, and by 1880 the members of the movement were already branching out into styles of their own. Impressionism has remained a favorite style for decades, and the works of major Impressionist painters bring huge sums at art auctions.

feeling of depth to a picture. Both Mary Cassatt and [9] (he, *him*) learned from the Japanese the principle of cutting figures at the edge of the canvas to achieve a snapshot-like quality. As you can see, the Japanese technique of juxtaposing different patterned fabrics appealed to Mary Cassatt, and this technique was used by Pierre Bonnard as well as by [10] (*she*, her).

REVIEW C Proofreading Sentences for Correct Pronoun Forms

For each of the following sentences that contains an incorrect pronoun form, identify the error, and then give the correct form. If a sentence is correct, write *C*.

EXAMPLE **1. Neither Karl nor myself could find the book.**
1. *myself—I*

1. Many farm workers voted for Cesar Chavez, who they believed would fight for their rights. **1.** C
2. Both her father and ~~herself~~ have artistic talent. **2.** she
3. I can't understand his dropping out of the band during his senior year. **3.** C
4. The new exchange students, Michelle and ~~her~~, already speak some English. **4.** she
5. Robert's parents have no objection to ~~him~~ trying to get a job after school. **5.** his
6. I thought that Beth and ~~her~~ would make the best officers. **6.** she
7. They have many more cassette tapes than ~~us~~. **7.** we
8. The title of salutatorian goes to ~~whomever~~ has the second highest academic average. **8.** whoever
9. Who is supposed to sit in this empty seat between Lauren and ~~I~~? **9.** me
10. Who do you suppose won the traditional dance contest at the powwow? **10.** C

REVIEW D Selecting Correct Forms of Pronouns

Choose the correct form of each pronoun in parentheses in the following paragraph. Be prepared to explain your choices.

EXAMPLE **You have the same features in almost exactly the same positions as [1] (*I*, *me*), yet nearly anyone can easily tell our faces apart.**
1. *I*

USAGE

USAGE

WRITING APPLICATION

OBJECTIVE

- To write a persuasive letter in which *who* and *whom* are used correctly

[1] (*Who, Whom*) do you think the picture on the left is a portrait of? Reuben thought it was a woman, and I told him I couldn't believe [2] (*him, his*) not recognizing [3] (*who, whom*) it was! You should give [4] (*you, yourself*) a round of applause if you guessed George Washington. Both of these pictures were created when a scientist named Leon D. Harmon asked [5] (*him, himself*) how much information people actually needed to recognize a face. [6] (*He, Him*) and his colleagues took photographs of famous portraits, divided each photo into squares, and then averaged the color and brightness inside each square into a single tone. The computer-generated image gives you and [7] (*I, me*) very little information—there are no features and no outlines, only a pattern of colored blocks. Even though we can't see the eyes, nose, and mouth, the chances of [8] (*us, our*) recognizing a particular human face are very high. For the picture on the right, Reuben was a better guesser than [9] (*I, me*), especially when he held the page a few feet away from his eyes. Suddenly, he saw the [10] (*Mona Lisa, Mona Lisa's*) looking back at him!

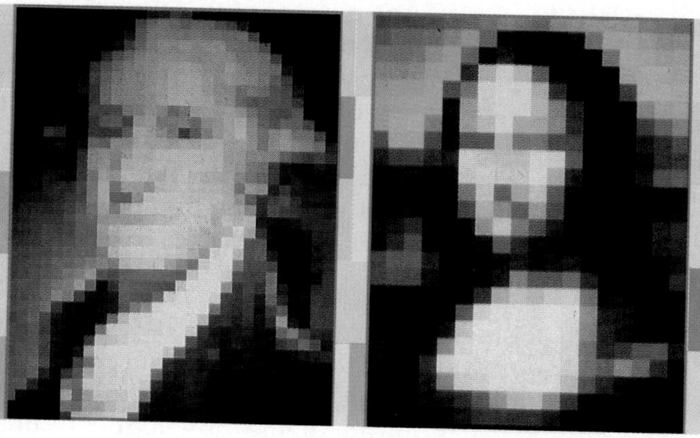

Blocpix image by Ed Manning, Stratford, CT 06497.

USAGE

WRITING APPLICATION

Using *Who* and *Whom* Correctly in Formal English

Distinctions between *who* and *whom* are more important in formal English than in informal English. In a casual conversation or a note to a friend, it's usually acceptable to use

ANSWERS

Review D

1. object of preposition *of*
2. possessive case with gerund
3. predicate nominative
4. reflexive pronoun
5. reflexive pronoun
6. subject
7. indirect object
8. possessive case with gerund
9. elliptical construction (than I was)
10. direct object modified by a present participle

USAGE

WRITING APPLICATION

The most difficult part of this assignment for students will be including the prescribed number of pronouns in the letter. You can help students by demonstrating sentence-combining techniques using *who* and *whom*. For example, two sentences like "This person volunteers five hours each week in a nursing home" and "This person is a starting player on the soccer team" can be combined as "This person, who is a starting player on the soccer team, volunteers five hours each week in a nursing home."

CRITICAL THINKING
Evaluation

To choose traits and examples of activities to illustrate that certain people are outstanding students, your students will have to evaluate the people they are considering. They will have to use a set of criteria on which to base their evaluations. You can help your students to develop criteria by leading a discussion on the characteristics students consider to be outstanding. Point out to students that their criteria will differ because different people will value different characteristics.

USAGE

who rather than *whom*. But in an essay, a business letter, or a formal speech, you should be sure to use the correct case form of the pronoun.

INFORMAL The character who I like best in "The First Seven Years" is Sobel.
FORMAL The character **whom** I like best in "The First Seven Years" is Sobel.

INFORMAL Who did you nominate?
FORMAL **Whom** did you nominate?

WRITING ACTIVITY

Your school's newspaper is planning a special feature on outstanding students and is looking for some suggestions. Write a letter to the editor, describing a student at your school and explaining what makes him or her outstanding. In your letter, use *who* (or *whoever*) three times and *whom* (or *whomever*) twice.

Prewriting Being an outstanding student doesn't necessarily mean getting the best grades or belonging to the most clubs. You may know people who are outstanding for their integrity, their humor or wit, or their helpfulness to other people. Decide who you think is the most outstanding student at your school. Then jot down some notes on the qualities and achievements that make this person special. Note a few specific examples of that person's behavior that illustrate these qualities.

Writing Remember that your goal is to persuade the editors of the newspaper that your classmate is outstanding. Begin by naming the person and telling briefly why he or she should be featured in the newspaper. Then give the examples you listed in your notes. Or, you may want to tell an anecdote about the person that shows his or her special qualities.

Evaluating and Revising Ask a friend to read your paragraph and pretend he or she is the editor of the newspaper. Is your letter clear and convincing? If not, you'll need to revise your examples or replace them with more engaging ones. Be sure each of your examples works to support your description of the person. Does your letter follow one of the

SEGMENT 7 *(pp. 697–698)*

REVIEW: POSTTEST

OBJECTIVE

- To proofread sentences and a paragraph for correct pronoun forms

correct forms for a business letter? (See pages 994–1001 for more about business correspondence.) Check that you've used the pronoun *who* and *whom* (or *whoever* and *whomever*) correctly.

Proofreading and Publishing Remember that errors in grammar, usage, or mechanics may distract your readers from your message. Proofread your paragraph carefully. Take extra care with pronouns, making sure they're in the correct case. You and your classmates may want to create your own "Wall of Fame." Collect your letters and, perhaps, some photographs of the outstanding students you've written about and arrange the letters and photos in a bulletin-board display.

Review: Posttest

A. Proofreading Sentences for Correct Pronoun Forms

For each of the following sentences that contains an incorrect pronoun form, identify the error and then give the correct form. If a sentence is correct, write *C*.

EXAMPLE **1. Manuel and him are on the soccer team.**
1. *him—he*

1. Garvin thinks that Debbie is planning a surprise party for Marita and ~~I~~. 1. me
2. Please send Anna and me a copy of the rough draft that you and she wrote. 2. C
3. You and I should probably ask Mr. Beauvais because no one else speaks French better than ~~him~~. 3. he
4. Tamisha hopes it will be ~~her~~ and Pete who are appointed to the student council. 4. she
5. But seriously, ~~whom~~ did you expect would win the blue ribbon? 5. who
6. ~~Who~~ did Justin give that autographed picture of Maria Tallchief to? 6. Whom

PROOFREADING

For help with the form and guidelines for a letter to the editor, you may want to refer your students to ***Chapter 8, Writing to Persuade,*** p. 317.

7. she

7. Danielle and I had our Bat Mitzvahs in the same month, and ~~her~~ and I both did very well reading from the Torah.
8. Mrs. Kitts says that our knowing facts is less important than our knowing where to find them. 8. C 9. your
9. I really appreciated ~~you~~ picking me up after school today.
10. All of us students, especially ~~myself~~, feel much more confident about repairing autos after taking this course.

10. me

USAGE

B. Proofreading a Paragraph for Correct Pronoun Forms

Identify each incorrect pronoun form in the following sentences, and then give the correct form. [Note: There may be more than one error in a sentence.] If a sentence is correct, write *C*.

EXAMPLE **[1] Meriwether Lewis hired me when him and William Clark set out to explore the Louisiana Purchase.**
1. *him—he*

11. I
12. We
13. me
14. whom
15. me
16. she
17. him
18. C
19. us
20. he/they

[11] My cousin John and ~~me~~ were proud to be included in the group that went along with Lewis and Clark. **[12]** ~~Us~~ cousins were jacks-of-all-trades; both of us did everything from loading pack animals to building campfires. **[13]** For John and ~~I~~, one of the best things about the trip was getting to know the other members of the group. **[14]** Someone ~~who~~ we became good friends with was York, a strong, friendly African American. **[15]** Everyone, including ~~myself~~, found York to be one of the most valuable members of the expedition. **[16]** Many people know that Sacagawea, a Shoshone woman, was an interpreter on the expedition, but York was just as valuable an interpreter as ~~her~~. **[17]** In fact, communicating with Native Americans would have been practically impossible without both Sacagawea and ~~himself~~. **[18]** Whenever the expedition met with Native Americans, Sacagawea would tell her French husband Charbonneau what was said between her and them. **[19]** Charbonneau would then repeat the message in French to York, who would translate the French into English for Lewis, Clark, and the rest of ~~we~~ expedition members. **[20]** When we needed food and horses, York himself did much of the trading with Native Americans because ~~him~~ and ~~them~~ got along very well.

SEGMENT 1 *(pp. 699–701)*

DIAGNOSTIC TEST

OBJECTIVE

- To revise sentences by correcting unclear references

23 CLEAR REFERENCE

Pronouns and Antecedents

USAGE

Diagnostic Test

A. Revising Sentences by Correcting Unclear References

Most of the following sentences contain pronouns without clear antecedents. Revise each sentence to correct any unclear pronoun references. [Note: Although sentences can be corrected in more than one way, you need to give only one revision.] If a sentence is correct, write *C.*

EXAMPLE 1. Aaron had not yet seen the new aerobics video, so he had a difficult time doing any of them.
1. *Aaron had not yet seen the new aerobics video, so he had a difficult time doing any of the exercises.*

1. In the magazine article, they explain how microprocessors are used in the electrical stimulation of paralyzed muscles.
2. Lucia wrote to Sara every week while she was visiting her aunt and uncle in Guadalajara, Mexico.

Teacher's ResourceBank™

RESOURCES

FOR THE WHOLE CHAPTER

- Chapter Review Form A 263–264
- Chapter Review Form B 265–266
- Assessment Portfolio
  - Usage Pretests 571–578
  - Usage Mastery Tests 597–604

CHAPTER OVERVIEW

This chapter deals with pronoun-reference clarity. It contains segments on ambiguous reference, general reference, weak reference, and indefinite reference. Each segment contains rules, examples, and exercises.

USING THE DIAGNOSTIC TEST

If students seem to be having problems with clear reference in their compositions, you can use the **Diagnostic Test** to identify those students who need concentrated work on the material in this chapter. Students who miss three or more of the items should probably work through the explanatory material and the exercises.

USAGE

ANSWERS

Diagnostic Test: Part A

Revisions will vary. Here are some possibilities:

1. The magazine article explains how microprocessors are used in the electrical stimulation of paralyzed muscles.
2. While Lucia was visiting her aunt and uncle in Guadalajara, Mexico, she wrote to Sara every week.

3. The star of the play was sick, two other actors had not memorized their lines, and the stage manager was out of town. These problems caused the director to cancel rehearsals.

4. Zack likes to browse in music stores but seldom buys anything there.

5. In many families today, parents have opened savings accounts or have bought stock to help pay their children's college expenses.

6. After the architect had made changes on the blueprint, she discussed the changes with the contractor.

7. We were disappointed that we couldn't ride the mules to Phantom Ranch at the bottom of the Grand Canyon.

8. C

9. The glass bowl shattered when it landed on the floor.

10. C

3. The star of the play was sick, two other actors had not memorized their lines, and the stage manager was out of town. This caused the director to cancel rehearsals.

4. Zack likes to browse in music stores but seldom buys any of them.

5. In many families today, you will find that parents have opened savings accounts or have bought stock to help pay their children's college expenses.

6. The architect discussed with the contractor the changes she had just made on the blueprint.

7. We couldn't ride the mules to Phantom Ranch at the bottom of the Grand Canyon, which was disappointing.

8. It is raining again, but the state highway department crew is working to repair the bridge.

9. When the glass bowl landed on the floor, it shattered.

10. He told many of his own original jokes, one of which was about a penguin on its first visit to Times Square.

B. Revising Sentences by Correcting Unclear References

Most of the following sentences contain pronouns without clear antecedents. Revise each sentence to correct any unclear pronoun references. [Note: Although sentences can be corrected in more than one way, you need to give only one revision.] If a sentence is correct, write *C*. Revisions will vary.

EXAMPLE **1.** **Ferris studied the Chinese poet T'ao Ch'ien in his world literature class last semester.**

1. ***In his world literature class last semester, Ferris studied the Chinese poet T'ao Ch'ien.***

11. T'ao ~~Ch'ien loved to work~~ in his garden, ~~which~~ is evident in his poetry. 1. Ch'ien's love for working

12. T'ao Ch'ien's topics came from his own simple life. One of these was worrying about his five sons. 12. topics

13. ~~In our~~ literature book ~~it~~ states that the Chinese consider Tu Fu to be their greatest poet. 13. Our

14. Many people admire poetry, but most people don't think ~~they~~ can be used for medicinal purposes. 14. poetry

15. ~~In this book, you will find~~ a story about Tu Fu's suggesting that his poetry could cure malarial fever. 15. This book contains

16. That more than a thousand of Tu Fu's poems survive is amazing. 16. C

SEGMENT 2 *(pp. 701–705)*

AMBIGUOUS REFERENCE AND GENERAL REFERENCE Rules 23b, 23c

OBJECTIVES

- To revise sentences by correcting ambiguous references
- To revise sentences by correcting general references

17. The poet Li Po liked to travel and to enjoy nature. ~~This~~ gave him many poetry subjects but no family life. 17. These interests
18. Ms. Johnson explained to Alicia the meaning of the Li Po poem ~~she~~ had just read. 18. Alicia
19. John Jay liked Po Chu-i's poetry, and ~~he~~ wanted to copy one of the poems.
20. Darnell took almost the whole class period to describe the tragic love story related in Po Chu-i's narrative poem *The Song of Everlasting Regret.* ~~It~~ went by very quickly. 20. The period

USAGE

A pronoun has no definite meaning in itself. Its meaning is clear only when the reader knows what word it stands for. This word is called the ***antecedent*** of the pronoun.

23a. A pronoun should always refer clearly to its antecedent.

In the following examples, arrows point from the pronouns to their antecedents.

EXAMPLES The Pope asked **Leonardo** to do the sculpture, but **he** refused.

The math teacher gave **us** a problem that **we** couldn't solve.

After trying on the long blue **dress,** Mary said, **"This** fits perfectly."

Ambiguous Reference

23b. Avoid an ***ambiguous reference,*** which occurs when a pronoun refers to either of two antecedents.

AMBIGUOUS Colleen called Alicia while she was doing her homework. [The antecedent of *she* and *her* is unclear. Who was doing her homework, Colleen or Alicia?]

CLEAR While Colleen was doing her homework, she called Alicia.

CLEAR While Alicia was doing her homework, Colleen called her.

Teacher's ResourceBank™

RESOURCES

AMBIGUOUS REFERENCE AND GENERAL REFERENCE

- Problems in Pronoun Reference A 261

QUICK REMINDER

Write the following sentences on the chalkboard and ask students to identify and correct the problems:

1. Eloise praised Anna, and she looked confused. [The antecedent of *she* is unclear. Anna looked confused when Eloise praised her.]
2. The road department is paving the street, which causes problems. [*Which* has no specific antecedent. The paving of the street by the road department causes problems.]
3. Fishing licenses have gone up in price, and this means fewer people will go fishing. [*This* has no specific antecedent. Fishing licenses have gone up in price. This price hike means fewer people will go fishing.]

MEETING INDIVIDUAL NEEDS

LEP/ESL

General Strategies. Explain to students that in revising sentences with ambiguous reference, the first task is to identify the antecedent for the pronoun. In sentences such as the ones in **Exercise 1,** making an arbitrary decision about which antecedent the pronoun is referring to is often necessary.

USAGE

AMBIGUOUS The ship's officer explained to the passenger the meaning of the regulation he had just read. [The antecedent of *he* is unclear. Who had just read the regulation?]

CLEAR After the ship's officer read the regulation, he explained its meaning to the passenger.

CLEAR After reading the regulation, the ship's officer explained its meaning to the passenger.

CLEAR After the passenger read the regulation, the ship's officer explained its meaning to him.

USAGE

EXERCISE 1 **Revising Sentences by Correcting Ambiguous References**

Revise each of the following sentences, correcting the ambiguous pronoun references. [Note: Although sentences can be corrected in more than one way, you need to give only one revision.]

EXAMPLE **1. When the ship struck the dock, it burst into flames.**

1. *When it struck the dock, the ship burst into flames.*

or

The dock burst into flames when the ship struck it.

1. The loyal forces fought the guerrillas until they were almost entirely destroyed.
2. The police officer told the sergeant that she lost a button from her uniform.
3. The guide explained to the tourist the value of the stone she had found.
4. Leon told Carlos that his report would be better if he were to add more details about Cesar Chavez.
5. When Anna brought Lena to the conference, we asked her for her credentials.
6. Since the show was scheduled for the same night as the intramural playoff game, it had to be postponed.
7. The manager told the dishwasher that he would have to replace all broken dishes.
8. When the ambassador emerged from a long conference with the foreign minister, reporters thought he looked confident.
9. When the truck hit the wall, it was hardly damaged.
10. A copy of the Black History Month schedule was posted on the board, but somebody took it.

USAGE

ANSWERS

Exercise 1

Revisions will vary. Here are some possibilities:

1. The loyal forces fought the guerrillas until the guerrillas were almost entirely destroyed.
2. After noticing that a button was lost from the sergeant's uniform, the police officer told the sergeant about it.
3. The guide explained to the tourist the value of the stone the tourist had found.
4. Leon told Carlos that Carlos could make his report better by adding more details about Cesar Chavez.
5. We asked Lena for her credentials when Anna brought her to the conference.
6. Since the show was scheduled for the same night as the intramural playoff game, the show had to be postponed.
7. The manager told the dishwasher that the dishwasher would have to replace all broken dishes.
8. Reporters thought the ambassador looked confident when he emerged from a long conference with the foreign minister.
9. The truck was hardly damaged when it hit the wall.
10. Somebody took the copy of the Black History Month schedule that was posted on the board.

23c

General Reference

23c. Avoid a ***general reference,*** which occurs when a pronoun refers to a general idea rather than to a specific noun.

The pronouns commonly used in making general references are *it, this, that, which,* and *such.*

GENERAL The wind rose, and dark clouds rolled in from the distant hills. This prompted the campers to seek shelter. [*This* has no specific antecedent.]

CLEAR The wind rose, and dark clouds began rolling in from the distant hills. These ominous conditions prompted the campers to seek shelter.

CLEAR As the wind rose and dark clouds began rolling in from the distant hills, the campers sought shelter.

GENERAL More than 20 percent of those who enter college fail to graduate, which is a shame. [*Which* has no specific antecedent.]

CLEAR That more than 20 percent of those who enter college fail to graduate is a shame.

EXERCISE 2 **Revising Sentences by Correcting General References**

Revise each of the following sentences, correcting the general pronoun reference. [Note: Although these sentences can be corrected in more than one way, you need to give only one revision.]

Revisions will vary.

EXAMPLE **1.** England invaded France in 1337. It began a series of wars known as the Hundred Years' War.

1. *England's invasion of France in 1337 began a series of wars known as the Hundred Years' War.*

or

When England invaded France in 1337, a series of wars known as the Hundred Years' War began.

1. On California's San Miguel Island, ~~we had~~ a guided tour by a ranger, ~~which~~ made the visit especially interesting.

2. A great many young people have already left Hastings Corners to work in the city, ~~which~~ is unfortunate for this town. **2.** That

INTEGRATING THE LANGUAGE ARTS

Literature Link. John Crowe Ransom uses ambiguous pronoun references in the fourth and fifth stanzas of his poem "Parting, Without a Sequel." If your literature textbook contains the poem, ask your students to read the selection and to comment on the antecedents of the words *who, his,* and *he* in the fourth stanza and on the antecedents of *his* and *he* in the fifth. How does the meaning of the poem change if the pronouns refer to the tree rather than to the father? [Answers will vary. The poem deals with a young woman's ambivalence about sending a scolding letter. If the pronouns refer to the tree, the poem may mean that even nature knows she's making a mistake. If the pronouns refer to the father, the meaning may be that he knows his daughter will soon regret her letter.]

USAGE

REVIEW A

OBJECTIVE

- To revise sentences by correcting ambiguous and general references

3. to make a difficult decision about

3. The guidance counselor asked me whether I wanted to take German, French, or Spanish, ~~which was difficult to decide.~~ 4. These changes 5. This damage
4. My parents bought a new carpet and new curtains, and they hired someone to paint the walls and ceiling. ~~That~~ certainly improved the appearance of the room.
5. After the storm last weekend, the trail to the top of the mountain was washed out in some spots and was blocked in many places with fallen branches. ~~It~~ made the ascent nerve-racking. 6. Having all three subjects on the test
6. The first part of the test will be on chemistry, the second on mathematics, the third on physics. ~~This~~ will make it very difficult. 7. The conflicting descriptions
7. Several of the eyewitnesses described the man as short, others said he was tall, and yet others said he was "about average." ~~It~~ confused the police investigators.
8. The principal said that the play will have to be given in the old auditorium unless by some miracle the new auditorium can be completed ahead of schedule, ~~which~~ will be a blow to the Maude Adams Drama Club.
9. We hiked all morning and then went skiing at Gates of the Arctic National Park and Preserve, ~~which~~ made us all extremely tired. 9. . This activity
10. I received a notice that three of my library books were overdue, ~~which~~ was ~~a complete surprise.~~ 10. When/I/ completely surprised.

8. . Having to use the old auditorium

REVIEW A **Revising Sentences by Correcting Ambiguous and General References**

Most of the following sentences contain ambiguous or general pronoun references. Revise each faulty sentence. [Note: Although these sentences can be corrected in more than one way, you need to give only one revision.] If a sentence is correct, write *C*. Revisions will vary.

EXAMPLE
1. Some people still haven't heard about the Civil Rights Memorial, which is unfortunate.
1. *That some people still haven't heard about the Civil Rights Memorial is unfortunate.*

1. ~~Tonya sent a postcard to Alice~~ After ~~she~~ saw the Civil Rights Memorial at the Southern Poverty Law Center in Montgomery, Alabama. 1. Tonya/, she sent a postcard to Alice.

USAGE

2. Morris S. Dees, cofounder of the Law Center, and other center officials wanted to find a top architect to create a special memorial. This^led them to Maya Lin. **2. desire**
3. My mother remembers reading about Lin at the time^~~she~~ was chosen to design the Vietnam Veterans Memorial in Washington, D.C. **3. Lin**
4. Before she made up her mind, Lin researched the history of the civil rights movement.^~~That~~ convinced her to accept the project. **4. Her research**
5. As you can see here, the granite memorial consists of two distinct parts: a wall with an engraved quotation and a round tabletop. This^makes a simple but striking effect. **5. design**

6. Engraving the events and names associated with the civil rights movement on the tabletop was an inspired idea. **6. C**
7. Water^~~flows~~ down the wall and over the tabletop of the memorial, ~~which~~ adds a sense of calm and continuity. **7. flowing**
8. Mrs. Bledsoe told Tamisha about some of the forty entries ^~~she~~ had just read on the tabletop. **8. Tamisha**
9. When the Law Center dedicated^~~the memorial~~ in 1989,^~~it~~ became a popular tourist stop. **9. it/the memorial**
10. Nowadays, many people come to Montgomery especially to see the Civil Rights Memorial^~~which~~, of course, benefits the city. **10. . This increased tourism**

USAGE

VISUAL CONNECTIONS

Exploring the Subject. The Civil Rights Memorial is constructed out of black Canadian granite, and it forms the entrance plaza of the Southern Poverty Law Center. The inscription that dominates the large vertical wall is a paraphrase of a verse from the Book of Amos in the Bible, and Martin Luther King, Jr., used it at least twice in famous speeches.

USAGE

SEGMENT 3 *(pp. 706–710)*

WEAK REFERENCE AND INDEFINITE REFERENCE Rules 23d, 23e

OBJECTIVES

- To revise sentences by correcting weak pronoun references
- To write a paragraph consisting of a description and an evaluation of a work of art
- To revise sentences by correcting indefinite pronoun references

Teacher's ResourceBank™

RESOURCES

WEAK REFERENCE AND INDEFINITE REFERENCE

- Problems in Pronoun Reference B 262

QUICK REMINDER

Write the following sentences on the chalkboard. Ask students to identify weak or indefinite references and to revise the sentences.

1. Joan painted whenever she could find time, but she never sold any of them. [The antecedent of *them* is not expressed. Joan painted whenever she could find time, but she never sold any of her paintings.]
2. In the directions it says to preheat the oven. [*It* is not necessary to the meaning of the sentence. The directions say to preheat the oven.]
3. Antoine is an accomplished pianist, but he doesn't own one. [The antecedent of *one* is not identified. Antoine is an accomplished pianist, but he doesn't own a piano.]
4. I grow a lot of vegetables and consider it an enjoyable hobby. [The antecedent of *it* is not identified. I consider growing a lot of vegetables an enjoyable hobby.]
5. In some schools, you will see students wearing uniforms. [*You* has no clear antecedent in the sentence. In some schools, students wear uniforms.]

USAGE

Weak Reference

23d. Avoid a ***weak reference,*** which occurs when a pronoun refers to an antecedent that has not been expressed.

WEAK Every time a circus came to town, my sister Erin wanted to become one of them. [The antecedent of *them* is not expressed.]

CLEAR Every time a circus came to town, my sister Erin wanted to become one of the troupe.

WEAK He was a very superstitious person. One of these was that walking under a ladder would bring bad luck. [The antecedent of *these* is not expressed.]

CLEAR He was a very superstitious person. One of his superstitions was that walking under a ladder would bring bad luck.

CLEAR He believed in many superstitions. One of these was that walking under a ladder would bring bad luck.

CLEAR He believed in many superstitions, one of which was that walking under a ladder would bring bad luck.

EXERCISE 3 Revising Sentences by Correcting Weak References

Revise each of the following sentences, correcting the weak pronoun reference. [Note: Although some of these sentences can be corrected in more than one way, you need to give only one revision.] Revisions will vary.

EXAMPLE
1. Mom is very interested in psychiatry, but she does not believe they know all the answers.
1. *Mom is very interested in psychiatry, but she does not believe that psychiatrists know all the answers.*

1. Sir Arthur Conan Doyle began his career as a doctor, and ~~it~~ explains his interest in careful observation. 1. his medical training
2. She is a careful gardener, watering ~~them~~ whenever the soil gets dry. 2. the plants
3. They planned to eat dinner outdoors by candlelight, but a strong wind kept blowing ~~them~~ out. 3. the candles.
4. For years after seeing the Alvin Ailey American Dance Theater perform, Leah dreamed of joining ~~them.~~ 4. the troupe.

5. Even though it rained on the night of the concert, Eric went because his favorite^ ~~ones~~ were scheduled to be played. **5.** musical numbers
6. My brother has an anthology of Japanese literature for his college course, but he hasn't read any of^ ~~them~~ yet. **6.** the selections
7. Although Bradley enjoys reading poetry, he has never written^ ~~one.~~ **7.** a poem.
8. Sarah's uncle has a huge vegetable garden, and he keeps ^~~them~~ supplied with fresh vegetables all summer long. **8.** Sarah's family
9. He spent more than an hour at the clothing store but did not try^ ~~any on.~~ **9.** on any clothes.
10. Deep-sea fishing isn't very enjoyable to me unless I catch at least one^ **10.** fish.

USAGE

Indefinite Reference

23e. In formal writing, avoid the indefinite use of the pronouns *it, they,* and *you.*

An ***indefinite reference*** occurs when a pronoun refers to no particular person or thing. Such a pronoun is unnecessary to the meaning of the sentence.

INDEFINITE In the newspaper it reported that a volcano had erupted in the Indian Ocean. [*It* is not necessary to the meaning of the sentence.]

CLEAR The newspaper reported that a volcano had erupted in the Indian Ocean.

INDEFINITE In this history book, they refer to the American Civil War as the War Between the States. [*They* does not refer to any specific persons.]

CLEAR This history book refers to the American Civil War as the War Between the States.

INDEFINITE In some nineteenth-century novels, you will find the vocabulary quite difficult. [*You* has no clear antecedent in the sentence.]

CLEAR In some nineteenth-century novels, the vocabulary is quite difficult.

NOTE: The indefinite use of *it* in familiar expressions such as *it is snowing, it is early,* and *it seems* is acceptable.

USAGE

MEETING INDIVIDUAL NEEDS

LEP/ESL

General Strategies. Because ESL students will no doubt hear the indefinite use of pronouns quite often in everyday speech, **Rule 23e** may be confusing. You might want to emphasize that the rule says "In formal writing. . . ." In speaking and in informal writing, the usage is considered acceptable.

A DIFFERENT APPROACH

Your advanced students may benefit from practice in locating and correcting weak and indefinite references in their own writing. They can go back to previous writing assignments, look for problems in pronoun reference, and revise any problem sentences.

PICTURE THIS

Descriptions should be organized logically, such as by spatial order. Students should describe the head, the box, the arms, and the contents of the box. Evaluations will vary.

VISUAL CONNECTIONS

About the Artwork. *Memorial to the Idea of Man If He Was an Idea* by H. C. Westermann, is a surrealistic sculpture. In this work, as in others of its genre, bits and pieces of common objects are transformed into art.

Westermann's sculpture consists of a box made of laminated wood and shaped to resemble a person by the addition of arms and a one-eyed head. Westermann creates an air of fun about his work by adding things like openings to look through, drawers and doors that open, and mirrors to create reflected images.

USAGE

USAGE

PICTURE THIS

You are the art critic for the local newspaper, and you're reviewing a new exhibit of modern sculpture. You discover this work by H. C. Westermann to be as surprising and intriguing as its title: *Memorial to the Idea of Man If He Was an Idea.* Write a paragraph about the sculpture to include in your review. In your paragraph, describe the sculpture and give your opinion of it. Should your readers go to see the sculpture for themselves? Tell why or why not. In your review, use clear pronoun references so that your readers aren't confused.

Subject:	a modern sculpture
Audience:	readers of the local newspaper
Purpose:	to inform; to evaluate a sculpture in an exhibit

H.C. Westermann, "Memorial to the Idea of Man If He Was an Idea." Collection of Susan and Lewis Manilow.

EXERCISE 4 **Revising Sentences by Correcting Indefinite Pronoun References**

Revise each of the following sentences, correcting the indefinite use of *it, they,* or *you.* [Note: Although these sentences can be corrected in more than one way, you need to give only one revision.] Revisions will vary.

EXAMPLE **1.** In Japan they have the world's tallest roller coaster.
1. *Japan has the world's tallest roller coaster.*
or
The world's tallest roller coaster is in Japan.

REVIEW B

OBJECTIVE

• To revise sentences by correcting weak and indefinite references

1. ~~In~~ *The Diary of Anne Frank* ~~it~~ shows a young Jewish girl's courage during two years of hiding from the Nazis.
2. Everyone is excited about graduation because ~~you~~ have worked so hard for it. **2.** the seniors
3. In some parts of Africa, ~~they~~ mine diamonds and sell them to jewelers to be cut. **3.** prospectors
4. ~~In~~ the sports sections of the daily newspapers, ~~it tells~~ all about the day's events in sports. **4.** tell
5. When Grandpa was a child, ~~you~~ were supposed to be absolutely silent at the table. **5.** children
6. ~~In~~ the movie guide, ~~it~~ states that *The Long Walk Home* is almost a documentary about civil rights.
7. ~~On~~ the book jacket, ~~they say~~ that the authors themselves experienced these thrilling adventures. **7.** says
8. ~~They had whirled~~ so fast ~~it~~ made them dizzy. **8.** Whirling
9. One of the attractions of the tour was that ~~they~~ listed free admissions to all places of interest. **9.** the sponsors
10. When the Neville Brothers come to town next week, ~~it~~ will be ~~a sold-out show.~~ **10.** their show/sold out.

USAGE

REVIEW B **Revising Sentences by Correcting Weak and Indefinite References**

Most of the following sentences contain weak and indefinite pronoun references. Revise each faulty sentence. [Note: Although sentences can be corrected in more than one way, you need to give only one revision.] If a sentence is correct, write *C*.

Revisions will vary.

EXAMPLE **1. In the newspaper they ran an article about English actor Jeremy Brett as the detective Sherlock Holmes.**
1. *The newspaper ran an article about English actor Jeremy Brett as the detective Sherlock Holmes.*

1. Every time I see Sherlock Holmes on public television's *Mystery!* series, I want to read some more of ~~them.~~ **1.** the Sherlock Holmes mysteries.
2. ~~In~~ the article, ~~they talk~~ about Brett's authentic Holmes wardrobe, an example of which ~~you~~ can ~~see~~ in the picture on the next page. **2.** talks/be seen
3. In some old movies, ~~you will find~~ Holmes ~~wearing~~ a deerstalker hat, but he never does in the stories by Sir Arthur Conan Doyle. **3.** wears
4. Holmes is a very theatrical person. One of ~~these~~ is ~~using~~ disguises, such as that of a priest in "Final Problem." **4.** example/his theatrical bent/his use of

USAGE

MEETING **INDIVIDUAL** NEEDS

LEARNING STYLES

Auditory Learners. Some of the auditory learners in your class may benefit from working with partners on **Review B.** Ask the partners to read each sentence aloud as the auditory learners follow the text. Then both students in each pair can work together to revise the sentences, with both members responsible for explaining why the revisions were made.

USAGE

> **TIMESAVER**
> **Parts A** and **B** of the **Posttest** deal with the same concepts. You can save grading time for this activity if you let your students do **Part A** one day in class and **Part B** later if it appears that students need reteaching. You can set a criterion ahead of time for determining whether your students have mastered the concepts in the chapter. For example, you can use a score of 80 as the cutoff point for determining which students need reteaching.

SEGMENT 4 *(pp. 710–712)*

REVIEW: POSTTEST

OBJECTIVE

- To revise sentences by correcting faulty pronoun references

USAGE

5. In the *Mystery!* series, Brett was given the opportunity to play Holmes as Conan Doyle created the character. 5. C
6. Throughout Conan Doyle's stories ~~they present~~ Holmes ^ as confident, fair, and dramatic but also as restless, temperamental, and moody. 6. is presented
7. When we heard that Brett starred as Sherlock Holmes on the London stage, we wanted to see ^ ~~it.~~ 7. his performance.
8. ~~In~~ the reviews of *Mystery!* ~~they~~ state that Brett is widely considered the best Sherlock Holmes ever.
9. I joined the local chapter of the Baker Street Irregulars, which is a kind of Sherlock Holmes fan club. 9. C
10. From 1887 to 1927, Conan Doyle chronicled the life of Holmes, writing more than fifty ^ ~~of them.~~ 10. Sherlock Holmes stories.

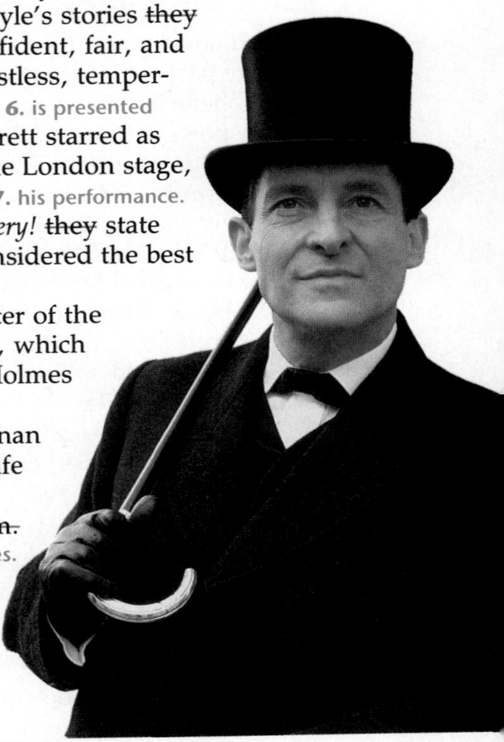

Review: Posttest

A. Revising Sentences by Correcting Faulty Pronoun References

The following sentences contain examples of ambiguous, general, weak, and indefinite references. Revise each sentence, correcting the faulty pronoun reference. [Note: Although sentences can be corrected in more than one way, you need to give only one revision.] Revisions will vary.

EXAMPLE 1. My grandparents walk five miles every day. It is one of the best forms of exercise.
1. *My grandparents walk five miles every day. Walking is one of the best forms of exercise.*

1. I heard ~~the owl~~ hoot from a tree nearby, ~~but~~ I couldn't see ~~it.~~ 1. Though/it/the owl.
2. ~~In~~ small print on the insurance policy, ~~it~~ said that ~~they were~~ not responsible for damage caused by floods. 2. The/the company was
3. We hiked almost fourteen miles to the campsite, pitched our tents, arranged our sleeping bags, and then made our supper. This so exhausted us that we immediately went to sleep. 3. activity
4. Many of our presidents began their political careers as minor public officials, ~~which~~ is a good thing. 4. That
5. Isaac Bashevis Singer was one of the best-known Jewish novelists of the twentieth century, and I always enjoy ~~them~~ very much. 5. his novels
6. ~~In~~ *Mama's Bank Account*, ~~it~~ describes how a Norwegian American family lives in San Francisco.
7. When we saw the flock of geese, ~~they~~ told us that ~~they~~ had flown all the way from northern Canada. 7. the guides/the geese
8. Jan liked the Wynton Marsalis tape but was disappointed that it didn't include her favorite ~~one.~~ 8. song.
9. The shipwrecked men paddled their raft with their hands day after day, but this brought them no closer to land. 9. effort
10. Out in the country, far away from city lights, ~~they~~ say ~~you can frequently see~~ the aurora borealis. 10. people/can frequently be seen.

B. Revising Sentences by Correcting Faulty Pronoun References

Most of the following sentences contain ambiguous, general, weak, or indefinite references. Revise each faulty sentence. If a sentence is correct, write *C*. [Note: Although sentences can be corrected in more than one way, you need to give only one revision.] Revisions will vary.

EXAMPLE **1. Carl Sagan praised Stephen W. Hawking after he wrote *A Brief History of Time*.**

1. *Carl Sagan praised Stephen W. Hawking after Hawking wrote A Brief History of Time.*

11. ~~In~~ the review of the book, ~~it~~ calls Hawking one of the greatest physicists of the twentieth century.
12. Hawking's 1988 book about physics and the universe became a best-seller, ~~which~~ was surprising. 12. That

USAGE

MEETING INDIVIDUAL NEEDS

AT-RISK STUDENTS

Many at-risk students have erratic school attendance and may miss school on the day you use the **Posttest** in class. You can help students to complete this work by allowing them to do the **Posttest** at home. Even if you use the scores as a test grade, the items are such that using the text of the chapter for help won't invalidate the scores.

USAGE

13. Rick

13. Jamie told Rick that ~~he~~ should have read Hawking's chapter about black holes in space before writing his report.
14. Whenever Francine reads a good book about science she always wants to become ~~one of them.~~ 14. a scientist.
15. According to Hawking, Galileo was a talented science writer. One of ~~these~~ was the work *Two New Sciences*, the basis of modern physics. 15. Galileo's books
16. ~~In~~ Hawking's book, ~~you will find~~ concepts about quantum mechanics, ~~which~~ can be difficult for nonscientists to understand. 16. contains/a subject that
17. ~~In~~ this magazine article on Hawking, ~~they tell~~ about his personal battle with motor neuron disease. 17. tells
18. Because the disease affects his speech and movement, Hawking wrote his book by using a voice synthesizer and a personal computer on his wheelchair. 18. C
19. Even though Hawking carefully explains his theories on the thermodynamic and cosmological arrows of time, ~~it~~ still ~~confuses~~ some readers. 19. the theories/confuse
20. That Hawking apparently understands the applications of Einstein's theories to time and the universe does not seem astonishing. 20. C

USAGE

USAGE

SEGMENT 1 (pp. 713–714)

DIAGNOSTIC TEST

OBJECTIVES

- To choose the correct verb forms in sentences
- To revise verb voice or mood

24 CORRECT VERB USAGE

Principal Parts; Tense, Voice, Mood

Diagnostic Test

A. Choosing the Correct Verb Forms

For each of the following sentences, choose the correct form of the verb in parentheses.

EXAMPLE 1. (*Sit, Set*) this pitcher of juice on the table, please.
1. *Set*

1. A beautiful oak banister (*rises, raises*) along the staircase.
2. If you (*would have, had*) visited Mexico City, you would have seen the great pyramids at Tenochtitlan.
3. Tammie says that yesterday she should have (*went, gone*) to the beach.

USAGE

Teacher's ResourceBank™

RESOURCES

FOR THE WHOLE CHAPTER

- Chapter Review Form A 276–277
- Chapter Review Form B 278–279
- Assessment Portfolio
  - Usage Pretests 571–578
  - Usage Mastery Tests 597–604

CHAPTER OVERVIEW

The material in this chapter will clarify for students the sometimes confusing nature of verbs. Principal parts of regular and irregular verbs, verb tense, active and passive voice, and mood are all thoroughly discussed. Additional explanation for troublesome verbs such as *lie* and *lay, sit* and *set,* and *rise* and *raise* is provided and is reinforced by multiple exercises. In the **Writing Application,** students are asked to use active and passive voice in writing a few paragraphs of a story.

You may want to refer to this chapter when you teach composition. A quick review of verb usage before the revision stage can provide students the help they need to make their compositions clear and effective.

USAGE

USING THE DIAGNOSTIC TEST

The first part of the **Diagnostic Test** deals with tenses of irregular verbs. You may want to let your students take **Part A** so that you can evaluate how well they understand basic concepts. If students appear to need an extensive review of verb usage, you may want to postpone giving the second part of the **Diagnostic Test** until you have finished teaching the first six segments of the chapter. You can give **Part B** when you are ready to assess students' mastery of voice and mood.

USAGE

USAGE

4. Edward said that he wanted (*to go*, *to have gone*) to the Diez y Seis party, where his friends were celebrating Mexico's independence from Spain.
5. One of the statues has (*fell*, *fallen*) off its base.
6. How long did it (*lie*, *lay*) on the floor?
7. Since last September I (*missed*, *have missed*) only one day of school.
8. The U.S. Census Bureau has predicted that by the year 2000 the Hispanic population in the United States (*will grow*, *will have grown*) to more than 25 million.
9. Fortunately, I have never been (*stinged*, *stung*) by a bee.
10. The unusual pattern in this wool material was (*weaved*, *woven*) by Seamus MacMhuiris, an artist who uses bold geometric designs.
11. The house became very quiet after everyone (*left*, *had left*).
12. I (*began*, *begun*) this homework assignment an hour ago.
13. My parents' old car has (*broke*, *broken*) down again.
14. Everyone who (*saw*, *seen*) Greg Louganis dive in the 1988 Olympics recognized his superior talent.
15. He likes to (*sit*, *set*) on the porch in his rocking chair.

B. Revising Verb Voice or Mood

Revise the following sentences by correcting verbs that use an awkward passive voice or verbs that are not in the appropriate mood. Answers may vary.

16. If I ~~was~~ you, I would not skate on that lake; the ice is too thin. **16.** were **17.** The dog caught the ball that I threw.
17. ~~The ball that was thrown by me was caught by the dog.~~
18. He now wishes that he ~~was~~ on the field trip to the Diego Rivera exhibit. **18.** were
19. The quilt that ~~was made by me~~ won second prize at the county fair. **19.** I made **20.** crowd enjoyed the
20. The half-time show ~~was enjoyed by the crowd.~~

REFERENCE NOTE: Depending on their function, verbs may be classified as *action verbs* or *linking verbs* and as *main verbs* or *helping verbs*. For a discussion of these different kinds of verbs, see pages 565–567.

SEGMENT 2 *(pp. 715–730)*

THE PRINCIPAL PARTS OF VERBS

Rules 24a–24c

OBJECTIVE

- To use the past and past participle forms of regular and irregular verbs in sentences

The Principal Parts of Verbs

24a. Every verb has four basic forms called the ***principal parts:*** the *infinitive,* the *present participle,* the *past,* and the *past participle.* All other forms of a verb are derived from these principal parts.

The following examples include *is* and *have* in parentheses to indicate that helping verbs (forms of *be* and *have*) are used with the present participle and past participle forms of verbs.

INFINITIVE	PRESENT PARTICIPLE	PAST	PAST PARTICIPLE
receive	(is) receiving	received	(have) received
join	(is) joining	joined	(have) joined
bring	(is) bringing	brought	(have) brought
sing	(is) singing	sang	(have) sung
hurt	(is) hurting	hurt	(have) hurt

All verbs form the present participle in the same way: by adding *–ing* to the infinitive form. All verbs, however, do not form the past and past participle in the same way.

Regular Verbs

24b. A ***regular verb*** is one that forms its past and past participle by adding *–d* or *–ed* to the infinitive form.

INFINITIVE	PRESENT PARTICIPLE	PAST	PAST PARTICIPLE
use	(is) using	used	(have) used
revise	(is) revising	revised	(have) revised
outline	(is) outlining	outlined	(have) outlined
watch	(is) watching	watched	(have) watched
happen	(is) happening	happened	(have) happened
rush	(is) rushing	rushed	(have) rushed

Teacher's ResourceBank™

RESOURCES

THE PRINCIPAL PARTS OF VERBS

QUICK REMINDER

Write the following sentences on the chalkboard and ask students to identify the verb in each sentence. Then have students give the present participle, past, and past participle forms of each verb.

1. Gina and Laurie sing their duets off-key. [sing—(are) singing, sang, (have) sung]
2. Jim tells me tall tales about the Old West. [tells—(is) telling, told, (has) told]
3. I comb my cat's tail. [comb—(am) combing, combed, (have) combed]

MEETING INDIVIDUAL NEEDS

LEP/ESL

General Strategies. Students may not realize that a past-tense verb form that they hear every day is spelled with a *–d* or an *–ed.* This confusion arises because native speakers of English often barely pronounce the *d* or even pronounce it as a *t.* Point out this discrepancy between spelling and pronunciation and have students pay particular attention to these past and past participle forms.

USAGE

A few regular verbs have alternative past and past participle forms ending in *–t.*

INFINITIVE	PRESENT PARTICIPLE	PAST	PAST PARTICIPLE
burn	(is) burning	burned *or* burnt	(have) burned *or* burnt
dream	(is) dreaming	dreamed *or* dreamt	(have) dreamed *or* dreamt
leap	(is) leaping	leaped *or* leapt	(have) leaped *or* leapt

NOTE: The regular verbs *deal* and *mean* always form the past and past participle by adding *–t: dealt, (have) dealt; meant, (have) meant.*

When forming the past and past participle of regular verbs, avoid omitting the *–d* or *–ed* ending. Pay particular attention to the forms of the verbs *ask, attack, drown, prejudice, risk, suppose,* and *use.*

NONSTANDARD The firefighter risk his life to save the valuable artifacts.
STANDARD The firefighter **risked** his life to save the valuable artifacts.

NONSTANDARD We should have ask for directions.
STANDARD We should have **asked** for directions.

REFERENCE NOTE: For a discussion of standard and nonstandard English, see page 478.

Irregular Verbs

24c. An ***irregular verb*** forms the past and the past participle in some other way than by adding *–d* or *–ed* to the infinitive form.

The best way to learn the principal parts of irregular verbs is to memorize them. No single usage rule applies to the different ways that these verbs form their past and past participle forms.

USAGE

However, there are some general guidelines that you can use. Irregular verbs form the past and past participle by

- changing vowels *or* consonants
- changing vowels *and* consonants
- making no change

INFINITIVE	PRESENT PARTICIPLE	PAST	PAST PARTICIPLE
swim	(is) swimming	swam	(have) swum
bend	(is) bending	bent	(have) bent
teach	(is) teaching	taught	(have) taught
burst	(is) bursting	burst	(have) burst

When forming the past and the past participle of irregular verbs, avoid these common errors:

(1) using the past form with a helping verb

NONSTANDARD I have never swam in this lake before.
STANDARD I **have** never **swum** in this lake before.

(2) using the past participle form without a helping verb

NONSTANDARD She swum to shore to get help.
STANDARD She **swam** to shore to get help.

(3) adding *–d, –ed,* or *–t* to the infinitive form

NONSTANDARD We bursted into laughter as soon as we saw the comedian.
STANDARD We **burst** into laughter as soon as we saw the comedian.

NOTE: If you are not sure about the principal parts of a verb, look in a dictionary. Entries for irregular verbs give the principal parts.

The alphabetical lists on pages 718–724 contain the principal parts of many common irregular verbs. You may use these lists as a reference; however, keep in mind that the lists do not include every irregular verb.

The irregular verbs in the first list, Group 1, form their past and past participle in a similar way.

USAGE

COMMON ERROR

Problem. Students sometimes use the regular *–d* or *–ed* endings for irregular verbs and thus create words such as *runned, catched, gived,* and *shaked.*

Solution. Because students learn to speak by hearing and imitating, they will benefit from oral drills of irregular forms. Try holding a conjugation bee, or let students conjugate verbs to a rap beat. These activities will help students develop an ear for correct verb forms.

USAGE

MEETING
INDIVIDUAL
NEEDS

LESS-ADVANCED STUDENTS

As they work through the exercises in this chapter, have students list irregular verbs that are problematic for them. Students could make charts with the infinitive, past, and past participle forms of the verbs and keep the charts in their notebooks for reference when they are completing writing assignments.

USAGE

USAGE

COMMON IRREGULAR VERBS

GROUP I: Each of these irregular verbs has the same form for its past and past participle.

INFINITIVE	PRESENT PARTICIPLE	PAST	PAST PARTICIPLE
bind	(is) binding	bound	(have) bound
bring	(is) bringing	brought	(have) brought
build	(is) building	built	(have) built
buy	(is) buying	bought	(have) bought
catch	(is) catching	caught	(have) caught
creep	(is) creeping	crept	(have) crept
feel	(is) feeling	felt	(have) felt
fight	(is) fighting	fought	(have) fought
find	(is) finding	found	(have) found
fling	(is) flinging	flung	(have) flung
have	(is) having	had	(have) had
hold	(is) holding	held	(have) held
keep	(is) keeping	kept	(have) kept
lay	(is) laying	laid	(have) laid
lead	(is) leading	led	(have) led
leave	(is) leaving	left	(have) left
lend	(is) lending	lent	(have) lent
lose	(is) losing	lost	(have) lost
make	(is) making	made	(have) made
meet	(is) meeting	met	(have) met
pay	(is) paying	paid	(have) paid
say	(is) saying	said	(have) said
seek	(is) seeking	sought	(have) sought
sell	(is) selling	sold	(have) sold
send	(is) sending	sent	(have) sent
sit	(is) sitting	sat	(have) sat
spend	(is) spending	spent	(have) spent
spin	(is) spinning	spun	(have) spun
stand	(is) standing	stood	(have) stood
sting	(is) stinging	stung	(have) stung
swing	(is) swinging	swung	(have) swung

(continued)

COMMON IRREGULAR VERBS *(continued)*			
GROUP I			
INFINITIVE	PRESENT PARTICIPLE	PAST	PAST PARTICIPLE
teach	(is) teaching	taught	(have) taught
tell	(is) telling	told	(have) told
think	(is) thinking	thought	(have) thought
win	(is) winning	won	(have) won

EXERCISE 1 **Using the Past and Past Participle Forms of Verbs**

For each of the following sentences, give the correct form (past or past participle) of the verb in parentheses.

EXAMPLE **1. Bob and Terri have (*lead*) our class in math scores for two years.**
1. *led*

1. The movie monster (*swing*) around and lunged into the woods. **1. swung**
2. Have you (*teach*) your little brother Bobby how to throw a curveball yet? **2. taught**
3. Mrs. Torres (*tell*) us yesterday that Mexican ballads are called *corridos*. **3. told**
4. Ever since we met last year, Kitty and I have (*sit*) together in assembly. **4. sat**
5. When we got to the new video store at the mall, you had just (*leave*). **5. left**
6. Unfortunately, I have already (*spend*) most of my weekly allowance. **6. spent**
7. In an earlier scene, Tarzan had (*catch*) hold of a vine and used it to swing through the trees. **7. caught**
8. Those two paintings by Horace Pippin really (*hold*) our interest. **8. held**
9. Not only had he juggled six oranges, but he had (*spin*) two plates on sticks. **9. spun**
10. The tiger-striped cat (*creep*) down the hallway and into the dark room. **10. crept**

USAGE

TIMESAVER
You may want to organize a team of several students who have demonstrated mastery of regular and irregular verb forms. The team can correct the exercises in this segment and provide tutoring for students having difficulty.

USAGE

A DIFFERENT APPROACH

Ask students to think of examples of irregular verbs that form their past tenses and past participles in the following ways:

1. by changing a vowel [*sit, begin*]
2. by changing vowels for the past form and adding *–en* for the past participle form [*take, give*]
3. by changing the complete word [*fly, go*]
4. by making no change [*set, bid*]

USAGE

EXERCISE 2 **Using the Past and Past Participle Forms of Irregular Verbs**

Many people like to play with the English language. Some enjoy word games. Others, like the author of the following silly poem, break the rules of standard usage just for fun. Each couplet in the poem contains an incorrect past or past participle form of an irregular verb. For each incorrect form shown in italics, provide the correct form. [Note: The poem will no longer rhyme.]

EXAMPLE **Bake, baked; make, [1] *maked?* Hold it—not so fast! Verbs that rhyme in the present form may not rhyme in the past!**
1. *made*

USAGE

Today we fling the same old ball that yesterday we flung;
Today we bring the same good news that yesterday we
[1] *brung*. 1. brought

And we still mind our parents, the folks we've always
minded; 2. found
And I may find a dime, just like the dime you [2] *finded*.

I smell the crimson rose, the very rose you smelled; 3. told
I tell a silly joke today, the same joke you once [3] *telled*.

4. won
You grin to hear me tell it now, just as last week you grinned;
You win our game of checkers, just as last week you [4] *winned*.

I peek into your closet now, and yesterday I peeked; 5. sought
I seek my birthday present, as every year I've [5] *seeked*.

6. taught
You reach to take my hand in yours; it was not I who reached;
You teach me to be friendly, as always you have [6] *teached*.

7. kept
I beep my horn to warn you; I'm sure my horn just beeped;
I keep all my appointments, the ones I should have [7] *keeped*.

I scream all day, I yell all night, I've screamed and I have
yelled
To sell all my newspapers, and today's batch I [8] *selled*. 8. sold

I wink my eye at you today, as yesterday I winked; 9. thought
I think I like you very much, as yesterday I [9] *thinked*.

I lose my train of thought sometimes; my train of thought
I've [10] *losed*. 10. lost
But I can use my verbs with care; just see the ones I've used!

COMMON IRREGULAR VERBS			
GROUP II:	Each of these irregular verbs has a different form for its past and past participle.		
INFINITIVE	**PRESENT PARTICIPLE**	**PAST**	**PAST PARTICIPLE**
arise	(is) arising	arose	(have) arisen
be	(is) being	was, were	(have) been
bear	(is) bearing	bore	(have) borne
beat	(is) beating	beat	(have) beaten *or* beat
become	(is) becoming	became	(have) become
begin	(is) beginning	began	(have) begun
bite	(is) biting	bit	(have) bitten
blow	(is) blowing	blew	(have) blown
break	(is) breaking	broke	(have) broken
choose	(is) choosing	chose	(have) chosen
come	(is) coming	came	(have) come
dive	(is) diving	dove *or* dived	(have) dived
do	(is) doing	did	(have) done
draw	(is) drawing	drew	(have) drawn
drink	(is) drinking	drank	(have) drunk
drive	(is) driving	drove	(have) driven
eat	(is) eating	ate	(have) eaten
fall	(is) falling	fell	(have) fallen
fly	(is) flying	flew	(have) flown
forbid	(is) forbidding	forbade *or* forbad	(have) forbidden
forget	(is) forgetting	forgot	(have) forgotten *or* forgot
forsake	(is) forsaking	forsook	(have) forsaken
freeze	(is) freezing	froze	(have) frozen
get	(is) getting	got	(have) gotten *or* got
give	(is) giving	gave	(have) given
go	(is) going	went	(have) gone
grow	(is) growing	grew	(have) grown
hide	(is) hiding	hid	(have) hidden

(continued)

USAGE

INTEGRATING THE LANGUAGE ARTS

Usage and Dictionary Skills. Point out to students that when they have questions about the principal parts of verbs, they can look the verbs up in a dictionary. Explain that the entry word in a dictionary is the infinitive form and that the past, past participle, and present participle forms are listed following the entry word. For example, if students look up *sing,* they will find *sang, sung,* and *singing* listed after *sing.* Have each student choose two or three irregular verbs to look up in a dictionary. Students should write each verb's principal parts.

USAGE

COOPERATIVE LEARNING

Conjugating verbs to a rhythmic beat can help students remember verb forms. Divide the class into mixed-ability groups of three or four students. Assign each group ten irregular verbs and have the groups prepare rhythmic oral presentations that include the present, past, and past participle forms of the verbs. The presentations can be poems, songs, stories, or prose recitations, and students can use movement to keep the beat or to act out their verbs. Even if students just chant the verb forms, they should do it to some form of beat or rhythm.

USAGE

COMMON IRREGULAR VERBS *(continued)*

GROUP II

INFINITIVE	PRESENT PARTICIPLE	PAST	PAST PARTICIPLE
know	(is) knowing	knew	(have) known
lie	(is) lying	lay	(have) lain
ride	(is) riding	rode	(have) ridden
ring	(is) ringing	rang	(have) rung
rise	(is) rising	rose	(have) risen
run	(is) running	ran	(have) run
see	(is) seeing	saw	(have) seen
shake	(is) shaking	shook	(have) shaken
show	(is) showing	showed *or* shown	(have) showed *or* shown
shrink	(is) shrinking	shrank *or* shrunk	(have) shrunk
sing	(is) singing	sang	(have) sung
sink	(is) sinking	sank	(have) sunk
slay	(is) slaying	slew	(have) slain
speak	(is) speaking	spoke	(have) spoken
spring	(is) springing	sprang *or* sprung	(have) sprung
steal	(is) stealing	stole	(have) stolen
strike	(is) striking	struck	(have) struck *or* stricken
strive	(is) striving	strove *or* strived	(have) striven *or* strived
swear	(is) swearing	swore	(have) sworn
swim	(is) swimming	swam	(have) swum
take	(is) taking	took	(have) taken
tear	(is) tearing	tore	(have) torn
throw	(is) throwing	threw	(have) thrown
wake	(is) waking	wakened *or* woke	(have) wakened, waked, *or* woken
wear	(is) wearing	wore	(have) worn
weave	(is) weaving	wove	(have) woven
write	(is) writing	wrote	(have) written

REVIEW A

OBJECTIVE

- To use past and past participle forms of verbs correctly

EXERCISE 3 **Using Past and Past Participle Forms of Verbs**

For each of the following sentences, give the correct form (past or past participle) of the verb in parentheses.

EXAMPLE **1. Aunt Barbara (*freeze*) fourteen pints of corn.**
1. *froze*

1. Your friends have (*come*) to see you. 1. come
2. He (*do*) his best on the PSAT last Saturday. 2. did
3. Elizabeth has finally (*begin*) to understand the value of proofreading. 3. begun
4. One of the poems I submitted to the contest was (*choose*) to receive a prize. 4. chosen
5. The tour group had (*come*) far into the desert to see the ancient Pueblo dwellings. 5. come
6. Strong winds (*drive*) the Dutch galleon off its course. 6. drove
7. The silence was (*break*) by a sudden clap of thunder. 7. broken
8. West Side High's team easily (*beat*) its opponents. 8. beat
9. Miguel (*blow*) up balloons and made decorations for his sister's *quinceañera* party, the celebration of her fifteenth birthday. 9. blew
10. When I soaked my new jeans in hot water, they (*shrink*) a little. 10. shrank [*or* shrunk]

USAGE

REVIEW A **Using Past and Past Participle Forms of Verbs Correctly**

In the following paragraph, decide whether each italicized verb is correct. If it is not, give the correct verb form. If a verb is correct, write *C*.

If you have [1] *seen* the maturity and intensity of perform- 1. C
ances by the young woman shown on the next page, you know
firsthand that she has [2] ~~*stealed*~~ the hearts of many music 2. stolen
lovers. Excited fans have [3] ~~*brung*~~ down the house with 3. brought
applause and have [4] ~~*threw*~~ bouquets of roses at her feet. Barely 4. thrown
out of her teens, Midori has [5] ~~*knew*~~ the joys and struggles of 5. known
being a professional concert violinist ever since she was a small
girl. Whenever she has [6] ~~*spoke*~~ to the press, Midori has 6. spoken
[7] ~~*showed*~~ an outgoing and unaffected personality. Her violin 7. shown
teacher at the Juilliard School, Dorothy DeLay, had also
[8] *taught* such stars as Itzhak Perlman and Joshua Bell. When 8. C

USAGE

USAGE

VISUAL CONNECTIONS

Exploring the Subject. Midori, who was born in October, 1971, received her first violin for her third birthday. It was only one sixteenth the size of an ordinary violin, but the size didn't stop this child prodigy from learning to play it brilliantly. Initially, Midori trained under the direction of her mother, who is herself a renowned violinist. Midori later trained at Julliard. She gained worldwide fame at the age of fourteen. Midori limits herself to about eighty-five concerts a year. She lives with her family in New York City.

USAGE

Midori was eleven, the famous conductor Zubin Mehta [9] ~~*brung*~~ her onstage as a surprise guest soloist with the New York Philharmonic. Ever since, Midori has [10] ~~*finded*~~ the concert hall a wonderful place; in fact, she says that she loves "the feeling of standing on a stage, whether there is an audience present or not."

9. brought

10. found

COMMON IRREGULAR VERBS			
GROUP III:	Each of these irregular verbs has the same form for its infinitive, past, and past participle.		
INFINITIVE	**PRESENT PARTICIPLE**	**PAST**	**PAST PARTICIPLE**
burst	(is) bursting	burst	(have) burst
cost	(is) costing	cost	(have) cost
cut	(is) cutting	cut	(have) cut
hit	(is) hitting	hit	(have) hit
hurt	(is) hurting	hurt	(have) hurt
let	(is) letting	let	(have) let
put	(is) putting	put	(have) put
read	(is) reading	read	(have) read
set	(is) setting	set	(have) set
spread	(is) spreading	spread	(have) spread

REVIEWS B–F

OBJECTIVES

- To proofread sentences for correct verb forms
- To use the past and past participle forms of verbs correctly
- To proofread a paragraph for the correct use of irregular verbs

EXERCISE 4 **Using the Past and the Past Participle Forms of Verbs**

Most of the following sentences contain an incorrect verb form. If a verb form is incorrect, give the correct form. If a sentence is correct, write *C*.

1. The crowded roots of the plant had ~~bursted~~ the flowerpot. 1. burst
2. Nancy set the antipasto salad in the center of the dining table. 2. C
3. After we've cut the grass, we'll weed the garden. 3. C
4. The angry hornet stung me right on the end of my nose, and it ~~hurted~~ all afternoon. 4. hurt
5. Hussein ~~spreaded~~ his pita bread with a thick layer of tasty hummus. 5. spread
6. Where have I ~~putted~~ my notebook? 6. put
7. You must have read the assignment too quickly. 7. C
8. As soon as the robin was well, we ~~letted~~ it go free. 8. let
9. Skateboards ~~costed~~ less last year. 9. cost
10. Both Felina and Fernanda ~~hitted~~ home runs in last week's softball game. 10. hit

USAGE

REVIEW B **Proofreading Sentences for Correct Verb Forms**

For the following sentences, give the correct form for each incorrect verb form. If a sentence is correct, write *C*.

EXAMPLE 1. When my art class went to the museum of African American art, I seen some collages that Romare Bearden had maked.
1. *saw; made*

1. Seeing the unusual medium of collage has ~~letted~~ me think about art in a new way. 1. let
2. Bearden ~~growed~~ up in North Carolina and then ~~spended~~ time studying in New York, Pittsburgh, and Paris. 2. grew/spent
3. Since the 1930s, when his art career ~~begun~~, he has gotten a reputation as a leading abstract artist. 3. began
4. Instead of specializing in painting or drawing, Bearden ~~finded~~ his niche in the somewhat unusual medium of collage. 4. found
5. He fashions his artworks out of pieces of colored paper that have been ~~cutted~~ or ~~teared~~ into small shapes. 5. cut/torn

USAGE

USAGE

6. Often, he has ~~gave~~ his collages more variety by using pieces from black-and-white or color photographs. 6. given
7. If you examine his *Blue Interior, Morning* (shown below), you can see that Bearden has built this composition around a family eating breakfast. 7. C
8. The materials that he assembled were ~~chose~~ for their textural harmony and for their ability to be ~~wove~~ into the blue color scheme. 8. chosen/woven
9. In his work, Bearden has often depicted universal human figures whose composite nature is clearly ~~showed~~ by their different-colored fingers or legs. 9. shown
10. I could have ~~swore~~ it was impossible to create a pleasing composition with all the figures way down in one corner, but Bearden has certainly succeeded. 10. sworn

Romare Bearden, "Blue Interior, Morning", 1968. Collage on board, 44 × 56". Collection of The Chase Manhattan Bank, N.A./Courtesy the Estate of Romare Bearden.

REVIEW C **Using the Past and Past Participle Forms of Verbs**

For each of the following sentences, give the correct form (past or past participle) of the verb in parentheses.

EXAMPLE 1. The pitcher (*strike*) out eleven batters in a row.
1. *struck*

1. Have you ever (*read*) anything by Gwendolyn Brooks, the lifetime poet laureate of Illinois? 1. read
2. We (*drink*) tomato juice with last night's dinner. 2. drank
3. How many of you (*see*) Fernando Valenzuela pitch? 3. saw

USAGE

VISUAL CONNECTIONS

Related Expression Skills. Students might like to try their hands at creating collages in the manner of Romare Bearden. You can tie this activity into a study of literature by asking students to create collages illustrating the theme of a short story or poem. Students can use colored construction paper, pictures cut from magazines, and a host of other materials. You may want to ask an art teacher at your school to give you and your students some pointers on how to get started.

4. I thought my skates had been (*steal*), but then I finally found them. 4. stolen
5. He had (*write*) a play about his experience in Vietnam. 5. written
6. Garrett's dad has (*sing*) in a barbershop quartet for years. 6. sung
7. We would have bought those Detroit Pistons tickets no matter how much they had (*cost*). 7. cost
8. Female rap groups like Salt-N-Pepa have (*become*) quite popular lately. 8. become
9. Don't you think that the dough for the bread has (*rise*) enough to bake? 9. risen
10. LaToya says she has never (*ride*) on a roller coaster. 10. ridden
11. Have you ever (*fly*) a Japanese dragon kite? 11. flown
12. I shivered and (*shake*) after I dented the front fender of Mom's car. 12. shook
13. When Mrs. Isayama called my name, I (*swing*) around. 13. swung
14. My father has (*forbid*) my younger sister to use his power tools without supervision. 14. forbidden
15. Wanda (*burst*) into the room to greet her friends. 15. burst
16. Yesterday, Nguyen and I each (*hit*) about two hundred tennis balls. 16. hit
17. Darius had (*fall*) when he went in for the layup. 17. fallen
18. The government class has (*go*) to observe the city council in session. 18. gone
19. I was not aware that the telephone had (*ring*). 19. rung
20. Have you (*have*) a taste of that delicious tabbouleh salad from North Africa yet? 20. had

USAGE

REVIEW D **Using the Past and Past Participle Forms of Verbs** Answers may vary.

The following paragraph contains ten numbered blanks. For each blank, choose an appropriate verb from the box below and give its correct past or past participle form.

bring	find	spread	see
become	creep	seek	begin
make	spin	let	think

EXAMPLE Suppose you were a farmer, and one morning you went out to your fields and [1] ____ a 300-foot-long pattern like the ones shown on the next page!
1. *found*

USAGE

1. began
2. became
3. made
4. spread
5. brought
6. thought
7. sought
8. crept
9. spun
10. let

Many circular flattened areas like these [1] ____ to appear in fields across southern England in the late 1970s. The phenomenon soon [2] ____ one of the most popular mysteries the world had ever known. People calling themselves "cereologists" insisted that no human being could have [3] ____ these unusual patterns. The idea quickly [4] ____ that the circles were the landing spots of UFOs that had [5] ____ visitors from space. Respected scientists [6] ____ that the weird designs resulted from ball lightning, whirling columns of air, or other strange weather conditions. When it was reported that circle researchers had [7] ____ public funding, two British landscape painters came forward with the truth. David Chorley and Douglas Bower confessed that they had [8] ____ into the fields at night with a ball of string and a wooden plank and had [9] ____ the plank in a circle to create the flattened areas of grain. Before Chorley and Bower spoke up, millions of people had [10] ____ themselves believe that the crop circles were formed by extraterrestrials—and even now, thousands of diehards still do.

VISUAL CONNECTIONS

Ideas for Writing. Ask students to write letters to David Chorley and Douglas Bower to express opinions about the hoax the two men committed with the crop circles. Have students follow the guidelines for business letters in **Chapter 38: "Letters and Forms"** and ask them to back up their opinions with reasons, examples, or explanations. If several students favor the hoax and several oppose it, you may want to have students on opposite sides debate the matter before the class.

REVIEW E

Using the Past and Past Participle Forms Correctly

For each of the following sentences, decide whether the italicized verb is correct. If it is not, give the correct verb form. If a sentence is correct, write *C*.

1. American shoppers have certainly *grew* accustomed to the convenience of paper grocery bags. 1. grown

2. In recent years, many Americans have ~~*went*~~ right on using them—at the rate of forty billion bags a year! **2.** gone
3. Have you ever ~~*thinked*~~ about the history of the standard flat-bottomed grocery bag with pleated sides? **3.** thought
4. Someone must have ~~*cutted*~~ out and pasted together the first flat-bottomed paper bag. **4.** cut
5. Actually, I have *read* that the inventor of these bags was a man named Charles Stilwell. **5.** C
6. After he had ~~*fighted*~~ in the Civil War, he returned home and began to tinker with inventions. **6.** fought
7. He created a machine to fold and glue brown paper into bags, a job that had previously been ~~*did*~~ by hand. **7.** done
8. Earlier bags had V-shaped bottoms, which meant that they had not ~~*standed*~~ up by themselves. **8.** stood
9. I have certainly ~~*putted*~~ Charles Stilwell's bags to use in my after-school supermarket job. **9.** put
10. Many other everyday items that we have always ~~*took*~~ for granted, such as safety pins and eyeglasses, have interesting histories, too. **10.** taken

USAGE

REVIEW F

Proofreading a Paragraph for the Correct Use of Irregular Verbs

Most of the sentences in the following paragraph contain an error in the use of irregular verbs. If a verb is incorrect, supply the correct form. If a sentence is correct, write *C*.

[1] Pioneers on their way to California had always ~~losed~~ much time when they hit the rugged Sierra Nevada. [2] Wagon trains had turned and ~~drived~~ many miles out of their way, searching for a trail their oxen and horses could take through these mountains. [3] Then James Beckwourth, an African American frontiersman and explorer, discovered an important route between the forbidding peaks. [4] Have you ~~finded~~ Beckwourth Pass on the map on the next page? [5] Other routes, including Donner Pass, had already been discovered, but soon wagonmasters ~~seen~~ that Beckwourth Pass was the lowest in elevation and, therefore, the easiest to cross. [6] James Beckwourth was a versatile man; he ~~been~~ a trapper, trader, explorer, and mountain man. [7] He even ~~fighted~~ in the Second Seminole War as an army scout. [8] During the Gold Rush, he caught gold fever and ~~spended~~ some time prospecting in California. [9] Beckwourth always ~~gotten~~ along quite well with Native

1. lost
2. driven
3. C
4. found
5. saw
6. was
7. fought
8. spent
9. got

USAGE

SEGMENT 3 *(pp. 730–736)*

SIX TROUBLESOME VERBS

OBJECTIVES

- To choose the correct forms of *lie* and *lay* in sentences
- To write sentences containing correct forms of *lie* and *lay*
- To use the forms of *sit* and *set* correctly in sentences
- To use the forms of *rise* and *raise* correctly in sentences

USAGE

Teacher's ResourceBank™

RESOURCES

SIX TROUBLESOME VERBS

QUICK REMINDER

You may find it helpful to write the verbs *lie, lay, sit, set, rise,* and *raise* on the chalkboard and ask students to each compose one sentence for each verb. When students finish writing, list on the chalkboard a brief definition of each word. Then ask a few volunteers to read their sentences aloud. If anyone gets confused about a verb's meaning, he or she can refer to the definitions on the chalkboard.

Americans—especially the Crow people, who adopted him. [10] By the end of his life, he had ~~became~~ such a good friend to the Crow that they gave him the chance to be a chief!

10. become

USAGE

Six Troublesome Verbs

Lie and *Lay*

The verb *lie* means "to rest" or "to stay, to recline, or to remain in a certain state or position." *Lie* never takes an object.

The verb *lay* means "to put [something] in a place." *Lay* usually takes an object.

INFINITIVE	PRESENT PARTICIPLE	PAST	PAST PARTICIPLE
lie (to rest)	(is) lying	lay	(have) lain
lay (to put)	(is) laying	laid	(have) laid

• To choose the correct forms of *lie* and *lay, sit* and *set,* and *rise* and *raise* in sentences

EXAMPLES The printout **is lying** there next to the computer. [no object]

The secretary **is laying** a copy of the report on everyone's desk. [*Copy* is the object of *is laying.*]

The explorers saw that a vast wilderness **lay** before them. [no object]

She carefully **laid** the holiday decorations in the box. [*Decorations* is the object of *laid.*]

My basset hound **has lain** in front of the fireplace since early this morning. [no object]

Tranh **has** already **laid** the fishing gear in the boat. [*Gear* is the object of *has laid.*]

EXERCISE 5 **Choosing the Forms of *Lie* and *Lay***

For each of the following sentences, choose the correct verb form in parentheses. Be prepared to explain your choices.

EXAMPLE **1.** The construction workers are (*laying, lying*) the foundation now.
1. *laying*

1. The old stereoscope had (*lain, laid*) in my grandmother's attic for years.
2. The interstate (*lays, lies*) north of town.
3. The rake is (*laying, lying*) in a pile of leaves.
4. When was that tile in the foyer (*laid, lain*)?
5. Judy and Adrian (*lay, laid*) their books on the table.
6. She read the paper as she (*laid, lay*) in the recliner.
7. The key to success (*lays, lies*) in determination.
8. (*Lie, Lay*) here and relax before going on.
9. Ms. Collins (*laid, lay*) the study guides on the table.
10. Jack stole the hen that (*lay, laid*) golden eggs.

EXERCISE 6 **Writing Sentences Using the Forms of *Lie* and *Lay***

For each numbered item at the top of the next page, use the subject and verb form given to write a correct sentence. Be sure to add an object to forms of *lay*. For participle forms, you will need to supply helping verbs. When two forms are spelled the same, the information in parentheses tells you which meaning or form to use.

USAGE

MEETING INDIVIDUAL NEEDS

LEP/ESL

General Strategies. Students need to be reminded that there are two strategies they can employ when wrestling with the six troublesome verbs. The first strategy is to look for a direct object in the sentence. If the verb has a direct object, then *lay, set,* or *raise* is probably the appropriate choice. As a second strategy, students should look for a prepositional phrase immediately following the verb. That configuration indicates that *lie, sit,* or *rise* is the correct choice. Concerning the past and participial forms of these verbs, there is probably only one strategy, however—memorization.

USAGE

ANSWERS

Exercise 6

Answers will vary. Here are some possibilities:

1. The detectives lay the blame for the accident on the slick roads.
2. The sparrow laid her eggs in the oak tree in my neighbor's yard.
3. My father will be laying carpet in our new den this weekend.
4. That dog has lain there quietly for three hours.
5. The children at the preschool lie down for a nap after lunch each day.
6. The butler has laid the table with the best silver for dinner tonight.
7. Mr. Hill lay down for a nap after school yesterday.
8. Books are lying all around my room, so I should pick them up before my mother gets home.
9. Miami lies south of Ft. Lauderdale.
10. The mechanic lays his tools on this workbench every day at closing time.

USAGE

USAGE

EXAMPLE SUBJECT VERB FORM
1. package lying
1. *The package was lying on the doormat when we got home.*

	SUBJECT	VERB FORM
1.	detectives	lay (to put)
2.	sparrow	laid (past)
3.	father	laying
4.	dog	lain
5.	children	lie
6.	butler	laid (past participle)
7.	Mr. Hill	lay (to rest)
8.	books	lying
9.	Miami	lies
10.	mechanic	lays

Sit and *Set*

The verb *sit* means "to rest in an upright seated position." *Sit* seldom takes an object.

The verb *set* means "to put [something] in a place." *Set* usually takes an object.

INFINITIVE	PRESENT PARTICIPLE	PAST	PAST PARTICIPLE
sit (to rest)	(is) sitting	sat	(have) sat
set (to put)	(is) setting	set	(have) set

EXAMPLES **May I sit** here? [no object]
May I set the chair here? [*Chair* is the object of *May set.*]

We **sat** in the theater for an hour, waiting for the play to begin. [no object]
Kishi **set** the candles on the piano. [*Candles* is the object of *set.*]

EXERCISE 7 **Using the Forms of *Sit* and *Set***

Complete each of the following sentences by supplying the correct form of *sit* or *set*.

EXAMPLE **1.** Carrie is ____ in the rocking chair, reading the newspaper.
1. *sitting*

1. I ____ in the doctor's waiting room for an hour yesterday morning. **1.** sat
2. We ____ in the front row at the Gloria Estefan concert. **2.** sat
3. ____ the carton down near the door. **3.** Set
4. We were ____ so high up in the theater that the stage looked no bigger than a postage stamp. **4.** sitting
5. If we had ____ any longer, we would have been late for class. **5.** sat
6. Let's ____ that pot of hot-and-sour soup on the buffet. **6.** set
7. Jonathan is ____ aside five dollars each week so that he can buy a CD player. **7.** setting
8. You shouldn't ____ on the damp ground. **8.** sit
9. I hope that Trish and Brandon haven't ____ those plants too close to the radiator. **9.** set
10. We all ____ around the campfire last night. **10.** sat

USAGE

Rise and *Raise*

The verb *rise* means "to go up" or "to get up." *Rise* never takes an object.

The verb *raise* means "to cause [something] to rise" or "to lift up." *Raise* usually takes an object.

INFINITIVE	PRESENT PARTICIPLE	PAST	PAST PARTICIPLE
rise (to go up)	(is) rising	rose	(have) risen
raise (to lift up)	(is) raising	raised	(have) raised

EXAMPLES She **rose** from the wheelchair and walked toward the door. [no object]
Willis **raised** the window blinds to brighten the room. [*Window blinds* is the object of *raised.*]

The prices of fresh fruit and vegetables **have risen** considerably because of the drought. [no object]
Salim **has** already **raised** the flag. [*Flag* is the object of *has raised.*]

USAGE

A DIFFERENT APPROACH

Tell students that one trick for remembering the difference between *rise* and *raise* is to memorize the sentence "All rise and raise the window." People rise; windows are raised. *Raise* is a regular verb (past tense and past participle formed by adding *–d*), so the only problem is remembering the forms of the irregular *rise:* "I rise now, but she rose then, and they have risen many times in the past."

MEETING INDIVIDUAL NEEDS

ADVANCED STUDENTS

You may want to have students develop rules for using other verb pairs that frequently cause problems, such as *learn* and *teach* and *leave* and *let.* Ask students to write explanations of each of the verbs and to include in their rules sentences that are examples of the correct usage. Then have the students present the material to the rest of the class.

USAGE

USAGE

EXERCISE 8 Using *Rise* and *Raise* Correctly

For each of the following sentences, decide whether the italicized verb is correct. If it is not, give the correct verb form. If a sentence is correct, write C.

EXAMPLE **1. Everyone *raised* for the pledge of allegiance.**
1. *rose*

1. The cost of a ticket to see a Kentucky Headhunters concert ~~*has raised*~~. 1. has risen
2. The student council president *will raise* the flag. 2. C
3. The Bunsen burner flame ~~*has raised*~~ too high. 3. has risen
4. While fishing with my uncle Thibeaux in Louisiana, I saw an alligator slowly ~~*raise*~~ out of the mud. 4. rise
5. The curling smoke *rose* from the pile of leaves. 5. C
6. The sun *was rising* behind Pikes Peak. 6. C
7. The woman who *is rising* now to address the audience has been nominated for vice-president. 7. C
8. How much *has* the price of gasoline ~~*raised*~~ since the end of the Persian Gulf Conflict? 8. risen
9. The cost of a dozen eggs *has been raised*, but you can use this coupon. 9. C
10. *Has* the popularity of video games *risen*? 10. C

EXERCISE 9 Choosing the Forms of *Lie-Lay, Sit-Set,* and *Rise-Raise*

For each of the following sentences, choose the correct verb form in parentheses. Be prepared to explain your choices.

EXAMPLE **1. I think I will (*lay, lie*) here and rest awhile.**
1. *lie*

1. They (*sit*, *set*) the yearbooks in Mr. Cohen's office.
2. The thermostat should have kept the temperature from (*rising*, *raising*).
3. Where was Emily (*sitting*, *setting*) at the end of *Our Town*?
4. Is the number of traffic fatalities still (*raising*, *rising*)?
5. San Francisco (*lays*, *lies*) southwest of Sacramento.
6. Let's (*set*, *sit*) down and talk about the problem.
7. The price of citrus fruit (*rises*, *raises*) after a freeze.
8. Hours of driving (*lay*, *laid*) ahead of us.
9. A replica of *The Thinker* is (*setting*, *sitting*) there.
10. The helium-filled balloon (*rose*, *raised*) into the air.

REVIEW G

OBJECTIVE

- To proofread a paragraph for correct verb usage

EXERCISE 10 **Choosing the Forms of *Lie-Lay, Sit-Set,* and *Rise-Raise***

Many familiar expressions and sayings include forms of *lie, lay, sit, set, rise,* or *raise.* Complete each expression below by choosing the correct form from the pair given.

1. Let sleeping dogs ___. (*lie, lay*)
2. ___ down your burden. (*Lie, Lay*)
3. Those who would deceive the fox must ___ early in the morning. (*rise, raise*)
4. I'm ___ on top of the world. (*setting, sitting*)
5. If you can't ___ the bridge, lower the river. (*rise, raise*)
6. He who ___ down with dogs gets up with fleas. (*lies, lays*)
7. Cream always ___ to the top. (*rises, raises*)
8. ___ down—you're rocking the boat! (*Set, Sit*)
9. Whenever possible, ___ to the occasion. (*rise, raise*)
10. ___ high standards. (*Set, Sit*)

USAGE

REVIEW G **Proofreading a Paragraph for Correct Verb Usage**

Most of the sentences in the following paragraph have one or more errors in verb usage. For each error, write the correct form of the verb. If a sentence is correct, write *C.* Be prepared to explain your answers.

EXAMPLE [1] As a child, Frida Kahlo had often thinked she would become an explorer.
1. *thought*

[1] You have probably ~~saw~~ pictures of murals painted by Diego Rivera, the famous Mexican painter. [2] But you may never have ~~came~~ across the paintings by Frida Kahlo, his wife. [3] Kahlo ~~shined~~ in her own right as a powerful painter, although she often ~~standed~~ in the shadow of her more renowned husband. [4] She ~~taked~~ up painting during her recovery from a streetcar accident in which she had ~~broke~~ several bones. [5] Other medical problems ~~arised~~ from time to time throughout her life, and though sometimes she had to paint from her wheelchair, Kahlo always painted straight from her heart. [6] In fact, she ~~gived~~ this image literal expression in one of her paintings in which she portrays herself using a heart as her palette. [7] Kahlo never ~~forgetted~~ her childhood dream of

1. seen
2. come
3. shone/stood
4. took/broken
5. arose
6. gave
7. forgot

USAGE

SEGMENT 4 *(pp. 736–743)*

TENSE Rules 24d, 24e

OBJECTIVES

- To identify the six tenses of verbs in sentences
- To write sentences in the perfect tenses
- To use correct verb tenses in writing questions and answers for an interview

Frida Kahlo (1907–54), "Self Portrait as a Tehuana (Diego on my Mind)". Oil on canvas. $29\frac{7}{8}'' \times 24''$ (76 × 61 cm). Private collection, Mexico City. Photograph courtesy of The Metropolitan Museum of Art.

8. struck

exploration and, instead of seas and mountains, explored the territory of the human spirit. [8] Frida Kahlo ~~striked~~ everyone who met her as an elegant, intense, and talented woman. [9] Although she sometimes found life painful, she was full of fun, high spirits, and love. [10] Kahlo is especially noted for her self-portraits, in which she sometimes ~~choosed~~ to paint herself with a tiny portrait of Rivera on her forehead, as in the painting shown here.

9. C

10. chose

Tense

24d. The *tense* of a verb indicates the time of the action or state of being expressed by the verb.

Every verb has six tenses: *present, past, future, present perfect, past perfect,* and *future perfect.* These tenses are formed from the four principal parts of a verb.

The Forms of Verbs According to Tense

Listing all of the forms of a verb according to tense is called ***conjugating*** a verb.

CONJUGATION OF THE VERB *SEE*			
PRINCIPAL PARTS			
INFINITIVE	PRESENT PARTICIPLE	PAST	PAST PARTICIPLE
see	seeing	saw	seen

Teacher's ResourceBank™

RESOURCES

TENSE

- Verb Tense 272

QUICK REMINDER

Write the following sentences on the chalkboard. Have students correct the tense of the verbs in the underlined phrases.

1. I will talk yesterday to the football coach about my position. [talked]
2. He has already run out of gasoline when he called. [had already run]
3. Tomorrow we have thought about everything. [will think]

24d

CONJUGATION OF THE VERB *SEE* *(continued)*	
PRESENT TENSE	
SINGULAR	***PLURAL***
I see	we see
you see	you see
he, she, it sees	they see
PAST TENSE	
SINGULAR	***PLURAL***
I saw	we saw
you saw	you saw
he, she, it saw	they saw
FUTURE TENSE (*will* or *shall* + infinitive)	
SINGULAR	***PLURAL***
I will (shall) see	we will (shall) see
you will see	you will see
he, she, it will see	they will see
PRESENT PERFECT TENSE (*have* or *has* + past participle)	
SINGULAR	***PLURAL***
I have seen	we have seen
you have seen	you have seen
he, she, it has seen	they have seen
PAST PERFECT TENSE (*had* + past participle)	
SINGULAR	***PLURAL***
I had seen	we had seen
you had seen	you had seen
he, she, it had seen	they had seen
FUTURE PERFECT TENSE (*will have* or *shall have* + past participle)	
SINGULAR	***PLURAL***
I will (shall) have seen	we will (shall) have seen
you will have seen	you will have seen
he, she, it will have seen	they will have seen

USAGE

MEETING INDIVIDUAL NEEDS

LEP/ESL

General Strategies. Students probably will have trouble with the present perfect verb tense. One common way the present perfect is used is in the question "Have you ever . . . ?" A helpful exercise can take the form of a survey. Give each student a question to ask the other members of the class. Students might ask one of the following questions:

1. Have you ever studied Chinese?
2. Have you ever been to Europe?
3. Have you ever slept outside?
4. Have you ever seen a flamingo?
5. Have you ever had the mumps?

The rhythmic repetition of a phrase is a key method of language learning and will help ESL students fix this construction in their minds.

USAGE

Each tense also has a ***progressive form,*** which expresses continuing action or state of being. The progressive form consists of the appropriate tense of *be* plus the present participle.

Present Progressive	am, is, are seeing
Past Progressive	was, were seeing
Future Progressive	will (shall) be seeing
Present Perfect Progressive	has been, have been seeing
Past Perfect Progressive	had been seeing
Future Perfect Progressive	will (shall) have been seeing

Only the present and the past tenses have another form called the ***emphatic form,*** which shows emphasis. In the present tense, the emphatic form of a verb consists of *do* or *does* plus the infinitive. In the past tense, the emphatic form consists of *did* plus the infinitive.

Present Emphatic	do, does see
Past Emphatic	did see

The conjugation of the verb *be* differs from that of other verbs. Only the present and past tenses of *be* have the progressive form and none of the tenses has the emphatic form.

CONJUGATION OF THE VERB *BE*

PRINCIPAL PARTS

INFINITIVE	PRESENT PARTICIPLE	PAST	PAST PARTICIPLE
be	being	was, were	been

PRESENT TENSE

SINGULAR	***PLURAL***
I am	we are
you are	you are
he, she, it is	they are

Present Progressive: am, are, is being

PAST TENSE

SINGULAR	***PLURAL***
I was	we were
you were	you were
he, she, it was	they were

Past Progressive: was, were being

(continued)

USAGE

CONJUGATION OF THE VERB *BE* (continued)	
FUTURE TENSE (*will* or *shall* + infinitive)	
SINGULAR	***PLURAL***
I will (shall) be	we will (shall) be
you will be	you will be
he, she, it will be	they will be
PRESENT PERFECT TENSE (*have* or *has* + past participle)	
SINGULAR	***PLURAL***
I have been	we have been
you have been	you have been
he, she, it has been	they have been
PAST PERFECT TENSE (*had* + past participle)	
SINGULAR	***PLURAL***
I had been	we had been
you had been	you had been
he, she, it had been	they had been
FUTURE PERFECT TENSE (*will have* or *shall have* + past participle)	
SINGULAR	***PLURAL***
I will (shall) have been	we will (shall) have been
you will have been	you will have been
he, she, it will have been	they will have been

The Uses of the Tenses

24e. Each of the six tenses has its own special uses.

(1) The ***present tense*** is used mainly to express an action (or a state of being) that is occurring now.

EXAMPLES Martina **races** down the court and **shoots** the ball. [present]
The fans **are cheering** wildly. [present progressive]
Martina and her teammates **do look** confident. [present emphatic]

MEETING INDIVIDUAL NEEDS

LEP/ESL

Asian Languages. Some languages, such as Chinese, Lao, Indonesian, and Vietnamese, do not use verb tenses to indicate time. Instead, a speaker will use either context or an adverb to establish the time of the events being discussed. The idea of specifying tense in every sentence might seem redundant to some students; therefore, they might use only the present tense. Emphasize that in English, the correct tense must be used in every sentence.

USAGE

The present tense is also used

- to show a customary or habitual action or state of being
- to convey a general truth—something that is always true
- to make a historical event seem current (such use is called the *historical present*)
- to summarize the plot or subject matter of a literary work (such use is called the *literary present*)
- to express future time

EXAMPLES For breakfast I usually **eat** some cereal and **drink** orange juice. [customary action]
The earth **revolves** around the sun, which **is** the central star in our solar system. [general truth]
In a surprise move, the Greeks **construct** a huge wooden horse and **leave** it outside the walls of Troy. [historical present]
The Dark Child **tells** the story of a boy growing up in an African village. [literary present]
The workshop that **begins** tomorrow **continues** for two weeks. [future time]

USAGE

(2) The ***past tense*** is used to express an action (or a state of being) that occurred in the past but did not continue into the present.

EXAMPLES In the last lap the runner **fell** and **injured** his knee. [past]
He **was trying** to break the record for that event. [past progressive]
The injury **did prevent** him from competing in the relay race. [past emphatic]

NOTE: A past action or state of being may also be shown in another way.

EXAMPLE I **used to hate** spicy food.

(3) The ***future tense*** is used to express an action (or a state of being) that will occur. The future tense is formed with *will* or *shall* and the infinitive.

EXAMPLES The president **will** not **return** to Washington today. [future]
The president **will be holding** a press conference at noon. [future progressive]

A future action or state of being may also be expressed by using

- the present tense of *be* followed by *going to* and the infinitive form of a verb
- the present tense of *be* followed by *about to* and the infinitive form of a verb
- the present tense of a verb with a word or phrase that expresses future time

EXAMPLES My cousins **are going to visit** Japan in July.
Ms. Scheirer **is about to announce** the winners.
The boxer **defends** his title **next Friday night.**

(4) The present perfect tense is used mainly to express an action (or a state of being) that occurred at some indefinite time in the past. The present perfect tense always includes the helping verb *have* or *has.*

EXAMPLES Miguel already **has entered** the information into the computer. [present perfect]
Who **has been using** this computer? [present perfect progressive]

USAGE

NOTE: Avoid the use of the present perfect tense to express a *specific* time in the past. Instead, use the past tense.

NONSTANDARD They have bought a computer last week. [*Last week* indicates a specific time in the past.]
STANDARD They **bought** a computer last week. [past tense]

The present perfect tense is also used to express an action (or a state of being) that began in the past and continues into the present.

EXAMPLES Mr. Steele **has taught** school for twenty-one years. [present perfect]
He **has been coaching** soccer since 1986. [present perfect progressive]

(5) The ***past perfect tense*** is used to express an action (or a state of being) that was completed in the past before some other past occurrence. The past perfect tense always includes the helping verb *had.*

EXAMPLES Paul **had traveled** several miles before he realized his mistake. [past perfect]
He discovered that he **had been misreading** the road map. [past perfect progressive]

USAGE

ANSWERS

Exercise 11

1. a. has reported, have adjusted—present perfect
   b. had reported—past perfect; have adjusted—present perfect
2. a. took—past
   b. have taken—present perfect
3. a. will do—future
   b. will have done—future perfect
4. a. has reported—present perfect
   b. had reported—past perfect
5. a. Do know—present emphatic; originated—past
   b. Did know—past emphatic; originated—past
6. a. have sent—present perfect
   b. had sent—past perfect
7. a. will make—future
   b. will have made—future perfect
8. a. think—present; have seen—present perfect
   b. thought—past; had seen—past perfect
9. a. Did reach—past emphatic
   b. Has reached—present perfect
10. a. was—past
    b. has been—present perfect

(6) The ***future perfect tense*** is used to express an action (or a state of being) that will be completed in the future before some other future occurrence. The future perfect tense always includes the helping verbs *will have* or *shall have.*

EXAMPLES By the time school begins in August, you **will have saved** enough money to buy the car. [future perfect]
By then, you **will have been working** here a year. [future perfect progressive]

EXERCISE 11 **Understanding the Uses of the Six Tenses**

Identify the tenses of the verbs in each of the following pairs of sentences. Be prepared to explain how these differences in tense alter the meanings of the sentences.

1. **a.** Channel 5 News has reported on how successfully Asians have adjusted to life in America.
   b. Channel 5 News had reported on how successfully Asians have adjusted to life in America.
2. **a.** I took piano lessons for three years.
   b. I have taken piano lessons for three years.
3. **a.** We will do our research on Friday.
   b. We will have done our research on Friday.
4. **a.** Jane has reported on recent fossil discoveries.
   b. Jane had reported on recent fossil discoveries.
5. **a.** Do you know that the secret ballot method of voting originated in Australia?
   b. Did you know that the secret ballot method of voting originated in Australia?
6. **a.** We have sent out invitations.
   b. We had sent out invitations.
7. **a.** I will make a time line of the Middle Ages before this weekend.
   b. I will have made a time line of the Middle Ages before this weekend.
8. **a.** I think that I have seen her somewhere before.
   b. I thought that I had seen her somewhere before.
9. **a.** Did the jury reach a verdict?
   b. Has the jury reached a verdict?
10. **a.** Ms. Wong was the club sponsor for five years.
    b. Ms. Wong has been the club sponsor for five years.

EXERCISE 12 **Writing Sentences in the Present Perfect, Past Perfect, and Future Perfect Tenses**

Write ten original sentences according to the following directions.

1. Using different verbs in the *present perfect tense,* write three sentences about a story you have read.
2. Using different verbs in the *past perfect tense,* write three sentences about a movie you have seen.
3. Using different verbs in the *future perfect tense,* write four sentences about a place you would like to visit.

PICTURE THIS

Your friend's science project went berserk! Yesterday she took home her new plant fertilizer and tested it on an ordinary rosebush. Overnight, the little plant produced this enormous rose bloom. You're the star reporter for your school's newspaper, and your friend has agreed to let you interview her. Think of at least five questions to ask your friend about her experiment and about her plans for her amazing discovery. Then use your imagination to record your friend's answers and comments. Be sure to use the correct tenses of verbs in your questions and in your friend's responses.

Subject: your friend's science experiment
Audience: readers of the school newspaper
Purpose: to record an important discovery; to inform

René Magritte, Le Tombeau des Lutteurs, ©1960 c. Herscovici/Art Resource, New York.

ANSWERS

Exercise 12

Sentences will vary. Each sentence should have a main verb or a verb in a subordinate clause in the tense specified. All of the verbs should consist of the appropriate helping verbs and the correct past participles.

PICTURE THIS

Students who don't know anything about rosebushes might need to be told that ordinarily a rose blossom takes weeks to develop as the bush puts on new growth. So, the results yielded by the new fertilizer are truly amazing.

As a prewriting activity, discuss with the class how the inventor could test her product on other plants besides roses.

USAGE

SEGMENT 5 *(pp. 744–748)*

SPECIAL PROBLEMS IN THE USE OF TENSES Rules 24f–24k

OBJECTIVE

- To use tenses correctly in sentences

Teacher's ResourceBank™

RESOURCES

SPECIAL PROBLEMS IN THE USE OF TENSES

- Special Problems in the Use of Tenses 273

QUICK REMINDER

Write the following sentences on the chalkboard and ask students to identify the verb that denotes which event in each sentence occurred first.

1. André refused to read aloud the short story he had written for the contest. [had written]
2. If we had asked him before he arrived at the party, he would have agreed to read it. [had asked]
3. By the time we have our next party, the story will have been sent to the contest officials. [will have been sent]

Special Problems in the Use of Tenses

Sequence of Tenses

24f. Use tense forms carefully to show the correct relationship between verbs in a sentence.

(1) When describing events that occur at the same time, use verbs in the same tense.

EXAMPLES The coach **blows** the whistle, and the swimmers **dive** into the pool. [present tense]

The coach **blew** the whistle, and the swimmers **dived** into the pool. [past tense]

(2) When describing events that occur at different times, use verbs in different tenses to show the order of events.

EXAMPLES She now **works** for *The New York Times,* but she **worked** for the *Wall Street Journal* earlier this year. [Because her work for *The New York Times* is occurring now, the present tense form *works* is the correct form. Her work for the *Wall Street Journal* occurred at a specific time in the past and preceded her work at the *Times;* therefore, the past tense form *worked* is the correct form.]

Since the new band director **took** over, our band **has won** all of its contests. [Because the new director took over at a specific time in the past, the use of the past tense is correct. The winning has taken place over a period of time and continues into the present; therefore, the present perfect tense is used.]

The tense you use depends on the meaning that you want to express.

EXAMPLES I **think** I **have** a B average in math. [Both verbs are in the present tense to indicate that both actions are occurring now.]

I **think** I **had** a B average in math. [The change to the past tense in the second verb implies that I no longer have a B average in math.]

Lia said that she **lived** near the park. [Both verbs are in the past tense to indicate that both actions no longer occur.]

Lia said that she **will live** near the park. [The change in the second verb implies that Lia did not live near the park at the time she made the statement but that she planned to live there.]

24g. Avoid the use of *would have* in "if clauses" that express the earlier of two past actions. Use the past perfect tense.

NONSTANDARD If she would have handed in her application, she would have gotten the job.
STANDARD If she **had handed** in her application, she would have gotten the job.

NONSTANDARD If Felita would have asked her parents, she probably could have gone with us.
STANDARD If Felita **had asked** her parents, she probably could have gone with us.

EXERCISE 13 **Using Tenses Correctly**

Each of the following sentences contains an error in the use of tenses. Identify the error, and then give the correct form of the verb.

EXAMPLE 1. The holidays will begin by the time we arrive in Miami.
1. *will begin—will have begun*

1. Francesca promised to bring the Papago basket that she ^bought in Arizona. 1. had
2. Who found that the earth ^~~revolved~~ around the sun? 2. revolves
3. By the time we get to the picnic area, the rain will ^~~stop~~. 3. have stopped
4. In July my parents will ^~~be~~ married for twenty-five years. 4. have been
5. If the books ^~~have been~~ cataloged last week, why haven't they been placed on the shelves? 5. were
6. I would have agreed if you ^~~would have~~ asked me sooner. 6. had
7. Val claims that cats ^~~made~~ the best pets. 7. make
8. We studied *Macbeth* after we ^learned about the English Renaissance and the Globe Theatre. 8. had
9. The graduation valedictory will ^~~be~~ delivered by then. 9. have been
10. As a witness to the accident, Pam told what ^happened. 10. had

USAGE

MEETING INDIVIDUAL NEEDS

LESS-ADVANCED STUDENTS

Extra practice may help students learn the correct sequence for tenses in sentences with "if clauses." Have students work in pairs. Ask one student in each pair to write an "if clause," and ask the partner to complete the sentence by using the past perfect tense. After three sentences, have partners switch roles. Circulate among the pairs to monitor their work.

USAGE

COMMON ERROR

Problem. Many people in speaking use a sound that resembles *of* rather than *have,* as in "She would of gotten the job." Confusion between the two words often arises through oral use of the contraction *would've.*

Solution. Point out that while *would've* may sound like *would of,* it is actually the contracted form of *would have.* The *have* or *–'ve* must not be confused with *of* in writing.

USAGE

The Present Infinitive and the Present Perfect Infinitive

Infinitives have present and present perfect tenses.

PRESENT INFINITIVE	to see	to be	to change
PRESENT PERFECT INFINITIVE	to have seen	to have been	to have changed

USAGE

24h. The ***present infinitive*** is used to express an action (or a state of being) that follows another action (or state of being).

EXAMPLES Latrice hopes **to attend** the Super Bowl. [The action expressed by *to attend* follows the action expressed by *hopes.*]

Latrice had planned **to go** to the game with her brother. [The action expressed by *to go* follows the action expressed by *had planned.*]

24i. The ***present perfect infinitive*** is used to express an action (or a state of being) that precedes another action (or state of being).

EXAMPLES The divers claim **to have located** an ancient sailing vessel. [The action expressed by *to have located* precedes the action expressed by *claim.*]

They claimed **to have spent** three weeks exploring the ship. [The action expressed by *to have spent* precedes the action expressed by *claimed.*]

The Present Participle and the Present Perfect Participle

Participles have present and present perfect tenses.

PRESENT PARTICIPLE	seeing	being	changing
PRESENT PERFECT PARTICIPLE	having seen	having been	having changed

REVIEW H

OBJECTIVE

- To use verb tenses correctly in sentences

24j. The ***present participle*** is used to express an action (or a state of being) that occurs at the same time as another action (or state of being).

EXAMPLES **Gazing** through the telescope, I saw the rings around Saturn. [The action expressed by *Gazing* occurs at the same time as the action expressed by *saw.*]
Studying the night sky, I identified some celestial objects without the use of a telescope. [The action expressed by *Studying* occurs at the same time as the action expressed by *identified.*]

24k. The ***present perfect participle*** is used to express an action (or a state of being) that precedes another action (or state of being).

EXAMPLES **Having completed** her outline, Kate wrote the first draft of her research paper. [The action expressed by *Having completed* precedes the action expressed by *wrote.*]
Having proofread her research paper, Kate typed the final draft. [The action expressed by *Having proofread* precedes the action expressed by *typed.*]

USAGE

REVIEW H **Using Tenses Correctly**

Each of the following sentences contains an error in the use of verbs. Identify the error and then give the correct form of the verb.

EXAMPLE **1.** I would have taken more money on my trip to Japan if I would have known what the exchange rate was.
1. *would have known—had known*

1. When you charge the battery in the car, be sure to ~~have protected~~ your eyes and hands from the sulfuric acid in the battery. **1.** protect
2. ~~Deciding~~ to attend the concert at Boyer Hall, we bought four tickets for Saturday night. **2.** Having decided
3. Before Friday is over, we will ~~hear~~ some great music. **3.** have heard
4. If I ~~would have~~ known about the free offer, I would have sent in a coupon. **4.** had
5. My old skates ~~lay~~ in my closet for the past two years. **5.** have lain
6. I would have liked to ~~have gone~~ swimming yesterday. **6.** go

USAGE

SEGMENT 6 *(pp. 748–754)*

ACTIVE VOICE AND PASSIVE VOICE Rule 241

OBJECTIVE

- To revise sentences in the passive voice

Teacher's ResourceBank™

RESOURCES

ACTIVE AND PASSIVE VOICE

- Active and Passive Voice 274

QUICK REMINDER

To show how changing passive voice to active voice makes writing clearer and more forceful, write the following recipe on the chalkboard. Ask students to rewrite the sentences by changing the verbs to active voice.

The oven should be preheated to 350 degrees F. A pizza pan should be greased. One package of dry yeast is sprinkled in 1 cup of hot water. The yeast is stirred until it dissolves. Two and a half cups of flour, 1 teaspoon of salt, and 1 teaspoon of sugar are combined and added to the hot water. Two tablespoons of vegetable oil should be added, and the mixture is then set aside for five minutes. Then it is spread on the pizza pan and baked for twenty minutes.

USAGE

7. After ~~singing~~ the aria, Jessye Norman received a standing ovation. **7.** having sung
8. If I had the address, I would have been able to deliver the package myself. **8.** had
9. Dave should have ~~went~~ to the dentist three months ago when his tooth began to hurt. **9.** gone
10. I'll just ~~set~~ here for a while until Dr. López returns. **10.** sit

Active Voice and Passive Voice

Voice is the form a transitive verb takes to indicate whether the subject of the verb performs or receives the action.

REFERENCE NOTE: For more discussion of transitive verbs, see page 565.

When the subject of a verb performs the action, the verb is in the ***active voice.*** When the subject receives the action, the verb is in the ***passive voice.***

The verb in a passive construction always includes a form of *be* and the past participle of a transitive verb. Notice in the following conjugation of the verb *see* in the passive voice that the form of *be* determines the tense of the passive verb.

REFERENCE NOTE: The conjugation of see in the active voice is on pages 736–737.

As the examples after the following chart show, transitive verbs in the active voice have objects, and verbs in the passive voice do not.

CONJUGATION OF THE VERB *SEE* IN THE PASSIVE VOICE	
PRESENT TENSE	
SINGULAR	***PLURAL***
I am seen	we are seen
you are seen	you are seen
he, she, it is seen	they are seen
Present Progressive: am, are, is being seen	

(continued)

USAGE

CONJUGATION OF THE VERB *SEE* IN THE PASSIVE VOICE (*continued*)	
PAST TENSE	
SINGULAR	***PLURAL***
I was seen	we were seen
you were seen	you were seen
he, she, it was seen	they were seen
Past Progressive: was, were being seen	
FUTURE TENSE	
SINGULAR	***PLURAL***
I will (shall) be seen	we will (shall) be seen
you will be seen	you will be seen
he, she, it will be seen	they will be seen
Future Progressive: will (shall) be being seen	
PRESENT PERFECT TENSE	
SINGULAR	***PLURAL***
I have been seen	we have been seen
you have been seen	you have been seen
he, she, it has been seen	they have been seen
PAST PERFECT TENSE	
SINGULAR	***PLURAL***
I had been seen	we had been seen
you had been seen	you had been seen
he, she, it had been seen	they had been seen
FUTURE PERFECT TENSE	
SINGULAR	***PLURAL***
I will (shall) have been seen	we will (shall) have been seen
you will have been seen	you will have been seen
he, she, it will have been seen	they will have been seen

ACTIVE VOICE Gloria Naylor **wrote** *The Women of Brewster Place.* [*The Women of Brewster Place* is the direct object.]

PASSIVE VOICE *The Women of Brewster Place* **was written** by Gloria Naylor.

USAGE

MEETING INDIVIDUAL NEEDS

ADVANCED STUDENTS

Write ten interesting action verbs on the chalkboard. You could choose ten from the list of irregular verbs in this chapter.

Ask students to incorporate the verbs into short, expressive narratives. The narratives can be on any topic students choose, but they must be written in the active voice. If time permits, you can ask students to read their narratives aloud in class.

USAGE

ACTIVE VOICE The optometrist **adjusted** the eyeglasses. [*Eyeglasses* is the direct object.]
PASSIVE VOICE The eyeglasses **were adjusted** by the optometrist.

ACTIVE VOICE Carol **has adopted** the two puppies. [*Puppies* is the direct object.]
PASSIVE VOICE The two puppies **have been adopted** by Carol.
PASSIVE VOICE The two puppies **have been adopted.**

From these examples, you can see how an active construction can become a passive construction. The verb from the active sentence becomes a past participle preceded by a form of *be.* The object of the verb becomes the subject of the verb in a passive construction. The subject in an active construction becomes the object of the preposition *by* in a passive construction. As the last example shows, this prepositional phrase is not always necessary.

USAGE

USAGE

The Retained Object

A transitive verb in the active voice often has an indirect object as well as a direct object. Either object can become the subject or can remain a complement in the passive construction.

S V I.O. D.O.
ACTIVE Ms. Ribas gave each student a thesaurus.
PASSIVE Each student was given a thesaurus (by Ms. Ribas).
PASSIVE A thesaurus was given each student (by Ms. Ribas).

As you can see, the indirect object *student* in the active construction becomes the subject in the first passive construction, and the direct object *thesaurus* remains a complement. In the second passive construction, *thesaurus* is the subject, and *student* is the complement. A complement in a passive construction is called a ***retained object,*** not a direct object or an indirect object.

The Uses of the Passive Voice

Choosing between the active voice and the passive voice is a matter of style, not correctness. In general, however, the passive voice is less direct, less forceful, and less concise than the active voice. In fact, the passive voice may produce an awkward effect.

AWKWARD PASSIVE	Last night, the floor **was scrubbed** by my father, and the faucet **was fixed** by my mother.
ACTIVE	Last night, my father **scrubbed** the floor, and my mother **fixed** the faucet.
AWKWARD PASSIVE	The first wristwatch **was created** by a court jeweler when a watch set in a bracelet **was requested** by Empress Josephine.
ACTIVE	When Empress Josephine **requested** a watch set in a bracelet, a court jeweler **created** the first wristwatch.

Notice that the use of the passive voice in a long passage is particularly awkward.

AWKWARD PASSIVE	When my mother **was asked** by the local camera club to give a lecture on modern photography, she **was amazed** by the request. Mom **had** never **been chosen** to do anything like this before. Since I **am considered** by my mother to be the most imaginative member of our family, I **was given** by her the task of choosing the topics that **would be presented** by her. Dad **was asked** by her to select the slides that **would be shown** to the amateur photographers. Within a few days, the lecture **had been prepared** by Mom. On the night of the presentation, everyone in the audience **was impressed** by Mom's knowledge of modern photography.
ACTIVE	When the local camera club **asked** my mother to give a lecture on modern photography, the request **amazed** her. No one **had** ever **chosen** Mom to do anything like this before. Since my mother **considers** me the most imaginative member of our family, she **gave** me the task of choosing the topics that she **would present.** She **asked** Dad to select the slides that she **would show** to the amateur photographers. Within a few days, Mom **had prepared** the lecture. On the night of the presentation, Mom's knowledge of modern photography **impressed** everyone in the audience.

USAGE

INTEGRATING THE LANGUAGE ARTS

Technology Link. There are computer programs available that can check writing for overuse of passive voice. If your school's computer department has such a program, you may want to encourage students to use it.

USAGE

USAGE

ANSWERS

Exercise 14

1. At first, these people gathered and ate roots and berries.
2. They may have accidentally made the discovery that certain foods can be improved by cooking.
3. Hunters and gatherers may have left slaughtered animals or piles of edible roots near the fire.
4. They noticed that when food was cooked, it tasted better.
5. C

USAGE

24l. The passive voice should be used sparingly. Use the passive voice in the following situations.

(1) When you do not know the performer of the action

EXAMPLES Asbestos **was used** for making fireproof materials.
An anonymous letter **had been sent** to the police chief.

(2) When you do not want to reveal the performer of the action

EXAMPLES Many careless errors **were made** in some of these essays.
The missing paintings **have been returned** to the museum.

(3) When you want to emphasize the receiver of the action

EXAMPLES Penicillin **was discovered** accidentally.
This book **has been translated** into more than one hundred languages.

EXERCISE 14 Revising Sentences in the Passive Voice

Revise the following sentences by changing the passive voice to active voice wherever the change is desirable. If the passive is preferable, write *C*.

EXAMPLE **1.** A variety of cooking methods and utensils were invented by early humans.
1. *Early humans invented a variety of cooking methods and utensils.*

1. At first, roots and berries were gathered and eaten by these people.
2. The discovery that certain foods can be improved by cooking may have accidentally been made by them.
3. Slaughtered animals or piles of edible roots may have been left near the fire by hunters and gatherers.
4. It was noticed by them that when food was cooked, it tasted better.
5. The first ovens were formed from pits lined with stones and hot coals.

WRITING APPLICATION

OBJECTIVE

- To write a two- or three-paragraph opening for an adventure story

6. It wasn't long before ovens were built above the ground with some kind of chimney to carry away the smoke.
7. Primitive kettles were made by early humans by smearing clay over reed baskets and drying them in the sun.
8. Liquid foods could then be kept in such a basket for short periods without leaking.
9. When a clay-coated basket was placed near the flames by a prehistoric cook to heat its contents, sometimes the clay was baked by the high temperature into a pottery shell.
10. Once the simple physics of making pottery was mastered by early people, they learned to create the pottery shell without the basket.

USAGE

WRITING APPLICATION

Using Active Voice and Passive Voice Effectively

Most authorities on writing advise people to use the active voice. In general, this advice is sound—active voice verbs do help to make writing direct and lively. They clearly show who or what performed the action of the verb. Passive voice verbs, on the other hand, de-emphasize the identity of the person or thing performing the action. Consequently, the choice between active and passive voice in a particular sentence is a matter of style. The decision about which voice to use rests on what the writer wants to emphasize. Compare the following sentences.

SENTENCE 1 The rescue team found the trapped miner and quickly cleared away the debris. [active voice]

SENTENCE 2 The trapped miner was found, and the debris was quickly cleared away. [passive voice]

What does each sentence emphasize? Which sentence might you use in a news update on a mining accident? in a story about emergency rescue workers? Explain your choices.

6. C
7. Early humans made primitive kettles by smearing clay over reed baskets and drying them in the sun.
8. C
9. When a prehistoric cook placed a clay-coated basket near the flames to heat its contents, sometimes the high temperature baked the clay into a pottery shell.
10. Once early people mastered the simple physics of making pottery, they learned to create the pottery shell without the basket.

WRITING APPLICATION You may want to review with students the kinds of external conflicts that occur in stories (a person versus another person, a person versus some force in nature, or a person versus society) to refresh students' memories and to help them get ideas for their stories.

USAGE

CRITICAL THINKING
Evaluation

In addition to emphasizing that students should use active and passive voice appropriately, suggest that students consider the following points as they evaluate their paragraphs:

1. Are the verbs action verbs rather than forms of *to be*?
2. Are precise nouns used whenever possible? Are adjectives and adverbs sharp and vivid?
3. If dialogue is used, does it sound natural? Does the dialogue help to develop the kinds of characters the writer wants to create?
4. Do the paragraphs contain hints or events that arouse suspense?

You can use these criteria to evaluate students' work.

USAGE

WRITING ACTIVITY

A writer's club is holding a contest for the most exciting opening of an adventure story. The winner of the contest will get to publish his or her completed story in an upcoming issue of a national magazine. To enter the contest, write a two- or three-paragraph opening for an adventure story. Use active voice verbs to make your sentences lively and concise. Use passive voice verbs wherever they are needed for style or for emphasis.

Prewriting A good adventure story centers around a gripping conflict, a life-or-death problem that the hero must overcome. Brainstorm some ideas for an exciting conflict. Then create a brief plot outline for a story based on the conflict you think would lead to the greatest adventure. (For help with developing a short-story plot, see pages 166–167.) Think of a way to begin your story. You may want to begin at an exciting point in the middle of the action, or you may want to tell the story as a flashback. Jot down interesting details that will grab your readers' attention.

Writing Use your prewriting notes to help you write a first draft. Expand on your original ideas, adding details as you think of them.

Evaluating and Revising Ask a friend to read your story opener. Is the opening interesting and exciting? Can your friend predict what will happen next? Note down any revision suggestions. After you've revised the content of your story opener, focus on your writing style. Have you used active voice and passive voice verbs effectively? Use a thesaurus to help you replace any bland verbs with precise, imaginative ones.

Proofreading Remember that writers from all across the country will be entering the contest. Submit your best writing and check carefully for mistakes in grammar, usage, spelling, and punctuation. Be sure that you've used the correct forms of irregular verbs.

USAGE

SEGMENT 7 *(pp. 755–759)*
MOOD Rules 24m–24o

OBJECTIVE

- To identify the mood of verbs in sentences

Mood

Mood is the form a verb takes to indicate the attitude of the person using the verb. Verbs may be in one of three moods: the *indicative,* the *imperative,* or the *subjunctive.*

24m. The ***indicative mood*** is used to express a fact, an opinion, or a question.

EXAMPLES Andrei Sakharov **was** the nuclear physicist who **won** the Nobel Prize for peace in 1975.
All of us **think** that baseball team **is** the best one in the state.
Can you **explain** the difference between a meteor and a meteorite?

REFERENCE NOTE: For examples of all of the tense forms in the indicative mood, see the conjugations on pages 736–737 and 738–739.

24n. The ***imperative mood*** is used to express a direct command or request.

The imperative mood of a verb has only one form. It is the same as the infinitive form of a verb.

EXAMPLES **Explain** the difference between a meteor and a meteorite.
Please **fasten** your seat belt.

GREETING CARDS
CARDS
I NEED A GET-WELL CARD FOR MY OLD ENGLISH TEACHER. DO YOU HAVE ONE THAT CAJOLES IN THE INDICATIVE MOOD RATHER THAN COMMANDS IN THE IMPERATIVE?
© 1977 by NEA, Inc., T.M. Reg. U.S. Pat. Off.
8-1 THAVES

USAGE

Teacher's ResourceBank™
RESOURCES

MOOD
- Mood 275

QUICK REMINDER

Write the following sentences on the chalkboard and ask students to select the correct verb in parentheses. (Correct verbs are underscored.)

1. If I (was, were) you, I'd buy a used car and save on depreciation.
2. If it (was, were) to stop raining, maybe we could have a picnic in the park.
3. It's essential that he (attend, attends) class every day.
4. I wish she (was, were) more patient.

Point out to students that all of these sentences require the subjunctive mood, which they'll study in this segment.

USAGE

MEETING INDIVIDUAL NEEDS

LEP/ESL

General Strategies. Speakers of Spanish, French, Italian, Portuguese, and other Romance languages are probably more familiar with the subjunctive mood than are native speakers of English. These languages use the subjunctive mood more often and for more reasons than English does.

Ask students who speak Romance languages to translate the following sentences into their native languages and to demonstrate how the subjunctive form differs from the indicative:

1. We don't know whether the rain will stop.
2. We know that the rain will stop.

You can have students write the sentences on the chalkboard to demonstrate the differences for the whole class.

ADVANCED STUDENTS

Advanced students who are studying Romance languages may already understand the concept of subjunctive mood. You may want to have students do **Exercise 15** as a pretest for this segment to determine whether or not students need to study the textbook material on mood.

USAGE

USAGE

24o. The ***subjunctive mood*** is used to express a suggestion, a necessity, a condition contrary to fact, or a wish.

Only the present and past tenses have distinctive subjunctive forms. The other tense forms in the subjunctive mood are the same as those in the indicative mood.

The following partial conjugation of *be* shows how the present and past tense forms in the subjunctive mood differ from those in the indicative mood. [Note: The use of *that* and *if,* which are shown in parentheses, is explained at the bottom of this page and on the next page.]

PRESENT INDICATIVE		PRESENT SUBJUNCTIVE	
SINGULAR	*PLURAL*	*SINGULAR*	*PLURAL*
I am	we are	(that) I be	(that) we be
you are	you are	(that) you be	(that) you be
he, she, it is	they are	(that) he, she, it be	(that) they be
PAST INDICATIVE		**PAST SUBJUNCTIVE**	
I was	we were	(if) I were	(if) we were
you were	you were	(if) you were	(if) you were
he, she, it was	they were	(if) he, she, it were	(if) they were

Notice in the conjugation that the present subjunctive form of a verb is the same as the infinitive form. For all verbs except *be,* the past subjunctive form is the same as the past form. The verb *be* has two past tense forms. As you can see, however, the past tense form *was* in the indicative mood becomes *were* in the subjunctive mood. Therefore, *were* is the only past subjunctive form of *be.*

(1) The ***present subjunctive*** is used to express a suggestion or a necessity.

Generally, the verb in a subordinate clause beginning with *that* is in the subjunctive mood when the independent clause contains a word indicating a suggestion (such as *ask, request, suggest,* or *recommend*) or a word indicating a necessity (such as *necessary* or *essential*).

EXAMPLES Ms. Chávez suggested that he **apply** for the job.
The moderator at the convention requested that the state delegates **be seated.**
It is necessary that she **attend** the convention.
It is required that you **be** here on time.

(2) The *past subjunctive* is used to express a condition contrary to fact or to express a wish.

In general, a clause beginning with *if, as if,* or *as though* expresses a condition contrary to fact—something that is not true. In such a clause, use the past subjunctive. Remember that *were* is the only past subjunctive form of *be.*

EXAMPLES If I **were** you, I'd have those tires checked.
If he **were** to proofread his writing, he would make fewer errors.
Because of the bad telephone connection, Gregory sounded as though [as if] he **were** ten thousand miles away.

Similarly, use the past subjunctive to express a wish—a condition that is desirable.

EXAMPLES I wish I **were** more patient than I am.
Reiko wishes that her best friend **were**n't moving away.

EXERCISE 15 **Identify the Mood of Verbs**

For each of the following sentences, identify the mood of the italicized verb as *indicative, imperative,* or *subjunctive.*

1. Theo, *stand* back a safe distance while I try again to start this lawnmower. **1.** imperative
2. Did you know that Tamisha's mother *is* the new manager at the supermarket? **2.** indicative
3. Bradley says that if he *were* president, he'd take steps to reduce the federal deficit. **3.** subjunctive
4. I suggest that these young maple trees *be* planted quickly before they wilt. **4.** subjunctive
5. *Were* you and your two brothers excited about visiting your birthplace in Mexico? **5.** indicative
6. This Lenni-Lenape moccasin *was* found near Matawan, New Jersey. **6.** indicative

USAGE

USAGE

REVIEWS I and J

OBJECTIVES

- To proofread sentences for correct verb usage
- To proofread a paragraph for the correct use of verbs

7. Stay there and *be* a good dog while I go into the bakery, Molly. 7. imperative
8. When my dad saw the dented fender, he looked as if he *were* ready to explode. 8. subjunctive
9. "I wish that you *were* not moving so far away," muttered my best friend Bao. 9. subjunctive
10. Mr. Darwin requested that you *be* the bus monitor on our next class trip. 10. subjunctive

REVIEW I

Proofreading Sentences for Correct Verb Usage

Most of the following sentences contain errors in the use of verbs. If a sentence has a verb error, identify the error, and then give the correct verb form. If a sentence is correct, write C.

EXAMPLE **1. After he had passed the jewelry store, he wished he went into it.**

1. *went—had gone*

1. The rock group had finished the concert, but the audience called for another set. 1. C
2. Do you think that she would have ~~volunteer~~ to help us if she ~~weren't~~ highly qualified? 2. volunteered/had not been
3. If Sherrie ~~would~~ not ~~have~~ missed the printer's deadline, the yearbook delivery would have been on time. 3. had
4. Although I thought I planned my trip down to the last detail, there was one thing I ~~had forgotten~~. 4. had/forgot [or C]
5. If you ~~would have~~ remembered to bring along something to read, you would not have been so bored. 5. had
6. The smell from the paper mill ~~laid~~ over the town like a blanket. 6. lay
7. Sarah says she enjoyed working on the kibbutz in Israel last summer, but she hardly got a chance to ~~set~~ down the whole time. 7. sit
8. By the time they ~~had~~ smelled the smoke, the flames had already begun to spread.
9. I am glad to have the opportunity to revise my essay for a higher grade. 9. C
10. If Emiliano Zapata ~~would have~~ known the invitation was a trap, he would not have been ambushed at a farm near Cuautla. 10. had

USAGE

USAGE

REVIEW J — Proofreading a Paragraph for Correct Use of Verbs

Most of the sentences in the following paragraph contain errors in the use of verbs. If a sentence has an error, identify the error and then supply the correct verb form. If a sentence is correct, write *C*.

EXAMPLE [1] **After he had lit the candle, Dad begun to recite the first principle of Kwanzaa.**

1. *begun—began*

[1] Kwanzaa has been being celebrated by African Americans for more than twenty-five years. [2] This holiday has been created in 1966 by Maulanga Karenga, a professor of black studies at California State University. [3] Dr. Karenga wished that there was a nonreligious holiday especially for black Americans. [4] If he has not treasured his own background, we would not have this inspiring celebration to enjoy. [5] Professor Karenga has believed that people's heritage should be celebrated by them. [6] Recently, more and more African Americans have began to reserve the seven-day period immediately following Christmas for Kwanzaa. [7] If you would have joined my family for Kwanzaa last year, you would have heard my grandfather's talk about family values and about African Americans who have fought for freedom and honor. [8] We all wore items of traditional African clothing like these and displayed a red, black, and green flag to symbolize Africa. [9] Mom lay out a wonderful feast each night, and we lit a candle and talked about one of the seven principles of Kwanzaa. [10] I wish I asked you to our house last year for Kwanzaa, and I will definitely invite you this year.

USAGE

ANSWERS

Review J

1. has been being celebrated — has been celebrated
2. has been — was
3. was — were
4. has treasured — had treasured
5. has believed — believed; people's heritage should be celebrated by them — people should celebrate their heritage
6. have began — have begun
7. would have joined — had joined
8. C
9. lay — laid
10. asked — had asked

USAGE

SEGMENT 8 *(pp. 760–761)*

REVIEW: POSTTEST

OBJECTIVE

- To proofread sentences for correct verb usage

USAGE

Review: Posttest

A. Proofreading Sentences for Correct Verb Usage

Most of the following sentences contain errors in the use of verbs. If a sentence has a verb error, revise the sentence, using the correct verb form. If a sentence is correct, write *C*.

EXAMPLE **1. If I would have seen the accident, I would have reported it.**

1. ***If I had seen the accident, I would have reported it.***

1. If modern society ~~was~~ an agricultural one, more of us would know about farming and about the difficulties faced by farmers. **1. were**
2. According to the latest census tally at that time, more than 39,000 Native Americans ~~had been~~ currently living in Wisconsin. **2. were**
3. How many of us possess the skills to ~~have survived~~ on our own without the assistance of store-bought items? **3. survive**
4. If you ~~would have~~ taken the nutrition class, you would have learned how to shop wisely for food. **4. had**
5. Wacky, my pet hamster, was acting as if she ~~was~~ trying to tell me something. **5. were**
6. Yesterday, ~~Dad's pickup truck was~~ washed and waxed ~~by my brother.~~ **6. my brother/Dad's pickup truck**
7. According to this news article, the concert last Saturday night ~~is~~ "a resounding success." **7. was**
8. Janet Jackson's concerts have ~~broke~~ all attendance records at the City Arena. **8. broken**
9. Because of the excessive amount of rain this spring, the water in the dam has ~~raised~~ to a dangerous level. **9. risen**
10. After ~~spending~~ the entire morning working in the garden, Jim is ~~laying~~ down for a rest. **10. having spent/lying**

B. Proofreading Sentences for Correct Verb Usage

Most of the following sentences contain errors in the use of verbs. If a sentence has a verb error, revise the sentence, using the correct verb form. If a sentence is correct, write *C*.

USAGE

EXAMPLE 1. From our studies we had concluded that women had played many critical roles in the history of our nation.

1. *From our studies we have concluded that women have played many critical roles in the history of our nation.*

11. In Daytona Beach, Florida, Mary McLeod Bethune had founded a tiny school, which ~~become~~ Bethune-Cookman College. **11.** became
12. Jane Addams founded Hull House in Chicago to educate the poor and to acquaint immigrants with American ways; for her efforts she ~~had~~ received the Nobel Prize for peace in 1931.
13. In 1932, after a flight lasting almost fifteen hours, Amelia Earhart became the first woman to have flown solo across the Atlantic Ocean. **13.** C
14. Pearl Buck, a recipient of the Nobel Prize for literature in 1938, ~~strived~~ to bring understanding and peace to people all over the world. **14.** strove
15. When the Republican National Convention met in San Francisco in 1964, Margaret Chase Smith, senator from Maine, received twenty-seven delegate votes for the presidential nomination. **15.** C
16. Lorraine Hansberry wrote the successful play *A Raisin in the Sun*, which ~~had~~ been translated into thirty languages. **16.** has
17. Have you ever heard of Belva Lockwood, a woman whose accomplishments paved the way for women in politics? **17.** C
18. In 1879, a short time after Lockwood was admitted to the bar, she became the first woman lawyer to ~~have argued~~ a case before the United States Supreme Court. **18.** argue (*or* C)
19. Although Lockwood is not well known nowadays, she did receive more than four thousand votes for the presidency in 1884. **19.** C
20. By the time you leave high school, you will ~~learn~~ many interesting facts about history. **20.** have learned

USAGE

USAGE

Teacher's ResourceBank™

RESOURCES

FOR THE WHOLE CHAPTER

- Chapter Review Form A 290–291
- Chapter Review Form B 292–293
- Assessment Portfolio
  - Usage Pretests 571–578
  - Usage Mastery Tests 597–604

CHAPTER OVERVIEW

The first part of this chapter helps students to identify adjective and adverb modifiers and to correctly use the troublesome pairs *bad* and *badly, good* and *well,* and *slow* and *slowly.* The second part focuses on making comparisons by correctly using comparative and superlative forms, both regular and irregular.

You may want to refer students to this chapter when teaching **Chapter 14: "Writing Clear Sentences," Chapter 15: "Combining Sentences,"** and **Chapter 16: "Improving Sentence Style."** The material could be introduced with any of the composition chapters, especially in segments that deal with evaluation and revision. This chapter could also be used as a resource by students who use modifiers incorrectly in their writing.

USAGE

SEGMENT 1 *(pp. 762–763)*

DIAGNOSTIC TEST

OBJECTIVES

- To select correct modifiers to complete sentences
- To proofread a paragraph and revise the incorrect modifiers

USAGE

25 CORRECT USE OF MODIFIERS

Forms and Uses of Adjectives and Adverbs; Comparison

Diagnostic Test

A. Selecting Modifiers to Complete Sentences

Select the correct modifier in parentheses for each of the following sentences.

EXAMPLE **1. When you feel (*nervous, nervously*), take a deep breath and concentrate on relaxing images.**
1. *nervous*

1. When Rosa and I had the flu, Rosa was (*sicker, sickest*).
2. As a student, Edmonia Lewis watched (*careful, carefully*) when her teacher demonstrated sculpting techniques.
3. As you approach the next intersection, drive (*cautious, cautiously*).
4. This car is roomier than (*any, any other*) car we ever had.
5. The leaders of the Underground Railroad acted (*quick, quickly*) to help runaway slaves.

6. If you look at the two kittens carefully, you will see that the smaller one is (*healthier*, *healthiest*).
7. It was obvious from his response at the press conference that the candidate had prepared his answers (*well*, *good*).
8. This must be the (*baddest*, *worst*) movie ever made.
9. You will drive more (*steady*, *steadily*) if you keep your eyes on the road.
10. Mr. Yan thinks that Jacinto Quirarte is the (*better*, *best*) authority on Mexican American and pre-Columbian art.

B. Proofreading a Paragraph for Incorrect Modifiers

Most of the sentences in the following paragraph contain errors in the use of modifiers. Identify each error and give the correct form. If a sentence is correct, write *C*.

EXAMPLE **[1]** The slogan of Chicago's most largest hands-on museum is "We've got fun down to a science."
1. *most largest—largest*

[11] Malcolm and I went to visit Chicago's interestingest museum, the Museum of Science and Industry. **[12]** Although the museum houses more than two thousand displays, we decided to go slow even if it meant we could see only a few exhibits. **[13]** To see certain special displays, we planned our day careful. **[14]** First, we walked through an incredible model of a beating heart. **[15]** The thumping and swishing of the heart were better than any sound effects we'd ever heard. **[16]** Next, Malcolm went to play computer games while I decided to explore more livelier happenings at the farm exhibit. **[17]** When we met later for lunch, I asked him which computer game was hardest to win, tic tac toe or the money game. **[18]** As we headed for the Omnimax Theater to view the most advanced film projection system in the world, Malcolm admitted that he hadn't done good at either game. **[19]** We spent the rest of the day looking at a submarine, a lunar module, and, the funniest thing of all—ourselves on television! **[20]** We both agreed that the Museum of Science and Industry is better than any museum we've ever visited.

11. most interesting
12. slowly
13. carefully
14. C
15. other
17. harder
18. well
19. C
20. other

USAGE

USING THE DIAGNOSTIC TEST

If you find that some students are having difficulty in using modifiers correctly in their writing, you can use the **Diagnostic Test** to define their specific strengths and weaknesses. An assessment of students' responses should help you group students to meet individual needs or to make special assignments.

USAGE

SEGMENT 2 *(pp. 764–767)*

FORMS OF MODIFIERS Rules 25a, 25b

OBJECTIVE

- To select correct modifiers to complete sentences

Teacher's ResourceBank™

RESOURCES

FORMS OF MODIFIERS

- Adjective and Adverb Modifiers 285

QUICK REMINDER

Remind students that adverbs tell *where, when, how,* and *to what extent.* Adjectives tell *what kind, which one,* and *how many.*

Write the following sentences on the chalkboard. Have students classify each underlined word as an adjective or an adverb; then have them identify what it tells.

1. Just before the tornado hit, the air was surprisingly calm. (adverb; tells extent of being calm)
2. The sputtering barge churned huge green waves in the river. (adjective; tells what kind of barge)
3. Her eyes blinked rapidly as she spoke. (adverb; tells how her eyes blinked)
4. The candidates had a lively debate. (adjective; tells what kind of debate)

Forms of Modifiers

A ***modifier*** is a word that limits the meaning of another word. The two kinds of modifiers are the *adjective* and the *adverb.*

An ***adjective*** limits the meaning of a noun or a pronoun.

EXAMPLES **strong** wind **an** alligator
a loud voice **the original** one

An ***adverb*** limits the meaning of a verb, an adjective, or another adverb.

EXAMPLES drives **carefully** **suddenly** stopped
extremely important **rather** quickly

Most modifiers with an *–ly* ending are used as adverbs. In fact, many adverbs are formed by adding *–ly* to adjectives.

ADJECTIVES	perfect	clear	quiet	abrupt
ADVERBS	perfectly	clearly	quietly	abruptly

However, some modifiers ending in *–ly* may be used as adjectives.

EXAMPLES a **daily** lesson an **early** breakfast a **lively** discussion

A few modifiers have the same form whether used as adjectives or as adverbs.

ADJECTIVES	ADVERBS
a **hard** job	works **hard**
a **late** start	started **late**
an **early** arrival	arriving **early**
a **fast** walk	to walk **fast**

Uses of Modifiers

25a. Use an adjective to modify the subject of a linking verb.

The most common linking verbs are the forms of *be: am, is, are, was, were, be, been,* and *being.* A linking verb is often followed by a *predicate adjective*—a word that modifies the subject.

EXAMPLES Our new computer system is **efficient.**
The governor's comments on the controversial issue were **candid.**

REFERENCE NOTE: For more about predicate adjectives, see pages 560 and 595.

25b. Use an adverb to modify an action verb.

Action verbs are often modified by adverbs—words that tell *how, when, where,* or *to what extent* an action is performed.

EXAMPLES Our new computer system is operating **efficiently.**
The governor **candidly** expressed her view on the controversial issue.

Some verbs may be used as linking verbs or as action verbs.

EXAMPLES Carmen looked **frantic.** [*Looked* is a linking verb. The modifier following it is an adjective, *frantic.*]
Carmen looked **frantically** for her class ring. [*Looked* is an action verb. The modifier following it is an adverb, *frantically.*]

To help you determine whether a verb is a linking verb or an action verb, replace the verb with a form of *seem.* If the substitution sounds reasonable, the original verb is a linking verb. If the substitution sounds absurd, the original verb is an action verb.

EXAMPLES Carmen looked frantic. [Since *Carmen seemed frantic* sounds reasonable, *looked* is a linking verb.]
Carmen looked frantically for her class ring. [Since *Carmen seemed frantically for her class ring* sounds absurd, *looked* is an action verb.]

REFERENCE NOTE: For more information about linking verbs and action verbs, see pages 565–567.

Like main verbs, verbals may be modified by adverbs.

EXAMPLES Barking **loudly,** the dog frightened the burglar. [The adverb *loudly* modifies the participle *barking.*]
Not fastening the bracket **tightly** will enable you to adjust it **later.** [The adverbs *not* and *tightly* modify the gerund *fastening.* The adverb *later* modifies the infinitive *to adjust.*]

REFERENCE NOTE: For more about verbals, see pages 611–617.

USAGE

MEETING INDIVIDUAL NEEDS

LEP/ESL

Spanish. Because adjectives in Spanish generally follow the nouns they modify, you may want to have the students pay special attention to adjective placement. Write several example sentences on the chalkboard and draw arrows from the adjectives to the nouns they modify. For example, illustrate the first sentence on p. 765 as follows:

Our new computer system is efficient.

Students should see that the pattern in English of nouns preceded by adjectives or of adjectives following linking verbs is generally different from adjective placement in their native language.

INTEGRATING THE LANGUAGE ARTS

Literature Link. The way a writer uses modifiers can contribute greatly to his or her style. Ask students to read one of Ernest Hemingway's short stories, such as "In Another Country," and to notice his use of adjectives. [He uses adjectives sparingly; those he uses are generally predicate adjectives.] Ask students to discuss the effect that using few adjectives has on Hemingway's writing. [His writing is straightforward and precise. His descriptions often rely on strong verbs.]

USAGE

EXERCISE 1 **Selecting Modifiers to Complete Sentences**

Select the correct modifier in parentheses for each of the following sentences.

EXAMPLE **1. When you look (*careful, carefully*) at these pots, you can see the tiny figures etched on them.**
1. *carefully*

1. The woman in the picture is Rosemary Apple Blossom Lonewolf, an artist whose style remains (*unique, uniquely*) among Native American potters.
2. Lonewolf combines (*traditional, traditionally*) and modern techniques to create her miniature pottery.
3. In crafting her pots, Lonewolf uses dark red clay that is (*ready, readily*) available around the Santa Clara Pueblo in New Mexico, where she lives.

4. These miniatures have a detailed and (*delicate, delicately*) etched surface called sgraffito.
5. Because of the (*extreme, extremely*) intricate detail on its surface, a single pot may take many months to finish.
6. The subjects for most of Lonewolf's pots combine ancient Pueblo myths and traditions with (*current, currently*) ideas or events.

USAGE

VISUAL CONNECTIONS

Ideas for Writing. Tell students to imagine what a day in Rosemary Lonewolf's studio might involve—sketching an idea, firing pots, or carefully etching a design. Have students write informative descriptions based on the pictures and on what they imagined. Students should use adverb and adjective modifiers correctly. You may wish to have students work in pairs to share their descriptions.

SEGMENT 3 *(pp. 767–770)*

SIX TROUBLESOME MODIFIERS

OBJECTIVES

- To determine the correct use of *bad* and *badly, good* and *well,* and *slow* and *slowly* in sentences
- To write a journal entry that includes adjectives and linking verbs

7. One pot called *Half-Breed's Horizons* (*clear, clearly*) depicts a Pueblo corn dancer walking down a city street lined with skyscrapers.
8. Lonewolf uses such images to show that Native Americans can and do adapt (*real, really*) well to new ways.
9. At first known only in the Southwest, Lonewolf's work is now shown throughout the United States because the appeal of her subjects is quite (*broad, broadly*).
10. Rosemary Lonewolf's talented family includes her father, grandfather, and son, who are all (*high, highly*) skilled potters.

USAGE

Six Troublesome Modifiers

Bad and *Badly*

Bad is an adjective. *Badly* is an adverb. In standard English, only the adjective form should follow a sense verb or other linking verb.

NONSTANDARD If the meat smells badly, don't eat it.
STANDARD If the meat smells **bad,** don't eat it.

NOTE: Although the expression *feel badly* has become acceptable in informal situations, use *feel bad* in formal speaking and writing.

Good and *Well*

Good is an adjective. *Well* may be used as an adjective or as an adverb. Avoid using *good* to modify an action verb. Instead, use *well,* an adverb meaning "capably" or "satisfactorily."

NONSTANDARD The school orchestra played good.
STANDARD The school orchestra played **well.**

NONSTANDARD Although she was nervous, Aretha performed quite good.
STANDARD Although she was nervous, Aretha performed quite **well.**

Used as an adjective, *well* means "in good health" or "satisfactory in appearance or condition."

EXAMPLES He says that he feels **well.**
She looks **well** in that band uniform.
It's midnight, and all is **well.**

Teacher's ResourceBank™

RESOURCES

SIX TROUBLESOME MODIFIERS

QUICK REMINDER

Write the following sentences on the chalkboard. Have students fill in the blanks with *good* or *well.*

1. Lola drives fairly ____. [well]
2. She can drive as ____ as I can. [well]
3. However, we both could use a ____ teacher. [good]

Remind students that *good* modifies a noun or a pronoun and that *well* most often modifies a verb.

USAGE

MEETING INDIVIDUAL NEEDS

LEP/ESL

General Strategies. When native speakers of English are asked how they are doing, they often respond by saying "good" rather than "well." Because most ESL students put a great deal of faith in the spoken forms they hear, they appreciate knowing why these forms often deviate from the textbook. You could tell them that the use of *good* in response to a greeting is a casual, informal use of English that is common in everyday speech.

COOPERATIVE LEARNING

After initial discussion of the three troublesome modifier pairs, let students teach each other the material. Set up six-member teams. Two members will teach *bad* and *badly,* two will teach *good* and *well,* and two will teach *slow* and *slowly.* Each pair of students is also responsible for writing a six-sentence practice exercise on their material for the other members.

A DIFFERENT APPROACH

You may want students to practice before they work on **Exercise 2.** Divide the class into two teams and have each team create sentences that call for a choice between *bad* and *badly, good* and *well,* and *slow* and *slowly* (six sentences per pair of words, eighteen sentences per team).

Alternating between teams, have a team member read a sentence and give thirty seconds for the opposing team to choose the correct modifier and to explain the reasoning behind the choice. An incorrect explanation gives the other team a chance to respond. Teams receive a point for each correct answer and lose a point for each incorrect answer.

USAGE

Slow and *Slowly*

Slow is an adjective. *Slowly* is an adverb. Avoid the common error of using *slow* to modify an action verb.

NONSTANDARD Do sloths always move that slow?
STANDARD Do sloths always move that **slowly**?

NOTE: The expressions *drive slow* and *go slow* have become acceptable in informal situations. In formal speaking and writing, however, use *drive slowly* and *go slowly.*

USAGE

EXERCISE 2 **Determining the Correct Use of *Bad* and *Badly, Well* and *Good,* and *Slow* and *Slowly***

Each of the following sentences contains an italicized modifier. If the modifier is incorrect, give the correct form. If the modifier is correct, write C.

EXAMPLE 1. When I painted the house, I fell off the ladder and hurt my right arm *bad.*
1. *badly*

1. The renowned conductor Leonard Bernstein led the New York Philharmonic Orchestra *well* for many years. 1. C
2. Despite the immense size and tremendous power of this airplane, the engines start up ~~*slow*~~. 2. slowly
3. I can hit the ball ~~*good*~~ if I keep my eye on it. 3. well
4. Before Uncle Chet's hip-replacement surgery, his gait was painful and *slow.* 4. C
5. After studying French for the past three years in high school, we were pleased to discover how ~~*good*~~ we spoke and understood it on our trip to Quebec. 5. well
6. Some of the experiments that the chemistry class has conducted have made the corridors smell ~~*badly*~~. 6. bad
7. During the Han dynasty in China, candidates who did ~~*bad*~~ on civil service tests did not become government officials. 7. badly
8. Whenever I watch the clock, the time seems to go ~~*slow*~~. 8. slowly
9. When my parents correct my little sister, they tell her not to behave ~~*bad*~~. 9. badly
10. After hearing how her Navajo ancestors overcame many problems, Anaba felt ~~*well*~~. 10. good

REVIEW A

OBJECTIVE

- To proofread a paragraph and determine the correct use of modifiers

ANSWERS

Review A

1. C
2. C
3. Huge
4. tremendously
5. C
6. slowly
7. rapidly
8. bad
9. C
10. wonderfully

REVIEW A **Determining the Correct Use of Modifiers**

Proofread the following paragraph, correcting any errors in the use of modifiers. If a sentence is correct, write *C.*

EXAMPLE [1] **Some volcanoes rest quiet for many years.**
1. *quietly*

[1] More than five hundred active volcanoes exist on land, and thousands more are found in the sea. [2] Eruptions of these volcanoes are often spectacularly violent. [3] ~~Hugely~~ reddish clouds rise from the volcano, while bright rivers of lava pour down the mountainside. [4] Beyond the eerie, beautiful spectacle that the eye sees, however, is the ~~tremendous~~ destructive force of the volcano. [5] A volcano begins as magma, a river of rock melted by the extreme heat inside the earth. [6] The rock melts ~~slow,~~ forming a gas that, together with the magma, causes the volcano to erupt. [7] Lava flows from the eruption site, sometimes quite ~~rapid~~, destroying everything in its path. [8] After a volcano erupts, observers usually feel ~~badly~~ because the heat and ash created by the eruption can seriously threaten not only the environment but also the lives and property of people living nearby. [9] On the other hand, volcanoes can also have a positive effect on the environment. [10] Lava and volcanic ash gradually mix with the soil to make it ~~wonderful~~ rich in minerals.

USAGE

PICTURE THIS

Just look at all these beautifully wrapped presents! This holiday season you and many other volunteers worked for an organization that distributes gifts to needy children. The most enjoyable part of your job was wrapping these gifts with colorful paper and ribbons. Now you want to remember

PICTURE THIS

Provide the class with a prewriting activity by asking students to close their eyes and to imagine that they are working as volunteers wrapping gifts such as those shown in the picture. What do they see? What do they hear? How do the paper and ribbons look and feel? How do the volunteers feel about the work they are doing? After a few moments, students might jot down thoughts and details that come to them.

USAGE

SEGMENT 4 *(pp. 770–777)*

COMPARISON OF MODIFIERS Rules 25c–25f

OBJECTIVES

- To write the comparative and superlative forms of modifiers
- To revise sentences by correcting errors in the use of the comparative and superlative forms of modifiers

USAGE

Teacher's ResourceBank™

RESOURCES

COMPARISON OF MODIFIERS

QUICK REMINDER

Write the following sentences on the chalkboard. Have students decide which choice offered in parentheses better completes each sentence.

1. The singing contest will determine the (better, best) voices in the large chorus. [best]
2. That is the (most beautiful, beautifulest) song of the night. [most beautiful]
3. He has the (most deep, deepest) voice in the bass section. [deepest]

You may want to remind students that the number of syllables in the modifier can help determine whether to add *–er*/*–est* or to use *more*/*most*.

this special time as clearly as possible. Write a journal entry describing the work you did. Tell how you felt when the last present was wrapped. In your journal entry, use at least four adjectives with linking verbs.

Subject: holiday volunteer work
Audience: you
Purpose: to record events; to express your feelings

USAGE

Comparison of Modifiers

25c. ***Comparison*** refers to the change in the form of an adjective or an adverb to show increasing or decreasing degrees in the quality the modifier expresses.

There are three degrees of comparison: *positive, comparative,* and *superlative.*

	POSITIVE	COMPARATIVE	SUPERLATIVE
ADJECTIVES	neat	neater	neatest
	careful	more careful	most careful
	optimistic	less optimistic	least optimistic
	good	better	best
ADVERBS	soon	sooner	soonest
	calmly	more calmly	most calmly
	commonly	less commonly	least commonly
	well	better	best

Regular Comparison

(1) Most one-syllable modifiers form the comparative and superlative degrees by adding *–er* and *–est.*

25c

POSITIVE	COMPARATIVE	SUPERLATIVE
soft	softer	softest
clean	cleaner	cleanest
fast	faster	fastest
long	longer	longest

REFERENCE NOTE: For information on determining the syllables in a word, see page 976.

(2) Some two-syllable modifiers form the comparative and superlative degrees by adding *–er* and *–est.* Other two-syllable modifiers form the comparative and superlative degrees by using *more* and *most.*

POSITIVE	COMPARATIVE	SUPERLATIVE
simple	simpler	simplest
likely	likelier	likeliest
cautious	more cautious	most cautious
freely	more freely	most freely

If you are not sure how a two-syllable modifier is compared, use a dictionary.

REFERENCE NOTE: For guidelines on spelling modifiers with *–er* and *–est,* see pages 906–907.

(3) Modifiers of more than two syllables form the comparative and superlative degrees by using *more* and *most.*

POSITIVE	COMPARATIVE	SUPERLATIVE
efficient	more efficient	most efficient
punctual	more punctual	most punctual
frequently	more frequently	most frequently
skillfully	more skillfully	most skillfully

USAGE

MEETING INDIVIDUAL NEEDS

LEP/ESL

General Strategies. The strategy of counting the syllables of an adjective in order to know how to form its comparative and superlative degrees applies to few if any other languages. In many languages, syllables have nothing to do with grammar. Some ESL students might be unaccustomed to thinking about syllables and might be unsure of what they are. If students have trouble with the exercises in this segment, be sure they know how to consult a dictionary to check the division of words into syllables.

AT-RISK STUDENTS

To motivate students, allow them to use a multisensory approach in areas that interest them. Ask students to use magazine or newspaper photos to illustrate degrees of comparison for adjectives and adverbs. For example, students might find advertisements for three different athletic shoes, mount them on paper, and identify the different shoes as versatile, more versatile, most versatile. Other possible areas for comparison include music, movies, occupations, foods, and sports.

USAGE

USAGE

(4) To show a decrease in the qualities they express, all modifiers form the comparative and superlative degrees by using *less* and *least.*

POSITIVE	COMPARATIVE	SUPERLATIVE
proud	less proud	least proud
honest	less honest	least honest
patiently	less patiently	least patiently
reasonably	less reasonably	least reasonably

Irregular Comparison

Some modifiers do not follow the regular methods of forming the comparative and superlative degrees.

POSITIVE	COMPARATIVE	SUPERLATIVE
bad	worse	worst
good	better	best
well	better	best
little	less	least
many	more	most
much	more	most

EXERCISE 3 **Writing the Comparative and Superlative Forms of Modifiers**

Write the comparative and the superlative forms of each of the following modifiers.

EXAMPLE **1.** stubborn
1. *more (less) stubborn; most (least) stubborn*

1. anxious
2. hard
3. cheerful
4. eager
5. quick
6. well
7. cold
8. stealthily
9. expensive
10. enthusiastically

USAGE

ANSWERS

Exercise 3

1. more (less) anxious; most (least) anxious
2. harder (less hard); hardest (least hard)
3. more (less) cheerful; most (least) cheerful
4. more (less) eager; most (least) eager
5. quicker (less quick); quickest (least quick)
6. better (worse); best (worst)
7. colder (less cold); coldest (least cold)
8. more (less) stealthily; most (least) stealthily
9. more (less) expensive; most (least) expensive
10. more (less) enthusiastically; most (least) enthusiastically

Uses of Comparative and Superlative Forms

25d. Use the comparative degree when comparing two things. Use the superlative degree when comparing more than two.

COMPARATIVE Although both puppies look cute, the **more active** one seems **healthier.** [comparison of two puppies]
After reading *King Lear* and *A Winter's Tale,* I can understand why *King Lear* is **more widely** praised. [comparison of two plays]

SUPERLATIVE Of the four plays that we saw, I think *Death of a Salesman* was the **most moving.** [comparison of four plays]
I sat in the front row because it provided the **best** view of the chemistry experiment. [comparison of many views]

NOTE: In informal situations the superlative degree is sometimes used to emphasize the comparison of only two things. Avoid such use of the superlative degree in formal speaking and writing.

INFORMAL Which was hardest to learn, French or Spanish?
FORMAL Which was **harder** to learn, French or Spanish?

The superlative degree is also used to compare two things in some idiomatic expressions.

EXAMPLE Put your best foot forward.

25e. Include the word *other* or *else* when comparing one member of a group with the rest of the group.

NONSTANDARD Anita has hit more home runs this season than any member of the team. [Anita is a member of the team. Logically, Anita could not have hit more home runs than herself.]
STANDARD Anita has hit more home runs this season than any **other** member of the team.
NONSTANDARD I think that Jean-Pierre Rampal plays the flute better than anyone. [The pronoun *anyone* includes Rampal. Logically, Jean-Pierre Rampal cannot play better than himself.]
STANDARD I think Jean-Pierre Rampal plays the flute better than anyone **else.**

USAGE

A DIFFERENT APPROACH

Brainstorming in small groups, students might practice using positive, comparative, and superlative forms of modifiers to create three-line slogans such as "Listening to music is enjoyable. Practicing music is more enjoyable. Performing music is most enjoyable." Students could make posters and illustrate the slogans.

INTEGRATING THE LANGUAGE ARTS

Literature Link. Initiate a brief discussion of the importance of word choice to poets. Explain that poetry's condensed form and poets' use of words to create images make word choice particularly important in poetry. Have students read "Success is counted sweetest" by Emily Dickinson, and ask them why they think the poet used the superlative form *sweetest* in the first line (which is used as the title). [Students might say that the superlative form indicates the level to which people who fail elevate the meaning of success. It sets the stage for the powerful analogy she uses in the second and third stanzas: the heightened impact of the victory song on the ears of the defeated, dying soldier.]

USAGE

INTEGRATING THE LANGUAGE ARTS

Technology Link. Some word-processing programs include electronic dictionaries that students might use to check comparative and superlative forms.

Spell-check programs might also help students choose correct forms. For example, if they are unsure whether *beautifuler* or *more beautiful* is the correct comparative form, they could see whether *beautifuler* is listed in their spell-check program. Because it is not listed, *beautifuler* is incorrect; *more beautiful* is correct.

Usage and Speaking. Provide, or have students bring to class, pictures of sports events such as swim team competitions, track meets, or basketball games. Have students work in pairs; one student can hold up a picture while the other student plays the role of a sports announcer and provides a brief commentary on some imaginary sports event. Then have students reverse roles. The object is to use correctly as many comparative and superlative forms of modifiers as possible. You may wish to make this a game in which the pair of students using correctly the most comparative and superlative forms of modifiers wins a prize.

USAGE

USAGE

25f. Avoid double comparisons.

A ***double comparison*** is the use of two comparative forms (usually *–er* and *more*) or two superlative forms (usually *–est* and *most*) to modify the same word.

NONSTANDARD	This week's program is more funnier than last week's.
STANDARD	This week's program is **funnier** than last week's.
NONSTANDARD	In our school, the most farthest you can go in math is Calculus II.
STANDARD	In our school, the **farthest** you can go in math is Calculus II.

EXERCISE 4 Using the Comparative and Superlative Forms of Modifiers

Revise the following sentences by correcting the errors in the use of the comparative and superlative forms of modifiers.

EXAMPLE **1.** It seems I spend more time doing my biology homework than anyone in my class.
1. *It seems I spend more time doing my biology homework than anyone else in my class.*

1. Which is the ~~most~~ famous Russian ballet company, the Kirov or the Bolshoi? **1. more**
2. When Barbara Rose Collins served as a state representative in Michigan, my aunt thought that she fought harder than anyone for key legislation to help minorities. **2. else** **3. othe**
3. According to the National Weather Service, Hurricane Andrew did more damage than any hurricane this century.
4. Although both cars appear to be well constructed, I think that the ~~most~~ desirable one is the one that gets better gas mileage. **4. more** **5. farther**
5. Which of these two hotels is ~~farthest~~ from the airport?
6. I know this shade of blue is a closer match than that one, but we still haven't found the ~~better~~ match. **6. best**
7. In the dance marathon, Anton and Inez managed to stay awake and keep moving longer than any couple on the dance floor. **7. other** **8. else**
8. Of all the women singers of the 1960s and 1970s, Joan Baez participated in more peace rallies than anyone.

WRITING APPLICATION

OBJECTIVE

- To use comparisons in persuasive writing

9. Lucia has the most ~~uncommonest~~ hobby I've ever heard of—collecting insects. 9. uncommon 10. other
10. The newscaster said that the pollen count this morning was higher than any count taken in the past ten years.

WRITING APPLICATION

Using Comparisons in Persuasive Writing

USAGE

From time to time, you've probably tried to persuade other people to see or do things differently. You likely gave specific reasons why they should change their minds. You may even have presented these reasons as comparisons.

EXAMPLE *Return of the Star Warriors* is **more believable** and has **better** special effects than *Space Creeps.*

WRITING ACTIVITY

How can producers of television shows make their programs more appealing to teenagers? You've decided to write to one of the major networks expressing your opinion on the subject. Write a letter pointing out how producers can better address the interests and concerns of teenage viewers. To support your opinion, draw a comparison between two current television shows—one that you and your friends like and one that you don't like. Explain why one show is more appealing to you than the other. In your letter, use at least five comparative forms of modifiers.

Prewriting You may already have a clear idea of the kinds of shows you like to see. If not, you can get started by listing several current TV programs aimed at teenage audiences. Ask a few friends to tell you what they like or dislike about each show. Jot down your friends' responses along with your own opinions. Then narrow down the list to the most-liked and the least-liked shows. Use your notes to help you identify the kinds of characters, situations, and themes that do and do not appeal to teenage viewers.

WRITING APPLICATION

This assignment gives students the opportunity to practice writing a business letter to express an opinion. Discuss with students the basic elements of writing persuasively: an opinion or opinions (opinions about what teenagers do and do not like in selected, current television programs), a purpose (to convince a producer to make changes in programming), reasons and evidence (examples of what does and does not succeed), and credibility (reasons why producers should listen to students).

USAGE

CRITICAL THINKING

Synthesis

Explain to students that a clear method of organization will help to communicate their ideas. Refer students to the information on pp. 217–218 that covers the point-by-point method and the block method for organizing comparisons. Have students decide which of the two methods would work better in their letters.

REVIEW B

OBJECTIVE

- To revise a paragraph by identifying and correcting errors in the use of modifiers

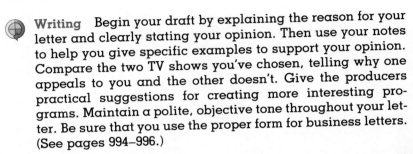

USAGE

TIMESAVER To lessen your grading time, have students help you to develop an evaluation scale. You could suggest the following example and see if students agree with the assigned point values.

EVALUATION SCALE

Category	Possible Points	Your Score
Effective introduction	10	
Appropriate letter form	15	
Concise style	15	
Polite, objective tone	15	
Adequate support for opinion	20	
Use of comparative forms	15	
Effective conclusion	10	
Total	100	

USAGE

Writing Begin your draft by explaining the reason for your letter and clearly stating your opinion. Then use your notes to help you give specific examples to support your opinion. Compare the two TV shows you've chosen, telling why one appeals to you and the other doesn't. Give the producers practical suggestions for creating more interesting programs. Maintain a polite, objective tone throughout your letter. Be sure that you use the proper form for business letters. (See pages 994–996.)

Evaluating and Revising Ask an adult friend or relative to help you evaluate your letter. Is your opinion statement clear? Are your reasons specific and convincing? Remember you are writing to a busy executive. Revise your letter to make it as concise and direct as you can. Be sure that you've used at least five comparative forms of modifiers.

Proofreading and Publishing Make sure you've used the appropriate form for business letters. Proofread your letter for any errors in grammar, spelling, or punctuation. Pay special attention to modifiers, and revise any double comparisons. To publish your letter, you can mail it to the television network. First, find out the address of the network and, if possible, the name of the person to whom you should write. Then, retype or recopy the letter neatly. You and your classmates may want to collect your letters and send them all together, along with a cover note.

REVIEW B **Using Modifiers Correctly**

Proofread the following paragraph, correcting any errors in the use of modifiers. If a sentence is correct, write *C.*

EXAMPLE [1] Of the two forts, this one is the oldest.
1. *older*

[1] St. Augustine, Florida, is the home of *Castillo de San Marcos*, the ~~most~~ oldest standing fort in the United States. [2] Earlier wood forts had been extremely difficult to defend, but *Castillo*

2. C

de San Marcos, as you can see, was built of stone. [3] Before the construction of this fort, Spain had no strong military base that could withstand a ~~real~~ fierce enemy assault. [4] In fact, previous battles with the British had proved that of the two countries, Spain had the ~~least~~ defensible forts. [5] Begun in 1672, the building of *Castillo de San Marcos* went ~~slow~~, taking several decades to complete. [6] Replacing the existing nine wood forts in St. Augustine, the new stone fort fared ~~good~~ against attacks. [7] Today, no one is sure which fort was ~~easiest~~ to protect, Spain's *Castillo de San Marcos* or the British fort in Charleston, South Carolina. [8] However, *Castillo de San Marcos,* with its 16-foot-thick walls and 40-foot-wide moat, proved to be one of the ~~most~~ strongest forts in the South and was never taken by force. [9] When Florida finally did come under British control, the Spanish felt especially ~~badly~~ about leaving their impressive fort in the hands of their old enemies. [10] *Castillo de San Marcos* is now a National Monument and stands today as a memorial to all those who fought so ~~courageous~~ to guard St. Augustine long ago.

3. really
4. less
5. slowly
6. well
7. easier
9. bad
10. courageously

USAGE

USAGE

VISUAL CONNECTIONS

Ideas for Writing. Have each student write an expressive paragraph describing an incident in the huge fort. Students can imagine they are standing guard in the night as they see a British fleet sailing up the river to attack the fort. Or they can imagine they are working on the construction of the fort. Students should pay special attention to using correct modifiers as they proofread.

SEGMENT 5 *(pp. 778–779)*

REVIEW: POSTTEST

OBJECTIVE

- To revise sentences and a paragraph by correcting errors in the use of modifiers

Review: Posttest

A. Using Modifiers Correctly

Most of the following sentences contain errors in the use of modifiers. If the sentence is incorrect, revise it to eliminate the error. If it is correct, write *C*.

EXAMPLE **1.** Steve, who is the most brightest student in the physics class, is also a whiz in chemistry.
1. *Steve, who is the brightest student in the physics class, is also a whiz in chemistry.*

USAGE

1. After listening to "The Battle of the Bands," we thought that the jazz band performed even ~~more~~ better than the rock group.
2. When the treasurer presented the annual report, most of the statistics showed that the company had done ~~badder~~ this year than last. **2.** worse
3. Megan shoots foul shots so ~~good~~ that she has made the varsity team. **3.** well
4. The more ~~even~~ you distribute the work load among the group members, the more satisfied everyone will be. **4.** evenly
5. In 1949, Jackie Robinson was voted the Most Valuable Player in the National League. **5.** C
6. Last night the weather forecaster announced that this has been the ~~most rainy~~ spring season the area has had in the past decade. **6.** rainiest
7. This is the ~~most tasty~~ piece of sourdough bread I have ever eaten. **7.** tastiest
8. After receiving a rare coin for my birthday, I began to take coin collecting more seriously. **8.** C
9. Before taking a computer course, I couldn't program at all, but now I program very ~~good~~. **9.** well
10. When she danced at the Paris Opera, American ballet star Maria Tallchief was received ~~enthusiastic~~ by French audiences. **10.** enthusiastically

B. Proofreading for the Correct Use of Modifiers

Proofread the following paragraph, correcting any errors in the use of modifiers.

USAGE

EXAMPLE **[1] When in doubt, dress conservative rather than stunningly for a job interview.**

1. *conservatively*

[11] No matter whether three or three hundred candidates apply for a job, a smart employer tries to find the ~~more~~ qualified applicant. **[12]** If you heed the following simple guidelines, you will likely create a more favorable impression than ~~any~~ candidate in your job-hunting market. **[13]** First, a well-prepared data sheet, or résumé, always helps to make a ~~better~~ impression before the interview. **[14]** Second, a ~~proper~~ dressed candidate appears neat and well groomed during the interview. **[15]** Your clothes do not have to be ~~more fancier~~ or more expensive than any other candidate's, but they should look just as professional. **[16]** Third, before your interview, you should try to imagine the most ~~common~~ asked questions for your field. **[17]** There is no ~~worst~~ way to make a lasting impression than to provide poorly thought-out answers to an interviewer's questions. **[18]** Finally, learning all you can about a company is one of the ~~effectivest~~ ways to impress a future employer. **[19]** When two well-qualified candidates apply for the same position, often the one with the ~~greatest~~ knowledge of the company is hired. **[20]** If you follow these guidelines and still don't get the job, try not to feel too ~~badly~~; instead, set your sights on succeeding at your next job interview.

USAGE

ANSWERS

Review: Posttest Part B

11. most
12. any other
13. good
14. properly
15. fancier *or* more fancy
16. commonly
17. worse
18. most effective
19. greater
20. bad

USAGE

Teacher's ResourceBank™

RESOURCES

FOR THE WHOLE CHAPTER

CHAPTER OVERVIEW

The first part of this chapter covers the correct placement of modifying phrases and clauses in sentences. The second part covers the recognition and correction of dangling modifiers.

The material in this chapter could be introduced with any of the composition chapters, especially in segments that deal with evaluation and revision. The information in the chapter could also be used as a resource by students who use modifiers incorrectly in their compositions.

USAGE

ANSWERS

Diagnostic Test: Part A

Revisions may vary. Here are some possibilities:

1. Computer owners use animation programs to show cartoon characters racing across their screen.
2. Grant and Lee rode on horses to Appomattox Court House to make an agreement that ended the Civil War.
3. C
4. In his laboratory, Lue Gim Gong developed a type of orange that could resist frost.

SEGMENT 1 *(pp. 780–782)*

DIAGNOSTIC TEST

OBJECTIVE

- To revise sentences by correcting faulty modifiers

USAGE

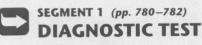

26 PLACEMENT OF MODIFIERS

Misplaced and Dangling Modifiers

Diagnostic Test

A. Revising Sentences by Correcting Faulty Modifiers

Most of the following sentences contain errors in the use of modifiers. Revise each faulty sentence so that its meaning is clear. If a sentence is correct, write *C.*

EXAMPLE **1. Without access to fresh bamboo, the giant panda's proper diet cannot be maintained.**
1. ***Without access to fresh bamboo, the giant panda cannot maintain its proper diet.***

1. Racing across their screens, computer owners use animation programs to show cartoon characters.
2. Grant and Lee rode to Appomattox Court House to make an agreement on horses that ended the Civil War.
3. To honor inventor Jan Ernst Matzeliger, the U.S. Postal Service issued a new stamp in the Black Heritage Series.
4. Lue Gim Gong developed a type of orange that could resist frost in his laboratory.

5. Attacking at just the right time, Pensacola was captured by Louisiana Governor Bernardo de Gálvez during the Revolutionary War.
6. The detective writer said that he would introduce a new villain on page one.
7. Scientists have planned carefully to ensure that the space station *Freedom* will soon take flight in all departments of Huntsville's Marshall Space Flight Center.
8. When proofreading on a computer, screen format should be checked as well as spelling.
9. The mayoral candidate stated in a full-page newspaper advertisement an apology would be forthcoming.
10. Did you know that Navajo advisers helped to develop a system of codes that the U.S. Army used while fighting World War II in New Mexico?

USAGE

B. Revising Sentences by Correcting Faulty Modifiers

Most of the following sentences contain errors in the use of modifiers. Revise each faulty sentence so that its meaning is clear. If a sentence is correct, write *C*. Revisions will vary.

EXAMPLE
1. Carrie Green dreamed of touring Virginia's Historic Triangle while reading travel brochures.
1. *While reading travel brochures, Carrie Green dreamed of touring Virginia's Historic Triangle.*

11. On the spur of the moment,

11. The Greens and the Alvarezes decided to visit the historic town of Williamsburg, Virginia, which has been painstakingly restored ~~on the spur of the moment.~~
12. ~~Decorated in colonial style,~~ the two families registered at a quaint inn 12. decorated in colonial style.
13. After resting for an hour or so, the Governor's Palace, the College of William and Mary, the Capitol, and many other sites ~~were visited.~~ 13. they visited
14. Joel Green quickly snapped a great shot of a candlemaker ~~focusing his camera.~~ 14. Focusing his camera,
15. A tour guide at DeWitt Wallace Decorative Arts Gallery explained how eighteenth-century costumes were sewn. 15. C
16. The tour guide said ~~when the families asked~~ she would be happy to go into greater detail. 16. When the families asked,

5. Attacking at just the right time, Louisiana Governor Bernardo de Gálvez captured Pensacola during the Revolutionary War.
6. The detective writer said on page one that he would introduce a new villain.
7. In all departments of Huntsville's Marshall Space Flight Center, scientists have planned carefully to ensure that the space station *Freedom* will soon take flight.
8. When proofreading on a computer, you should check screen format as well as spelling.
9. In a full-page newspaper advertisement, the mayoral candidate stated an apology would be forthcoming.
10. Did you know that Navajo advisers in New Mexico helped to develop a system of codes that the U. S. Army used while fighting World War II?

USAGE

USING THE DIAGNOSTIC TEST

If you find that some students are having difficulty using modifiers correctly in their writing, you can use the **Diagnostic Test** to define specific strengths and weaknesses. An assessment of students' responses should help you group students for special assignments to meet their individual needs.

MISPLACED MODIFIERS Rule 26a

OBJECTIVES

- To revise sentences by correcting misplaced modifiers
- To write picture captions with modifying phrases and clauses

Teacher's ResourceBank™

RESOURCES

MISPLACED MODIFIERS

- Misplaced Modifiers 299

QUICK REMINDER

Write the following sentences on the chalkboard and have students revise them. Remind students to place modifying phrases and clauses as close as possible to the word or words being modified.

1. Shawna read that the chili contest would be held on Saturday in the local paper.
   [Shawna read in the local paper that the chili contest would be held on Saturday.]
2. The café delivered fresh, hot pizza to Carlos in a cardboard box.
   [The café delivered fresh, hot pizza in a cardboard box to Carlos.]

MEETING INDIVIDUAL NEEDS

LEARNING STYLES

Visual Learners. Students might need some visual reinforcement for placing phrases and clauses close to the words they modify. Choose some example sentences from the textbook to write on the chalkboard. Use colored chalk to circle the modifying phrase or clause in each sentence; then draw an arrow to the word it modifies. Have students follow the same procedure when revising sentences in the exercises.

USAGE

17. Dressed in colonial garb, a woman at the Raleigh Tavern asked the families to imagine how eighteenth-century residents may have spread news. **17.** C
18. Having seen enough for the day, a quiet dinner at the inn ~~was enjoyed by all of them.~~ **18.** they all enjoyed
19. Kevin dipped his spoon into a bowl of peanut butter soup ~~filled with great apprehension.~~ **19.** Filled with great apprehension,
20. With fond memories and many photographs, the trip to Williamsburg ~~will not soon be forgotten.~~ **20.** the families will not soon forget

USAGE

Misplaced Modifiers

A modifying phrase or clause that sounds awkward because it modifies the wrong word or group of words is called a ***misplaced modifier.***

26a. Avoid using a misplaced modifier.

To correct a misplaced modifier, place the phrase or clause as close as possible to the word or words you intend it to modify.

MISPLACED Uncle Bill saw a dog gnawing a bone on his way to work. [Was the dog on his way to work?]
CLEAR **On his way to work,** Uncle Bill saw a dog gnawing a bone.

MISPLACED They were delighted to see a field of daffodils climbing up the hill.
CLEAR **Climbing up the hill,** they were delighted to see a field of daffodils.

MISPLACED The anxious hunter watched the raging lion come charging at him while readying a bow and arrow.
CLEAR **While readying a bow and arrow,** the anxious hunter watched the raging lion come charging at him.

Two-Way Modifiers

Avoid placing a phrase or clause so that it seems to modify either of two words. Such a misplaced modifier is often called a ***two-way,*** or ***squinting, modifier.***

26a

MISPLACED The prime minister said in the press interview her opponent spoke honestly. [Did the prime minister speak in the press interview, or did her opponent?]

CLEAR **In the press interview,** the prime minister said her opponent spoke honestly.

CLEAR The prime minister said her opponent spoke honestly **in the press interview.**

MISPLACED The mayor said when the city council met he would discuss the proposed budget.

CLEAR **When the city council met,** the mayor said he would discuss the proposed budget.

CLEAR The mayor said he would discuss the proposed budget **when the city council met.**

MISPLACED The manager told the two rookies after the game to report to the dugout.

CLEAR **After the game,** the manager told the two rookies to report to the dugout.

CLEAR The manager told the two rookies to report to the dugout **after the game.**

USAGE

EXERCISE 1 **Revising Sentences by Correcting Misplaced Modifiers**

The following sentences contain misplaced modifiers. Revise each sentence so that its meaning is clear and correct.

Answers may vary.

EXAMPLE **1.** We listened eagerly to the stories told by Scheherazade in the *Arabian Nights,* munching peanuts and crackers.

1. *Munching peanuts and crackers, we listened eagerly to the stories told by Scheherazade in* The Arabian Nights.

1. Louise projected^ the photographs ~~on a large screen~~ that she had taken at the zoo. **1.** on a large screen
2. Mr. Martínez promised ~~in the morning~~ he would tell a Native American trickster tale^. **2.** in the morning.
3. ^I pointed to the fish tank and showed my friends my new puffer, ~~swelling with pride.~~ **3.** Swelling with pride,
4. ^Ralph Ellison said ~~during an interview~~ Richard Wright gave him inspiration to become a writer. **4.** During an interview,
5. I talked^ about the problem I had in writing my first draft^, ~~with Megan,~~ and she said she had the same problem. **5.** with Megan

MEETING INDIVIDUAL NEEDS

STUDENTS WITH SPECIAL NEEDS

Because copying is generally labor-intensive for students with learning disabilities, you could duplicate the exercises in this segment. Then have students circle modifiers and draw arrows as suggested for visual learners.

CRITICAL THINKING
Analysis and Synthesis

To correct misplaced modifying phrases or clauses, students must first carefully analyze each sentence. You may want to suggest the following procedure for sentence analysis:

1. Find the simple subject and the simple predicate of the main clause.
2. Identify any objects or subject complements.
3. Bracket all modifying phrases and clauses and determine what word or words they modify in the sentence.

Students then can synthesize the information and revise the sentences by placing the modifying phrases or clauses near the words they modify.

USAGE

USAGE

PICTURE THIS

As part of prewriting, you may want to have students study captions in sources such as textbooks, magazines, and newspapers.

You may also want to organize students into small groups to discuss the content of the photographs and to brainstorm ideas for captions.

6. Filled with a sense of accomplishment,

6. My aunt had finally mastered the art of making stuffed cabbage, ~~filled with a sense of accomplishment.~~

7. I like to walk along the beach at low tide, ~~digging~~ for clams ~~without a care in the world.~~

8. Mrs. Jennings sang some folk songs about working on the railroad ~~in the Lincoln School auditorium.~~

9. There is a bracelet ~~in the museum~~ that is four thousand years old. **8.** In the Lincoln School auditorium, **9.** In the museum

10. I found a good book about Virginia Woolf written by her husband ~~at a garage sale.~~ **10.** At a garage sale

7. Without a care in the world, /and dig

USAGE

PICTURE THIS

You've heard the saying many times: A picture is worth a thousand words. As the photo editor for a current-events magazine, you take this proverb to heart. You know that incredible photographs like the ones below help make news stories come alive.

However, a photograph doesn't mean much if your readers don't know its *context*. Write a concise, two- or three-line caption for each photograph above. Tell where and when the

SEGMENT 3 *(pp. 785–787)*

DANGLING MODIFIERS Rule 26b

OBJECTIVE

- To revise sentences by correcting dangling modifiers

photograph was taken, and try to sum up its significance. In your captions, use a total of five modifying phrases and clauses. Be sure that each modifier is placed correctly.

Subject: photographs of current events
Audience: magazine readers
Purpose: to inform

USAGE

Dangling Modifiers

A modifying phrase or clause that does not sensibly modify any word or words in a sentence is called a ***dangling modifier.***

26b. Avoid using a dangling modifier.

You may correct a dangling modifier by adding a word or words that the phrase or clause can sensibly refer to or by adding a word or words to the phrase or clause.

DANGLING Having selected a college, a trip to the campus was planned. [Who selected a college?]
CLEAR **Having selected a college,** my friend and I planned a trip to the campus.
CLEAR **After we selected a college,** my friend and I planned a trip to the campus.

DANGLING After winning the Pulitzer Prize for poetry, the novel *Maud Martha* was written.
CLEAR **After winning the Pulitzer Prize for poetry,** Gwendolyn Brooks wrote the novel *Maud Martha.*
CLEAR **After Gwendolyn Brooks won the Pulitzer Prize for poetry,** she wrote the novel *Maud Martha.*

DANGLING While correcting papers, the message came from the principal.
CLEAR **While correcting papers,** the teacher received the message from the principal.
CLEAR **While the teacher was correcting papers,** the message came from the principal.

Teacher's ResourceBank™
RESOURCES

DANGLING MODIFIERS
- Dangling Modifiers 300

USAGE

QUICK REMINDER

Write the following sentences on the chalkboard and have students revise them:

1. While answering the phone, the doorbell rang.
   [While I was answering the phone, the doorbell rang.]
2. To learn how to use a computer, familiarity with typing is helpful.
   [When you learn how to use a computer, you will find that familiarity with typing is helpful.]

MEETING **INDIVIDUAL** NEEDS

LESS-ADVANCED STUDENTS

Misplaced and dangling modifiers often occur in the early drafts of writing assignments when students write hurriedly and add information to the ends of sentences as afterthoughts.

Suggest that students work in pairs when revising to edit each other's papers and to look specifically for logical order and for closeness of each modifier to the word modified.

USAGE

NOTE: A few dangling modifiers have become standard in idiomatic expressions.

EXAMPLES **Generally speaking,** Americans now have a longer life expectancy than ever before.
To be honest, the party was rather boring.

REFERENCE NOTE: For more information about idiomatic expressions, see pages 486–487. For information about using a comma after introductory words, phrases, and clauses, see pages 853–854.

EXERCISE 2 **Revising Sentences by Correcting Dangling Modifiers**

The following sentences contain dangling modifiers. Revise each sentence so that its meaning is clear and correct. **Revisions will vary.**

EXAMPLE **1.** Waiting at the bus stop, my older brother drove by in his new car.
1. *While I was waiting at the bus stop, my older brother drove by in his new car.*

1. Frightened by our presence, the ~~rabbit's ears~~ perked up and its nose ~~twitched.~~ **1. rabbit/its ears/twitched**
2. To interpret this poem, a knowledge of mythology ~~is helpful.~~ **2. you need**
3. All bundled up in a blanket, the ~~baby's~~ first outing ~~was a brief one.~~ **3. baby had a brief**
4. When performing onstage, the microphone ~~should not be placed~~ too near the speaker cones. **4. do not place**
5. To be a good opera singer, clear enunciation ~~is extremely important.~~ **5. you need**
6. To help colonial soldiers during the Revolutionary War, Haym ~~Solomon's efforts~~ raised money to buy food and clothing. **6. Solomon**
7. Before moving to Sacramento, Pittsburgh ~~had been their home~~ for ten years. **7. they had lived in**
8. While ~~reaching~~ into his pocket for change, ~~the~~ car rolled into the side of the tollbooth. **8. the driver reached/his**
9. ~~To work efficiently without sticking,~~ be sure to use the proper solvent and machine oil.
10. When ~~discussing~~ colonial American writers, the contributions of the African American poet Phillis Wheatley ~~should not be forgotten.~~ **10. you discuss/do not forget**

9. to keep the mechanism working efficiently without sticking.

USAGE

REVIEW

OBJECTIVE

- To revise sentences by correcting faulty modifiers

REVIEW

Revising Sentences by Correcting Faulty Modifiers

Most of the following sentences contain errors in the use of modifiers. Revise each faulty sentence so that its meaning is clear and correct. If a sentence is correct, write *C*.

EXAMPLE **1. I described my trip to Hawaii to my friends who had never been there when I got back.**
1. ***When I got back, I described my trip to Hawaii to my friends, who had never been there.***

1. Visitors soon learn how important one man can be on vacation in Hawaii.
2. Born in the mid-1700s, the Hawaiian people were united under one government by Kamehameha I.
3. After capturing Maui, Molokai, and Lanai, Oahu was soon another of Kamehameha's conquests.
4. Kamehameha assured the Hawaiian people when he became the ruler of the entire island they would see peace.
5. By 1810, Kamehameha was certain his conquest would be successful.
6. Having won Kauai and Niihau, Kamehameha's dream of a united country was realized.
7. A hero to his people, Kamehameha's government ruled Hawaii for many years.
8. A statue to honor the great ruler was crafted by Thomas Gould.
9. While being transported by sea, the Hawaiian people lost their beloved statue.
10. Though still at the bottom of the ocean, the sculptor made the duplicate shown here.

USAGE

ANSWERS

Review

Revisions will vary. Here are some possibilities:

1. On vacation in Hawaii, visitors soon learn how important one man can be.
2. The Hawaiian people were united under one government by Kamehameha I, born in the mid-1700s.
3. After his conquest of Maui, Molokai, and Lanai, Kamehameha soon captured Oahu.
4. Kamehameha assured the Hawaiian people they would see peace when he became ruler of the entire island.
5. C
6. When he won Kauai and Niihau, Kamehameha's dream of a united country was realized.
7. Kamehameha was a hero to his people, and his government ruled Hawaii for many years.
8. C
9. The Hawaiian people lost their beloved statue while transporting it by sea.
10. Although the original is still at the bottom of the ocean, the sculptor made the duplicate shown here.

USAGE

SEGMENT 4 *(pp. 788–789)*

REVIEW: POSTTEST

OBJECTIVE

- To revise sentences by correcting faulty modifiers

USAGE

ANSWERS

Review: Posttest Part A

Revisions will vary. Here are some possibilities:

1. Having eaten the remains of the zebra, the lion licked its chops as we watched.
2. To honor his guests, a Northwest Native American host gave away almost all of his possessions at an elaborate party called a potlatch.
3. Sitting on the porch last night, the girls counted thirteen shooting stars.
4. To do well on examinations, you need to develop good study habits.
5. When touring the South, you should plan a visit to the new Civil Rights Memorial in Montgomery, Alabama.
6. The leader of the safari promised we would see a herd of eland in the morning.
7. While I was running for the bus, my wallet must have dropped out of my pocket.
8. The crowd rose to their feet and cheered as she caught the pop fly with her usual skill.
9. She traveled to Paris on the train especially to see the *Venus de Milo.*
10. We found the castle quite dilapidated after crumbling for a hundred years.

USAGE

Review: Posttest

A. Revising Sentences by Correcting Faulty Modifiers

The following sentences contain errors in the use of modifiers. Revise each sentence so that its meaning is clear and correct.

EXAMPLE **1. Attached to my application, you will find a transcript of my grades.**
1. *You will find a transcript of my grades attached to my application.*

1. Having eaten the remains of the zebra, we watched the lion lick its chops.
2. To honor his guests, almost all of the possessions of the Northwest Native American host were given away at an elaborate party called a potlatch.
3. The girls counted thirteen shooting stars sitting on the porch last night.
4. To do well on examinations, good study habits should be developed.
5. When touring the South, a visit to the new Civil Rights Memorial in Montgomery, Alabama, should be planned.
6. The leader of the photo safari promised in the morning we would see a herd of eland.
7. While running for the bus, my wallet must have dropped out of my pocket.
8. Catching the pop fly with her usual skill, the crowd rose to their feet and cheered.
9. She traveled to Paris especially to see the *Venus de Milo* on the train.
10. After crumbling for a hundred years, we found the castle quite dilapidated.

B. Using Modifiers Correctly

Most of the following sentences contain errors in the use of modifiers. Revise each faulty sentence so that its meaning is clear and correct. If a sentence is correct, write *C*.

EXAMPLE **1. Before they had computers, all newspaper layout work was done by hand.**

1. ***Before they had computers, newspaper editors did all layout work by hand.***

11. Computer whiz Kim Montgomery said in the computer resource center anyone can learn to master basic desktop publishing.

12. To prove her point, the editor of the school newspaper was asked to give desktop publishing a try.

13. Kim led Terri, a novice computer user, to an unoccupied terminal with an encouraging smile.

14. In a short tutorial session, Kim emphasized the need to practice adding, deleting, and moving paragraphs.

15. While looking over her shoulder, Terri hit various keys to call up menus on the computer screen.

16. Terri sometimes stared blankly at the computer screen, not knowing what to do next.

17. In need of more information, the tutor was asked many questions by the pupil.

18. "To prepare professional-quality illustrations, a graphics package is what you need," Kim said.

19. Kim said when the computer sounded an error warning she would be happy to offer assistance.

20. Kim was pleased to see Terri confidently keyboarding information as she went to help another student.

USAGE

ANSWERS

Review: Posttest Part B

Revisions will vary. Here are some possibilities:

11. Computer whiz Kim Montgomery said anyone can learn to master basic desktop publishing in the computer resource center.

12. To prove her point, Kim asked the editor of the school newspaper to give desktop publishing a try.

13. With an encouraging smile, Kim led Terri, a novice computer user, to an unoccupied terminal.

14. C

15. While Kim looked over Terri's shoulder, Terri hit various keys to call up menus on the computer screen.

16. Not knowing exactly what to do next, Terri sometimes stared blankly at the computer screen.

17. The pupil needed more information and asked the tutor many questions.

18. "To prepare professional-quality illustrations, you need a graphics package," Kim said.

19. When the computer sounded an error warning, Kim said she would be happy to offer assistance.

20. As she went to help another student, Kim was happy to see Terri confidently keyboarding information.

USAGE

SEGMENT 1 *(pp. 790–792)*

DIAGNOSTIC TEST

OBJECTIVE

- To identify correct usage by selecting words to complete sentences

Teacher's ResourceBank™

RESOURCES

FOR THE WHOLE CHAPTER

CHAPTER OVERVIEW

This chapter uses an alphabetical format to address common usage problems of speech and writing. It explains how a glossary is arranged and includes a brief discussion of standard and nonstandard and formal and informal language.

Some of the usage problems featured include distinguishing between similar-sounding words such as *accept/except* and distinguishing between words that refer to singular and plural nouns such as between/among. It includes words that are used incorrectly because of meaning, such as bring/take. It also addresses incorrect usage, such as *off of,* that can influence the impression someone makes. And it includes information on double negatives. The **Writing Application** focuses on using standard English in writing a local history.

After evaluating students' needs, select the information most useful for your class and focus on it. You might refer to this chapter when students are evaluating and revising compositions. It may also be used with **Chapter 12: "English: History and Development,"** which explores the origins and usage of English. In addition, this chapter can be useful to students who are reviewing for standardized tests.

USAGE

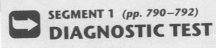

27 A GLOSSARY OF USAGE

Common Usage Problems

Diagnostic Test

A. Identifying Correct Usage

Choose the correct word or words in parentheses in each of the following sentences. [Note: A sentence may contain more than one choice.]

EXAMPLE 1. When my math teacher announced the rules for the year, she said she would not (*except, accept*) any papers written in ink.

1. *accept*

1. All of the members of Congress (*except*, *accept*), I believe, Representative Carpenter voted to retain the present tax structure for another year.
2. My grandparents have (*affected*, *effected*) all of us with their generosity, hope, and faith in the future.

3. I (*couldn't*, *could*) hardly believe my eyes when I saw a 90 on my geometry test; I must (*of*, *have*) remembered the formulas better than I thought I would.
4. (*This*, *This here*) plane was designed by the world-famous paper-airplane expert Dr. Yasuaki Ninomiya.
5. Does this poem make an (*allusion*, *illusion*) to the *Iliad*?
6. (*Being that*, *Because*) Jennifer had never learned to swim, she was afraid to go on the boat ride.
7. At the end of the nineteenth century, two of my great-grandparents (*emigrated*, *immigrated*) from Ireland to the United States.
8. When Trini Lopez recorded the hit folk song "If I Had a Hammer," he (*had no*, *didn't have no*) way of knowing that it would sell $4.5 million worth of records.
9. (*Can't none*, *Can't any*) of the people in town see that the mayor is appointing political cronies to patronage jobs?
10. The (*Gallaghers they*, *Gallaghers*) have worked for years to increase voter registration in (*this*, *this here*) town.

USAGE

B. Identifying Correct Usage

For each sentence in the following paragraph, choose the correct item from the pair given in parentheses.

EXAMPLE **Whenever I walk into Montsho Books, I can't help [1] (*feeling*, *but feel*) proud to be black.**
1. *feeling*

Do you want to know where this bookstore **[11]** (*is*, *is at*)? I should **[12]** (*of*, *have*) mentioned that it's in Orlando, Florida, just a short **[13]** (*way*, *ways*) from the Orlando Arena. Ms. Perkins, **[14]** (*which*, *who*) runs the store, told me **[15]** (*where*, *that*) *montsho* means "black" in Tswana, an African language. When Ms. Perkins was a schoolteacher, she noticed that there **[16]** (*were*, *weren't*) hardly any children's books that featured African Americans. At first, she thought that she would write children's books about the black experience, but then Ms. Perkins decided she **[17]** (*had ought*, *ought*) to open a store that sold books exclusively by and about blacks. **[18]** (*Beside*, *Besides*) poetry and fiction by African Americans, the shop offers all kinds of nonfiction selections including books on philosophy, history, health, humor, and cooking. Montsho Books is quite an unusual **[19]** (*kind of*, *kind of a*) bookstore; it has become a

USING THE DIAGNOSTIC TEST

The **Diagnostic Test** will help gauge students' ability to identify correct usage by having them select the correct words or phrases in sentences. You might use this test to determine if any of your students rely heavily on nonstandard English.

USAGE

SEGMENT 2 (pp. 792–795)

A, AN—AT

OBJECTIVE

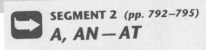

- To identify correct usage by selecting words to complete sentences

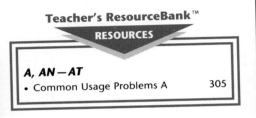

Teacher's ResourceBank™

RESOURCES

A, AN—AT

- Common Usage Problems A 305

USAGE

QUICK REMINDER

To compare the uses of *affect* and *effect,* write the following sentences on the chalkboard:

1. "... it is the right of the people ... to institute new government ... organizing its powers in such form, as to them shall seem most likely to effect their safety and happiness." (the Declaration of Independence)
2. Reading the document will affect me.

Have students suggest what the difference between the two words is and elicit that when *effect* is used as a verb form, it means "to bring about"; *affect* means "to influence." Suggest to students that in most everyday usage they can "stick to the *a* for action" and use *affect* as a verb.

true cultural center for Orlando's black community. The shop even sponsors the Montsho Sphinxes, a Brain Bowl Black History team of seventh- through twelfth-graders, which looks **[20]** (*like, as if*) it might win the state grand prize some year soon!

A ***glossary*** is an alphabetical list of special terms or expressions with definitions, explanations, and examples. On the following pages is a short glossary of English usage.

You'll notice that some examples in this glossary are labeled *standard, nonstandard, formal,* or *informal.* The label ***standard*** or ***formal*** identifies usage that is appropriate in serious writing and speaking (such as in compositions for school and speeches). The label ***informal*** indicates standard English that is generally used in conversation and in everyday writing such as personal letters. The label ***nonstandard*** identifies usage that does not follow the guidelines of standard English usage.

USAGE

REFERENCE NOTE: For more about standard English, see page 478.

a, an These ***indefinite articles*** refer to one of the members of a general group. *A* is used before words beginning with a consonant sound. *An* is used before words beginning with a vowel sound.

EXAMPLES "New African" is **a** poignant story about **a** young African American girl growing up in Philadelphia during the early 1960s.

The teacher read from the novel **an** excerpt that describes the grandfather as **an** honorable man. [Notice that the *h* in *honorable* is silent; therefore, the word begins with a vowel sound.]

accept, except *Accept* is a verb meaning "to receive." *Except* may be either a verb or a preposition. As a verb, *except* means "to leave out." As a preposition, *except* means "excluding."

EXAMPLES I will **accept** another yearbook assignment.
Should the military services **except** women from combat duty? [verb]
She typed everything **except** the bibliography. [preposition]

affect, effect *Affect* is a verb meaning "to influence." *Effect* may be used as a verb or a noun. As a verb, *effect* means "to bring about [a desired result]," or "to accomplish." As a noun, *effect* means "the result [of an action]."

EXAMPLES Decisions of the United States Supreme Court **affect** the lives of many people.
Some of the decisions **effect** great social change. [verb]
In history class, did you learn what far-reaching **effects** the *Brown v. Board of Education of Topeka, Kansas* decision had? [noun]

all the farther, all the faster Avoid these expressions by using *as far as* and *as fast as,* respectively.

NONSTANDARD The first act was all the farther we had read in *A Raisin in the Sun.*
STANDARD The first act was **as far as** we had read in *A Raisin in the Sun.*

allusion, illusion An *allusion* is an indirect reference to something. An *illusion* is a mistaken idea or a misleading appearance.

EXAMPLES Flannery O'Connor makes numerous biblical **allusions** in her stories.
Illusions of success haunted Willy Loman.
Makeup can be used to create an **illusion.**

alumni, alumnae *Alumni* (pronounced ə lum′ nī) is the plural of *alumnus* (a male graduate). *Alumnae* (pronounced ə lum′ nē) is the plural of *alumna* (a female graduate). Considered as a single group, the graduates of a coeducational school are referred to as *alumni.*

EXAMPLES Each year the **alumni** have provided two athletic scholarships.
Did the administration ask the **alumnae** how they felt about admitting men to the school?
Men and women from the first graduating class attended the **alumni** reunion.

NOTE: In informal usage the graduates from a women's college may be called *alumni.* In formal situations, however, the plural *alumnae* should be used.

among See **between, among.**

USAGE

MEETING INDIVIDUAL NEEDS

LEP/ESL

Spanish. Because *a* and *an* are often slurred over in spoken English, ESL students may benefit from hearing the pronunciation of both words so that they can recognize the words in speech. Tell students that *a* is pronounced as *uh* (or ə, the schwa sound). *An* is pronounced as *un* (or *ən*), but the word is often pronounced so quickly that the vowel sound is not apparent and the word sounds like *'n.* Pronounce the words slowly and at normal speed and use them in sentences.

COMMON ERROR

Problem. Students sometimes fail to use the articles *a* and *an* correctly in their writing.

Solution. Remind students that they must listen for a vowel sound, not just look for a vowel letter. Suggest that they read aloud words that begin with *h, u,* and *eu* before they choose the correct article. (*Hour/horse, umbrella/university,* and *European* are good examples.)

USAGE

MEETING INDIVIDUAL NEEDS

AT-RISK STUDENTS

Students who need language practice often become bored when writing sentences. Many times they need training in oral language because that is where their underlying usage problems begin. Ask some good speakers from the class to tape several examples of glossary entries used in sentences. Listening to passages that use words correctly can be a good way to improve speech and therefore to improve writing.

LEARNING STYLES

Visual Learners. Several of the words in this segment are nouns that can be visually represented, such as *allusion/illusion* and *alumni/alumnae*. Have visual learners illustrate the concepts on index cards that can be alphabetized and used as references. (There are several other noun entries in other segments of the glossary, so have students glance ahead.)

USAGE

USAGE

amount, number Use *amount* to refer to a singular word. Use *number* to refer to a plural word.

EXAMPLES A large **amount** of work is done in the library. [*Amount* refers to the singular word *work*.]
A large **number** of books have been checked out of our library. [*Number* refers to the plural word *books*.]

and etc. *Etc.* is an abbreviation of the Latin words *et cetera,* meaning "and others" or "and so forth." Since *and* is included in the definition of *etc.*, using *and* with *etc.* is unnecessary.

EXAMPLE We are studying twentieth-century American novelists: Ernest Hemingway, Margaret Walker, Jean Toomer, Pearl Buck, **etc.** [not *and etc.*]

anyways, anywheres Omit the final *s* in these words and in similar words such as *everywheres* and *nowheres*.

EXAMPLES I couldn't take both band and art **anyway** [not *anyways*].
Are your grandparents going camping **anywhere** [not *anywheres*] this summer?

as See **like, as.**

as if See **like, as if.**

at Avoid using *at* after a construction beginning with *where*.

NONSTANDARD Where is the Crow Canyon Archaeological Center located at?
STANDARD Where is the Crow Canyon Archaeological Center located?

EXERCISE 1 **Identifying Correct Usage**

Choose the correct word or words in parentheses in each sentence in the following paragraph.

EXAMPLE [1] My mother and Ms. Wang, both (*alumnae, alumni*) of Pratt Institute, went there to see an exhibition of paintings.
1. *alumnae*

[1] In 1988, the artist Chuck Close suffered spinal-artery collapse, and even though he never fully recovered, he kept painting (*anyway, anyways*). [2] Partially paralyzed, he learned to

work from a wheelchair, with (*a, an*) handy arrangement of straps to hold his brush in place. [3] As he had done before his illness, Close still painted large frontal portraits of friends, fellow artists, (*and etc., etc.*) [4] The picture on the left is an example of how Close often painted before 1988, dividing a photo of a person into a large (*amount, number*) of tiny squares. [5] He would first rule the canvas or paper into a grid, and then he would copy the photo's colors, bit by bit, into the small squares to create the type of (*allusion, illusion*) you see here. [6] A single painting might contain (*anywhere, anywheres*) from a few hundred to several thousand squares. [7] The overall effect is much like a certain kind of computer graphic, (*accept, except*) that the painting is not quite as mechanical. [8] The photograph on the right shows Close in 1991 working on a self-portrait that has a similar (*affect, effect*), but his style is bolder and more colorful. [9] At first glance, you may be surprised by his newer paintings and wonder where that computerlike quality (*is, is at*)! [10] But you soon realize that Close had never gone (*all the farther, as far as*) he could with his grid technique and that his recent paintings are simply a logical extension of his earlier style.

USAGE

Chuck Close, "Alex" 1987. Oil on Canvas, 100 × 84" John Back/Photograph courtesy of The Pace Gallery.

Chuck Close, *Self-Portrait*, 1991. Oil on canvas, 100 × 84" (work in progress), Bill Jacobson Studio/Photograph courtesy of The Pace Gallery.

USAGE

VISUAL CONNECTIONS
Alex

About the Artwork. Chuck Close's portrait of Alex is an example of an art form that creates the illusion of a whole by skillful analysis and reproduction of individual parts. Students might enjoy analyzing the work of other artists, such as Picasso and other artists of the Cubism movement, who use analysis of parts to create a whole.

SEGMENT 3 *(pp. 796–802)*

BAD, BADLY—GOOD, WELL

OBJECTIVES

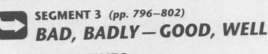

- To write a descriptive advertisement containing the correct usage of five specific words and expressions
- To identify correct usage by selecting words to complete sentences
- To revise sentences to correct errors in usage

Teacher's ResourceBank™

RESOURCES

BAD, BADLY—GOOD, WELL

- Common Usage Problems B 306

QUICK REMINDER

Write *between* and *among* on the chalkboard along with the sentences below. Have students decide upon one of the two words for each sentence.

1. I can't decide ____ the two books. [between]
2. Can you see any similarities ____ the mysteries of Agatha Christie, Dorothy Sayers, and Josephine Tey? [between]
3. I split my reading time ____ the three. [among]

Point out that the second sentence is the type that gives most people problems. In addition to referring to only two items, *between* is also used when all items are compared to each other. When comparative words such as *difference* and *similarity* are used, *between* is the appropriate word.

MEETING INDIVIDUAL NEEDS

LEP/ESL

General Strategies. ESL students often learn English by talking with classmates who may misuse *good* and *well,* so you may want to give ESL students more examples of the correct uses of the two. A fill-in-the-blank exercise composed by students might make the lesson more relevant.

USAGE

bad, badly See page 767.

because In formal situations, do not use the construction *reason . . . because.* Instead, use *reason . . . that.*

INFORMAL The reason for the eclipse is because the moon has come between the earth and the sun.

FORMAL The **reason** for the eclipse is **that** the moon has come between the earth and the sun.

being as, being that Avoid using either of these expressions for *because* or *since.*

EXAMPLE **Because** [not *Being as*] Ms. Ribas is a gemologist, she may know the value of these gemstones.

beside, besides *Beside* is a preposition meaning "by the side of." *Besides* may be used as a preposition or an adverb. As a preposition, *besides* means "in addition to." As an adverb, it means "moreover."

EXAMPLES He set the plate of sandwiches **beside** the bowl of fruit punch.

Besides fringe benefits, the job offered a high salary. [preposition]

I am not in the mood to go shopping; **besides,** I have an English test tomorrow. [adverb]

between, among Use *between* when referring to only two items or to more than two when each item is being compared to each other item.

EXAMPLES The money from the sale of the property was divided **between** Sasha and Antonio.

Do you know the difference **between** a simile, a metaphor, and an analogy?

Use *among* when you are referring to more than two items and are not considering each item in relation to each of the others.

EXAMPLE The money from the sale of the property was divided **among** the four relatives.

bring, take *Bring* means "to come carrying something." *Take* means "to go carrying something."

EXAMPLES I will **bring** my Wynton Marsalis tapes when I come over.

USAGE

Please **take** the model of the Globe Theatre to the library.
You may **take** my softball glove to school today, but please **bring** it home this afternoon.

bust, busted Avoid using these words as verbs. Use a form of *break* or *burst,* depending on the meaning you intend.

EXAMPLES One of the headlights on the van is **broken** [not *busted*].
A pipe in the apartment above ours **burst** [not *busted*].

but, only See **The Double Negative,** pages 811–812.

can't hardly, can't scarcely See **The Double Negative,** pages 811–812.

could of See **of.**

done *Done* is the past participle of *do.* Avoid using *done* for *did,* which is the past form of *do* and does not require an auxiliary verb.

NONSTANDARD He done all of his homework over the weekend.
STANDARD He **did** all of his homework over the weekend.
STANDARD He **had done** all of his homework over the weekend.

don't, doesn't *Don't* is the contraction of *do not. Doesn't* is the contraction of *does not.* Use *doesn't,* not *don't,* with singular subjects except *I* and *you.*

EXAMPLES She **doesn't** [not *don't*] like seafood.
The bookstore **doesn't** [not *don't*] have any copies of Faith Ringgold's *Tar Beach* in stock.

PICTURE THIS

The year is 1820. After experimenting for months, you have built the wonderful hot-air balloon shown on the next page. To introduce your fellow townspeople to this new form of

USAGE

COOPERATIVE LEARNING

Have students select partners. Assign one student in each pair as the "between" person and the other as the "among" person. Then write a narrative prologue, such as the following sentence, on the chalkboard:

The two expedition teams met with strange occurrences in the Antarctic—eerie lights, howling winds, and a visit by a hairy creature named Fuzz.

Have each pair compose a short fantasy using the sentence as the opening line. Tell students that they must write the stories with their partners, but that each student is responsible for using his or her assigned word correctly at least three times in the story. You may want to post the stories on a bulletin board to share with other classes.

INTEGRATING THE LANGUAGE ARTS

Usage and Vocabulary. To reinforce the concept that English is not used the same way on all occasions, have students make lists of polite slang expressions they commonly use. Then have the class compile a combined list of expressions. Discuss with the class occasions when more formal language would be useful and occasions when formal language would be required. Then generate a directory of formal ways to say each slang expression. You could reinforce the concept that a speaker's and a writer's audience will influence the choice of vocabulary.

USAGE

PICTURE THIS

Remind students that when they are writing advertising flyers, all the information does not have to be in complete sentences. Often advertisements use a few catchy phrases in display type to call attention to the body of the advertisement and to emphasize what the illustration shows. Before students write, you might want to familiarize them with the history of hot-air balloons and get them intrigued with the adventure that these balloons presented when they were first introduced.

VISUAL CONNECTIONS

About the Subject. Although inventors were interested in hot-air balloons as far back as the thirteenth century, balloons were not invented until the late 1700s. Two French brothers, the Montgolfiers, experimented with filling cloth bags with hot air, which caused the bags to rise. Their experiments began a curiosity that became popular as a means of transportation. The balloons float because the hot air inside is lighter than the surrounding cooler air.

The first manned balloon flight across the English Channel occurred in 1785. A French flyer, J. P. Blanchard, made an ascent at Philadelphia in 1793. From 1794 until 1945, balloons were used in wartime for observation and communication. More recently, hot-air balloons have been used for scientific exploration and, of course, for recreation.

USAGE

USAGE

transportation, you're going to sell balloon rides at the County Fair. Create a flyer advertising your incredible flying balloon. In your flyer, describe the amazing sensations of a balloon ride, and convince potential customers that the balloon is safe. Use at least five of the following words and expressions correctly.

as far as	don't
as fast as	doesn't
as if	effect
bring	affect
take	beside

Subject: a hot-air balloon
Audience: potential customers
Purpose: to persuade

effect See **affect, effect.**

emigrate, immigrate Emigrate is a verb meaning "to leave a country or region to settle elsewhere." *Immigrate* is a verb meaning "to come into a country or region to settle there."

EXAMPLES Thousands of people **emigrated** from Germany during the 1870s.
Most of the German refugees **immigrated** to the United States.

NOTE: The nouns that correspond to *emigrate* and *immigrate* are *emigrant* (one who goes away from a country or region) and *immigrant* (one who comes into a country or region).

etc. See **and etc.**

everywheres See **anyways, anywheres.**

except See **accept, except.**

fewer, less Use *fewer,* which tells "how many," to modify a plural noun. Use *less,* which tells "how much," to modify a singular noun.

EXAMPLES **Fewer** students are going out for football this year.
I find that I have a lot more fun now that I spend **less** time watching TV.

good, well See page 767.

USAGE

EXERCISE 2 **Identifying Correct Usage**

Choose the correct word or words in parentheses in each of the following sentences.

1. There isn't one state that (*doesn't, don't*) have numerous place names derived from Native American words.
2. Your mistakes will be (*fewer, less*) if you proofread your paper.
3. The assignments on Greek philosophers were divided (*among, between*) the juniors in the humanities class.
4. Marcus did (*good, well*) on his driver's exam.
5. Will you (*bring, take*) these books to our study session tomorrow night?
6. (*Being that, Since*) she has passed all the tests, she should be a likely candidate for the military academy.
7. The junkyard just outside the city limits certainly looked (*bad, badly*), didn't it?
8. Chen Rong was a famous Chinese artist who (*did, done*) many beautiful paintings of dragons.
9. (*Beside, Besides*) *The Scarlet Letter* and *The Red Badge of Courage,* we read *The Joy-Luck Club* and *Tortuga.*
10. During the nineteenth century, many people (*emigrated, immigrated*) from Asia to the United States.

COMMON ERROR

Problem. Students often confuse *immigrate* and *emigrate.*

Solution. Tell students that an easy way to remember the difference between these words is to use the initial letters to create a mnemonic device. Explain that the *e* in *emigrate* can stand for *exit,* and the *i* in *immigrate* can stand for *in.* Then have students create their own examples. [*Exile* and *exodus* or *integrate* and *initiate* are possibilities.]

INTEGRATING THE LANGUAGE ARTS

Technology Link. Have students check for proper grammar and usage in their writing by using a grammar-check computer program. Grammar-check features can readily catch a number of mistakes, including double negatives and nonstandard usage such as *being that, anywheres,* and *bust.* Emphasize that the programs aren't foolproof, but that they often note the potential for error and query the user about usage. Then it is up to the writer to refer to a glossary or grammar source.

TIMESAVER

Group students in threes to complete **Exercises 2–4.** Have one student in each group be responsible for answering one set of exercises. Then have the three exchange papers. Tell each student to check the paper. Next, have the second student pass the paper to a third and correct the exercises with the class. Having students work this way allows all students to be exposed to all the questions in all three exercises and saves grading time.

USAGE

REVIEW A

OBJECTIVE

- To identify correct usage by selecting words to complete sentences

INTEGRATING THE LANGUAGE ARTS

Literature Link. You might want to explain to students that residents of different geographical regions often speak unique dialects that differ from standard speech. Sometimes writers who want to capture the full flavor of the cultures they're writing about use this informal English to portray characters.

Writers like Mark Twain and Lorraine Hansberry exemplify this craft of writing dialect. You might have students read portions of *The Adventures of Huckleberry Finn* or *A Raisin in the Sun* to discuss the informal language. Have students identify examples of regional dialect to discover how dialect helps build characterization. Explain to students that language that may otherwise be considered incorrect grammatically can be valuable in creating vivid characters.

USAGE

USAGE

REVIEW A Completing Sentences with Correct Usage

Choose an item from the colored box to complete each of the following sentences correctly. [Note: Be careful! Some of the items in the box are nonstandard usages.]

except	accept	held at	number
being as	busted	is that	is because
immigrate	alumni	alumnae	took
anywheres	held	amount	anywhere
brought	emigrate	since	broke

EXAMPLE 1. Two years ago, my Uncle Koichi decided to ____ to this country from Japan.
1. *immigrate*

1. Fortunately, he ____ along his marvelous kite-making skills and his keen business sense. **1. brought**
2. At first it was hard for Uncle Koichi to ____ the fact that kite-flying isn't as popular here as it is in Japan. **2. accept**
3. I did some research for him and found out where the big kite festivals are ____. **3. held**
4. He decided to settle right here in Southern California ____ plenty of kite enthusiasts live here all year round. **4. since**

5. First, Uncle Koichi built a small ____ of beautiful kites, and then he started giving kite-flying lessons. 5. number
6. All three of my older brothers are enthusiastic ____ of Koichi's Kite Kollege. 6. alumni
7. The reason that Uncle Koichi's shop is successful ____ he loves his work and is very good at it. 7. is that
8. My first kite ____ into pieces when I crashed it into a tree, but Uncle Koichi built me another one. 8. broke
9. I took these photographs of his magnificent dragon kite, which takes ____ from three to five people to launch, depending on wind conditions. 9. anywhere
10. My uncle's customers and friends all hope that he will never ____ from the United States and take his glorious kites back to Japan. 10. emigrate

USAGE

EXERCISE 3 **Correcting Errors in Usage**

Most of the following sentences contain errors in usage. If a sentence contains an error, revise the sentence. If a sentence is correct, write *C.*

EXAMPLE **1. The five starting players have twenty fouls between them.**
1. *The five starting players have twenty fouls among them.*

1. It ~~don't~~ look as if the rain will stop this afternoon. 1. doesn't
2. Sometimes I can get so absorbed in a movie that I forget where ~~I'm at~~. 2. I am 3. C 4. affected
3. Would you bring your guitar when you come to visit us?
4. The drought seriously ~~effected~~ the lettuce crop. 5. accept
5. You must learn to ~~except~~ criticism if you want to improve.
6. ~~Being as~~ the Black History Month essay contest ends next week, we need to submit our entries soon. 6. Because
7. The reason that many Irish people moved to France and Argentina after the unsuccessful Irish rebellion in 1798 is ~~because~~ they refused to live under English rule. 7. that
8. Although I did badly on the quiz, I did very well on the exam. 8. C 9. allusion
9. The title of James Baldwin's *Notes of a Native Son* is an ~~illusion~~ to Richard Wright's famous novel *Native Son.*
10. ~~Beside~~ you and me, who else is going on the hike? 10. Besides

A DIFFERENT APPROACH

If students have difficulty distinguishing between pairs of words, such as *accept/except, emigrate/immigrate, alumnae/alumni,* and *affect/effect,* have students compose sentences that include both words used correctly in the same sentence, as in "I didn't want to accept any apology except one made with sincerity." You might have students write their completed sentences on index cards and post the cards around the room.

USAGE

REVIEW B

OBJECTIVE

- To proofread sentences to correct errors in usage

MEETING INDIVIDUAL NEEDS

STUDENTS WITH SPECIAL NEEDS

Reading sentences presented as in **Review B** may be difficult for learning disabled students with visual-processing deficits. If possible, duplicate the exercises on a handout and leave room after each sentence for students to rewrite the correct form. Challenging students to handle too many variables in one exercise is counterproductive to success and does not improve students' grammatical usage.

USAGE

REVIEW B **Proofreading a Paragraph for Correct Usage**

For each sentence in the following paragraph, identify the incorrect word or phrase. Then write the correct form. If a sentence is correct, write *C*.

EXAMPLE [1] If you think you can jump rope as good as these girls, find out if there's a branch of the American Double Dutch League near you.

1. *good—well*

1. anywhere
2. C
3. Because
4. as fast as
5. etc.
6. C
7. number
8. illusion
9. take
10. doesn't

[1] Double Dutch is a fast-action rope-jumping style that's been popular on U.S. playgrounds for ~~anywheres~~ from fifty to a hundred years. [2] In double Dutch, turners twirl two ropes alternately in opposite directions, creating an eggbeater effect. [3] ~~Being that~~ the two ropes are going so fast, jumpers have to jump double-fast. [4] Their feet fly at over three hundred steps a minute—about half that number is ~~all the faster~~ I can go! [5] To make things even more interesting, two jumpers often perform together to rhymes or music, doing flips, twists, cartwheels, ~~and etc~~. [6] Besides competing in local meets, jumpers can participate in competitions organized by the American Double Dutch League, the sport's official governing body. [7] In competition, all teams must perform the same ~~amount~~ of tests, including the speed test, the compulsory-tricks test, and the freestyle test. [8] This photo isn't an optical ~~allusion~~—the two jumpers are twins as well as being a double Dutch doubles team! [9] Not only did these girls win their divisional title in the American Double Dutch League World Championships, but also they were chosen to ~~bring~~ their sport to the Moscow International Folk Festival. [10] Olympic athlete Florence "Flo Jo" Joyner enthusiastically supports Double Dutch, and it ~~don't~~ surprise me at all that she likes to jump double Dutch herself!

SEGMENT 4 *(pp. 803–806)*

HAD OF—MIGHT OF, MUST OF

OBJECTIVE

- To identify correct usage by selecting words to complete sentences

had of See **of.**

had ought, hadn't ought Do not use *had* or *hadn't* with *ought.*

NONSTANDARD	His test scores had ought to be back by now.
STANDARD	His test scores **ought** to be back by now.
NONSTANDARD	She hadn't ought to have turned here.
STANDARD	She **ought not** to have turned here.

hardly See **The Double Negative,** pages 811–812.

he, she, it, they Avoid using a pronoun along with its antecedent as the subject of a verb. Such an error is sometimes called a ***double subject.***

NONSTANDARD	The computer system it is down today.
STANDARD	The **computer system is** down today.
NONSTANDARD	Fay Stanley and Diane Stanley they wrote a biography of the Hawaiian princess Ka'iulani.
STANDARD	**Fay Stanley and Diane Stanley wrote** a biography of the Hawaiian princess Ka'iulani.

illusion See **allusion, illusion.**

immigrate See **emigrate, immigrate.**

imply, infer *Imply* means "to suggest." *Infer* means "to interpret" or "to draw as a conclusion."

EXAMPLES The governor **implied** in her speech that she would support a statewide testing program.
I **inferred** from the governor's speech that she would support a statewide testing program.

in, into *In* means "within." *Into* means "from the outside to the inside." In formal situations, avoid using *in* for *into.*

INFORMAL	He threw the scraps of paper in the litter basket.
FORMAL	He threw the scraps of paper **into** the litter basket.

it See **he, she, it, they.**

kind(s), sort(s), type(s) With the singular form of each of these nouns, use *this* or *that.* With the plural form, use *these* or *those.*

EXAMPLES **This kind** of gas is dangerous; **those kinds** are harmless.
These types of reading assignments are always challenging.

USAGE

Teacher's ResourceBank™

RESOURCES

HAD OF—MIGHT OF, MUST OF

- Common Usage Problems C 307

QUICK REMINDER

To emphasize the difference between formal and informal language, write the sentences below on the chalkboard. Ask students to determine which sound like remarks they might overhear [1 and 3] and which sound like the formal language they might hear on a weather report [2 and 4].

1. It looks like it's going to rain again tomorrow.
2. It looks as though rain may be in the forecast for tomorrow.
3. What kind of a day is it going to be?
4. What kind of weather should you plan for today?

MEETING INDIVIDUAL NEEDS

LEP/ESL

Spanish. Because Spanish does not have as many helping verbs as English, Spanish-speakers may need an explanation of the use of helping verbs. If they learn distinctly the word *have,* they can avoid using *of* as a helping verb.

USAGE

COMMON ERROR

Problem. Students often confuse *of* with *have* because they do not hear the difference between the two words when they are used in speech.

Solution. Have students slowly read sentences that correctly use *have* as a helping verb. Tell the students to exaggerate the way the word sounds so that it will be imprinted on their memories and will not become a slurred-over word.

USAGE

USAGE

kind of, sort of In formal situations, avoid using *kind of* for the adverb *somewhat* or *rather*.

INFORMAL Jackie was kind of disappointed when she did not make the basketball team.
FORMAL Jackie was **somewhat** [or *rather*] disappointed when she did not make the basketball team.

kind of a, sort of a In formal situations, omit the *a*.

INFORMAL What kind of a car do you drive?
FORMAL What **kind of** car do you drive?

leave, let *Leave* means "to go away." *Let* means "to permit" or "to allow." Avoid using *leave* for *let*.

EXAMPLES **Let** [not *leave*] them stay where they are.
They **let** [not *left*] Jaime out early for a dentist appointment.

less See **fewer, less.**

lie, lay See pages 730–731.

like, as *Like* is a preposition. In formal situations, do not use *like* for the conjunction *as* to introduce a subordinate clause.

INFORMAL Placido Domingo sings like Caruso once did.
FORMAL Placido Domingo sings **as** Caruso once did.

REFERENCE NOTE: For more information about subordinate clauses, see pages 629–637.

like, as if In formal situations, avoid using the preposition *like* for the conjunction *as if* or *as though* to introduce a subordinate clause.

INFORMAL The singers sounded like they had not rehearsed.
FORMAL The singers sounded **as if** [or *as though*] they had not rehearsed.

might of, must of See **of.**

EXERCISE 4 Identifying Correct Usage

Choose the correct word or words in parentheses in each of the following sentences.

1. (*These*, *This*) kinds of questions require more thought than (*this*, *these*) kind.
2. I (*had ought*, *ought*) to check out a good library book.

REVIEW C

OBJECTIVE

- To identify correct usage by selecting words to complete sentences

3. It looks (*like*, *as if*) we'll be able to attend the powwow.
4. Will the coach (*leave*, *let*) you skip soccer practice today?
5. He serves the ball exactly (*as*, *like*) the coach showed him.
6. I (*implied*, *inferred*) from Dad's remark about "slovenliness" that my sister and I had forgotten to clean our room.
7. When Jay Gatsby walked (*in*, *into*) the room, everyone stared at him.
8. (*Leave*, *Let*) Rosetta explain the trigonometry problem.
9. Did Mr. Stokes (*imply*, *infer*) that he was pleased with my research paper on Mexican American authors?
10. What sort (*of*, *of a*) culture did the Phoenicians have?

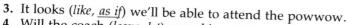

REVIEW C Identifying Correct Usage

Each sentence in the following paragraphs contains at least one pair of italicized items. Choose the correct item from each pair to complete the sentence.

EXAMPLE [1] While we were driving through the Appalachian Mountains, (*my father*, *my father he*) suddenly started chuckling and pulled over to the side of the road.
1. *my father*

[1] Dad said that we really (*had ought*, *ought*) to get out of the car and see the amazing mailbox that somebody had built. [2] Neither Ivy nor I was especially interested in mailboxes, but when we saw the fanciful metal figure that Dad was pointing to, we both smiled just (*as*, *like*) he had. [3] We jumped out to take the middle photo shown on the next page, and while we were standing (*beside*, *besides*) the road, a man came out of the house. [4] He introduced himself as Charlie Lucas and said he had built the mailbox man by welding together scraps from (*broken*, *busted*) machinery. [5] We started chatting with him, and the next thing we knew, he had invited us (*in*, *into*) the house to see more of his figures. [6] The house was (*kind of*, *rather*) like an art museum: there were dinosaurs made from colorful twisted wire, a fiddle-player with a head made from a shovel, and an alligator whose body (*might have*, *might of*) once been a crankshaft.

[7] "Dad, are these figures art?" Ivy whispered, and Dad's answer (*inferred*, *implied*) that they were. [8] He said that art (*don't*, *doesn't*) always have to be stuffy and serious or made

USAGE

MEETING INDIVIDUAL NEEDS

ADVANCED STUDENTS

Some students will benefit from exposure to usage errors not covered in this chapter. Have students review other grammar textbooks, other parts of this textbook, or other manuals of style. Although many sources employ an alphabetical order, readers should become familiar with any idiosyncrasies in presentation of material so that answers to specific questions can be easily located. Students might create handbooks that include frequently confused words and then assemble the handbooks for the class. Encourage students to refer to these handbooks when they are checking writing for errors.

USAGE

SEGMENT 5 *(pp. 806–810)*

NO, NONE, NOTHING—WOULD OF

OBJECTIVE

- To identify correct usage by selecting words to complete sentences

USAGE

Teacher's ResourceBank™

RESOURCES

NO, NONE, NOTHING—WOULD OF

- Common Usage Problems D 308

QUICK REMINDER

Write the sentence below on the chalkboard. Have students rewrite it on their papers in standard English.

If I had of known he would be here, I would of asked him to take care of this here problem. [If I had known he would be here, I would have asked him to take care of this problem.]

After students have rewritten the sentence, discuss their answers and explain any errors they might have made.

from bronze or marble and that true artists aren't always (*alumnae, alumni*) of famous art schools. [9] (*Mr. Lucas he, Mr. Lucas*) agreed with Dad that (*these kind, these kinds*) of sculptures and all other kinds of folk art are of great value to human beings. [10] Folk art comes straight from the heart; it often recycles cast-off materials that most people (*would have, would of*) considered junk; it offers a different perspective on life; and it makes people smile!

Charlie Lucas, *Old Buddy.*

Charlie Lucas, *Twisted Wire Dinosaur.*

USAGE

no, none, nothing See **The Double Negative,** pages 811–812.

nor See **or, nor.**

nowheres See **anyways, anywheres.**

number See **amount, number.**

of *Of* is a preposition. Do not use *of* in place of *have* after verbs such as *could, should, would, might,* and *must.*

NONSTANDARD	He could of had a summer job if he had applied earlier.
STANDARD	He **could have** had a summer job if he had applied earlier.

NONSTANDARD You ought to of taken a foreign language.
STANDARD You **ought to have** taken a foreign language.

Also do not use *of* after *had*.

NONSTANDARD If I had of known the word *raze*, I would have made a perfect score.
STANDARD If I **had** known the word *raze*, I would have made a perfect score.

Avoid using *of* after other prepositions such as *inside, off,* and *outside.*

EXAMPLE Chian-Chiu dived **off** [not *off of*] the side of the pool into the water.

off, off of Do not use *off* or *off of* in place of *from.*

NONSTANDARD You can get a program off of the usher.
STANDARD You can get a program **from** the usher.

or, nor Use *or* with *either;* use *nor* with *neither.*

EXAMPLES On Tuesdays the school cafeteria offers a choice for lunch of **either** a taco salad **or** a pizza.
I wonder why **neither** Ralph Ellison **nor** Robert Frost was given the Nobel Prize for literature.

ought to of See **of.**

raise, rise See page 733.

reason . . . is because See **because.**

scarcely See **The Double Negative,** pages 811–812.

she See **he, she, it, they.**

should of See **of.**

sit, set See page 732.

slow, slowly See page 768.

some, somewhat In formal situations, avoid using *some* to mean "to some extent." Use *somewhat.*

INFORMAL My grades have improved some during the past month.
FORMAL My grades have improved **somewhat** during the past month.

somewheres See **anyways, anywheres.**

sort(s) See **kind(s), sort(s), type(s)** and **kind of a, sort of a.**

USAGE

MEETING INDIVIDUAL NEEDS

LEP/ESL

General Strategies. While students are learning English, they may hesitate to speak, for fear of making errors. Calling too much attention to word choice can make students too critical of themselves and hinder their fluency. You might want to emphasize to students that as they learn the language, they should expect errors and that only practice will improve their use of English. Encourage them to ask questions of native speakers about usage problems and to refer to a glossary for assistance.

USAGE

COMMON ERROR

Problem. Students often confuse the conjunction *than* with the adverb *then.*

Solution. Explain to students that they should use *then* only when an expression tells when. Write the following reminder on the chalkboard:

THEN = WHEN

At all other times, students should use *than,* which compares or contrasts. Write this reminder on the chalkboard:

THAN = COMPARE or CONTRAST

USAGE

USAGE

sort of See **kind of, sort of.**

take See **bring, take.**

than, then *Than* is a conjunction used in comparisons. *Then* is an adverb telling when.

EXAMPLES He is a better cook **than** I am.
Let the sauce simmer for ten minutes, and **then** stir in two cups of cooked mixed vegetables.

that See **who, which, that.**

them Do not use *them* as an adjective. Use *those.*

EXAMPLE All of **those** [not *them*] paintings are by Carmen Lomas Garza.

they See **he, she, it, they.**

this here, that there Avoid using *here* or *there* after *this* or *that.*

EXAMPLE **This** [not *This here*] story tells about the Hmong people of Laos.

this, that, these, those See **kind(s), sort(s), types(s).**

type(s) See **kind(s), sort(s), type(s).**

type, type of Avoid using *type* as an adjective. Add *of* after *type.*

NONSTANDARD I prefer this type shirt.
STANDARD I prefer this **type of** shirt.

ways Use *way,* not *ways,* in referring to distance.

INFORMAL My home, in Wichita, is a long ways from Tokyo, where my pen pal lives.
FORMAL My home, in Wichita, is a long **way** from Tokyo, where my pen pal lives.

well, good See page 767.

when, where Do not use *when* or *where* to begin a definition.

NONSTANDARD A spoonerism is when you switch the beginning sounds of two words.
STANDARD A spoonerism is **a slip of the tongue in which the beginning sounds of two words are switched.**

NONSTANDARD A thesaurus is where you can find synonyms and antonyms of words.
STANDARD A thesaurus is **a book in which you can find synonyms and antonyms of words.**

where Do not use *where* for *that*.

EXAMPLE I read **that** [not *where*] Demosthenes learned to enunciate by practicing with pebbles in his mouth.

where . . . at See **at.**

who, which, that *Who* refers to persons only. *Which* refers to things only. *That* may refer to either persons or things.

EXAMPLES Wasn't Beethoven the composer **who** [or *that*] continued to write music after he had become deaf?

First editions of Poe's first book, **which** was titled *Tamerlane and Other Poems,* are worth thousands of dollars.

Is Emily Dickinson the poet **that** [or *who*] wrote on scraps of paper?

Is this the only essay **that** James Baldwin wrote?

who, whom See pages 690–692.

would of See **of.**

USAGE

EXERCISE 5 Identifying Correct Usage

Choose the correct word or words in parentheses in each of the following sentences.

1. I read in a newspaper article (*that, where*) dogs are being trained to help people with hearing impairments.
2. The earliest female author in United States literature who wrote frankly about women's concerns was neither Willa Cather (*or, nor*) Edith Wharton; she was Kate Chopin.
3. Jack London must (*of, have*) led an adventurous life.
4. Our teacher assigned us (*this, this here*) chapter to read.
5. Joe had the flu last week, but he's feeling (*some, somewhat*) better today.
6. As we passed Shreveport and crossed the Texas line, El Paso seemed a long (*way, ways*) away.
7. For advice, I go to Ms. Sanchez, (*which, who*) is a very understanding guidance counselor.
8. This (*type, type of*) short story has appealed to readers for many years.
9. Pass me (*them, those*) notes on the experiment, please.
10. He did a flip turn and pushed (*off, off of*) the pool wall.

A DIFFERENT APPROACH

To keep drill from becoming monotonous, use a quiz-show format to practice correct usage. Select a student to serve as emcee and have students provide the material for the quiz. Have them write sentences requiring the contestants to select the correct usage. Then have the emcee ask contestants to complete the sentences. Use the activity on those days when you have a few minutes to spare. You might keep a running score for students.

USAGE

REVIEW D

OBJECTIVE

- To identify correct usage by selecting words to complete sentences

MEETING **INDIVIDUAL** NEEDS

LEARNING STYLES

Visual Learners. When you teach correct usage, you may occasionally require your students to generate their own sentences to use for practice. Visual learners might find it easier to get involved in the activity if you provide artwork or other visual stimuli like **Picture This** to get them started. Having identified subjects in front of students can help inspire ideas.

USAGE

USAGE

REVIEW D **Identifying Correct Usage**

Each sentence in the following paragraph has a pair of italicized items. Choose the correct item from each pair to complete the sentence.

EXAMPLE [1] Have you read (*where, that*) Vietnamese refugees are working hard to succeed in the United States?
1. *that*

[1] When Vietnamese immigrants stepped (*off, off of*) the planes that had brought them from refugee camps all over Asia, they didn't know what to expect in America. [2] However, like previous immigrants, they were people (*which, who*) managed to succeed against all odds. [3] The boat people neither spoke English (*or, nor*) understood much about life in the United States. [4] Grateful just to be alive, they could (*have, of*) contented themselves with simple survival. [5] Instead, many of (*them, those*) Vietnamese families have encouraged their children to achieve academic excellence. [6] According to one study, half of the refugee children earn a B average overall and half also receive A's in math; (*that, that there*) study also places these students near the national average in English. [7] One reason Vietnamese students do so well is (*because, that*) they believe that success comes from hard work, not from luck or natural aptitude. [8] Consequently, rather (*than, then*) watch television or go to the mall, families like the one shown here spend weeknights doing homework together. [9] Even parents who do not speak English (*good, well*) help by not assigning chores during study time. [10] Younger children get extra instruction (*from, off of*) older brothers and sisters, and all this effort is helping the Vietnamese become one of the most successful immigrant groups in the United States.

SEGMENT 6 *(pp. 811–815)*

THE DOUBLE NEGATIVE

OBJECTIVE

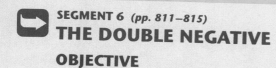

- To revise sentences to eliminate double negatives

Teacher's ResourceBank™

RESOURCES

THE DOUBLE NEGATIVE

- The Double Negative 309

The Double Negative

A ***double negative*** is a construction in which two negative words are used where one is enough. Although acceptable until Shakespeare's time, double negatives are now considered nonstandard.

NONSTANDARD She has not read none of Nadine Gordimer's books.
STANDARD She has **not** read **any** of Nadine Gordimer's books.
STANDARD She has read **none** of Nadine Gordimer's books.

NONSTANDARD I do not know nothing about the Peloponnesian War.
STANDARD I do **not** know **anything** about the Peloponnesian War.
STANDARD I know **nothing** about the Peloponnesian War.

NONSTANDARD Grandma said that she hadn't never seen another pumpkin that was as large as this one.
STANDARD Grandma said that she **hadn't ever** seen another pumpkin that was as large as this one.
STANDARD Grandma said that she had **never** seen another pumpkin that was as large as this one.

Common Negative Words

barely	never	not (n't)
but (meaning "only")	no	nothing
	nobody	nowhere
hardly	none	only
neither	no one	scarcely

NOTE: Avoid the common error of using *n't,* the contraction of *not,* with another negative word, especially *barely, hardly,* or *scarcely.*

NONSTANDARD I can't hardly take another step in these new boots.
STANDARD I can **hardly** take another step in these new boots.

NONSTANDARD The film is so long that we couldn't scarcely see it in one class period.
STANDARD The film is so long that we could **scarcely** see it in one class period.

USAGE

QUICK REMINDER

Write the following sentences on the chalkboard or on a transparency. Have students rewrite them correctly.

1. The museum was so crowded that I didn't hardly get to see the Chinese soldiers. [The museum was so crowded that I hardly got to see the Chinese soldiers.]
2. I never get to see nothing in a crowd because I'm so short. [I never get to see anything in a crowd because I'm so short.]
3. I don't know nothing about the exhibit except what I read in the brochure. [I know nothing about the exhibit except what I read in the brochure.]

MEETING INDIVIDUAL NEEDS

LEP/ESL

Spanish. Double and even triple negatives in the same sentence are used in Spanish. You will probably want to work closely with Spanish-speaking students to help them avoid double negatives in their writing.

USAGE

The words *but* and *only* are considered negative words when they are used as adverbs meaning "no more than." In such cases, the use of another negative word with *but* or *only* is considered informal.

INFORMAL Whenever I see you, I can't help but smile.
FORMAL Whenever I see you, I can't help smiling.

USAGE

EXERCISE 6 **Revising Sentences to Eliminate Double Negatives**

Revise each of the following sentences to eliminate the double negative. Although the following sentences can be corrected in more than one way, you need to give only one revision.

Revisions will vary.

EXAMPLE 1. He hadn't no pencils on his desk.
1. *He had no pencils on his desk.*
or
He hadn't any pencils on his desk.

1. any
2. any
3. anybody
4. have
5. anything
6. could
7. any
8. feeling
9. any
10. anything

1. Tom didn't have ~~no~~ time to buy the books.
2. Haven't ~~none~~ of you seen the dog?
3. Isn't ~~nobody~~ else interested in going to visit the pueblo at Tesuque this morning?
4. We ~~haven't~~ but one day to visit the fair.
5. She didn't contribute ~~nothing~~ to the project.
6. The lights were so dim that we ~~couldn't~~ barely see.
7. They said that they didn't think they'd have ~~no~~ time to go to the post office.
8. In the mountains you can't help ~~but feel~~ calm.
9. Can't ~~none~~ of them come to the party?
10. José Martí was sentenced to six years in prison, and he hadn't done ~~nothing~~ but write a letter that the Spanish government didn't like.

"CONFOUNDED DOUBLE NEGATIVES."

USAGE

ANSWERS
Review E
Revisions will vary. Here are some possibilities:

1. A New Year's Eve Watch is an African American gathering to welcome the new year by singing, chanting, and shouting.
2. She didn't do too badly on the quiz.

REVIEW E

OBJECTIVE

- To proofread sentences to correct errors in usage

REVIEW E **Correcting Errors in Usage**

Most of the following sentences contain errors in usage. If a sentence contains an error or errors, revise the sentence. If a sentence is correct, write *C*.

EXAMPLE 1. Can't none of the staff sort the yearbook pictures?
1. *Can't any of the staff sort the yearbook pictures?*

1. A New Year's Eve Watch is when African Americans join together to welcome the new year by singing, chanting, and shouting.
2. She didn't do too bad on the quiz.
3. We should of paid closer attention to the instructions.
4. I wonder how many Americans realize the importance of the Minutemen, which were true champions of freedom during the American Revolution.
5. Being as my parents prefer tapes, they don't hardly ever play their records.
6. A large amount of people contributed to the charity drive.
7. Swimming is the type of sport that requires daily training.
8. Did Mr. Jackson mean to infer that we might have a pop quiz tomorrow, or was he just joking?
9. I don't think he knows where he's at.
10. Some speakers make illusions to the "good old days."
11. Remind me to bring my beaded doeskin shirt to the dry cleaner's so that it will be ready in time for the powwow on Saturday.
12. I don't know whether to except his invitation or not.
13. The reason we left the party early is because we had to catch the six o'clock train the next morning.
14. I can't help but think of *The Sound of Music* when I hear the song "Edelweiss."
15. There weren't none of us who were finished with our final copy.
16. I think these kind of stereo speakers give a better sound.
17. I couldn't hardly remember the names of all the states.
18. I infer from your research paper that Gutenberg had a great affect on the way books were printed.
19. My Chinese name, Wan Ju, means "someone who never lets nothing stand in the way of her success."
20. Miguel Castañeda has played ice hockey for Mexico besides being the first competitive speed skater to represent that country.

USAGE

3. We should have paid closer attention to the instructions.
4. I wonder how many Americans realize the importance of the Minutemen, who were true champions of freedom during the American Revolution.
5. Because my parents prefer tapes, they hardly ever play their records.
6. A large number of people contributed to the charity drive.
7. C
8. Did Mr. Jackson mean to imply that we might have a pop quiz tomorrow, or was he just joking?
9. I don't think he knows where he is.
10. Some speakers make allusions to the "good old days."
11. Remind me to take my beaded doeskin shirt to the dry cleaner's so that it will be ready in time for the powwow on Saturday.
12. I don't know whether to accept his invitation or not.
13. The reason we left the party early is that we had to catch the six o'clock train the next morning.
14. I can't help thinking of *The Sound of Music* when I hear the song "Edelweiss."
15. There weren't any of us who were finished with our final copy.
16. I think this kind of stereo speakers gives a better sound.
17. I could hardly remember the names of all the states.
18. I infer from your research paper that Gutenberg had a great effect on the way books were printed.
19. My Chinese name, Wan Ju, means "someone who never lets anything stand in the way of her success."
20. C

USAGE

WRITING APPLICATION

OBJECTIVES

- To write an informal local history containing dialect in direct quotations
- To write a letter that uses standard English to tell a story

WRITING APPLICATION

The **Writing Application** gives students a dual opportunity—to use conversational English to make their storytelling lively and to present conversational English in a formal context in a letter. You might want to review the proper form for a business letter in **Chapter 38: "Letters and Forms."**

CRITICAL THINKING

Synthesis

In the **Writing Application,** students are asked to collect anecdotal information for an informal history. The story may include regional or cultural dialects and may be written informally. However, students are asked to present the information in a formal letter. By bringing together these two types of writing into one composition, students will be integrating information and using synthesis skills.

USAGE

PREWRITING

You might want to brainstorm with the class to think of stories students have heard about the community. If you have historical societies in your community, you might invite a speaker to come, or you could plan a trip to a historical-society library if possible. Make sure students understand that personal experiences and family anecdotes are also appropriate.

WRITING APPLICATION

Using Standard English in Writing a Local History

Variety is the spice of life—and of language. In casual conversation you hear many usages that don't follow the rules and guidelines of standard formal English. Often, these usages are part of a *dialect*—a variety of English unique to the speaker's geographical region or cultural group. (For more about dialects, see pages 475–477.) Dialects make conversational English lively and expressive. In writing, they help capture the particular flavor of a speaker's words. When paraphrasing, however, it's best to use standard English.

USAGE

QUOTATION	Great-aunt Celia said, "Don't you pay him no mind."
PARAPHRASE	Great-aunt Celia said that I shouldn't pay any attention to him.

WRITING ACTIVITY

Dr. Yolanda Washington, a professor at the nearby community college, is compiling an informal history of your area. She has invited students in American history classes at local high schools to submit historical accounts of local people, places, and events to be included in this project. Write a letter to Dr. Washington, telling a true story about your block, your neighborhood, or your town. You may use dialect in direct quotations, but be sure to use standard English in the rest of your letter. Use the **Glossary of Usage** to check any words or phrases you're not sure about.

Prewriting First, think of some of the stories you may have heard about your community. Maybe the story of how a particular geographical feature got its name springs to mind. Or you might choose to tell about your parents', grandparents', or great-grandparents' arrival in the area. Some local stories might even have taken place during larger historical events such as the Civil War. If you don't know any stories about your community's history, ask an older family member, a friend, or a neighbor to tell you some. Then choose the

SEGMENT 7 *(pp. 815–817)*

REVIEW: POSTTEST

OBJECTIVE

- To proofread sentences to correct errors in usage

best story to send to Dr. Washington. Jot down as many concrete details as you can. Record a few good quotations and paraphrases that capture the local flavor of the story.

Writing Follow the standard form for business letters (pages 994–1002). Begin your draft by greeting Dr. Washington and explaining that you'd like to contribute to her local history project. Then set the scene for your story by indicating the time period and setting. Write down the events of the story in a clear, straightforward order. Include as many details as you can.

Evaluating and Revising Check with someone who knows the story to be sure you've recorded the facts accurately. Ask for additional details that may make the story more interesting and informative. As you revise, check words and expressions in the **Glossary of Usage** to make sure they're formal standard English. Avoid nonstandard usages in paraphrases. If you've included quotations, check them for correct punctuation. (For more about punctuating quotations, see pages 878–881.)

Proofreading and Publishing Proofread your letter carefully for errors in grammar, usage, or mechanics. Be sure you've used the correct form for business letters. You and other members of your class may want to compile an informal history of your community. You can publish your stories by collecting them in a booklet and giving copies of the booklet to a local historical society, a tourist information center, school and public libraries, or any other people or organizations that might enjoy them.

Review: Posttest

A. Correcting Errors in Usage

Most of the following sentences contain errors in usage. If a sentence contains an error, revise the sentence. If a sentence is correct, write *C*.

WRITING

Remind students to organize the letters so that the stories can flow within them. Emphasize that errors can be corrected in the evaluation stage.

USAGE

PROOFREADING AND PUBLISHING

Allow students to exchange letters with one another so that more than one person has a chance to proofread the letters. Plan to collect the stories and publish them for other classes in the school, for family members, or for persons with historical interest in the community.

INTEGRATING THE LANGUAGE ARTS

Usage and Writing. Remind students that while the glossary looks like a lot to learn, no one has to worry about every entry. Explain that most people have a few usage errors that show up in their speech or writing. The trick is to learn when to look something up for formal writing or speech. Students might even want to start keeping personal glossaries that contain reminders of their particular usage problems.

USAGE

EXAMPLE **1.** Many of us felt badly when our class trip was canceled.

1. *Many of us felt bad when our class trip was canceled.*

1. Do sloths always move that ~~slow~~? **1.** slowly
2. I inferred from what Julio said that he has ~~excepted~~ my apology. **2.** accepted
3. Over eighty years ago my great-grandfather ~~immigrated~~ from Mexico. **3.** emigrated
4. He talked persuasively for an hour, but his words had no ~~affect.~~ **4.** effect.
5. The Seminoles of Florida piece together colorful fabrics to create striking dresses, shirts, skirts, ~~and~~ etc.
6. The sizable ~~amount~~ of hours I have spent studying has really helped my grades. **6.** number
7. Are you implying that you noticed nothing unusual in the cafeteria today? **7.** C
8. When La Toya, Tamisha, and I ate at the new Ethiopian restaurant, the food was served in communal bowls, and we divided it ~~between~~ ourselves. **8.** among
9. The reason the book was so difficult to understand was ~~because~~ the writing was unclear. **9.** that
10. If you kept ~~less~~ fish in your tank, they would live longer. **10.** fewer

USAGE

B. Correcting Errors in Usage

Most of the sentences in the following paragraph contain errors in usage. Identify the error or errors in each incorrect sentence and write the correct form. If a sentence is correct, write *C.*

EXAMPLE **[1]** In-line skates provide such a smooth, fast ride that they give the allusion that you're ice-skating.

1. *allusion—illusion*

11. have
12. somewhere
13. that
14. into/any

[11] Almost no one could ~~of~~ predicted the revolution that took place in skating equipment a few years ago. **[12]** Surprisingly, the very first in-line rollerskates were invented ~~somewheres~~ in the Netherlands in the 1700s. **[13]** I read in the newspaper ~~where~~ in 1769 a London instrument maker and mechanic wore in-line skates with metal wheels to a party. **[14]** Playing a violin, he came gliding ~~in~~ the room on the skates, but he made a crash landing because he didn't have ~~no~~ idea how to stop. **[15]** Maybe that's why nobody really excepted the newfangled skates in them days. **[16]** Later, an American inventor devised the four-wheeled skate, which became popular, and it looked like in-line skates weren't never going to succeed. **[17]** Finally, in 1980, two Minneapolis brothers noticed that hockey players hated being off of the ice during the summer. **[18]** Thinking that in-line skates would be a perfect cross-training tool to keep hockey players in shape all year, the brothers started building the new skates in their basement. **[19]** The idea might of stopped right there if other people hadn't found out that beside being a good training tool, in-line skating is just plain fun. **[20]** In-line skating offers a great low-impact aerobic workout, and it's safe—as long as skaters wear the right type protective gear and learn how to stop!

15. accepted/those

16. as if/ ever

18. C

19. have/ besides

20. of

USAGE

USAGE

SEGMENT 1 *(pp. 818–819)*

DIAGNOSTIC TEST

OBJECTIVES

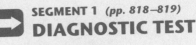

- To recognize and correct errors of capitalization in sentences
- To proofread a paragraph for correct capitalization

Teacher's ResourceBank™

RESOURCES

FOR THE WHOLE CHAPTER

• Chapter Review Form A	323–324
• Chapter Review Form B	325–326
• Assessment Portfolio	
Mechanics Pretests	579–586
Mechanics Mastery Tests	605–612

CHAPTER OVERVIEW

This chapter presents the rules of capitalization within the context of preferred current usage. In the **Writing Application**, students will apply the rules in this chapter to a friendly letter that they draft and revise.

The chapter defines each rule, gives examples of each, and explains frequently encountered applications. **Reference Notes** direct students to other parts of the textbook for clarification of key terms used in the chapter. As you use the chapter, you might have students suggest examples of their own to enhance their awareness of the rules of standard usage for capitals.

You may want to refer students to this chapter when they are proofreading any writing assignment. The **Summary Style Review**, pp. 838–839, may be a useful reference tool.

MECHANICS

MECHANICS

28 CAPITALIZATION

Rules of Standard Usage

Diagnostic Test

A. Recognizing Correctly Capitalized Sentences

For each of the following sentences, write the words that should be capitalized. If a sentence is correct, write *C*.

EXAMPLE **1. After Dan finishes shopping, he'll meet us in front of Calvert's grocery.**
1. *Grocery*

1. In the fall, aunt Lisa's play will be staged by the Captain Philip Weston theater.
2. We were surprised to find that the film was in spanish, although english subtitles were provided.
3. Was Artemis the Greek goddess who ruled the hunt? 3. C
4. Pablo's favorite board game is *Trivial pursuit* because he always wins.
5. Have you seen *A raisin in the sun* yet?
6. Leon stood at the card counter for a full hour, trying to choose just the right card for Valentine's day.

7. The opening speech will be given by ex-Senator Preston. 7. C
8. Alnaba's new brother was delivered at Memorial hospital just before dawn.
9. Come to see our fantastic selection of top-quality stereo equipment at our new location just south of interstate 4 and River Road!
10. Can you name four countries located on the continent of Africa? 10. C

B. Proofreading for Correct Capitalization

Proofread the following paragraph for errors in capitalization. In each sentence, change lowercase letters to capitals or capital letters to lowercase as necessary. If a sentence is correct, write *C*. Words that should be lowercased or capitalized are underscored.

EXAMPLE **[1]** As humanity has developed more and more of the Earth's wilderness areas, many animal species have become extinct or endangered.

1. *earth's*

[11] Last year, in a special Ecology course at Charlotte High School, I found out about some endangered North American animals. **[12]** I learned that conservationists here in the south are particularly concerned about the fate of the Florida panther. **[13]** All of that classroom discussion didn't have much impact on me, however, until early one Saturday morning last Spring, when I was lucky enough to sight one of these beautiful creatures. **[14]** My Uncle and I were driving to Big Bass Lake for some fishing, and I saw what looked like a large dog crossing the road some distance ahead of us. **[15]** Suddenly, Uncle Billy stopped his old ford truck and reached for the field glasses in the glove compartment. **[16]** As he handed them to me, he said, "look closely, Chris. You probably won't see a panther again any time soon." **[17]** Standing in the middle of Collingswood avenue, the cat turned and looked straight at us. **[18]** When those brown eyes met mine, I knew I had the title for my term paper—"Hello And Goodbye." **[19]** Then the big cat leisurely turned and crossed the road and loped off into the woods east of Sunshine Mall. **[20]** As the panther disappeared back into the wilds of Charlotte county, Uncle Billy said, "May god go with you, pal." 19. C

MECHANICS

USING THE DIAGNOSTIC TEST

The **Diagnostic Test** contains two parts. **Part A** asks students to identify words that should be capitalized in sentences. **Part B** checks students' abilities to proofread a paragraph for correct capitalization. You may use the results to determine which chapter segments will require special emphasis. Have students inventory their own weaknesses to help them plan and manage their study time.

MECHANICS

SEGMENT 2 *(pp. 820–827)*

FIRST WORDS, THE PRONOUN *I*, THE INTERJECTION *O*, PROPER NOUNS, AND PROPER ADJECTIVES Rules 28a–28c

OBJECTIVES

- To identify in phrases words that should be capitalized
- To write a fictitious interview that includes five proper nouns

Teacher's ResourceBank™

RESOURCES

FIRST WORDS, THE PRONOUN *I*, THE INTERJECTION *O*, PROPER NOUNS, AND PROPER ADJECTIVES

QUICK REMINDER

Write the following sentences on the chalkboard. Have students copy them and correct errors in capitalization. Lowercase letters that should be capitalized and capital letters that should be changed to lowercase are underlined.

1. the wind swirled around my head, and my hat blew away.
2. if you see her before i do, tell her i'll meet her at the dance.
3. One of my favorite poems is "o Captain! My Captain!"
4. Ms. barker called to tell me i had won the writing contest.
5. It was hard work but, Oh, so rewarding.

You may want to tell students that *O* has a more dramatic effect than the word *oh* and *O* is used almost exclusively in poetry such as Walt Whitman's "O Captain! My Captain!" and Langston Hughes's "O God of Dust."

SELECTION AMENDMENT

Description of change: excerpted

Rationale: to focus on the concept of capitalization presented in this chapter

In your reading, you'll notice variations in the use of capitalization. Most writers, however, follow the rules presented in this chapter. In your own writing, following these rules will help you communicate clearly with the widest possible audience.

28a. Capitalize the first word in every sentence.

EXAMPLES **A**uthor Leslie Marmon Silko was born in Albuquerque, New Mexico, and grew up on the Laguna Pueblo Reservation.
When he missed the bus, my brother asked, "**W**ill you drive me to school?"

Traditionally, the first word of a line of poetry is capitalized.

EXAMPLE
Joy may be shy, unique,
Friendly to a few,
Sorrow never scorned to speak
To any who
Were false or true.

Countee Cullen, "Any Human to Another"

NOTE: Some modern writers, for reasons of style, do not follow this rule. When you quote from a writer's work, always use capital letters exactly as the writer uses them.

REFERENCE NOTE: See page 878 for more information about using capital letters in quotations.

MECHANICS

28b. Capitalize the interjection *O* and the pronoun *I*.

The interjection *O* is usually used only for invocations and is followed by the name of the person or thing being addressed. Don't confuse it with the common interjection *oh*, which is capitalized only when it appears at the beginning of a sentence and is always followed by punctuation.

EXAMPLES Walt Whitman's tribute to Abraham Lincoln begins, "**O** Captain! my Captain!"
What **I** meant was—**oh,** never mind.

28c. Capitalize *proper nouns* and *proper adjectives.*

A ***common noun*** names one member of a group of people, places, or things. A ***proper noun*** names a particular person, place, or thing. ***Proper adjectives*** are formed from proper nouns.

☞ REFERENCE NOTE: For more information about proper nouns and common nouns, see pages 553–554. See pages 559–561 for more on proper adjectives.

Common nouns are capitalized only if they

- begin a sentence (also, in most cases, a line of poetry)

  or
- begin a direct quotation

  or
- are part of a title

COMMON NOUNS	PROPER NOUNS	PROPER ADJECTIVES
a writer	Dickens	Dickensian characters
a country	Brazil	Brazilian coastline
a president	Jefferson	Jeffersonian ideals
an island	Hawaii	Hawaiian climate

In proper nouns made up of two or more words, all articles, coordinating conjunctions, and short prepositions (those with fewer than five letters) are not capitalized.

EXAMPLES **Queen of Spain**
American Society for the Prevention of Cruelty to Animals

The parts of a compound word are capitalized as if each part stood alone.

EXAMPLES **African American** **Central American nations** **Chinese checkers** **English-speaking tourists**

NOTE: Proper nouns and proper adjectives may lose their capitals after long usage.

EXAMPLES **madras** **sandwich** **watt** **puritan**

When you're not sure whether to capitalize a word, check a dictionary.

(1) Capitalize the names of persons.

GIVEN NAMES	**Patricia**	**Brian**	**Toshio**	**Aretha**
SURNAMES	**Sánchez**	**Goldblum**	**Williams**	**Ozawa**

MECHANICS

MEETING INDIVIDUAL NEEDS

LEP/ESL

Vietnamese and Spanish. In some languages, days of the week, months, and nationalities used as adjectives are lowercased as in "On the first monday in april, we're going to watch a french film." Your acknowledgment to students that they are being asked to reverse rules they may already have mastered in their native languages may help them deal with this change independently.

MECHANICS

INTEGRATING THE LANGUAGE ARTS

Technology Link. Use the examples of proper nouns and proper adjectives shown in this chapter along with examples relevant to your students to compose an exercise of a few paragraphs on the computer. Or you could have advanced students compose the exercise. Have students take turns (as computers are available) capitalizing the proper nouns and adjectives. You could have students print their answers and then check them against a file showing the correct capitalization.

MECHANICS

NOTE: Some names contain more than one capital letter. Usage varies in the capitalization of *van, von, du, de la,* and other parts of many multiword names. Always verify the spelling of a name with the person, or check the name in a reference source.

EXAMPLES **La Fontaine** **McEwen** **O'Connor** **Van Doren** **Yellow Thunder** **Ibn Ezra** **Villa-Lobos** **van Gogh**

Abbreviations such as *Ms., Mr., Dr., Gen., Jr. (junior),* and *Sr. (senior)* should always be capitalized.

EXAMPLES **Ms. Gloria Steinem** **Gordon Parks, Jr.** **Dr. Antonia Novello** **Martin Luther King, Sr.**

REFERENCE NOTE: For more about punctuating abbreviations, see pages 844–845.

MECHANICS

(2) Capitalize geographical names.

TYPE OF NAME	EXAMPLES	
Towns, Cities	Boston Tokyo	South Bend Rio de Janeiro
Counties, Townships	Marion County Lawrence Township	Lafayette Parish Nottinghamshire
States	Wisconsin New Hampshire	Oklahoma North Carolina
Regions	the East the Southwest	Northern Hemisphere New England

NOTE: Words such as *north, western,* and *southeast* are not capitalized when they indicate direction.

EXAMPLES **east of the river** **driving south** **western Iowa**

REFERENCE NOTE: The abbreviations of names of states are always capitalized. For more about using and punctuating such abbreviations, see page 845.

TYPE OF NAME	EXAMPLES	
Countries	Mozambique Costa Rica	United States of America

(continued)

TYPE OF NAME	EXAMPLES	
Continents	North America Africa	Asia Europe
Islands	Catalina Island Greater Antilles	Isle of Pines Florida Keys
Mountains	Blue Ridge Mountains Sierra Nevada	Mount McKinley Humphrey's Peak
Other Land Forms and Features	Cape Cod Mojave Desert Mississippi Valley	Isthmus of Panama Horse Cave Point Sur
Bodies of Water	Pacific Ocean Strait of Hormuz	Great Lakes Saint Lawrence Seaway
Parks	Point Reyes National Seashore	Gates of the Arctic National Park
Roads, Highways, Streets	Route 30 Interstate 55 Pennsylvania Turnpike	Michigan Avenue North Tenth Street Morningside Drive

REFERENCE NOTE: In addresses, abbreviations such as *St., Ave., Dr.,* and *Blvd.* are capitalized. For more about abbreviations, see pages 844–845.

NOTE: The second word in a hyphenated number begins with a small letter.

EXAMPLE Forty-second Street

Words such as *city, island, street,* and *park* are capitalized only when they are part of a name.

PROPER NOUNS	COMMON NOUNS
a rodeo in Carson City	a rodeo in a nearby city
a ferry to Block Island	a ferry to a resort island
swimming in Clear Lake	swimming in the lake
along Canal Street	along a neighborhood street

MECHANICS

MEETING INDIVIDUAL NEEDS

LEARNING STYLES

Visual Learners. Have students create charts similar to the geographical names charts on pp. 822–823. Ask students to add examples to each category, using places that are familiar to them. When they finish, let them discuss their choices and check their charts for errors.

MECHANICS

EXERCISE 1 Capitalizing Words and Names Correctly

If a word or words in the following phrases should be capitalized, write the entire phrase correctly. If a phrase is correct, write *C*. Words that should be capitalized are underscored.

1. the far west
2. a city north of louisville
3. the utah salt flats
4. the cape of good hope
5. chris o'malley 5. O'Malley
6. hoover dam
7. southern illinois
8. lock the door!
9. the kalahari desert
10. the northeast
11. gulf of Alaska 12. McLeod
12. mary mcleod bethune
13. a mountain people 13. C
14. tom delaney, jr.
15. hawaiian volcanoes state park
16. a north american actor
17. san francisco bay
18. skiing on the lake 18. C
19. turned west at the corner
20. a tibetan yak 19. C
21. mexican gold
22. the delaware
23. east indian curry
24. decatur street north
25. fifty-sixth street

MECHANICS

PICTURE THIS

What a story! It's 1932, and this pilot, Amelia Earhart, has just completed a record-setting flight. She is the first woman to successfully fly solo across the Atlantic Ocean. However, due to mechanical problems and bad weather, she did not land at her intended destination, Paris. As the map on the next page shows, she has landed instead near Londonderry, Ireland. You are a newspaper reporter covering this exciting story, and Miss Earhart has granted you a brief interview. Write down some questions to ask her, and use your imagination to record her answers. In your interview, include at least five proper nouns. Be sure to capitalize each proper noun you use.

MECHANICS

PICTURE THIS

Before students begin this assignment, ask them to watch a TV interview. Then review and discuss using the *5W–How?* questions as an interview tool. Explain that good writers always research background information before conducting personal interviews. The class can share any knowledge they have acquired from outside sources about Earhart's life and accomplishments. When students finish, have them exchange their written interviews to check for correct capitalization.

Subject: Amelia Earhart's solo transatlantic flight
Audience: newspaper readers
Purpose: to inform

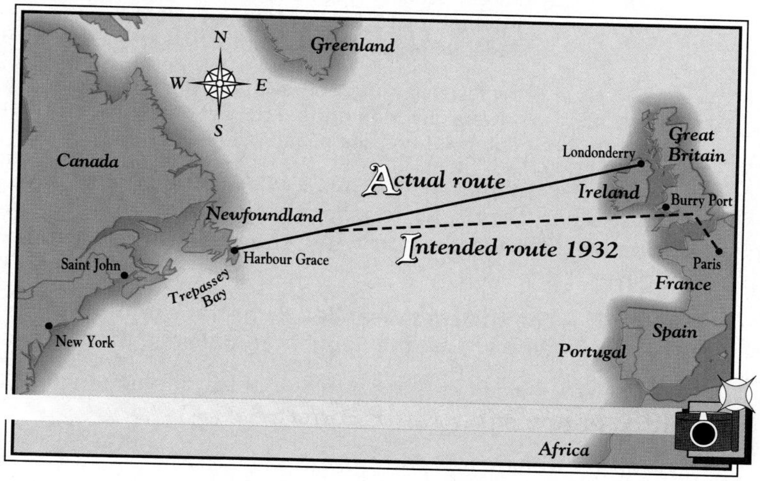

(3) Capitalize the names of organizations, teams, business firms, institutions, buildings, and government bodies.

TYPE OF NAME	EXAMPLES	
Organizations	American Dental Association Future Farmers of America National Science Foundation	
Teams	Detroit Pistons San Diego Padres	Miami Dolphins Cedar Hill Hawks
Business Firms	Roth's Optical Diesel Engine Specialists	Hip-Hop Music, Inc. American Broadcasting Corporation
Institutions, Buildings	Duke University Century Center Rialto Theater	Mayo Clinic Meadowlawn High School
Government Bodies	Department of State Atomic Energy Commission	Congress House of Representatives

MEETING **INDIVIDUAL** NEEDS

ADVANCED STUDENTS

Students who have mastered capitalization rules can research and compare the design and capabilities of Earhart's plane with those of modern aircraft. Ask them to imagine how Earhart might react to the recent developments in aviation if she were alive today. They should also consider ways in which Earhart's final trip might have been different if undertaken today. Ask students to present their reports to the class. You could have the class list all the proper nouns and proper adjectives used in each report.

A DIFFERENT APPROACH

Collect copies of different kinds of application forms such as job applications, applications for college, and applications for school grants. Applications often require only phrases to complete the forms, and because rules for sentence structure are suspended, applicants become lax about what to capitalize. Remind students that even though they may answer questions without writing complete sentences, they should use the rules for proper nouns and proper adjectives. Titles, business firms, and government bodies are important to the people evaluating applications. Have students fill out applications and check each other's forms for correct capitalization.

MECHANICS

INTEGRATING THE LANGUAGE ARTS

Mechanics and Dictionary Skills. Explain to students that acronyms are abbreviations composed of the first letters of a series of words. They are written in capital letters (FBI, IBM). Some acronyms eventually enter common usage as words and then are no longer written in capital letters. Have students look up the following words in a dictionary and report on their origins as acronyms:

1. radar [radio detecting and ranging]
2. sonar [sound navigation and ranging]
3. scuba [self-contained underwater breathing apparatus]
4. laser [light amplification (by) stimulated emission of radiation]

A recent trend has been for organizations to create acronyms in which the letters form or sound like an existing word. Share these examples:

NOW (National Organization for Women)
MADD (Mothers Against Drunk Driving)
SADD (Students Against Drunk Driving)

Have the class discuss why these organizations chose those particular words and ask students to give other examples of this kind of acronym.

MECHANICS

REFERENCE NOTE: The names of organizations, businesses, and government bodies are often abbreviated to a series of capital letters.

EXAMPLES	**P**arent-**T**eacher **A**ssociation	**PTA**
	International **B**usiness **M**achines	**IBM**
	Federal **B**ureau of **I**nvestigation	**FBI**

Usually the letters in such abbreviations are not followed by periods, but always check an up-to-date dictionary to be sure. For more about abbreviations, see pages 844–845.

Do not capitalize words such as *democratic, republican,* and *socialist* when they refer to principles or forms of government. Capitalize such words only when they refer to a specific political party.

EXAMPLES The citizens demanded **d**emocratic reforms.
Who will be the **R**epublican nominee for governor?

The word *party* in the name of a political party may be capitalized or not; either way is correct.

EXAMPLE **Democratic party**
or
Democratic Party

REFERENCE NOTE: Do not capitalize words such as *building, hospital, theater, high school, university,* and *post office* unless they are part of a proper noun. For more on the differences between common nouns and proper nouns, see pages 553–554 and 820–821.

MECHANICS

(4) Capitalize the names of historical events and periods, special events, and holidays and other calendar items.

TYPE OF NAME	EXAMPLES	
Historical Events and Periods	Boston Tea Party Battle of Saratoga Reign of Terror	Middle Ages French Revolution Mesozoic Era
Special Events	Olympics New York Marathon	Ohio State Fair Pan-American Games
Holidays and Other Calendar Items	Wednesday September Kwanzaa	Fourth of July Memorial Day Mother's Day

NOTE: Do not capitalize the name of a season unless the season is being personified or unless it is used in a proper noun.

EXAMPLES The **w**inter was unusually warm.
Overnight, **W**inter crept in, trailing her snowy veil.
We plan to attend the school's **W**inter **C**arnival.

(5) Capitalize the names of nationalities, races, and peoples.

EXAMPLES **Lithuanian** **Haitian** **Jewish** **Asian**
Caucasian **Hispanic** **Bantu** **Zuni**

(6) Capitalize the brand names of business products.

EXAMPLES **B**orden milk **C**olonial bread **Z**enith television

Notice that the noun that may follow a brand name is not capitalized: a Xerox **m**achine.

(7) Capitalize the names of ships, monuments, awards, planets, and any other particular places, things, or events.

TYPE OF NAME	EXAMPLES	
Ships, Trains	*Monitor*	*Zephyr*
Aircraft and Spacecraft	*Air Force One* **M**inuteman	*Columbia* *Enola Gay*
Monuments, Memorials, Awards	**N**avaho **N**ational **M**onument **M**ount **R**ushmore **N**ational **M**emorial **C**ongressional **M**edal of **H**onor	
Planets, Stars, Constellations	**J**upiter **U**rsa **M**inor	**R**igel **L**ittle **D**ipper

NOTE: Do not capitalize the words *sun* and *moon*. Do not capitalize the word *earth* unless it is used along with the names of other heavenly bodies that are capitalized.

EXAMPLES The **m**oon reflects light from the **s**un.
This orchid grows wild in only one place on **e**arth.
Venus is closer to the sun than **E**arth is.

MECHANICS

MEETING INDIVIDUAL NEEDS

STUDENTS WITH SPECIAL NEEDS

Students with learning disabilities often have difficulty processing information. They frequently benefit from the use of mnemonic aids, such as well designed charts, guides, and handbooks that make use of strong visual presentations. Because this chapter is interrupted by exercises and examples, you might want to design a chart that includes all the rules, a handbook that serves as a glossary of capitalization rules, or some other visual memory device. You might also pair students with students who can read through the rules and effectively discuss the exceptions with them.

MECHANICS

SEGMENT 3 *(pp. 828–836)*

LANGUAGES, SPECIFIC COURSE NAMES, AND TITLES Rules 28d, 28e

OBJECTIVE

- To capitalize words, names and titles correctly

Teacher's ResourceBank™

RESOURCES

LANGUAGES, SPECIFIC COURSE NAMES, AND TITLES

- Titles 322

QUICK REMINDER

Write the following sentences on the chalkboard and ask students to correct the capitalization errors:

1. I admire the way doctor stephen hawking has continued scientific research despite his serious disease. [Doctor Stephen Hawking]
2. Is uncle bill coming for sunday dinner? [Uncle Bill, Sunday]
3. This year I am taking algebra, english, and biology I. [English, Biology I.]
4. I heard ex-president carter speak at my sister's graduation. [ex-President Carter]

EXERCISE 2

Teaching Note. Although departments and other organizational divisions are often capitalized inside the offices of an organization, there is no general rule requiring capitalization for these bodies.

MECHANICS

MECHANICS

28d. Do *not* capitalize the names of school subjects, except for names of languages and course names followed by a number.

EXAMPLES				
	history	**a**rt	**p**hysics	**g**eometry
	Spanish	**L**atin	**A**lgebra I	**C**hemistry II

NOTE: Do not capitalize the class names *senior, junior, sophomore,* and *freshman* unless they are part of a proper noun.

EXAMPLES The **j**uniors are planning a surprise for **S**enior **D**ay.
The **F**reshman **F**ollies was a big success.

EXERCISE 2 Capitalizing Words and Names Correctly

Write the following words and phrases, using capital letters where they are needed. If a word or phrase is correct, write *C*. Words that should be capitalized are underscored.

1. the science department
2. north atlantic treaty organization
3. st. patrick's cathedral
4. *city of new orleans* (train)
5. the federal reserve bank
6. the normandy invasion
7. classes in auto mechanics 7. C
8. the world cup
9. chinese cuisine
10. cherokee history
11. midtown traffic 11. C
12. jones and drake, inc.
13. spaceflight to mars
14. on labor day
15. *ariadne* (boat)
16. at holiday inn
17. the louisiana world exposition
18. early summer 18. C
19. gold medal flour
20. an american history class

REVIEW A Proofreading a Paragraph for Correct Capitalization

For each sentence in the following paragraph, write the word or words that should be capitalized. If a word is improperly capitalized, write the word correctly. Words that should be lowercased or capitalized are underscored.

EXAMPLE [1] Even if you don't know much about horses, you can likely appreciate the beauty of the arabian horses shown on the next page.
1. *Arabian*

[1] Perhaps no other breed of horses can conjure up such images of romance as these beautiful animals from Northern

REVIEW A

OBJECTIVE

- To proofread a paragraph for correct capitalization

Africa. [2] Their distinctive and colorful trappings bring to mind the nomadic lives of wandering tribes and the exciting exploits of their bedouin chieftains. [3] Smaller and lighter than many breeds, with proportionally large hooves, these horses are perfectly suited to the hot sands of the Sahara or the Arabian desert. [4] Some evidence suggests that north African peoples may have been breeding these horses as long ago as seven thousand years. [5] Arabians characteristically have elegant heads and necks as well as large, lustrous eyes, features that have been prized by breeders all over the Earth. [6] These horses have played their part in many historical events far from the Continent of Africa. [7] During the Revolutionary war, for instance, George Washington rode a gray said to be the offspring of a famous Arabian stallion. [8] America's love affair with the Arabian horse has continued from the early days of our nation right through to the Present. [9] Today, the Arabian Horse club has thousands of names on its roster. [10] Some of the newer importers include W. R. Brown of Berlin, New Hampshire, and Spencer Bade of Fall river, Massachusetts.

Arabian horses in action.

MECHANICS

VISUAL CONNECTIONS

Exploring the Subject. The Arabian horse is known to have existed in the Middle East as early as the 7th century A.D., but its actual history has been obscured by many legends. The race horses known as Thoroughbreds trace their origins to crossbreeding between European and Arabian horses.

MEETING
INDIVIDUAL
NEEDS

LEP/ESL

General Strategies. You may need to explain the term *title* to students. Before you begin your explanation, be sure students understand that this word is used for both people and documents. Students might get a clearer picture if you draw a stick figure, a book, and a painting on the chalkboard and show how each has a title. For example, you may write *Dr. Nguyen* under the stick figure, *Shadows on the Rock* under the book, and *The Horse Fair* under the painting.

LESS-ADVANCED STUDENTS

When giving examples of titles to capitalize, try to use names and titles that are familiar to students. These may include names or titles of businesses, teachers, and public buildings. You may want to brainstorm with the students and list their suggestions on the chalkboard.

MECHANICS

28e. Capitalize titles.

(1) Capitalize a title belonging to a particular person when it comes before the person's name.

EXAMPLES **General Davis** **Dr. Ramírez** **President Kennedy**

In general, do not capitalize a title used alone or following a name. Some titles, however, are by tradition capitalized. If you are unsure of whether or not to capitalize a title, check in a dictionary.

EXAMPLES Who is the **g**overnor of Kansas?
Sherian Grace Cadoria, a **b**rigadier **g**eneral, is the highest-ranking African American woman in the U.S. Armed Forces.
The **S**peaker of the **H**ouse rose to greet the **Q**ueen of England.

A title is usually capitalized when it is used alone in direct address.

EXAMPLES Have you reached your decision, **G**overnor?
We're honored to welcome you, **M**s. **M**ayor.
Please come in, **S**ir [or **s**ir].

NOTE: For special emphasis or clarity, writers sometimes capitalize a title used alone or following a person's name.

EXAMPLES The **G**overnor was in the last car in the parade.
Did the **P**resident veto the bill?

Do not capitalize *ex–*, *–elect*, *former*, or *late* when they are used with a title.

EXAMPLES **ex-G**overnor Walsh the president-**e**lect

(2) Capitalize words showing family relationships when used with a person's name but *not* when preceded by a possessive.

EXAMPLES **A**unt **A**my **U**ncle **H**ector **G**randmother **G**uttman
my **s**ister your **c**ousin **T**helma's **n**ephew

(3) Capitalize the first and last words and all important words in titles of books, periodicals, poems, stories, plays, historical documents, movies, radio and television programs, works of art, and musical compositions.

MECHANICS

Unimportant words in a title include

- articles: *a, an, the*
- short prepositions (fewer than five letters): *of, to, in, for, from, with*
- coordinating conjunctions: *and, but, for, nor, or, so, yet*

TYPE OF TITLE	EXAMPLES
Books	***The Call of the Wild*** ***The Way to Rainy Mountain*** ***One Hundred Years of Solitude***
Periodicals	***Car and Driver*** ***Louisville Courier-Journal***
Poems	**"Tonight I Can Write"** **"Most Satisfied by Snow"**
Stories	**"In Another Country"** **"The Catch in the Shadow of the Sunrise"**
Plays	***Song of Sheba*** ***Watch on the Rhine*** ***The Importance of Being Earnest***
Historical Documents	**Declaration of Independence** **Mayflower Compact** **Treaty of Versailles**
Movies	***Children of a Lesser God*** ***No Place to Be Somebody*** ***Come See the Paradise***
Radio and Television Programs	**"Adventures in Good Music"** ***In Living Color*** ***WKRP in Cincinnati***
Works of Art	***Woman Before a Mirror*** ***Prelude to Farewell***
Musical Compositions	**"Lift Every Voice and Sing"** ***Into the Light*** ***Three Places in New England***

MECHANICS

A DIFFERENT APPROACH

Have each student in a team of four quickly list as many titles as possible in response to your prompts. Prompts might include titles of books, songs, movies, poems, plays, and works of art. After two minutes have students on each team confer and compile a list of the members' responses. Then have teams tally the number of responses in each category. You could declare a winning team and winners in each category.

COMMON ERROR

Problem. Students might be confused about when to capitalize familial titles that follow possessive forms.

Solution. Remind students that words for family relationships aren't capitalized when they follow possessive forms unless the person's name is included. Write these examples on the chalkboard and note the difference between them. "That is my uncle." "This is my Uncle Ed." Ask students to suggest other examples.

MECHANICS

INTEGRATING THE LANGUAGE ARTS

Literature Link. In literature, students will frequently encounter the names of gods and goddesses from Greek and Roman mythology. You may want to have students do research and prepare charts showing the names these two cultures gave to deities that oversaw various regions (earth, sea, sky) or activities (love, war, agriculture). Have partners exchange charts and check for correct capitalization. Tell students to save their charts for reference when reading literature.

MECHANICS

NOTE: The article *the* is often written before a title but is not capitalized unless it is the first word of the title.

EXAMPLES **the** *Austin American-Statesman*
The Atlantic

REFERENCE NOTE: For information about which titles should be italicized and which should be enclosed in quotation marks, see pages 875–876 and 882–883.

(4) Capitalize the names of religions and their followers, holy days and celebrations, holy writings, and specific deities.

TYPE OF NAME	EXAMPLES	
Religions and Followers	Christianity Hinduism Judaism	Buddhist Muslim Presbyterian
Holy Days and Celebrations	Epiphany Ramadan Rosh Hashanah	Easter Passover Potlatch
Holy Writings	the Bible the Koran the Talmud	Rig-Veda Genesis the Pentateuch
Specific Deities	Allah Brahma	God the Holy Spirit

The words *god* and *goddess* are not capitalized when they refer to the deities of ancient mythology. The names of specific mythological deities are capitalized, however.

EXAMPLE **The Greek god of the sea was Poseidon.**

NOTE: Some writers capitalize all pronouns that refer to a deity. Others capitalize such pronouns only if necessary to prevent confusion.

EXAMPLE Through Moses, God commanded the pharaoh to let His people go.

MECHANICS

REVIEWS B and C

OBJECTIVES

- To write a press release that includes correctly capitalized titles
- To proofread paragraphs for correct capitalization

EXERCISE 3 Capitalizing Names and Titles Correctly

Write the following items, using capital letters where they are needed. If an item is correct, write *C*. Words that should be capitalized are underscored.

1. the washington post
2. ex-senator Margaret Chase Smith
3. soul train (TV program) 4. C
4. captain of the fencing team
5. emancipation proclamation
6. the first chapter in *the grapes of wrath*
7. the teachings of islam
8. the late Bessie Smith 8. C
9. "Come with me, dad."
10. the new testament

REVIEW B Using Capital Letters in a Press Release

You and your classmates have written and produced a play about the plight of homeless people in America. The money that you raise from the sale of tickets will be donated to a local homeless shelter and job-training program. Because you are eager to raise as much money as possible, you have decided to issue a press release to local newspapers and radio stations to announce your class's theatrical debut. Write a short paragraph that includes the following information:

Title of the play
Date(s) and time(s) of the performance(s)
Where the performance will take place
Name(s) of the lead player(s)
The name of the organization that will receive the profits from the play

REVIEW C Proofreading a Paragraph for Correct Capitalization

For each sentence in the following paragraphs, change lowercase letters to capitals and capital letters to lowercase as necessary. If a sentence is correct, write *C*.

Words that should be lowercased or capitalized are underscored.

[1] Among the many unusual scenes that captain Christopher Columbus witnessed in the New World was that of native Hispaniolans playing games with balls made of latex, the white liquid that oozes from plants like the rubber tree, guayule, milkweed, and dandelion. [2] Latex balls were also used by the mayas, but unlike the ball games that you may have played

MECHANICS

COOPERATIVE LEARNING

You might divide the class into groups of three or four to complete **Review B.** Have each group use personal experiences to brainstorm for ideas. Each member should contribute two sentences to the group's paragraph. Ask each group to create a poster that can accompany its press release.

ANSWERS

Review B

Paragraphs will vary, but each should include information that is correctly capitalized. Students might use theatrical reviews or the entertainment sections of news magazines and local newspapers for ideas and format.

MECHANICS

with your Brother or Sister, Mayan games were sacred rituals. [3] According to the *Book Of counsel*, an ancient Mayan document, the games reenacted the story of twins who became immortal. [4] Ball games were so important to the Mayan culture that, along with stately masks of their gods, Mayan artists rendered statues of ball players, and builders erected large stone stadiums for playing. [5] Although columbus did not note his encounters with latex, other explorers did, and one recorded the fascinating use of Latex shown here—the Mayan practice of coating their feet with a protective layer of the milky liquid. 4. C

[6] Latex does not hold up well in extreme temperatures, and it was used in europe only for rubbing out pencil marks (hence the term *rubber*), until Charles Goodyear became fascinated with the substance and declared that "elastic gum" glorified god. [7] Goodyear's discovery of vulcanization enabled the successful commercial production of rubber and earned him the public admiration of emperor Napoleon III. [8] In the next decades Brazil increased its rubber production thousands of times over, as Eric R. Wolf points out in *Europe And The People Without History*. [9] Indeed, rubber became such an essential part of our lives that the U.S. army once asked a young Major named Eisenhower to study the matter. [10] Wisely, the Late President Eisenhower advised the military to maintain its own source of this valuable commodity.

MECHANICS

WRITING APPLICATION

OBJECTIVE

- To write a pen-pal letter that uses correct capitalization

WRITING APPLICATION

Using Capitalization in a Letter

Why does one person eat with a knife and fork, another with chopsticks, and still another with his or her hands? Each one is following the social conventions of his or her culture. Like conventions of social behavior, conventions of language are practices that have become standardized over time. For example, the conventions of capitalization taught in this chapter are important because readers of English everywhere expect capital letters to be used in certain ways. Nonstandard capitalization may confuse readers by suggesting a meaning that wasn't intended. Compare the following sentences. How does the use of capital letters and lowercase letters affect the meaning of each?

EXAMPLES Mom and I spend each New Year's Day watching the rose bowl with our relatives in west Virginia.
Mom and I spend each New Year's Day watching the Rose Bowl with our relatives in West Virginia.

WRITING ACTIVITY

You've just started corresponding with a teenager in Japan. You and your pen pal are eager to learn more about each other's cultures, including customs, holidays, food, schools, and recreational activities. Write a letter to your pen pal describing some custom or practice that is unique to American culture or special to your family. In your letter, follow the rules of capitalization given in this chapter.

Prewriting List some typically American holidays, customs, and practices that you think might interest your pen pal. For each item on your list, brainstorm as many descriptive details as you can. For example, if you're describing the Fourth of July, you'll want to give specific details about how you celebrate the holiday—what you eat, whether you watch fireworks, how your town decorates for the holiday, and so forth. Choose one item from your list to write about. You may want to use an encyclopedia to look up any historical information you're not sure about.

MECHANICS

WRITING APPLICATION

You may wish to refer your students to **Chapters 6** and **7** for information about writing to inform and to explain, as well as about the use of descriptive detail. Encourage students to research the origins of national or local holidays. They might also ask relatives how their own family traditions began.

CRITICAL THINKING
Analysis

Remind students that their pen pals will probably be interested in aspects of American culture and customs that we take for granted. In the prewriting stage, students could list as many holidays, customs, and practices as possible. Once they have selected a topic from this list, students could imagine that they are Japanese and that they have no knowledge of this experience. Students should select precise, descriptive details that will give their pen pals the feeling of participating in the event.

MECHANICS

SEGMENT 4 *(pp. 836–839)*

REVIEW: POSTTEST

OBJECTIVE

- To capitalize words and phrases correctly

WRITING

Remind students that their audience will probably not be familiar with American idioms and colloquialisms. The literal translations of these expressions often do not convey the meaning intended. Descriptive phrases must be clear and precise.

EVALUATING AND REVISING

If your students use style-check or grammar-check features on computers when they are revising, remind them that these programs are not foolproof. Some systems may incorrectly question the correct use of capital letters in proper nouns and adjectives. These systems may also incorrectly identify sentence beginnings in some constructions.

Writing As you write your draft, organize your information clearly. Add facts, examples, and details as you think of them. Use clear, straightforward language, and try to avoid colloquialisms and idioms that your friend may not recognize. (For more about colloquialisms and idioms, see pages 486–487.) Be sure to capitalize proper nouns, including the names of geographical areas, historical events, and holidays.

Evaluating and Revising Put yourself in the place of your pen pal, who may not be familiar with the custom you're describing. Be sure you've included enough information to help your pen pal understand the meaning behind the holiday or other special event. Also add descriptive, sensory details to help your reader vividly picture the celebration or custom.

Proofreading Proofread your letter for any errors in grammar, usage, and mechanics. Take special care with capitalization of proper nouns. Be sure that you have followed the guidelines on page 1004 for writing personal letters.

MECHANICS

Review: Posttest

Capitalizing Words and Phrases Correctly

For each of the following sentences, write the words that should be capitalized. If a sentence is correct, write *C*.

EXAMPLE **1. The rotary club has invited representative William Bashone to speak at tonight's annual banquet.**
1. ***Rotary Club; Representative***

1. According to Zack Johnson, the company's representative, you shouldn't buy just any car; you should buy a saturn.
2. One of the earliest cars made by Henry Ford was called the Model T; it had a four-cylinder, twenty-horsepower engine. 2. C
3. On our vacation we toured several states in the south.

4. Johnson's bake shop and deli is just north of state street on highway 143.
5. Before you can take this computer course, you must pass algebra II.
6. Aren't they planning a parade to celebrate Martin Luther King, jr., day?
7. Because we cheered so loudly at the special olympics, ms. Andrews made Bill and me honorary cheerleaders for her special education class.
8. In a nationally televised press conference, the president warned that he would veto any tax increase.
9. The british poet Ted Hughes was married to Sylvia Plath, who was an american writer.
10. The only man in American history who was not elected to be vice-president or president, yet held both positions, is ex-president Gerald Ford.
11. My mother asked me to walk to the supermarket and buy a quart container of farmingbury milk and two pounds of pinto beans.
12. When we toured eastern Tennessee, we visited the Oak Ridge Laboratory, where atomic research was carried out during World War II. 12. C
13. The Spanish-american Club has planned a festival for late summer; it will be held at the north end of the city.
14. If you are looking for the best apples in the state, follow route 14 until you see the signs for Peacock's Orchard.
15. In a controversial debate on the Panama canal, the United States voted to relinquish its control of the canal to the Panamanian government.
16. When my Aunt Janice visited England last summer, she toured buckingham palace and tried to catch a glimpse of queen Elizabeth.
17. Mayor-elect Sabrena Willis will speak to the public about her proposals to upgrade the city's bilingual education program. 17. C
18. Earl and Jamie were lucky to get tickets to see the Indigo girls at the Erwin center.
19. When spring arrives, I know it's time to start thinking about where to look for a summer job. 19. C
20. Although the east room of the White house is now used for press conferences, it was once a place where Abigail Adams aired the president's laundry.

MECHANICS

REVIEW: POSTTEST

Teaching Note. In the past the word *president* was always capitalized when it referred to the head of a nation. However, most newspapers capitalize the word only as a formal title before names. There may be some difference of opinion on questions 8, 10, and 20. If disagreement occurs, refer to **Rule 28e** on p. 830 and have students verbalize the reasoning for their choices.

MECHANICS

A DIFFERENT APPROACH

Divide the class into groups of four (two students on one team and two students on another). Team A should give a common-noun prompt, such as *woman, building, book,* or *song.* Team B should answer with a proper noun in that category. Then Team B should give a prompt and Team A should answer.

MECHANICS

MECHANICS

SUMMARY STYLE REVIEW	
Names of Persons	
Mrs. Martin A. LaForge, Sr.	a neighbor
Louise Brown	a girl in my class
Mr. Peter Echohawk	a math teacher
Geographical Names	
Sioux City	a city in Iowa
Orange County	a county in Florida
Staten Island	an island in New York Harbor
Allegheny Mountains	a mountain range
Pacific Ocean	across the ocean
Forty-third Street	a one-way street
Sequoia National Park	a national park
in the East, North, Midwest	heading east, north, south
Organizations, Business Firms, Institutions, Government Bodies	
New York Philharmonic	a symphony orchestra
Something from the Oven	a bakery
Madison High School	a large high school
Supreme Court	a district court
Department of the Interior	a department of government
Historical Events and Periods, Special Events, Calendar Items	
the Korean War	a veteran of the war
the Stone Age	a prehistoric age
the Super Bowl	a championship game
Father's Day	a national holiday
April, July, October, January	spring, summer, autumn, winter
Nationalities, Races, Religions	
Cambodian	a nationality
Caucasian	a race
Judaism	a religion
God	myths about the Roman gods
Brand Names	
Stutz Bearcat	an antique automobile
Pac-Man	a video game

(continued)

SUMMARY STYLE REVIEW *(continued)*	
Other Particular Places, Things, Events, Awards	
***N**iña*	a ship
***M**etroliner*	a train
***G**alileo*	a spacecraft
Springarn **M**edal	an award
the **M**ilky **W**ay	a galaxy
Earth, **V**enus, **S**aturn	from the earth
the **C**oronado **M**emorial	a **m**emorial in **A**rizona
Senior **P**rom	a **s**enior in high school
Silver **S**tar	a **m**edal for heroism
Specific Courses, Languages	
Bookkeeping I	after **b**ookkeeping class
Spanish	a foreign language
Geometry II	a **g**eometry test
Titles	
Mayor **D**ixon	a **m**ayor
President of the **U**nited **S**tates	**p**resident of the club
the **D**uke of **E**dinburgh	a **d**uke's title
Aunt **R**osa	my **a**unt
***T**he **P**iano **L**esson*	a **p**lay
the ***O**akland **T**ribune*	a daily **n**ewspaper
Holy **B**ible	a religious **b**ook

MECHANICS

MECHANICS

SEGMENT 1 *(pp. 840–841)*

DIAGNOSTIC TEST

OBJECTIVES

- To correct sentences by adding or deleting end marks and commas
- To revise a paragraph for correct comma usage

Teacher's ResourceBank™

RESOURCES

FOR THE WHOLE CHAPTER

CHAPTER OVERVIEW

This chapter begins with a discussion of end marks—periods, question marks, and exclamation points. The chapter then discusses the use of commas with series, independent clauses, nonessential clauses and phrases, introductory elements, and interrupters. The chapter also discusses the conventional use of commas in dates, addresses, and letters. In the **Writing Application** students practice the correct use of interrupters by writing brief essays about their favorite fictional characters.

You may want to use this chapter when your students need a review of punctuation. During the proofreading stage of composition, have students refer to the chapter for specific problems. It may also be useful to review the chapter when students prepare to take standardized tests.

MECHANICS

MECHANICS

29 PUNCTUATION

End Marks and Commas

Diagnostic Test

A. Correcting Sentences by Adding or Deleting End Marks and Commas

Add or delete end marks or commas to correct each of the following sentences.

EXAMPLE **1.** Do you think that it will rain today Brian.
1. *Do you think that it will rain today, Brian?*

1. Gov. Jameston, a well-known Democrat, does not plan to run for another term.
2. This year, I am taking courses in English, Spanish, algebra, and history.

3. When I joined the staff of the newspaper, I was taught to write short, powerful headlines.
4. The essay, that Ms. Hughes assigned yesterday, is due next Monday.
5. Would you send me a postcard from Hawaii while you're there on vacation?
6. Bravo, what a great solo!
7. Geometry, which I took last year, was not an easy subject for me.
8. Peg asked, "Have you read, for example, *Animal Farm* by George Orwell"?
9. Please send this package to Mrs. Rose Sanchez, 116 East Elm Street, Allentown, P, A, 18001.
10. The letter was dated June 16, 1993, and was mailed from Washington, D.C.,

B. Proofreading a Paragraph for Correct Comma Usage

Add or delete commas to correct each sentence in the following paragraph.

[11] One of the most dangerous assignments for a pilot is to fly over the cold, barren stretches of snow and ice north of the Arctic Circle. **[12]** Ellen Paneok, an Inupiat pilot, should know. **[13]** Even before she learned to drive a car, Paneok was flying over the tundra far from her hometown of Kotzebue, in Alaska. **[14]** Traveling in the Arctic, a bush pilot must be alert to the dangers of fatigue, vertigo, and the northern lights. **[15]** Caught in dense fog or a snowstorm, a pilot can easily lose his or her bearings and become a victim of vertigo. **[16]** Furthermore, the pilot, who stares at the northern lights too long, can wind up buried in a snowbank. **[17]** Paneok, therefore, keeps a sharp lookout for objects on the ground. **[18]** A glimpse of a caribou, a patch of brush, a jutting ice dome, etc., will help her regain her sense of direction and will also break the boredom. **[19]** Soaring over the tundra, she provides many rural people with produce, and transportation. **[20]** Paneok loves to fly, for the beauty of Alaska, and the needs of her fellow Alaskans make the risk worthwhile.

MECHANICS

USING THE DIAGNOSTIC TEST

Use the results of this test to determine how much instruction and practice students need to use end marks and commas correctly.

MECHANICS

SEGMENT 2 *(pp. 842–846)*

END MARKS Rules 29a–29e

OBJECTIVES

- To correct sentences by adding appropriate end marks
- To write dialogue for a comic strip and to use the appropriate end marks

Teacher's ResourceBank™

RESOURCES

END MARKS

• Using End Marks	331

QUICK REMINDER

Ask each student to compose a question, a statement, an exclamation, a request, and a command and to punctuate each sentence correctly. You might write examples like the following sentences on the chalkboard:

1. What sports do you enjoy? (question)
2. I enjoy soccer, tennis, and football. (statement)
3. What great games they are! (exclamation)
4. Please remember the rules. (request)
5. Kick the ball. (command)

Point out to students that the period and the exclamation point are sometimes interchangeable, depending upon the level of emotion expressed in the sentence.

MECHANICS

In speaking, the tone and pitch of your voice, the pauses in your speech, and the gestures and expressions you use all help to make your meaning clear. In writing, marks of punctuation such as end marks and commas tell readers where these verbal and nonverbal cues occur. However, if the meaning of a sentence is unclear in the first place, punctuation will not usually clarify it. Whenever you find yourself struggling to punctuate a sentence correctly, take a closer look at your arrangement of phrases or your choice of words. Often you can eliminate the punctuation problem by recasting the sentence.

End Marks

29a. A statement (or declarative sentence) is followed by a period.

EXAMPLE October is Hispanic Heritage Month in the United States**.**

29b. A question (or interrogative sentence) is followed by a question mark.

EXAMPLES Did you get the leading role**?**
When is your first performance**?**

(1) Do not use a question mark after a declarative sentence containing an indirect question.

EXAMPLE Katie wondered who would win the award**.**

(2) Orders and requests are often put in question form even when they aren't actually questions. In that case, they may be followed by either a period or a question mark.

EXAMPLES Will you please complete this brief questionnaire**?**
or
Will you please complete this brief questionnaire**.**

(3) A question mark should be placed inside the closing quotation marks when the quotation itself is a question. Otherwise, a question mark should be placed outside the closing quotation marks.

EXAMPLES To avoid answering a personal question, simply reply, "Why do you ask**?**" [The quotation is a question.]
Did Mr. Shields actually say, "Your reports are due in three days"**?** [The quotation is not a question, but the sentence as a whole is.]

29c. An imperative sentence is followed by either a period or an exclamation point.

EXAMPLES Turn the music down, please**.**
Turn the music down**!**

An imperative sentence may be stated as a question. However, since its purpose is to give a command or make a request, it should be followed by a period or an exclamation point.

EXAMPLES May we get through, please**.**
Will you let us through**!**

29d. An exclamation is followed by an exclamation point.

EXAMPLES I can't believe that**!**
Don't cross that line**!**

An exclamation mark should be placed inside the closing quotation marks when the quotation itself is an exclamation. Otherwise, it should be placed outside the quotation marks.

EXAMPLES "Down in front**!**" yelled the crowd.
Ms. Chen couldn't have said, "No homework"**!**

REFERENCE NOTE: For information on how sentences are classified according to purpose, see rule 18m on pages 597–598. For more discussion on the placement of end marks with closing quotation marks, see rule 30m (4) on pages 879–880.

An interjection at the beginning of a sentence is usually followed by a comma.

USUAL Hey**,** don't do that**!**
INFREQUENT Hey**!** Don't do that**!**

Notice in the examples above that an exclamation point may be used after a single word as well as after a sentence.

NOTE: Do not overuse exclamation points. Use an exclamation mark only when a statement is obviously emphatic.

MECHANICS

MEETING INDIVIDUAL NEEDS

LEP/ESL

Spanish. In Spanish, exclamation points and question marks are used at the beginnings of sentences as well as at the ends, and they are inverted in the beginning position. Some students may need reminders to become accustomed to the English use of exclamation points and question marks only at the ends of sentences.

LEARNING STYLES

Auditory Learners. It may be easier for some students to hear the differences in sentence types than to recognize them visually. Give students oral examples of each type. Then have students identify each sentence type and its proper end mark.

CRITICAL THINKING

Analysis

End marks let readers know whether the writer is making a statement, asking a question, or expressing strong feelings. Write the following sentences on the chalkboard:

1. I made the highest grade.
2. I made the highest grade?
3. I made the highest grade!

Ask students to analyze and explain how the purpose and meaning of the sentence changes according to the end mark used.

MECHANICS

EXERCISE 1 **Correcting Sentences by Adding End Marks**

Write each word that should be followed by an end mark in the following sentences; then add the appropriate end mark. If quotation marks should precede or follow the end mark, write them in the proper place.

EXAMPLES
1. Mom asked, "When did you receive the letter
1. *letter?"*
2. Terrific What a throw
2. *Terrific! throw!*

1. When do you want to take your vacation?
2. I did have enough money to go to the movies.
3. Wow! Did you see that liftoff?
4. Willie, are you ready to give your report on Thurgood Marshall?
5. Carefully set the Ming vase on the display stand.
6. Mom wants to know why you did not buy a newspaper.
7. What a downpour!
8. Leave the theater immediately!
9. He yelled across the field, "Hurry!"
10. Didn't you hear her say "I'm not ready yet"?

29e. An abbreviation is usually followed by a period.

MECHANICS

TYPES OF ABBREVIATIONS	EXAMPLES		
Personal Names	Susan B. Anthony S. I. Hayakawa		
Organizations and Companies	Assn. Co.	Corp. Inc.	Ltd.
Titles Used with Names	Dr. Jr.	Mr. Mrs.	Ms. Ph. D.
Units of Measure	ft. in.	oz. qt.	mi. yd.
Time of Day	A.M. *(or* a.m.*)*	P.M. *(or* p.m.*)*	
Years	B.C. *(written after the date)* A.D. *(written before the date)*		
Addresses	Ave. Blvd.	Dr. Pkwy.	Rd. St.
States	Ark. Calif.	Fla. Penn.	S. Car. N. Mex.

NOTE: Two-letter state codes are used only when the ZIP code is included. The state codes are not followed by periods.

EXAMPLE Springfield, MA 01101

When an abbreviation that ends with a period is the last word in a statement, do not add another period as an end mark. *Do* add a question mark or an exclamation point if one is needed.

EXAMPLES Mr. Rodríguez lives in Fargo, N. Dak.
Isn't he originally from Dover, Del.?

Some common abbreviations are written without periods.

EXAMPLES AC, CORE, FBI, GI, IOU, MTV, OK, PC, ROTC, SOS
cc, db, ft, l, lb, kw, ml, psi, rpm

NOTE: As a rule, an abbreviation is capitalized only if the words that it stands for are capitalized. If you're not sure whether to use periods with an abbreviation or whether to capitalize it, check a dictionary.

MECHANICS

COMMON ERROR

Problem. All states can be abbreviated in two different ways, but only one of the abbreviations uses a period. Students often punctuate state abbreviations incorrectly because of confusion.

Solution. Display the following list used by the United States Postal Service for students to refer to throughout the year. Remind students that the two-letter abbreviations are followed by ZIP codes, not by periods.

AL Alabama
AK Alaska
AZ Arizona
AR Arkansas
CA California
CO Colorado
CT Connecticut
DE Delaware
FL Florida
GA Georgia
HI Hawaii
ID Idaho
IL Illinois
IN Indiana
IA Iowa
KS Kansas
KY Kentucky
LA Louisiana
ME Maine
MD Maryland
MA Massachusetts
MI Michigan
MN Minnesota
MS Mississippi
MO Missouri
MT Montana
NE Nebraska
NV Nevada
NH New Hampshire
NJ New Jersey
NM New Mexico
NY New York
NC North Carolina
ND North Dakota
OH Ohio
OK Oklahoma
OR Oregon
PA Pennsylvania
RI Rhode Island
SC South Carolina
SD South Dakota
TN Tennessee
TX Texas
UT Utah
VT Vermont
VA Virginia
WA Washington
WV West Virginia
WI Wisconsin
WY Wyoming

MECHANICS

SEGMENT 3 *(pp. 846–861)*

COMMAS Rules 29f–29m

OBJECTIVE

- To correct sentences by adding commas

PICTURE THIS

You may want to allow students to draw their own cartoons and to develop dialogue for them, or students could take an existing comic strip and replace the dialogue with their own. If students do the latter, be sure that they create their own dialogue.

Teacher's ResourceBank™

RESOURCES

COMMAS

MECHANICS

QUICK REMINDER

Write the following sentences on the chalkboard without commas and have students tell where commas should be added:

1. We need to ride to the stadium [,] buy our tickets [,] and find our seats before the show starts.
2. The show starts at noon [,] but the bus leaves at 9:00.
3. Reginald [,] the band's drummer [,] grew up in my home town.
4. Running for the bus [,] Jefferson dropped his backpack.
5. In addition to losing his tickets [,] he lost his bus fare.

MECHANICS

PICTURE THIS

You're a cartoonist developing a comic strip for the funny papers. You've drawn these cartoon frames; now you need to add the dialogue in word balloons. Write at least one line of dialogue for each frame. In your comic strip, correctly punctuate at least one of each of the four types of sentences—declarative, interrogative, imperative, and exclamatory. Also, begin at least one sentence with an interjection.

Subject: a cartoon
Audience: readers of the funny papers
Purpose: to entertain

Commas

Items in a Series

29f. Use commas to separate items in a series.

EXAMPLES The basketball coach recommended that she practice dribbling, shooting, weaving, and passing. [words]
We can meet before English class, during lunch, or after school. [phrases]
After school I must make sure that my room is clean, that my little brother is home from his piano lesson, and that the garbage has been emptied. [clauses]

(1) When *and, or,* or *nor* joins the last two items in a series, you may omit the comma before the conjunction. Never omit the final comma, however, if such an omission would make the sentence unclear.

UNCLEAR Phyllis, Ken and Matt formed a rock band. [It looks as though Phyllis is being addressed.]

CLEAR Phyllis, Ken, and Matt formed a rock band. [Phyllis is clearly a member of the band.]

Some writers prefer always to use the comma before the *and* in a series. Follow your teacher's instructions on this point.

NOTE: Some words—such as *bread and butter* and *law and order*—are paired so often that they may be considered a single item.

EXAMPLE For lunch we had soup, salad, bread and butter, and milk.

(2) If all the items in a series are linked by *and, or,* or *nor,* do not use commas to separate them.

EXAMPLES Tyrone **and** Earlene **and** Lily won awards for their sculptures.
Should we walk **or** ride our bikes **or** take the bus?

(3) Do not place a comma before or after a series.

INCORRECT I enjoy, gymnastics, basketball, and wrestling.

CORRECT I enjoy gymnastics, basketball, and wrestling.

NOTE: The abbreviation *etc.* (meaning "and so forth") at the end of a series is always followed by a comma unless it falls at the end of a sentence.

EXAMPLES Randy bought hamburger, buns, onions, etc., for the cookout.
For the cookout Randy bought hamburger, buns, onions, etc.

29g. Use a comma to separate two or more adjectives preceding a noun.

EXAMPLE Lucia is an intelligent, thoughtful, responsible student.

When the last adjective before the noun is thought of as part of the noun, the comma before the adjective is omitted.

EXAMPLES Let's play this new video game.
I've finally found a decent, affordable used car.

MECHANICS

MEETING INDIVIDUAL NEEDS

STUDENTS WITH SPECIAL NEEDS

Students with disabilities in processing information often have difficulties if they are required to learn too many new concepts at one time. The numerous rules of comma usage presented in this segment may be frustrating to students if the rules are presented all at once. Be prepared to spend time reinforcing each rule before proceeding to the next one. You might also compare related rules frequently, especially when an exception is presented.

LEARNING STYLES

Kinetic Learners. Some students may learn comma usage more quickly by working at the chalkboard than by working at their desks. You may want to use the sentences in one of the exercises for this purpose. Read the sentences aloud and ask students to write the sentences on the chalkboard and to insert commas where needed.

MECHANICS

INTEGRATING THE LANGUAGE ARTS

Literature Link. Students often become confused when they read literature in which authors seem to disregard punctuation rules. Have students read and discuss a short story such as "The Notorious Jumping Frog of Calaveras County" by Mark Twain. Ask them to find examples of comma use that contradict a rule shown in the textbook. Then point out to students that creative writers often experiment with punctuation, and that, possibly as a result of such experimentation, the rules for punctuation change over time.

Remind students that the English language is not static; it changes to meet the communication needs of the changing world.

MEETING INDIVIDUAL NEEDS

LEP/ESL

General Strategies. Comma placement is not universal from language to language. Turkish, Dutch, and Arabic languages use commas without linking words to join independent clauses. Students who speak these languages may use comma splices such as "My hometown is not large, it is very pretty." When you correct such comma splices, acknowledge that you are asking students to change rules they have already mastered in their native languages.

MECHANICS

Compound nouns such as *video game* and *used car* are considered single units rather than two separate words. You can use two tests to determine whether an adjective and a noun form a unit.

TEST 1: Insert the word *and* between the adjectives. If *and* fits sensibly between the adjectives, use a comma. In the first example above, *and* cannot be logically inserted: *new and video game.* In the second sentence, *and* sounds sensible between the first two adjectives (*decent and affordable*) but not between the second and third (*affordable and used*).

TEST 2: Change the order of the adjectives. If the order of the adjectives can be reversed sensibly, use a comma. *Affordable, decent used car* makes sense, but *used decent car* and *video new game* do not.

Independent Clauses

29h. Use a comma before *and, but, or, nor, for, so,* and *yet* when they join independent clauses.

EXAMPLES I read a review of David Henry Hwang's *M. Butterfly*, and now I want to see the play.
Amy followed the recipe carefully, for she had never made paella before.

NOTE: Always use a comma before *yet, so,* or *for* joining independent clauses. The comma may be omitted before *and, but, or,* and *nor* if the independent clauses are very short and if the sentence is not confusing or unclear without it.

EXAMPLES The phone rang and I answered it.
We can go in the morning or we can leave now.

The teacher called on Maria and John began to answer. [awkward without comma]
The teacher called on Maria, and John began to answer. [clear with comma]

Don't confuse a compound sentence with a simple sentence that has a compound verb.

SIMPLE SENTENCE My sister had been accepted at Howard University but then decided to attend Grambling University instead. [one independent clause with a compound verb]

MECHANICS

29h

COMPOUND SENTENCE My sister had been accepted at Howard University, but then she decided to attend Grambling University instead. [two independent clauses]

Also, keep in mind that compound subjects and compound objects are not separated by commas.

EXAMPLES What he is saying today and what he said yesterday are two different things. [two subordinate clauses serving as a compound subject]
Television crews covered the Daytona 500 and the Indianapolis 500. [compound object]

REFERENCE NOTE: For more about compound subjects and compound verbs, see pages 585–586.

EXERCISE 2 Correcting Sentences by Adding Commas

Write each word in the following sentences that should be followed by a comma, and add the comma. If a sentence is correct, write *C*.

1. The photograph showed a happy, mischievous little boy.
2. Barbara will bring potato salad to the picnic, and Marc will bring the cold cuts.
3. Alain Leroy Locke was a Rhodes scholar, taught philosophy, created one of the foremost collections of African art, and mentored many black writers.
4. We studied the following authors in English class this semester: F. Scott Fitzgerald, Lorraine Hansberry, and Rudolfo Anaya.
5. The introduction of the hardy sweet potato helped the Chinese to alleviate the famines that plagued them. 5. C
6. The committee has suggested that the cafeteria serve a different selection daily, that classes not be interrupted by announcements, and that pep rallies always be held during sixth period.
7. Students will receive paper, pencils, rulers, etc., at the beginning of the test.
8. April liked the ballet, but Jenny thought it was boring.
9. Last winter was abnormally cold, icy, and snowy.
10. The concert consisted of African American music and featured jazz, rhythm and blues, spirituals, and several gospel songs.

MECHANICS

A DIFFERENT APPROACH

You might have small groups of students work together to create a classroom handbook on commas. The entries should include the rules, illustrations of the rules in original sentences, and the most difficult aspects of understanding the rules.

When each group has completed its part of the project, your class will have its own handbook for proofreading. Students can add to the handbook as they learn new comma rules.

TIMESAVER

As students complete the exercises in this chapter, suggest that they use colored ink for the punctuation. The different color will make the punctuation more visually striking and easier to grade.

MECHANICS

REVIEW A

OBJECTIVE

- To proofread a paragraph and insert commas and end marks as needed

REVIEW A **Proofreading for the Correct Use of End Marks and Commas**

Add or delete end marks and commas to correct each sentence in the following paragraph.

[1] Known as Stonehenge, the great circle of stones shown here is located in England, and remains one of the most mysterious structures of the ancient world. [2] Much of the riddle of Stonehenge concerns the transport of the awesome massive blue stones that stand in the monument's inner circle. [3] These rocks are indigenous to Wales and many people have asked, "How did these huge stones travel two hundred miles
3. ? to England." [4] Do you remember Merlin from the stories of King Arthur's legendary court. [5] This wily, and powerful sorcerer is said to have moved the stones by magic. [6] The story of Merlin may be fascinating but modern astronomers anthropologists, and other scientists are searching for a more rational explanation. [7] Some theorists believe that many of the gigantic blue Welsh monoliths were shipped by raft through dangerous tidal waters, but other scientists scoff and say, "That's impossible?" [8] Still other theorists wonder if glaciers may have lifted moved, and deposited the stones so far from their home? [9] Visitors to Stonehenge are no longer allowed within the monument and venturing inside the protected area will draw a polite but authoritative, "Will you please step back" [10] So far, Stonehenge has not yielded a solution to the mystery of the blue stones yet a section of the site remains unexplored and may contain clues as to how they got there.

MECHANICS

MECHANICS

Nonessential Clauses and Phrases

29i. Use commas to set off nonessential clauses and nonessential participial phrases.

A *nonessential* (or *nonrestrictive*) clause or participial phrase is one containing information that isn't needed to understand the main idea of the sentence.

NONESSENTIAL CLAUSES Lydia Cabrera**, who was born in Cuba,** wrote many books about African Cuban culture.
Did the Senate hearings**, which were televised,** attract a large audience?

NONESSENTIAL PHRASES Lee**, noticing my confusion,** rephrased her question.
Willie Herenton**, defeating the incumbent in 1991,** became the first African American mayor of Memphis.

Each nonessential clause or phrase in the examples above can be left out without changing the main idea of the sentence.

EXAMPLES Lydia Cabrera wrote many books about African Cuban culture.
Did the Senate hearings attract a large audience?
Lee rephrased her question.
Willie Herenton became the first African American mayor of Memphis.

An *essential* (or *restrictive*) clause or phrase is one that can't be left out without changing the meaning of the sentence. Essential clauses and phrases are *not* set off by commas. Notice how leaving out the essential clause or phrase would change the meaning of each of the following sentences.

ESSENTIAL CLAUSES The juniors **who were selected for Boys State and Girls State** were named.
Material **that is quoted verbatim** should be placed in quotation marks.

ESSENTIAL PHRASES Those **participating in the food drive** should bring their donations by Friday.
The election **won by Willie Herenton** took place in October 1991.

NOTE: Adjective clauses beginning with *that,* like the one in the second example above, are nearly always essential.

MECHANICS

MEETING INDIVIDUAL NEEDS

LEARNING STYLES

Visual Learners. To help students decide if a clause or phrase is essential or nonessential, suggest that students bracket or mark out the clause or phrase in question. If the sentence retains its meaning without the bracketed information, the clause or phrase is nonessential and should be set off by commas.

MECHANICS

Some clauses and participial phrases may be either essential or nonessential. The presence or absence of commas tells the reader how the clause or phrase relates to the main idea of the sentence.

NONESSENTIAL CLAUSE Una's cousin**, who wants to be an astronaut,** attended a space camp in Huntsville, Alabama, last summer. [Una has only one cousin. Her only cousin attended the space camp.]

ESSENTIAL CLAUSE Una's cousin **who wants to be an astronaut** attended a space camp in Huntsville, Alabama, last summer. [Una has more than one cousin. The one who wants to be an astronaut attended the space camp.]

NONESSENTIAL PHRASE Your cat**, draped along the back of the couch,** seems contented. [You have only one cat. It seems contented.]

ESSENTIAL PHRASE Your cat **draped along the back of the couch** seems contented. [You have more than one cat. The one on the back of the couch seems contented.]

REFERENCE NOTE: See pages 628–637 for more information on clauses and page 612 for more information on participial phrases.

MECHANICS

EXERCISE 3 Correcting Sentences by Adding Commas

For each of the following sentences, write each word that should be followed by a comma, and add the comma. If a sentence is correct, write *C*.

1. All students going on the trip tomorrow will meet in the auditorium after school today. 1. C
2. The White River Bridge, which closed today for resurfacing, will not be open for traffic until mid-October.
3. The symphony that Beethoven called the *Eroica* was composed to celebrate the memory of a great man. 3. C
4. From the composer's letters, we learn that this "great man" whom he had in mind was Napoleon Bonaparte. 4. C
5. Natalie Curtis, always interested in the music of Native Americans, was an early recorder of their songs.

MECHANICS

6. The driver who caused the wreck was going too fast. 6. C
7. The musician who founded the annual music festival in Puerto Rico was Pablo Casals. 7. C
8. Semantics, which is concerned with the meanings of words, is an interesting subject of study for high school students.
9. My car, which is seven years old, simply refuses to start on cold mornings.
10. All contestants submitting photographs for the contest must sign a release form. 10. C

Introductory Elements

29j. Use a comma after certain introductory elements.

(1) Use commas to set off interjections such as *well, oh, why,* and *hey.* Other introductory words such as *yes* and *no* are also followed by commas.

EXAMPLES Well, I guess so.
Yikes, are we late!
Yes, I heard your question.

(2) Use a comma after an introductory participial phrase.

EXAMPLES Looking poised and calm, Jill walked to the podium.
Exhausted after the five-mile hike, the scouts took a break.

NOTE: Don't confuse a gerund phrase used as the subject of a sentence with an introductory participial phrase.

EXAMPLES **Following directions** can sometimes be difficult. [The gerund phrase *Following directions* is the subject of the sentence.]
Following directions, I began to assemble the bike. [*Following directions* is an introductory participial phrase modifying *I*.]

(3) Use a comma after two or more introductory prepositional phrases.

EXAMPLE In the first round of the golf tournament, I played one of the best golfers in the state.

MECHANICS

COMMON ERROR

Problem. Many students fail to add commas after introductory phrases or clauses and as a result, they create sentences that are difficult to understand.

Solution. To demonstrate how important the placement of commas can be after introductory phrases and clauses, write the following incorrect sentence on the chalkboard:

After eating my dog Sophie goes to sleep.

Ask students to think of similar sentences with introductory phrases or clauses that need to be set off by commas. Ask students to write these examples on the chalkboard. Have students check their writing for similar comma omissions.

MECHANICS

REVIEW B

OBJECTIVE

- To correct comma errors in a paragraph

COOPERATIVE LEARNING

To give students extra practice with introductory elements, pair students and have them collect interesting magazine pictures. Each pair could write descriptive paragraphs about the pictures by using sentences with introductory words, introductory prepositional phrases, introductory verbal phrases, and introductory adverb clauses.

Allow class time for revision and proofreading. Ask volunteers to read their paragraphs and show their pictures.

TIMESAVER

You may want students to read aloud the sentences in **Review B** and to tell where the commas are needed.

MECHANICS

A single introductory prepositional phrase does not require a comma unless the sentence is awkward to read without one or unless the phrase is parenthetical.

EXAMPLES At the track meet our school's team placed first.
At the track**,** meet me in front of the snack bar. [The comma is needed to avoid reading "track meet."]
By the way**,** I need to borrow a quarter. [The comma is needed because *By the way* is parenthetical.]

REFERENCE NOTE: See rule 29k (3) on page 856 for more information on using commas with parenthetical elements.

(4) Use a comma after an introductory adverb clause.

An introductory adverb clause may appear at the beginning of a sentence or before any independent clause in the sentence.

EXAMPLES After I had locked the car door**,** I remembered that the keys were still in the ignition.
Fortunately, I had a spare set of keys with me; if I hadn't**,** I would have had to walk home.

NOTE: An adverb clause that follows an independent clause is usually not set off by a comma.

EXAMPLE Thousands of homes in the Philippines were destroyed **when Mt. Pinatubo erupted in 1991.**

MECHANICS

REVIEW B **Using Commas in a Paragraph**

For each sentence in the following paragraph, write each word that should be followed by a comma, and add the comma. If a sentence is correct, write *C*.

[1] Have you ever had a dream that seemed absolutely real, but, as you awoke, you realized how outlandish it had been?
2. C [2] An artist painting a surrealistic picture can sometimes generate that same dreamlike feeling in an audience. [3] For example, this painting, which is one of many surreal landscapes by Salvador Dali, conveys the strange experience of a dream. [4] In a dream, time has a different meaning, and the bizarre can seem ordinary. [5] While only five minutes may actually have passed, events requiring hours or days may have taken place in a dream. [6] Dali's clocks, drooping as limply as a sleeper, show that the rigid march of time can relax in a dream. [7] In the liquid time and unearthly space of dreams, not even solid reality can

29k

be certain. [8] Objects far more fantastic and incredible than the creature who reclines on the sand can seem in dreams to be as familiar as your own face. [9] Sleeping peacefully, Dali's strange creature does not seem to realize that it is saddled with the burden of time. [10] Well, until the alarm clock wakes you from your own dreams, you probably don't realize it either.

8. C

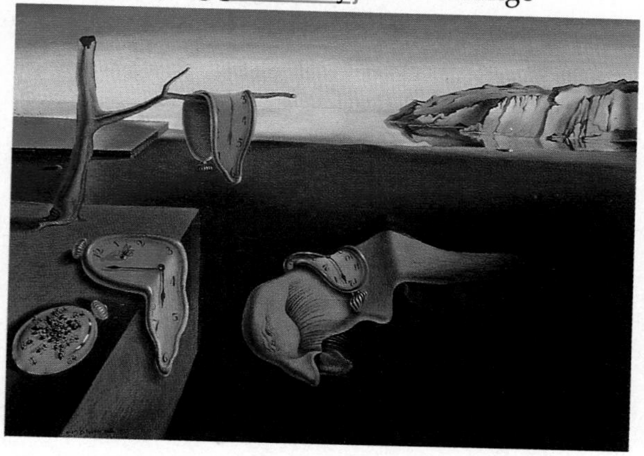

Salvador Dali, The Persistence of Memory (Persistance de la memoire), 1931. Oil on canvas, 9 1/2 × 13" (24.1 × 33 cm). Collection, The Museum of Modern Art, New York. Given Anonymously.

Interrupters

29k. Use commas to set off elements that interrupt a sentence.

(1) Appositives and appositive phrases are usually set off by commas.

An ***appositive*** is a noun or pronoun that follows another noun or a pronoun to identify or explain it. An ***appositive phrase*** consists of an appositive and its modifiers.

EXAMPLES My favorite book by Claude McKay, *Banjo*, was first published in 1929.
Is that he, the one with the red hair?

Sometimes an appositive is so closely related to the word preceding it that it should not be set off by commas. Such an appositive is called a *restrictive appositive.*

EXAMPLES my nephew Jim
the young American gymnast Lanna Apisukh
the saying "Haste makes waste"

REFERENCE NOTE: See page 621 for more information on appositives and appositive phrases.

MECHANICS

VISUAL CONNECTIONS
The Persistence of Memory

About the Artist. Salvador Dali was born in Catalonia, Spain, in 1904, and died in 1989. Dali used self-induced hallucinatory states to explore subconscious imagery. He became the world's best-known Surrealist artist. He also wrote many autobiographical works and collaborated on film projects. His paintings were done in a carefully precise style.

MEETING INDIVIDUAL NEEDS

LEARNING STYLES

Auditory Learners. Some students may be able to hear parenthetical expressions more easily than they can spot them on a page. You might read aloud sentences with parenthetical expressions and then read the same sentences without the parenthetical expressions. Students should recognize that the sentences make sense without the parenthetical expressions. Stress that parenthetical expressions always interrupt the flow of the sentence and that this interruption indicates the need for commas.

MECHANICS

(2) Words used in direct address are set off by commas.

EXAMPLES **Mom, have you called Mrs. Johnson yet?**
Your essay, Theo, was well organized.
Will you answer the question, Monica?

(3) Parenthetical expressions are set off by commas.

Parenthetical expressions are remarks that add incidental information or relate ideas to each other.

Commonly Used Parenthetical Expressions

after all	I believe (hope, etc.)	naturally
at any rate	incidentally	nevertheless
by the way	in fact	of course
consequently	in general	on the contrary
for example	in the first place	on the other hand
for instance	meanwhile	that is
however	moreover	therefore

MECHANICS

EXAMPLES Incidentally, I won't be home for supper.
Simón Bolívar liberated much of South America from Spanish rule, and, moreover, he became the most powerful man on the continent.
It's too late to call now, I believe.

REFERENCE NOTE: Parentheses and dashes are sometimes used to set off parenthetical expressions. See pages 872–874.

Some of these expressions do not have to be used parenthetically. When they are not, don't set them off with commas.

EXAMPLES **By the way,** she is in my vocal music class. [parenthetical, meaning "incidentally"]
You can tell **by the way** she sings that she enjoys the class. [not parenthetical, meaning "by the manner in which"]

NOTE: A contrasting expression introduced by *not* is parenthetical and must be set off by commas.

EXAMPLE Margaret Walker**, not Alice Walker,** wrote the novel *Jubilee.*

MECHANICS

291

EXERCISE 4 Correcting Sentences by Adding Commas

For each of the following sentences, write each word that should be followed by a comma, and add the comma. If a sentence is correct, write *C*.

1. As a matter of fact, your lateness is your own fault since you knew what time the bus would be leaving.
2. Have you seen Mr. Welch, our new accounting teacher?
3. Zimbabwe's stone ruins, once a stronghold for an ancient empire, attest to the skill of those early stonemasons.
4. Please listen, class, while Jim makes an announcement.
5. Texans have a right to be proud of men such as Sergeants José Mendoza López and Macario García, who earned the Congressional Medal of Honor.
6. Our neighbor, Mrs. Kirby, gets our mail when we are away.
7. The expressive brushstrokes of Chinese calligraphy make it not only beautiful but also complex, perhaps the most complex of all written languages.
8. Mr. Beck, the yearbook photographer, always tries, I think, to place each person in the most flattering pose.
9. It is the pressure of getting work in on time, not the work itself, that gets on my nerves.
10. It's the phone that's ringing, Suzanne, not the doorbell.

Conventional Uses

29l. Use a comma in certain conventional situations.

(1) Use a comma to separate items in dates and addresses.

EXAMPLES On Friday, October 23, 1991, my niece Leslie was born.
Please address all inquiries to 92 Keystone Crossings, Indianapolis, IN 46240.

Notice that no comma separates the month from the day, the house number from the street name, or the ZIP code from the two-letter state code.

If the day is given before the month or only the month and the year are given, no comma is used.

EXAMPLES On 15 June 1924 Congress approved a law making all Native Americans U.S. citizens.
Will our new school be open by August 1996?

MECHANICS

INTEGRATING THE LANGUAGE ARTS

Mechanics and Writing. Have each student write three sentences that use the interrupters discussed in this segment. Then pair students and have them rewrite their partners' sentences so that there are no interrupters. Initiate a class discussion about how the placement or removal of interrupters affects writing style. Ask students to decide if their sentences are better with or without interrupters.

MECHANICS

REVIEW C

OBJECTIVE

- To correct sentences by adding end marks and commas

COMMON ERROR

Problem. Students tend to use too many commas rather than too few.

Solution. Explain to students that they must have a definite rule or reason for placing every comma or mark of punctuation that they use. When there is no rule requiring punctuation and the meaning is clear without it, advise students not to insert punctuation marks. When you go over the exercises in class, you might have students identify the rules that apply to each comma they add.

MECHANICS

NOTE: No comma is needed when items in an address or a date are joined by a preposition.

EXAMPLE The play is at the Melrose Theater **on** Broad Avenue **in** Midland Heights.

(2) Use a comma after the salutation of a friendly letter and after the closing of any letter.

EXAMPLES Dear Rosa, Sincerely yours,

(3) Use a comma after a name followed by an abbreviation such as *Jr., Sr.,* or *M.D.* and also after the abbreviation when the name and abbreviation are used together in a sentence.

EXAMPLES Coretta Jones, M.D.
Is Juan Fuentes, Jr., your cousin?

Unnecessary Commas

29m. Do not use unnecessary commas.

Using too many commas can be confusing. Use a comma only if a rule requires one or if the meaning is unclear without one.

INCORRECT The teacher in the room across the hall, is Cam's aunt. [*Teacher* is the subject; it must not be separated by a comma from the verb *is*.]

CORRECT The teacher in the room across the hall is Cam's aunt.

MECHANICS

REVIEW C Correcting Sentences by Adding End Marks and Commas

Write each of the following sentences, adding end marks and commas where they are needed.

1. Wow! Little Bear, who taught you to draw a bow like that?
2. First performed on March 11, 1959, on Broadway in New York City, Lorraine Hansberry's play *A Raisin in the Sun*, which was later made into a movie, was awarded the New York Drama Critics Circle Award.
3. Although the house was a mess, Mom said that if we all helped put away toys and books, picked up all the clothes lying around, dusted the furniture, and vacuumed the rug, it would look presentable by the time Grandma arrived.

WRITING APPLICATION

OBJECTIVE

- To write a descriptive essay containing correctly punctuated interrupters

4. After all, you could look at the map to see if there is an exit off of Interstate 70 to a state road that will take us south to Greenville, Illinois, instead of just complaining because I don't know the way.
5. On her way to work each morning, she saw young people on their paper routes, children waiting for school buses, mail carriers beginning their deliveries, and the inevitable joggers puffing along on their morning workouts.
6. City buses can be a pleasant way to travel, but why do they run so infrequently, and when they do arrive, why are they in bunches of three or four or more?
7. Gen. Benjamin O. Davis, Sr the first African American who was promoted to the rank of lieutenant general in the U.S. Army, was the grandson of a slave. 7. Sr.,
8. If you are going to paint window frames, cover the panes of glass with masking tape, which will protect the glass from being spattered.
9. On a beautiful fall day in New England, it is wise to go for a walk, play a game outdoors, or go for a drive; for it won't be long until everything is bleak, cold, and dreary.
10. If I had my way, I would live in a climate where it would be warm, not hot, in the daytime and cool in the evening all year round.

WRITING APPLICATION

Using Interrupters Correctly

Sometimes you feel as though you just have to interrupt. In conversation, you listen for a pause—a chance to slip in a comment at just the right moment. Interruptions in writing have to be carefully placed, too. Avoid awkward phrasing by reading a sentence aloud and listening for the most natural place to insert an interrupter.

AWKWARD Bob enjoys fishing, so he decided to write, naturally, about Santiago in *The Old Man and the Sea.*

BETTER Bob enjoys fishing, so**, naturally,** he decided to write about Santiago in *The Old Man and the Sea.*

WRITING APPLICATION This activity involves many concepts. Each student will have to use commas correctly in an essay about a favorite fictional hero and to include at least two apositives and three parenthetical expressions. Point out to students that they might want to use an expressive or informative aim to write this descriptive essay.

CRITICAL THINKING
Evaluation

Students will need to evaluate how well they have followed directions in using commas in appositives and parenthetical expressions. You might have students exchange essays in the proofreading stage and have their peers use a list of the rules presented in the textbook to evaluate their peers' work.

PREWRITING

You may want to brainstorm with the class to discover possible characters that they are familiar with from novels, stories, and poems and then you could list these characters on the chalkboard.

WRITING

As students work on developing paragraphs, suggest that they circle each appositive and parenthetical expression. This reminder will help students keep track of the expressions and help them focus on correct comma usage.

MECHANICS

Always use commas to set off interrupters. Commas signal a shift in thought and help avoid confusion.

CONFUSING Because I like comic strips, I'm going to write my essay I believe on Calvin of *Calvin and Hobbes*. [Does the writer intend to write on Calvin?]

CLEAR Because I like comic strips, I'm going to write my essay, I believe, on Calvin of *Calvin and Hobbes*.

WRITING ACTIVITY

Next Friday, your English class will celebrate Literary Heroes Day. Your teacher has asked you to write a brief essay (two or three paragraphs long) about your favorite fictional character. Describe the character and explain why the character is your hero. In your essay use at least two appositives and three parenthetical expressions. Be sure to use commas correctly with each interrupter.

Prewriting First, you'll need to decide on a character to write about. If one doesn't come to mind right away, think back on the novels, stories, and poems that you've read or heard. Next, jot down the names of the three characters you remember most clearly. Then, from your list, choose the character that impressed or entertained you the most. You may then want to skim the work that the character appears in to find passages that give important information about the character. In your notes, be sure to include the character's strongest and most interesting traits.

Writing Use your notes to help you write your first draft. Begin by describing the character and noting some of the most important traits that make this person your hero. Illustrate these traits by giving at least two examples of things the character does or says. Wherever appropriate, use appositives and parenthetical expressions to add information to your sentences.

Evaluating and Revising Ask a friend or relative to read your essay. Does your description give a vivid picture of the character? Is it clear why this character is your hero? If not, add or revise details to help make your point more clearly. Be sure that you've used at least two appositives and three parenthetical expressions.

MECHANICS

SEGMENT 4 *(pp. 861–863)*

REVIEW: POSTTEST

OBJECTIVES

- To correct sentences by adding or deleting end marks and commas
- To proofread and edit a letter for the correct use of end marks and commas

Proofreading and Publishing Proofread your essay for any errors in grammar, usage, or mechanics. Pay special attention to commas before and after parenthetical expressions. You and your classmates may want to celebrate Literary Heroes Day by creating a bulletin board display. Place a typed or neatly written copy of each essay on the bulletin board along with illustrations of the different characters.

Review: Posttest

A. Correcting Sentences by Adding or Deleting End Marks and Commas

Write the following sentences, adding or deleting end marks and commas as necessary. If a sentence is correct, write *C*.

EXAMPLE **1. Sally asked, "Where do you want to go after the recital"?**
1. ***Sally asked, "Where do you want to go after the recital?"***

1. Who was it who said, "I only regret that I have but one life to give for my country?"
2. Startled, we heard a high-pitched, whining, noise just outside the window.
3. Any student, who has not signed up for the contest by three o'clock, will not be eligible to participate.
4. My friend Esteban, running up the stairs two at a time, yelled out the good news. 4. C
5. "Why does the telephone always ring just as soon as I sit down to work," she asked?
6. My parents are trading in their car a two-door model with a sunroof bucket seats and air conditioning.
7. I have drilled practiced trained and exercised for weeks and now I am too tired to compete.
8. "Well Coach I can promise you that I'll be ready for the game next week," Kit said.

MECHANICS

TIMESAVER

You may want to have students circle each of the commas in their **Writing Application** papers. You can then quickly check to see that students understand the different uses of the comma.

MECHANICS

9. James King, an Iroquois guide, used to conduct tours of the Somers Mountain Indian Museum in Somers, Connecticut.
10. "Where should the question mark be placed in a quoted sentence?" Yolanda inquired.

B. Proofreading a Letter for the Correct Use of End Marks and Commas

Add or delete end marks or commas to correct each sentence in the following letter.

EXAMPLE [1] Dear Toni
1. *Dear Toni,*

[11] As she promised, our friend Takara and her family were waiting for us at the Osaka airport on Monday, June 16. **[12]** I'm so glad that you introduced us and that I could come to visit such a kind, generous, and friendly family.

[13] Wow! I love their house; it's totally different from any home that I've ever seen before, and my favorite part of it is the garden! **[14]** In the middle of the house and down one step, a large rectangular courtyard lies open to the sun and air; the garden is in the courtyard. **[15]** Rocks, not plants and trees, dominate the space, and clean, white sand, instead of grass, covers the ground. **[16]** I wonder who carefully rakes the sand every day, leaving small rows of lines covering the ground? **[17]** Takara told me that the sand represents the ocean, the lines are like waves, and the rocks stand for islands. **[18]** Sitting in the garden, I believe she is right, for the garden is as peaceful as any deserted beach.

13. [or]

[19] My flight, by the way, will be arriving in Portland in ten short days; if you're free, would you please meet me at the airport?

[20] Sincerely yours,

Ramona

MECHANICS

SUMMARY OF COMMA USES

29f	Use commas to separate items in a series.
29g	Use a comma to separate two or more adjectives preceding a noun.
29h	Use a comma before *and, but, or, nor, for, so,* and *yet* when they join independent clauses.
29i	Use commas to set off nonessential clauses and nonessential participial phrases.
29j	Use a comma after certain introductory elements. (1) After interjections and after introductory words such as *yes* and *no* (2) After an introductory participial phrase (3) After two or more introductory prepositional phrases (4) After an introductory adverb clause
29k	Use commas to set off elements that interrupt a sentence. (1) Appositives and appositive phrases (2) Words in direct address (3) Parenthetical expressions
29l	Use a comma in certain conventional situations. (1) To separate items in dates and addresses (2) After the salutation of a friendly letter and the closing of any letter (3) After a name followed by an abbreviation such as *Jr., Sr.,* or *M.D.*
29m	Do not use unnecessary commas.

MECHANICS

MECHANICS

SEGMENT 1 *(pp. 864–866)*

DIAGNOSTIC TEST

OBJECTIVE

- To proofread and correct sentences with errors of punctuation in the use of semicolons, colons, dashes, parentheses, brackets, italics (underlining), quotation marks, apostrophes, and hyphens

Teacher's ResourceBank™

RESOURCES

FOR THE WHOLE CHAPTER

• Chapter Review Form A	358–360
• Chapter Review Form B	361–363
• Assessment Portfolio	
Mechanics Pretests	579–586
Mechanics Mastery Tests	605–612

CHAPTER OVERVIEW

This chapter discusses the use of semicolons, colons, dashes, parentheses, brackets, italics, quotation marks, ellipsis points, apostrophes, and hyphens. The **Writing Application** asks students to write dialogue using apostrophes correctly. A **Review: Posttest** is included at the end of the chapter for checking students' mastery of the use of the punctuation marks discussed.

After evaluating students' needs, select and focus on the information most useful for your class. You might want to teach elements of this chapter when students are reviewing for standardized tests. You could use this chapter as a ready reference when students proofread their papers.

MECHANICS

MECHANICS

30 PUNCTUATION

Other Marks of Punctuation

Diagnostic Test

A. Proofreading Sentences for Correct Punctuation

The following sentences contain errors in the use of semicolons, colons, dashes, parentheses, brackets, italics (underlining), quotation marks, apostrophes, and hyphens. Rewrite each sentence correctly. [Note: A sentence may contain more than one error.] Hyphens are indicated by the ‸ symbol.

EXAMPLE 1. "This job", the employment director said, requires some experience with computers, dont apply for it unless you know BASIC.".

1. *"This job," the employment director said, "requires some experience with computers; don't apply for it unless you know BASIC."*

1. She learned the word daube from working the crossword puzzle in the New York Times.
2. "I like everything about my new car—it's design, color, and smooth ride," Cari said.

3. Our school has had exchange students from: Denmark, Liberia, Korea, Uruguay, and France.
4. Our flight will land in Rio de Janeiro by 8:00 P.M.; more-over, our hotel reservations have already been confirmed.
5. The presidency of Franklin Delano Roosevelt (1933–1945) was the longest one in American history.
6. Did you hear about the student council's decision that the class song must be chosen by a three-fourths majority?
7. Last year "The Dance"—do you know that song?—was chosen overwhelmingly.
8. The guide added, "Rosa Bonheur, a French artist, painted Buffalo Bill on his favorite horse."
9. Nancy asked, "Can you remember whether there are two c's or two s's in occasion"?
10. Mr. Elliott's favorite books are Atlas Shrugged, by Ayn Rand; East of Eden, by John Steinbeck; and Beloved, by Toni Morrison.

B. Proofreading Paragraphs for Correct Punctuation

The following paragraphs of conversation contain errors in the use of semicolons, colons, dashes, parentheses, italics (under-lining), quotation marks, apostrophes, and hyphens. Rewrite each paragraph, correcting the errors. **Hyphens are indicated by the ^ symbol.**

EXAMPLE **[1]** "The Renaissance Festival will open at 10 30 in the morning, therefore, we should be in line for tickets by 9 30, Janice said.

1. *"The Renaissance Festival will open at 10:30 in the morning; therefore, we should be in line for tickets by 9:30," Janice said.*

[11] "What in the world—please don't think me too uninformed—is a Renaissance festival"? Leroy asked.

[12] "It's a fair that celebrates Europe's Renaissance, which lasted from about A.D. 1300 to around A.D. 1600," Janice said.

[13] "Well, I'm ready to go; I know what to expect because I've seen the movies Camelot and The Princess Bride," Leroy said.

[14] "Even so, you'll be amazed," Janice said, "because you'll see people dressed up as: kings and queens, jesters, peasants, knights and ladies, wizards, and even dragons."

MECHANICS

USING THE DIAGNOSTIC TEST

You may want to administer the **Diagnostic Test** to determine which uses of punctuation discussed in this chapter might give students difficulty. An analysis of how well students complete the **Diagnostic Test** will help you decide how to approach the material in this chapter.

MECHANICS

SEGMENT 2 *(pp. 866–869)*

SEMICOLONS Rules 30a–30d

OBJECTIVE

- To locate and correct semicolon errors in sentences

DIAGNOSTIC TEST: PART B

Teaching Note. Some students may hyphenate *apple-and-pineapple* in sentence 19.

[15] "I suppose Id better mind my ps and qs with wizards and dragons around Leroy exclaimed.

[16] "Oh, all the wizards's manners are good and the fierce looking dragons actually are friendly," Janice said.

[17] "And there are many other sights to see, too jousts, mazes, elephants and camels, games of strength, music, and all kinds of crafts

[18] Leroy asked, "Isnt there any Renaissance food?

[19] "Plenty!" Janice said. "My favorites are bagels, which are sold from traveling carts, soup served in bread bowls, which are freshly baked, and apple and pineapple fritters."

[20] "I've been to several Renaissance fairs, including big ones in Texas and Missouri, but, of course, I think theyre all great," Janice added.

Teacher's ResourceBank™

RESOURCES

SEMICOLONS

- Semicolons 349

MECHANICS

QUICK REMINDER

Write the following sentences on the chalkboard and ask students to insert semicolons where needed:

1. I looked at my watch as I hurried toward the classroom I was tardy again. [classroom; I]
2. Mr. Farr smiled as I tried to slip into my seat however, he was not pleased with me. [seat; however]
3. After class when it was time to go home, Neal, Matt, and Susan were waiting for me instead, I had to finish my project. [me; instead]

MECHANICS

Semicolons

30a. Use a semicolon between independent clauses that are closely related in thought and are not joined by *and, but, for, nor, or, so,* or *yet.*

EXAMPLES The rain had finally stopped**;** a few rays of sunshine were pushing their way through breaks in the clouds.

"Tart words make no friends**;** a spoonful of honey will catch more flies than a gallon of vinegar."

Benjamin Franklin, *Poor Richard's Almanack*

Do not join independent clauses unless there is a close relationship between the main ideas of the clauses.

NONSTANDARD For Ramón, oil painting is a difficult medium to master; when he was younger, he had enjoyed taking photographs.

STANDARD For Ramón, oil painting is a difficult medium to master**.** When he was younger, he had enjoyed taking photographs.

30b. Use a semicolon between independent clauses joined by a conjunctive adverb or a transitional expression.

30 a–c

A ***conjunctive adverb*** or a ***transitional expression*** indicates the relationship of the independent clauses that it joins.

EXAMPLES The snowfall made traveling difficult**; nevertheless,** we arrived home safely.
Denisa plays baseball well**; in fact,** she would like to try out for a major-league team.

Commonly Used Conjunctive Adverbs

accordingly	however	moreover
besides	indeed	nevertheless
consequently	instead	otherwise
furthermore	meanwhile	therefore

Commonly Used Transitional Expressions

as a result	for instance	in other words
for example	in fact	that is

NOTE: When a conjunctive adverb or a transitional expression is used *between* independent clauses, it is preceded by a semicolon and followed by a comma. When used *within* a clause, a conjunctive adverb or a transitional expression is set off by commas.

EXAMPLES Most members of Congress favor the new tax bill**; however,** the president does not support it.
Most members of Congress favor the new tax bill; the president**, however,** does not support it.

REFERENCE NOTE: For more information about conjunctive adverbs and transitional expressions, see pages 640–641.

30c. Use a semicolon (rather than a comma) before a coordinating conjunction to join independent clauses that contain commas.

EXAMPLE During the seventeenth century—the era of such distinguished prose writers as Sir Thomas Browne**,** John Donne**,** and Jeremy Taylor—the balanced compound sentence using commas and semicolons reached a high degree of perfection and popularity**;** but the tendency today is to use a fast-moving style with shorter sentences and fewer commas and semicolons. [commas within the first clause]

MECHANICS

MEETING INDIVIDUAL NEEDS

LEP/ESL

Spanish. In Spanish, it is not necessary for the relationship between two independent clauses joined with a semicolon to be as close as the relationship is in English. If some students are overusing semicolons, you may want to meet with them and discuss the need for close relationships between independent clauses joined by semicolons in English sentences.

A DIFFERENT APPROACH

If students need additional practice in semicolon use, collect a few sentences from several essays and have students correct some of the comma splices and other punctuation errors by inserting semicolons. Or you may want to enter students' sentences into a word processor and have students make corrections on the screen by using the insert function to add semicolons.

MECHANICS

30d. Use a semicolon between items in a series if the items contain commas.

EXAMPLES The president of the club has appointed the following to chair the standing committees: Richard Stokes, planning; Rebecca Hartley, membership; Salvador Berrios, financial; and Ann Jeng, legal.

The summer reading list includes *Behind the Trail of Broken Treaties,* by Vine Deloria; *House Made of Dawn,* by N. Scott Momaday; and *Blue Highways: A Journey into America,* by William Least Heat-Moon.

EXERCISE 1 **Using Semicolons Correctly**

Add semicolons where they are needed in the following sentences.

EXAMPLE 1. The great American humorist Will Rogers was proud of his Cherokee heritage he often referred to it in his talks and writings.

1. *The great American humorist Will Rogers was proud of his Cherokee heritage; he often referred to it in his talks and writings.*

1. William Penn Adair Rogers was born in 1879 in Oologah, Indian Territory, which is now Oklahoma; and he spent his childhood on his father's ranch, a prosperous holding of about sixty thousand acres.
2. As a youth, Will Rogers liked to learn and practice rope tricks; he often could be found roping instead of attending to his chores.
3. Rogers was captivated by professional roping performers at the Chicago World's Fair in 1893; in fact, that experience probably marked the start of his interest in show business.
4. He went on to do some roping and humorous speaking at fairs and other public gatherings; however, his actual show business debut came in 1902.
5. That year Rogers joined Texas Jack's Wild West Show as a "fancy lasso artist"; he also rode horses and performed in various western scenes during the show.
6. Notice how confident the young Rogers appears in the publicity photo on the next page; his expression, stance, and costume suggest an accomplished performer.

COOPERATIVE LEARNING

Pair students to work on **Exercise 1** with advanced and less-advanced students working together. Instruct students to identify the subjects and verbs of all independent clauses before deciding where to place the semicolons.

Often instruction from peers is accepted more readily than advice from a teacher, and being able to formulate understandable explanations benefits advanced students by enabling them to use their knowledge to explain.

TIMESAVER

Before students turn in **Exercise 1,** have them underline the subject of each independent clause once and the verb of each independent clause twice. Then have them circle each semicolon. This should help you to quickly check their work to see that it meets the requirements for using semicolons.

MECHANICS

SEGMENT 3 *(pp. 869–872)*

COLONS Rules 30e–30f

OBJECTIVE

- To write sentences that contain colons

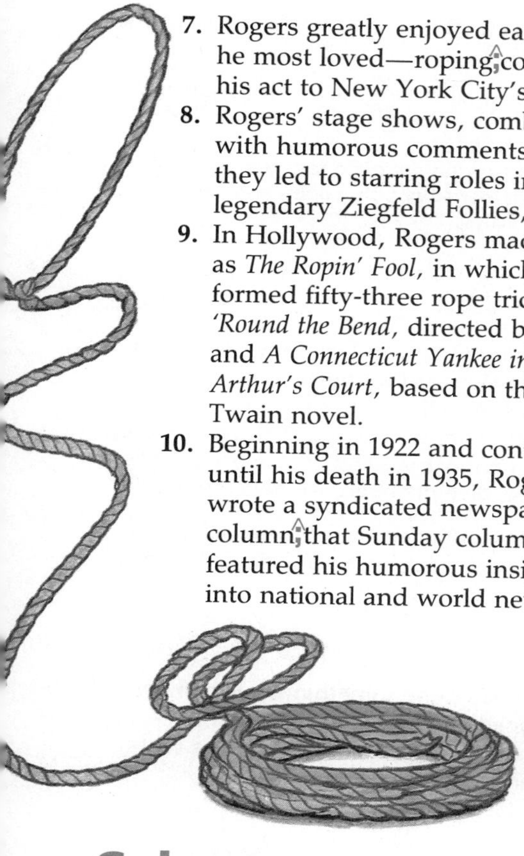

7. Rogers greatly enjoyed earning his living by doing what he most loved—roping; consequently, he decided to take his act to New York City's vaudeville theaters.
8. Rogers' stage shows, combining his roping with humorous comments, were popular; they led to starring roles in musicals, the legendary Ziegfeld Follies, and movies.
9. In Hollywood, Rogers made such films as *The Ropin' Fool,* in which he performed fifty-three rope tricks; *Steamboat 'Round the Bend,* directed by John Ford; and *A Connecticut Yankee in King Arthur's Court,* based on the Mark Twain novel.
10. Beginning in 1922 and continuing until his death in 1935, Rogers wrote a syndicated newspaper column; that Sunday column featured his humorous insights into national and world news.

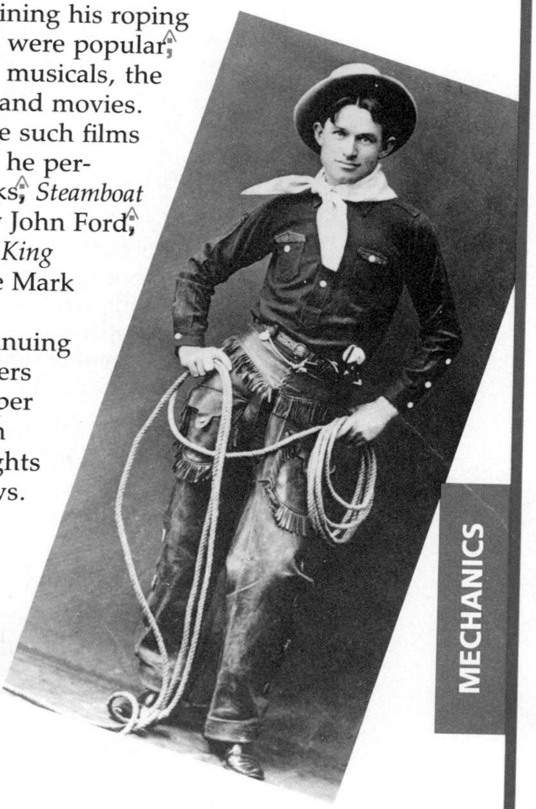

Colons

30e. Use a colon to mean "note what follows."

(1) Use a colon before a list of items, especially after expressions such as *as follows* and *the following.*

EXAMPLES Prior to 1722, the Iroquois Confederation consisted of five Native American nations**:** Mohawk, Oneida, Onondago, Cayuga, and Seneca.

The magazine article profiles the following famous women of nineteenth-century America**:** Mary Baker Eddy, Clara Barton, Maria Mitchell, Mary Church Terrell, Susan B. Anthony, and Sarah Winnemucca.

Teacher's ResourceBank™

RESOURCES

COLONS	
• Colons	350

QUICK REMINDER

Write the following sentences on the chalkboard and ask for volunteers to tell where the sentences need colons:

1. I always enjoy myself on vacation because I take the following items extra shirts, my favorite pillow, my oldest jeans, and my dad's credit card. [items:]
2. When I was on vacation in Oklahoma, I visited the tribal capitals of several tribes, the Choctaws, the Cherokees, the Arapaho, and the Cheyenne. [tribes:]

MEETING INDIVIDUAL NEEDS

LEP/ESL

General Strategies. Students might get confused when they try to use the expressions *as follows* and *the following*. Showing two of the structures for these expressions might be helpful:

1. Noun + Linking Verb + *as follows:* "Supplies are as follows: . . . ." "The qualities she likes most in a person are as follows: . . . ."
2. Verb + *the following* + Noun: "Bring the following supplies: . . . ." "Learn to spell the following new words: . . . ."

LESS-ADVANCED STUDENTS

Some students might confuse the colon with the semicolon or think that they are interchangeable. Tell your class that ordinarily a colon is a kind of sign or pointer to the part of a sentence the writer wants to emphasize, whereas a semicolon helps the reader avoid confusion by separating ideas or items.

MECHANICS

NOTE: Do not use a colon before a list that directly follows a verb or a preposition.

EXAMPLES **The emergency kit included safety flares, jumper cables, and a flashlight.** [The list directly follows the verb *included.*]

Each student taking the math test was provided with two sharpened pencils, paper, and a ruler. [The list directly follows the preposition *with.*]

(2) Use a colon before a long, formal statement or quotation.

EXAMPLE **Patrick Henry concluded his revolutionary speech before the Virginia House of Burgesses with these ringing words: "Is life so dear, or peace so sweet as to be purchased at the price of chains and slavery? Forbid it, Almighty God! I know not what course others may take, but as for me, give me liberty or give me death!"**

REFERENCE NOTE: For more information about using long quotations, see page 880.

(3) Use a colon between independent clauses when the second clause explains or restates the idea of the first.

EXAMPLES **Lois felt that she had done something worthwhile: she had designed and sewn her first quilt.**

Thomas Jefferson had many talents: he was a writer, a politician, an architect, and an inventor.

MECHANICS

EXERCISE 2 Writing Sentences Using Colons

For your American history class, you're writing a report on the women's suffrage movement in the United States during the early 1900s. In the process of researching your topic, you have collected the pictures shown on the next page and have made the accompanying preliminary notes. Use the pictures and notes to write five sentences for your report. Include a colon in each sentence; give at least one example of each of the three uses of colons presented in this chapter so far.

EXAMPLE 1. *Major leaders in the women's suffrage movement included the following: Carrie Chapman Catt, Susan B. Anthony, Lucretia Mott, and Elizabeth Cady Stanton.*

NOTES

Marches—such demonstrations common, helped influence people. Describe marchers?

Wyoming, Utah, Colorado, Idaho—granted full voting rights to women by 1900. Seven more states did so by 1914.

The women who did get to vote organized demonstrations, organized marches, pressured Congress, formed associations (state and national), participated in World War I efforts

Carrie Lane Chapman Catt—president of National American Women's Suffrage Association, 1900–1904. Also a founder and honorary chair of National League of Women Voters. Had been a school superintendent in Mason City, Iowa. Intelligent and informed. Active in women's rights in Iowa in 1880s. Spoke throughout U.S. and world.

Some other early feminist leaders—Susan B. Anthony, Lucretia Mott, Elizabeth Cady Stanton

Nineteenth Amendment to the U.S. Constitution (ratified Aug. 26, 1920):
"The right of citizens of the United States to vote shall not be denied or abridged by the United States or by any State on account of sex.
"Congress shall have power to enforce this article by appropriate legislation."

MECHANICS

ANSWERS

Exercise 2

Sentences will vary. Here are some possibilities:

1. Carrie Lane Chapman Catt held the following positions: president of the National American Women's Suffrage Association, founder and honorary chair of the National League of Women Voters, and school superintendent in Mason City, Iowa.
2. Four states granted full voting rights to women by 1900: Wyoming, Utah, Colorado, and Idaho.
3. Women were determined to secure voting rights: they organized demonstrations and marches, pressured Congress, formed associations, and participated in World War I efforts.
4. The women who participated in the marches and demonstrations had the following characteristics: determination, stamina, and conviction.
5. The Nineteenth Amendment guaranteed women the right to vote with these words: "The right of citizens of the United States to vote shall not be denied or abridged by the United States or by any State on account of sex."

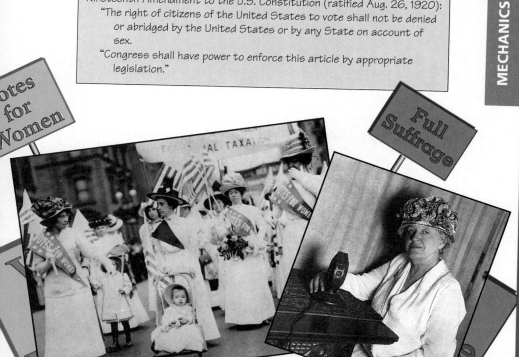

MECHANICS

SEGMENT 4 *(pp. 872–875)*

DASHES, PARENTHESES, and BRACKETS

Rules 30g–30j

OBJECTIVE

- To write a paragraph to express a character's thoughts and feelings that includes dashes, parentheses, and brackets

Teacher's ResourceBank™

RESOURCES

DASHES, PARENTHESES, and BRACKETS

- Dashes, Parentheses, and Brackets 351

MECHANICS

QUICK REMINDER

Write the following sentences on the chalkboard and ask students to insert dashes, parentheses, or brackets where needed:

1. The success of the project depended on one thing the development of a precise set of directions. [Place a dash between *thing* and *the*.]
2. The Ming dynasty of China 1368–1644 is famous for naval expeditions to Africa. [Put parentheses around 1368–1644.]
3. George Orwell (pen name of Eric Arthur Blair 1903–1950) is best known for his novels *Animal Farm* and *1984*. [Put brackets around 1903–1950.]

30f. Use a colon in certain conventional situations.

(1) Use a colon between the hour and the minute.

EXAMPLES **5:20** P.M. **8:45 in the morning**

(2) Use a colon between chapter and verse in referring to passages from the Bible.

EXAMPLES **Proverbs 10:1** **Deuteronomy 5:6–21**

(3) Use a colon between a title and subtitle.

EXAMPLES ***Another View: To Be Black in America*** [book]
Superman IV: The Quest for Peace [movie]
Impression: Sunrise [painting]

(4) Use a colon after the salutation of a business letter.

EXAMPLES **Dear Mrs. Rodríguez:** **To Whom It May Concern:**
Dear Sir or Madam: **Dear Service Manager:**

NOTE: Use a comma after the salutation of a friendly letter.

EXAMPLE **Dear Mom and Dad,**

MECHANICS

Dashes

30g. Use a dash to indicate an abrupt break in thought.

EXAMPLES **The poor condition of this road—it really needs to be paved—makes this route unpopular.**
The real villain turns out to be—but I don't want to spoil the ending for those of you who have not yet seen the movie.

30h. Use a dash to mean *namely, in other words, that is,* and similar expressions that come before an explanation.

EXAMPLES **Amanda joined the chorus for only one reason—she loves to sing.**
Very few people in this class—three, to be exact—have completed their projects.

Parentheses

30i. Use parentheses to enclose informative or explanatory material of minor importance.

EXAMPLES Harriet Tubman **(***ca.* 1820–1913**)** is remembered for her work in the Underground Railroad.
A *roman à clef* **(**literally, "novel with a key"**)** is a novel about real people to whom the novelist has assigned fictitious names.

Be sure that the material enclosed in parentheses can be omitted without losing important information or changing the basic meaning and construction of the sentence.

IMPROPER USE OF PARENTHESES George Eliot (whose real name was Mary Ann Evans) was one of many women in nineteenth-century England who wrote under a masculine pseudonym. [The information in parentheses clarifies that George Eliot was a woman. Each parenthesis should be replaced by a comma.]

Follow these guidelines for capitalizing and punctuating parenthetical sentences.

(1) A parenthetical sentence that falls within another sentence

- should not begin with a capital letter unless it begins with a word that should always be capitalized
- should not end with a period but may end with a question mark or an exclamation point

EXAMPLES The Malay Archipelago **(see the map on page 350)** includes the Philippines.
Legendary jazz musician Louis "Satchmo" Armstrong **(have you heard of him?)** was born in Louisiana.

(2) A parenthetical sentence that stands by itself

- should begin with a capital letter
- should end with a period, a question mark, or an exclamation point before the closing parenthesis

EXAMPLES The Malay Archipelago includes the Philippines. **(See the map on page 350.)**
Legendary jazz musician Louis "Satchmo" Armstrong was born in Louisiana. **(That's a coincidence! My hero Harry Connick, Jr., was born there, too.)**

MECHANICS

MEETING INDIVIDUAL NEEDS

LEP/ESL

General Strategies. Deciding whether to place punctuation marks inside or outside parentheses can be difficult for ESL students. You could give sentences that require students to determine where to place other punctuation marks when parentheses are used. Have students work in pairs or small groups; place less-advanced students with those who have higher-level English skills.

STUDENTS WITH SPECIAL NEEDS

Students with visual-processing disorders might have difficulty reading and copying the sentences in several of the exercises in this chapter. Suggest that students use index cards above and below the lines of text they are reading to help them focus. It also may be helpful to engage a peer tutor to read exercises aloud to a student as the student follows in the textbook.

MECHANICS

INTEGRATING THE LANGUAGE ARTS

Literature Link. E. E. Cummings often uses parentheses in his poetry. Ask students to read and analyze one of Cummings's poems that contains parentheses. Ask students to write paragraphs telling how the poem would be affected if the parentheses were not used. Ask students to give specific examples of the changes in meaning that would occur.

PICTURE THIS

Students may confuse stream-of-consciousness writing with interior monologue. In general, stream-of-consciousness writing is characterized by the use of association, reiteration of motifs, apparent incoherence, confused syntax, and punctuation that simulates a free flow of a character's mental processes. Interior monologue refers to thoughts presented in a more controlled manner, closer to direct verbalization.

When parenthetical material falls within a sentence, punctuation should never come before the opening parenthesis but may follow the closing parenthesis.

INCORRECT The first professional baseball team, the Cincinnati Red Stockings, (the Reds), was formed in 1869.

CORRECT The first professional baseball team, the Cincinnati Red Stockings **(**the Reds**),** was formed in 1869.

Brackets

30j. Use brackets to enclose an explanation within quoted or parenthetical material.

EXAMPLES The newspaper article stated that "at the time of that Democratic National Convention **[**in Chicago in 1968**]** there were many protest groups operating in the United States."

I think that Hilda Doolittle (more commonly known as H.D. **[**1886–1961**]**) is best remembered for her Imagist poetry.

PICTURE THIS

What a great day for people watching! It's a warm Saturday morning, and you're taking a leisurely walk through the park in this photograph. As you pass each person, you can't help but wonder what he or she is thinking and feeling. The scene gives you an idea for a *stream-of-consciousness* story, a story that records the natural, continuous flow of a character's thoughts and feelings.

SEGMENT 5 *(pp. 875–877)*

ITALICS Rules 30k, 30l

OBJECTIVE

- To revise sentences by adding semicolons, colons, dashes, parentheses, brackets, and italics (underlining)

Write the first paragraph or two of a story about one of the people in the park. Record whatever you imagine is going through the person's mind. In your story, use at least two pairs of dashes, two pairs of parentheses, and one pair of brackets to help express the many levels of your character's thoughts and feelings.

Subject: a character's thoughts and feelings
Audience: readers of a fictional story
Purpose: to reveal the character's thoughts; to entertain

Italics

Italics are printed characters that slant to the right. To indicate italics in handwritten or typewritten work, use underlining.

PRINTED *The Heart is a Lonely Hunter* was written by Carson McCullers.

HANDWRITTEN <u>The Heart is a Lonely Hunter</u> was written by Carson McCullers.

NOTE: If you use a personal computer, you may be able to set words in italics. Most word processing software and many printers are capable of producing italic type.

30k. Use italics (underlining) for titles of books, plays, periodicals, newspapers, works of art, films, television programs, long musical compositions, trains, ships, aircraft, and spacecraft.

TYPE OF NAME	EXAMPLES	
Books	*The Scarlet Letter* *Invisible Man*	*Fifth Chinese Daughter*
Plays	*The Crucible*	*West Side Story*
Periodicals	*Reader's Digest*	*Newsweek*

(continued)

MECHANICS

Teacher's ResourceBank™

RESOURCES

ITALICS

QUICK REMINDER

Write the following list on the chalkboard and ask the class which items would be italicized in sentences:

1. The Catcher in the Rye
2. National Geographic
3. Dances with Wolves
4. American Gothic
5. 60 Minutes
6. Voyager
7. mea culpa

[All of the items should be italicized in sentences.]

MECHANICS

MEETING INDIVIDUAL NEEDS

LESS-ADVANCED STUDENTS

Because some students may have difficulty distinguishing between titles that should be italicized (underlined) and those that should be placed in quotation marks, you might teach **Rules 30k** and **30n** (pp. 875 and 882) together. Directly compare the two lists following the rules and point out that titles that are italicized (underlined) tend to name longer works or works that are complete in themselves. Titles placed in quotation marks usually name shorter works or portions of longer ones.

Present on an overhead projector, one item at a time, a scrambled list of items covered by these two rules. As each item is uncovered, have students call out either "italics" or "quotation marks."

LEP/ESL

General Strategies. Some students will do better on tasks like **Exercise 3** if they are paired with native English speakers. Collaboration can facilitate learning the rules for punctuation and can stimulate discussions of cultural information imbedded in the language.

MECHANICS

TYPE OF NAME	EXAMPLES	
Newspapers	*Dallas Morning News* *Philadelphia Inquirer*	*San Francisco Examiner*
Works of Art	*The Kiss*	*Starry Night*
Films	*Rain Man* *It's a Wonderful Life*	*Stand and Deliver* *Out of Africa*
TV Programs	*Jeopardy!* *American Playhouse*	*Star Trek: The Next Generation*
Long Musical Compositions	*Liverpool Oratorio* *The Planets*	*Hiawatha's Wedding Feast*
Trains, Ships	*Century Limited*	*Queen Mary*
Aircraft, Spacecraft	*Solar Challenger* *Graf Zeppelin*	*Apollo 11* *Landsat-1*

NOTE: The article *the* before the title of a newspaper is neither italicized nor capitalized when written within a sentence.

EXAMPLE I found this information in the *New York Times.*

REFERENCE NOTE: For examples of titles that are not italicized but are enclosed in quotation marks, see pages 882–883.

MECHANICS

30l. Use italics (underlining) for words, letters, and symbols referred to as such and for foreign words.

EXAMPLES Should the use of *their* for *there* be considered a spelling error or a usage error?
The teacher couldn't tell whether I had written a script *S* or an *&.*
Some U.S. coins were stamped with the inscription *E pluribus unum.*

EXERCISE 3 Revising Sentences by Adding Semicolons, Colons, Dashes, Parentheses, Brackets, and Italics (Underlining)

Revise the following sentences by adding semicolons, colons, dashes, parentheses, brackets, and italics (underlining) where they are needed.

EXAMPLE 1. Did you watch World of Discovery last night?
1. *Did you watch World of Discovery last night?*

1. Les Brown—be sure to watch his show—is a tremendous motivational speaker who encourages people to make positive changes in their lives.
2. First aid for a snake bite is as follows: keep the victim still; if the bite is in an arm or a leg, place the limb below the level of the heart; if a hospital is less than thirty minutes away, take the victim there immediately.
3. Providing visuals (pictures, charts, maps, or graphs) can often help an audience understand technical information more easily.
4. The citizen who spoke before the Nuclear Regulatory Commission stated, "If you permit this project [the new Marblehead nuclear plant] to be completed, you will be creating another Three Mile Island."
5. *The Little Foxes,* a play by Lillian Hellman—its title, by the way, is taken from the Song of Solomon 2:15—had a truly remarkable effect upon Maxine last year; it may have been the reading of this play that helped her decide to major in drama in college.
6. Engineers' quests for the ideal high-fidelity speaker—*ideal* means the ability to reproduce exactly whatever recorded signals are fed to a speaker—have led to many innovative designs; for instance, electrostatic panels and truncated pyramids have been offered as alternatives to the traditional box-shaped enclosure.
7. We're looking forward to spending tomorrow at the Alabama-Coushatta Indian Reservation in East Texas; however, we won't arrive until around 10:30.
8. While reading a history book called The Rise and Fall of Nazi Germany, I used my dictionary to look up the definitions of the following terms: Anschluss, Luftwaffe, and Wehrmacht.
9. When you talk in front of an audience, remember these four principles: speak loudly and clearly; refrain from nervous habits and gestures; look directly at your audience; and above all, have something to say.
10. There was an article in Omni about Arthur C. Clarke's 2001: A Space Odyssey and the similarities to our own space flights; the article also reviewed Clarke's 2010: Odyssey Two.

MECHANICS

COMMON ERROR

Problem. Students write unclear sentences because they fail to use italics for words and letters, as in **Rule 30 l.**

Solution. Write the following sentence on the chalkboard:

She forgot an and wrote other.

Show students that when they italicize (underline) *an* and *other,* the sentence is easier to understand. Write the following rule on the chalkboard and have students refer to the rule when they proofread their written work:

If you see the words *the word, the letter,* or *the figure* before a particular word, letter, or figure—or if you could add such a phrase to a sentence without changing the sentences' meaning—italicize (underline) the word, letter, or figure. You might leave this rule on the chalkboard as students do **Exercise 3.**

MECHANICS

SEGMENT 6 *(pp. 878–885)*

QUOTATION MARKS Rules 30m–30o

OBJECTIVE

- To add quotation marks, other punctuation marks, and capital letters where needed in a dialogue and in sentences

Teacher's ResourceBank™

RESOURCES

QUOTATION MARKS

• Quotation Marks A	353
• Quotation Marks B	354

QUICK REMINDER

To emphasize how quotation marks help understanding, write this dialogue between two students, Tula and Mario, on the chalkboard as a single paragraph without quotation marks. Have students read the passage to determine who is speaking. Show students where paragraphing would occur and where quotation marks should be placed. Have students discuss the conventions for making dialogue understandable.

"Hello," said Tula, "where are you going? I'm going to chemistry class."

"I'm going to speech class. Have you done your English homework?"

"Sure."

"When did you do it?" Mario asked. "I finished it last night."

MECHANICS

SELECTION AMENDMENT

Description of change: excerpted

Rationale: to focus on the concept of quotation marks presented in this chapter

Quotation Marks

30m. Use quotation marks to enclose a ***direct quotation***—a person's exact words.

Be sure to place quotation marks both before and after a person's exact words.

EXAMPLES Chief Joseph said, after his surrender in 1877, "The earth is the mother of all people, and all people should have equal rights upon it."

"The track meet is canceled because of the unusually cold weather," announced Coach Griffey.

Do not use quotation marks to enclose an ***indirect quotation***—a rewording of a direct quotation.

DIRECT QUOTATION Aaron said, "I can type ninety-five words a minute."

INDIRECT QUOTATION Aaron said that he can type ninety-five words a minute.

MECHANICS

(1) A direct quotation begins with a capital letter.

EXAMPLE The poet Emily Dickinson wrote in a letter to Thomas Wentworth Higginson, her literary advisor, "If I feel physically as if the top of my head were taken off, I know *that* is poetry."

However, when the quotation is only a part of a sentence, do not begin it with a capital letter.

EXAMPLE In her essay "On the Mall," Joan Didion describes shopping malls as "toy gardens in which no one lives."

(2) When the expression identifying the speaker divides a quoted sentence, the second part begins with a small letter.

EXAMPLE "I really have to leave now," said Gwen, "so that I will be on time." [Notice that each part of a divided quotation is enclosed in quotation marks.]

When the second part of a divided quotation is a sentence, it begins with a capital letter.

EXAMPLE "Teddy Roosevelt was the first U.S. President who was concerned about the depletion of the nation's natural resources," explained Mr. Fuentes. "He established a conservation program that expanded the national park system and created many wildlife sanctuaries."

NOTE: When a direct quotation of two or more sentences is not divided, only one set of quotation marks is used.

EXAMPLE **"**Teddy Roosevelt was the first U.S. President who was concerned about the depletion of the nation's natural resources. He established a conservation program that expanded the national park system and created many wildlife sanctuaries,**"** explained Mr. Fuentes.

(3) A direct quotation is set off from the rest of the sentence by a comma, a question mark, or an exclamation point, but not by a period.

EXAMPLES "I nominate Pilar for class president**,**" said Erin.
"What is the capital of Thailand**?**" asked Mr. Klein.
"This chili is too spicy**!**" exclaimed Brian.

NOTE: If the quotation is only a word or a phrase, do not set it off with commas.

EXAMPLE When Clara tried to keep the crystal vase from falling off the shelf and knocked over the china plates in the process, she knew what "clumsy as an ox" meant.

(4) When used with quotation marks, the other marks of punctuation are placed according to the following rules:

- Commas and periods are always placed inside the closing quotation marks.

EXAMPLE **"**On the other hand**,"** he said, **"**your decision may be correct**."**

- Semicolons and colons are always placed outside the closing quotation marks.

EXAMPLES My neighbor said, **"**Of course I'll buy a magazine subscription**";** it was lucky that I asked her on payday.
Edna St. Vincent Millay uses these devices in her poem **"**Spring**":** alliteration, slant rhyme, and personification.

MECHANICS

MEETING INDIVIDUAL NEEDS

AT-RISK STUDENTS

Students in danger of failing to complete their educations are often more motivated when the material they must learn seems relevant to their own experiences and goals. Direct quotations used in school often are contrived and seem inapplicable to everyday writing.

You might remind students that because a lot of business is transacted by telephone, they might need to use direct and indirect quotations from these conversations when they file complaints with a utility company, consumer-protection agency, union, labor department, or work supervisor.

STUDENTS WITH SPECIAL NEEDS

Some students with learning disabilities have difficulty distinguishing direct quotations from indirect quotations. The newspaper is a good source for examples of both kinds. Point out that reporters often paraphrase what a person says to make room for other information. Have students highlight examples of direct and indirect quotations using two different colors. Analyze their examples in small groups. Point out clues to direct and indirect quotations and emphasize the placement of punctuation.

MECHANICS

INTEGRATING THE LANGUAGE ARTS

Literature Link. Students might not be aware that other types of literature—plays and screenplays, for example—use different conventions for presenting dialogue. Have students examine a play to identify the techniques used for dialogue and to discuss why methods are different for plays than for other works of literature. [In play scripts, the person speaking is clearly identified and all text except for stage directions is intended to be spoken aloud; no quotation marks are needed.]

SELECTION AMENDMENT
Description of change: excerpted
Rationale: to focus on the concept of using quotation marks presented in this chapter

MECHANICS

- Question marks and exclamation points are placed inside the closing quotation marks if the quotation itself is a question or an exclamation. Otherwise, they are placed outside.

EXAMPLES "Dad, will you please call the doctor tomorrow morning?" I asked.
"Move those golf clubs right now!" yelled my mother.
Did Langston Hughes write the line "My soul has grown deep like rivers"?
I'm sick of hearing "This is so boring"!

Notice in the last two examples given above that the end mark belonging with each quotation has been omitted. In a question or an exclamation that ends with a quotation, only the question mark or exclamation point is necessary, and it is placed outside the closing quotation marks.

(5) When quoting a passage that consists of more than one paragraph, put quotation marks at the beginning of each paragraph and at the end of only the last paragraph in the passage.

EXAMPLE "The water was thick and heavy and the color of a mirror in a dark room. Minnows broke the surface right under the wharf. I jumped. I couldn't help it.

"And I got to thinking that something might come out of the water. It didn't have a name or a shape. But it was there."

Shirley Ann Grau, "The Land and the Water"

NOTE: A long passage quoted from a printed source is often set off from the rest of the text. The entire passage may be indented or set in smaller type. The passage is sometimes single-spaced instead of double-spaced, though Modern Language Association guidelines call for double-spacing. When a quotation is set off in any of these ways, no quotation marks are necessary.

(6) Use single quotation marks to enclose a quotation within a quotation.

EXAMPLES The teacher requested, "Jorge, please explain what Emerson meant when he said, 'To be great is to be misunderstood.' " [Notice that the period is placed inside the single quotation mark.]

MECHANICS

The teacher asked, "Jorge, do you understand what Emerson meant when he said, 'To be great is to be misunderstood'?" [The question mark is placed inside the double quotation marks, not the single quotation mark, because the entire quotation of the teacher's words is a question.]

(7) When writing ***dialogue*** (a conversation), begin a new paragraph every time the speaker changes, and enclose the speaker's words in quotation marks.

EXAMPLE "But what kind of authentic and valuable information do you require?" asked Klapaucius.

"All kinds, as long as it's true," replied the pirate. "You never can tell what facts may come in handy. I already have a few hundred wells and cellars full of them, but there's room for twice again as much. So out with it; tell me everything you know, and I'll jot it down. But make it snappy!"

"A fine state of affairs," Klapaucius whispered in Trurl's ear. "He could keep us here for an eon or two before we tell him everything we know. Our knowledge is colossal!!"

"Wait," whispered Trurl, "I have an idea."

Stanislaw Lem, from "The Sixth Sally"

EXERCISE 4 Using Quotation Marks with Other Marks of Punctuation

Add quotation marks and other punctuation marks where they are needed in the following dialogue. Also correct any errors in the use of capitalization, and begin a new paragraph each time the speaker changes.

EXAMPLE [1] You can tell from this picture Lloyd said that people have a lot of fun during the Juneteenth holiday. [2] But I don't get it

[1] *"You can tell from this picture," Lloyd said, "that people have a lot of fun during the Juneteenth holiday. [2] But I don't get it."*

[1] Do you mean Janelle asked that you don't understand having fun or you don't understand Juneteenth [2] Lloyd, who didn't like being misunderstood, quickly replied stop joking around [3] Janelle said I'll be glad to tell you what Juneteenth is;

MECHANICS

COMMON ERROR

Problem. When writing dialogue, many students fail to begin new paragraphs when there is a change of speaker.

Solution. Explain to students that just as play scripts guide actors, dialogue in writing should guide readers in interpretation. A new paragraph on the page should serve to indicate where each character begins speaking.

Explain to students that paragraphing allows a writer to compose several lines of dialogue without adding *she said* or *he asked.* You might remind students that when they write dialogue and their speaker changes, they might lightly write each speaker's name in the margin and check to make sure that each time the speaker changes, a new paragraph begins.

MECHANICS

ANSWERS

Exercise 4

[1] "Do you mean," Janelle asked, "that you don't understand having fun or you don't understand Juneteenth?"

[2] Lloyd, who didn't like being misunderstood, quickly replied, "Stop joking around."

[3] Janelle said, "I'll be glad to tell you what Juneteenth is"; she hadn't meant to upset Lloyd. **[4]** "Juneteenth is

SELECTION AMENDMENT

Description of change: excerpted
Rationale: to focus on the concept of writing dialogue presented in this chapter

celebrated every year on June 19," she continued, "to mark the day in 1865 when a Union general proclaimed the slaves in Texas to be free. **[5]** It's celebrated not only in Texas but also throughout the South."

[6] Lloyd interrupted, "Why were the Texas slaves proclaimed free so long after Lincoln's Emancipation Proclamation?"

[7] "Remember that Lincoln gave his proclamation in 1863, but the Civil War continued until April 9, 1865," Janelle replied, "and then it took a while for news to spread."

[8] Janelle thought that her explanations had satisfied Lloyd, but then he asked, "So how is Juneteenth celebrated?"

[9] "Now that's a question you don't need to ask," she replied, "because you go to the Juneteenth parade every year. **[10]** It's celebrated much the same everywhere," she added, "with families enjoying picnics, parades, games, and music."

INTEGRATING THE LANGUAGE ARTS

Mechanics and Writing. Have students create guides to keep in their notebooks for reference when punctuating titles in their writing. With the class, compile a list that includes the items in **Rule 30k** and **Rule 30n.** The class might brainstorm to add other categories to the list. Then have students alphabetize the list and designate beside each category which punctuation—italics or quotation marks—it requires.

MECHANICS

she hadn't meant to upset Lloyd. [4] Juneteenth is celebrated every year on June 19 she continued to mark the day in 1865 when a Union general proclaimed the slaves in Texas to be free. [5] It's celebrated not only in Texas but also throughout the South [6] Lloyd interrupted why were the Texas slaves proclaimed free so long after Lincoln's Emancipation Proclamation [7] Remember that Lincoln gave his proclamation in 1863, but the Civil War continued until April 9, 1865 Janelle replied and then it took a while for news to spread [8] Janelle thought that her explanations had satisfied Lloyd, but then he asked So how is Juneteenth celebrated [9] Now that's a question you don't need to ask she replied Because you go to the Juneteenth parade every year. [10] It's celebrated much the same everywhere she added With families enjoying picnics, parades, games, and music.

30n. Use quotation marks to enclose titles of short works, such as short stories, poems, essays, articles, songs, episodes of television series, and chapters and other parts of books.

TYPE OF NAME	EXAMPLES	
Short Stories	"The Open Boat"	"The Tell-Tale Heart"
Poems	"Guitarreros"	"Thanatopsis"
Essays	"On the Mall"	"The Creative Process"
Articles	"Old Poetry and Modern Music" "How to Improve Your Grades"	

(continued)

TYPE OF NAME	EXAMPLES
Songs	"On Top of Old Smoky" "Wind Beneath My Wings"
TV Episodes	"The Flight of the Condor" "Tony's Surprise Party"
Chapters and Parts of Books	"The World Was New" "The Colonies' Struggle for Freedom"

REFERENCE NOTE: For examples of titles that are italicized, see pages 875–876.

30o. Use quotation marks to enclose slang words, invented words, technical terms, and dictionary definitions of words.

EXAMPLES Chloe reached for a high note and hit a "clinker."
The newspaper reporter described the Halloween festival as "spooktacular."
Although I am not familiar with computer language, I do know that to "boot" a disk does not mean to kick it.
The verb *recapitulate* means "to repeat briefly" or "to summarize."

NOTE: Avoid using slang words in formal speaking and writing. When using technical terms, be sure to explain their meanings. If you are not sure whether a word is appropriate or its meaning is clear, consult an up-to-date dictionary.

MECHANICS

EXERCISE 5 Correcting Sentences by Adding Quotation Marks, Other Punctuation Marks, and Capitalization

Revise the following sentences by adding quotation marks, other marks of punctuation, and capitalization.

EXAMPLE 1. In one of his books, Mark Twain wrote It is easier to stay out than get out
1. *In one of his books, Mark Twain wrote, "It is easier to stay out than get out."*

1. The section called "People in the News" in this book has some interesting facts about celebrities.

CRITICAL THINKING
Application

A simple reminder to avoid both slang words and technical terms in writing helps students avoid excessive informality and jargon. But it is also important for students to recognize legitimate uses of both slang and technical language.

Stories and personal narratives are forms that use slang to create believable characterization. Research reports and literary analyses may need technical terms for a clear presentation. Students should learn to choose the best words to suit the purpose, tone, and audience of their writing. Ask students to write down three instances in which slang would be appropriate in writing.

MECHANICS

REVIEW A

OBJECTIVE

- To correct punctuation and capitalization in a dialogue

2. Are you going to the Greek Festival asked Mr. Doney or didn't you know that it's scheduled for this weekend
3. Our teacher quoted Willa Cather's words there are only two or three human stories, and they go on repeating themselves as fiercely as if they had never happened before.
4. How do I find out who wrote the poem Dream Deferred Jill asked her English teacher
5. The phrase frosting on the cake has nothing to do with dessert it refers to something additional that is a pleasant surprise.
6. I'm still hungry complained Donna after finishing a plate of stew that baked apple looks tempting
7. When faced with a frightening situation, I often recite Psalm 23 4, which starts Yea, though I walk through the valley of the shadow of death, I will fear no evil.
8. Perhaps the finest memorial to Abraham Lincoln is the poem When Lilacs Last in the Dooryard Bloom'd in Walt Whitman's book Sequel to Drum-Taps.
9. Are you saying I don't know the answer or I don't understand the question
10. Ms. Hammer warned us that the movie was, to use her words, a parody of the novel furthermore she advised us not to waste our money and time by seeing it.

MECHANICS

MECHANICS

REVIEW A **Proofreading a Dialogue for Correct Punctuation**

In the following dialogue, correct any errors in the use of quotation marks and other marks of punctuation. Also correct any errors in the use of capitalization, and regroup sentences to form a new paragraph each time the speaker changes.

Carets indicate paragraph breaks.

EXAMPLE [1] I think The Weeping Woman would be a good title for my new song Tomás told Jim. can you guess what it's about

1. *"I think 'The Weeping Woman' would be a good title for my new song," Tomás told Jim. "Can you guess what it's about?"*

[1] Well, I once read a magazine article titled La Llorona, the Weeping Woman about a popular Mexican American legend, Jim replied. [2] That's the legend I'm talking about Tomás

SEGMENT 7 *(pp. 885–887)*

ELLIPSIS POINTS Rule 30p

OBJECTIVE

- To use ellipsis points to punctuate omissions in a written passage

exclaimed. I first heard it when I was a little boy growing up in southern California.

[3] I think Jim commented, People in the music business would call the song a tear-jerker because it tells a sad story.

[4] I'll say it's sad Tomás replied it's about a poor, wronged woman who goes crazy, drowns her children, and kills herself; then she returns as a ghost to look for them forever.

[5] It's frightening to hear when you're young because La Llorona is usually described as a headless woman dressed all in white.

[6] Isn't she usually seen around water Jim asked. [7] Yes, Tomás said but you didn't mention one of the scariest things: her fingernails look like knives.

[8] Didn't your mother ever say, Don't believe those horrible stories, ~~son asked~~ Jim. **8.** son,'?" asked

[9] Oh, sure Tomás replied. to tell the truth, I never did really believe them. But they are great stories.

[10] Well, maybe, but give me a humorous story like The Catbird Seat any day Jim said.

Ellipsis Points

30p. Use ellipsis points (. . .) to mark omissions from quoted material and pauses in a written passage.

Omissions from Quoted Material

ORIGINAL Sitting here tonight, many years later, with more time than money, I think about those faces that pass before my eyes like it was yesterday. They remind me of the chances and temptations to become an outlaw. I sure came through a tough mill. I see those men as they stood in those old days of the Golden West—some of them in the springtime of their manhood, so beautiful and strong that it makes you wonder, because their hearts are as black as night, and they are cruel, treacherous and merciless as a man-eating tiger of the jungle.

Andrew García, from *Tough Trip Through Paradise*

MECHANICS

Teacher's ResourceBank™

RESOURCES

ELLIPSIS POINTS

- Ellipsis Points 355

QUICK REMINDER

Write the following sentence on the chalkboard and ask students to replace the underlined part with ellipsis points:

When I go to college, I plan to <u>take many interesting courses, join a service fraternity, play intramural sports, and</u> experience as much as I can.

[When I go to college, I plan to . . . experience as much as I can.]

Ask students to think of at least two reasons why ellipsis points might be used [space constraints, deleting unnecessary material].

SELECTION AMENDMENT

Description of change: excerpted

Rationale: to focus on the concept of using ellipsis points presented in this chapter

MECHANICS

MEETING INDIVIDUAL NEEDS

LEP/ESL

General Strategies. Some students may have trouble deciding which words in a sentence or passage can be replaced with ellipsis points. You may want to discuss summarization and the difference between general and specific details. The discussion will help students understand when to use ellipsis points and how to replace unnecessary details.

SELECTION AMENDMENT
Description of change: excerpted
Rationale: to focus on the concept of using ellipsis points presented in this chapter

MECHANICS

(1) If the quoted material that comes before the ellipsis points is not a complete sentence, use three ellipsis points with a space before the first point.

EXAMPLE In his autobiography, *Tough Trip Through Paradise,* Andrew García reflects, "Sitting here tonight, . . . I think about those faces that pass before my eyes like it was yesterday."

(2) If the quoted material that comes before or after the ellipsis points is a complete sentence, use an end mark before the ellipsis points.

EXAMPLE García observes, "I see those men as they stood in those old days of the Golden West—some of them in the springtime of their manhood. . . ." [The period is placed before the ellipsis points.]

(3) If one sentence or more is omitted, ellipsis points follow the end mark that precedes the omitted material.

EXAMPLE Recalling his youth, Andrew García writes, "Sitting here tonight, many years later, with more time than money, I think about those faces that pass before my eyes like it was yesterday. . . . I sure came through a tough mill." [The period precedes the ellipsis points.]

To show that a full line or more of poetry has been omitted, use an entire line of spaced periods.

EXAMPLE A single flow'r he sent me, since we met.
All tenderly his messenger he chose;
. . . .
Why is it no one ever sent me yet
One perfect limousine, do you suppose?

Dorothy Parker, from "One Perfect Rose"

MECHANICS

Pauses in Written Passages

(4) To indicate a pause in a written passage, use three ellipsis points with a space before the first point.

EXAMPLE "Well . . . I can't really say," hedged the company's representative.

SEGMENT 8 *(pp. 887–895)*

APOSTROPHES Rules 30q–30s

OBJECTIVES

- To proofread for and to correct incorrect possessive forms
- To use apostrophes to form possessive nouns and pronouns
- To proofread for errors in contractions and plurals

EXERCISE 6 Using Ellipsis Points Correctly

Omit the italicized parts of the following passages. Use ellipsis points to punctuate each omission correctly.

1. Yet El Hoyo is not an outpost of a few families against the world. *It fights for no cause except those which soothe its immediate angers.* It laughs and cries with the same amount of passion in times of plenty and of want.

   1. world. . . . It

   Mario Suárez, from "Tucson, Arizona: El Hoyo"

2. Yellowstone, it seemed to me, was the top of the world, *a region of deep lakes and dark timber, canyons and waterfalls.* But beautiful as it is, one might have the sense of confinement there.

   N. Scott Momaday, from the Introduction to *The Way to Rainy Mountain*

   2. world, ... But

3. A cloud, *the exact color of the boy's hat and shaped like a turnip,* had descended over the sun, and another, worse looking, crouched behind the car.

   3. cloud, . . . had

   Flannery O'Connor, from "The Life You Save May Be Your Own"

4. I am silver and exact. I have no preconceptions.
   Whatever I see I swallow immediately
   Just as it is, unmisted by love or dislike.
   I am not cruel, only truthful—

   Sylvia Plath, from "Mirror"

5. What would happen to me here? *Would I survive?* My expectations were modest. I wanted only a job.

   5. here? . . . My

   Richard Wright, from *American Hunger*

4. I am silver and exact. I have no preconceptions.
. . . .
I am not cruel, only truthful —

Apostrophes

Possessive Case

The ***possessive case*** of a noun or a pronoun shows ownership or relationship.

OWNERSHIP	the **performers'** costumes	**Ellen Zwilich's** music
	Grandmother's recipe	**your** responsibility
RELATIONSHIP	the **team's** coach	ten **dollars'** worth
	my best **friend's** sister	**our** cousins

MECHANICS

EXERCISE 6

Teaching Note. You may want to point out to students that usage varies as to retaining a comma before an ellipsis.

Teacher's ResourceBank™

RESOURCES

APOSTROPHES

- Apostrophes 356

QUICK REMINDER

Write the following sentences on the chalkboard and ask students to rewrite them so that apostrophes are needed:

1. She enjoys the class taught by Ms. Defoyd. [She enjoys Ms. Defoyd's class.]
2. We agree with the ideas of the other students. [We agree with the other students' ideas.]
3. This car is owned by my sister-in-law. [This is my sister-in-law's car.]
4. They like the music of Ravel and Mozart. [They like Ravel's and Mozart's music.]
5. The soup is not ready. [The soup isn't ready.]

AMENDMENTS TO SELECTIONS

Description of change: excerpted
Rationale: to focus on the concept of using ellipsis points presented in this chapter

MECHANICS

MEETING INDIVIDUAL NEEDS

LEP/ESL

Spanish. Spanish has a possessive form for pronouns but does not use a possessive form for nouns. For example, instead of *José's book,* Spanish uses *the book of Jose.* To provide extra practice in using the possessive form, give students statements that they can rephrase to include a possessive noun. An example is "This book belongs to José. It is . . . ." [José's book]

MECHANICS

30q. Use an apostrophe in forming the possessive of nouns and indefinite pronouns.

(1) To form the possessive of a singular noun, add an apostrophe and an *s.*

EXAMPLES	a **bird's** nest	**Ross's** opinion
	the **principal's** office	**everyone's** responsibility

NOTE: When forming the possessive of a singular noun ending in an *s* sound, add only an apostrophe if the noun has two or more syllables and if the addition of *'s* will make the noun awkward to pronounce. Otherwise, add *'s.*

EXAMPLES	for **conscience'** sake	Ms. **Schwartz's** car
	Hercules' strength	the **witness's** testimony

(2) To form the possessive of a plural noun ending in *s,* add only the apostrophe.

EXAMPLES	the **girls'** gym	the **Joneses'** house
	the **players'** uniforms	the **volunteers'** efforts

The few plural nouns that do not end in *s* form the possessive by adding an apostrophe and an *s.*

EXAMPLES **men's** fashions **children's** toys

NOTE: Do not use an apostrophe to form the plural of a noun. Remember that an apostrophe indicates ownership or relationship, not number.

INCORRECT Carl Lewis has won six Olympic gold medal's.
CORRECT Carl Lewis has won six Olympic gold **medals.**

MECHANICS

(3) Do not use an apostrophe with possessive personal pronouns or with the possessive pronoun *whose.*

Possessive Personal Pronouns	
my, mine	our, ours
your, yours	their, theirs
his, her, hers, its	

INCORRECT The books were her's.
CORRECT The books were **hers.**

INCORRECT The leopard can't change it's spots.
CORRECT The leopard can't change **its** spots.

INCORRECT Marjorie is the girl who's mother I met.
CORRECT Marjorie is the girl **whose** mother I met.

REFERENCE NOTE: Do not confuse the possessive pronouns *its, your, their, theirs,* and *whose* with the contractions *it's, you're, they're, there's,* and *who's.* See pages 892, 919, 924, and 925. For more about possessive pronouns, see pages 674–675 and 683–684.

(4) To form the possessive of an indefinite pronoun, add an apostrophe and an *s.*

EXAMPLES Each **one's** time is recorded separately.
He seems to need **everybody's** attention.

Indefinite Pronouns in the Possessive Case			
another's	everybody's	no one's	somebody's
anybody's	everyone's	one's	someone's
anyone's	nobody's	other's	

NOTE: In such forms as *anyone else* and *somebody else,* the correct possessives are *anyone else's* and *somebody else's.*

EXERCISE 7 Proofreading for Correct Possessive Forms

Most of the following items contain an incorrect possessive form. For each error, give the correct form of the word. If an item is correct, write *C.*

MEETING INDIVIDUAL NEEDS

STUDENTS WITH SPECIAL NEEDS

To eliminate the need for students to copy all the exercises, you may want to enlarge individual copies of the exercises in this segment and give them to students. This procedure will enable students to focus their efforts on placement of apostrophes rather than on the difficult process of copying.

MECHANICS

A DIFFERENT APPROACH

To help students become more familiar with the use of apostrophes, divide the class into groups of three and have each group search through newspapers, magazines, or other texts for examples of different uses of apostrophes. After an allotted time, spokespersons from each group can report on their findings.

MECHANICS

EXAMPLE **1.** Chris' tapes
1. *Chris's tapes*

1. It is her's.
2. womens department
3. that boys radio
4. Who's is it? **4.** Whose
5. fly's wings **5.** C
6. scissors' blades **6.** C
7. mice's tails **7.** C
8. childrens program
9. no ones fault
10. the Harlem Globetrotters's game
11. San Jose's industries **11.** C
12. a Buddhist's beliefs **12.** C
13. leaves' color **13.** C
14. It is somebody's else. **14.** somebody else's.
15. soldiers' rations **15.** C
16. it's shiny surface
17. That is their's.
18. churches spire
19. the Siouxs land
20. a horses hooves

(5) Form the possessive of only the last word in a compound word, in the name of an organization or business firm, or in a word group showing joint possession.

EXAMPLES father-in-**law's** gloves
Taylor, Sanders, and **Weissman's** law office
Roz and **Denise's** idea

REFERENCE NOTE: For more information about compound nouns, see pages 554–555.

When a possessive pronoun is part of a word group showing joint possession, each noun in the word group is also possessive.

EXAMPLE Chen**'s,** Ramona**'s,** and **my** project

(6) Form the possessive of each noun in a word group showing individual possession of similar items.

EXAMPLES **Baldwin's** and **Ellison's** writings
the **doctor's** and **dentist's** fees

(7) When used in the possessive form, words indicating time, such as *minute, hour, day, week, month,* and *year,* and words indicating amounts in cents or dollars require apostrophes.

EXAMPLES a **week's** vacation — four **weeks'** vacation
a **dollar's** worth — five **dollars'** worth

MECHANICS

EXERCISE 8 Forming Possessive Nouns and Pronouns

Each of the following phrases expresses a possessive relationship. Revise each word group so that a possessive noun or pronoun expresses the same relationship.

EXAMPLE 1. promise of my sister-in-law
1. *my sister-in-law's promise*

1. party of Juan and Geraldo
2. clothes of babies
3. jobs of my brothers-in-law
4. village of Inuits
5. pay of two weeks
6. restaurant of Charlie and Barney
7. worth of one dollar
8. coats of the gentlemen
9. singing of the birds
10. plans of the school board
11. victory of the players
12. languages of Sumer and Egypt
13. delay of six months
14. testimonies of the clerk and the customer
15. streets of West Baden
16. name of it
17. flooding of the Guadalupe River
18. hope of everyone else
19. opinions of the people
20. route of our mail carrier

Contractions

30r. Use an apostrophe to show where letters, words, or numbers have been omitted in a contraction.

A ***contraction*** is a shortened form of a word, word group, or figure in which an apostrophe takes the place of all the letters, words, or numbers that are omitted.

EXAMPLES

I am	**I'm**	they had	**they'd**
let us	**let's**	where is	**where's**
of the clock	**o'clock**	we are	**we're**
she would	**she'd**	you will	**you'll**
1992	**'92**	Pat is	**Pat's**

The word *not* can be shortened to *n't* and added to a verb, usually without any change in the spelling of the verb.

EXAMPLES	is not	**isn't**	has not	**hasn't**
	do not	**don't**	should not	**shouldn't**
	does not	**doesn't**	were not	**weren't**
EXCEPTIONS	will not	**won't**	can not	**can't**

ANSWERS

Exercise 8

1. Juan and Geraldo's party
2. babies' clothes
3. my brothers-in-law's jobs
4. Inuits' village
5. two weeks' pay
6. Charlie and Barney's restaurant
7. one dollar's worth
8. the gentlemen's coats
9. the birds' singing
10. the school board's plans
11. the players' victory
12. Sumer's and Egypt's languages
13. six months' delay
14. the clerk's and the customer's testimonies
15. West Baden's streets
16. its name
17. the Guadalupe River's flooding
18. everyone else's hope
19. the people's opinions
20. our mail carrier's route

COMMON ERROR

Problem. Because some contractions and possessive pronouns sound alike (*who's/whose; it's/its; you're/your; they're/their; there's/theirs*), students may confuse them when writing.

Solution. Make a list of confusing contraction/possessive pronoun pairs. Suggest that students read all constructions with apostrophes as if they were two words. If the expanded phrase makes sense, the word is a contraction and should be written with an apostrophe.

WRITING APPLICATION

OBJECTIVE

- To use contractions in informal dialogue

WRITING APPLICATION

In this assignment, students are asked to use contractions to write informal dialogue. As they write a scene for a play, students will have an opportunity to apply what they have learned about using apostrophes in contractions.

Do not confuse contractions with possessive pronouns.

CONTRACTIONS	POSSESSIVE PRONOUNS
It's [*It is*] late. **It's** [*It has*] been an exciting week.	**Its** wing is broken.
Who's [*Who is*] in charge? **Who's** [*Who has*] been keeping score?	**Whose** ticket is this?
You're [*You are*] a good student.	**Your** shoe is untied.
They're [*They are*] in the library. **There's** [*There is*] no one at home.	**Their** house is for sale. Those dogs are **theirs.**

WRITING APPLICATION

Using Contractions in Informal Dialogue

In casual conversation, people often take shortcuts. For example, how many times have you heard "how's it going" for *how is it going* and "there're" for *there are*? Writers use apostrophes to help show these shortened forms, called *contractions,* in written dialogue. Using contractions makes a written work sound more like natural speech. In the following passage, notice how the contractions help make the conversation between two friends, Jean and Berenger, more believable.

> BERENGER: [*admiringly*] You always look so immaculate.
> JEAN: [*continuing his inspection of* BERENGER] Your clothes are all crumpled, they're a disgrace! Your shirt is downright filthy, and your shoes . . . [BERENGER *tries to hide his feet under the table.*] Your shoes haven't been touched. What a mess you're in! And look at your shoulders . . .
> BERENGER: What's the matter with my shoulders?
> JEAN: Turn round! Come on, turn round! You've been leaning against some wall. [BERENGER *holds his hand*

> *out docilely to* JEAN.] No, I haven't got a brush with me; it would make my pockets bulge. [*Still docile,* BERENGER *flicks his shoulders to get rid of the white dust;* JEAN *averts his head.*] Heavens! Where did you get all that from?
>
> Eugène Ionesco, from *Rhinoceros*

Although contractions are a natural part of speech, they are inappropriate in formal writing such as research papers, business letters, and reports. (For more about the differences between formal and informal English, see pages 484–488.)

WRITING ACTIVITY

For your final project in drama class, you've decided to write and produce a short play. You've already drafted a scene-by-scene outline of the play. In one scene, the two main characters will have a heated discussion about something that's important to them. Write the dialogue for your scene. Use contractions to make the characters' speech sound natural and realistic.

Prewriting First, brainstorm some ideas for your main characters. Are they two teenagers? an older and a younger brother or sister? a parent and a child? Once you decide who your characters are, think about the sort of discussion they might have. You can make their argument silly, humorous, serious, dramatic, or whatever you wish. Jot down some notes for the dialogue. Decide how the characters will resolve their argument at the end of the scene. Before you begin your draft, you may want to look at the **Writing Workshop** on pages 193–196 for help with writing dialogue for plays.

Writing Follow the form for presenting dialogue in a play (pages 193–196). In your first draft, concentrate on getting down the basic content of your characters' conversation. You can polish the dialogue later as you evaluate and revise. Be sure that your dialogue focuses on a specific topic or issue and that you maintain a consistent tone throughout.

Evaluating and Revising To help you evaluate the dialogue, you might ask two friends to read the parts of the

MECHANICS

CRITICAL THINKING
Synthesis

After students have written their informal dialogues, ask them to rewrite the dialogues by changing all contractions to their formal constructions. Discuss with students the effect that removing the contractions has on the dialogue. [The removal will probably cause the language to sound stilted and unnatural.]

PREWRITING

Explain to students that often an author will create tension and conflict by giving the characters totally different personalities. Because the assignment asks for dialogue of a heated discussion, creating characters that will naturally be in opposition to each other is important. Ask students to brainstorm possible personalities that might clash.

SELECTION AMENDMENT

Description of change: excerpted
Rationale: to focus on the concept of contractions in conversation presented in this chapter

MECHANICS

PROOFREADING AND PUBLISHING

Have students dramatize their dialogues for the class. Some students might also enjoy adding stage directions to their dialogues.

MECHANICS

characters. As you listen, ask yourself these questions. Does each line of dialogue sound natural? Does your dialogue have the tone you want? Do the characters resolve their argument in a realistic way? If not, add, cut, or revise words, phrases, or entire lines to achieve the effect you want. Use contractions to help make your dialogue sound like an actual discussion between two people.

Proofreading and Publishing Because they're small, apostrophes and other punctuation marks are easy to miss. Proofread your dialogue carefully for correct punctuation. Make sure you've begun a new paragraph each time the speaker changes. With your teacher's permission, you may want to produce your scene for the class. Cast two volunteer actors for the roles, and work with them to get the dialogue just right. Decide what actions and gestures should accompany the dialogue. Use simple props to help make the scene realistic.

MECHANICS

Plurals

30s. Use an apostrophe and an *s* to form the plurals of all lowercase letters, some uppercase letters, and some words referred to as words.

EXAMPLES There are two ***r*'s** and two ***s*'s** in *embarrassed*.
Try not to use so many ***I*'s** in your cover letter. [Without the apostrophe, the plural of the pronoun *I* would spell *Is*.]
After the happy couple said their ***I do*'s**, everyone cheered.

You may add only an *s* to form the plurals of such items—except lowercase letters—if the plural forms will not cause misreading.

EXAMPLE Compact discs **(CDs)** were introduced more than ten years ago.

NOTE: Use apostrophes consistently.

EXAMPLE **On her report card were three A's and three B's.**
[Without the apostrophe, the plural of *A* would spell *As.* The apostrophe in the plural of *B* is unnecessary but is included for consistency.]

REFERENCE NOTE: For more about forming these kinds of plurals and the plurals of numbers, see page 912.

EXERCISE 9 Proofreading for Errors in Contractions and Plurals

Add or delete apostrophes as needed in the following sentences. [Note: You may need to change the spelling of some words.]

EXAMPLE **1. Lets try to find a modern puzzle maze that wont be too difficult for us to explore.**
1. *Let's; won't*

1. ~~Your~~ lucky if you've ever been through an old-fashioned hedge maze such as the one pictured below. **1. You're**
2. It's like a maze from an English castle; in fact, we can't help being reminded of the maze at Hampton Court Palace.
3. From above, some of the bushes look like h's, t's, and other letters.
4. Don't you wonder if these people will find ~~they're~~ way out by dusk or even ten o'clock? **4. their**
5. I've read that mazes like this one became popular in Europe during the 1500s and 1600s; however, my uncle said that he's read about mazes that were built two thousand years ago.

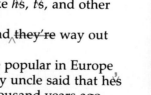

MECHANICS

SEGMENT 9 *(pp. 896–899)*

HYPHENS Rules 30t–30x

OBJECTIVE

- To write sentences that contain hyphens

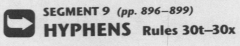

Teacher's ResourceBank™

RESOURCES

HYPHENS

- Hyphens 357

QUICK REMINDER

Write the following words on the chalkboard and ask students to divide the words with hyphens as if the words were at the end of a line of text:

1. fingernail [finger-nail]
2. passenger [pas-sen-ger]
3. enough [should not be divided]
4. twenty-one [twenty-one]

Point out that using hyphens to divide words isn't always a matter of common sense.

MEETING INDIVIDUAL NEEDS

LEP/ESL

General Strategies. English differs from Romance languages such as Spanish, French, and Italian because English speakers can create new words by inventing compound adjectives. You may want to point this out to ESL students. You may also want to explain that the words in compound adjectives are often joined by hyphens. Ask students to practice forming compound adjectives like these in the following phrases:

1. a tree-climbing boy
2. reddish-brown leaves
3. a hair-raising experience

MECHANICS

Hyphens

30t. Use a hyphen to divide a word at the end of a line.

When dividing a word at the end of a line, remember the following rules:

- Do not divide a one-syllable word.

INCORRECT The treaty that ended the war was signed in Paris in 1783.

CORRECT The treaty that ended the war was signed in Paris in 1783.

- Divide a word only between syllables.

INCORRECT Shashona wrote a story about the endangered gray wolf.

CORRECT Shashona wrote a story about the endangered gray wolf.

NOTE: When you are not sure about the division of a word, look in a dictionary.

- Divide an already hyphenated word at the hyphen.

INCORRECT Among Elena's drawings were two self-portraits.

CORRECT Among Elena's drawings were two self-
portraits.

- Do not divide a word so that one letter stands alone.

INCORRECT Most of the buildings there are made of a-
dobe.

CORRECT Most of the buildings there are made of adobe.

MECHANICS

30u. Use a hyphen with compound numbers from *twenty-one* to *ninety-nine* and with fractions used as modifiers.

EXAMPLES six hundred **twenty-five**
a **three-fourths** quorum [*Three-fourths* is an adjective modifying *quorum.*]
three fourths of the audience [*Three fourths* is not a modifier. *Fourths* is a noun modified by the adjective *three.*]

30v. Use a hyphen with the prefixes *ex–*, *self–*, and *all–*, with the suffix *–elect*, and with all prefixes before a proper noun or proper adjective.

EXAMPLES	**ex-**mayor	**pre-**Civil War
	self-improvement	**mid-**Atlantic
	governor**-elect**	**trans-**Siberian
	all-star	**pro-**American

REFERENCE NOTE: For more guidelines on adding prefixes and suffixes to words, see pages 905–907.

30w. Hyphenate a compound adjective when it precedes the noun it modifies.

EXAMPLES	a **well-designed** engine	an engine that is **well designed**
	a **world-famous** skier	a skier who is **world famous**

Do not use a hyphen if one of the modifiers is an adverb ending in *–ly*.

EXAMPLE a **partly finished** research paper

NOTE: Some compound adjectives are always hyphenated, whether they precede or follow the words they modify.

EXAMPLES	an **up-to-date** dictionary	a dictionary that is **up-to-date**
	a **well-informed** debater	a debater who is **well-informed**

If you are unsure about whether a compound adjective is hyphenated, look up the word in a dictionary.

30x. Use a hyphen to prevent awkwardness or confusion.

EXAMPLES **de-emphasize** [prevents awkwardness of two identical vowels]
anti-inflammatory [prevents awkwardness of two identical vowels]
re-cover a chair [prevents confusion with *recover*]
a **re-creation** of the event [prevents confusion with *recreation*]

MECHANICS

INTEGRATING THE LANGUAGE ARTS

Technology Link. Because most computer programs simply move words that are too long to the next line or automatically insert hyphens to divide words, students may question the purpose of studying the rules for hyphens. Point out that to proofread computer-generated text accurately and to be able to write by hand when computers are not available, students need to know the rules for dividing words and to use a dictionary when they are unsure.

MECHANICS

REVIEWS B and C

OBJECTIVES

- To revise groups of words by adding apostrophes and hyphens
- To proofread a paragraph and insert correct punctuation and capitalization where needed

ANSWERS

Exercise 10

Sentences will vary. Here are some possibilities:

1. Our new teacher is twenty-three years old.
2. The vote passed by a two-thirds majority.
3. The ex-governor is now a lawyer.
4. He is a well-known fashion model.
5. The skier flew down the mountain-side.

REVIEW C

Teaching Note. Answers requiring parentheses and dashes may vary. Dashes are generally used to indicate the most abrupt break in thought, whereas parentheses are used for explanatory material. Usually the writer determines the emphasis.

MECHANICS

EXERCISE 10 **Writing Sentences Using Hyphens**

Write five sentences according to the following guidelines. In your sentences, use a variety of subjects and verbs.

1. Write a sentence with a compound number.
2. Write a sentence with a fraction used as an adjective.
3. Write a sentence containing a word with the prefix *ex–*.
4. Write a sentence with a compound adjective preceding the word it modifies.
5. Write a sentence in which you break a word at the end of a line.

REVIEW B **Using Apostrophes and Hyphens**

Revise the following groups of words by adding apostrophes and hyphens where needed. If a word group is correct, write *C*.
Hyphens are indicated by the ^ symbol.

EXAMPLE **1. post World War II Europe**
1. *post-World War II Europe*

1. my sister-in-law's new pickup truck
2. trans-Alaskan
3. Achilles' heel
4. You're from Peru, aren't you?
5. one third of the class 5. C
6. Isn't soda bread Irish?
7. Who are all of these *you*'s and *they*'s?
8. three-quarter-length sleeves
9. There are three *a*'s in *alphabetical*.
10. It's theirs, not ours.
11. remark the boundary lines 11. re-mark
12. politics in the 1960s 12. C [*or* 1960's]
13. dotted all of your *i*'s
14. Didn't Anthony make your piñata?
15. self-appointed critic
16. It's after five o'clock.
17. part-time job
18. Why didn't someone an-swer the phone?
19. That's all there is to know. 19. C
20. Where's the Shaker box you bought?

REVIEW C **Proofreading a Paragraph for Correct Punctuation and Capitalization**

Most of the sentences in the following paragraph contain errors in the use of punctuation and capitalization. Rewrite each incorrect sentence, adding the necessary punctuation and capitalization. If a sentence is correct, write *C*. Answers may vary.

MECHANICS

SEGMENT 10 *(pp. 899–901)*

REVIEW: POSTTEST

OBJECTIVE

- To proofread and correct sentences and paragraphs with errors in the use of semicolons, colons, dashes, parentheses, italics, quotation marks, apostrophes, and hyphens

EXAMPLE [1] **Can we be sure sports historians arent that Abner Doubleday invented baseball, that Princeton and Rutgers played the first football game, or that golf originated in China in the second century B.C.?**

1. ***Can we be sure (sports historians aren't) that Abner Doubleday invented baseball, that Princeton and Rutgers played the first football game, or that golf originated in China in the second century B.C.?***

[1] The origins of most sports are unknown: try as we may, we cannot say exactly when or where or how such games as baseball, football, and golf were first played. [2] There is, however, one exception to this rule—the game of basketball. [3] Historians of sports know precisely where basketball began; they know precisely when it began; and, perhaps the most interesting fact of all, they know the name of the man who invented it—Dr. James Naismith. [4] In the winter of 1891–1892, Naismith, who was then an instructor at the YMCA Training College (now called Springfield College) in Springfield, Massachusetts, had a problem on his hands. [5] The football season was over; the baseball season had not yet begun. [6] His students needed indoor exercise at a competitive sport; however, no such sport existed. [7] Working with the materials at hand, Naismith set himself the task of creating a new indoor sport. [8] He fastened two peach baskets to the walls at opposite ends of his gymnasium, and, using a soccer ball, he devised the game that we call basketball today. [9] He started with eighteen available players, and the first rule he wrote read as follows: "There shall be nine players on each side." [10] Imagine eighteen players set loose on a modern basketball court! **10.** C

7. C

MECHANICS

Review: Posttest

A. Proofreading Sentences for Correct Punctuation

The following sentences contain errors in the use of semicolons, colons, dashes, parentheses, brackets, italics (underlining), quotation marks, apostrophes, and hyphens. Rewrite the

MECHANICS

sentences correcting the errors. [Note: There may be more than one error in a sentence. You may have to add punctuation where it is needed, or you may have to delete punctuation that is incorrectly used.] Hyphens are indicated by the ‸ symbol.

EXAMPLE **1. Did you say "that you want to join us"?**
1. ***Did you say that you want to join us?***

1. ~~Ed~~ and Jim's essays were both titled "Kwanzaa: A Special Time for African Americans." **1. Ed's**
2. "Among the writers in America today, he (Galway Kinnell) has earned his reputation as an outstanding poet," noted the critic in <u>Newsweek</u>.
3. The circus audience applauded and cheered as the acro-bats performed the perfectly-timed stunt. **4. stated, 'Turn**
4. Paula said in a desperate tone, "I know Sue's directions ~~stated, "Turn~~ right when you get to the gas station,' but, unfortunately, I'm not sure which gas station she meant."
5. William Butler Yeats (1865–1939), an Irish poet who won the Nobel Prize for literature, was once a member of the Irish parliament.
6. I couldn't get along in school without the following: a college dictionary, a thesaurus, and a pocket calculator.
7. My driver's license won't expire for another two weeks.
8. "Well, I don't know," Lauren said. "Where do you think all this soot comes from?"
9. Several people I respect think <u>Raintree County</u> by Ross Lockridge, Jr., is the greatest American ~~novel, I~~ plan to read it soon. **9. novel; I**
10. Here's my telephone number; call me if you decide to go to the movie.

B. Proofreading Paragraphs for Correct Punctuation

The following paragraphs of conversation contain errors in the uses of semicolons, colons, dashes, parentheses, italics (underlining), quotation marks, apostrophes, and hyphens. Rewrite each paragraph, correcting the errors. **Hyphens are indicated by the ‸ symbol.**

EXAMPLE **[1] "You may like mystery, comedy, and science fiction movies, but my favorite movies are those about real peoples lives, Ben said."**

1. *"You may like mystery, comedy, and science fiction movies; but my favorite movies are those about real people's lives," Ben said.*

[11] Tell me we've got time some of your all time favorites, then," Tani said.

[12] "I recently saw Mountains of the Moon for the first time I really learned a lot about the life of Sir Richard Burton from it," Ben replied.

[13] Whats his claim to fame? Tani asked.

[14] "Sir Richard Burton was a man of many talents he was an explorer, an author, a scholar, a linguist, and a diplomat."

[15] "Did the movie try to show all those talents?" Tani asked. That would seem difficult to do."

[16] "The movie is mostly an African adventure, its about Burtons search for the source of the Nile River," Ben said.

[17] "Some of my other favorites include, Gandhi, about the Indian independence leader, Amadeus, about Mozart's life, and *The Spirit of St. Louis,* a really old film about Charles Lindbergh."

[18] "I'll bet three fourths of our friends have never heard of most of the movies youve seen," Tani said.

[19] "The downtown video store the one owned by Ross' brother has them all," Ben said. **19. Ross's**

[20] "Biographical movies well researched ones, anyway are a good way to learn about famous people," Tani said.

MECHANICS

MECHANICS

SEGMENT 1 *(pp. 902–903)*
IMPROVING YOUR SPELLING

OBJECTIVE
- To divide words into syllables

Teacher's ResourceBank™
RESOURCES

FOR THE WHOLE CHAPTER

• Chapter Review Form A	376–377
• Chapter Review Form B	378–379
• Assessment Portfolio	
Mechanics Pretests	579–586
Mechanics Mastery Tests	605–612

CHAPTER OVERVIEW
After a few suggestions for improving spelling, the chapter takes up the most common rules governing spelling in English. The third segment of the chapter deals with words that are often confused with each other, and the chapter ends with a list of three hundred useful spelling words.

Teacher's ResourceBank™
RESOURCES

IMPROVING YOUR SPELLING

• Proofreading for Spelling Errors	371

QUICK REMINDER
Write the following words on the chalkboard and ask your students to divide them into syllables:

1. consideration [con sid er a tion]
2. custodial [cus to di al]
3. forbidden [for bid den]
4. hypocrisy [hy poc ri sy]
5. hypocrite [hyp o crite]

Ask students to check dictionaries if necessary.

31 SPELLING

Improving Your Spelling

Good Spelling Habits

Using the following techniques will improve your spelling:

1. **Pronounce words carefully.**

   EXAMPLES ath • lete [not *ath • e • lete*]
   ac • ci • den • tal • ly [not *ac • ci • dent • ly*]
   can • di • date [not *can • i • date*]

2. **Spell by syllables.** A ***syllable*** is a word part that can be pronounced by itself.

   EXAMPLES per • ma • nent [three syllables]
   op • ti • mis • tic [four syllables]
   oc • ca • sion • al • ly [five syllables]

3. **Use a dictionary.** By using a dictionary, you will become familiar with the correct pronunciations and divisions of words. In fact, using a dictionary to check the spelling of one word may help you spell other words. For example, checking the spelling of *democracy* may help you spell other words ending in *–cracy*, such as *theocracy*, *autocracy*, and *aristocracy*.

4. **Proofread for careless spelling errors.** Always reread what you have written so that you can eliminate careless spelling errors, such as typos (*thier* for *their*), missing letters (*familar* for *familiar*), and the misuse of similar-sounding words (*affect* for *effect*).

5. **Keep a spelling notebook.** Divide each page into four columns.

COLUMN 1 Write correctly any word you find troublesome.
COLUMN 2 Write the word again, dividing it into syllables and marking the stressed syllable(s). (You will likely need to use a dictionary.)
COLUMN 3 Write the word again, circling the part(s) that cause you trouble.
COLUMN 4 Jot down any comments that will help you remember the correct spelling.

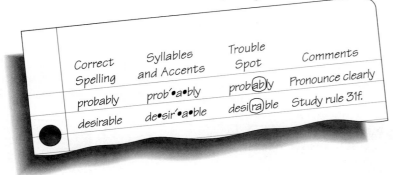

Correct Spelling	Syllables and Accents	Trouble Spot	Comments
probably	prob′•a•bly	prob(ab)ly	Pronounce clearly
desirable	de•sir′•a•ble	desi(ra)ble	Study rule 31f.

MECHANICS

EXERCISE 1 Dividing Words into Syllables

Write the syllables of each of the following words, using hyphens between the syllables. Do not look up the words in a dictionary. Be sure that the division of each word includes all of the letters of the word. When you have finished, use a dictionary to check your work. Vertical lines indicate syllable breaks.

EXAMPLE 1. accommodate
1. *ac-com-mo-date*

1. ad|ver|sa|ry
2. a|li|as
3. bar|ba|rous
4. chim|ney
5. cos|tume
6. def|i|cit
7. gen|u|ine
8. in|ci|den|tal|ly
9. pro|cras|ti|nate
10. tem|per|a|ture

MEETING INDIVIDUAL NEEDS

LEP/ESL

General Strategies. One of the keys to good spelling is correct pronunciation. Students who are at the beginning stage of learning English may need repeated drills with the pronunciation of some words, especially words with silent letters. You can work with small groups of students to drill them each day on the pronunciation of ten words. The list of spelling words at the end of the chapter can be useful for this purpose.

STUDENTS WITH SPECIAL NEEDS

Many students with special needs have a great deal of difficulty with spelling. You can help students develop strategies for circumventing such difficulties; encourage students to keep spelling notebooks and to have someone else proofread their written work. The proofreader can circle misspelled words, and the student can look them up in his or her spelling notebook or in a dictionary.

MECHANICS

TIMESAVER

You can save time by having your students do **Exercise 1** orally. One way to ensure participation by everyone in the class is to have students write their responses to each item; then call on students at random to tell the class what they wrote.

SPELLING RULES Rules 31a–31o

OBJECTIVES

- To spell *ie* and *ei* words
- To spell words with prefixes and suffixes
- To spell the plural forms of nouns

Teacher's ResourceBank™

RESOURCES

SPELLING RULES

QUICK REMINDER

Each of the misspelled words in the following sentences violates one of the spelling rules in this segment. Have students find and correct the misspelled words.

1. Carmen's soccer team had to forfiet its last game of the season. [forfeit]
2. Councilman Ortega's opponent conceeded the election at two o'clock in the morning. [conceded]
3. High school achievment tests will be given Tuesday morning. [achievement]
4. In many offices, computers are prefered. [preferred]
5. James and Thomas are brother-in-laws. [brothers-in-law]

MECHANICS

Spelling Rules

ie and *ei*

31a. Write *ie* when the sound is long *e*, except after *c*.

EXAMPLES	**believe**	**field**	**conceit**	**ceiling**	**receive**	**niece**
EXCEPTIONS	**either**	**leisure**	**neither**	**seize**	**weird**	

31b. Write *ei* when the sound is not long *e*.

EXAMPLES	**forfeit**	**freight**	**eight**	**neighbor**	**weigh**
EXCEPTIONS	**ancient**	**view**	**friend**	**mischief**	**conscience**

MECHANICS

EXERCISE 2 **Spelling *ie* and *ei* Words**

1. gr. ie .f	6. counterf. ei .t	11. p. ie .rce	16. shr. ie .k
2. th. ei .r	7. dec. ei .ve	12. l. ei .sure	17. f. ie .rce
3. v. ei .l	8. ch. ie .ftain	13. th. ie .f	18. . ei .ght
4. h. ei .r	9. perc. ei .ve	14. sl. ei .gh	19. cash. ie .r
5. bel. ie .f	10. rec. ei .pt	15. bes. ie .ge	20. y. ie .ld

HATTIE, YOU'RE HAVING TROUBLE SPELLING WORDS WITH "I" AND "E" IN THEM... I HAVE SOMETHING TO HELP...
ALL YOU HAVE TO DO IS REMEMBER THIS SIMPLE RULE: "I" BEFORE "E" EXCEPT AFTER "C"... WELL, WHAT DO YOU SAY?
WEIRD

BORN LOSER reprinted by permission of NEA, Inc.

–*cede*, –*ceed*, and –*sede*

31c. The only English word ending in –*sede* is *supersede.* The only words ending in –*ceed* are *exceed, proceed,* and *succeed.* All other words with this sound end in –*cede.*

EXAMPLES **accede** **concede** **intercede** **precede** **recede** **secede**

Adding Prefixes

A ***prefix*** is a letter or group of letters added to the beginning of a word to create a new word with a different meaning.

EXAMPLES il + legible = **il**legible pre + historic = **pre**historic
in + correct = **in**correct un + certain = **un**certain

31d. When adding a prefix, do not change the spelling of the original word.

EXAMPLES dis + satisfy = **dis**satisfy im + mature = **im**mature
mis + spell = **mis**spell re + adjust = **re**adjust

REFERENCE NOTE: For a listing of prefixes, see pages 984–986.

Adding Suffixes

A ***suffix*** is a letter or group of letters added to the end of a word to create a new word with a different meaning.

EXAMPLES help + less = help**less** work + ed = work**ed**
move + ment = move**ment** hope + ful = hope**ful**

31e. When adding the suffix *–ness* or *–ly,* do not change the spelling of the original word.

EXAMPLES plain + ness = plain**ness** casual + ly = casual**ly**
gentle + ness = gentle**ness** final + ly = final**ly**

EXCEPTION For most words ending in *y,* change the *y* to *i* before adding *–ness* or *–ly.*

empty + ness = empt**iness** busy + ly = bus**ily**
heavy + ness = heav**iness** ready + ly = read**ily**

NOTE: One-syllable adjectives ending in *y* generally follow rule 31e.

EXAMPLES dry + ness = dry**ness** shy + ly = shy**ly**

REFERENCE NOTE: For a listing of suffixes, see pages 986–987.

EXERCISE 3 **Spelling Words with Prefixes and Suffixes**

Spell each of the following words, adding the prefix or suffix given.

MECHANICS

MEETING INDIVIDUAL NEEDS

LEP/ESL

General Strategies. A review of dictionary skills may be helpful to students. To ensure that they understand the abbreviations and other keys to pronunciation and meaning, you can create a simple key as a handout. Although your mainstream students may have perfected these skills, it's important not to assume that LEP/ESL students have learned them.

MECHANICS

ANSWERS

Exercise 3

1. misinform
2. habitually
3. illegal
4. happiness
5. stubbornness
6. craftily
7. inanimate
8. immovable
9. disappear
10. dissimilar

MEETING **INDIVIDUAL** NEEDS

LEARNING STYLES

Auditory Learners. Students might benefit from deliberately mispronouncing some words while they're learning how to spell them; for example, students could pronounce any silent consonants, such as the *w* in *answer.*

MECHANICS

1. mis + inform
2. habitual + ly
3. il + legal
4. happy + ness
5. stubborn + ness
6. crafty + ly
7. in + animate
8. im + movable
9. dis + appear
10. dis + similar

31f. Drop the final silent *e* before a suffix beginning with a vowel.

EXAMPLES care + ing = car**ing** dose + age = dos**age**
love + able = lov**able** simple + er = simpl**er**

EXCEPTIONS Keep the final silent *e*
- in a word ending in *ce* or *ge* before a suffix beginning with *a* or *o:* peace**able;** courage**ous**
- in *dye* before *–ing:* dye**ing**
- in *mile* before *–age:* mile**age**

31g. Keep the final silent *e* before a suffix beginning with a consonant.

EXAMPLES hope + ful = hope**ful** love + ly = love**ly**
care + less = care**less** place + ment = place**ment**

EXCEPTIONS awe + ful = aw**ful** whole + ly = whol**ly**
argue + ment = argu**ment** nine + th = nin**th**
judge + ment = judg**ment** true + ly = tru**ly**
acknowledge + ment = acknowledg**ment** *or* acknowledge**ment**

31h. For words ending in *y* preceded by a consonant, change the *y* to *i* before any suffix that does not begin with *i.*

EXAMPLES thirsty + est = thirst**iest**
plenty + ful = plent**iful**
modify + ing = modif**ying**
accompany + ment = accompan**iment**

31i. For words ending in *y* preceded by a vowel, keep the *y* when adding a suffix.

EXAMPLES gray + est = gray**est** obey + ing = obey**ing**
play + ed = play**ed** enjoy + ment = enjoy**ment**

EXCEPTIONS day—dai**ly** lay—lai**d** pay—pai**d** say—sai**d**

MECHANICS

REVIEWS A and B

OBJECTIVES

- To spell words with suffixes
- To proofread a paragraph for spelling errors

EXERCISE 4 **Spelling Words with Suffixes**

Spell each of the following words, adding the suffix given.

1. employ + ment
2. thrifty + ness
3. beauty + fy
4. modify + cation
5. sure + ly
6. lively + er
7. share + ing
8. glide + ed
9. loose + est
10. play + ful

31j. Double the final consonant before a suffix that begins with a vowel if the word *both* (1) has only one syllable or has the accent on the last syllable *and* (2) ends in a single consonant preceded by a single vowel.

EXAMPLES thin + est = **thinnest** occur + ence = **occurrence**
rap + ing = **rapping** refer + ed = **referred**

Do not double the final consonant unless the word satisfies both of the conditions.

EXAMPLES prevent + ing = **preventing** [has accent on the last syllable but does not end in a single consonant preceded by a single vowel]
mellow + er = **mellower** [ends in a single consonant preceded by a single vowel but does not have accent on the last syllable]
refer + ence = **reference** [satisfies both conditions but addition of suffix causes shift in accent]

NOTE: The final consonant of some words may or may not be doubled. Either spelling is acceptable.

EXAMPLES cancel + ed = **canceled** *or* **cancelled**
travel + er = **traveler** *or* **traveller**

If you are not sure whether you should double the final consonant, follow rule 31j, or consult a dictionary.

REVIEW A **Spelling Words with Suffixes**

Spell each of the following words, adding the suffix given.

1. plan + ed
2. prefer + ence
3. friendly + er
4. achieve + ment
5. propel + er
6. seize + ure
7. definite + ly
8. joy + ful
9. argue + ment
10. prepare + ed

MECHANICS

ANSWERS

Exercise 4

1. employment
2. thriftiness
3. beautify
4. modification
5. surely
6. livelier
7. sharing
8. glided
9. loosest
10. playful

ANSWERS

Review A

1. planned
2. preference
3. friendlier
4. achievement
5. propeller
6. seizure
7. definitely
8. joyful
9. argument
10. prepared

MECHANICS

REVIEW B Proofreading a Paragraph for Spelling Errors

Proofread the following paragraph and correct each misspelled word.

1. scientist
2. leaving
3. management
4. succeeded
5. notified
6. permitted/dimming
7. reevaluated
8. safely
9. paid
10. received

[1] The ~~sceintist~~ Granville T. Woods (below, center) was quite an inventor. [2] After ~~leaveing~~ school at the age of ten, Woods worked on the railroads in Missouri. [3] However, his love of electrical and mechanical devices led him to study engineering and later to open a factory where his ~~managment~~ skills and knowledge served him well. [4] Later, Woods ~~succeded~~ in devising a telegraph that allowed stationmasters to communicate with engineers on moving trains. [5] With this device, speeding trains could be ~~notifyed~~ of any problems along the track, and train engineers could quickly alert stations to dangerous situations. [6] His successes ~~permited~~ Woods to relocate to New York City, and there he learned that the method theaters used for ~~diming~~ lights was responsible for many fires. [7] Woods ~~revaluated~~ the design and devised a new system. [8] This new lighting system operated ~~safly~~ and was, at the same time, 40 percent more efficient than the old one. [9] Not surprisingly, companies like American Bell Telephone and General Electric ~~payed~~ generous sums for Woods' inventions. [10] In all, Woods ~~recieved~~ over 150 patents for his inventions, and many of them, such as the electrified rail for New York City's subway, are still in use.

MECHANICS

The Granger Collection, New York

MECHANICS

Forming the Plurals of Nouns

31k. Remembering the following rules will help you spell the plural forms of nouns.

(1) For most nouns, add *–s.*

SINGULAR	player	beagle	ship	island	senator	Jefferson
PLURAL	**players**	**beagles**	**ships**	**islands**	**senators**	**Jeffersons**

(2) For nouns ending in *s, x, z, ch,* or *sh,* add *–es.*

SINGULAR	class	tax	waltz	match	brush	Chávez
PLURAL	**classes**	**taxes**	**waltzes**	**matches**	**brushes**	**Chávezes**

(3) For nouns ending in *y* preceded by a vowel, add *–s.*

SINGULAR	monkey	journey	alloy	decoy	tray	McKay
PLURAL	**monkeys**	**journeys**	**alloys**	**decoys**	**trays**	**McKays**

(4) For nouns ending in *y* preceded by a consonant, change the *y* to *i* and add *–es.*

SINGULAR	fly	country	comedy	trophy	cavity	theory
PLURAL	**flies**	**countries**	**comedies**	**trophies**	**cavities**	**theories**

EXCEPTION For proper nouns, add *–s.*
Kennedy—**Kennedys** Gregory—**Gregorys**

(5) For some nouns ending in *f* or *fe,* add *–s.* For others, change the *f* or *fe* to *v* and add *–es.*

SINGULAR	gulf	roof	belief	leaf	shelf	knife
PLURAL	**gulfs**	**roofs**	**beliefs**	**leaves**	**shelves**	**knives**

NOTE: If you are not sure how to spell the plural of a word ending in *f* or *fe,* look in a dictionary.

(6) For nouns ending in *o* preceded by a vowel, add *–s.*

SINGULAR	studio	radio	cameo	stereo	igloo	Ignacio
PLURAL	**studios**	**radios**	**cameos**	**stereos**	**igloos**	**Ignacios**

(7) For nouns ending in *o* preceded by a consonant, add *–es.*

SINGULAR	torpedo	tomato	hero	veto	potato
PLURAL	**torpedoes**	**tomatoes**	**heroes**	**vetoes**	**potatoes**

MECHANICS

MEETING INDIVIDUAL NEEDS

LEP/ESL

General Strategies. Not all languages form the plurals of nouns by changing the endings of words. Swahili, for example, forms plurals by changing prefixes. If you have students in your class who speak other languages, involve them in this lesson by asking them how plurals are formed in their native languages.

MECHANICS

A DIFFERENT APPROACH

Have students work in small groups to generate lists of the the plural forms of the last names of students in the class. Students may need to refer to the rules in this segment to complete the activity. After each group has a complete list, go over it to make certain each name is correct.

As an alternative to this activity, provide phone books or other directories and have each group list twenty-five names and their plurals.

MECHANICS

For some common nouns ending in *o* preceded by a consonant, especially those referring to music, and for proper nouns, add only an *–s*.

SINGULAR	taco	photo	piano	solo	alto	Ibo	Suro
PLURAL	tacos	photos	pianos	solos	altos	Ibos	Suros

NOTE: For some nouns ending in *o* preceded by a consonant, you may add either *–s* or *–es*.

SINGULAR	motto	tornado	mosquito	zero	banjo
PLURAL	mottos	tornados	mosquitos	zeros	banjos
	or	*or*	*or*	*or*	*or*
	mottoes	tornadoes	mosquitoes	zeroes	banjoes

If you are ever in doubt about the plural form of a noun ending in *o* preceded by a consonant, check the spelling in a dictionary.

(8) The plural of a few nouns is formed in irregular ways.

SINGULAR	tooth	goose	woman	mouse	foot	child
PLURAL	teeth	geese	women	mice	feet	children

(9) For a few nouns, the singular and the plural forms are the same.

SINGULAR AND PLURAL	sheep	deer	trout	salmon
	moose	species	Japanese	Sioux

(10) For most compound nouns, form the plural of only the last word of the compound.

SINGULAR	notebook	bookshelf	baby sitter	ten-year-old
PLURAL	notebooks	bookshelves	baby sitters	ten-year-olds

(11) For compound nouns in which one of the words is modified by the other word or words, form the plural of the noun modified.

SINGULAR	sister-in-law	runner-up	mountain goat
PLURAL	sisters-in-law	runners-up	mountain goats

NOTE: Some compound nouns have two acceptable plural forms.

SINGULAR	attorney general	court-martial	notary public
PLURAL	attorney generals	court-martials	notary publics
	or	*or*	*or*
	attorneys general	courts-martial	notaries public

MECHANICS

NOTE: Check an up-to-date dictionary whenever you are in doubt about the plural form of a compound noun.

(12) For some nouns borrowed from other languages, the plural is formed as in the original languages.

SINGULAR	**alumnus** [male]	**alumna** [female]	**phenomenon**
PLURAL	**alumni** [male]	**alumnae** [female]	**phenomena**

A few nouns borrowed from other languages have two plural forms. For each of the following nouns, the plural form preferred in English is given first.

SINGULAR	**index**	**appendix**	**formula**	**cactus**
PLURAL	**indexes**	**appendixes**	**formulas**	**cactuses**
	or	*or*	*or*	*or*
	indices	**appendices**	**formulae**	**cacti**

NOTE: Whenever you are in doubt about which spelling to use, remember that a dictionary lists the most frequently used spelling first.

"I don't know, Harry. This has the ring of authenticity."

MECHANICS

MECHANICS

REVIEW C

OBJECTIVE

- To explain the spelling of words by referring to rules

ANSWERS

Exercise 5

1. gulfs
2. pennies
3. fathers-in-law
4. rights of way
5. 1700s *or* 1700's
6. sopranos
7. lives
8. larvae *or* larvas
9. bunches
10. Murphys
11. valleys
12. tries
13. boxes
14. halves
15. echoes
16. elk
17. *o*'s
18. politics
19. nieces
20. turkeys

ANSWERS

Review C

Students should identify the appropriate rule for each word and paraphrase the rules to show how they apply to the words.

1. 31k (11)
2. 31k (8)
3. 31k (10)
4. 31k (12)
5. 31a
6. 31f
7. 31a
8. 31d
9. 31f
10. 31e
11. 31k (5)
12. 31e
13. 31d
14. 31c
15. 31j
16. 31c
17. 31k (1)
18. 31k (13)
19. 31k (6)
20. 31e

MECHANICS

(13) To form the plural of figures, most uppercase letters, signs, and words used as words, add an *–s* or both an apostrophe and an *–s.*

SINGULAR	*8*	1990	*C*	*&*	*and*
PLURAL	*8*s	1990s	*C*s	*&*s	*and*s
	or	or	or	or	or
	8's	1990's	*C*'s	*&*'s	*and*'s

To prevent confusion, add both an apostrophe and an *–s* to form the plural of all lowercase letters, certain uppercase letters, and some words used as words.

EXAMPLES The word *Mississippi* contains four *s*'s and four *i*'s. [Without an apostrophe, the plural of *s* would look awkward, and the plural of *i* could be confused with *is*.]

Sebastian usually makes straight A's. [Without an apostrophe, the plural of *A* could be confused with *As*.]

Because I mistakenly thought Evelyn Waugh was a woman, I used *her*'s instead of *his*'s in my paragraph. [Without an apostrophe, the plural of *her* would look like the possessive pronoun *hers* and the plural of *his* would look like the word *hiss*.]

REFERENCE NOTE: For more information about forming these kinds of plurals, see pages 894–895.

MECHANICS

EXERCISE 5 Spelling the Plural Forms of Nouns

Spell the plural form of each of the following nouns.

1. gulf
2. penny
3. father-in-law
4. right of way
5. 1700
6. soprano
7. life
8. larva
9. bunch
10. Murphy
11. valley
12. try
13. box
14. half
15. echo
16. elk
17. *o*
18. politics
19. niece
20. turkey

REVIEW C Understanding the Spelling Rules

By referring to the rules on the previous pages, explain the spelling of each of the following words.

1. senators-elect
2. parentheses
3. teaspoonfuls
4. data
5. handkerchief
6. obligation
7. conceive
8. immature
9. changeable
10. liberally
11. wharves
12. iciness
13. illegible
14. proceed
15. biggest
16. secede
17. wheels
18. *c*'s
19. rodeos
20. lovely

Writing Numbers

31l. Spell out a ***cardinal number***—a number that shows how many—that can be expressed in one or two words. Otherwise, use numerals.

EXAMPLES	**seven** juniors	**fifty-one** votes	**one thousand** miles
	203 juniors	**421** votes	**1,242** miles

REFERENCE NOTE: For information about hyphenating numbers, see page 896.

NOTE: Do not spell out some numbers and use numerals for others in the same context. Be consistent by using numerals to express all of the numbers.

INCONSISTENT William Shakespeare wrote thirty-seven plays and 154 sonnets.

CONSISTENT William Shakespeare wrote **37** plays and **154** sonnets.

However, to distinguish between numbers appearing beside each other, spell out one number, and use numerals for the other.

EXAMPLES I need to buy **ten 29**-cent stamps.
Corey sold **135 five**-dollar tickets.

31m. Spell out a number that begins a sentence.

EXAMPLES **Eighty-eight** senators voted in favor of the bill.
Three hundred thirty-two tickets were sold.

If the number appears awkward when spelled out, revise the sentence so that it does not begin with the number.

AWKWARD Two thousand five hundred sixty-four pounds is the combined weight of those seven sumo wrestlers.

IMPROVED The combined weight of those seven sumo wrestlers is **2,564** pounds.

31n. Always spell out an ***ordinal number***—a number that expresses order.

EXAMPLES Thurgood Marshall was the **first** [not *1st*] African American to serve on the U.S. Supreme Court.
The Rio Grande is the **twenty-second** [not *22nd*] longest river in the world.

MECHANICS

COMMON ERROR

Problem. Some students are confused about when to use hyphens with numbers that are spelled out.

Solution. The numbers *twenty-one* to *ninety-nine* are spelled with hyphens. Beyond ninety-nine, no additional hyphen is used. For example, in writing a check for $132.00, the number should be written as "one hundred thirty-two."

MECHANICS

REVIEW D

OBJECTIVE

- To proofread a paragraph for spelling errors

31o. Use numerals to express numbers in conventional situations.

TYPES OF NUMBERS	EXAMPLES		
Identification Numbers	Chapter **26** Interstate **20**	pages **41–54** lines **10–14**	Act **5** Channel **8**
Measurements/ Statistics	**98.6** degrees **14.6** ounces	**42** years old ratio of **5** to **1**	**8** percent $4\frac{1}{2}$ feet
Addresses	**512** Willow Drive Arrowhead, DE **34322–0422**		
Dates	July **7, 1993**	**44** B.C.	A.D. **145**
Times of Day	**6:20** P.M. (*or* p.m.)	**8:00** A.M. (*or* a.m.)	

NOTE: Spell out a number used with *o'clock*.

EXAMPLE **nine** o'clock

REVIEW D **Proofreading a Paragraph for Spelling Errors**

Proofread the following paragraph and correct each misspelled word.

1. monkeys 2. flies

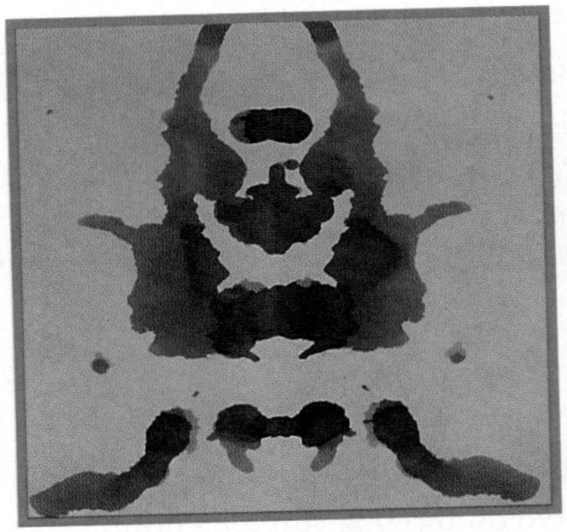

[1] Does this inkblot remind you of ~~monkies~~? [2] Maybe you see two Eskimos in igloos perched on the back of a polar bear fishing for salmon in a trout stream full of ~~flys~~. [3] Then again, ~~may be~~ four geese chasing a dozen mice down Interstate ~~Four~~ is the image that comes to your mind as you gaze at the dark shapes and white spaces. [4] To psychiatrists and psychologists who

3. maybe/4

MECHANICS

VISUAL CONNECTIONS

Exploring the Subject. The Rorschach inkblot test is widely used throughout the world by mental health professionals to diagnose psychological conditions, but its inventor, the Swiss psychiatrist Hermann Rorschach (1884–1922), intended it primarily as a research tool in studying perception. Rorschach was interested in determining how much subtlety people were able to perceive by looking quickly at each symmetrical inkblot. For example, did they notice subtle shadings and color variations? Were they able to see small details? The Rorschach inkblot test is often slighted in movies and TV shows because it seems rather mysterious or even silly, but trained mental-health professionals use it for very serious purposes.

MECHANICS

SEGMENT 3 *(pp. 915–929)*

WORDS OFTEN CONFUSED

OBJECTIVE

- To distinguish between words often confused

have taken special ~~class's~~, the pictures you imagine are really images of your own mind. [5] ~~1~~ of ten standard inkblots, this design is part of a special psychological test devised by Hermann Rorschach. [6] Although Rorschach was not the ~~1st~~ to study inkblots and the imagination, his inkblots are one of the most famous methods of gaining insights into people's minds. [7] As you might suspect, a group of five-~~years~~-olds will see very different images in these inkblots than a group of adults would. [8] By having a person describe what he or she saw in each inkblot, Rorschach was able to infer a great deal about that person's fears, ~~beliefes~~, desires, and hopes. [9] For example, what does it mean if you see seven tacos playing banjos made of white ~~potatos~~, waltzing with two walruses on loaves of bread? [10] Maybe you're hungry, or maybe you feel like dancing, and it's time to put your tap ~~shoe's~~ on.

4. classes **5.** One **6.** first **7.** year **8.** beliefs **9.** potatoes **10.** shoes

Words Often Confused

all ready	*all prepared* Are you *all ready* for the exam?
already	*previously* We have *already* studied that chapter.
all together	*everyone in the same place* My family will be *all together* during this Thanksgiving holiday.
altogether	*entirely* The president is *altogether* opposed to the bill.
altar	[noun] *a table or stand at which religious rites are performed* This is the *altar* used in the Communion service.
alter	[verb] *to change* Do not *alter* your plans on my account.

MECHANICS

Teacher's ResourceBank™

RESOURCES

WORDS OFTEN CONFUSED

QUICK REMINDER

Have students choose the word in parentheses that correctly completes each sentence. The correct choice is underlined.

1. My mother has (all ready, <u>already</u>) invited people to the party.
2. On his eighteenth birthday Calvin said, "Hooray! I'm no longer a (<u>minor</u>, miner)."
3. The seventh-grade class traveled to Washington to see the U.S. (Capital, <u>Capitol</u>) building.
4. The cactus and other plants in the (<u>desert</u>, dessert) burst into bloom after the thunderstorm.
5. Hortense's tooth was so (lose, <u>loose</u>) she feared she would (<u>lose</u>, loose) it.

MECHANICS

MEETING INDIVIDUAL NEEDS

ADVANCED STUDENTS

Some of the pairs of words often confused have similar origins. *Counsel* and *council,* for example, both come from the Latin word *concilium,* meaning "group of people" or "meeting." Suggest that students use a dictionary to find out which pairs of words have similar etymologies and which do not. After they have finished, ask students if they might have predicted the results.

ascent	[noun] *a rise; a climb* The climbers' *ascent* was a slow one.
assent	[verb] *to agree;* [noun] *consent* Will they *assent* to our proposal? Our last proposal won their *assent.*
born	*given life* Ynes Mexia was *born* in Washington, D.C.
borne	*carried; endured* They have *borne* their troubles better than we thought they would.
brake	[verb] *to stop or slow down;* [noun] *a device for stopping or slowing down* He *braked* the car and swerved to avoid hitting the child. An automobile *brake* will overheat if used too often.
break	[verb] *to cause to come apart; to shatter;* [noun] *a fracture* If you're not careful, you'll *break* the mirror. The *break* in the bone will heal in six weeks.
capital	[noun] *a city that is the seat of government of a country or state; money or property;* [adjective] *punishable by death; an uppercase letter; of major importance* Manila is the *capital* of the Philippines. The company has *capital* of $100,000. *Capital* punishment was the subject of the debate. A proper noun begins with a *capital* letter. That is a *capital* suggestion.
capitol	[noun] *building in which a legislature meets* [capitalized when it refers to the building where the U.S. Congress meets] The *capitol* in Austin is a popular tourist attraction. Our Senate and House of Representatives meet in the *Capitol* in Washington.

MECHANICS

MECHANICS

clothes	*wearing apparel* I'd like to buy some summer *clothes.*
cloths	*pieces of fabric* Use these *cloths* to clean the car.

EXERCISE 6 **Distinguishing Between Words Often Confused**

From the choices in parentheses, select the correct word or words for each of the following sentences.

1. The governor said that the roof of the (*capital, capitol*) needs to be repaired.
2. We have finished packing and are (*all ready, already*) to go.
3. Saying nothing, the major gave a nod of (*ascent, assent*).
4. At night, Tokyo, the (*capital, capitol*) of Japan, is filled with vivid neon lights advertising all sorts of shops, clubs, and products.
5. You called us after we had (*all ready, already*) left.
6. Please keep your foot on the (*brake, break*).
7. The expenditures will be (*born, borne*) by the taxpayers.
8. Seminole jackets are made from long, narrow strips of different-colored (*cloths, clothes*) carefully sewn together to make one garment.
9. The new dam will (*altar, alter*) the course of the river.
10. Your arguments are not (*all together, altogether*) convincing.

coarse	[adjective] *rough; crude* The driveway was covered with *coarse* sand. His *coarse* language and manners prevented him from getting the job.
course	[noun] *path of action; passage or way; study or group of studies; part of a meal;* [also used with *of* to mean *naturally* or *certainly*] What *course* do you think I should follow? Geraldo's parents go to the golf *course* every Saturday. The *course* in world history lasts a full year. My favorite main *course* is bolichi. Of *course,* you may go with us.

MECHANICS

COMMON ERROR

Problem. Students might have problems with spelling words that sound alike (homophones) but that are different in meaning.

Solution. The quickest way to master these troublesome pairs (or threesomes) is to memorize the words and their spellings. Mnemonic devices can sometimes work. For example, the *–er* in *letter* and *paper* could help the student remember *stationery* (writing paper), as opposed to *stationary* (not moving). The *o* in *dome* may be associated with the *o* in *capitol* (a government building that often has a dome).

MECHANICS

complement	[noun] *something that makes whole or complete;* [verb] *to make whole or complete* The diagram shows that the angle *WXY* is the *complement* of the angle *YXZ*. A good shortstop would *complement* the team.
compliment	[noun] *praise; respect;* [verb] *to express praise or respect* The performer was pleased and flattered by the critic's *compliments*. Did the critics *compliment* all of the other performers, too?
consul	[noun] *a person appointed by a government to serve its citizens in a foreign country* The Israeli *consul* held a press conference to pledge his support for the peace talks.
council	[noun] *a group assembled for conferences or legislation* The student *council* meets this afternoon.
councilor	[noun] *a member of a council* The queen's *councilors* met together for several hours but could not agree.
counsel	[noun] *advice;* [verb] *to advise* Shandra sought *counsel* from Mr. Nakai. Mr. Nakai *counseled* her to apply for the scholarship.
counselor	[noun] *one who gives advice* Shandra's guidance *counselor* helped her complete the application.
des´ert	[noun] *a dry region* Irrigation has brought new life to the *desert*.
desert´	[verb] *to leave or abandon* A good soldier never *deserts* his or her post.
dessert´	[noun] *the final course of a meal* My favorite *dessert* is frozen yogurt with strawberries on top.

MECHANICS

formally	*in a strict or dignified manner* Mayor Pérez will *formally* open the new recreation center on Wednesday.
formerly	*previously* Mrs. Ling was *formerly* the head of the math department at Leland High School.
ingenious	*clever; resourceful; skillful* Carla has an *ingenious* plan to earn some money this summer.
ingenuous	*innocent; trusting; frank* Ian is as *ingenuous* as a five-year-old child.
its	[possessive form of *it*] Our city must increase *its* water supply.
it's	[contraction of *it is* or *it has*] *It's* almost time for the bell to ring. *It's* been nice talking to you.
later	[adjective] *more late;* [adverb] *at a subsequent time* I wasn't on time, but you were even *later.* I'll see you *later.*
latter	[adjective] *the second of two* (as opposed to *former*) Dr. Edwards can see you in the morning or the afternoon, but the *latter* time is more convenient for her.
lead	[verb, pronounced "leed"] *to go first; to guide* Who will *lead* the discussion group?
led	[verb, past tense of *lead*] Elaine *led* the band onto the field.
lead	[noun, pronounced "led"] *a heavy metal; graphite in a pencil* The mechanic used small weights made of *lead* to balance the wheel. My pencil *lead* broke during the test.

MECHANICS

COMMON ERROR

Problem. *Its* and *it's* continue to confuse students and often appear on lists of commonly misspelled words.

Solution. This confusion can be avoided if you encourage students to think *it is* instead of *it's* when they write. Remind them that the apostrophe isn't needed to show possession with *its.* To reinforce the fact that *it's* is a contraction, tell students to think of the apostrophe as a replacement for the second *i* in *it is.*

MECHANICS

A DIFFERENT APPROACH

You may want to introduce students to several word pairs that are spelled in exactly the same way but that are used as different parts of speech, are pronounced differently, and carry different meanings (such as *desert* and *desert*). When such a word is used as a noun or adjective, the stress is on the first syllable. When the word is used as a verb, the stress falls on the second syllable. Other examples include *address—address, conflict—conflict, content—content, permit—permit, present—present,* and *produce—produce.* Ask students to work with partners and to use the word pairs to create sentences such as "My father won't permit me to get a driving permit until next year."

MECHANICS

EXERCISE 7 Distinguishing Between Words Often Confused

In the following sentences, select the correct word from each pair in parentheses.

1. Court is (*formally, formerly*) opened with a bailiff's cry of "Oyez, Oyez!"
2. When her painting was purchased by the museum, the artist received many (*complements, compliments*).
3. One of my father's favorite sayings is "What's next—(*desert, dessert*) or (*desert, dessert*) the table?"
4. The discovery and development of synthetic fibers must have required an (*ingenious, ingenuous*) mind.
5. I enjoy both chicken and steak but prefer the (*later, latter*).
6. One of the guidance (*councilor's, counselor's*) jobs is to (*lead, led*) students to take the proper (*coarse, course*) of study.
7. Have you tried out the new public golf (*coarse, course*)?
8. Ebenezer D. Basset, the first African American diplomat, was appointed minister to Haiti by President Grant; Basset later served as Haiti's (*Consul, Council*) General.
9. Do you know the song "(*Its, It's*) Later Than You Think"?
10. The stark simplicity of the sand painting forms a perfect (*complement, compliment*) to its complex spiritual meaning.

MECHANICS

loose [adjective, pronounced "loos"] *not firmly fastened; not tight*
The front wheel on your bike is *loose.*
Clothes with a *loose* fit are stylish now.

lose [verb, pronounced "looz"] *to suffer loss*
The trees will *lose* their leaves soon.

miner [noun] *a worker in a mine*
American *miners* lead the world in the production of coal.

minor [noun] *a person under legal age;* [adjective] *of small importance* (as opposed to *major*)
Normally, a *minor* is not permitted to sign a legal paper.
Let's not list any of the *minor* objections to the plan.

moral	[adjective] *good; virtuous;* [noun] *a lesson of conduct derived from a story or event* Good conduct is based upon *moral* principles. The *moral* of this old folk tale is "Be true to yourself."
morale	[noun] *spirit; mental condition* Teamwork is impossible without good *morale.*
peace	*calmness* (as opposed to *strife* or *war*) Disarmament is an important step toward *peace.*
piece	*a part of something* Four *pieces* of the puzzle are missing.
personal	[adjective] *individual; private* My *personal* opinion has nothing to do with the case. Do you feel that details of the candidates' *personal* lives should be made public?
personnel	[noun] *a group of people employed in the same work or service* Most large companies prefer to recruit their executive *personnel* from among college graduates.
plain	[adjective] *not fancy; undecorated; clear;* [noun] *a large area of flat land* Although the new uniforms are *plain,* they are quite attractive. Does my explanation make things *plain* to you? Many Western movies are set on the Great *Plains.*
plane	[noun] *a flat surface; a woodworking tool; an airplane* Some problems in physics deal with the mechanical advantage of an inclined *plane.* Use this *plane* to make the wood smooth. We watched the *plane* circle for its landing.

MECHANICS

MECHANICS

INTEGRATING THE LANGUAGE ARTS

Spelling and Vocabulary. Introducing prefixes that modify the meanings of words may help students build vocabulary. The following prefixes are grouped according to meaning:

Prefixes showing quantity:	
half	*semi*circle
	*hemi*sphere
one	*uni*cycle
	*mono*mial
thousand	*kilo*gram
Prefixes showing negation:	
not	*un*happy
	*il*legal
without, no,	*dis*respect
opposite to	*counter*feit
against	*ant*acid
	*contra*dict
Prefixes showing time:	
before	*ante*cedent
	*fore*cast
	*pre*cede
after	*post*war
again	*re*write
Prefixes showing direction or position:	
above, over	*super*vise
across, over	*trans*port
with	*co*exist
	*com*municate
	*sym*pathy

MECHANICS

principal	[noun] *the head of a school;* [adjective] *main; most important* The *principal* will address the entire student body tomorrow. Florida and California are our *principal* citrus-growing states.
principle	[noun] *a rule of conduct; a fact or a general truth* The *principle* of the Golden Rule is found in many religions. This machine operates on a new *principle.*
quiet	[adjective] *still; silent* The library is usually a *quiet* place to study.
quite	[adverb] *completely; rather; very* Are you *quite* finished? We are *quite* proud of Angel's achievements.
rout	[noun] *a disorderly flight;* [verb] *to put to flight; to defeat overwhelmingly* What began as an orderly retreat ended as a *rout.* The coach predicts that his Bears will *rout* the Wildcats in the playoffs.
route	*a road; a way to go* This highway is the shortest *route* to the mountains.

EXERCISE 8 Distinguishing Between Words Often Confused

In the following sentences, select the correct word from each pair in parentheses.

1. As Surgeon General of the United States, the (*principal, principle*) duty of Dr. Antonia Novello is to safeguard the health of Americans.
2. Automated methods of extracting ore have put thousands of (*miners, minors*) out of work.
3. Coral has a sign that she puts on her desk in the library; it reads: "(*Quiet, Quite*) please. Genius at work."

4. When Kurt's (*plain*, *plane*) failed to return, the (*moral*, *morale*) of his squadron sank to zero.
5. The accident that completely demolished the car was caused by a (*loose*, *lose*) cotter pin worth ten cents.
6. Follow the marked (*rout*, *route*), or you will surely (*loose*, *lose*) your way.
7. The (*principal*, *principle*) that underlies that company's choice of (*personal*, *personnel*) is "An educated person is usually willing to learn more."
8. The columnist described the game as a (*rout*, *route*) for our team.
9. To prevent infection, always apply first aid to (*miner*, *minor*) cuts.
10. For his contribution in bringing an end to the first Arab-Israeli war, Dr. Ralph J. Bunche was awarded the Nobel Prize for (*piece*, *peace*) in 1950.

stationary	[adjective] *in a fixed position* The new state power plant contains large *stationary* engines.
stationery	[noun] *writing paper* I always save my best *stationery* for important letters.
straight	[adjective] *not crooked or curved; direct* Draw a *straight* line that connects points A and B.
strait	[noun] *channel connecting two large bodies of water;* [usually plural] *difficulty; distress* The *Strait* of Gibraltar links the Atlantic Ocean and the Mediterranean Sea. His family always helped him when he was in bad *straits*.
than	[conjunction, used for comparisons] Loretta is taller *than* I.
then	[adverb] *at that time; next* We lived on Garden Street until last year; *then* we moved to our new house.

(continued)

MECHANICS

INTEGRATING THE LANGUAGE ARTS

Mechanics and Dictionary Skills. Sometimes misspellings result because students spell a word as it sounds. For example, a student might write *captain gown* for *cap and gown,* as in "I look forward to walking across the stage in my captain gown at graduation." Use anonymous examples from students' papers or make up some examples to demonstrate the difference between the heard word and the written word. Other examples include *pairashoot* for *parachute, collage* for *college, row model* for *role model, pedal stool* for *pedestal,* and *mirrow* for *mirror.*

Knowing the etymologies of words can help students to remember the correct spellings. Divide the class into mixed-ability groups of three or four and have each group look up the etymologies of some of the words. Then have groups report their findings to the class.

MECHANICS

MECHANICS

their	[possessive form of *they*] The performers are studying *their* lines.
there	[adverb] *at that place;* [expletive, used to fill out the meaning of a sentence] I will be *there* after rehearsal. *There* will be four performances of the play.
they're	[contraction of *they are*] *They're* performing a play by Sonia Sánchez.
to	[preposition; part of the infinitive form of a verb] Let's go *to* the movies. After the rain, the birds began *to* sing.
too	[adverb] *more than enough; also* Is it *too* far to walk? You, *too,* are invited to the sports banquet.
two	[adjective] *one plus one;* [noun] *the number between one and three; a pair* They serve *two* flavors: vanilla and chocolate. *Two* of my favorite writers are Nadine Gordimer and Ntozake Shange.
waist	*the midsection of the body* These slacks are too tight at the *waist.*
waste	[noun] *useless spending; unused or useless material;* [verb] *to use foolishly* The movie was simply a *waste* of time. Don't *waste* your money on movies like that.
weather	[noun] *atmospheric conditions* We had good *weather* for the picnic.
whether	[conjunction, used to express an alternative] I don't know *whether* Denzel will help us or not.
who's	[contraction of *who is* or *who has*] *Who's* going to portray the Navajo detective in the play? *Who's* been using my typewriter?
whose	[possessive form of *who*] *Whose* artwork is this?

REVIEW E

OBJECTIVE

- To proofread a paragraph for spelling errors

your	[possessive form of *you*] Is this *your* book?
you're	[contraction of *you are*] I hope *you're* able to come to my graduation.

EXERCISE 9 Distinguishing Between Words Often Confused

In the following sentences, select the correct word or words from the choices given in parentheses.

1. (*Their*, *There*) Great Dane is taller and heavier (*than*, *then*) (*your*, *you're*) Irish wolfhound.
2. Since the roof of the stadium is not (*stationary*, *stationery*), we can put it up or take it down as needed.
3. If the (*weather*, *whether*) isn't (*to*, *too*, *two*) awful, we will go (*to*, *too*, *two*) the game.
4. The Mexican women over (*there*, *their*, *they're*) are wearing *rebozos*, versatile shawls worn over the head, around the shoulders, or about the (*waist*, *waste*).
5. (*Who's*, *Whose*) planning to write a term paper about Ida Tarbell?
6. If that is not (*your*, *you're*) car, then (*who's*, *whose*) is it—(*there's*, *theirs*)?
7. Half of India's population could be fed on the food that is (*waisted*, *wasted*) every year in the United States.
8. What did (*your*, *you're*) family say when you told them about the scholarship (*your*, *you're*) going to get?
9. What styles of (*stationary*, *stationery*) did you order for the class project?
10. Deep in the jungles of Cambodia lies a maze of (*straight*, *strait*) roads and canals that were part of the ancient Khmer capital of Angkor Thom.

MECHANICS

REVIEW E Proofreading Paragraphs for Spelling Errors

Proofread the following paragraphs and correct each misspelled word.

1. Plains

[1] Last winter, as we flew over the Nazca ~~Planes~~ of Peru, I took photographs of the eighteen famous bird images that

MECHANICS

have puzzled archaeologists for years. [2] Excitement rippled
2. desert through the aircraft as the ~~dessert~~ seemed to come alive with
mysterious images like this one. [3] Although the group of fig-

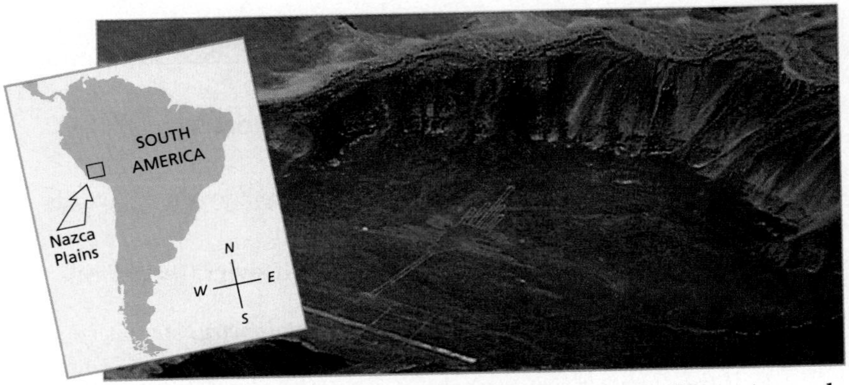

ures covers two hundred square miles, each figure is made
3. loose only of ~~lose~~ mounds of rocks and pebbles. [4] The dry ~~whether~~
4. weather in the region has preserved these fragile messages for more
than fifteen hundred years.

[5] Because many of the designs cannot be perceived from
5. ascent the ground, some people believe that the Nazca had aircraft,
perhaps balloons or huge kites, capable of an ~~assent~~ to a thousand feet or more. [6] To test this hypothesis, one group of
investigators actually constructed a crude hot-air balloon made
6. coarse of ~~course~~ vegetable fiber. [7] A violent gust threw the balloon
7. its and ~~it's~~ passengers to the ground before carrying them some
three miles away.

[8] One of the more astounding theories about the designs is
8. straight that the ~~strait~~ lines were landing strips for spaceships. [9] Other
9. routes theorists wonder if the flight ~~routs~~ of the birds represented by
the patterns helped warn the Nazca of cold winds and rain.
[10] Maria Reiche, an astronomer and mathematician who has
10. ingenious studied the area, believes that the lines form an ~~ingenuous~~ calendar. [11] However, a computer analysis of lunar and solar
11. led patterns has ~~lead~~ astronomers to doubt this theory.

12. all ready [12] As our plane landed, we tourists were ~~already~~ for a
closer look at these weird figures. [13] Early the next day, we
met our tour guide in front of the hotel and boarded a small
13. then bus; ~~than~~ we headed for the Nazca lines.

[14] Our guide told us that parts of the fragile figures have
14. already ~~all ready~~ been ruined by car and foot traffic. [15] Following the

MECHANICS

MECHANICS

~~consul~~ of Maria Reiche, the Peruvian government no longer allows tourists to walk or drive over the area. [16] Consequently, we could view the figures only from an observation tower that had been built close ~~too~~ them. [17] Nevertheless, we were ~~quiet~~ impressed by the amount of planning and work that must have been required to create these fascinating lines.

15. counsel **16.** to **17.** quite

[18] When our guide signaled us back to the bus, I picked up a stone and, for a moment, held a ~~peace~~ of history in my hand; then I carefully placed the stone back where I had found it. [19] ~~Latter~~, I sat in my hotel room and thought about the Nazca and the unusual images they'd made. [20] Who, I wondered, were these ancient people ~~who's~~ achievements continue to baffle modern science?

18. piece **19.** Later **20.** whose

300 Spelling Words

The following list contains three hundred commonly misspelled words. The words are grouped so that you can study them ten at a time. To master any words that give you difficulty, follow the five-step procedure given at the beginning of this chapter (see pages 902–903).

accidentally	arctic	benefited
accommodate	argument	bicycle
accurate	arrangement	biscuit
acknowledgment	assassinate	bookkeeper
acquaintance	association	bracelet
across	athletics	breathe
aerial	atomic	bruise
aisle	attach	bulletin
all right	attention	bureau
always	attitude	business
amateur	auxiliary	calendar
analyze	awful	campaign
announce	awkward	candidate
anonymous	bachelor	catastrophe
apologize	background	cellophane
appearance	banana	cemetery
appreciate	bargain	ceremony
approaching	beggar	challenge
appropriate	beginning	chaperon
approval	believe	classroom

MECHANICS

MEETING INDIVIDUAL NEEDS

ADVANCED STUDENTS

Some students won't have many problems spelling the words in the **300 Spelling Words** list. Allow such students to work as a group to compile a list of words that they have encountered in their reading and that they have difficulty spelling. Students can then study the words from the list they have compiled instead of spending time studying words they already know how to spell.

LEP/ESL

General Strategies. If possible, let ESL students put accent marks over the stressed syllables of the words in the **300 Spelling Words** list. If students stress syllables correctly when speaking, they will recognize the words more readily in print. Recognition will lead to better speaking.

MECHANICS

COOPERATIVE LEARNING

One of the most troubling aspects of English spelling is the prevalence of words with silent letters. For example, *a* is silent in the word *head; b* is silent in the word *numb;* and the first *c* is silent in the word *science.*

Have students work in groups of four or five to locate, in the **300 Spelling Words** list, words with silent letters. Groups should record all such words they find and should identify the silent letters in each word. The group that correctly identifies the most silent letters wins.

MECHANICS

college
colonel
colossal
column
commission
committee
comparatively
compel
competition
completely

complexion
concentrate
conscience
conscientious
contemptible
convenience
copies
cordially
corps
correspondence

corroborate
courageous
courteous
criticism
criticize
cylinder
decide
decision
defense
definitely

dependent
descendant
descent
description
desirable
develop
dictionary
different
dining
dinosaur

disappear
disappoint
discipline
discuss
disease
dissatisfied
divided
doesn't
economical
efficient

eighth
elementary
eligible
embarrass
emphasize
endeavor
environment
equipment
especially
etiquette

exaggerate
excellent
excitement
exercise
exhausted
existence
expense
experienced
extraordinary
familiar

fascinating
fatigue
February
feminine
fiery
financial
foreign
forfeit
fourth
fragile

generally
genius
government
governor
grammar
grateful
guarantee
guard
gymnasium
handkerchief

happened
harass
haven't
height
heroes
hindrance
hoping
horizon
hospital
humorous

imitation
immediately
incident
inconvenience
indispensable
inevitable
influence
initial
interpreted
interrupted

irrelevant
irresistible
jewelry
laboratory
leisure
license
lightning
likelihood
literacy
loneliness

MECHANICS

losing
luxurious
maintenance
maneuver
marriage
matinee
meant
medicine
medieval
mentioned

microphone
minimum
mischievous
missile
misspelled
movable
municipal
necessary
neighbors
nickel

ninety
ninth
nonsense
noticeable
nuclear
nuisance
occasionally
occur
occurred
omitted

opinion
opportunity
optimistic
pamphlet
parallel
parliament
particularly
pastime
permanent
permissible

perseverance
personally
personnel
perspiration
persuade
playwright
pleasant
pneumonia
possess
possibility

potato
practice
preference
prejudice
privilege
probably
procedure
professor
pronunciation
propaganda

propeller
prophecy
psychology
pursue
questionnaire
realize
receive
recognize
recommend
referral

rehearse
reign
relief
repetition
representative
restaurant
rhythm
satisfactorily
schedule
scissors

seize
semester
separate
sergeant
shiny
siege
similar
sincerely
souvenir
straight

strategy
subtle
successful
sufficient
suppress
surprised
suspension
syllable
sympathy
synonym

tariff
television
temperament
temperature
thoroughly
tomorrow
tournament
traffic
tragedy
transferred

twelfth
tyranny
undoubtedly
unforgettable
unfortunately
unnecessary
vacuum
valuable
villain
weird

MECHANICS

PART THREE

RESOURCES

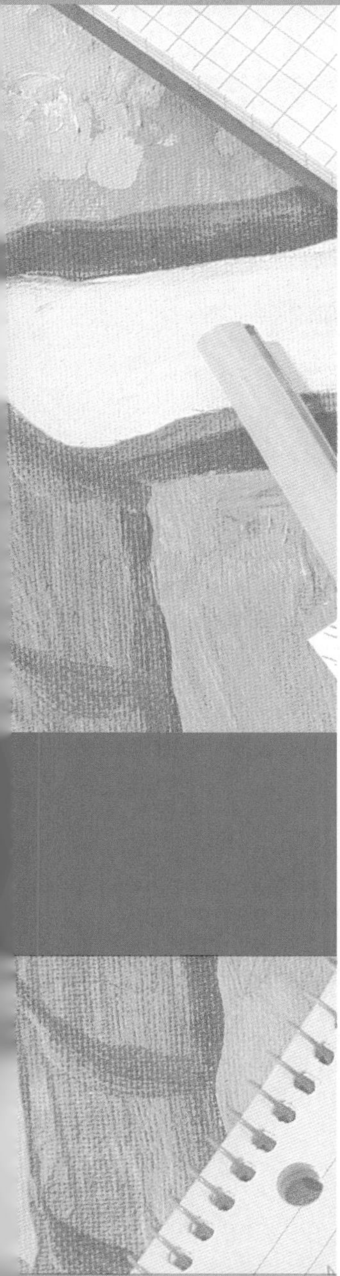

FORMAL SPEAKING AND DEBATE *(pp. 932–947)*

OBJECTIVES

- To prepare and give a speech by using note cards and visuals
- To listen critically to a short speech, to take notes, and to answer questions about the speech
- To prepare for and conduct a debate

Teacher's ResourceBank™

RESOURCES

FORMAL SPEAKING AND DEBATE

CHAPTER OVERVIEW

Teaching spoken expression skills is a natural and integral part of English instruction that helps students in many contexts, both in and outside school. This chapter can help students develop speaking skills for formal situations and for debates.

The speaking skills strengthened include preparing and delivering speeches and engaging in active listening. By following the established procedures, each student will learn to select a topic, analyze the audience, organize speech notes and materials, practice giving a speech, and deliver a speech with effective speaking techniques. As listeners, students will learn to use the LQ2R method and to listen critically to speeches. The chapter also includes debate preparations and strategies including refuting opposing arguments and building a rebuttal.

QUICK REMINDER

Give the class a controversial topic and related proposition for debate, such as these examples: all buildings should be equipped for the handicapped; public schools should all become profit-making enterprises; the

RESOURCES

32 FORMAL SPEAKING AND DEBATE

Skills and Strategies

A formal speech is one that takes place at a specified time and location. You will use this type of public speaking in many different settings on many different occasions, but whenever you make a formal speech, you will usually have time to prepare the exact message you want to deliver at the appointed time.

Becoming an Effective Speaker

For every type of formal speaking, there are specific techniques and strategies you can use to help you effectively communicate your intended message to your audience and to evaluate and respond to a speech effectively when you are a member of an audience.

The more you prepare, plan, and practice for a speech, the more likely you are to be successful in accomplishing your purpose for speaking. Several important factors that you should consider in planning your speech include

- your purpose for speaking
- the topic you are speaking about
- the occasion for your speech and the audience you will be speaking to

RESOURCES

Preparing a Speech

A good speech doesn't just happen. You have to analyze the situation to decide what will be appropriate, then make your plans and prepare your speech. The first step in preparing your speech is to identify your purpose for speaking. Some of the most common purposes are to inform, to persuade, or to entertain your audience.

PURPOSE	DESCRIPTION OF SPEECH	EXAMPLES OF SPEECH TITLES
To inform	gives facts *or* explains how to do something	New Ideas in Computer Technology How to Publish Your First Novel
To persuade	attempts to change an opinion *or* attempts to get listeners to act	Why Beagles Make Good Pets Why We Should Live Without Television
To entertain	relates to an amusing story or incident	The Dinner Date Disaster

Selecting a Topic

Sometimes your speech topic will be assigned, but often you will be able to choose your own topic. If so, remember to focus on something you're interested in. If you're not interested in your subject, your audience will also lose interest. In selecting your topic, you will probably consider the answers to the following questions.

- *What is your overall purpose in speaking?* Do you want to inform, persuade, or entertain your listeners?
- *What is the occasion for the speech?* Will the topic you have chosen fit the occasion?
- *How much time will you have?* Have you limited your speech topic to a manageable length?

RESOURCES

criminal justice system should be more severe on repeat offenders. Have each student list several reasons why the proposition should be adopted or rejected.

MEETING INDIVIDUAL NEEDS

LEP/ESL

General Strategies. Students may worry about using correct grammar in front of an audience of native English speakers. They may be relieved to find out that listeners focus more on message than on form. Advise ESL students that if they suddenly realize they have made a mistake, they should keep going rather than back up and call attention to the mistake. Remind them that few people are likely to have noticed. Listeners prefer information presented with uninterrupted content rather than with perfect grammar.

A DIFFERENT APPROACH

Many students find that the hardest part of preparing a speech is selecting a topic, and they sometimes discount their own experiences. Suggest to students that hobbies, unusual interests, and personal experiences often make excellent topics. An interest in a subject can add to a speaker's credibility and add enough vitality to the speech to make it memorable.

RESOURCES

CRITICAL THINKING

Analysis

In **Analyzing Your Audience,** students learn to consider the audience's knowledge about and interest in a subject. Students could also analyze other factors that affect the audience's response, such as age, sex, cultural background, educational level, and group membership. They might use charts, Venn diagrams, or graphs to present their considerations about an audience for a particular debate proposition.

COMMON ERROR

Problem. Students often prepare the wording of their extemporaneous speeches so exactly that they end up trying to memorize their speeches. As a consequence, they race through the material without much spontaneity or variety.

Solution. Stress that the key ideas written on note cards should be represented by signal words or short phrases, not by complete sentences. This will help to encourage spontaneous, natural speaking and will eliminate hasty presentations and forgetful pauses.

RESOURCES

Analyzing Your Audience

In planning your speech and focusing your topic, you will also need to consider your audience's needs and interests.

AUDIENCE CONSIDERATIONS

QUESTIONS ABOUT AUDIENCE	EVALUATION	YOUR SPEECH WILL NEED
What does the audience already know about this subject?	very little	to provide background or details to better inform your listeners
	a little	to include some background details
	a lot	to focus on interesting aspects or issues
How interested will the audience be in this subject?	very interested	to maintain their interest
	somewhat interested	to focus on aspects that most interest them
	uninterested	to focus on persuading your listeners that this topic is important

RESOURCES

Organizing Speech Notes and Materials

Once you have identified and focused the topic for your speech so that it suits your overall purpose, you will need to gather and organize the information you plan to present.

REFERENCE NOTE: For more details about researching information, see pages 412–417 and 959–966.

The most common type of speech, the one most often used by experienced public speakers, is an ***extemporaneous speech*** that is prepared but not memorized. When you organize your materials for an extemporaneous speech, you first write out a complete outline of your speech. Then you prepare note cards that you can refer to when you are presenting your speech.

GUIDELINES FOR SPEECH NOTE CARDS

1. Put only one key idea, possibly accompanied by a brief example or detail, on each card.
2. Make a special note card for material that you plan to read word for word, such as a quotation, a series of dates, or a list of statistics.
3. Make a special note card to indicate when you should pause to show a visual, such as a chart, diagram, graph, picture, or model.
4. Number your completed cards to keep them in order.

Practicing Your Speech

Once you have written your outline and made your speech notes, you're ready to practice delivering your speech. To give a successful speech, you'll need to rehearse your presentation. Remember that there are only three aspects of your speech that your audience can judge by, and that you can improve all of these with practice: your ideas, your body, and your voice.

Your Ideas. These are expressed in your written speech outline and transferred onto your speech notes. Practice until you are comfortable and familiar with what you plan to say. Try to use expressive words that help your listeners visualize clearly what you want them to understand.

Your Body. Your speech will be more effective if you use "body language" that reinforces the impression you intend to make.

- *Stand confidently.* Look alert and interested in what you're saying.
- *Use natural gestures.* Use relaxed, normal gestures as you speak.

MEETING **INDIVIDUAL** NEEDS

STUDENTS WITH SPECIAL NEEDS

Because many learning disabled students have difficulties in organizing material, you may want to work with students in preparing and organizing their note cards for speaking. Students who are comfortable speaking but who have difficulties reading might use a limited number of cue cards with only a few words when they plan speeches. Students who are easily distracted or careless might color-code their note cards or number the backs with large numerals.

COMMON ERROR

Problem. When it is time for students to present their speeches, they sometimes reveal their reluctance through facial expressions and body language.

Solution. Remind students that their attitudes before they begin to speak influence how the audience will respond. The speaking occasion begins the moment a student leaves his or her seat.

RESOURCES

A DIFFERENT APPROACH

Each person hears his or her voice uniquely—differently than how the rest of the world hears it. Because sound vibration from a speaker's vocal cords affects hearing, speakers often think they are using more vocal variety than they actually are. Encourage more variety by having students record their speeches to listen to how they sound. Have students exaggerate their use of volume, pitch, stress, and rate.

COMMON ERROR

Problem. Speakers sometimes stare at the back wall or deliver their speeches to only one person.

Solution. Tell students that if making eye contact while they are speaking makes them nervous, they might look at people's foreheads or at the tops of their heads. To help students direct their speeches to the entire audience, suggest that they write reminders on some of their note cards to look at specific people in different areas of the room.

RESOURCES

- *Make direct eye contact with your audience.* When you look at various people in your audience, it makes them feel that you are speaking *with* them rather than speaking *at* them.

Your Voice. Speak clearly and loudly enough so everyone in the audience can hear. Use a normal variety of vocal patterns so that your voice is interesting to listen to.

- *Volume.* You always need to be loud enough to be heard, but you can also raise and lower your volume for emphasis as you speak.
- *Pitch.* Use the natural rise and fall of your voice to emphasize various ideas and avoid a monotone.
- *Stress.* Emphasize important words or phrases.
- *Rate.* Generally, you should speak at a comfortable, relaxed pace, although you can vary your rate or pause briefly where it's effective for emphasis.

Delivering a Speech

There are several methods that you can use to present a speech. The speaking occasion usually determines the type of method that you should choose when you present a speech.

METHODS OF DELIVERING A SPEECH

TYPE OF SPEECH	ADVANTAGES	DISADVANTAGES
Manuscript speech (read to audience word for word from a prepared script)	provides exact words you wish to say; less chance of errors or omissions	doesn't permit audience feedback; tends to be dull
Memorized speech (memorized word for word from a script and recited to the audience)	gives speaker freedom to move around and look at audience	may not sound natural; requires much practice and memorization; risk of forgetting speech

(continued)

RESOURCES

METHODS OF DELIVERING A SPEECH *(continued)*		
TYPE OF SPEECH	ADVANTAGES	DISADVANTAGES
Extemporaneous speech (outlined and carefully prepared, but not memorized; speech notes often used)	sounds natural; allows speaker to respond to audience in a natural manner	requires practice and preparation
Impromptu speech (given on the spur of the moment, without preparation or notes)	sounds very natural	can sound disorganized, not suited for formal speech

Speeches given on radio or television often use the manuscript method in order to stay within rigid time limits. Speeches given in contests or for formal programs are often memorized. Impromptu speeches are given whenever an unexpected short speech is required.

However, for a prepared speech delivered to a live audience, the extemporaneous method is usually the most effective. Audiences respond best to extemporaneous speeches because they sound natural and provide more opportunities for interaction between the speaker and the audience.

Speaking Effectively

It's normal to feel nervous before you give your speech. But it's important not to allow nervousness to distract you or affect your speaking. Here are some suggestions that can help.

1. *Be prepared.* Avoid excessive nervousness by organizing and being familiar with your speech notes and visuals.
2. *Practice your speech.* Rehearse as if you're giving your actual presentation.
3. *Focus on your purpose for speaking.* Think about what you want your listeners to do, believe, or feel as a result of your speech.

RESOURCES

COOPERATIVE LEARNING

Before your students give their speeches, you may wish to assign each student a partner who will have the task of announcing that person as a speaker.

A DIFFERENT APPROACH

Try to schedule a short question-and-answer period after each speech. The questioning period can keep the class involved and give speakers an immediate response to their speeches. It also helps develop confidence, as students tend to forget their nervousness while fielding questions.

MEETING INDIVIDUAL NEEDS

LESS-ADVANCED STUDENTS

To combat students' nervousness before and during their speeches, do not assign grades to the first few speeches students give. Knowing that the speech will not be evaluated may help relieve some of the pressure. Also, a frank and open discussion of the common symptoms of stage fright may help students realize that it is a natural phenomenon.

RESOURCES

MEETING INDIVIDUAL NEEDS

LEP/ESL

General Strategies. When students are learning a new language, they have trouble listening for information. In an unfamiliar language, a listener may have trouble determining when one word or sentence ends and another begins. A student may also have trouble understanding related ideas.

Strategies that will improve listening skills include small group discussions, visuals related to the topic, exposure to questions about material before any activity, discussions of answers after listening, multiple-choice questions after listening a second time, and answering true-false questions after a third listening session.

INTEGRATING THE LANGUAGE ARTS

Literature Link. Students can gain skill in active listening by listening to essays being read aloud as well as by listening to speeches. When you read aloud an essay, have students listen to discover the purpose of the essay, the main ideas or opinions developed, the method the writer uses to support the ideas, and the tone the writer adopts.

You might use essays like E. B. White's "Death of a Pig," Russell Baker's "School vs. Education," Maxine Hong Kingston's "The Girl Who Wouldn't Talk," or speeches like William Faulkner's Nobel Prize Acceptance Speech if your literature textbook contains these selections.

RESOURCES

Active Listening

Hearing is a passive process, but listening requires you to think as well as hear. There are some specific procedures that you can follow to help you listen effectively to a speaker and evaluate what you hear.

Listening Politely

When you listen to a speaker, you need to be sure that you have given the speaker a fair opportunity to express his or her message. The speaker responds to you as a listener, depending on how well it appears you are paying attention.

Here's how to be a courteous and encouraging listener.

1. *Respect the speaker.* Be tolerant of individual differences. Show respect for the speaker's cultural background, such as customs, race, or religion.
2. *Don't interrupt.* Wait until the speaker finishes.
3. *Pay attention.* Don't distract others.
4. *Keep an open mind.* Try to understand the speaker's point of view. Also, be aware of how your own point of view affects the way you evaluate the opinions and values of others.
5. *Don't judge too soon.* Wait to hear the speaker's whole message before you make judgments about the speech.

Using the LQ2R Method

The LQ2R study method is especially helpful when you are listening to a speaker who is giving information.

L *Listen* carefully to material as it is being presented. Focus your attention on the speaker.

Q *Question* yourself as you listen. Make a list, mentally or by taking notes, of questions that occur to you.

R *Recite* in your own words the information as it is being presented. Summarize information in your mind or jot down notes as you listen.

R *Re-listen* as the speaker concludes the presentation. Major points may be reemphasized.

RESOURCES

Listening Critically

When you listen in order to evaluate a speech, you are listening critically. Critical listening is important whenever a speaker is presenting information that is new to you or when a speaker is trying to persuade you to accept his or her opinions about an issue.

To sway their listeners, speakers may use *propaganda devices*. ***Propaganda devices*** are statements, often based on invalid arguments, that attempt to convince listeners to believe in something or to take some action. The mass media, such as television, radio, and newspapers, often feature paid advertisements that use propaganda or persuasive devices to influence you. If you learn to recognize propaganda devices, you will be able to weigh the evidence of a speaker's arguments without being swayed by misleading appeals. (See pages 288–292 for more about persuasive methods.)

When you listen to a speech, you can't possibly remember every word the speaker says. However, if you listen critically, you'll be able to find the parts of the speaker's message that are most important.

GUIDELINES FOR LISTENING CRITICALLY	
Find main ideas.	What are the most important points? Listen for clue words a speaker might use, such as *major, main, most important,* or similar words.
Identify significant details.	What dates, names, or facts does the speaker use to support the main points of the speech? What kinds of examples or explanations are used to support the main ideas?
Distinguish between facts and opinions.	A fact is a statement that can be proved to be true. An opinion is a belief or a judgment about something; it cannot be proved to be true.

RESOURCES

CRITICAL THINKING
Analysis

After discussing **Guidelines for Listening Critically,** have students experiment to analyze which method is more helpful for them in remembering more information—listening or reading. Read aloud an informative article from a newspaper or a magazine and have students listen carefully and take notes.

Then hand out another article and ask students to take notes as they read the article. After students finish reading, ask them questions about each article that pertain to the main idea, significant details, cause-and-effect relationships, and other questions requiring comprehension skills.

Have students determine whether they retained more information by listening to an article or by reading one.

RESOURCES

MEETING INDIVIDUAL NEEDS

STUDENTS WITH SPECIAL NEEDS

Sometimes students with learning disabilities need visual reminders to help them to listen carefully. Before asking students to listen, you might write on the chalkboard a set of questions that can help students focus on specific information while they listen.

COMMON ERROR

Problem. If a proposition contains more than one central idea, there can be confusion. For example, "Resolved: That both the national debt and the prospect of global warming threaten the future of the United States."

Solution. Ensure that debate propositions contain only one central idea. For example: "Resolved: That the increasing national debt threatens the economic future of the United States."

RESOURCES

GUIDELINES FOR LISTENING CRITICALLY *(continued)*	
Identify the order of organization.	What kind of order does the speaker use to arrange the presentation—time sequence, spatial order, order of importance?
Note comparisons and contrasts.	What details are compared or contrasted with others?
Understand cause and effect.	What events are related to or affect others?
Predict outcomes and draw conclusions.	What reasonable conclusions can you make from the facts and evidence from the speech?

REFERENCE NOTE: For help with interpreting and analyzing information, see pages 1010–1012.

RESOURCES

Debating

A formal debate involves two groups, or teams, who publicly discuss a controversial topic in a systematic way. The topic under discussion is called the ***proposition.*** One team, the *affirmative team,* argues that the proposition should be accepted or adopted. The other side, the *negative team,* argues that the proposition should be rejected. To win the debate, the affirmative side must present enough proof to establish its case.

Stating a Debate Proposition

The central issue in a debate is stated as a proposition that is phrased as a resolution and limited to a specific idea. The proposition should be an issue that is actually debatable, and should offer each side an equal chance to build a reasonable case. The proposition should be clearly stated in language that is understandable to the debaters and to the audience.

DEBATE PROPOSITIONS

TYPE	DEFINITION	EXAMPLE
Proposition of fact	determines what is true or false	*Resolved:* That the ozone layer is depleted by synthetic products.
Proposition of value	states the value of a person, place, or thing	*Resolved:* That American students can compete with foreign students in all areas of study.
Proposition of policy	determines what action should be taken	*Resolved:* That the United States should adopt national health insurance for all citizens.

Preparing a Debate Brief

To be an effective debater you must prepare thoroughly: you must research the proposition and plan a strategy for the debate.

1. *Research the proposition.* Consult reference books to obtain information. Record facts and evidence on note cards.
2. *Identify specific issues.* The ***issues*** in a debate are the main differences between the affirmative and the negative positions. Every debatable proposition rests on several issues. To prove your proposition, list all the arguments you have for supporting your side of the proposition. To refute your opposition, list all the reasons you think your opponents will give for disagreeing with your views.
3. *Support your arguments.* Based on the information gathered during your research, identify evidence that supports your arguments—examples, quotations, statistics, expert opinions, analogies, and logic. Also, find evidence that will refute arguments your opponents are likely to use.

RESOURCES

COMMON ERROR

Problem. Debate propositions that contain emotional language or loaded words may unfairly skew the debate in favor of one side. For example, "Resolved: That drug dealers are scum who should be locked up for good."

Solution. Explain to students that they must use objective, unemotional language so that the debate revolves around issues. For example, "Resolved: That convicted drug dealers should receive mandatory life sentences."

INTEGRATING THE LANGUAGE ARTS

Library Link. Effective debaters present up-to-date information. To help students to keep up-to-date, maintain a classroom file of current newsmagazines and encourage students to read newspapers and to clip items that may be useful in debates. Suggest that students research periodical indexes after they have chosen debate topics.

As students research their debate topics, have them carefully record all their sources. Although informal classroom debates may not call for sources to be cited, formal debaters are expected to document their sources, and failure to do so can cause the debater to lose.

RESOURCES

COMMON ERROR

Problem. Students tend to favor one side of a proposition and may neglect to build arguments for the opposing side.

Solution. Emphasize that the successful debater puts personal biases aside and is prepared to argue either side with equal effectiveness.

RESOURCES

4. *Build a brief.* A ***brief*** is an outline for debate. It contains a logical arrangement of all the arguments needed to prove or disprove a proposition, as well as the evidence you have gathered to support your arguments.

EXCERPT OF A BRIEF—OPPOSING ARGUMENTS

Resolved: That the U.S. jury system should be significantly changed.

Affirmative

I. Jury trials in civil cases cause unfair delay and clog the courts.
   A. Only a few jury cases can be heard at a time; others must await trial. A survey by the Institute of Judicial Administration showed an average delay of 13.3 months.
   B. Delay only helps wrongdoers.
      1. The memory and the availability of witnesses diminishes.
      2. Delays may cause wronged parties to give up their cases.
   C. Delays force the innocent to wait before clearing themselves.

II. Jury trials waste time and money.
   A. They take the time of courts, participants, and jurors.
   B. They add to court costs, including juror payment.
   C. In New York city alone, jury service each year is equal to 50,000 people taken from their jobs for ten days--a huge loss of time and money to jurors' businesses.

III. Juries should be composed of fewer than twelve members.
   A. There is no specific reason for having twelve jurors.
   B. States that use smaller juries--with eight or even six jurors--report no reduction in the administration of justice.
   C. If juries were smaller, fewer jury members would need to be challenged: costs would be cut and verdicts reached sooner.

Negative

I. Court congestion is not caused by jury trial alone but by
   A. Increasing population
   B. Government failure to provide enough judges and courts.

II. The jury system does not waste time, money, or human energy.
   A. It costs little compared to other government expenditures.
   B. Jury expense represents only 1/170 of 1% of total costs in Federal courts, or only $1 for each $17,000 spent.
   C. In a University of Chicago survey of jurors, 94% said they'd serve again, 3% were very willing, and only 3% were unwilling.

III. The proposal to reduce the size of juries hides many dangers.
   A. It might represent a first step in eliminating juries entirely.
   B. Ethnically diverse citizens are less likely to be represented.

RESOURCES

Refuting the Opposing Arguments

In addition to building a strong case for or against the proposition, each of the teams in a debate must argue against its opponents' case. To refute, or attack, your opponents' arguments, you should

- state clearly the arguments you are going to refute
- tell the audience how you plan to refute the argument
- present proof to refute the argument by using facts, statistics, quotations, and other supporting data or evidence
- explain how the proof you have presented effectively refutes your opponents' arguments

Building a Rebuttal

The rebuttal should attempt to rebuild your case. This part of the debate allows each of the opposing sides a chance to repair the arguments that have been attacked by their opponents during the refutation. An effective rebuttal should

- restate your original arguments
- state your position on the issues your opponents have already attacked
- present proof that supports your arguments
- point out any weaknesses in your opponents' arguments
- summarize your original arguments and present any additional evidence you have gathered that supports your position

Participating in a Debate

Good debaters are courteous. Ridicule, sarcasm, or personal attacks are not acceptable. Do not deliberately misquote your opponents or attempt to distract or disturb them. A debate should be won or lost only on the basis of reasoned argument and convincing delivery.

It is customary to refer to participants in a debate by using, instead of names, polite terms such as "The first affirmative speaker," "My worthy opponents," "My colleagues," or "My teammates."

REFUTING THE OPPOSING ARGUMENTS

When building their cases, skilled debaters will often anticipate opposing arguments and refute these arguments in advance. This has the effect of weakening the oppositions's position.

BUILDING A REBUTTAL

Encourage your debaters to end positively. After refuting an opponent's arguments, a debater should add constructive material that will lead the audience to think positively about the arguments supporting the debater's own position.

PARTICIPATING IN A DEBATE

Remind your students that when they participate in a debate, they are in full view of the judge or judges at all times. How they behave when they are not speaking may influence judges and therefore is important.

A DIFFERENT APPROACH

While the cross-examination format has now largely replaced the standard format in contest, you may wish to start novice debaters with the standard format. After they have developed some debating skill, they will be ready for the cut and thrust of cross-examination debate.

CROSS-EXAMINATION DEBATE FORMAT

During cross-examination, questions should be brief and should attempt to elicit brief responses. To avoid unpleasant surprises, skilled debaters normally ask only questions to which they can anticipate the answers.

Speaking Order for a Debate

Most debates are divided into two parts. During the first part, both teams make ***constructive speeches,*** attempting to "build" their cases by presenting their arguments for or against the proposition, and attempting to refute, or disprove, the points they believe will be raised by the opposing team. After an intermission, the second part of the debate begins, and both teams make ***rebuttal speeches,*** trying to reply to damaging arguments raised by the opposing team in their closing speeches. Specific time limits are assigned for each speech, although these limits vary, depending on the type of debate.

ORDER OF SPEAKING FOR A STANDARD DEBATE	
1. CONSTRUCTIVE SPEECHES a. First affirmative b. First negative c. Second affirmative d. Second negative	2. REBUTTAL SPEECHES a. First negative b. First affirmative c. Second negative d. Second affirmative

Cross-Examination Debate Format. Opposing teams, in a cross-examination debate, have the opportunity to question the opponents' major points immediately after each constructive speech. This style of debate tests a debater's ability to think critically and respond quickly.

ORDER OF SPEAKING FOR A CROSS-EXAMINATION DEBATE
1. CONSTRUCTIVE SPEECHES a. First affirmative constructive b. Cross-examination by second negative c. First negative constructive d. Cross-examination by first affirmative e. Second affirmative constructive f. Cross-examination by first negative g. Second negative constructive h. Cross-examination by second affirmative

(continued)

RESOURCES

RESOURCES

ORDER OF SPEAKING FOR A CROSS-EXAMINATION DEBATE *(continued)*
2. REBUTTAL SPEECHES a. First negative rebuttal b. First affirmative rebuttal c. Second negative rebuttal d. Second affirmative rebuttal

Lincoln-Douglas Debate. A Lincoln-Douglas debate has only one speaker on each team. Also, propositions in this type of debate are always propositions of value rather than propositions of fact or policy.

This one-on-one debate format is often used when opposing candidates for political office debate in the presence of voters. The name commemorates the sensational series of debates between rival political candidates, Abraham Lincoln and Stephen Douglas.

ORDER OF SPEAKING FOR A LINCOLN-DOUGLAS DEBATE
1. CONSTRUCTIVE SPEECH a. Affirmative constructive b. Cross-examination by negative c. Negative constructive d. Cross-examination by affirmative 2. REBUTTAL SPEECHES a. Affirmative rebuttal b. Negative rebuttal c. Affirmative rebuttal

Conducting and Judging a Debate

A chairperson often presides during the debate. A speaker may appeal to the chairperson if he or she believes that any debating procedures or time limits have been violated by the opposing team.

RESOURCES

ORDER OF SPEAKING FOR A LINCOLN-DOUGLAS DEBATE

This format permits three speeches for the affirmative to two for the negative. When deciding on time limits, be sure that each debater have the same total time to present his or her case.

CONDUCTING AND JUDGING A DEBATE

In addition to ensuring that debaters speak in the proper order and that the debate is conducted in a courteous atmosphere, the chairperson should arrange for a competent timekeeper who will inform the debaters of the time they have remaining by means of flash cards.

Judges should be careful to judge the debate as it was presented and not as it might have been. A judge may have superior knowledge of a proposition and awareness of deficiencies in the cases, but should not let this prejudice him or her in favor of one side or the other.

RESOURCES

The most common method of determining the winner of a debate is by decision of three appointed judges. The judges are expected to base their decision on the merits of the debate and not on their own views of the proposition. Occasionally, an audience may vote to determine the winning team.

Review

EXERCISE 1 Preparing and Giving a Speech

Choose a topic for a three- to five-minute speech to present to your English class, considering the occasion and the interests of your listeners when selecting a topic. Identify your purpose for speaking. Gather material, make an outline, and prepare note cards. Include at least one visual. Then deliver your speech, using effective speaking techniques.

EXERCISE 2 Listening Critically

Listen to a short speech presented by a classmate, by your teacher, or on television or radio. Take brief notes. Then answer the following questions about the speech.

1. Identify the purpose of the speech.
2. What are the main ideas expressed in the speech?
3. What details support or explain the key ideas in the speech?
4. In what ways did the speaker's body language and voice contribute to the message of the speech?
5. Did the speaker achieve the purpose he or she intended? Explain why or why not.

EXERCISE 3 Preparing a Debate Brief

Divide the class into groups of four or six members. Each group will either select one of the following general topics or choose their own. Then the group will write a specific debate proposition. Each group will then divide into affirmative and negative teams, research the topic, and prepare written debate briefs, using the example on page 942 as a model.

RESOURCES

ANSWERS

Exercise 1

Speeches will vary but should follow the guidelines in the textbook for preparing and giving a speech. You might go over students' outlines, note cards, and visuals with them to make suggestions before they give their speeches.

ANSWERS

Exercise 2

Answers will vary according to the speech presented. Students should answer each of the five questions after listening critically.

ANSWERS

Exercise 3

Students should follow guidelines for conducting and participating in a debate. The briefs should be judged in terms of logical arrangement, identification of all the relevant issues, and completeness of supporting evidence. Sources should be adequately documented.

RESOURCES

1. Animal rights
2. Lie detector tests
3. Equal rights amendment
4. Year-round school year
5. Crime and law enforcement
6. Censorship of music
7. Raising the driving age
8. Energy conservation
9. Compulsory military service
10. Mass transit

EXERCISE 4 Conducting a Debate

Stage a debate, using the affirmative and negative teams, the debate proposition, and the briefs developed for Exercise 3. Select one of the debate formats discussed on pages 944–946 for conducting a debate and assign specific time limits for each stage of the procedure. Appoint a chairperson to preside over the debate. Either select judges or create a ballot for use by the whole class when deciding the outcome of the debate.

RESOURCES

ANSWERS

Exercise 4

Judges should be warned to be as objective as possible when evaluating the debate and when deciding on the winning side. You may want to follow the debate with an evaluation session. During the evaluation consider analysis, evidence, reasoning, organization, refutation, and delivery.

RESOURCES

COMMUNICATION SKILLS *(pp. 948–958)*

OBJECTIVES

- To design a checklist for conducting an interview that includes interview questions
- To prepare for a job interview by planning questions
- To practice for a college interview by planning questions
- To select a topic, to hold a group discussion, and to convey findings to the class

Teacher's ResourceBank™

RESOURCES

COMMUNICATION SKILLS

CHAPTER OVERVIEW

This chapter can help students to apply the communication skills developed for composition to other communication activities. It explains the communication cycle and gives suggestions for giving and receiving information. The chapter discusses techniques for conducting an interview and for being interviewed. Students are asked to prepare questions for conducting and for participating in interviews.

Both informal and formal group discussions are included with responsibilities for participants and rules of order given. The section on oral interpretation shows students how to adapt material for presentation and how to present interpretations. Students are then asked to participate in group discussions and to present oral interpretations.

QUICK REMINDER

Pair students and give them a few minutes to interview one another about any outstanding (positive) traits that define their partners. Students should try to discover what makes their partners unique and interesting. After students interview their partners, have each pair go to the front of the class to introduce each other.

RESOURCES

33 COMMUNICATION SKILLS

Types and Techniques

Communicating requires skill in both speaking and listening. You might think that communicating simply means talking. However, communication is complex. It occurs in many different settings and under a variety of circumstances, but its purpose is always the same: to share information or ideas. To improve your ability to communicate, you can practice your speaking skills.

The Communication Cycle

Communication is a two-way process. A speaker expresses feelings or ideas, and the listener (or listeners) responds to the speaker's message. This response is called ***feedback.*** Listener feedback may be in the form of a verbal response (words) or a nonverbal response (gestures, facial expressions, body language, or nonword sounds such as sighs or giggles).

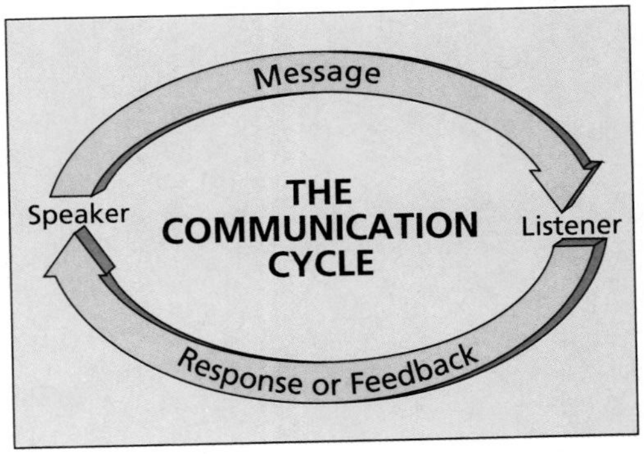

- To select a literary work and to present an oral interpretation to the class

Giving and Receiving Information

In some of the simplest communication situations, the purpose is to transmit specific items of information. For situations of this type, successful communication takes place whenever the speaker is clear and precise and whenever the listener clearly understands the information that the speaker is attempting to convey. This type of communication exchange includes occasions when someone is giving or receiving instructions or directions and giving or receiving telephone messages. The following chart contains suggestions for improving your effectiveness in situations of this type whether you are the speaker or the listener.

GIVING AND RECEIVING DIRECTIONS

Giving	Receiving
Make each step as simple and easy to understand as possible. Explain the steps in an order that makes sense.	Listen to each step. Look for transitional words that tell you when each step of the process ends and the next one begins, such as *first, second, next, then, last,* and *finally*.
Remember to include every step or all the necessary information.	Listen carefully so that you can keep track of the number of steps and their order. In your mind, picture yourself doing each step. Take notes if necessary.
Repeat all directions or instructions so that the other person can remember them.	Make sure you have all the necessary information and that you understand the directions. Ask questions if you are unclear about any steps.

RESOURCES

MEETING INDIVIDUAL NEEDS

LEP/ESL

General Strategies. Some ESL students go through years of school without the opportunity to speak their native languages in the classroom. Ask students to give presentations both in English and in their native languages. This language presentation also allows native English speakers an opportunity to appreciate and understand linguistic differences.

COOPERATIVE LEARNING

Have students work in groups of four on **Giving and Receiving Directions.** Assign each group a process to analyze, such as playing a sport, gardening, or starting a club. Students should give directions or instructions to explain the steps of the process.

A member of each group could introduce the other group members to the class and announce the subject of the group's report. Then each speaker should present a part of the process to the class.

RESOURCES

INTEGRATING THE LANGUAGE ARTS

Technology Link. When students make telephone calls, they may have to leave messages on answering machines. Remind students that when they leave recorded messages, they need to identify themselves clearly, give their telephone numbers, and keep their messages brief.

If you have students who have not had experience with leaving messages on answering machines, you could have students time each other as they pretend to leave messages. Or you might bring a tape recorder to class to practice leaving messages.

RESOURCES

CONDUCTING AN INTERVIEW

Tell your class that many experienced interviewees make it a habit to write brief thank-you notes. Ask the class why this habit might be desirable. [It creates goodwill in case a follow-up interview is needed; it helps the interviewer remember the interviewee's name.]

Here are suggestions for improving your effectiveness when you are giving or receiving telephone messages.

GIVING AND RECEIVING TELEPHONE MESSAGES	
Making Calls	**Receiving Calls**
If you reach the wrong number, tell the person who answers that you are sorry for the disturbance.	Be understanding if someone dials your number in error. Everyone makes mistakes.
Avoid calling early in the morning, late at night, or at mealtimes.	If someone calls at an inconvenient time, ask if you may return the call later.
Say who you are as soon as the person answers. If the person you're calling is not there, leave your name and number and a short message.	Say hello when you answer. Take a message if the call is for someone who is out. Repeat the message to make sure you wrote it correctly.
Don't stay on the phone too long. If you place the call, it's your responsibility to end it.	If you need to end the call, say politely that you need to go. You might offer to call back at another time.

RESOURCES

Interviewing

An *interview* is a communication situation in which the object is to exchange ideas or information. You might take part in an interview to gather information, apply for a job, or apply for admission to a college.

Conducting an Interview

At times when you are preparing a research paper, a class report, a speech, or a newspaper article, you may need to interview certain people for firsthand information. Some suggestions about how you can be an effective interviewer follow.

Preparing for the Interview

- Make arrangements well in advance. Set up a time that is convenient for the other person to meet with you.
- Make a list of questions to ask. Make sure the questions are arranged in a logical order and require more than yes or no answers.

Participating in the Interview

- Arrive on time and be polite and patient.
- Ask the other person's permission if you plan to take notes or use a tape recorder.
- Avoid argument. Be tactful and courteous. Remember, the interview was granted at your request.
- Listen carefully and ask follow-up questions if you do not understand an answer or if you think you need more information.

Following up on the Interview

- Review your notes to refresh your memory, and then make a summary of the material you have gathered.
- Send a note expressing your appreciation for the interview.

Interviewing for a Position

When you apply for a position such as a job, an employer will usually require an interview with you before agreeing to hire you. Other situations for which you may be interviewed for a position require the same general preparations.

HOW TO INTERVIEW FOR A POSITION

1. *Arrange an appointment.* Write a business letter of application in which you request an interview for the job. If you are granted an interview, be prompt for your appointment.
2. *Bring a résumé.* If you haven't already submitted a résumé, take your résumé to the interview and give it to the interviewer.

(continued)

INTEGRATING THE LANGUAGE ARTS

Library Link. Remind students that preparation before an interview is one of the best ways to ensure that the interview goes smoothly. Although asking questions is the goal of an interview, the more knowledge one has before the interview begins, the better the questions will be and as a result, more knowledge will be gained.

Remind students that professional interviewers plan their questions by researching as much about their subjects as they can ahead of time. Students may need to ask themselves preliminary questions and they may need to spend some time in the library polishing their questions. Many libraries have collections of information about companies and colleges that are very useful when students are planning for job or college interviews.

RESOURCES

COOPERATIVE LEARNING

You might have students practice job or college interviews with each other. Pair students and allow them time to research interview questions. Then have each student take a turn at interviewing and at being interviewed.

After students have had time to practice, have volunteers present their interviews before the class. The class could make suggestions as to how the volunteers could improve their interview techniques.

MEETING INDIVIDUAL NEEDS

RESOURCES

STUDENTS WITH SPECIAL NEEDS

Students with learning disabilities might find the idea of speaking before a group very intimidating. Encourage students to become comfortable in group discussions before they give individual speeches. Suggest that students work with partners before they give speeches before an audience. You might also suggest that they practice their deliveries beforehand by tape-recording their speeches and evaluating themselves.

HOW TO INTERVIEW FOR A POSITION *(continued)*

3. *Be neat and well-groomed.* It's important to look your best when you are interviewing to apply for any type of job.
4. *Answer questions clearly and honestly.* Answer the questions the interviewer asks, adding any additional information that might inform the employer that you are the right person for the job.
5. *Ask questions.* Questions that job applicants usually ask include requests for information about work hours, salary, or chances for advancement. By your questions, show that you know something about the company or business.
6. *Be prepared to be tested.* The employer may require you to take tests that demonstrate your skills, intelligence, or personality.
7. *Follow up the interview.* After the interview, write a short thank-you note. Tell the interviewer that you appreciated the opportunity for the interview and that you look forward to hearing from the company in the near future.

REFERENCE NOTE: For more about writing a letter of application and preparing a résumé, see pages 999–1001.

RESOURCES

Group Discussions

Groups of every kind—cooperative learning groups, school clubs, city councils, parent and teacher groups, community organizations, labor unions, legislative assemblies—communicate through group discussions.

There are many types of group discussions. However, each group discussion has a specific purpose. Some of the most common purposes for group discussions are

- to share ideas
- to suggest solutions for solving a problem
- to make an evaluation, decision, or recommendation

When a group is establishing the purpose to be accomplished by its discussion, one important factor to be considered is the time available. If there is a specific limit on the time for discussion, the group will need to set a goal that can be accomplished in the time allowed.

Informal Group Discussions

An informal group discussion is one that usually takes place between members of a group small enough to allow everyone to participate without using parliamentary procedures.

Effective group discussions require that each participant play a role. In a discussion each role has specific responsibilities. For example, a chairperson may be elected (or appointed) whose task is to keep the discussion moving smoothly. Another group member may serve as secretary, or reporter, taking notes during the discussion.

In its discussion, a group may follow a prepared outline, or ***agenda,*** of topics in the order they will be discussed. In some groups, the chairperson sets the agenda; in others, the agenda is established by a preliminary discussion and is agreed upon by the members.

Here are some of the responsibilities of members of a group discussion.

A Chairperson's Responsibilities

1. Announce the topic and explain the agenda.
2. Follow the agenda, keeping the discussion on the topics to be considered.
3. Encourage participation by each member.
4. Avoid disagreements by being objective and settling conflicts or confusions fairly.

A Secretary's or Reporter's Responsibilities

1. Make notes of significant information or actions.
2. Prepare a final report.

A Participant's Responsibilities

1. Take part in the discussion.
2. Cooperate with other members, being fair and considerate of others' opinions and suggestions.

RESOURCES

A DIFFERENT APPROACH

Students might want to establish a special-interest group, such as a network of students looking for part-time jobs or a club devoted to learning about colleges. Have the students follow the guidelines for group discussion. Encourage the chairperson to plan an agenda that promotes participation by each member. Have the secretary or reporter post the notes of the meeting so that the information will be available to all students.

RESOURCES

FORMAL GROUP DISCUSSIONS

Students may be interested in knowing why the rules for conducting meetings are known as parliamentary procedure. Tell students that these rules are based on customs established over the centuries by the British Parliament.

According to rules of parliamentary procedure, each member of a group has the right to vote and each vote counts equally. Normally, a simple majority is sufficient to carry a motion. Sometimes, however, especially when a motion involves infringement of personal rights, two thirds of those voting must affirm a motion for it to pass.

Many groups establish a minimum number of members to be present before business can be transacted to prevent a tiny minority from making decisions that are disapproved of by the true majority. The quorum can be any figure, but it is normally set somewhere between forty and sixty percent.

A DIFFERENT APPROACH

Have students brainstorm to list the formal uses for parliamentary procedure. Have students include the business, government, educational, and social uses that require parliamentary procedure.

RESOURCES

Formal Group Discussions

Clubs, organizations, and other groups often meet on a regular basis to discuss issues of importance to the entire group. To conduct effective meetings, formal groups often follow an established set of rules known as ***parliamentary procedure.*** The single most authoritative source is a book called *Robert's Rules of Order, Revised* by Henry Robert.

The basic principles of parliamentary procedure as found in *Robert's Rules of Order* protect the rights of individual members of the group while providing a systematic means for dealing with issues that come before the group for a decision.

Here are some of the basic principles of parliamentary procedure:

- The majority decides.
- The minority has the right to be heard.
- Decisions are made by voting.

The benefit of parliamentary procedure is that it allows a group of individuals to deal in an orderly, organized way with issues that are raised and decisions that the group needs to make about those issues. This system of organized procedures provides the following advantages:

- Only one issue is decided at a time.
- Everyone is assured of the chance to be heard, everyone has the right to vote, and all votes are counted as equal.
- All sides of an issue are debated in open discussion.

RESOURCES

ORDER OF BUSINESS

A formal group meeting usually follows the standard order of business suggested in *Robert's Rules of Order:*

1. *Call to order:* The chairperson says, "The meeting will come to order."
2. *Reading and approval of the minutes:* The chairperson says, "The secretary (or recorder) will read the minutes from our last meeting." The secretary reads these minutes, and the chairperson inquires, "Are there any additions or corrections to the minutes?" The minutes are then approved, or they are corrected and then approved.

(continued)

ORDER OF BUSINESS *(continued)*
3. *Officers' reports:* The chairperson calls for a report from other officers who need to report, as by saying, "Will the treasurer please give us a report?"
4. *Committee reports:* The chairperson may ask the presiding officer of standing committees and then of special committees to make reports to the group.
5. *Old business:* Any issues that have not been fully resolved at the last meeting may now be discussed. The chairperson may ask the group, "Is there any old business to be discussed?"
6. *New business:* Any new issues that have not previously been discussed may now be addressed.
7. *Announcements:* The chairperson may ask the members, "Are there any announcements?"
8. *Adjournment:* The chairperson ends the meeting, saying, "The meeting is now adjourned."

PROCEDURES FOR DISCUSSION OF BUSINESS
The meeting follows specific procedures for discussion of business.
1. Anyone who wishes to speak must be recognized by the chairperson.
2. A participant may introduce a motion, or proposal, for discussion, by beginning "I move that . . . "
3. To support the motion, another member must second it, saying "I second the motion." A motion that is not seconded is dropped.
4. A motion that has been seconded may be discussed by the group.
5. Other motions made by members may amend the motion under consideration; may postpone, limit, or extend debate or discussion; or may refer the motion to a committee for further research.
6. After discussion, the group votes on the motion. The chairperson usually votes only in the case of a tie.

RESOURCES

ORDER OF BUSINESS

Tell students that while the order of business suggested in *Robert's Rules of Order* is the usual order of business, any group can adopt bylaws that will permit alternative orders of business. Also, with the consent of the majority, items of business can be shifted from the set order.

PROCEDURES FOR DISCUSSION OF BUSINESS

If a group is following rules of order, no discussion is in order unless it has been preceded by a motion.

If a motion is made to amend a main motion, that motion must be voted on before voting occurs on the main motion.

RESOURCES

INTEGRATING THE LANGUAGE ARTS

Literature Link. Reader's theater allows students to develop skills in oral interpretation and awareness of drama. After selecting several short one-act plays, such as *Trifles* by Susan Glaspell or *Where the Cross Is Made* by Eugene O'Neill, divide your class into groups. If a play has several small speaking parts, a student might be assigned to read more than one part. After the groups have familiarized themselves with their plays, they can take turns performing for each other.

Another possible activity for oral interpretation is a poetry reading. A dramatic monologue is effective when read aloud to an audience, as is narrative poetry. Students might use dramatic monologues, such as T. S. Eliot's "The Love Song of J. Alfred Prufrock" or selections from narrative poems, such as Edgar Lee Masters's *Spoon River Anthology* or Longfellow's *Evangeline.*

RESOURCES

Oral Interpretation

Oral interpretation involves the presentation of a work of literature to a group of listeners in order to express the meaning contained in the literary work. You might use acting as well as speaking skills—vocal techniques, facial expression, body language, and gestures—to express the overall meaning of the literary work.

Adapting Material

When you are adapting material for an oral interpretation, you usually have a specific purpose and audience in mind. Every occasion has its own requirements. Be sure you have thought about factors such as the length of time that will be allowed for your presentation and your audience's interests. As a general rule, no props or costumes are provided for oral interpretations; instead, performers usually rely on the imagination of the audience to provide the scenery and other dramatic enhancements.

For your oral interpretation, you will need to make an abbreviated version, or *cutting,* of a work of fiction or nonfiction, a long poem, or a play.

HOW TO MAKE A CUTTING

1. Follow the story line of the literary work in time order.
2. Delete dialogue tags such as *she replied sadly.* Instead, use these clues to tell you how to interpret the character's words as you express them.
3. Delete passages that don't contribute to the overall effect or impression you intend to create with your oral interpretation.

RESOURCES

Presenting an Oral Interpretation

For your interpretation you may need to write an introduction that sets the scene, tells something about the author, or gives some necessary details about what has already taken place in the story.

The common practice, when presenting an oral interpretation, is to prepare a *reading script*. A reading script is usually typed (double-spaced) and can be marked to assist you in your interpretive reading. For example, you might underline words to remind you to use special emphasis, or mark a slash (/) to indicate where you'd like a dramatic pause.

Once you have developed a reading script, rehearse several different interpretations until you are satisfied that you have chosen the most effective manner of expressing the meaning of the selection.

Use your voice in a manner that suits your presentation. Pronounce words carefully. You can use your body and your voice to show that you are portraying different characters. Use body language and gestures to emphasize the meaning or to reveal traits of the major characters in the story as you narrate and act out what they say and do.

Review

EXERCISE 1 Planning an Interview

Select a topic that requires firsthand information from an individual. Design a checklist that includes setting up the interview, doing research, and preparing questions to ask the person being interviewed. Make sure that your questions are organized, and clear, and that they require thoughtful responses.

EXERCISE 2 Preparing for a Job Interview

Check the classified section of a local newspaper and find a job that you might like and for which you are qualified. List the questions that you would expect an interviewer to ask you and the answers you would provide. Also, make a list of questions you would ask the interviewer about the job or position.

EXERCISE 3 Practicing a College Interview

Working with a partner, make a list of questions you would likely be asked by a college admissions officer. Then make a list

INTEGRATING THE LANGUAGE ARTS

Reading and Speaking. Students might enjoy staging an oral interpretation recital. Each member of the class could read a short poem, or the class could read poems in chorus, with one or two students acting as narrators to link each poem with the next.

ANSWERS

Exercise 1

Checklists and questions will vary. Students should follow the guidelines for preparing for an interview as well as the guidelines for conducting an interview. Check to see that questions are well organized and thought provoking.

ANSWERS

Exercise 2

Questions and answers will vary. Students should follow the guidelines for participating in an interview and the guidelines for being interviewed for a position. Check students' lists of questions to see if students have included pertinent, appropriate questions.

ANSWERS

Exercise 3

Questions and presentations will vary. Students should follow the general guidelines for interviewing and being interviewed. Encourage students to project their own individuality into the presentations.

RESOURCES

ANSWERS

Exercise 4

Group discussions will vary according to the topics chosen, but each student should follow the guidelines for group discussions and should narrow the focus to a specific topic that lends itself to a problem with solutions.

ANSWERS

Exercise 5

Presentations and scripts will vary, but students should follow the guidelines for adapting material for presenting an oral interpretation.

RESOURCES

of questions you might ask this representative of the college you might attend. Have one person act as the interviewer and the other as the person being interviewed. Present the interview in class and respond to the feedback from your classmate.

EXERCISE 4 Presenting a Group Discussion

Your class is to select one of the following broad subjects and narrow the focus to a specific topic. The purpose of this discussion should be to share ideas and suggest solutions to a problem. Work in groups small enough to allow thorough discusion of the topic. Select a reporter to convey your group's findings to the class.

1. Choosing a career
2. Professional vs. amateur sports
3. Vandalism
4. Prejudice
5. American foreign policy

EXERCISE 5 Presenting an Oral Interpretation

Select a portion of a literary work suitable for an oral presentation and adapt the material for a short presentation to your class. First, prepare a reading script. Second, write an introduction that tells the author and title of the selection and that provides enough background information so that your audience can understand the meaning of the scene. Then, present your material in class.

RESOURCES

THE LIBRARY/MEDIA CENTER *(pp. 959–966)*

OBJECTIVES

- To use the card catalog to find specific information
- To locate specific information in the *Readers' Guide*
- To create a diagram of the school library

34 The Library/ Media Center

Finding and Using Information

For centuries, libraries have been storehouses for information recorded in manuscripts, books, newspapers, and other written forms. In the past few decades, information has also become increasingly available in other forms, such as audio and video recordings and computer programs. With the addition of these nonprint forms, the library is now often called a media center or media resource center.

The Librarian

To find books in the library, you need to know how they're classified and arranged. If you need help finding specific information, don't hesitate to ask your librarian. Librarians are professionals trained to track down information; they can show you how to use the library's resources effectively. Also, a librarian may be able to find information for you by borrowing sources from other libraries.

Teacher's ResourceBank™

RESOURCES

THE LIBRARY/MEDIA CENTER

CHAPTER OVERVIEW

This chapter covers organization of the library, arrangement of books by the Dewey decimal system and the Library of Congress system, use of the card catalog and on-line catalog, and the use of reference materials—the *Readers' Guide,* the vertical file, microforms, computer databases, and recorded materials. You may want to refer students to this chapter throughout the year, especially in conjunction with **Chapter 11: "Writing a Research Paper."**

QUICK REMINDER

To start students thinking about how to find information in the library, ask them to name topics they would like to know more about. List these on the chalkboard. Then ask students how they would go about finding information about these subjects. Lead students to understand that the sources in a library have been arranged so that people can easily find information.

RESOURCES

MEETING INDIVIDUAL NEEDS

LEP/ESL

General Strategies. Because reading is a good way to strengthen language proficiency, you may want to encourage leisure reading by arranging regular trips to the library. Give students a brief introductory tour and guide them toward interesting books geared to their reading levels. Support this practice by periodically setting aside ten minutes for leisure reading during class. You could pair students and have them take turns reading to each other.

ADVANCED STUDENTS

Have small groups of students prepare oral reports about libraries. Possible topics include the history of public libraries in the United States, services offered by public libraries, library careers, nonprint media, or famous libraries.

RESOURCES

Finding Books in the Library

The Call Number

In most libraries, books are assigned ***call numbers*** to identify each book and indicate where it's shelved. Call numbers are assigned according to one of two classification systems: the *Dewey decimal system* or the *Library of Congress system.*

The Dewey Decimal System

Nonfiction. In the Dewey decimal system, nonfiction books and some works of literature are grouped by subject into ten general subject areas, each assigned a range of numbers. Within this range, subgroups of numbers identify more specific categories.

DEWEY DECIMAL CLASSIFICATION SYSTEM

NUMBERS	SUBJECT AREAS	EXAMPLES OF SUBDIVISIONS
000–099	General Works	encyclopedias, periodicals, bibliographies
100–199	Philosophy	psychology, ethics, personality
200–299	Religion	theology, bibles, mythology
300–399	Social Science	economics, education, government, law
400–499	Philology or Language	grammar, dictionaries, foreign languages
500–599	Science	biology, chemistry, geology, mathematics
600–699	Technology	agriculture, engineering, health, medical science, environment
700–799	The Arts	motion pictures, music, painting, photography, sports
800–899	Literature	criticism, drama, essays, poetry
900–999	History	archaeology, geography, travel, collective biographies

NOTE: Some libraries use the letter *R* before the call numbers of reference books in any of these categories.

RESOURCES

Fiction. The Dewey decimal system groups books of fiction together in alphabetical order according to the authors' last names. Works of fiction by the same author are arranged alphabetically by the first important word of the title (excluding *A, An,* and *The*). Collections of short stories may be grouped separately from novels.

NOTE: Authors' names that begin with *Mc* are alphabetized as *Mac.* Names beginning with *St.* are alphabetized as *Saint.*

The Library of Congress System

The Library of Congress system uses code letters to identify subject categories. The first letter of a book's call number tells the general category. The second letter tells the subcategory. The librarian can provide you with a complete list of letter codes for Library of Congress categories and subcategories.

LIBRARY OF CONGRESS CLASSIFICATION SYSTEM

GENERAL CATEGORIES

A	General Works	M	Music
B	Philosophy, Psychology, Religion	N	Fine Arts
C–F	History	P	Language and Literature
G	Geography, Anthropology, Recreation	Q	Science
H	Social Science	R	Medicine
J	Political Science	S	Agriculture
K	Law	T	Technology
L	Education	U	Military Science
		V	Naval Science
		Z	Bibliography and Library Science

The Card Catalog

The ***card catalog*** is a cabinet of drawers filled with alphabetically arranged cards: *title cards, author cards,* and *subject cards.* You may also find cross-reference cards that advise you where to look for additional information. Catalog cards may give publication facts, list the number of pages, and tell whether the book contains illustrations or diagrams.

RESOURCES

CRITICAL THINKING
Analysis

Have students analyze the way you have arranged the books in your classroom. If your class library is extensive, students could prepare a floor plan detailing the arrangement. You could also challenge students to devise a more useful arrangement.

A DIFFERENT APPROACH

When students are using the card catalog to research a subject, suggest that they pay attention to similarities in the call numbers. If students find several books with approximately the same call number, they may have found a whole category of books about a subject. Going to the shelves at this point may be more productive than continuing to search through the card catalog.

RESOURCES

MEETING INDIVIDUAL NEEDS

LESS-ADVANCED STUDENTS

To give students hands-on practice with the card catalog, ask them each to list on a piece of paper three topics of interest. Direct students to subject cards in the school library and ask students to locate and write down the title and call numbers of a book for each subject. If they are interested in reading these books, allow students time to locate and check out their choices.

RESOURCES

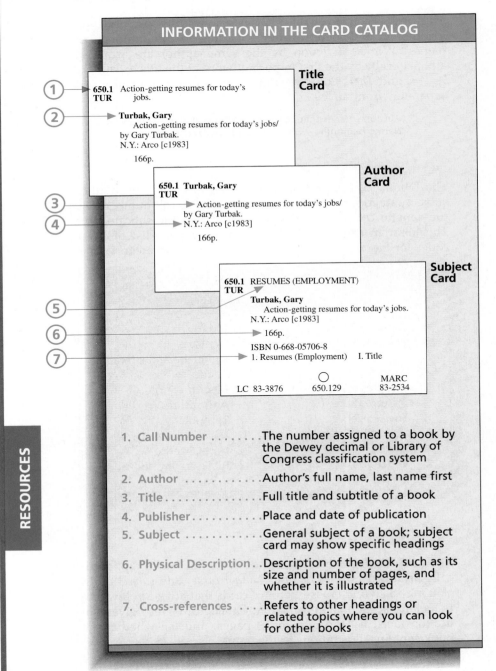

INFORMATION IN THE CARD CATALOG

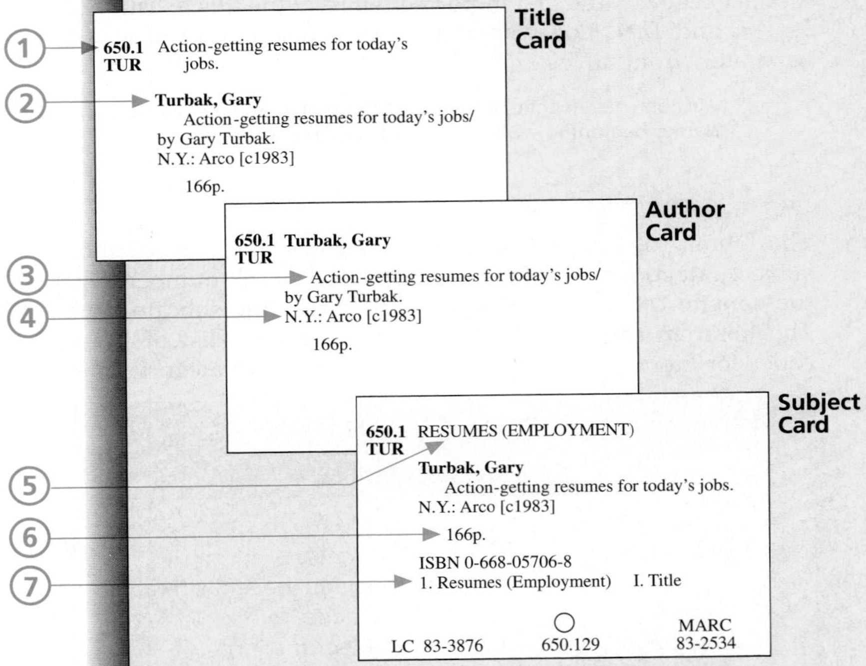

Title Card
650.1 TUR Action-getting resumes for today's jobs.
Turbak, Gary
Action-getting resumes for today's jobs/ by Gary Turbak.
N.Y.: Arco [c1983]
166p.
Author Card
650.1 TUR Turbak, Gary
Action-getting resumes for today's jobs/ by Gary Turbak.
N.Y.: Arco [c1983]
166p.
Subject Card
650.1 TUR RESUMES (EMPLOYMENT)
Turbak, Gary
Action-getting resumes for today's jobs.
N.Y.: Arco [c1983]
166p.
ISBN 0-668-05706-8
1. Resumes (Employment) I. Title
LC 83-3876
650.129
MARC 83-2534
1
2
3
4
5
6
7

1. Call Number .... The number assigned to a book by the Dewey decimal or Library of Congress classification system
2. Author .... Author's full name, last name first
3. Title .... Full title and subtitle of a book
4. Publisher .... Place and date of publication
5. Subject .... General subject of a book; subject card may show specific headings
6. Physical Description . . Description of the book, such as its size and number of pages, and whether it is illustrated
7. Cross-references .... Refers to other headings or related topics where you can look for other books

The On-line Catalog

The ***on-line catalog*** is a computerized version of the card catalog. To view a catalog listing on a library's computer, you type in an author's name, a title, or a subject on the keyboard. The computer then displays on the screen the information that you'd find if you looked under this heading in the card catalog. The on-line catalog can locate information quickly and may tell you if a book you are looking for is checked out or if it is available at another library.

Using Reference Materials

The *Readers' Guide*

When you need to find a magazine article, use the *Readers' Guide to Periodical Literature*. It indexes articles, poems, and stories from more than one hundred magazines. As you can see in the following excerpt, the *Readers' Guide* gives a great amount of information in a very compact space.

(1) **MOIZE, ELIZABETH A.**
(2) Austin [cover story] il *National Geographic*
(3) 177:50–71 Je '90
MOJAVE DESERT (CALIF.)
(4) *See also*
Mojave National Park (Calif.)
Faults in the Mojave Desert, California, as revealed
(5) on enhanced Landsat images [cover story] J. P.
Ford and others. bibl f il *Science* 248:1000–3
(6) My 25 '90
(7) **MOJAVE NATIONAL PARK (CALIF.)**
A poet, a painter, and the Lonesome Triangle
[ranchers and environmentalists battle over
(8) Mojave Desert proposal] K. Heacox. il map
Audubon 92:66–77 My '90
MOLDEA, DAN E., 1950–
about
Author charges libel in 'N.Y. Times' book review.
(9) H. Fields. *Publishers Weekly* 237:10 S 7 '90
MOLECULAR BEAMS
New mechanisms for chemistry at surfaces. S.T.
Ceyer bibl f il *Science* 249:113-9 Jl 13 '90

1. **Author entry**
2. **Title of article**
3. **Page reference**
4. **Subject cross-reference**
5. **Name of magazine**
6. **Volume number of magazine**
7. **Subject entry**
8. **Date of magazine**
9. **Author of article**

RESOURCES

INTEGRATING THE LANGUAGE ARTS

Technology Link. If your school has an on-line catalog, ask the librarian to show your class how to use it. Then give students time to use the on-line catalog to locate information. You might suggest that students keep note cards with simple step-by-step instructions. When they see how easy it is to use the on-line catalog, they might develop interest in learning more about computers.

Library Skills and Writing. One way to combine use of the *Readers' Guide* with writing for a real audience is to have each student write a letter to a prominent public figure. First, have each student read the articles indexed in the *Readers' Guide* that pertain to the chosen person. Students should look for information on which to base their letters. For example, a student might congratulate a public figure who actively supports environmental issues. Encourage students to include specific details in their letters. After students have carefully edited and proofread their letters, suggest that they mail the letters. A few of the public figures may even answer.

RESOURCES

SELECTION AMENDMENT
Description of change: excerpted
Rationale: to focus on the concept of *Readers' Guide* presented in this chapter

MEETING INDIVIDUAL NEEDS

STUDENTS WITH SPECIAL NEEDS

Students with reading disabilities might have trouble with the reduced print and condensed form of the *Readers' Guide.* You could pair such students with partners of good reading ability. In addition, when such students are reading small print in other sources, use of highlighter pens (as appropriate), colored transparency sheets, straight edges, and magnifiers may be helpful.

Throughout the year, paperback editions of the *Readers' Guide* are published. Each issue lists materials published two to four weeks previously. The paperback issues are then bound into a single, hardcover volume at the end of the year.

As the sample entry on page 963 shows, magazine articles are listed by subject and by author but not by title. The *Readers' Guide* also gives *"see"* and *"see also"* references. A key at the front of the *Readers' Guide* explains the meaning of the abbreviations used in entries.

The Vertical File

The ***vertical file*** is a file cabinet containing a variety of up-to-date materials. Libraries generally keep current pictures, pamphlets, newspaper clippings, and catalogs in special folders in the vertical file. Organized by subject, these materials often consist of government, business, or educational publications. Ask the librarian to help you use the vertical file to find current materials.

Microforms

To save space, many libraries photographically reduce periodicals and newspapers and store them on ***microforms.*** The two most common kinds of microforms are *microfilm* (a roll or reel of film) and *microfiche* (a sheet of film). The librarian can tell you if your library stores periodicals on microforms and, if so, where they are kept, and how you can view them.

Computers

Computer systems have become information networks. Large volumes of printed and visual materials can be stored on optical storage devices. In some libraries, you can access reference information on computers. Like the on-line catalog, reference materials are available in ***databases***—collections of information that are stored on a computer for easy retrieval. The kinds of information you can find on a computer depend on what database systems the library has or is connected to.

RESOURCES

Recorded Materials

Your library may have audiovisual materials that you can use to help you whenever you need to do research. For example, you might find audiocassettes of famous speeches or of well-known poets reading their works. On videotapes, you might find documentaries and other educational programs that relate to your research topic. Ask the librarian what audiovisual materials are available in the library.

Review

EXERCISE 1 Using the Card Catalog

Use the card catalog to find the following books. For each book, give its title, author or editor, and call number.

1. a biography of Benjamin Franklin
2. a collection of plays by one of the following authors: Amiri Baraka, Tennessee Williams, or Lillian Hellman
3. a guide to colleges and universities
4. a collection of essays about American history
5. a recent book on movie making

EXERCISE 2 Using the *Readers' Guide*

In your school or neighborhood library find answers to the following questions about the *Readers' Guide*. Responses will vary.

1. Where are the volumes of the *Readers' Guide* kept in this library?
2. What is the date of the most recent monthly issue of the *Readers' Guide* found in this library?
3. In the *Readers' Guide*, find a heading for an article on the subject of recycling. Write the title of the article, the name of the author, the name of the magazine, the date the article was published, and the page numbers listed for this article. In addition, list any *"see"* or *"see also"* references you find for this heading.

CRITICAL THINKING
Analysis

As students study the various media available in the library, you might want to have the class analyze the effects of the mass media on society. Start by having students define *media* and then have them brainstorm to discover how the mass media affect people's everyday decisions. For example, you could discuss how the various media educate, inform, persuade, entertain, and solve problems. On the negative side, have students analyze how the media homogenize people's thinking and foster reliance on the media's authority.

ANSWERS
Exercise 1

Answers will vary. Here are some possibilities:

1. *Benjamin Franklin* by Chris Looby; *Benjamin Franklin* by Thomas J. Fleming
2. *Selected Plays and Prose of Amiri Baraka/Le Roi Jones; Tennessee Williams: Four Plays; Lillian Hellman, The Collected Plays*
3. *Comparative Guide to American Colleges* by James Cass and Max Birnbaum; *Barron's Guide to the Best, Most Popular, and Most Exciting Colleges*
4. *Essays in Afro-American History* by Philip S. Foner; *The Culture of Consumption: Critical Essays in American History, 1880–1980* edited by Richard Wightman Fox and T. J. Jackson Lears
5. *Feature Filmmaking at Used-Car Prices* by Rick Schmidt; *Making Movies* by John Russo

RESOURCES

4. Check in the *Readers' Guide* under a subject heading of a career that interests you. Write down the title, author, magazine, date, and page numbers for three articles listed.
5. List the title, author, name of the magazine, date, and page numbers of an entry for a review of a recent television program or movie that interests you.

EXERCISE 3 Learning the Arrangement of Your Library

Draw a diagram of your school library, labeling the areas where the following resources are found. List, below your diagram, any items that you could not find.

1. the card catalog (or on-line catalog)
2. the fiction section
3. the reference section
4. the *Readers' Guide*
5. current magazines
6. the librarian's desk
7. the vertical file
8. microforms
9. computers
10. the checkout and return desk

ANSWERS

Exercise 3

Diagrams should accurately reflect the school library. You will probably want to check the lists of items that students could not find. If your library contains these items, help students locate them.

RESOURCES

REFERENCE WORKS *(pp. 967–974)*

OBJECTIVES

- To identify appropriate reference works to find specific information
- To locate reference books and to provide specific information about each book

35 REFERENCE WORKS

Principal References and Their Uses

In the library you will find a special, separate section known as the *reference section.* Reference works contain facts and information organized in a way that makes it easier to find whatever information you need. If you are familiar with your library's reference books and other resources, you will have a wealth of information at your disposal.

The Reference Section of the Library

Through its many reference works, your library can give you answers to almost any question you can imagine. Become familiar with the location of the reference section in your library. Learn to be a more resourceful researcher, able to find information from a variety of sources.

Your library may contain references in a variety of forms. The most common type of references are found in books, but your library may also provide reference sources in other forms, such as on a computer database or in the form of microfilm or microfiche. Ask your librarian to tell you about the various types of reference works found in your library.

Teacher's ResourceBank™

RESOURCES

REFERENCE WORKS

CHAPTER OVERVIEW

This chapter provides students with an overview of common reference books. Charts provide examples and descriptions of the following categories: books of synonyms, encyclopedias, biographical reference books, literary biographies, special field biographies, atlases, historical atlases, almanacs and yearbooks, indexes and bibliographies, books of quotations, references to literature, literature and author directories, current events resources, special references for specific subjects, and college reference books. A familiarity with the information in this chapter could help students to research information across the curriculum.

RESOURCES

QUICK REMINDER

Ask students to name types of reference works used to find the following information:

1. a list of last year's winners of the Nobel Prizes [an almanac]
2. the important rivers and mountains in Nepal [atlas or encyclopedia]
3. a brief list of facts about Eleanor Roosevelt [encyclopedia or biographical dictionary]

Point out that there are many specific reference works students can use to locate information.

MEETING INDIVIDUAL NEEDS

LEP/ESL

General Strategies. Thesauruses and books of synonyms may be particularly helpful to students who have limited English vocabularies. You may want to work individually or in small groups with students to explain how to use these reference books.

LESS-ADVANCED STUDENTS

A quick survey of your class may disclose that many students have relied primarily on dictionaries and encyclopedias as reference tools. This reliance is probably due to an unfamiliarity with alternatives. If possible, show students the reference books listed in the charts throughout this chapter. Hands-on experience may make a difference.

RESOURCES

Common Reference Books

BOOKS OF SYNONYMS	
EXAMPLES	DESCRIPTION
Roget's International Thesaurus	uses a categorized index system of synonyms; words grouped into categories and subcategories
The New Roget's Thesaurus in Dictionary Form *Webster's New Dictionary of Synonyms*	list entries alphabetically, as in a dictionary

ENCYCLOPEDIAS	
EXAMPLES	DESCRIPTION
Collier's Encyclopedia *The Encyclopedia Americana* *The Encyclopaedia Britannica* *The World Book Encyclopedia*	multivolume works; articles arranged alphabetically by subject; may contain an index or an annual supplement
Lincoln Library of Essential Information *The New Columbia Encyclopedia* *The Random House Encyclopedia*	single-volume works; articles are briefer and less comprehensive in coverage than in multivolume encyclopedias

GENERAL BIOGRAPHICAL REFERENCE BOOKS	
EXAMPLE	DESCRIPTION
Biography Index	tells where to find books and periodicals with biographical information about specific, prominent people

RESOURCES

OTHER BIOGRAPHICAL REFERENCE BOOKS	
EXAMPLES	DESCRIPTION
Current Biography Yearbook	monthly issues, bound at year end; often has photographs
The International Who's Who *Webster's New Biographical Dictionary*	profile of famous people from many nationalities; give details about their birth, careers, and accomplishments
Who's Who in America *Who's Who Among Black Americans*	profiles of famous people, their lives, and their major accomplishments

LITERARY BIOGRAPHIES	
EXAMPLES	DESCRIPTION
American Authors 1600–1900 *American Women Writers* (series) Magill's *Cyclopedia of World Authors* *Dictionary of Literary Biography* *Twentieth Century Authors*	profiles of authors; usually have details about dates of authors' birth or death, titles of major works and dates when they were published, awards or honors won

SPECIAL FIELD BIOGRAPHIES	
EXAMPLES	DESCRIPTION
American Men & Women of Science *Biographical Dictionary of American Sports* (series) *Biographical Dictionary of Film* Vasari's *Lives of the Most Eminent Painters, Sculptors, and Architects*	profiles of individuals who are famous for their distinctions or accomplishments in a specific field or career

RESOURCES

INTEGRATING THE LANGUAGE ARTS

Literature Link. Explain that events and places from writers' lives often influence their works. For example, have students read a story by Isaac Bashevis Singer such as "The Key." Have them read some biographical information about Singer and ask them to identify influences from his life that are found in his writing. [In "The Key" the setting and the main character—the lonely, crotchety Bessie—spring naturally from Singer's street knowledge of the Upper West Side of New York, his home for many years.]

Then ask students to identify the reference books that would be helpful in finding biographical information about authors of other selections the class has read. You may want to have students form groups to reread particular selections and then to research the lives of the writers. Have the groups report any information that sheds light on the author's choice of plot, setting, theme, or characters.

Library Skills and Writing. The reference section of the library can be an invaluable source for students who are searching for topics for their writing. Suggest that students spend some time just browsing.

RESOURCES

COOPERATIVE LEARNING

To provide students with an overview of the reference materials that are available in the school library, divide the class into small groups and assign each group a major category from the charts in the chapter. (You may want to combine some of the categories.) Have students explore the library for everything available in their categories. Then ask each group to prepare and present a report in which they list the available works, describe the works' locations, describe the contents, and suggest possible uses. Then the groups could combine their information to create a booklet or chart for class members to use as they research topics throughout the year.

RESOURCES

ATLASES	
EXAMPLES	DESCRIPTION
Goode's World Atlas *Hammond Medallion World Atlas* *National Geographic Atlas of the World* *The New York Times Atlas of the World*	primarily, provide maps; may also give statistics about industries, raw materials, exports and imports, or climate of various countries or regions of the world

HISTORICAL ATLASES	
EXAMPLES	DESCRIPTION
The American Heritage Pictorial Atlas of United States History *Atlas of World Cultures* Heyden's *Atlas of the Classical World* *Rand McNally Atlas of World History*	give graphic representations of significant historical changes, such as the rise and fall of empires, movement of peoples, and spread of cultures

ALMANACS AND YEARBOOKS	
EXAMPLES	CONTENTS
The World Almanac and Book of Facts	summary of year's notable events; index in front
Information Please Almanac: Atlas & Yearbook	less formal and complete than *World Almanac;* articles may be more comprehensive
The International Year Book and Statesmen's Who's Who	facts about international organizations, nations of the world, and sketches of world leaders
Statistical Abstract of the United States	statistics on many topics, such as population, health and nutrition, education

RESOURCES

INDEXES AND BIOGRAPHIES	
EXAMPLES	DESCRIPTION
Art Index *Biography Index* *General Sciences Index* *The National Geographic Magazine Cumulative Index* *The New York Times Index* *Social Sciences Index*	provide information as a guide to articles found in periodicals or other information sources
A Biographical Guide to the Study of Western American Literature *Three Centuries of English and American Plays: A Checklist* *World Historical Fiction Guide*	lists of books or articles; grouped by subject, author, or time period; annotated bibliographies include descriptions and notes

BOOKS OF QUOTATIONS	
EXAMPLES	DESCRIPTION
Bartlett's *Familiar Quotations* Flesch's *The New Book of Unusual Quotations* *The Oxford Dictionary of Quotations*	famous quotations; usually indexed by subject; some are arranged by author or time period; often tell author, date, and source of quotation

REFERENCES TO LITERATURE	
EXAMPLES	DESCRIPTION
Granger's Index to Poetry	tells where to find specific poems; entries indexed by subject, by title, and by first line
Subject Index to Literature	tells where to find short stories and poems in collections or anthologies; entries indexed by subject

RESOURCES

INTEGRATING THE LANGUAGE ARTS

Library Skills and Writing. Show students a book of quotations such as *The International Thesaurus of Quotations,* which classifies quotations by subject. Explain to students that speakers and writers can enlarge ideas of their own by quoting famous people. For example, a quotation about physical fitness could introduce an essay or a speech about the benefits of exercise. You will probably want to emphasize the importance of correctness in quotations and sources.

MEETING INDIVIDUAL NEEDS

LEP/ESL

General Strategies. A recent edition of *Granger's Index to Poetry* lists over fifty collections of translated poetry from Africa, India, Mexico, and other countries. In addition, *The Home Book of Verse* contains poems both in original languages and in English translations. Using such sources, ESL students might locate and share poems reflecting their heritage.

RESOURCES

COMMON ERROR

Problem. When working on research projects, students may fail to record information about each source they use.

Solution. Have students make a note card for each source they use. The cards should contain the following information: author or authors (complete names as listed on the title page), complete title (including subtitle), publisher's name and city where publisher is located, and date of publication.

INTEGRATING THE LANGUAGE ARTS

Technology Link. Some word processing programs have excellent systems for handling footnotes and bibliographies. Students who use computers for their compositions should familiarize themselves with their programs' capabilities. You may want to suggest practice work before the research paper deadline.

RESOURCES

OTHER LITERATURE REFERENCE GUIDES	
EXAMPLES	DESCRIPTION
Benét's Reader's Encyclopedia	contains information about works of literature, such as plots, main characters; also gives summaries of poems, descriptions of operas
Book Review Digest *Book Review Index* *Brewer's Dictionary of Phrase and Fable* *Essay and General Literature Index* *An Index to One-Act Plays* *Play Index* *Short Story Index*	guides to book reviews, essays, short stories, plays, poems, and other literary works that may be found in periodicals or in collections or anthologies

LITERATURE AND AUTHOR DIRECTORIES	
EXAMPLES	DESCRIPTION
The Cambridge History of American Literature *Harper's Dictionary of Classical Literature and Antiquities* *The Oxford Companion to American Literature* *The Oxford Companion to English Literature*	contain information about authors and their major works; may include brief critiques of best-known works by specific authors or plot outlines of selected works; may offer information on literary movements or genres

CURRENT EVENTS RESOURCES	
EXAMPLES	DESCRIPTION
Social Issues Resources Series (SIRS) (audiotapes, videotapes, reprints of newspaper and magazine articles, photographs, letters, and posters)	up-to-date information on a number of important subjects, such as crime or family issues, scientific discoveries, or documents from the National Archives

RESOURCES

SPECIAL REFERENCES FOR SPECIFIC SUBJECTS	
EXAMPLES	DESCRIPTION
The Encyclopedia of American Facts and Dates *The Encyclopedia of Religion* *The International Encyclopedia of the Social Sciences* *Facts on File* (series of books and yearbooks) *The New Grove Dictionary of Music and Musicians* (series) *McGraw-Hill Encyclopedia of Science & Technology* *The Sports Encyclopedia* *Webster's New Geographical Dictionary*	contain information related to specific topics or of interest to researchers in specific fields; may include short biographies of major figures or evaluations of a person's major contributions to the particular field

COLLEGE REFERENCE BOOKS	
EXAMPLES	DESCRIPTION
Barron's Index of College Majors	arranged by state; highlights majors offered at each school
Barron's Profile of American Colleges *Peterson's Guide to Two-Year Colleges* *Peterson's Guide to Four-Year Colleges*	profile most accredited, four-year colleges; include articles on choosing a college, taking entrance exams, preparing applications; give information about student life, application deadlines, and financial aid
The Directory of Educational Institutions	covers business schools that offer programs in secretarial science, business administration, accounting
Technical, Trade, and Business School Data Handbook	divided into regional volumes; includes community and junior colleges; has index of programs and index of schools

RESOURCES

MEETING INDIVIDUAL NEEDS

ADVANCED STUDENTS

If you are teaching a college preparatory class, call attention to the reference books on colleges and universities. You may want students to locate these books, to look through them, and to report orally on their findings. Usually the books will be available in the school library; if not, copies will probably be found in the guidance counselor's office or in the principal's office.

RESOURCES

CAREER GUIDES	
EXAMPLES	DESCRIPTION
The Encyclopedia of Careers and Vocational Guidance *The Dictionary of Occupational Titles* *Occupational Outlook Handbook* *Career Opportunities Series* *Guide to Federal Jobs*	contain information about various industries and occupations, such as job descriptions, projected figures for employment for specific occupations, and job-related education requirements

Review

EXERCISE 1 Selecting Reference Books

Name a reference book you could use to find each of the following items of information.

1. international records in track events
2. the source of the expression "All the world's a stage"
3. a description of the climate of the Falkland Islands
4. a critique of a prominent author's works
5. entrance requirements for Yale, Harvard, and Princeton

EXERCISE 2 Finding Reference Books

Find and list three books in your library from one of the following categories. For each book, give the title, describe the contents and arrangement of the information in the book, and explain when students should use it.

biographical reference books
literature reference books
guides to colleges and universities
reference books on history or science
books about authors
books of quotations
almanacs
reference books on art or music

RESOURCES

ANSWERS

Exercise 1

Responses may vary. Here are some possibilities:

1. an almanac such as *The World Almanac and Book of Facts*
2. a book of quotations such as Bartlett's *Familiar Quotations*
3. an encyclopedia such as *Collier's Encyclopedia* or an atlas such as *Goode's World Atlas*
4. a literature and author directory such as *American Authors and Books*
5. a college reference book such as *Barron's Profile of American Colleges*

ANSWERS

Exercise 2

Responses will vary but should correctly reflect the collection in the school library.

RESOURCES

THE DICTIONARY *(pp. 975–979)*

OBJECTIVES

- To use a dictionary to find information
- To use a dictionary to trace the etymologies of words

36 THE DICTIONARY

Arrangement and Contents

Dictionaries record how words are used in the English language. A dictionary shows how most English speakers say or spell a word and what the word means to different people under particular circumstances. In a dictionary you will also find information such as word histories and various forms a word can appear in.

Types of Dictionaries

There are many kinds of dictionaries. Each of the different kinds offers a particular range and amount of information about the words it contains. Two of the most common types of dictionaries, the ones most often used as references on word usage by the majority of speakers of the English language, are *unabridged dictionaries* and *abridged* (or *college*) dictionaries. Unabridged dictionaries are large books, usually found in libraries. Abridged dictionaries are more likely to be found in homes or in school classrooms.

RESOURCES

RESOURCES

THE DICTIONARY

CHAPTER OVERVIEW

This chapter describes different types of dictionaries and familiarizes students with the ten parts of a dictionary entry. Review exercises at the end of the chapter give students the opportunity to make use of different dictionary features.

You might refer students to this chapter when they revise or proofread their writing. You might also want to integrate this chapter with a study of vocabulary and spelling.

QUICK REMINDER

To familiarize students with specialized dictionaries, bring to the classroom a variety of dictionaries covering specific areas such as medicine, science, law, crosswords, rhyming words, foreign languages, slang, music, art, or mythology. Write on the chalkboard some words that relate to the dictionaries you have, and ask students to choose the dictionary best suited to provide the information needed about each word.

RESOURCES

MEETING INDIVIDUAL NEEDS

LEP/ESL

General Strategies. Students who are not acquainted with bilingual dictionaries may benefit from working with those that translate both a foreign language to English and English to a foreign language. To help students become proficient in the use of bilingual dictionaries, have ESL students with the same native languages take turns selecting words to be looked up.

Native speakers could take part by choosing English words for the ESL students to look up. If several foreign languages are represented in your classroom, an English word and the equivalent word from each language could be researched and posted in the classroom.

LEARNING STYLES

Auditory Learners. Students who are auditory learners may have trouble relating the diacritical marks in the dictionary to the sounds of the spoken word. You may want to read the pronunciation key from the classroom dictionary into a tape recorder and have students listen to the tape as they look at the pronunciation key. Encourage students to stop the tape frequently and to repeat the sounds out loud.

Contents of a Dictionary Entry

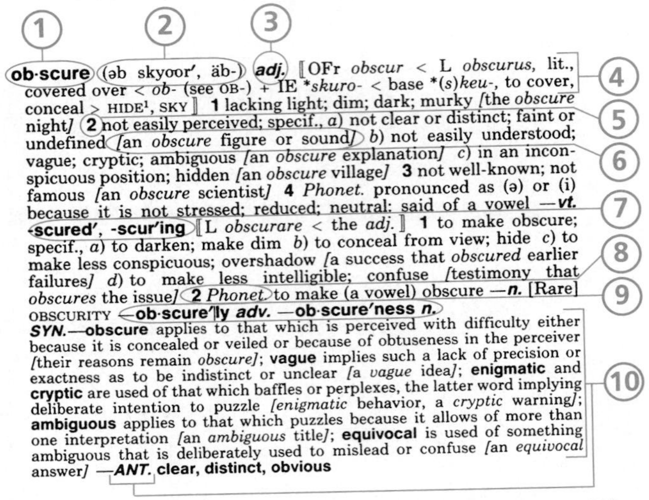

ob·scure (əb skyoor′, äb-) ***adj.*** ⟦OFr *obscur* < L *obscurus,* lit., covered over < *ob-* (see OB-) + IE **skuro-* < base *(*s*)*keu-*, to cover, conceal > HIDE¹, SKY⟧ **1** lacking light; dim; dark; murky *[the obscure night]* **2** not easily perceived; specif., *a*) not clear or distinct; faint or undefined *[an obscure figure or sound]* *b*) not easily understood; vague; cryptic; ambiguous *[an obscure explanation]* *c*) in an inconspicuous position; hidden *[an obscure village]* **3** not well-known; not famous *[an obscure scientist]* **4** *Phonet.* pronounced as (ə) or (i) because it is not stressed; reduced; neutral: said of a vowel —***vt.*** **-scured′, -scur′ing** ⟦L *obscurare* < the *adj.*⟧ **1** to make obscure; specif., *a*) to darken; make dim *b*) to conceal from view; hide *c*) to make less conspicuous; overshadow *[a success that obscured earlier failures]* *d*) to make less intelligible; confuse *[testimony that obscures the issue]* **2** *Phonet.* to make (a vowel) obscure —***n.*** [Rare] OBSCURITY —**ob·scure′ly** ***adv.*** —**ob·scure′ness** ***n.***

SYN.—**obscure** applies to that which is perceived with difficulty either because it is concealed or veiled or because of obtuseness in the perceiver *[their reasons remain obscure]*; **vague** implies such a lack of precision or exactness as to be indistinct or unclear *[a vague idea]*; **enigmatic** and **cryptic** are used of that which baffles or perplexes, the latter word implying deliberate intention to puzzle *[enigmatic behavior, a cryptic warning]*; **ambiguous** applies to that which puzzles because it allows of more than one interpretation *[an ambiguous title]*; **equivocal** is used of something ambiguous that is deliberately used to mislead or confuse *[an equivocal answer]* —***ANT.*** **clear, distinct, obvious**

1. **Entry word.** The boldfaced entry word shows how the word is spelled and how it is divided into syllables. The entry word may also show capitalization and provide alternate spellings.
2. **Pronunciation.** The pronunciation is shown by the use of accent marks and either diacritical marks or phonetic respelling. A pronunciation key explains the sounds represented by these symbols.
3. **Part-of-speech labels.** These labels (usually in abbreviated form) indicate how the entry word should be used in a sentence. Some words may be used as more than one part of speech. In this case, a part-of-speech label is given before each numbered (or lettered) series of definitions.
4. **Etymology.** The etymology is the origin and history of a word. It tells how the word (or its parts) came into English, tracing the word from its earliest known form in the language it came from.
5. **Definitions.** If there is more than one meaning for a word, the definitions are numbered or lettered. Most dictionaries list definitions in order of frequency of use,

but some order definitions according to the date when the word came to have each meaning. Read your dictionary's introduction to be sure you know how a word's definitions are listed.

6. **Examples.** Phrases or sentences may demonstrate how the defined word is to be used.
7. **Other forms.** Your dictionary may show spellings for other forms of the word. Full or partial spellings of plural forms of nouns, different tenses of verbs, or the comparison forms of adjectives and adverbs may be given.
8. **Special usage labels.** These labels may show that a definition is limited to certain forms of speech (such as [archaic] or [slang]). Or, the labels may indicate that a definition is used only in a certain field, such as *Law, Med.* (medicine), or *Chem.* (chemistry). Your dictionary will have a key for abbreviations used.
9. **Related word forms.** These are various forms of the entry word, usually created by adding suffixes or prefixes.
10. **Synonyms and antonyms.** Synonyms and antonyms may appear at the end of some word entries. You may also find synonyms included within the list of definitions, printed in capital letters.

Information Found in Dictionaries

Unabridged Dictionaries

An ***unabridged dictionary*** is the most comprehensive source for finding information about a word. Unabridged dictionaries offer more word entries, including words that are relatively rare. In addition, they usually give more information, such as fuller word histories or longer lists of synonyms or antonyms.

The Oxford English Dictionary is the largest unabridged dictionary. The *OED,* as it is often called, attempts to list and define every word in the English language. Consisting of many large volumes, the *OED* gives the approximate date of a word's first appearance in English and shows, in a quotation, how the word was used at that time. The *OED* also traces the changes in

MEETING INDIVIDUAL NEEDS

LEP/ESL

General Strategies. Students with limited English proficiency may benefit from having access to dictionaries designed for younger students. *The Lincoln Writing Dictionary for Children* (Harcourt Brace Jovanovich) has a simple, easily understood format and includes many attractive pictures and features. Students may find the book's definitions easier to grasp because most definitions are accompanied by interesting sentences that illustrate the uses of the words. Often the sentences link the word to literature.

STUDENTS WITH SPECIAL NEEDS

Because learning disabled students often have trouble working with cluttered information and small print, you might want to enlarge a dictionary entry onto individual charts for students. Use different colors of highlighters to identify each of the different kinds of information found in the entry. Using their charts as guides, students could practice using several different kinds of dictionaries to locate information.

INTEGRATING THE LANGUAGE ARTS

Literature Link. Many writers, such as the poet Emily Dickinson, capitalize words to emphasize them. You could assign one of Dickinson's short poems, such as "Apparently with No Surprise" or "Some Keep the Sabbath Going to Church," and have students look up the capitalized words in the poem to see if the words are capitalized in the dictionary. Then ask students to discuss why they think the poet chose to capitalize those particular words.

COOPERATIVE LEARNING

Have students work in pairs and assign each pair a different word to look up first in an unabridged and then in an abridged dictionary. Have each pair of students make a chart that uses the ten parts of a dictionary entry to compare the information from the two dictionaries. Students should then compare their charts to see if the differences in information are consistent in the dictionaries.

A DIFFERENT APPROACH

Class members that have special interests could create short dictionaries of words that are specific to their interests. They might consider many different areas: creative endeavors such as music, dance, or art; hobbies such as collections, crafts, or needlework; recreational and sports activities; computer programming; or other personal interests. Students could include jargon and slang appropriate to the activity.

RESOURCES

spelling or meaning that a word has had over the centuries. Because its entries emphasize a word's history instead of its current meanings, the *OED* is not used like most dictionaries.

Unabridged dictionaries commonly consist of one large volume. One well-known, single-volume unabridged dictionary is *Webster's Third New International Dictionary*. It is called an *international* dictionary because it contains words (with variations in spelling and meaning) that occur in several English-speaking countries. Another widely used unabridged dictionary is the *Random House Dictionary of the English Language*.

Abridged Dictionaries

An ***abridged*** or ***college dictionary*** is the most commonly used reference book in America. Abridged dictionaries do not contain as many entries or as much information about entry words as unabridged dictionaries. However, abridged dictionaries are revised frequently, so they give the most up-to-date information on meanings and uses of words. Besides word entries, most abridged dictionaries contain other useful information, such as tables of commonly used abbreviations, selected biographical entries, or tables of signs and symbols.

Specialized Dictionaries

A ***specialized dictionary*** contains entries that relate to a specific subject or field. For example, there are specialized dictionaries for terms used in art, music, sports, gardening, mythology, and many other subjects.

Specialized dictionaries are useful when you want information about a word or term that might not be included in a general dictionary or that might have a different meaning when the term is used in a particular context. Other dictionaries of special terms include dictionaries for slang words and idioms.

Another type of specialized dictionary contains ordinary words grouped or arranged to suit a particular purpose. For example, there are rhyming dictionaries (often used by poets) that group words according to the sound of their last syllable.

Foreign language dictionaries are specialized dictionaries that contain foreign words and phrases. They may also contain lists of irregular verbs and rules of grammar or punctuation.

RESOURCES

Review

EXERCISE 1 Finding Information in the Dictionary

Using an unabridged or a college dictionary, find the answers to the following questions. Answers will vary according to the dictionary used. These are from *Webster's New World Dictionary*, Third College Edition.

1. Copy the correct pronunciation of *foliicolous*, including diacritical marks. Be sure that you are able to pronounce the word correctly. 1. fō′lē ik′ ə ləs
2. How many different meanings are given in your dictionary for the word *gauge*? 2. 11
3. What is the height of Mount Everest? 3. 29,028 feet (8,848 meters)
4. How did *guinea* get its meaning?
5. From what language is the word *pajamas* derived? 5. Hindi

4. The gold from which guineas were first made came from Guinea, a coastal country of west Africa.

EXERCISE 2 Finding Information in the Dictionary

Using an abridged or college dictionary, look up the answers to the following questions.

1. What was Galileo's full name? 1. Galileo Galilei
2. What is the scientific notation for pyridoxine? 2. $C_8H_{11}NO_3$
3. What is the meaning of the Latin phrase *mare liberum*? 3. free sea
4. When was the Great Wall of China constructed? 4. third century B.C.
5. From what language is *pest* derived? 5. Latin

EXERCISE 3 Finding the Etymologies of Words

Using an abridged or college dictionary, look up the etymologies of the following words. [Note: Refer to the guide at the front of your dictionary for the meanings of abbreviations and symbols.]

1. office
2. velvet
3. cave
4. library
5. oil
6. quick
7. hospitable
8. boral
9. tea
10. tarnish

RESOURCES

ANSWERS

Exercise 3

Answers will vary. These are from *Webster's New World Dictionary*, Third College Edition. The < symbol means "derived from."

1. OFr < L *officium* < *opificium*, doing of work < *opifex*, a worker < *opus*, a work + *facere*, to do
2. ME < OFr *veluotte* < VL *villutus* < L *villus*, shaggy hair
3. ME & OFr < L *cava*, fem. of *cavus*, hollow < IE base **keu-*, a swelling, arch, cavity
4. ME *librarie* < OFr < *libraire*, copyist < L *librarius*, *n.*, transcriber of books, *adj.*, of books < *liber*, a book, orig. inner bark or rind of a tree (which was written on) < IE base **leubh-*, to peel off > LEAF, Gr *lepein*, to strip off rind
5. ME *oile* < OFr < L *oleum*, oil, olive oil < Gr *elaion*, (olive) oil, akin to *elaia*, OLIVE
6. ME *quik*, lively, alive < OE *cwicu*, living
7. MFr < ML *hospitabilis* < *hospitare*, to receive as a guest < *hospes*, host, guest
8. BOR(ON) + AL(UMINUM)
9. Amoy Chin *t'e* (Mandarin *ch'a*)
10. < Fr *terniss-*, inflectional stem of *ternir*, to make dim < MFr, prob. < OHG *tarnjan*, to conceal < *tarni*, hidden

RESOURCES

VOCABULARY *(pp. 980–993)*

OBJECTIVES

- To use context clues in sentences to determine word meanings
- To use context and a dictionary to determine definitions
- To use roots, prefixes, and suffixes to discover meanings of words
- To choose word pairs to complete analogies

Teacher's ResourceBank™

RESOURCES

VOCABULARY

CHAPTER OVERVIEW

This chapter discusses ways for students to expand their vocabularies by adding to word banks. It also explains methods to determine the meanings of new words, such as using context clues; recognizing roots, prefixes, and suffixes; and understanding denotative and connotative differences. The relationships in analogies are presented in charts that illustrate the ways to answer analogy questions commonly found on standardized tests. Review exercises at the end of the chapter give students the opportunity to test their mastery of these concepts.

Because the exercises require students to use dictionaries, you could teach this chapter in conjunction with **Chapter 36: "The Dictionary."** The material on word origins in **Chapter 12: "English: History and Development"** can add another dimension to students' understanding of word roots.

RESOURCES

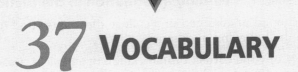

37 VOCABULARY

Learning and Using New Words

An effective vocabulary increases the power and persuasiveness of what you write and say. Studies have shown that a large vocabulary is an important indicator of your success in high school, in college, and in your future career. College entrance examinations place great emphasis on vocabulary, and many job tests have sections devoted to word knowledge.

RESOURCES

Adding to Your Word Bank

One method of increasing your vocabulary is to make a habit of collecting words. You can expand your knowledge with each addition to your word bank. Whenever you find new words in your reading or in school, write these words in your notebook along with their definitions. Then consult your dictionary to be sure you have understood the meaning of each word.

Using Context Clues

Frequently, you can figure out the meaning of unfamiliar words that are used in conversation or in reading passages by analyzing how these words are used. Determining the meaning of new words in this way is known as using ***context clues.*** The ***context*** of a word is made up of the phrases and sentences that surround it. Look at all of the circumstances in which a word is used so that you can find clues to its meaning.

The following chart shows examples of some of the most common types of context clues.

TYPES OF CONTEXT CLUES

TYPE OF CLUE	EXPLANATION
Definitions and Restatements	Look for words that define or restate the meaning of a word. ■ Vonelle studied *ethnology,* that is, the science dealing with the cultures of various people.
Examples	A word may be accompanied by an example that illustrates its meaning. ■ His acts of *benevolence* were well-known, especially his generous donations to children's hospitals.
Synonyms	Look for clues that indicate an unfamiliar word is similar in meaning to a familiar word. ■ Rosita has always been so dependably prompt that she has been given a special award by her employer for her consistent *punctuality.*
Comparisons	Sometimes an unknown word may be compared with a more familiar word. ■ Registration procedures for the *symposium* will be similar to those of other conferences.

(continued)

RESOURCES

QUICK REMINDER

Write this sentence on the chalkboard:

For the talent show we formed a musical group; and since all eight of us play musical instruments, we decided the *octet* we formed should be an instrumental one.

Ask students this question: If you did not already know, how could you tell from the sentence what the meaning of *octet* is in this sentence? [It is identified as a musical group made up of eight people playing musical instruments.]

Tell students that when they use the words next to or related to unknown words in a sentence to determine the meanings of these words, they are using context clues.

MEETING INDIVIDUAL NEEDS

LEP/ESL

General Strategies. Using context clues is a valuable way to expand vocabulary in any new language. You might go over **Types of Context Clues** in greater detail with students and emphasize and possibly restate concepts and examples. Encourage students to refer to the chart as they add to their word banks.

RESOURCES

COMMON ERROR

Problem. Making wrong inferences from context clues can lead students to erroneous definitions.

Solution. Before students add new words to their word banks, suggest that they verify the definitions they inferred from the context clues by looking words up in a dictionary. Encourage students to learn other meanings of each new word to expand their vocabularies even more.

MEETING INDIVIDUAL NEEDS

STUDENTS WITH SPECIAL NEEDS

Students with learning disabilities may have reading difficulties that limit their vocabulary development and that therefore limit their ability to make inferences about new words.

Help familiarize students with any words in passages with which they have difficulty. Relate unfamiliar words to known words and connect vocabulary to students' knowledge base. You may want to ask them to restate passages in their own words so that you can check their understanding.

RESOURCES

TYPES OF CONTEXT CLUES *(continued)*

TYPE OF CLUE	EXPLANATION
Contrast	An unfamiliar word may sometimes be contrasted with a more familiar word. ■ Everyone from the largest *metropolis* to the smallest village participated in the nationwide peace effort.
Cause and Effect	Look for clues that indicate an unfamiliar word is related to the cause, or is the result of, an action, feeling, or idea. ■ Since the instructions were given in the wrong order, it's not surprising that most of the students looked quite *flummoxed.*

Determining Meanings from the General Context

Sometimes context clues are subtle. You may need to read an entire passage to understand the meaning of an unfamiliar word. In such a case, you must infer the meaning of the unfamiliar word by drawing on your own knowledge of the general topic or by making connections between the unfamiliar word and the other information provided in the material.

RESOURCES

Using Word Parts

In general, English words are of two kinds: those that can be divided into smaller parts (*unthinkable, displeased*) and those that cannot (*youth, money*). Words that stand alone and are complete by themselves are ***base words.*** Words that can be divided are made up of two or more word parts. The three types of word parts are

- roots
- prefixes
- suffixes

Learning the meanings of some of the most commonly used word parts can often help you determine the meanings of unfamiliar words.

Roots

A word's ***root*** is the part that carries the core meaning of the word. When other word parts are added to a word root, new words are formed.

The English language contains many words formed from Greek and Latin roots. A knowledge of these roots and meanings can help you determine the meanings of many words.

COMMON WORD ROOTS

ROOT	MEANING	EXAMPLES
GREEK		
–anthrop–	human	anthropology, anthropomorphic
–bio–	life	biography, bionic
–chrom–	color	chromatic, monochrome
–dem–	people	demagogue, democrat
–derm–	skin	dermatology, epidermis
–graph–	write, writing	calligraphy, autograph
–hydr–	water	hydrant, hydroelectric
–log–, –logy–	study, word	logic, theology
–ortho–	straight	orthodox, orthography
–phil–	like, love	philosophy, philanthropy
–zo–	life, animal	zoo, zoology
LATIN		
–audi–	hear	audio, auditorium
–ben–, –bene–	good	benign, beneficial
–cent–	hundred	centennial, century

(continued)

RESOURCES

INTEGRATING THE LANGUAGE ARTS

Literature Link. If your literature book contains the selection, ask students to read and discuss Abraham Lincoln's Gettysburg Address. Then ask them to look up the meanings of *dedicate* [to set apart for special use], *consecrate* [to declare or set apart as sacred], and *hallow* [to make or set apart as holy]. Ask students why Lincoln may have used three words of such similar meaning. [He may have used them because of their different and increasingly strong connotations and to emphasize the solemnity of what the battlefield represented.]

MEETING INDIVIDUAL NEEDS

ADVANCED STUDENTS

Students who are studying Latin, Greek, or one of the Romance languages will find many connections to roots, prefixes, and suffixes in English words. Ask students who are taking Latin to make a list of additional Latin roots and prefixes that can be found in English. Ask students of Latin, French, Spanish, or Italian to make a list of ten foreign-language words that can be found in English in virtually the same forms.

RESOURCES

MEETING INDIVIDUAL NEEDS

LEP/ESL

General Strategies. Point out to students that eighty percent of the English language is of foreign origin. Although many roots are Latin and Greek, others come from nearly every language in Europe, the Middle East, Africa, Asia, and Polynesia.

Encourage students to look for cognates in words and word roots. Remind students that the roots of many English words come from the same roots as words in their native languages. Although the meanings of the words may not be identical, relationships exist. Recognition of related meanings, combined with context clues, can aid in students' assimilation of new words and in vocabulary expansion.

RESOURCES

COMMON WORD ROOTS *(continued)*

ROOT	MEANING	EXAMPLES
–cogn–	know	cognizant, recognize
–duc–, –duct–	draw, lead	induce, deduct
–loc–	place	locality, locate
–magn–	large, grand	magnify, magnitude
–man–	hand	manicure, manual
–mater–, –matr–	mother	maternal, matriarch
–mor–, –mort–	death	moribund, mortal
–omni–	all	omnipresent, omniscient
–pater–, –patr–	father	paternal, patriarchy
–prim–	early	primeval, primitive
–solv–	loosen, accomplish	dissolve, solvent
–spir–	breath	expire, inspire
–uni–	one	unify, universe
–vid–, –vis–	see	video, vision

Prefixes

A ***prefix*** is a word part that is added onto the beginning of a word or in front of a word root to form a new word. The new word's meaning reflects the combined meanings of its parts.

RESOURCES

COMMON PREFIXES

PREFIX	MEANING	EXAMPLES
GREEK		
a–	lacking, without	amorphous, atheistic
anti–	against, opposing	antipathy, antithesis
dia–	through, across	diagnose, diameter
hyper–	excessive	hypersensitive, hypertension
hypo–	under, below	hypodermic, hypothermia

(continued)

COMMON PREFIXES *(continued)*		
PREFIX	MEANING	EXAMPLES
mon–, mono–	one	monandry, monotheism
para–	beside, beyond	paradox, paralegal
peri–	around	perimeter, periscope
psych–, psycho–	mind	psychic, psychopath
sym–	with, together	sympathy, symphony
LATIN AND FRENCH		
ab–	from, away	abdicate, abjure
contra–	against	contradict, contravene
de–	away, from, off	deflect, defrost
dif–, dis–	away, not, opposing	differ, disappoint
e–, ef–, ex–	away, from, out	emigrate, effront, extract
in–, im–	in, into, within	infer, insurgent, impression
inter–	among, between	intercede, interrupt
intra–	within	intramural, intrastate
per–	through	perceive, permit
post–	after, following	postpone, postscript
pre–	before	preclude, prevent
pro–	forward, favoring	produce, pronoun
re–	back, backward, again	recur, replant, revoke
retro–	back, backward	retrograde, retrospect
semi–	partly	semiofficial, semiprivate
ultra–	beyond, excessively	ultramodern, ultraviolet

(continued)

RESOURCES

MEETING INDIVIDUAL NEEDS

LEARNING STYLES

Kinetic and Visual Learners. Students might benefit from transferring each root, prefix, and suffix from the chart to an individual index card. Ask students to color-code each card—perhaps using red for roots, yellow for prefixes, and blue for suffixes. Then tell them to see how many words they can create by using different combinations of the cards. When they are unsure of a word, encourage students to use a dictionary.

LESS-ADVANCED STUDENTS

For review of material up to this point, ask students to refer to the prefixes chart to explain how the italicized prefixes change the meanings of the following words:

1. *mis–* + match [not matched]
2. *retro–* + rocket [rocket that fires backwards from other rockets on a spacecraft]
3. *de–* + frost [take frost off]
4. *semi–* + soft [half soft]
5. *hyper–* + active [excessively active]

RESOURCES

INTEGRATING THE LANGUAGE ARTS

Technology Link. Students can use computers to reinforce their awareness of word parts. Have students working in pairs use one of their own compositions or some other material that is already on a computer disk.

One student should choose a root, prefix, or suffix of any common word. The other student then can use the global-search function to locate the word part in the composition. Students can take turns choosing word parts and operating the computer.

RESOURCES

COMMON PREFIXES *(continued)*

PREFIX	MEANING	EXAMPLES
OLD ENGLISH		
be–	around, about	belay, bemoan
for–	away, off, from	forgo, forswear
mis–	not, badly, wrongly	miscalculate, mismatch
over–	above, excessively	oversee, overdo
un–	not, reverse of	unhappy, unlock

REFERENCE NOTE: For guidelines on spelling when adding prefixes, see page 905.

Suffixes

A ***suffix*** is a word part that is added onto the end of a word or after a word root to form a new word. There are two main kinds of suffixes: those that provide a grammatical signal of some kind but do not greatly change the basic meaning of the word (*–s, –ed, –ing*) and those that create new words. The suffixes listed below are primarily those that create new words.

COMMON SUFFIXES

NOUN SUFFIXES	MEANING	EXAMPLES
GREEK, LATIN, AND FRENCH		
–ance, –ence	act, condition	acceptance, turbulence
–cy	state, condition	accuracy, currency
–er, –or	doer, action	baker, donor
–ism	act, doctrine, manner	barbarism, cubism, patriotism
–tude	quality, state	aptitude, quietude
–ty, –y	quality, state, action	beauty, enmity, inquiry
–ure	act, result, means	culture, signature

(continued)

RESOURCES

COMMON SUFFIXES *(continued)*		
NOUN SUFFIXES	MEANING	EXAMPLES
OLD ENGLISH		
–dom	state, rank, condition	serfdom, wisdom
–hood	state, condition	statehood, womanhood
–ness	quality, state	kindness, shortness
ADJECTIVE SUFFIXES	MEANING	EXAMPLES
GREEK, LATIN, AND FRENCH		
–able, –ible	able, likely	tolerable, possible
–ate	having, characteristic of	desolate, separate
–esque	in the style of, like	humoresque, picturesque
–fic	making, causing	beatific, terrific
–ous	marked by, given to	religious, riotous
OLD ENGLISH		
–en	like, made of	ashen, wooden
–ful	full of, marked by	thankful, zestful
–less	lacking, without	countless, hopeless
–ly	like, characteristic of	kingly, yearly
–some	apt to, showing	lonesome, tiresome
–ward	in the direction of	downward, outward
VERB SUFFIXES	MEANING	EXAMPLES
GREEK, LATIN, AND FRENCH		
–ate	become, cause to be	animate, sublimate
–esce	become, grow, continue	acquiesce, obsolesce
–fy	make, cause to have	fortify, glorify
–ize	make, cause to be	criticize, motorize
OLD ENGLISH		
–en	cause to be, become	blacken, weaken

REFERENCE NOTE: For guidelines on spelling when adding suffixes, see pages 905–907.

RESOURCES

A DIFFERENT APPROACH

Let each student pick a suffix to use in a limerick or a poem. Choose a student to compose a first line that ends with the chosen suffix. Each student in turn then will add a line. At the end of each limerick or poem, a new suffix should be chosen. Example words on the chart may be used, but encourage students to be creative while keeping lines appropriate for the classroom. In the case of limericks, the suffix should occur at the end of the first, second, and fifth lines, but couplets and *aabb* rhyme schemes could also be created.

RESOURCES

MEETING INDIVIDUAL NEEDS

AT-RISK STUDENTS

Point out to working students that nearly every job has its own vocabulary—words used in ways that are specific to the work, materials, or place. Some jobs have words that evolved through combining, shortening, blending, and shifting to express job-related ideas or processes. Explain that these also are vocabulary words, even if they are not found in dictionaries. Ask working students to make lists of words that are specific to their workplaces and have them note the meanings of the words. Lists could be shared with the class.

RESOURCES

Other Ways to Form New Words

New words are constantly added to the English language. The most common way new words are formed is by a process of combination. ***Affixes,*** prefixes or suffixes, are usually added to a base word or to a word root to make a new word. Sometimes, however, two base words can be combined or put together with a hyphen to make a new word. Here are some of the most common ways new words are made.

PROCESS	DESCRIPTION	EXAMPLES
combining	combining two base words to make a compound or combining a word with an affix	doorway, high-rise unfold, wonderful
shortening	omitting part of an original word to shorten it or to change it to another part of speech	telephone → phone burglar → burgle nuclear → nuke
blending	shortening and combining two words	breakfast + lunch = brunch smoke + fog = smog
shifting	changing the meaning or usage of a word	host (n.) → host (v.) farm (n.) → farm (v.)

RESOURCES

Choosing the Appropriate Word

Using the Dictionary

Whether you are writing or speaking, it's very important that the words you choose match your purpose. Most words in the English language have a number of different meanings. Whenever you look in a dictionary for the definition of a word, be sure to scan *all* the definitions given. Keep in mind the context in which you originally encountered the word. Then try the various definitions in the same context until you find the one that fits best.

To help you, dictionaries often provide sample contexts. Compare these sample contexts to the context in which you first heard or read the word to make sure you've found the correct meaning.

Choosing the Right Synonym

Synonyms are words that have the same or nearly the same meaning. However, synonyms often have subtle shades of differences in meaning. Use a dictionary or thesaurus to make sure you understand the exact differences in meanings between synonyms.

Many words have two kinds of meaning: *denotative* and *connotative.* The ***denotative*** meaning of a word is the meaning given by a dictionary. The ***connotative*** meaning of a word is the feeling or tone associated with it. For example, the words *smirk* and *grin* both mean "to smile." However, the word *grin* has a more positive connotation than *smirk,* which suggests an affected, insincere, or annoying smile. When you read, listen, or speak, be aware of both the denotative and connotative meanings of words.

REFERENCE NOTE: For more information about denotative and connotative meanings, see page 492.

RESOURCES

Analogies

Analogies provide a special type of context in which you are asked to analyze the relationship between one pair of words in order to identify or to supply a second pair of words that has the same relationship.

Analogy questions frequently appear on standardized tests because they measure your command of vocabulary as well as your ability to identify the relationships and patterns among

MEETING INDIVIDUAL NEEDS

LESS-ADVANCED STUDENTS

Some students may have a difficult time with the concept of analogies. You may want to help illustrate the idea by using props to show simple relationships such as old/new, large/small, tall/short, shiny/dull, smooth/rough, high/low, heavy/light, and light/dark. Set up two props and then let students choose other items to arrange in an order that completes the analogy.

RESOURCES

words. On standardized tests, analogies are frequently presented in multiple-choice form, as in the following example.

EXAMPLE **1.** INCH : FOOT : : ______________

A quart: measure
B weight: peck
(C) ounce: pound
D meter: yard

HOW TO ANSWER ANALOGY QUESTIONS	
Analyze the first pair of words.	Identify the relationship between the first two items. In the example given, an *inch* is a measurement, part of a *foot.*
Express the analogy in sentence or question form.	The example given above could be read as "An *inch* has the same relationship to a *foot* as . . . (what other pair of items among the choices given?)."
Find the best available choice to complete the analogy.	■ If multiple choices are given, select the pair of words that has the same type of relationship between them as the first pair given in the question. (In this example, only choice *C* shows the same relationship, which is that of a part to a whole unit of measurement.) ■ If you are required to fill in the blank to complete the analogy, you are often given one word of the second pair of items, and you are expected to supply the final word.

RESOURCES

Although there are many different relationships that can be represented in analogies, a smaller number of specific relationships are fairly common. Examples of these common types are shown in the following chart.

TYPES OF ANALOGY RELATIONSHIPS	
TYPE	EXAMPLE
Word to synonym	NEWS : TIDINGS :: adage : proverb
Word to antonym	RECKLESS : CAUTIOUS :: rash : prudent
Cause to effect	VIRUS : FLU :: tension : headache
Part to whole	FLOOR : BUILDING :: step : staircase
Whole to part	WEEK : DAY :: decade : year
Item to category	ALLIGATOR : REPTILE :: mosquito : insect
Time sequence	TUESDAY : THURSDAY :: June : August
Object to function	PEN : WRITING :: chisel : sculpturing
Action to object	CUTTING : KNIFE :: pruning : shears
Action to performer	PAINTING : ARTIST :: paddling : canoeist

Review

EXERCISE 1 **Using Context Clues**

For the italicized word in each of the following sentences, write a short definition based on the clues you find in the context. Check your definitions with the dictionary. Answers may vary.

1. Instead of *ameliorating* the skin condition, the treatment seemed to be worsening it. **1.** improving
2. The amount of *arable* land—that is, land that can be cultivated—is very small. **2.** fit for cultivation
3. Watch for *concomitants* of a severe head cold, such as a feeling of tiredness accompanied by aches and pains in the joints and muscles. **3.** accompanying or attendant conditions, circumstances, or things

RESOURCES

TIMESAVER

When students have finished **Exercise 1,** have them trade papers; then ask for volunteers to supply the answers. The class can discuss the context clues that led to the correct answers. The students then can mark any incorrect answers on the papers.

RESOURCES

4. agitated with anxiety

4. Mr. Ryko always seemed so nervous and confused that he irritated co-workers with his tendency to be *distraught*.
5. Since Dixie is *taciturn* by nature, our attempts to get her to join in the conversation were in vain. 5. untalkative

EXERCISE 2 Using the General Context to Determine Meaning

For each italicized word, write your own definition or synonym. Then check the dictionary's definitions of each word. If you guessed incorrectly, check the context again.

Along with the [1] *proliferation* of fax machines in the United States, there has also been an increase in what is called "junk fax mail." Many businesses commonly use fax machines when they want to [2] *disseminate* their advertisements. However, this practice sometimes [3] *impedes* the everyday business of companies who use the machines to [4] *expedite* business transactions. Important documents can be [5] *dispatched* and returned in a matter of minutes rather than days. Many businesses have found themselves missing [6] *acute* deadlines because their fax machines were tied up with incoming advertisements. For example, it was [7] *imperative* for a Baltimore law firm to fax the news of a concluded deal by exactly 5 P.M. But they missed this critical deadline because their fax machine was receiving a multiple-page fax from a nearby restaurant. State legislatures are attempting the task of [8] *appeasing* two demands that [9] *inevitably* clash. Some states have considered [10] *remedial* measures, such as requiring businesses who fax ads to first consult a list of people who have requested not to receive advertisements on their fax machines.

EXERCISE 3 Learning New Words with Latin and Greek Roots

Underline the root or roots in each of the following words. Using your dictionary, write a brief definition of the word.

1. benevolent
2. graphology
3. incognito
4. biosphere
5. misanthrope
6. magnate
7. solvent
8. dermatitis
9. chromophil
10. omnivorous

RESOURCES

ANSWERS

Exercise 2

Answers may vary.

1. production or creation in profusion
2. spread far and wide
3. obstructs or delays
4. speed up or make easy the progress or action of
5. sent out promptly
6. crucial; critical
7. absolutely necessary; urgent
8. satisfying
9. unavoidably; certainly
10. providing or intending to provide a remedy

ANSWERS

Exercise 3

Answers will vary according to dictionaries used.

1. meaning: inclined to do good; kind
2. meaning: study of handwriting
3. meaning: unknown identity
4. meaning: the zone of planet earth where life naturally occurs; the living organisms of the earth
5. meaning: person who despises other human beings
6. meaning: powerful person
7. meaning: capable of dissolving another substance
8. meaning: skin inflammation
9. meaning: readily stained with dye
10. meaning: eating both animal and vegetable

RESOURCES

EXERCISE 4 Understanding the Meanings of Prefixes

Give the meaning of each of the following words. Then identify the prefix in each word and its meaning. Be prepared to explain the link between the meaning of the prefix and the meaning of the whole word.

EXAMPLE **1.** antithesis
1. *meaning: direct contrast or opposition of ideas prefix: anti– (against, opposing)*

1. hyperventilate
2. promotion
3. misgiving
4. retroactive
5. intervene

EXERCISE 5 Identifying Suffixes and Defining Words

For each word, identify the suffix and guess what the whole word means. Use a dictionary to check your answers.

EXAMPLE **1.** novelty
1. *–ty; the state or condition of being novel (new or unusual)*

1. forbearance
2. conductor
3. collegiate
4. constancy
5. toilsome

EXERCISE 6 Completing Analogies

In the following items, choose the pair of words whose relationship is most similar to that of the first pair given.

1. SPEAK : COMMUNICATE :: **(a)** swim : sink **(b)** sing : enthrall **(c)** gaze : observe **(d)** walk : move
2. RELEVANT : PERTINENT :: **(a)** wasteful : efficient **(b)** thoughtful : pensive **(c)** implicit : explicit **(d)** quiet : slow
3. ENCOURAGE : PROHIBIT :: **(a)** endorse : approve **(b)** gyrate : maneuver **(c)** bless : redeem **(d)** nurture : reject
4. QUIVER : ARROW :: **(a)** movie : scene **(b)** pitcher : water **(c)** governor : pardon **(d)** scholarship : college
5. ERASER : PENCIL :: **(a)** scabbard : sword **(b)** mountain : ore **(c)** crown : queen **(d)** tree : limb

RESOURCES

ANSWERS
Exercise 4

1. meaning: to breathe abnormally fast or deeply
prefix: hyper (excessive)
2. meaning: advancement in rank, grade, or position; furtherance of an enterprise, cause, etc.
prefix: pro (forward, favoring)
3. meaning: a feeling of apprehension
prefix: mis (not, badly, wrongly)
4. meaning: applying to a period prior to enactment
prefix: retro (back, backward)
5. meaning: to come, be, or lie between; to take place between two points of time, events, etc.; to come or be in between as an influencing force
prefix: inter (between)

ANSWERS
Exercise 5

1. –ance; condition of being forbearing (showing restraint)
2. –or; one who conducts (leads)
3. –ate; characteristic of college
4. –cy; state of being constant; steady, faithful, or dependable
5. –some; apt to toil (labor)

RESOURCES

LETTERS AND FORMS *(pp. 994–1005)*

OBJECTIVES

- To write business letters of request, complaint, appreciation, and application
- To write a personal résumé
- To complete forms and applications
- To write informal and social letters, including thank-you notes, invitations, and letters of regret

Teacher's ResourceBank™

RESOURCES

LETTERS AND FORMS

CHAPTER OVERVIEW

This chapter shows students how to write various business letters and how to address business envelopes. Both the block form and modified block form for letters are included. A sample of a personal résumé is included as an aid to students who are applying for jobs.

Eleventh-graders will learn how to correctly complete job and college application forms they are probably confronting currently. Social correspondence is presented through instructions for thank-you letters, invitations, and letters of regret.

QUICK REMINDER

Introduce the chapter by writing a business person's name and address on the chalkboard. Briefly explain or demonstrate the difference between block and modified block form, and let students choose the form they prefer.

Then ask each student to set up a business letter on a piece of notebook paper. Have students use their own paper. Have students use their own addresses and today's date for the heading, the name and address you wrote on the chalkboard for the inside address and salutation, squiggly lines for the

RESOURCES

38 LETTERS AND FORMS

Style and Contents

Letters can be an effective means of communicating for a variety of purposes. You may want to request information, order products, make a complaint, convey your appreciation, or apply for a job. You will also need to write letters of social correspondence. Or, you may need to complete printed forms. Your letters and completed forms will be judged on their content as well as on their appearance.

The Appearance of a Business Letter

Business letters follow certain standards of style and format.

- Use plain paper ($8\frac{1}{2}'' \times 11''$).
- Type your letter if possible (single-spaced, leaving an extra line between paragraphs). Otherwise, write legibly, using black or blue ink.
- Center your letter on the page with equal margins, usually one inch, on all sides.
- Use only one side of the paper. If you need a second page, leave a one-inch margin at the bottom of the first page and carry over at least two lines to the second page.
- Avoid markouts, erasures, or other careless marks. Check for typing errors and misspellings.

Writing Business Letters

The Parts of a Business Letter

A business letter contains six parts:

(1) the heading
(2) the inside address
(3) the salutation
(4) the body
(5) the closing
(6) the signature

Block Style

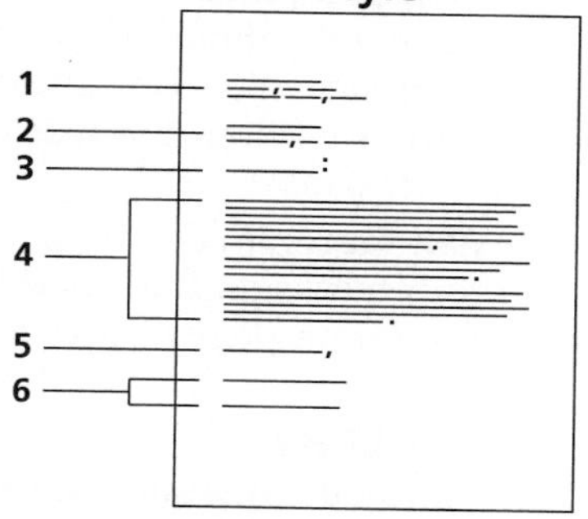

There are two styles used frequently for business letters. With the ***block form,*** every part of the letter begins at the left-hand margin, and paragraphs are not indented. In the ***modified block form,*** the heading, the closing, and the signature are aligned along an imaginary line just to the right of the center of the page. The other parts of the letter begin at the left-hand margin. All paragraphs are indented.

Modified Block Style

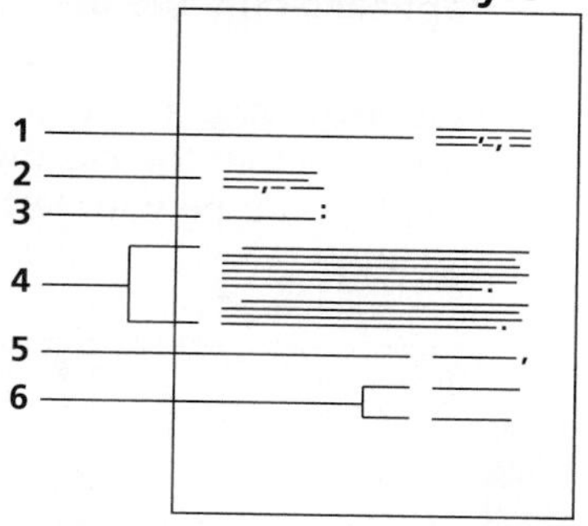

The Heading. The heading usually consists of three lines:

- your street address (or post office box number)
- your city, state, and ZIP code
- the date that you wrote the letter

The Inside Address. The inside address shows the name and address of the person or organization you are writing. If you're writing to a specific person, use a courtesy title (such as *Mr., Ms., Mrs.,* or *Miss*) or a professional title (such as *Dr.* or *Professor*) in front of the person's name. After the person's name, include the person's business or job title (such as *Owner* or *Sales Manager*), followed by the name of the company or organization and the address.

RESOURCES

body, an acceptable closing, and their own signatures. (You may want to mention that real business letters should be written or typed on unlined paper, not on notebook paper.)

Looking over the papers will give you an idea of what percentage of the class is familiar with basic business-letter writing.

MEETING INDIVIDUAL NEEDS

LEP/ESL

General Strategies. Students need to be familiar with phrases and abbreviations that traditionally appear in business correspondence. You might make lists of opening and closing phrases, such as "It has come to my attention . . ."; "In regard to . . ."; "Your attention to this matter will be appreciated"; and "Thank you for your interest and support . . . ." These examples could be used in students' letters. You could also include abbreviations used in titles, addresses, and company names. Then ask volunteers to explain how the phrases and abbreviations should be used in letters.

RESOURCES

MEETING INDIVIDUAL NEEDS

STUDENTS WITH SPECIAL NEEDS

Students who have problems with written expression may have difficulty in visualizing the forms of business letters. You may want to help by collecting some examples of actual business letters in a folder or notebook. You might annotate them with notes about spacing, alignment, and capitalization usage. Students may then use the letters as references for the correct form while creating their own letters.

COOPERATIVE LEARNING

To give students practice in using the **Guidelines for the Contents of a Business Letter,** divide the class into four or five groups. Ask each group to think of a reason for writing a business letter. Then ask each group to write at least three sentences that could appear in the letter. Together, the sentences should exemplify all four of the guidelines. Tell students they will be reading the sentences aloud and explaining how the guidelines are being used.

RESOURCES

The Salutation. The salutation is your greeting. If you are writing to a specific person, begin with *Dear,* followed by a courtesy title or a professional title and the person's last name. End the salutation with a colon.

If you don't have the name of a specific person, you can use a general salutation, such as *Dear Sir or Madam* or *Ladies and Gentlemen.* You can also use a department or a position title, with or without the word *Dear.*

The Body. The body, or main part, of your letter contains your message. If the body of your letter contains more than one paragraph, leave a space between paragraphs.

The Closing. In closing, you should end your letter in a courteous manner. Closings often used in business letters include *Sincerely, Yours truly, Respectfully yours,* and *Regards.* Capitalize only the first word of the closing.

The Signature. Your signature should be written in ink, directly below the closing. Sign your full name. Do not use a title. If you type your letter, type your name neatly below your signature.

RESOURCES

GUIDELINES FOR THE CONTENTS OF A BUSINESS LETTER

Business letters usually follow a few simple guidelines.

- *Use a courteous, positive, and professional tone.* Maintain a respectful, constructive tone—even if you're angry. Rude or insulting letters are counterproductive.
- *Use formal, standard English.* Avoid slang, dialect, contractions, or abbreviations. Business letters are usually formal in tone and use of language.
- *State your purpose clearly and quickly.* Assume that the person reading your letter is busy. Tell why you are writing in the first or second sentence of the letter.
- *Include all necessary information.* Provide all the information your reader needs to understand and respond appropriately to your letter.

Types of Business Letters

Request or Order Letters

Occasionally you may require something that you can obtain by writing a ***request letter.*** For example, you might write to a college to request a catalog of courses offered, or you might write to a state's tourism agency to request a brochure about a travel destination. An ***order letter*** is a special kind of request letter that is written to order merchandise by mail, especially when you do not have a printed order form.

Here is the body of a sample request letter. The writer is asking a college to send information and an admission form.

> Please send me a catalog of courses as well as an application form for admission to Stanville College. I am a junior in high school and beginning to consider my choices among colleges.
>
> Along with the catalog and application, please also send a list of the admissions requirements for both the School of Liberal Arts and the School of Engineering.

When you are writing a request or order letter, follow these guidelines.

1. State your request clearly.
2. If you're asking for information, enclose a self-addressed, stamped envelope.
3. If you're asking an individual for a special request, make sure your request is reasonable and that you have allowed enough time for the person to answer you well in advance of the time you must have the information.
4. If you're ordering something, include all important details, such as the size, color, style, and price. You might include information about the magazine or newspaper in which you saw the item advertised. Compute correctly if there are costs involved, including any necessary sales tax or shipping charges.

MEETING INDIVIDUAL NEEDS

LESS-ADVANCED STUDENTS

Students may need extra help in addressing envelopes. You could prepare sheets with envelope-sized rectangles printed on them to hand out, along with a list of U.S. Postal Service state abbreviations. Explain to students that the post office now has machines that speed up mail sorting and delivery by "reading" addresses that are printed or typed in black ink. Ask students to practice printing their return addresses and a variety of business addresses, using proper form and including state abbreviations and Zip Code numbers.

MEETING INDIVIDUAL NEEDS

ADVANCED STUDENTS

Students could use their knowledge of business-letter forms to write letters to the editor of either the school or the community newspaper. The letters should offer either praise or complaint about some current event or issue. If the letters are published, the newspaper pages could then be posted on a bulletin board.

INTEGRATING THE LANGUAGE ARTS

Literature Link. Have students read Robert E. Lee's letter to his son. The letter is found in many eleventh-grade literature textbooks. After students have read the letter, ask them to compare and contrast it with typical modern correspondance—both business and personal letters. You might want to discuss purpose, tone, use of language, and format.

RESOURCES

Complaint or Adjustment Letters

The purpose of a ***complaint*** or ***adjustment letter*** is to report a problem and to request a satisfactory resolution of the difficulty. This type of letter calls attention to errors that you feel need to be addressed by the organization responsible.

Here is the body of a sample adjustment letter. The writer is reporting a problem and is telling the company how she believes the problem should be resolved.

On October 25, I bought a silk button-down shirt at your store for $42.26. The shirt was charged to my mother's account. Since the size I wanted was not in stock, the shirt was later delivered to my home. When the shirt arrived, on October 28, the package had split open and the shirt was stained.

I am returning the shirt and would like the full amount of $42.26 credited to my mother's account. The account is under the name of Sabrina Tallwood. Her account number is 55-432-6591-2.

When you are writing a complaint or adjustment letter, follow these suggestions.

1. Register your complaint as soon as possible after noticing the problem.
2. Explain exactly what is wrong. Necessary information might include
   - what product or service you ordered or that you expected
   - why you are not satisfied (for example: because of damaged goods, incorrect merchandise, or bad service)
   - how you were affected (for example: because you lost time or money)
   - what you want the individual, company, or organization to do about it
3. Keep the tone of your letter calm and courteous. Despite your possible frustration about the mistake or error, you will be much more effective if you are cool-headed and communicate clearly about the problem.

RESOURCES

Appreciation or Commendation Letters

An ***appreciation*** or ***commendation letter*** is written to compliment or to express appreciation to a person, group, or an organization. For example, you might write to a television network, telling how much you like a particular program and encouraging the network not to cancel it. Or, you might write to a restaurant where you enjoyed a particularly good meal to express your appreciation. Your appreciation or commendation letters are usually most effective when you are very clear about exactly why you are pleased.

Here is the body of a sample appreciation letter. The writer is expressing appreciation for a specific television program.

On Tuesday, June 13, I watched the first show in your series about the problems facing today's teens. I wanted to let you know that I especially appreciate your broadcast of "Teenagers in the 90's."

As a teenager, I considered your portrayal of some of the problems we face very accurate. But instead of focusing only on the dilemmas of modern adolescence, your program gave helpful--and hopeful--suggestions about where teens like me might find information, resources, or support as we deal with these crucial concerns.

Many parents, such as my own, rarely hear about these issues from an unbiased source. I hope your network will continue to broadcast programs such as this one that help to increase people's understanding of one another's concerns. We need more programs like yours that contribute to frank and open talks about serious issues.

Letters of Application

You write a ***letter of application*** to provide a selection committee or a possible employer enough information to determine whether you are a good candidate for a position. This position may be a job, membership in an organization, or a scholarship.

On the next page is a sample of a job application letter.

MEETING INDIVIDUAL NEEDS

LEARNING STYLES

Visual Learners. On an overhead projector, show the class examples of letters and forms. Ask students to identify them one at a time. Examples could include a business letter, a personal thank-you note, a job application form, a change-of-address form, a letter of regret, a scholarship application form, a catalog order form, a résumé, a selective service form, a voter-registration form, a credit-card application form, a medical form, and a bank deposit slip. Ask students for guidelines for filling out some of the different forms. [General guidelines include typing or printing neatly in black ink, filling in all blanks, having the right information in the right blank, and being sure all information is correct.]

INTEGRATING THE LANGUAGE ARTS

Technology Link. Students who have access to word processors may prefer to use them to write letters. Most word processing programs have business-letter templates, which simplify entering the correct information. Remind students to center their letters by adjusting margins, so that letters, regardless of their length, look balanced on the printed pages.

COMMON ERROR

Problem. The differences between the parts of business and personal letters often confuse students.

Solution. Have students compare and contrast the two types of letters by listing what parts each type of letter contains. Remind students that personal letters are always less formal than business letters and therefore include fewer parts.

Personal letter: modified block form, a heading with the date only, a salutation with a name followed by a comma, a closing that uses a friendly term

Business letter: either block or modified block form; a heading with the sender's address and the date; an inside address with a courtesy title, name, business title, and address; a salutation with a courtesy or professional title followed by a colon; a formal closing, such as *Sincerely,* or *Yours truly*

321 Fifth Street
Riverside, MO 64168
May 26, 1992

Personnel Director
Value Insurance Company
41 Bank Street
Riverside, MO 64168

Dear Personnel Director:

Please consider me an applicant for the summer stenographer position advertised in Sunday's Herald.

I am seventeen years old and a junior at Central High School. My course of study has included business classes such as typing, bookkeeping, and business English. I can take dictation at the rate of ninety words a minute and can type either from shorthand notes or recordings at a rate of about fifty words a minute.

Last summer I was employed as a fill-in stenographer for the Superior Trucking Company. I did filing and billing, and performed other tasks as well as regular stenographic work. I feel at home in a business office and enjoy responsibility.

I will gladly supply you with references who can tell you about my qualifications for this position.

I am available for a personal interview at your convenience. My telephone number is 555-7023. I can be reached most evenings after 5:00 p.m.

Very truly yours,

Veronica Harjo

Veronica Harjo

When you are writing a letter of application, remember the following points.

1. Identify the job or position you are applying for. Mention how you heard about it.
2. Depending on the position you are applying for, you might include
   - your age, grade in school, or grade-point average
   - your experience, or your activities, awards, and honors
   - personal qualities or characteristics that make you a good choice for the position
   - the date or times you are available

3. Offer to provide references. Your references should include two or three responsible adults (usually not relatives) who have agreed to recommend you. Be prepared to supply their addresses and telephone numbers.

The Personal Résumé

A ***résumé*** is a summary of your background and experience. For many job positions, you submit a résumé along with your letter of application. There are many different styles of arranging the information on a résumé. Whatever style you select, be sure your résumé looks neat and businesslike.

JOHN L. ZENO

1632 Garden View Drive
Allentown, PA 18103
Telephone: (215) 555-6160

EDUCATION:	Junior, St. Timothy High School Major studies: College preparatory courses in business and foreign languages Grade-point average: 3.0 (B)	
WORK EXPERIENCE:	Summer 1991	Camp counselor Camp Holiday Beaver Lake, PA
	Summer 1990	Volunteer office worker YMCA Allentown, PA
SKILLS:	Shorthand:	120 words a minute
	Typing:	70 words a minute
	Business machines:	dictating, calculating, and duplicating machines
	Languages:	Can speak and translate Spanish fluently
	Extracurricular activities:	Vice President, Future Business Leaders of America; member, Spanish Club
REFERENCES:	Dr. Walter A. Smidt, Principal St. Timothy High School Allentown, PA	(215) 555-1019
	Mary Francis Tate, Teacher St. Timothy High School Allentown, PA	(215) 555-1019
	Mr. Glen Ramos, Director Camp Holiday Beaver Lake, PA	(215) 555-4593

RESOURCES

COMMON ERROR

Problem. Students often fold letters in unacceptable ways.

Solution. Demonstrate the correct way to fold letters. Show that business letters are folded into thirds—bottom third up first, then top third folded down—and inserted into large envelopes. For personal letters on $8\frac{1}{2}'' \times 11''$ paper that are put into small envelopes, the sheets are folded first in half and then in thirds.

MEETING INDIVIDUAL NEEDS

LEP/ESL

General Strategies. You may want to point out that, although in some countries the return address is written on the back of the envelope, the U.S. Postal Service prefers that return addresses always be positioned in the upper left corner of the front of the envelope. Also remind students to put dates in business correspondence in month-day-year order, rather than the day-month-year order to which they may be accustomed.

Addressing an Envelope

A business letter should be sent in a plain business envelope. Write or type your name and address in the upper left-hand corner of the envelope. Write or type the name and address of the person or organization to whom you are writing (the addressee) on the center of the envelope. The addressee's name and address should exactly match the inside address on the letter. Use the two-letter postal service abbreviations for state names, and be sure to include correct ZIP codes.

Completing Printed Forms and Applications

As you enter the work force or begin applying to colleges, you'll be asked to fill out a variety of forms and applications. The person or organization who receives your form or application will be able to help you best if you fill the form out neatly, completely, and legibly.

RESOURCES

GUIDELINES FOR COMPLETING FORMS

1. Always read the entire form to make sure you understand exactly what items of information you are being asked to supply.
2. Type neatly or print legibly, using a pen or pencil as directed.
3. Include all information requested. If a question does not apply to you, write *N.A.* or *not applicable* instead of leaving the space blank.
4. Keep the form neat and clean. Avoid smudges or cross-outs.
5. When you have completed the form, proofread it carefully in order to correct any spelling, grammar, punctuation, or factual errors.
6. Submit the form to the correct person or mail it to the correct address.

Application for Employment

Personal Information

1. Social Security Number *034-38-3151* Date *5/20/94*
2. Name *COHEN* (Last) *SARAH* (First) *LYNN* (Middle)
3. Present Address *10226 Zenith Lane* (street) *Omaha* (city) *Nebraska 68154* (state ZIP)
4. Permanent Address *same as above*
5. Phone No. *(402) 555-3376* 6. Date of Birth *9/19/76*
7. Height *5' 3"* Color of Hair *Brown*
   Color of Eyes *Brown*
8. If related to anyone in our employ, state name and department. *N/A*
   Referred by *Ms. Bernie Schulman*

Employment Desired

9. Position *Sales Clerk* Date you can start *6/8/92* Salary Desired *$5.25/hr*
10. Are you employed now? *yes*
    If so, may we inquire of your present employer? *yes*
11. Ever applied to this company before? *no* Where When

Education

12. Name and Location of Last School *Lincoln High School* *Omaha, NE*
    Years Attended *91–present* Date Graduated *N/A*
    Subjects Studied *Academic*

Former Employers (List below last two employers, beginning with most recent.)

13. Date Month/Year	Name and Address of Employer	Salary	Position	Reason for leaving
6/91–	*Mrs. Richard Lance, 1225 N. Washington, Omaha, NE*	*$4.25/hr*	*Yard Work*	*None*
3/89–7/91	*Minneapolis Tribune, Minneapolis, MN*	*$2.50/hr*	*Paper Carrier*	*Moved to Nebraska*

References: List the names of three persons not related to you, whom you have known at least one year.

	Name	Address	Business	Years Aquainted
14.	*Dr. Yolanda Torres*	*208 De Kalb, Omaha, NE 61851*	*Veterinarian*	*1*
15.	*Mr. Howard Dannenberg*	*535 S. Fifth St., Omaha, NE 61854*	*Nurse (Retired)*	*1*
16.	*Mrs. Gretchen Musich*	*104 York Lane, Omaha, NE 61853*	*Beautician*	*1*

Signature: *Sarah L. Cohen* **Date:** *5/20/94*

RESOURCES

A DIFFERENT APPROACH

Ask students to imagine what they will be doing in ten years or what they hope they will be doing then. Then ask them to project themselves into the future and apply for that job. Have them either create résumés that include what they foresee their education and work entries will include, or have them write letters of application for their dream jobs that also reflect the intervening years. To add a spark of interest, allow students to include a touch of humor. Volunteers could then read their résumés or letters to the class.

RESOURCES

MEETING INDIVIDUAL NEEDS

LEARNING STYLES

Kinetic Learners. You may want to tell students that although strict form needs to be followed in business letters, personal correspondence is open to creativity. Encourage students to design stationery, note cards, or greeting cards by cutting, folding, drawing, and painting with pencils, markers, or paint and brushes. Explain that envelopes also may be created by folding typing paper and using decorations. Remind students not to obscure the places for address and return address if the envelope is to go through the mail.

RESOURCES

ANSWERS

Exercise 1

Each letter should follow either the block or modified block form. Letters should contain all six parts of a business letter and should be courteous in tone. Letters should also include all pertinent information.

Writing Informal or Social Letters

Occasionally, the most appropriate way to communicate with people you know personally is through the mail. When you want to thank someone formally, congratulate someone for an accomplishment, send an invitation, or respond to an invitation extended to you, you should write a social letter.

Social letters are much less formal in style than business letters. For example, social letters don't include an inside address and most use the modified block form.

Thank-you Letters. The purpose of a thank-you letter is to express appreciation for a gift or a favor someone gave you. Try to say more than just "thank you": Give details about how the person's gift or efforts were helpful or appreciated.

Invitations. An invitation should contain specific information about a planned event, such as the occasion, the time and place, and any other special details guests might need to know.

Letters of Regret. If you have been invited to a party or function and will be unable to attend, it's polite to send a letter of regret. A written reply is especially appropriate if you were sent a written invitation with the letters *R.S.V.P.* (in French, these letters are an abbreviation for "please reply").

RESOURCES

Review

EXERCISE 1 **Writing Business Letters**

Write two of the following business letters. Using either block or modified block form, place the parts of the business letter correctly on the page. Use your own return address and today's date, but make up any other information you need.

1. In a letter, order two tickets (at $8.00 each) for the June 17 performance of *The Piano Lesson* at the Summer Stock Playhouse; P.O. Box 15; Slaughter Beach, Delaware 19963.

2. Write a letter of adjustment or complaint. Inform a store's credit department that items (specify them) you ordered but returned to the store have not been credited to your account; ask that your account balance be adjusted.
3. Write a letter to a local radio station expressing your delight over a new talk show the station has added to its programming. State exactly why you find the program appealing.
4. Write to a local, state, or national elected official explaining your position on a public issue; request a response.
5. Write a letter of application answering a help-wanted advertisement in your local newspaper.

EXERCISE 2 Writing a Résumé

Choose a job that interests you. Then write a personal résumé that shows you are qualified for such a position. Include a short letter explaining how you heard about the job and requesting a personal interview.

EXERCISE 3 Completing Forms

Choose one of the following activities.

1. Obtain an application form for a driver's license or a learner's permit and complete it correctly.
2. Complete an auto insurance application form, using information about your car or a car owned by a friend or relative.
3. Complete an application form for employment with a company.
4. Locate a mail-order catalog and select several items to order. Complete the mail-order form in the catalog, indicating the items you have chosen.

EXERCISE 4 Writing Social Letters

Write a social letter for one of the following situations.

1. Write a thank-you letter expressing appreciation for a gift or favor you have received.
2. Write an invitation letter for an upcoming event you are planning.
3. Write a letter of regret explaining that you will not be able to attend an event to which you have been invited.

ANSWERS
Exercise 2

Résumés should follow a standard form and use the style on p. 1001 as a guideline. Work experience should begin with one's current job and work backward in time. The cover letter should explain how the applicant heard of the job and should include a request for an interview. Completed assignments should be neat and error free.

ANSWERS
Exercise 3

Forms will vary but should be completed correctly and neatly. Make sure students follow directions as requested on the forms, such as using ink or printing responses.

ANSWERS
Exercise 4

Letters will vary but should follow the form for personal correspondence. They should include all necessary information; have an informal, friendly tone; and be neatly written.

RESOURCES

Teacher's ResourceBank™

RESOURCES

FOR THE WHOLE CHAPTER

- Chapter Review Form A 475–476
- Chapter Review Form B 477–478

CHAPTER OVERVIEW

Because the information in this chapter can prove immediately useful to students and can help them grasp the material covered in other chapters, you may want to cover this section during the first week or two of the school year. If your students intend to take the Preliminary Scholastic Aptitude Test in October, you may want to teach the second segment closer to the test date.

RESOURCES

39 STUDYING AND TEST TAKING

Using Skills and Strategies

As you continue your high school studies and prepare for college or a career, you need to develop skills and strategies that will make your studying and test taking more effective. The ability to study efficiently is a skill that you will find valuable no matter what profession you pursue. When you have learned productive study methods, you will have mastered techniques for analyzing, evaluating, and utilizing information that are necessary skills in almost every career.

RESOURCES

Following a Study Plan

All studying has two basic purposes. First, you study to acquire information, and then to apply it. Developing good study habits is enormously important. To study effectively

- keep track of your assignments and due dates
- select a time and place to study free from distractions
- break large assignments into smaller steps and then schedule time to complete each step
- allow a reasonable amount of study time to complete each of your assignments

SEGMENT 1 *(pp. 1006–1024)*

STRENGTHENING STUDY SKILLS

OBJECTIVES

- To practice using study skills
- To paraphrase a poem
- To write a précis

Strengthening Study Skills

Reading and Understanding

To read productively, you need to determine your purpose for reading. Then adjust your reading rate to suit the material and your purpose for reading.

READING RATES ACCORDING TO PURPOSE		
READING RATE	PURPOSE	EXAMPLE
Scanning	Reading for specific details or points of reference	Searching a short story for the name of the main character's pen pal
Skimming	Reading for main points	Reviewing characteristics of an economic theory to prepare for an essay test
Reading for mastery	Reading to understand and remember	Reading a new chapter in your history book before outlining it

Writing to Learn

Writing contributes many benefits to the learning process. Writing helps you to focus your thoughts, respond to ideas, record your observations, and plan your work. Writing can also help you recall and understand information and provide you with ideas that you might use for future assignments.

TYPE OF WRITING	PURPOSE	EXAMPLE
Freewriting	To help you focus your thoughts	Writing to connect ideas between a class lecture and assigned readings

(continued)

RESOURCES

Teacher's ResourceBank™

RESOURCES

STRENGTHENING STUDY SKILLS

QUICK REMINDER

Ask students to tell you three reading rates, three purposes for reading, and what *SQ3R* stands for [three reading rates: scanning, skimming, and reading for mastery; purposes for reading: for details, for main points, and for understanding and remembering information; SQ3R: survey, question, read, recite, review]

MEETING INDIVIDUAL NEEDS

ADVANCED STUDENTS

If students have heard about speed reading they might be curious about the process. Tell them that in speed-reading programs that focus on speed alone, comprehension may be impaired. If they take speed-reading courses, students should look for ones that develop both speed and comprehension. Remind them that good readers read certain material slowly instead of trying to speed read it. A reader who speeds through a great work of literature, for instance, may miss much of the subtlety that makes the literature great.

RESOURCES

TYPE OF WRITING	PURPOSE	EXAMPLE
Autobiographical Sketches	To help you examine and express the meaning of key events in your life	Writing about your impressions on the day your brother left home to go to college
Diaries	To help you recall your impressions and express your feelings	Writing about a problem you faced and overcame in one of your classes
Journals and Learning Logs	To help you record your observations, descriptions, solutions, and questions	Writing to keep a record of each step in the progress of a team project
	To help you present a problem, analyze it, and propose a solution	Writing about the issues you plan to raise during an upcoming group discussion

Using a Word Processor as a Writing Tool

The word processor makes it easier to produce written work because it eliminates many time-consuming tasks. Although it can't do the job for you, word processing can help you produce your best writing; it offers benefits at each stage of the writing process.

Prewriting. You can freewrite and brainstorm ideas easily on the computer. Then you can fill in notes or outlines without having to type them in again.

Writing First Drafts. After a little practice, you can compose your thoughts quickly on the word processor.

Evaluating. Because changes are easy to make, the word processor is great for analyzing work in progress. You can save a copy of your document and then insert and delete text freely.

RESOURCES

MEETING INDIVIDUAL NEEDS

LEP/ESL

General Strategies. The information concerning word processors might need a more thorough explanation. Many students may not have access to this equipment at home, while others will not be familiar with personal computers. Therefore, if possible, plan a field trip either to the school's computer lab or to a nearby facility, such as a community college. Students should be guided individually through the simple procedure of opening a new file and naming it, creating a short document and saving it, and printing out a hard copy of the document.

RESOURCES

If you decide you don't like the changes, you still have your original document saved.

Revising. A word processor is a great time-saver for revisions. You can insert, move, or delete text easily. Then you can print out a clean copy without having to repeat steps.

Proofreading. You can use a spell-checking function on most word processors to find errors. You may also have a search-and-replace function that you can use to correct a specific type of error wherever it occurs throughout your document.

Writing the Final Version. After you have made all your revisions and have proofread and made all corrections, you can print out one or more final copies.

Using the SQ3R Method

One frequently used method of study, called *SQ3R,* was developed by an educational psychologist named Francis Robinson. The SQ3R study method is made up of five simple steps.

S *Survey* the entire study assignment to understand the general scope of the material. Read all titles, headings, subheadings, and terms in boldface and italic type. Also, look over any charts, outlines, and summaries.

Q *Question* yourself. What should you know after completing your reading? Make a list of questions to be answered. Also, look at any questions provided at the end of a reading selection.

R *Read* the material carefully. Think of answers to your questions as you read.

R *Recite* in your own words answers to each question.

R *Review* the material by rereading quickly, looking over the questions, and recalling the answers.

REFERENCE NOTE: For study techniques to help with listening skills, see page 938.

RESOURCES

INTEGRATING THE LANGUAGE ARTS

Technology Link. Some authorities on writing suggest that students use a hard copy of a document for revision. A hard copy allows students to see a great deal more of the composition at one time. Monitors for computers and word processors permit writers to see only a few lines at a time. It is difficult to notice when the same word has been used frequently within a few lines, when problems of parallelism exist, when paragraphs are longer than they should be, and when sentences are too long.

CRITICAL THINKING

Evaluation

There are variations of the SQ3R study method. The PQ6R method, developed by Francis Robinson and adapted by Norma Kahn in *More Learning in Less Time* includes the following steps: Preview, Question, Read, Recite, Write, Review, Reflect, and Review. If a copy of Kahn's book is available, have students compare the two methods to decide which one they think would be most helpful to them. Students should define the criteria they use to make their judgments.

RESOURCES

Interpreting and Analyzing Information

Finding the Main Idea

To understand a passage of reading, you must determine what it means and how the information it contains fits together. An important first step is to determine the main idea of the selection.

Stated Main Idea. The main idea is often stated directly in a thesis statement or can be found in one or two specific sentences in a passage.

Implied Main Idea. The main idea is not always easy to find. Sometimes the main idea of a reading passage may be implied, or suggested, rather than stated directly. To find an implied main idea in a passage, you must analyze all of the supporting details and decide what overall meaning these details combine to express.

HOW TO FIND THE MAIN IDEA

- Identify the overall topic. (What is the passage about?)
- Identify what the passage reveals about the topic. (What's the message of the passage as a whole?)
- Sum up the meaning of the passage in one clear, effective sentence.
- Review the passage. (If you have correctly identified the main idea, all of the other details included in the passage will support it.)

REFERENCE NOTE: For additional information on finding the main idea, whether stated or implied, see pages 64–66.

Recognizing Relationships Among Details

After you have identified the main idea of a reading passage, you will need to identify the details that support the main idea and evaluate how they are related to the main idea and to each other.

RESOURCES

FINDING RELATIONSHIPS AMONG DETAILS	
Identify specific details.	What details answer specific questions such as *Who? What? When? Where? Why?* and *How?* (*5W-How?* questions)?
Distinguish between fact and opinion.	What information can be proved true or false (facts)? What statements express a personal belief or attitude (opinions)?
Identify similarities and differences.	Are any details shown to be similar to or different from one another?
Understand cause and effect.	Do prior events have an impact on, or affect, later events?
Identify an order of organization.	In what order are the details arranged—chronological order, spatial order, order of importance, or any other ordered pattern?

Reading Passage

When the great Italian conductor Arturo Toscanini heard Marian Anderson sing, he proclaimed that her voice was of a quality that is heard only once in a hundred years. Although she came to be regarded as perhaps the greatest contralto of the twentieth century, Marian Anderson, an African American, struggled against discrimination for many years.

Born to poor parents in Philadelphia in 1902, Marian Anderson first gained notice in a children's church choir. Soon she was performing in a number of churches. Money was scarce, but numerous supporters contributed toward her operatic training. Eventually, she began

Sample Analysis

OPINION: What did Arturo Toscanini think of Marian Anderson's singing?
ANSWER: *He said that a voice like hers was heard only once in a hundred years.*

FACT: Where did Ms. Anderson first receive public recognition?
ANSWER: *She gained recognition in a children's church choir.*

RESOURCES

MEETING INDIVIDUAL NEEDS

LESS-ADVANCED STUDENTS

Setting aside time each day for independent reading will show students that you think reading is important and will also give students time to practice their reading skills. Allow students to bring reading material to class each day and allot ten minutes of class time for independent reading. On some days you may even want to allow students to read independently during the whole class period. You will probably want to have plenty of high-interest selections available for those who forget to bring anything to read.

RESOURCES

COMMON ERROR

Problem. When students read aloud in class, you may notice that they sometimes read words that aren't there or transpose the words in some way.

Solution. When students change or transpose words, especially if the meaning doesn't change, they may actually be showing signs of growth as readers. Instead of reading word for word, they are reading for meaning. If the missed word doesn't detract from the overall meaning, refrain from correcting students. If it's necessary to clarify meaning after a student has finished reading, do so without calling direct attention to the fact that the student misread a word.

RESOURCES

making concert appearances. However, she continually faced discrimination. Many music schools and concert halls were closed to her. Also, while making concert appearances in the South, Ms. Anderson was forced to endure the indignity of inferior, segregated railroad and hotel accommodations.

Frustrated, Ms. Anderson left the United States in the mid-1930s for study and concert tours in Europe. There she finally received critical and popular success. Ms. Anderson returned to the United States as a triumphant concert star.

Yet even at the height of her success, Marian Anderson continued to face discrimination at home. In one incident in Washington, D.C., the Daughters of the American Revolution (DAR) refused Ms. Anderson permission to perform at Constitution Hall. Many Americans protested this action, and many women, including First Lady Eleanor Roosevelt, resigned their memberships in the DAR.

In a public show of support for Marian Anderson, Secretary of the Interior Harold L. Ickes invited her to sing from the steps of the Lincoln Memorial on Easter Sunday, 1939. Over 75,000 people attended Anderson's brilliant, historic performance.

In 1955, Marian Anderson became the first black soloist ever to sing at the Metropolitan Opera House in New York City. In 1958, she was named to serve as a delegate to the United Nations, and she received the Presidential Medal of Freedom in 1963.

In the course of her operatic career, Marian Anderson's talent and courage helped to remove discriminatory barriers for other African American artists.

CONTRAST: How did Anderson's success in Europe contrast with her earlier career in the United States?
ANSWER: *In Europe, Anderson became very successful.*

CAUSE AND EFFECT: What was the effect of the DAR's refusal to allow Anderson to sing at Constitution Hall?
ANSWER: *Many people protested the DAR's actions, including members who resigned from the organization. Anderson then performed at the Lincoln Memorial.*

DETAIL: How many people attended Anderson's Easter Concert at the Lincoln Memorial?
ANSWER: *Over 75,000 people attended her concert at the Lincoln Memorial.*

ORDER: What honor did Marian Anderson receive eight years after she sang at the Metropolitan Opera?
ANSWER: *She received the Presidential Medal of Freedom.*

RESOURCES

Applying Reasoning Skills

You can draw conclusions by evaluating, interpreting, and analyzing the facts and evidence presented in a reading passage. A ***valid conclusion*** is one that is firmly grounded in facts, evidence, or logic. An ***invalid conclusion,*** however, is one that is not consistent with the evidence presented. For example, it is invalid to conclude that Marian Anderson achieved success effortlessly. This conclusion conflicts with details in the reading passage, such as Ms. Anderson's early poverty and her having to leave the United States to prove her talent and to escape the discriminatory treatment she had faced here.

HOW TO DRAW CONCLUSIONS OR MAKE INFERENCES	
Gather all the evidence.	What facts or details have you learned about the subject?
Evaluate the evidence.	Do you know enough to make a few observations based on facts or reasonable assumptions?
Make appropriate connections.	What can you reasonably conclude or infer from the evidence you have gathered and evaluated?

Analyzing Graphics and Illustrations

Informational materials frequently include graphics, such as diagrams, maps, and charts. Graphics visually organize bodies of information that might be difficult to understand in written form. For example, the graph on page 1014 shows the relationship between the amounts of several types of waste generated by urban areas of the United States and the projections for the amounts generated in the future.

Suppose you are a city manager trying to find ways to reduce the amount of solid waste being dumped in the city landfill. By looking at the graph, you would see that a major paper recycling campaign could be the single most important factor in slowing the rate of increase in future landfill costs.

A DIFFERENT APPROACH

You may want to relate the process of drawing conclusions to the experiments students perform in their science classes. Ask a volunteer to describe an experiment and the conclusion that was reached and to explain the thought processes that were involved in reaching the conclusion.

RESOURCES

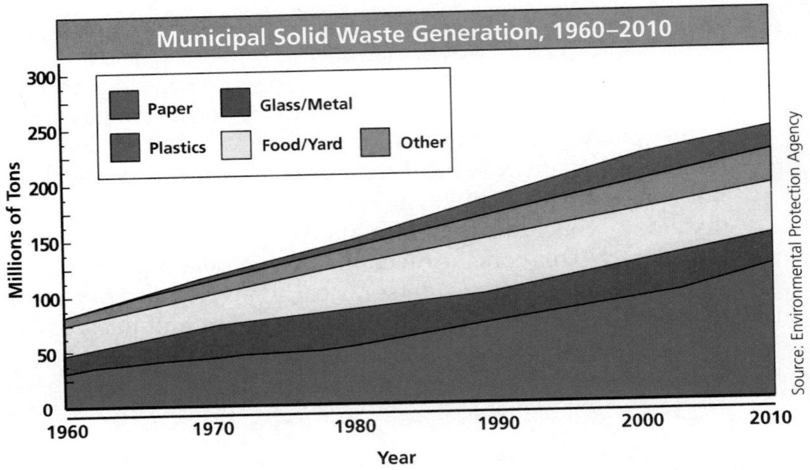

Graphs such as the one above help you make decisions because you can see relationships among items of data.

Applying Study Methods

Various study methods can be used to organize and process information. Among the most common study methods are

- taking notes
- classifying
- organizing information visually
- outlining
- paraphrasing
- summarizing
- writing a précis
- memorizing

Taking Notes

Careful note taking can help you remember what you read or hear in a lecture. Note taking also helps you organize information for studying, taking tests, and writing research papers.

Look at the study notes on pages 1015–1016. These notes cover the reading passage on pages 1011–1012. The main points in the passage are identified and arranged in groups. Then each of these groups is given a heading that indicates the key idea.

RESOURCES

RESOURCES

HOW TO TAKE STUDY NOTES	
Recognize and record main points.	Set off main points as headings in your notes. ■ In a lecture, key words such as *major* or *most important* may indicate main points. ■ In a textbook, chapter headings and subheadings are usually reliable indicators of main ideas.
Summarize.	Don't record every detail. Summarize or abbreviate, using single words or phrases to record key ideas and supporting details.
Note important examples.	A few vivid examples can help you recall the main ideas.

Marion Anderson

Biography

- *African American; born 1902 in Philadelphia, PA*
- *sang in church choir; supporters paid for opera training*

Discriminatory Treatment

- *many music schools and some concert halls closed to her*
- *segregated railroad coaches and hotels*
- *DAR refused to let her perform at Constitution Hall*

Successes

- *DAR ban on Constitution Hall concert protested; many resigned DAR (e.g. Eleanor Roosevelt)*

MEETING INDIVIDUAL NEEDS

LEP/ESL

General Strategies. Note taking for lectures can prove difficult and frustrating because the student cannot ask the speaker to slow down. In addition, students may have difficulty following what they are hearing because the vocabulary is unfamiliar. They may try to record the lecture verbatim, which can result in further frustration. To provide practice and reinforcement for this skill, have students work with peer tutors in interview or dictation situations.

RESOURCES

MEETING INDIVIDUAL NEEDS

LESS-ADVANCED STUDENTS

Some students may have difficulty understanding the explanation of *classification.* To make the concept more accessible, collect a variety of items from around the classroom and place them on a table. Items can include books, pencils, chalk, tablets, clothing, small art pieces, games, calendars, diskettes, charts, and so on. Organize students into mixed-ability groups of five or six. Ask groups to list all the ways they can classify the items on the table. For example, they can classify by size, purpose, or color.

Successes (cont.)

- *in 1930s, studied in Europe; concerts praised*
- *Cabinet member invited her to sing at Lincoln Memorial on Easter Sunday, 1939; over 75,000 attended*
- *1st black soloist at Metropolitan Opera*
- *conductor Arturo Toscanini said her voice quality heard only every 100 yrs.*
- *some called her greatest contralto of 20th century*
- *1958, delegate to U.N.; 1963, Pres. Medal of Freedom*
- *career inspired other black artists*

Classifying

Classification is a method of organizing by arranging items into categories. For example, you use classification when you make an outline, determining the ideas that fit together under a specific heading. When you group items, you identify relationships among them.

EXAMPLE What do each of the following have in common?
ostriches, rheas, emus, penguins, kiwis

ANSWER They are all flightless birds.

You also classify when you recognize patterns. For example, look at the following sequence of numbers.

What's the next number in the series?

105 111 118 126 135 ___?___

ANSWER To the first number (105), *6* is added to produce the second number (111). To the second number, *7* is added to produce the third number (118); *8* is added to the third number, and *9* is added to the fourth (126). So: *10* should be added to the fifth number (135) to produce the answer, which should be *145.*

Organizing Information Visually

You may find it helpful to reorganize information from a reading passage into a chart, map, or diagram. For example, the passage that follows presents facts about early automobile history.

> Inventors from several countries contributed to the development of the automobile. Nicolas Cugnot, a French engineer, built a steam-powered road vehicle in 1769 that crashed on its trial run. In 1801, Richard Trevithick, an Englishman, tested another steam-powered horseless carriage. Unlike Cugnot's invention, however, Trevithick's ran. Shortly after the trial run of Trevithick's steam engine, the American inventor Oliver Evans built a steam-powered machine used to clear sediment from waterways: the amphibious digger. Completed in 1805, it was the first steam-powered vehicle that could travel on land *and* water. Once the internal-combustion engine was developed in France in the middle of the nineteenth century, work on the automobile accelerated. In 1886, Gottlieb Daimler, a German inventor, designed an engine that ran on gasoline. Then, in the 1890s, a French engineer, Émile Levassor, produced a chassis that fit Daimler's engine. The car, the first gasoline-powered vehicle with the engine in front, is considered the forerunner of today's automobile.

By making a table similar to the one below, you would find the information in the paragraph easier to recall.

INVENTOR'S NAME	COUNTRY OF ORIGIN	DATE OF INVENTION	CONTRIBUTION
Nicolas Cugnot	France	1769	steam-powered road vehicle
Richard Trevithick	England	1801	first successful steam auto
Oliver Evans	U.S.A.	1805	amphibious digger
Gottlieb Daimler	Germany	1886	engine that ran on gasoline
Émile Levassor	France	1890s	chassis for Daimler's engine

RESOURCES

A DIFFERENT APPROACH

The word *outline* may cause some students to think of a very formal and rigid style. They might be unsure of exactly how to make a formal outline and might believe that without knowing the conventions of formal outlining, they can't use outlining to study or take notes.

Reassure students that although there is a formal style for outlining, students do not necessarily need to use it when taking notes. Explain that the important thing is that they understand the notes they take.

Outlining

An outline can help you organize ideas and information. When you write an outline, you identify and record major concepts and supporting details. You also group these ideas in an organized pattern that shows their order and their relationship.

If you are taking lecture notes, however, you might want to use an informal outline form. This method helps you organize information quickly. (See the sample notes on pages 1015–1016.)

FORMAL OUTLINE FORM

I. Main Point
  A. Supporting Point
    1. Detail
      a. Information or detail

INFORMAL OUTLINE FORM

Main Idea
  Supporting detail
  Supporting detail
  Supporting detail

Paraphrasing

A ***paraphrase*** is a restatement of someone's ideas in your own words. Paraphrasing helps you understand what you read, especially if the original is written in poetic or elaborate language. A paraphrase is often about the same length as the original, so this technique is rarely used for long passages.

Paraphrasing a Literary Selection. At times you may write a paraphrase of a poem or a literary passage in order to express in simpler terms the meaning of a complex work.

For example, in language arts classes, you may be asked to paraphrase a poem like the one that follows.

Ozymandias
by Percy Bysshe Shelley

I met a traveler from an antique land
Who said: Two vast and trunkless legs of stone
Stand in the desert . . . Near them, on the sand,
Half sunk, a shattered visage lies, whose frown,
And wrinkled lip, and sneer of cold command,
Tell that its sculptor well those passions read
Which yet survive, stamped on these lifeless things,

RESOURCES

The hand that mocked them, and the heart that fed;
And on the pedestal these words appear:
"My name is Ozymandias, king of kings;
Look on my works, ye Mighty, and despair!"
Nothing beside remains. Round the decay
Of that colossal wreck, boundless and bare
The lone and level sands stretch far away.

As an example, here is a possible paraphrase of this poem.

The speaker in this poem repeats a traveler's tale about something the traveler saw in a land that had been inhabited by people since ancient times. While in the desert, the traveler came across the legs of what had once been a complete stone statue of a king. Next to the legs, partly covered by sand, lay the broken pieces of the statue's face. The traveler could tell from the harsh and proud expression carved on the face that the artist had skillfully captured the character of the king. However, the king's passions, as well as the heart that held them and the hand that carried them out, were long outlived by the stone that recorded them. The statue's pedestal bore an inscription declaring that the king, Ozymandias, considered himself the greatest of rulers and commanding that other monarchs should observe the kingdom he built and thereupon lose hope of ever equaling its splendor. Of Ozymandias's self-proclaimed accomplishments, there is nothing left. The giant, ruined statue is surrounded by a huge, lonely desert.

Paraphrasing Prose. At times you may need to paraphrase a portion of an essay, an article, or another type of prose work. For instance, you may need to paraphrase information you find in an essay in order to fit it smoothly into a report.

For example, the following is an excerpt from *Novum Organum,* an essay by Francis Bacon, published in 1620.

The human understanding is no dry light, but receives an infusion from the will and affections; whence proceed sciences which may be called "sciences as one would." For what a man had rather were true he more readily believes.

INTEGRATING THE LANGUAGE ARTS

Literature Link. To give students practice in paraphrasing, have them each write a line-by-line paraphrase of a poem such as "The Steeple-Jack" by Marianne Moore. Lead a discussion of how students' paraphrases differ from the poem. Students might notice that their paraphrases don't evoke the same mood that the poem does. Help students see how the poet's choice of words affects the mood of the poem.

INTEGRATING THE LANGUAGE ARTS

Study Skills and Mechanics. Remind students that while paraphrased material doesn't contain direct quotations from the original source, credit still has to be given to the original writer for his or her ideas. Failure to give credit for ideas is considered to be plagiarism. If verbatim phrases or words with special significance from the original source are used directly, they must be enclosed in quotation marks. Making sure to correctly enclose directly quoted information in quotation marks is important during note taking. Consistently following this procedure helps the writer trust the accuracy of notes and of subsequent paraphrasing when working in the research process.

RESOURCES

> Therefore he rejects difficult things from impatience of research; sober things, because they narrow hope; the deeper things of nature, from superstition; the light of experience, from arrogance and pride, lest his mind should seem to be occupied with things mean and transitory; things not commonly believed, out of deference to the opinion of the vulgar. Numberless in short are the ways, and sometimes imperceptible, in which the affections color and infect the understanding.

Here's how you might paraphrase this passage and incorporate your paraphrase into a report.

> Although modern scientists have available the most advanced technology, the greatest single obstacle to new discoveries is the human tendency to ignore information if it challenges people's preconceived notions. This human limit is as much an obstruction to the advance of science as it was in 1620, when Francis Bacon commented in his *Novum Organum* that no one's knowledge is pure; it is strongly affected by human desires and emotions. Bacon commented that science could be described as the study of what people wanted to believe. Bacon complained that humans decline things that are hard because they grow impatient or frustrated; things that are serious because they prefer to feel happily hopeful; things that are mysterious because people are superstitious; things that have been gained through experience because of their smug, vain belief that past events are of little importance; and things that are new and different because of fear that others will disagree. Bacon concluded by saying that there are many ways, some of them not easily noticeable, that people's ideas can be influenced by their own beliefs and wishes.

RESOURCES

HOW TO PARAPHRASE

1. **Read the entire selection to get the overall meaning before you begin writing your paraphrase.**
2. **Identify the main idea of the selection. Keep it in mind while you write your paraphrase.**

(continued)

HOW TO PARAPHRASE *(continued)*

3. Identify the speaker in fictional material. (Is the poet or author speaking, or is it a character?)
4. Write your paraphrase in your own words, using complete sentences and standard paragraph form.
5. Review the selection to be sure that your paraphrase expresses the same ideas as the original.

Summarizing

A ***summary*** is a restatement in condensed form of main ideas. Summarizing is a useful way to record the basic meaning of a selection you are studying. In addition, writing a summary helps you think critically; you have to analyze the material, identify the most important ideas, and eliminate details that can be left out.

HOW TO SUMMARIZE

1. Review the material carefully, identifying the main ideas and supporting details.
2. Condense the material. Focus only on key ideas, removing unnecessary details, examples, or repetitions. Write a sentence in your own words about each main idea.
3. Use your list of sentences to write your summary in paragraph form. If necessary, add transitional words to show how the ideas are related.
4. Revise your summary. Be sure it covers the most important points, that the information is clearly expressed, and that your words remain faithful to the author's intent.

Here is a sample summary of the article on pages 404–406.

> In 1583, Galileo Galilei, observing an altar lamp, discovered isochronism—the idea that the time it takes a pendulum to swing depends on how long it is, not how widely it swings. Galileo's discovery was part of the new

RESOURCES

CRITICAL THINKING
Analysis

Point out to students that when they summarize material, they have to analyze the material to identify the main ideas and to eliminate everything but the key points. Tell the class that knowing how to write a good summary is a skill that they will use in writing research reports, taking notes, writing reviews, and writing synopses.

RESOURCES

science that involved direct observation rather than the study of other people's teachings. Galileo's discovery also led to the precision clock that allowed worldwide synchronization and standardization of time. Since the earth spins on its axis, every point on the planet experiences a 24-hour day, with 15° of spin being an hour of time. The time difference between two points depends on the number of degrees of longitude in between.

Writing a Précis

A ***précis*** is a written summary. When you write a précis, you shorten a piece of writing—a reading passage, a chapter, an article, a report—to its bare essentials. Most of the techniques that you use for writing a précis are the same as summarizing skills. However, there are certain standard practices that you should follow when you are writing a précis.

GUIDELINES FOR WRITING A PRÉCIS

1. *Be brief.* A précis is seldom more than a third as long as the material being summarized, often less.
2. *Don't paraphrase.* If you merely put each sentence of the original version in slightly different words, you will wind up with as much material as the original.
3. *Stick to the central points.* Avoid examples, unnecessary adjectives, and repetitions.
4. *Use your own wording.* Don't just take phrases or sentences from the original.
5. *Be faithful to the author's points and views.* Don't add your own comments, and don't use such expressions as "The author says" or "The paragraph means."

RESOURCES

Following is a paragraph from which to write a précis.

Rapidity in reading has an obvious direct bearing on success in college work because of the large amount of reading which must be covered in nearly all college courses. But it is probably also a direct measure of the special kind of aptitude that can be called bookish, because rapidity of reading usually correlates with comprehension and retention. Generally speaking, the more rapidly a reader reads, the more effectively he grasps and retains. The normal reading speed of college freshmen has been found to be around 250 words a minute on ordinary reading matter, and a student who reads more slowly than that will certainly have difficulty in completing his college tasks within reasonable study periods. To be a really good college risk under this criterion, one should readily and habitually cover not fewer than 300 words a minute on ordinary reading matter. [143 words]

The chart below shows errors to be avoided in a précis.

COMMON ERRORS IN PRÉCIS-WRITING

ERROR	EXAMPLE FROM FAULTY PRÉCIS
uses phrases taken directly from original	Reading speed has a direct bearing on success in college since college classes often demand much reading. Rapidity of reading usually means a student has better comprehension and retention.
précis misses the point of the original; emphasizes unimportant points	Great amounts of reading are required in most college courses. It's important to read fast to have success in college. A person who reads slowly won't have enough time to get all the work done.
writer of précis injected own ideas	For college success, reading speed is important since college classes, such as history and English, often demand much reading. Surprisingly, students who read quickly retain and recall material better than slower readers, who may flunk out if they can't keep up with their homework.

The following précis is acceptable; it is an appropriate length, and it is stated in the writer's own words.

RESOURCES

SEGMENT 2 *(pp. 1024–1041)*

IMPROVING TEST-TAKING SKILLS

OBJECTIVE

- To prepare for tests of verbal expression and of critical reading skills

MEETING INDIVIDUAL NEEDS

LEARNING STYLES

Kinetic Learners. Suggest that students move around when they are memorizing. For example, a student who is memorizing a poem might want to find a quiet place to walk back and forth while reciting the material aloud. The need to refer to notes should gradually lessen. By connecting the movement with the material, the student should later be able to remember the feeling and hence to recapture the words.

RESOURCES

Teacher's ResourceBank™

RESOURCES

IMPROVING TEST-TAKING SKILLS

For college success, reading speed is important; college classes often demand much reading. Students who read quickly retain and recall material better than slower readers. The average college freshman's speed is 250 words a minute, but higher achievers read faster than 300 words a minute. [45 words]

Memorizing

You are more likely to retain information if you follow these guidelines.

1. *Condense the information.* A chapter, for example, can often be summarized or condensed.
2. *Rehearse the material in several different ways.* Use several different senses to commit the material to memory. Write or copy the material so you can see it and use touch and muscle movements. Say the material out loud so you can hear it.
3. *Use memory games.* Use the first letter of each word in a series to form a new word. Make a rhyme to help you remember dates or facts. Associate information with a vivid mental image.
4. *Repeat the material.* Recite the material frequently in short sessions.

RESOURCES

Improving Test-Taking Skills

Preparing for Tests

To improve your performance on all types of tests, you need to prepare carefully and learn various test-taking strategies. For example, one of the most important factors that affect your performance on a test is your attitude. If you think that you can do well and know that you have prepared to the best of your ability, you will be more likely to focus your energies on the test and concentrate on doing well. Most people feel nervous before a big test, but you can learn how to channel that energy into useful effort.

Kinds of Tests

Classroom Tests. The purpose of the typical classroom test is to measure your ability to use key academic skills or to demonstrate your knowledge of specific academic subjects. Classroom tests often combine several types of test questions. For example, a test might be made up of twenty multiple-choice questions worth four points each and two essay questions worth ten points each. Many different combinations of test questions and scoring methods may be used.

The best way to prepare for classroom tests is to be sure that you are familiar with the material or that you have practiced the skill you must demonstrate at the time of testing. Apply the study skills suggested earlier in this chapter to improve your performance on classroom tests.

Standardized Tests. A standardized test is one in which your score is evaluated according to a "standard" or "norm" compiled from the scores of other students who have taken the same test. Some standardized tests may be developed by a school district or state. The best-known tests of this type are those given to students across the entire United States.

- the *Preliminary Scholastic Aptitude Test (PSAT)*
- the *National Merit Scholars Qualifying Test (NMSQT)*
- the *Scholastic Aptitude Test (SAT-I Reasoning Test)*
- the *Scholastic Aptitude Test (SAT-II Subject Test)*
- the *American College Testing Program (ACT)*

There are two basic types of standardized tests: those testing aptitude and those testing achievement.

Aptitude (or Reasoning) Tests	▪ intended to evaluate basic skills or reasoning abilities needed in various general areas of study ▪ often cover material you have learned during many years of study (such as verbal expression skills and critical thinking ability)
Achievement (or Academic Subject) Tests	▪ intended to measure knowledge of specific subjects (such as history, literature, sciences, mathematics, or foreign languages)

QUICK REMINDER

Ask your students to brainstorm a list of the kinds of classroom tests they take in each of their classes. Write the list on the chalkboard as students suggest ideas. Then ask students to develop a chart with the kinds of tests listed down the left-hand column and the subjects they take in a row across the top. Have them make check marks in the chart to indicate the kinds of tests they have in each subject. You can also do this on the chalkboard. Lead students in a discussion of the kinds of tests they find most difficult.

RESOURCES

MEETING **INDIVIDUAL** NEEDS

STUDENTS WITH SPECIAL NEEDS

While standardized tests are scored and evaluated in terms of a standard, they're also called standardized because they must be given according to standardized procedures with regard to time limits, directions, the use of calculators or dictionaries, and the like. Some state and national standardized tests, such as the SAT, permit deviations from the standardized administration procedures for students with special needs. Your guidance counselor can probably give you detailed information about permitted modifications for specific tests. You can discuss these modifications with the students, their parents, test administrators, and others involved in the testing process.

RESOURCES

HOW TO PREPARE FOR STANDARDIZED TESTS

1. *Learn what specific abilities will be tested.* Information booklets may be provided. Practice with these or with published study guides.
2. *Know what materials you will need.* On the day of the test, you may need to bring specific materials, such as your official test registration card, number 2 pencils, or lined paper for writing an essay answer.
3. *Determine how the test is evaluated.* If there is no penalty for wrong answers, make your best guess on all questions possible. However, if wrong answers are penalized, make guesses only if you are fairly sure of the correct answer.

Taking Standardized Tests

One purpose of standardized tests is to give a prediction of how well you may perform in the college environment. They test your ability to identify and correct problems with verbal expression as well as your ability to analyze and interpret the meaning, purpose, and organization of reading passages.

Kinds of Test Questions

Most test questions are either limited-response questions or open-response questions.

Limited-Response Questions. Limited-response questions give you a limited number of choices from which you select the most appropriate answer. Questions of this type include

- multiple-choice questions
- true/false questions
- matching questions

Open-Response Questions. Open-response questions require you to provide a written response to a specific prompt. These responses may vary widely in their length:

- fill-in-the-blank questions
- short-answer questions
- essay questions

RESOURCES

Tests of Verbal Expression

Standardized tests often contain limited-response questions that measure your understanding of written expression and expression of meaning clearly and with grammatical correctness.

MATERIAL COVERED ON VERBAL EXPRESSION TESTS	
Grammar Questions	You identify the most correct answer, using standard grammar and usage rules. These test items often cover correct use of ■ subject-verb agreement (649–664) ■ principal parts of verbs (713–730) ■ pronouns (672–698)
Punctuation Questions	You identify use of correct punctuation. These test items often cover correct use of ■ end marks and commas (840–863) ■ dashes, semicolons, and colons (866–872) ■ parentheses and quotation marks (873–883) ■ apostrophes and hyphens (887–898)
Sentence Structure Questions	You demonstrate knowledge of what is (and what is not) a complete sentence. These test items often cover correction of ■ fragments and run-on sentences (515–523) ■ combining sentences (526–538) ■ modifiers (762–779) ■ verb usage (713–754) ■ parallel structure (512–514) ■ transitional words (79–81, 117–118)
Revision-in-Context Questions	You show appropriate revision to a part of or to an entire composition. These test items often cover correct use of ■ composition structure (96–123) ■ unity and coherence (72–81) ■ tone (34–37) ■ arranging ideas (38–42)
Rhetorical Strategies Questions	You show an understanding of strategies used by writers to express ideas and opinions. These test items often cover ■ strategies of development (82–89) ■ sequence of ideas (75–78) ■ style and tone (482–483)

RESOURCES

A DIFFERENT APPROACH

One widely used test of verbal expression skills is the Test of Standard Written English (TSWE) that is given as part of the SAT. Scores on the TSWE aren't used to calculate students' total verbal score on the SAT, but TSWE scores are reported along with SAT scores.

Every year the College Board publishes a free booklet that contains a sample SAT and TSWE that students can use for practice. The American College Testing Service publishes a free booklet that contains a sample ACT. These booklets are usually available from guidance counselors. You can obtain a classroom set of these booklets and let your students familiarize themselves with the tests' formats and with the kinds of skills the tests cover. If your students seem to need review or instruction in a particular skill covered on a test, you can provide help beforehand. The College Board also publishes collections of old tests that can be used for additional practice.

For the best-known national tests, these multiple-choice, verbal expression questions are not asked in isolated form. Instead, they appear in the context of a reading passage. You are given a sample passage, usually a long paragraph, with several words and phrases underlined and numbered. Then you are given a series of test items related to the passage. You are expected to pick the choice that best expresses the meaning, is most grammatically correct, or is more consistent with the style and tone of the passage.

Here is a sample test passage with sample questions.

Sample Verbal Expression Test Passage

In an Age of Science—and among all the periods of history, none of them merits [1] that name better than our own—trained scientists are fortunate people. Their training is a matter of national concern, because [2] our nation badly needs more scientists than it has. They can often advance quickly. They can climb as far in science as their ambitions and talents permit. Most important is that they stand [3] at the very center of the forces that are conquering and remaking the world around us. Their futures are bright. It is small wonder that so many young people dream of entering one of the scientific professions.

SAMPLE VERBAL EXPRESSION QUESTIONS	
1. **A.** NO CHANGE B. are meriting C. meriting D. merit	[This is a question about grammar; it requires you to know the correct subject-verb agreement.]
2. A. NO CHANGE B. concern; because C. concern. Because **D.** concern because	[This is a question about punctuation; it requires you to know which mark of punctuation is appropriate here.]

(continued)

SAMPLE VERBAL EXPRESSION QUESTIONS *(continued)*	
3. How should the third and fourth sentences be combined? A. In science, because they can often advance quickly, they can climb as far as their ambitions and talents permit. (B.) They can often advance as fast and as far in science as their ambitions and talents permit. C. They can often advance quickly and far in science, because of their ambitions and talents. D. As quickly and as far in science as their ambitions and talents will permit them, they can advance.	[This is a question about sentence structure; it requires you to know how to combine sentences effectively.]
4. Which is the best revision of the portion of the passage indicated by the number 3? (A.) Most important, they stand B. It is most important that they stand C. It is most important; they stand D. Most importantly that they stand	[This is a revision-in-context question; it requires you to use revision skills to best express the ideas in the passage.]
5. This passage might next discuss A. how our government should provide grants to help scientific research. B. why science is not respected in other nations. (C.) specific occupations for young people in the sciences. D. why there are not enough scientists.	[This is a question about rhetorical strategies; it requires you to use your knowledge of writing strategy, organization, and style in order to draw conclusions and make inferences about the passage.]

RESOURCES

MEETING INDIVIDUAL NEEDS

LESS-ADVANCED STUDENTS

Many standardized tests of achievement in science and social studies are really tests of students' abilities to read material drawn from a particular content area. Point out that in tests of this type, students aren't expected to possess the knowledge the questions call for. Instead, the information requested by the questions is stated or implied in the reading passages in the test.

RESOURCES

As you can see, there are only two basic types of questions used to test verbal expression on the most current, best-known national tests.

MOST COMMON TYPES OF VERBAL EXPRESSION TEST ITEMS	
"NO CHANGE" Items	■ give list of suggested revisions of underlined, numbered portions of passage ■ always contain one "NO CHANGE" choice (these words are often printed in capital letters) among list of choices; selected if indicated part is correct as is
Critical Thinking Items	■ ask you to analyze and evaluate the passage as a whole ■ ask you to make inferences about portions of a passage as related to the whole

Tests of Critical Reading

Standardized tests may contain a number of limited-response questions that measure your ability to analyze and interpret a piece of writing. These questions require you to look critically at a particular piece of writing to find the meaning, purpose, and organization of the selection. In addition, these questions require you to evaluate the effectiveness of the passage in conveying the meaning intended by the writer.

Questions used in tests of critical reading and critical analysis cover the following subject matter:

CRITICAL READING
- organization
- evaluation
- interpretation
- synthesis
- vocabulary in context
- style

CRITICAL ANALYSIS
- analogies
- logic

RESOURCES

MATERIAL COVERED ON CRITICAL READING TESTS	
Organization Questions	You identify the organizational techniques used by the writer of a passage. These test items often cover identification of ■ author's use of particular writing strategies (82–89) ■ the main idea of a passage (1010) ■ arrangement of supporting details (64–70) ■ transitional devices that make the passage coherent (79–81) ■ techniques used to conclude the passage (119–121)
Evaluation Questions	You judge the effectiveness of techniques used by the author of a passage. These test items often cover identification of ■ the author's opinion (1011) ■ the author's intended audience (33–37) ■ the author's tone or point of view (33–37) ■ the author's purpose (33–37)
Interpretation Questions	You draw conclusions or make inferences about the meaning of information presented in a passage. These test items often cover identification of ■ ambiguities in information (503–525) ■ conclusions or inferences based on given material (1013) ■ specific conclusions or inferences that can be drawn about the author or the topic of a passage (1013)
Synthesis Questions	You demonstrate knowledge of how parts of a passage fit together into a whole. These test items often cover interpretation of ■ techniques used to unify details (72–74) ■ the cumulative meaning of details in a passage (1010–1012)

(continued)

RESOURCES

RESOURCES

CRITICAL THINKING
Analysis

One useful procedure for students to use in taking standardized tests is to look over the questions before they read the reading passages. By looking over the questions, students can figure out what kinds of information they will be expected to obtain from the passage. It will probably still be necessary for them to go back to the passage as they answer the questions, but a quick analysis of the questions before reading can alert them to the kinds of things to watch for.

RESOURCES

MATERIAL COVERED ON CRITICAL READING TESTS *(continued)*	
Vocabulary in Context Questions	You infer the meaning of an unfamiliar word by an analysis of its context. These test items often cover determination of ■ the meaning of a passage to learn the meaning of a word (981–982) ■ the meaning of an unfamiliar word, using context clues (1043–1044)
Style Questions	You analyze a passage to evaluate the author's use of style (480–497). These test items often cover identification of ■ the author's style ■ the author's voice and tone ■ the author's intended audience

Here is a sample reading passage with sample questions.

Sample Reading Passage

By the end of 1855, Walt Whitman was seeing his "wonderous and ponderous book," *Leaves of Grass,* through its final stages. He read the typeset pages by candlelight. When the poet Hart Crane began working on *The Bridge* some sixty years later, he worked under an electric light. Before 1920, few major American cities had been electrified. By the 1930s, nearly every American city was illuminated.

Henry Adams saw his first electric generator, or dynamo, in Paris at the Great Exposition of 1900. Because they could produce cheap electricity, these dynamos had commercial use. In time they were used to generate the brilliant arc lights of San Francisco, New York, and Philadelphia, thus replacing gas street lamps that were the hallmark of American cities in the nineteenth century.

Yet arc lights were simply unsuitable for home use because of their intense brightness. Credit for the discovery and promotion of the incandescent light used in household light bulbs must go to Thomas Alva Edison. Financed by a group of wealthy backers, Edison and his team designed an entire system to provide electricity: filaments, wiring, efficient dynamos, safety features, and even the sockets themselves. In 1881, Edison unveiled his famous Pearl Street Station in New York

RESOURCES

City. Edison's men laid the wires to the square mile around 257 Pearl Street, and they wired individual households and installed meters to measure electricity use. Edison's stations would eventually supply power to over 400,000 lamps in places such as Chicago and Milan, New Orleans, and Berlin.

At the outset, electricity for the home was an expensive luxury for the elite. In 1907, for example, only 8% of American homes had electricity. However, large-scale generators and greater consumption gradually allowed the costs to drop. By 1920, 34% of American homes had electricity, and by 1941 nearly 80% were supplied with electricity. Today, we simply take electricity for granted.

By candlelight, Whitman handwrote his poetry. By fluorescent light, a modern poet keystrokes poetry into a computer. Electrification, communication, urbanization—all are processes and systems that affect our lives. Only by understanding the history of these technological developments can we truly understand their importance.

SAMPLE CRITICAL READING QUESTIONS

1. According to the passage, in which order (from earliest to latest) did the following events occur?

I. Eighty percent of American homes have electricity.
II. Walt Whitman writes *Leaves of Grass.*
III. Henry Adams sees the dynamo at the Great Exposition.
IV. Edison begins operation of the Pearl Street Station in New York.

(A.) II, IV, III, I
B. II, III, IV, I
C. II, I, III, IV
D. II, IV, I, III

[This is an organization question; it requires you to identify the time sequence of these events and to arrange them in the correct historical time order.]

2. The word *elite* in the fourth paragraph may be defined as
A. a variety of type found on a typewriter.
B. a group of arrogant, stubborn people.
C. the last people to agree to a new idea.
(D.) the wealthiest members of a social group.

[This is a vocabulary-in-context question; it requires you to examine the context in which the word appears in the passage in order to determine the appropriate definition.]

(continued)

RESOURCES

RESOURCES

COMMON ERROR

Problem. Some students choose the first answer that seems to be correct and fail to read and evaluate the other options.

Solution. The directions for most standardized tests say that students should choose the best answer from all of the alternatives that are given. Sometimes more than one answer is partially correct. Remind students to make sure that they read all of the answers before choosing one.

RESOURCES

SAMPLE CRITICAL READING QUESTIONS *(continued)*

3. Imagine that after reading the passage your classmate wrote the following paragraph.

   In the home, women were thought to be the benefactors of electrification. Irons, vacuum cleaners, hot water heaters, clothes washers, and refrigerators—all were hailed as inventions that would make women's lives easier. But they also reinforced the idea that the woman's place was in the home. These gadgets were indeed labor-saving devices, but only if someone remained in the home to use them. Only recently have we questioned whether these so-called technological advances were advantages at all.

   You could assume that your classmate is critical of the idea that technological advances

   A. are often invisible.
   B. are inexpensive.
   (C.) are beneficial to everyone.
   D. exist independently of each other.

   [This is an evaluation question; it requires you to identify the main points of the original passage and to recognize which of these points your classmate disputed.]

4. The phrase "keystrokes poetry into a computer" is best taken to mean that electrification is a form of progress that

   A. jeopardizes our historical awareness.
   (B.) influences daily the way we live our lives.
   C. improves our ability to compose poetry.
   D. most affects students.

   [This is an interpretation question; you are asked to examine the context of the word noted in order to explain its meaning in the passage.]

5. It can be inferred from the description of Thomas Alva Edison that he was

   A. a man who represented the nineteenth century.
   B. a man who changed his ideas frequently.
   (C.) an organized, driven man.
   D. a capitalist concerned only for his own welfare.

   [This is a synthesis question; it requires you to read, in the passage as a whole, about the efforts needed to electrify a small urban area. Then you can infer that Edison, the project director, was a driven man of great organizational powers.]

(continued)

RESOURCES

SAMPLE CRITICAL READING QUESTIONS *(continued)*

6. Readers of this passage are likely to describe it as
A. informal.
(B.) historical.
C. inspirational.
D. biographical.

[This is a question of style; it requires you to analyze the way the passage is written to determine the category or type of writing it represents.]

Tests of Critical Analysis

Standardized tests may contain a number of limited-response questions that measure your ability to recognize specific kinds of relationships.

MATERIAL COVERED ON CRITICAL ANALYSIS TESTS	
Analogy Questions	These ask you to analyze the relationship between a pair of words and to use reasoning skills to identify a second pair of words that have the same relationship (989–991). EXAMPLE: SEW : CUT :: ____________ A. paint : brush B. willow : tree (C.) plaster : break D. wind : moan
Logic Questions	These ask you to analyze a sentence or a brief passage to fill in one or more blanks with the most appropriate word or words given. EXAMPLE: Because electrification began to gain ____ at the turn of the century, this era signals an important ____ in American history. A. mediocrity . . . collapse (B.) momentum . . . juncture C. patents . . . tragedy D. popularity . . . rendezvous

RESOURCES

RESOURCES

COOPERATIVE LEARNING

One way to study for an essay test is to anticipate the questions that may possibly be on the test and to develop answers to these questions. Let your students work in groups of four to develop sample questions for an essay test on a unit of material you've covered in literature. Let a reporter from each group share the group's questions with the rest of the class. You can also duplicate all of the questions and let students use them as a study guide for the test.

RESOURCES

Essay Tests

Essay tests require you to think about and express your understanding of selected material in an organized way. Because essay tests call for critical thinking and writing skills, answers can vary. However, a well-written essay must be complete, organized according to the directions, and supported with sufficient detail.

Essay questions usually ask you to perform specific tasks. Each of these tasks is expressed with a verb. Each task requires a specific response that you can prepare for by becoming familiar with the key terms and the kinds of information called for.

ESSAY TEST QUESTIONS

KEY VERB	TASK	SAMPLE QUESTION
analyze	Take something apart to see how each part works.	Analyze the main character in Nathaniel Hawthorne's "The Minister's Black Veil."
argue	Take a viewpoint on an issue and give reasons to support this opinion.	Argue whether or not your school should forbid students to work on weekday evenings.
compare	Point out likenesses.	Compare the British Parliament with the U.S. Congress as law-making bodies.
contrast	Point out differences.	Contrast organic farming methods with traditional procedures.
define	Give specific details that make something unique.	Define the term *osmosis* as it relates to the permeability of membranes.

(continued)

RESOURCES

ESSAY TEST QUESTIONS *(continued)*		
KEY VERB	TASK	SAMPLE QUESTION
demonstrate (also illustrate, present, show)	Provide examples to support a point.	Demonstrate that an electrical charge is conducted by metal.
describe	Give a picture in words.	Describe an incident in *Othello* that features Iago.
discuss	Examine in detail.	Discuss the term *Romanticism.*
explain	Give reasons.	Explain why congruent angles are complementary.
identify	Point out specific persons, places, things, or characteristics.	Identify members of the presidential cabinet and their duties.
interpret	Give the meaning or significance of something.	Interpret the importance of the dismantling of the Berlin Wall.
list (also outline, trace)	Give all steps in order or all details about a subject.	List events leading to the Persian Gulf Conflict.
summarize	Give a brief overview of the main points.	Summarize the plot of F. Scott Fitzgerald's *The Great Gatsby.*

Before you start writing on an essay test, scan the questions quickly. Determine how many answers you are expected to write. If you have a choice between several items, decide which of them you can answer best. Then plan how much time to spend on each answer, and stay on this schedule.

RESOURCES

Read the essay question carefully. There may be several parts to the question that you need to answer.

Pay attention to important terms in the question. Find the key verbs; these identify tasks you must accomplish in your essay.

Take a moment to use prewriting strategies. On scratch paper, make notes or a simple outline to help you decide what to write.

Evaluate and revise as you write. You will not be able to redraft your whole essay, but you can edit to strengthen specific parts.

QUALITIES OF A GOOD ESSAY ANSWER

- The essay is well organized.
- The main ideas and supporting points are clear.
- The sentences are complete and well written.
- There are no distracting errors in spelling, punctuation, or grammar.

Review

EXERCISE 1 **Using Study Skills**

The following numbered items suggest ways for you to practice using the study skills discussed on pages 1009–1016.

1. In a brief paragraph, identify ways that you use different rates of reading, such as those noted on page 1007, in order to accomplish different purposes.
2. Choose a magazine article or a textbook chapter. Read the selection, using the SQ3R method outlined on page 1009. List at least five questions and write brief answers to each one.
3. Working with a group of two or three classmates, write a list of critical reading questions about Chief Joseph's "An Indian's View of Indian Affairs" (pages 278–280). Use the sample analysis of the reading passage on pages 1011–1012 as a model. Let each group's members ask their questions to test the rest of the class.

RESOURCES

ANSWERS

Exercise 1

Answers will vary. Here are some guidelines for evaluation:

1. Students' responses will vary. Each student should list at least one example of each of the three reading rates.
2. Students' questions should deal with significant facts or ideas in the selection, and answers should be complete and accurate.
3. Questions should demonstrate use of the information in the **Finding Relationships Among Details** chart on p. 1011. For example: How does Chief Joseph say a man is like a horse?

RESOURCES

4. Find a passage in a textbook, a nonfiction book, a magazine, or a newspaper that gives information that you can express in graphic form. Using the information and example on page 1017 as a model, make a diagram, chart, or other visual arrangement of the most pertinent information from the passage.
5. Select a chapter from one of your textbooks that you have been assigned as homework and take study notes, using the strategies explained on pages 1014–1016.

EXERCISE 2 **Paraphrasing a Poem**

Write a paraphrase of "The New Colossus" by Emma Lazarus (page 11). Follow the guidelines on pages 1018–1019.

EXERCISE 3 **Writing a Précis**

Write a précis of the essay by James West Davidson, "The Frontier Kitchen of the Plains" (pages 256–259). Follow the guidelines on pages 1022–1024.

EXERCISE 4 **Preparing for Tests of Verbal Expression**

Read the passage, then answer the questions that follow, using the guidelines on pages 1027–1030.

> Planes of the future may be held together by glue instead of by thousands of rivets or metal bolts. Experiments conducted by American aircraft manufacturers and the Air Force revealed that a glued aircraft would have several advantages over a riveted one. It would weigh 15 percent less. It would also cost 20 percent less to build and maintain. Structural tests on a glued fuselage showed that it could survive 120,000 hours of <u>flight; four times</u> (1) the life of the average riveted aircraft. Furthermore, the glued fuselage proved to be less likely to <u>develop cracks and the glue</u> (2) even retarded the growth of cracks cut into the fuselage deliberately. Encouragement was also found in the results from tests of the plane's resistance to environmental stresses such as salt air, high humidity, and freezing temperatures.

RESOURCES

4. Students' graphics should include titles, and the information in the graphics should be accurate and pertinent.
5. The study notes should include all of the main ideas and sufficient details to support the main ideas. The notes should be concise.

ANSWERS
Exercise 2

Paraphrases will vary. Paraphrases should be in the students' own words. They should be written in complete sentences and in standard paragraph form. Each paraphrase should identify the speaker of the poem and should contain the same ideas as the poem.

ANSWERS
Exercise 3

Précis will vary. The précis should be brief, written in the students' own words, faithful to the author's point of view, and concerned only with the central points.

RESOURCES

1. A. NO CHANGE
   B. flight, four times
   C. flight. Four times
   D. flight, and four times

2. A. NO CHANGE
   B. develop cracks; the glue
   C. develop cracks. And the glue
   D. develop cracks, and the glue

3. How should the third and fourth sentences be combined?
   A. It would weigh and cost 20 percent less for building and maintenance.
   B. In addition to less weight by 15 percent, it would cost 20 percent less as building and maintenance.
   C. It would weigh 15 percent less, and it would cost 20 percent less to build and maintain.
   D. Because it would weigh 15 percent less, it would cost 20 percent less to build it and maintain it.

4. Which of the following is the best revision of the last sentence?
   A. Encouragement was also found in the results from tests of the plane's resistance to environmental stresses such as: salt air; high humidity; and freezing temperatures.
   B. The results from tests of the plane's resistance to environmental stresses such as salt air, high humidity, and freezing temperatures were also encouraging.
   C. The resulting tests of the plane's resistance to environmental stresses such as salt air, high humidity, and freezing temperatures were also encouraged.
   D. Resulting from tests of the plane's resistance to environmental stresses such as salt air, high humidity, and freezing temperatures were also encouraged.

5. In telling about the various tests that the glued plane was subjected to, the writer is
   A. giving concrete examples to prove the plane's durability.
   B. using the extremes of the environmental factors to create a humorous effect.
   C. giving the reader an idea of how frustrating these tests were for the scientists.
   D. using description to make the reader feel a part of the scene.

RESOURCES

RESOURCES

EXERCISE 5 Preparing for Tests of Critical Reading Skills

Using the sample test passage on pages 1032–1033, answer the following questions.

1. What idea does this passage show best?
   - **A.** the conflict between people and technology
   - **B.** the drawbacks of technology
   - **C.** the effect of technological change on American cities
   - **D.** the difficulty in finding financial backing for new inventions
2. The word *electrification* in the final paragraph may be defined as
   - **A.** a shock or jolt.
   - **B.** an increase in excitement.
   - **C.** decay of the cities.
   - **D.** conversion to electric power.
3. The author's predominant attitude about the subject seems to be
   - **A.** criticism of the rate of technological change.
   - **B.** distrust of power companies.
   - **C.** approval of technological change.
   - **D.** interest in how electrification affected Whitman's poetry.
4. Which of the following interpretations is suggested by the second paragraph?
   - **A.** In 1900, Henry Adams saw possibilities for the dynamo.
   - **B.** In 1900, American cities had arc lights but needed cheap electricity to run them.
   - **C.** Gas lamps were not used in Europe.
   - **D.** Gas lamps were less expensive than electric light.
5. This passage most probably has the purpose of
   - **A.** persuading the reader.
   - **B.** giving information to the reader.
   - **C.** expressing the author's creativity.
   - **D.** entertaining the reader.

RESOURCES

Glossary of Terms

A

Action verb Expresses physical or mental activity. (See page 565.)

Active voice The voice a verb is in when it expresses an action done *by* its subject. (See page 748.)

Adjective Modifies a noun or a pronoun. (See page 559.)

Adjective clause A subordinate clause that modifies a noun or a pronoun. (See page 630.)

Adjective phrase A prepositional phrase that modifies a noun or a pronoun. (See page 605.)

Adverb Modifies a verb, an adjective, or another adverb. (See page 568.)

Adverb clause A subordinate clause that modifies a verb, an adjective, or an adverb. (See page 636.)

Adverb phrase A prepositional phrase that modifies a verb, an adjective, or an adverb. (See page 607.)

Agreement The correspondence, or match, between grammatical forms. (See Chapter 21.)

Aim One of the four basic purposes, or reasons, for writing. (See pages 7 and 20.)

Ambiguous reference Occurs when a pronoun refers to either of two antecedents. (See page 701.)

Antecedent The word that a pronoun stands for. (See page 555.)

Appositive A noun or a pronoun placed beside another noun or pronoun to identify or explain it. (See page 621.)

Appositive phrase Consists of an appositive and its modifiers. (See page 621.)

Article *A, an,* and *the,* the most frequently used adjectives. (See page 560.)

C

Case The form of a noun or pronoun that shows how it is used in a sentence. (See page 674.)

Cause-and-effect explanation A form of writing in which a writer explains the causes and/or effects of a situation. (See Chapter 7.)

Chronological order A way of arranging ideas in a paragraph or composition according to when events happen. (See pages 39 and 75.)

Classification A strategy of development: looking at a subject as it relates to other subjects in a group. (See page 86.)

Clause A group of words that contains a verb and its subject and is used as part of a sentence. (See page 628.)

Coherence A quality achieved when all the ideas in a paragraph or composition are clearly arranged and connected. (See pages 75 and 117.)

Comparison Refers to the change in the form of an adjective or an adverb to show increasing or decreasing degrees in the quality the modifier expresses. (See page 770.)

Comparison/Contrast essay A form of writing in which a writer discusses similarities or differences (or both) between two subjects. (See Chapter 6.)

Complement A word or group of words that completes the meaning of a verb. (See page 591.)

Complex sentence Has one independent clause and at least one subordinate clause. (See page 641.)

Compound-complex sentence Has two or more independent clauses and at least one subordinate clause. (See page 641.)

Compound sentence Has two or more independent clauses but no subordinate clauses. (See page 640.)

Conjunction Joins words or groups of words. (See page 574.)

D

Dangling modifier A modifying word, phrase, or clause that does not clearly and sensibly modify a word or a group of words in a sentence. (See page 785.)

Declarative sentence Makes a statement and is followed by a period. (See page 597.)

Description A strategy of development: using sensory details and spatial order to describe individual features of a specific subject. (See page 83.)

Direct object A word or word group that receives the action of the verb or shows the result of the action, telling *whom* or *what* after a transitive verb. (See page 592.)

Direct reference Connects ideas in a paragraph or composition by referring to a noun or pronoun used earlier. (See page 79.)

Double negative The use of two negative words when one is enough. (See page 811.)

E

Elliptical clause A clause from which words have been omitted. (See page 637.)

Essential clause/Essential phrase Also called **restrictive:** is necessary to the meaning of a sentence; not set off by commas. (See page 851.)

Evaluating A stage in the writing process: making judgments about a composition's strengths and weaknesses in content, organization, and style. (See pages 6 and 45.)

Evaluation A strategy of development: making judgments about a subject in an attempt to determine its value. (See page 89.)

Exclamatory sentence Expresses strong feeling and is followed by an exclamation point. (See page 598.)

Expository writing Aims at being informative, explanatory, or exploratory. (See page 7.)

G

General reference Occurs when a pronoun refers to a general idea rather than to a specific noun. (See page 703.)

Gerund A verb form ending in *–ing* that is used as a noun. (See page 614.)

Gerund phrase Consists of a gerund and its modifiers and complements. (See page 615.)

I

Imperative mood Used to express a direct command or request. (See page 755.)

Imperative sentence Gives a command or makes a request and is followed by either a period or an exclamation point. (See page 598.)

Indefinite reference Occurs when a pronoun refers to no particular person or thing. (See page 707.)

Independent clause Also called a **main clause:** expresses a complete thought and can stand by itself as a sentence. (See page 628.)

Indicative mood Used to express a fact, an opinion, or a question. (See page 755.)

Indirect object A word or word group that comes between a transitive verb and object and tells *to whom* or *to what* or *for whom* or *for what* the action of a verb is done. (See page 592.)

Infinitive (1) One of the principal parts of a verb. (See page 715.) **(2)** A verb form usually preceded by *to,* used as a noun, an adjective, or an adverb. (See page 616.)

Infinitive phrase Consists of an infinitive and its modifiers and complements. (See page 619.)

Interjection Expresses emotion and has no grammatical relation to the rest of the sentence. (See page 576.)

Interrogative sentence Asks a question and is followed by a question mark. (See page 597.)

Intransitive verb An action verb that does not take an object. (See page 565.)

L

Linking verb Connects the subject with a word that identifies or describes it. (See page 565.)

Literary analysis A form of writing in which a writer examines and responds to a piece of literature critically. (See Chapter 10.)

Literary writing Aims at creating imaginative works. (See page 7.)

Logical order A way of arranging details in a paragraph or composition according to what makes logical sense, such as grouping related ideas together. (See pages 39 and 76.)

M

Misplaced modifier A word, phrase, or clause that makes a sentence awkward because it seems to modify the wrong word or group of words. (See page 782.)

Modifier A word that limits the meaning of another word. (See page 764.)

Mood The form a verb takes to indicate the attitude of the person using the verb. (See page 755.)

N

Narration A strategy of development: relating events or actions over a period of time, usually using chronological order. (See page 84.)

Nonessential clause/Nonessential phrase Also called **nonrestrictive:** adds information not necessary to the main idea in the sentence and is set off by commas. (See page 851.)

Noun Names a person, place, thing, or idea. (See page 553.)

Noun clause A subordinate clause used as a noun. (See page 634.)

Number The form of a word that indicates whether the word is singular or plural. (See page 649.)

O

Objective complement A word or word group that helps complete the meaning of a transitive verb by identifying or modifying the direct object. (See page 593.)

Object of a preposition The noun or pronoun that ends a prepositional phrase. (See page 605.)

Order of importance A way of arranging details, in a paragraph or composition, from least to most important or from most to least important. (See pages 39 and 76.)

P

Participial phrase Consists of a participle and its complements and modifiers. (See page 612.)

Participle A verb form used as an adjective. (See page 611.)

Passive voice The voice a verb is in when it expresses an action done *to* its subject. (See page 748.)

Personal essay A form of writing in which an author explores and shares the meaning of an experience that was especially important to him or her. (See Chapter 4.)

Persuasive essay A form of writing in which a writer supports an opinion and tries to persuade an audience. (See Chapter 8.)

Persuasive writing Aims at convincing people to accept an idea or to take action. (See page 7.)

Phrase A group of related words used as a single part of speech and does not contain a verb and its subject. (See page 605.)

Point of view The vantage point, or position, from which a writer tells a story or describes a subject. (See page 169.)

Predicate The part of a sentence that says something about the subject. (See page 584.)

Predicate adjective An adjective that follows a linking verb and modifies the subject of the verb. (See page 595.)

Predicate nominative A word or word group that follows a linking verb and refers to the same person or thing as the subject of the verb. (See page 595.)

Preposition Shows the relationship of a noun or a pronoun to some other word in a sentence. (See page 571.)

Prepositional phrase A group of words beginning with a preposition and ending with an object (a noun or a pronoun). (See page 605.)

Prewriting The first stage of the writing process: thinking and planning, deciding what to write about, collecting ideas and details, and making a plan for presenting ideas. (See pages 6 and 22.)

Problem-solution essay A form of exploratory writing in which a writer explains a problem and proposes an effective solution. (See Chapter 9.)

Pronoun Is used in place of a noun or more than one noun. (See page 555.)

Proofreading A stage of the writing process: carefully reading a revised draft to correct mistakes in grammar, usage, and mechanics. (See pages 6 and 50.)

Publishing The last stage of the writing process: making a final, clean copy of a paper and sharing it with an audience. (See pages 6 and 51.)

Purpose A reason for writing or speaking. (See pages 7 and 21.)

R

Research report A form of writing in which a writer presents factual information discovered through exploration and research. (See Chapter 11.)

Revising A stage of the writing process: making changes in a composition's content, organization, and style in order to improve it. (See pages 6 and 45.)

S

Self-Expressive writing Aims at expressing a writer's feelings and thoughts. (See page 7.)

Sentence A group of words that contains a subject and a verb and expresses a complete thought. (See page 582.)

Simple sentence Has one independent clause and no subordinate clauses. (See page 640.)

Spatial order A way of arranging details in a paragraph or composition according to location. (See pages 39 and 75.)

Style A writer's unique way of adapting language to suit different occasions. (See Chapter 13.)

Subject Tells whom or what a sentence is about. (See page 584.)

Subject complement A word or word group that completes the meaning of a linking verb and identifies or modifies the subject. (See page 595.)

Subjunctive mood Used to express a suggestion, a necessity, a condition contrary to fact, or a wish. (See page 756.)

Subordinate clause Also called a **dependent clause:** does not express a complete thought and cannot stand alone as a sentence. (See page 629.)

Supporting sentences Give specific details or information to support a main idea. (See page 67.)

T

Tense Indicates the time of an action or state of being expressed by a verb. (See page 736.)

Theme The underlying meaning or message a writer wants to communicate to readers. (See page 172.)

Thesis statement Announces the limited topic of a composition and the main, or unifying, idea about that topic. (See page 102.)

Tone The feeling or attitude a writer conveys about a topic. (See page 34.)

Topic sentence Expresses the main idea of a paragraph. (See page 64.)

Transitional expressions Words and phrases that indicate relationships between ideas in a paragraph or composition. (See page 79.)

Transitive verb An action verb that takes an object. (See page 565.)

U

Unity A quality achieved when all the sentences or paragraphs in a composition work together as a unit to express or support one main idea. (See pages 72 and 117.)

V

Verb Expresses an action or a state of being. (See page 565.)

Verbal A form of a verb used as a noun, an adjective, or an adverb. (See page 611.)

Verbal phrase Consists of a verbal and its modifiers and complements. (See page 611.)

Verb phrase Consists of a main verb preceded by at least one helping verb. (See page 611.)

Voice (1) The unique sound and rhythm of a writer's language. (See page 482.) **(2)** The form a transitive verb takes to indicate whether the subject of the verb performs or receives the action. (See page 748.)

W

Weak reference Occurs when a pronoun refers to an antecedent that has not been expressed. (See page 706.)

Writing A stage of the writing process: putting ideas into words, following a plan that organizes the ideas. (See pages 6 and 43.)

Writing process The series of stages, or steps, that a writer goes through to develop ideas and to communicate them clearly in a piece of writing. (See pages 6 and 21.)

Glossary

This glossary is a short dictionary of words found in the professional writing models in this textbook. The words are defined according to their meanings in the context of the writing models.

Pronunciation Key

Symbol	Key Words
a	asp, fat, parrot
ā	ape, date, play, break, fail
ä	ah, car, father, cot
e	elf, ten, berry
ē	even, meet, money, flea, grieve
i	is, hit, mirror
ī	ice, bite, high, sky
ō	open, tone, go, boat
ô	all, horn, law, oar
oo	look, pull, moor, wolf
o͞o	ooze, tool, crew, rule
yo͞o	use, cute, few
yoo	cure, globule
oi	oil, point, toy
ou	out, crowd, plow
u	up, cut, color, flood
ʉr	urn, fur, deter, irk
ə	a in ago
	e in agent
	i in sanity
	o in comply
	u in focus
ər	perhaps, murder

Symbol	Key Words
b	bed, fable, dub, ebb
d	dip, beadle, had, dodder
f	fall, after, off, phone
g	get, haggle, dog
h	he, ahead, hotel
j	joy, agile, badge
k	kill, tackle, bake, coat, quick
l	let, yellow, ball
m	met, camel, trim, summer
n	not, flannel, ton
p	put, apple, tap
r	red, port, dear, purr
s	sell, castle, pass, nice
t	top, cattle, hat
v	vat, hovel, have
w	will, always, swear, quick
y	yet, onion, yard
z	zebra, dazzle, haze, rise
ch	chin, catcher, arch, nature
sh	she, cushion, dash, machine
th	thin, nothing, truth
th	then, father, lathe
zh	azure, leisure, beige
ŋ	ring, anger, drink

Abbreviation Key

adj. adjective
adv. adverb
n. noun
vi. intransitive verb
vt. transitive verb

A

a • cute [ə kyo͞ot′] *adj.* Sharp and quick.

an • nals [an′əlz] *n.* A written history in chronological order.

an • tiq • ui • ty [an tik′wə tē] *n.* The condition of being very old.

ar • ti • fice [ärt′ə fis] *n.* Craft.

B

bluff [bluf] **n.** A high, steep cliff.

bois • ter • ous [bois′tər əs] *adj.* Loud and lively.

C

cir • cum • vent [sur′kəm vent′] *vt.* To get the better of someone by cleverness.

com • pli • ance [kəm plī′əns] *n.* Giving in to a request.

crass [kras] *adj.* Extremely stupid.

D

dec • o • rous [dek′ə rəs] *adj.* Proper.

de • lin • e • ate [di lin′ē āt′] *vt.* To describe in words.

de • rail [dē rāl′] *vt.* To cause to go off course.

Di • vine Prov • i • dence [də vīn′ präv′ ə dəns] *n.* Guidance from God.

E

en • deav • or [en dev′ər] *n.* A serious effort.

en • dow • ment [en dou′mənt] *n.* Talent.

es • chew [es cho͞o′] *vt.* To avoid.

F

fa • ce • tious • ly [fə sē′shəs lē] *adv.* Jokingly.

fan • cy [fan′sē] *vt.* To form an idea.

G

grave • ly [grāv′lē] *adv.* Seriously.

H

his • tri • on • ic [his′trē än′ik] *adj.* Overly dramatic.

I

id • i • o • syn • cra • sy [id′ē o′ siŋ′ krə sē] *n.* A peculiarity.

im • pe • cu • ni • ous [im′pi kyo͞o′ nē əs] *adj.* Poor.

in • ces • sant [in ses′ənt] *adj.* Seemingly endless.

in • cur • sion [in kur′zhən] *n.* A raid.

M

mal • a • dy [mal′ə dē] *n.* A disease.

mar • tial [mär′shəl] *adj.* Having to do with war.

min • strel [min′strəl] *n.* A performer of the mid-1800s who blackened his face and sang and told jokes.

moor [moor] *vt.* To hold in place with ropes or cables.

N

no • mad • ic [nō mad′ik] *adj.* Having no permanent home; moving constantly.

O

oc • tave [äk′tiv] ***n.*** Seven tones above or below any given tone on the music scale.

Om • nip • o • tence [äm nip′ə təns] ***n.*** God.

P

pen • du • lous [pen′dyo͞o ləs] ***adj.*** Hanging and swinging freely.

per • func • to • ri • ly [pər fuŋk′tə rə lē] ***adv.*** Done out of routine.

per • il [per′əl] ***n.*** Danger.

plau • si • bly [plô′zə blē] ***adv.*** In a seemingly true manner.

pneu • mat • ic drill [no͞o mat′ik dril] ***n.*** A hole-boring device operated by compressed air.

pri • mal [prī′məl] ***adj.*** Original.

pro • di • gious [prō dij′əs] ***adj.*** Enormous.

R

rasp [rasp] ***vt.*** To scrape.

ring • er [riŋ′ər] ***n.*** A person substituted for another in a competition.

ru • di • ment [ro͞o′də mənt] ***n.*** The basic principles of a subject.

S

scur • vy [skʉr′vē] ***n.*** A disease caused by a lack of vitamin C resulting in weakness and bleeding gums.

sheep dip [shēp′ dip′] ***n.*** A chemical mixture to rid sheep of insects.

slov • en • li • ness [sluv′ən lē nes] ***n.*** Untidiness.

stand • pipe [stand′pīp′] ***n.*** A cylinder for storing water supply.

sub • sist • ence [səb sis′təns] ***n.*** That which provides essential support such as food.

suf • fice [sə fīs′] ***vi.*** To be good enough.

sur • plus • age [sʉr′plus′ij] ***n.*** Unnecessary words.

syn • chro • nize [siŋ′krə nīz′] ***vt.*** To make to agree in time.

T

thrum [thrum] ***n.*** A drumming sound.

tu • to • ri • al [to͞o tôr′ē əl] ***adj.*** Of or about individualized teaching, especially for helping students overcome learning problems.

V

ven • er • a • ble [ven′ər ə bəl] ***adj.*** Honorable because of age.

vi • car • i • ous [vī ker′ē əs] ***adj.*** Feeling as if one is taking part in something that is actually happening to someone else.

W

waft [wäft] ***vi.*** To float.

wane [wān] ***vi.*** To decrease in amount.

wist • ful [wist′fəl] ***adj.*** Longing.

Index

A

INDEX

1051

B

C

INDEX

INDEX

INDEX

INDEX

D

INDEX

INDEX

E

INDEX

INDEX

INDEX

F

INDEX

1059

INDEX

INDEX

INDEX

J

K

L

INDEX

INDEX

M

INDEX

INDEX

INDEX

INDEX

N

O

INDEX

INDEX

P

INDEX

INDEX

1067

INDEX

INDEX

INDEX

Q

INDEX

INDEX

R

INDEX

1071

S

INDEX

INDEX

INDEX

INDEX

INDEX

INDEX

T

INDEX
1076

U

V

INDEX

W

INDEX

INDEX

Y

Z

INDEX

1079

Acknowledgments

For permission to reprint copyrighted material, grateful acknowledgment is made to the following sources:

Andrews and McMeel, a Universal Press Syndicate Company: From "Star Wars" from *Roger Ebert's Movie Home Companion 1988 Edition* by Roger Ebert. Copyright © 1988 by Roger Ebert. From *The Far Side Gallery* by Gary Larson. Copyright © 1985 by Universal Press Syndicate.

Isaac Asimov: "Learning Science" from *The Tyrannosaurus Prescription and 100 Other Essays* by Isaac Asimov. Copyright © 1981 by American Chemical Society.

Atheneum Publishers: From "Beware: Do Not Read This Poem" from *New and Collected Poems* by Ishmael Reed. Copyright © 1968, 1970 by Ishmael Reed.

Augsburg Fortress: From "It's Up to You" from *Straight from the Heart* by Jesse Jackson. Copyright © 1987 by Jesse Jackson.

Bantam Books, a division of Bantam Doubleday Dell Publishing Group, Inc.: From *Yeager: An Autobiography* by General Chuck Yeager and Leo Janos. Copyright © 1985 by Yeager, Inc.

Beacon Press: From *Thousand Pieces of Gold* by Ruthanne Lum McCunn. Copyright © 1981 by Ruthanne Lum McCunn.

BOA Editions, Ltd., 92 Park Ave., Brockport, NY 14420: "the thirty eighth year" (Retitled: "An Ordinary Woman") from *good woman: poems and a memoir 1969–1980* by Lucille Clifton. Copyright © 1987 by Lucille Clifton.

Georges Borchardt, Inc.: From "Introduction" by John Lahr from *Baby, That Was Rock and Roll* by Robert Palmer. Copyright © 1978 by John Lahr. From "On Rewriting" by Richard Selzer. Copyright © 1979 by Richard Selzer. First appeared in *The New York Times.*

The Boston Globe: From "Lax regulation, inadequate laws promote insider-lending abuse" by Mitchell Zuckoff from *The Boston Globe,* vol. 240, no. 68, September 6, 1991. Copyright © 1991 by *The Boston Globe.*

Brandt & Brandt Literary Agency, Inc.: From "You Are Now Entering the Human Heart" by Janet Frame from *The New Yorker.* Copyright © 1969 by The New Yorker Magazine, Inc. From "The Land and the Water" from *The Wind Shifting West* by Shirley Ann Grau. Copyright © 1973 by Shirley Ann Grau.

Clarion Books, an imprint of Houghton Mifflin Company: From *From Top Hats to Baseball Caps, From Bustles to Blue Jeans* by Lila Perl. Text copyright © 1990 by Lila Perl. All rights reserved.

Don Congdon Associates, Inc.: From "The Toynbee Convector" from *The Toynbee Convector* by Ray Bradbury. Copyright © 1988 by Ray Bradbury.

The Crossroad/Continuum Publishing Group: From "The Sixth Sally" from *The Cyberiad: Fables for the Cybernetic Age* by Stanislaw Lem, translated from the Polish by Michael Kandel. Copyright © 1974 by The Seabury Press, Inc.

The Crown Publishing Group: From *Life, The Universe and Everything* by Douglas Adams. Copyright © 1982 by Douglas Adams.

Darhansoff & Verrill Agency: From "The World in Its Extreme" by William Langewiesche from *The Atlantic,* vol. 268, no. 5, November 1991. Copyright © by William Langewiesche.

Delacorte Press/Seymour Lawrence, a division of Bantam Doubleday Dell Publishing Group, Inc.: From "Tom Edison's Shaggy Dog" from *Welcome to the Monkey House* by Kurt Vonnegut, Jr. Copyright © 1953 by Kurt Vonnegut, Jr. Originally published in *Colliers.*

Doubleday, a division of Bantam Doubleday Dell Publishing Group, Inc.: From "Dogs that have known me" from *Please don't eat the daisies* by Jean Kerr. Copyright © 1957 by Jean Kerr. "Once Is Not Enough" from *Magic in the Movies: The Story of Special Effects* by Jane O'Connor and Katy Hall. Copyright © 1980 by Jane O'Connor. From "Animal Senses" from *The Living World* by Tony Seddon and Jill Bailey. Copyright © 1986 by BLA Publishing, Ltd.

Ebony Magazine: From "Black, Blue and Gray: The Other Civil War" from *Ebony*, vol. XLVI, no. 4, February 1991. Copyright © 1991 by Johnson Publishing Company, Inc.

Anita Endrezze: "Sunset at Twin Lake" by Anita Endrezze from *Harper's Anthology of 20th Century Native American Poetry*, edited by Duane Niatum.

Farrar, Straus and Giroux, Inc.: From *The Magic Barrel* by Bernard Malamud. Copyright © 1954, 1958 and copyright renewed © 1986 by Bernard Malamud.

The Feminist Press: From "To Da-Duh in Memoriam" from *Reena and Other Stories* by Paule Marshall. Copyright © 1983 by The Feminist Press at The City University of New York.

The Georgia Review: "The Gift" by Louis Dollarhide. Copyright © 1969 by The University of Georgia. First appeared in *The Georgia Review.*

Gibbs Smith Publisher: From "A Flight of Geese" from *The Girl from Cardigan* by Leslie Norris. Copyright © 1988 by Leslie Norris.

Grove Press, Inc.: From "Rhinoceros" from *Rhinoceros and Other Plays* by Eugéne Ionesco, translated by Derek Prouse. Copyright © 1960 by John Calder (Publishers) Ltd.

Harcourt Brace Jovanovich, Inc.: From "The Life You Save May Be Your Own" from *A Good Man Is Hard to Find and Other Stories* by Flannery O'Connor. Copyright 1953 by Flannery O'Connor; copyright renewed © 1981 by Regina O'Connor. From "The Jilting of Granny Weatherall" from *The Flowering Judas and Other Stories* by Katherine Anne Porter. Copyright 1930 and renewed © 1958 by Katherine Anne Porter.

Harmony Books, a Division of Crown Publishers, Inc.: From *Labyrinth: Solving the Riddle of the Maze* by Adrian Fisher & Georg Gerster. Text copyright © 1990 by Adrian Fisher. Compilation copyright © 1990 by Adrian Fisher and Georg Gerster.

HarperCollins Publishers: From *Pilgrim at Tinker Creek* by Annie Dillard. Copyright © 1974 by Annie Dillard. From *Dust Tracks on a Road* by Zora Neale Hurston. Copyright 1942 by Zora Neale Hurston, renewed copyright © 1970 by John C. Hurston. From *Jonah's Gourd Vine* by Zora Neale Hurston. Copyright 1934 by Zora Neale Hurston; copyright renewed © 1962 by John C. Hurston. From "Mirror" from *The Collected Poems of Sylvia Plath*, edited by Ted Hughes. Copyright © 1963 by Ted Hughes. From *Seven Arrows* by Hyemeyohsts Storm. Copyright © 1972 by Hyemeyohsts Storm. From *American Hunger* by Richard Wright. Copyright 1944 by Richard Wright; copyright renewed © 1977 by Ellen Wright.

Harvard University Press and the Trustees of Amherst College: From "A Narrow Fellow in the Grass" from *The Poems of Emily Dickinson*, edited by Thomas H. Johnson. Copyright 1951, © 1955, 1979, 1983 by the President and Fellows of Harvard College. Published by the Belknap Press of Harvard University Press, Cambridge, MA.

Hendrick-Long Publishing Company: From *Dinosaur Days in Texas* by Tom and Jane D. Allen with Savannah Waring Walker. Copyright © 1989 by Hendrick-Long Publishing Company, Dallas, TX.

Hill and Wang, a division of Farrar, Straus and Giroux, Inc.: From *I Wonder As I Wander* by Langston Hughes. Copyright © 1956 by Langston Hughes. From *What's That Pig Outdoors? A Memoir of Deafness* by Henry Kisor. Copyright © 1990 by Henry Kisor.

Henry Holt and Company, Inc.: From *A Yellow Raft in Blue Water* by Michael Dorris. Copyright © by Michael Dorris.

The Horn Book, Inc., 14 Beacon St., Boston, MA 02108: "Why I Am a Writer" by Pat Mora from *The Horn Book Magazine*, vol LXVI, no. 4, July/August 1990, pp. 436–437.

Alton Hornsby, Jr.: From *The Black Almanac* by Alton Hornsby. Copyright © 1972 by Alton Hornsby.

Houghton Mifflin Company: From *Tough Trip Through Paradise* by Andrew García. Copyright © 1967 by the Rock Foundation.

Congressman Andy Jacobs, Jr.: "Replace 'The Star Spangled Banner'" by Andy Jacobs, Jr. from *USA Today*, August 1, 1990, p. 10A. Copyright © 1990 by Andy Jacobs, Jr.

Johnson Publishing Company, Inc.: From "Marigolds" by Eugenia Collier from *Negro Digest*, November 1969. Copyright © 1969 by Johnson Publishing Company, Inc.

Henry J. Kaiser Family Foundation: Quotation by Henry J. Kaiser.

Knight-Ridder Tribune News: From "Car-Buying: The Compleat Guide" by Dave Barry from *The Washington Post*, January 21, 1990. Copyright © 1990 by Dave Barry.

Alfred A. Knopf, Inc.: From pp. 26–28 from *Running Tide* by Joan Benoit. Copyright © 1987 by Joan Benoit Samuelson. From *Alistair Cooke's America* by Alistair Cooke. Copyright © 1973 by Alistair Cooke. From "The Negro Speaks of Rivers" from *Selected Poems of Langston Hughes*. Copyright 1926 by Alfred A. Knopf, Inc.; copyright renewed 1954 by Langston Hughes. "Ex-Basketball Player" from *The Carpentered Hen and Other Tame Creatures* by John Updike. Copyright © 1982 by John Updike. From "Men at War: An Interview with Shelby Foote" from *The Civil War: An Illustrated History* by Geoffrey C. Ward. Copyright © 1990 by American Documentaries, Inc.

James Kotsilibas-Davis: From "Sands of Time" by James Kotsilibas-Davis from *Travel-Holiday*, January 1990, pp. 47–48. Copyright © 1990 by James Kotsilibas-Davis.

Little, Brown and Company, Inc.: From *Blue Highways: A Journey into America* by William Least Heat Moon. Copyright © 1982 by William Least Heat Moon.

Harold Matson Company, Inc.: From *All Creatures Great and Small* by Daniel Mannix. Copyright © 1963 by Daniel P. Mannix.

McGraw-Hill, Inc.: From "The Frontier Kitchen of the Plains" from *Nation of Nations: A Narrative History of the American Republic* by James West Davidson, William E. Gienapp, Christine Leigh Heyrman, Mark H. Lytle, and Michael B. Stoff. Copyright © 1990 by McGraw-Hill, Inc.

MD Magazine: From a note by Catherine Drinker Bowen from *MD*, July 1981. Copyright © 1981 by MD Magazine.

Morrow Junior Books, a division of William Morrow & Company, Inc.: From *Dogs: All About Them* by Alvin and Virginia Silverstein. Copyright © 1986 by Alvin and Virginia Silverstein.

National Geographic Society: From "Whatzat? An Odd Bird With a Cow's Stomach" from "Geographica" from *National Geographic*, vol. 178, no. 1, July 1990. Copyright © 1990 by National Geographic Society.

John Neary and Life Magazine: From "Eliot Porter" from *Life*, February 1991, vol. 14, no. 2. Copyright © 1991 by John Neary.

New Directions Publishing Corporation: "The Great Figure" from *Collected Poems, Volume I, 1909–1939* by William Carlos Williams. Copyright 1938 by New Directions Publishing Corporation.

New Jersey Monthly: "A Sit-Down Tour" by Matt Tomlinson from *New Jersey Monthly*, September 1991. Copyright © 1991 by New Jersey Monthly.

The New York Review of Books: From "In Sorrow's Kitchen" by Zora Neale Hurston from *The New York Review of Books*, vol. XXV, no. 20, December 21, 1978. Copyright © 1978 by Nyrev, Inc.

The New York Times Company: Quote by Doris Lessing from *The New York Times*, April 22, 1984. Copyright © 1984 by The New York Times Company. From "On rewriting" by Richard Selzer from *The New York Times*, September 28, 1979. Copyright © 1979 by The New York Times Company. From a review of *Their Eyes Were Watching God* by Zora Neale Hurston from "Books of the Times" by Ralph Thompson from *The New York Times*, October 6, 1937. Copyright 1937 by The New York Times Company. From "Típica Sound of Cuba" by Peter Watrous from *The New York Times*, February 28, 1991. Copyright © 1991 by The New York Times Company.

The New Yorker Magazine, Inc.: From "Notes and Comment" from "The Talk of the Town" from *The New Yorker*, July 15, 1991. Copyright © 1991 by The New Yorker Magazine, Inc. From "Blue Spruce" by David Long from *The New Yorker*, November 12, 1990. Copyright © 1990 by David Long.

Newsweek, Inc.: From "Dances with Garbage" by Mary Hager, Bill Harlan, Michael Mason, and Andrew Murr from *Newsweek*, vol. CXVII, no. 17, p. 36, April 29, 1991. Copyright © 1991 by Newsweek, Inc. All rights reserved. From "The Last Days of Eden" by Spencer Reiss from *Newsweek*, vol. CXVI, no. 23, p. 48, December 3, 1990. Copyright © 1990 by Newsweek, Inc. All rights reserved.

W. W. Norton & Company, Inc.: From "The Making of a Scientist" from *"What do YOU Care What Other People Think?": Further Adventures of a Curious Character* by Richard P. Feynman, as told to Ralph Leighton. Copyright © 1988 by Gweneth Feynman and Ralph Leighton.

Pantheon Books, a division of Random House, Inc.: From "The Moustache" from *Eight Plus One* by Robert Cormier. Copyright © 1975 by Robert Cormier.

Publishers Weekly: Quote by Gloria Steinem from *Publishers Weekly*, August 12, 1983. Copyright © 1983 by Publishers Weekly.

The Putnam Publishing Group: From "Rules of the Game" from *The Joy Luck Club* by Amy Tan. Copyright © 1989 by Amy Tan. From the back cover from *Riding the Iron Rooster: By Train Through China* by Paul Theroux. Copyright © 1988 by Cape Cod Scriveners Co.

The Rainbow Coalition: From a speech given by Jesse Jackson at a Teen Conference in Atlanta, Georgia, in 1978 from *Jesse Jackson: Still Fighting for the Dream* by Brenda Wilkinson. Copyright © 1978 by Jesse Jackson.

Random House, Inc.: From "Graduation" from *I Know Why the Caged Bird Sings* by Maya Angelou. Copyright © 1969 by Maya Angelou. From "Making Time Portable" from *The Discoverers* by Daniel Boorstin. Copyright © 1983 by Daniel Boorstin. From *A Raisin in the Sun* by Lorraine Hansberry. Copyright © 1958 by Robert Nemiroff, as an unpublished work. Copyright © 1959, 1966, 1984 by Robert Nemiroff. From "New African" from *Sarah Phillips* by Andrea Lee. Copyright © 1983 by Andrea Lee. From "The Wheelbarraow" from *Selected Stories* by V.S. Pritchett. Copyright © 1978 by V. S. Pritchett.

St. Martin's Press, Inc.: "Wheelchair Hell: A Look at Campus Accessibility" from *The Great American Bologna Festival and other student essays* by Elizabeth Rankin. Copyright © 1991 by St. Martin's Press, Inc.

Michael Schumacher: From "Jay McInerney" by Michael Schumacher. Copyright © 1984 by Michael Schumacher.

Charles Scribner's Sons, an imprint of Macmillan Publishing Company: From "In Another Country" from *Men Without Women* by Ernest Hemingway. Copyright 1927 by Charles Scribner's Sons; copyright renewed © 1955 by Ernest Hemingway. From "Becoming a Writer" from *Kaffir Boy in America: An Encounter with Apartheid* by Mark Mathabane. Copyright © 1989 by Mark Mathabane.

Simon & Schuster, Inc.: From "Visual Displays" from *The Birder's Handbook* by Paul R. Ehrlich, David S. Dobkin, and Darryl Wheye. Copyright © 1988 by Paul R. Ehrlich, David S. Dobkin, and Darryl Wheye. From "Insert Flap 'A' and Throw Away" from *The Most of S. J. Perelman* by S. J. Perelman. Copyright © 1930, 1931, 1932, 1933, 1935, 1936, 1953, 1955, 1956, 1958 by S. J. Perelman; copyright renewed © 1986 by Adam and Abby Perelman.

Smithsonian Institution: "The engaging habits of chameleons suggest mirth more than menace" (Retitled: "Chameleon Comedians") by James Martin from *Smithsonian,* Vol. 21, No. 3, June 1990. Copyright © 1990 by Smithsonian Institution.

The Society of Authors as representative of the Literary Trustees of Walter de la Mare: From "Sam" by Walter de la Mare.

Gary Soto: From "The Jacket" from *Small Faces* by Gary Soto. Copyright © 1986 by Gary Soto.

Mario Suárez: From "Tuscon, Arizona: El Hoyo" by Mario Súárez from *Aztlán: An Anthology of Mexican American Literature,* edited by Luis Valdez and Stan Steiner. Published by Alfred A. Knopf, Inc., 1972.

Sabine Ulibarrí: From "My Wonder Horse" from *Tierra Amarilla: Stories of New Mexico* by Sabine Ulibarrí. Copyright © 1971 by The University of New Mexico Press.

Universe Publishing: From "An Indian's View of Indian Affairs" by Chief Joseph from *Red & White: Indian Views of the White Man, 1492–1982* by Annett Rosenstiel. Copyright © 1983 by Annette Rosenstiel.

University of Illinois Press: From *Zora Neale Hurston: A Literary Biography* by Robert E. Hemenway. Copyright © 1977 by the Board of Trustees of the University of Illinois.

The University of New Mexico Press: From "The Way to Rainy Mountain" from *The Way to Rainy Mountain* by N. Scott Momaday. Copyright © 1969 by The University of New Mexico Press. Originally published in *The Reporter,* January 26, 1967.

University of Notre Dame Press: From *Barrio Boy* by Ernesto Galarza. Copyright © 1971 by University of Notre Dame Press.

University Press of New England: From "Leisure" from *The Complete Poems of W. H., Davies.* Copyright © 1963 by Jonathan Cape Limited.

USA Today: "Wyoming dinosaur find may be a fossil first" by Linda Kanamine from *USA Today,* September 26, 1991, p. 3A. Copyright © 1991 by *USA Today.*

Viking Penguin, a division of Penguin Books USA Inc.: From "Pencils" from *Reading The Numbers* by Mary Blocksma. Copyright © 1989 by Mary Blocksma. From *The Floating World* by Cynthia Kadohata. Copyright © 1989 by Cynthia Kadohata. From "From Japlish to Franglais" from *The Story of English* by Robert McCrum, William Cran, and Robert MacNeil. Copyright © 1986 by Robert McCrum, William Cran, and Robert MacNeil. "One Perfect Rose" from *The Portable Dorothy Parker,* Introduction by Brendan Gill. Copyright 1928 and copyright renewed © 1956 by Dorothy Parker. From pp. 63–64 (selection by Mike Montgomery) from *It Was a Dark and Stormy Night: The Best (?) from the Bulwer-Lytton Contest,* edited by Scott Rice. Copyright © 1984 by Scott Rice. From "Flight" from *The*

Long Valley by John Steinbeck. Copyright 1938 and copyright renewed © 1966 by John Steinbeck. From *The Red Pony* by John Steinbeck. Copyright 1933, 1937, 1938 and copyright renewed © 1961, 1965, 1966 by John Steinbeck. From an Interview with E. B. White from *Writers at Work: The Paris Review Interviews,* Eighth Series, edited by George Plimpton, Introduction by Joyce Carol Oates.

Wallace Literary Agency, Inc.: From "On the Mall" from *The White Album* by Joan Didion. Copyright © 1979 by Joan Didion.

Fred Ward: From "The Timeless Mystique of Emeralds" by Fred Ward from *National Geographic,* July 1990. Copyright © 1990 by Fred Ward.

Webster's New World Dictionaries, a Division of Simon & Schuster, New York: From the entry "obscure" from *Webster's New World Dictionary, Third College Edition.* Copyright © 1988 by Simon & Schuster, Inc.

Vicki Williams: From "Keep 'The Star Spangled Banner'" by Vicki Williams from *USA Today,* August 1, 1990, p. 10A. Copyright © 1990 by Vicki Williams.

The H. W. Wilson Company: Entries from "Moisturizers" through "Moldings (Architecture)" from *Readers' Guide to Periodical Literature,* 1990. Copyright © 1990, 1991 by The H. W. Wilson Company.

Workman Publishing Company, Inc.: From "Three Great Homemade Props" from "Get Ready" from *Be A Clown!* by Turk Pipkin. Copyright © 1989 by Turk Pipkin.

Photo Credits

Abbreviations used: (t) top, (c) center, (b) bottom, (l) left, (r) right.

COVER: Ralph J. Brunke Photograph.

TABLE OF CONTENTS: Page vi, Murray & Associates, Inc./The Stock Market; vii, Schomburg Center for Research in Black Culture. The New York Public Library. Astor, Lenox & Tilden Foundations/Photographed by Andrew J. Figueroa.; viii, Kay Chernush/The Image Bank; ix, UPI/ Bettmann; x, The Stock Market; xi, © Robert Foothorap; xii(t), UPI/Bettmann; xii(c), FPG International; xii(b), UPI/Bettmann; xiii, Culver Pictures, Inc.; xiv, M. Richards/PhotoEdit; xv, David R. Frazier Photolibrary; xvii, Charlene Smith/ProFiles West; xviii, HRW Photo by Michelle Bridwell; xix(l), The Bettmann Archive; xx, HRW Photo by Lisa Davis; xxii(t), Paul J. Sutton/Duomo; xxii(b), Mel Gigiacomo/The Image Bank; xxiv, HRW Photo by Joe Jaworski; xxv, Photograph from "Native America Portraits" by Nancy Hathaway and Kurt Koegler, copyright © 1990. Published by Chronicle Books. xxvi, R.R. Production/SuperStock; xxvii, Folkart Carving by Margarito Melchor/Photograph by Vicki Ragan; xxviii, Carol Friedman, Courtesy Sony Classical Records; xxix, Jerry Jacka Photography; xxx(l), Stephane Compoint/ Sygma; xxx(c), S. Franklin/Mangum; xxx(r), Louis Gubb/JB Pictures; xxxii, Courtesy Will Rogers Memorial Archives; xxxiii(t), xxxiii(b), Culver Pictures, Inc.; xxxiv(t), Susan Gaetz; xxxiv(b), HRW Photo by Michael Lyon; xxxv, Uniphoto Picture Agency; xxxvii, HRW Photo by Michael Lyon; xxxviii, Melanie Carr/Zephyr Pictures; xxxix, Steve Dunwell/The Image Bank.

CHAPTER 0: Page 2, © 1989, Comstock,Inc.; 4, Uniphoto Picture Agency; 5, Peter Beck/The Stock Market; 6, R.R. Production/SuperStock; 7, Susan Gaetz; 11, Joseph Drivas/The Image Bank.

CHAPTER 1: Page 16, Photo Courtesy of Pat Mora; 24(l), Melanie Carr/Zephyr Pictures; 24(r), Skjold; 25, HRW Photo by Lisa Davis; 28(l), Junio Owaki/The Stock Market; 28(r), J. Lambert-Malson/The Image Bank; 29(l), Sophia Smith Collection, Smith College Library/HRW Photo Research Library; 29(c), The Bettmann Archive; 29(cr), HRW Photo Research Library/UPI/ Bettmann Newsphotos; 29(r), Schomburg Center for Research in Black Culture. The New York Public Library. Astor, Lenox & Tilden Foundations/Photographed by Andrew J. Figueroa ; 31, David Brownell/The Image Bank; 32, David Barnes/The Stock Market; 35, 36, © Art Wolfe; 40(l), Ted Kaufman/The Stock Market; 40(r), Murray & Associates, Inc./The Stock Market; 42, DiMaggio/Kalish/The Stock Market; 44(tl), UPI/ Bettmann; 44(tr), AFP/Archive Photos; 44(bl), 44(br), Everett Collection, Inc.; 46, HRW Photo by Michael Lyon; 51(t), David deLossy/The Image Bank; 51(b), Roy Morsch/The Stock Market.

CHAPTER 2: Page 58(t), 58(b), 59, 60, David Madison/Duomo; 63, Skjold; 65, Michael Putland /© Retna Ltd.; 66, The Bettmann Archive; 68, HRW Photo by Lisa Davis; 69, Jean-Francois Podevin/The Image Bank; 70(t), Phil McCarten/ PhotoEdit; 70(b), The Stock Market; 71(l), Sobel/ Klonsky/The Image Bank; 71(br), John Kelly/The Image Bank; 71(inset), Phil Lauro/ProFiles West; 74, Photographed by Jim Fowler; 76, Schomburg Center for Research in Black Culture. The New York Public Library. Astor, Lenox & Tilden Foundations/Photographed by Andrew J. Figueroa.; 77(t), Warner Bros./SuperStock; 77(b), David W. Hamilton/The Image Bank; 78, Jeff Gnass/The Stock Market; 79, HRW Photo by Lisa Davis; 81, Photographed By: © 1991, Lisa Ebright; 87(l), Alan Oddie/PhotoEdit; 87(r), Lynne M. Stone/The Image Bank; 88(l), © Uniphoto; 88(tr), Norbert Wu/AllStock; 88(br), Jeffrey L. Rotman/Peter Arnold, Inc.; 93(l), Myrleen Ferguson/PhotoEdit; 93(c), Momatiuk/Eastcott/Woodfin Camp; 93(r), John A. Sawyer/ProFiles West; 94, Tom Tracy/ The Stock Market.

CHAPTER 3: Page 98, Tony Freeman/Photo-Edit; 99(t), A.M. Rosario/The Image Bank; 99(b), SuperStock; 100(t), Palmer/Kane Inc./The Stock Market; 100(b), Gabe Palmer/The Stock Market; 101, Kay Chernush/The Image Bank; 102, Morton Kravitz/SuperStock; 104, (c)Lightscapes/The Stock Market; 105, Schomburg Center for Research in Black Culture. The New York Public Library. Astor, Lenox & Tilden Foundations/Photographed by Andrew J. Figueroa; 107, David Young-Wolff/PhotoEdit; 108, Michael Yada/ Zephyr Pictures; 109, Tony Freeman/PhotoEdit; 111, HRW Photo by Michael Lyon; 112, Joan Neary; 113, Stuart D. Strahl/WCI - New York Zoological Society; 114, HRW Photo by Michael Lyon; 115, Wide World Photos; 118, The Bettmann Archive; 119, Paul Conklin/PhotoEdit; 120, Claudia Parks ©/The Stock Market; 123(l), Kewn Akers/Zephyr Pictures; 123(r), P.R. Production/ SuperStock.

CHAPTER 4: Page 126, US Army Installation, Carlisle Barracks, PA/Photographed by Leib Image Archives; 127, Cook Collection/The Valentine Museum, Richmond, Virginia; 128, Culver Pictures, Inc.; 131(t), Bob Daemmrich Photography; 131(c), Tony Freeman/PhotoEdit; 131(b), Allen Russell/ProFiles West; 133, Richard Hutchings/InfoEdit; 134(tl), G. Outerbridge/Super-Stock; 134(tr), © 1990 Tony Freeman/PhotoEdit; 134(bl), Richard Hutchings/Info Edit; 134(br), A. Scapinl/SuperStock; 136(l), Wiley/Wales/ProFiles West; 136(r), Wiley/Wales/ProFiles West; 137, Glod Collection/SuperStock; 139, Sy Seidman/ HRW Photo Library; 146, HRW Photo by Lisa Davis; 153, UPI/Bettmann; 155, Miller Collection/

SuperStock; 156(l), ProFiles West; 156(r), Nawrocki Stock Photo.

CHAPTER 5: Page 162, Costa Manos/Magnum; 164(l), Orion/Shooting Star; 164(tr), Shooting Star; 164(br), Shooting Star; 165, HRW Photo by Lisa Davis; 168(l), Allen Russell/ProFiles West; 168(r), Michael J. Howell/ProFiles West; 173, Stuart N. Dee/The Image Bank; 175, R. Llewellyn/SuperStock; 183, 185, 186, Del Valle High School, Del Valle, Texas/HRW Photo by Michelle Bridwell; 192, Raymond and Tirza Martin High School, Laredo, TX/HRW Photo by Michelle Bridwell; 193, Melanie Carr/Zephyr Pictures; 194, UPI/Bettmann Newsphotos; 196, Nawrocki Stock Photo; 200, The Stock Market; 202(l), HRW Photo Research Library; 202(tc), Everett Collection Inc.; 202(bc), Hackett/Archive Photos; 202(r), Frederick Hill Meserve, Litt D./HRW Photo Research Library.

CHAPTER 6: Page 208, © Robert Foothorap; 211(l), 211(r), The Bettmann Archive; 212(l), Doc Pele/Stills/Retna Ltd.,; 212(c), SuperStock; 212(r), D. Strohmeyer/Allsport; 215(t), Richard Steedman/The Stock Market; 215(b), Mauritius/SuperStock; 217(l), 217(r), The Bettmann Archive; 219, Farrar, Straus & Girous, Inc./© John H. White; 221, Jane Brown/Camela Press/Globe Photos; 223(t), Peter Vadnai/The Stock Market; 223(c), 223(cr), Michael Kevin Daly/The Stock Market; 223(b), R. Llewellyn/SuperStock; 225, The Bettmann Archive; 230, Culver Pictures, Inc.; 235, Anthony Edgeworth/The Stock Market; 236(l), P. Barry Levy/ProFiles West; 236(r), Myrleen Ferguson/PhotoEdit; 239(t), Runk/Schoenberger/Grant Heilman Photography; 239(c), 239(b), Custom Medical Stock Photo.

CHAPTER 7: Page 242, UPI/Bettmann; 243(tl), FPG International; 243(c), 243(tr), 243(bl),243(br), UPI/Bettmann; 244, Gary Gershoff/Retna Ltd; 245, Courtesy of Charles Scribner's Sons/MacMillian Publishing Company; 247, Richard Hutchings/InfoEdit; 248, P. Rivera/SuperStock; 253(l), 253(r), HRW Photo by Michelle Bridwell; 254, Zig Leszczynski/Animals, Animals; 259(l), 259(r), Sears & Roebuck Catalogue, 1897 Reprint/HRW Photo By Michelle Bridwell; 261, Alan Oddie/PhotoEdit; 264(l), C. Dallas/SuperStock; 264(r), Chris Jones/The Stock Market; 269, Bob Daemmrich Photography; 271, Everett Collection.

CHAPTER 8: Page 279, Culver Pictures, Inc.; 285(l), H. Alexander/SuperStock; 285(r), Freda Leinwand; 287(r), Joe Sohn/Chronosohn/The Stock Market; 287(l), Barbara Kirk/The Stock Market; 289(l), P. Barry Levy/ProFiles West; 289(cl), Tony Freeman/PhotoEdit; 289(cr), Allen Russell/ProFiles West; 289(r), Tony Freeman/PhotoEdit; 295, George Rose/Gamma Liaison Network; 297, R. King/SuperStock; 299(l), 299(r), HRW Photo by Lisa Davis; 304, The Stock Market; 308, Anderson High School/HRW Photo By Michelle Bridwell; 309, HRW Photo by Lisa Davis; 310, Mary Kate Denny/PhotoEdit; 312, Thomas Craig/FPG International.

CHAPTER 9: Page 325(l), © Melanie Carr/Zephyr Pictures; 325(r), HRW Photo by Michelle Bridwell; 326, Anderson High School, Austin, TX/HRW photo by Michelle Bridwell; 328(l), Rainer Drexel/Bildererg/The Stock Market; 328(r), Bill Strode/Woodfin Camp; 336, HRW Photo by Michael Lyon; 337, David R. Frazier Photolibrary; 339, © Mary Kate Denny/PhotoEdit; 341, PhotoEdit; 343(l), 343(r), HRW Photo By Michael Lyon; 345, Richard Hutchings/Info Edit; 351, Steve Dunwell/The Image Bank; 352, United High School, Laredo, TX/HRW Photo by Michelle Bridwell; 355, 356, The Stock Market; 357, Jim Wright/Zephyr Pictures.

CHAPTER 10: Page 362, The Bettmann Archive; 365, The Bettmann Archive; 370, UPI/Bettmann Newsphotos; 377, The Stock Market; 379, Courtesy of St. Mary's College; 382, PhotoEdit; 385, David R. Frazier Photolibrary; 387, T. Rosenthal/SuperStock; 389(t), HRW Photo By Lisa Davis; 389(b), © Todd Powell/ProFiles West; 396(l), Archive Photos; 396(r), Everett Collection; 398, Schuster/SuperStock; 400, Reprinted by permission of The Putnam Publishing Group from RIDING THE IRON ROOSTER by Paul Theroux Copyright ©1988 by Cape Cod Scriveners Company.

CHAPTER 11: Page 410, James Weldon Johnson Collection/Yale Collection of American Literature, Beinecke Rare Book & Manuscript Library, Yale University/Courtesy of the Estate of Carl Van Vechten, Joseph Solomon, Executor; 417, David R. Frazier Photolibray; 421, Photographed by Eric Beggs; 423, H. Kanus/SuperStock; 425, The Stock Market; 426(l), James Weldon Johnson Collection/Yale Collection of American Literature, Beinecke Rare Book & Manuscript Library, Yale University/Courtesy of the Estate of Carl Van Vechten, Joseph Solomon, Executor; 426(c), UPI/Bettmann; 426(r), The Bettmann Archive; 427, © George Gerster/© 1989 Comstock, Inc.; 436(l), David R. Frazier Photolibrary; 436(r), Alan Oddie/PhotoEdit; 438, Archive Photos; 451, © Spencer Grant/New England Stock Photo; 453 (l), 453(r), Photographed by Eric Beggs; 455(t), David Young-Wolff/PhotoEdit; 455(bl), Deborah Davis/PhotoEdit; 455(br), R. Llewellyn/SuperStock; 458, T. Algire/SuperStock; 459, UPI/Bettmann.

CHAPTER 12: Page 463, Charlene Smith/ProFiles West; 477(l), 477(r), ©Mavournea Hay/Michelle Bridwell Photography.

CHAPTER 13: Page 482, HRW Photo By Michelle Bridwell.

CHAPTER 14: Page 504, James Newberry; 509, Archive Photos; 511(l), HRW Photo by Stan Byers; 511(r), Keystone View Co./Courtesy Museum of New Mexico; 512, HRW Photo by Lisa Davis; 514(l), David Madison/Bruce Coleman; 514(r), Archive Photos; 517(l), Bettmann Archive; 517(c), FPG International; 517(r), Culver Pictures; 520(l), The Bettmann Archive.

CHAPTER 15: Page 528, Patrick Aventturier/Gamma Liaison; 530, John White/HRW Photo Research Library; 533, Paul Steel/The Stock Market; 534, Nathan Benn/Woodfin Camp Associates; 539, Paul S. Howell/Gamma Liaison.

CHAPTER 16: Page 541, Hillel Burger/Peabody Museum of Archaeology and Ethnology; 546, Camermann International, Ltd; 549, HRW Photo by Lisa Davis.

CHAPTER 17: Page 571, Dan Bosler/Tony Stone Worldwide/Chicago Ltd.; 573(tl), Mel Gigiacomo/The Image Bank; 573(tr), Paul J. Sutton/Duomo; 573(bl), Harry J. Landon/Shooting Star; 573(br), Archive Photos; 578, James Valentine.

CHAPTER 18: Page 583, The Bettmann Archive; 597, Jon Reis/The Stock Market; 599, Phil Schofield/AllStock.

CHAPTER 19: Page 606(l), 606(r), © B. Lyon / Valan Photos; 606(c), © Albert Kuhnigk/Valan Photos; 610, HRW Photo By Joe Jaworski; 619, Copyright © 1992 by Harcourt Brace Jovanovich, Publishers. Reprinted under license by Holt, Rinehart and Winston Inc.; 623(c), Copyright 1991, Comstock; 623(bl), Robbi Newman/The Image Bank; 623(bc), © Franklin Viola/Copyright 1991, Comstock; 623(br), Martha Stradiotto/The Image Bank; 623(tl), Copr. William W. Bacon, III/Allstock; 623(tr), © Kelvin Aitken/Peter Arnold, Inc.

CHAPTER 20: Page 630(tc), 630(tr), 630(bc), Congdon Egg Farm, Lockhart, Texas/Lisa Davis; 630(tl), 630(br), J.C. Allen & Son, Inc.; 633, 633(inset), Colha Pre Classic Project/Courtesy of Dr. Tom Hester, Texas Archeological Research Laboratory. The University of Texas at Austin; 636(l), © Lee Watson/Unicorn Stock Photos; 636(r), Jack S. Grove/PhotoEdit; 639(t), 639(b), Photograph from "Native America Portraits" by Nancy Hathaway and Kurt Koegler, Copyright © 1990. Published by Chronicle Books.

CHAPTER 21: Page 663, Wide World Photos; 669(t), Photographs by Zheng Zhensun copyright © 1991/Copyright © 1991 Byron Preiss Visual Publications, Inc. & New China Pictures Company/All rights Reserved. Published by Scholastic Inc.

CHAPTER 22: Page 678, Charles L. Blockson/Afro American Collection, Sullivan Hall, Temple University, Philadelphia, PA; 682(l), Folkart Carving by Adrian Xuana/Photograph by Vicki Ragan; 682(c), Folkart Carving by Ventura Fabian/Photograph by Vicki Ragan; 682(r), Folkart Carving by Margarito Melchor/Photograph by Vicki Ragan; 685, HRW Photo by Michelle Bridwell.

CHAPTER 23: Page 705(t), 705(b), Courtesy of Martin Luther King Civil Rights Memorial /Photograph by Paul Roberton.; 710, Everett Collection, Inc.

CHAPTER 24: Page 724, Carol Friedman, Courtesy Sony Classical Records; 728, Terence Meaden/Sipa Press; 730, Colorado Historical Society; 759(l), 759(c), 759(r), African American Cultural Center, Los Angeles, CA.

CHAPTER 25: Page 766(t), 766 (b), Jerry Jacka Photography; 769, © Bob Daemmrich Photography; 777, A. Hyde Jr. /SuperStock.

CHAPTER 26: Page 784(l), Stephane Compoint/Sygma.784(c), S. Franklin/Magnum; 784(r), Louise Gubb/JB Pictures; 787, Ron Watts/Westlight.

CHAPTER 27: Page 800(l), 800 (r), Gene Stein/Westlight; 802(r), Paul J. Sutton/Duomo; 802(l), Daniel R. Westergren/© National Geographic Society; 806(l), 806(c), 806(r), Paul Rocheleau Photographer; 810, Michael Newman/PhotoEdit.

CHAPTER 28: Page 824, Seaver Center for Western History Research, Natural History Museum of Los Angeles County; 829, © Jason Laure, 1980.

CHAPTER 29: Page 850, Copyright © Christian Vioujard/Gamma Liaison.

CHAPTER 30: Page 869, Courtesy Will Rogers Memorial Archives; 871(l), HRW Photo Research Library; 871(r), Culver Pictures, Inc.; 874, R. Llewellyn/SuperStock; 882, Kolvoord/TexaStock; 895, Mark Hess/The Image Bank.

CHAPTER 31: Page 908(c), 908(r), Culver Pictures, Inc.; 914, Custom Medical Stock Photo; 926, Larry Dale Gordon/The Image Bank.

ILLUSTRATION CREDITS

Linda Blackwell—154, 227, 320, 323, 334, 367, 384, 441, 449, 534; Keith Bowden—475; Stephen Brayfield—xix, 84, 281, 520, 528, 530, 544, 834; Neesa Becker—375, 394; Rondi Collette—594, 829, 888; Chris Ellison—177, 178, 180; Richard Erickson—55, 263, 275, 466, 540; Janice Fried—798; Tom Gianni—xxxii, 44, 113, 146, 148, 153, 230, 509, 606, 777, 869, 882; Tom Herzberg—276–277; Mary Jones—315, 316, 470, 487; Linda Kelen—xvii, 25, 191, 464, 468, 494, 500, 846; Susan Kemnitz—145, 155, 156; Rich Lo—xx, 42, 115, 355, 423, 438, 472, 479, 501, 512, 521, 549, 844, 911; Yoshi Miyake—xxiii, 533, 588; Pamela Paulsrud—313, 408; Precision Graphics—471, 535, 825, 926; Doug Schneider—105, 119, 137, 360, 506, 546, 571, 597, 661, 678, 730; Jack Scott—165, 357; Steve Shock—206, 207, 208, 237, 257, 258, 405, 406; Chuck Solway—226; Troy Thomas—160–161, 162, 320–321; Nancy Tucker—483

Acknowledgments

For permission to reprint copyrighted material in the Annotated Teacher's Edition, grateful acknowledgment is made to the following sources:

Alumnae of College of Saint Teresa: Quotation by Flannery O'Connor from "Censer" from *Conversations with Flannery O'Connor*, edited by Rosemary M. Magee. Copyright © 1960 by College of Saint Teresa.

American Association of University Women: From a speech by Rachel Carson for the "American Association of University Women," June 22, 1956. Copyright © 1956 by American Association of University Women.

Carol Brissie on behalf of William K. Zinsser: From *On Writing Well*, Second Edition, p. 71, by William K. Zinsser. Copyright © 1980 by William K. Zinsser.

Curtis Brown Ltd.: From *Reading Over Your Shoulder* by Robert Graves and Alan Hodge. Copyright © 1943 and renewed © 1971 by Robert Graves and Alan Hodge. From "Forward" from *Reeling* by Pauline Kael. Copyright © 1976 by Pauline Kael.

Doubleday, a division of Bantam Doubleday Dell Publishing Group, Inc.: From "Salvation is the Issue" by Toni Cade Bambara and "An Answer to Some Questions on How I Write" by Nikki Giovanni from *Black Women Writers (1950–1980)*, edited by Mari Evans. Copyright © 1983 by Mari Evans. Quotations by Maxine Hong Kingston, Toni Morrison, and Richard Rodriguez from *A World of Ideas II* by Bill Moyers, edited by Andie Tucher Copyright © 1990 by Public Affairs Television, Inc.

Harcourt Brace Jovanovich, Inc.: From *The Modern Researcher*, Fourth Edition by Jacques Barzun and Henry F. Graff. Copyright © 1985 by Harcourt Brace Jovanovich, Inc.

HarperCollins Publishers, Inc.: From *Black Elk: The Secret Ways of a Lakota* by Wallace H. Black Elk and William S. Lyon. Copyright © 1990 by Wallace H. Black Elk and William S. Lyon. From *Word Origins and their Romantic Stories* by Wilfred Funk. Copyright 1950 by Wilfred Funk, Inc. From *The Passionate State of Mind*, no. 266, by Eric Hoffer. Copyright © 1955 by Eric Hoffer and HarperCollins Publishers.

Harvard University Press: From "The Raison d'Etre of Criticism in the Arts" has appeared in this country under the title of "On Criticism in the Arts, Especially Music" in *Music and Criticism: A Symposium*, edited by Richard Frederic French. Copyright 1948 by the Harvard University Press.

Holmes & Meier Publishers, Inc.: From "Diane Johnson," interviewed by Janet Todd from *Women Writers Talking*, edited by Janet Todd (New York: Holmes & Meier, 1983), p. 132. Copyright © 1983 by Holmes & Meier Publishers, Inc.

Henry Holt and Company, Inc.: From *The Public Years* by Bernard M. Baruch. Copyright © 1960 by Bernard M. Baruch. Copyright © 1988 by Renee B. Samstag. Originally published in *Reader's Digest*. From "The Figure a Poem Makes" from *Selected Prose of Robert Frost*, edited by Hyde Cox and Edward Connery Lathem. Copyright 1939, © 1967 by Holt, Rinehart and Winston; copyright 1946 by Robert Frost.

Alfred A. Knopf, Inc.: From "Miss Jewett" from *Not Under Forty* by Willa Cather. Copyright 1936 by Willa Cather. From *Practicing History, Selected Essays* by Barbara A. Tuchman. Copyright 1936, 1937, © 1959, 1962, 1964, 1965, 1966, 1967, 1968, 1971, 1972, 1973, 1974, 1976, 1977, 1979, 1980, 1981 by Alma Tuchman, Lucy T. Eisenberg, and Jessica Tuchman Matthews. Introduction copyright © 1981 by Barbara Tuchman.

Little, Brown and Company: From Dialogues by Alfred North Whitehead. Copyright 1953 by Alfred North Whitehead.

Macmillan Publishing Co., Inc.: From "Elementary Principles of Composition" from *The Elements of Style*, Third Edition by William Strunk Jr. and E. B. White. Copyright © 1979 by Macmillan Publishing Company.

New American Library, a division of Penguin Books USA Inc.: From *The Lively Art of Writing* by Lucile Vaughan Payne. Copyright © 1965 by Follett Publishing Company.

Harold Ober Associates, Inc.: Quotation by F. Scott Fitzgerald from *Beloved Infidel* by Sheila Graham and Gerold Frank. Copyright © 1959 by Sheila Graham and Gerold Frank.

Oxford University Press: From *A Dictionary of Modern English Usage* by H. W. Fowler. Copyright © 1965 by Oxford University Press.

People Weekly: "Hell on Wheels" from the "Up Front" section of *People Weekly*, September 16, 1991, vol. 36, no. 10. Copyright © 1991 by People Weekly.

David Petersen: From "Erasing the Blue Pencil Blues" by David Petersen from *The Writer's Handbook*, edited by Sylvia K. Burack. Copyright © 1988 by David Petersen.

Prentice-Hall: From *The Writer's Work: Guide to Effective Composition* by Dean Memering and Frank O'Hare. Copyright © 1980 by Prentice-Hall, Inc. From *Writing with Style* by John R. Trimble. Copyright © 1975 by Prentice-Hall, Inc.

Random House, Inc.: From *The Dyer's Hand and other essays* by W. H. Auden. Copyright 1948, 1950, 1952, 1953, 1954, © 1956, 1957, 1958, 1960, 1962 by W. H. Auden.

Reader's Digest: Quotation by Bernard Baruch from *Reader's Digest*, March 1948, and in *Bernard Baruch, The Public Years.* Copyright 1948 and copyright renewed © 1960 by Bernard Baruch.

Lady Meriel Richardson: Quotation attributed to Sir Ralph Richardson from *The Texas Observer*, December 18, 1977.

Running Press Book Publishers, 125 S. 22nd Street, Philadelphia, PA: Quotations by Truman Capote, E. L. Doctorow, E. M. Forster, Anatole France, Alfred Kazin, Karl Kraus, George Bernard Shaw, Wallace Stevens, and Robert Stone from *Writers on Writing*, selected and compiled by Jon Winokur. Copyright © 1989, 1990 by Jon Winokur.

Russell & Volkening as agents for the Estate of Jessamyn West: From the Introduction of *The Quaker Reader* by Jessamyn West. Copyright © 1962 by Jessamyn West, renewed © 1990 by Harry McPherson.

Scott, Foresman and Company, a subsidiary of HarperCollins Publishers: From *Style: Ten Lessons in Clarity & Grace* by Joseph M. Williams. Copyright © 1985, 1981 by Scott, Foresman and Company.

Shambhala Publications, 300 Massachusetts Ave., Boston, MA 02115: From "Writing as a Practice" from *Writing Down the Bones, Freeing the Writer Within* by Natalie Goldberg. Copyright © 1986 by Natalie Goldberg.

William Stott: From "Getting It Down" from *Write to the Point* by Bill Stott. Copyright © 1991 by Bill Stott. Published by Columbia University Press.

Swallow Press: Quotation by Marvin Bell from *Finding the Words: Conversations With Writers Who Teach* by Nancy L. Bunge. Copyright © 1985 by Nancy L. Bunge.

Think Magazine: Quotation by Alfred Kazin from *Think,* February 1963. Copyright © 1963 by Think Magazine.

University of Arkansas Press: Quotation by Colleen McElroy from *The Writers Mind: Interview with American Authors,* vol. III by Irv Broughton. Copyright © 1990 by University of Arkansas Press.

University of California Press: From "English at Its Twilight" from *State of the Language,* 1990 Edition, edited by Christopher Ricks and Leonard Michaels. Copyright © 1989 by The Regents of the University of California.

University of Tennessee Press: Quotation by Sherwood Anderson from *Sherwood Anderson: Selected Letters,* edited by Charles E. Modlin. Copyright © 1984 by The University of Tennessee Press/Knoxville.

University of Virginia Press: Quotation by William Faulkner from *Faulkner in the University,* edited by Frederick L. Gwynn and Joseph L. Blotner. Copyright © 1959 by University of Virginia Press.

University Press of Mississippi: From *Conversations with Flannery O'Connor,* edited by Rosemary M. Magee. Copyright © 1987 by University Press of Mississippi.

Van Nostrand Reinhold Company: From *Toward a Psychology of Being,* Second Edition by Abraham H. Maslow. Copyright © 1968 by Litton Educational Publishing Inc.

Viking Penguin, a division of Penguin Books USA Inc.: From "Lillian Hellman" from *Writers at Work: Third Series,* edited by George A. Plimpton. Copyright © 1967 by The Paris Review, Inc.

PHOTO CREDITS *(Annotated Teacher's Edition)*

Abbreviations used: (t) top, (c) center, (b) bottom, (l) left, (r) right.

COVER: Ralph J. Brunke Photography

TABLE OF CONTENTS: Page T6(l) Larry Ford; (tr) Dennis Carlyle Darling; (c) Larry Ford; (br) J. Alexander Newberry.

PROFESSIONAL ESSAYS: Page T36–T77, border by M. Angelo/Westlight; T36(t), Dennis Carlyle Darling; T36(c), T36(b), T37(tl), Larry Ford; T37(tr), J. Alexander Newberry; T37(cl), Larry Ford; T37(cr) Dennis Carlyle Darling; T37(bl), T37 (br), James Newberry; T38, T39, T42, Dennis Carlyle Darling; T45, T47, T48, Larry Ford; T51, Dennis Carlyle Darling; T53, T55, Larry Ford; T57, Dennis Carlyle Darling; T62, T65, J. Alexander Newberry; T66, T67, T68, T69, James Newberry; T72, T73, Larry Ford.

ILLUSTRATION CREDITS: *(Annotated Teacher's Edition)*

Jane Thurmond Design—Page 13A, 61A, 103A, 131A, 165A, 201A, 247A, 283A, 321A, 361A, 405A, 420A, 440A

Edd Patton—Page T39, T40, T41, T44, T46, T49, T50, T53, T54, T57, T58, T59, T60, T61, T63, T64, T66, T67, T69, T71, T72, T74, T75, T76, T77

Front Matter Design—Maeder Design
Icons—Mike Krone